Pro C# 7

With .NET and .NET Core

Eighth Edition

Andrew Troelsen

Philip Japikse

Apress®

Pro C# 7: With .NET and .NET Core

Andrew Troelsen
Minneapolis, Minnesota, USA

Philip Japikse
West Chester, Ohio, USA

ISBN-13 (pbk): 978-1-4842-3017-6
https://doi.org/10.1007/978-1-4842-3018-3

ISBN-13 (electronic): 978-1-4842-3018-3

Library of Congress Control Number: 2017958717

Cover image by Freepik (`www.freepik.com`)

Managing Director: Welmoed Spahr
Editorial Director: Todd Green
Acquisitions Editor: Gwenan Spearing
Development Editor: Laura Berendson
Technical Reviewers: Eric Potter, Lee Brandt, and Sean Whitesell
Coordinating Editor: Mark Powers
Copy Editor: Kim Wimpsett

Distributed to the book trade worldwide by Springer Science+Business Media New York, 233 Spring Street, 6th Floor, New York, NY 10013. Phone 1-800-SPRINGER, fax (201) 348-4505, e-mail `orders-ny@springer-sbm.com`, or visit `www.springeronline.com`. Apress Media, LLC is a California LLC and the sole member (owner) is Springer Science + Business Media Finance Inc (SSBM Finance Inc). SSBM Finance Inc is a **Delaware** corporation.

For information on translations, please e-mail `rights@apress.com`, or visit `www.apress.com/rights-permissions`.

Apress titles may be purchased in bulk for academic, corporate, or promotional use. eBook versions and licenses are also available for most titles. For more information, reference our Print and eBook Bulk Sales web page at `www.apress.com/bulk-sales`.

Any source code or other supplementary material referenced by the author in this book is available to readers on GitHub via the book's product page, located at `www.apress.com/9781484230176`. For more detailed information, please visit `www.apress.com/source-code`.

Printed on acid-free paper

Contents at a Glance

Contents

About the Authors

Andrew Troelsen has more than 20 years of experience in the software industry. During this time he has worked as a developer, educator, author, public speaker, team lead, and now a manager at Thomson Reuters in the big data platform. He is the author of numerous books in the Microsoft universe covering C++-based COM development with ATL, COM and .NET interoperability, Visual Basic, and the award-winning C# and the .NET platform (which would be this book right here). He has a master of science degree in software engineering (MSSE) from the University of St. Thomas and is working on a second master of science degree in computational linguistics (CLMS) from the University of Washington.

Philip Japikse is an international speaker, Microsoft MVP, ASPInsider, MCSD, CSM, and CSP, and passionate member of the developer community. Phil has been working with .NET since the first betas, developing software for more than 30 years, and heavily involved in the agile community since 2005. Phil is the lead director for the Cincinnati .NET User's Group (www.cinnug.org), founded the Cincinnati Day of Agile (www.dayofagile.org), and volunteers for the National Ski Patrol. Phil is also a published author with LinkedIn Learning (https://www.lynda.com/Phil-Japikse/7908546-1.html). During the day, Phil works as an enterprise consultant and agile coach for large to medium firms throughout the United States. Phil enjoys to learn new tech and is always striving to improve his craft. You can follow Phil on Twitter via www.twitter.com/skimedic and read his blog at www.skimedic.com/blog.

About the Technical Reviewers

Eric Potter is a software architect for Aptera Software and a Microsoft MVP for Visual Studio and development technologies. He works primarily in the .NET web platform but loves opportunities to try other stacks. He has been developing high-quality custom software solutions since 2001. At Aptera, he has successfully delivered solutions for clients in a wide variety of industries. In his spare time, he loves to tinker with Arduino projects. He fondly remembers what it was like to develop software for the Palm OS. He has an amazing wife and five wonderful children. He blogs at http://humbletoolsmith.com/, and you can follow him on Twitter as @pottereric.

After almost two decades writing software professionally (and a few years unprofessionally before that), **Lee Brandt** still continues to learn every day. He has led teams in small and large companies and always manages to keep the business needs at the forefront of software development efforts. He speaks internationally about software development, from both a technical and business perspective, and loves to teach others what he learns. Lee writes software in Objective-C, JavaScript, and C#... mostly. He is a Microsoft Most Valuable Professional in Visual Studio and development technologies and one of the directors of the Kansas City Developer Conference (KCDC). Lee is also a decorated Gulf War veteran, a husband, and a proud pet parent and loves to play the drums whenever he gets any spare time.

Sean Whitesell is a software developer in Tulsa, Oklahoma, with more than 17 years of experience in client-server, web, embedded, and electronics development. He is the president of the Tulsa .NET User Group and frequently speaks at area user groups and conferences. His passions are in solving problems programmatically, coding craftsmanship, and teaching. He is also a chaplain and sound engineer at his church and teaches self-defense classes for children.

Acknowledgments

As always, I would like to offer a heartfelt thank-you to the entire team at Apress. I have been lucky to have worked with Apress on a variety of books since 2001. Beyond publishing high-quality technical material, the staff is excellent, and without them this book would not be possible. Thanks, everyone!

I also want to thank my co-author Philip Japikse. Thanks, Phil, for working hard to maintain the same approachable vibe of the book, while still adding your own personal expertise and voice. I believe our book (and those who read it) will most certainly benefit from this new partnership!

Last but not least, I want to thank my wife, Mandy, and my son, Soren, for supporting me.

—Andrew Troelsen

I also want to thank Apress and the entire team involved in writing this book. As I've come to expect with all of my books for Apress, I am very impressed with the dedication and level of support we received during the writing process. I want to thank you, the reader, for reading this book and hope that you will find it as helpful in your career as it has been in mine. Lastly, I couldn't have done this without my family and the support I've had from them. Between reading my work and proofing it and their understanding of the time involved, I couldn't have done it without you! Love you all!

—Philip Japikse

Introduction

We're a Team That Includes *You*

Technology authors write for a demanding group of people (for the best of possible reasons). You know that building software solutions using any platform or language is extremely complicated and is specific to your department, company, client base, and subject matter. Perhaps you work in the electronic publishing industry, develop systems for the state or local government, or work at NASA or a branch of the military. Collectively, we have worked in a variety of industries, including developing children's educational software (Oregon Trail/Amazon Trail), various enterprise systems, and projects within the medical and financial industries. The chances are almost 100 percent that the code you write at your place of employment has little to do with the code we have authored over the years.

Therefore, in this book, we have deliberately chosen to avoid creating demonstrations that tie the example code to a specific industry or vein of programming. Given this, we explain C#, OOP, the CLR, and the .NET base class libraries using industry-agnostic examples. Rather than having every blessed example fill a grid with data, calculate payroll, or whatnot, we stick to subject matter we can all relate to: automobiles (with some geometric structures and employee payroll systems thrown in for good measure). And that's where you come in.

Our job is to explain the C# programming language and the core aspects of the .NET platform the best we possibly can. As well, we will do everything we can to equip you with the tools and strategies you need to continue your studies at this book's conclusion.

Your job is to take this information and apply it to your specific programming assignments. We obviously understand that your projects most likely don't revolve around automobiles with friendly pet names (Zippy the BMW or a Yugo named Clunker, among others), but that's what applied knowledge is all about!

Rest assured, once you understand the topics and concepts presented within this text, you will be in a perfect position to build .NET solutions that map to your own unique programming environment.

An Overview of This Book

Pro C# 7.0 is logically divided into nine distinct parts, each of which contains a number of related chapters. Here is a part-by-part and chapter-by-chapter breakdown of the text.

Part I: Introducing C# and the .NET Platform

The purpose of Part I is to acclimate you to the nature of the .NET platform and various development tools used during the construction of .NET applications.

Chapter 1: The Philosophy of .NET

This first chapter functions as the backbone for the remainder of the text. The primary goal of this chapter is to acquaint you with a number of .NET-centric building blocks, such as the Common Language Runtime, Common Type System, Common Language Specification, and base class libraries. Here, you will take an initial look at the C# programming language and the .NET assembly format. We wrap up by examining the platform-independent nature of the .NET platform.

Chapter 2: Building C# Applications

The goal of this chapter is to introduce you to the process of compiling C# source code files. Here, you will learn about the completely free (and fully functional) Visual Studio Community edition upon which this book is based as well as learn about the Professional and Enterprise editions of Visual Studio 2017. You will also learn how to configure your development machine using the new workload-based Visual Studio installation process, enabling C# 7.1 features in your projects, as well as installing the all-important .NET 4.7 and .NET Core 2.0 frameworks.

Part II: Core C# Programming

The topics presented in this part of the book are quite important because you will use them regardless of which type of .NET software you intend to develop (e.g., web applications, desktop GUI applications, code libraries, or Windows services). Here, you will learn about the fundamental data types of .NET, work with text manipulation, and learn the role of various C# parameter modifiers (including optional and named arguments).

Chapter 3: Core C# Programming Constructs, Part I

This chapter begins your formal investigation of the C# programming language. Here, you will learn about the role of the `Main()` method and numerous details regarding the intrinsic data types of the .NET platform and variable declaration, and you will work with and manipulate textual data using `System.String` and `System.Text.StringBuilder`. You will also examine iteration and decision constructs, narrowing and widening operations, and the `unchecked` keyword.

Chapter 4: Core C# Programming Constructs, Part II

This chapter completes your examination of the core aspects of C#, beginning with creating and manipulating arrays of data. Next you examine how to construct overloaded type methods and define parameters using the `out`, `ref`, and `params` keywords. You will also learn about the enum type, structures, and nullable data types, and you will understand the distinction between value types and reference types. Finally, you will learn about tuples, a new feature in C# 7.

Part III: Object-Oriented Programming with C#

In this part, you will come to understand the core constructs of the C# language, including the details of object-oriented programming. This part will also examine how to process runtime exceptions and will dive into the details of working with strongly typed interfaces.

Chapter 5: Understanding Encapsulation

This chapter begins your examination of object-oriented programming (OOP) using the C# programming language. After you are introduced to the pillars of OOP (encapsulation, inheritance, and polymorphism), the remainder of this chapter will show you how to build robust class types using constructors, properties, static members, constants, and read-only fields. You will wrap up with an examination of partial type definitions, object initialization syntax, and automatic properties.

Chapter 6: Understanding Inheritance and Polymorphism

Here, you will examine the remaining pillars of OOP (inheritance and polymorphism), which allow you to build families of related class types. As you do this, you will examine the role of virtual methods, abstract methods (and abstract base classes), and the nature of the polymorphic interface. Then you will explore pattern matching, new in C# 7. Last but not least, this chapter will explain the role of the supreme base class of the .NET platform, System.Object.

Chapter 7: Understanding Structured Exception Handling

The point of this chapter is to discuss how to handle runtime anomalies in your codebase through the use of structured exception handling. Not only will you learn about the C# keywords that allow you to handle such problems (try, catch, throw, when, and finally), but you will also come to understand the distinction between application-level and system-level exceptions. In addition, this chapter will examine various tools within Visual Studio that allow you to debug the exceptions that escape your notice.

Chapter 8: Working with Interfaces

The material in this chapter builds upon your understanding of object-based development by covering the topic of interface-based programming. Here, you will learn how to define classes and structures that support multiple behaviors, how to discover these behaviors at runtime, and how to selectively hide particular behaviors using explicit interface implementation. In addition to creating a number of custom interfaces, you will also learn how to implement standard interfaces found within the .NET platform. You will use these to build objects that can be sorted, copied, enumerated, and compared.

Part IV: Advanced C# Programming

This part of the book will deepen your understanding of the C# language by walking you through a number of more advanced (but important) concepts. Here, you will complete your examination of the .NET type system by investigating interfaces and delegates. You will also learn about the role of generics, take a first look at Language Integrated Query, and examine a number of more advanced features of C# (e.g., extension methods, partial methods, pointer manipulation, and object lifetime).

Chapter 9: Collections and Generics

This chapter explores the topic of *generics*. As you will see, generic programming gives you a way to create types and type members, which contain various *placeholders* that can be specified by the caller. In a nutshell, generics greatly enhance application performance and type safety. Not only will you explore various generic types within the System.Collections.Generic namespace, but you will also learn how to build your own generic methods and types (with and without constraints).

Chapter 10: Delegates, Events, and Lambda Expressions

The purpose of Chapter 10 is to demystify the delegate type. Simply put, a .NET delegate is an object that points to other methods in your application. Using this type, you can build systems that allow multiple objects to engage in a two-way conversation. After you have examined the use of .NET delegates, you will then be introduced to the C# event keyword, which you can use to simplify the manipulation of raw delegate programming. You will wrap up this chapter by investigating the role of the C# lambda operator (=>) and exploring the connection between delegates, anonymous methods, and lambda expressions.

Chapter 11: Advanced C# Language Features

This chapter deepens your understanding of the C# programming language by introducing you to a number of advanced programming techniques. Here, you will learn how to overload operators and create custom conversion routines (both implicit and explicit) for your types. You will also learn how to build and interact with type indexers, as well as work with extension methods, anonymous types, partial methods, and C# pointers using an unsafe code context.

Chapter 12: LINQ to Objects

This chapter begins your examination of Language Integrated Query (LINQ). LINQ allows you to build strongly typed query expressions that can be applied to a number of LINQ targets to manipulate data in the broadest sense of the word. Here, you will learn about LINQ to Objects, which allows you to apply LINQ expressions to containers of data (e.g., arrays, collections, and custom types). This information will serve you well as you encounter a number of additional LINQ APIs throughout the remainder of this book.

Chapter 13: Understanding Object Lifetime

The final chapter of this part examines how the CLR manages memory using the .NET garbage collector. Here, you will come to understand the role of application roots, object generations, and the System.GC type. Once you understand the basics, you will examine the topics of disposable objects (using the IDisposable interface) and the finalization process (using the System.Object.Finalize() method). This chapter will also investigate the Lazy<T> class, which allows you to define data that will not be allocated until requested by a caller. As you will see, this feature can be helpful when you want to ensure you do not clutter the heap with objects that are not actually required by your programs.

Part V: Programming with .NET Assemblies

Part V dives into the details of the .NET assembly format. Not only will you learn how to deploy and configure .NET code libraries, but you will also come to understand the internal composition of a .NET binary image. This part also explains the role of .NET attributes and the role of resolving type information at runtime. This section will also explain the role of the Dynamic Language Runtime (DLR) and the C# dynamic keyword. Later chapters will examine some fairly advanced topics regarding assemblies, such as application domains, the syntax of Common Intermediate Language (CIL), and the construction of in-memory assemblies.

Chapter 14: Building and Configuring Class Libraries

At a high level, *assembly* is the term used to describe a *.dll or *.exe binary file created with a .NET compiler. However, the true story of .NET assemblies is far richer than that. Here, you will learn the distinction between single-file and multifile assemblies, as well as how to build and deploy each entity.

You'll also examine how you can configure private and shared assemblies using XML-based *.config files and publisher policy assemblies. Along the way, you will investigate the internal structure of the global assembly cache (GAC).

Chapter 15: Type Reflection, Late Binding, and Attribute-Based Programming

Chapter 15 continues your examination of .NET assemblies by checking out the process of runtime type discovery using the System.Reflection namespace. Using the types of this namespace, you can build applications that can read an assembly's metadata on the fly. You will also learn how to load and create types at runtime dynamically using late binding. The final topic of this chapter will explore the role of .NET attributes (both standard and custom). To illustrate the usefulness of each of these topics, the chapter shows you how to construct an extendable Windows Forms application.

Chapter 16: Dynamic Types and the Dynamic Language Runtime

.NET 4.0 introduced a new aspect of the .NET runtime environment called the *dynamic language runtime*. Using the DLR and the C# 2010 dynamic keyword, you can define data that is not truly resolved until runtime. Using these features simplifies some complex .NET programming tasks dramatically. In this chapter, you will learn some practical uses of dynamic data, including how to leverage the .NET reflection APIs in a streamlined manner, as well as how to communicate with legacy COM libraries with a minimum of fuss and bother.

Chapter 17: Processes, AppDomains, and Object Contexts

Now that you have a solid understanding of assemblies, this chapter dives deeper into the composition of a loaded .NET executable. The goal of this chapter is to illustrate the relationship between processes, application domains, and contextual boundaries. These topics provide the proper foundation for Chapter 19, where you will examine the construction of multithreaded applications.

Chapter 18: Understanding CIL and the Role of Dynamic Assemblies

The goal of the final chapter in this section is twofold. In the first half (more or less), you will examine the syntax and semantics of CIL in much greater detail than in previous chapters. The remainder of this chapter will cover the role of the System.Reflection.Emit namespace. You can use these types to build software that can generate .NET assemblies in memory at runtime. Formally speaking, assemblies defined and executed in memory are termed *dynamic assemblies*.

Part VI: Introducing the .NET Base Class Libraries

By this point in the text, you have a solid handle on the C# language and the details of the .NET assembly format. Part VI leverages your newfound knowledge by exploring a number of commonly used services found within the base class libraries, including the creation of multithreaded applications, file I/O, and database access using ADO.NET. This part also covers the construction of distributed applications using Windows Communication Foundation and the LINQ to XML API.

Chapter 19: Multithreaded, Parallel, and Async Programming

This chapter examines how to build multithreaded applications and illustrates a number of techniques you can use to author thread-safe code. The chapter opens by revisiting the .NET delegate type to ensure, explaining a delegate's intrinsic support for asynchronous method invocations. Next, you will investigate the types within the System.Threading namespace. The next section covers the Task Parallel Library (TPL). Using the TPL, .NET developers can build applications that distribute their workload across all available CPUs in a wickedly simple manner. At this point, you will also learn about the role of Parallel LINQ, which provides a way to create LINQ queries that scale across multiple machine cores. The remainder of the chapter covers creating nonblocking calls using the async/await keywords, introduced in C# 5, and local functions and generalized async return types, both new in C# 7.

Chapter 20: File I/O and Object Serialization

The System.IO namespace allows you to interact with a machine's file and directory structure. Over the course of this chapter, you will learn how to create (and destroy) a directory system programmatically. You will also learn how to move data into and out of various streams (e.g., file based, string based, and memory based). The latter part of this chapter will examine the object serialization services of the .NET platform. Simply put, serialization allows you to persist the state of an object (or a set of related objects) into a stream for later use. Deserialization (as you might expect) is the process of plucking an object from the stream into memory for consumption by your application. After you understand the basics, you will learn how to customize the serialization process using the ISerializable interface and a set of .NET attributes.

Chapter 21: Data Access with ADO.NET

In this first of two database-centric chapters using the full .NET Framework, you will take your first look at the database access API of the .NET platform, ADO.NET. Specifically, this chapter will introduce you to the role of .NET data providers and how to communicate with a relational database using the connected layer of ADO.NET, which is represented by connection objects, command objects, transaction objects, and data reader objects.

Chapter 22: Introducing Entity Framework 6

This chapter wraps up your investigation of ADO.NET by examining the role of Entity Framework (EF) 6. EF is an object-relational mapping (ORM) framework that provides a way to author data-access code using strongly typed classes that directly map to your business model. Here, you will come to understand the role of the EF DbContext, using data annotations and the Fluent API to shape your database, implementing repositories for encapsulating common code, transactions, migrations, concurrency checking, and command interception. While doing so, you will learn to interact with relational databases using LINQ to Entities. You will also build the custom data access library (AutoLotDAL.dll), which you will use in several of the remaining chapters of the book.

Chapter 23: Introducing Windows Communication Foundation

Until this point in the book, all the sample applications have executed on a single computer. In this chapter, you will learn about the Windows Communication Foundation (WCF) API that allows you to build distributed applications in a symmetrical manner, regardless of their underlying plumbing. This chapter will expose you to the construction of WCF services, hosts, and clients, as well as using XML-based configuration files to specify addresses, bindings, and contracts declaratively.

Part VII: Windows Presentation Foundation

The initial desktop GUI API supported by the .NET platform was termed Windows Forms. While this API is still fully supported in the full .NET Framework, .NET 3.0 introduced programmers to an amazing API called Windows Presentation Foundation (WFP). Unlike Windows Forms, this supercharged UI framework integrates a number of key services, including data binding, 2D and 3D graphics, animations, and rich documents, into a single, unified object model. This is all accomplished using a declarative markup grammar called Extensible Application Markup Language (XAML). Furthermore, the WPF control architecture provides a trivial way to restyle the look and feel of a typical control radically using little more than some well-formed XAML.

Chapter 24: Introducing Windows Presentation Foundation and XAML

In this chapter, you will begin by examining the motivation behind the creation of WPF (when there was already a desktop development framework in .NET). Then, you will learn about the syntax of XAML and, finally, take a look at the Visual Studio support for building WPF applications.

Chapter 25: WPF Controls, Layouts, Events, and Data Binding

This chapter will expose you to the process of using intrinsic WPF controls and layout managers. For example, you will learn to build menu systems, splitter windows, toolbars, and status bars. This chapter will also introduce you to a number of WPF APIs (and their related controls), including the WPF Ink API, commands, routed events, the data-binding model, and dependency properties.

Chapter 26: WPF Graphics Rendering Services

WPF is a graphically intensive API; given this fact, WPF provides three ways to render graphics: shapes, drawings and geometries, and visuals. In this chapter, you will evaluate each option and learn about a number of important graphics primitives (e.g., brushes, pens, and transformations) along the way. This chapter will also examine ways to incorporate vector images into your WPF graphics, as well as how to perform hit-testing operations against graphical data.

Chapter 27: WPF Resources, Animations, Styles, and Templates

This chapter will introduce you to three important (and interrelated) topics that will deepen your understanding of the Windows Presentation Foundation API. The first order of business is to learn the role of logical resources. As you will see, the logical resource (also termed an *object resource*) system provides a way for you to name and refer to commonly used objects within a WPF application. Next, you will learn how to define, execute, and control an animation sequence. Despite what you might be thinking, however, WPF animations are not limited to the confines of video games or multimedia applications. You will wrap up the chapter by learning about the role of WPF styles. Similar to a web page that uses CSS or the ASP.NET theme engine, a WPF application can define a common look and feel for a set of controls.

Chapter 28: WPF Notifications, Commands, Validation, and MVVM

This chapter begins by examining three core WPF framework capabilities: notifications, validation, and commands. In the notifications section, you will learn about observable models and collections and how they keep your application data and UI in sync. Next, you will dig deeper into commands, building custom commands to encapsulate your code. In the validation section, you will learn how to use the several validation mechanisms available to use in WPF applications. The chapter closes with an examination of the Model-View-ViewModel (MVVM) pattern and ends by creating an application that demonstrates the MVVM pattern in action.

Part VIII: ASP.NET

Part VIII is devoted to an examination of constructing web applications using the ASP.NET programming API. Microsoft designed ASP.NET MVC to leverage the Model-View-Controller pattern and is a lightweight framework for building web applications. ASP.NET Web API 2.2 is based on (and similar to) ASP.NET MVC and is a framework for building RESTful services.

Chapter 29: Introducing ASP.NET MVC

This chapter covers ASP.NET MVC. ASP.NET MVC is based on the Model-View-Controller (MVC) pattern, and after getting an understanding of the MVC pattern, you will build an MVC application. You will learn about Visual Studio scaffolding, routing, controllers, actions, and views. Then you will build an ASP.NET MVC application using the data access layer you built in Chapter 22.

Chapter 30: Introducing ASP.NET Web API

In this chapter, you build a RESTful service using ASP.NET Web API 2.2. This service handles all create, read, update, and delete (CRUD) operations on the Inventory data, again using the data access layer you built in Chapter 22. Finally, you will update your ASP.NET MVC5 application to use the RESTful service as its data access layer.

Part IX: .NET Core

Part IX is dedicated to .NET Core, the cross-platform rewrite of .NET. After learning about .NET Core in general, the motivation, and the differences between .NET Core and the full .NET Framework, you will re-create the AutoLot data access layer in Entity Framework Core. The final two chapters cover building ASP.NET Core web applications and ASP.NET Core RESTful services.

Chapter 31: The Philosophy of .NET Core

This chapter introduces you to .NET Core, the revolutionary cross-platform version of .NET. You will learn about the goals of .NET Core, the different parts (like the CoreCLR and CoreFX), and the .NET Core support life cycle. After installing (and confirming the installation of) .NET Core, you will finish the chapter by comparing .NET to the full .NET Framework.

Chapter 32: Introducing Entity Framework Core

This chapter covers the .NET Core version of the Entity Framework. While many of the EF concepts still hold true, there are some notable and important differences between EF 6 and EF Core. You will begin the chapter by comparing EF 6 to EF Core and then dive right into creating AutoLotDAL_Core2, the EF Core version of the data access layer you created in Chapter 22. This updated data access layer will be used by the remaining chapters in this book.

Chapter 33: Introducing ASP.NET Core Web Applications

This is the first of two chapters on ASP.NET Core and deals with building MVC-style web applications. You will start by using the new ASP.NET Core Web Application template to create the AutoLotMVC_Core2 application, and then you will dive into what's new in ASP.NET Core (compared to ASP.NET MVC5), including dependency injection support, a new configuration system, environmental awareness, tag helpers, and view components. You will finish the chapter by building the ASP.NET Core version of the AutoLotMVC application (from Chapter 29), using AutoLotDAL_Core2 for the data access layer.

Chapter 34: Introducing ASP.NET Core Service Applications

This chapter concludes your look at ASP.NET Core by building a RESTful service using ASP.NET Core. Instead of a separate (but similar) framework, services and web applications use the same codebase in ASP.NET Core, with MVC and WEB API together at last. Just like the service you built in Chapter 30, AutoLotAPI_Core2 handles all of the CRUD operations on the Inventory data using the AutoLotDAL_Core2 data access layer from Chapter 32. Finally, you will update your ASP.NET Core web application to use the new service instead of calling AutoLotDAL_Core2 directly.

Downloadable Appendixes

In addition to the printed material, the GitHub repo contains the source code for this book (accessible via www.apress.com/9781484230176) and additional appendixes distributed as PDFs. These bonus appendixes cover a number of additional APIs in the .NET platform that you might find useful in your line of work. Specifically, you will find the following bonus material:

- Appendix A, "ADO.NET Data Sets, Data Tables, and Data Adapters"

- Appendix B, "Introducing LINQ to XML"

- Appendix C, "Introducing ASP.NET Web Forms"

- Appendix D, "ASP.NET Web Controls, Master Pages, and Themes"

- Appendix E, "ASP.NET State Management Techniques"

Obtaining This Book's Source Code

You can find all the code examples contained in this book available at the public GitHub repo (XX). You will find that the code projects have been partitioned on a chapter-by-chapter basis.

On a related note, be aware that you will find "Source Code" notes, such as the following, in all the book's chapters. These notes serve as your visual cue that you can load the example under discussion into Visual Studio for further examination and modification.

■ **Source Code**   This is a source code note that refers you to a specific directory in the GitHub repo.

To open a solution into Visual Studio, use the File ➤ Open ➤ Project/Solution menu option and then navigate to the correct *.sln file within the correct subdirectory of the unzipped archive.

Obtaining Updates for This Book

As you read through this text, you might find an occasional grammatical or code error (although we sure hope not). If this is the case, please accept our apologies. Being human, a glitch or two might be present, despite our best efforts. If this is the case, you can obtain the current errata list from the book's page on the Apress web site at www.apress.com. As well, you can use this area to notify us of any errors you might find.

■ ■ ■

PART I

Introducing C# and the .NET Platform

CHAPTER 1

■ ■ ■

The Philosophy of .NET

Microsoft's .NET platform (and the related C# programming language) were formally introduced circa 2002 and have quickly become a mainstay of modern-day software development. As mentioned in the book's introduction, the goal of this text is twofold. The first order of business is to provide you with a deep and detailed examination of the syntax and semantics of C#. The second (equally important) order of business is to illustrate the use of numerous .NET APIs, including database access with ADO.NET and the Entity Framework (EF), user interfaces with Windows Presentation Foundation (WPF), service-oriented applications with Windows Communication Foundation (WCF), and web service and web site development using ASP.NET MVC. The last part of this book covers the newest member of the .NET family, .NET Core, which is the cross-platform version of the .NET platform. As they say, the journey of a thousand miles begins with a single step; and with this I welcome you to Chapter 1.

The point of this first chapter is to lay the conceptual groundwork for the remainder of the book. Here you will find a high-level discussion of a number of .NET-related topics such as assemblies, the Common Intermediate Language (CIL), and just-in-time (JIT) compilation. In addition to previewing some keywords of the C# programming language, you will also come to understand the relationship between various aspects of the .NET Framework, such as the Common Language Runtime (CLR), the Common Type System (CTS), and the Common Language Specification (CLS).

This chapter also provides you with a survey of the functionality supplied by the .NET base class libraries, sometimes abbreviated as BCLs. Here, you will get an overview of the language-agnostic and platform-independent nature of the .NET platform. As you would hope, many of these topics are explored in further detail throughout the remainder of this text.

An Initial Look at the .NET Platform

Before Microsoft released the C# language and .NET platform, software developers who created applications for the Windows family of operating system frequently made use of the COM programming model. COM (which stands for the Component Object Model) allowed individuals to build libraries of code that could be shared across diverse programming languages. For example, a C++ programmer could build a COM library that could be used by a Visual Basic developer. The language-independent nature of COM was certainly useful; however, COM was plagued by a complicated infrastructure and a fragile deployment model and was possible only on the Windows operating system.

Despite the complexity and limitations of COM, countless applications have been successful created with this architecture. However, nowadays, the majority of applications created for the Windows family of operating systems are not created with COM. Rather, desktop applications, web sites, OS services, and libraries of reusable data access/business logic are created using the .NET platform.

Electronic supplementary material The online version of this chapter (https://doi.org/10.1007/978-1-4842-3018-3_1) contains supplementary material, which is available to authorized users.

Some Key Benefits of the .NET Platform

As mentioned, C# and the .NET platform were first introduced to the world in 2002 and were intended to offer a much more powerful, more flexible, and simpler programming model than COM. As you will see during the remainder of this book, the .NET Framework is a software platform for building systems on the Windows family of operating systems, as well as on numerous non-Microsoft operating systems such as macOS, iOS, Android, and various Unix/Linux distributions. To set the stage, here is a quick rundown of some core features provided courtesy of .NET:

- *Interoperability with existing code*: This is (of course) a good thing. Existing COM software can commingle (i.e., interop) with newer .NET software, and vice versa. As of .NET 4.0 onward, interoperability has been further simplified with the addition of the dynamic keyword (covered in Chapter 16).

- *Support for numerous programming languages*: .NET applications can be created using any number of programming languages (C#, Visual Basic, F#, and so on).

- *A common runtime engine shared by all .NET-aware languages*: One aspect of this engine is a well-defined set of types that each .NET-aware language understands.

- *Language integration:* .NET supports cross-language inheritance, cross-language exception handling, and cross-language debugging of code. For example, you can define a base class in C# and extend this type in Visual Basic.

- *A comprehensive base class library*: This library provides thousands of predefined types that allow you to build code libraries, simple terminal applications, graphical desktop applications, and enterprise-level web sites.

- *A simplified deployment model*: Unlike COM, .NET libraries are not registered into the system registry. Furthermore, the .NET platform allows multiple versions of the same *.dll to exist in harmony on a single machine.

You will see each of these topics (and many more) examined in the chapters to come.

Introducing the Building Blocks of the .NET Platform (the CLR, CTS, and CLS)

Now that you know some of the major benefits provided by .NET, let's preview three key (and interrelated) topics that make it all possible: the CLR, CTS, and CLS. From a programmer's point of view, .NET can be understood as a runtime environment and a comprehensive base class library. The runtime layer is properly referred to as the *Common Language Runtime*, or *CLR*. The primary role of the CLR is to locate, load, and manage .NET objects on your behalf. The CLR also takes care of a number of low-level details such as memory management, application hosting, coordinating threads, and performing basic security checks (among other low-level details).

Another building block of the .NET platform is the *Common Type System*, or *CTS*. The CTS specification fully describes all possible data types and all programming constructs supported by the runtime, specifies how these entities can interact with each other, and details how they are represented in the .NET metadata format (more information on metadata later in this chapter; see Chapter 15 for complete details).

Understand that a given .NET-aware language might not support every feature defined by the CTS. The *Common Language Specification*, or *CLS*, is a related specification that defines a subset of common types and programming constructs that all .NET programming languages can agree on. Thus, if you build .NET types that expose only CLS-compliant features, you can rest assured that all .NET-aware languages can consume them. Conversely, if you make use of a data type or programming construct that is outside of the bounds of the CLS, you cannot guarantee that every .NET programming language can interact with your .NET code library. Thankfully, as you will see later in this chapter, it is simple to tell your C# compiler to check all of your code for CLS compliance.

The Role of the Base Class Libraries

In addition to the CLR, CTS, and CLS specifications, the .NET platform provides a base class library that is available to all .NET programming languages. Not only does this base class library encapsulate various primitives such as threads, file input/output (I/O), graphical rendering systems, and interaction with various external hardware devices, but it also provides support for a number of services required by most real-world applications.

The base class libraries define types that can be used to build any type of software application. For example, you can use ASP.NET to build web sites and REST services, WCF to build distributed systems, WPF to build desktop GUI applications, and so forth. As well, the base class libraries provide types to interact with the directory and file system on a given computer, communicate with relational databases (via ADO.NET), and so forth. From a high level, you can visualize the relationship between the CLR, CTS, CLS, and the base class library, as shown in Figure 1-1.

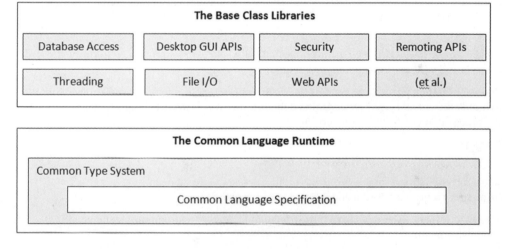

Figure 1-1. *The CLR, CTS, CLS, and base class library relationship*

What C# Brings to the Table

C# is a programming language whose core syntax looks *very* similar to the syntax of Java. However, calling C# a Java clone is inaccurate. In reality, both C# and Java are members of the C family of programming languages (e.g., C, Objective C, C++) and, therefore, share a similar syntax.

The truth of the matter is that many of C#'s syntactic constructs are modeled after various aspects of Visual Basic (VB) and C++. For example, like VB, C# supports the notion of class properties (as opposed to traditional getter and setter methods) and optional parameters. Like C++, C# allows you to overload operators, as well as create structures, enumerations, and callback functions (via delegates).

Moreover, as you work through this text, you will quickly see that C# supports a number of features traditionally found in various functional languages (e.g., LISP or Haskell) such as lambda expressions and anonymous types. Furthermore, with the advent of *Language Integrated Query* (LINQ), C# supports a

number of constructs that make it quite unique in the programming landscape. Nevertheless, the bulk of C#
is indeed influenced by C-based languages.

Because C# is a hybrid of numerous languages, the result is a product that is as syntactically clean
(if not cleaner) as Java, is about as simple as VB, and provides just about as much power and flexibility as C++.
Here is a partial list of core C# features that are found in all versions of the language:

- No pointers required! C# programs typically have no need for direct pointer
  manipulation (although you are free to drop down to that level if absolutely
  necessary, as shown in Chapter 11).

- Automatic memory management through garbage collection. Given this, C# does not
  support a `delete` keyword.

- Formal syntactic constructs for classes, interfaces, structures, enumerations, and
  delegates.

- The C++-like ability to overload operators for a custom type, without the complexity
  (e.g., making sure to "return *this to allow chaining" is not your problem).

- Support for attribute-based programming. This brand of development allows you
  to annotate types and their members to further qualify their behavior. For example,
  if you mark a method with the `[Obsolete]` attribute, programmers will see your
  custom warning message print out if they attempt to make use of the decorated
  member.

With the release of .NET 2.0 (circa 2005), the C# programming language was updated to support
numerous new bells and whistles, most notability the following:

- The ability to build generic types and generic members. Using generics, you are able
  to build efficient and type-safe code that defines numerous *placeholders* specified at
  the time you interact with the generic item.

- Support for anonymous methods, which allow you to supply an inline function
  anywhere a delegate type is required.

- The ability to define a single type across multiple code files (or, if necessary, as an
  in-memory representation) using the `partial` keyword.

.NET 3.5 (released circa 2008) added even more functionality to the C# programming language,
including the following features:

- Support for strongly typed queries (e.g., LINQ) used to interact with various forms of
  data. You will first encounter LINQ in Chapter 12.

- Support for anonymous types that allow you to model the *structure* of a type (rather
  than its behavior) on the fly in code.

- The ability to extend the functionality of an existing type (without subclassing) using
  extension methods.

- Inclusion of a lambda operator (=>), which even further simplifies working with .NET
  delegate types.

- A new object initialization syntax, which allows you to set property values at the time
  of object creation.

.NET 4.0 (released in 2010) updated C# yet again with a handful of features.

- Support for optional method parameters, as well as named method arguments.

- Support for dynamic lookup of members at runtime via the dynamic keyword. As you will see in Chapter 18, this provides a unified approach to invoking members on the fly, regardless of which framework the member implemented.

- Working with generic types is much more intuitive, given that you can easily map generic data to and from general System.Object collections via covariance and contravariance.

With the release of .NET 4.5, C# received a pair of new keywords (async and await), which greatly simplify multithreaded and asynchronous programming. If you have worked with previous versions of C#, you might recall that calling methods via secondary threads required a fair amount of cryptic code and the use of various .NET namespaces. Given that C# now supports language keywords that handle this complexity for you, the process of calling methods asynchronously is almost as easy as calling a method in a synchronous manner. Chapter 19 will cover these topics in detail.

C# 6 was released with .NET 4.6 and introduced a number of minor features that help streamline your codebase. Here are is a quick rundown of some of the features found in C# 6:

- Inline initialization for automatic properties as well as support for read-only automatic properties

- Single-line method implementations using the C# lambda operator

- Support of static imports to provide direct access to static members within a namespace

- A null conditional operator, which helps check for null parameters in a method implementation

- A new string-formatting syntax termed *string interpolation*

- The ability to filter exceptions using the new when keyword

- Using await in catch and finally blocks

- nameOf expressions to return a string representation of symbols

- Index initializers

- Improved overload resolution

This brings me to the current major release of C#, which was released with .NET 4.7 in March 2017. Similar to C# 6, version 7 introduces additional features for streamlining your codebase, and it adds some more significant features (such as tuples and ref locals and returns) that developers have been asking to have included in the language specification for quite some time. These will be detailed throughout the remainder of this book; however, here is a quick rundown of the new features in C# 7:

- Declaring out variables as inline arguments

- Nesting functions inside other functions to limit scope and visibility

- Additional expression-bodied members

- Generalized async return types

- New tokens to improve readability for numeric constants

- Lightweight unnamed types (called *tuples*) that contain multiple fields

- Updates to logic flow using type matching in addition to value checking (pattern matching)

- Returning a reference to a value, instead of just the value itself (`ref` locals and returns)

- The introduction of lightweight throwaway varials (called *discards*)

- Throw expressions, allowing the throw to be executed in more places, such as conditional expressions, lambdas, and others

Not long after C# 7 was released, C# 7.1 was released in August 2017. This minor release added the following features:

- The ability to have a program's main method be `async`.

- A new literal, `default`, that allows for initialization of any type.

- Correction of an issue with pattern matching that prevented using generics with the new pattern matching feature.

- Like anonymous methods, tuple names can be inferred from the projection that creates them.

Managed vs. Unmanaged Code

It is important to note that the C# language can be used only to build software that is hosted under the .NET runtime (you could never use C# to build a native COM server or an unmanaged C/C++-style application). Officially speaking, the term used to describe the code targeting the .NET runtime is *managed code*. The binary unit that contains the managed code is termed an *assembly* (more details on assemblies in just a bit). Conversely, code that cannot be directly hosted by the .NET runtime is termed *unmanaged code.*

As mentioned previously (and detailed later in this chapter and the next), the .NET platform can run on a variety of operating systems. Thus, it is quite possible to build a C# application on a Windows machine using Visual Studio and run the program on a macOS machine using the .NET Core runtime. As well, you could build a C# application on Linux using Xamarin Studio and run the program on Windows, macOS and so on. With the most recent release of Visual Studio 2017, you can also build .NET Core applications on a Mac to be run on Windows, macOS or Linux. To be sure, the notion of a managed environment makes it possible to build, deploy, and run .NET programs on a wide variety of target machines.

Additional .NET-Aware Programming Languages

Understand that C# is not the only language that can be used to build .NET applications. Out of the box, Visual Studio provides you with five managed languages, specifically, C#, Visual Basic, C++/CLI, JavaScript, and F#.

■ **Note** F# is a .NET language based on the syntax of functional languages. While F# can be used as a purely functional language, it also has support for OOP constructs and the .NET base class libraries. If you are interested in learning more about this managed language, navigate to the official F# home page at `http://msdn.microsoft.com/fsharp`.

In addition to the managed languages provided by Microsoft, there are .NET compilers for Smalltalk, Ruby, Python, COBOL, and Pascal (to name a few). Although this book focuses almost exclusively on C#, you might want to consult the following Wikipedia page, which lists a large number of programming languages that target the .NET Framework:

https://en.wikipedia.org/wiki/List_of_CLI_languages

While I assume you are primarily interested in building .NET programs using the syntax of C#, I encourage you to visit this site, as you are sure to find many .NET languages worth investigating at your leisure (LISP.NET, anyone?).

Life in a Multilanguage World

As developers first come to understand the language-agnostic nature of .NET, numerous questions arise. The most prevalent of these questions would have to be, "If all .NET languages compile down to managed code, why do we need more than one language/compiler?"

There are a number of ways to answer this question. First, we programmers are a very particular lot when it comes to our choice of programming language. Some of us prefer languages full of semicolons and curly brackets with as few language keywords as possible. Others enjoy a language that offers more *human-readable* syntactic tokens (such as Visual Basic). Still others might want to leverage their mainframe skills while moving to the .NET platform (via the COBOL .NET compiler).

Now, be honest. If Microsoft were to build a single "official" .NET language derived from the BASIC family of languages, can you really say all programmers would be happy with this choice? Or, if the only "official" .NET language was based on Fortran syntax, imagine all the folks out there who would ignore .NET altogether. Because the .NET runtime couldn't care less which language was used to build a block of managed code, .NET programmers can stay true to their syntactic preferences and share the compiled code among teammates, departments, and external organizations (regardless of which .NET language others choose to use).

Another excellent by-product of integrating various .NET languages into a single, unified software solution is the simple fact that all programming languages have their own sets of strengths and weaknesses. For example, some programming languages offer excellent intrinsic support for advanced mathematical processing. Others offer superior support for financial calculations, logical calculations, interaction with mainframe computers, and so forth. When you take the strengths of a particular programming language and then incorporate the benefits provided by the .NET platform, everybody wins.

Of course, in reality the chances are quite good that you will spend much of your time building software using your .NET language of choice. However, once you master the syntax of one .NET language, it is easy to learn another. This is also quite beneficial, especially to the software consultants of the world. If your language of choice happens to be C# but you are placed at a client site that has committed to Visual Basic, you are still able to leverage the functionality of the .NET Framework, and you should be able to understand the overall structure of the codebase with minimal fuss and bother.

An Overview of .NET Assemblies

Regardless of which .NET language you choose to program with, understand that despite .NET binaries taking the same file extension as unmanaged Windows binaries (*.dll or *.exe), they have absolutely no internal similarities. Specifically, .NET binaries do not contain platform-specific instructions but rather platform-agnostic *Intermediate Language* (*IL*) and type metadata. Figure 1-2 shows the big picture of the story thus far.

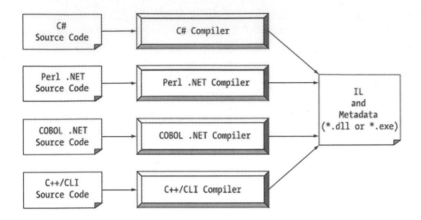

Figure 1-2. All .NET-aware compilers emit IL instructions and metadata

---

■ **Note**   IL is also known as Microsoft Intermediate Language (MSIL) or alternatively as the Common Intermediate Language (CIL). Thus, as you read the .NET literature, understand that IL, MSIL, and CIL are all describing essentially the same concept. In this book, I will use the abbreviation CIL to refer to this low-level instruction set.

When a *.dll or *.exe has been created using a .NET-aware compiler, the binary blob is termed an *assembly*. You will examine numerous details of .NET assemblies in Chapter 14. However, to facilitate the current discussion, you do need to understand some basic properties of this new file format.

As mentioned, an assembly contains CIL code, which is conceptually similar to Java bytecode in that it is not compiled to platform-specific instructions until absolutely necessary. Typically, "absolutely necessary" is the point at which a block of CIL instructions (such as a method implementation) is referenced for use by the .NET runtime.

In addition to CIL instructions, assemblies also contain *metadata* that describes in vivid detail the characteristics of every "type" within the binary. For example, if you have a class named SportsCar, the type metadata describes details such as SportsCar's base class, specifies which interfaces are implemented by SportsCar (if any), and gives full descriptions of each member supported by the SportsCar type. .NET metadata is always present within an assembly and is automatically generated by a .NET-aware language compiler.

Finally, in addition to CIL and type metadata, assemblies themselves are also described using metadata, which is officially termed a *manifest*. The manifest contains information about the current version of the assembly, culture information (used for localizing string and image resources), and a list of all externally referenced assemblies that are required for proper execution. You'll examine various tools that can be used to examine an assembly's types, metadata, and manifest information over the course of the next few chapters.

The Role of the Common Intermediate Language

Let's examine CIL code, type metadata, and the assembly manifest in a bit more detail. CIL is a language that sits above any particular platform-specific instruction set. For example, the following C# code models a trivial calculator. Don't concern yourself with the exact syntax for now, but do notice the format of the Add() method in the Calc class.

```
// Calc.cs
using System;
namespace CalculatorExample
{
  // This class contains the app's entry point.
  class Program
  {
    static void Main()
    {
      Calc c = new Calc();
      int ans = c.Add(10, 84);
      Console.WriteLine("10 + 84 is {0}.", ans);
      // Wait for user to press the Enter key before shutting down.
      Console.ReadLine();
    }
  }

  // The C# calculator.
  class Calc
  {
    public int Add(int x, int y)
    { return x + y; }
  }
}
```

After you compile this code file using the C# compiler (csc.exe), you end up with a single-file *.exe assembly that contains a manifest, CIL instructions, and metadata describing each aspect of the Calc and Program classes.

■ **Note**   Chapter 2 examines how to use graphical integrated development environments (IDEs), such as Visual Studio Community, to compile your code files.

For example, if you were to open this assembly using ildasm.exe (examined a little later in this chapter), you would find that the Add() method is represented using CIL such as the following:

```
.method public hidebysig instance int32 Add(int32 x,
   int32 y) cil managed
{
  // Code size 9 (0x9)
  .maxstack 2
  .locals init (int32 V_0)
  IL_0000: nop
  IL_0001: ldarg.1
  IL_0002: ldarg.2
  IL_0003: add
  IL_0004: stloc.0
  IL_0005: br.s IL_0007
  IL_0007: ldloc.0
  IL_0008: ret
} // end of method Calc::Add
```

Don't worry if you are unable to make heads or tails of the resulting CIL for this method—Chapter 18 will describe the basics of the CIL programming language. The point to concentrate on is that the C# compiler emits CIL, not platform-specific instructions.

Now, recall that this is true of all .NET-aware compilers. To illustrate, assume you created this same application using Visual Basic, rather than C#.

```vb
' Calc.vb
Imports System

Namespace CalculatorExample
  ' A VB "Module" is a class that contains only
  ' static members.
  Module Program
    Sub Main()
      Dim c As New Calc
      Dim ans As Integer = c.Add(10, 84)
      Console.WriteLine("10 + 84 is {0}.", ans)
      Console.ReadLine()
    End Sub
  End Module

  Class Calc
    Public Function Add(ByVal x As Integer, ByVal y As Integer) As Integer
      Return x + y
    End Function
  End Class
End Namespace
```

If you examine the CIL for the Add() method, you find similar instructions (slightly tweaked by the Visual Basic compiler, vbc.exe).

```
.method public instance int32 Add(int32 x,
  int32 y) cil managed
{
  // Code size 8 (0x8)
  .maxstack 2
  .locals init (int32 V_0)
  IL_0000: ldarg.1
  IL_0001: ldarg.2
  IL_0002: add.ovf
  IL_0003: stloc.0
  IL_0004: br.s IL_0006
  IL_0006: ldloc.0
  IL_0007: ret
} // end of method Calc::Add
```

■ **Source Code**   You can find the Calc.cs and Calc.vb code files in the Chapter 1 subdirectory.

Benefits of CIL

At this point, you might be wondering exactly what is gained by compiling source code into CIL rather than directly to a specific instruction set. One benefit is language integration. As you have already seen, each .NET-aware compiler produces nearly identical CIL instructions. Therefore, all languages are able to interact within a well-defined binary arena.

Furthermore, given that CIL is platform-agnostic, the .NET Framework itself is platform-agnostic, providing the same benefits Java developers have grown accustomed to (e.g., a single codebase running on numerous operating systems). In fact, there is an international standard for the C# language, and a large subset of the .NET platform and implementations already exists for many non-Windows operating systems (more details at the conclusion of this chapter).

Compiling CIL to Platform-Specific Instructions

Because assemblies contain CIL instructions rather than platform-specific instructions, CIL code must be compiled on the fly before use. The entity that compiles CIL code into meaningful CPU instructions is a JIT compiler, which sometimes goes by the friendly name of *jitter*. The .NET runtime environment leverages a JIT compiler for each CPU targeting the runtime, each optimized for the underlying platform.

For example, if you are building a .NET application to be deployed to a handheld device (such as a Windows Phone device), the corresponding jitter is well equipped to run within a low-memory environment. On the other hand, if you are deploying your assembly to a back-end company server (where memory is seldom an issue), the jitter will be optimized to function in a high-memory environment. In this way, developers can write a single body of code that can be efficiently JIT compiled and executed on machines with different architectures.

Furthermore, as a given jitter compiles CIL instructions into corresponding machine code, it will cache the results in memory in a manner suited to the target operating system. In this way, if a call is made to a method named `PrintDocument()`, the CIL instructions are compiled into platform-specific instructions on the first invocation and retained in memory for later use. Therefore, the next time `PrintDocument()` is called, there is no need to recompile the CIL.

■ **Note**   It is also possible to perform a "pre-JIT" of an assembly when installing your application using the `ngen.exe` command-line tool that ships with the .NET Framework SDK. Doing so can improve startup time for graphically intensive applications.

The Role of .NET Type Metadata

In addition to CIL instructions, a .NET assembly contains full, complete, and accurate metadata, which describes every type (e.g., class, structure, enumeration) defined in the binary, as well as the members of each type (e.g., properties, methods, events). Thankfully, it is always the job of the compiler (not the programmer) to emit the latest and greatest type metadata. Because .NET metadata is so wickedly meticulous, assemblies are completely self-describing entities.

To illustrate the format of .NET type metadata, let's take a look at the metadata that has been generated for the `Add()` method of the C# `Calc` class you examined previously (the metadata generated for the Visual Basic version of the `Add()` method is similar; again, more on the use of `ildasm.exe` in just a bit).

```
TypeDef #2 (02000003)
-----------------------------------------------------------
  TypDefName: CalculatorExample.Calc (02000003)
  Flags      : [NotPublic] [AutoLayout] [Class]
  [AnsiClass] [BeforeFieldInit] (00100001)
  Extends    : 01000001 [TypeRef] System.Object
  Method #1 (06000003)
-----------------------------------------------------------
  MethodName: Add (06000003)
  Flags      : [Public] [HideBySig] [ReuseSlot] (00000086)
  RVA        : 0x00002090
  ImplFlags  : [IL] [Managed] (00000000)
  CallCnvntn: [DEFAULT]
  hasThis
  ReturnType: I4
    2 Arguments
    Argument #1:   I4
    Argument #2:   I4
    2 Parameters
    (1) ParamToken : (08000001) Name : x flags: [none] (00000000)
    (2) ParamToken : (08000002) Name : y flags: [none] (00000000)
```

Metadata is used by numerous aspects of the .NET runtime environment, as well as by various development tools. For example, the IntelliSense feature provided by tools such as Visual Studio is made possible by reading an assembly's metadata at design time. Metadata is also used by various object- browsing utilities, debugging tools, and the C# compiler itself. To be sure, metadata is the backbone of numerous .NET technologies including WCF, reflection, late binding, and object serialization. Chapter 15 will formalize the role of .NET metadata.

The Role of the Assembly Manifest

Last but not least, remember that a .NET assembly also contains metadata that describes the assembly itself (technically termed a *manifest*). Among other details, the manifest documents all external assemblies required by the current assembly to function correctly, the assembly's version number, copyright information, and so forth. Like type metadata, it is always the job of the compiler to generate the assembly's manifest. Here are some relevant details of the manifest generated when compiling the Calc.cs code file shown earlier in this chapter (assume you instructed the compiler to name your assembly Calc.exe):

```
.assembly extern mscorlib
{
  .publickeytoken = (B7 7A 5C 56 19 34 E0 89 )
  .ver 4:0:0:0
}
.assembly Calc
{
  .hash algorithm 0x00008004
  .ver 0:0:0:0
}
.module Calc.exe
.imagebase 0x00400000
.subsystem 0x00000003
.file alignment 0x00000200
.corflags 0x00000001
```

In a nutshell, this manifest documents the set of external assemblies required by `Calc.exe` (via the `.assembly extern` directive) as well as various characteristics of the assembly itself (e.g., version number, module name). Chapter 14 will examine the usefulness of manifest data in much more detail.

Understanding the Common Type System

A given assembly may contain any number of distinct types. In the world of .NET, *type* is simply a general term used to refer to a member from the set {class, interface, structure, enumeration, delegate}. When you build solutions using a .NET-aware language, you will most likely interact with many of these types. For example, your assembly might define a single class that implements some number of interfaces. Perhaps one of the interface methods takes an enumeration type as an input parameter and returns a structure to the caller.

Recall that the CTS is a formal specification that documents how types must be defined in order to be hosted by the CLR. Typically, the only individuals who are deeply concerned with the inner workings of the CTS are those building tools and/or compilers that target the .NET platform. It is important, however, for all .NET programmers to learn about how to work with the five types defined by the CTS in their language of choice. The following is a brief overview.

CTS Class Types

Every .NET-aware language supports, at the least, the notion of a *class type*, which is the cornerstone of object-oriented programming (OOP). A class may be composed of any number of members (such as constructors, properties, methods, and events) and data points (fields). In C#, classes are declared using the `class` keyword, like so:

```
// A C# class type with 1 method.
class Calc
{
  public int Add(int x, int y)
  {
    return x + y;
  }
}
```

Chapter 5 will begin your formal examination of building class types with C#; however, Table 1-1 documents a number of characteristics pertaining to class types.

Table 1-1. *CTS Class Characteristics*

Class Characteristic	Meaning in Life
Is the class sealed?	Sealed classes cannot function as a base class to other classes.
Does the class implement any interfaces?	An interface is a collection of abstract members that provides a contract between the object and object user. The CTS allows a class to implement any number of interfaces.
Is the class abstract or concrete?	Abstract classes cannot be directly instantiated but are intended to define common behaviors for derived types. Concrete classes can be instantiated directly.
What is the visibility of this class?	Each class must be configured with a visibility keyword such as `public` or `internal`. Basically, this controls whether the class may be used by external assemblies or only from within the defining assembly.

CTS Interface Types

Interfaces are nothing more than a named collection of abstract member definitions, which may be supported (i.e., implemented) by a given class or structure. In C#, interface types are defined using the `interface` keyword. By convention, all .NET interfaces begin with a capital letter *I*, as in the following example:

```
// A C# interface type is usually
// declared as public, to allow types in other
// assemblies to implement their behavior.
public interface IDraw
{
  void Draw();
}
```

On their own, interfaces are of little use. However, when a class or structure implements a given interface in its unique way, you are able to request access to the supplied functionality using an interface reference in a polymorphic manner. Interface-based programming will be fully explored in Chapter 8.

CTS Structure Types

The concept of a structure is also formalized under the CTS. If you have a C background, you should be pleased to know that these user-defined types (UDTs) have survived in the world of .NET (although they behave a bit differently under the hood). Simply put, a *structure* can be thought of as a lightweight class type having value-based semantics. For more details on the subtleties of structures, see Chapter 4. Typically, structures are best suited for modeling geometric and mathematical data and are created in C# using the `struct` keyword, as follows:

```
// A C# structure type.
struct Point
{
  // Structures can contain fields.
  public int xPos, yPos;

  // Structures can contain parameterized constructors.
  public Point(int x, int y)
  { xPos = x; yPos = y;}

  // Structures may define methods.
  public void PrintPosition()
  {
    Console.WriteLine("({0}, {1})", xPos, yPos);
  }
}
```

CTS Enumeration Types

Enumerations are a handy programming construct that allow you to group name-value pairs. For example, assume you are creating a video game application that allows the player to select one of three character categories (Wizard, Fighter, or Thief). Rather than keeping track of simple numerical values to represent each possibility, you could build a strongly typed enumeration using the enum keyword.

```
// A C# enumeration type.
enum CharacterType
{
  Wizard = 100,
  Fighter = 200,
  Thief = 300
}
```

By default, the storage used to hold each item is a 32-bit integer; however, it is possible to alter this storage slot if need be (e.g., when programming for a low-memory device such as a mobile device). Also, the CTS demands that enumerated types derive from a common base class, System.Enum. As you will see in Chapter 4, this base class defines a number of interesting members that allow you to extract, manipulate, and transform the underlying name-value pairs programmatically.

CTS Delegate Types

Delegates are the .NET equivalent of a type-safe, C-style function pointer. The key difference is that a .NET delegate is a *class* that derives from System.MulticastDelegate, rather than a simple pointer to a raw memory address. In C#, delegates are declared using the delegate keyword.

```
// This C# delegate type can "point to" any method
// returning an int and taking two ints as input.
delegate int BinaryOp(int x, int y);
```

Delegates are critical when you want to provide a way for one object to forward a call to another object and provide the foundation for the .NET event architecture. As you will see in Chapters 10 and 19, delegates have intrinsic support for multicasting (i.e., forwarding a request to multiple recipients) and asynchronous method invocations (i.e., invoking the method on a secondary thread).

CTS Type Members

Now that you have previewed each of the types formalized by the CTS, realize that most types take any number of *members*. Formally speaking, a type member is constrained by the set {constructor, finalizer, static constructor, nested type, operator, method, property, indexer, field, read-only field, constant, event}.

The CTS defines various *adornments* that may be associated with a given member. For example, each member has a given visibility trait (e.g., public, private, protected). Some members may be declared as abstract (to enforce a polymorphic behavior on derived types) as well as virtual (to define a canned, but overridable, implementation). Also, most members may be configured as static (bound at the class level) or instance (bound at the object level). The creation of type members is examined over the course of the next several chapters.

■ **Note** As described in Chapter 9, the C# language also supports the creation of generic types and generic members.

Intrinsic CTS Data Types

The final aspect of the CTS to be aware of for the time being is that it establishes a well-defined set of fundamental data types. Although a given language typically has a unique keyword used to declare a fundamental data type, all .NET language keywords ultimately resolve to the same CTS type defined in an assembly named `mscorlib.dll`. Consider Table 1-2, which documents how key CTS data types are expressed in various .NET languages.

Table 1-2. *The Intrinsic CTS Data Types*

CTS Data Type	VB Keyword	C# Keyword	C++/CLI Keyword
System.Byte	Byte	byte	unsigned char
System.SByte	SByte	sbyte	signed char
System.Int16	Short	short	short
System.Int32	Integer	int	int or long
System.Int64	Long	long	__int64
System.UInt16	UShort	ushort	unsigned short
System.UInt32	UInteger	uint	unsigned int or unsigned long
System.UInt64	ULong	ulong	unsigned __int64
System.Single	Single	float	float
System.Double	Double	double	double
System.Object	Object	object	object^
System.Char	Char	char	wchar_t
System.String	String	string	String^
System.Decimal	Decimal	decimal	Decimal
System.Boolean	Boolean	bool	bool

Given that the unique keywords of a managed language are simply shorthand notations for a real type in the `System` namespace, you no longer have to worry about overflow/underflow conditions for numerical data or how strings and Booleans are internally represented across different languages. Consider the following code snippets, which define 32-bit numerical variables in C# and Visual Basic, using language keywords as well as the formal CTS data type:

```
// Define some "ints" in C#.
int i = 0;
System.Int32 j = 0;

' Define some  "ints" in VB.
Dim i As Integer = 0
Dim j As System.Int32 = 0
```

Understanding the Common Language Specification

As you are aware, different languages express the same programming constructs in unique, language-specific terms. For example, in C# you denote string concatenation using the plus operator (+), while in VB you typically make use of the ampersand (&). Even when two distinct languages express the same programmatic idiom (e.g., a function with no return value), the chances are good that the syntax will appear quite different on the surface.

```
// C# method returning nothing.
public void MyMethod()
{
  // Some interesting code...
}
```

```
' VB method returning nothing.
Public Sub MyMethod()
  ' Some interesting code...
End Sub
```

As you have already seen, these minor syntactic variations are inconsequential in the eyes of the .NET runtime, given that the respective compilers (csc.exe or vbc.exe, in this case) emit a similar set of CIL instructions. However, languages can also differ with regard to their overall level of functionality. For example, a .NET language might or might not have a keyword to represent unsigned data and might or might not support pointer types. Given these possible variations, it would be ideal to have a baseline to which all .NET-aware languages are expected to conform.

The CLS is a set of rules that describe in vivid detail the minimal and complete set of features a given .NET-aware compiler must support to produce code that can be hosted by the CLR, while at the same time be accessed in a uniform manner by all languages that target the .NET platform. In many ways, the CLS can be viewed as a *subset* of the full functionality defined by the CTS.

The CLS is ultimately a set of rules that compiler builders must conform to if they intend their products to function seamlessly within the .NET universe. Each rule is assigned a simple name (e.g., CLS Rule 6) and describes how this rule affects those who build the compilers as well as those who (in some way) interact with them. The crème de la crème of the CLS is Rule 1.

> *Rule 1:* CLS rules apply only to those parts of a type that are exposed outside the defining assembly.

Given this rule, you can (correctly) infer that the remaining rules of the CLS do not apply to the logic used to build the inner workings of a .NET type. The only aspects of a type that must conform to the CLS are the member definitions themselves (i.e., naming conventions, parameters, and return types). The implementation logic for a member may use any number of non-CLS techniques, as the outside world won't know the difference.

To illustrate, the following C# Add() method is not CLS compliant, as the parameters and return values make use of unsigned data (which is not a requirement of the CLS):

```
class Calc
{
  // Exposed unsigned data is not CLS compliant!
  public ulong Add(ulong x, ulong y)
  {
    return x + y;
  }
}
```

However, if you were to only make use of unsigned data internally in a method, as follows:

```
class Calc
{
  public int Add(int x, int y)
  {
    // As this ulong variable is only used internally,
    // we are still CLS compliant.
    ulong temp = 0;
    ...
    return x + y;
  }
}
```

you have still conformed to the rules of the CLS and can rest assured that all .NET languages are able to invoke the Add() method.

Of course, in addition to Rule 1, the CLS defines numerous other rules. For example, the CLS describes how a given language must represent text strings, how enumerations should be represented internally (the base type used for storage), how to define static members, and so forth. Luckily, you don't have to commit these rules to memory to be a proficient .NET developer. Again, by and large, an intimate understanding of the CTS and CLS specifications is typically of interest only to tool/compiler builders.

Ensuring CLS Compliance

As you will see over the course of this book, C# does define a number of programming constructs that are not CLS compliant. The good news, however, is that you can instruct the C# compiler to check your code for CLS compliance using a single .NET attribute.

```
// Tell the C# compiler to check for CLS compliance.
[assembly: CLSCompliant(true)]
```

Chapter 15 dives into the details of attribute-based programming. Until then, simply understand that the [CLSCompliant] attribute will instruct the C# compiler to check every line of code against the rules of the CLS. If any CLS violations are discovered, you receive a compiler error and a description of the offending code.

Understanding the Common Language Runtime

In addition to the CTS and CLS specifications, the final three-letter abbreviation (TLA) to contend with at the moment is the CLR. Programmatically speaking, the term *runtime* can be understood as a collection of services that are required to execute a given compiled unit of code. For example, when Java developers deploy software to a new computer, they need to ensure the Java virtual machine (JVM) has been installed on the machine in order to run their software.

The .NET platform offers yet another runtime system. The key difference between the .NET runtime and the various other runtimes I just mentioned is that the .NET runtime provides a single, well-defined runtime layer that is shared by *all* languages and platforms that are .NET-aware.

The crux of the CLR is physically represented by a library named mscoree.dll (aka the Common Object Runtime Execution Engine). When an assembly is referenced for use, mscoree.dll is loaded automatically, which in turn loads the required assembly into memory. The runtime engine is responsible for a number of tasks. First, it is the agent in charge of resolving the location of an assembly and finding the requested type within the binary by reading the contained metadata. The CLR then lays out the type in memory, compiles the associated CIL into platform-specific instructions, performs any necessary security checks, and then executes the code in question.

In addition to loading your custom assemblies and creating your custom types, the CLR will also interact with the types contained within the .NET base class libraries when required. Although the entire base class library has been broken into a number of discrete assemblies, the key assembly is mscorlib.dll, which contains a large number of core types that encapsulate a wide variety of common programming tasks, as well as the core data types used by all .NET languages. When you build .NET solutions, you automatically have access to this particular assembly.

Figure 1-3 illustrates the high-level workflow that takes place between your source code (which is making use of base class library types), a given .NET compiler, and the .NET execution engine.

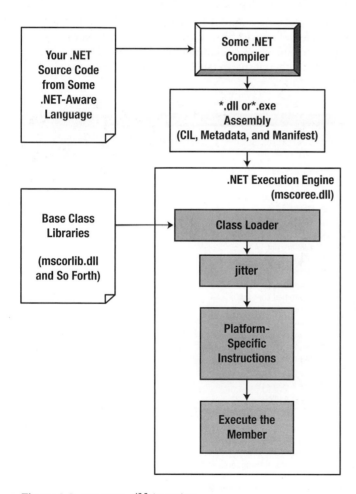

Figure 1-3. mscoree.dll *in action*

The Assembly/Namespace/Type Distinction

Each of us understands the importance of code libraries. The point of framework libraries is to give developers a well-defined set of existing code to leverage in their applications. However, the C# language does not come with a language-specific code library. Rather, C# developers leverage the language- neutral .NET libraries. To keep all the types within the base class libraries well organized, the .NET platform makes extensive use of the *namespace* concept.

A namespace is a grouping of semantically related types contained in an assembly or possibly spread across multiple related assemblies. For example, the System.IO namespace contains file I/O–related types, the System.Data namespace defines basic database types, and so on. It is important to point out that a single assembly (such as mscorlib.dll) can contain any number of namespaces, each of which can contain any number of types.

To clarify, Figure 1-4 shows the Visual Studio Object Browser utility (which can be found under the View menu). This tool allows you to examine the assemblies referenced by your current project, the namespaces within a particular assembly, the types within a given namespace, and the members of a specific type. Note that the mscorlib.dll assembly contains many different namespaces (such as System.IO), each with its own semantically related types (e.g., BinaryReader).

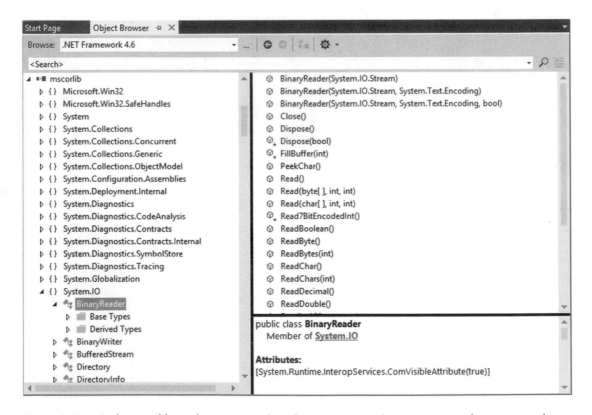

Figure 1-4. *A single assembly can have any number of namespaces, and namespaces can have any number of types*

The key difference between this approach and a language-specific library is that any language targeting the .NET runtime uses the *same* namespaces and *same* types. For example, the following three programs all illustrate the ubiquitous Hello World application, written in C#, VB, and C++/CLI:

```
// Hello World in C#.
using System;

public class MyApp
{
  static void Main()
  {
    Console.WriteLine("Hi from C#");
  }
}
```

```
' Hello World in VB.
Imports System
Public Module MyApp
  Sub Main()
    Console.WriteLine("Hi from VB")
  End Sub
End Module
```

```
// Hello World in C++/CLI.
#include "stdafx.h"
using namespace System;

int main(array<System::String ^> ^args)
{
  Console::WriteLine(L"Hi from C++/CLI");
  return 0;
}
```

Notice that each language is using the Console class defined in the System namespace. Beyond some obvious syntactic variations, these three applications look and feel very much alike, both physically and logically.

Clearly, once you are comfortable with your .NET programming language of choice, your next goal as a .NET developer is to get to know the wealth of types defined in the (numerous) .NET namespaces. The most fundamental namespace to get your head around initially is named System. This namespace provides a core body of types that you will need to leverage time and again as a .NET developer. In fact, you cannot build any sort of functional C# application without at least making a reference to the System namespace, as the core data types (e.g., System.Int32, System.String) are defined here. Table 1-3 offers a rundown of some (but certainly not all) of the .NET namespaces grouped by related functionality.

Table 1-3. *A Sampling of .NET Namespaces*

.NET Namespace	Meaning in Life
System	Within System, you find numerous useful types dealing with intrinsic data, mathematical computations, random number generation, environment variables, and garbage collection, as well as a number of commonly used exceptions and attributes.
System.Collections System.Collections.Generic	These namespaces define a number of stock container types, as well as base types and interfaces that allow you to build customized collections.
System.Data System.Data.Common System.Data.EntityClient System.Data.SqlClient	These namespaces are used for interacting with relational databases using ADO.NET.
System.IO System.IO.Compression System.IO.Ports	These namespaces define numerous types used to work with file I/O, compression of data, and port manipulation.
System.Reflection System.Reflection.Emit	These namespaces define types that support runtime type discovery as well as dynamic creation of types.
System.Runtime.InteropServices	This namespace provides facilities to allow .NET types to interact with unmanaged code (e.g., C-based DLLs and COM servers), and vice versa.
System.Drawing System.Windows.Forms	These namespaces define types used to build desktop applications using .NET's original UI toolkit (Windows Forms).
System.Windows System.Windows.Controls System.Windows.Shapes	The System.Windows namespace is the root for several namespaces that represent the Windows Presentation Foundation (WPF) UI toolkit.
System.Linq System.Xml.Linq System.Data.DataSetExtensions	These namespaces define types used when programming against the LINQ API.
System.Web	This is one of many namespaces that allows you to build ASP.NET web applications.
System.Web.Http	This is one of many namespaces that allows you to build RESTful web services.
System.ServiceModel	This is one of many namespaces used to build distributed applications using the Windows Communication Foundation API.
System.Workflow.Runtime System.Workflow.Activities	These are two of many namespaces that define types used to build "workflow-enabled" applications using the Windows Workflow Foundation API.
System.Threading System.Threading.Tasks	This namespace defines numerous types to build multithreaded applications that can distribute workloads across multiple CPUs.
System.Security	Security is an integrated aspect of the .NET universe. In the security-centric namespaces, you find numerous types dealing with permissions, cryptography, and so on.
System.Xml	The XML-centric namespaces contain numerous types used to interact with XML data.

The Role of the Microsoft Root Namespace

You probably noticed while reading over the listings in Table 1-3 that System is the root namespace for a majority of nested namespaces (e.g., System.IO, System.Data). As it turns out, however, the .NET base class library defines a number of topmost root namespaces beyond System, the most useful of which is named Microsoft.

Any namespace nested within Microsoft (e.g., Microsoft.CSharp, Microsoft.ManagementConsole, Microsoft.Win32) contains types that are used to interact with services unique to the Windows operating system. Given this point, you should not assume that these types could be used successfully on other .NET-enabled operating systems such as macOS. For the most part, this text will not dig into the details of the Microsoft rooted namespaces, so be sure to consult the .NET Framework 4.7 SDK documentation if you are interested.

■ **Note** Chapter 2 will illustrate the use of the .NET Framework 4.7 SDK documentation, which provides details regarding every namespace, type, and member within the base class libraries.

Accessing a Namespace Programmatically

It is worth reiterating that a namespace is nothing more than a convenient way for us mere humans to logically understand and organize related types. Consider again the System namespace. From your perspective, you can assume that System.Console represents a class named Console that is contained within a namespace called System. However, in the eyes of the .NET runtime, this is not so. The runtime engine sees only a single class named System.Console.

In C#, the using keyword simplifies the process of referencing types defined in a particular namespace. Here is how it works. Let's say you are interested in building a graphical desktop application using the WPF API. While learning the types each namespace contains takes study and experimentation, here are some possible candidates to reference in your program:

```
// Here are some possible namespaces used to build a WPF application.
using System;                    // General base class library types.
using System.Windows.Shapes;     // Graphical rendering types.
using System.Windows.Controls;   // Windows Forms GUI widget types.
using System.Data;               // General data-centric types.
using System.Data.SqlClient;     // MS SQL Server data-access types.
```

Once you have specified some number of namespaces (and set a reference to the assemblies that define them), you are free to create instances of the types they contain. For example, if you are interested in creating an instance of the Button class (defined in the System.Windows.Controls namespace), you can write the following:

```
// Explicitly list the namespaces used by this file.
using System;
using System.Windows.Controls;
```

```
class MyGUIBuilder
{
  public void BuildUI()
  {
    // Create a button control.
    Button btnOK = new Button();
    ...
  }
}
```

Because your code file is importing the System.Windows.Controls namespace, the compiler is able to resolve the Button class as a member of this namespace. If you did not import the System.Windows.Controls namespace, you would be issued a compiler error. However, you are free to declare variables using a *fully qualified name* as well.

```
// Not listing System.Windows.Controls namespace!
using System;

class MyGUIBuilder
{
  public void BuildUI()
  {
    // Using fully qualified name.
    System.Windows.Controls.Button btnOK =
      new System.Windows.Controls.Button();
    ...
  }
}
```

While defining a type using the fully qualified name provides greater readability, I think you'd agree that the C# using keyword reduces keystrokes. In this text, we will avoid the use of fully qualified names (unless there is a definite ambiguity to be resolved) and opt for the simplified approach of the C# using keyword.

However, always remember that the using keyword is simply a shorthand notation for specifying a type's fully qualified name, and either approach results in the same underlying CIL (given that CIL code always uses fully qualified names) and has no effect on performance or the size of the assembly.

Referencing External Assemblies

In addition to specifying a namespace via the C# using keyword, you need to tell the C# compiler the name of the assembly containing the actual CIL implementation for the referenced type. As mentioned, many core .NET namespaces are defined within mscorlib.dll. However, by way of example, the System.Drawing.Bitmap class is contained within a separate assembly named System.Drawing.dll. A vast majority of the .NET Framework assemblies are located under a specific directory termed the *global assembly cache* (GAC). On a Windows machine, this can be located by default under C:\Windows\Assembly\GAC, as shown in Figure 1-5.

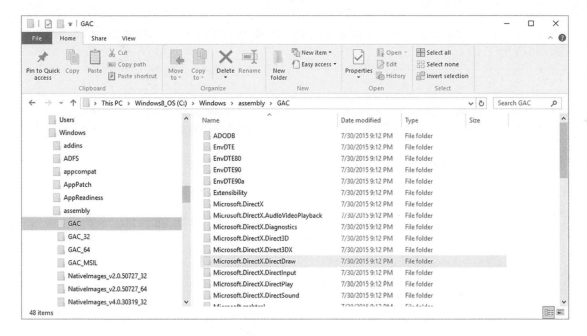

Figure 1-5. *Many .NET libraries reside in the GAC*

Depending on the development tool you are using to build your .NET applications, you will have various ways to inform the compiler which assemblies you want to include during the compilation cycle. You'll examine how to do so in Chapter 2, so I'll hold off on the details for now.

■ **Note** As you will see in Chapter 14, a Windows OS has multiple locations where framework libraries can be installed; however, this is generally encapsulated from the developer. On a non-Windows machine (such as macOS or Linux), the location of the GAC depends on the .NET distribution.

Exploring an Assembly Using ildasm.exe

If you are beginning to feel a tad overwhelmed at the thought of gaining mastery over every namespace in the .NET platform, just remember that what makes a namespace unique is that it contains types that are somehow *semantically related*. Therefore, if you have no need for a user interface beyond a simple console application, you can forget all about the desktop and web namespaces (among others). If you are building a painting application, the database namespaces are most likely of little concern. Like any new set of prefabricated code, you learn as you go.

The Intermediate Language Disassembler utility (`ildasm.exe`), which ships with the .NET Framework, allows you to load up any .NET assembly and investigate its contents, including the associated manifest, CIL code, and type metadata. This tool allows you to dive deeply into how their C# code maps to CIL and ultimately helps you understand the inner workings of the .NET platform. While you never *need* to use `ildasm.exe` to become a proficient .NET programmer, I highly recommend you fire up this tool from time to time to better understand how your C# code maps to runtime concepts.

■ **Note**   You can easily run `ildasm.exe` by opening a Visual Studio command prompt and typing **ildasm** followed by the Enter key.

After you launch `ildasm.exe`, proceed to the File ➤ Open menu command and navigate to an assembly you want to explore. By way of illustration, Figure 1-6 shows the `Calc.exe` assembly generated based on the `Calc.cs` file shown earlier in this chapter. `ildasm.exe` presents the structure of an assembly using a familiar tree-view format.

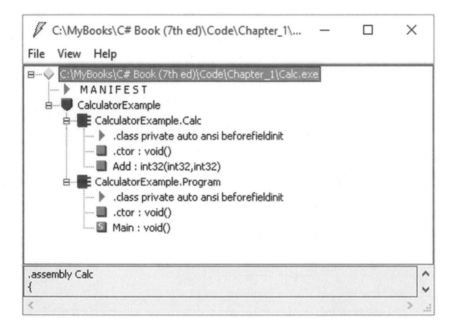

Figure 1-6. `ildasm.exe` allows you to see the CIL code, manifest, and metadata within a .NET assembly

Viewing CIL Code

In addition to showing the namespaces, types, and members contained in a given assembly, `ildasm.exe` allows you to view the CIL instructions for a given member. For example, if you were to double-click the `Main()` method of the `Program` class, a separate window would display the underlying CIL (see Figure 1-7).

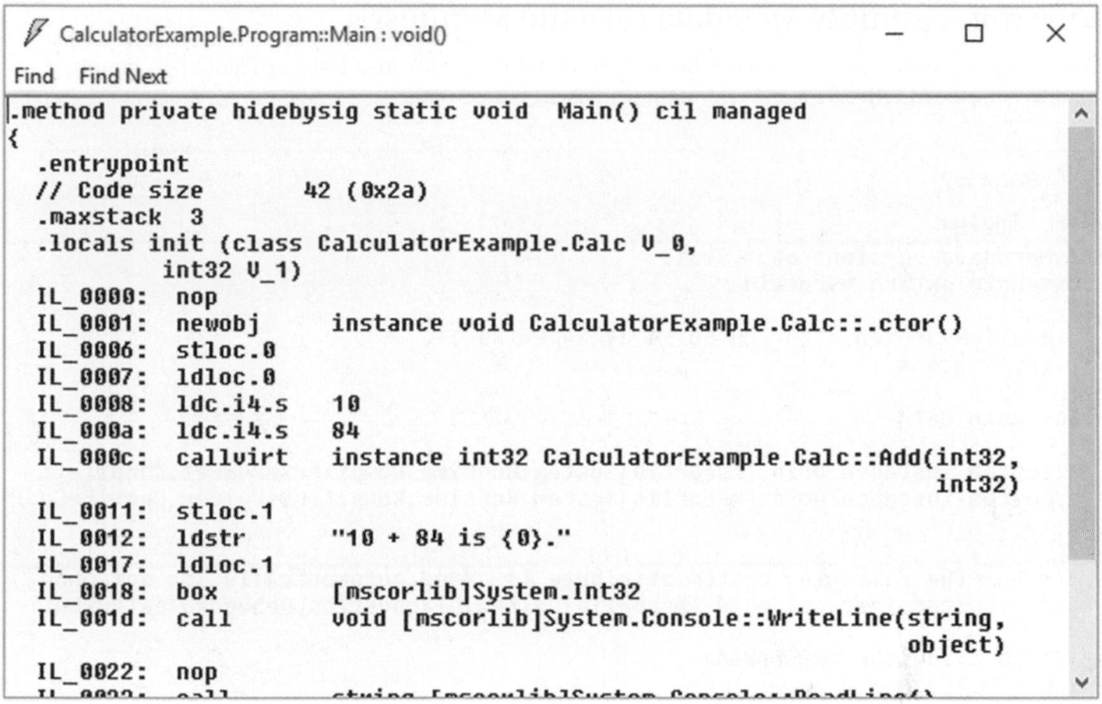

```
CalculatorExample.Program::Main : void()                      —    □    ✕
Find   Find Next
.method private hidebysig static void  Main() cil managed      ^
{
  .entrypoint
  // Code size        42 (0x2a)
  .maxstack  3
  .locals init (class CalculatorExample.Calc V_0,
           int32 V_1)
  IL_0000:  nop
  IL_0001:  newobj      instance void CalculatorExample.Calc::.ctor()
  IL_0006:  stloc.0
  IL_0007:  ldloc.0
  IL_0008:  ldc.i4.s    10
  IL_000a:  ldc.i4.s    84
  IL_000c:  callvirt     instance int32 CalculatorExample.Calc::Add(int32,
                                                                   int32)

  IL_0011:  stloc.1
  IL_0012:  ldstr       "10 + 84 is {0}."
  IL_0017:  ldloc.1
  IL_0018:  box         [mscorlib]System.Int32
  IL_001d:  call        void [mscorlib]System.Console::WriteLine(string,
                                                                 object)

  IL_0022:  nop
  IL_0023:  call        string [mscorlib]System.Console::ReadLine()    ⌄
```

Figure 1-7. *Viewing the underlying CIL*

Viewing Type Metadata

If you want to view the type metadata for the currently loaded assembly, press Ctrl+M. Figure 1-8 shows the metadata for the Calc.Add() method.

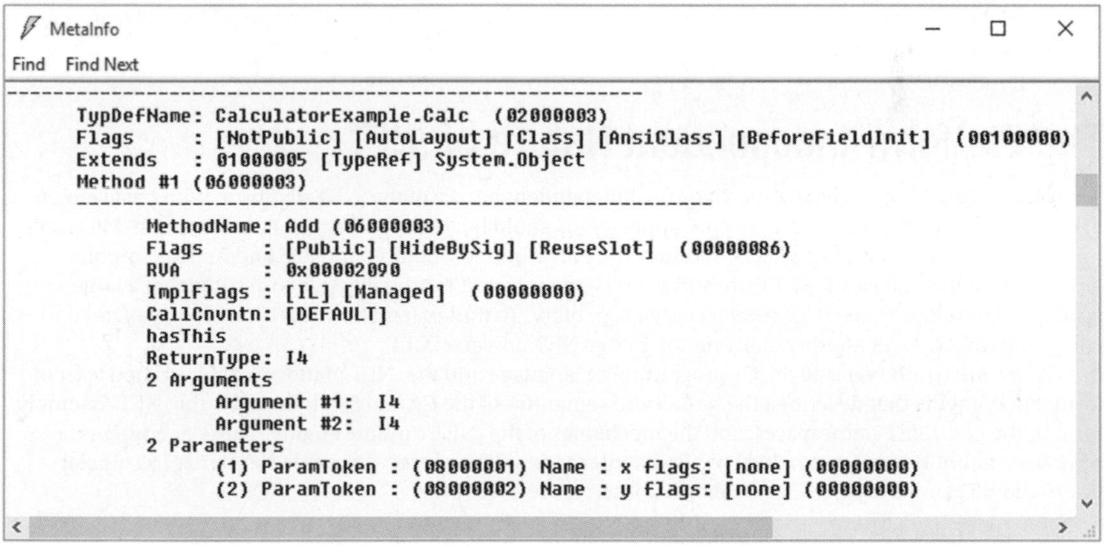

```
MetaInfo                                                      —    □    ✕
Find   Find Next
------------------------------------------------------------  ^
    TypDefName: CalculatorExample.Calc  (02000003)
    Flags     : [NotPublic] [AutoLayout] [Class] [AnsiClass] [BeforeFieldInit]  (00100000)
    Extends   : 01000005 [TypeRef] System.Object
    Method #1 (06000003)
    ------------------------------------------------------------
        MethodName: Add (06000003)
        Flags     : [Public] [HideBySig] [ReuseSlot]  (00000086)
        RVA       : 0x00002090
        ImplFlags : [IL] [Managed]  (00000000)
        CallCnvntn: [DEFAULT]
        hasThis
        ReturnType: I4
        2 Arguments
            Argument #1:  I4
            Argument #2:  I4
        2 Parameters
            (1) ParamToken : (08000001) Name : x flags: [none] (00000000)
            (2) ParamToken : (08000002) Name : y flags: [none] (00000000)   ⌄
<                                                                       >
```

Figure 1-8. *Viewing type metadata via ildasm.exe*

Viewing Assembly Metadata (aka the Manifest)

Finally, if you are interested in viewing the contents of the assembly's manifest (see Figure 1-9), simply double-click the MANIFEST icon in the main window of ildasm.exe.

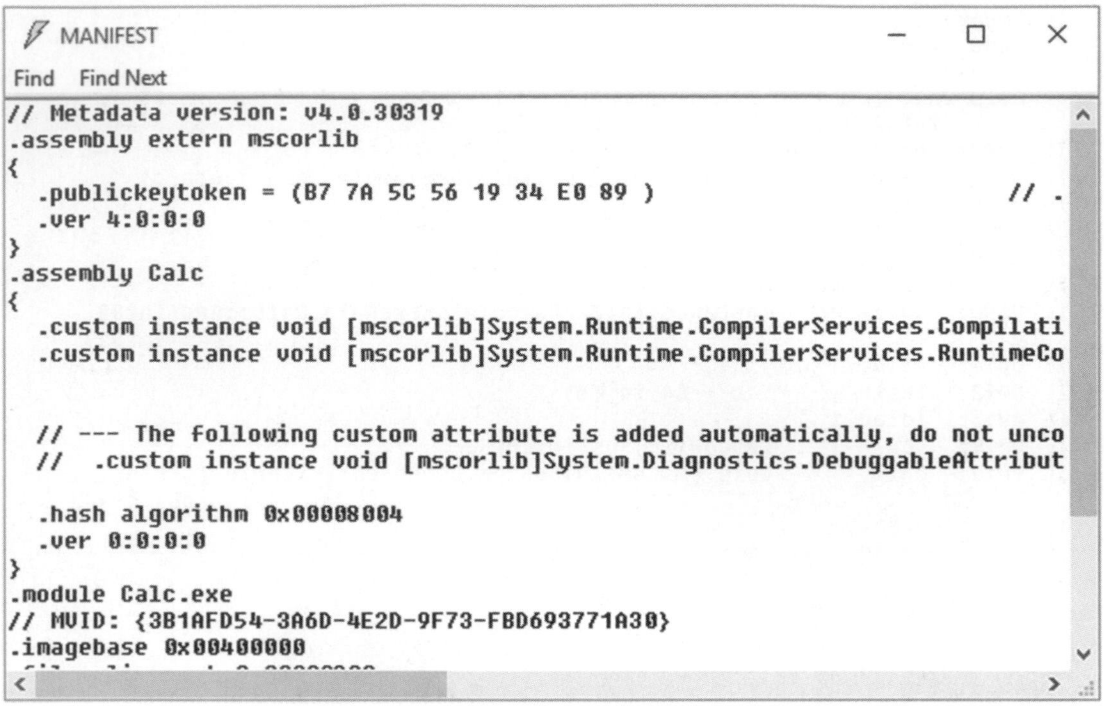

```
// Metadata version: v4.0.30319
.assembly extern mscorlib
{
  .publickeytoken = (B7 7A 5C 56 19 34 E0 89 )                              // .
  .ver 4:0:0:0
}
.assembly Calc
{
  .custom instance void [mscorlib]System.Runtime.CompilerServices.Compilati
  .custom instance void [mscorlib]System.Runtime.CompilerServices.RuntimeCo


  // --- The following custom attribute is added automatically, do not unco
  //   .custom instance void [mscorlib]System.Diagnostics.DebuggableAttribut

  .hash algorithm 0x00008004
  .ver 0:0:0:0
}
.module Calc.exe
// MVID: {3B1AFD54-3A6D-4E2D-9F73-FBD693771A30}
.imagebase 0x00400000
```

Figure 1-9. *Viewing manifest data via* ildasm.exe

To be sure, ildasm.exe has more options than shown here, and we will illustrate additional features of the tool where appropriate in the text.

The Platform-Independent Nature of .NET

Allow me to briefly comment on the platform-independent nature of the .NET platform. With past versions of .NET, it wasn't widely known that .NET applications could be developed and executed on non-Microsoft operating systems, including macOS, various Linux distributions, Solaris, and iOS and Android mobile devices. With the release of .NET Core and the related fanfare, it is probably safe to assume that a large number of developers are at least *aware* of the capability. To understand how this is possible, you need to come to terms with yet another abbreviation in the .NET universe: CLI.

When Microsoft released the C# programming language and the .NET platform, it also crafted a set of formal documents that described the syntax and semantics of the C# and CIL languages, the .NET assembly format, the core .NET namespaces, and the mechanics of the .NET runtime engine. These documents have been submitted to (and ratified by) Ecma International (www.ecma-international.org) as official international standards. The specifications of interest are as follows:

> *ECMA-334*: The C# Language Specification

> *ECMA-335*: The Common Language Infrastructure (CLI)

The importance of these documents becomes clear when you understand that they enable third parties to build distributions of the .NET platform for any number of operating systems and/or processors. ECMA-335 is the "meatier" of the two specifications, so much so that it has been broken into various partitions, including those shown in Table 1-4.

Table 1-4. *Partitions of the CLI*

Partitions of ECMA-335	Meaning in Life
Partition I: Concepts and Architecture	Describes the overall architecture of the CLI, including the rules of the CTS and CLS and the mechanics of the .NET runtime engine.
Partition II: Metadata Definition and Semantics	Describes the details of .NET metadata and the assembly format.
Partition III: CIL Instruction Set	Describes the syntax and semantics of CIL code.
Partition IV: Profiles and Libraries	Gives a high-level overview of the minimal and complete class libraries that must be supported by a .NET distribution.
Partition V: Binary Formats	Describes a standard way to interchange debugging information between CLI producers and consumers.
Partition VI: Annexes	Provides a collection of odds-and-ends details such as class library design guidelines and the implementation details of a CIL compiler.

Be aware that Partition IV (Profiles and Libraries) defines only a *minimal* set of namespaces that represent the core services expected by a CLI distribution (e.g., collections, console I/O, file I/O, threading, reflection, network access, core security needs, XML data manipulation). The CLI does *not* define namespaces that facilitate web development (ASP.NET), database access (ADO.NET), or desktop graphical user interface (GUI) application development (Windows Presentation Foundation or Windows Forms).

The good news, however, is that the alternative .NET distribution (termed Mono) extends the CLI libraries with Microsoft-compatible equivalents of ASP.NET implementations, ADO.NET implementations, and various desktop GUI implementations to provide full-featured, production-level development platforms. To date, there are three major implementations of the CLI beyond Microsoft's Windows-specific .NET platform. See Table 1-5.

Table 1-5. *Open Source .NET Distributions*

Distribution	Meaning in Life
The Mono project	The Mono project is an open source distribution of the CLI that targets various Linux distributions (e.g., SuSe, Fedora), macOS, iOS devices (iPad, iPhone), Android devices, and (surprise!) Windows.
Xamarin SDK	Xamarin grew from the Mono project and allows for developing cross-platform GUI applications for mobile devices. The SDK is open sourced, while the full Xamarin product is not.
.NET Core	In addition to the Windows-centric .NET Framework, Microsoft also supports a cross-platform version of .NET, which focuses on the construction of code libraries, data access, web services, and web applications.

The Mono Project

The Mono project is an excellent choice if you want to build .NET software that can run on a variety of operating systems. In addition to all the key .NET namespaces, Mono provides additional libraries to allow the construction of GUI-based desktop software, ASP.NET web applications, and software-targeting mobile devices (iPad, iPhone, and Android). You can download the Mono distribution from the following URL:

`www.mono-project.com/`

Out of the box, the Mono project consists of a number of command-line tools and all of the associated code libraries. However, as you will see in Chapter 2, there is a full-fledged graphical IDE typically used with Mono named Xamarin Studio. In fact, Microsoft Visual Studio projects can be loaded into Xamarin Studio projects, and vice versa. Again, you can find more information in Chapter 2, but you might want to check out the Xamarin web site for more details.

`http://xamarin.com/`

Xamarin

Xamarin descended from the Mono project and was created by many of the same engineers who created the Mono project. While the Mono project is still alive and well, ever since Xamarin was purchased by Microsoft and started shipping with Visual Studio 2017, Xamarin has become the default framework for creating cross-platform GUI applications, especially for mobile devices. The Xamarin SDK ships with all versions of Visual Studio 2017, and Visual Studio 2017 Enterprise license holders also get Xamarin Enterprise.

Microsoft .NET Core

The other major cross-platform distribution of .NET comes from Microsoft. Beginning in 2014, Microsoft announced an open source version of its full-scale (Windows-specific) .NET 4.7 Framework called .NET Core. The .NET Core distribution is *not* a complete carbon copy of the .NET 4.7 Framework. Rather, .NET Core focuses on the construction of ASP.NET web applications that can run on Linux, macOS, and Windows. Thus, you can essentially consider .NET Core to be a subset of the full .NET Framework. You can find a good article that compares and contrasts the full .NET Framework to the .NET Core framework on the MSDN .NET Blog site. Here is a direct link (but if this changes, just do a web search for .*NET Core is Open Source*):

`http://blogs.msdn.com/b/dotnet/archive/2014/11/12/net-core-is-open-source.aspx`

As luck would have it, all the features of C#, as well as a number of key libraries, are included in .NET Core. Therefore, a majority of this book will map directly to this distribution. Recall, though, that .NET Core is focused on building RESTful services and web applications and does not provide implementations of desktop GUI APIs (such as WPF or Windows Forms). If you need to build cross-platform GUI applications, then Xamarin is the better choice.

.NET Core is covered in detail in Part IX of this book, including the philosophy of .NET Core, Entity Framework Core, ASP.NET Core services, and ASP.NET Core web applications.

It is also worth noting that Microsoft has also released a free, lightweight, and cross-platform code editor to help support development with .NET Core. This editor is simply named Visual Studio Code. While it is certainly not as full featured as Microsoft Visual Studio or Xamarin Studio, it is a useful tool to edit C# code in a cross-platform manner. While this text will not use Visual Studio Code, you might want to learn more at the following web site:

```
https://code.visualstudio.com/
```

Summary

The point of this chapter was to lay out the conceptual framework necessary for the remainder of this book. I began by examining a number of limitations and complexities found within the technologies prior to .NET and followed up with an overview of how .NET and C# attempt to simplify the current state of affairs.

.NET basically boils down to a runtime execution engine (`mscoree.dll`) and base class library (`mscorlib.dll` and associates). The Common Language Runtime is able to host any .NET binary (aka assembly) that abides by the rules of managed code. As you saw, assemblies contain CIL instructions (in addition to type metadata and the assembly manifest) that are compiled to platform-specific instructions using a just-in-time compiler. In addition, you explored the role of the Common Language Specification and Common Type System. This was followed by an examination of the `ildasm.exe` object browsing tool.

In the next chapter, you will take a tour of the common integrated development environments you can use when you build your C# programming projects. You will be happy to know that in this book, you will use completely free (and feature-rich) IDEs, so you can start exploring the .NET universe with no money down.

CHAPTER 2

■ ■ ■

Building C# Applications

As a C# programmer, you can choose from among numerous tools to build .NET applications. The tool (or tools) you select will be based primarily on three factors: any associated costs, the OS you are using to develop the software, and the computing platforms you are targeting. The point of this chapter is to provide a survey of the most common integrated development environments (IDEs) that support the C# language. Do understand that this chapter will *not* go over every single detail of each IDE; it will give you enough information to select your programming environment as you work through this text and give you a foundation to build on.

The first part of this chapter will examine a set of IDEs from Microsoft that enable development of .NET applications on a Windows operating system (7, 8.*x*, and 10). As you will see, some of these IDEs can be used to build Windows-centric applications only, while others support the construction of C# apps for alternative operating systems and devices (such as macOS, Linux, or Android). The latter part of this chapter will then examine some IDEs that can *run* on a non-Windows OS. This enables developers to build C# programs using Apple computers as well as Linux distributions.

■ **Note**   This chapter will give you an overview of a good number of IDEs. However, this book will assume you are using the (completely free) Visual Studio 2017 Community IDE. If you want to build your applications on a different OS (macOS or Linux), this chapter will guide you in the right direction; however, your IDE will differ from the various screenshots in this text.

Building .NET Applications on Windows

As you will see over the course of this chapter, you can choose from a variety of IDEs to build C# applications; some come from Microsoft, and others come from third-party (many of which are open source) vendors. Now, despite what you might be thinking, many Microsoft IDEs are completely free. Thus, if your primary interest is to build .NET software on the Windows operating system (7, 8.*x*, or 10), you will find the following major options:

- Visual Studio Community

- Visual Studio Professional

- Visual Studio Enterprise

The Express editions have been removed, leaving three versions of Visual Studio 2017. The Community and Professional editions are *essentially* the same, with the main technical difference being that Professional has CodeLens and Community does not. The more significant difference is in the licensing model.

© Andrew Troelsen and Philip Japikse 2017

A. Troelsen and P. Japikse, *Pro C# 7*, https://doi.org/10.1007/978-1-4842-3018-3_2

Community is licensed for open source, academic, and small-business uses. Professional is licensed for enterprise development. As one would expect, the Enterprise edition has many additional features above the Professional edition.

■ **Note**   For specific licensing details, please go to `https://www.visualstudio.com`. Licensing Microsoft products can be complex, and this book does not cover the details. For the purposes of writing (and following along with) this book, Community is legal to use.

Each IDE ships with sophisticated code editors, key database designers, integrated visual debuggers, GUI designers for desktop and web applications, and so forth. Since they all share a common core set of features, the good news is that it is easy to move between them and feel quite comfortable with their basic operation.

Installing Visual Studio 2017

Before using Visual Studio 2017 to develop, execute, and debug C# applications, you need to get it installed. The installation experience is dramatically different from previous versions and is worth discussing in more detail.

■ **Note**   You can download Visual Studio 2017 Community from `https://www.visualstudio.com/downloads`.

The Visual Studio 2017 installation process is now broken down into application-type workloads. This allows you to install just the components you need for the work you plan on doing. For example, if you are going to build web applications, you would install the "ASP.NET and web development" workload.

Another (extremely) significant change is that Visual Studio 2017 supports true side-by-side installation. Note that I am not referring to just previous versions of Visual Studio but to Visual Studio 2017 itself! On my main workstation, I have Visual Studio 2017 Enterprise installed. For this book, I will be using Visual Studio Community. With Visual Studio 2015 (and the previous edition of this book), I had to use a different machine than the one I use to service clients. Now, it's all on the same machine. If you have Professional or Enterprise supplied by your employer, you can still install the Community edition to work on the open source projects (or the code in this book).

When you launch the installer for Visual Studio 2017 Community, you are presented with the screen shown in Figure 2-1. This screen has all of the workloads available, the option to select individual components, and a summary on the right side showing what has been selected. Notice the red warning at the bottom stating "A nickname must be provided to disambiguate this install." This is because I have other installs of Visual Studio 2017 on my machine. If this is your first install, you won't see this.

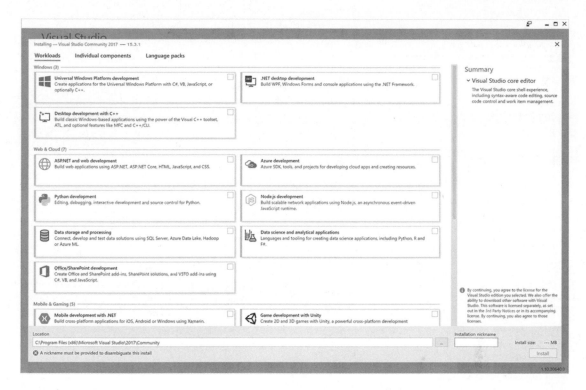

Figure 2-1. *The new Visual Studio installer*

For this book, you will want to install the following workloads:

- .NET desktop development

- ASP.NET and web development

- Data storage and processing

- .NET Core cross-platform development

I also had to add an installation nickname, ProC#. These selections are shown in Figure 2-2.

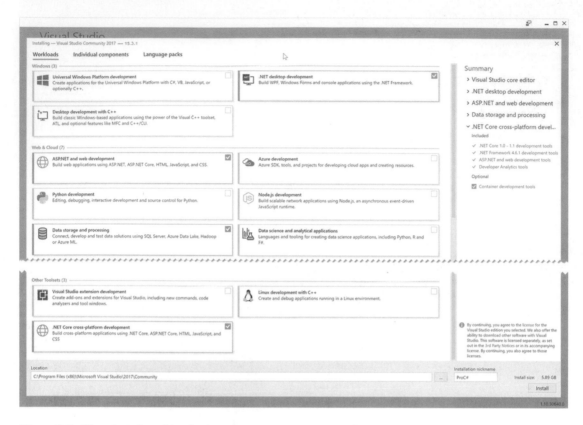

Figure 2-2. *The selected workloads*

Select Individual Components from the top of the installer, and select the following additional items:

- .NET Core runtime
- .NET Framework 4.6.2 SDK
- .NET Framework 4.6.2 targeting pack
- .NET Framework 4.7 SDK
- .NET Framework 4.7 targeting pack
- Class Designer
- Testing tools core features
- Visual Studio Tools for Office (VSTO)

Once you have all of them selected, click Install. This will provide you with everything you need to work through the examples in this book, including the new section on .NET Core.

Taking Visual Studio 2017 for a Test-Drive

Visual Studio 2017 is a one-stop shop for software development with the .NET platform and C#. Let's take a quick look at Visual Studio by building a simple Windows console application.

Building .NET Applications

To get your feet wet, let's take some time to build a simple C# application and keep in mind that the topics illustrated here will be useful for all editions of Visual Studio.

The New Project Dialog Box and C# Code Editor

Now that you have installed Visual Studio, activate the File ➤ New Project menu option. As you can see in Figure 2-3, this IDE has support for console apps, WPF/Windows Forms apps, Windows services, and many more. To start, create a new C# Console Application project named SimpleCSharpConsoleApp, making sure to change the Framework version to 4.7.

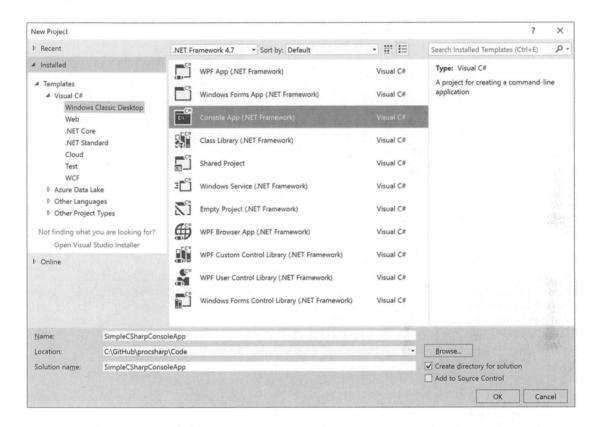

Figure 2-3. *The New Project dialog box*

As you can see from Figure 2-3, Visual Studio is capable of creating a variety of application types, including Windows Desktop, Web, .NET Core, and many more. These will be covered throughout this book.

■ **Note** If you don't see an option for .NET Framework 4.7, you will need to install the 4.7 Developer Pack, available at https://www.microsoft.com/en-us/download/details.aspx?id=55168. You can also click the "Install other frameworks..." option in drop-down list to get the Developer Pack.

Once the project has been created, you will see that the initial C# code file (named Program.cs) has been opened in the code editor. Add the following C# code to your Main() method. You'll notice as you type that IntelliSense will kick in as you apply the dot operator.

```
static void Main(string[] args)
{
  // Set up Console UI (CUI)
  Console.Title = "My Rocking App";
  Console.ForegroundColor = ConsoleColor.Yellow;
  Console.BackgroundColor = ConsoleColor.Blue;
  Console.WriteLine("***********************************");
  Console.WriteLine("***** Welcome to My Rocking App *****");
  Console.WriteLine("***********************************");
  Console.BackgroundColor = ConsoleColor.Black;

  // Wait for Enter key to be pressed.
  Console.ReadLine();
}
```

Here, you are using the Console class defined in the System namespace. Because the System namespace has been automatically included at the top of your file via a using statement, you have no need to qualify the namespace before the class name (e.g., System.Console.WriteLine()). This program does not do anything too interesting; however, note the final call to Console.ReadLine(). This is in place simply to ensure the user must press a key to terminate the application. If you did not do this, the program would disappear almost instantly when debugging the program!

Using C# 7.1 Features

At the time of this writing, Visual Studio doesn't have direct support for creating C# 7.1 projects. To use the new features, there are two options. The first is to update the project file manually, and the second is to let the Visual Studio help (in the form of the quick-fix light bulb) update your project file for you. While the latter sounds easiest, it's not currently reliable, but I am certain it will get better in upcoming Visual Studio releases.

To update the project file, open the SimpleCSharpConsoleApp.csproj file in any text editor (except Visual Studio), and update the Debug and Release property groups to the following:

```
<PropertyGroup Condition=" '$(Configuration)|$(Platform)' == 'Debug|AnyCPU' ">
  <PlatformTarget>AnyCPU</PlatformTarget>
  <DebugSymbols>true</DebugSymbols>
  <DebugType>full</DebugType>
  <Optimize>false</Optimize>
  <OutputPath>bin\Debug\</OutputPath>
  <DefineConstants>DEBUG;TRACE</DefineConstants>
  <ErrorReport>prompt</ErrorReport>
  <WarningLevel>4</WarningLevel>
  <LangVersion>7.1</LangVersion>
</PropertyGroup>
<PropertyGroup Condition=" '$(Configuration)|$(Platform)' == 'Release|AnyCPU' ">
  <PlatformTarget>AnyCPU</PlatformTarget>
  <DebugType>pdbonly</DebugType>
  <Optimize>true</Optimize>
```

```
    <OutputPath>bin\Release\</OutputPath>
    <DefineConstants>TRACE</DefineConstants>
    <ErrorReport>prompt</ErrorReport>
    <WarningLevel>4</WarningLevel>
    <LangVersion>7.1</LangVersion>
  </PropertyGroup>
```

Running and Debugging Your Project

Now, to run your program and see the output, you can simply press the Ctrl+F5 keyboard command (which is also accessed from the Debug ➤ Start Without Debugging menu option). Once you do, you will see a Windows console window pop on the screen with your custom (and colorful) message. Be aware that when you "run" your program, you bypass the integrated debugger.

If you need to debug your code (which will certainly be important when building larger programs), your first step is to set breakpoints at the code statement you want to examine. Although there isn't much code in this example, set a breakpoint by clicking the leftmost gray bar of the code editor (note that breakpoints are marked with a red dot icon; see Figure 2-4).

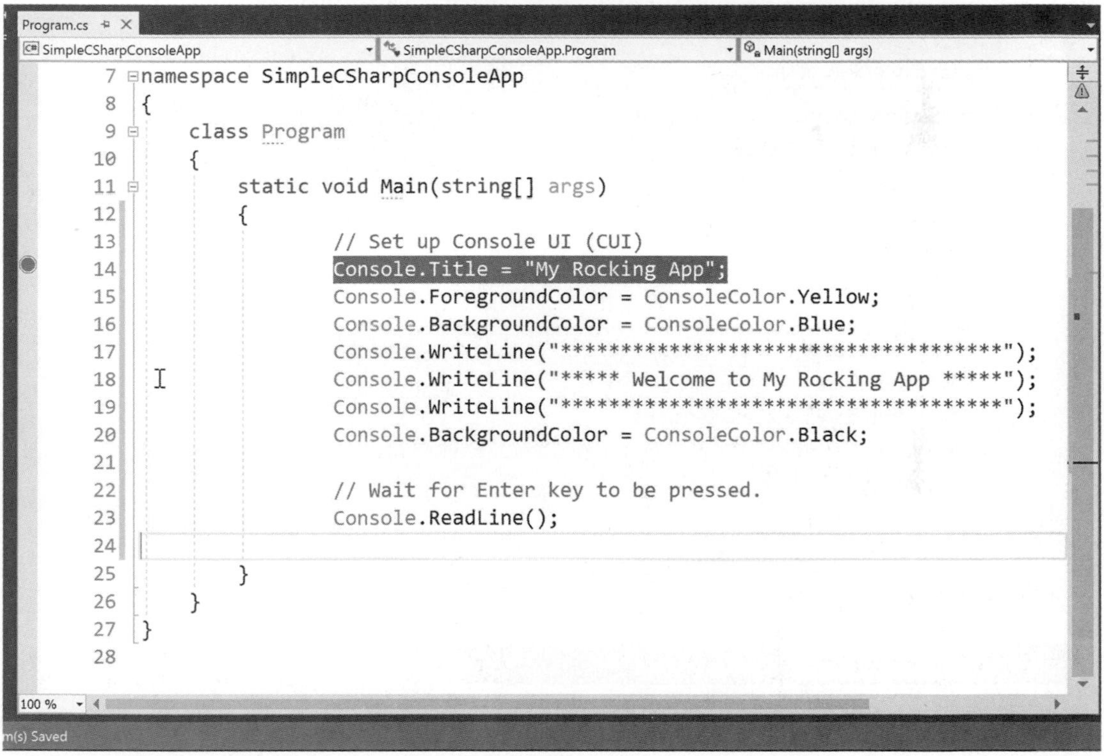

Figure 2-4. *Setting breakpoints*

If you now press the F5 key (or use the Debug ➤ Start Debugging menu option or click the green arrow with Start next to it in the toolbar), your program will halt at each breakpoint. As you would expect, you can interact with the debugger using the various toolbar buttons and menu options of the IDE. Once you have evaluated all breakpoints, the application will eventually terminate once Main() has completed.

■ **Note**   Microsoft IDEs have sophisticated debuggers, and you will learn about various techniques over the chapters to come. For now, be aware that when you are in a debugging session, a large number of useful options will appear under the Debug menu. Take a moment to verify this for yourself.

Solution Explorer

If you look at the right of the IDE, you will see a window named Solution Explorer, which shows you a few important things. First, notice that the IDE has created a solution with a single project (see Figure 2-5). This can be confusing at first, as they both have been given the same name (SimpleCSharpConsoleApp). The idea here is that a "solution" can contain multiple projects that all work together. For example, your solution might include three class libraries, one WPF application, and one WCF web service. The earlier chapters of this book will always have a single project; however, when you build some more complex examples, you'll see how to add new projects to your initial solution space.

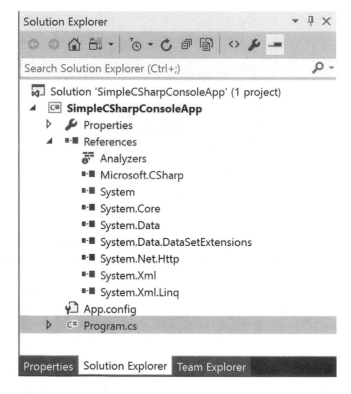

Figure 2-5. *Solution Explorer*

■ **Note**   Be aware that when you select the topmost solution in the Solution Explorer window, the IDE's menu system will show you a different set of choices than when you select a project. If you ever find yourself wondering where a certain menu item has disappeared to, double-check you did not accidentally select the wrong node.

You will also notice a References icon. You can use this node when your application needs to reference additional .NET libraries beyond what are included for a project type by default. Because you have created a C# Console Application project, you will notice a number of libraries have been automatically added such as System.dll, System.Core.dll, System.Data.dll, and so forth (note the items listed under the References node don't show the .dll file extension). You will see how to add libraries to a project shortly.

■ **Note**   Recall from Chapter 1 that all .NET projects have access to a foundational library named mscorlib.dll. This library is so necessary that it is not even listed explicitly in Solution Explorer.

The Object Browser

If you were to right-click any library under the References node and select View in Object Browser, you will open the integrated Object Browser (you can also open this using the View menu). Using this tool, you can see the various namespaces in an assembly, the types in a namespace, and the members of each type. Figure 2-6 shows some namespaces of the always-present mscorlib.dll assembly.

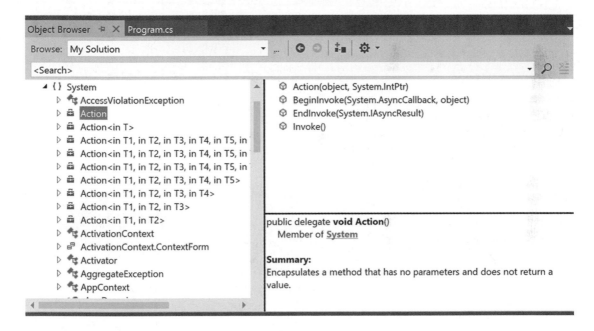

Figure 2-6.   *The Object Browser*

This tool can be useful when you want to see the internal organization of a .NET library as well as when you want to get a brief description of a given item. Also notice the <Search> bar at the top of the window. This can be helpful when you know the name of a type you want to use but have no idea where it might be located. On a related note, keep in mind that the search feature will search only the libraries used in your current solution by default (you can search the entire .NET Framework by changing the selection in the Browse drop-down box).

Referencing Additional Assemblies

To continue your test, let's add an assembly (aka code library) not automatically included in a Console Application project. To do so, right-click the References tab of Solution Explorer and select Add Reference (or select the Project ➤ Add Reference menu option). From the resulting dialog box, find a library named System.Windows.Forms.dll (again, you won't see the file extension here) and check it off (Figure 2-7).

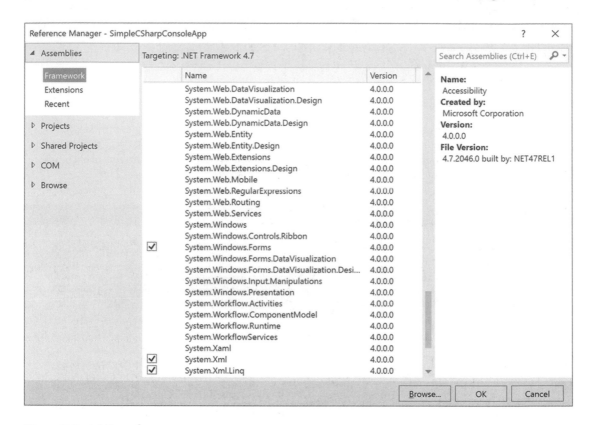

Figure 2-7. *Adding references*

Once you click the OK button, this new library is added to your reference set (you'll see it listed under the References node). As explained in Chapter 1, however, referencing a library is only the first step. To use the types in a given C# code file, you need to define a using statement. Add the following line to the using directives in your code file:

```
using System.Windows.Forms;
```

Then add the following line of code directly after the call to Console.ReadLine() in your Main() method:

```
MessageBox.Show("All done!");
```

When you run or debug your program once again, you will find a simple message box appears before the program terminates.

Viewing Project Properties

Next, notice an icon named Properties within Solution Explorer. When you double-click this item, you are presented with a sophisticated project configuration editor. For example, in Figure 2-8, notice how you can change the version of the .NET Framework you are targeting for the solution.

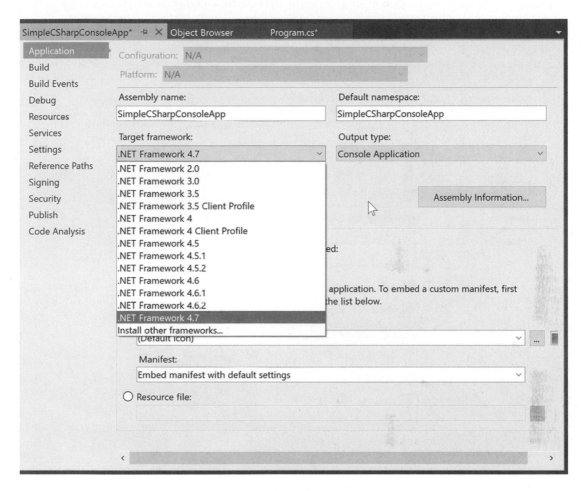

Figure 2-8. *The Project Properties window*

You will see various aspects of the Project Properties window as you progress through this book. However, if you take some time to poke around, you will see that you can establish various security settings, strongly name your assembly (see Chapter 14), deploy your application, insert application resources, and configure pre- and post-build events.

The Visual Class Designer

Visual Studio also gives you the ability to design classes and other types (such as interfaces or delegates) in a visual manner. The Class Designer utility allows you to view and modify the relationships of the types (classes, interfaces, structures, enumerations, and delegates) in your project. Using this tool, you are able to visually add (or remove) members to (or from) a type and have your modifications reflected in the corresponding C# file. Also, as you modify a given C# file, changes are reflected in the class diagram.

To access the visual type designer tools, the first step is to insert a new class diagram file. To do so, activate the Project ➤ Add New Item menu option and locate the Class Diagram type (Figure 2-9).

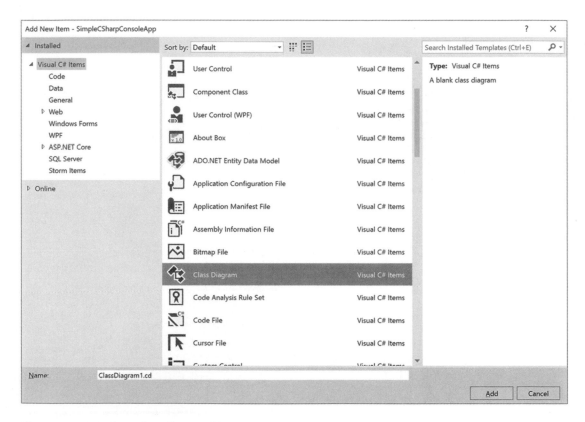

Figure 2-9. *Inserting a class diagram file into the current project*

Initially, the designer will be empty; however, you can drag and drop files from your Solution Explorer window on the surface. For example, once you drag `Program.cs` onto the designer, you will find a visual representation of the `Program` class. If you click the arrow icon for a given type, you can show or hide the type's members (see Figure 2-10).

Figure 2-10. *The Class Diagram viewer*

■ **Note**   Using the Class Designer toolbar, you can fine-tune the display options of the designer surface.

The Class Designer utility works in conjunction with two other aspects of Visual Studio: the Class Details window (activated using the View ➤ Other Windows menu) and the Class Designer Toolbox (activated using the View ➤ Toolbox menu item). The Class Details window not only shows you the details of the currently selected item in the diagram but also allows you to modify existing members and insert new members on the fly (see Figure 2-11).

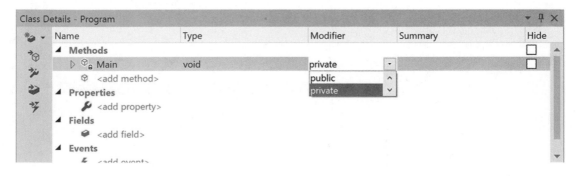

Figure 2-11. *The Class Details window*

The Class Designer Toolbox, which can also be activated using the View menu, allows you to insert new types (and create relationships between these types) into your project visually (see Figure 2-12). (Be aware you must have a class diagram as the active window to view this toolbox.) As you do so, the IDE automatically creates new C# type definitions in the background.

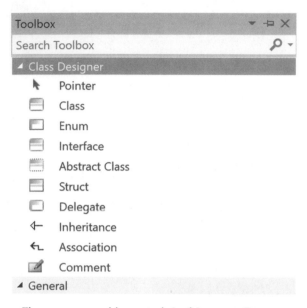

Figure 2-12. *The Class Designer Toolbox*

By way of example, drag a new class from the Class Designer Toolbox onto your Class Designer. Name this class Car in the resulting dialog box. This will result in the creation of a new C# file named Car.cs that is automatically added to your project. Now, using the Class Details window, add a public string field named PetName (see Figure 2-13).

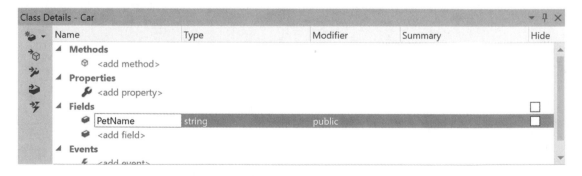

Figure 2-13. *Adding a field with the Class Details window*

If you now look at the C# definition of the Car class, you will see it has been updated accordingly (minus the additional code comments shown here).

```csharp
public class Car
{
    // Public data is typically a bad idea; however,
    // it keeps this example simple.
    public string PetName;
}
```

Now, activate the designer file once again and drag another new class onto the designer and name it SportsCar. Select the Inheritance icon from the Class Designer Toolbox and click the top of the SportsCar icon. Next, click the mouse on top of the Car class icon. If you performed these steps correctly, you have just derived the SportsCar class from Car (see Figure 2-14).

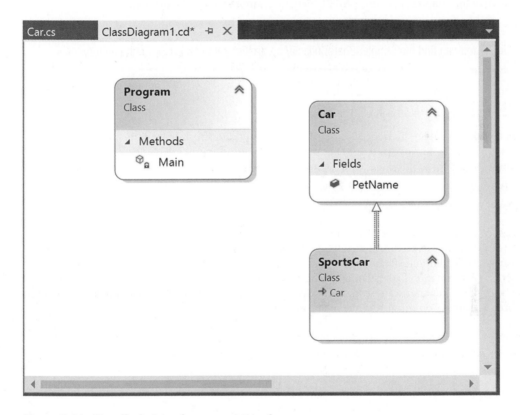

Figure 2-14. *Visually deriving from an existing class*

■ **Note**   The concept of inheritance will be fully examined in Chapter 6.

To complete this example, update the generated `SportsCar` class with a public method named `GetPetName()`, authored as follows:

```
public class SportsCar : Car
{
   public string GetPetName()
   {
     PetName = "Fred";
     return PetName;
   }
}
```

As you would expect, the visual type designer is one of the many features of Visual Studio Community. As mentioned earlier, this edition of the book will assume you are using Visual Studio Community as your IDE of choice. Over the chapters to come, you will learn many more features of this tool.

■ **Source Code**   You can find the SimpleCSharpConsoleApp project in the Chapter 2 subdirectory.

Visual Studio 2017 Professional

As mentioned earlier, the main difference between Community and Professional editions is the allowable usage scenarios. If you are currently employed as a software engineer, the chances are good your company has purchased a copy of this edition for you as your tool of choice.

Visual Studio 2017 Enterprise

To wrap up your examination of the Visual Studio editions that run on Windows, let's take a quick look at Visual Studio 2017 Enterprise. Visual Studio 2017 Enterprise has all the same features found in Visual Studio Professional, as well as additional features geared toward corporate-level collaborative development and full support for cross-platform mobile development with Xamarin.

I won't be saying much more about Visual Studio 2017 Enterprise edition. For the purposes of this book, any of the three versions (Community, Professional, and Enterprise) will work.

■ **Note**   You can find a side-by-side comparison of Community vs. Professional vs. Enterprise at https://www.visualstudio.com/vs/compare/.

The .NET Framework Documentation System

The final aspect of Visual Studio you *must* be comfortable with from the outset is the fully integrated help system. The .NET Framework documentation is extremely good, very readable, and full of useful information. Given the huge number of predefined .NET types (which number well into the thousands), you must be willing to roll up your sleeves and dig into the provided documentation. If you resist, you are doomed to a long, frustrating, and painful existence as a .NET developer.

You can view the .NET Framework SDK documentation at the following web address:

```
https://docs.microsoft.com/en-us/dotnet/
```

■ **Note**   It would not be surprising if Microsoft someday changes the location of the online .NET Framework Class Library documentation. If this is the case, a web search for the same topic (.*NET Framework Class Library documentation*) should quickly help you find the current location.

Once you are on this main page, click "Switch to the Library TOC view." This will change the page to a view that is easier to navigate. Locate the .NET Development node in the TOC, and click the arrow to expand the TOC. Next, click the arrow next to the .NET Framework 4.7, 4.6, and 4.5 node. Finally, click the ".NET Framework class library" entry. At this point, you can use the tree navigation window to view each namespace, type, and member of the platform. See Figure 2-15 for an example of viewing the types of the System namespace.

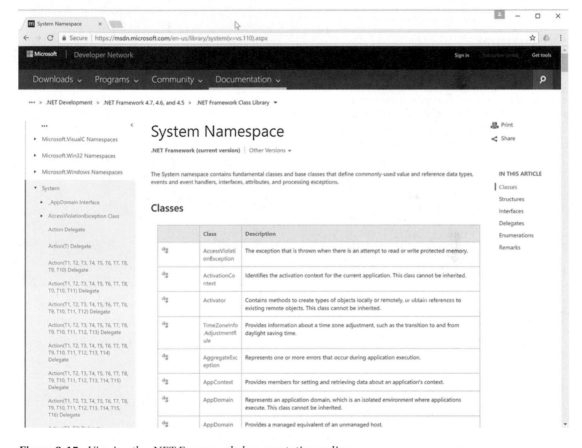

Figure 2-15. *Viewing the .NET Framework documentation online*

■ **Note**   At the risk of sounding like a broken record, I can't emphasize enough how important it is that you learn to use the .NET Framework SDK documentation. No book, no matter how lengthy, can cover every aspect of the .NET platform. Make sure you take some time to get comfortable using the help system—you'll thank yourself later.

Building.NET Applications on a Non-Windows OS

There are several options for building .NET applications on non-Windows operating systems. In addition to Xamarin Studio, there are also Visual Studio for the Mac and Visual Studio Code (which also runs on Linux). The types of applications that can be built with these development environments are limited to applications that are being developed either using .NET Core (Visual Studio Code and Visual Studio for the Mac) or for mobile (Visual Studio for the Mac, Xamarin Studio).

That is all I will mention about the non-Windows development tools in this book. But rest assured that Microsoft is embracing all developers, not just developers who own Windows-based computers.

Summary

As you can see, you have many new toys at your disposal! The point of this chapter was to provide you with a tour of the major programming tools a C# programmer may leverage during the development process. As mentioned, if you are interested only in building .NET applications on a Windows development machine, your best bet is to download Visual Studio Community. As also mentioned, this edition of the book will use this particular IDE going forward. Thus, the forthcoming screenshots, menu options, and visual designers will all assume you are using Visual Studio Community.

If you want to build .NET Core applications or cross-platform mobile application on a non-Windows OS, then Visual Studio for the Mac, Visual Studio Code, or Xamarin Studio will be your best choice.

■ ■ ■

PART II

Core C# Programing

CHAPTER 3

■ ■ ■

Core C# Programming Constructs, Part I

This chapter begins your formal investigation of the C# programming language by presenting a number of bite-sized, stand-alone topics you must be comfortable with as you explore the .NET Framework. The first order of business is to understand how to build your program's *application object* and to examine the composition of an executable program's entry point: the Main() method. Next, you will investigate the fundamental C# data types (and their equivalent types in the System namespace) including an examination of the System.String and System.Text.StringBuilder classes.

After you know the details of the fundamental .NET data types, you will then examine a number of data type conversion techniques, including narrowing operations, widening operations, and the use of the checked and unchecked keywords.

This chapter will also examine the role of the C# var keyword, which allows you to *implicitly* define a local variable. As you will see later in this book, implicit typing is extremely helpful, if not occasionally mandatory, when working with the LINQ technology set. You will wrap up this chapter by quickly examining the C# keywords and operators that allow you to control the flow of an application using various looping and decision constructs.

The Anatomy of a Simple C# Program

C# demands that all program logic be contained within a type definition (recall from Chapter 1 that *type* is a general term referring to a member of the set {class, interface, structure, enumeration, delegate}). Unlike many other languages, in C# it is not possible to create global functions or global points of data. Rather, all data members and all methods must be contained within a type definition. To get the ball rolling, create a new Console Application project named SimpleCSharpApp. You might agree that the code within the initial Program.cs file is rather uneventful.

```
using System;
using System.Collections.Generic;
using System.Linq;
using System.Text;
using System.Threading.Tasks;
```

© Andrew Troelsen and Philip Japikse 2017
A. Troelsen and P. Japikse, *Pro C# 7*, https://doi.org/10.1007/978-1-4842-3018-3_3

```
namespace SimpleCSharpApp
{
  class Program
  {
    static void Main(string[] args)
    {
    }
  }
}
```

Given this, update the Main() method of your Program class with the following code statements:

```
class Program
{
  static void Main(string[] args)
  {
    // Display a simple message to the user.
    Console.WriteLine("***** My First C# App *****");
    Console.WriteLine("Hello World!");
    Console.WriteLine();

    // Wait for Enter key to be pressed before shutting down.
    Console.ReadLine();
  }
}
```

■ **Note**   C# is a case-sensitive programming language. Therefore, *Main* is not the same as *main*, and *Readline* is not the same as *ReadLine*. Be aware that all C# keywords are lowercase (e.g., public, lock, class, dynamic), while namespaces, types, and member names begin (by convention) with an initial capital letter and have capitalized the first letter of any embedded words (e.g., Console.WriteLine, System.Windows. MessageBox, System.Data.SqlClient). As a rule of thumb, whenever you receive a compiler error regarding "undefined symbols," be sure to check your spelling and casing first!

The previous code contains a definition for a class type that supports a single method named Main(). By default, Visual Studio names the class defining Main() Program; however, you are free to change this if you so choose. Every executable C# application (console program, Windows desktop program, or Windows service) must contain a class defining a Main() method, which is used to signify the entry point of the application.

Formally speaking, the class that defines the Main() method is termed the *application object*. While it is possible for a single executable application to have more than one application object (which can be useful when performing unit tests), you must inform the compiler which Main() method should be used as the entry point via the /main option of the command-line compiler or via the Startup Object drop- down list box, located on the Application tab of the Visual Studio project properties window (see Chapter 2).

Note that the signature of Main() is adorned with the static keyword, which will be examined in detail in Chapter 5. For the time being, simply understand that static members are scoped to the class level (rather than the object level) and can thus be invoked without the need to first create a new class instance.

In addition to the static keyword, this Main() method has a single parameter, which happens to be an array of strings (string[] args). Although you are not currently bothering to process this array, this parameter may contain any number of incoming command-line arguments (you'll see how to access them momentarily). Finally, this Main() method has been set up with a void return value, meaning you do not explicitly define a return value using the return keyword before exiting the method scope.

The logic of Program is within Main(). Here, you make use of the Console class, which is defined within the System namespace. Among its set of members is the static WriteLine(), which, as you might assume, sends a text string and carriage return to the standard output. You also make a call to Console.ReadLine() to ensure the command prompt launched by the Visual Studio IDE remains visible during a debugging session until you press the Enter key. (If you did not add this line, your application would terminate immediately during a debugging session and you could not read the output!) You will learn more about the System. Console class shortly.

Variations on the Main( ) Method

By default, Visual Studio will generate a Main() method that has a void return value and an array of string types as the single input parameter. This is not the only possible form of Main(), however. It is permissible to construct your application's entry point using any of the following signatures (assuming it is contained within a C# class or structure definition):

```
// int return type, array of strings as the parameter.
static int Main(string[] args)
{
  // Must return a value before exiting!
  return 0;
}

// No return type, no parameters.
static void Main()
{
}

// int return type, no parameters.
static int Main()
{
  // Must return a value before exiting!
  return 0;
}
```

■ **Note**　The Main() method may also be defined as public as opposed to private, which is assumed if you do not supply a specific access modifier. Visual Studio automatically defines a program's Main() method as implicitly private.

Obviously, your choice of how to construct Main() will be based on two questions. First, do you want to return a value to the system when Main() has completed and your program terminates? If so, you need to return an int data type rather than void. Second, do you need to process any user-supplied, command-line parameters? If so, they will be stored in the array of strings. Let's examine all of the options in more detail.

Async Main Methods (New)

With the release of C# 7.1, the Main() method can now be asynchronous. Async programming is covered in Chapter 19, but for now realize there are four additional signatures.

```
static Task Main()
static Task<int> Main()
static Task Main(string[])
static Task<int> Main(string[])
```

These will be covered in greater detail in Chapter 19.

Specifying an Application Error Code

While a vast majority of your Main() methods will return void as the return value, the ability to return an int from Main() keeps C# consistent with other C-based languages. By convention, returning the value 0 indicates the program has terminated successfully, while another value (such as -1) represents an error condition (be aware that the value 0 is automatically returned, even if you construct a Main() method prototyped to return void).

On the Windows operating system, an application's return value is stored within a system environment variable named %ERRORLEVEL%. If you were to create an application that programmatically launches another executable (a topic examined in Chapter 18), you can obtain the value of %ERRORLEVEL% using the static System.Diagnostics.Process.ExitCode property.

Given that an application's return value is passed to the system at the time the application terminates, it is obviously not possible for an application to obtain and display its final error code while running. However, to illustrate how to view this error level upon program termination, begin by updating the Main() method, as follows:

```
// Note we are now returning an int, rather than void.
static int Main(string[] args)
{
  // Display a message and wait for Enter key to be pressed.
  Console.WriteLine("***** My First C# App *****");
  Console.WriteLine("Hello World!");
  Console.WriteLine();
  Console.ReadLine();

  // Return an arbitrary error code.
  return -1;
}
```

Now let's capture the return value of Main() with the help of a batch file. Using Windows Explorer, navigate to the folder containing your solution file (for example, C:\SimpleCSharpApp\). Add a new text file (named SimpleCSharpApp.bat) to that folder containing the following instructions (if you have not authored *.bat files before, don't concern yourself with the details; this is a test . . . this is only a test):

```
@echo off

rem A batch file for SimpleCSharpApp.exe
rem which captures the app's return value.
```

```
.\SimpleCSharpApp\bin\debug\SimpleCSharpApp
@if "%ERRORLEVEL%" == "0" goto success

:fail
  echo This application has failed!
  echo return value = %ERRORLEVEL%
  goto end
:success
  echo This application has succeeded!
  echo return value = %ERRORLEVEL%
  goto end
:end
echo All Done.
```

At this point, open a command prompt and navigate to the folder containing your executable and new *.bat file. Execute the batch logic by typing its name and pressing the Enter key. You should find the output shown next, given that your Main() method is returning -1. Had the Main() method returned 0, you would see the message "This application has succeeded!" print to the console.

```
***** My First C# App *****

Hello World!

This application has failed!
return value = -1
All Done.
```

Again, a vast majority (if not all) of your C# applications will use void as the return value from Main(), which, as you recall, implicitly returns the error code of zero. To this end, the Main() methods used in this text (beyond the current example) will indeed return void (and the remaining projects will certainly not need to make use of batch files to capture return codes).

Processing Command-Line Arguments

Now that you better understand the return value of the Main() method, let's examine the incoming array of string data. Assume that you now want to update your application to process any possible command-line parameters. One way to do so is using a C# for loop. (Note that C#'s iteration constructs will be examined in some detail near the end of this chapter.)

```
static int Main(string[] args)
{
...
  // Process any incoming args.
  for(int i = 0; i < args.Length; i++)
    Console.WriteLine("Arg: {0}", args[i]);

  Console.ReadLine();
  return -1;
}
```

Here, you are checking to see whether the array of strings contains some number of items using the Length property of System.Array. As you'll see in Chapter 4, all C# arrays actually alias the System.Array class and, therefore, share a common set of members. As you loop over each item in the array, its value is printed to the console window. Supplying the arguments at the command line is equally simple, as shown here:

```
C:\SimpleCSharpApp\bin\Debug>SimpleCSharpApp.exe /arg1 -arg2

***** My First C# App *****
Hello World!
Arg: /arg1
Arg: -arg2
```

As an alternative to the standard for loop, you may iterate over an incoming string array using the C# foreach keyword. Here is some sample usage (but again, you will see specifics of looping constructs later in this chapter):

```
// Notice you have no need to check the size of the array when using "foreach".
static int Main(string[] args)
{
...
  // Process any incoming args using foreach.
  foreach(string arg in args)
    Console.WriteLine("Arg: {0}", arg);

  Console.ReadLine();
  return -1;
}
```

Finally, you are also able to access command-line arguments using the static GetCommandLineArgs() method of the System.Environment type. The return value of this method is an array of strings. The first index identifies the name of the application itself, while the remaining elements in the array contain the individual command-line arguments. Note that when using this approach, it is no longer necessary to define Main() as taking a string array as the input parameter, although there is no harm in doing so.

```
static int Main(string[] args)
{
...
  // Get arguments using System.Environment.
  string[] theArgs = Environment.GetCommandLineArgs();
  foreach(string arg in theArgs)
    Console.WriteLine("Arg: {0}", arg);

  Console.ReadLine();
  return -1;
}
```

Of course, it is up to you to determine which command-line arguments your program will respond to (if any) and how they must be formatted (such as with a - or / prefix). Here, I simply passed in a series of options that were printed directly to the command prompt. Assume, however, you were creating a new video game and programmed your application to process an option named -godmode. If the user starts your application with the flag, you know he is, in fact, *a cheater*, and you can take an appropriate course of action.

Specifying Command-Line Arguments with Visual Studio

In the real world, an end user has the option of supplying command-line arguments when starting a program. However, during the development cycle, you might want to specify possible command-line flags for testing purposes. To do so with Visual Studio, double-click the Properties icon in Solution Explorer and select the Debug tab on the left side. From there, specify values using the "Command line arguments" text box (see Figure 3-1) and save your changes.

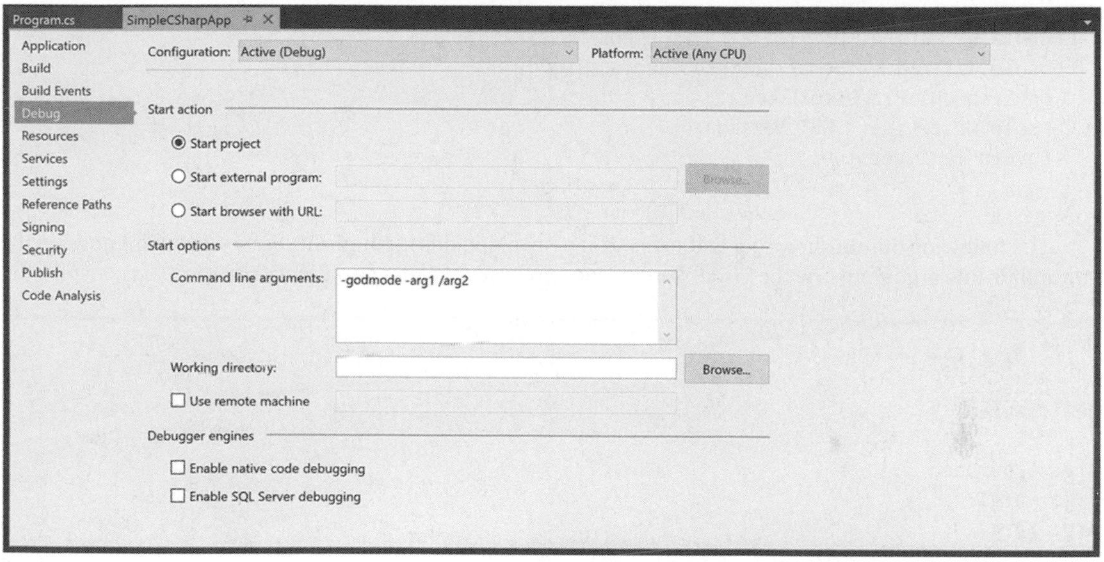

Figure 3-1. *Setting command arguments via Visual Studio*

After you have established such command-line arguments, they will automatically be passed to the `Main()` method when debugging or running your application within the Visual Studio IDE.

An Interesting Aside: Some Additional Members of the System.Environment Class

The `Environment` class exposes a number of extremely helpful methods beyond `GetCommandLineArgs()`. Specifically, this class allows you to obtain a number of details regarding the operating system currently hosting your .NET application using various static members. To illustrate the usefulness of `System.Environment`, update your `Main()` method to call a helper method named `ShowEnvironmentDetails()`.

```
static int Main(string[] args)
{
...
  // Helper method within the Program class.
  ShowEnvironmentDetails();

  Console.ReadLine();
  return -1;
}
```

Implement this method within your Program class to call various members of the Environment type.

```
static void ShowEnvironmentDetails()
{
  // Print out the drives on this machine,
  // and other interesting details.
  foreach (string drive in Environment.GetLogicalDrives())
    Console.WriteLine("Drive: {0}", drive);

  Console.WriteLine("OS: {0}", Environment.OSVersion);
  Console.WriteLine("Number of processors: {0}",
    Environment.ProcessorCount);
  Console.WriteLine(".NET Version: {0}",
    Environment.Version);
}
```

The following output shows a possible test run of invoking this method. Of course, if you did not specify command-line arguments via the Visual Studio Debug tab, you will not find them printed to the console.

```
***** My First C# App *****

Hello World!

Arg: -godmode
Arg: -arg1
Arg: /arg2

Drive: C:\
Drive: D:\
OS: Microsoft Windows NT 6.2.9200.0
Number of processors: 8
.NET Version: 4.0.30319.42000
```

The Environment type defines members other than those shown in the previous example. Table 3-1 documents some additional properties of interest; however, be sure to check out the .NET Framework 4.7 SDK documentation for full details.

Table 3-1. *Select Properties of System.Environment*

Property	Meaning in Life
ExitCode	Gets or sets the exit code for the application
Is64BitOperatingSystem	Returns a bool to represent whether the host machine is running a 64-bit OS
MachineName	Gets the name of the current machine
NewLine	Gets the newline symbol for the current environment
SystemDirectory	Returns the full path to the system directory
UserName	Returns the name of the user that started this application
Version	Returns a Version object that represents the version of the .NET platform

---

■ **Source Code**   You can find the SimpleCSharpApp project in the Chapter 3 subdirectory.

The System.Console Class

Almost all the example applications created over the course of the initial chapters of this book make extensive use of the System.Console class. While it is true that a console user interface (CUI) may not be as enticing as a graphical user interface (GUI) or web application, restricting the early examples to console programs will allow you to keep focused on the syntax of C# and the core aspects of the .NET platform, rather than dealing with the complexities of building desktop GUIs or web sites.

As its name implies, the Console class encapsulates input, output, and error-stream manipulations for console-based applications. Table 3-2 lists some (but definitely not all) members of interest. As you can see, the Console class does provide some members that can spice up a simple command-line application, such as the ability to change background and foreground colors and issue beep noises (in a variety of frequencies!).

Table 3-2. *Select Members of System.Console*

Member	Meaning in Life
Beep()	This method forces the console to emit a beep of a specified frequency and duration.
BackgroundColor	These properties set the background/foreground colors for the current output.
ForegroundColor	They may be assigned any member of the ConsoleColor enumeration.
BufferHeight	These properties control the height/width of the console's buffer area.
BufferWidth	
Title	This property gets or sets the title of the current console.
WindowHeight	These properties control the dimensions of the console in relation to the established buffer.
WindowWidth	
WindowTop	
WindowLeft	
Clear()	This method clears the established buffer and console display area.

Basic Input and Output with the Console Class

In addition to the members in Table 3-2, the Console type defines a set of methods to capture input and output, all of which are static and are, therefore, called by prefixing the name of the class (Console) to the method name. As you have seen, WriteLine() pumps a text string (including a carriage return) to the output stream. The Write() method pumps text to the output stream without a carriage return. ReadLine() allows you to receive information from the input stream up until the Enter key is pressed, while Read() is used to capture a single character from the input stream.

To illustrate basic I/O using the Console class, create a new Console Application project named BasicConsoleIO and update your Main() method to call a helper method named GetUserData().

```
class Program
{
  static void Main(string[] args)
  {
    Console.WriteLine("***** Basic Console I/O *****");
    GetUserData();
    Console.ReadLine();
  }

  private static void GetUserData()
  {
  }
}
```

■ **Note**   Visual Studio supports a number of "code snippets" that will insert code once activated. The cw code snippet is quite useful during the early chapters of this text, in that it will automatically expand to Console. WriteLine()! To test this for yourself, type in cw somewhere within your Main() method and hit the Tab key twice (sadly, there is no code snippet for Console.ReadLine()). To see all code snippets, right-click in a C# code file and choose the Insert Snippet menu option.

Implement this method within the Program class with logic that prompts the user for some bits of information and echoes each item to the standard output stream. For example, you could ask the user for a name and age (which will be treated as a text value for simplicity, rather than the expected numerical value), as follows:

```
static void GetUserData()
{
  // Get name and age.
  Console.Write("Please enter your name: ");
  string userName = Console.ReadLine();
  Console.Write("Please enter your age: ");
  string userAge = Console.ReadLine();

  // Change echo color, just for fun.
  ConsoleColor prevColor = Console.ForegroundColor;
  Console.ForegroundColor = ConsoleColor.Yellow;

  // Echo to the console.
  Console.WriteLine("Hello {0}! You are {1} years old.",
  userName, userAge);

  // Restore previous color.
  Console.ForegroundColor = prevColor;
}
```

Not surprisingly, when you run this application, the input data is printed to the console (using a custom color to boot!).

Formatting Console Output

During these first few chapters, you might have noticed numerous occurrences of tokens such as {0} and {1} embedded within various string literals. The .NET platform supports a style of string formatting slightly akin to the `printf()` statement of C. Simply put, when you are defining a string literal that contains segments of data whose value is not known until runtime, you are able to specify a placeholder within the literal using this curly-bracket syntax. At runtime, the values passed into `Console.WriteLine()` are substituted for each placeholder.

The first parameter to `WriteLine()` represents a string literal that contains optional placeholders designated by {0}, {1}, {2}, and so forth. Be aware that the first ordinal number of a curly-bracket placeholder always begins with 0. The remaining parameters to `WriteLine()` are simply the values to be inserted into the respective placeholders.

■ **Note** If you have more uniquely numbered curly-bracket placeholders than fill arguments, you will receive a format exception at runtime. However, if you have more fill arguments than placeholders, the unused fill arguments are ignored.

It is permissible for a given placeholder to repeat within a given string. For example, if you are a Beatles fan and want to build the string `"9, Number 9, Number 9"`, you would write this:

```
// John says...
Console.WriteLine("{0}, Number {0}, Number {0}", 9);
```

Also, know that it is possible to position each placeholder in any location within a string literal, and it need not follow an increasing sequence. For example, consider the following code snippet:

```
// Prints: 20, 10, 30
Console.WriteLine("{1}, {0}, {2}", 10, 20, 30);
```

Formatting Numerical Data

If you require more elaborate formatting for numerical data, each placeholder can optionally contain various format characters. Table 3-3 shows the most common formatting options.

Table 3-3. *.NET Numerical Format Characters*

String Format Character	Meaning in Life
C or c	Used to format currency. By default, the flag will prefix the local cultural symbol (a dollar sign [$] for U.S. English).
D or d	Used to format decimal numbers. This flag may also specify the minimum number of digits used to pad the value.
E or e	Used for exponential notation. Casing controls whether the exponential constant is uppercase (E) or lowercase (e).
F or f	Used for fixed-point formatting. This flag may also specify the minimum number of digits used to pad the value.
G or g	Stands for *general*. This character can be used to format a number to fixed or exponential format.
N or n	Used for basic numerical formatting (with commas).
X or x	Used for hexadecimal formatting. If you use an uppercase X, your hex format will also contain uppercase characters.

These format characters are suffixed to a given placeholder value using the colon token (e.g., {0:C}, {1:d}, {2:X}). To illustrate, update the Main() method to call a new helper function named FormatNumericalData(). Implement this method in your Program class to format a fixed numerical value in a variety of ways.

```
// Now make use of some format tags.
static void FormatNumericalData()
{
  Console.WriteLine("The value 99999 in various formats:");
  Console.WriteLine("c format: {0:c}", 99999);
  Console.WriteLine("d9 format: {0:d9}", 99999);
  Console.WriteLine("f3 format: {0:f3}", 99999);
  Console.WriteLine("n format: {0:n}", 99999);

  // Notice that upper- or lowercasing for hex
  // determines if letters are upper- or lowercase.
  Console.WriteLine("E format: {0:E}", 99999);
  Console.WriteLine("e format: {0:e}", 99999);
  Console.WriteLine("X format: {0:X}", 99999);
  Console.WriteLine("x format: {0:x}", 99999);
}
```

The following output shows the result of calling the FormatNumericalData() method:

```
The value 99999 in various formats:

c format: $99,999.00
d9 format: 000099999
f3 format: 99999.000
n format: 99,999.00
E format: 9.999900E+004
e format: 9.999900e+004
X format: 1869F
x format: 1869f
```

You'll see additional formatting examples where required throughout this text; however, if you are interested in digging into .NET string formatting further, look up the topic "Formatting Types" within the .NET Framework 4.7 SDK documentation.

■ **Source Code**   You can find the BasicConsoleIO project in the Chapter 3 subdirectory.

Formatting Numerical Data Beyond Console Applications

On a final note, be aware that the use of the .NET string formatting characters is not limited to console programs. This same formatting syntax can be used when calling the static string.Format() method. This can be helpful when you need to compose textual data at runtime for use in any application type (e.g., desktop GUI app, ASP.NET web app, and so forth).

The string.Format() method returns a new string object, which is formatted according to the provided flags. After this point, you are free to use the textual data as you see fit. For example, assume you are building a graphical WPF desktop application and need to format a string for display in a message box. The following code illustrates how to do so, but be aware that this code will not compile until you reference the PresentationFramework.dll assembly for use by your project (see Chapter 2 for information on referencing libraries using Visual Studio).

```
static void DisplayMessage()
{
  // Using string.Format() to format a string literal.
  string userMessage = string.Format("100000 in hex is {0:x}", 100000);

  // You need to reference PresentationFramework.dll
  // in order to compile this line of code!
  System.Windows.MessageBox.Show(userMessage);
}
```

■ **Note**   .NET 4.6 and C# 6 introduced an alternative syntax to the curly-bracket placeholders termed *string interpolation syntax*. You will examine this approach later in the chapter.

System Data Types and Corresponding C# Keywords

Like any programming language, C# defines keywords for fundamental data types, which are used to represent local variables, class data member variables, method return values, and parameters. Unlike other programming languages, however, these keywords are much more than simple compiler- recognized tokens. Rather, the C# data type keywords are actually shorthand notations for full-blown types in the System namespace. Table 3-4 lists each system data type, its range, the corresponding C# keyword, and the type's compliance with the Common Language Specification (CLS).

Table 3-4. *The Intrinsic Data Types of C#*

C# Shorthand	CLS Compliant?	System Type	Range	Meaning in Life
bool	Yes	System.Boolean	true or false	Represents truth or falsity
sbyte	No	System.SByte	–128 to 127	Signed 8-bit number
byte	Yes	System.Byte	0 to 255	Unsigned 8-bit number
short	Yes	System.Int16	–32,768 to 32,767	Signed 16-bit number
ushort	No	System.UInt16	0 to 65,535	Unsigned 16-bit number
int	Yes	System.Int32	–2,147,483,648 to 2,147,483,647	Signed 32-bit number
uint	No	System.UInt32	0 to 4,294,967,295	Unsigned 32-bit number
long	Yes	System.Int64	–9,223,372,036,854,775, 808 to 9,223,372,036,854, 775,807	Signed 64-bit to number
ulong	No	System.UInt64	0 to 18,446,744,073,709, 551,615	Unsigned 64-bit number
char	Yes	System.Char	U+0000 to U+ffff	Single 16-bit Unicode character
float	Yes	System.Single	$-3.4 \ 10^{38}$ to $+3.4 \ 10^{38}$	32-bit floating-point number
double	Yes	System.Double	$\pm 5.0 \ 10^{-324}$ to $\pm 1.7 \ 10^{308}$	64-bit floating-point number
decimal	Yes	System.Decimal	$(-7.9 \times 10^{28}$ to $7.9 \times 10^{28})/$ $(10^{0 \ to \ 28})$	128-bit signed number
string	Yes	System.String	Limited by system memory	Represents a set of Unicode characters
Object	Yes	System.Object	Can store any data type in an object variable	The base class of all types in the .NET universe

■ **Note** Recall from Chapter 1 that CLS-compliant .NET code can be used by any managed programming language. If you expose non-CLS-compliant data from your programs, other .NET languages might not be able to make use of it.

By default, a floating-point number is treated as a `double`. To declare a `float` variable, use the suffix f or F to the raw numerical value (`5.3F`), and use the suffix m or M to a floating-point number to declare a decimal (`300.5M`). Finally, raw whole numbers default to an `int` data type. To set the underlying data type to a `long`, suffix l or L (`4L`).

Variable Declaration and Initialization

When you are declaring a local variable (e.g., a variable within a member scope), you do so by specifying the data type followed by the variable's name. To begin, create a new Console Application project named BasicDataTypes. Update the `Program` class with the following helper method that is called from within `Main()`:

```
static void LocalVarDeclarations()
{
  Console.WriteLine("=> Data Declarations:");
  // Local variables are declared as so:
  // dataType varName;
  int myInt;
  string myString;
  Console.WriteLine();
}
```

Be aware that it is a *compiler error* to make use of a local variable before assigning an initial value. Given this, it is good practice to assign an initial value to your local data points at the time of declaration. You may do so on a single line or by separating the declaration and assignment into two code statements.

```
static void LocalVarDeclarations()
{
  Console.WriteLine("=> Data Declarations:");
  // Local variables are declared and initialized as follows:
  // dataType varName = initialValue;
  int myInt = 0;

  // You can also declare and assign on two lines.
  string myString;
  myString = "This is my character data";

  Console.WriteLine();
}
```

It is also permissible to declare multiple variables of the same underlying type on a single line of code, as in the following three bool variables:

```
static void LocalVarDeclarations()
{
  Console.WriteLine("=> Data Declarations:");
  int myInt = 0;
  string myString;
  myString = "This is my character data";

  // Declare 3 bools on a single line.
  bool b1 = true, b2 = false, b3 = b1;
  Console.WriteLine();
}
```

Since the C# bool keyword is simply a shorthand notation for the System.Boolean structure, it is also possible to allocate any data type using its full name (of course, the same point holds true for any C# data type keyword). Here is the final implementation of LocalVarDeclarations(), which illustrates various ways to declare a local variable:

```
static void LocalVarDeclarations()
{
  Console.WriteLine("=> Data Declarations:");
  // Local variables are declared and initialized as follows:
  // dataType varName = initialValue;
  int myInt = 0;

  string myString;
  myString = "This is my character data";

  // Declare 3 bools on a single line.
  bool b1 = true, b2 = false, b3 = b1;

  // Use System.Boolean data type to declare a bool.
  System.Boolean b4 = false;

  Console.WriteLine("Your data: {0}, {1}, {2}, {3}, {4}, {5}",
      myInt, myString, b1, b2, b3, b4);
  Console.WriteLine();
}
```

The default Literal (New)

The default literal is a new feature in C# 7.1 that allows for assigning a variable the default value for its data type. This works for standard data types as well as custom classes (Chapter 5) and generic types (Chapter 9). Create a new method named DefaultDeclarations() and add the following code:

```
static void DefaultDeclarations()
{
  Console.WriteLine("=> Default Declarations:");
  int myInt = default;
}
```

Unless you manually configured the project to use C# 7.1, the project will not compile. If you hover over the default keyword, the Visual Studio light bulb will enable you to upgrade your project to C# 7.1, as shown in Figure 3-2.

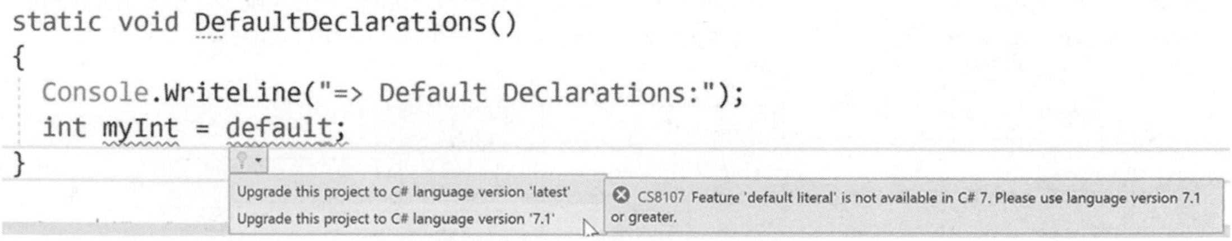

```
static void DefaultDeclarations()
{
  Console.WriteLine("=> Default Declarations:");
  int myInt = default;
}
```

| Upgrade this project to C# language version 'latest' | ⊗ CS8107 Feature 'default literal' is not available in C# 7. Please use language version 7.1 |
| Upgrade this project to C# language version '7.1' | or greater. |

Figure 3-2. *Upgrading the project to C# 7.1*

Intrinsic Data Types and the new Operator

All intrinsic data types support what is known as a *default constructor* (see Chapter 5). This feature allows you to create a variable using the new keyword, which automatically sets the variable to its default value.

- bool variables are set to false.
- Numeric data is set to 0 (or 0.0 in the case of floating-point data types).
- char variables are set to a single empty character.
- BigInteger variables are set to 0.
- DateTime variables are set to 1/1/0001 12:00:00 AM.
- Object references (including strings) are set to null.

■ **Note**   The BigInteger data type mentioned in the previous list will be explained in just a bit.

Although it is more cumbersome to use the new keyword when creating a basic data type variable, the following is syntactically well-formed C# code:

```
static void NewingDataTypes()
{
  Console.WriteLine("=> Using new to create variables:");
  bool b = new bool();            // Set to false.
  int i = new int();              // Set to 0.
  double d = new double();        // Set to 0.
  DateTime dt = new DateTime();   // Set to 1/1/0001 12:00:00 AM
  Console.WriteLine("{0}, {1}, {2}, {3}", b, i, d, dt);
  Console.WriteLine();
}
```

The Data Type Class Hierarchy

It is interesting to note that even the primitive .NET data types are arranged in a *class hierarchy*. If you are new to the world of inheritance, you will discover the full details in Chapter 6. Until then, just understand that types at the top of a class hierarchy provide some default behaviors that are granted to the derived types. The relationship between these core system types can be understood as shown in Figure 3-3.

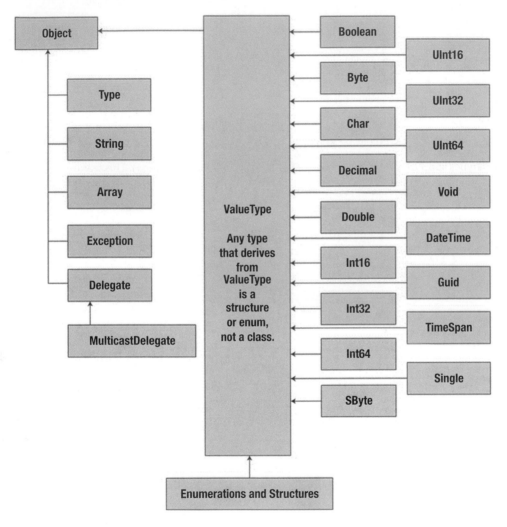

Figure 3-3. *The class hierarchy of system types*

Notice that each type ultimately derives from System.Object, which defines a set of methods (e.g., ToString(), Equals(), GetHashCode()) common to all types in the .NET base class libraries (these methods are fully detailed in Chapter 6).

Also note that many numerical data types derive from a class named System.ValueType. Descendants of ValueType are automatically allocated on the stack and, therefore, have a predictable lifetime and are quite efficient. On the other hand, types that do not have System.ValueType in their inheritance chain (such as System.Type, System.String, System.Array, System.Exception, and System.Delegate) are not allocated on the stack but on the garbage-collected heap. (You can find more information on this distinction in Chapter 4.)

Without getting too hung up on the details of System.Object and System.ValueType, just understand that because a C# keyword (such as int) is simply shorthand notation for the corresponding system type (in this case, System.Int32), the following is perfectly legal syntax, given that System.Int32 (the C# int) eventually derives from System.Object and, therefore, can invoke any of its public members, as illustrated by this additional helper function:

```
static void ObjectFunctionality()
{
  Console.WriteLine("=> System.Object Functionality:");

  // A C# int is really a shorthand for System.Int32,
  // which inherits the following members from System.Object.
  Console.WriteLine("12.GetHashCode() = {0}", 12.GetHashCode());
  Console.WriteLine("12.Equals(23) = {0}", 12.Equals(23));
  Console.WriteLine("12.ToString() = {0}", 12.ToString());
  Console.WriteLine("12.GetType() = {0}", 12.GetType());
  Console.WriteLine();
}
```

If you were to call this method from within Main(), you would find the output shown here:

```
=> System.Object Functionality:

12.GetHashCode() = 12
12.Equals(23) = False
12.ToString() = 12
12.GetType() = System.Int32
```

Members of Numerical Data Types

To continue experimenting with the intrinsic C# data types, understand that the numerical types of .NET support MaxValue and MinValue properties that provide information regarding the range a given type can store. In addition to the MinValue/MaxValue properties, a given numerical system type may define further useful members. For example, the System.Double type allows you to obtain the values for epsilon and infinity (which might be of interest to those of you with a mathematical flare). To illustrate, consider the following helper function:

```
static void DataTypeFunctionality()
{
  Console.WriteLine("=> Data type Functionality:");

  Console.WriteLine("Max of int: {0}", int.MaxValue);
  Console.WriteLine("Min of int: {0}", int.MinValue);
  Console.WriteLine("Max of double: {0}", double.MaxValue);
  Console.WriteLine("Min of double: {0}", double.MinValue);
  Console.WriteLine("double.Epsilon: {0}", double.Epsilon);
```

```
  Console.WriteLine("double.PositiveInfinity: {0}",
    double.PositiveInfinity);
  Console.WriteLine("double.NegativeInfinity: {0}",
    double.NegativeInfinity);
  Console.WriteLine();
}
```

Members of System.Boolean

Next, consider the System.Boolean data type. The only valid assignment a C# bool can take is from the set {true | false}. Given this point, it should be clear that System.Boolean does not support a MinValue/MaxValue property set but rather TrueString/FalseString (which yields the string "True" or "False", respectively). Here's an example:

```
Console.WriteLine("bool.FalseString: {0}", bool.FalseString);
Console.WriteLine("bool.TrueString: {0}", bool.TrueString);
```

Members of System.Char

C# textual data is represented by the string and char keywords, which are simple shorthand notations for System.String and System.Char, both of which are Unicode under the hood. As you might already know, a string represents a contiguous set of characters (e.g., "Hello"), while the char can represent a single slot in a string (e.g., 'H').

The System.Char type provides you with a great deal of functionality beyond the ability to hold a single point of character data. Using the static methods of System.Char, you are able to determine whether a given character is numerical, alphabetical, a point of punctuation, or whatnot. Consider the following method:

```
static void CharFunctionality()
{
  Console.WriteLine("=> char type Functionality:");
  char myChar = 'a';
  Console.WriteLine("char.IsDigit('a'): {0}", char.IsDigit(myChar));
  Console.WriteLine("char.IsLetter('a'): {0}", char.IsLetter(myChar));
  Console.WriteLine("char.IsWhiteSpace('Hello There', 5): {0}",
    char.IsWhiteSpace("Hello There", 5));
  Console.WriteLine("char.IsWhiteSpace('Hello There', 6): {0}",
    char.IsWhiteSpace("Hello There", 6));
  Console.WriteLine("char.IsPunctuation('?'): {0}",
    char.IsPunctuation('?'));
  Console.WriteLine();
}
```

As illustrated in the previous method, many members of System.Char have two calling conventions: a single character or a string with a numerical index that specifies the position of the character to test.

Parsing Values from String Data

The .NET data types provide the ability to generate a variable of their underlying type given a textual equivalent (e.g., parsing). This technique can be extremely helpful when you want to convert some user input data (such as a selection from a GUI-based, drop-down list box) into a numerical value. Consider the following parsing logic within a method named `ParseFromStrings()`:

```
static void ParseFromStrings()
{
  Console.WriteLine("=> Data type parsing:");
  bool b = bool.Parse("True");
  Console.WriteLine("Value of b: {0}", b);
  double d = double.Parse("99.884");
  Console.WriteLine("Value of d: {0}", d);
  int i = int.Parse("8");
  Console.WriteLine("Value of i: {0}", i);
  char c = Char.Parse("w");
  Console.WriteLine("Value of c: {0}", c);
  Console.WriteLine();
}
```

Using TryParse to Parse Values from String Data

One issue with the preceding code is that an exception will be thrown if the string cannot be cleanly converted to the correct data type. For example, the following will fail at runtime:

```
bool b = bool.Parse("Hello");
```

   One solution is to wrap each call to `Parse()` in a `try-catch` block (exception handling is covered in detail in Chapter 7), which can add a lot of code, or use a `TryParse()` statement. The `TryParse()` statement takes an out parameter (the out modifier is covered in detail in the Chapter 4) and returns a `bool` if the parsing was successful. Create a new method named `ParseFromStringWithTryParse()` and add the following code:

```
static void ParseFromStringsWithTryParse()
{
  Console.WriteLine("=> Data type parsing with TryParse:");
  if (bool.TryParse("True", out bool b));
  {
    Console.WriteLine("Value of b: {0}", b);
  }
  string value = "Hello";
  if (double.TryParse(value, out double d))
  {
    Console.WriteLine("Value of d: {0}", d);
  }
  else
  {
    Console.WriteLine("Failed to convert the input ({0}) to a double",value);
  }
  Console.WriteLine();
}
```

If you are new to programming and don't know how if-else statements work, they are covered later in this chapter in detail. The important item to note from the preceding example is that if a string can be converted to the requested datatype, the TryParse() method returns true and assigns the parsed value to the variable passed into the method. If the value cannot be parsed, the variable is assigned its default value, and the TryParse() method returns false.

System.DateTime and System.TimeSpan

The System namespace defines a few useful data types for which there are no C# keywords, such as the DateTime and TimeSpan structures. (I'll leave the investigation of System.Guid and System.Void, as shown in Figure 3-2, to interested readers, but do be aware that these two data types in the System namespace are seldom useful in most applications.)

The DateTime type contains data that represents a specific date (month, day, year) and time value, both of which may be formatted in a variety of ways using the supplied members. The TimeSpan structure allows you to easily define and transform units of time using various members.

```
static void UseDatesAndTimes()
{
  Console.WriteLine("=> Dates and Times:");

  // This constructor takes (year, month, day).
  DateTime dt = new DateTime(2015, 10, 17);

  // What day of the month is this?
  Console.WriteLine("The day of {0} is {1}", dt.Date, dt.DayOfWeek);

  // Month is now December.
  dt = dt.AddMonths(2);
  Console.WriteLine("Daylight savings: {0}", dt.IsDaylightSavingTime());

  // This constructor takes (hours, minutes, seconds).
  TimeSpan ts = new TimeSpan(4, 30, 0);
  Console.WriteLine(ts);

  // Subtract 15 minutes from the current TimeSpan and
  // print the result.
  Console.WriteLine(ts.Subtract(new TimeSpan(0, 15, 0)));
}
```

The System.Numerics.dll Assembly

The System.Numerics namespace defines a structure named BigInteger. As its name implies, the BigInteger data type can be used when you need to represent *humongous* numerical values, which are not constrained by a fixed upper or lower limit.

■ **Note**   The System.Numerics namespace defines a second structure named Complex, which allows you to model mathematically complex numerical data (e.g., imaginary units, real data, hyperbolic tangents). Consult the .NET Framework 4.7 SDK documentation if you are interested.

While many of your .NET applications might never need to make use of the BigInteger structure, if you do find the need to define a massive numerical value, your first step is to reference the System.Numerics.dll assembly into your project. If you want to follow along with the current example, perform the following tasks:

1. Select the Project ➤ Add Reference menu option of Visual Studio.

2. Locate and select the System.Numerics.dll assembly within the list of presented libraries found in the Framework tab on the left side.

3. Click the OK button.

After you have done so, add the following using directive to the file, which will be using the BigInteger data type:

```
// BigInteger lives here!
using System.Numerics;
```

At this point, you can create a BigInteger variable using the new operator. Within the constructor, you can specify a numerical value, including floating-point data. However, recall that when you define a literal whole number (such as 500), the runtime will default the data type to an int. Likewise, literal floating-point data (such as 55.333) will default to a double. How, then, can you set BigInteger to a massive value while not overflowing the default data types used for raw numerical values?

The simplest approach is to establish the massive numerical value as a text literal, which can be converted into a BigInteger variable via the static Parse() method. If required, you can also pass in a byte array directly to the constructor of the BigInteger class.

■ **Note**   After you assign a value to a BigInteger variable, you cannot change it, as the data is immutable. However, the BigInteger class defines a number of members that will return new BigInteger objects based on your data modifications (such as the static Multiply() method used in the preceding code sample).

In any case, after you have defined a BigInteger variable, you will find this class defines similar members as other intrinsic C# data types (e.g., float, int). In addition, the BigInteger class defines several static members that allow you to apply basic mathematical expressions (such as adding and multiplying) to BigInteger variables. Here is an example of working with the BigInteger class:

```
static void UseBigInteger()
{
  Console.WriteLine("=> Use BigInteger:");
  BigInteger biggy =
    BigInteger.Parse("9999999999999999999999999999999999999999999999");
  Console.WriteLine("Value of biggy is {0}", biggy);
  Console.WriteLine("Is biggy an even value?: {0}", biggy.IsEven);
  Console.WriteLine("Is biggy a power of two?: {0}", biggy.IsPowerOfTwo);
  BigInteger reallyBig = BigInteger.Multiply(biggy,
    BigInteger.Parse("8888888888888888888888888888888888888888888888"));
  Console.WriteLine("Value of reallyBig is {0}", reallyBig);
}
```

It is also important to note that the BigInteger data type responds to C#'s intrinsic mathematical operators, such as +, -, and *. Therefore, rather than calling BigInteger.Multiply() to multiply two huge numbers, you could author the following code:

```
BigInteger reallyBig2 = biggy * reallyBig;
```

At this point, I hope you understand that the C# keywords representing basic data types have a corresponding type in the .NET base class libraries, each of which exposes a fixed functionality. While I have not detailed each member of these data types, you are in a great position to dig into the details as you see fit. Be sure to consult the .NET Framework 4.7 SDK documentation for full details regarding the various .NET data types—you will likely be surprised at the amount of built-in functionality.

■ **Source Code**   You can find the BasicDataTypes project in the Chapter 3 subdirectory.

Digit Separators (New)

Sometimes when assigning large numbers to a numeric variable, there are more digits than the eye can keep track of. C# 7 introduces the underscore (_) as a digit separator (for integer, long, decimal, or double data types). Here's an example of using the new digit separator:

```
static void DigitSeparators()
{
  Console.WriteLine("=> Use Digit Separators:");
  Console.Write("Integer:");
  Console.WriteLine(123_456);
  Console.Write("Long:");
  Console.WriteLine(123_456_789L);
  Console.Write("Float:");
  Console.WriteLine(123_456.1234F);
  Console.Write("Double:");
  Console.WriteLine(123_456.12);
  Console.Write("Decimal:");
  Console.WriteLine(123_456.12M);
}
```

Binary Literals (New)

C# 7 introduces a new literal for binary values, for example, for creating bit masks. Now, binary numbers can be written as you would expect. Here's an example:

```
0b0001_0000
```

The new digit separator also works with binary literals. Here is a method that shows using the new literals with the digit separator:

```
private static void BinaryLiterals()
{
  Console.WriteLine("=> Use Binary Literals:");
  Console.WriteLine("Sixteen: {0}",0b0001_0000);
  Console.WriteLine("Thirty Two: {0}",0b0010_0000);
  Console.WriteLine("Sixty Four: {0}",0b0100_0000);
}
```

Working with String Data

System.String provides a number of methods you would expect from such a utility class, including methods that return the length of the character data, find substrings within the current string, and convert to and from uppercase/lowercase. Table 3-5 lists some (but by no means all) of the interesting members.

Table 3-5. *Select Members of System.String*

String Member	Meaning in Life
Length	This property returns the length of the current string.
Compare()	This static method compares two strings.
Contains()	This method determines whether a string contains a specific substring.
Equals()	This method tests whether two string objects contain identical character data.
Format()	This static method formats a string using other primitives (e.g., numerical data, other strings) and the {0} notation examined earlier in this chapter.
Insert()	This method inserts a string within a given string.
PadLeft() PadRight()	These methods are used to pad a string with some characters.
Remove() Replace()	These methods are used to receive a copy of a string with modifications (characters removed or replaced).
Split()	This method returns a String array containing the substrings in this instance that are delimited by elements of a specified char array or string array.
Trim()	This method removes all occurrences of a set of specified characters from the beginning and end of the current string.
ToUpper() ToLower()	These methods create a copy of the current string in uppercase or lowercase format, respectively.

Basic String Manipulation

Working with the members of System.String is as you would expect. Simply declare a string variable and make use of the provided functionality via the dot operator. Be aware that a few of the members of System.String are static members and are, therefore, called at the class (rather than the object) level. Assume you have created a new Console Application project named FunWithStrings. Author the following method, which should be called from within Main():

```
static void BasicStringFunctionality()
{
  Console.WriteLine("=> Basic String functionality:");
  string firstName = "Freddy";
  Console.WriteLine("Value of firstName: {0}", firstName);
  Console.WriteLine("firstName has {0} characters.", firstName.Length);
  Console.WriteLine("firstName in uppercase: {0}", firstName.ToUpper());
  Console.WriteLine("firstName in lowercase: {0}", firstName.ToLower());
  Console.WriteLine("firstName contains the letter y?: {0}",
    firstName.Contains("y"));
  Console.WriteLine("firstName after replace: {0}", firstName.Replace("dy", ""));
  Console.WriteLine();
}
```

There's not too much to say here, as this method simply invokes various members, such as ToUpper() and Contains(), on a local string variable to yield various formats and transformations. Here is the initial output:

```
***** Fun with Strings *****

=> Basic String functionality:
Value of firstName: Freddy
firstName has 6 characters.
firstName in uppercase: FREDDY
firstName in lowercase: freddy
firstName contains the letter y?: True
firstName after replace: Fred
```

While this output might not seem too surprising, the output seen via calling the Replace() method is a bit misleading. In reality, the firstName variable has not changed at all; rather, you receive a new string in a modified format. You will revisit the immutable nature of strings in just a few moments.

String Concatenation

string variables can be connected to build larger strings via the C# + (as well as +=) operator. As you might know, this technique is formally termed *string concatenation*. Consider the following new helper function:

```
static void StringConcatenation()
{
  Console.WriteLine("=> String concatenation:");
  string s1 = "Programming the ";
```

```
  string s2 = "PsychoDrill (PTP)";
  string s3 = s1 + s2;
  Console.WriteLine(s3);
  Console.WriteLine();
}
```

You might be interested to know that the C# + symbol is processed by the compiler to emit a call to the static `String.Concat()` method. Given this, it is possible to perform string concatenation by calling `String.Concat()` directly (although you really have not gained anything by doing so—in fact, you have incurred additional keystrokes!).

```
static void StringConcatenation()
{
  Console.WriteLine("=> String concatenation:");
  string s1 = "Programming the ";
  string s2 = "PsychoDrill (PTP)";
  string s3 = String.Concat(s1, s2);
  Console.WriteLine(s3);
  Console.WriteLine();
}
```

Escape Characters

As in other C-based languages, C# string literals may contain various *escape characters*, which qualify how the character data should be printed to the output stream. Each escape character begins with a backslash, followed by a specific token. In case you are a bit rusty on the meanings behind these escape characters, Table 3-6 lists the more common options.

***Table 3-6.** String Literal Escape Characters*

Character	Meaning in Life
\'	Inserts a single quote into a string literal.
\"	Inserts a double quote into a string literal.
\\	Inserts a backslash into a string literal. This can be quite helpful when defining file or network paths.
\a	Triggers a system alert (beep). For console programs, this can be an audio clue to the user.
\n	Inserts a new line (on Windows platforms).
\r	Inserts a carriage return.
\t	Inserts a horizontal tab into the string literal.

For example, to print a string that contains a tab between each word, you can make use of the \t escape character. Or assume you want to create a string literal that contains quotation marks, another that defines a directory path, and a final string literal that inserts three blank lines after printing the character data. To do so without compiler errors, you would need to make use of the \", \\, and \n escape characters.

Also, to annoy any person within a 10-foot radius from you, notice that I have embedded an alarm within each string literal (to trigger a beep). Consider the following:

```
static void EscapeChars()
{
  Console.WriteLine("=> Escape characters:\a");
  string strWithTabs = "Model\tColor\tSpeed\tPet Name\a ";
  Console.WriteLine(strWithTabs);

  Console.WriteLine("Everyone loves \"Hello World\"\a ");
  Console.WriteLine("C:\\MyApp\\bin\\Debug\a ");

  // Adds a total of 4 blank lines (then beep again!).
  Console.WriteLine("All finished.\n\n\n\a ");
  Console.WriteLine();
}
```

Defining Verbatim Strings

When you prefix a string literal with the @ symbol, you have created what is termed a *verbatim string*. Using verbatim strings, you disable the processing of a literal's escape characters and print out a string as is. This can be most useful when working with strings representing directory and network paths. Therefore, rather than making use of \\ escape characters, you can simply write the following:

```
// The following string is printed verbatim,
// thus all escape characters are displayed.
Console.WriteLine(@"C:\MyApp\bin\Debug");
```

Also note that verbatim strings can be used to preserve white space for strings that flow over multiple lines.

```
// White space is preserved with verbatim strings.
string myLongString = @"This is a very
    very
        very
            long string";
Console.WriteLine(myLongString);
```

Using verbatim strings, you can also directly insert a double quote into a literal string by doubling the " token.

```
Console.WriteLine(@"Cerebus said ""Darrr! Pret-ty sun-sets""");
```

Strings and Equality

As fully explained in Chapter 4, a *reference type* is an object allocated on the garbage-collected managed heap. By default, when you perform a test for equality on reference types (via the C# == and != operators), you will be returned true if the references are pointing to the same object in memory. However, even though the string data type is indeed a reference type, the equality operators have been redefined to compare the *values* of string objects, not the object in memory to which they refer.

```
static void StringEquality()
{
  Console.WriteLine("=> String equality:");
  string s1 = "Hello!";
  string s2 = "Yo!";
  Console.WriteLine("s1 = {0}", s1);
  Console.WriteLine("s2 = {0}", s2);
  Console.WriteLine();

  // Test these strings for equality.
  Console.WriteLine("s1 == s2: {0}", s1 == s2);
  Console.WriteLine("s1 == Hello!: {0}", s1 == "Hello!");
  Console.WriteLine("s1 == HELLO!: {0}", s1 == "HELLO!");
  Console.WriteLine("s1 == hello!: {0}", s1 == "hello!");
  Console.WriteLine("s1.Equals(s2): {0}", s1.Equals(s2));
  Console.WriteLine("Yo.Equals(s2): {0}", "Yo!".Equals(s2));
  Console.WriteLine();
}
```

The C# equality operators by default perform a case-sensitive, culture-insensitive, character-by-character equality test on `string` objects. Therefore, "Hello!" is not equal to "HELLO!", which is also different from "hello!". Also, keeping the connection between `string` and `System.String` in mind, notice that you are able to test for equality using the `Equals()` method of `String` as well as the baked-in equality operators. Finally, given that every string literal (such as "Yo") is a valid `System.String` instance, you are able to access string-centric functionality from a fixed sequence of characters.

Modifying String Comparison Behavior

As mentioned, the string equality operators (`Compare()`, `Equals()`, and `==`) as well as the `IndexOf()` function are by default case-sensitive and culture-insensitive. This can cause a problem if your program doesn't care about case. One way to overcome this is to convert everything to uppercase or lowercase and then compare, like this:

```
if (firstString.ToUpper() == secondString.ToUpper())
{
  //Do something
}
```

This makes a copy of each string with all lowercase letters. It's probably not an issue in most cases but could be a performance hit with a significantly large string. Even if it's not a performance issue, it is a bit of a pain to write each time. And what if you forget to call `ToUpper()`? That could lead to a hard-to-find bug in your program.

A much better practice is to use the overloads of the methods listed earlier that take a value of the `StringComparison` enumeration to control exactly how the comparisons are done. Table 3-7 describes the `StringComparison` values.

Table 3-7. *Values of the StringComparison Enumeration*

C# Equality/Relational Operator	Meaning in Life
CurrentCulture	Compares strings using culture-sensitive sort rules and the current culture
CurrentCultureIgnoreCase	Compares strings using culture-sensitive sort rules and the current culture and ignores the case of the strings being compared
InvariantCulture	Compares strings using culture-sensitive sort rules and the invariant culture
InvariantCultureIgnoreCase	Compares strings using culture-sensitive sort rules and the invariant culture and ignores the case of the strings being compared
Ordinal	Compares strings using ordinal (binary) sort rules
OrdinalIgnoreCare	Compares strings using ordinal (binary) sort rules and ignores the case of the strings being compared

The see the effect of using the StringComparison option, create a new method named StringEqualitySpecifyingCompareRules() and add the following code:

```
static void StringEqualitySpecifyingCompareRules()
{
  Console.WriteLine("=> String equality (Case Insensitive:");
  string s1 = "Hello!";
  string s2 = "HELLO!";
  Console.WriteLine("s1 = {0}", s1);
  Console.WriteLine("s2 = {0}", s2);
  Console.WriteLine();

  // Check the results of changing the default compare rules.
  Console.WriteLine("Default rules: s1={0},s2={1}s1.Equals(s2): {2}", s1, s2,
  s1.Equals(s2));
  Console.WriteLine("Ignore case: s1.Equals(s2, StringComparison.OrdinalIgnoreCase): {0}",
    s1.Equals(s2, StringComparison.OrdinalIgnoreCase));
  Console.WriteLine("Ignore case, Invarariant Culture: s1.Equals(s2, StringComparison.
  InvariantCultureIgnoreCase): {0}",
    s1.Equals(s2, StringComparison.InvariantCultureIgnoreCase));
  Console.WriteLine();
  Console.WriteLine("Default rules: s1={0},s2={1} s1.IndexOf(\"E\"): {2}", s1, s2,
  s1.IndexOf("E"));
  Console.WriteLine("Ignore case: s1.IndexOf(\"E\", StringComparison.OrdinalIgnoreCase):
  {0}", s1.IndexOf("E",
    StringComparison.OrdinalIgnoreCase));
  Console.WriteLine("Ignore case, Invarariant Culture: s1.IndexOf(\"E\", StringComparison.
  InvariantCultureIgnoreCase): {0}",
    s1.IndexOf("E", StringComparison.InvariantCultureIgnoreCase));
  Console.WriteLine();
}
```

While the examples here are simple ones and use the same letters across most cultures, if your application needed to take into account different culture sets, using the StringComparison options is a must.

Strings Are Immutable

One of the interesting aspects of System.String is that after you assign a string object with its initial value, the character data *cannot be changed*. At first glance, this might seem like a flat-out lie, given that you are always reassigning strings to new values and because the System.String type defines a number of methods that appear to modify the character data in one way or another (such as uppercasing and lowercasing). However, if you look more closely at what is happening behind the scenes, you will notice the methods of the string type are, in fact, returning you a new string object in a modified format.

```
static void StringsAreImmutable()
{
  // Set initial string value.
  string s1 = "This is my string.";
  Console.WriteLine("s1 = {0}", s1);

  // Uppercase s1?
  string upperString = s1.ToUpper();
  Console.WriteLine("upperString = {0}", upperString);

  // Nope! s1 is in the same format!
  Console.WriteLine("s1 = {0}", s1);
}
```

If you examine the relevant output that follows, you can verify that the original string object (s1) is not uppercased when calling ToUpper(). Rather, you are returned a *copy* of the string in a modified format.

```
s1 = This is my string.
upperString = THIS IS MY STRING.
s1 = This is my string.
```

The same law of immutability holds true when you use the C# assignment operator. To illustrate, implement the following StringsAreImmutable2() method:

```
static void StringsAreImmutable2()
{
  string s2 = "My other string";
  s2 = "New string value";
}
```

Now, compile your application and load the assembly into ildasm.exe (see Chapter 1). The following output shows what you would find if you were to generate CIL code for the StringsAreImmutable2() method:

```
.method private hidebysig static void StringsAreImmutable2() cil managed
{
  // Code size 14 (0xe)
  .maxstack 1
  .locals init ([0] string s2)
  IL_0000:  nop
  IL_0001:  ldstr       "My other string"
  IL_0006:  stloc.0
  IL_0007:  ldstr       "New string value"
  IL_000c:  stloc.0
  IL_000d:  ret
} // end of method Program::StringAreImmutable2
```

Although you have yet to examine the low-level details of the CIL, note the numerous calls to the ldstr (load string) opcode. Simply put, the ldstr opcode of the CIL loads a new string object on the managed heap. The previous string object that contained the value "My other string" will eventually be garbage collected.

So, what exactly are you to gather from this insight? In a nutshell, the string class can be inefficient and result in bloated code if misused, especially when performing string concatenation or working with huge amounts of text data. If you need to represent basic character data such as a U.S. Social Security number, first or last names, or simple bits of text used within your application, the string class is the perfect choice.

However, if you are building an application that makes heavy use of frequently changing textual data (such as a word processing program), it would be a bad idea to represent the word processing data using string objects, as you will most certainly (and often indirectly) end up making unnecessary copies of string data. So, what is a programmer to do? Glad you asked.

The System.Text.StringBuilder Type

Given that the string type can be inefficient when used with reckless abandon, the .NET base class libraries provide the System.Text namespace. Within this (relatively small) namespace lives a class named StringBuilder. Like the System.String class, the StringBuilder defines methods that allow you to replace or format segments, for example. When you want to use this type in your C# code files, your first step is to make sure the following namespace is imported into your code file (this should already be the case for a new Visual Studio project):

```
// StringBuilder lives here!
using System.Text;
```

What is unique about the StringBuilder is that when you call members of this type, you are directly modifying the object's internal character data (making it more efficient), not obtaining a copy of the data in a modified format. When you create an instance of the StringBuilder, you can supply the object's initial startup values via one of many *constructors*. If you are new to the topic of constructors, simply understand that constructors allow you to create an object with an initial state when you apply the new keyword. Consider the following usage of StringBuilder:

```
static void FunWithStringBuilder()
{
  Console.WriteLine("=> Using the StringBuilder:");
  StringBuilder sb = new StringBuilder("**** Fantastic Games ****");
  sb.Append("\n");
  sb.AppendLine("Half Life");
  sb.AppendLine("Morrowind");
  sb.AppendLine("Deus Ex" + "2");
  sb.AppendLine("System Shock");
  Console.WriteLine(sb.ToString());
  sb.Replace("2", " Invisible War");
  Console.WriteLine(sb.ToString());
  Console.WriteLine("sb has {0} chars.", sb.Length);
  Console.WriteLine();
}
```

Here, I have constructed a StringBuilder set to the initial value "**** Fantastic Games ****". As you can see, I am appending to the internal buffer and am able to replace or remove characters at will. By default, a StringBuilder is only able to initially hold a string of 16 characters or fewer (but will expand automatically if necessary); however, this default starting value can be changed via an additional constructor argument.

```
// Make a StringBuilder with an initial size of 256.
StringBuilder sb = new StringBuilder("**** Fantastic Games ****", 256);
```

If you append more characters than the specified limit, the StringBuilder object will copy its data into a new instance and grow the buffer by the specified limit.

String Interpolation

The curly bracket syntax illustrated within this chapter ({0}, {1}, and so on) has existed within the .NET platform since version 1.0. Starting with the release of C# 6, C# programmers can use an alternative syntax to build string literals that contain placeholders for variables. Formally, this is called *string interpolation*. While the output of the operation is identical to traditional string formatting syntax, this new approach allows you to directly embed the variables themselves, rather than tacking them on as a comma-delimited list.

Consider the following additional method of your Program class (StringInterpolation()), which builds a string variable using each approach:

```
static void StringInterpolation()
{
    // Some local variables we will plug into our larger string
    int age = 4;
    string name = "Soren";

    // Using curly bracket syntax.
    string greeting = string.Format("Hello {0} you are {1} years old.", name, age);

    // Using string interpolation
    string greeting2 = $"Hello {name} you are {age} years old.";
}
```

In the greeting2 variable, notice how the string you are constructing begins with a dollar sign ($) prefix. Next, notice that the curly brackets still are used to mark a variable placeholder; however, rather than using a numerical tag, you are able to place the variable directly into the scope. The assumed advantage is that this new formatting syntax is a bit easier to read in a linear (left-to-right) fashion, given that you are not required to "jump to the end" to see the list of values to plug in at runtime.

There is another interesting aspect of this new syntax: the curly brackets used in string interpolation are a valid scope. Therefore, you can use the dot operation on the variables to change their state. Consider updates to each assembled string variable.

```
string greeting = string.Format("Hello {0} you are {1} years old.", name.ToUpper(), age);
string greeting2 = $"Hello {name.ToUpper()} you are {age} years old.";
```

Here, I have uppercased the name via a call to ToUpper(). Do note that in the string interpolation approach, you do *not* add a semicolon terminator when calling this method. Given this, you cannot use the curly-bracket scope as a fully blown method scope that contains numerous lines of executable code. Rather, you can invoke a single member on the object using the dot operator as well as define a simple general expression such as {age += 1}.

It is also worth noting that you can still use escape characters in the string literal within this new syntax. Thus, if you wanted to insert a tab, you can prefix a \t token as so:

```
string greeting = string.Format("\tHello {0} you are {1} years old.", name.ToUpper(), age);
string greeting2 = $"\tHello {name.ToUpper()} you are {age} years old.";
```

As you might expect, you are free to use either approach when building your string variables on the fly. Do keep in mind, however, that if you are using an earlier version of the .NET platform, string interpolation syntax will result in a compiler error. Thus, if you need to ensure your C# code will compile under multiple versions of the compiler, it is safer to stick to the traditional numerical placeholder approach.

■ **Source Code**   You can find the FunWithStrings project in the Chapter 3 subdirectory.

Narrowing and Widening Data Type Conversions

Now that you understand how to work with intrinsic C# data types, let's examine the related topic of *data type conversion*. Assume you have a new Console Application project named TypeConversions that defines the following class:

```
class Program
{
  static void Main(string[] args)
  {
    Console.WriteLine("***** Fun with type conversions *****");

    // Add two shorts and print the result.
    short numb1 = 9, numb2 = 10;
    Console.WriteLine("{0} + {1} = {2}",
      numb1, numb2, Add(numb1, numb2));
    Console.ReadLine();
  }
```

```
static int Add(int x, int y)
{
  return x + y;
}
}
```

Notice that the Add() method expects to be sent two int parameters. However, the Main() method is, in fact, sending in two short variables. While this might seem like a complete and total mismatch of data types, the program compiles and executes without error, returning the expected result of 19.

The reason the compiler treats this code as syntactically sound is because there is no possibility for loss of data. Given that the maximum value of a short (32,767) is well within the maximum range of an int (2,147,483,647), the compiler implicitly *widens* each short to an int. Formally speaking, *widening* is the term used to define an implicit *upward cast* that does not result in a loss of data.

■ **Note**   Look up "Type Conversion Tables" in the .NET Framework 4.7 SDK documentation if you want to see permissible widening (and narrowing, discussed next) conversions for each C# data type.

Although this implicit widening worked in your favor for the previous example, other times this "feature" can be the source of compile-time errors. For example, assume you have set values to numb1 and numb2 that (when added together) overflow the maximum value of a short. Also, assume you are storing the return value of the Add() method within a new local short variable, rather than directly printing the result to the console.

```
static void Main(string[] args)
{
  Console.WriteLine("***** Fun with type conversions *****");

  // Compiler error below!
  short numb1 = 30000, numb2 = 30000;
  short answer = Add(numb1, numb2);

  Console.WriteLine("{0} + {1} = {2}",
    numb1, numb2, answer);
  Console.ReadLine();
}
```

In this case, the compiler reports the following error:

```
Cannot implicitly convert type 'int' to 'short'. An explicit conversion exists (are you
missing a cast?)
```

The problem is that although the Add() method is capable of returning an int with the value 60,000 (as this fits within the range of a System.Int32), the value cannot be stored in a short, as it overflows the bounds of this data type. Formally speaking, the CLR was unable to apply a *narrowing operation*. As you can guess, narrowing is the logical opposite of widening, in that a larger value is stored within a smaller data type variable.

It is important to point out that all narrowing conversions result in a compiler error, even when you can reason that the narrowing conversion should indeed succeed. For example, the following code also results in a compiler error:

```
// Another compiler error!
static void NarrowingAttempt()
{
  byte myByte = 0;
  int myInt = 200;
  myByte = myInt;

  Console.WriteLine("Value of myByte: {0}", myByte);
}
```

Here, the value contained within the int variable (myInt) is safely within the range of a byte; therefore, you would expect the narrowing operation to not result in a runtime error. However, given that C# is a language built with type safety in mind, you do indeed receive a compiler error.

When you want to inform the compiler that you are willing to deal with a possible loss of data because of a narrowing operation, you must apply an *explicit cast* using the C# casting operator, ( ). Consider the following update to the Program type:

```
class Program
{
  static void Main(string[] args)
  {
    Console.WriteLine("***** Fun with type conversions *****");
    short numb1 = 30000, numb2 = 30000;

    // Explicitly cast the int into a short (and allow loss of data).
    short answer = (short)Add(numb1, numb2);

    Console.WriteLine("{0} + {1} = {2}",
      numb1, numb2, answer);
    NarrowingAttempt();
    Console.ReadLine();
  }

  static int Add(int x, int y)
{
    return x + y;
}

  static void NarrowingAttempt()
{
    byte myByte = 0;
    int myInt = 200;

    // Explicitly cast the int into a byte (no loss of data).
    myByte = (byte)myInt;
    Console.WriteLine("Value of myByte: {0}", myByte);
  }
}
```

At this point, the code compiles; however, the result of the addition is completely incorrect.

```
***** Fun with type conversions *****
30000 + 30000 = -5536
Value of myByte: 200
```

As you have just witnessed, an explicit cast allows you to force the compiler to apply a narrowing conversion, even when doing so may result in a loss of data. In the case of the NarrowingAttempt() method, this was not a problem because the value 200 can fit snuggly within the range of a byte. However, in the case of adding the two shorts within Main(), the end result is completely unacceptable (30,000 + 30,000 = –5536?).

If you are building an application where loss of data is always unacceptable, C# provides the checked and unchecked keywords to ensure data loss does not escape undetected.

The checked Keyword

Let's begin by learning the role of the checked keyword. Assume you have a new method within Program that attempts to add two bytes, each of which has been assigned a value that is safely below the maximum (255). If you were to add the values of these types (casting the returned int to a byte), you would assume that the result would be the exact sum of each member.

```
static void ProcessBytes()
{
  byte b1 = 100;
  byte b2 = 250;
  byte sum = (byte)Add(b1, b2);

  // sum should hold the value 350. However, we find the value 94!
  Console.WriteLine("sum = {0}", sum);
}
```

If you were to view the output of this application, you might be surprised to find that sum contains the value 94 (rather than the expected 350). The reason is simple. Given that a System.Byte can hold a value only between 0 and 255 (inclusive, for a grand total of 256 slots), sum now contains the overflow value (350 – 256 = 94). By default, if you take no corrective course of action, overflow/underflow conditions occur without error.

To handle overflow or underflow conditions in your application, you have two options. Your first choice is to leverage your wits and programming skills to handle all overflow/underflow conditions manually. Of course, the problem with this technique is the simple fact that you are human, and even your best attempts might result in errors that have escaped your eyes.

Thankfully, C# provides the checked keyword. When you wrap a statement (or a block of statements) within the scope of the checked keyword, the C# compiler emits additional CIL instructions that test for overflow conditions that may result when adding, multiplying, subtracting, or dividing two numerical data types.

If an overflow has occurred, you will receive a runtime exception: System.OverflowException. Chapter 7 will examine all the details of structured exception handling and the use of the try and catch keywords. Without getting too hung up on the specifics at this point, observe the following update:

```
static void ProcessBytes()
{
  byte b1 = 100;
  byte b2 = 250;

  // This time, tell the compiler to add CIL code
  // to throw an exception if overflow/underflow
  // takes place.
  try
  {
    byte sum = checked((byte)Add(b1, b2));
    Console.WriteLine("sum = {0}", sum);
  }
  catch (OverflowException ex)
  {
    Console.WriteLine(ex.Message);
  }
}
```

Notice that the return value of Add() has been wrapped within the scope of the checked keyword. Because the sum is greater than a byte, this triggers a runtime exception. Notice the error message printed out via the Message property.

```
Arithmetic operation resulted in an overflow.
```

If you want to force overflow checking to occur over a block of code statements, you can do so by defining a "checked scope" as follows:

```
try
{
  checked
  {
    byte sum = (byte)Add(b1, b2);
    Console.WriteLine("sum = {0}", sum);
  }
}
catch (OverflowException ex)
{
  Console.WriteLine(ex.Message);
}
```

In either case, the code in question will be evaluated for possible overflow conditions automatically, which will trigger an overflow exception if encountered.

Setting Project-wide Overflow Checking

If you are creating an application that should never allow silent overflow to occur, you might find yourself in the annoying position of wrapping numerous lines of code within the scope of the checked keyword. As an alternative, the C# compiler supports the /checked flag. When enabled, all your arithmetic will be evaluated for overflow without the need to make use of the C# checked keyword. If overflow has been discovered, you will still receive a runtime exception.

To enable this flag using Visual Studio, open your project's property page and click the Advanced button on the Build tab. From the resulting dialog box, select the "Check for arithmetic overflow/underflow" check box (see Figure 3-4).

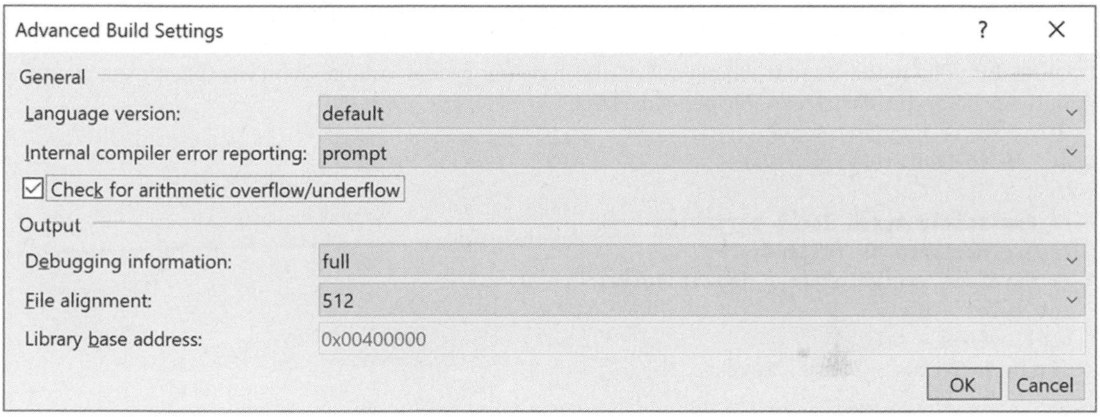

Figure 3-4. Enabling project-wide overflow/underflow data checking

Enabling this setting can be helpful when you're creating a debug build. After all the overflow exceptions have been squashed out of the codebase, you're free to disable the /checked flag for subsequent builds (which can increase the runtime performance of your application).

The unchecked Keyword

Now, assuming you have enabled this project-wide setting, what are you to do if you have a block of code where data loss *is* acceptable? Given that the /checked flag will evaluate all arithmetic logic, C# provides the unchecked keyword to disable the throwing of an overflow exception on a case-by-case basis. This keyword's use is identical to that of the checked keyword in that you can specify a single statement or a block of statements.

```
// Assuming /checked is enabled,
// this block will not trigger
// a runtime exception.
unchecked
{
  byte sum = (byte)(b1 + b2);
  Console.WriteLine("sum = {0} ", sum);
}
```

So, to summarize the C# checked and unchecked keywords, remember that the default behavior of the .NET runtime is to ignore arithmetic overflow/underflow. When you want to selectively handle discrete statements, make use of the checked keyword. If you want to trap overflow errors throughout your application, enable the /checked flag. Finally, the unchecked keyword can be used if you have a block of code where overflow is acceptable (and thus should not trigger a runtime exception).

■ **Source Code**   You can find the TypeConversions project in the Chapter 3 subdirectory.

Understanding Implicitly Typed Local Variables

Up until this point in the chapter, when you have been defining local variables, you've *explicitly* specified the underlying data type of each variable being declared.

```
static void DeclareExplicitVars()
{
  // Explicitly typed local variables
  // are declared as follows:
  // dataType variableName = initialValue;
  int myInt = 0;
  bool myBool = true;
  string myString = "Time, marches on...";
}
```

While many (including yours truly) would argue that it is always good practice to explicitly specify the data type of each variable, the C# language does provide for *implicitly typing* of local variables using the var keyword. The var keyword can be used in place of specifying a specific data type (such as int, bool, or string). When you do so, the compiler will automatically infer the underlying data type based on the initial value used to initialize the local data point.

To illustrate the role of implicit typing, create a new Console Application project named ImplicitlyTypedLocalVars. Notice how the local variables within the previous method can now be declared as follows:

```
static void DeclareImplicitVars()
{
  // Implicitly typed local variables
  // are declared as follows:
  // var variableName = initialValue;
  var myInt = 0;
  var myBool = true;
  var myString = "Time, marches on...";
}
```

■ **Note**   Strictly speaking, var is not a C# keyword. It is permissible to declare variables, parameters, and fields named var without compile-time errors. However, when the var token is used as a data type, it is contextually treated as a keyword by the compiler.

In this case, the compiler is able to infer, given the initially assigned value, that myInt is, in fact, a System.Int32, myBool is a System.Boolean, and myString is indeed of type System.String. You can verify this by printing the type name via *reflection*. As you will see in much more detail in Chapter 15, *reflection* is the act of determining the composition of a type at runtime. For example, using reflection, you can determine the data type of an implicitly typed local variable. Update your method with the following code statements:

```
static void DeclareImplicitVars()
{
  // Implicitly typed local variables.
  var myInt = 0;
  var myBool = true;
  var myString = "Time, marches on...";

  // Print out the underlying type.
  Console.WriteLine("myInt is a: {0}", myInt.GetType().Name);
  Console.WriteLine("myBool is a: {0}", myBool.GetType().Name);
  Console.WriteLine("myString is a: {0}", myString.GetType().Name);
}
```

■ **Note** Be aware that you can use this implicit typing for any type including arrays, generic types (see Chapter 9), and your own custom types. You'll see other examples of implicit typing over the course of this book.

If you were to call the DeclareImplicitVars() method from within Main(), you'd find the output shown here:

```
***** Fun with Implicit Typing *****

myInt is a: Int32
myBool is a: Boolean
myString is a: String
```

Restrictions on Implicitly Typed Variables

There are various restrictions regarding the use of the var keyword. First, implicit typing applies *only* to local variables in a method or property scope. It is illegal to use the var keyword to define return values, parameters, or field data of a custom type. For example, the following class definition will result in various compile-time errors:

```
class ThisWillNeverCompile
{
  // Error! var cannot be used as field data!
  private var myInt = 10;

  // Error! var cannot be used as a return value
  // or parameter type!
  public var MyMethod(var x, var y){}
}
```

Also, local variables declared with the var keyword *must* be assigned an initial value at the exact time of declaration and *cannot* be assigned the initial value of null. This last restriction should make sense, given that the compiler cannot infer what sort of type in memory the variable would be pointing to based only on null.

```
// Error! Must assign a value!
var myData;

// Error! Must assign value at exact time of declaration!
var myInt;
myInt = 0;

// Error! Can't assign null as initial value!
var myObj = null;
```

It is permissible, however, to assign an inferred local variable to null after its initial assignment (provided it is a reference type).

```
// OK, if SportsCar is a reference type!
var myCar = new SportsCar();
myCar = null;
```

Furthermore, it is permissible to assign the value of an implicitly typed local variable to the value of other variables, implicitly typed or not.

```
// Also OK!
var myInt = 0;
var anotherInt = myInt;

string myString = "Wake up!";
var myData = myString;
```

Also, it is permissible to return an implicitly typed local variable to the caller, provided the method return type is the same underlying type as the var-defined data point.

```
static int GetAnInt()
{
  var retVal = 9;
  return retVal;
}
```

Implicit Typed Data Is Strongly Typed Data

Be aware that implicit typing of local variables results in *strongly typed data*. Therefore, use of the var keyword is *not* the same technique used with scripting languages (such as JavaScript or Perl) or the COM Variant data type, where a variable can hold values of different types over its lifetime in a program (often termed *dynamic typing*).

■ **Note**   C# does allow for dynamic typing in C# using a keyword called—surprise, surprise—dynamic. You will learn about this aspect of the language in Chapter 16.

Rather, type inference keeps the strongly typed aspect of the C# language and affects only the declaration of variables at compile time. After that, the data point is treated as if it were declared with that type; assigning a value of a different type into that variable will result in a compile-time error.

```csharp
static void ImplicitTypingIsStrongTyping()
{
  // The compiler knows "s" is a System.String.
  var s = "This variable can only hold string data!";
  s = "This is fine...";

  // Can invoke any member of the underlying type.
  string upper = s.ToUpper();

  // Error! Can't assign numerical data to a string!
  s = 44;
}
```

Usefulness of Implicitly Typed Local Variables

Now that you have seen the syntax used to declare implicitly typed local variables, I am sure you are wondering when to make use of this construct. First, using var to declare local variables simply for the sake of doing so brings little to the table. Doing so can be confusing to others reading your code because it becomes harder to quickly determine the underlying data type and, therefore, more difficult to understand the overall functionality of the variable. So, if you know you need an int, declare an int!

However, as you will see beginning in Chapter 12, the LINQ technology set makes use of *query expressions* that can yield dynamically created result sets based on the format of the query itself. In these cases, implicit typing is extremely helpful because you do not need to explicitly define the type that a query may return, which in some cases would be literally impossible to do. Without getting hung up on the following LINQ example code, see whether you can figure out the underlying data type of subset:

```csharp
static void LinqQueryOverInts()
{
  int[] numbers = { 10, 20, 30, 40, 1, 2, 3, 8 };

  // LINQ query!
  var subset = from i in numbers where i < 10 select i;

  Console.Write("Values in subset: ");
  foreach (var i in subset)
  {
    Console.Write("{0} ", i);
  }
  Console.WriteLine();

  // Hmm...what type is subset?
  Console.WriteLine("subset is a: {0}", subset.GetType().Name);
  Console.WriteLine("subset is defined in: {0}", subset.GetType().Namespace);
}
```

You might be assuming that the subset data type is an array of integers. That seems to be the case, but, in fact, it is a low-level LINQ data type that you would never know about unless you have been doing LINQ for a long time or you open the compiled image in ildasm.exe. The good news is that when you are using LINQ, you seldom (if ever) care about the underlying type of the query's return value; you will simply assign the value to an implicitly typed local variable.

In fact, it could be argued that the *only time* you would make use of the var keyword is when defining data returned from a LINQ query. Remember, if you know you need an int, just declare an int! Overuse of implicit typing (via the var keyword) is considered by most developers to be poor style in production code.

■ **Source Code**   You can find the ImplicitlyTypedLocalVars project in the Chapter 3 subdirectory.

C# Iteration Constructs

All programming languages provide ways to repeat blocks of code until a terminating condition has been met. Regardless of which language you have used in the past, I would guess the C# iteration statements should not raise too many eyebrows and should require little explanation. C# provides the following four iteration constructs:

- for loop
- foreach/in loop
- while loop
- do/while loop

Let's quickly examine each looping construct in turn, using a new Console Application project named IterationsAndDecisions.

■ **Note**   I will keep this section of the chapter short and to the point, as I am assuming you have experience using similar keywords (if, for, switch, etc.) in your current programming language. If you require more information, look up the topics "Iteration Statements (C# Reference)," "Jump Statements (C# Reference)," and "Selection Statements (C# Reference)" within the .NET Framework 4.7 SDK documentation.

The for Loop

When you need to iterate over a block of code a fixed number of times, the for statement provides a good deal of flexibility. In essence, you are able to specify how many times a block of code repeats itself, as well as the terminating condition. Without belaboring the point, here is a sample of the syntax:

```
// A basic for loop.
static void ForLoopExample()
{
  // Note! "i" is only visible within the scope of the for loop.
  for(int i = 0; i < 4; i++)
```

```
  {
    Console.WriteLine("Number is: {0} ", i);
  }
  // "i" is not visible here.
}
```

All your old C, C++, and Java tricks still hold when building a C# for statement. You can create complex terminating conditions, build endless loops, loop in reverse (via the -- operator), and use the goto, continue, and break jump keywords.

The foreach Loop

The C# foreach keyword allows you to iterate over all items in a container without the need to test for an upper limit. Unlike a for loop, however, the foreach loop will walk the container only in a linear (n+1) fashion (thus, you cannot go backward through the container, skip every third element, or whatnot).

However, when you simply need to walk a collection item by item, the foreach loop is the perfect choice. Here are two examples using foreach—one to traverse an array of strings and the other to traverse an array of integers. Notice that the data type before the in keyword represents the type of data in the container.

```
// Iterate array items using foreach.
static void ForEachLoopExample()
{
  string[] carTypes = {"Ford", "BMW", "Yugo", "Honda" };
  foreach (string c in carTypes)
    Console.WriteLine(c);

  int[] myInts = { 10, 20, 30, 40 };
  foreach (int i in myInts)
  Console.WriteLine(i);
}
```

The item after the in keyword can be a simple array (seen here) or, more specifically, any class implementing the IEnumerable interface. As you will see in Chapter 9, the .NET base class libraries ship with a number of collections that contain implementations of common abstract data types (ADTs). Any of these items (such as the generic List<T>) can be used within a foreach loop.

Use of Implicit Typing Within foreach Constructs

It is also possible to use implicit typing within a foreach looping construct. As you would expect, the compiler will correctly infer the correct "type of type." Recall the LINQ example method shown earlier in this chapter. Given that you don't know the exact underlying data type of the subset variable, you can iterate over the result set using implicit typing.

```
static void LinqQueryOverInts()
{
  int[] numbers = { 10, 20, 30, 40, 1, 2, 3, 8 };

  // LINQ query!
  var subset = from i in numbers where i < 10 select i;
  Console.Write("Values in subset: ");
```

```
  foreach (var i in subset)
  {
    Console.Write("{0} ", i);
  }
}
```

The while and do/while Looping Constructs

The while looping construct is useful should you want to execute a block of statements until some terminating condition has been reached. Within the scope of a while loop, you will need to ensure this terminating event is indeed established; otherwise, you will be stuck in an endless loop. In the following example, the message "In while loop" will be continuously printed until the user terminates the loop by entering yes at the command prompt:

```
static void WhileLoopExample()
{
  string userIsDone = "";

  // Test on a lower-class copy of the string.
  while(userIsDone.ToLower() != "yes")
  {
    Console.WriteLine("In while loop");
    Console.Write("Are you done? [yes] [no]: ");
    userIsDone = Console.ReadLine();
  }
}
```

Closely related to the while loop is the do/while statement. Like a simple while loop, do/while is used when you need to perform some action an undetermined number of times. The difference is that do/while loops are guaranteed to execute the corresponding block of code at least once. In contrast, it is possible that a simple while loop may never execute if the terminating condition is false from the onset.

```
static void DoWhileLoopExample()
{
  string userIsDone = "";

  do
  {
    Console.WriteLine("In do/while loop");
    Console.Write("Are you done? [yes] [no]: ");
    userIsDone = Console.ReadLine();
  }while(userIsDone.ToLower() != "yes"); // Note the semicolon!
}
```

Decision Constructs and the Relational/Equality Operators

Now that you can iterate over a block of statements, the next related concept is how to control the flow of program execution. C# defines two simple constructs to alter the flow of your program, based on various contingencies.

- The if/else statement
- The switch statement

■ **Note** C# 7 extends the is expression and switch statements with a technique called *pattern matching*. Both of these extensions and how these changes affect if/else and switch statements will be addressed in Chapter 6 after covering base class/derived class rules, casting, and the standard is operator.

The if/else Statement

First up is the if/else statement. Unlike in C and C++, the if/else statement in C# operates only on Boolean expressions, not ad hoc values such as –1 or 0.

Equality and Relational Operators

C# if/else statements typically involve the use of the C# operators shown in Table 3-8 to obtain a literal Boolean value.

Table 3-8. *C# Relational and Equality Operators*

C# Equality/Relational Operator	Example Usage	Meaning in Life
==	if(age == 30)	Returns true only if each expression is the same
!=	if("Foo" != myStr)	Returns truc only if each expression is different
<	if(bonus < 2000)	Returns true if expression A (bonus) is less than, greater than, less than or equal to, or greater than or equal to expression B (2000)
>	if(bonus > 2000)	
<=	if(bonus <= 2000)	
>=	if(bonus >= 2000)	

Again, C and C++ programmers need to be aware that the old tricks of testing a condition for a value not equal to zero will not work in C#. Let's say you want to see whether the string you are working with is longer than zero characters. You might be tempted to write this:

```
static void IfElseExample()
{
  // This is illegal, given that Length returns an int, not a bool.
  string stringData = "My textual data";
  if(stringData.Length)
  {
    Console.WriteLine("string is greater than 0 characters");
  }
  else
  {
    Console.WriteLine("string is not greater than 0 characters");
  }
  Console.WriteLine();
}
```

If you want to use the String.Length property to determine truth or falsity, you need to modify your conditional expression to resolve to a Boolean.

```
// Legal, as this resolves to either true or false.
If (stringData.Length > 0)
{
  Console.WriteLine("string is greater than 0 characters");
}
```

The Conditional Operator

The conditional operator (?:) is a shorthand method of writing a simple if-else statement. The syntax works like this:

```
condition ? first_expression : second_expression;
```

The condition is the conditional test (the if part of the if-else statement). If the test passes, then the code immediately after the question mark (?) is executed. If the test does not evaluate to true, the code after the colon (the else part of the if-else statement) is executed. The previous code example can be written using the conditional operator like this:

```
private static void ExecuteIfElseUsingConditionalOperator()
{
  string stringData = "My textual data";
  Console.WriteLine(stringData.Length > 0
    ? "string is greater than 0 characters"
    : "string is not greater than 0 characters");
  Console.WriteLine();
}
```

There are some restrictions to the conditional operator. First, both types of `first_expression` and `second_expression` must be the same. Second, the conditional operator can be used only in assignment statements. The following code will result in the compiler error "Only assignment, call, increment, decrement, and new object expressions can be used as a statement":

```
stringData.Length > 0
  ? Console.WriteLine("string is greater than 0 characters")
  : Console.WriteLine("string is not greater than 0 characters");
```

Logical Operators

An `if` statement may be composed of complex expressions as well and can contain `else` statements to perform more complex testing. The syntax is identical to C (and C++) and Java. To build complex expressions, C# offers an expected set of logical operators, as shown in Table 3-9.

Table 3-9. C# Logical Operators

Operator	Example	Meaning in Life
&&	if(age == 30 && name == "Fred")	AND operator. Returns true if all expressions are true.
||	if(age == 30 || name == "Fred")	OR operator. Returns true if at least one expression is true.
!	if(!myBool)	NOT operator. Returns true if false, or false if true.

■ **Note** The && and || operators both "short-circuit" when necessary. This means that after a complex expression has been determined to be false, the remaining subexpressions will not be checked. If you require all expressions to be tested regardless, you can use the related & and | operators.

The switch Statement

The other simple selection construct offered by C# is the `switch` statement. As in other C-based languages, the `switch` statement allows you to handle program flow based on a predefined set of choices. For example, the following `Main()` logic prints a specific string message based on one of two possible selections (the `default` case handles an invalid selection):

```
// Switch on a numerical value.
static void SwitchExample()
{
  Console.WriteLine("1 [C#], 2 [VB]");
  Console.Write("Please pick your language preference: ");

  string langChoice = Console.ReadLine();
  int n = int.Parse(langChoice);
```

```
switch (n)
{
  case 1:
    Console.WriteLine("Good choice, C# is a fine language.");
    break;
  case 2:
    Console.WriteLine("VB: OOP, multithreading, and more!");
    break;
  default:
    Console.WriteLine("Well...good luck with that!");
    break;
}
}
```

■ **Note** C# demands that each case (including `default`) that contains executable statements have a terminating `return`, `break`, or `goto` to avoid falling through to the next statement.

One nice feature of the C# `switch` statement is that you can evaluate `string` data in addition to numeric data. In fact, all version of C# can evaluate `char`, `string`, `bool`, `int`, `long`, and `enum` data types. As you will see in the next section, C# 7 adds additional capabilities. Here is an updated `switch` statement that evaluates a string variable:

```
static void SwitchOnStringExample()
{
  Console.WriteLine("C# or VB");
  Console.Write("Please pick your language preference: ");

  string langChoice = Console.ReadLine();
  switch (langChoice)
  {
    case "C#":
      Console.WriteLine("Good choice, C# is a fine language.");
      break;
    case "VB":
      Console.WriteLine("VB: OOP, multithreading and more!");
      break;
    default:
      Console.WriteLine("Well...good luck with that!");
      break;
  }
}
```

It is also possible to switch on an enumeration data type. As you will see in Chapter 4, the C# `enum` keyword allows you to define a custom set of name-value pairs. To whet your appetite, consider the following final helper function, which performs a `switch` test on the `System.DayOfWeek` enum. You'll notice some syntax I have not yet examined, but focus on the issue of switching over the enum itself; the missing pieces will be filled in over the chapters to come.

```
static void SwitchOnEnumExample()
{
  Console.Write("Enter your favorite day of the week: ");
  DayOfWeek favDay;

  try
  {
    favDay = (DayOfWeek) Enum.Parse(typeof(DayOfWeek), Console.ReadLine());
  }
  catch (Exception)
  {
    Console.WriteLine("Bad input!");
    return;
  }

  switch (favDay)
  {
    case DayOfWeek.Sunday:
      Console.WriteLine("Football!!");
      break;
    case DayOfWeek.Monday:
      Console.WriteLine("Another day, another dollar");
      break;
    case DayOfWeek.Tuesday:
      Console.WriteLine("At least it is not Monday");
      break;
    case DayOfWeek.Wednesday:
      Console.WriteLine("A fine day.");
      break;
    case DayOfWeek.Thursday:
      Console.WriteLine("Almost Friday...");
      break;
    case DayOfWeek.Friday:
      Console.WriteLine("Yes, Friday rules!");
      break;
    case DayOfWeek.Saturday:
      Console.WriteLine("Great day indeed.");
      break;
  }
  Console.WriteLine();
}
```

Falling through from one case statement to another case statement is not allowed, but what if multiple case statements should produce the same result? Fortunately, they can be combined, as the following code snippet demonstrates:

```
case DayOfWeek.Saturday:
case DayOfWeek.Saunday:
  Console.WriteLine("It's the weekend!");
  break;
```

If any code was included between the case statements, the compiler would throw an error. As long as they are consecutive statements, as shown earlier, case statements can be combined to share common code.

In addition to the return and break statements shown in the previous code samples, the switch statement also supports using a goto to exit a case condition and execute another case statement. While this is supported, it's generally thought of as an anti-pattern and not generally used. Here is an example of using the goto statement in a switch block:

```
public static void SwitchWithGoto()
{
  var foo = 5;
  switch (foo)
  {
    case 1:
      //do something
      goto case 2;
    case 2:
      //do something else
      break;
    case 3:
      //yet another action
      goto default;
    default:
      //default action
      break;
  }
}
```

Using Pattern Matching in Switch Statements (New)

Prior to C# 7, match expressions in switch statements were limited to comparing a variable to constant values, sometimes referred to as the *constant pattern*. In C# 7, switch statements can also employ the *type pattern*, where case statements can evaluate the *type* of the variable being checked and case expressions are no longer limited to constant values. The rule that each case statement must be terminated with a return or break still applies; however, goto statements are not supported using the type pattern.

■ **Note** If you are new to object-oriented programming, this section might be a little confusing. It will all come together in Chapter 6, when you revisit the new pattern matching features of C# 7 in the context of classes and base classes. For now, just understand that there is a powerful new way to write switch statements.

Add another method named ExecutePatternMatchingSwitch() and add the following code:

```
static void ExecutePatternMatchingSwitch()
{
  Console.WriteLine("1 [Integer (5)], 2 [String (\"Hi\")], 3 [Decimal (2.5)]");
  Console.Write("Please choose an option: ");
  string userChoice = Console.ReadLine();
  object choice;
```

```
//This is a standard constant pattern switch statement to set up the example
switch (userChoice)
{
  case "1":
    choice = 5;
    break;
  case "2":
    choice = "Hi";
    break;
  case "3":
    choice = 2.5;
    break;
  default:
    choice = 5;
    break;
}
//This is new the pattern matching switch statement
switch (choice)
{
  case int i:
    Console.WriteLine("Your choice is an integer.");
    break;
  case string s:
    Console.WriteLine("Your choice is a string.");
    break;
  case decimal d:
    Console.WriteLine("Your choice is a decimal.");
    break;
  default:
    Console.WriteLine("Your choice is something else");
    break;
}
  Console.WriteLine();
}
```

The first switch statement is using the standard constant pattern and is included merely to set up this (very trivial) example. In the second switch statement, the variable is typed as object and, based on the input from the user, can be parsed into an int, string, or decimal data type. Based on the *type* of the variable, different case statements are matched. In addition to checking the data type, a variable is assigned in each of the case statements (except for the default case). Update the code to the following to use the values in the variables:

```
//This is new the pattern matching switch statement
switch (choice)
{
  case int i:
    Console.WriteLine("Your choice is an integer {0}.",i);
    break;
  case string s:
    Console.WriteLine("Your choice is a string. {0}", s);
    break;
```

```
  case decimal d:
    Console.WriteLine("Your choice is a decimal. {0}", d);
    break;
  default:
    Console.WriteLine("Your choice is something else");
    break;
}
```

In addition to evaluating on the type of the match expression, when clauses can be added to the case statements to evaluate conditions on the variable. In this example, in addition to checking the type, the value of the converted type is also checked for a match:

```
static void ExecutePatternMatchingSwitchWithWhen()
{
  Console.WriteLine("1 [C#], 2 [VB]");
  Console.Write("Please pick your language preference: ");

  object langChoice = Console.ReadLine();
  var choice = int.TryParse(langChoice.ToString(), out int c) ? c : langChoice;

  switch (choice)
  {
    case int i when i == 2:
    case string s when s.Equals("VB", StringComparison.OrdinalIgnoreCase):
      Console.WriteLine("VB: OOP, multithreading, and more!");
      break;
    case int i when i == 1:
    case string s when s.Equals("C#", StringComparison.OrdinalIgnoreCase):
      Console.WriteLine("Good choice, C# is a fine language.");
      break;
    default:
      Console.WriteLine("Well...good luck with that!");
      break;
  }
  Console.WriteLine();
}
```

This adds a new dimension to the switch statement as the order of the case statements is now significant. With the constant pattern, each case statement had to be unique. With the type pattern, this is no longer the case. For example, the following code will match every integer in the first case statement and will never execute the second or the third (in fact, the following code will fail to compile):

```
  switch (choice)
  {
      case int i:
        //do something
        break;
      case int i when i == 0:
        //do something
        break;
```

```
    case int i when i == -1:
        // do something
        break;
}
```

With the initial release of C# 7, there was a small glitch with pattern matching when pattern matching using generic types. This has been resolved with C# 7.1.

■ **Source Code** You can find the IterationsAndDecisions project in the Chapter 3 subdirectory.

Summary

The goal of this chapter was to expose you to numerous core aspects of the C# programming language. You examined the commonplace constructs in any application you may be interested in building. After examining the role of an application object, you learned that every C# executable program must have a type defining a Main() method, which serves as the program's entry point. Within the scope of Main(), you typically create any number of objects that work together to breathe life into your application.

Next, you dove into the details of the built-in data types of C# and came to understand that each data type keyword (e.g., int) is really a shorthand notation for a full-blown type in the System namespace (System.Int32, in this case). Given this, each C# data type has a number of built-in members. Along the same vein, you also learned about the role of *widening* and *narrowing,* as well as the role of the checked and unchecked keywords.

The chapter wrapped up by covering the role of implicit typing using the var keyword. As discussed, the most useful place for implicit typing is when working with the LINQ programming model. Finally, you quickly examined the various iteration and decision constructs supported by C#.

Now that you have an understanding of some of the basic nuts and bolts, the next chapter (Chapter 4) will complete your examination of core language features. After that, you will be well prepared to examine the object-oriented features of C# beginning in Chapter 5.

CHAPTER 4

■ ■ ■

Core C# Programming Constructs, Part II

This chapter picks up where Chapter 3 left off and completes your investigation of the core aspects of the C# programming language. You will start with an investigation of the details behind manipulating arrays using the syntax of C# and get to know the functionality contained within the related System.Array class type.

Next, you will examine various details regarding the construction of C# methods, exploring the out, ref, and params keywords. Along the way, you will also examine the role of optional and named parameters. I finish the discussion on methods with a look at *method overloading*.

Next, this chapter discusses the construction of enumeration and structure types, including a fairly detailed examination of the distinction between a *value type* and a *reference type*. This chapter wraps up by examining the role of *nullable* data types and the related operators.

After you have completed this chapter, you will be in a perfect position to learn the object-oriented capabilities of C#, beginning in Chapter 5.

Understanding C# Arrays

As I would guess you are already aware, an *array* is a set of data items, accessed using a numerical index. More specifically, an array is a set of contiguous data points of the same type (an array of ints, an array of strings, an array of SportsCars, and so on). Declaring, filling, and accessing an array with C# are all quite straightforward. To illustrate, create a new Console Application project named FunWithArrays that contains a helper method named SimpleArrays(), invoked from within Main().

```
class Program
{
  static void Main(string[] args)
  {
    Console.WriteLine("***** Fun with Arrays *****");
    SimpleArrays();
    Console.ReadLine();
  }
  static void SimpleArrays()
  {
    Console.WriteLine("=> Simple Array Creation.");
    // Create an array of ints containing 3 elements indexed 0, 1, 2
    int[] myInts = new int[3];
```

© Andrew Troelsen and Philip Japikse 2017
A. Troelsen and P. Japikse, *Pro C# 7*, https://doi.org/10.1007/978-1-4842-3018-3_4

```
    // Create a 100 item string array, indexed 0 - 99
    string[] booksOnDotNet = new string[100];
    Console.WriteLine();
  }
}
```

Look closely at the previous code comments. When declaring a C# array using this syntax, the number used in the array declaration represents the total number of items, not the upper bound. Also note that the lower bound of an array always begins at 0. Thus, when you write int[] myInts = new int[3], you end up with an array holding three elements, indexed at positions 0, 1, and 2.

After you have defined an array variable, you are then able to fill the elements index by index, as shown here in the updated SimpleArrays() method:

```
static void SimpleArrays()
{
  Console.WriteLine("=> Simple Array Creation.");
  // Create and fill an array of 3 Integers
  int[] myInts = new int[3];
  myInts[0] = 100;
  myInts[1] = 200;
  myInts[2] = 300;

  // Now print each value.
  foreach(int i in myInts)
    Console.WriteLine(i);
  Console.WriteLine();
}
```

■ **Note** Do be aware that if you declare an array but do not explicitly fill each index, each item will be set to the default value of the data type (e.g., an array of bools will be set to false or an array of ints will be set to 0).

C# Array Initialization Syntax

In addition to filling an array element by element, you are able to fill the items of an array using C# *array initialization syntax*. To do so, specify each array item within the scope of curly brackets ({}). This syntax can be helpful when you are creating an array of a known size and want to quickly specify the initial values. For example, consider the following alternative array declarations:

```
static void ArrayInitialization()
{
  Console.WriteLine("=> Array Initialization.");

  // Array initialization syntax using the new keyword.
  string[] stringArray = new string[]
    { "one", "two", "three" };
  Console.WriteLine("stringArray has {0} elements", stringArray.Length);
```

```
// Array initialization syntax without using the new keyword.
bool[] boolArray = { false, false, true };
Console.WriteLine("boolArray has {0} elements", boolArray.Length);

// Array initialization with new keyword and size.
int[] intArray = new int[4] { 20, 22, 23, 0 };
Console.WriteLine("intArray has {0} elements", intArray.Length);
Console.WriteLine();
}
```

Notice that when you make use of this "curly-bracket" syntax, you do not need to specify the size of the array (seen when constructing the stringArray variable), given that this will be inferred by the number of items within the scope of the curly brackets. Also notice that the use of the new keyword is optional (shown when constructing the boolArray type).

In the case of the intArray declaration, again recall the numeric value specified represents the number of elements in the array, not the value of the upper bound. If there is a mismatch between the declared size and the number of initializers (whether you have too many or too few initializers), you are issued a compile-time error. The following is an example:

```
// OOPS! Mismatch of size and elements!
int[] intArray = new int[2] { 20, 22, 23, 0 };
```

Implicitly Typed Local Arrays

In Chapter 3, you learned about the topic of implicitly typed local variables. Recall that the var keyword allows you to define a variable, whose underlying type is determined by the compiler. In a similar vein, the var keyword can be used to define *implicitly typed local arrays*. Using this technique, you can allocate a new array variable without specifying the type contained within the array itself (note you must use the new keyword when using this approach).

```
static void DeclareImplicitArrays()
{
  Console.WriteLine("=> Implicit Array Initialization.");

  // a is really int[].
  var a = new[] { 1, 10, 100, 1000 };
  Console.WriteLine("a is a: {0}", a.ToString());

  // b is really double[].
  var b = new[] { 1, 1.5, 2, 2.5 };
  Console.WriteLine("b is a: {0}", b.ToString());

  // c is really string[].
  var c = new[] { "hello", null, "world" };
  Console.WriteLine("c is a: {0}", c.ToString());
  Console.WriteLine();
}
```

Of course, just as when you allocate an array using explicit C# syntax, the items in the array's initialization list must be of the same underlying type (e.g., all ints, all strings, or all SportsCars). Unlike what you might be expecting, an implicitly typed local array does not default to System.Object; thus, the following generates a compile-time error:

```
// Error! Mixed types!
var d = new[] { 1, "one", 2, "two", false };
```

Defining an Array of Objects

In most cases, when you define an array, you do so by specifying the explicit type of item that can be within the array variable. While this seems quite straightforward, there is one notable twist. As you will come to understand in Chapter 6, System.Object is the ultimate base class to every type (including fundamental data types) in the .NET type system. Given this fact, if you were to define an array of System.Object data types, the subitems could be anything at all. Consider the following ArrayOfObjects() method (which again can be invoked from Main() for testing):

```
static void ArrayOfObjects()
{
  Console.WriteLine("=> Array of Objects.");

  // An array of objects can be anything at all.
  object[] myObjects = new object[4];
  myObjects[0] = 10;
  myObjects[1] = false;
  myObjects[2] = new DateTime(1969, 3, 24);
  myObjects[3] = "Form & Void";
  foreach (object obj in myObjects)
  {
    // Print the type and value for each item in array.
    Console.WriteLine("Type: {0}, Value: {1}", obj.GetType(), obj);
  }
  Console.WriteLine();
}
```

Here, as you are iterating over the contents of myObjects, you print the underlying type of each item using the GetType() method of System.Object, as well as the value of the current item. Without going into too much detail regarding System.Object.GetType() at this point in the text, simply understand that this method can be used to obtain the fully qualified name of the item (Chapter 15 examines the topic of type information and reflection services in detail). The following output shows the result of calling ArrayOfObjects():

```
=> Array of Objects.
Type: System.Int32, Value: 10
Type: System.Boolean, Value: False
Type: System.DateTime, Value: 3/24/1969 12:00:00 AM
Type: System.String, Value: Form & Void
```

Working with Multidimensional Arrays

In addition to the single-dimension arrays you have seen thus far, C# also supports two varieties of multidimensional arrays. The first of these is termed a *rectangular array*, which is simply an array of multiple dimensions, where each row is of the same length. To declare and fill a multidimensional rectangular array, proceed as follows:

```
static void RectMultidimensionalArray()
{
  Console.WriteLine("=> Rectangular multidimensional array.");
  // A rectangular MD array.
  int[,] myMatrix;
  myMatrix = new int[3,4];

  // Populate (3 * 4) array.
  for(int i = 0; i < 3; i++)
    for(int j = 0; j < 4; j++)
      myMatrix[i, j] = i * j;

  // Print (3 * 4) array.
  for(int i = 0; i < 3; i++)
  {

    for(int j = 0; j < 4; j++)
      Console.Write(myMatrix[i, j] + "\t");
    Console.WriteLine();
  }
  Console.WriteLine();
}
```

The second type of multidimensional array is termed a *jagged array*. As the name implies, jagged arrays contain some number of inner arrays, each of which may have a different upper limit. Here's an example:

```
static void JaggedMultidimensionalArray()
{
  Console.WriteLine("=> Jagged multidimensional array.");
  // A jagged MD array (i.e., an array of arrays).
  // Here we have an array of 5 different arrays.
  int[][] myJagArray = new int[5][];

  // Create the jagged array.
  for (int i = 0; i < myJagArray.Length; i++)
    myJagArray[i] = new int[i + 7];

  // Print each row (remember, each element is defaulted to zero!).
  for(int i = 0; i < 5; i++)
  {
    for(int j = 0; j < myJagArray[i].Length; j++)
      Console.Write(myJagArray[i][j] + " ");
    Console.WriteLine();
  }
  Console.WriteLine();
}
```

The output of calling each of the RectMultidimensionalArray() and JaggedMultidimensionalArray() methods within Main() is shown next:

```
=> Rectangular multidimensional array:

0       0       0       0
0       1       2       3
0       2       4       6

=> Jagged multidimensional array:

0 0 0 0 0 0 0
0 0 0 0 0 0 0 0
0 0 0 0 0 0 0 0 0
0 0 0 0 0 0 0 0 0 0
0 0 0 0 0 0 0 0 0 0 0
```

Arrays As Arguments or Return Values

After you have created an array, you are free to pass it as an argument or receive it as a member return value. For example, the following PrintArray() method takes an incoming array of ints and prints each member to the console, while the GetStringArray() method populates an array of strings and returns it to the caller:

```
static void PrintArray(int[] myInts)
{
  for(int i = 0; i < myInts.Length; i++)
    Console.WriteLine("Item {0} is {1}", i, myInts[i]);
}

static string[] GetStringArray()
{
  string[] theStrings = {"Hello", "from", "GetStringArray"};
  return theStrings;
}
```

These methods may be invoked as you would expect.

```
static void PassAndReceiveArrays()
{
  Console.WriteLine("=> Arrays as params and return values.");
  // Pass array as parameter.
  int[] ages = {20, 22, 23, 0} ;
  PrintArray(ages);

  // Get array as return value.
  string[] strs = GetStringArray();
  foreach(string s in strs)
    Console.WriteLine(s);

  Console.WriteLine();
}
```

At this point, you should feel comfortable with the process of defining, filling, and examining the contents of a C# array variable. To complete the picture, let's now examine the role of the System.Array class.

The System.Array Base Class

Every array you create gathers much of its functionality from the System.Array class. Using these common members, you are able to operate on an array using a consistent object model. Table 4-1 gives a rundown of some of the more interesting members (be sure to check the .NET Framework 4.7 SDK documentation for full details).

Table 4-1. *Select Members of System.Array*

Member of Array Class	Meaning in Life
Clear()	This static method sets a range of elements in the array to empty values (0 for numbers, null for object references, false for Booleans).
CopyTo()	This method is used to copy elements from the source array into the destination array.
Length	This property returns the number of items within the array.
Rank	This property returns the number of dimensions of the current array.
Reverse()	This static method reverses the contents of a one-dimensional array.
Sort()	This static method sorts a one-dimensional array of intrinsic types. If the elements in the array implement the IComparer interface, you can also sort your custom types (see Chapter 9).

Let's see some of these members in action. The following helper method makes use of the static Reverse() and Clear() methods to pump out information about an array of string types to the console:

```
static void SystemArrayFunctionality()
{
  Console.WriteLine("=> Working with System.Array.");
  // Initialize items at startup.
  string[] gothicBands = {"Tones on Tail", "Bauhaus", "Sisters of Mercy"};

  // Print out names in declared order.
  Console.WriteLine("-> Here is the array:");
  for (int i = 0; i < gothicBands.Length; i++)
  {
    // Print a name.
    Console.Write(gothicBands[i] + ", ");
  }
  Console.WriteLine("\n");

  // Reverse them...
  Array.Reverse(gothicBands);
  Console.WriteLine("-> The reversed array");
```

```
// ... and print them.
for (int i = 0; i < gothicBands.Length; i++)
{
  // Print a name.
  Console.Write(gothicBands[i] + ", ");
}
Console.WriteLine("\n");

// Clear out all but the first member.
Console.WriteLine("-> Cleared out all but one...");
Array.Clear(gothicBands, 1, 2);

for (int i = 0; i < gothicBands.Length; i++)
{
  // Print a name.
  Console.Write(gothicBands[i] + ", ");
}
Console.WriteLine();
}
```

If you invoke this method from within Main(), you will get the output shown here:

```
=> Working with System.Array.
-> Here is the array:
Tones on Tail, Bauhaus, Sisters of Mercy,

-> The reversed array
Sisters of Mercy, Bauhaus, Tones on Tail,

-> Cleared out all but one...
Sisters of Mercy, , ,
```

Notice that many members of System.Array are defined as static members and are, therefore, called at the class level (for example, the Array.Sort() and Array.Reverse() methods). Methods such as these are passed in the array you want to process. Other members of System.Array (such as the Length property) are bound at the object level; thus, you are able to invoke the member directly on the array.

■ **Source Code** You can find the FunWithArrays application in the Chapter 4 subdirectory.

Methods and Parameter Modifiers

To begin this section, let's examine the details of defining methods. Just like the Main() method (see Chapter 3), your custom methods may or may not take parameters and may or may not return values to the caller. As you will see over the next several chapters, methods can be implemented within the scope of classes or structures (as well as prototyped within interface types) and may be decorated with various keywords (e.g., static, virtual, public, new) to qualify their behavior. At this point in the text, each of your methods has followed the following basic format:

```
// Recall that static methods can be called directly
// without creating a class instance.
class Program
{
  // static returnType MethodName(paramater list) { /* Implementation */ }
  static int Add(int x, int y)
  {
    return x + y;
  }
}
```

Return Values and Expression Bodied Members (Updated)

You already learned about simple methods that return values, such as the Add() method. C# 6 introduced expression-bodied members that shorten the syntax for single-line methods. For example, Add() can be rewritten using the following syntax:

```
static int Add(int x, int y) => x + y;
```

This is what is commonly referred to as *syntactic sugar*, meaning that the generated IL is no different. It's just another way to write the method. Some find it easier to read, and others don't, so the choice is yours (or your team's) which style you prefer.

This syntax also works with read-only member properties (classes and member properties are covered in Chapter 5).

C# 7 expanded this capability to include single-line constructors, finalizers, and get and set accessors on properties and indexers (all covered later in this book, starting with Chapter 5). Throughout this book you will see a mixture of using expression-bodied members as well as the more traditional approach.

■ **Note** Don't be alarmed by the => operator. This is a lambda operation, which is covered in great detail in Chapter 10. That chapter also explains exactly *how* expression-bodied members work. For now, just consider them a shortcut to writing single-line statements.

Method Parameter Modifiers

The default manner in which a parameter is sent into a function is *by value*. Simply put, if you do not mark an argument with a parameter modifier, a copy of the data is passed into the function. As explained later in this chapter, exactly *what* is copied will depend on whether the parameter is a value type or a reference type.

While the definition of a method in C# is quite straightforward, you can use a handful of methods to control how arguments are passed to the method in question, as listed in Table 4-2.

Table 4-2. *C# Parameter Modifiers*

Parameter Modifier	Meaning in Life
(None)	If a parameter is not marked with a parameter modifier, it is assumed to be passed by value, meaning the called method receives a copy of the original data.
out	Output parameters must be assigned by the method being called and, therefore, are passed by reference. If the called method fails to assign output parameters, you are issued a compiler error.
ref	The value is initially assigned by the caller and may be optionally modified by the called method (as the data is also passed by reference). No compiler error is generated if the called method fails to assign a ref parameter.
params	This parameter modifier allows you to send in a variable number of arguments as a single logical parameter. A method can have only a single params modifier, and it must be the final parameter of the method. In reality, you might not need to use the params modifier all too often; however, be aware that numerous methods within the base class libraries do make use of this C# language feature.

To illustrate the use of these keywords, create a new Console Application project named FunWithMethods. Now, let's walk through the role of each keyword.

Discards

Discards are temporary, dummy variables that are intentionally unused. They are unassigned, don't have a value, and might not even allocate any memory. This can provide a performance benefit but, at the least, can make your code more readable. Discards can be used with out parameters, with tuples, with pattern matching (Chapters 6 and 8), or even as stand-alone variables.

You might wonder why you would use assign a value to a throwaway variable. It comes in handy with async programming, as you will see Chapter 19.

The Default by Value Parameter-Passing Behavior

The default manner in which a parameter is sent into a function is *by value*. Simply put, if you do not mark an argument with a parameter modifier, a copy of the data is passed into the function. As explained later in this chapter, exactly *what* is copied will depend on whether the parameter is a value type or a reference type. For the time being, assume the following method within the Program class operates on two numerical data types passed by value:

```
// Arguments are passed by value by default.
static int Add(int x, int y)
{
  int ans = x + y;
  // Caller will not see these changes
  // as you are modifying a copy of the
  // original data.
  x = 10000;
  y = 88888;
  return ans;
}
```

Numerical data falls under the category of *value types*. Therefore, if you change the values of the parameters within the scope of the member, the caller is blissfully unaware, given that you are changing the values on a *copy* of the caller's original data.

```
static void Main(string[] args)
{
  Console.WriteLine("***** Fun with Methods *****\n");

  // Pass two variables in by value.
  int x = 9, y = 10;
  Console.WriteLine("Before call: X: {0}, Y: {1}", x, y);
  Console.WriteLine("Answer is: {0}", Add(x, y));
  Console.WriteLine("After call: X: {0}, Y: {1}", x, y);
  Console.ReadLine();
}
```

As you would hope, the values of x and y remain identical before and after the call to Add(), as shown in the following output, as the data points were sent in by value. Thus, any changes on these parameters within the Add() method are not seen by the caller, as the Add() method is operating on a copy of the data.

```
***** Fun with Methods *****

Before call: X: 9, Y: 10
Answer is: 19
After call: X: 9, Y: 10
```

The out Modifier (Updated)

Next, you have the use of *output parameters*. Methods that have been defined to take output parameters (via the out keyword) are under obligation to assign them to an appropriate value before exiting the method scope (if you fail to do so, you will receive compiler errors).

To illustrate, here is an alternative version of the Add() method that returns the sum of two integers using the C# out modifier (note the physical return value of this method is now void):

```
// Output parameters must be assigned by the called method.
static void Add(int x, int y, out int ans)
{
  ans = x + y;
}
```

Calling a method with output parameters also requires the use of the out modifier. However, the local variables that are passed as output variables are not required to be assigned before passing them in as output arguments (if you do so, the original value is lost after the call). The reason the compiler allows you to send in seemingly unassigned data is because the method being called *must* make an assignment. Starting with C# 7, out parameters do not need to be declared before using them. In other words, they can be declared inside the method call, like this:

```
Add(90, 90, out int ans);
```

The following code is an example of calling a method with an inline declaration of the out parameter:

```
static void Main(string[] args)
{
  Console.WriteLine("***** Fun with Methods *****");
...
  // No need to assign initial value to local variables
  // used as output parameters, provided the first time
  // you use them is as output arguments.
  // C# 7 allows for out parameters to be declared in the method call
  Add(90, 90, out int ans);
  Console.WriteLine("90 + 90 = {0}", ans);
  Console.ReadLine();
}
```

The previous example is intended to be illustrative in nature; you really have no reason to return the value of your summation using an output parameter. However, the C# out modifier does serve a useful purpose: it allows the caller to obtain multiple outputs from a single method invocation.

```
// Returning multiple output parameters.
static void FillTheseValues(out int a, out string b, out bool c)
{
  a = 9;
  b = "Enjoy your string.";
  c = true;
}
```

The caller would be able to invoke the FillTheseValues() method. Remember that you must use the out modifier when you invoke the method, as well as when you implement the method.

```
static void Main(string[] args)
{
  Console.WriteLine("***** Fun with Methods *****");
...
  int i; string str; bool b;
  FillTheseValues(out i, out str, out b);

  Console.WriteLine("Int is: {0}", i);
  Console.WriteLine("String is: {0}", str);
  Console.WriteLine("Boolean is: {0}", b);
  Console.ReadLine();
}
```

■ **Note** C# 7 introduces tuples, which are another way to return multiple values out of a method call. You'll learn more about that later in this chapter.

Always remember that a method that defines output parameters must assign the parameter to a valid value before exiting the method scope. Therefore, the following code will result in a compiler error, as the output parameter has not been assigned within the method scope:

```
static void ThisWontCompile(out int a)
{
  Console.WriteLine("Error! Forgot to assign output arg!");
}
```

Finally, if you don't care about the value of an out parameter, you can use a discard as a placeholder. For example, if you want to determine whether a string is a valid date format but don't care about the parsed date, you could write the following code:

```
if (DateTime.TryParse(dateString, out _)
{
  //do something
}
```

The ref Modifier

Now consider the use of the C# ref parameter modifier. Reference parameters are necessary when you want to allow a method to operate on (and usually change the values of) various data points declared in the caller's scope (such as a sorting or swapping routine). Note the distinction between output and reference parameters.

- Output parameters do not need to be initialized before they are passed to the method. The reason for this is that the method must assign output parameters before exiting.

- Reference parameters must be initialized before they are passed to the method. The reason for this is that you are passing a reference to an existing variable. If you don't assign it to an initial value, that would be the equivalent of operating on an unassigned local variable.

Let's check out the use of the ref keyword by way of a method that swaps two string variables (of course, any two data types could be used here, including int, bool, float, and so on).

```
// Reference parameters.
public static void SwapStrings(ref string s1, ref string s2)
{
  string tempStr = s1;
  s1 = s2;
  s2 = tempStr;
}
```

This method can be called as follows:

```
static void Main(string[] args)
{
  Console.WriteLine("***** Fun with Methods *****");
...
  string str1 = "Flip";
  string str2 = "Flop";
  Console.WriteLine("Before: {0}, {1} ", str1, str2);
```

```
  SwapStrings(ref str1, ref str2);
  Console.WriteLine("After: {0}, {1} ", str1, str2);
  Console.ReadLine();
}
```

Here, the caller has assigned an initial value to local string data (str1 and str2). After the call to SwapStrings() returns, str1 now contains the value "Flop", while str2 reports the value "Flip".

```
Before: Flip, Flop
After: Flop, Flip
```

■ **Note**   The C# ref parameter modifier keyword will be revisited later in this chapter in the section "Understanding Value Types and Reference Types." As you will see, the behavior of this keyword changes just a bit depending on whether the argument is a value type or reference type.

ref Locals and Returns (New)

In addition to modifying parameters with the ref keyword, C# 7 introduces the ability to use and return references to variables defined elsewhere. Before showing how that works, let's look at the following method:

```
// Returns the value at the array position.
public static string SimpleReturn(string[] strArray, int position)
{
  return strArray[position];
}
```

A string array is passed in (by value), along with a position value. Then the value of the array at that position is returned. If the string that is returned from the method is modified outside of this method, you would expect the array to still hold the original values. As the following code demonstrates, that is exactly what happens:

```
#region Ref locals and params
string[] stringArray = { "one", "two", "three" };
int pos = 1;
Console.WriteLine("=> Use Simple Return");
Console.WriteLine("Before: {0}, {1}, {2} ", stringArray[0], stringArray[1], stringArray[2]);
var output = SimpleReturn(stringArray, pos);
output = "new";
Console.WriteLine("After: {0}, {1}, {2} ", stringArray[0], stringArray[1], stringArray[2]);
#endregion
```

The result of this code outputs the following to the console:

```
=> Use Simple Return
Before: one, two, three
After: one, two, three
```

But what if you didn't want the *value* of the array position but instead a *reference* to the array position? This could certainly be achieved prior to C# 7, but the new capabilities using the ref keyword makes it much simpler.

There are two changes that need to be made to the simple method. The first is that instead of a straight return [value to be returned], the method must do a return ref [reference to be returned]. The second change is that the method declaration must also include the ref keyword. Create a new method called SampleRefReturn like this:

```
// Returning a reference.
public static ref string SampleRefReturn(string[] strArray, int position)
{
  return ref strArray[position];
}
```

This is essentially the same method as before, with the addition of the two instances of the ref keyword. This now returns a reference to the position in the array, instead of the value held in the position of the array. Calling this method also requires the use of the ref keyword, both for the return variable and for the method call itself, like this:

```
ref var refOutput = ref SampleRefReturn(stringArray, pos);
```

Any changes to the reference returned will then also update the array, as the following code demonstrates:

```
#region Ref locals and params
Console.WriteLine("=> Use Ref Return");
Console.WriteLine("Before: {0}, {1}, {2} ", stringArray[0], stringArray[1], stringArray[2]);
ref var refOutput = ref SampleRefReturn(stringArray, pos);
refOutput = "new";
Console.WriteLine("After: {0}, {1}, {2} ", stringArray[0], stringArray[1], stringArray[2]);
```

Printing the array values to the console shows the effect of changing the value of the reference variable returned from the new method:

```
=> Use Ref Return
Before: one, two, three
After: one, new, three
```

There are some rules around this new feature that are worth noting here:

- Standard method results cannot be assigned to a ref local variable. The method must have been created as a ref return method.

- A local variable inside the ref method can't be returned as a ref local variable. The following code does not work:

```
ThisWillNotWork(string[] array)
{
  int foo = 5;
  return ref foo;
}
```

- This new feature doesn't work with async methods (covered in Chapter 19).

The params Modifier

C# supports the use of *parameter arrays* using the params keyword. To understand this language feature, you must (as the name implies) understand how to manipulate C# arrays. If this is not the case, you might want to return to this section after you read the section "Understanding C# Arrays" later in this chapter.

The params keyword allows you to pass into a method a variable number of identically typed parameters (or classes related by inheritance) as a *single logical parameter*. As well, arguments marked with the params keyword can be processed if the caller sends in a strongly typed array or a comma- delimited list of items. Yes, this can be confusing! To clear things up, assume you want to create a function that allows the caller to pass in any number of arguments and return the calculated average.

If you were to prototype this method to take an array of doubles, this would force the caller to first define the array, then fill the array, and finally pass it into the method. However, if you define CalculateAverage()to take a params of double[] data types, the caller can simply pass a comma- delimited list of doubles. The .NET runtime will automatically package the set of doubles into an array of type double behind the scenes.

```
// Return average of "some number" of doubles.
static double CalculateAverage(params double[] values)
{
  Console.WriteLine("You sent me {0} doubles.", values.Length);

  double sum = 0;
  if(values.Length == 0)
    return sum;
  for (int i = 0; i < values.Length; i++)
    sum += values[i];
  return (sum / values.Length);
}
```

This method has been defined to take a parameter array of doubles. What this method is in fact saying is, "Send me any number of doubles (including zero), and I'll compute the average." Given this, you can call CalculateAverage() in any of the following ways:

```csharp
static void Main(string[] args)
{
  Console.WriteLine("***** Fun with Methods *****");
...
  // Pass in a comma-delimited list of doubles...
  double average;
  average = CalculateAverage(4.0, 3.2, 5.7, 64.22, 87.2);
  Console.WriteLine("Average of data is: {0}", average);

  // ...or pass an array of doubles.
  double[] data = { 4.0, 3.2, 5.7 };
  average = CalculateAverage(data);
  Console.WriteLine("Average of data is: {0}", average);

  // Average of 0 is 0!
  Console.WriteLine("Average of data is: {0}", CalculateAverage());
  Console.ReadLine();
}
```

If you did not make use of the params modifier in the definition of CalculateAverage(), the first invocation of this method would result in a compiler error, as the compiler would be looking for a version of CalculateAverage() that took five double arguments.

■ **Note**   To avoid any ambiguity, C# demands a method support only a single params argument, which must be the final argument in the parameter list.

As you might guess, this technique is nothing more than a convenience for the caller, given that the array is created by the CLR as necessary. By the time the array is within the scope of the method being called, you are able to treat it as a full-blown .NET array that contains all the functionality of the System.Array base class library type. Consider the following output:

```
You sent me 5 doubles.
Average of data is: 32.864
You sent me 3 doubles.
Average of data is: 4.3
You sent me 0 doubles.
Average of data is: 0
```

Defining Optional Parameters

C# allows you to create methods that can take *optional arguments*. This technique allows the caller to invoke a single method while omitting arguments deemed unnecessary, provided the caller is happy with the specified defaults.

■ **Note** As you will see in Chapter 16, a key motivation for adding optional arguments to C# is to simplify interacting with COM objects. Several Microsoft object models (e.g., Microsoft Office) expose their functionality via COM objects, many of which were written long ago to make use of optional parameters, which earlier versions of C# did not support.

To illustrate working with optional arguments, assume you have a method named EnterLogData(), which defines a single optional parameter.

```
static void EnterLogData(string message, string owner = "Programmer")
{
  Console.Beep();
  Console.WriteLine("Error: {0}", message);
  Console.WriteLine("Owner of Error: {0}", owner);
}
```

Here, the final string argument has been assigned the default value of "Programmer", via an assignment within the parameter definition. Given this, you can call EnterLogData() from within Main() in two ways.

```
static void Main(string[] args)
{
  Console.WriteLine("***** Fun with Methods *****");
...
  EnterLogData("Oh no! Grid can't find data");
  EnterLogData("Oh no! I can't find the payroll data", "CFO");

  Console.ReadLine();
}
```

Because the first invocation of EnterLogData() did not specify a second string argument, you would find that the programmer is the one responsible for losing data for the grid, while the CFO misplaced the payroll data (as specified by the second argument in the second method call).

One important thing to be aware of is that the value assigned to an optional parameter must be known at compile time and cannot be resolved at runtime (if you attempt to do so, you'll receive compile-time errors!). To illustrate, assume you want to update EnterLogData() with the following extra optional parameter:

```
// Error! The default value for an optional arg must be known
// at compile time!
static void EnterLogData(string message,
           string owner = "Programmer", DateTime timeStamp = DateTime.Now)
{
  Console.Beep();
  Console.WriteLine("Error: {0}", message);
  Console.WriteLine("Owner of Error: {0}", owner);
  Console.WriteLine("Time of Error: {0}", timeStamp);
}
```

This will not compile because the value of the Now property of the DateTime class is resolved at runtime, not compile time.

■ **Note**   To avoid ambiguity, optional parameters must always be packed onto the *end* of a method signature. It is a compiler error to have optional parameters listed before nonoptional parameters.

Invoking Methods Using Named Parameters

Another language feature found in C# is support for *named arguments*. To be honest, at first glance, this language construct might appear to do little more than result in confusing code. And to continue being completely honest, this could be the case! Similar to optional arguments, including support for named parameters is partially motivated by the desire to simplify the process of working with the COM interoperability layer (again, see Chapter 16).

Named arguments allow you to invoke a method by specifying parameter values in any order you choose. Thus, rather than passing parameters solely by position (as you will do in most cases), you can choose to specify each argument by name using a colon operator. To illustrate the use of named arguments, assume you have added the following method to the Program class:

```
static void DisplayFancyMessage(ConsoleColor textColor,
  ConsoleColor backgroundColor, string message)
{
  // Store old colors to restore after message is printed.
  ConsoleColor oldTextColor = Console.ForegroundColor;
  ConsoleColor oldbackgroundColor = Console.BackgroundColor;

  // Set new colors and print message.
  Console.ForegroundColor = textColor;
  Console.BackgroundColor = backgroundColor;
  Console.WriteLine(message);

  // Restore previous colors.
  Console.ForegroundColor = oldTextColor;
  Console.BackgroundColor = oldbackgroundColor;
}
```

Now, the way DisplayFancyMessage() was written, you would expect the caller to invoke this method by passing two ConsoleColor variables followed by a string type. However, using named arguments, the following calls are completely fine:

```
static void Main(string[] args)
{
  Console.WriteLine("***** Fun with Methods *****");
...
  DisplayFancyMessage(message: "Wow! Very Fancy indeed!",
    textColor: ConsoleColor.DarkRed,
    backgroundColor: ConsoleColor.White);
```

```
  DisplayFancyMessage(backgroundColor: ConsoleColor.Green,
    message: "Testing...",
    textColor: ConsoleColor.DarkBlue);
  Console.ReadLine();
}
```

One minor "gotcha" regarding named arguments is that if you begin to invoke a method using positional parameters, you must list them before any named parameters. In other words, named arguments must always be packed onto the end of a method call. The following code is an example:

```
// This is OK, as positional args are listed before named args.
DisplayFancyMessage(ConsoleColor.Blue,
  message: "Testing...",
  backgroundColor: ConsoleColor.White);

// This is an ERROR, as positional args are listed after named args.
DisplayFancyMessage(message: "Testing...",
  backgroundColor: ConsoleColor.White,
  ConsoleColor.Blue);
```

This restriction aside, you might still be wondering when you would ever want to use this language feature. After all, if you need to specify three arguments to a method, why bother flipping around their positions?

Well, as it turns out, if you have a method that defines optional arguments, this feature can actually be really helpful. Assume DisplayFancyMessage() has been rewritten to now support optional arguments, as you have assigned fitting defaults.

```
static void DisplayFancyMessage(ConsoleColor textColor = ConsoleColor.Blue,
  ConsoleColor backgroundColor = ConsoleColor.White,
  string message = "Test Message")
{
   ...
}
```

Given that each argument has a default value, named arguments allow the caller to specify only the parameters for which they do not want to receive the defaults. Therefore, if the caller wants the value "Hello!" to appear in blue text surrounded by a white background, they can simply specify the following:

```
DisplayFancyMessage(message: "Hello!");
```

Or, if the caller wants to see "Test Message" print out with a green background containing blue text, they can invoke DisplayFancyMessage().

```
DisplayFancyMessage(backgroundColor: ConsoleColor.Green);
```

As you can see, optional arguments and named parameters tend to work hand in hand. To wrap up your examination of building C# methods, I need to address the topic of *method overloading*.

■ **Source Code**   You can find the FunWithMethods application in the Chapter 4 subdirectory.

Understanding Method Overloading

Like other modern object-oriented languages, C# allows a method to be *overloaded*. Simply put, when you define a set of identically named methods that differ by the number (or type) of parameters, the method in question is said to be *overloaded*.

To understand why overloading is so useful, consider life as an old-school Visual Basic 6.0 (VB6) developer. Assume you are using VB6 to build a set of methods that return the sum of various incoming data types (Integers, Doubles, and so on). Given that VB6 does not support method overloading, you would be required to define a unique set of methods that essentially do the same thing (return the sum of the arguments).

```
' VB6 code examples.
Public Function AddInts(ByVal x As Integer, ByVal y As Integer) As Integer
  AddInts = x + y
End Function

Public Function AddDoubles(ByVal x As Double, ByVal y As Double) As Double
  AddDoubles = x + y
End Function

Public Function AddLongs(ByVal x As Long, ByVal y As Long) As Long
  AddLongs = x + y
End Function
```

Not only can code such as this become tough to maintain, but the caller must now be painfully aware of the name of each method. Using overloading, you are able to allow the caller to call a single method named Add(). Again, the key is to ensure that each version of the method has a distinct set of arguments (methods differing only by return type are not unique enough).

■ **Note**   As explained in Chapter 9, it is possible to build generic methods that take the concept of overloading to the next level. Using generics, you can define *type placeholders* for a method implementation that are specified at the time you invoke the member in question.

To check this out firsthand, create a new Console Application project named MethodOverloading. Now, consider the following class definition:

```
// C# code.
class Program
{
  static void Main(string[] args)
  {
  }

  // Overloaded Add() method.
  static int Add(int x, int y)
  { return x + y; }

  static double Add(double x, double y)
  { return x + y; }
```

```
  static long Add(long x, long y)
  { return x + y; }
}
```

The caller can now simply invoke Add() with the required arguments, and the compiler is happy to comply, given that the compiler is able to resolve the correct implementation to invoke with the provided arguments.

```
static void Main(string[] args)
{
  Console.WriteLine("***** Fun with Method Overloading *****\n");

  // Calls int version of Add()
  Console.WriteLine(Add(10, 10));

  // Calls long version of Add() (using the new digit separator)
  Console.WriteLine(Add(900_000_000_000, 900_000_000_000));

  // Calls double version of Add()
  Console.WriteLine(Add(4.3, 4.4));

  Console.ReadLine();
}
```

The Visual Studio IDE provides assistance when calling overloaded methods to boot. When you type in the name of an overloaded method (such as your good friend Console.WriteLine()), IntelliSense will list each version of the method in question. Note that you are able to cycle through each version of an overloaded method using the up and down arrow keys shown in Figure 4-1.

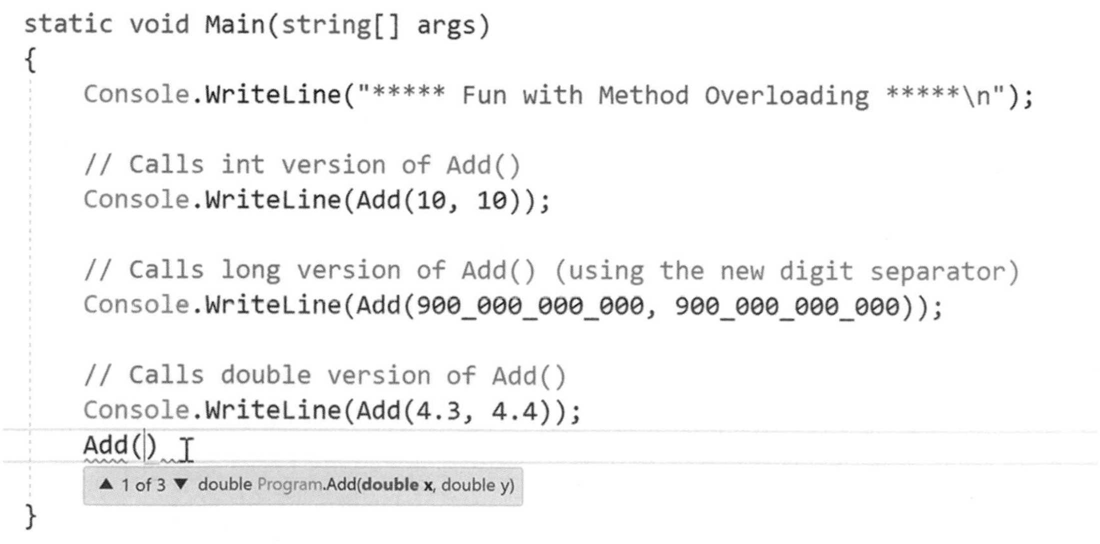

Figure 4-1. *Visual Studio IntelliSense for overloaded methods*

■ **Source Code**   You can find the MethodOverloading application in the Chapter 4 subdirectory.

Local Functions (New)

Another new feature introduced in C# 7 is the ability to create methods within methods, referred to officially as *local functions*. A local function is a function declared inside another function.

■ **Note**   Up to this point in the text, we've used the term *method*. Why all of a sudden am I introducing the term *function*? Is that something different than a method? Academically speaking, one can argue that they are different. Practically speaking, they are used interchangeably. For this text, consider a method and a function as equivalent. The new feature is officially named *local functions*, and I didn't want to change the name just for consistency in this text. From here on out, I am back to calling them *methods*.

To see how this works, create a new Console Application project named FunWithLocalFunctions. As an example, let's say you want to extend the Add() example from the previous section by including validation of the inputs. There are many ways to accomplish this, and one simple way is to add the validation directly into the Add() method. Let's go with that and update the previous example to the following:

```
static int Add(int x, int y)
{
  //Do some validation here
  return x + y;
}
```

As you can see, there are no big changes. There's just a comment indicating that real code should do something. What if you wanted to separate the actual reason for the method (returning the sum of the arguments) from the validation of the arguments? You could create additional methods and call them from the Add() method. But that would require creating another method just for use by one other method. Maybe that's overkill. This new feature allows you to do the validation first and then encapsulate the real goal of the method defined inside the AddWrapper() method, as shown here:

```
static int AddWrapper(int x, int y)
{
  //Do some validation here
  return Add();

  int Add()
  {
    return x + y;
  }
}
```

The contained Add() method can be called only from the wrapping AddWrapper() method. So, the question I'm sure you are thinking is, "What did this buy me?" The answer for this example, quite simply, is little (if anything). This feature was added into the C# specification for custom iterator methods (Chapter 8) and asynchronous methods (Chapter 19), and you will see the benefit when you get to those topics.

133

■ **Source Code**   You can find the LocalFunctions application in the Chapter 4 subdirectory.

That wraps up the initial examination of building methods using the syntax of C#. Next, let's check out how to build and manipulate enumerations and structures.

Understanding the enum Type

Recall from Chapter 1 that the .NET type system is composed of classes, structures, enumerations, interfaces, and delegates. To begin exploration of these types, let's check out the role of the *enumeration* (or simply, enum) using a new Console Application project named FunWithEnums.

■ **Note**   Do not confuse the term *enum* with *enumerator*; they are completely different concepts. An enum is a custom data type of name-value pairs. An enumerator is a class or structure that implements a .NET interface named IEnumerable. Typically, this interface is implemented on collection classes, as well as the System.Array class. As you will see in Chapter 8, objects that support IEnumerable can work within the foreach loop.

When building a system, it is often convenient to create a set of symbolic names that map to known numerical values. For example, if you are creating a payroll system, you might want to refer to the type of employees using constants such as vice president, manager, contractor, and grunt. C# supports the notion of custom enumerations for this very reason. For example, here is an enumeration named EmpType (you can define this in the same file as your Program class, right before the class definition):

```
// A custom enumeration.
enum EmpType
{
  Manager,       // = 0
  Grunt,         // = 1
  Contractor,    // = 2
  VicePresident  // = 3
}
```

The EmpType enumeration defines four named constants, corresponding to discrete numerical values. By default, the first element is set to the value zero (0), followed by an n+1 progression. You are free to change the initial value as you see fit. For example, if it made sense to number the members of EmpType as 102 through 105, you could do so as follows:

```
// Begin with 102.
enum EmpType
{
  Manager = 102,
  Grunt,         // = 103
  Contractor,    // = 104
  VicePresident  // = 105
}
```

Enumerations do not necessarily need to follow a sequential ordering and do not need to have unique values. If (for some reason or another) it makes sense to establish your EmpType as shown here, the compiler continues to be happy:

```
// Elements of an enumeration need not be sequential!
enum EmpType
{
  Manager = 10,
  Grunt = 1,
  Contractor = 100,
  VicePresident = 9
}
```

Controlling the Underlying Storage for an enum

By default, the storage type used to hold the values of an enumeration is a System.Int32 (the C# int); however, you are free to change this to your liking. C# enumerations can be defined in a similar manner for any of the core system types (byte, short, int, or long). For example, if you want to set the underlying storage value of EmpType to be a byte rather than an int, you can write the following:

```
// This time, EmpType maps to an underlying byte.
enum EmpType : byte
{
  Manager = 10,
  Grunt = 1,
  Contractor = 100,
  VicePresident = 9
}
```

Changing the underlying type of an enumeration can be helpful if you are building a .NET application that will be deployed to a low-memory device and need to conserve memory wherever possible. Of course, if you do establish your enumeration to use a byte as storage, each value must be within its range! For example, the following version of EmpType will result in a compiler error, as the value 999 cannot fit within the range of a byte:

```
// Compile-time error! 999 is too big for a byte!
enum EmpType : byte
{
  Manager = 10,
  Grunt = 1,
  Contractor = 100,
  VicePresident = 999
}
```

Declaring enum Variables

Once you have established the range and storage type of your enumeration, you can use it in place of so- called magic numbers. Because enumerations are nothing more than a user-defined data type, you are able to use them as function return values, method parameters, local variables, and so forth. Assume you have a method named AskForBonus(), taking an EmpType variable as the sole parameter. Based on the value of the incoming parameter, you will print out a fitting response to the pay bonus request.

```csharp
class Program
{
  static void Main(string[] args)
  {
    Console.WriteLine("**** Fun with Enums *****");
    // Make an EmpType variable.
    EmpType emp = EmpType.Contractor;
    AskForBonus(emp);
    Console.ReadLine();
  }

  // Enums as parameters.
  static void AskForBonus(EmpType e)
  {
    switch (e)
    {
      case EmpType.Manager:
        Console.WriteLine("How about stock options instead?");
        break;
      case EmpType.Grunt:
        Console.WriteLine("You have got to be kidding...");
        break;
      case EmpType.Contractor:
        Console.WriteLine("You already get enough cash...");
        break;
      case EmpType.VicePresident:
        Console.WriteLine("VERY GOOD, Sir!");
        break;
    }
  }
}
```

Notice that when you are assigning a value to an enum variable, you must scope the enum name (EmpType) to the value (Grunt). Because enumerations are a fixed set of name-value pairs, it is illegal to set an enum variable to a value that is not defined directly by the enumerated type.

```csharp
static void ThisMethodWillNotCompile()
{
  // Error! SalesManager is not in the EmpType enum!
  EmpType emp = EmpType.SalesManager;

  // Error! Forgot to scope Grunt value to EmpType enum!
  emp = Grunt;
}
```

The System.Enum Type

The interesting thing about .NET enumerations is that they gain functionality from the System.Enum class type. This class defines a number of methods that allow you to interrogate and transform a given enumeration. One helpful method is the static Enum.GetUnderlyingType(), which, as the name implies, returns the data type used to store the values of the enumerated type (System.Byte in the case of the current EmpType declaration).

```
static void Main(string[] args)
{
  Console.WriteLine("**** Fun with Enums *****");
  // Make a contractor type.
  EmpType emp = EmpType.Contractor;
  AskForBonus(emp);

  // Print storage for the enum.
  Console.WriteLine("EmpType uses a {0} for storage",
    Enum.GetUnderlyingType(emp.GetType()));
  Console.ReadLine();
}
```

If you were to consult the Visual Studio Object Browser, you would be able to verify that the Enum.GetUnderlyingType() method requires you to pass in a System.Type as the first parameter. As fully examined in Chapter 15, Type represents the metadata description of a given .NET entity.

One possible way to obtain metadata (as shown previously) is to use the GetType() method, which is common to all types in the .NET base class libraries. Another approach is to use the C# typeof operator. One benefit of doing so is that you do not need to have a variable of the entity you want to obtain a metadata description of.

```
// This time use typeof to extract a Type.
Console.WriteLine("EmpType uses a {0} for storage",
    Enum.GetUnderlyingType(typeof(EmpType)));
```

Dynamically Discovering an enum's Name-Value Pairs

Beyond the Enum.GetUnderlyingType() method, all C# enumerations support a method named ToString(), which returns the string name of the current enumeration's value. The following code is an example:

```
static void Main(string[] args)
{
  Console.WriteLine("**** Fun with Enums *****");
  EmpType emp = EmpType.Contractor;
  AskForBonus(emp);

  // Prints out "emp is a Contractor".
  Console.WriteLine("emp is a {0}.", emp.ToString());
  Console.ReadLine();
}
```

If you are interested in discovering the value of a given enumeration variable, rather than its name, you can simply cast the enum variable against the underlying storage type. The following is an example:

```
static void Main(string[] args)
{
  Console.WriteLine("**** Fun with Enums *****");
  EmpType emp = EmpType.Contractor;
  ...

  // Prints out "Contractor = 100".
  Console.WriteLine("{0} = {1}", emp.ToString(), (byte)emp);
  Console.ReadLine();
}
```

■ **Note**   The static `Enum.Format()` method provides a finer level of formatting options by specifying a desired format flag. Consult the .NET Framework 4.7 SDK documentation for full details of the `System.Enum.Format()` method.

`System.Enum` also defines another static method named `GetValues()`. This method returns an instance of `System.Array`. Each item in the array corresponds to a member of the specified enumeration. Consider the following method, which will print out each name-value pair within any enumeration you pass in as a parameter:

```
// This method will print out the details of any enum.
static void EvaluateEnum(System.Enum e)
{
  Console.WriteLine("=> Information about {0}", e.GetType().Name);

  Console.WriteLine("Underlying storage type: {0}",
    Enum.GetUnderlyingType(e.GetType()));

  // Get all name-value pairs for incoming parameter.
  Array enumData = Enum.GetValues(e.GetType());
  Console.WriteLine("This enum has {0} members.", enumData.Length);

  // Now show the string name and associated value, using the D format
  // flag (see Chapter 3).
  for(int i = 0; i < enumData.Length; i++)
  {
    Console.WriteLine("Name: {0}, Value: {0:D}",
      enumData.GetValue(i));
  }
  Console.WriteLine();
}
```

To test this new method, update your Main() method to create variables of several enumeration types declared in the System namespace (as well as an EmpType enumeration for good measure). The following code is an example:

```
static void Main(string[] args)
{
  Console.WriteLine("**** Fun with Enums *****");
  ...
  EmpType e2 = EmpType.Contractor;

  // These types are enums in the System namespace.
  DayOfWeek day = DayOfWeek.Monday;
  ConsoleColor cc = ConsoleColor.Gray;

  EvaluateEnum(e2);
  EvaluateEnum(day);
  EvaluateEnum(cc);
  Console.ReadLine();
}
```

Some partial output is shown here:

```
=> Information about DayOfWeek
Underlying storage type: System.Int32
This enum has 7 members.
Name: Sunday, Value: 0
Name: Monday, Value: 1
Name: Tuesday, Value: 2
Name: Wednesday, Value: 3
Name: Thursday, Value: 4
Name: Friday, Value: 5
Name: Saturday, Value: 6
```

As you will see over the course of this text, enumerations are used extensively throughout the .NET base class libraries. For example, ADO.NET makes use of numerous enumerations to represent the state of a database connection (e.g., opened or closed) or the state of a row in a DataTable (e.g., changed, new, or detached). Therefore, when you make use of any enumeration, always remember that you are able to interact with the name-value pairs using the members of System.Enum.

■ **Source Code**   You can find the FunWithEnums project in the Chapter 4 subdirectory.

Understanding the Structure (aka Value Type)

Now that you understand the role of enumeration types, let's examine the use of .NET *structures* (or simply *structs*). Structure types are well suited for modeling mathematical, geometrical, and other "atomic" entities in your application. A structure (such as an enumeration) is a user-defined type; however, structures are not simply a collection of name-value pairs. Rather, structures are types that can contain any number of data fields and members that operate on these fields.

■ **Note** If you have a background in OOP, you can think of a structure as a "lightweight class type," given that structures provide a way to define a type that supports encapsulation but cannot be used to build a family of related types. When you need to build a family of related types through inheritance, you will need to make use of class types.

On the surface, the process of defining and using structures is simple, but as they say, the devil is in the details. To begin understanding the basics of structure types, create a new project named FunWithStructures. In C#, structures are defined using the struct keyword. Define a new structure named Point, which defines two member variables of type int and a set of methods to interact with said data.

```
struct Point
{
  // Fields of the structure.
  public int X;
  public int Y;

  // Add 1 to the (X, Y) position.
  public void Increment()
  {
    X++; Y++;
  }

  // Subtract 1 from the (X, Y) position.
  public void Decrement()
  {
    X--; Y--;
  }

  // Display the current position.
  public void Display()
  {
    Console.WriteLine("X = {0}, Y = {1}", X, Y);
  }
}
```

Here, you have defined your two integer fields (X and Y) using the public keyword, which is an access control modifier (Chapter 5 furthers this discussion). Declaring data with the public keyword ensures the caller has direct access to the data from a given Point variable (via the dot operator).

■ **Note** It is typically considered bad style to define public data within a class or structure. Rather, you will want to define *private* data, which can be accessed and changed using *public* properties. These details will be examined in Chapter 5.

Here is a `Main()` method that takes the `Point` type out for a test-drive:

```
static void Main(string[] args)
{
  Console.WriteLine("***** A First Look at Structures *****\n");

  // Create an initial Point.
  Point myPoint;
  myPoint.X = 349;
  myPoint.Y = 76;
  myPoint.Display();

  // Adjust the X and Y values.
  myPoint.Increment();
  myPoint.Display();
  Console.ReadLine();
}
```

The output is as you would expect.

```
***** A First Look at Structures *****

X = 349, Y = 76
X = 350, Y = 77
```

Creating Structure Variables

When you want to create a structure variable, you have a variety of options. Here, you simply create a `Point` variable and assign each piece of public field data before invoking its members. If you do *not* assign each piece of public field data (X and Y in this case) before using the structure, you will receive a compiler error.

```
// Error! Did not assign Y value.
Point p1;
p1.X = 10;
p1.Display();

// OK! Both fields assigned before use.
Point p2;
p2.X = 10;
p2.Y = 10;
p2.Display();
```

As an alternative, you can create structure variables using the C# new keyword, which will invoke the structure's *default constructor*. By definition, a default constructor does not take any arguments. The benefit of invoking the default constructor of a structure is that each piece of field data is automatically set to its default value.

141

```
// Set all fields to default values
// using the default constructor.
Point p1 = new Point();

// Prints X=0,Y=0.
p1.Display();
```

It is also possible to design a structure with a *custom constructor*. This allows you to specify the values of field data upon variable creation, rather than having to set each data member field by field. Chapter 5 will provide a detailed examination of constructors; however, to illustrate, update the Point structure with the following code:

```
struct Point
{
  // Fields of the structure.
  public int X;
  public int Y;

  // A custom constructor.
  public Point(int XPos, int YPos)
  {
    X = XPos;
    Y = YPos;
  }
...
}
```

With this, you could now create Point variables, as follows:

```
// Call custom constructor.
Point p2 = new Point(50, 60);

// Prints X=50,Y=60.
p2.Display();
```

As mentioned, working with structures on the surface is quite simple. However, to deepen your understanding of this type, you need to explore the distinction between a .NET value type and a .NET reference type.

■ **Source Code**   You can find the FunWithStructures project in the Chapter 4 subdirectory.

Understanding Value Types and Reference Types

■ **Note**   The following discussion of value types and reference types assumes that you have a background in object-oriented programming. If this is not the case, you might want to skip to the "Understanding C# Nullable Types" section of this chapter and return to this section after you have read Chapters 5 and 6.

Unlike arrays, strings, or enumerations, C# structures do not have an identically named representation in the .NET library (that is, there is no System.Structure class) but are implicitly derived from System.ValueType. Simply put, the role of System.ValueType is to ensure that the derived type (e.g., any structure) is allocated on the *stack*, rather than the garbage-collected *heap*. Simply put, data allocated on the stack can be created and destroyed quickly, as its lifetime is determined by the defining scope. Heap-allocated data, on the other hand, is monitored by the .NET garbage collector and has a lifetime that is determined by a large number of factors, which will be examined in Chapter 13.

Functionally, the only purpose of System.ValueType is to override the virtual methods defined by System.Object to use value-based versus reference-based semantics. As you might know, overriding is the process of changing the implementation of a virtual (or possibly abstract) method defined within a base class. The base class of ValueType is System.Object. In fact, the instance methods defined by System.ValueType are identical to those of System.Object.

```
// Structures and enumerations implicitly extend System.ValueType.
public abstract class ValueType : object
{
  public virtual bool Equals(object obj);
  public virtual int GetHashCode();
  public Type GetType();
  public virtual string ToString();
}
```

Given that value types are using value-based semantics, the lifetime of a structure (which includes all numerical data types [int, float], as well as any enum or structure) is predictable. When a structure variable falls out of the defining scope, it is removed from memory immediately.

```
// Local structures are popped off
// the stack when a method returns.
static void LocalValueTypes()
{
  // Recall! "int" is really a System.Int32 structure.
  int i = 0;

  // Recall! Point is a structure type.
  Point p = new Point();
} // "i" and "p" popped off the stack here!
```

Value Types, References Types, and the Assignment Operator

When you assign one value type to another, a member-by-member copy of the field data is achieved. In the case of a simple data type such as System.Int32, the only member to copy is the numerical value. However, in the case of your Point, the X and Y values are copied into the new structure variable. To illustrate, create a new Console Application project named ValueAndReferenceTypes and then copy your previous Point definition into your new namespace. Next, add the following method to your Program type:

```
// Assigning two intrinsic value types results in
// two independent variables on the stack.
static void ValueTypeAssignment()
```

```
{
  Console.WriteLine("Assigning value types\n");

  Point p1 = new Point(10, 10);
  Point p2 = p1;

  // Print both points.
  p1.Display();
  p2.Display();

  // Change p1.X and print again. p2.X is not changed.
  p1.X = 100;
  Console.WriteLine("\n=> Changed p1.X\n");
  p1.Display();
  p2.Display();
}
```

Here, you have created a variable of type Point (named p1) that is then assigned to another Point (p2). Because Point is a value type, you have two copies of the MyPoint type on the stack, each of which can be independently manipulated. Therefore, when you change the value of p1.X, the value of p2.X is unaffected.

```
Assigning value types
X = 10, Y = 10
X = 10, Y = 10
=> Changed p1.X
X = 100, Y = 10
X = 10, Y = 10
```

In stark contrast to value types, when you apply the assignment operator to reference types (meaning all class instances), you are redirecting what the reference variable points to in memory. To illustrate, create a new class type named PointRef that has the same members as the Point structures, beyond renaming the constructor to match the class name.

```
// Classes are always reference types.
class PointRef
{
  // Same members as the Point structure...
  // Be sure to change your constructor name to PointRef!
  public PointRef(int XPos, int YPos)
  {
    X = XPos;
    Y = YPos;
  }
}
```

Now, use your PointRef type within the following new method. Note that beyond using the PointRef class, rather than the Point structure, the code is identical to the ValueTypeAssignment() method.

```
static void ReferenceTypeAssignment()
{
  Console.WriteLine("Assigning reference types\n");
  PointRef p1 = new PointRef(10, 10);
  PointRef p2 = p1;

  // Print both point refs.
  p1.Display();
  p2.Display();

  // Change p1.X and print again.
  p1.X = 100;
  Console.WriteLine("\n=> Changed p1.X\n");
  p1.Display();
  p2.Display();
}
```

In this case, you have two references pointing to the same object on the managed heap. Therefore, when you change the value of X using the p1 reference, p2.X reports the same value. Assuming you have called this new method within Main(), your output should look like the following:

```
Assigning reference types
X = 10, Y = 10
X = 10, Y = 10
=> Changed p1.X
X = 100, Y = 10
X = 100, Y = 10
```

Value Types Containing Reference Types

Now that you have a better feeling for the basic differences between value types and reference types, let's examine a more complex example. Assume you have the following reference (class) type that maintains an informational string that can be set using a custom constructor:

```
class ShapeInfo
{
  public string InfoString;
  public ShapeInfo(string info)
  {
    InfoString = info;
  }
}
```

Now assume that you want to contain a variable of this class type within a value type named `Rectangle`. To allow the caller to set the value of the inner `ShapeInfo` member variable, you also provide a custom constructor. Here is the complete definition of the `Rectangle` type:

```
struct Rectangle
{
  // The Rectangle structure contains a reference type member.
  public ShapeInfo RectInfo;

  public int RectTop, RectLeft, RectBottom, RectRight;

  public Rectangle(string info, int top, int left, int bottom, int right)
  {
    RectInfo = new ShapeInfo(info);
    RectTop = top; RectBottom = bottom;
    RectLeft = left; RectRight = right;
  }

  public void Display()
  {
    Console.WriteLine("String = {0}, Top = {1}, Bottom = {2}, " +
      "Left = {3}, Right = {4}",
      RectInfo.infoString, RectTop, RectBottom, RectLeft, RectRight);
  }
}
```

At this point, you have contained a reference type within a value type. The million-dollar question now becomes, what happens if you assign one `Rectangle` variable to another? Given what you already know about value types, you would be correct in assuming that the integer data (which is indeed a structure— `System.Int32`) should be an independent entity for each `Rectangle` variable. But what about the internal reference type? Will the object's *state* be fully copied, or will the reference to that object be copied? To answer this question, define the following method and invoke it from `Main()`:

```
static void ValueTypeContainingRefType()
{
  // Create the first Rectangle.
  Console.WriteLine("-> Creating r1");
  Rectangle r1 = new Rectangle("First Rect", 10, 10, 50, 50);

  // Now assign a new Rectangle to r1.
  Console.WriteLine("-> Assigning r2 to r1");
  Rectangle r2 = r1;

  // Change some values of r2.
  Console.WriteLine("-> Changing values of r2");
  r2.RectInfo.InfoString = "This is new info!";
  r2.RectBottom = 4444;

  // Print values of both rectangles.
  r1.Display();
  r2.Display();
}
```

The output is shown here:

```
-> Creating r1
-> Assigning r2 to r1
-> Changing values of r2
String = This is new info!, Top = 10, Bottom = 50, Left = 10, Right = 50
String = This is new info!, Top = 10, Bottom = 4444, Left = 10, Right = 50
```

As you can see, when you change the value of the informational string using the r2 reference, the r1 reference displays the same value. By default, when a value type contains other reference types, assignment results in a copy of the references. In this way, you have two independent structures, each of which contains a reference pointing to the same object in memory (i.e., a shallow copy). When you want to perform a deep copy, where the state of internal references is fully copied into a new object, one approach is to implement the ICloneable interface (as you will do in Chapter 8).

■ **Source Code**   You can find the ValueAndReferenceTypes project in the Chapter 4 subdirectory.

Passing Reference Types by Value

Reference types or value types can, obviously, be passed as parameters to methods. However, passing a reference type (e.g., a class) by reference is quite different from passing it by value. To understand the distinction, assume you have a simple Person class defined in a new Console Application project named RefTypeValTypeParams, defined as follows:

```
class Person
{
  public string personName;
  public int personAge;

  // Constructors.
  public Person(string name, int age)
  {
    personName = name;
    personAge = age;
  }
  public Person(){}

  public void Display()
  {
    Console.WriteLine("Name: {0}, Age: {1}", personName, personAge);
  }
}
```

Now, what if you create a method that allows the caller to send in the Person object by value (note the lack of parameter modifiers, such as out or ref)?

```
static void SendAPersonByValue(Person p)
{
  // Change the age of "p"?
  p.personAge = 99;

  // Will the caller see this reassignment?
  p = new Person("Nikki", 99);
}
```

Notice how the SendAPersonByValue() method attempts to reassign the incoming Person reference to a new Person object, as well as change some state data. Now let's test this method using the following Main() method:

```
static void Main(string[] args)
{
  // Passing rcf-types by value.
  Console.WriteLine("***** Passing Person object by value *****");
  Person fred = new Person("Fred", 12);
  Console.WriteLine("\nBefore by value call, Person is:");
  fred.Display();

  SendAPersonByValue(fred);
  Console.WriteLine("\nAfter by value call, Person is:");
  fred.Display();
  Console.ReadLine();
}
```

The following is the output of this call:

```
***** Passing Person object by value *****

Before by value call, Person is:
Name: Fred, Age: 12

After by value call, Person is:
Name: Fred, Age: 99
```

As you can see, the value of personAge has been modified. This behavior seems to fly in the face of what it means to pass a parameter by value. Given that you were able to change the state of the incoming Person, what was copied? The answer: a copy of the reference to the caller's object. Therefore, as the SendAPersonByValue() method is pointing to the same object as the caller, it is possible to alter the object's state data. What is not possible is to reassign what the reference *is pointing to*.

Passing Reference Types by Reference

Now assume you have a SendAPersonByReference() method, which passes a reference type by reference (note the ref parameter modifier).

```
static void SendAPersonByReference(ref Person p)
{
  // Change some data of "p".
  p.personAge = 555;

  // "p" is now pointing to a new object on the heap!
  p = new Person("Nikki", 999);
}
```

As you might expect, this allows complete flexibility of how the callee is able to manipulate the incoming parameter. Not only can the callee change the state of the object, but if it so chooses, it may also reassign the reference to a new Person object. Now ponder the following updated Main() method:

```
static void Main(string[] args)
{
  // Passing ref-types by ref.
  Console.WriteLine("***** Passing Person object by reference *****");
  ...

  Person mel - new Person("Mel", 23);
  Console.WriteLine("Before by ref call, Person is:");
  mel.Display();

  SendAPersonByReference(ref mel);
  Console.WriteLine("After by ref call, Person is:");
  mel.Display();
  Console.ReadLine();
}
```

Notice the following output:

```
***** Passing Person object by reference *****
Before by ref call, Person is:
Name: Mel, Age: 23
After by ref call, Person is:
Name: Nikki, Age: 999
```

As you can see, an object named Mel returns after the call as an object named Nikki, as the method was able to change what the incoming reference pointed to in memory. The golden rule to keep in mind when passing reference types is the following:

- If a reference type is passed by reference, the callee may change the values of the object's state data, as well as the object it is referencing.

- If a reference type is passed by value, the callee may change the values of the object's state data but *not* the object it is referencing.

■ **Source Code**   You can find the RefTypeValTypeParams project in the Chapter 4 subdirectory.

Final Details Regarding Value Types and Reference Types

To wrap up this topic, consider the information in Table 4-3, which summarizes the core distinctions between value types and reference types.

Table 4-3. *Value Types and Reference Types Comparison*

Intriguing Question	Value Type	Reference Type
Where are objects allocated?	Allocated on the stack.	Allocated on the managed heap.
How is a variable represented?	Value type variables are local copies.	Reference type variables are pointing to the memory occupied by the allocated instance.
What is the base type?	Implicitly extends System.ValueType.	Can derive from any other type (except System.ValueType), as long as that type is not "sealed" (more details on this in Chapter 6).
Can this type function as a base to other types?	No. Value types are always sealed and cannot be inherited from.	Yes. If the type is not sealed, it may function as a base to other types.
What is the default parameter passing behavior?	Variables are passed by value (i.e., a copy of the variable is passed into the called function).	For reference types, the reference is copied by value.
Can this type override System.Object.Finalize()?	No.	Yes, indirectly (more details on this in Chapter 13).
Can I define constructors for this type?	Yes, but the default constructor is reserved (i.e., your custom constructors must all have arguments).	But, of course!
When do variables of this type die?	When they fall out of the defining scope.	When the object is garbage collected.

Despite their differences, value types and reference types both have the ability to implement interfaces and may support any number of fields, methods, overloaded operators, constants, properties, and events.

Understanding C# Nullable Types

Let's examine the role of the *nullable data type* using a Console Application project named NullableTypes. As you know, C# data types have a fixed range and are represented as a type in the System namespace. For example, the System.Boolean data type can be assigned a value from the set {true, false}. Now, recall that all the numerical data types (as well as the Boolean data type) are *value types*. Value types can never be assigned the value of null, as that is used to establish an empty object reference.

```
static void Main(string[] args)
{
  // Compiler errors!
  // Value types cannot be set to null!
  bool myBool = null;
  int myInt = null;

  // OK! Strings are reference types.
  string myString = null;
}
```

C# supports the concept of *nullable data types*. Simply put, a nullable type can represent all the values of its underlying type, plus the value null. Thus, if you declare a nullable bool, it could be assigned a value from the set {true, false, null}. This can be extremely helpful when working with relational databases, given that it is quite common to encounter undefined columns in database tables. Without the concept of a nullable data type, there is no convenient manner in C# to represent a numerical data point with no value.

To define a nullable variable type, the question mark symbol (?) is suffixed to the underlying data type. Do note that this syntax is legal only when applied to value types. If you attempt to create a nullable reference type (including strings), you are issued a compile-time error. Like a non-nullable variable, local nullable variables must be assigned an initial value before you can use them.

```
static void LocalNullableVariables()
{
  // Define some local nullable variables.
  int? nullableInt = 10;
  double? nullableDouble = 3.14;
  bool? nullableBool = null;
  char? nullableChar = 'a';
  int?[] arrayOfNullableInts = new int?[10];

  // Error! Strings are reference types!
  // string? s = "oops";
}
```

In C#, the ? suffix notation is a shorthand for creating an instance of the generic System.Nullable<T> structure type. Although you will not examine generics until Chapter 9, it is important to understand that the System.Nullable<T> type provides a set of members that all nullable types can make use of.

For example, you are able to programmatically discover whether the nullable variable indeed has been assigned a null value using the HasValue property or the != operator. The assigned value of a nullable type may be obtained directly or via the Value property. In fact, given that the ? suffix is just a shorthand for using Nullable<T>, you could implement your LocalNullableVariables() method as follows:

```
static void LocalNullableVariablesUsingNullable()
{
  // Define some local nullable types using Nullable<T>.
  Nullable<int> nullableInt = 10;
  Nullable<double> nullableDouble = 3.14;
  Nullable<bool> nullableBool = null;
  Nullable<char> nullableChar = 'a';
  Nullable<int>[] arrayOfNullableInts = new Nullable<int>[10];
}
```

151

Working with Nullable Types

As stated, nullable data types can be particularly useful when you are interacting with databases, given that columns in a data table may be intentionally empty (e.g., undefined). To illustrate, assume the following class, which simulates the process of accessing a database that has a table containing two columns that may be null. Note that the GetIntFromDatabase() method is not assigning a value to the nullable integer member variable, while GetBoolFromDatabase() is assigning a valid value to the bool? member.

```
class DatabaseReader
{
  // Nullable data field.
  public int? numericValue = null;
  public bool? boolValue = true;

  // Note the nullable return type.
  public int? GetIntFromDatabase()
  { return numericValue; }

  // Note the nullable return type.
  public bool? GetBoolFromDatabase()
  { return boolValue; }
}
```

Now, assume the following Main() method, which invokes each member of the DatabaseReader class and discovers the assigned values using the HasValue and Value members, as well as using the C# equality operator (not equal, to be exact):

```
static void Main(string[] args)
{
  Console.WriteLine("***** Fun with Nullable Data *****\n");
  DatabaseReader dr = new DatabaseReader();

  // Get int from "database".
  int? i = dr.GetIntFromDatabase();
  if (i.HasValue)
    Console.WriteLine("Value of 'i' is: {0}", i.Value);
  else
    Console.WriteLine("Value of 'i' is undefined.");
  // Get bool from "database".
  bool? b = dr.GetBoolFromDatabase();
  if (b != null)
    Console.WriteLine("Value of 'b' is: {0}", b.Value);
  else
    Console.WriteLine("Value of 'b' is undefined.");
  Console.ReadLine();
}
```

The Null Coalescing Operator

The next aspect to be aware of is any variable that might have a null value (i.e., a reference-type variable or a nullable value-type variable) can make use of the C# ?? operator, which is formally termed the *null coalescing operator*. This operator allows you to assign a value to a nullable type if the retrieved value is in fact null. For this example, assume you want to assign a local nullable integer to 100 if the value returned from GetIntFromDatabase() is null (of course, this method is programmed to always return null, but I am sure you get the general idea).

```
static void Main(string[] args)
{
  Console.WriteLine("***** Fun with Nullable Data *****\n");
  DatabaseReader dr = new DatabaseReader();
...
  // If the value from GetIntFromDatabase() is null,
  // assign local variable to 100.
  int myData = dr.GetIntFromDatabase() ?? 100;
  Console.WriteLine("Value of myData: {0}", myData);
  Console.ReadLine();
}
```

The benefit of using the ?? operator is that it provides a more compact version of a traditional if/else condition. However, if you want, you could have authored the following functionally equivalent code to ensure that if a value comes back as null, it will indeed be set to the value 100:

```
// Long-hand notation not using ?? syntax.
int? moreData = dr.GetIntFromDatabase();
if (!moreData.HasValue)
    moreData = 100;
Console.WriteLine("Value of moreData: {0}", moreData);
```

The Null Conditional Operator

When you are writing software, it is common to check incoming parameters, which are values returned from type members (methods, properties, indexers), against the value null. For example, let's assume you have a method that takes a string array as a single parameter. To be safe, you might want to test for null before proceeding. In that way, you will not get a runtime error if the array is empty. The following would be a traditional way to perform such a check:

```
static void TesterMethod(string[] args)
{
  // We should check for null before accessing the array data!
  if (args != null)
  {
    Console.WriteLine($"You sent me {args.Length} arguments.");
  }
}
```

Here, you use a conditional scope to ensure that the Length property of the string array will not be accessed if the array is null. If the caller failed to make an array of data and called your method like so, you are still safe and will not trigger a runtime error:

```
TesterMethod(null);
```

With the current release of the C# language, it is now possible to leverage the null conditional operator token (a question mark placed after a variable type but before an access operator) to simplify the previous error checking. Rather than explicitly building a conditional statement to check for null, you can now write the following:

```
static void TesterMethod(string[] args)
{
  // We should check for null before accessing the array data!
  Console.WriteLine($"You sent me {args?.Length} arguments.");
}
```

In this case, you are not using a conditional statement. Rather, you are suffixing the ? operator directly after the string array variable. If this is null, its call to the Length property will not throw a runtime error. If you want to print an actual value, you could leverage the null coalescing operator to assign a default value as so:

```
Console.WriteLine($"You sent me {args?.Length ?? 0} arguments.");
```

There are some additional areas of coding where the new C# 6.0 null conditional operator will be quite handy, especially when working with delegates and events. However, since those topics are not addressed until later in the book (see Chapter 10), you will hold on any additional use cases. With this, your initial investigation of the C# programming language is complete! In Chapter 5, you will begin to dig into the details of object-oriented development.

■ **Source Code** You can find the NullableTypes application in the Chapter 4 subdirectory.

Tuples (New)

To wrap up this chapter, let's examine the role of tuples using a final Console Application project named FunWithTuples. As mentioned earlier in this chapter, one way to use out parameters is to retrieve more than one value from a method call. While doing that certainly works, it's a bit of a hack. It's much better to use a construct *designed* for this.

Tuples, which are lightweight data structures that contain multiple fields, were actually added in C# 6 but in a very limited way. The fields are not validated, you cannot define your own methods, and (perhaps) more importantly each property is a reference type, potentially causing memory and performance issues.

In C# 7, tuples use the new ValueTuple data type instead of reference types, potentially saving significant memory. The ValueTuple data type creates different structs based on the number of properties for a tuple. An additional feature added in C# 7 is that each property in a tuple can be assigned a specific name (just like variables), greatly enhancing the usability.

Getting Started with Tuples

Enough theory, let's write some code! To create a tuple, simply enclose the values to be assigned to the tuple in parentheses, as follows:

```
("a", 5, "c")
```

Notice that they don't all have to be the same data type. The parenthetical construct is also used to assign the tuple to a variable (or you can use the var keyword and the compiler will assign the data types for you). To assign the previous example to a variable, the following two lines achieve the same thing. The values variable will be a tuple with two string properties and an int property.

```
(string, int, string) values = ("a", 5, "c");
var values = ("a", 5, "c");
```

■ **Note**   If the preceding code doesn't compile, you will need to install the System.ValueTuple NuGet package. Right-click the project name in Solution Explorer, select Manage NuGet Packages, and when the NuGet Package Manager loads, click Browse in the top-left corner. Next, enter System.ValueTuple in the search box and then click install. I'm running VS 2017 Community edition on Windows 10 and didn't need to install it for tuple support. However, your configuration may be different.

By default, the compiler assigns each property the name ItemX, where X represents the one based position in the tuple. For the previous example, the property names are Item1, Item2, and Item3. Accessing them is done as follows:

```
Console.WriteLine($"First item: {values.Item1}");
Console.WriteLine($"Second item: {values.Item2}");
Console.WriteLine($"Third item: {values.Item3}");
```

Specific names can also be added to each property in the tuple on either the right side or the left side of the statement. While it is not a compiler error to assign names on both sides of the statement, if you do, the right side will be ignored, and only the left-side names are used. The following two lines of code show setting the names on the left and the right and achieve the same end:

```
(string FirstLetter, int TheNumber, string SecondLetter) valuesWithNames = ("a", 5, "c");
var valuesWithNames2 = (FirstLetter: "a", TheNumber: 5, SecondLetter: "c");
```

Now the properties on the tuple can be accessed using the field names as well as the ItemX notation, as shown in the following code:

```
Console.WriteLine($"First item: {valuesWithNames.FirstLetter}");
Console.WriteLine($"Second item: {valuesWithNames.TheNumber}");
Console.WriteLine($"Third item: {valuesWithNames.SecondLetter}");
//Using the item notation still works!
Console.WriteLine($"First item: {valuesWithNames.Item1}");
Console.WriteLine($"Second item: {valuesWithNames.Item2}");
Console.WriteLine($"Third item: {valuesWithNames.Item3}");
```

155

Note that when setting the names on the right, you must use the keyword var. Setting the data types specifically (even without custom names) triggers the compiler to use the left side, assign the properties using the ItemX notation, and ignore any of the custom names set on the right. The following two examples ignore the Custom1 and Custom2 names:

```
(int, int) example = (Custom1:5, Custom2:7);
(int Field1, int Field2) example = (Custom1:5, Custom2:7);
```

It is also important to call out that the custom field names exist only at compile time and aren't available when inspecting the tuple at runtime using reflection (reflection is covered in Chapter 15).

Inferred Variable Names (C# 7.1)

New in C# 7.1 is the ability for C# to infer the variable names of tuples under certain conditions. However, 7.1 must be enabled for this to work. For example, the following code will initially give compile errors with the tuple property names (on the final line):

```
Console.WriteLine("=> Inferred Tuple Names");
var foo = new {Prop1 = "first", Prop2 = "second"};
var bar = (foo.Prop1, foo.Prop2);
Console.WriteLine($"{bar.Prop1};{bar.Prop2}");
```

Hover over the error, and let Visual Studio update the project to use C# 7.1 (or change it manually as you did in Chapter 2). Once the project is updated, the tuple infers the property names when the tuple is created.

Tuples As Method Return Values

Earlier in this chapter, out parameters were used to return more than one value from a method call. There are additional ways to do this, such as creating a class or structure specifically to return the values. But if this class or struct is only to be used as a data transport for one method, that is extra work and extra code that doesn't need to be developed. Tuples are perfectly suited for this task, are lightweight, and are easy to declare and use.

This is the one of the examples from the out parameter section. It returns three values but requires three parameters passed in as transport mechanisms for the calling code.

```
static void FillTheseValues(out int a, out string b, out bool c)
{
  a = 9;
  b = "Enjoy your string.";
  c = true;
}
```

By using a tuple, you can remove the parameters and still get the three values back.

```
static (int a,string b,bool c) FillTheseValues()
{
  return (9,"Enjoy your string.",true);
}
```

Calling this method is as simple as calling any other method.

```
var samples = FillTheseValues();
Console.WriteLine($"Int is: {samples.a}");
Console.WriteLine($"String is: {samples.b}");
Console.WriteLine($"Boolean is: {samples.c}");
```

Perhaps a better example is deconstructing a full name into its individual parts (first, middle, last). The following code takes in a full name and returns a tuple with the different parts:

```
static (string first, string middle, string last) SplitNames(string fullName)
{
  //do what is needed to split the name apart
  return ("Philip", "F", "Japikse");
}
```

Discards with Tuples

Following up on the SplitNames() example, suppose you know that you need only the first and last names and don't care about the first. By providing variable names for the values you want returned and filling in the unneeded values with an underscore (_) placeholder, you can refine the return value like this:

```
var (first, _, last) = SplitNames("Philip F Japikse");
Console.WriteLine($"{first}:{last}");
```

The middle name value of the tuple is discarded.

Deconstructing Tuples

Deconstructing is the term given when separating out the properties of a tuple to be used individually. FillTheseValues did just that. But there is another use for this pattern that can be helpful, and that is deconstructing custom types.

Take a shorter version of the Point structure used earlier in this chapter. A new method named Deconstruct() has been added to return the individual properties of the Point instance as a tuple with properties named XPos and YPos.

```
struct Point
{
  // Fields of the structure.
  public int X;
  public int Y;

  // A custom constructor.
  public Point(int XPos, int YPos)
  {
    X = XPos;
    Y = YPos;
  }

  public (int XPos, int YPos) Deconstruct() => (X, Y);
}
```

157

Notice the new Deconstruct() method, shown in bold in the previous code listing. This method can be named anything, but by convention it is typically named Deconstruct(). This allows a single method call to get the individual values of the structure by returning a tuple.

```
Point p = new Point(7,5);
var pointValues = p.Deconstruct();
Console.WriteLine($"X is: {pointValues.XPos}");
Console.WriteLine($"Y is: {pointValues.YPos}");
```

■ **Source Code**   You can find the FunWithTuples application in the Chapter 4 subdirectory.

Summary

This chapter began with an examination arrays. Then we discussed the C# keywords that allow you to build custom methods. Recall that by default parameters are passed by value; however, you may pass a parameter by reference if you mark it with ref or out. You also learned about the role of optional or named parameters and how to define and invoke methods taking parameter arrays.

After you investigated the topic of method overloading, the bulk of this chapter examined several details regarding how enumerations and structures are defined in C# and represented within the .NET base class libraries. Along the way, you examined several details regarding value types and reference types, including how they respond when passing them as parameters to methods and how to interact with nullable data types and variables that might be null (e.g., reference-type variables and nullable value-type variables) using the ? and ?? operators.

The final section of the chapter looked into a long-anticipated feature in C#, tuples. After getting an understanding of what they are and how they work, you used them to return multiple values from methods as well as to deconstruct custom types.

■ ■ ■

PART III

Object-Oriented Programming with C#

CHAPTER 5

■ ■ ■

Understanding Encapsulation

In Chapters 3 and 4, you investigated a number of core syntactical constructs that are commonplace to any .NET application you might be developing. Here, you will begin your examination of the object-oriented capabilities of C#. The first order of business is to examine the process of building well-defined class types that support any number of *constructors*. After you understand the basics of defining classes and allocating objects, the remainder of this chapter will examine the role of *encapsulation*. Along the way, you will learn how to define class properties and come to understand the details of the `static` keyword, object initialization syntax, read-only fields, constant data, and partial classes.

Introducing the C# Class Type

As far as the .NET platform is concerned, the most fundamental programming construct is the *class type*. Formally, a class is a user-defined type that is composed of field data (often called *member variables*) and members that operate on this data (such as constructors, properties, methods, events, and so forth). Collectively, the set of field data represents the "state" of a class instance (otherwise known as an *object*). The power of object-oriented languages, such as C#, is that by grouping data and related functionality in a unified class definition, you are able to model your software after entities in the real world.

To get the ball rolling, create a new C# Console Application project named SimpleClassExample. Next, insert a new class file (named `Car.cs`) into your project using the Project ➤ Add Class menu selection. Choose the Class icon from the resulting dialog box, as shown in Figure 5-1, and click the Add button.

© Andrew Troelsen and Philip Japikse 2017
A. Troelsen and P. Japikse, *Pro C# 7*, https://doi.org/10.1007/978-1-4842-3018-3_5

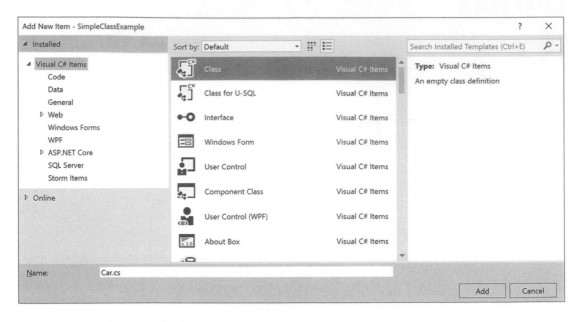

Figure 5-1. *Inserting a new C# class type*

A class is defined in C# using the class keyword. Here is the simplest possible declaration:

```
class Car
{
}
```

After you have defined a class type, you will need to consider the set of member variables that will be used to represent its state. For example, you might decide that cars maintain an int data type to represent the current speed and a string data type to represent the car's friendly pet name. Given these initial design notes, update your Car class as follows:

```
class Car
{
  // The 'state' of the Car.
  public string petName;
  public int currSpeed;
}
```

Notice that these member variables are declared using the public access modifier. Public members of a class are directly accessible once an object of this type has been created. Recall the term *object* is used to describe an instance of a given class type created using the new keyword.

■ **Note**   Field data of a class should seldom (if ever) be defined as public. To preserve the integrity of your state data, it is a far better design to define data as private (or possibly protected) and allow controlled access to the data via properties (as shown later in this chapter). However, to keep this first example as simple as possible, public data fits the bill.

162

After you have defined the set of member variables representing the state of the class, the next design step is to establish the members that model its behavior. For this example, the Car class will define one method named SpeedUp() and another named PrintState(). Update your class as so:

```
class Car
{
  // The 'state' of the Car.
  public string petName;
  public int currSpeed;

// The functionality of the Car.
// Using the expression-bodied member syntax introduced in C# 6
public void PrintState()
  => Console.WriteLine("{0} is going {1} MPH.", petName, currSpeed);

public void SpeedUp(int delta)
  => currSpeed += delta;
}
```

PrintState() is more or less a diagnostic function that will simply dump the current state of a given Car object to the command window. SpeedUp() will increase the speed of the Car object by the amount specified by the incoming int parameter. Now, update your Main() method in the Program class with the following code:

```
static void Main(string[] args)
{
  Console.WriteLine("***** Fun with Class Types *****\n");

  // Allocate and configure a Car object.
  Car myCar = new Car();
  myCar.petName = "Henry";
  myCar.currSpeed = 10;

  // Speed up the car a few times and print out the
  // new state.
  for (int i = 0; i <= 10; i++)
  {
    myCar.SpeedUp(5);
    myCar.PrintState();
  }
  Console.ReadLine();
}
```

After you run your program, you will see that the Car variable (myCar) maintains its current state throughout the life of the application, as shown in the following output:

```
***** Fun with Class Types *****

Henry is going 15 MPH.
Henry is going 20 MPH.
Henry is going 25 MPH.
Henry is going 30 MPH.
Henry is going 35 MPH.
Henry is going 40 MPH.
Henry is going 45 MPH.
Henry is going 50 MPH.
Henry is going 55 MPH.
Henry is going 60 MPH.
Henry is going 65 MPH.
```

Allocating Objects with the new Keyword

As shown in the previous code example, objects must be allocated into memory using the new keyword. If you do not use the new keyword and attempt to use your class variable in a subsequent code statement, you will receive a compiler error. For example, the following Main() method will not compile:

```
static void Main(string[] args)
{
  Console.WriteLine("***** Fun with Class Types *****\n");

  // Compiler error! Forgot to use 'new' to create object!
  Car myCar;
  myCar.petName = "Fred";
}
```

To correctly create an object using the new keyword, you may define and allocate a Car object on a single line of code.

```
static void Main(string[] args)
{
  Console.WriteLine("***** Fun with Class Types *****\n");
  Car myCar = new Car();
  myCar.petName = "Fred";
}
```

As an alternative, if you want to define and allocate a class instance on separate lines of code, you may do so as follows:

```
static void Main(string[] args)
{
  Console.WriteLine("***** Fun with Class Types *****\n");
  Car myCar;
```

```
  myCar = new Car();
  myCar.petName = "Fred";
}
```

Here, the first code statement simply declares a reference to a yet-to-be-determined Car object. It is not until you assign a reference to an object that this reference points to a valid object in memory.

In any case, at this point you have a trivial class that defines a few points of data and some basic operations. To enhance the functionality of the current Car class, you need to understand the role of *constructors*.

Understanding Constructors

Given that objects have state (represented by the values of an object's member variables), a programmer will typically want to assign relevant values to the object's field data before use. Currently, the Car class demands that the petName and currSpeed fields be assigned on a field-by-field basis. For the current example, this is not too problematic, given that you have only two public data points. However, it is not uncommon for a class to have dozens of fields to contend with. Clearly, it would be undesirable to author 20 initialization statements to set 20 points of data!

Thankfully, C# supports the use of *constructors*, which allow the state of an object to be established at the time of creation. A constructor is a special method of a class that is called indirectly when creating an object using the new keyword. However, unlike a "normal" method, constructors never have a return value (not even void) and are always named identically to the class they are constructing.

The Role of the Default Constructor

Every C# class is provided with a "freebie" *default constructor* that you can redefine if need be. By definition, a default constructor never takes arguments. After allocating the new object into memory, the default constructor ensures that all field data of the class is set to an appropriate default value (see Chapter 3 for information regarding the default values of C# data types).

If you are not satisfied with these default assignments, you may redefine the default constructor to suit your needs. To illustrate, update your C# Car class as follows:

```
class Car
{
  // The 'state' of the Car.
  public string petName;
  public int currSpeed;

  // A custom default constructor.
  public Car()
  {
    petName = "Chuck";
    currSpeed = 10;
  }
...
}
```

In this case, you are forcing all Car objects to begin life named Chuck at a rate of 10 mph. With this, you are able to create a Car object set to these default values as follows:

```
static void Main(string[] args)
{
  Console.WriteLine("***** Fun with Class Types *****\n");

  // Invoking the default constructor.
  Car chuck = new Car();

  // Prints "Chuck is going 10 MPH."
  chuck.PrintState();
...
}
```

Defining Custom Constructors

Typically, classes define additional constructors beyond the default. In doing so, you provide the object user with a simple and consistent way to initialize the state of an object directly at the time of creation. Ponder the following update to the Car class, which now supports a total of three constructors:

```
class Car
{
  // The 'state' of the Car.
  public string petName;
  public int currSpeed;

  // A custom default constructor.
  public Car()
  {
    petName = "Chuck";
    currSpeed = 10;
  }

  // Here, currSpeed will receive the
  // default value of an int (zero).
  public Car(string pn)
  {
    petName = pn;
  }

  // Let caller set the full state of the Car.
  public Car(string pn, int cs)
  {
    petName = pn;
    currSpeed = cs;
  }
...
}
```

Keep in mind that what makes one constructor different from another (in the eyes of the C# compiler) is the number of and/or type of constructor arguments. Recall from Chapter 4, when you define a method of the same name that differs by the number or type of arguments, you have *overloaded* the method. Thus, the Car class has overloaded the constructor to provide a number of ways to create an object at the time of declaration. In any case, you are now able to create Car objects using any of the public constructors. Here's an example:

```
static void Main(string[] args)
{
  Console.WriteLine("***** Fun with Class Types *****\n");

  // Make a Car called Chuck going 10 MPH.
  Car chuck = new Car();
  chuck.PrintState();

  // Make a Car called Mary going 0 MPH.
  Car mary = new Car("Mary");
  mary.PrintState();

  // Make a Car called Daisy going 75 MPH.
  Car daisy = new Car("Daisy", 75);
  daisy.PrintState();
...
}Encapsulation:constructors:
```

Constructors as Expression-Bodied Members (New)

C# 7 builds on the C# 6 expression-bodied member style, adding additional uses for the new style. Constructors, finalizers, and get/set accessors on properties and indexers now accept the new syntax. With this in mind, the previous constructor can be written like this:

```
// Here, currSpeed will receive the
// default value of an int (zero).
public Car(string pn) => petName = pn;
```

The second constructor is not a valid candidate, since expression bodied members are designed for one-line methods.

The Default Constructor Revisited

As you have just learned, all classes are provided with a free default constructor. Thus, if you insert a new class into your current project named Motorcycle, defined like so:

```
class Motorcycle
{
  public void PopAWheely()
  {
    Console.WriteLine("Yeeeeeee Haaaaaeewww!");
  }
}
```

you are able to create an instance of the Motorcycle type via the default constructor out of the box.

```
static void Main(string[] args)
{
  Console.WriteLine("***** Fun with Class Types *****\n");
  Motorcycle mc = new Motorcycle();
  mc.PopAWheely();
...
}
```

However, as soon as you define a custom constructor with any number of parameters, the default constructor is silently removed from the class and is no longer available. Think of it this way: if you do not define a custom constructor, the C# compiler grants you a default in order to allow the object user to allocate an instance of your type with field data set to the correct default values. However, when you define a unique constructor, the compiler assumes you have taken matters into your own hands.

Therefore, if you want to allow the object user to create an instance of your type with the default constructor, as well as your custom constructor, you must *explicitly* redefine the default. To this end, understand that in a vast majority of cases, the implementation of the default constructor of a class is intentionally empty, as all you require is the ability to create an object with default values. Consider the following update to the Motorcycle class:

```
class Motorcycle
{
  public int driverIntensity;

  public void PopAWheely()
  {
    for (int i = 0; i <= driverIntensity; i++)
    {
      Console.WriteLine("Yeeeeeee Haaaaaeewww!");
    }
  }

  // Put back the default constructor, which will
  // set all data members to default values.
  public Motorcycle() {}

  // Our custom constructor.
  public Motorcycle(int intensity)
  {
    driverIntensity = intensity;
  }
}
```

■ **Note**   Now that you better understand the role of class constructors, here is a nice shortcut. The Visual Studio IDE provides the ctor code snippet. When you type **ctor** and press the Tab key twice, the IDE will automatically define a custom default constructor. You can then add custom parameters and implementation logic. Give it a try.

The Role of the this Keyword

C# supplies a this keyword that provides access to the current class instance. One possible use of the this keyword is to resolve scope ambiguity, which can arise when an incoming parameter is named identically to a data field of the class. Of course, you could simply adopt a naming convention that does not result in such ambiguity, however; to illustrate this use of the this keyword, update your Motorcycle class with a new string field (named name) to represent the driver's name. Next, add a method named SetDriverName() implemented as follows:

```
class Motorcycle
{
  public int driverIntensity;

  // New members to represent the name of the driver.
  public string name;
  public void SetDriverName(string name)
  {
    name = name;
  }
...
}
```

Although this code will compile just fine, Visual Studio will display a warning message informing you that you have assigned a variable back to itself! To illustrate, update Main() to call SetDriverName() and then print out the value of the name field. You might be surprised to find that the value of the name field is an empty string!

```
// Make a Motorcycle with a rider named Tiny?
Motorcycle c = new Motorcycle(5);
c.SetDriverName("Tiny");
c.PopAWheely();
Console.WriteLine("Rider name is {0}", c.name); // Prints an empty name value!
```

The problem is that the implementation of SetDriverName() is assigning the incoming parameter *back to itself* given that the compiler assumes name is referring to the variable currently in the method scope rather than the name field at the class scope. To inform the compiler that you want to set the current object's name data field to the incoming name parameter, simply use this to resolve the ambiguity.

```
public void SetDriverName(string name)
{
  this.name = name;
}
```

Do understand that if there is no ambiguity, you are not required to make use of the this keyword when a class wants to access its own data fields or members, as this is implied. For example, if you rename the string data member from name to driverName (which will also require you to update your Main() method), the use of this is optional as there is no longer a scope ambiguity.

```
class Motorcycle
{
  public int driverIntensity;
  public string driverName;
```

```
public void SetDriverName(string name)
{
  // These two statements are functionally the same.
  driverName = name;
  this.driverName = name;
}
...
}
```

Even though there is little to be gained when using this in unambiguous situations, you might still find this keyword useful when implementing class members, as IDEs such as Visual Studio will enable IntelliSense when this is specified. This can be helpful when you have forgotten the name of a class member and want to quickly recall the definition. Consider Figure 5-2.

Figure 5-2. *The IntelliSense of this*

Chaining Constructor Calls Using this

Another use of the this keyword is to design a class using a technique termed *constructor chaining*. This design pattern is helpful when you have a class that defines multiple constructors. Given that constructors often validate the incoming arguments to enforce various business rules, it can be quite common to find redundant validation logic within a class's constructor set. Consider the following updated Motorcycle:

```
class Motorcycle
{
  public int driverIntensity;
  public string driverName;

  public Motorcycle() { }
```

```
  // Redundant constructor logic!
  public Motorcycle(int intensity)
  {
    if (intensity > 10)
    {
      intensity = 10;
    }
    driverIntensity = intensity;
  }

  public Motorcycle(int intensity, string name)
  {
    if (intensity > 10)
    {
      intensity = 10;
    }
    driverIntensity = intensity;
    driverName = name;
  }
...
}
```

Here (perhaps in an attempt to ensure the safety of the rider) each constructor is ensuring that
the intensity level is never greater than 10. While this is all well and good, you do have redundant code
statements in two constructors. This is less than ideal, as you are now required to update code in multiple
locations if your rules change (for example, if the intensity should not be greater than 5 rather than 10).

One way to improve the current situation is to define a method in the Motorcycle class that will validate
the incoming argument(s). If you were to do so, each constructor could make a call to this method before
making the field assignment(s). While this approach does allow you to isolate the code you need to update
when the business rules change, you are now dealing with the following redundancy:

```
class Motorcycle
{
    public int driverIntensity;
    public string driverName;

    // Constructors.
    public Motorcycle() { }

    public Motorcycle(int intensity)
    {
      SetIntensity(intensity);
    }

    public Motorcycle(int intensity, string name)
    {
      SetIntensity(intensity);
      driverName = name;
    }
```

```
  public void SetIntensity(int intensity)
  {
    if (intensity > 10)
    {
      intensity = 10;
    }
    driverIntensity = intensity;
  }
...
}
```

A cleaner approach is to designate the constructor that takes the *greatest number of arguments* as the "master constructor" and have its implementation perform the required validation logic. The remaining constructors can make use of the this keyword to forward the incoming arguments to the master constructor and provide any additional parameters as necessary. In this way, you need to worry only about maintaining a single constructor for the entire class, while the remaining constructors are basically empty.

Here is the final iteration of the Motorcycle class (with one additional constructor for the sake of illustration). When chaining constructors, note how the this keyword is "dangling" off the constructor's declaration (via a colon operator) outside the scope of the constructor itself.

```
class Motorcycle
{
    public int driverIntensity;
    public string driverName;

    // Constructor chaining.
    public Motorcycle() {}
    public Motorcycle(int intensity)
      : this(intensity, "") {}
    public Motorcycle(string name)
      : this(0, name) {}

    // This is the 'master' constructor that does all the real work.
    public Motorcycle(int intensity, string name)
    {
      if (intensity > 10)
      {
        intensity = 10;
      }
      driverIntensity - intensity;
      driverName = name;
    }
...
}
```

Understand that using the this keyword to chain constructor calls is never mandatory. However, when you make use of this technique, you do tend to end up with a more maintainable and concise class definition. Again, using this technique, you can simplify your programming tasks, as the real work is delegated to a single constructor (typically the constructor that has the most parameters), while the other constructors simply "pass the buck."

■ **Note**   Recall from Chapter 4 that C# supports optional parameters. If you use optional parameters in your class constructors, you can achieve the same benefits as constructor chaining, with considerably less code. You will see how to do so in just a moment.

Observing Constructor Flow

On a final note, do know that once a constructor passes arguments to the designated master constructor (and that constructor has processed the data), the constructor invoked originally by the caller will finish executing any remaining code statements. To clarify, update each of the constructors of the Motorcycle class with a fitting call to Console.WriteLine().

```
class Motorcycle
{
  public int driverIntensity;
  public string driverName;

  // Constructor chaining.
  public Motorcycle()
  {
    Console.WriteLine("In default ctor");
  }

  public Motorcycle(int intensity)
     : this(intensity, "")
  {
    Console.WriteLine("In ctor taking an int");
  }

  public Motorcycle(string name)
     : this(0, name)
  {
    Console.WriteLine("In ctor taking a string");
  }

  // This is the 'master' constructor that does all the real work.
  public Motorcycle(int intensity, string name)
  {
    Console.WriteLine("In master ctor ");
    if (intensity > 10)
    {
      intensity = 10;
    }
    driverIntensity = intensity;
    driverName = name;
  }
...
}
```

Now, ensure your `Main()` method exercises a `Motorcycle` object as follows:

```
static void Main(string[] args)
{
  Console.WriteLine("***** Fun with class Types *****\n");

  // Make a Motorcycle.
  Motorcycle c = new Motorcycle(5);
  c.SetDriverName("Tiny");
  c.PopAWheely();
  Console.WriteLine("Rider name is {0}", c.driverName);
  Console.ReadLine();
}
```

With this, ponder the output from the previous `Main()` method.

```
***** Fun with class Types *****

In master ctor
In ctor taking an int
Yeeeeeee Haaaaaaeewww!
Yeeeeeee Haaaaaaeewww!
Yeeeeeee Haaaaaaeewww!
Yeeeeeee Haaaaaaeewww!
Yeeeeeee Haaaaaaeewww!
Yeeeeeee Haaaaaaeewww!
Rider name is Tiny
```

As you can see, the flow of constructor logic is as follows:

- You create your object by invoking the constructor requiring a single `int`.

- This constructor forwards the supplied data to the master constructor and provides any additional startup arguments not specified by the caller.

- The master constructor assigns the incoming data to the object's field data.

- Control is returned to the constructor originally called and executes any remaining code statements.

The nice thing about using constructor chaining is that this programming pattern will work with any version of the C# language and .NET platform. However, if you are targeting .NET 4.0 and higher, you can further simplify your programming tasks by making use of optional arguments as an alternative to traditional constructor chaining.

Revisiting Optional Arguments

In Chapter 4, you learned about optional and named arguments. Recall that optional arguments allow you to define supplied default values to incoming arguments. If the caller is happy with these defaults, they are not required to specify a unique value; however, they may do so to provide the object with custom data.

Consider the following version of `Motorcycle`, which now provides a number of ways to construct objects using a *single* constructor definition:

```
class Motorcycle
{
  // Single constructor using optional args.
  public Motorcycle(int intensity = 0, string name = "")
  {
    if (intensity > 10)
    {
      intensity = 10;
    }
    driverIntensity = intensity;
    driverName = name;
  }
...
}
```

With this one constructor, you are now able to create a new `Motorcycle` object using zero, one, or two arguments. Recall that named argument syntax allows you to essentially skip over acceptable default settings (see Chapter 3).

```
static void MakeSomeBikes()
{
    // driverName = "", driverIntensity = 0
    Motorcycle m1 = new Motorcycle();
    Console.WriteLine("Name= {0}, Intensity= {1}",
      m1.driverName, m1.driverIntensity);

    // driverName = "Tiny", driverIntensity = 0
    Motorcycle m2 = new Motorcycle(name:"Tiny");
    Console.WriteLine("Name= {0}, Intensity= {1}",
      m2.driverName, m2.driverIntensity);

    // driverName = "", driverIntensity = 7
    Motorcycle m3 = new Motorcycle(7);
    Console.WriteLine("Name= {0}, Intensity= {1}",
      m3.driverName, m3.driverIntensity);
}
```

In any case, at this point you are able to define a class with field data (aka member variables) and various operations such as methods and constructors. Next up, let's formalize the role of the `static` keyword.

■ **Source Code**   You can find the SimpleClassExample project in the `Chapter 5` subdirectory.

Understanding the static Keyword

A C# class may define any number of *static members*, which are declared using the static keyword. When you do so, the member in question must be invoked directly from the class level, rather than from an object reference variable. To illustrate the distinction, consider your good friend System.Console. As you have seen, you do not invoke the WriteLine() method from the object level, as shown here:

```
// Compiler error! WriteLine() is not an object level method!
Console c = new Console();
c.WriteLine("I can't be printed...");
```

but instead simply prefix the class name to the static WriteLine() member.

```
// Correct! WriteLine() is a static method.
Console.WriteLine("Much better! Thanks...");
```

Simply put, static members are items that are deemed (by the class designer) to be so commonplace that there is no need to create an instance of the class before invoking the member. While any class can define static members, they are quite commonly found within *utility classes*. By definition, a utility class is a class that does not maintain any object-level state and is not created with the new keyword. Rather, a utility class exposes all functionality as class-level (aka static) members.

For example, if you were to use the Visual Studio Object Browser (via the View ➤ Object Browser menu item) to view the System namespace of mscorlib.dll, you would see that all the members of the Console, Math, Environment, and GC classes (among others) expose all their functionality via static members. These are but a few utility classes found within the .NET base class libraries.

Again, be aware that static members are not only found in utility classes; they can be part of any class definition at all. Just remember that static members promote a given item to the class level rather than the object level. As you will see over the next few sections, the static keyword can be applied to the following:

- Data of a class

- Methods of a class

- Properties of a class

- A constructor

- The entire class definition

- In conjunction with the C# using keyword

Let's see each of our options, beginning with the concept of static data.

■ **Note**   You will examine the role of static properties later in this chapter, while examining the properties themselves.

Defining Static Field Data

Most of the time when designing a class, you define data as instance-level data or, said another way, as nonstatic data. When you define instance-level data, you know that every time you create a new object, the object maintains its own independent copy of the data. In contrast, when you define *static* data of a class, the memory is shared by all objects of that category.

To see the distinction, create a new Console Application project named StaticDataAndMembers. Now, insert a new class into your project named SavingsAccount. Begin by defining a point of instance-level data (to model the current balance) and a custom constructor to set the initial balance.

```
// A simple savings account class.
class SavingsAccount
{
  // Instance-level data.
  public double currBalance;

  public SavingsAccount(double balance)
  {
    currBalance = balance;
  }
}
```

When you create SavingsAccount objects, memory for the currBalance field is allocated for each object. Thus, you could create five different SavingsAccount objects, each with their own unique balance. Furthermore, if you change the balance on one account, the other objects are not affected.

Static data, on the other hand, is allocated once and shared among all objects of the same class category. Add a static point of data named currInterestRate to the SavingsAccount class, which is set to a default value of 0.04.

```
// A simple savings account class.
class SavingsAccount
{
  // Instance-level data.
  public double currBalance;

  // A static point of data.
  public static double currInterestRate = 0.04;

  public SavingsAccount(double balance)
  {
    currBalance = balance;
  }
}
```

If you were to create three instances of SavingsAccount in Main() as follows:

```
static void Main(string[] args)
{
  Console.WriteLine("***** Fun with Static Data *****\n");
  SavingsAccount s1 = new SavingsAccount(50);
  SavingsAccount s2 = new SavingsAccount(100);
  SavingsAccount s3 = new SavingsAccount(10000.75);
  Console.ReadLine();
}
```

the in-memory data allocation would look something like Figure 5-3.

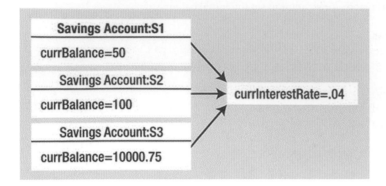

Figure 5-3. *Static data is allocated once and shared among all instances of the class*

Here, the assumption is that all saving accounts should have the same interest rate. Because static data is shared by all objects of the same category, if you were to change it in any way, all objects will "see" the new value the next time they access the static data, as they are all essentially looking at the same memory location. To understand how to change (or obtain) static data, you need to consider the role of static methods.

Defining Static Methods

Let's update the SavingsAccount class to define two static methods. The first static method (GetInterestRate()) will return the current interest rate, while the second static method (SetInterestRate()) will allow you to change the interest rate.

```
// A simple savings account class.
class SavingsAccount
{
  // Instance-level data.
  public double currBalance;

  // A static point of data.
  public static double currInterestRate = 0.04;

  public SavingsAccount(double balance)
  {
    currBalance = balance;
  }

  // Static members to get/set interest rate.
  public static void SetInterestRate(double newRate)
  { currInterestRate = newRate; }

  public static double GetInterestRate()
  { return currInterestRate; }
}
```

Now, observe the following usage:

```
static void Main(string[] args)
{
  Console.WriteLine("***** Fun with Static Data *****\n");
  SavingsAccount s1 = new SavingsAccount(50);
  SavingsAccount s2 = new SavingsAccount(100);

  // Print the current interest rate.
  Console.WriteLine("Interest Rate is: {0}", SavingsAccount.GetInterestRate());

  // Make new object, this does NOT 'reset' the interest rate.
  SavingsAccount s3 = new SavingsAccount(10000.75);
  Console.WriteLine("Interest Rate is: {0}", SavingsAccount.GetInterestRate());

  Console.ReadLine();
}
```

The output of the previous Main() is shown here:

```
***** Fun with Static Data *****

Interest Rate is: 0.04
Interest Rate is: 0.04
```

As you can see, when you create new instances of the SavingsAccount class, the value of the static data is not reset, as the CLR will allocate the static data into memory exactly one time. After that point, all objects of type SavingsAccount operate on the same value for the static currInterestRate field.

When designing any C# class, one of your design challenges is to determine which pieces of data should be defined as static members and which should not. While there are no hard-and-fast rules, remember that a static data field is shared by all objects of that type. Therefore, if you are defining a point of data that *all* objects should share between them, static is the way to go.

Consider what would happen if the interest rate variable were *not* defined using the static keyword. This would mean every SavingsAccount object would have its own copy of the currInterestRate field. Now, assume you created 100 SavingsAccount objects and needed to change the interest rate. That would require you to call the SetInterestRate() method 100 times! Clearly, this would not be a useful way to model "shared data." Again, static data is perfect when you have a value that should be common to all objects of that category.

■ **Note**   It is a compiler error for a static member to reference nonstatic members in its implementation. On a related note, it is an error to use the this keyword on a static member because this implies an object!

Defining Static Constructors

A typical constructor is used to set the value of an object's instance-level data at the time of creation. However, what would happen if you attempted to assign the value of a static point of data in a typical constructor? You might be surprised to find that the value is reset each time you create a new object!

179

To illustrate, assume you have updated the SavingsAccount class constructor as follows (also note you are no longer assigning the currInterestRate field inline):

```
class SavingsAccount
{
  public double currBalance;
  public static double currInterestRate;

  // Notice that our constructor is setting
  // the static currInterestRate value.
  public SavingsAccount(double balance)
  {
    currInterestRate = 0.04; // This is static data!
    currBalance = balance;
  }
...
}
```

Now, assume you have authored the following code in Main():

```
static void Main( string[] args )
{
  Console.WriteLine("***** Fun with Static Data *****\n");

  // Make an account.
  SavingsAccount s1 = new SavingsAccount(50);

  // Print the current interest rate.
  Console.WriteLine("Interest Rate is: {0}", SavingsAccount.GetInterestRate());

  // Try to change the interest rate via property.
  SavingsAccount.SetInterestRate(0.08);

  // Make a second account.
  SavingsAccount s2 = new SavingsAccount(100);

  // Should print 0.08...right??
  Console.WriteLine("Interest Rate is: {0}", SavingsAccount.GetInterestRate());
  Console.ReadLine();
}
```

If you executed the previous Main() method, you would see that the currInterestRate variable is reset each time you create a new SavingsAccount object, and it is always set to 0.04. Clearly, setting the value of static data in a normal instance-level constructor sort of defeats the whole purpose. Every time you make a new object, the class-level data is reset! One approach to setting a static field is to use member initialization syntax, as you did originally.

```
class SavingsAccount
{
  public double currBalance;
```

```
  // A static point of data.
  public static double currInterestRate = 0.04;
...
}
```

This approach will ensure the static field is assigned only once, regardless of how many objects you create. However, what if the value for your static data needed to be obtained at runtime? For example, in a typical banking application, the value of an interest rate variable would be read from a database or external file. Performing such tasks usually requires a method scope such as a constructor to execute the code statements.

For this reason, C# allows you to define a static constructor, which allows you to safely set the values of your static data. Consider the following update to your class:

```
class SavingsAccount
{
  public double currBalance;
  public static double currInterestRate;

  public SavingsAccount(double balance)
  {
    currBalance = balance;
  }

  // A static constructor!
  static SavingsAccount()
  {
    Console.WriteLine("In static ctor!");
    currInterestRate = 0.04;
  }
...
}
```

Simply put, a static constructor is a special constructor that is an ideal place to initialize the values of static data when the value is not known at compile time (e.g., you need to read in the value from an external file, read in the value from a database, generate a random number, or whatnot). If you were to rerun the previous Main() method, you would find the output you expect. Note that the message "In static ctor!" prints only one time, as the CLR calls all static constructors before the first use (and never calls them again for that instance of the application).

```
***** Fun with Static Data *****

In static ctor!
Interest Rate is: 0.04
Interest Rate is: 0.08
```

Here are a few points of interest regarding static constructors:

- A given class may define only a single static constructor. In other words, the static constructor cannot be overloaded.

- A static constructor does not take an access modifier and cannot take any parameters.

- A static constructor executes exactly one time, regardless of how many objects of the type are created.

- The runtime invokes the static constructor when it creates an instance of the class or before accessing the first static member invoked by the caller.

- The static constructor executes before any instance-level constructors.

Given this modification, when you create new SavingsAccount objects, the value of the static data is preserved, as the static member is set only one time within the static constructor, regardless of the number of objects created.

■ **Source Code** The StaticDataAndMembers project is included in the Chapter 5 subdirectory.

Defining Static Classes

It is also possible to apply the static keyword directly on the class level. When a class has been defined as static, it is not creatable using the new keyword, and it can contain only members or data fields marked with the static keyword. If this is not the case, you receive compiler errors.

■ **Note** Recall that a class (or structure) that exposes only static functionality is often termed a *utility class*. When designing a utility class, it is good practice to apply the static keyword to the class definition.

At first glance, this might seem like a fairly odd feature, given that a class that cannot be created does not appear all that helpful. However, if you create a class that contains nothing but static members and/or constant data, the class has no need to be allocated in the first place! To illustrate, create a new Console Application project named SimpleUtilityClass. Next, define the following class:

```
// Static classes can only
// contain static members!
static class TimeUtilClass
{
  public static void PrintTime()
    => Console.WriteLine(Now.ToShortTimeString());

  public static void PrintDate()
    => Console.WriteLine(Today.ToShortDateString());
}
```

Given that this class has been defined with the static keyword, you cannot create an instance of TimeUtilClass using the new keyword. Rather, all functionality is exposed from the class level.

```
static void Main(string[] args)
{
  Console.WriteLine("***** Fun with Static Classes *****\n");
```

```
// This is just fine.
TimeUtilClass.PrintDate();
TimeUtilClass.PrintTime();

// Compiler error! Can't create instance of static classes!
TimeUtilClass u = new TimeUtilClass ();

Console.ReadLine();
}
```

Importing Static Members via the C# using Keyword

C# 6 added support for importing static members with the using keyword. To illustrate, consider the C# file currently defining the utility class. Because you are making calls to the WriteLine() method of the Console class, as well as the Now property of the DateTime class, you must have a using statement for the System namespace. Since the members of these classes are all static, you could alter your code file with the following static using directives:

```
// Import the static members of Console and DateTime.
using static System.Console;
using static System.DateTime;
```

With these "static imports," the remainder of your code file is able to directly use the static members of the Console and DateTime class, without the need to prefix the defining class (although that would still be just fine, provided that you have imported the System namespace). For example, you could update your utility class like so:

```
static class TimeUtilClass
{
  public static void PrintTime() => WriteLine(Now.ToShortTimeString());

  public static void PrintDate() => WriteLine(Today.ToShortDateString());
}
```

You could argue that this iteration of the class is a bit cleaner in that you have a slightly smaller codebase. A more realistic example of code simplification might involve a C# class that is making substantial use of the System.Math class (or some other utility class). Since this class has nothing but static members, it could be somewhat easier to have a static using statement for this type and then directly call into the members of the Math class in your code file.

However, be aware that overuse of static import statements could result in potential confusion. First, what if multiple classes define a WriteLine() method? The compiler is confused and so are others reading your code. Second, unless a developer is familiar with the .NET code libraries, he or she might not know that WriteLine() is a member of the Console class. Unless a person were to notice the set of static imports at the top of a C# code file, they might be quite unsure where this method is actually defined. For these reasons, I will limit the use of static using statements in this text.

In any case, at this point in the chapter, you should feel comfortable defining simple class types containing constructors, fields, and various static (and nonstatic) members. Now that you have the basics of class construction under your belt, you can formally investigate the three pillars of object-oriented programming.

■ **Source Code**   You can find the SimpleUtilityClass project in the Chapter 5 subdirectory.

Defining the Pillars of OOP

All object-oriented languages (C#, Java, C++, Visual Basic, etc.) must contend with three core principles, often called the *pillars* of object-oriented programming (OOP).

- *Encapsulation*: How does this language hide an object's internal implementation details and preserve data integrity?

- *Inheritance*: How does this language promote code reuse?

- *Polymorphism*: How does this language let you treat related objects in a similar way?

Before digging into the syntactic details of each pillar, it is important that you understand the basic role of each. Here is an overview of each pillar, which will be examined in full detail over the remainder of this chapter and the next.

The Role of Encapsulation

The first pillar of OOP is called *encapsulation*. This trait boils down to the language's ability to hide unnecessary implementation details from the object user. For example, assume you are using a class named DatabaseReader, which has two primary methods, named Open() and Close().

```
// Assume this class encapsulates the details of opening and closing a database.
DatabaseReader dbReader = new DatabaseReader();
dbReader.Open(@"C:\AutoLot.mdf");

// Do something with data file and close the file.
dbReader.Close();
```

The fictitious DatabaseReader class encapsulates the inner details of locating, loading, manipulating, and closing a data file. Programmers love encapsulation, as this pillar of OOP keeps coding tasks simpler. There is no need to worry about the numerous lines of code that are working behind the scenes to carry out the work of the DatabaseReader class. All you do is create an instance and send the appropriate messages (e.g., "Open the file named AutoLot.mdf located on my C drive").

Closely related to the notion of encapsulating programming logic is the idea of data protection. Ideally, an object's state data should be specified using the private (or possibly protected) keyword. In this way, the outside world must ask politely in order to change or obtain the underlying value. This is a good thing, as publicly declared data points can easily become corrupted (ideally by accident rather than intent!). You will formally examine this aspect of encapsulation in just a bit.

The Role of Inheritance

The next pillar of OOP, *inheritance*, boils down to the language's ability to allow you to build new class definitions based on existing class definitions. In essence, inheritance allows you to extend the behavior of a base (or *parent*) class by inheriting core functionality into the derived subclass (also called a *child class*). Figure 5-4 shows a simple example.

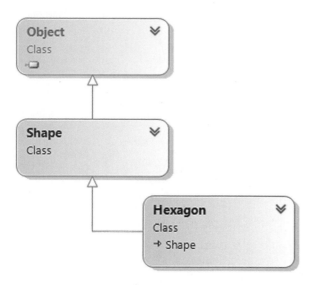

Figure 5-4. *The "is-a" relationship*

You can read the diagram in Figure 5-4 as "A Hexagon is-a Shape that is-an Object." When you have classes related by this form of inheritance, you establish *"is-a" relationships* between types. The "is-a" relationship is termed *inheritance*.

Here, you can assume that Shape defines some number of members that are common to all descendants (maybe a value to represent the color to draw the shape and other values to represent the height and width). Given that the Hexagon class extends Shape, it inherits the core functionality defined by Shape and Object, as well as defines additional hexagon-related details of its own (whatever those may be).

■ **Note**   Under the .NET platform, System.Object is always the topmost parent in any class hierarchy, which defines some general functionality for all types (fully described in Chapter 6).

There is another form of code reuse in the world of OOP: the containment/delegation model also known as the *"has-a" relationship* or aggregation. This form of reuse is not used to establish parent-child relationships. Rather, the "has-a" relationship allows one class to define a member variable of another class and expose its functionality (if required) to the object user indirectly.

For example, assume you are again modeling an automobile. You might want to express the idea that a car "has-a" radio. It would be illogical to attempt to derive the Car class from a Radio, or vice versa (a Car "is-a" Radio? I think not!). Rather, you have two independent classes working together, where the Car class creates and exposes the Radio's functionality.

```
class Radio
{
  public void Power(bool turnOn)
  {
    Console.WriteLine("Radio on: {0}", turnOn);
  }
}
```

```
class Car
{
  // Car 'has-a' Radio.
  private Radio myRadio = new Radio();

  public void TurnOnRadio(bool onOff)
  {
    // Delegate call to inner object.
    myRadio.Power(onOff);
  }
}
```

Notice that the object user has no clue that the Car class is using an inner Radio object.

```
static void Main(string[] args)
{
  // Call is forwarded to Radio internally.
  Car viper = new Car();
  viper.TurnOnRadio(false);
}
```

The Role of Polymorphism

The final pillar of OOP is *polymorphism*. This trait captures a language's ability to treat related objects in a similar manner. Specifically, this tenant of an object-oriented language allows a base class to define a set of members (formally termed the *polymorphic interface*) that are available to all descendants. A class's polymorphic interface is constructed using any number of *virtual* or *abstract* members (see Chapter 6 for full details).

In a nutshell, a *virtual member* is a member in a base class that defines a default implementation that may be changed (or more formally speaking, *overridden*) by a derived class. In contrast, an *abstract method* is a member in a base class that does not provide a default implementation but does provide a signature. When a class derives from a base class defining an abstract method, it *must* be overridden by a derived type. In either case, when derived types override the members defined by a base class, they are essentially redefining how they respond to the same request.

To preview polymorphism, let's provide some details behind the shapes hierarchy shown in Figure 5-5. Assume that the Shape class has defined a virtual method named Draw() that takes no parameters. Given that every shape needs to render itself in a unique manner, subclasses such as Hexagon and Circle are free to override this method to their own liking (see Figure 5-5).

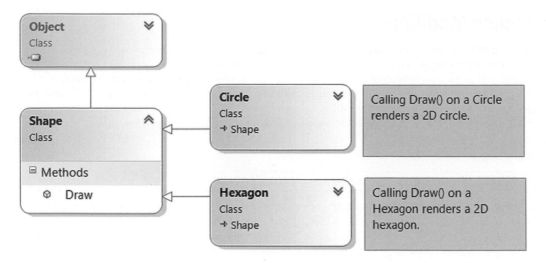

Figure 5-5. *Classical polymorphism*

After a polymorphic interface has been designed, you can begin to make various assumptions in your code. For example, given that Hexagon and Circle derive from a common parent (Shape), an array of Shape types could contain anything deriving from this base class. Furthermore, given that Shape defines a polymorphic interface to all derived types (the Draw() method in this example), you can assume each member in the array has this functionality.

Consider the following Main() method, which instructs an array of Shape-derived types to render themselves using the Draw() method:

```
class Program
{
  static void Main(string[] args)
  {
    Shape[] myShapes = new Shape[3];
    myShapes[0] = new Hexagon();
    myShapes[1] = new Circle();
    myShapes[2] = new Hexagon();

    foreach (Shape s in myShapes)
    {
      // Use the polymorphic interface!
      s.Draw();
    }
    Console.ReadLine();
  }
}
```

This wraps up our brisk overview of the pillars of OOP. Now that you have the theory in your mind, the remainder of this chapter explores further details of how encapsulation is handled under C#. Chapter 6 will tackle the details of inheritance and polymorphism.

C# Access Modifiers

When working with encapsulation, you must always take into account which aspects of a type are visible to various parts of your application. Specifically, types (classes, interfaces, structures, enumerations, and delegates) as well as their members (properties, methods, constructors, and fields) are defined using a specific keyword to control how "visible" the item is to other parts of your application. Although C# defines numerous keywords to control access, they differ on where they can be successfully applied (type or member). Table 5-1 documents the role of each access modifier and where it may be applied.

Table 5-1. *C# Access Modifiers*

C# Access Modifier	May Be Applied To	Meaning in Life
public	Types or type members	Public items have no access restrictions. A public member can be accessed from an object, as well as any derived class. A public type can be accessed from other external assemblies.
private	Type members or nested types	Private items can be accessed only by the class (or structure) that defines the item.
protected	Type members or nested types	Protected items can be used by the class that defines it and any child class. However, protected items cannot be accessed from the outside world using the C# dot operator.
internal	Types or type members	Internal items are accessible only within the current assembly. Therefore, if you define a set of internal types within a .NET class library, other assemblies are not able to use them.
protected internal	Type members or nested types	When the protected and internal keywords are combined on an item, the item is accessible within the defining assembly, within the defining class, and by derived classes.

In this chapter, you are concerned only with the public and private keywords. Later chapters will examine the role of the internal and protected internal modifiers (useful when you build .NET code libraries) and the protected modifier (useful when you are creating class hierarchies).

The Default Access Modifiers

By default, type members are *implicitly private* while types are *implicitly internal*. Thus, the following class definition is automatically set to internal, while the type's default constructor is automatically set to private (however, as you would suspect, there are few times you would want a private class constructor):

```
// An internal class with a private default constructor.
class Radio
{
  Radio(){}
}
```

If you want to be explicit, you could add these keywords yourself with no ill effect (beyond a few additional keystrokes).

```
// An internal class with a private default constructor.
internal class Radio
{
  private Radio(){}
}
```

To allow other parts of a program to invoke members of an object, you must define them with the public keyword (or possibly with the protected keyword, which you will learn about in the next chapter). As well, if you want to expose the Radio to external assemblies (again, useful when building .NET code libraries; see Chapter 14), you will need to add the public modifier.

```
// A public class with a public default constructor.
public class Radio
{
  public Radio(){}
}
```

Access Modifiers and Nested Types

As mentioned in Table 5-1, the private, protected, and protected internal access modifiers can be applied to a *nested type*. Chapter 6 will examine nesting in detail. What you need to know at this point, however, is that a nested type is a type declared directly within the scope of class or structure. By way of example, here is a private enumeration (named CarColor) nested within a public class (named SportsCar):

```
public class SportsCar
{
  // OK! Nested types can be marked private.
  private enum CarColor
  {
    Red, Green, Blue
  }
}
```

Here, it is permissible to apply the private access modifier on the nested type. However, non-nested types (such as the SportsCar) can be defined only with the public or internal modifiers. Therefore, the following class definition is illegal:

```
// Error! Nonnested types cannot be marked private!
private class SportsCar
{}
```

The First Pillar: C#'s Encapsulation Services

The concept of encapsulation revolves around the notion that an object's data should not be directly accessible from an object instance. Rather, class data is defined as private. If the object user wants to alter the state of an object, it does so indirectly using public members. To illustrate the need for encapsulation services, assume you have created the following class definition:

```
// A class with a single public field.
class Book
{
  public int numberOfPages;
}
```

The problem with public data is that the data itself has no ability to "understand" whether the current value to which it is assigned is valid with regard to the current business rules of the system. As you know, the upper range of a C# int is quite large (2,147,483,647). Therefore, the compiler allows the following assignment:

```
// Humm. That is one heck of a mini-novel!
static void Main(string[] args)
{
  Book miniNovel = new Book();
  miniNovel.numberOfPages = 30_000_000;
}
```

Although you have not overflowed the boundaries of an int data type, it should be clear that a mini novel with a page count of 30,000,000 pages is a bit unreasonable. As you can see, public fields do not provide a way to trap logical upper (or lower) limits. If your current system has a business rule that states a book must be between 1 and 1,000 pages, you are at a loss to enforce this programmatically. Because of this, public fields typically have no place in a production-level class definition.

■ **Note**   To be more specific, members of a class that represent an object's state should not be marked as public. As you will see later in this chapter, public constants and public read-only fields are quite useful.

Encapsulation provides a way to preserve the integrity of an object's state data. Rather than defining public fields (which can easily foster data corruption), you should get in the habit of defining *private data*, which is indirectly manipulated using one of two main techniques.

- You can define a pair of public accessor (get) and mutator (set) methods.

- You can define a public .NET property.

Whichever technique you choose, the point is that a well-encapsulated class should protect its data and hide the details of how it operates from the prying eyes of the outside world. This is often termed *black-box programming*. The beauty of this approach is that an object is free to change how a given method is implemented under the hood. It does this without breaking any existing code making use of it, provided that the parameters and return values of the method remain constant.

Encapsulation Using Traditional Accessors and Mutators

Over the remaining pages in this chapter, you will be building a fairly complete class that models a general employee. To get the ball rolling, create a new Console Application project named EmployeeApp and insert a new class file (named Employee.cs) using the Project Add class menu item. Update the Employee class with the following fields, methods, and constructors:

```
class Employee
{
  // Field data.
  private string empName;
  private int empID;
  private float currPay;

  // Constructors.
  public Employee() {}
  public Employee(string name, int id, float pay)
  {
    empName = name;
    empID = id;
    currPay = pay;
  }

  // Methods.
  public void GiveBonus(float amount)
  {
    currPay += amount;
  }

  public void DisplayStats()
  {
    Console.WriteLine("Name: {0}", empName);
    Console.WriteLine("ID: {0}", empID);
    Console.WriteLine("Pay: {0}", currPay);
  }
}
```

Notice that the fields of the Employee class are currently defined using the private keyword. Given this, the empName, empID, and currPay fields are not directly accessible from an object variable. Therefore, the following logic in Main() would result in compiler errors:

```
static void Main(string[] args)
{
  Employee emp = new Employee();

  // Error! Cannot directly access private members
  // from an object!
  emp.empName = "Marv";
}
```

If you want the outside world to interact with a worker's full name, a traditional approach (which is common in Java) is to define an accessor (get method) and a mutator (set method). The role of a get method is to return to the caller the current value of the underlying state data. A set method allows the caller to change the current value of the underlying state data, as long as the defined business rules are met.

To illustrate, let's encapsulate the empName field. To do so, add the following public methods to the Employee class. Notice that the SetName() method performs a test on the incoming data to ensure the string is 15 characters or less. If it is not, an error prints to the console and returns without making a change to the empName field.

■ **Note**   If this were a production-level class, you would also make to check the character length for an employee's name within your constructor logic. Ignore this detail for the time being, as you will clean up this code in just a bit when you examine .NET property syntax.

```
class Employee
{
  // Field data.
  private string empName;
  ...

  // Accessor (get method).
  public string GetName()
  {
    return empName;
  }

  // Mutator (set method).
  public void SetName(string name)
  {
    // Do a check on incoming value
    // before making assignment.
    if (name.Length > 15)
      Console.WriteLine("Error! Name length exceeds 15 characters!");
    else
      empName = name;
  }
}
```

This technique requires two uniquely named methods to operate on a single data point. To test your new methods, update your Main() method as follows:

```
static void Main(string[] args)
{
  Console.WriteLine("***** Fun with Encapsulation *****\n");
  Employee emp = new Employee("Marvin", 456, 30_000);
  emp.GiveBonus(1000);
  emp.DisplayStats();
```

```
  // Use the get/set methods to interact with the object's name.
  emp.SetName("Marv");
  Console.WriteLine("Employee is named: {0}", emp.GetName());
  Console.ReadLine();
}
```

Because of the code in your SetName() method, if you attempted to specify more than 15 characters (see the following), you would find the hard-coded error message printed to the console:

```
static void Main(string[] args)
{
  Console.WriteLine("***** Fun with Encapsulation *****\n");
...
  // Longer than 15 characters! Error will print to console.
  Employee emp2 = new Employee();
  emp2.SetName("Xena the warrior princess");

  Console.ReadLine();
}
```

So far, so good. You have encapsulated the private empName field using two public methods named GetName() and SetName(). If you were to further encapsulate the data in the Employee class, you would need to add various additional methods (such as GetID(), SetID(), GetCurrentPay(), SetCurrentPay()). Each of the mutator methods could have within it various lines of code to check for additional business rules. While this could certainly be done, the C# language has a useful alternative notation to encapsulate class data.

Encapsulation Using .NET Properties

Although you can encapsulate a piece of field data using traditional get and set methods, .NET languages prefer to enforce data encapsulation state data using *properties*. First, understand that properties are just a simplification for "real" accessor and mutator methods. Therefore, as a class designer, you are still able to perform any internal logic necessary before making the value assignment (e.g., uppercase the value, scrub the value for illegal characters, check the bounds of a numerical value, and so on).

Here is the updated Employee class, now enforcing encapsulation of each field using property syntax rather than traditional get and set methods:

```
class Employee
{
  // Field data.
  private string empName;
  private int empID;
  private float currPay;

  // Properties!
  public string Name
  {
    get { return empName; }
    set
```

```
    {
      if (value.Length > 15)
        Console.WriteLine("Error! Name length exceeds 15 characters!");
      else
        empName = value;
    }
  }

  // We could add additional business rules to the sets of these properties;
  // however, there is no need to do so for this example.
  public int ID
  {
    get { return empID; }
    set { empID = value; }
  }
  public float Pay
  {
    get { return currPay; }
    set { currPay = value; }
  }
  ...
}
```

A C# property is composed by defining a get scope (accessor) and set scope (mutator) directly within the property itself. Notice that the property specifies the type of data it is encapsulating by what appears to be a return value. Also take note that, unlike a method, properties do not make use of parentheses (not even empty parentheses) when being defined. Consider the following commentary on your current ID property:

```
// The 'int' represents the type of data this property encapsulates.
public int ID // Note lack of parentheses.
{
  get { return empID; }
  set { empID = value; }
}
```

Within a set scope of a property, you use a token named value, which is used to represent the incoming value used to assign the property by the caller. This token is *not* a true C# keyword but is what is known as a *contextual keyword*. When the token value is within the set scope of the property, it always represents the value being assigned by the caller, and it will always be the same underlying data type as the property itself. Thus, notice how the Name property can still test the range of the string as so:

```
public string Name
{
  get { return empName; }
  set
  {
    // Here, value is really a string.
    if (value.Length > 15)
      Console.WriteLine("Error! Name length exceeds 15 characters!");
    else
      empName = value;
  }
}
```

After you have these properties in place, it appears to the caller that it is getting and setting a *public point* of data; however, the correct get and set block is called behind the scenes to preserve encapsulation.

```
static void Main(string[] args)
{
  Console.WriteLine("***** Fun with Encapsulation *****\n");
  Employee emp = new Employee("Marvin", 456, 30000);
  emp.GiveBonus(1000);
  emp.DisplayStats();

  // Reset and then get the Name property.
  emp.Name = "Marv";
  Console.WriteLine("Employee is named: {0}", emp.Name);
  Console.ReadLine();
}
```

Properties (as opposed to accessor and mutator methods) also make your types easier to manipulate, in that properties are able to respond to the intrinsic operators of C#. To illustrate, assume that the Employee class type has an internal private member variable representing the age of the employee. Here is the relevant update (notice the use of constructor chaining):

```
class Employee
{
...
  // New field and property.
  private int empAge;
  public int Age
  {
    get { return empAge; }
    set { empAge = value; }
  }

  // Updated constructors.
  public Employee() {}
  public Employee(string name, int id, float pay)
  :this(name, 0, id, pay){}

  public Employee(string name, int age, int id, float pay)
  {
    empName = name;
    empID = id;
    empAge = age;
    currPay = pay;
  }

  // Updated DisplayStats() method now accounts for age.
  public void DisplayStats()
  {
    Console.WriteLine("Name: {0}", empName);
    Console.WriteLine("ID: {0}", empID);
```

```
        Console.WriteLine("Age: {0}", empAge);
        Console.WriteLine("Pay: {0}", currPay);
    }
}
```

Now assume you have created an Employee object named joe. On his birthday, you want to increment the age by one. Using traditional accessor and mutator methods, you would need to write code such as the following:

```
Employee joe = new Employee();
joe.SetAge(joe.GetAge() + 1);
```

However, if you encapsulate empAge using a property named Age, you are able to simply write this:

```
Employee joe = new Employee();
joe.Age++;
```

Properties as Expression-Bodied Members (New)

As mentioned previously, property get and set accessors can also be written as expression-bodied members. The rules and syntax are the same: single-line methods can be written using the new syntax. So, the Age property could be written like this:

```
public int Age
{
  get => empAge;
  set => empAge = value;
}
```

Both syntaxes compile down to the same IL, so which syntax you use is completely up to you. In this text, you will see a mix of both styles to keep visibility on them, not because I am adhering to a specific code style.

Using Properties Within a Class Definition

Properties, specifically the set portion of a property, are common places to package up the business rules of your class. Currently, the Employee class has a Name property that ensures the name is no more than 15 characters. The remaining properties (ID, Pay, and Age) could also be updated with any relevant logic.

While this is well and good, also consider what a class constructor typically does internally. It will take the incoming parameters, check for valid data, and then make assignments to the internal private fields. Currently, your master constructor does *not* test the incoming string data for a valid range, so you could update this member as so:

```
public Employee(string name, int age, int id, float pay)
{
    // Humm, this seems like a problem...
    if (name.Length > 15)
      Console.WriteLine("Error! Name length exceeds 15 characters!");
```

```
  else
    empName = name;

    empID = id;
    empAge = age;
    currPay = pay;
}
```

I am sure you can see the problem with this approach. The Name property and your master constructor are performing the same error checking. If you were also making checks on the other data points, you would have a good deal of duplicate code. To streamline your code and isolate all of your error checking to a central location, you will do well if you *always* use properties within your class whenever you need to get or set the values. Consider the following updated constructor:

```
public Employee(string name, int age, int id, float pay)
{
    // Better! Use properties when setting class data.
    // This reduces the amount of duplicate error checks.
    Name = name;
    Age = age;
    ID = id;
    Pay = pay;
}
```

Beyond updating constructors to use properties when assigning values, it is good practice to use properties throughout a class implementation to ensure your business rules are always enforced. In many cases, the only time when you directly make reference to the underlying private piece of data is within the property itself. With this in mind, here is your updated Employee class:

```
class Employee
{
    // Field data.
    private string empName;
    private int empID;
    private float currPay;
    private int empAge;

    // Constructors.
    public Employee() { }
    public Employee(string name, int id, float pay)
      :this(name, 0, id, pay){}
    public Employee(string name, int age, int id, float pay)
    {
      Name = name;
      Age = age;
      ID = id;
      Pay = pay;
    }
```

```
// Methods.
public void GiveBonus(float amount)
{ Pay += amount; }

public void DisplayStats()
{
  Console.WriteLine("Name: {0}", Name);
  Console.WriteLine("ID: {0}", ID);
  Console.WriteLine("Age: {0}", Age);
  Console.WriteLine("Pay: {0}", Pay);
}

// Properties as before...
...
}
```

Read-Only and Write-Only Properties

When encapsulating data, you might want to configure a *read-only property*. To do so, simply omit the set block. Likewise, if you want to have a *write-only property*, omit the get block. For example, assume you have a new property named SocialSecurityNumber, which encapsulates a private string variable named empSSN. If you want to make this a read-only property, you could write this:

```
public string SocialSecurityNumber
{
  get { return empSSN; }
}
```

Now assume your class constructor has a new parameter to let the caller set the SSN of the object. Since the SocialSecurityNumber property is read-only, you cannot set the value as so:

```
public Employee(string name, int age, int id, float pay, string ssn)
{
  Name = name;
  Age = age;
  ID = id;
  Pay = pay;

  // OOPS! This is no longer possible if the property is read only.
  SocialSecurityNumber = ssn;
}
```

Unless you are willing to redesign the property as read-write, your only choice would be to use the underlying empSSN member variable within your constructor logic as so:

```
public Employee(string name, int age, int id, float pay, string ssn)
{
  ...
  // Check incoming ssn parameter as required and then set the value.
  empSSN = ssn;
}
```

198

■ **Source Code**   You can find the EmployeeApp project in the Chapter 5 subdirectory.

Revisiting the static Keyword: Defining Static Properties

Earlier in this chapter, you examined the role of the static keyword. Now that you understand the use of C#
property syntax, you can formalize static properties. In the StaticDataAndMembers project created earlier
in this chapter, your SavingsAccount class had two public static methods to get and set the interest rate.
However, it would be more standard to wrap this data point in a static property. Here's an example (note the
use of the static keyword):

```
// A simple savings account class.
class SavingsAccount
{
  // Instance-level data.
  public double currBalance;

  // A static point of data.
  private static double currInterestRate = 0.04;

  // A static property.
  public static double InterestRate
  {
    get { return currInterestRate; }
    set { currInterestRate = value; }
  }
...
}
```

If you want to use this property in place of the previous static methods, you could update your Main()
method as so:

```
// Print the current interest rate via property.
Console.WriteLine("Interest Rate is: {0}", SavingsAccount.InterestRate);
```

Understanding Automatic Properties

When you are building properties to encapsulate your data, it is common to find that the set scopes
have code to enforce business rules of your program. However, in some cases you may not need any
implementation logic beyond simply getting and setting the value. This means you can end up with a lot of
code looking like the following:

```
// A Car type using standard property
// syntax.
class Car
{
  private string carName = "";
  public string PetName
```

```
  {
    get { return carName; }
    set { carName = value; }
  }
}
```

In these cases, it can become rather verbose to define private backing fields and simple property definitions multiple times. By way of an example, if you are modeling a class that requires nine private points of field data, you end up authoring nine related properties that are little more than thin wrappers for encapsulation services.

To streamline the process of providing simple encapsulation of field data, you may use *automatic property syntax*. As the name implies, this feature will offload the work of defining a private backing field and the related C# property member to the compiler using a new bit of syntax. To illustrate, create a new Console Application project named AutoProps. Now, consider the reworking of the Car class, which uses this syntax to quickly create three properties:

```
class Car
{
    // Automatic properties!No need to define backing fields.
    public string PetName { get; set; }
    public int Speed { get; set; }
    public string Color { get; set; }
}
```

■ **Note** Visual Studio provides the prop code snippet. If you type **prop** inside a class definition and press the Tab key twice, the IDE will generate starter code for a new automatic property. You can then use the Tab key to cycle through each part of the definition to fill in the details. Give it a try!

When defining automatic properties, you simply specify the access modifier, underlying data type, property name, and empty get/set scopes. At compile time, your type will be provided with an autogenerated private backing field and a fitting implementation of the get/set logic.

■ **Note** The name of the autogenerated private backing field is not visible within your C# codebase. The only way to see it is to make use of a tool such as ildasm.exe.

Since C# version 6, it is possible to define a "read-only automatic property" by omitting the set scope. However, it is not possible to define a write-only property. To solidify, consider the following:

```
// Read-only property? This is OK!
public int MyReadOnlyProp { get; }

// Write only property? Error!
public int MyWriteOnlyProp { set; }
```

Interacting with Automatic Properties

Because the compiler will define the private backing field at compile time (and given that these fields are not directly accessible in C# code), the class-defining automatic properties will always need to use property syntax to get and set the underlying value. This is important to note because many programmers make direct use of the private fields *within* a class definition, which is not possible in this case. For example, if the Car class were to provide a DisplayStats() method, it would need to implement this method using the property name.

```
class Car
{
  // Automatic properties!
  public string PetName { get; set; }
  public int Speed { get; set; }
  public string Color { get; set; }

  public void DisplayStats()
  {
    Console.WriteLine("Car Name: {0}", PetName);
    Console.WriteLine("Speed: {0}", Speed);
    Console.WriteLine("Color: {0}", Color);
  }
}
```

When you are using an object defined with automatic properties, you will be able to assign and obtain the values using the expected property syntax.

```
static void Main(string[] args)
{
  Console.WriteLine("***** Fun with Automatic Properties *****\n");

  Car c = new Car();
  c.PetName = "Frank";
  c.Speed = 55;
  c.Color = "Red";

  Console.WriteLine("Your car is named {0}? That's odd...",
    c.PetName);
  c.DisplayStats();

  Console.ReadLine();
}
```

Automatic Properties and Default Values

When you use automatic properties to encapsulate numerical or Boolean data, you are able to use the autogenerated type properties straightaway within your codebase, as the hidden backing fields will be assigned a safe default value (false for Booleans and 0 for numerical data). However, be aware that if you use automatic property syntax to wrap another class variable, the hidden private reference type will also be set to a default value of null (which can prove problematic if you are not careful).

Let's insert into your current project a new class named Garage, which makes use of two automatic properties (of course, a real garage class might maintain a collection of Car objects; however, ignore that detail here).

```
class Garage
{
   // The hidden int backing field is set to zero!
   public int NumberOfCars { get; set; }

   // The hidden Car backing field is set to null!
   public Car MyAuto { get; set; }
}
```

Given C#'s default values for field data, you would be able to print out the value of NumberOfCars as is (as it is automatically assigned the value of zero), but if you directly invoke MyAuto, you will receive a "null reference exception" at runtime, as the Car member variable used in the background has not been assigned to a new object.

```
static void Main(string[] args)
{
   ...
   Garage g = new Garage();

   // OK, prints default value of zero.
   Console.WriteLine("Number of Cars: {0}", g.NumberOfCars);

   // Runtime error! Backing field is currently null!
   Console.WriteLine(g.MyAuto.PetName);
   Console.ReadLine();
}
```

To solve this problem, you could update the class constructors to ensure the object comes to life in a safe manner. Here's an example:

```
class Garage
{
   // The hidden backing field is set to zero!
   public int NumberOfCars { get; set; }

   // The hidden backing field is set to null!
   public Car MyAuto { get; set; }

   // Must use constructors to override default
   // values assigned to hidden backing fields.
   public Garage()
   {
     MyAuto = new Car();
     NumberOfCars = 1;
   }
```

```
  public Garage(Car car, int number)
  {
    MyAuto = car;
    NumberOfCars = number;
  }
}
```

With this modification, you could now place a Car object into the Garage object as so:

```
static void Main(string[] args)
{
  Console.WriteLine("***** Fun with Automatic Properties *****\n");

  // Make a car.
  Car c = new Car();
  c.PetName = "Frank";
  c.Speed = 55;
  c.Color = "Red";
  c.DisplayStats();

  // Put car in the garage.
  Garage g = new Garage();
  g.MyAuto = c;
  Console.WriteLine("Number of Cars in garage: {0}", g.NumberOfCars);
  Console.WriteLine("Your car is named: {0}", g.MyAuto.PetName);

  Console.ReadLine();
}
```

Initialization of Automatic Properties

While the previous approach works just fine, since the release of C# 6, you are provided with a language feature that can simplify how an automatic property receives its initial value assignment. Recall from the onset of this chapter, a data field of a class can be directly assigned an initial value upon declaration. Here's an example:

```
class Car
{
  private int numberOfDoors = 2;
}
```

In a similar manner, C# now allows you to assign an initial value to the underlying backing field generated by the compiler. This alleviates you from the hassle of adding additional code statements in class constructors to ensure property data comes to life as intended.

Here is an updated version of the Garage class that is initializing automatic properties to fitting values. Note you no longer need to add additional logic to your default class constructor to make safe assignments. In this iteration, you are directly assigning a new Car object to the MyAuto property.

```
class Garage
{
    // The hidden backing field is set to 1.
    public int NumberOfCars { get; set; } = 1;

    // The hidden backing field is set to a new Car object.
    public Car MyAuto { get; set; } = new Car();

    public Garage(){}
    public Garage(Car car, int number)
    {
        MyAuto = car;
        NumberOfCars = number;
    }
}
```

As you may agree, automatic properties are a nice feature of the C# programming language, as you can define a number of properties for a class using a streamlined syntax. Be aware of course that if you are building a property that requires additional code beyond getting and setting the underlying private field (such as data validation logic, writing to an event log, communicating with a database, etc.), you will be required to define a "normal" .NET property type by hand. C# automatic properties never do more than provide simple encapsulation for an underlying piece of (compiler-generated) private data.

■ **Source Code**   You can find the AutoProps project in the Chapter 5 subdirectory.

Understanding Object Initialization Syntax

As shown throughout this chapter, a constructor allows you to specify startup values when creating a new object. On a related note, properties allow you to get and set underlying data in a safe manner. When you are working with other people's classes, including the classes found within the .NET base class library, it is not too uncommon to discover that there is not a single constructor that allows you to set every piece of underlying state data. Given this point, a programmer is typically forced to pick the best constructor possible, after which the programmer makes assignments using a handful of provided properties.

To help streamline the process of getting an object up and running, C# offers *object initializer syntax*. Using this technique, it is possible to create a new object variable and assign a slew of properties and/or public fields in a few lines of code. Syntactically, an object initializer consists of a comma-delimited list of specified values, enclosed by the { and } tokens. Each member in the initialization list maps to the name of a public field or public property of the object being initialized.

To see this syntax in action, create a new Console Application project named ObjectInitializers. Now, consider a simple class named Point, created using automatic properties (which is not mandatory for object initialization syntax but helps you write some concise code).

```
class Point
{
    public int X { get; set; }
    public int Y { get; set; }
```

```
  public Point(int xVal, int yVal)
  {
    X = xVal;
    Y = yVal;
  }
  public Point() { }

  public void DisplayStats()
  {
    Console.WriteLine("[{0}, {1}]", X, Y);
  }
}
```

Now consider how you can make Point objects using any of the following approaches:

```
static void Main(string[] args)
{
  Console.WriteLine("***** Fun with Object Init Syntax *****\n");

  // Make a Point by setting each property manually.
  Point firstPoint = new Point();
  firstPoint.X = 10;
  firstPoint.Y = 10;
  firstPoint.DisplayStats();

  // Or make a Point via a custom constructor.
  Point anotherPoint = new Point(20, 20);
  anotherPoint.DisplayStats();

  // Or make a Point using object init syntax.
  Point finalPoint = new Point { X = 30, Y = 30 };
  finalPoint.DisplayStats();
  Console.ReadLine();
}
```

The final Point variable is not making use of a custom constructor (as one might do traditionally) but is rather setting values to the public X and Y properties. Behind the scenes, the type's default constructor is invoked, followed by setting the values to the specified properties. To this end, object initialization syntax is just shorthand notation for the syntax used to create a class variable using a default constructor and to set the state data property by property.

Calling Custom Constructors with Initialization Syntax

The previous examples initialized Point types by implicitly calling the default constructor on the type.

```
// Here, the default constructor is called implicitly.
Point finalPoint = new Point { X = 30, Y = 30 };
```

If you want to be clear about this, it is permissible to explicitly call the default constructor as follows:

```
// Here, the default constructor is called explicitly.
Point finalPoint = new Point() { X = 30, Y = 30 };
```

Do be aware that when you are constructing a type using initialization syntax, you are able to invoke *any* constructor defined by the class. Your Point type currently defines a two-argument constructor to set the (x, y) position. Therefore, the following Point declaration results in an X value of 100 and a Y value of 100, regardless of the fact that the constructor arguments specified the values 10 and 16:

```
// Calling a custom constructor.
Point pt = new Point(10, 16) { X = 100, Y = 100 };
```

Given the current definition of your Point type, calling the custom constructor while using initialization syntax is not terribly useful (and more than a bit verbose). However, if your Point type provides a new constructor that allows the caller to establish a color (via a custom enum named PointColor), the combination of custom constructors and object initialization syntax becomes clear. Assume you have updated Point as follows:

```
enum PointColor
{ LightBlue, BloodRed, Gold }

class Point
{
    public int X { get; set; }
    public int Y { get; set; }
    public PointColor Color{ get; set; }

    public Point(int xVal, int yVal)
    {
      X = xVal;
      Y = yVal;
      Color = PointColor.Gold;
    }

    public Point(PointColor ptColor)
    {
      Color = ptColor;
    }

    public Point()
      : this(PointColor.BloodRed){ }

    public void DisplayStats()
    {
      Console.WriteLine("[{0}, {1}]", X, Y);
      Console.WriteLine("Point is {0}", Color);
    }
}
```

With this new constructor, you can now create a gold point (positioned at 90, 20) as follows:

```
// Calling a more interesting custom constructor with init syntax.
Point goldPoint = new Point(PointColor.Gold){ X = 90, Y = 20 };
goldPoint.DisplayStats();
```

Initializing Data with Initialization Syntax

As briefly mentioned earlier in this chapter (and fully examined in Chapter 6), the "has-a" relationship allows you to compose new classes by defining member variables of existing classes. For example, assume you now have a Rectangle class, which makes use of the Point type to represent its upper-left/bottom-right coordinates. Since automatic properties set all fields of class variables to null, you will implement this new class using "traditional" property syntax.

```
class Rectangle
{
    private Point topLeft = new Point();
    private Point bottomRight = new Point();

    public Point TopLeft
    {
      get { return topLeft; }
      set { topLeft = value; }
    }
    public Point BottomRight
    {
      get { return bottomRight; }
      set { bottomRight = value; }
    }

    public void DisplayStats()
    {
      Console.WriteLine("[TopLeft: {0}, {1}, {2} BottomRight: {3}, {4}, {5}]",
        topLeft.X, topLeft.Y, topLeft.Color,
        bottomRight.X, bottomRight.Y, bottomRight.Color);
    }
}
```

Using object initialization syntax, you could create a new Rectangle variable and set the inner Points as follows:

```
// Create and initialize a Rectangle.
Rectangle myRect = new Rectangle
{
    TopLeft = new Point { X = 10, Y = 10 },
    BottomRight = new Point { X = 200, Y = 200}
};
```

207

Again, the benefit of object initialization syntax is that it basically decreases the number of keystrokes (assuming there is not a suitable constructor). Here is the traditional approach to establishing a similar Rectangle:

```
// Old-school approach.
Rectangle r = new Rectangle();
Point p1 = new Point();
p1.X = 10;
p1.Y = 10;
r.TopLeft = p1;
Point p2 = new Point();
p2.X = 200;
p2.Y = 200;
r.BottomRight = p2;
```

While you might feel object initialization syntax can take a bit of getting used to, once you get comfortable with the code, you'll be quite pleased at how quickly you can establish the state of a new object with minimal fuss and bother.

■ **Source Code**   You can find the ObjectInitilizers project in the Chapter 5 subdirectory.

Working with Constant Field Data

C# offers the const keyword to define constant data, which can never change after the initial assignment. As you might guess, this can be helpful when you are defining a set of known values for use in your applications that are logically connected to a given class or structure.

Assume you are building a utility class named MyMathClass that needs to define a value for pi (which you will assume to be 3.14 for simplicity). Begin by creating a new Console Application project named ConstData. Given that you would not want to allow other developers to change this value in code, pi could be modeled with the following constant:

```
namespace ConstData
{
  class MyMathClass
  {
    public const double PI = 3.14;
  }

  class Program
  {
    static void Main(string[] args)
    {
      Console.WriteLine("***** Fun with Const *****\n");
      Console.WriteLine("The value of PI is: {0}", MyMathClass.PI);
      // Error! Can't change a constant!
      // MyMathClass.PI = 3.1444;
```

```
        Console.ReadLine();
      }
    }
}
```

Notice that you are referencing the constant data defined by MyMathClass using a class name prefix (i.e., MyMathClass.PI). This is because constant fields of a class are implicitly *static*. However, it is permissible to define and access a local constant variable within the scope of a method or property. Here's an example:

```
static void LocalConstStringVariable()
{
    // A local constant data point can be directly accessed.
    const string fixedStr = "Fixed string Data";
    Console.WriteLine(fixedStr);

    // Error!
    // fixedStr = "This will not work!";
}
```

Regardless of where you define a constant piece of data, the one point to always remember is that the initial value assigned to the constant must be specified at the time you define the constant. Thus, if you were to modify your MyMathClass in such a way that the value of pi is assigned in a class constructor as follows:

```
class MyMathClass
{
    // Try to set PI in ctor?
    public const double PI;

    public MyMathClass()
    {
        // Not possible- must assign at time of declaration.
        PI = 3.14;
    }
}
```

you would receive a compile-time error. The reason for this restriction has to do with the fact the value of constant data must be known at compile time. Constructors (or any other method), as you know, are invoked at runtime.

Understanding Read-Only Fields

Closely related to constant data is the notion of *read-only field data* (which should not be confused with a read-only property). Like a constant, a read-only field cannot be changed after the initial assignment. However, unlike a constant, the value assigned to a read-only field can be determined at runtime and, therefore, can legally be assigned within the scope of a constructor but nowhere else.

This can be helpful when you don't know the value of a field until runtime, perhaps because you need to read an external file to obtain the value but want to ensure that the value will not change after that point. For the sake of illustration, assume the following update to MyMathClass:

```
class MyMathClass
{
    // Read-only fields can be assigned in ctors,
    // but nowhere else.
    public readonly double PI;

    public MyMathClass ()
    {
      PI = 3.14;
    }
}
```

Again, any attempt to make assignments to a field marked readonly outside the scope of a constructor results in a compiler error.

```
class MyMathClass
{
    public readonly double PI;
    public MyMathClass ()
    {
      PI = 3.14;
    }

    // Error!
    public void ChangePI()
    { PI = 3.14444;}
}
```

Static Read-Only Fields

Unlike a constant field, read-only fields are not implicitly static. Thus, if you want to expose PI from the class level, you must explicitly use the static keyword. If you know the value of a static read-only field at compile time, the initial assignment looks similar to that of a constant (however, in this case, it would be easier to simply use the const keyword in the first place, as you are assigning the data field at the time of declaration).

```
class MyMathClass
{
    public static readonly double PI = 3.14;
}

class Program
{
    static void Main(string[] args)
    {
      Console.WriteLine("***** Fun with Const *****");
      Console.WriteLine("The value of PI is: {0}", MyMathClass.PI);
      Console.ReadLine();
    }
}
```

However, if the value of a static read-only field is not known until runtime, you must use a static constructor as described earlier in this chapter.

```
class MyMathClass
{
    public static readonly double PI;

    static MyMathClass()
    { PI = 3.14; }
}
```

■ **Source Code**   You can find the ConstData project in the Chapter 5 subdirectory.

Understanding Partial Classes

Last but not least, it is important to understand the role of the C# partial keyword. A production-level class could easily consist of hundreds and hundreds (if not thousands) of lines of code within a single *.cs file. As it turns out, when you are creating your classes, it is often the case that much of the boilerplate code can be basically ignored after it is accounted for. For example, field data, properties, and constructors tend to remain as is during production, while methods tend to be modified quite often to account for updated algorithms and so forth.

In C#, you can partition a single class across multiple code files to isolate the boilerplate code from more readily useful (and complex) members. To illustrate where partial classes could be useful, open the EmployeeApp project you created previously in this chapter in Visual Studio, and then open the Employee. cs file for editing. As you recall, this single file contains code of all aspects of the class.

```
class Employee
{
    // Field Data

    // Constructors

    // Methods

    // Properties
}
```

Using partial classes, you could choose to move (for example) the properties, constructors, and field data into a new file named Employee.Core.cs (the name of the file is irrelevant). The first step is to add the partial keyword to the current class definition and cut the code to be placed into the new file.

```
// Employee.cs
partial class Employee
{
    // Methods

    // Properties
}
```

Next, assuming you have inserted a new class file into your project, you can move the data fields and constructors to the new file using a simple cut-and-paste operation. In addition, you *must* add the partial keyword to this aspect of the class definition. Here's an example:

```
// Employee.Core.cs
partial class Employee
{
    // Field data

    // Constructors
}
```

■ **Note** Remember that every aspect of a partial class definition must be marked with the partial keyword!

After you compile the modified project, you should see no difference whatsoever. The whole idea of a partial class is realized only during design time. After the application has been compiled, there is just a single, unified class within the assembly. The only requirement when defining partial types is that the type's name (Employee in this case) is identical and defined within the same .NET namespace.

Use Cases for Partial Classes?

Now that you understand the mechanics of how to define a partial class, you may be wondering exactly when (and if) you will ever need to do so. To be honest, you may not need to make use of partial class definitions too often. However, Visual Studio uses them in the background all the time. For example, if you are building a graphical user interface using Windows Presentation Foundation (WPF), you will note that Visual Studio places all the designer-generated code into a dedicated partial class file, leaving you to focus on your custom programming logic (without the designer-generated code getting in the way).

■ **Source Code** You can find the EmployeeAppPartial project in the Chapter 5 subdirectory.

Summary

The point of this chapter was to introduce you to the role of the C# class type. As you have seen, classes can take any number of *constructors* that enable the object user to establish the state of the object upon creation. This chapter also illustrated several class design techniques (and related keywords). Recall that the this keyword can be used to obtain access to the current object, the static keyword allows you to define fields and members that are bound at the class (not object) level, and the const keyword (and readonly modifier) allows you to define a point of data that can never change after the initial assignment.

The bulk of this chapter dug into the details of the first pillar of OOP: encapsulation. You learned about the access modifiers of C# and the role of type properties, object initialization syntax, and partial classes. With this behind you, you are now able to turn to the next chapter where you will learn to build a family of related classes using inheritance and polymorphism.

CHAPTER 6

■ ■ ■

Understanding Inheritance and Polymorphism

Chapter 5 examined the first pillar of OOP: encapsulation. At that time, you learned how to build a single well-defined class type with constructors and various members (fields, properties, methods, constants, and read-only fields). This chapter will focus on the remaining two pillars of OOP: inheritance and polymorphism.

First, you will learn how to build families of related classes using *inheritance*. As you will see, this form of code reuse allows you to define common functionality in a parent class that can be leveraged, and possibly altered, by child classes. Along the way, you will learn how to establish a *polymorphic interface* into class hierarchies using virtual and abstract members, as well as the role of explicit casting.

The chapter will wrap up by examining the role of the ultimate parent class in the .NET base class libraries: `System.Object`.

The Basic Mechanics of Inheritance

Recall from Chapter 5 that inheritance is an aspect of OOP that facilitates code reuse. Specifically speaking, code reuse comes in two flavors: inheritance (the "is-a" relationship) and the containment/delegation model (the "has-a" relationship). Let's begin this chapter by examining the classical inheritance model of the "is-a" relationship.

When you establish "is-a" relationships between classes, you are building a dependency between two or more class types. The basic idea behind classical inheritance is that new classes can be created using existing classes as a starting point. To begin with a simple example, create a new Console Application project named BasicInheritance. Now assume you have designed a class named Car that models some basic details of an automobile.

```
// A simple base class.
class Car
{
  public readonly int maxSpeed;
  private int currSpeed;

  public Car(int max)
  {
    maxSpeed = max;
  }
}
```

```
  public Car()
  {
    maxSpeed = 55;
  }
  public int Speed
  {
    get { return currSpeed; }
    set
    {
      currSpeed = value;
      if (currSpeed > maxSpeed)
      {
        currSpeed = maxSpeed;
      }
    }
  }
}
```

Notice that the Car class is using encapsulation services to control access to the private currSpeed field using a public property named Speed. At this point, you can exercise your Car type as follows:

```
static void Main(string[] args)
{
  Console.WriteLine("***** Basic Inheritance *****\n");
  // Make a Car object and set max speed.
  Car myCar = new Car(80);

  // Set the current speed, and print it.
  myCar.Speed = 50;
  Console.WriteLine("My car is going {0} MPH", myCar.Speed);
  Console.ReadLine();
}
```

Specifying the Parent Class of an Existing Class

Now assume you want to build a new class named MiniVan. Like a basic Car, you want to define the MiniVan class to support data for a maximum speed, a current speed, and a property named Speed to allow the object user to modify the object's state. Clearly, the Car and MiniVan classes are related; in fact, it can be said that a MiniVan "*is-a*" type of Car. The "is-a" relationship (formally termed *classical inheritance*) allows you to build new class definitions that extend the functionality of an existing class.

The existing class that will serve as the basis for the new class is termed a *base class, superclass,* or *parent class.* The role of a base class is to define all the common data and members for the classes that extend it. The extending classes are formally termed *derived* or *child* classes. In C#, you make use of the colon operator on the class definition to establish an "is-a" relationship between classes. Assume you have authored the following new MiniVan class:

```
// MiniVan "is-a" Car.
class MiniVan : Car
{
}
```

Currently, this new class has not defined any members whatsoever. So, what have you gained by extending your MiniVan from the Car base class? Simply put, MiniVan objects now have access to each public member defined within the parent class.

■ **Note**   Although constructors are typically defined as public, a derived class never inherits the constructors of a parent class. Constructors are used to construct only the class that they are defined within, although they can be called by a derived class through constructor chaining. This will be covered shortly.

Given the relation between these two class types, you could now make use of the MiniVan class like so:

```
static void Main(string[] args)
{
  Console.WriteLine("***** Basic Inheritance *****\n");
...
  // Now make a MiniVan object.
  MiniVan myVan = new MiniVan();
  myVan.Speed = 10;
  Console.WriteLine("My van is going {0} MPH",
    myVan.Speed);
  Console.ReadLine();
}
```

Again, notice that although you have not added any members to the MiniVan class, you have direct access to the public Speed property of your parent class and have thus reused code. This is a far better approach than creating a MiniVan class that has the same members as Car, such as a Speed property. If you did duplicate code between these two classes, you would need to now maintain two bodies of code, which is certainly a poor use of your time.

Always remember that inheritance preserves encapsulation; therefore, the following code results in a compiler error, as private members can never be accessed from an object reference:

```
static void Main(string[] args)
{
  Console.WriteLine("***** Basic Inheritance *****\n");
...
  // Make a MiniVan object.
  MiniVan myVan = new MiniVan();
    myVan.Speed = 10;
  Console.WriteLine("My van is going {0} MPH",
  myVan.Speed);

  // Error! Can't access private members!
  myVan.currSpeed = 55;
  Console.ReadLine();
}
```

On a related note, if the MiniVan defined its own set of members, it would still not be able to access any private member of the Car base class. Remember, private members can be accessed *only* by the class that defines it. For example, the following method in MiniVan would result in a compiler error:

```
// MiniVan derives from Car.
class MiniVan : Car
{
  public void TestMethod()
  {
    // OK! Can access public members
    // of a parent within a derived type.
    Speed = 10;

    // Error! Cannot access private
    // members of parent within a derived type.
    currSpeed = 10;
  }
}
```

Regarding Multiple Base Classes

Speaking of base classes, it is important to keep in mind that C# demands that a given class have exactly *one* direct base class. It is not possible to create a class type that directly derives from two or more base classes (this technique, which is supported in unmanaged C++, is known as *multiple inheritance*, or simply *MI*). If you attempted to create a class that specifies two direct parent classes, as shown in the following code, you would receive compiler errors:

```
// Illegal! C# does not allow
// multiple inheritance for classes!
class WontWork
  : BaseClassOne, BaseClassTwo
{}
```

As you will see in Chapter 8, the .NET platform does allow a given class, or structure, to implement any number of discrete interfaces. In this way, a C# type can exhibit a number of behaviors while avoiding the complexities associated with MI. On a related note, while a class can have only one direct base class, it is permissible for an interface to directly derive from multiple interfaces. Using this technique, you can build sophisticated interface hierarchies that model complex behaviors (again, see Chapter 8).

The sealed Keyword

C# supplies another keyword, sealed, that prevents inheritance from occurring. When you mark a class as sealed, the compiler will not allow you to derive from this type. For example, assume you have decided that it makes no sense to further extend the MiniVan class.

```
// The MiniVan class cannot be extended!
sealed class MiniVan : Car
{
}
```

If you (or a teammate) were to attempt to derive from this class, you would receive a compile-time error.

```
// Error! Cannot extend
// a class marked with the sealed keyword!
class DeluxeMiniVan
  : MiniVan
{}
```

Most often, sealing a class makes the best sense when you are designing a utility class. For example, the System namespace defines numerous sealed classes. You can verify this for yourself by opening the Visual Studio Object Browser (via the View menu) and selecting the String class within the System namespace of the mscorlib.dll assembly. Notice in Figure 6-1 the icon used to denote a sealed class.

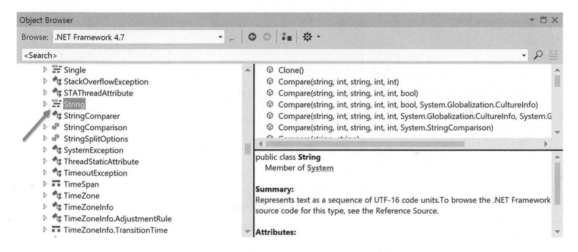

Figure 6-1. *The base class libraries define numerous sealed types, such as* System.String

Thus, just like the MiniVan, if you attempt to build a new class that extends System.String, you will receive a compile-time error.

```
// Another error! Cannot extend
// a class marked as sealed!
class MyString
  : String
{}
```

■ **Note**   In Chapter 4, you learned that C# structures are always implicitly sealed (see Table 4-3). Therefore, you can never derive one structure from another structure, a class from a structure, or a structure from a class. Structures can be used to model only stand-alone, atomic, user-defined data types. If you want to leverage the is-a relationship, you must use classes.

As you would guess, there are many more details to inheritance that you will come to know during the remainder of this chapter. For now, simply keep in mind that the colon operator allows you to establish base/derived class relationships, while the `sealed` keyword prevents subsequent inheritance from occurring.

Revisiting Visual Studio Class Diagrams

In Chapter 2, I briefly mentioned that Visual Studio allows you to establish base/derived class relationships visually at design time. To leverage this aspect of the IDE, your first step is to include a new class diagram file into your current project. To do so, access the Project ➤ Add New Item menu option and click the Class Diagram icon (in Figure 6-2, I renamed the file from `ClassDiagram1.cd` to `Cars.cd`).

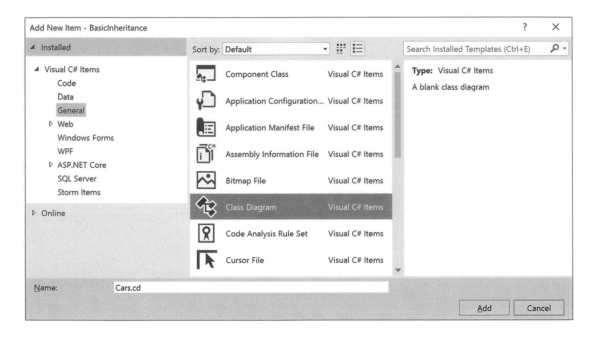

Figure 6-2. *Inserting a new class diagram*

After you click the Add button, you will be presented with a blank designer surface. To add types to a class designer, simply drag each file from the Solution Explorer window onto the surface. Also recall that if you delete an item from the visual designer (simply by selecting it and pressing the Delete key), this will not destroy the associated source code but simply remove the item off the designer surface. Figure 6-3 shows the current class hierarchy.

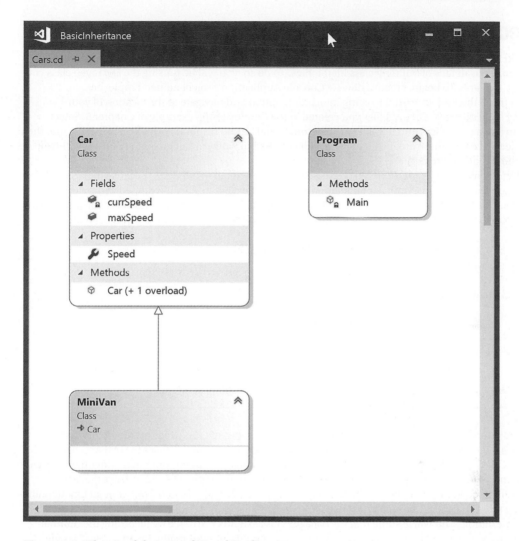

Figure 6-3. *The visual designer of Visual Studio*

Beyond simply displaying the relationships of the types within your current application, recall from Chapter 2 that you can also create new types and populate their members using the Class Designer toolbox and Class Details window.

If you want to make use of these visual tools during the remainder of the book, feel free. However, always make sure you analyze the generated code so you have a solid understanding of what these tools have done on your behalf.

■ **Source Code**   You can find the BasicInheritance project in the Chapter 6 subdirectory.

The Second Pillar of OOP: The Details of Inheritance

Now that you have seen the basic syntax of inheritance, let's create a more complex example and get to know the numerous details of building class hierarchies. To do so, you will be reusing the Employee class you designed in Chapter 5. To begin, create a new C# Console Application project named Employees.

Next, activate the Project ➤ Add Existing Item menu option and navigate to the location of your Employee.cs and Employee.Core.cs files you created in the EmployeeApp example of Chapter 5. Select each of them (via a Ctrl+click) and click the Add button. Visual Studio responds by copying each file into the current project (because these are full copies, you will not need to worry about changing the original work you did in the Chapter 5 project).

Before you start to build some derived classes, you have one detail to attend to. Because the original Employee class was created in a project named EmployeeApp, the class has been wrapped within an identically named .NET namespace. Chapter 14 will examine namespaces in detail; however, for simplicity, rename the current namespace (in both file locations) to Employees to match your new project name.

```
// Be sure to change the namespace name in both C# files!
namespace Employees
{
  partial class Employee
  {...}
}
```

■ **Note**   As a sanity check, compile and run your new project by pressing Ctrl+F5. The program will not do anything at this point; however, this will ensure you do not have any compiler errors.

Your goal is to create a family of classes that model various types of employees in a company. Assume you want to leverage the functionality of the Employee class to create two new classes (SalesPerson and Manager). The new SalesPerson class "is-an" Employee (as is a Manager). Remember that under the classical inheritance model, base classes (such as Employee) are used to define general characteristics that are common to all descendants. Subclasses (such as SalesPerson and Manager) extend this general functionality while adding more specific functionality.

For your example, you will assume that the Manager class extends Employee by recording the number of stock options, while the SalesPerson class maintains the number of sales made. Insert a new class file (Manager.cs) that defines the Manager class with the following automatic property:

```
// Managers need to know their number of stock options.
class Manager : Employee
{
  public int StockOptions { get; set; }
}
```

Next, add another new class file (SalesPerson.cs) that defines the SalesPerson class with a fitting automatic property.

```
// Salespeople need to know their number of sales.
class SalesPerson : Employee
{
  public int SalesNumber { get; set; }
}
```

220

Now that you have established an "is-a" relationship, SalesPerson and Manager have automatically inherited all public members of the Employee base class. To illustrate, update your Main() method as follows:

```
// Create a subclass object and access base class functionality.
static void Main(string[] args)
{
  Console.WriteLine("***** The Employee Class Hierarchy *****\n");
  SalesPerson fred = new SalesPerson();
  fred.Age = 31;
  fred.Name = "Fred";
  fred.SalesNumber = 50;
  Console.ReadLine();
}
```

Controlling Base Class Creation with the base Keyword

Currently, SalesPerson and Manager can be created only using the "freebie" default constructor (see Chapter 5). With this in mind, assume you have added a new six-argument constructor to the Manager type, which is invoked as follows:

```
static void Main(string[] args)
{
...
  // Assume Manager has a constructor matching this signature:
  // (string fullName, int age, int empID,
  // float currPay, string ssn, int numbOfOpts)
  Manager chucky = new Manager("Chucky", 50, 92, 100000, "333-23-2322", 9000);
  Console.ReadLine();
}
```

If you look at the parameter list, you can clearly see that most of these arguments should be stored in the member variables defined by the Employee base class. To do so, you might implement this custom constructor on the Manager class as follows:

```
public Manager(string fullName, int age, int empID,
            float currPay, string ssn, int numbOfOpts)
{
  // This property is defined by the Manager class.
  StockOptions = numbOfOpts;

  // Assign incoming parameters using the
  // inherited properties of the parent class.
  ID = empID;
  Age = age;
  Name = fullName;
  Pay = currPay;

  // OOPS! This would be a compiler error,
  // if the SSN property were read-only!
  SocialSecurityNumber = ssn;
}
```

The first issue with this approach is that if you defined any property as read-only (for example, the SocialSecurityNumber property), you are unable to assign the incoming string parameter to this field, as shown in the final code statement of this custom constructor.

The second issue is that you have indirectly created a rather inefficient constructor, given that under C#, unless you say otherwise, the default constructor of a base class is called automatically before the logic of the derived constructor is executed. After this point, the current implementation accesses numerous public properties of the Employee base class to establish its state. Thus, you have really made seven hits (five inherited properties and two constructor calls) during the creation of a Manager object!

To help optimize the creation of a derived class, you will do well to implement your subclass constructors to explicitly call an appropriate custom base class constructor, rather than the default. In this way, you are able to reduce the number of calls to inherited initialization members (which saves processing time). First, ensure your Employee parent class has the following five-argument constructor:

```csharp
// Add to the Employee base class.
public Employee(string name, int age, int id, float pay, string ssn)
  :this(name, age, id, pay)
{
    empSSN = ssn;
}
```

Now, let's retrofit the custom constructor of the Manager type to do this very thing using the base keyword.

```csharp
public Manager(string fullName, int age, int empID,
               float currPay, string ssn, int numbOfOpts)
  : base(fullName, age, empID, currPay, ssn)
{
  // This property is defined by the Manager class.
  StockOptions = numbOfOpts;
}
```

Here, the base keyword is hanging off the constructor signature (much like the syntax used to chain constructors on a single class using the this keyword, as was discussed in Chapter 5), which always indicates a derived constructor is passing data to the immediate parent constructor. In this situation, you are explicitly calling the five-parameter constructor defined by Employee and saving yourself unnecessary calls during the creation of the child class. The custom SalesPerson constructor looks almost identical.

```csharp
// As a general rule, all subclasses should explicitly call an appropriate
// base class constructor.
public SalesPerson(string fullName, int age, int empID,
  float currPay, string ssn, int numbOfSales)
  : base(fullName, age, empID, currPay, ssn)
{
  // This belongs with us!
  SalesNumber = numbOfSales;
}
```

■ **Note**   You may use the base keyword whenever a subclass wants to access a public or protected member defined by a parent class. Use of this keyword is not limited to constructor logic. You will see examples using base in this manner during the examination of polymorphism, later in this chapter.

Finally, recall that once you add a custom constructor to a class definition, the default constructor is silently removed. Therefore, be sure to redefine the default constructor for the SalesPerson and Manager types. Here's an example:

```
// Add back the default ctor
// in the Manager class as well.
public SalesPerson() {}
```

Keeping Family Secrets: The protected Keyword

As you already know, public items are directly accessible from anywhere, while private items can be accessed only by the class that has defined them. Recall from Chapter 5 that C# takes the lead of many other modern object languages and provides an additional keyword to define member accessibility: protected.

When a base class defines protected data or protected members, it establishes a set of items that can be accessed directly by any descendant. If you want to allow the SalesPerson and Manager child classes to directly access the data sector defined by Employee, you can update the original Employee class definition as follows:

```
// Protected state data.
partial class Employee
{
  // Derived classes can now directly access this information.
  protected string empName;
  protected int empID;
  protected float currPay;
  protected int empAge;
  protected string empSSN;
...
}
```

The benefit of defining protected members in a base class is that derived types no longer have to access the data indirectly using public methods or properties. The possible downfall, of course, is that when a derived type has direct access to its parent's internal data, it is possible to accidentally bypass existing business rules found within public properties. When you define protected members, you are creating a level of trust between the parent class and the child class, as the compiler will not catch any violation of your type's business rules.

Finally, understand that as far as the object user is concerned, protected data is regarded as private (as the user is "outside" the family). Therefore, the following is illegal:

```
static void Main(string[] args)
{
  // Error! Can't access protected data from client code.
  Employee emp = new Employee();
  emp.empName = "Fred";
}
```

■ **Note** Although protected field data can break encapsulation, it is quite safe (and useful) to define protected methods. When building class hierarchies, it is common to define a set of methods that are only for use by derived types and are not intended for use by the outside world.

Adding a Sealed Class

Recall that a *sealed* class cannot be extended by other classes. As mentioned, this technique is most often used when you are designing a utility class. However, when building class hierarchies, you might find that a certain branch in the inheritance chain should be "capped off," as it makes no sense to further extend the linage. For example, assume you have added yet another class to your program (PTSalesPerson) that extends the existing SalesPerson type. Figure 6-4 shows the current update.

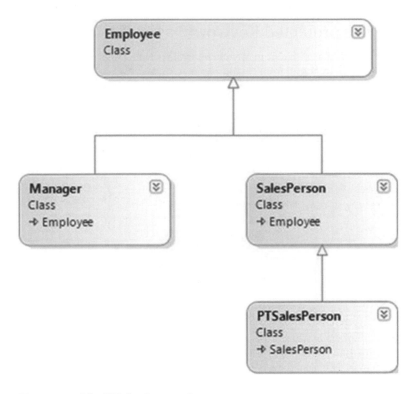

Figure 6-4. *The PTSalesPerson class*

PTSalesPerson is a class representing, of course, a part-time salesperson. For the sake of argument, let's say you want to ensure that no other developer is able to subclass from PTSalesPerson. (After all, how much more part-time can you get than "part-time"?) Again, to prevent others from extending a class, use the sealed keyword.

```
sealed class PTSalesPerson : SalesPerson
{
  public PTSalesPerson(string fullName, int age, int empID,
                       float currPay, string ssn, int numbOfSales)
    :base (fullName, age, empID, currPay, ssn, numbOfSales)
  {
  }
    // Assume other members here...
}
```

Programming for Containment/Delegation

Recall that code reuse comes in two flavors. You have just explored the classical "is-a" relationship. Before you examine the third pillar of OOP (polymorphism), let's examine the "has-a" relationship (also known as the *containment/delegation model* or *aggregation*). Assume you have created a new class that models an employee benefits package, as follows:

```
// This new type will function as a contained class.
class BenefitPackage
{
  // Assume we have other members that represent
  // dental/health benefits, and so on.
  public double ComputePayDeduction()
  {
    return 125.0;
  }
}
```

Obviously, it would be rather odd to establish an "is-a" relationship between the BenefitPackage class and the employee types. (Employee "is-a" BenefitPackage? I don't think so.) However, it should be clear that some sort of relationship between the two could be established. In short, you would like to express the idea that each employee "has-a" BenefitPackage. To do so, you can update the Employee class definition as follows:

```
// Employees now have benefits.
partial class Employee
{
  // Contain a BenefitPackage object.
  protected BenefitPackage empBenefits = new BenefitPackage();
...
}
```

At this point, you have successfully contained another object. However, exposing the functionality of the contained object to the outside world requires delegation. *Delegation* is simply the act of adding public members to the containing class that use the contained object's functionality.

For example, you could update the Employee class to expose the contained empBenefits object using a custom property, as well as make use of its functionality internally using a new method named GetBenefitCost().

```
partial class Employee
{
  // Contain a BenefitPackage object.
  protected BenefitPackage empBenefits = new BenefitPackage();

  // Expose certain benefit behaviors of object.
  public double GetBenefitCost()
  { return empBenefits.ComputePayDeduction(); }
```

```
  // Expose object through a custom property.
  public BenefitPackage Benefits
  {
    get { return empBenefits; }
    set { empBenefits = value; }
  }
...
}
```

In the following updated Main() method, notice how you can interact with the internal BenefitsPackage type defined by the Employee type:

```
static void Main(string[] args)
{
  Console.WriteLine("***** The Employee Class Hierarchy *****\n");
  ...
  Manager chucky = new Manager("Chucky", 50, 92, 100000, "333-23-2322", 9000);
  double cost = chucky.GetBenefitCost();
  Console.ReadLine();
}
```

Understanding Nested Type Definitions

Chapter 5 briefly mentioned the concept of nested types, which is a spin on the "has-a" relationship you have just examined. In C# (as well as other .NET languages), it is possible to define a type (enum, class, interface, struct, or delegate) directly within the scope of a class or structure. When you have done so, the nested (or "inner") type is considered a member of the nesting (or "outer") class and in the eyes of the runtime can be manipulated like any other member (fields, properties, methods, and events). The syntax used to nest a type is quite straightforward.

```
public class OuterClass
{
  // A public nested type can be used by anybody.
  public class PublicInnerClass {}

  // A private nested type can only be used by members
  // of the containing class.
  private class PrivateInnerClass {}
}
```

Although the syntax is fairly clear, understanding why you would want to do this might not be readily apparent. To understand this technique, ponder the following traits of nesting a type:

- Nested types allow you to gain complete control over the access level of the inner type because they may be declared privately (recall that non-nested classes cannot be declared using the private keyword).

- Because a nested type is a member of the containing class, it can access private members of the containing class.

- Often, a nested type is useful only as a helper for the outer class and is not intended for use by the outside world.

When a type nests another class type, it can create member variables of the type, just as it would for any point of data. However, if you want to use a nested type from outside the containing type, you must qualify it by the scope of the nesting type. Consider the following code:

```
static void Main(string[] args)
{
  // Create and use the public inner class. OK!
  OuterClass.PublicInnerClass inner;
  inner = new OuterClass.PublicInnerClass();

  // Compiler Error! Cannot access the private class.
  OuterClass.PrivateInnerClass inner2;
  inner2 = new OuterClass.PrivateInnerClass();
}
```

To use this concept within the employees example, assume you have now nested the BenefitPackage directly within the Employee class type.

```
partial class Employee
{
  public class BenefitPackage
  {
    // Assume we have other members that represent
    // dental/health benefits, and so on.
    public double ComputePayDeduction()
    {
      return 125.0;
    }
  }
...
}
```

The nesting process can be as "deep" as you require. For example, assume you want to create an enumeration named BenefitPackageLevel, which documents the various benefit levels an employee may choose. To programmatically enforce the tight connection between Employee, BenefitPackage, and BenefitPackageLevel, you could nest the enumeration as follows:

```
// Employee nests BenefitPackage.
public partial class Employee
{
  // BenefitPackage nests BenefitPackageLevel.
  public class BenefitPackage
  {
    public enum BenefitPackageLevel
    {
      Standard, Gold, Platinum
    }
```

```
    public double ComputePayDeduction()
    {
      return 125.0;
    }
  }
...
}
```

Because of the nesting relationships, note how you are required to make use of this enumeration:

```
static void Main(string[] args)
{
...
  // Define my benefit level.
  Employee.BenefitPackage.BenefitPackageLevel myBenefitLevel =
    Employee.BenefitPackage.BenefitPackageLevel.Platinum;
  Console.ReadLine();
}
```

Excellent! At this point, you have been exposed to a number of keywords (and concepts) that allow you to build hierarchies of related types via classical inheritance, containment, and nested types. If the details aren't crystal clear right now, don't sweat it. You will be building a number of additional hierarchies over the remainder of this book. Next up, let's examine the final pillar of OOP: polymorphism.

The Third Pillar of OOP: C#'s Polymorphic Support

Recall that the Employee base class defined a method named GiveBonus(), which was originally implemented as follows:

```
public partial class Employee
{
  public void GiveBonus(float amount)
  {
    Pay += amount;
  }
...
}
```

Because this method has been defined with the public keyword, you can now give bonuses to salespeople and managers (as well as part-time salespeople).

```
static void Main(string[] args)
{
  Console.WriteLine("***** The Employee Class Hierarchy *****\n");

  // Give each employee a bonus?
  Manager chucky = new Manager("Chucky", 50, 92, 100000, "333-23-2322", 9000);
  chucky.GiveBonus(300);
  chucky.DisplayStats();
  Console.WriteLine();
```

```
SalesPerson fran = new SalesPerson("Fran", 43, 93, 3000, "932-32-3232", 31);
fran.GiveBonus(200);
fran.DisplayStats();
Console.ReadLine();
}
```

The problem with the current design is that the publicly inherited GiveBonus() method operates identically for all subclasses. Ideally, the bonus of a salesperson or part-time salesperson should take into account the number of sales. Perhaps managers should gain additional stock options in conjunction with a monetary bump in salary. Given this, you are suddenly faced with an interesting question: "How can related types respond differently to the same request?" Again, glad you asked!

The virtual and override Keywords

Polymorphism provides a way for a subclass to define its own version of a method defined by its base class, using the process termed *method overriding*. To retrofit your current design, you need to understand the meaning of the virtual and override keywords. If a base class wants to define a method that *may be* (but does not have to be) overridden by a subclass, it must mark the method with the virtual keyword.

```
partial class Employee
{
  // This method can now be "overridden" by a derived class.
  public virtual void GiveBonus(float amount)
  {
    Pay += amount;
  }
...
}
```

■ **Note**   Methods that have been marked with the virtual keyword are (not surprisingly) termed *virtual methods*.

When a subclass wants to change the implementation details of a virtual method, it does so using the override keyword. For example, the SalesPerson and Manager could override GiveBonus() as follows (assume that PTSalesPerson will not override GiveBonus() and, therefore, simply inherits the version defined by SalesPerson):

```
class SalesPerson : Employee
{
...
  // A salesperson's bonus is influenced by the number of sales.
  public override void GiveBonus(float amount)
  {
    int salesBonus = 0;
    if (SalesNumber >= 0 && SalesNumber <= 100)
      salesBonus = 10;
    else
```

```
    {
      if (SalesNumber >= 101 && SalesNumber <= 200)
        salesBonus = 15;
      else
        salesBonus = 20;
    }
    base.GiveBonus(amount * salesBonus);
  }
}

class Manager : Employee
{
...
  public override void GiveBonus(float amount)
  {
    base.GiveBonus(amount);
    Random r = new Random();
    StockOptions += r.Next(500);
  }
}
```

Notice how each overridden method is free to leverage the default behavior using the base keyword. In this way, you have no need to completely reimplement the logic behind GiveBonus() but can reuse (and possibly extend) the default behavior of the parent class.

Also assume that the current DisplayStats() method of the Employee class has been declared virtually.

```
public virtual void DisplayStats()
{
    Console.WriteLine("Name: {0}", Name);
    Console.WriteLine("ID: {0}", ID);
    Console.WriteLine("Age: {0}", Age);
    Console.WriteLine("Pay: {0}", Pay);
    Console.WriteLine("SSN: {0}", SocialSecurityNumber);
}
```

By doing so, each subclass can override this method to account for displaying the number of sales (for salespeople) and current stock options (for managers). For example, consider the Manager's version of the DisplayStats() method (the SalesPerson class would implement DisplayStats() in a similar manner to show the number of sales).

```
public override void DisplayStats()
{
  base.DisplayStats();
  Console.WriteLine("Number of Stock Options: {0}", StockOptions);
}
```

Now that each subclass can interpret what these virtual methods mean for itself, each object instance behaves as a more independent entity.

```
static void Main(string[] args)
{
  Console.WriteLine("***** The Employee Class Hierarchy *****\n");

  // A better bonus system!
  Manager chucky = new Manager("Chucky", 50, 92, 100000, "333-23-2322", 9000);
  chucky.GiveBonus(300);
  chucky.DisplayStats();
  Console.WriteLine();

  SalesPerson fran = new SalesPerson("Fran", 43, 93, 3000, "932-32-3232", 31);
  fran.GiveBonus(200);
  fran.DisplayStats();
  Console.ReadLine();
}
```

The following output shows a possible test run of your application thus far:

```
***** The Employee Class Hierarchy *****

Name: Chucky
ID: 92
Age: 50
Pay: 100300
SSN: 333-23-2322
Number of Stock Options: 9337

Name: Fran
ID: 93
Age: 43
Pay: 5000
SSN: 932-32-3232
Number of Sales: 31
```

Overriding Virtual Members Using the Visual Studio IDE

As you might have already noticed, when you are overriding a member, you must recall the type of every parameter—not to mention the method name and parameter passing conventions (ref, out, and params). Visual Studio has a helpful feature that you can make use of when overriding a virtual member. If you type the word override within the scope of a class type (then hit the spacebar), IntelliSense will automatically display a list of all the overridable members defined in your parent classes, as you see in Figure 6-5.

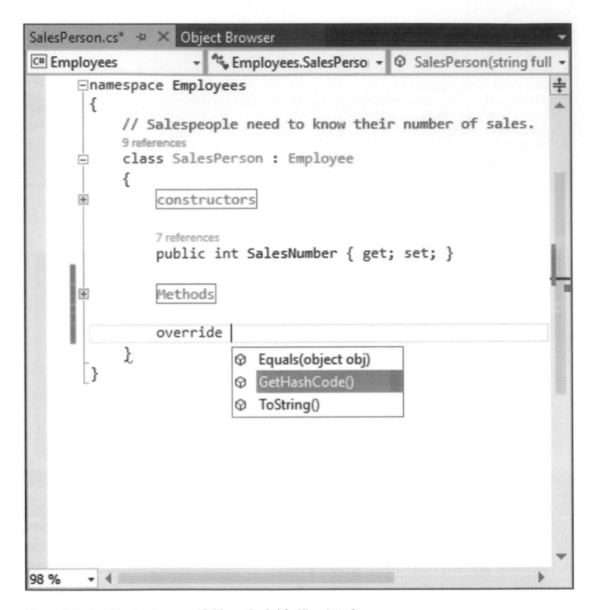

Figure 6-5. *Quickly viewing overridable methods à la Visual Studio*

When you select a member and hit the Enter key, the IDE responds by automatically filling in the method stub on your behalf. Note that you also receive a code statement that calls your parent's version of the virtual member (you are free to delete this line if it is not required). For example, if you used this technique when overriding the DisplayStats() method, you might find the following autogenerated code:

```
public override void DisplayStats()
{
  base.DisplayStats();
}
```

Sealing Virtual Members

Recall that the sealed keyword can be applied to a class type to prevent other types from extending its behavior via inheritance. As you might remember, you sealed PTSalesPerson because you assumed it made no sense for other developers to extend this line of inheritance any further.

On a related note, sometimes you might not want to seal an entire class but simply want to prevent derived types from overriding particular virtual methods. For example, assume you do not want part-time salespeople to obtain customized bonuses. To prevent the PTSalesPerson class from overriding the virtual GiveBonus() method, you could effectively seal this method in the SalesPerson class as follows:

```
// SalesPerson has sealed the GiveBonus() method!
class SalesPerson : Employee
{
...
  public override sealed void GiveBonus(float amount)
  {
    ...
  }
}
```

Here, SalesPerson has indeed overridden the virtual GiveBonus() method defined in the Employee class; however, it has explicitly marked it as sealed. Thus, if you attempted to override this method in the PTSalesPerson class, you would receive compile-time errors, as shown in the following code:

```
sealed class PTSalesPerson : SalesPerson
{
  public PTSalesPerson(string fullName, int age, int empID,
                       float currPay, string ssn, int numbOfSales)
    :base (fullName, age, empID, currPay, ssn, numbOfSales)
  {
  }

  // Compiler error! Can't override this method
  // in the PTSalesPerson class, as it was sealed.
  public override void GiveBonus(float amount)
  {
  }
}
```

Understanding Abstract Classes

Currently, the Employee base class has been designed to supply various data members for its descendants, as well as supply two virtual methods (GiveBonus() and DisplayStats()) that may be overridden by a given descendant. While this is all well and good, there is a rather odd byproduct of the current design; you can directly create instances of the Employee base class.

```
// What exactly does this mean?
Employee X = new Employee();
```

In this example, the only real purpose of the Employee base class is to define common members for all subclasses. In all likelihood, you did not intend anyone to create a direct instance of this class, reason being that the Employee type itself is too general of a concept. For example, if I were to walk up to you and say, "I'm an employee!" I would bet your first question to me would be, "What *kind* of employee are you?" Are you a consultant, trainer, admin assistant, copyeditor, or White House aide?

Given that many base classes tend to be rather nebulous entities, a far better design for this example is to prevent the ability to directly create a new Employee object in code. In C#, you can enforce this programmatically by using the abstract keyword in the class definition, thus creating an *abstract base class*.

```
// Update the Employee class as abstract
// to prevent direct instantiation.
abstract partial class Employee
{
  ...
}
```

With this, if you now attempt to create an instance of the Employee class, you are issued a compile-time error.

```
// Error! Cannot create an instance of an abstract class!
Employee X = new Employee();
```

At first glance, it might seem strange to define a class that you cannot directly create an instance of. Recall, however, that base classes (abstract or not) are useful, in that they contain all the common data and functionality of derived types. Using this form of abstraction, you are able to model that the "idea" of an employee is completely valid; it is just not a concrete entity. Also understand that although you cannot *directly* create an instance of an abstract class, it is still assembled in memory when derived classes are created. Thus, it is perfectly fine (and common) for abstract classes to define any number of constructors that are called *indirectly* when derived classes are allocated.

At this point, you have constructed a fairly interesting employee hierarchy. You will add a bit more functionality to this application later in this chapter when examining C# casting rules. Until then, Figure 6-6 illustrates the crux of your current design.

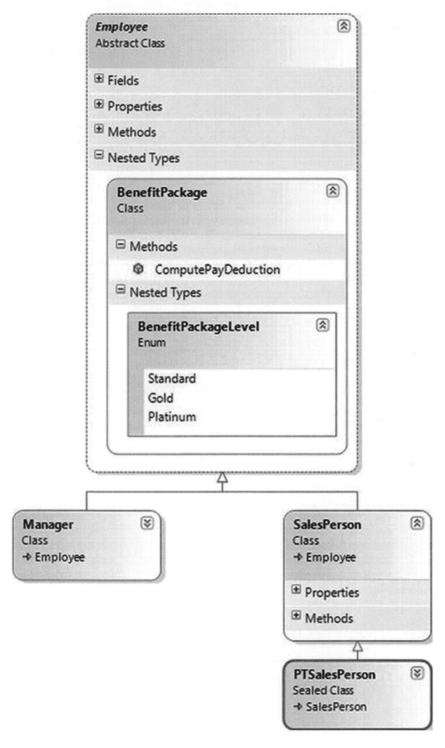

Figure 6-6. *The Employee hierarchy*

■ **Source Code**   You can find the Employees project in the `Chapter 6` subdirectory.

Understanding the Polymorphic Interface

When a class has been defined as an abstract base class (via the `abstract` keyword), it may define any number of *abstract members*. Abstract members can be used whenever you want to define a member that does *not* supply a default implementation but *must* be accounted for by each derived class. By doing so, you enforce a *polymorphic interface* on each descendant, leaving them to contend with the task of providing the details behind your abstract methods.

Simply put, an abstract base class's polymorphic interface simply refers to its set of virtual and abstract methods. This is much more interesting than first meets the eye because this trait of OOP allows you to build easily extendable and flexible software applications. To illustrate, you will be implementing (and slightly modifying) the hierarchy of shapes briefly examined in Chapter 5 during the overview of the pillars of OOP. To begin, create a new C# Console Application project named Shapes.

In Figure 6-7, notice that the `Hexagon` and `Circle` types each extend the `Shape` base class. Like any base class, `Shape` defines a number of members (a `PetName` property and `Draw()` method, in this case) that are common to all descendants.

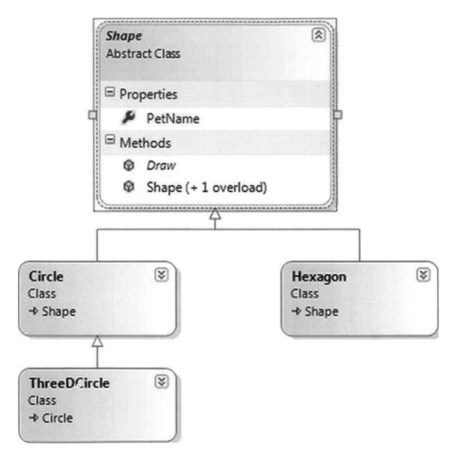

Figure 6-7. *The shapes hierarchy*

Much like the employee hierarchy, you should be able to tell that you don't want to allow the object user to create an instance of Shape directly, as it is too abstract of a concept. Again, to prevent the direct creation of the Shape type, you could define it as an abstract class. As well, given that you want the derived types to respond uniquely to the Draw() method, let's mark it as virtual and define a default implementation.

```
// The abstract base class of the hierarchy.
abstract class Shape
{
  public Shape(string name = "NoName")
  { PetName = name; }

  public string PetName { get; set; }

  // A single virtual method.
  public virtual void Draw()
  {
    Console.WriteLine("Inside Shape.Draw()");
  }
}
```

Notice that the virtual Draw() method provides a default implementation that simply prints out a message that informs you that you are calling the Draw() method within the Shape base class. Now recall that when a method is marked with the virtual keyword, the method provides a default implementation that all derived types automatically inherit. If a child class so chooses, it *may* override the method but does not *have* to. Given this, consider the following implementation of the Circle and Hexagon types:

```
// Circle DOES NOT override Draw().
class Circle : Shape
{
  public Circle() {}
  public Circle(string name) : base(name){}
}

// Hexagon DOES override Draw().
class Hexagon : Shape
{
  public Hexagon() {}
  public Hexagon(string name) : base(name){}
  public override void Draw()
  {
    Console.WriteLine("Drawing {0} the Hexagon", PetName);
  }
}
```

The usefulness of abstract methods becomes crystal clear when you once again remember that subclasses are *never required* to override virtual methods (as in the case of Circle). Therefore, if you create an instance of the Hexagon and Circle types, you'd find that the Hexagon understands how to "draw" itself correctly or at least print out an appropriate message to the console. The Circle, however, is more than a bit confused.

```
static void Main(string[] args)
{
  Console.WriteLine("***** Fun with Polymorphism *****\n");

  Hexagon hex = new Hexagon("Beth");
  hex.Draw();
  Circle cir = new Circle("Cindy");
  // Calls base class implementation!
  cir.Draw();
  Console.ReadLine();
}
```

Now consider the following output of the previous Main() method:

```
***** Fun with Polymorphism *****

Drawing Beth the Hexagon
Inside Shape.Draw()
```

Clearly, this is not an intelligent design for the current hierarchy. To force each child class to override the Draw() method, you can define Draw() as an abstract method of the Shape class, which by definition means you provide no default implementation whatsoever. To mark a method as abstract in C#, you use the abstract keyword. Notice that abstract members do not provide any implementation whatsoever.

```
abstract class Shape
{
  // Force all child classes to define how to be rendered.
  public abstract void Draw();
  ...
}
```

■ **Note** Abstract methods can be defined only in abstract classes. If you attempt to do otherwise, you will be issued a compiler error.

Methods marked with abstract are pure protocol. They simply define the name, return type (if any), and parameter set (if required). Here, the abstract Shape class informs the derived types that "I have a method named Draw() that takes no arguments and returns nothing. If you derive from me, you figure out the details."

Given this, you are now obligated to override the Draw() method in the Circle class. If you do not, Circle is also assumed to be a noncreatable abstract type that must be adorned with the abstract keyword (which is obviously not useful in this example). Here is the code update:

```
// If we did not implement the abstract Draw() method, Circle would also be
// considered abstract, and would have to be marked abstract!
class Circle : Shape
{
  public Circle() {}
  public Circle(string name) : base(name) {}
```

```
  public override void Draw()
  {
    Console.WriteLine("Drawing {0} the Circle", PetName);
  }
}
```

The short answer is that you can now assume that anything deriving from Shape does indeed have a unique version of the Draw() method. To illustrate the full story of polymorphism, consider the following code:

```
static void Main(string[] args)
{
  Console.WriteLine("***** Fun with Polymorphism *****\n");

  // Make an array of Shape-compatible objects.
  Shape[] myShapes = {new Hexagon(), new Circle(), new Hexagon("Mick"),
    new Circle("Beth"), new Hexagon("Linda")};

  // Loop over each item and interact with the
  // polymorphic interface.
  foreach (Shape s in myShapes)
  {
    s.Draw();
  }
  Console.ReadLine();
}
```

Here is the output from the modified Main() method:

```
***** Fun with Polymorphism *****

Drawing NoName the Hexagon
Drawing NoName the Circle
Drawing Mick the Hexagon
Drawing Beth the Circle
Drawing Linda the Hexagon
```

This Main() method illustrates polymorphism at its finest. Although it is not possible to *directly* create an instance of an abstract base class (the Shape), you are able to freely store references to any subclass with an abstract base variable. Therefore, when you are creating an array of Shapes, the array can hold any object deriving from the Shape base class (if you attempt to place Shape-incompatible objects into the array, you receive a compiler error).

Given that all items in the myShapes array do indeed derive from Shape, you know they all support the same "polymorphic interface" (or said more plainly, they all have a Draw() method). As you iterate over the array of Shape references, it is at runtime that the underlying type is determined. At this point, the correct version of the Draw() method is invoked in memory.

This technique also makes it simple to safely extend the current hierarchy. For example, assume you derived more classes from the abstract Shape base class (Triangle, Square, etc.). Because of the polymorphic interface, the code within your foreach loop would not have to change in the slightest, as the compiler enforces that only Shape-compatible types are placed within the myShapes array.

Understanding Member Shadowing

C# provides a facility that is the logical opposite of method overriding, termed *shadowing*. Formally speaking, if a derived class defines a member that is identical to a member defined in a base class, the derived class has shadowed the parent's version. In the real world, the possibility of this occurring is the greatest when you are subclassing from a class you (or your team) did not create yourself (such as when you purchase a third-party .NET software package).

For the sake of illustration, assume you receive a class named ThreeDCircle from a co-worker (or classmate) that defines a subroutine named Draw() taking no arguments.

```
class ThreeDCircle
{
  public void Draw()
  {
    Console.WriteLine("Drawing a 3D Circle");
  }
}
```

You figure that a ThreeDCircle "is-a" Circle, so you derive from your existing Circle type.

```
class ThreeDCircle : Circle
{
  public void Draw()
  {
    Console.WriteLine("Drawing a 3D Circle");
  }
}
```

After you recompile, you find the following warning:

```
'ThreeDCircle.Draw()' hides inherited member 'Circle.Draw()'. To make the current member
override that implementation, add the override keyword. Otherwise add the new keyword.
```

The problem is that you have a derived class (ThreeDCircle) that contains a method that is identical to an inherited method. To address this issue, you have a few options. You could simply update the parent's version of Draw() using the override keyword (as suggested by the compiler). With this approach, the ThreeDCircle type is able to extend the parent's default behavior as required. However, if you don't have access to the code defining the base class (again, as would be the case in many third- party libraries), you would be unable to modify the Draw() method as a virtual member, as you don't have access to the code file!

As an alternative, you can include the new keyword to the offending Draw() member of the derived type (ThreeDCircle, in this example). Doing so explicitly states that the derived type's implementation is intentionally designed to effectively ignore the parent's version (again, in the real world, this can be helpful if external .NET software somehow conflicts with your current software).

```
// This class extends Circle and hides the inherited Draw() method.
class ThreeDCircle : Circle
{
  // Hide any Draw() implementation above me.
  public new void Draw()
```

```
  {
    Console.WriteLine("Drawing a 3D Circle");
  }
}
```

You can also apply the new keyword to any member type inherited from a base class (field, constant, static member, or property). As a further example, assume that ThreeDCircle wants to hide the inherited PetName property.

```
class ThreeDCircle : Circle
{
  // Hide the PetName property above me.
  public new string PetName { get; set; }

  // Hide any Draw() implementation above me.
  public new void Draw()
  {
    Console.WriteLine("Drawing a 3D Circle");
  }
}
```

Finally, be aware that it is still possible to trigger the base class implementation of a shadowed member using an explicit cast, as described in the next section. The following code shows an example:

```
static void Main(string[] args)
{
...
  // This calls the Draw() method of the ThreeDCircle.
  ThreeDCircle o = new ThreeDCircle();
  o.Draw();

  // This calls the Draw() method of the parent!
  ((Circle)o).Draw();
  Console.ReadLine();
}
```

■ **Source Code**   You can find the Shapes project in the Chapter 6 subdirectory.

Understanding Base Class/Derived Class Casting Rules

Now that you can build a family of related class types, you need to learn the rules of class *casting operations*. To do so, let's return to the Employees hierarchy created earlier in this chapter and add some new methods to the Program class (if you are following along, open the Employees project in Visual Studio). As described later in this chapter, the ultimate base class in the system is System.Object. Therefore, everything "is-an" Object and can be treated as such. Given this fact, it is legal to store an instance of any type within an object variable.

```
static void CastingExamples()
{
  // A Manager "is-a" System.Object, so we can
  // store a Manager reference in an object variable just fine.
  object frank = new Manager("Frank Zappa", 9, 3000, 40000, "111-11-1111", 5);
}
```

In the Employees project, Managers, SalesPerson, and PTSalesPerson types all extend Employee, so you can store any of these objects in a valid base class reference. Therefore, the following statements are also legal:

```
static void CastingExamples()
{
  // A Manager "is-a" System.Object, so we can
  // store a Manager reference in an object variable just fine.
  object frank = new Manager("Frank Zappa", 9, 3000, 40000, "111-11-1111", 5);

  // A Manager "is-an" Employee too.
  Employee moonUnit = new Manager("MoonUnit Zappa", 2, 3001, 20000, "101-11-1321", 1);

  // A PTSalesPerson "is-a" SalesPerson.
  SalesPerson jill = new PTSalesPerson("Jill", 834, 3002, 100000, "111-12-1119", 90);
}
```

The first law of casting between class types is that when two classes are related by an "is-a" relationship, it is always safe to store a derived object within a base class reference. Formally, this is called an *implicit cast*, as "it just works" given the laws of inheritance. This leads to some powerful programming constructs. For example, assume you have defined a new method within your current Program class.

```
static void GivePromotion(Employee emp)
{
  // Increase pay...
  // Give new parking space in company garage...

  Console.WriteLine("{0} was promoted!", emp.Name);
}
```

Because this method takes a single parameter of type Employee, you can effectively pass any descendant from the Employee class into this method directly, given the "is-a" relationship.

```
static void CastingExamples()
{
  // A Manager "is-a" System.Object, so we can
  // store a Manager reference in an object variable just fine.
  object frank = new Manager("Frank Zappa", 9, 3000, 40000, "111-11-1111", 5);

  // A Manager "is-an" Employee too.
  Employee moonUnit = new Manager("MoonUnit Zappa", 2, 3001, 20000, "101-11-1321", 1);
  GivePromotion(moonUnit);
```

```
// A PTSalesPerson "is-a" SalesPerson.
SalesPerson jill = new PTSalesPerson("Jill", 834, 3002, 100000, "111-12-1119", 90);
GivePromotion(jill);
}
```

The previous code compiles given the implicit cast from the base class type (Employee) to the derived type. However, what if you also wanted to promote Frank Zappa (currently stored in a general System. Object reference)? If you pass the frank object directly into this method, you will find a compiler error as follows:

```
object frank = new Manager("Frank Zappa", 9, 3000, 40000, "111-11-1111", 5);
// Error!
GivePromotion(frank);
```

The problem is that you are attempting to pass in a variable that is not declared as an Employee but a more general System.Object. Given that object is higher up the inheritance chain than Employee, the compiler will not allow for an implicit cast, in an effort to keep your code as type-safe as possible.

Even though you can figure out that the object reference is pointing to an Employee-compatible class in memory, the compiler cannot, as that will not be known until runtime. You can satisfy the compiler by performing an *explicit cast*. This is the second law of casting: you can, in such cases, explicitly downcast using the C# casting operator. The basic template to follow when performing an explicit cast looks something like the following:

(ClassIWantToCastTo)referenceIHave

Thus, to pass the object variable into the GivePromotion() method, you could author the following code:

```
// OK!
GivePromotion((Manager)frank);
```

The C# as Keyword

Be aware that explicit casting is evaluated at *runtime*, not compile time. For the sake of argument, assume your Employees project had a copy of the Hexagon class created earlier in this chapter. For simplicity, you could add the following class to the current project:

```
class Hexagon
{
  public void Draw() { Console.WriteLine("Drawing a hexagon!"); }
}
```

Although casting the employee object to a shape object makes absolutely no sense, code such as the following could compile without error:

```
// Ack! You can't cast frank to a Hexagon, but this compiles fine!
object frank = new Manager();
Hexagon hex = (Hexagon)frank;
```

However, you would receive a runtime error, or, more formally, a *runtime exception*. Chapter 7 will examine the full details of structured exception handling; however, it is worth pointing out, for the time being, that when you are performing an explicit cast, you can trap the possibility of an invalid cast using the try and catch keywords (again, see Chapter 7 for full details).

```
// Catch a possible invalid cast.
object frank = new Manager();
Hexagon hex;
try
{
  hex = (Hexagon)frank;
}
catch (InvalidCastException ex)
{
  Console.WriteLine(ex.Message);
}
```

Obviously this is a contrived example; you would never bother casting between these types in this situation. However, assume you have an array of System.Object types, only a few of which contain Employee-compatible objects. In this case, you would like to determine whether an item in an array is compatible to begin with and, if so, perform the cast.

C# provides the as keyword to quickly determine at runtime whether a given type is compatible with another. When you use the as keyword, you are able to determine compatibility by checking against a null return value. Consider the following:

```
// Use "as" to test compatibility.
object[] things = new object[4];
things[0] = new Hexagon();
things[1] = false;
things[2] = new Manager();
things[3] = "Last thing";

foreach (object item in things)
{
  Hexagon h = item as Hexagon;
  if (h == null)
    Console.WriteLine("Item is not a hexagon");
  else
  {
    h.Draw();
  }
}
```

Here you loop over each item in the array of objects, checking each one for compatibility with the Hexagon class. If (and only if!) you find a Hexagon-compatible object, you invoke the Draw() method. Otherwise, you simply report the items are not compatible.

The C# is Keyword (Updated)

In addition to the as keyword, the C# language provides the is keyword to determine whether two items are compatible. Unlike the as keyword, however, the is keyword returns false, rather than a null reference, if the types are incompatible. Currently, the GivePromotion() method has been designed to take any possible type derived from Employee. Consider the following update, which now checks to see exactly which "type of employee" you have been passed:

```
static void GivePromotion(Employee emp)
{
  Console.WriteLine("{0} was promoted!", emp.Name);
  if (emp is SalesPerson)
  {
    Console.WriteLine("{0} made {1} sale(s)!", emp.Name,
      ((SalesPerson)emp).SalesNumber);
    Console.WriteLine();
  }
  if (emp is Manager)
  {
    Console.WriteLine("{0} had {1} stock options...", emp.Name,
      ((Manager)emp).StockOptions);
    Console.WriteLine();
  }
}
```

Here, you are performing a runtime check to determine what the incoming base class reference is actually pointing to in memory. After you determine whether you received a SalesPerson or Manager type, you are able to perform an explicit cast to gain access to the specialized members of the class. Also notice that you are not required to wrap your casting operations within a try/catch construct, as you know that the cast is safe if you enter either if scope, given your conditional check.

New in C# 7, the is keyword can also assign the converted type to a variable if the cast works. This cleans up the preceding method by preventing the "double-cast" problem. In the preceding example, the first cast is done when checking to see whether the type matches, and if it does, then the variable has to be cast again. Consider this update to the preceding method:

```
static void GivePromotion(Employee emp)
{
  Console.WriteLine("{0} was promoted!", emp.Name);
  //Check if is SalesPerson, assign to variable s
  if (emp is SalesPerson s)
  {
    Console.WriteLine("{0} made {1} sale(s)!", emp.Name, s.SalesNumber);
    Console.WriteLine();
  }
  //Check if is Manager, if it is, assign to variable m
  if (emp is Manager m)
  {
    Console.WriteLine("{0} had {1} stock options...", emp.Name, m.StockOptions);
    Console.WriteLine();
  }
}
```

Discards with the is Keyword (New)

The is keyword can also be used in conjunction with the new discard variable placeholder. If you want to create a catchall in your if or switch statement, you can do so as follows:

```
if (obj is var _)
{
//do something
}
```

This will match everything, so be careful about the order in which you use the comparer with the discard.

Pattern Matching Revisited (New)

Chapter 3 introduced the C# 7 feature of pattern matching. Now that you have a firm understanding of casting, it's time for a better example. The preceding example can now be cleanly updated to use a pattern matching switch statement, as follows:

```
static void GivePromotion(Employee emp)
{
  Console.WriteLine("{0} was promoted!", emp.Name);
  switch (emp)
  {
    case SalesPerson s:
      Console.WriteLine("{0} made {1} sale(s)!", emp.Name, s.SalesNumber);
      break;
    case Manager m:
      Console.WriteLine("{0} had {1} stock options...", emp.Name, m.StockOptions);
      break;
  }
  Console.WriteLine();
}
```

When adding a when clause to the **case** statement, the full definition of the object *as it is cast* is available for use. For example, the SalesNumber property exists only on the SalesPerson class, and not the Employee class. If the cast in the first case statement succeeds, the variable s will hold an instance of a SalesPerson class, so the case statement could be updated to the following:

```
case SalesPerson s when s.SalesNumber > 5:
```

These new additions to the is and switch statements provide nice improvements that help reduce the amount of code to perform matching, as the previous examples demonstrated.

Discards with switch Statements (New)

Discards can also be used in switch statements, as shown in the following code:

```
switch (emp)
{
  case SalesPerson s when s.SalesNumber > 5:
    Console.WriteLine("{0} made {1} sale(s)!", emp.Name, s.SalesNumber);
    break;
  case Manager m:
    Console.WriteLine("{0} had {1} stock options...", emp.Name, m.StockOptions);
    break;
  case Intern _:
    //Ignore interns
    break;
  case null:
    //Do something when null
    break;
}
```

The Master Parent Class: System.Object

To wrap up this chapter, I'd like to examine the details of the master parent class in the .NET platform: Object. As you were reading the previous section, you might have noticed that the base classes in your hierarchies (Car, Shape, Employee) never explicitly specify their parent classes.

```
// Who is the parent of Car?
class Car
{...}
```

In the .NET universe, every type ultimately derives from a base class named System.Object, which can be represented by the C# object keyword (lowercase *o*). The Object class defines a set of common members for every type in the framework. In fact, when you do build a class that does not explicitly define its parent, the compiler automatically derives your type from Object. If you want to be clear in your intentions, you are free to define classes that derive from Object as follows (however, again, there is no need to do so):

```
// Here we are explicitly deriving from System.Object.
class Car : object
{...}
```

Like any class, System.Object defines a set of members. In the following formal C# definition, note that some of these items are declared virtual, which specifies that a given member may be overridden by a subclass, while others are marked with static (and are therefore called at the class level):

```
public class Object
{
  // Virtual members.
  public virtual bool Equals(object obj);
  protected virtual void Finalize();
  public virtual int GetHashCode();
  public virtual string ToString();
```

```
// Instance-level, nonvirtual members.
public Type GetType();
protected object MemberwiseClone();

// Static members.
public static bool Equals(object objA, object objB);
public static bool ReferenceEquals(object objA, object objB);
}
```

Table 6-1 offers a rundown of the functionality provided by some of the methods you're most likely to use.

Table 6-1. *Core Members of* `System.Object`

Instance Method of Object Class	Meaning in Life
`Equals()`	By default, this method returns `true` only if the items being compared refer to the same item in memory. Thus, `Equals()` is used to compare object references, not the state of the object. Typically, this method is overridden to return `true` only if the objects being compared have the same internal state values (that is, value-based semantics).
	Be aware that if you override `Equals()`, you should also override `GetHashCode()`, as these methods are used internally by `Hashtable` types to retrieve subobjects from the container.
	Also recall from Chapter 4 that the `ValueType` class overrides this method for all structures, so they work with value-based comparisons.
`Finalize()`	For the time being, you can understand this method (when overridden) is called to free any allocated resources before the object is destroyed. I talk more about the CLR garbage collection services in Chapter 9.
`GetHashCode()`	This method returns an `int` that identifies a specific object instance.
`ToString()`	This method returns a string representation of this object, using the `<namespace>.<type name>` format (termed the *fully qualified name*). This method will often be overridden by a subclass to return a tokenized string of name/value pairs that represent the object's internal state, rather than its fully qualified name.
`GetType()`	This method returns a Type object that fully describes the object you are currently referencing. In short, this is a Runtime Type Identification (RTTI) method available to all objects (discussed in greater detail in Chapter 15).
`MemberwiseClone()`	This method exists to return a member-by-member copy of the current object, which is often used when cloning an object (see Chapter 8).

To illustrate some of the default behavior provided by the Object base class, create a final C# Console Application project named ObjectOverrides. Insert a new C# class type that contains the following empty class definition for a type named Person:

```
// Remember! Person extends Object.
class Person {}
```

Now, update your Main() method to interact with the inherited members of System.Object as follows:

```
class Program
{
  static void Main(string[] args)
  {
    Console.WriteLine("***** Fun with System.Object *****\n");
    Person p1 = new Person();

    // Use inherited members of System.Object.
    Console.WriteLine("ToString: {0}", p1.ToString());
    Console.WriteLine("Hash code: {0}", p1.GetHashCode());
    Console.WriteLine("Type: {0}", p1.GetType());

    // Make some other references to p1.
    Person p2 = p1;
    object o = p2;
    // Are the references pointing to the same object in memory?
    if (o.Equals(p1) && p2.Equals(o))
    {
      Console.WriteLine("Same instance!");
    }
    Console.ReadLine();
  }
}
```

Here is the output of the current Main() method:

```
***** Fun with System.Object *****

ToString: ObjectOverrides.Person
Hash code: 46104728
Type: ObjectOverrides.Person
Same instance!
```

Notice how the default implementation of ToString() returns the fully qualified name of the current type (ObjectOverrides.Person). As you will see later during the examination of building custom namespaces in Chapter 14, every C# project defines a "root namespace," which has the same name of the project itself. Here, you created a project named ObjectOverrides; thus, the Person type and the Program class have both been placed within the ObjectOverrides namespace.

The default behavior of Equals() is to test whether two variables are pointing to the same object in memory. Here, you create a new Person variable named p1. At this point, a new Person object is placed on the managed heap. p2 is also of type Person. However, you are not creating a *new* instance but rather assigning this variable to reference p1. Therefore, p1 and p2 are both pointing to the same object in memory, as is the variable o (of type object, which was thrown in for good measure). Given that p1, p2, and o all point to the same memory location, the equality test succeeds.

Although the canned behavior of System.Object can fit the bill in a number of cases, it is quite common for your custom types to override some of these inherited methods. To illustrate, update the Person class to support some properties representing an individual's first name, last name, and age, each of which can be set by a custom constructor.

```
// Remember! Person extends Object.
class Person
{
  public string FirstName { get; set; } = "";
  public string LastName { get; set; } = "";
  public int Age { get; set; }

  public Person(string fName, string lName, int personAge)
  {
    FirstName = fName;
    LastName = lName;
    Age = personAge;
  }
  public Person(){}
}
```

Overriding System.Object.ToString()

Many classes (and structures) that you create can benefit from overriding ToString() in order to return a string textual representation of the type's current state. This can be quite helpful for purposes of debugging (among other reasons). How you choose to construct this string is a matter of personal choice; however, a recommended approach is to separate each name-value pair with semicolons and wrap the entire string within square brackets (many types in the .NET base class libraries follow this approach). Consider the following overridden ToString() for your Person class:

```
public override string ToString() => $"[First Name: {FirstName}; Last Name: {LastName};
Age: {Age}]";
```

This implementation of ToString() is quite straightforward, given that the Person class has only three pieces of state data. However, always remember that a proper ToString() override should also account for any data defined *up the chain of inheritance*.

When you override ToString() for a class extending a custom base class, the first order of business is to obtain the ToString() value from your parent using the base keyword. After you have obtained your parent's string data, you can append the derived class's custom information.

Overriding System.Object.Equals()

Let's also override the behavior of Object.Equals() to work with value-based semantics. Recall that by default, Equals() returns true only if the two objects being compared reference the same object instance in memory. For the Person class, it may be helpful to implement Equals() to return true if the two variables being compared contain the same state values (e.g., first name, last name, and age).

First, notice that the incoming argument of the Equals() method is a general System.Object. Given this, your first order of business is to ensure the caller has indeed passed in a Person object and, as an extra safeguard, to make sure the incoming parameter is not a null reference.

After you have established the caller has passed you an allocated Person, one approach to implement Equals() is to perform a field-by-field comparison against the data of the incoming object to the data of the current object.

```
public override bool Equals(object obj)
{
  if (obj is Person && obj != null)
  {
    Person temp;
    temp = (Person)obj;
    if (temp.FirstName == this.FirstName
      && temp.LastName == this.LastName
      && temp.Age == this.Age)
    {
     return true;
    }
    else
    {
      return false;
    }
  }
  return false;
}
```

Here, you are examining the values of the incoming object against the values of your internal values (note the use of the this keyword). If the name and age of each are identical, you have two objects with the same state data and, therefore, return true. Any other possibility results in returning false.

While this approach does indeed work, you can certainly imagine how labor intensive it would be to implement a custom Equals() method for nontrivial types that may contain dozens of data fields. One common shortcut is to leverage your own implementation of ToString(). If a class has a prim-and-proper implementation of ToString() that accounts for all field data up the chain of inheritance, you can simply perform a comparison of the object's string data (checking for null).

```
// No need to cast "obj" to a Person anymore,
// as everything has a ToString() method.
public override bool Equals(object obj) => obj?.ToString() == ToString();
```

Notice in this case that you no longer need to check whether the incoming argument is of the correct type (a Person, in this example), as everything in .NET supports a ToString() method. Even better, you no longer need to perform a property-by-property equality check, as you are not simply testing the value returned from ToString().

Overriding System.Object.GetHashCode()

When a class overrides the Equals() method, you should also override the default implementation of GetHashCode(). Simply put, a *hash code* is a numerical value that represents an object as a particular state. For example, if you create two string variables that hold the value Hello, you would obtain the same hash code. However, if one of the string objects were in all lowercase (hello), you would obtain different hash codes.

251

By default, System.Object.GetHashCode() uses your object's current location in memory to yield the hash value. However, if you are building a custom type that you intend to store in a Hashtable type (within the System.Collections namespace), you should always override this member, as the Hashtable will be internally invoking Equals() and GetHashCode() to retrieve the correct object.

■ **Note** To be more specific, the System.Collections.Hashtable class calls GetHashCode() internally to gain a general idea where the object is located, but a subsequent (internal) call to Equals() determines the exact match.

Although you are not going to place your Person into a System.Collections.Hashtable, for completion let's override GetHashCode(). There are many algorithms that can be used to create a hash code—some fancy, others not so fancy. Most of the time, you are able to generate a hash code value by leveraging the System.String's GetHashCode() implementation.

Given that the String class already has a solid hash code algorithm that is using the character data of the String to compute a hash value, if you can identify a piece of field data on your class that should be unique for all instances (such as a Social Security number), simply call GetHashCode() on that point of field data. Thus, if the Person class defined an SSN property, you could author the following code:

```
// Assume we have an SSN property as so.
class Person
{
  public string SSN {get; set;} = "";

  // Return a hash code based on a point of unique string data.
  public override int GetHashCode() => SSN.GetHashCode();
}
```

If you cannot find a single point of unique string data but you have overridden ToString(), call GetHashCode() on your own string representation.

```
// Return a hash code based on the person's ToString() value.
public override int GetHashCode() => ToString().GetHashCode();
```

Testing Your Modified Person Class

Now that you have overridden the virtual members of Object, update Main() to test your updates.

```
static void Main(string[] args)
{
  Console.WriteLine("***** Fun with System.Object *****\n");

  // NOTE: We want these to be identical to test
  // the Equals() and GetHashCode() methods.
  Person p1 = new Person("Homer", "Simpson", 50);
  Person p2 = new Person("Homer", "Simpson", 50);
```

```
  // Get stringified version of objects.
  Console.WriteLine("p1.ToString() = {0}", p1.ToString());
  Console.WriteLine("p2.ToString() = {0}", p2.ToString());

  // Test overridden Equals().
  Console.WriteLine("p1 = p2?: {0}", p1.Equals(p2));

  // Test hash codes.
  Console.WriteLine("Same hash codes?: {0}", p1.GetHashCode() == p2.GetHashCode());
  Console.WriteLine();

  // Change age of p2 and test again.
  p2.Age = 45;
  Console.WriteLine("p1.ToString() = {0}", p1.ToString());
  Console.WriteLine("p2.ToString() = {0}", p2.ToString());
  Console.WriteLine("p1 = p2?: {0}", p1.Equals(p2));
  Console.WriteLine("Same hash codes?: {0}", p1.GetHashCode() == p2.GetHashCode());
  Console.ReadLine();
}
```

The output is shown here:

```
***** Fun with System.Object *****

p1.ToString() = [First Name: Homer; Last Name: Simpson; Age: 50]
p2.ToString() = [First Name: Homer; Last Name: Simpson; Age: 50]
p1 = p2?: True
Same hash codes?: True

p1.ToString() = [First Name: Homer; Last Name: Simpson; Age: 50]
p2.ToString() = [First Name: Homer; Last Name: Simpson; Age: 45]
p1 = p2?: False
Same hash codes?: False
```

The Static Members of System.Object

In addition to the instance-level members you have just examined, System.Object does define two (very helpful) static members that also test for value-based or reference-based equality. Consider the following code:

```
static void StaticMembersOfObject()
{
  // Static members of System.Object.
  Person p3 = new Person("Sally", "Jones", 4);
  Person p4 = new Person("Sally", "Jones", 4);
  Console.WriteLine("P3 and P4 have same state: {0}", object.Equals(p3, p4));
  Console.WriteLine("P3 and P4 are pointing to same object: {0}",
    object.ReferenceEquals(p3, p4));
}
```

Here, you are able to simply send in two objects (of any type) and allow the System.Object class to determine the details automatically.

■ **Source Code**   You can find the ObjectOverrides project in the Chapter 6 subdirectory.

Summary

This chapter explored the role and details of inheritance and polymorphism. Over these pages you were introduced to numerous new keywords and tokens to support each of these techniques. For example, recall that the colon token is used to establish the parent class of a given type. Parent types are able to define any number of virtual and/or abstract members to establish a polymorphic interface. Derived types override such members using the override keyword.

In addition to building numerous class hierarchies, this chapter also examined how to explicitly cast between base and derived types and wrapped up by diving into the details of the cosmic parent class in the .NET base class libraries: System.Object.

CHAPTER 7

■ ■ ■

Understanding Structured Exception Handling

In this chapter, you will learn how to handle runtime anomalies in your C# code through the use of *structured exception handling*. Not only will you examine the C# keywords that allow you to handle such matters (try, catch, throw, finally, when), but you will also come to understand the distinction between application-level and system-level exceptions, as well as the role of the System.Exception base class. This discussion will lead into the topic of building custom exceptions and, finally, to a quick look at some exception-centric debugging tools of Visual Studio.

Ode to Errors, Bugs, and Exceptions

Despite what our (sometimes inflated) egos may tell us, no programmer is perfect. Writing software is a complex undertaking, and given this complexity, it is quite common for even the best software to ship with various *problems*. Sometimes the problem is caused by bad code (such as overflowing the bounds of an array). Other times, a problem is caused by bogus user input that has not been accounted for in the application's codebase (e.g., a phone number input field assigned to the value Chucky). Now, regardless of the cause of the problem, the end result is that the application does not work as expected. To help frame the upcoming discussion of structured exception handling, allow me to provide definitions for three commonly used anomaly-centric terms.

- *Bugs*: These are, simply put, errors made by the programmer. For example, suppose you are programming with unmanaged C++. If you fail to delete dynamically allocated memory, resulting in a memory leak, you have a bug.

- *User errors*: User errors, on the other hand, are typically caused by the individual running your application, rather than by those who created it. For example, an end user who enters a malformed string into a text box could very well generate an error *if* you fail to handle this faulty input in your codebase.

- *Exceptions*: Exceptions are typically regarded as runtime anomalies that are difficult, if not impossible, to account for while programming your application. Possible exceptions include attempting to connect to a database that no longer exists, opening a corrupted XML file, or trying to contact a machine that is currently offline. In each of these cases, the programmer (or end user) has little control over these "exceptional" circumstances.

© Andrew Troelsen and Philip Japikse 2017

A. Troelsen and P. Japikse, *Pro C# 7*, https://doi.org/10.1007/978-1-4842-3018-3_7

Given these definitions, it should be clear that .NET structured *exception* handling is a technique for dealing with runtime *exceptions*. However, even for the bugs and user errors that have escaped your view, the CLR will often generate a corresponding exception that identifies the problem at hand. By way of a few examples, the .NET base class libraries define numerous exceptions, such as FormatException, IndexOutOfRangeException, FileNotFoundException, ArgumentOutOfRangeException, and so forth.

Within the .NET nomenclature, an *exception* accounts for bugs, bogus user input, and runtime errors, even though programmers may view each of these as a distinct issue. However, before I get too far ahead of myself, let's formalize the role of structured exception handling and check out how it differs from traditional error-handling techniques.

■ **Note**   To make the code examples used in this book as clean as possible, I will not catch every possible exception that may be thrown by a given method in the base class libraries. In your production-level projects, you should, of course, make liberal use of the techniques presented in this chapter.

The Role of .NET Exception Handling

Prior to .NET, error handling under the Windows operating system was a confused mishmash of techniques. Many programmers rolled their own error-handling logic within the context of a given application. For example, a development team could define a set of numerical constants that represented known error conditions and make use of them as method return values. By way of an example, consider the following partial C code:

```
/* A very C-style error trapping mechanism. */
#define E_FILENOTFOUND 1000

int UseFileSystem()
{
  // Assume something happens in this function
  // that causes the following return value.
  return E_FILENOTFOUND;
}

void main()
{
  int retVal = UseFileSystem();
  if(retVal == E_FILENOTFOUND)
    printf("Cannot find file...");
}
```

This approach is less than ideal, given that the constant E_FILENOTFOUND is little more than a numerical value and is far from being a helpful agent regarding how to deal with the problem. Ideally, you would like to wrap the error's name, a descriptive message, and other helpful information about this error condition into a single, well-defined package (which is exactly what happens under structured exception handling). In addition to a developer's ad hoc techniques, the Windows API defines hundreds of error codes that come by way of #defines, HRESULTs, and far too many variations on the simple Boolean (bool, BOOL, VARIANT_BOOL, and so on).

The obvious problem with these older techniques is the tremendous lack of symmetry. Each approach is more or less tailored to a given technology, a given language, and perhaps even a given project. To put an end to this madness, the .NET platform provides a standard technique to send and trap runtime errors: structured exception handling. The beauty of this approach is that developers now have a unified approach to error handling, which is common to all languages targeting the .NET platform. Therefore, the way in which a C# programmer handles errors is syntactically similar to that of a VB programmer, or a C++ programmer using C++/CLI.

As an added bonus, the syntax used to throw and catch exceptions across assemblies and machine boundaries is identical. For example, if you use C# to build a Windows Communication Foundation (WCF) service, you can throw a SOAP fault to a remote caller, using the same keywords that allow you to throw an exception between methods in the same application.

Another bonus of .NET exceptions is that rather than receiving a cryptic numerical value, exceptions are objects that contain a human-readable description of the problem, as well as a detailed snapshot of the call stack that triggered the exception in the first place. Furthermore, you are able to give the end user help-link information that points the user to a URL that provides details about the error, as well as custom programmer-defined data.

The Building Blocks of .NET Exception Handling

Programming with structured exception handling involves the use of four interrelated entities.

- A class type that represents the details of the exception

- A member that *throws* an instance of the exception class to the caller under the correct circumstances

- A block of code on the caller's side that invokes the exception-prone member

- A block of code on the caller's side that will process (or *catch*) the exception, should it occur

The C# programming language offers five keywords (try, catch, throw, finally, and when) that allow you to throw and handle exceptions. The object that represents the problem at hand is a class extending System.Exception (or a descendent thereof). Given this fact, let's check out the role of this exception-centric base class.

The System.Exception Base Class

All exceptions ultimately derive from the System.Exception base class, which in turn derives from System.Object. Here is the crux of this class (note that some of these members are virtual and may thus be overridden by derived classes):

```
public class Exception : ISerializable, _Exception
{
  // Public constructors
  public Exception(string message, Exception innerException);
  public Exception(string message);
  public Exception();
...

  // Methods
  public virtual Exception GetBaseException();
  public virtual void GetObjectData(SerializationInfo info,
    StreamingContext context);
```

```
// Properties
public virtual IDictionary Data { get; }
public virtual string HelpLink { get; set; }
public Exception InnerException { get; }
public virtual string Message { get; }
public virtual string Source { get; set; }
public virtual string StackTrace { get; }
public MethodBase TargetSite { get; }
...
}
```

As you can see, many of the properties defined by System.Exception are read-only in nature. This is because derived types will typically supply default values for each property. For example, the default message of the IndexOutOfRangeException type is "Index was outside the bounds of the array."

■ **Note**   The Exception class implements two .NET interfaces. Although you have yet to examine interfaces (see Chapter 8), understand that the Exception interface allows a .NET exception to be processed by an unmanaged codebase (such as a COM application), while the ISerializable interface allows an exception object to be persisted across boundaries (such as a machine boundary).

Table 7-1 describes the most important members of System.Exception.

Table 7-1. *Core Members of the System.Exception Type*

System.Exception Property	Meaning in Life
Data	This read-only property retrieves a collection of key-value pairs (represented by an object implementing IDictionary) that provide additional, programmer-defined information about the exception. By default, this collection is empty.
HelpLink	This property gets or sets a URL to a help file or web site describing the error in full detail.
InnerException	This read-only property can be used to obtain information about the previous exceptions that caused the current exception to occur. The previous exceptions are recorded by passing them into the constructor of the most current exception.
Message	This read-only property returns the textual description of a given error. The error message itself is set as a constructor parameter.
Source	This property gets or sets the name of the assembly, or the object, that threw the current exception.
StackTrace	This read-only property contains a string that identifies the sequence of calls that triggered the exception. As you might guess, this property is useful during debugging or if you want to dump the error to an external error log.
TargetSite	This read-only property returns a MethodBase object, which describes numerous details about the method that threw the exception (invoking ToString() will identify the method by name).

The Simplest Possible Example

To illustrate the usefulness of structured exception handling, you need to create a class that will throw an exception under the correct (or one might say *exceptional*) circumstances. Assume you have created a new C# Console Application project (named SimpleException) that defines two class types (Car and Radio) associated by the "has-a" relationship. The Radio type defines a single method that turns the radio's power on or off.

```
class Radio
{
  public void TurnOn(bool on)
  {
    Console.WriteLine(on ? "Jamming..." : "Quiet time...");
  }
}
```

In addition to leveraging the Radio class via containment/delegation, the Car class (shown next) is defined in such a way that if the user accelerates a Car object beyond a predefined maximum speed (specified using a constant member variable named MaxSpeed), its engine explodes, rendering the Car unusable (captured by a private bool member variable named carIsDead).

Beyond these points, the Car type has a few properties to represent the current speed and a user supplied "pet name," as well as various constructors to set the state of a new Car object. Here is the complete definition (with code comments):

```
class Car
{
  // Constant for maximum speed.
  public const int MaxSpeed = 100;

  // Car properties.
  public int CurrentSpeed {get; set;} = 0;
  public string PetName {get; set;} = "";

  // Is the car still operational?
  private bool carIsDead;

  // A car has-a radio.
  private Radio theMusicBox = new Radio();

  // Constructors.
  public Car() {}
  public Car(string name, int speed)
  {
    CurrentSpeed = speed;
    PetName = name;
  }

  public void CrankTunes(bool state)
  {
    // Delegate request to inner object.
    theMusicBox.TurnOn(state);
  }
```

```
// See if Car has overheated.
public void Accelerate(int delta)
{
  if (carIsDead)
    Console.WriteLine("{0} is out of order...", PetName);
  else
  {
    CurrentSpeed += delta;
    if (CurrentSpeed > MaxSpeed)
    {
      Console.WriteLine("{0} has overheated!", PetName);
      CurrentSpeed = 0;
      carIsDead = true;
    }
    else
      Console.WriteLine("=> CurrentSpeed = {0}", CurrentSpeed);
  }
}
}
```

Now, if you implement a Main() method that forces a Car object to exceed the predefined maximum speed (set to 100, in the Car class) as shown here:

```
static void Main(string[] args)
{
  Console.WriteLine("***** Simple Exception Example *****");
  Console.WriteLine("=> Creating a car and stepping on it!");
  Car myCar = new Car("Zippy", 20);
  myCar.CrankTunes(true);

  for (int i = 0; i < 10; i++)
    myCar.Accelerate(10);
  Console.ReadLine();
}
```

you would see the following output:

```
***** Simple Exception Example *****
=> Creating a car and stepping on it!
Jamming...
=> CurrentSpeed = 30
=> CurrentSpeed = 40
=> CurrentSpeed = 50
=> CurrentSpeed = 60
=> CurrentSpeed = 70
=> CurrentSpeed = 80
=> CurrentSpeed = 90
=> CurrentSpeed = 100
Zippy has overheated!
Zippy is out of order...
```

Throwing a General Exception (Updated)

Now that you have a functional Car class, I'll demonstrate the simplest way to throw an exception. The current implementation of Accelerate() simply displays an error message if the caller attempts to speed up the Car beyond its upper limit.

To retrofit this method to throw an exception if the user attempts to speed up the automobile after it has met its maker, you want to create and configure a new instance of the System.Exception class, setting the value of the read-only Message property via the class constructor. When you want to send the exception object back to the caller, use the C# throw keyword. Here is the relevant code update to the Accelerate() method:

```
// This time, throw an exception if the user speeds up beyond MaxSpeed.
public void Accelerate(int delta)
{
  if (carIsDead)
    Console.WriteLine("{0} is out of order...", PetName);
  else
  {
    CurrentSpeed += delta;
    if (CurrentSpeed >= MaxSpeed)
    {
      carIsDead = true;
      CurrentSpeed = 0;

      // Use the "throw" keyword to raise an exception.
      throw new Exception($"{PetName} has overheated!");
    }
    else
      Console.WriteLine("=> CurrentSpeed = {0}", CurrentSpeed);
  }
}
```

Before examining how a caller would catch this exception, let's look at a few points of interest. First, when you are throwing an exception, it is always up to you to decide exactly what constitutes the error in question and when an exception should be thrown. Here, you are making the assumption that if the program attempts to increase the speed of a Car object beyond the maximum, a System.Exception object should be thrown to indicate the Accelerate() method cannot continue (which may or may not be a valid assumption; this will be a judgment call on your part based on the application you are creating).

Alternatively, you could implement Accelerate() to recover automatically without needing to throw an exception in the first place. By and large, exceptions should be thrown only when a more terminal condition has been met (for example, not finding a necessary file, failing to connect to a database, and the like). Deciding exactly what justifies throwing an exception is a design issue you must always contend with. For the current purposes, assume that asking a doomed automobile to increase its speed is cause to throw an exception.

In any case, if you were to rerun the application at this point using the previous logic in Main(), the exception will eventually be thrown. As shown in the following output, the result of not handling this error is less than ideal, given you receive a verbose error dump followed by the program's termination:

```
***** Simple Exception Example *****
=> Creating a car and stepping on it!
Jamming...
=> CurrentSpeed = 30
=> CurrentSpeed = 40
=> CurrentSpeed = 50
=> CurrentSpeed = 60
=> CurrentSpeed = 70
=> CurrentSpeed = 80
=> CurrentSpeed = 90

Unhandled Exception: System.Exception: Zippy has overheated!
   at SimpleException.Car.Accelerate(Int32 delta) in C:\MyBooks\C# Book (7th ed)
\Code\Chapter_7\SimpleException\Car.cs:line 62
   at SimpleException.Program.Main(String[] args) in C:\MyBooks\C# Book (7th ed)
\Code\Chapter_7\SimpleException\Program.cs:line 20
Press any key to continue . . .
```

Prior to C# 7, throw was a statement, which meant you could throw an exception only where statements are allowed. With C# 7, throw is available as an expression as well and can be called anywhere expressions are allowed.

Catching Exceptions

■ **Note** For those coming to .NET from a Java background, understand that type members are not prototyped with the set of exceptions they may throw (in other words, .NET does not support checked exceptions). For better or for worse, you are not required to handle every exception thrown from a given member.

Because the Accelerate() method now throws an exception, the caller needs to be ready to handle the exception, should it occur. When you are invoking a method that may throw an exception, you make use of a try/catch block. After you have caught the exception object, you are able to invoke the members of the exception object to extract the details of the problem.

What you do with this data is largely up to you. You might want to log this information to a report file, write the data to the Windows event log, e-mail a system administrator, or display the problem to the end user. Here, you will simply dump the contents to the console window:

```
// Handle the thrown exception.
static void Main(string[] args)
{
  Console.WriteLine("***** Simple Exception Example *****");
  Console.WriteLine("=> Creating a car and stepping on it!");
  Car myCar = new Car("Zippy", 20);
  myCar.CrankTunes(true);
```

```
// Speed up past the car's max speed to
// trigger the exception.
try
{
  for(int i = 0; i < 10; i++)
    myCar. Accelerate(10);
}
catch(Exception e)
{
  Console.WriteLine("\n*** Error! ***");
  Console.WriteLine("Method: {0}", e.TargetSite);
  Console.WriteLine("Message: {0}", e.Message);
  Console.WriteLine("Source: {0}", e.Source);
}

// The error has been handled, processing continues with the next statement.
Console.WriteLine("\n***** Out of exception logic *****");
Console.ReadLine();
}
```

In essence, a try block is a section of statements that may throw an exception during execution. If an exception is detected, the flow of program execution is sent to the appropriate catch block. On the other hand, if the code within a try block does not trigger an exception, the catch block is skipped entirely, and all is right with the world. The following output shows a test run of this program:

```
***** Simple Exception Example *****
=> Creating a car and stepping on it!
Jamming...
=> CurrentSpeed = 30
=> CurrentSpeed = 40
=> CurrentSpeed = 50
=> CurrentSpeed = 60
=> CurrentSpeed = 70
=> CurrentSpeed = 80
=> CurrentSpeed = 90

*** Error! ***
Method: Void Accelerate(Int32)
Message: Zippy has overheated!
Source: SimpleException

***** Out of exception logic *****
```

As you can see, after an exception has been handled, the application is free to continue on from the point after the catch block. In some circumstances, a given exception could be critical enough to warrant the termination of the application. However, in a good number of cases, the logic within the exception handler will ensure the application can continue on its merry way (although it could be slightly less functional, such as not being able to connect to a remote data source).

Configuring the State of an Exception

Currently, the System.Exception object configured within the Accelerate() method simply establishes a value exposed to the Message property (via a constructor parameter). As shown previously in Table 7-1, however, the Exception class also supplies a number of additional members (TargetSite, StackTrace, HelpLink, and Data) that can be useful in further qualifying the nature of the problem. To spruce up the current example, let's examine further details of these members on a case-by-case basis.

The TargetSite Property

The System.Exception.TargetSite property allows you to determine various details about the method that threw a given exception. As shown in the previous Main() method, printing the value of TargetSite will display the return type, name, and parameter types of the method that threw the exception. However, TargetSite does not return just a vanilla-flavored string but rather a strongly typed System.Reflection.MethodBase object. This type can be used to gather numerous details regarding the offending method, as well as the class that defines the offending method. To illustrate, assume the previous catch logic has been updated as follows:

```
static void Main(string[] args)
{
...
  // TargetSite actually returns a MethodBase object.
  catch(Exception e)
  {
    Console.WriteLine("\n*** Error! ***");
    Console.WriteLine("Member name: {0}", e.TargetSite);
    Console.WriteLine("Class defining member: {0}",
      e.TargetSite.DeclaringType);
    Console.WriteLine("Member type: {0}", e.TargetSite.MemberType);
    Console.WriteLine("Message: {0}", e.Message);
    Console.WriteLine("Source: {0}", e.Source);
  }
  Console.WriteLine("\n***** Out of exception logic *****");
  Console.ReadLine();
}
```

This time, you make use of the MethodBase.DeclaringType property to determine the fully qualified name of the class that threw the error (SimpleException.Car, in this case) as well as the MemberType property of the MethodBase object to identify the type of member (such as a property versus a method) where this exception originated. In this case, the catch logic would display the following:

```
*** Error! ***
Member name: Void Accelerate(Int32)
Class defining member: SimpleException.Car
Member type: Method
Message: Zippy has overheated!
Source: SimpleException
```

The StackTrace Property

The System.Exception.StackTrace property allows you to identify the series of calls that resulted in the exception. Be aware that you never set the value of StackTrace, as it is established automatically at the time the exception is created. To illustrate, assume you have once again updated your catch logic.

```
catch(Exception e)
{
  ...
  Console.WriteLine("Stack: {0}", e.StackTrace);
}
```

If you were to run the program, you would find the following stack trace is printed to the console (your line numbers and file paths may differ, of course):

```
Stack: at SimpleException.Car.Accelerate(Int32 delta)
in c:\MyApps\SimpleException\car.cs:line 65 at SimpleException.Program.Main()
in c:\MyApps\SimpleException\Program.cs:line 21
```

The string returned from StackTrace documents the sequence of calls that resulted in the throwing of this exception. Notice how the bottommost line number of this string identifies the first call in the sequence, while the topmost line number identifies the exact location of the offending member. Clearly, this information can be quite helpful during the debugging or logging of a given application, as you are able to "follow the flow" of the error's origin.

The HelpLink Property

While the TargetSite and StackTrace properties allow programmers to gain an understanding of a given exception, this information is of little use to the end user. As you have already seen, the System.Exception. Message property can be used to obtain human-readable information that can be displayed to the current user. In addition, the HelpLink property can be set to point the user to a specific URL or standard Windows help file that contains more detailed information.

By default, the value managed by the HelpLink property is an empty string. If you want to fill this property with a more interesting value, you need to do so before throwing the System.Exception object. Here are the relevant updates to the Car.Accelerate() method:

```
public void Accelerate(int delta)
{
  if (carIsDead)
    Console.WriteLine("{0} is out of order...", PetName);
  else
  {
    CurrentSpeed += delta;
    if (CurrentSpeed >= MaxSpeed)
    {
      carIsDead = true;
      CurrentSpeed = 0;
```

```
    // We need to call the HelpLink property, thus we need to
    // create a local variable before throwing the Exception object.
    Exception ex =
      new Exception($"{PetName} has overheated!");
    ex.HelpLink = "http://www.CarsRUs.com";
    throw ex;
  }
  else
    Console.WriteLine("=> CurrentSpeed = {0}", CurrentSpeed);
  }
}
```

The catch logic could now be updated to print this help link information as follows:

```
catch(Exception e)
{
  ...
  Console.WriteLine("Help Link: {0}", e.HelpLink);
}
```

The Data Property

The Data property of System.Exception allows you to fill an exception object with relevant auxiliary information (such as a timestamp). The Data property returns an object implementing an interface named IDictionary, defined in the System.Collections namespace. Chapter 8 examines the role of interface-based programming, as well as the System.Collections namespace. For the time being, just understand that dictionary collections allow you to create a set of values that are retrieved using a specific key. Observe the next update to the Car.Accelerate() method:

```
public void Accelerate(int delta)
{
  if (carIsDead)
    Console.WriteLine("{0} is out of order...", PetName);
  else
  {
    CurrentSpeed += delta;
    if (CurrentSpeed >= MaxSpeed)
    {
      carIsDead = true;
      CurrentSpeed = 0;

      // We need to call the HelpLink property, thus we need
      // to create a local variable before throwing the Exception object.
      Exception ex = new Exception($"{PetName} has overheated!");
      ex.HelpLink = "http://www.CarsRUs.com";

      // Stuff in custom data regarding the error.
      ex.Data.Add("TimeStamp",$"The car exploded at {DateTime.Now}");
      ex.Data.Add("Cause", "You have a lead foot.");
      throw ex;
    }
```

```
    else
      Console.WriteLine("=> CurrentSpeed = {0}", CurrentSpeed);
  }
}
```

To successfully enumerate over the key-value pairs, you must first make sure to specify a using directive for the System.Collections namespace since you will use a DictionaryEntry type in the file containing the class implementing your Main() method.

```
using System.Collections;
```

Next, you need to update the catch logic to test that the value returned from the Data property is not null (the default value). After that, you use the Key and Value properties of the DictionaryEntry type to print the custom data to the console.

```
catch (Exception e)
{
...
  Console.WriteLine("\n-> Custom Data:");
  foreach (DictionaryEntry de in e.Data)
    Console.WriteLine("-> {0}: {1}", de.Key, de.Value);
}
```

With this, here's the final output you'd see:

```
***** Simple Exception Example *****
=> Creating a car and stepping on it!
Jamming...
=> CurrentSpeed = 30
=> CurrentSpeed = 40
=> CurrentSpeed = 50
=> CurrentSpeed = 60
=> CurrentSpeed = 70
=> CurrentSpeed = 80
=> CurrentSpeed = 90

*** Error! ***
Member name: Void Accelerate(Int32)
Class defining member: SimpleException.Car
Member type: Method
Message: Zippy has overheated!
Source: SimpleException
Stack: at SimpleException.Car.Accelerate(Int32 delta)
       at SimpleException.Program.Main(String[] args)
Help Link: http://www.CarsRUs.com

-> Custom Data:
-> TimeStamp: The car exploded at 9/12/2015 9:02:12 PM
-> Cause: You have a lead foot.

***** Out of exception logic *****
```

The Data property is useful in that it allows you to pack in custom information regarding the error at hand, without requiring the building of a new class type to extend the Exception base class. As helpful as the Data property may be, however, it is still common for .NET developers to build strongly typed exception classes, which handle custom data using strongly typed properties.

This approach allows the caller to catch a specific exception-derived type, rather than having to dig into a data collection to obtain additional details. To understand how to do this, you need to examine the distinction between system-level and application-level exceptions.

■ **Source Code**   You can find the SimpleException project in the Chapter 7 subdirectory.

System-Level Exceptions (System.SystemException)

The .NET base class libraries define many classes that ultimately derive from System.Exception. For example, the System namespace defines core exception objects such as ArgumentOutOfRangeException, IndexOutOfRangeException, StackOverflowException, and so forth. Other namespaces define exceptions that reflect the behavior of that namespace. For example, System.Drawing.Printing defines printing exceptions, System.IO defines input/output-based exceptions, System.Data defines database-centric exceptions, and so forth.

Exceptions that are thrown by the .NET platform are (appropriately) called *system exceptions*. These exceptions are generally regarded as nonrecoverable, fatal errors. System exceptions derive directly from a base class named System.SystemException, which in turn derives from System.Exception (which derives from System.Object).

```
public class SystemException : Exception
{
  // Various constructors.
}
```

Given that the System.SystemException type does not add any additional functionality beyond a set of custom constructors, you might wonder why SystemException exists in the first place. Simply put, when an exception type derives from System.SystemException, you are able to determine that the .NET runtime is the entity that has thrown the exception, rather than the codebase of the executing application. You can verify this quite simply using the is keyword.

```
// True! NullReferenceException is-a SystemException.
NullReferenceException nullRefEx = new NullReferenceException();
Console.WriteLine("NullReferenceException is-a SystemException? : {0}",
                nullRefEx is SystemException);
```

Application-Level Exceptions (System.ApplicationException)

Given that all .NET exceptions are class types, you are free to create your own application-specific exceptions. However, because the System.SystemException base class represents exceptions thrown from the CLR, you might naturally assume that you should derive your custom exceptions from the System.Exception type. You could do this, but you could instead derive from the System.ApplicationException class.

```
public class ApplicationException : Exception
{
  // Various constructors.
}
```

Like `SystemException`, `ApplicationException` does not define any additional members beyond a set of constructors. Functionally, the only purpose of `System.ApplicationException` is to identify the source of the error. When you handle an exception deriving from `System.ApplicationException`, you can assume the exception was raised by the codebase of the executing application, rather than by the .NET base class libraries or .NET runtime engine.

■ **Note**   In practice, few .NET developers build custom exceptions that extend `ApplicationException`. Rather, it is more common to simply subclass `System.Exception`; however, either approach is technically valid.

Building Custom Exceptions, Take 1

While you can always throw instances of `System.Exception` to signal a runtime error (as shown in the first example), it is sometimes advantageous to build a *strongly typed exception* that represents the unique details of your current problem. For example, assume you want to build a custom exception (named `CarIsDeadException`) to represent the error of speeding up a doomed automobile. The first step is to derive a new class from `System.Exception/System.ApplicationException` (by convention, all exception classes end with the `Exception` suffix; in fact, this is a .NET best practice).

■ **Note**   As a rule, all custom exception classes should be defined as public classes (recall that the default access modifier of a non-nested type is internal). The reason is that exceptions are often passed outside of assembly boundaries and should therefore be accessible to the calling codebase.

Create a new Console Application project named CustomException, and copy the previous `Car.cs` and `Radio.cs` files into your new project using the Project Add Existing Item menu option (for clarity, be sure to change the namespace that defines the `Car` and `Radio` types from `SimpleException` to `CustomException`). Next, add the following class definition:

```
// This custom exception describes the details of the car-is-dead condition.
// (Remember, you can also simply extend Exception.)
public class CarIsDeadException : ApplicationException
{}
```

As with any class, you are free to include any number of custom members that can be called within the catch block of the calling logic. You are also free to override any virtual members defined by your parent classes. For example, you could implement `CarIsDeadException` by overriding the virtual `Message` property.

As well, rather than populating a data dictionary (via the `Data` property) when throwing the exception, the constructor allows the sender to pass in a timestamp and reason for the error. Finally, the time stamp data and cause of the error can be obtained using strongly typed properties.

```
public class CarIsDeadException : ApplicationException
{
  private string messageDetails = String.Empty;
  public DateTime ErrorTimeStamp {get; set;}
  public string CauseOfError {get; set;}

  public CarIsDeadException(){}
  public CarIsDeadException(string message,
    string cause, DateTime time)
  {
    messageDetails = message;
    CauseOfError = cause;
    ErrorTimeStamp = time;
  }

  // Override the Exception.Message property.
  public override string Message => $"Car Error Message: {messageDetails}";
}
```

Here, the CarIsDeadException class maintains a private field (messageDetails) that represents data regarding the current exception, which can be set using a custom constructor. Throwing this exception from the Accelerate() method is straightforward. Simply allocate, configure, and throw a CarIsDeadException type rather than a System.Exception (notice that, in this case, you no longer need to fill the data collection manually).

```
// Throw the custom CarIsDeadException.
public void Accelerate(int delta)
{
  CarIsDeadException ex =
    new CarIsDeadException($"{PetName} has overheated!",
    "You have a lead foot", DateTime.Now);
  ex.HelpLink = "http://www.CarsRUs.com";
  throw ex;
...
}
```

To catch this incoming exception, your catch scope can now be updated to catch a specific CarIsDeadException type (however, given that CarIsDeadException "is-a" System.Exception, it is still permissible to catch a System.Exception as well).

```
static void Main(string[] args)
{
  Console.WriteLine("***** Fun with Custom Exceptions *****\n");
  Car myCar = new Car("Rusty", 90);

  try
  {
    // Trip exception.
    myCar.Accelerate(50);
  }
```

```
catch (CarIsDeadException e)
{
  Console.WriteLine(e.Message);
  Console.WriteLine(e.ErrorTimeStamp);
  Console.WriteLine(e.CauseOfError);
}
Console.ReadLine();
}
```

So, now that you understand the basic process of building a custom exception, you might wonder when you are required to do so. Typically, you only need to create custom exceptions when the error is tightly bound to the class issuing the error (for example, a custom file-centric class that throws a number of file-related errors, a Car class that throws a number of car-related errors, a data access object that throws errors regarding a particular database table, and so forth). In doing so, you provide the caller with the ability to handle numerous exceptions on a descriptive error-by-error basis.

Building Custom Exceptions, Take 2

The current CarIsDeadException type has overridden the virtual System.Exception.Message property in order to configure a custom error message and has supplied two custom properties to account for additional bits of data. In reality, however, you are not required to override the virtual Message property, as you could simply pass the incoming message to the parent's constructor as follows:

```
public class CarIsDeadException : ApplicationException
{
  public DateTime ErrorTimeStamp { get; set; }
  public string CauseOfError { get; set; }

  public CarIsDeadException() { }

  // Feed message to parent constructor.
  public CarIsDeadException(string message, string cause, DateTime time)
    :base(message)
  {
    CauseOfError = cause;
    ErrorTimeStamp = time;
  }
}
```

Notice that this time you have *not* defined a string variable to represent the message and have *not* overridden the Message property. Rather, you are simply passing the parameter to your base class constructor. With this design, a custom exception class is little more than a uniquely named class deriving from System.ApplicationException (with additional properties if appropriate), devoid of any base class overrides.

Don't be surprised if most (if not all) of your custom exception classes follow this simple pattern. Many times, the role of a custom exception is not necessarily to provide additional functionality beyond what is inherited from the base classes but to supply a *strongly named type* that clearly identifies the nature of the error so the client can provide different handler logic for different types of exceptions.

Building Custom Exceptions, Take 3

If you want to build a truly prim-and-proper custom exception class, you want to make sure your type adheres to .NET best practices. Specifically, this requires that your custom exception does the following:

- Derives from Exception/ApplicationException

- Is marked with the [System.Serializable] attribute

- Defines a default constructor

- Defines a constructor that sets the inherited Message property

- Defines a constructor to handle "inner exceptions"

- Defines a constructor to handle the serialization of your type

Now, based on your current background with .NET, you might have no experience regarding the role of attributes or object serialization, which is just fine. I'll address these topics later (see Chapter 15 for information on attributes and Chapter 20 for details on serialization services). However, to complete your examination of building custom exceptions, here is the final iteration of CarIsDeadException, which accounts for each of these special constructors (the other custom properties and constructors would be as shown in the example in "Building Custom Exceptions, Take 2"):

```
[Serializable]
public class CarIsDeadException : ApplicationException
{
  public CarIsDeadException() { }
  public CarIsDeadException(string message) : base( message ) { }
  public CarIsDeadException(string message,
                           System.Exception inner)
    : base( message, inner ) { }
  protected CarIsDeadException(
    System.Runtime.Serialization.SerializationInfo info,
    System.Runtime.Serialization.StreamingContext context)
    : base( info, context ) { }
  // Any additional custom properties, constructors and data members...
}
```

Given that building custom exceptions that adhere to .NET best practices really differ by only their name, you will be happy to know that Visual Studio provides a code snippet template named Exception (see Figure 7-1) that will autogenerate a new exception class that adheres to .NET best practices. (Recall from Chapter 2 that a code snippet can be activated by typing its name, which is exception in this case, and pressing the Tab key twice.)

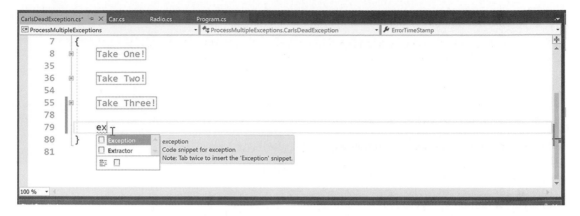

Figure 7-1. *The Exception code snippet template*

■ **Source Code** You can find the CustomException project in the Chapter 7 subdirectory.

Processing Multiple Exceptions

In its simplest form, a try block has a single catch block. In reality, though, you often run into situations where the statements within a try block could trigger *numerous* possible exceptions. Create a new C# Console Application project named ProcessMultipleExceptions; add the Car.cs, Radio.cs, and CarIsDeadException.cs files from the previous CustomException example into the new project (via Project ➤ Add Existing Item); and update your namespace names accordingly.

Now, update the Car's Accelerate() method to also throw a predefined base class library ArgumentOutOfRangeException if you pass an invalid parameter (which you can assume is any value less than zero). Note the constructor of this exception class takes the name of the offending argument as the first string, followed by a message describing the error.

```
// Test for invalid argument before proceeding.
public void Accelerate(int delta)
{
  if(delta < 0)
    throw new
      ArgumentOutOfRangeException("delta", "Speed must be greater than zero!");
  ...
}
```

The catch logic could now specifically respond to each type of exception.

```
static void Main(string[] args)
{
  Console.WriteLine("***** Handling Multiple Exceptions *****\n");
  Car myCar = new Car("Rusty", 90);
```

```
  try
  {
    // Trip Arg out of range exception.
    myCar.Accelerate(-10);
  }
  catch (CarIsDeadException e)
  {
    Console.WriteLine(e.Message);
  }
  catch (ArgumentOutOfRangeException e)
  {
    Console.WriteLine(e.Message);
  }
  Console.ReadLine();
}
```

When you are authoring multiple catch blocks, you must be aware that when an exception is thrown, it will be processed by the first appropriate catch. To illustrate exactly what the "first appropriate" catch means, assume you retrofitted the previous logic with an additional catch scope that attempts to handle all exceptions beyond CarIsDeadException and ArgumentOutOfRangeException by catching a general System.Exception as follows:

```
// This code will not compile!
static void Main(string[] args)
{
  Console.WriteLine("***** Handling Multiple Exceptions *****\n");
  Car myCar = new Car("Rusty", 90);

  try
  {
    // Trigger an argument out of range exception.
    myCar.Accelerate(-10);
  }
  catch(Exception e)
  {
    // Process all other exceptions?
    Console.WriteLine(e.Message);
  }
  catch (CarIsDeadException e)
  {
    Console.WriteLine(e.Message);
  }
  catch (ArgumentOutOfRangeException e)
  {
    Console.WriteLine(e.Message);
  }
  Console.ReadLine();
}
```

This exception-handling logic generates compile-time errors. The problem is that the first catch block can handle *anything* derived from System.Exception (given the "is-a" relationship), including the CarIsDeadException and ArgumentOutOfRangeException types. Therefore, the final two catch blocks are unreachable!

The rule of thumb to keep in mind is to make sure your catch blocks are structured such that the first catch is the most specific exception (i.e., the most derived type in an exception-type inheritance chain), leaving the final catch for the most general (i.e., the base class of a given exception inheritance chain, in this case System.Exception).

Thus, if you want to define a catch block that will handle any errors beyond CarIsDeadException and ArgumentOutOfRangeException, you could write the following:

```
// This code compiles just fine.
static void Main(string[] args)
{
  Console.WriteLine("***** Handling Multiple Exceptions *****\n");
  Car myCar = new Car("Rusty", 90);
  try
  {
    // Trigger an argument out of range exception.
    myCar.Accelerate(-10);
  }
  catch (CarIsDeadException e)
  {
    Console.WriteLine(e.Message);
  }
    catch (ArgumentOutOfRangeException e)
  {
    Console.WriteLine(e.Message);
  }
  // This will catch any other exception
  // beyond CarIsDeadException or
  // ArgumentOutOfRangeException.
  catch (Exception e)
  {
    Console.WriteLine(e.Message);
  }
  Console.ReadLine();
}
```

■ **Note** Where at all possible, always favor catching specific exception classes, rather than a general System.Exception. Though it might appear to make life simple in the short term (you may think, "Ah! This catches all the other things I don't care about."), in the long term you could end up with strange runtime crashes, as a more serious error was not directly dealt with in your code. Remember, a final catch block that deals with System.Exception tends to be very general indeed.

General catch Statements

C# also supports a "general" catch scope that does not explicitly receive the exception object thrown by a given member.

```
// A generic catch.
static void Main(string[] args)
{
  Console.WriteLine("***** Handling Multiple Exceptions *****\n");
  Car myCar = new Car("Rusty", 90);
  try
  {
    myCar.Accelerate(90);
  }
  catch
  {
    Console.WriteLine("Something bad happened...");
  }
  Console.ReadLine();
}
```

Obviously, this is not the most informative way to handle exceptions since you have no way to obtain meaningful data about the error that occurred (such as the method name, call stack, or custom message). Nevertheless, C# does allow for such a construct, which can be helpful when you want to handle all errors in a general fashion.

Rethrowing Exceptions

When you catch an exception, it is permissible for the logic in a try block to *rethrow* the exception up the call stack to the previous caller. To do so, simply use the throw keyword within a catch block. This passes the exception up the chain of calling logic, which can be helpful if your catch block is only able to partially handle the error at hand.

```
// Passing the buck.
static void Main(string[] args)
{
...
  try
  {
    // Speed up car logic...
  }
  catch(CarIsDeadException e)
  {
    // Do any partial processing of this error and pass the buck.
    throw;
  }
...
}
```

Be aware that in this example code, the ultimate receiver of CarIsDeadException is the CLR because it is the Main() method rethrowing the exception. Because of this, your end user is presented with a system-supplied error dialog box. Typically, you would only rethrow a partial handled exception to a caller that has the ability to handle the incoming exception more gracefully.

Notice as well that you are not explicitly rethrowing the CarIsDeadException object but rather making use of the throw keyword with no argument. You're not creating a new exception object; you're just rethrowing the original exception object (with all its original information). Doing so preserves the context of the original target.

Inner Exceptions

As you might suspect, it is entirely possible to trigger an exception at the time you are handling another exception. For example, assume you are handling a CarIsDeadException within a particular catch scope and during the process you attempt to record the stack trace to a file on your C: drive named carErrors.txt (you must specify you are using the System.IO namespace to gain access to these I/O-centric types).

```
catch(CarIsDeadException e)
{
  // Attempt to open a file named carErrors.txt on the C drive.
  FileStream fs = File.Open(@"C:\carErrors.txt", FileMode.Open);
  ...
}
```

Now, if the specified file is not located on your C: drive, the call to File.Open() results in a FileNotFoundException! Later in this book, you will learn all about the System.IO namespace where you'll discover how to programmatically determine whether a file exists on the hard drive before attempting to open the file in the first place (thereby avoiding the exception altogether). However, to stay focused on the topic of exceptions, assume the exception has been raised.

When you encounter an exception while processing another exception, best practice states that you should record the new exception object as an "inner exception" within a new object of the same type as the initial exception. (That was a mouthful!) The reason you need to allocate a new object of the exception being handled is that the only way to document an inner exception is via a constructor parameter. Consider the following code:

```
catch (CarIsDeadException e)
{
  try
  {
    FileStream fs = File.Open(@"C:\carErrors.txt", FileMode.Open);
    ...
  }
  catch (Exception e2)
  {
    // Throw an exception that records the new exception,
    // as well as the message of the first exception.
    throw new CarIsDeadException(e.Message, e2);
  }
}
```

Notice, in this case, I have passed in the FileNotFoundException object as the second parameter to the CarIsDeadException constructor. After you have configured this new object, you throw it up the call stack to the next caller, which in this case would be the Main() method.

Given that there is no "next caller" after Main() to catch the exception, you would be again presented with an error dialog box. Much like the act of rethrowing an exception, recording inner exceptions is usually useful only when the caller has the ability to gracefully catch the exception in the first place. If this is the case, the caller's catch logic can use the InnerException property to extract the details of the inner exception object.

The finally Block

A try/catch scope may also define an optional finally block. The purpose of a finally block is to ensure that a set of code statements will *always* execute, exception (of any type) or not. To illustrate, assume you want to always power down the car's radio before exiting Main(), regardless of any handled exception.

```
static void Main(string[] args)
{
  Console.WriteLine("***** Handling Multiple Exceptions *****\n");
  Car myCar = new Car("Rusty", 90);
  myCar.CrankTunes(true);
  try
  {
    // Speed up car logic.
  }
  catch(CarIsDeadException e)
  {
    // Process CarIsDeadException.
  }
  catch(ArgumentOutOfRangeException e)
  {
    // Process ArgumentOutOfRangeException.
  }
  catch(Exception e)
  {
    // Process any other Exception.
  }
  finally
  {
    // This will always occur. Exception or not.
    myCar.CrankTunes(false);
  }
  Console.ReadLine();
}
```

If you did not include a finally block, the radio would not be turned off if an exception were encountered (which might or might not be problematic). In a more real-world scenario, when you need to dispose of objects, close a file, or detach from a database (or whatever), a finally block ensures a location for proper cleanup.

Exception Filters

C# 6 introduced a new clause that can be placed on a catch scope, via the when keyword. When you add this clause, you have the ability to ensure that the statements within a catch block are executed only if some condition in your code holds true. This expression must evaluate to a Boolean (true or false) and can be obtained by using a simple code statement in the when definition itself or by calling an additional method in your code. In a nutshell, this approach allows you to add "filters" to your exception logic.

First, assume you have added a few custom properties to your CarIsDeadException.

```csharp
public class CarIsDeadException : ApplicationException
{
...
    // Custom members for our exception.
    public DateTime ErrorTimeStamp { get; set; }
    public string CauseOfError { get; set; }

    public CarIsDeadException(string message, string cause, DateTime time)
      : base(message)
    {
        CauseOfError = cause;
        ErrorTimeStamp = time;
    }
}
```

Also assume the Accelerate() method uses this new constructor when throwing the error.

```csharp
CarIsDeadException ex =
  new CarIsDeadException($"{PetName} has overheated!",
                        "You have a lead foot", DateTime.Now);
```

Now, consider the following modified exception logic. Here, I have added a when clause to the CarIsDeadException handler to ensure the catch block is never executed on a Friday (a contrived example, but who wants their automobile to break down on the weekend?). Notice that the single Boolean statement in the when clause must be wrapped in parentheses (also note you are now printing out a new message in this scope, which will output only when the when condition is true).

```csharp
catch (CarIsDeadException e) when (e.ErrorTimeStamp.DayOfWeek != DayOfWeek.Friday)
{
  // This new line will only print if the when clause evaluates to true.
  Console.WriteLine("Catching car is dead!");

  Console.WriteLine(e.Message);
}
```

While the chances are you will simply have a catch clause for a given error under any condition, as you can see, the new when keyword allows you to get much more granular when responding to runtime errors.

Debugging Unhandled Exceptions Using Visual Studio

Do be aware that Visual Studio supplies a number of tools that help you debug unhandled custom exceptions. Again, assume you have increased the speed of a Car object beyond the maximum but this time did not bother to wrap your call within a try block.

```
Car myCar = new Car("Rusty", 90);
myCar.Accelerate(2000);
```

If you start a debugging session within Visual Studio (using the Debug ➤ Start Debugging menu selection), Visual Studio automatically breaks at the time the uncaught exception is thrown. Better yet, you are presented with a window (see Figure 7-2) displaying the value of the Message property.

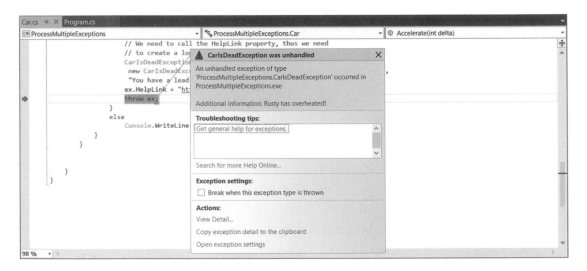

Figure 7-2. *Debugging unhandled custom exceptions with Visual Studio*

■ **Note**   If you fail to handle an exception thrown by a method in the .NET base class libraries, the Visual Studio debugger breaks at the statement that called the offending method.

If you click the View Detail link, you will find the details regarding the state of the object (see Figure 7-3).

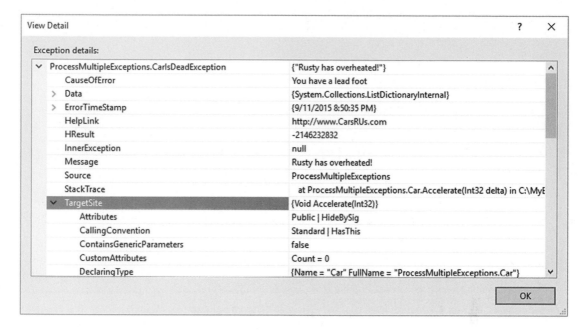

Figure 7-3. *Viewing exception details*

■ **Source Code**   You can find the ProcessMultipleExceptions project in the Chapter 7 subdirectory.

Summary

In this chapter, you examined the role of structured exception handling. When a method needs to send an error object to the caller, it will allocate, configure, and throw a specific System.Exception-derived type via the C# throw keyword. The caller is able to handle any possible incoming exceptions using the C# catch keyword and an optional finally scope. Since C# 6.0, the ability to create exception filters using the optional when keyword was added, and C# 7 has expanded the locations from where you can throw exceptions.

When you are creating your own custom exceptions, you ultimately create a class type deriving from System.ApplicationException, which denotes an exception thrown from the currently executing application. In contrast, error objects deriving from System.SystemException represent critical (and fatal) errors thrown by the CLR. Last but not least, this chapter illustrated various tools within Visual Studio that can be used to create custom exceptions (according to .NET best practices) as well as debug exceptions.

CHAPTER 8

■ ■ ■

Working with Interfaces

This chapter builds upon your current understanding of object-oriented development by examining the topic of interface-based programming. Here you'll learn how to define and implement interfaces and come to understand the benefits of building types that support multiple behaviors. Along the way, you will also examine a number of related topics, such as obtaining interface references, explicit interface implementation, and the construction of interface hierarchies. You'll also examine a number of standard interfaces defined within the .NET base class libraries. As you will see, your custom classes and structures are free to implement these predefined interfaces to support a number of useful behaviors, such as object cloning, object enumeration, and object sorting.

Understanding Interface Types

To begin this chapter, allow me to provide a formal definition of the *interface type*. An interface is nothing more than a named set of *abstract members*. Recall from Chapter 6 that abstract methods are pure protocol in that they do not provide a default implementation. The specific members defined by an interface depend on the exact behavior it is modeling. Said another way, an interface expresses a *behavior* that a given class or structure may choose to support. Furthermore, as you will see in this chapter, a class or structure can support as many interfaces as necessary, thereby supporting (in essence) multiple behaviors.

As you might guess, the .NET base class libraries ship with numerous predefined interface types that are implemented by various classes and structures. For example, as you will see in Chapter 21, ADO.NET ships with multiple data providers that allow you to communicate with a particular database management system. Thus, under ADO.NET, you have numerous connection objects to choose from (SqlConnection, OleDbConnection, OdbcConnection, etc.). In addition, third-party database vendors (as well as numerous open source projects) provide .NET libraries to communicate with a wide number of other databases (MySQL, Oracle, etc.), all of which contain objects implementing these interfaces.

Regardless of the fact that each connection class has a unique name, is defined within a different namespace, and (in some cases) is bundled within a different assembly, all connection classes implement a common interface named IDbConnection.

```
// The IDbConnection interface defines a common
// set of members supported by all connection objects.
public interface IDbConnection : IDisposable
{
    // Methods
    IDbTransaction BeginTransaction();
    IDbTransaction BeginTransaction(IsolationLevel il);
    void ChangeDatabase(string databaseName);
    void Close();
```

```
    IDbCommand CreateCommand();
    void Open();
    // Properties
    string ConnectionString { get; set;}
    int ConnectionTimeout { get; }
    string Database { get; }
    ConnectionState State { get; }
}
```

■ **Note**   By convention, .NET interfaces are prefixed with a capital letter *I*. When you are creating your own custom interfaces, it is considered a best practice to do the same.

Don't concern yourself with the details of what these members actually do at this point. Simply understand that the IDbConnection interface defines a set of members that are common to all ADO.NET connection classes. Given this, you are guaranteed that every connection object supports members such as Open(), Close(), CreateCommand(), and so forth. Furthermore, given that interface members are always abstract, each connection object is free to implement these methods in its own unique manner.

As you work through the remainder of this book, you'll be exposed to dozens of interfaces that ship with the .NET base class libraries. As you will see, these interfaces can be implemented on your own custom classes and structures to define types that integrate tightly within the framework. As well, once you understand the usefulness of the interface type, you will certainly find reasons to build your own.

Interface Types vs. Abstract Base Classes

Given your work in Chapter 6, the interface type might seem somewhat similar to an abstract base class. Recall that when a class is marked as abstract, it *may* define any number of abstract members to provide a polymorphic interface to all derived types. However, even when a class does define a set of abstract members, it is also free to define any number of constructors, field data, nonabstract members (with implementation), and so on. Interfaces, on the other hand, contain *only* member definitions.

The polymorphic interface established by an abstract parent class suffers from one major limitation in that *only derived types* support the members defined by the abstract parent. However, in larger software systems, it is common to develop multiple class hierarchies that have no common parent beyond System. Object. Given that abstract members in an abstract base class apply only to derived types, you have no way to configure types in different hierarchies to support the same polymorphic interface. By way of example, assume you have defined the following abstract class:

```
public abstract class CloneableType
{
    // Only derived types can support this
    // "polymorphic interface." Classes in other
    // hierarchies have no access to this abstract
    // member.
    public abstract object Clone();
}
```

Given this definition, only members that extend CloneableType are able to support the Clone() method. If you create a new set of classes that do not extend this base class, you can't gain this polymorphic interface. Also, you might recall that C# does not support multiple inheritance for classes. Therefore, if you wanted to create a MiniVan that is-a Car and is-a CloneableType, you are unable to do so.

```
// Nope! Multiple inheritance is not possible in C#
// for classes.
public class MiniVan : Car, CloneableType
{
}
```

As you might guess, interface types come to the rescue. After an interface has been defined, it can be implemented by any class or structure, in any hierarchy, and within any namespace or any assembly (written in any .NET programming language). As you can see, interfaces are *highly* polymorphic. Consider the standard .NET interface named ICloneable, defined in the System namespace. This interface defines a single method named Clone():

```
public interface ICloneable
{
    object Clone();
}
```

If you examine the .NET Framework 4.7 SDK documentation, you'll find that a large number of seemingly unrelated types (System.Array, System.Data.SqlClient.SqlConnection, System.OperatingSystem, System.String, etc.) all implement this interface. Although these types have no common parent (other than System.Object), you can treat them polymorphically via the ICloneable interface type.

For example, if you had a method named CloneMe() that took an ICloneable interface parameter, you could pass this method any object that implements said interface. Consider the following simple Program class defined within a Console Application project named ICloneableExample:

```
class Program
{
    static void Main(string[] args)
    {
        Console.WriteLine("***** A First Look at Interfaces *****\n");

        // All of these classes support the ICloneable interface.
        string myStr = "Hello";
        OperatingSystem unixOS = new OperatingSystem(PlatformID.Unix, new Version());
        System.Data.SqlClient.SqlConnection sqlCnn =
          new System.Data.SqlClient.SqlConnection();

        // Therefore, they can all be passed into a method taking ICloneable.
        CloneMe(myStr);
        CloneMe(unixOS);
        CloneMe(sqlCnn);
        Console.ReadLine();
    }

    private static void CloneMe(ICloneable c)
    {
        // Clone whatever we get and print out the name.
        object theClone = c.Clone();
        Console.WriteLine("Your clone is a: {0}",
          theClone.GetType().Name);
    }
}
```

When you run this application, the class name of each class prints to the console via the GetType() method you inherit from System.Object. As explained in Chapter 15, this method (and .NET reflection services) allows you to understand the composition of any type at runtime. In any case, the output of the previous program is shown next:

```
***** A First Look at Interfaces *****

Your clone is a: String
Your clone is a: OperatingSystem
Your clone is a: SqlConnection
```

■ **Source Code**   You can find the ICloneableExample project in the Chapter 8 subdirectory.

Another limitation of abstract base classes is that *each derived type* must contend with the set of abstract members and provide an implementation. To see this problem, recall the shapes hierarchy you defined in Chapter 6. Assume you defined a new abstract method in the Shape base class named GetNumberOfPoints(), which allows derived types to return the number of points required to render the shape.

```
abstract class Shape
{
...
  // Every derived class must now support this method!
  public abstract byte GetNumberOfPoints();
}
```

Clearly, the only class that has any points in the first place is Hexagon. However, with this update, *every* derived class (Circle, Hexagon, and ThreeDCircle) must now provide a concrete implementation of this function, even if it makes no sense to do so. Again, the interface type provides a solution. If you define an interface that represents the behavior of "having points," you can simply plug it into the Hexagon type, leaving Circle and ThreeDCircle untouched.

Defining Custom Interfaces

Now that you better understand the overall role of interface types, let's see an example of defining and implementing custom interfaces. To begin, create a new Console Application project named CustomInterface. Using the Project ➤ Add Existing Item menu option, insert the file (or files) containing your shape type definitions (Shapes.cs in the book's solution code) created in Chapter 6 during the Shapes example. After you have done so, rename the namespace that defines your shape-centric types to CustomInterface (simply to avoid having to import namespace definitions in your new project).

```
namespace CustomInterface
{
    // Your shape types defined here...
}
```

Now, insert a new interface into your project named IPointy using the Project ➤ Add New Item menu option, as shown in Figure 8-1.

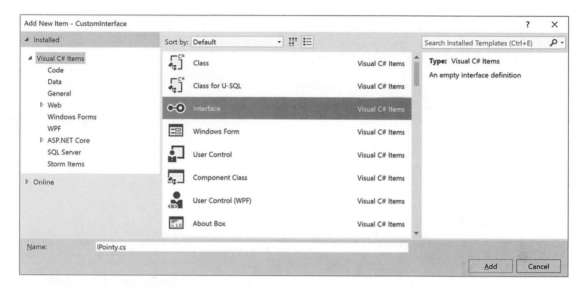

Figure 8-1. *Interfaces, like classes, can be defined in any* *.cs *file*

At a syntactic level, an interface is defined using the C# interface keyword. Unlike a class, interfaces never specify a base class (not even System.Object; however, as you will see later in this chapter, an interface can specify base interfaces). Moreover, the members of an interface never specify an access modifier (as all interface members are implicitly public and abstract). To get the ball rolling, here is a custom interface defined in C#:

```
// This interface defines the behavior of "having points."
public interface IPointy
{
    // Implicitly public and abstract.
    byte GetNumberOfPoints();
}
```

Remember that when you define interface members, you do not define an implementation scope for the members in question. Interfaces are pure protocol and, therefore, never define an implementation (that is up to the supporting class or structure). Hence, the following version of IPointy would result in various compiler errors:

```
// Ack! Errors abound!
public interface IPointy
{
    // Error! Interfaces cannot have data fields!
    public int numbOfPoints;

    // Error! Interfaces do not have constructors!
    public IPointy() { numbOfPoints = 0;}
```

```
   // Error! Interfaces don't provide an implementation of members!
   byte GetNumberOfPoints() { return numbOfPoints; }
}
```

In any case, this initial IPointy interface defines a single method. However, .NET interface types are also able to define any number of property prototypes. For example, let's update the IPointy interface to use a read-only property rather than a traditional accessor method.

```
// The pointy behavior as a read-only property.
public interface IPointy
{
   // A read-write property in an interface would look like:
   // retType PropName { get; set; }
   //
   // while a write-only property in an interface would be:
   // retType PropName { set; }

   byte Points { get; }
}
```

■ **Note**   Interface types can also contain event (see Chapter 10) and indexer (see Chapter 11) definitions.

Interface types are quite useless on their own, as they are nothing more than a named collection of abstract members. For example, you can't allocate interface types as you would a class or structure.

```
// Ack! Illegal to allocate interface types.
static void Main(string[] args)
{
   IPointy p = new IPointy(); // Compiler error!
}
```

Interfaces do not bring much to the table until they are implemented by a class or structure. Here, IPointy is an interface that expresses the behavior of "having points." The idea is simple: some classes in the shapes hierarchy have points (such as the Hexagon), while others (such as the Circle) do not.

Implementing an Interface

When a class (or structure) chooses to extend its functionality by supporting interfaces, it does so using a comma-delimited list in the type definition. Be aware that the direct base class must be the first item listed after the colon operator. When your class type derives directly from System.Object, you are free to simply list the interface (or interfaces) supported by the class, as the C# compiler will extend your types from System.Object if you do not say otherwise. On a related note, given that structures always derive from System.ValueType (see Chapter 4), simply list each interface directly after the structure definition. Ponder the following examples:

```
// This class derives from System.Object and
// implements a single interface.
public class Pencil : IPointy
{...}
```

```
// This class also derives from System.Object
// and implements a single interface.
public class SwitchBlade : object, IPointy
{...}

// This class derives from a custom base class
// and implements a single interface.
public class Fork : Utensil, IPointy
{...}

// This struct implicitly derives from System.ValueType and
// implements two interfaces.
public struct PitchFork : ICloneable, IPointy
{...}
```

Understand that implementing an interface is an all-or-nothing proposition. The supporting type is not able to selectively choose which members it will implement. Given that the IPointy interface defines a single read-only property, this is not too much of a burden. However, if you are implementing an interface that defines ten members (such as the IDbConnection interface shown earlier), the type is now responsible for fleshing out the details of all ten abstract members.

For this example, insert a new class type named Triangle that is-a Shape and supports IPointy. Note that the implementation of the read-only Points property simply returns the correct number of points (3).

```
// New Shape derived class named Triangle.
class Triangle : Shape, IPointy
{
    public Triangle() { }
    public Triangle(string name) : base(name) { }
    public override void Draw()
    { Console.WriteLine("Drawing {0} the Triangle", PetName); }

    // IPointy implementation.
    public byte Points
    {
      get { return 3; }
    }
}
```

Now, update your existing Hexagon type to also support the IPointy interface type.

```
// Hexagon now implements IPointy.
class Hexagon : Shape, IPointy
{
    public Hexagon(){ }
    public Hexagon(string name) : base(name){ }
    public override void Draw()
    { Console.WriteLine("Drawing {0} the Hexagon", PetName); }
```

```
// IPointy implementation.
public byte Points
{
    get { return 6; }
}
}
```

To sum up the story so far, the Visual Studio class diagram shown in Figure 8-2 illustrates IPointy-compatible classes using the popular "lollipop" notation. Notice again that Circle and ThreeDCircle do not implement IPointy, as this behavior makes no sense for these particular classes.

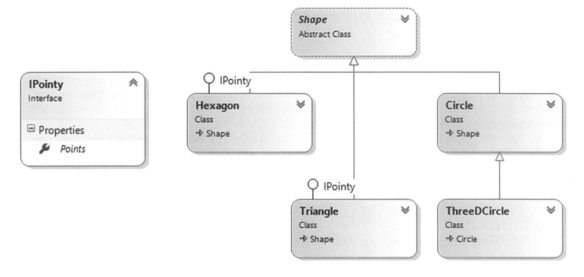

Figure 8-2. *The shapes hierarchy, now with interfaces*

■ **Note** To display or hide interface names in the class designer, right-click the interface icon and select the Collapse or Expand option.

Invoking Interface Members at the Object Level

Now that you have some classes that support the IPointy interface, the next question is how you interact with the new functionality. The most straightforward way to interact with functionality supplied by a given interface is to invoke the members directly from the object level (provided the interface members are not implemented explicitly; you can find more details later in the section "Explicit Interface Implementation"). For example, consider the following Main() method:

```
static void Main(string[] args)
{
    Console.WriteLine("***** Fun with Interfaces *****\n");
    // Call Points property defined by IPointy.
    Hexagon hex = new Hexagon();
```

```
    Console.WriteLine("Points: {0}", hex.Points);
    Console.ReadLine();
}
```

This approach works fine in this particular case, given that you are well aware that the Hexagon type has implemented the interface in question and, therefore, has a Points property. Other times, however, you might not be able to determine which interfaces are supported by a given type. For example, suppose you have an array containing 50 Shape-compatible types, only some of which support IPointy. Obviously, if you attempt to invoke the Points property on a type that has not implemented IPointy, you would receive an error. So, how can you dynamically determine whether a class or structure supports the correct interface?

One way to determine at runtime whether a type supports a specific interface is to use an explicit cast. If the type does not support the requested interface, you receive an InvalidCastException. To handle this possibility gracefully, use structured exception handling as in the following example:

```
static void Main(string[] args)
{
...
  // Catch a possible InvalidCastException.
  Circle c = new Circle("Lisa");
  IPointy itfPt = null;
  try
  {
    itfPt = (IPointy)c;
    Console.WriteLine(itfPt.Points);
  }
  catch (InvalidCastException e)
  {
    Console.WriteLine(e.Message);
  }
  Console.ReadLine();
}
```

While you could use try/catch logic and hope for the best, it would be ideal to determine which interfaces are supported before invoking the interface members in the first place. Let's see two ways of doing so.

Obtaining Interface References: The as Keyword

You can determine whether a given type supports an interface by using the as keyword, introduced in Chapter 6. If the object can be treated as the specified interface, you are returned a reference to the interface in question. If not, you receive a null reference. Therefore, be sure to check against a null value before proceeding.

```
static void Main(string[] args)
{
...
  // Can we treat hex2 as IPointy?
  Hexagon hex2 = new Hexagon("Peter");
  IPointy itfPt2 = hex2 as IPointy;
```

```
    if(itfPt2 != null)
      Console.WriteLine("Points: {0}", itfPt2.Points);
    else
      Console.WriteLine("OOPS! Not pointy...");
    Console.ReadLine();
}
```

Notice that when you use the as keyword, you have no need to use try/catch logic; if the reference is not null, you know you are calling on a valid interface reference.

Obtaining Interface References: The is Keyword (Updated)

You may also check for an implemented interface using the is keyword (also first discussed in Chapter 6). If the object in question is not compatible with the specified interface, you are returned the value false. On the other hand, if the type is compatible with the interface in question, you can safely call the members without needing to use try/catch logic.

To illustrate, assume you have an array of Shape types containing some members that implement IPointy. Notice how you are able to determine which items in the array support this interface using the is keyword, as shown in this retrofitted Main() method:

```
static void Main(string[] args)
{
    Console.WriteLine("***** Fun with Interfaces *****\n");

    // Make an array of Shapes.
    Shape[] myShapes = { new Hexagon(), new Circle(),
                        new Triangle("Joe"), new Circle("JoJo")} ;

    for(int i = 0; i < myShapes.Length; i++)
    {
      // Recall the Shape base class defines an abstract Draw()
      // member, so all shapes know how to draw themselves.
      myShapes[i].Draw();

      // Who's pointy?
      if (myShapes[i] is IPointy ip)
        Console.WriteLine("-> Points: {0}", ip.Points);
      else
        Console.WriteLine("-> {0}\'s not pointy!", myShapes[i].PetName);
      Console.WriteLine();
    }
    Console.ReadLine();
}
```

The output is as follows:

```
***** Fun with Interfaces *****

Drawing NoName the Hexagon
-> Points: 6

Drawing NoName the Circle
-> NoName's not pointy!

Drawing Joe the Triangle
-> Points: 3

Drawing JoJo the Circle
-> JoJo's not pointy!
```

■ **Note** This example uses the new feature in C# 7 to assign a variable (ip) to the interface instance in conjunction with checking for a match to the interface type. This is all part of the new pattern matching capabilities discussed in Chapters 3 and 6.

Interfaces As Parameters

Given that interfaces are valid .NET types, you may construct methods that take interfaces as parameters, as illustrated by the CloneMe() method earlier in this chapter. For the current example, assume you have defined another interface named IDraw3D.

```
// Models the ability to render a type in stunning 3D.
public interface IDraw3D
{
    void Draw3D();
}
```

Next, assume that two of your three shapes (ThreeDCircle and Hexagon) have been configured to support this new behavior.

```
// Circle supports IDraw3D.
class ThreeDCircle : Circle, IDraw3D
{
...
  public void Draw3D()
  { Console.WriteLine("Drawing Circle in 3D!"); }
}
```

```
// Hexagon supports IPointy and IDraw3D.
class Hexagon : Shape, IPointy, IDraw3D
{
...
  public void Draw3D()
  { Console.WriteLine("Drawing Hexagon in 3D!"); }
}
```

Figure 8-3 presents the updated Visual Studio class diagram.

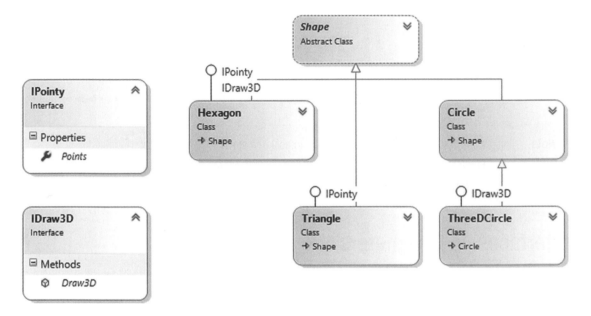

Figure 8-3. *The updated shapes hierarchy*

If you now define a method taking an IDraw3D interface as a parameter, you can effectively send in any object implementing IDraw3D. (If you attempt to pass in a type not supporting the necessary interface, you receive a compile-time error.) Consider the following method defined within your Program class:

```
// I'll draw anyone supporting IDraw3D.
static void DrawIn3D(IDraw3D itf3d)
{
  Console.WriteLine("-> Drawing IDraw3D compatible type");
  itf3d.Draw3D();
}
```

You could now test whether an item in the Shape array supports this new interface and, if so, pass it into the DrawIn3D() method for processing.

```
static void Main(string[] args)
{
  Console.WriteLine("***** Fun with Interfaces *****\n");
  Shape[] myShapes = { new Hexagon(), new Circle(),
                       new Triangle("Joe"), new Circle("JoJo") } ;
```

```
for(int i = 0; i < myShapes.Length; i++)
{
...
// Can I draw you in 3D?
if(myShapes[i] is IDraw3D)
  DrawIn3D((IDraw3D)myShapes[i]);
}
}
```

Here is the output of the updated application. Notice that only the Hexagon object prints out in 3D, as the other members of the Shape array do not implement the IDraw3D interface.

```
***** Fun with Interfaces *****

Drawing NoName the Hexagon
-> Points: 6
-> Drawing IDraw3D compatible type
Drawing Hexagon in 3D!

Drawing NoName the Circle
-> NoName's not pointy!

Drawing Joe the Triangle
-> Points: 3

Drawing JoJo the Circle
-> JoJo's not pointy!
```

Interfaces As Return Values

Interfaces can also be used as method return values. For example, you could write a method that takes an array of Shape objects and returns a reference to the first item that supports IPointy.

```
// This method returns the first object in the
// array that implements IPointy.
static IPointy FindFirstPointyShape(Shape[] shapes)
{
  foreach (Shape s in shapes)
  {
    if (s is IPointy ip)
      return ip;
  }
  return null;
}
```

You could interact with this method as follows:

```
static void Main(string[] args)
{
   Console.WriteLine("***** Fun with Interfaces *****\n");
   // Make an array of Shapes.
   Shape[] myShapes = { new Hexagon(), new Circle(),
                       new Triangle("Joe"), new Circle("JoJo")};

   // Get first pointy item.
   // To be safe, you'd want to check firstPointyItem for null before proceeding.
   IPointy firstPointyItem = FindFirstPointyShape(myShapes);
   Console.WriteLine("The item has {0} points", firstPointyItem.Points);
...
}
```

Arrays of Interface Types

Recall that the same interface can be implemented by numerous types, even if they are not within the same class hierarchy and do not have a common parent class beyond System.Object. This can yield some powerful programming constructs. For example, assume you have developed three new class types within your current project that model kitchen utensils (via Knife and Fork classes) and another modeling gardening equipment (à la PitchFork). Consider Figure 8-4.

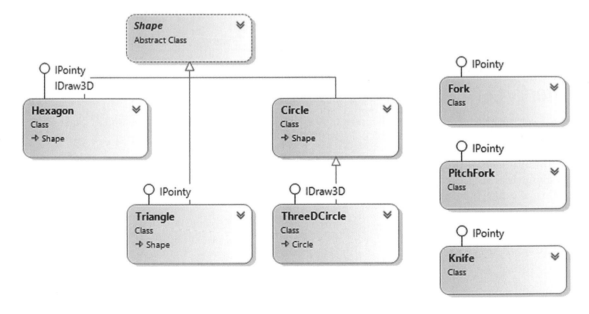

Figure 8-4. *Recall that interfaces can be "plugged into" any type in any part of a class hierarchy*

If you defined the PitchFork, Fork, and Knife types, you could now define an array of IPointy-compatible objects. Given that these members all support the same interface, you can iterate through the array and treat each item as an IPointy-compatible object, regardless of the overall diversity of the class hierarchies.

```
static void Main(string[] args)
{
...
    // This array can only contain types that
    // implement the IPointy interface.
    IPointy[] myPointyObjects = {new Hexagon(), new Knife(),
        new Triangle(), new Fork(), new PitchFork()};

    foreach(IPointy i in myPointyObjects)
    Console.WriteLine("Object has {0} points.", i.Points);
    Console.ReadLine();
}
```

Just to highlight the importance of this example, remember this: when you have an array of a given interface, the array can contain any class or structure that implements that interface.

Implementing Interfaces Using Visual Studio

Although interface-based programming is a powerful technique, implementing interfaces may entail a healthy amount of typing. Given that interfaces are a named set of abstract members, you are required to type in the definition and implementation for *each* interface method on *each* type that supports the behavior. Therefore, if you want to support an interface that defines a total of five methods and three properties, you need to account for all eight members (or else you will receive compiler errors).

As you would hope, Visual Studio supports various tools that make the task of implementing interfaces less burdensome. By way of a simple test, insert a final class into your current project named PointyTestClass. When you add an interface such as IPointy (or any interface for that matter) to a class type, you might have noticed that when you complete typing the interface's name (or when you position the mouse cursor on the interface name in the code window), the first letter is underlined (formally termed a *smart tag*). When you click the smart tag, you will be presented with a drop-down list that allows you to implement the interface (see Figure 8-5).

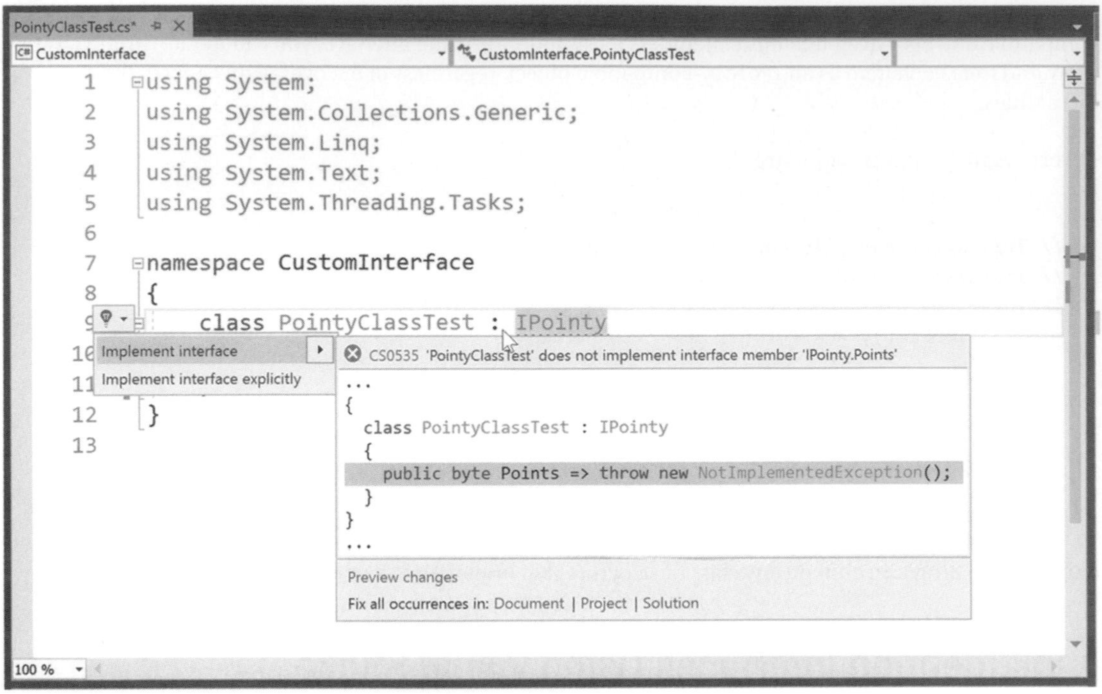

Figure 8-5. *Implementing interfaces using Visual Studio*

Notice you are presented with two options, the second of which (explicit interface implementation) will be examined in the next section. For the time being, select the first option, and you'll see that Visual Studio has generated stub code for you to update (note that the default implementation throws a System.NotImplementedException, which can obviously be deleted).

```
namespace CustomInterface
{
    class PointyTestClass : IPointy
    {
        public byte Points
        {
            get { throw new NotImplementedException(); }
        }
    }
}
```

■ **Note**   Visual Studio also supports extract interface refactoring, available from the Extract Interface option of the Quick Actions menu. This allows you to pull out a new interface definition from an existing class definition. For example, you might be halfway through writing a class when it dawns on you that you can generalize the behavior into an interface (and thereby open up the possibility of alternative implementations).

■ **Source Code**   You can find the CustomInterface project in the Chapter 8 subdirectory.

Explicit Interface Implementation

As shown earlier in this chapter, a class or structure can implement any number of interfaces. Given this, there is always the possibility you might implement interfaces that contain identical members and, therefore, have a name clash to contend with. To illustrate various manners in which you can resolve this issue, create a new Console Application project named InterfaceNameClash. Now design three interfaces that represent various locations to which an implementing type could render its output.

```
// Draw image to a form.
public interface IDrawToForm
{
    void Draw();
}

// Draw to buffer in memory.
public interface IDrawToMemory
{
    void Draw();
}

// Render to the printer.
public interface IDrawToPrinter
{
    void Draw();
}
```

Notice that each interface defines a method named Draw(), with the identical signature (which happen to be no arguments). If you now want to support each of these interfaces on a single class type named Octagon, the compiler would allow the following definition:

```
class Octagon : IDrawToForm, IDrawToMemory, IDrawToPrinter
{
    public void Draw()
    {
        // Shared drawing logic.
        Console.WriteLine("Drawing the Octagon...");
    }
}
```

Although the code compiles cleanly, you do have a possible problem. Simply put, providing a single implementation of the Draw() method does not allow you to take unique courses of action based on which interface is obtained from an Octagon object. For example, the following code will invoke the same Draw() method, regardless of which interface you obtain:

```
static void Main(string[] args)
{
    Console.WriteLine("***** Fun with Interface Name Clashes *****\n");
    // All of these invocations call the
    // same Draw() method!
    Octagon oct = new Octagon();
```

```
IDrawToForm itfForm = (IDrawToForm)oct;
itfForm.Draw();

IDrawToPrinter itfPriner = (IDrawToPrinter)oct;
itfPriner.Draw();

IDrawToMemory itfMemory = (IDrawToMemory)oct;
itfMemory.Draw();

Console.ReadLine();
}
```

Clearly, the sort of code required to render the image to a window is quite different from the code needed to render the image to a networked printer or a region of memory. When you implement several interfaces that have identical members, you can resolve this sort of name clash using *explicit interface implementation* syntax. Consider the following update to the Octagon type:

```
class Octagon : IDrawToForm, IDrawToMemory, IDrawToPrinter
{
    // Explicitly bind Draw() implementations
    // to a given interface.
    void IDrawToForm.Draw()
    {
        Console.WriteLine("Drawing to form...");
    }
    void IDrawToMemory.Draw()
    {
        Console.WriteLine("Drawing to memory...");
    }
    void IDrawToPrinter.Draw()
    {
        Console.WriteLine("Drawing to a printer...");
    }
}
```

As you can see, when explicitly implementing an interface member, the general pattern breaks down to this:

```
returnType InterfaceName.MethodName(params){}
```

Note that when using this syntax, you do not supply an access modifier; explicitly implemented members are automatically private. For example, the following is illegal syntax:

```
// Error! No access modifier!
public void IDrawToForm.Draw()
{
    Console.WriteLine("Drawing to form...");
}
```

Because explicitly implemented members are always implicitly private, these members are no longer available from the object level. In fact, if you were to apply the dot operator to an Octagon type, you would find that IntelliSense does not show you any of the Draw() members. As expected, you must use explicit casting to access the required functionality. Here's an example:

```
static void Main(string[] args)
{
  Console.WriteLine("***** Fun with Interface Name Clashes *****\n");
  Octagon oct = new Octagon();

  // We now must use casting to access the Draw()
  // members.
  IDrawToForm itfForm = (IDrawToForm)oct;
  itfForm.Draw();

  // Shorthand notation if you don't need
  // the interface variable for later use.
  ((IDrawToPrinter)oct).Draw();

  // Could also use the "is" keyword.
  If (oct is IDrawToMemory dtm)
    dtm.Draw();

  Console.ReadLine();
}
```

While this syntax is quite helpful when you need to resolve name clashes, you can use explicit interface implementation simply to hide more "advanced" members from the object level. In this way, when the object user applies the dot operator, the user will see only a subset of the type's overall functionality. However, those who require the more advanced behaviors can extract the desired interface via an explicit cast.

■ **Source Code**   You can find the InterfaceNameClash project in the Chapter 8 subdirectory.

Designing Interface Hierarchies

Interfaces can be arranged in an interface hierarchy. Like a class hierarchy, when an interface extends an existing interface, it inherits the abstract members defined by the parent (or parents). Of course, unlike class-based inheritance, derived interfaces never inherit true implementation. Rather, a derived interface simply extends its own definition with additional abstract members.

Interface hierarchies can be useful when you want to extend the functionality of an existing interface without breaking existing codebases. To illustrate, create a new Console Application project named InterfaceHierarchy. Now, let's design a new set of rendering-centric interfaces such that IDrawable is the root of the family tree.

```
public interface IDrawable
{
  void Draw();
}
```

Given that IDrawable defines a basic drawing behavior, you could now create a derived interface that extends this interface with the ability to render in modified formats. Here's an example:

```
public interface IAdvancedDraw : IDrawable
{
   void DrawInBoundingBox(int top, int left, int bottom, int right);
   void DrawUpsideDown();
}
```

Given this design, if a class were to implement IAdvancedDraw, it would now be required to implement every member defined up the chain of inheritance (specifically, the Draw(), DrawInBoundingBox(), and DrawUpsideDown() methods).

```
public class BitmapImage : IAdvancedDraw
{
   public void Draw()
   {
     Console.WriteLine("Drawing...");
   }

   public void DrawInBoundingBox(int top, int left, int bottom, int right)
   {
     Console.WriteLine("Drawing in a box...");
   }

   public void DrawUpsideDown()
   {
     Console.WriteLine("Drawing upside down!");
   }
}
```

Now, when you use the BitmapImage, you are able to invoke each method at the object level (as they are all public), as well as extract a reference to each supported interface explicitly via casting.

```
static void Main(string[] args)
{
  Console.WriteLine("***** Simple Interface Hierarchy *****");

  // Call from object level.
  BitmapImage myBitmap = new BitmapImage();
   myBitmap.Draw();
   myBitmap.DrawInBoundingBox(10, 10, 100, 150);
   myBitmap.DrawUpsideDown();

  // Get IAdvancedDraw explicitly.
   IAdvancedDraw iAdvDraw = myBitmap as IAdvancedDraw;
   if(iAdvDraw != null)
     iAdvDraw.DrawUpsideDown();
   Console.ReadLine();
}
```

■ **Source Code**   You can find the InterfaceHierarchy project in the Chapter 8 subdirectory.

Multiple Inheritance with Interface Types

Unlike class types, an interface can extend multiple base interfaces, allowing you to design some powerful and flexible abstractions. Create a new Console Application project named MIInterfaceHierarchy. Here is another collection of interfaces that model various rendering and shape abstractions. Notice that the IShape interface is extending both IDrawable and IPrintable.

```
// Multiple inheritance for interface types is a-okay.
interface IDrawable
{
    void Draw();
}

interface IPrintable
{
    void Print();
    void Draw(); // <-- Note possible name clash here!
}

// Multiple interface inheritance. OK!
interface IShape : IDrawable, IPrintable
{
    int GetNumberOfSides();
}
```

Figure 8-6 illustrates the current interface hierarchy.

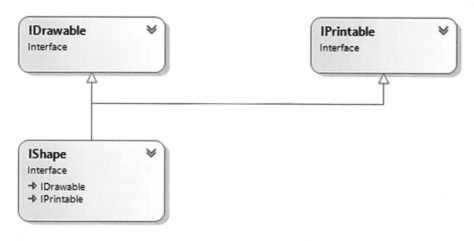

Figure 8-6. *Unlike classes, interfaces can extend multiple interface types*

At this point, the million-dollar question is, if you have a class supporting IShape, how many methods will it be required to implement? The answer: it depends. If you want to provide a simple implementation of the Draw() method, you need to provide only three members, as shown in the following Rectangle type:

```
class Rectangle : IShape
{
    public int GetNumberOfSides()
    { return 4; }

    public void Draw()
    { Console.WriteLine("Drawing..."); }

    public void Print()
    { Console.WriteLine("Printing..."); }
}
```

If you'd rather have specific implementations for each Draw() method (which in this case would make the most sense), you can resolve the name clash using explicit interface implementation, as shown in the following Square type:

```
class Square : IShape
{
    // Using explicit implementation to handle member name clash.
    void IPrintable.Draw()
    {
        // Draw to printer ...
    }
    void IDrawable.Draw()
    {
        // Draw to screen ...
    }
    public void Print()
    {
        // Print ...
    }

    public int GetNumberOfSides()
    { return 4; }
}
```

Ideally, at this point you feel more comfortable with the process of defining and implementing custom interfaces using the C# syntax. To be honest, interface-based programming can take a while to get comfortable with, so if you are in fact still scratching your head just a bit, this is a perfectly normal reaction.

Do be aware, however, that interfaces are a fundamental aspect of the .NET Framework. Regardless of the type of application you are developing (web-based, desktop GUIs, data-access libraries, etc.), working with interfaces will be part of the process. To summarize the story thus far, remember that interfaces can be extremely useful in the following cases:

- You have a single hierarchy where only a subset of the derived types supports a common behavior.

- You need to model a common behavior that is found across multiple hierarchies with no common parent class beyond System.Object.

Now that you have drilled into the specifics of building and implementing custom interfaces, the remainder of this chapter examines a number of predefined interfaces contained within the .NET base class libraries. As you will see, you can implement standard .NET interfaces on your custom types to ensure they integrate into the framework seamlessly.

■ **Source Code**   You can find the MlInterfaceHierarchy project in the Chapter 8 subdirectory.

The IEnumerable and IEnumerator Interfaces

To begin examining the process of implementing existing .NET interfaces, let's first look at the role of IEnumerable and IEnumerator. Recall that C# supports a keyword named foreach that allows you to iterate over the contents of any array type.

```
// Iterate over an array of items.
int[] myArrayOfInts = {10, 20, 30, 40};

foreach(int i in myArrayOfInts)
{
    Console.WriteLine(i);
}
```

While it might seem that only array types can use this construct, the truth of the matter is any type supporting a method named GetEnumerator() can be evaluated by the foreach construct. To illustrate, begin by creating a new Console Application project named CustomEnumerator. Next, add the Car.cs and Radio.cs files defined in the SimpleException example of Chapter 7 (via the Project ➤ Add Existing Item menu option).

■ **Note**   You might want to rename the namespace containing the Car and Radio types to CustomEnumerator to avoid having to import the CustomException namespace within this new project.

Now, insert a new class named Garage that stores a set of Car objects within a System.Array.

```
// Garage contains a set of Car objects.
public class Garage
{
    private Car[] carArray = new Car[4];

    // Fill with some Car objects upon startup.
    public Garage()
    {
        carArray[0] = new Car("Rusty", 30);
        carArray[1] = new Car("Clunker", 55);
        carArray[2] = new Car("Zippy", 30);
        carArray[3] = new Car("Fred", 30);
    }
}
```

Ideally, it would be convenient to iterate over the Garage object's subitems using the foreach construct, just like an array of data values.

```
// This seems reasonable ...
public class Program
{
    static void Main(string[] args)
    {
        Console.WriteLine("***** Fun with IEnumerable / IEnumerator *****\n");
        Garage carLot = new Garage();

        // Hand over each car in the collection?
        foreach (Car c in carLot)
        {

            Console.WriteLine("{0} is going {1} MPH",
                c.PetName, c.CurrentSpeed);
        }
        Console.ReadLine();
    }
}
```

Sadly, the compiler informs you that the Garage class does not implement a method named GetEnumerator(). This method is formalized by the IEnumerable interface, which is found lurking within the System.Collections namespace.

■ **Note**   In Chapter 9, you will learn about the role of generics and the System.Collections.Generic namespace. As you will see, this namespace contains generic versions of IEnumerable/IEnumerator that provide a more type-safe way to iterate over items.

Classes or structures that support this behavior advertise that they are able to expose contained items to the caller (in this example, the foreach keyword itself). Here is the definition of this standard .NET interface:

```
// This interface informs the caller
// that the object's items can be enumerated.
public interface IEnumerable
{
    IEnumerator GetEnumerator();
}
```

As you can see, the GetEnumerator() method returns a reference to yet another interface named System.Collections.IEnumerator. This interface provides the infrastructure to allow the caller to traverse the internal objects contained by the IEnumerable-compatible container.

```
// This interface allows the caller to
// obtain a container's items.
public interface IEnumerator
```

```
{
   bool MoveNext ();          // Advance the internal position of the cursor.
   object Current { get;}     // Get the current item (read-only property).
   void Reset ();             // Reset the cursor before the first member.
}
```

If you want to update the Garage type to support these interfaces, you could take the long road and implement each method manually. While you are certainly free to provide customized versions of GetEnumerator(), MoveNext(), Current, and Reset(), there is a simpler way. As the System.Array type (as well as many other collection classes) already implements IEnumerable and IEnumerator, you can simply delegate the request to the System.Array as follows (note you will need to import the System.Collections namespace into your code file):

```
using System.Collections;
...
public class Garage : IEnumerable
{
   // System.Array already implements IEnumerator!
   private Car[] carArray = new Car[4];

   public Garage()
   {
     carArray[0] = new Car("FeeFee", 200);
     carArray[1] = new Car("Clunker", 90);
     carArray[2] = new Car("Zippy", 30);
     carArray[3] = new Car("Fred", 30);
   }

   public IEnumerator GetEnumerator()
   {
     // Return the array object's IEnumerator.
     return carArray.GetEnumerator();
   }
}
```

After you have updated your Garage type, you can safely use the type within the C# foreach construct. Furthermore, given that the GetEnumerator() method has been defined publicly, the object user could also interact with the IEnumerator type.

```
// Manually work with IEnumerator.
IEnumerator i = carLot.GetEnumerator();
i.MoveNext();
Car myCar = (Car)i.Current;
Console.WriteLine("{0} is going {1} MPH", myCar.PetName, myCar.CurrentSpeed);
```

However, if you prefer to hide the functionality of IEnumerable from the object level, simply make use of explicit interface implementation.

```
IEnumerator IEnumerable.GetEnumerator()
{
    // Return the array object's IEnumerator.
    return carArray.GetEnumerator();
}
```

By doing so, the casual object user will not find the Garage's GetEnumerator() method, while the foreach construct will obtain the interface in the background when necessary.

■ **Source Code** You can find the CustomEnumerator project in the Chapter 8 subdirectory.

Building Iterator Methods with the yield Keyword

There's an alternative way to build types that work with the foreach loop via *iterators*. Simply put, an *iterator* is a member that specifies how a container's internal items should be returned when processed by foreach. To illustrate, create a new Console Application project named CustomEnumeratorWithYield and insert the Car, Radio, and Garage types from the previous example (again, renaming your namespace definitions to the current project if you like). Now, retrofit the current Garage type as follows:

```
public class Garage : IEnumerable
{
    private Car[] carArray = new Car[4];
    ...
    // Iterator method.

    public IEnumerator GetEnumerator()
    {
        foreach (Car c in carArray)
        {
            yield return c;
        }
    }
}
```

Notice that this implementation of GetEnumerator() iterates over the subitems using internal foreach logic and returns each Car to the caller using the yield return syntax. The yield keyword is used to specify the value (or values) to be returned to the caller's foreach construct. When the yield return statement is reached, the current location in the container is stored, and execution is restarted from this location the next time the iterator is called.

Iterator methods are not required to use the foreach keyword to return its contents. It is also permissible to define this iterator method as follows:

```
public IEnumerator GetEnumerator()
{
    yield return carArray[0];
    yield return carArray[1];
    yield return carArray[2];
    yield return carArray[3];
}
```

308

In this implementation, notice that the GetEnumerator() method is explicitly returning a new value to the caller with each pass through. Doing so for this example makes little sense, given that if you were to add more objects to the carArray member variable, your GetEnumerator() method would now be out of sync. Nevertheless, this syntax can be useful when you want to return local data from a method for processing by the foreach syntax.

Using a Local Function (New)

When the GetEnumerator() method is called, the code isn't executed until the value returned from the method is iterated. Update the method to the following code so that an exception is thrown on the first line:

```
public IEnumerator GetEnumerator()
{
  //This will not get thrown until MoveNext() is called
  throw new Exception("This won't get called");
  foreach (Car c in carArray)
  {
    yield return c;
  }
}
```

If you were to call the function like this and do *nothing else*, the exception will never be thrown:

```
IEnumerator carEnumerator = carLot.GetEnumerator();
```

It's not until MoveNext() is called that the code will execute and the exception is thrown. Depending on the needs of your program, that might be perfectly fine. But it might not. Recall from Chapter 4 the C# 7 local function feature; local functions are private functions inside other functions. One of the main uses for this new feature is to solve this problem (the other is for async methods, which will be covered in Chapter 19).
Update the method to this:

```
public IEnumerator GetEnumerator()
{
  //This will get thrown immediately
  throw new Exception("This will get called");

  return actualImplementation();

  //this is the private function
  IEnumerator actualImplementation()
  {
    foreach (Car c in carArray)
    {
      yield return c;
    }
  }
}
```

Building a Named Iterator

It is also interesting to note that the yield keyword can technically be used within any method, regardless of its name. These methods (which are technically called *named iterators*) are also unique in that they can take any number of arguments. When building a named iterator, be aware that the method will return the IEnumerable interface, rather than the expected IEnumerator-compatible type. To illustrate, you could add the following method to the Garage type (using a local function to encapsulate the iteration functionality):

```
public IEnumerable GetTheCars(bool returnReversed)
{
  //do some error checking here
  return actualImplementation();

  IEnumerable actualImplementation()
  {
    // Return the items in reverse.
    if (returnReversed)
    {
      for (int i - carArray.Length; i != 0; i--)
      {
        yield return carArray[i - 1];
      }
    }
    else
    {
      // Return the items as placed in the array.
      foreach (Car c in carArray)
      {
        yield return c;
      }
    }
  }
}
```

Notice that the new method allows the caller to obtain the subitems in sequential order, as well as in reverse order, if the incoming parameter has the value true. You could now interact with your new method as follows:

```
static void Main(string[] args)
{
  Console.WriteLine("***** Fun with the Yield Keyword *****\n");
  Garage carLot = new Garage();

  // Get items using GetEnumerator().
  foreach (Car c in carLot)
  {
    Console.WriteLine("{0} is going {1} MPH",
      c.PetName, c.CurrentSpeed);
  }

  Console.WriteLine();
```

```
// Get items (in reverse!) using named iterator.
foreach (Car c in carLot.GetTheCars(true))
{
  Console.WriteLine("{0} is going {1} MPH",
    c.PetName, c.CurrentSpeed);
}
Console.ReadLine();
}
```

As you might agree, named iterators are helpful constructs, in that a single custom container can define multiple ways to request the returned set.

So, to wrap up this look at building enumerable objects, remember that for your custom types to work with the C# foreach keyword, the container must define a method named GetEnumerator(), which has been formalized by the IEnumerable interface type. The implementation of this method is typically achieved by simply delegating it to the internal member that is holding onto the subobjects; however, it is also possible to use the yield return syntax to provide multiple "named iterator" methods.

■ **Source Code**   You can find the CustomEnumeratorWithYield project in the Chapter 8 subdirectory.

The ICloneable Interface

As you might recall from Chapter 6, System.Object defines a method named MemberwiseClone(). This method is used to obtain a *shallow copy* of the current object. Object users do not call this method directly, as it is protected. However, a given object may call this method itself during the *cloning* process. To illustrate, create a new Console Application project named CloneablePoint that defines a class named Point.

```
// A class named Point.
public class Point
{
    public int X {get; set;}
    public int Y {get; set;}

    public Point(int xPos, int yPos) { X = xPos; Y = yPos;}
    public Point(){}

    // Override Object.ToString().
    public override string ToString() => $"X = {X}; Y = {Y}";
}
```

Given what you already know about reference types and value types (see Chapter 4), you are aware that if you assign one reference variable to another, you have two references pointing to the same object in memory. Thus, the following assignment operation results in two references to the same Point object on the heap; modifications using either reference affect the same object on the heap:

```
static void Main(string[] args)
{
    Console.WriteLine("***** Fun with Object Cloning *****\n");
    // Two references to same object!
    Point p1 = new Point(50, 50);
```

311

```
    Point p2 = p1;
    p2.X = 0;
    Console.WriteLine(p1);
    Console.WriteLine(p2);
    Console.ReadLine();
}
```

When you want to give your custom type the ability to return an identical copy of itself to the caller, you may implement the standard ICloneable interface. As shown at the start of this chapter, this type defines a single method named Clone().

```
public interface ICloneable
{
    object Clone();
}
```

Obviously, the implementation of the Clone() method varies among your classes. However, the basic functionality tends to be the same: copy the values of your member variables into a new object instance of the same type and return it to the user. To illustrate, ponder the following update to the Point class:

```
// The Point now supports "clone-ability."
public class Point : ICloneable
{
    public int X { get; set; }
    public int Y { get; set; }

    public Point(int xPos, int yPos) { X = xPos; Y = yPos; }
    public Point() { }

    // Override Object.ToString().
    public override string ToString() => $"X = {X}; Y = {Y}";

    // Return a copy of the current object.
    public object Clone() => new Point(this.X, this.Y);
}
```

In this way, you can create exact stand-alone copies of the Point type, as illustrated by the following code:

```
static void Main(string[] args)
{
    Console.WriteLine("***** Fun with Object Cloning *****\n");
    // Notice Clone() returns a plain object type.
    // You must perform an explicit cast to obtain the derived type.
    Point p3 = new Point(100, 100);
    Point p4 = (Point)p3.Clone();

    // Change p4.X (which will not change p3.X).
    p4.X = 0;
```

```
   // Print each object.
   Console.WriteLine(p3);
   Console.WriteLine(p4);
   Console.ReadLine();
}
```

While the current implementation of Point fits the bill, you can streamline things just a bit. Because the Point type does not contain any internal reference type variables, you could simplify the implementation of the Clone() method as follows:

```
// Copy each field of the Point member by member.
public object Clone() => this.MemberwiseClone();
```

Be aware, however, that if the Point did contain any reference type member variables, MemberwiseClone() would copy the references to those objects (i.e., a *shallow copy*). If you want to support a true *deep copy*, you will need to create a new instance of any reference type variables during the cloning process. Let's see an example next.

A More Elaborate Cloning Example

Now assume the Point class contains a reference type member variable of type PointDescription. This class maintains a point's friendly name as well as an identification number expressed as a System.Guid (a globally unique identifier [GUID] is a statistically unique 128-bit number). Here is the implementation:

```
// This class describes a point.
public class PointDescription
{
   public string PetName {get; set;}
   public Guid PointID {get; set;}

   public PointDescription()
   {
     PetName = "No-name";
     PointID = Guid.NewGuid();
   }
}
```

The initial updates to the Point class itself included modifying ToString() to account for these new bits of state data, as well as defining and creating the PointDescription reference type. To allow the outside world to establish a pet name for the Point, you also update the arguments passed into the overloaded constructor.

```
public class Point : ICloneable
{
   public int X { get; set; }
   public int Y { get; set; }
   public PointDescription desc = new PointDescription();
```

```
  public Point(int xPos, int yPos, string petName)
  {
    X = xPos; Y = yPos;
    desc.PetName = petName;
  }
  public Point(int xPos, int yPos)
  {
    X = xPos; Y = yPos;
  }
  public Point() { }

  // Override Object.ToString().
  public override string ToString()
    => $"X = {X}; Y = {Y}; Name = {desc.PetName};\nID = {desc.PointID}\n";

  // Return a copy of the current object.
  public object Clone() => this.MemberwiseClone();
}
```

Notice that you did not yet update your Clone() method. Therefore, when the object user asks for a clone using the current implementation, a shallow (member-by-member) copy is achieved. To illustrate, assume you have updated Main() as follows:

```
static void Main(string[] args)
{
  Console.WriteLine("***** Fun with Object Cloning *****\n");
  Console.WriteLine("Cloned p3 and stored new Point in p4");
  Point p3 = new Point(100, 100, "Jane");
  Point p4 = (Point)p3.Clone();

  Console.WriteLine("Before modification:");
  Console.WriteLine("p3: {0}", p3);
  Console.WriteLine("p4: {0}", p4);
  p4.desc.PetName = "My new Point";
  p4.X = 9;

  Console.WriteLine("\nChanged p4.desc.petName and p4.X");
  Console.WriteLine("After modification:");
  Console.WriteLine("p3: {0}", p3);
  Console.WriteLine("p4: {0}", p4);
  Console.ReadLine();
}
```

Notice in the following output that while the value types have indeed been changed, the internal reference types maintain the same values, as they are "pointing" to the same objects in memory (specifically, note that the pet name for both objects is now "My new Point").

```
***** Fun with Object Cloning *****

Cloned p3 and stored new Point in p4
Before modification:
p3: X = 100; Y = 100; Name = Jane;
ID = 133d66a7-0837-4bd7-95c6-b22ab0434509

p4: X = 100; Y = 100; Name = Jane;
ID = 133d66a7-0837-4bd7-95c6-b22ab0434509

Changed p4.desc.petName  and p4.X
After modification:
p3: X = 100; Y = 100; Name = My new Point;
ID = 133d66a7-0837-4bd7-95c6-b22ab0434509

p4: X = 9; Y = 100; Name = My new Point;
ID = 133d66a7-0837-4bd7-95c6-b22ab0434509
```

To have your Clone() method make a complete deep copy of the internal reference types, you need to configure the object returned by MemberwiseClone() to account for the current point's name (the System.Guid type is in fact a structure, so the numerical data is indeed copied). Here is one possible implementation:

```
// Now we need to adjust for the PointDescription member.
public object Clone()
{
    // First get a shallow copy.
    Point newPoint = (Point)this.MemberwiseClone();

    // Then fill in the gaps.
    PointDescription currentDesc = new PointDescription();
    currentDesc.PetName = this.desc.PetName;
    newPoint.desc - currentDesc;
    return newPoint;
}
```

If you rerun the application once again and view the output (shown next), you see that the Point returned from Clone() does copy its internal reference type member variables (note the pet name is now unique for both p3 and p4).

```
***** Fun with Object Cloning *****

Cloned p3 and stored new Point in p4
Before modification:
p3: X = 100; Y = 100; Name = Jane;
ID = 51f64f25-4b0e-47ac-ba35-37d263496406

p4: X = 100; Y = 100; Name = Jane;
ID = 0d3776b3-b159-490d-b022-7f3f60788e8a

Changed p4.desc.petName  and p4.X
After modification:
p3: X = 100; Y = 100; Name = Jane;
ID = 51f64f25-4b0e-47ac-ba35-37d263496406

p4: X = 9; Y = 100; Name = My new Point;
ID = 0d3776b3-b159-490d-b022-7f3f60788e8a
```

To summarize the cloning process, if you have a class or structure that contains nothing but value types, implement your Clone() method using MemberwiseClone(). However, if you have a custom type that maintains other reference types, you might want to create a new object that takes into account each reference type member variable in order to get a "deep copy."

■ **Source Code**   You can find the CloneablePoint project in the Chapter 8 subdirectory.

The IComparable Interface

The System.IComparable interface specifies a behavior that allows an object to be sorted based on some specified key. Here is the formal definition:

```
// This interface allows an object to specify its
// relationship between other like objects.
public interface IComparable
{
   int CompareTo(object o);
}
```

■ **Note**   The generic version of this interface (IComparable<T>) provides a more type-safe manner to handle comparisons between objects. You'll examine generics in Chapter 9.

Let's assume you have a new Console Application project named ComparableCar that updates the Car class from Chapter 7 as so (notice that you have basically just added a new property to represent a unique ID for each car and a modified constructor):

```
public class Car
{
...
   public int CarID {get; set;}
   public Car(string name, int currSp, int id)
   {
     CurrentSpeed = currSp;
     PetName = name;
     CarID = id;
   }
   ...
}
```

Now assume you have an array of Car objects as follows:

```
static void Main(string[] args)
{
   Console.WriteLine("***** Fun with Object Sorting *****\n");

   // Make an array of Car objects.
   Car[] myAutos = new Car[5];
   myAutos[0] = new Car("Rusty", 80, 1);
   myAutos[1] = new Car("Mary", 40, 234);
   myAutos[2] = new Car("Viper", 40, 34);
   myAutos[3] = new Car("Mel", 40, 4);
   myAutos[4] = new Car("Chucky", 40, 5);

   Console.ReadLine();
}
```

The System.Array class defines a static method named Sort(). When you invoke this method on an array of intrinsic types (int, short, string, etc.), you are able to sort the items in the array in numeric/ alphabetic order, as these intrinsic data types implement IComparable. However, what if you were to send an array of Car types into the Sort() method as follows?

```
// Sort my cars? Not yet!
Array.Sort(myAutos);
```

If you run this test, you would get a runtime exception, as the Car class does not support the necessary interface. When you build custom types, you can implement IComparable to allow arrays of your types to be sorted. When you flesh out the details of CompareTo(), it will be up to you to decide what the baseline of the ordering operation will be. For the Car type, the internal CarID seems to be the logical candidate.

```
// The iteration of the Car can be ordered
// based on the CarID.
public class Car : IComparable
{
...
```

```
// IComparable implementation.
int IComparable.CompareTo(object obj)
{
  Car temp = obj as Car;
  if (temp != null)
  {
     if (this.CarID > temp.CarID)
       return 1;
     if (this.CarID < temp.CarID)
       return -1;
     else
       return 0;
  }
  else
    throw new ArgumentException("Parameter is not a Car!");
  }
}
```

As you can see, the logic behind CompareTo() is to test the incoming object against the current instance based on a specific point of data. The return value of CompareTo() is used to discover whether this type is less than, greater than, or equal to the object it is being compared with (see Table 8-1).

Table 8-1. *CompareTo() Return Values*

CompareTo() Return Value	Description
Any number less than zero	This instance comes before the specified object in the sort order.
Zero	This instance is equal to the specified object.
Any number greater than zero	This instance comes after the specified object in the sort order.

You can streamline the previous implementation of CompareTo() given that the C# int data type (which is just a shorthand notation for the CLR System.Int32) implements IComparable. You could implement the Car's CompareTo() as follows:

```
int IComparable.CompareTo(object obj)
{
   Car temp = obj as Car;
   if (temp != null)
     return this.CarID.CompareTo(temp.CarID);
   else
     throw new ArgumentException("Parameter is not a Car!");
}
```

In either case, so that your Car type understands how to compare itself to like objects, you can write the following user code:

```
// Exercise the IComparable interface.
static void Main(string[] args)
{
   // Make an array of Car objects.
```

```
...
  // Display current array.
  Console.WriteLine("Here is the unordered set of cars:");
  foreach(Car c in myAutos)
    Console.WriteLine("{0} {1}", c.CarID, c.PetName);

  // Now, sort them using IComparable!
  Array.Sort(myAutos);
  Console.WriteLine();

  // Display sorted array.
  Console.WriteLine("Here is the ordered set of cars:");
  foreach(Car c in myAutos)
    Console.WriteLine("{0} {1}", c.CarID, c.PctName);
  Console.ReadLine();
}
```

Here is the output from the previous `Main()` method:

```
***** Fun with Object Sorting *****

Here is the unordered set of cars:
1 Rusty
234 Mary
34 Viper
4 Mel
5 Chucky

Here is the ordered set of cars:
1 Rusty
4 Mel
5 Chucky
34 Viper
234 Mary
```

Specifying Multiple Sort Orders with IComparer

In this version of the Car type, you used the car's ID as the base for the sort order. Another design might have used the pet name of the car as the basis for the sorting algorithm (to list cars alphabetically). Now, what if you wanted to build a Car that could be sorted by ID *as well as* by pet name? If this is the type of behavior you are interested in, you need to make friends with another standard interface named IComparer, defined within the System.Collections namespace as follows:

```
// A general way to compare two objects.
interface IComparer
{
    int Compare(object o1, object o2);
}
```

■ **Note** The generic version of this interface (`IComparer<T>`) provides a more type-safe manner to handle comparisons between objects. You'll examine generics in Chapter 9.

Unlike the IComparable interface, IComparer is typically *not* implemented on the type you are trying to sort (i.e., the Car). Rather, you implement this interface on any number of helper classes, one for each sort order (pet name, car ID, etc.). Currently, the Car type already knows how to compare itself against other cars based on the internal car ID. Therefore, allowing the object user to sort an array of Car objects by pet name will require an additional helper class that implements IComparer. Here's the code (be sure to import the System.Collections namespace in the code file):

```
// This helper class is used to sort an array of Cars by pet name.
public class PetNameComparer : IComparer
{
   // Test the pet name of each object.
   int IComparer.Compare(object o1, object o2)
   {

   Car t1 = o1 as Car;
   Car t2 = o2 as Car;
   if(t1 != null && t2 != null)
      return String.Compare(t1.PetName, t2.PetName);
   else
     throw new ArgumentException("Parameter is not a Car!");
   }
}
```

The object user code is able to use this helper class. System.Array has a number of overloaded Sort() methods, one that just happens to take an object implementing IComparer.

```
static void Main(string[] args)
{
...
   // Now sort by pet name.
   Array.Sort(myAutos, new PetNameComparer());

   // Dump sorted array.
   Console.WriteLine("Ordering by pet name:");
   foreach(Car c in myAutos)
     Console.WriteLine("{0} {1}", c.CarID, c.PetName);
...
}
```

Custom Properties and Custom Sort Types

It is worth pointing out that you can use a custom static property to help the object user along when sorting your Car types by a specific data point. Assume the Car class has added a static read-only property named SortByPetName that returns an instance of an object implementing the IComparer interface (PetNameComparer, in this case; be sure to import System.Collections).

```
// We now support a custom property to return
// the correct IComparer interface.
public class Car : IComparable
{
    ...
    // Property to return the PetNameComparer.
    public static IComparer SortByPetName
    { get { return (IComparer)new PetNameComparer(); } }
}
```

The object user code can now sort by pet name using a strongly associated property, rather than just "having to know" to use the stand-alone PetNameComparer class type.

```
// Sorting by pet name made a bit cleaner.
Array.Sort(myAutos, Car.SortByPetName);
```

■ **Source Code**   You can find the ComparableCar project in the Chapter 8 subdirectory.

Ideally, at this point you not only understand how to define and implement your own interfaces but also understand their usefulness. To be sure, interfaces are found within every major .NET namespace, and you will continue working with various standard interfaces in the remainder of this book.

Summary

An interface can be defined as a named collection of *abstract members*. Because an interface does not provide any implementation details, it is common to regard an interface as a behavior that may be supported by a given type. When two or more classes implement the same interface, you can treat each type the same way (interface-based polymorphism) even if the types are defined within unique class hierarchies.

C# provides the interface keyword to allow you to define a new interface. As you have seen, a type can support as many interfaces as necessary using a comma-delimited list. Furthermore, it is permissible to build interfaces that derive from multiple base interfaces.

In addition to building your custom interfaces, the .NET libraries define a number of standard (i.e., framework-supplied) interfaces. As you have seen, you are free to build custom types that implement these predefined interfaces to gain a number of desirable traits such as cloning, sorting, and enumerating.

PART IV

Advanced C# Programming

CHAPTER 9

■ ■ ■

Collections and Generics

Any application you create with the .NET platform will need to contend with the issue of maintaining and manipulating a set of data points in memory. These data points can come from any variety of locations including a relational database, a local text file, an XML document, a web service call, or perhaps user-provided input.

When the .NET platform was first released, programmers frequently used the classes of the System. Collections namespace to store and interact with bits of data used within an application. In .NET 2.0, the C# programming language was enhanced to support a feature termed *generics*; and with this change, a new namespace was introduced in the base class libraries: System.Collections.Generic.

This chapter will provide you with an overview of the various collection (generic and nongeneric) namespaces and types found within the .NET base class libraries. As you will see, generic containers are often favored over their nongeneric counterparts because they typically provide greater type safety and performance benefits. After you've learned how to create and manipulate the generic items found in the framework, the remainder of this chapter will examine how to build your own generic methods and generic types. As you do this, you will learn about the role of *constraints* (and the corresponding C# where keyword), which allow you to build extremely type-safe classes.

The Motivation for Collection Classes

The most primitive container you could use to hold application data is undoubtedly the array. As you saw in Chapter 4, C# arrays allow you to define a set of identically typed items (including an array of System. Objects, which essentially represents an array of any type of data) of a fixed upper limit. Also recall from Chapter 4 that all C# array variables gather a good deal of functionality from the System.Array class. By way of a quick review, consider the following Main() method, which creates an array of textual data and manipulates its contents in various ways:

```
static void Main(string[] args)
{
  // Make an array of string data.
  string[] strArray = {"First", "Second", "Third" };

  // Show number of items in array using Length property.
  Console.WriteLine("This array has {0} items.", strArray.Length);
  Console.WriteLine();
```

© Andrew Troelsen and Philip Japikse 2017
A. Troelsen and P. Japikse, *Pro C# 7*, https://doi.org/10.1007/978-1-4842-3018-3_9

```
  // Display contents using enumerator.
  foreach (string s in strArray)
  {
    Console.WriteLine("Array Entry: {0}", s);
  }
  Console.WriteLine();

  // Reverse the array and print again.
  Array.Reverse(strArray);
  foreach (string s in strArray)
  {
    Console.WriteLine("Array Entry: {0}", s);
  }

  Console.ReadLine();
}
```

While basic arrays can be useful to manage small amounts of fixed-size data, there are many other times where you require a more flexible data structure, such as a dynamically growing and shrinking container or a container that can hold objects that meet only a specific criteria (e.g., only objects deriving from a specific base class or only objects implementing a particular interface). When you make use of a simple array, always remember they are "fixed size." If you make an array of three items, you get only three items; therefore, the following code would result in a runtime exception (an IndexOutOfRangeException, to be exact):

```
static void Main(string[] args)
{
  // Make an array of string data.
  string[] strArray = { "First", "Second", "Third" };

  // Try to add a new item at the end?? Runtime error!
  strArray[3] = "new item?";
...
}
```

■ **Note**   It is actually possible to change the size of an array using the generic Resize()<T> method. However, this will result in a copy of the data into a new array object and could be inefficient.

To help overcome the limitations of a simple array, the .NET base class libraries ship with a number of namespaces containing *collection classes*. Unlike a simple C# array, collection classes are built to dynamically resize themselves on the fly as you insert or remove items. Moreover, many of the collection classes offer increased type safety and are highly optimized to process the contained data in a memory-efficient manner. As you read over this chapter, you will quickly notice that a collection class can belong to one of two broad categories.

- Nongeneric collections (primarily found in the System.Collections namespace)

- Generic collections (primarily found in the System.Collections.Generic namespace)

Nongeneric collections are typically designed to operate on System.Object types and are, therefore, loosely typed containers (however, some nongeneric collections do operate only on a specific type of data, such as string objects). In contrast, generic collections are much more type-safe, given that you must specify the "type of type" they contain upon creation. As you will see, the telltale sign of any generic item is the "type parameter" marked with angled brackets (for example, List<T>). You will examine the details of generics (including the many benefits they provide) a bit later in this chapter. For now, let's examine some of the key nongeneric collection types in the System.Collections and System.Collections.Specialized namespaces.

The System.Collections Namespace

When the .NET platform was first released, programmers frequently used the nongeneric collection classes found within the System.Collections namespace, which contains a set of classes used to manage and organize large amounts of in-memory data. Table 9-1 documents some of the more commonly used collection classes of this namespace and the core interfaces they implement.

Table 9-1. *Useful Types of* System.Collections

System.Collections Class	Meaning in Life	Key Implemented Interfaces
ArrayList	Represents a dynamically sized collection of objects listed in sequential order	IList, ICollection, IEnumerable, and ICloneable
BitArray	Manages a compact array of bit values, which are represented as Booleans, where true indicates that the bit is on (1) and false indicates the bit is off (0)	ICollection, IEnumerable, and ICloneable
Hashtable	Represents a collection of key-value pairs that are organized based on the hash code of the key	IDictionary, ICollection, IEnumerable, and ICloneable
Queue	Represents a standard first-in, first-out (FIFO) collection of objects	ICollection, IEnumerable, and ICloneable
SortedList	Represents a collection of key-value pairs that are sorted by the keys and are accessible by key and by index	IDictionary, ICollection, IEnumerable, and ICloneable
Stack	A last-in, first-out (LIFO) stack providing push and pop (and peek) functionality	ICollection, IEnumerable, and ICloneable

The interfaces implemented by these collection classes provide huge insights into their overall functionality. Table 9-2 documents the overall nature of these key interfaces, some of which you worked with firsthand in Chapter 8.

Table 9-2. *Key Interfaces Supported by Classes of* `System.Collections`

System.Collections Interface	Meaning in Life
ICollection	Defines general characteristics (e.g., size, enumeration, and thread safety) for all nongeneric collection types
ICloneable	Allows the implementing object to return a copy of itself to the caller
IDictionary	Allows a nongeneric collection object to represent its contents using key-value pairs
IEnumerable	Returns an object implementing the IEnumerator interface (see next table entry)
IEnumerator	Enables foreach-style iteration of collection items
IList	Provides behavior to add, remove, and index items in a sequential list of objects

An Illustrative Example: Working with the ArrayList

Based on your experience, you might have some firsthand experience using (or implementing) some of these classic data structures such as stacks, queues, and lists. If this is not the case, I'll provide some further details on their differences when you examine their generic counterparts a bit later in this chapter. Until then, here is a Main() method making use of an ArrayList object. Notice that you can add (or remove) items on the fly and the container automatically resizes itself accordingly.

```
// You must import System.Collections to access the ArrayList.
static void Main(string[] args)
{
  ArrayList strArray = new ArrayList();
  strArray.AddRange(new string[] { "First", "Second", "Third" });

  // Show number of items in ArrayList.
  Console.WriteLine("This collection has {0} items.", strArray.Count);
  Console.WriteLine();

  // Add a new item and display current count.
  strArray.Add("Fourth!");
  Console.WriteLine("This collection has {0} items.", strArray.Count);

  // Display contents.
  foreach (string s in strArray)
  {
    Console.WriteLine("Entry: {0}", s);
  }
  Console.WriteLine();
}
```

As you would guess, the ArrayList class has many useful members beyond the Count property and AddRange() and Add() methods, so be sure you consult the .NET Framework documentation for full details. On a related note, the other classes of System.Collections (Stack, Queue, and so on) are also fully documented in the .NET help system.

However, it is important to point out that a majority of your .NET projects will most likely *not* make use of the collection classes in the `System.Collections` namespace! To be sure, these days it is far more common to make use of the generic counterpart classes found in the `System.Collections.Generic` namespace. Given this point, I won't comment on (or provide code examples for) the remaining nongeneric classes found in `System.Collections`.

A Survey of System.Collections.Specialized Namespace

`System.Collections` is not the only .NET namespace that contains nongeneric collection classes. The `System.Collections.Specialized` namespace defines a number of (pardon the redundancy) specialized collection types. Table 9-3 documents some of the more useful types in this particular collection-centric namespace, all of which are nongeneric.

Table 9-3. *Useful Classes of* `System.Collections.Specialized`

System.Collections.Specialized Type	Meaning in Life
HybridDictionary	This class implements IDictionary by using a ListDictionary while the collection is small and then switching to a Hashtable when the collection gets large.
ListDictionary	This class is useful when you need to manage a small number of items (ten or so) that can change over time. This class makes use of a singly linked list to maintain its data.
StringCollection	This class provides an optimal way to manage large collections of string data.
BitVector32	This class provides a simple structure that stores Boolean values and small integers in 32 bits of memory.

Beyond these concrete class types, this namespace also contains many additional interfaces and abstract base classes that you can use as a starting point for creating custom collection classes. While these "specialized" types might be just what your projects require in some situations, I won't comment on their usage here. Again, in many cases, you will likely find that the `System.Collections.Generic` namespace provides classes with similar functionality and additional benefits.

■ **Note**   There are two additional collection-centric namespaces (`System.Collections.ObjectModel` and `System.Collections.Concurrent`) in the .NET base class libraries. You will examine the former namespace later in this chapter, after you are comfortable with the topic of generics. `System.Collections.Concurrent` provides collection classes well-suited to a multithreaded environment (see Chapter 19 for information on multithreading).

The Problems of Nongeneric Collections

While it is true that many successful .NET applications have been built over the years using these nongeneric collection classes (and interfaces), history has shown that use of these types can result in a number of issues.

The first issue is that using the System.Collections and System.Collections.Specialized classes can result in some poorly performing code, especially when you are manipulating numerical data (e.g., value types). As you'll see momentarily, the CLR must perform a number of memory transfer operations when you store structures in any nongeneric collection class prototyped to operate on System.Objects, which can hurt runtime execution speed.

The second issue is that most of the nongeneric collection classes are not type-safe because (again) they were developed to operate on System.Objects, and they could therefore contain anything at all. If a .NET developer needed to create a highly type-safe collection (e.g., a container that can hold objects implementing only a certain interface), the only real choice was to create a new collection class by hand. Doing so was not too labor intensive, but it was a tad on the tedious side.

Before you look at how to use generics in your programs, you'll find it helpful to examine the issues of nongeneric collection classes a bit closer; this will help you better understand the problems generics intended to solve in the first place. If you want to follow along, create a new Console Application project named IssuesWithNonGenericCollections. Next, make sure you import the System.Collections namespace to the top of your C# code file.

```
using System.Collections;
```

The Issue of Performance

As you might recall from Chapter 4, the .NET platform supports two broad categories of data: value types and reference types. Given that .NET defines two major categories of types, you might occasionally need to represent a variable of one category as a variable of the other category. To do so, C# provides a simple mechanism, termed *boxing*, to store the data in a value type within a reference variable. Assume that you have created a local variable of type int in a method called SimpleBoxUnboxOperation(). If, during the course of your application, you were to represent this value type as a reference type, you would *box* the value, as follows:

```
static void SimpleBoxUnboxOperation()
{
  // Make a ValueType (int) variable.
  int myInt = 25;

  // Box the int into an object reference.
  object boxedInt = myInt;
}
```

Boxing can be formally defined as the process of explicitly assigning a value type to a System.Object variable. When you box a value, the CLR allocates a new object on the heap and copies the value type's value (25, in this case) into that instance. What is returned to you is a reference to the newly allocated heap-based object.

The opposite operation is also permitted through *unboxing*. Unboxing is the process of converting the value held in the object reference back into a corresponding value type on the stack. Syntactically speaking, an unboxing operation looks like a normal casting operation. However, the semantics are quite different. The CLR begins by verifying that the receiving data type is equivalent to the boxed type, and if so, it copies the value back into a local stack-based variable. For example, the following unboxing operations work successfully, given that the underlying type of the boxedInt is indeed an int:

```
static void SimpleBoxUnboxOperation()
{
  // Make a ValueType (int) variable.
  int myInt = 25;

  // Box the int into an object reference.
  object boxedInt = myInt;

  // Unbox the reference back into a corresponding int.
  int unboxedInt = (int)boxedInt;
}
```

When the C# compiler encounters boxing/unboxing syntax, it emits CIL code that contains the box/unbox op codes. If you were to examine your compiled assembly using ildasm.exe, you would find the following:

```
.method private hidebysig static void SimpleBoxUnboxOperation() cil managed
{
  // Code size 19 (0x13)
  .maxstack 1
  .locals init ([0] int32 myInt, [1] object boxedInt, [2] int32 unboxedInt)
  IL_0000: nop
  IL_0001: ldc.i4.s 25
  IL_0003: stloc.0
  IL_0004: ldloc.0
  IL_0005: box [mscorlib]System.Int32
  IL_000a: stloc.1
  IL_000b: ldloc.1
  IL_000c: unbox.any [mscorlib]System.Int32
  IL_0011: stloc.2
  IL_0012: ret
} // end of method Program::SimpleBoxUnboxOperation
```

Remember that unlike when performing a typical cast, you *must* unbox into an appropriate data type. If you attempt to unbox a piece of data into the incorrect data type, an InvalidCastException exception will be thrown. To be perfectly safe, you should wrap each unboxing operation in try/catch logic; however, this would be quite labor intensive to do for every unboxing operation. Consider the following code update, which will throw an error because you're attempting to unbox the boxed int into a long:

```
static void SimpleBoxUnboxOperation()
{
  // Make a ValueType (int) variable.
  int myInt = 25;

  // Box the int into an object reference.
  object boxedInt = myInt;
```

```
// Unbox in the wrong data type to trigger
// runtime exception.
try
{
  long unboxedInt = (long)boxedInt;
}
catch (InvalidCastException ex)
{
  Console.WriteLine(ex.Message);
}
}
```

At first glance, boxing/unboxing might seem like a rather uneventful language feature that is more academic than practical. After all, you will seldom need to store a local value type in a local object variable, as shown here. However, it turns out that the boxing/unboxing process is quite helpful because it allows you to assume everything can be treated as a System.Object, while the CLR takes care of the memory-related details on your behalf.

Let's look at a practical use of these techniques. Assume you have created a nongeneric System. Collections.ArrayList to hold onto a batch of numeric (stack-allocated) data. If you were to examine the members of ArrayList, you would find they are prototyped to operate on System.Object data. Now consider the Add(), Insert(), and Remove() methods, as well as the class indexer.

```
public class ArrayList : object,
  IList, ICollection, IEnumerable, ICloneable
{
...
  public virtual int Add(object value);
  public virtual void Insert(int index, object value);
  public virtual void Remove(object obj);
  public virtual object this[int index] {get; set; }
}
```

ArrayList has been built to operate on objects, which represent data allocated on the heap, so it might seem strange that the following code compiles and executes without throwing an error:

```
static void WorkWithArrayList()
{
  // Value types are automatically boxed when
  // passed to a method requesting an object.
  ArrayList myInts = new ArrayList();
  myInts.Add(10);
  myInts.Add(20);
  myInts.Add(35);
}
```

Although you pass in numerical data directly into methods requiring an object, the runtime automatically boxes the stack-based data on your behalf. Later, if you want to retrieve an item from the ArrayList using the type indexer, you must unbox the heap-allocated object into a stack-allocated integer using a casting operation. Remember that the indexer of the ArrayList is returning System.Objects, not System.Int32s.

```
static void WorkWithArrayList()
{
  // Value types are automatically boxed when
  // passed to a member requesting an object.
  ArrayList myInts = new ArrayList();
  myInts.Add(10);
  myInts.Add(20);
  myInts.Add(35);

  // Unboxing occurs when an object is converted back to
  // stack-based data.
  int i = (int)myInts[0];

  // Now it is reboxed, as WriteLine() requires object types!
  Console.WriteLine("Value of your int: {0}", i);
}
```

Again, note that the stack-allocated System.Int32 is boxed prior to the call to ArrayList.Add(), so it can be passed in the required System.Object. Also note that the System.Object is unboxed back into a System.Int32 once it is retrieved from the ArrayList via the casting operation, only to be boxed *again* when it is passed to the Console.WriteLine() method, as this method is operating on System.Object variables.

Boxing and unboxing are convenient from a programmer's viewpoint, but this simplified approach to stack/heap memory transfer comes with the baggage of performance issues (in both speed of execution and code size) and a lack of type safety. To understand the performance issues, ponder these steps that must occur to box and unbox a simple integer:

1. A new object must be allocated on the managed heap.

2. The value of the stack-based data must be transferred into that memory location.

3. When unboxed, the value stored on the heap-based object must be transferred back to the stack.

4. The now unused object on the heap will (eventually) be garbage collected.

Although this particular WorkWithArrayList() method won't cause a major bottleneck in terms of performance, you could certainly feel the impact if an ArrayList contained thousands of integers that your program manipulates on a somewhat regular basis. In an ideal world, you could manipulate stack-based data in a container without any performance issues. Ideally, it would be nice if you did not have to bother plucking data from this container using try/catch scopes (this is exactly what generics let you achieve).

The Issue of Type Safety

I touched on the issue of type safety when covering unboxing operations. Recall that you must unbox your data into the same data type it was declared as before boxing. However, there is another aspect of type safety you must keep in mind in a generic-free world: the fact that a majority of the classes of System.Collections can typically hold anything whatsoever because their members are prototyped to operate on System.Objects. For example, this method builds an ArrayList of random bits of unrelated data:

```
static void ArrayListOfRandomObjects()
{
  // The ArrayList can hold anything at all.
  ArrayList allMyObjects = new ArrayList();
  allMyObjects.Add(true);
```

```
  allMyObjects.Add(new OperatingSystem(PlatformID.MacOSX, new Version(10, 0)));
  allMyObjects.Add(66);
  allMyObjects.Add(3.14);
}
```

In some cases, you will require an extremely flexible container that can hold literally anything (as shown here). However, most of the time you desire a *type-safe* container that can operate only on a particular type of data point. For example, you might need a container that can hold only database connections, bitmaps, or IPointy-compatible objects.

Prior to generics, the only way you could address this issue of type safety was to create a custom (strongly typed) collection class manually. Assume you want to create a custom collection that can contain only objects of type Person.

```
public class Person
{
  public int Age {get; set;}
  public string FirstName {get; set;}
  public string LastName {get; set;}

  public Person(){}
  public Person(string firstName, string lastName, int age)
  {
    Age = age;
    FirstName = firstName;
    LastName = lastName;
  }

  public override string ToString()
  {
    return $"Name: {FirstName} {LastName}, Age: {Age}";
  }
}
```

To build a collection that can hold only Person objects, you could define a System.Collections.ArrayList member variable within a class named PersonCollection and configure all members to operate on strongly typed Person objects, rather than on System.Object types. Here is a simple example
(a production-level custom collection could support many additional members and might extend an abstract base class from the System.Collections or System.Collections.Specialized namespace):

```
public class PersonCollection : IEnumerable
{
  private ArrayList arPeople = new ArrayList();

  // Cast for caller.
  public Person GetPerson(int pos) => (Person)arPeople[pos];

  // Insert only Person objects.
  public void AddPerson(Person p)
  { arPeople.Add(p); }

  public void ClearPeople()
  { arPeople.Clear(); }
```

```
public int Count => arPeople.Count;

// Foreach enumeration support.
IEnumerator IEnumerable.GetEnumerator() => arPeople.GetEnumerator();
}
```

Notice that the PersonCollection class implements the IEnumerable interface, which allows a foreach-like iteration over each contained item. Also notice that your GetPerson() and AddPerson() methods have been prototyped to operate only on Person objects, not bitmaps, strings, database connections, or other items. With these types defined, you are now assured of type safety, given that the C# compiler will be able to determine any attempt to insert an incompatible data type.

```
static void UsePersonCollection()
{
  Console.WriteLine("***** Custom Person Collection *****\n");
  PersonCollection myPeople = new PersonCollection();
  myPeople.AddPerson(new Person("Homer", "Simpson", 40));
  myPeople.AddPerson(new Person("Marge", "Simpson", 38));
  myPeople.AddPerson(new Person("Lisa", "Simpson", 9));
  myPeople.AddPerson(new Person("Bart", "Simpson", 7));
  myPeople.AddPerson(new Person("Maggie", "Simpson", 2));

  // This would be a compile-time error!
  // myPeople.AddPerson(new Car());

  foreach (Person p in myPeople)
  Console.WriteLine(p);
}
```

While custom collections do ensure type safety, this approach leaves you in a position where you must create an (almost identical) custom collection for each unique data type you want to contain. Thus, if you need a custom collection that can operate only on classes deriving from the Car base class, you need to build a highly similar collection class.

```
public class CarCollection : IEnumerable
{
  private ArrayList arCars = new ArrayList();

  // Cast for caller.
  public Car GetCar(int pos) => (Car) arCars[pos];

  // Insert only Car objects.
  public void AddCar(Car c)
  { arCars.Add(c); }

  public void ClearCars()
  { arCars.Clear(); }

  public int Count => arCars.Count;

  // Foreach enumeration support.
  IEnumerator IEnumerable.GetEnumerator() => arCars.GetEnumerator();
}
```

However, a custom collection class does nothing to solve the issue of boxing/unboxing penalties. Even if you were to create a custom collection named IntCollection that you designed to operate only on System.Int32 items, you would have to allocate some type of object to hold the data (e.g., System.Array and ArrayList).

```
public class IntCollection : IEnumerable
{
  private ArrayList arInts = new ArrayList();

  // Get an int (performs unboxing!).
  public int GetInt(int pos) => (int)arInts[pos];

  // Insert an int (performs boxing)!
  public void AddInt(int i)
  { arInts.Add(i); }

  public void ClearInts()
  { arInts.Clear(); }

  public int Count => arInts.Count;}

  IEnumerator IEnumerable.GetEnumerator() => arInts.GetEnumerator();
}
```

Regardless of which type you might choose to hold the integers, you cannot escape the boxing dilemma using nongeneric containers.

A First Look at Generic Collections

When you use generic collection classes, you rectify all the previous issues, including boxing/unboxing penalties and a lack of type safety. Also, the need to build a custom (generic) collection class becomes quite rare. Rather than having to build unique classes that can contain people, cars, and integers, you can use a generic collection class and specify the type of type.

Consider the following method, which uses the generic List<T> class (in the System.Collections.Generic namespace) to contain various types of data in a strongly typed manner (don't fret the details of generic syntax at this time):

```
static void UseGenericList()
{
  Console.WriteLine("***** Fun with Generics *****\n");

  // This List<> can hold only Person objects.
  List<Person> morePeople = new List<Person>();
  morePeople.Add(new Person ("Frank", "Black", 50));
  Console.WriteLine(morePeople[0]);

  // This List<> can hold only integers.
  List<int> moreInts = new List<int>();
  moreInts.Add(10);
  moreInts.Add(2);
  int sum = moreInts[0] + moreInts[1];
```

```
// Compile-time error! Can't add Person object
// to a list of ints!
// moreInts.Add(new Person());
}
```

The first List<T> object can contain only Person objects. Therefore, you do not need to perform a cast when plucking the items from the container, which makes this approach more type-safe. The second List<T> can contain only integers, all of which are allocated on the stack; in other words, there is no hidden boxing or unboxing as you found with the nongeneric ArrayList. Here is a short list of the benefits generic containers provide over their nongeneric counterparts:

- Generics provide better performance because they do not result in boxing or unboxing penalties when storing value types.

- Generics are type safe because they can contain only the type of type you specify.

- Generics greatly reduce the need to build custom collection types because you specify the "type of type" when creating the generic container.

■ **Source Code**   You can find the IssuesWithNonGenericCollections project in the Chapter 9 subdirectory.

The Role of Generic Type Parameters

You can find generic classes, interfaces, structures, and delegates throughout the .NET base class libraries, and these might be part of any .NET namespace. Also be aware that generics have far more uses than simply defining a collection class. To be sure, you will see many different generics used in the remainder of this book for various reasons.

■ **Note**   Only classes, structures, interfaces, and delegates can be written generically; enum types cannot.

When you see a generic item listed in the .NET Framework documentation or the Visual Studio Object Browser, you will notice a pair of angled brackets with a letter or other token sandwiched within. Figure 9-1 shows the Visual Studio Object Browser displaying a number of generic items located within the System.Collections.Generic namespace, including the highlighted List<T> class.

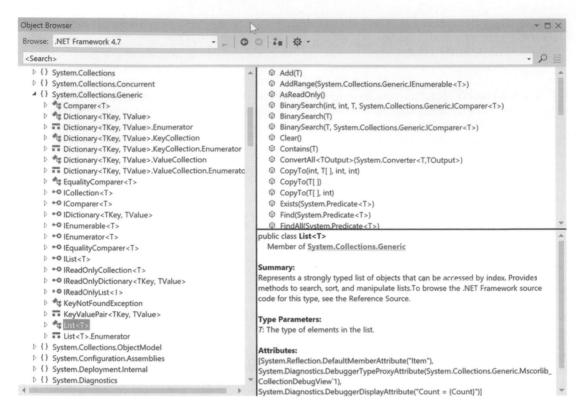

Figure 9-1. *Generic items supporting type parameters*

Formally speaking, you call these tokens *type parameters*; however, in more user-friendly terms, you can simply call them *placeholders*. You can read the symbol <T> as "of T." Thus, you can read IEnumerable<T> "as IEnumerable of T" or, to say it another way, "IEnumerable of type T."

■ **Note**   The name of a type parameter (placeholder) is irrelevant, and it is up to the developer who created the generic item. However, typically *T* is used to represent types, *TKey* or *K* is used for keys, and *TValue* or *V* is used for values.

When you create a generic object, implement a generic interface, or invoke a generic member, it is up to you to supply a value to the type parameter. You'll see many examples in this chapter and throughout the remainder of the text. However, to set the stage, let's see the basics of interacting with generic types and members.

Specifying Type Parameters for Generic Classes/Structures

When you create an instance of a generic class or structure, you specify the type parameter when you declare the variable and when you invoke the constructor. As you saw in the preceding code example, UseGenericList() defined two List<T> objects.

```
// This List<> can hold only Person objects.
List<Person> morePeople = new List<Person>();
```

You can read the preceding snippet as "a List<> of T, where T is of type Person." Or, more simply, you can read it as "a list of person objects." After you specify the type parameter of a generic item, it cannot be changed (remember, generics are all about type safety). When you specify a type parameter for a generic class or structure, all occurrences of the placeholder(s) are now replaced with your supplied value.

If you were to view the full declaration of the generic List<T> class using the Visual Studio Object Browser, you would see that the placeholder T is used throughout the definition of the List<T> type. Here is a partial listing (note the items in **bold**):

```
// A partial listing of the List<T> class.
namespace System.Collections.Generic
{
  public class List<T> :
    IList<T>, ICollection<T>, IEnumerable<T>, IReadOnlyList<T>
    IList, ICollection, IEnumerable
  {
...
    public void Add(T item);
    public ReadOnlyCollection<T> AsReadOnly();
    public int BinarySearch(T item);
    public bool Contains(T item);
    public void CopyTo(T[] array);
    public int FindIndex(System.Predicate<T> match);
    public T FindLast(System.Predicate<T> match);
    public bool Remove(T item);
    public int RemoveAll(System.Predicate<T> match);
    public T[] ToArray();
    public bool TrueForAll(System.Predicate<T> match);
    public T this[int index] { get; set; }
  }
}
```

When you create a List<T> specifying Person objects, it is as if the List<T> type were defined as follows:

```
namespace System.Collections.Generic
{
  public class List<Person> :
    IList<Person>, ICollection<Person>, IEnumerable<Person>, IReadOnlyList<Person>
    IList, ICollection, IEnumerable
  {
...
    public void Add(Person item);
    public ReadOnlyCollection<Person> AsReadOnly();
    public int BinarySearch(Person item);
```

```
    public bool Contains(Person item);
    public void CopyTo(Person[] array);
    public int FindIndex(System.Predicate<Person> match);
    public Person FindLast(System.Predicate<Person> match);
    public bool Remove(Person item);
    public int RemoveAll(System.Predicate<Person> match);
    public Person[] ToArray();
    public bool TrueForAll(System.Predicate<Person> match);
    public Person this[int index] { get; set; }
  }
}
```

Of course, when you create a generic List<T> variable, the compiler does not literally create a new implementation of the List<T> class. Rather, it will address only the members of the generic type you actually invoke.

Specifying Type Parameters for Generic Members

It is fine for a nongeneric class or structure to support generic properties. In these cases, you would also need to specify the placeholder value at the time you invoke the method. For example, System.Array supports a several generic methods. Specifically, the nongeneric static Sort() method now has a generic counterpart named Sort<T>(). Consider the following code snippet, where T is of type int:

```
int[] myInts = { 10, 4, 2, 33, 93 };

// Specify the placeholder to the generic
// Sort<>() method.
Array.Sort<int>(myInts);

foreach (int i in myInts)
{
  Console.WriteLine(i);
}
```

Specifying Type Parameters for Generic Interfaces

It is common to implement generic interfaces when you build classes or structures that need to support various framework behaviors (e.g., cloning, sorting, and enumeration). In Chapter 8, you learned about a number of nongeneric interfaces, such as IComparable, IEnumerable, IEnumerator, and IComparer. Recall that the nongeneric IComparable interface was defined like this:

```
public interface IComparable
{
  int CompareTo(object obj);
}
```

In Chapter 8, you also implemented this interface on your Car class to enable sorting in a standard array. However, the code required several runtime checks and casting operations because the parameter was a general System.Object.

```
public class Car : IComparable
{
...
  // IComparable implementation.
  int IComparable.CompareTo(object obj)
  {
    Car temp = obj as Car;
    if (temp != null)
    {
      if (this.CarID > temp.CarID)
        return 1;
      if (this.CarID < temp.CarID)
        return -1;
      else
        return 0;
    }
    else
      throw new ArgumentException("Parameter is not a Car!");
  }
}
```

Now assume you use the generic counterpart of this interface.

```
public interface IComparable<T>
{
  int CompareTo(T obj);
}
```

In this case, your implementation code will be cleaned up considerably.

```
public class Car : IComparable<Car>
{
...
  // IComparable<T> implementation.
  int IComparable<Car>.CompareTo(Car obj)
  {
    if (this.CarID > obj.CarID)
      return 1;
    if (this.CarID < obj.CarID)
      return -1;
    else
      return 0;
  }
}
```

Here, you do not need to check whether the incoming parameter is a Car because it can *only* be a Car!
If someone were to pass in an incompatible data type, you would get a compile-time error. Now that you
have a better handle on how to interact with generic items, as well as the role of type parameters
(aka placeholders), you're ready to examine the classes and interfaces of the System.Collections.Generic
namespace.

The System.Collections.Generic Namespace

When you are building a .NET application and need a way to manage in-memory data, the classes of System.Collections.Generic will most likely fit the bill. At the opening of this chapter, I briefly mentioned some of the core nongeneric interfaces implemented by the nongeneric collection classes. Not too surprisingly, the System.Collections.Generic namespace defines generic replacements for many of them.

In fact, you can find a number of the generic interfaces that extend their nongeneric counterparts. This might seem odd; however, by doing so, implementing classes will also support the legacy functionally found in their nongeneric siblings. For example, IEnumerable<T> extends IEnumerable. Table 9-4 documents the core generic interfaces you'll encounter when working with the generic collection classes.

Table 9-4. *Key Interfaces Supported by Classes of System.Collections.Generic*

System.Collections.Generic Interface	Meaning in Life
ICollection<T>	Defines general characteristics (e.g., size, enumeration, and thread safety) for all generic collection types
IComparer<T>	Defines a way to compare to objects
IDictionary<TKey, TValue>	Allows a generic collection objcct to represent its contents using key-value pairs
IEnumerable<T>	Returns the IEnumerator<T> interface for a given object
IEnumerator<T>	Enables foreach-style iteration over a generic collection
IList<T>	Provides behavior to add, remove, and index items in a sequential list of objects
ISet<T>	Provides the base interface for the abstraction of sets

The System.Collections.Generic namespace also defines several classes that implement many of these key interfaces. Table 9-5 describes some commonly used classes of this namespace, the interfaces they implement, and their basic functionality.

Table 9-5. *Classes of* System.Collections.Generic

Generic Class	Supported Key Interfaces	Meaning in Life
Dictionary<TKey, TValue>	ICollection<T>, IDictionary<TKey, TValue>, IEnumerable<T>	This represents a generic collection of keys and values.
LinkedList<T>	ICollection<T>, IEnumerable<T>	This represents a doubly linked list.
List<T>	ICollection<T>, IEnumerable<T>, IList<T>	This is a dynamically resizable sequential list of items.
Queue<T>	ICollection (Not a typo! This is the nongeneric collection interface), IEnumerable<T>	This is a generic implementation of a first-in, first-out list.
SortedDictionary<TKey, TValue>	ICollection<T>, IDictionary<TKey, TValue>, IEnumerable<T>	This is a generic implementation of a sorted set of key-value pairs.
SortedSet<T>	ICollection<T>, IEnumerable<T>, ISet<T>	This represents a collection of objects that is maintained in sorted order with no duplication.
Stack<T>	ICollection (Not a typo! This is the nongeneric collection interface), IEnumerable<T>	This is a generic implementation of a last-in, first-out list.

The System.Collections.Generic namespace also defines many auxiliary classes and structures that work in conjunction with a specific container. For example, the LinkedListNode<T> type represents a node within a generic LinkedList<T>, the KeyNotFoundException exception is raised when attempting to grab an item from a container using a nonexistent key, and so forth.

It is also worth pointing out that mscorlib.dll and System.dll are not the only assemblies that add new types to the System.Collections.Generic namespace. For example, System.Core.dll adds the HashSet<T> class to the mix. Be sure to consult the .NET Framework documentation for full details of the System.Collections.Generic namespace.

In any case, your next task is to learn how to use some of these generic collection classes. Before you do, however, allow me to illustrate a C# language feature (first introduced in .NET 3.5) that simplifies the way you populate generic (and nongeneric) collection containers with data.

Understanding Collection Initialization Syntax

In Chapter 4, you learned about *object initialization syntax*, which allows you to set properties on a new variable at the time of construction. Closely related to this is *collection initialization syntax*. This C# language feature makes it possible to populate many containers (such as ArrayList or List<T>) with items by using syntax similar to what you use to populate a basic array.

■ **Note**   You can apply collection initialization syntax only to classes that support an Add() method, which is formalized by the ICollection<T>/ICollection interfaces.

Consider the following examples:

```
// Init a standard array.
int[] myArrayOfInts = { 0, 1, 2, 3, 4, 5, 6, 7, 8, 9 };

// Init a generic List<> of ints.
List<int> myGenericList = new List<int> { 0, 1, 2, 3, 4, 5, 6, 7, 8, 9 };

// Init an ArrayList with numerical data.
ArrayList myList = new ArrayList { 0, 1, 2, 3, 4, 5, 6, 7, 8, 9 };
```

If your container is managing a collection of classes or a structure, you can blend object initialization syntax with collection initialization syntax to yield some functional code. You might recall the Point class from Chapter 5, which defined two properties named X and Y. If you wanted to build a generic List<T> of Point objects, you could write the following:

```
List<Point> myListOfPoints = new List<Point>
{
  new Point { X = 2, Y = 2 },
  new Point { X = 3, Y = 3 },
  new Point(PointColor.BloodRed){ X = 4, Y = 4 }
};

foreach (var pt in myListOfPoints)
{
  Console.WriteLine(pt);
}
```

Again, the benefit of this syntax is that you save yourself numerous keystrokes. While the nested curly brackets can become difficult to read if you don't mind your formatting, imagine the amount of code that would be required to fill the following List<T> of Rectangles if you did not have collection initialization syntax (you might recall from Chapter 4 that you created a Rectangle class that contained two properties encapsulating Point objects).

```
List<Rectangle> myListOfRects = new List<Rectangle>
{
  new Rectangle {TopLeft = new Point { X = 10, Y = 10 },
               BottomRight = new Point { X = 200, Y = 200}},
  new Rectangle {TopLeft = new Point { X = 2, Y = 2 },
               BottomRight = new Point { X = 100, Y = 100}},
  new Rectangle {TopLeft = new Point { X = 5, Y = 5 },
               BottomRight = new Point { X = 90, Y = 75}}
};

foreach (var r in myListOfRects)
{
  Console.WriteLine(r);
}
```

Working with the List<T> Class

Create a new Console Application project named FunWithGenericCollections. Note that your initial C# code file already imports the System.Collections.Generic namespace.

The first generic class you will examine is List<T>, which you've already seen once or twice in this chapter. The List<T> class is bound to be your most frequently used type in the System.Collections.Generic namespace because it allows you to resize the contents of the container dynamically. To illustrate the basics of this type, ponder the following method in your Program class, which leverages List<T> to manipulate the set of Person objects shown earlier in this chapter; you might recall that these Person objects defined three properties (Age, FirstName, and LastName) and a custom ToString() implementation:

```csharp
static void UseGenericList()
{
  // Make a List of Person objects, filled with
  // collection/object init syntax.
  List<Person> people = new List<Person>()
  {
    new Person {FirstName= "Homer", LastName="Simpson", Age=47},
    new Person {FirstName= "Marge", LastName="Simpson", Age=45},
    new Person {FirstName= "Lisa", LastName="Simpson", Age=9},
    new Person {FirstName= "Bart", LastName="Simpson", Age=8}
  };

  // Print out # of items in List.
  Console.WriteLine("Items in list: {0}", people.Count);

  // Enumerate over list.
  foreach (Person p in people)
  {
    Console.WriteLine(p);
  }

  // Insert a new person.
  Console.WriteLine("\n->Inserting new person.");
  people.Insert(2, new Person { FirstName = "Maggie", LastName = "Simpson", Age - 2 });
  Console.WriteLine("Items in list: {0}", people.Count);

  // Copy data into a new array.
  Person[] arrayOfPeople = people.ToArray();
  foreach (Person p in arrayOfPeople)
  {
    Console.WriteLine("First Names: {0}", p.FirstName);
  }
}
```

Here, you use initialization syntax to populate your List<T> with objects, as a shorthand notation for calling Add() *multiple* times. After you print out the number of items in the collection (as well as enumerate over each item), you invoke Insert(). As you can see, Insert() allows you to plug a new item into the List<T> at a specified index.

Finally, notice the call to the ToArray() method, which returns an array of Person objects based on the contents of the original List<T>. From this array, you loop over the items again using the array's indexer syntax. If you call this method from within Main(), you get the following output:

```
***** Fun with Generic Collections *****

Items in list: 4
Name: Homer Simpson, Age: 47
Name: Marge Simpson, Age: 45
Name: Lisa Simpson, Age: 9
Name: Bart Simpson, Age: 8

->Inserting new person.
Items in list: 5
First Names: Homer
First Names: Marge
First Names: Maggie
First Names: Lisa
First Names: Bart
```

The List<T> class defines many additional members of interest, so be sure to consult the .NET Framework documentation for more information. Next, let's look at a few more generic collections, specifically Stack<T>, Queue<T>, and SortedSet<T>. This should get you in a great position to understand your basic choices regarding how to hold your custom application data.

Working with the Stack<T> Class

The Stack<T> class represents a collection that maintains items using a last-in, first-out manner. As you might expect, Stack<T> defines members named Push() and Pop() to place items onto or remove items from the stack. The following method creates a stack of Person objects:

```
static void UseGenericStack()
{
  Stack<Person> stackOfPeople = new Stack<Person>();
  stackOfPeople.Push(new Person { FirstName = "Homer", LastName = "Simpson", Age = 47 });
  stackOfPeople.Push(new Person { FirstName = "Marge", LastName = "Simpson", Age = 45 });
  stackOfPeople.Push(new Person { FirstName = "Lisa", LastName = "Simpson", Age = 9 });

  // Now look at the top item, pop it, and look again.
  Console.WriteLine("First person is: {0}", stackOfPeople.Peek());
  Console.WriteLine("Popped off {0}", stackOfPeople.Pop());
  Console.WriteLine("\nFirst person is: {0}", stackOfPeople.Peek());
  Console.WriteLine("Popped off {0}", stackOfPeople.Pop());
  Console.WriteLine("\nFirst person item is: {0}", stackOfPeople.Peek());
  Console.WriteLine("Popped off {0}", stackOfPeople.Pop());

  try
  {
    Console.WriteLine("\nnFirst person is: {0}", stackOfPeople.Peek());
    Console.WriteLine("Popped off {0}", stackOfPeople.Pop());
  }
```

```
  catch (InvalidOperationException ex)
  {
    Console.WriteLine("\nError! {0}", ex.Message);
  }
}
```

Here, you build a stack that contains three people, added in the order of their first names: Homer, Marge, and Lisa. As you peek into the stack, you will always see the object at the top first; therefore, the first call to Peek() reveals the third Person object. After a series of Pop() and Peek() calls, the stack eventually empties, at which time additional Peek() and Pop() calls raise a system exception. You can see the output for this here:

```
***** Fun with Generic Collections *****

First person is: Name: Lisa Simpson, Age: 9
Popped off Name: Lisa Simpson, Age: 9

First person is: Name: Marge Simpson, Age: 45
Popped off Name: Marge Simpson, Age: 45

First person item is: Name: Homer Simpson, Age: 47
Popped off Name: Homer Simpson, Age: 47

Error! Stack empty.
```

Working with the Queue<T> Class

Queues are containers that ensure items are accessed in a first-in, first-out manner. Sadly, we humans are subject to queues all day long: lines at the bank, lines at the movie theater, and lines at the morning coffeehouse. When you need to model a scenario in which items are handled on a first-come, first-served basis, you will find the Queue<T> class fits the bill. In addition to the functionality provided by the supported interfaces, Queue defines the key members shown in Table 9-6.

Table 9-6. *Members of the Queue<T> Type*

Select Member of Queue<T>	Meaning in Life
Dequeue()	Removes and returns the object at the beginning of the Queue<T>
Enqueue()	Adds an object to the end of the Queue<T>
Peek()	Returns the object at the beginning of the Queue<T> without removing it

Now let's put these methods to work. You can begin by leveraging your Person class again and building a Queue<T> object that simulates a line of people waiting to order coffee. First, assume you have the following static helper method:

```
static void GetCoffee(Person p)
{
  Console.WriteLine("{0} got coffee!", p.FirstName);
}
```

Now assume you have this additional helper method, which calls GetCoffee() internally:

```
static void UseGenericQueue()
{
  // Make a Q with three people.
  Queue<Person> peopleQ = new Queue<Person>();
  peopleQ.Enqueue(new Person {FirstName= "Homer", LastName="Simpson", Age=47});
  peopleQ.Enqueue(new Person {FirstName= "Marge", LastName="Simpson", Age=45});
  peopleQ.Enqueue(new Person {FirstName= "Lisa", LastName="Simpson", Age=9});

  // Peek at first person in Q.
  Console.WriteLine("{0} is first in line!", peopleQ.Peek().FirstName);

  // Remove each person from Q.
  GetCoffee(peopleQ.Dequeue());
  GetCoffee(peopleQ.Dequeue());
  GetCoffee(peopleQ.Dequeue());
  // Try to de-Q again?
  try
  {
    GetCoffee(peopleQ.Dequeue());
  }
  catch(InvalidOperationException e)
  {
    Console.WriteLine("Error! {0}", e.Message);
  }
}
```

Here, you insert three items into the Queue<T> class using its Enqueue() method. The call to Peek() allows you to view (but not remove) the first item currently in the Queue. Finally, the call to Dequeue() removes the item from the line and sends it into the GetCoffee() helper function for processing. Note that if you attempt to remove items from an empty queue, a runtime exception is thrown. Here is the output you receive when calling this method:

```
***** Fun with Generic Collections *****

Homer is first in line!
Homer got coffee!
Marge got coffee!
Lisa got coffee!
Error! Queue empty.
```

Working with the SortedSet<T> Class

The SortedSet<T> class is useful because it automatically ensures that the items in the set are sorted when you insert or remove items. However, you do need to inform the SortedSet<T> class exactly *how* you want it to sort the objects, by passing in as a constructor argument an object that implements the generic IComparer<T> interface.

Begin by creating a new class named SortPeopleByAge, which implements IComparer<T>, where T is of type Person. Recall that this interface defines a single method named Compare(), where you can author whatever logic you require for the comparison. Here is a simple implementation of this class:

```
class SortPeopleByAge : IComparer<Person>
{
  public int Compare(Person firstPerson, Person secondPerson)
  {
    if (firstPerson?.Age > secondPerson?.Age)
    {
        return 1;
    }
    if (firstPerson?.Age < secondPerson?.Age)
    {
      return -1;
    }
    return 0;
  }
}
```

Now update your Program class with the following new method, which I assume you will call from Main():

```
static void UseSortedSet()
{
  // Make some people with different ages.
  SortedSet<Person> setOfPeople = new SortedSet<Person>(new SortPeopleByAge())
  {
    new Person {FirstName= "Homer", LastName="Simpson", Age=47},
    new Person {FirstName= "Marge", LastName="Simpson", Age=45},
    new Person {FirstName= "Lisa", LastName="Simpson", Age=9},
    new Person {FirstName= "Bart", LastName="Simpson", Age=8}
  };

  // Note the items are sorted by age!
  foreach (Person p in setOfPeople)
  {
    Console.WriteLine(p);
  }
    Console.WriteLine();

  // Add a few new people, with various ages.
  setOfPeople.Add(new Person { FirstName = "Saku", LastName = "Jones", Age = 1 });
  setOfPeople.Add(new Person { FirstName = "Mikko", LastName = "Jones", Age = 32 });

  // Still sorted by age!
  foreach (Person p in setOfPeople)
  {
    Console.WriteLine(p);
  }
}
```

When you run your application, the listing of objects is now always ordered based on the value of the Age property, regardless of the order you inserted or removed objects.

```
***** Fun with Generic Collections *****

Name: Bart Simpson, Age: 8
Name: Lisa Simpson, Age: 9
Name: Marge Simpson, Age: 45
Name: Homer Simpson, Age: 47

Name: Saku Jones, Age: 1
Name: Bart Simpson, Age: 8
Name: Lisa Simpson, Age: 9
Name: Mikko Jones, Age: 32
Name: Marge Simpson, Age: 45
Name: Homer Simpson, Age: 47
```

Working with the Dictionary<TKey, TValue> Class

Another handy generic collection is the Dictionary<TKey,TValue> type, which allows you to hold any number of objects that may be referred to via a unique key. Thus, rather than obtaining an item from a List<T> using a numerical identifier (for example, "Give me the second object"), you could use the unique text key (for example, "Give me the object I keyed as Homer").

Like other collection objects, you can populate a Dictionary<TKey,TValue> by calling the generic Add() method manually. However, you can also fill a Dictionary<TKey,TValue> using collection initialization syntax. Do be aware that when you are populating this collection object, key names must be unique. If you mistakenly specify the same key multiple times, you will receive a runtime exception.

Consider the following method that fills a Dictionary<K,V> with various objects. Notice when you create the Dictionary<TKey,TValue> object, you specify the key type (TKey) and underlying object type (TValue) as constructor arguments. Here, you are using a string data type as the key (although this is not required; the key can be any type) and a Person type as the value.

```
private static void UseDictionary()
{
    // Populate using Add() method
    Dictionary<string, Person> peopleA = new Dictionary<string, Person>();
    peopleA.Add("Homer", new Person { FirstName = "Homer", LastName = "Simpson", Age = 47 });
    peopleA.Add("Marge", new Person { FirstName = "Marge", LastName = "Simpson", Age = 45 });
    peopleA.Add("Lisa", new Person { FirstName = "Lisa", LastName = "Simpson", Age = 9 });

    // Get Homer.
    Person homer = peopleA["Homer"];
    Console.WriteLine(homer);

    // Populate with initialization syntax.
    Dictionary<string, Person> peopleB = new Dictionary<string, Person>()
    {
        { "Homer", new Person { FirstName = "Homer", LastName = "Simpson", Age = 47 } },
        { "Marge", new Person { FirstName = "Marge", LastName = "Simpson", Age = 45 } },
```

```
      { "Lisa", new Person { FirstName = "Lisa", LastName = "Simpson", Age = 9 } }
  };

  // Get Lisa.
  Person lisa = peopleB["Lisa"];
  Console.WriteLine(lisa);
}
```

It is also possible to populate a Dictionary<TKey,TValue> using a related initialization syntax introduced with the current version of .NET that is specific to this type of container (not surprisingly termed *dictionary initialization*). Similar to the syntax used to populate the personB object in the previous code example, you still define an initialization scope for the collection object; however, you can use the indexer to specify the key and assign this to a new object as so:

```
// Populate with dictionary initialization syntax.
Dictionary<string, Person> peopleC = new Dictionary<string, Person>()
{
    ["Homer"] = new Person { FirstName = "Homer", LastName = "Simpson", Age = 47 },
    ["Marge"] = new Person { FirstName = "Marge", LastName = "Simpson", Age = 45 },
    ["Lisa"] = new Person { FirstName = "Lisa", LastName = "Simpson", Age = 9 }
};
```

■ **Note** You can find the FunWithGenericCollections project in the Chapter 9 subdirectory.

The System.Collections.ObjectModel Namespace

Now that you understand how to work with the major generic classes, you can briefly examine an additional collection-centric namespace, System.Collections.ObjectModel. This is a relatively small namespace, which contains a handful of classes. Table 9-7 documents the two classes that you should most certainly be aware of.

Table 9-7. *Useful Members of System.Collections.ObjectModel*

System.Collections.ObjectModel Type	Meaning in Life
ObservableCollection<T>	Represents a dynamic data collection that provides notifications when items get added, when items get removed, or when the whole list is refreshed
ReadOnlyObservableCollection<T>	Represents a read-only version of ObservableCollection<T>

The ObservableCollection<T> class is useful in that it has the ability to inform external objects when its contents have changed in some way (as you might guess, working with ReadOnlyObservableCollection <T> is similar but read-only in nature).

Working with ObservableCollection<T>

Create a new Console Application project named FunWithObservableCollections and import the System.Collections.ObjectModel namespace into your initial C# code file. In many ways, working with ObservableCollection<T> is identical to working with List<T>, given that both of these classes implement the same core interfaces. What makes the ObservableCollection<T> class unique is that this class supports an event named CollectionChanged. This event will fire whenever a new item is inserted, a current item is removed (or relocated), or the entire collection is modified.

Like any event, CollectionChanged is defined in terms of a delegate, which in this case is NotifyCollectionChangedEventHandler. This delegate can call any method that takes an object as the first parameter and takes a NotifyCollectionChangedEventArgs as the second. Consider the following Main() method, which populates an observable collection containing Person objects and wires up the CollectionChanged event:

```
class Program
{
  static void Main(string[] args)
  {
    // Make a collection to observe and add a few Person objects.
    ObservableCollection<Person> people = new ObservableCollection<Person>()
    {
      new Person{ FirstName = "Peter", LastName = "Murphy", Age = 52 },
      new Person{ FirstName = "Kevin", LastName = "Key", Age = 48 },
    };

    // Wire up the CollectionChanged event.
    people.CollectionChanged += people_CollectionChanged;
  }

  static void people_CollectionChanged(object sender, System.Collections.Specialized.
  NotifyCollectionChangedEventArgs e)
  {
    throw new NotImplementedException();
  }
}
```

The incoming NotifyCollectionChangedEventArgs parameter defines two important properties, OldItems and NewItems, which will give you a list of items that were currently in the collection before the event fired and the new items that were involved in the change. However, you will want to examine these lists only under the correct circumstances. Recall that the CollectionChanged event can fire when items are added, removed, relocated, or reset. To discover which of these actions triggered the event, you can use the Action property of NotifyCollectionChangedEventArgs. The Action property can be tested against any of the following members of the NotifyCollectionChangedAction enumeration:

```
public enum NotifyCollectionChangedAction
{
  Add = 0,
  Remove = 1,
  Replace = 2,
  Move = 3,
  Reset = 4,
}
```

Here is an implementation of the CollectionChanged event handler that will traverse the old and new sets when an item has been inserted into or removed from the collection at hand:

```
static void people_CollectionChanged(object sender,
  System.Collections.Specialized.NotifyCollectionChangedEventArgs e)
{
  // What was the action that caused the event?
  Console.WriteLine("Action for this event: {0}", e.Action);

  // They removed something.
  if (e.Action == System.Collections.Specialized.NotifyCollectionChangedAction.Remove)
  {
    Console.WriteLine("Here are the OLD items:");
    foreach (Person p in e.OldItems)
    {
      Console.WriteLine(p.ToString());
    }
    Console.WriteLine();
  }

  // They added something.
  if (e.Action == System.Collections.Specialized.NotifyCollectionChangedAction.Add)
  {
    // Now show the NEW items that were inserted.
    Console.WriteLine("Here are the NEW items:");
    foreach (Person p in e.NewItems)
    {
      Console.WriteLine(p.ToString());
    }
  }
}
```

Now, assuming you have updated your Main() method to add and remove an item, you will see output similar to the following:

```
Action for this event: Add
Here are the NEW items:
Name: Fred Smith, Age: 32

Action for this event: Remove
Here are the OLD items:
Name: Peter Murphy, Age: 52
```

That wraps up the examination of the various collection-centric namespaces in the .NET base class libraries. To conclude the chapter, you will now examine how you can build your own custom generic methods and custom generic types.

■ **Source Code**   You can find the FunWithObservableCollection project in the Chapter 9 subdirectory.

Creating Custom Generic Methods

While most developers typically use the existing generic types within the base class libraries, it is also possible to build your own generic members and custom generic types. Let's look at how to incorporate custom generics into your own projects. The first step is to build a generic swap method. Begin by creating a new console application named CustomGenericMethods.

When you build custom generic methods, you achieve a supercharged version of traditional method overloading. In Chapter 2, you learned that overloading is the act of defining multiple versions of a single method, which differ by the number of, or type of, parameters.

While overloading is a useful feature in an object-oriented language, one problem is that you can easily end up with a ton of methods that essentially do the same thing. For example, assume you need to build some methods that can switch two pieces of data using a simple swap routine. You might begin by authoring a new method that can operate on integers, like this:

```
// Swap two integers.
static void Swap(ref int a, ref int b)
{
  int temp = a;
  a = b;
  b = temp;
}
```

So far, so good. But now assume you also need to swap two Person objects; this would require authoring a new version of Swap().

```
// Swap two Person objects.
static void Swap(ref Person a, ref Person b)
{
  Person temp = a;
  a = b;
  b = temp;
}
```

No doubt, you can see where this is going. If you also needed to swap floating-point numbers, bitmaps, cars, buttons, and whatnot, you would have to build even more methods, which would become a maintenance nightmare. You could build a single (nongeneric) method that operated on object parameters, but then you face all the issues you examined earlier in this chapter, including boxing, unboxing, a lack of type safety, explicit casting, and so on.

Whenever you have a group of overloaded methods that differ only by incoming arguments, this is your clue that generics could make your life easier. Consider the following generic Swap<T> method that can swap any two Ts:

```
// This method will swap any two items.
// as specified by the type parameter <T>.
static void Swap<T>(ref T a, ref T b)
{
  Console.WriteLine("You sent the Swap() method a {0}", typeof(T));
  T temp = a;
  a = b;
  b = temp;
}
```

Notice how a generic method is defined by specifying the type parameters after the method name but before the parameter list. Here, you state that the Swap<T>() method can operate on any two parameters of type <T>. To spice things up a bit, you also print out the type name of the supplied placeholder to the console using C#'s typeof() operator. Now consider the following Main() method, which swaps integers and strings:

```csharp
static void Main(string[] args)
{
  Console.WriteLine("***** Fun with Custom Generic Methods *****\n");

  // Swap 2 ints.
  int a = 10, b = 90;
  Console.WriteLine("Before swap: {0}, {1}", a, b);
  Swap<int>(ref a, ref b);
  Console.WriteLine("After swap: {0}, {1}", a, b);
  Console.WriteLine();

  // Swap 2 strings.
  string s1 = "Hello", s2 = "There";
  Console.WriteLine("Before swap: {0} {1}!", s1, s2);
  Swap<string>(ref s1, ref s2);
  Console.WriteLine("After swap: {0} {1}!", s1, s2);

  Console.ReadLine();
}
```

The output looks like this:

```
***** Fun with Custom Generic Methods *****

Before swap: 10, 90
You sent the Swap() method a System.Int32
After swap: 90, 10

Before swap: Hello There!
You sent the Swap() method a System.String
After swap: There Hello!
```

The major benefit of this approach is that you have only one version of Swap<T>() to maintain, yet it can operate on any two items of a given type in a type-safe manner. Better yet, stack-based items stay on the stack, while heap-based items stay on the heap!

Inference of Type Parameters

When you invoke generic methods such as Swap<T>, you can optionally omit the type parameter if (and only if) the generic method requires arguments because the compiler can infer the type parameter based on the member parameters. For example, you could swap two System.Boolean values by adding the following code to Main():

```
// Compiler will infer System.Boolean.
bool b1 = true, b2 = false;
Console.WriteLine("Before swap: {0}, {1}", b1, b2);
Swap(ref b1, ref b2);
Console.WriteLine("After swap: {0}, {1}", b1, b2);
```

Even though the compiler is able to discover the correct type parameter based on the data type used to declare b1 and b2, you should get in the habit of always specifying the type parameter explicitly.

```
Swap<string>(ref b1, ref b2);
```

This makes it clear to your fellow programmers that this method is indeed generic. Moreover, inference of type parameters works only if the generic method has at least one parameter. For example, assume you have the following generic method in your Program class:

```
static void DisplayBaseClass<T>()
{
  // BaseType is a method used in reflection,
  // which will be examined in Chapter 15
  Console.WriteLine("Base class of {0} is: {1}.", typeof(T), typeof(T).BaseType);
}
```

In this case, you must supply the type parameter upon invocation.

```
static void Main(string[] args)
{
...
  // Must supply type parameter if
  // the method does not take params.
  DisplayBaseClass<int>();
  DisplayBaseClass<string>();

  // Compiler error! No params? Must supply placeholder!
  // DisplayBaseClass();
  Console.ReadLine();
}
```

Currently, the generic Swap<T> and DisplayBaseClass<T> methods are defined within the application's Program class. Of course, as with any method, you are free to define these members in a separate class type (MyGenericMethods) if you would prefer to do it that way.

```
public static class MyGenericMethods
{
  public static void Swap<T>(ref T a, ref T b)
  {
    Console.WriteLine("You sent the Swap() method a {0}", typeof(T));
    T temp = a;
    a = b;
    b = temp;
  }

  public static void DisplayBaseClass<T>()
  {
    Console.WriteLine("Base class of {0} is: {1}.", typeof(T), typeof(T).BaseType);
  }
}
```

The static Swap<T> and DisplayBaseClass<T> methods have been scoped within a new static class type, so you need to specify the type's name when invoking either member, as in this example:

```
MyGenericMethods.Swap<int>(ref a, ref b);
```

Of course, generic methods do not need to be static. If Swap<T> and DisplayBaseClass<T> were instance level (and defined in a nonstatic class), you would simply make an instance of MyGenericMethods and invoke them using the object variable.

```
MyGenericMethods c = new MyGenericMethods();
c.Swap<int>(ref a, ref b);
```

■ **Source Code**   You can find the CustomGenericMethods project in the Chapter 9 subdirectory.

Creating Custom Generic Structures and Classes

Now that you understand how to define and invoke generic methods, it's time to turn your attention to the construction of a generic structure (the process of building a generic class is identical) within a new Console Application project named GenericPoint. Assume you have built a generic Point structure that supports a single type parameter that represents the underlying storage for the (x, y) coordinates. The caller can then create Point<T> types as follows:

```
// Point using ints.
Point<int> p = new Point<int>(10, 10);

// Point using double.
Point<double> p2 = new Point<double>(5.4, 3.3);
```

Here is the complete definition of Point<T>, with some analysis to follow:

```csharp
// A generic Point structure.
public struct Point<T>
{
  // Generic state date.
  private T xPos;
  private T yPos;

  // Generic constructor.
  public Point(T xVal, T yVal)
  {
    xPos = xVal;
    yPos = yVal;
  }

  // Generic properties.
  public T X
  {
    get { return xPos; }
    set { xPos = value; }
  }

  public T Y
  {
    get { return yPos; }
    set { yPos = value; }
  }

  public override string ToString() => $"[{xPOs}, {yPos}]";

  // Reset fields to the default value of the
  // type parameter.
  public void ResetPoint()
  {
    xPos = default(T);
    yPos = default(T);
  }
}
```

The default Keyword in Generic Code

As you can see, Point<T> leverages its type parameter in the definition of the field data, constructor arguments, and property definitions. Notice that, in addition to overriding ToString(), Point<T> defines a method named ResetPoint() that uses some new syntax you have not yet seen.

```csharp
// The "default" keyword is overloaded in C#.
// When used with generics, it represents the default
// value of a type parameter.
```

```
public void ResetPoint()
{
  X = default(T);
  Y = default(T);
}
```

With the introduction of generics, the C# default keyword has been given a dual identity. In addition to its use within a switch construct, it can also be used to set a type parameter to its default value. This is helpful because a generic type does not know the actual placeholders up front, which means it cannot safely assume what the default value will be. The defaults for a type parameter are as follows:

- Numeric values have a default value of 0.

- Reference types have a default value of null.

- Fields of a structure are set to 0 (for value types) or null (for reference types).

For Point<T>, you can set the X and Y values to 0 directly because it is safe to assume the caller will supply only numerical data. However, you can also increase the overall flexibility of the generic type by using the default(T) syntax. In any case, you can now exercise the methods of Point<T>.

```
static void Main(string[] args)
{
  Console.WriteLine("***** Fun with Generic Structures *****\n");

  // Point using ints.
  Point<int> p = new Point<int>(10, 10);
  Console.WriteLine("p.ToString()={0}", p.ToString());
  p.ResetPoint();
  Console.WriteLine("p.ToString()={0}", p.ToString());
  Console.WriteLine();

  // Point using double.
  Point<double> p2 = new Point<double>(5.4, 3.3);
  Console.WriteLine("p2.ToString()={0}", p2.ToString());
  p2.ResetPoint();
  Console.WriteLine("p2.ToString()={0}", p2.ToString());
  Console.ReadLine();
}
```

Here is the output:

```
***** Fun with Generic Structures *****

p.ToString()=[10, 10]
p.ToString()=[0, 0]

p2.ToString()=[5.4, 3.3]
p2.ToString()=[0, 0]
```

■ **Source Code**   You can find the GenericPoint project in the Chapter 9 subdirectory.

Constraining Type Parameters

As this chapter illustrates, any generic item has at least one type parameter that you need to specify at the time you interact with the generic type or member. This alone allows you to build some type-safe code; however, the .NET platform allows you to use the where keyword to get extremely specific about what a given type parameter must look like.

Using this keyword, you can add a set of constraints to a given type parameter, which the C# compiler will check at compile time. Specifically, you can constrain a type parameter as described in Table 9-8.

Table 9-8. *Possible Constraints for Generic Type Parameters*

Generic Constraint	Meaning in Life
where T : struct	The type parameter <T> must have System.ValueType in its chain of inheritance (i.e., <T> must be a structure).
where T : class	The type parameter <T> must not have System.ValueType in its chain of inheritance (i.e., <T> must be a reference type).
where T : new()	The type parameter <T> must have a default constructor. This is helpful if your generic type must create an instance of the type parameter because you cannot assume you know the format of custom constructors. Note that this constraint must be listed last on a multiconstrained type.
where T : NameOfBaseClass	The type parameter <T> must be derived from the class specified by NameOfBaseClass.
where T : NameOfInterface	The type parameter <T> must implement the interface specified by NameOfInterface. You can separate multiple interfaces as a comma-delimited list.

Unless you need to build some extremely type-safe custom collections, you might never need to use the where keyword in your C# projects. Regardless, the following handful of (partial) code examples illustrate how to work with the where keyword.

Examples Using the where Keyword

Begin by assuming that you have created a custom generic class, and you want to ensure that the type parameter has a default constructor. This could be useful when the custom generic class needs to create instances of the T because the default constructor is the only constructor that is potentially common to all types. Also, constraining T in this way lets you get compile-time checking; if T is a reference type, the programmer remembered to redefine the default in the class definition (you might recall that the default constructor is removed in classes when you define your own).

```
// MyGenericClass derives from object, while
// contained items must have a default ctor.
public class MyGenericClass<T> where T : new()
{
  ...
}
```

Notice that the where clause specifies which type parameter is being constrained, followed by a colon operator. After the colon operator, you list each possible constraint (in this case, a default constructor). Here is another example:

```
// MyGenericClass derives from object, while
// contained items must be a class implementing IDrawable
// and must support a default ctor.
public class MyGenericClass<T> where T : class, IDrawable, new()
{
  ...
}
```

In this case, T has three requirements. It must be a reference type (not a structure), as marked with the class token. Second, T must implement the IDrawable interface. Third, it must also have a default constructor. Multiple constraints are listed in a comma-delimited list; however, you should be aware that the new() constraint must always be listed last! Thus, the following code will not compile:

```
// Error! new() constraint must be listed last!
public class MyGenericClass<T> where T : new(), class, IDrawable
{
  ...
}
```

If you ever create a custom generic collection class that specifies multiple type parameters, you can specify a unique set of constraints for each, using separate where clauses.

```
// <K> must extend SomeBaseClass and have a default ctor,
// while <T> must be a structure and implement the
// generic IComparable interface.
public class MyGenericClass<K, T> where K : SomeBaseClass, new()
  where T : struct, IComparable<T>
{
  ...
}
```

You will rarely encounter cases where you need to build a complete custom generic collection class; however, you can use the where keyword on generic methods, as well. For example, if you want to specify that your generic Swap<T>() method can operate only on structures, you would update the method like this:

```
// This method will swap any structure, but not classes.
static void Swap<T>(ref T a, ref T b) where T : struct
{
  ...
}
```

Note that if you were to constrain the Swap() method in this manner, you would no longer be able to swap string objects (as is shown in the sample code) because string is a reference type.

The Lack of Operator Constraints

I want to make one more comment about generic methods and constraints as this chapter draws to a close. It might come as a surprise to you to find out that when creating generic methods, you will get a compiler error if you apply any C# operators (+, -, *, ==, etc.) on the type parameters. For example, imagine the usefulness of a class that can add, subtract, multiply, and divide generic types.

```
// Compiler error! Cannot apply
// operators to type parameters!
public class BasicMath<T>
{
  public T Add(T arg1, T arg2)
  { return arg1 + arg2; }
  public T Subtract(T arg1, T arg2)
  { return arg1 - arg2; }
  public T Multiply(T arg1, T arg2)
  { return arg1 * arg2; }
  public T Divide(T arg1, T arg2)
  { return arg1 / arg2; }
}
```

Unfortunately, the preceding BasicMath class will not compile. While this might seem like a major restriction, you need to remember that generics are generic. Of course, the numerical data can work just fine with the binary operators of C#. However, for the sake of argument, if <T> were a custom class or structure type, the compiler could assume the class supports the +, -, *, and / operators. Ideally, C# would allow a generic type to be constrained by supported operators, as in this example:

```
// Illustrative code only!
public class BasicMath<T> where T : operator +, operator -,
  operator *, operator /
{
  public T Add(T arg1, T arg2)
  { return arg1 + arg2; }
  public T Subtract(T arg1, T arg2)
  { return arg1 - arg2; }
  public T Multiply(T arg1, T arg2)
  { return arg1 * arg2; }
  public T Divide(T arg1, T arg2)
  { return arg1 / arg2; }
}
```

Alas, operator constraints are not supported under the current version of C#. However, it is possible (albeit it requires a bit more work) to achieve the desired effect by defining an interface that supports these operators (C# interfaces can define operators!) and then specifying an interface constraint of the generic class. In any case, this wraps up this book's initial look at building custom generic types. In Chapter 10, I will pick up the topic of generics once again in the course of examining the .NET delegate type.

Summary

This chapter began by examining the nongeneric collection types of System.Collections and System. Collections.Specialized, including the various issues associated with many nongeneric containers, including a lack of type safety and the runtime overhead of boxing and unboxing operations. As mentioned, for these very reasons, modern-day .NET programs will typically make use of the generic collection classes found in System.Collections.Generic and System.Collections.ObjectModel.

As you have seen, a generic item allows you to specify placeholders (type parameters) that you specify at the time of object creation (or invocation, in the case of generic methods). While you will most often simply use the generic types provided in the .NET base class libraries, you will also be able to create your own generic types (and generic methods). When you do so, you have the option of specifying any number of constraints (using the where keyword) to increase the level of type safety and ensure that you perform operations on types of a *known quantity* that are guaranteed to exhibit certain basic capabilities.

As a final note, remember that generics are found in numerous locations within the .NET base class libraries. Here, you focused specifically on generic collections. However, as you work through the remainder of this book (and when you dive into the platform on your own terms), you will certainly find generic classes, structures, and delegates located in a given namespace. As well, be on the lookout for generic members of a nongeneric class!

■ ■ ■

CHAPTER 10

Delegates, Events, and Lambda Expressions

Up to this point in the text, most of the applications you have developed added various bits of code to Main(), which, in some way or another, sent requests *to* a given object. However, many applications require that an object be able to communicate *back to* the entity that created it using a callback mechanism. While callback mechanisms can be used in any application, they are especially critical for graphical user interfaces in that controls (such as a button) need to invoke external methods under the correct circumstances (when the button is clicked, when the mouse enters the button surface, and so forth).

Under the .NET platform, the *delegate* type is the preferred means of defining and responding to callbacks within applications. Essentially, the .NET delegate type is a type-safe object that "points to" a method or a list of methods that can be invoked at a later time. Unlike a traditional C++ function pointer, however, .NET delegates are classes that have built-in support for multicasting and asynchronous method invocation.

In this chapter, you will learn how to create and manipulate delegate types, and then you'll investigate the C# event keyword, which streamlines the process of working with delegate types. Along the way, you will also examine several delegate- and event-centric language features of C#, including anonymous methods and method group conversions.

I wrap up this chapter by examining *lambda expressions*. Using the C# lambda operator (=>), you can specify a block of code statements (and the parameters to pass to those code statements) wherever a strongly typed delegate is required. As you will see, a lambda expression is little more than an anonymous method in disguise and provides a simplified approach to working with delegates. In addition, this same operation (as of .NET 4.6) can be used to implement a single-statement method or property using a concise syntax.

Understanding the .NET Delegate Type

Before formally defining .NET delegates, let's gain a bit of perspective. Historically, the Windows API made frequent use of C-style function pointers to create entities termed *callback functions,* or simply *callbacks*. Using callbacks, programmers were able to configure one function to report back to (call back) another function in the application. With this approach, Windows developers were able to handle button clicking, mouse moving, menu selecting, and general bidirectional communications between two entities in memory.

In the .NET Framework, callbacks are accomplished in a type-safe and object-oriented manner using *delegates*. In essence, a delegate is a type-safe object that points to another method (or possibly a list of methods)

© Andrew Troelsen and Philip Japikse 2017
A. Troelsen and P. Japikse, *Pro C# 7*, https://doi.org/10.1007/978-1-4842-3018-3_10

in the application, which can be invoked at a later time. Specifically, a delegate maintains three important pieces of information.

- The *address* of the method on which it makes calls

- The *parameters* (if any) of this method

- The *return type* (if any) of this method

■ **Note**   .NET delegates can point to either static or instance methods.

After a delegate object has been created and given the necessary information, it may dynamically invoke the method(s) it points to at runtime. Every delegate in the .NET Framework (including your custom delegates) is automatically endowed with the ability to call its methods *synchronously* or *asynchronously*. This fact greatly simplifies programming tasks, given that you can call a method on a secondary thread of execution without manually creating and managing a Thread object.

■ **Note**   You will examine the asynchronous behavior of delegate types during your investigation of threading and asynchronous calls in Chapter 19. In this chapter, you are concerned only with the synchronous aspects of the delegate type.

Defining a Delegate Type in C#

When you want to create a delegate type in C#, you use the delegate keyword. The name of your delegate type can be whatever you desire. However, you must define the delegate to match the signature of the method(s) it will point to. For example, the following delegate type (named BinaryOp) can point to any method that returns an integer and takes two integers as input parameters (you will build and use this delegate yourself a bit later in this chapter, so hang tight for now):

```
// This delegate can point to any method,
// taking two integers and returning an integer.
public delegate int BinaryOp(int x, int y);
```

When the C# compiler processes delegate types, it automatically generates a sealed class deriving from System.MulticastDelegate. This class (in conjunction with its base class, System.Delegate) provides the necessary infrastructure for the delegate to hold onto a list of methods to be invoked at a later time. For example, if you were to examine the BinaryOp delegate using ildasm.exe, you would find the class shown in Figure 10-1 (you will build this full example in just a moment if you want to check for yourself).

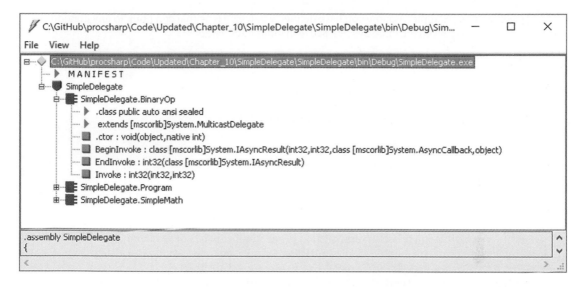

Figure 10-1. *The C# delegate keyword represents a sealed class deriving from* `System.MulticastDelegate`

As you can see, the compiler-generated `BinaryOp` class defines three public methods. `Invoke()` is perhaps the key method, as it is used to invoke each method maintained by the delegate object in a *synchronous* manner, meaning the caller must wait for the call to complete before continuing on its way. Strangely enough, the synchronous `Invoke()` method may not need to be called explicitly from your C# code. As you will see in just a bit, `Invoke()` is called behind the scenes when you use the appropriate C# syntax.

`BeginInvoke()` and `EndInvoke()` provide the ability to call the current method *asynchronously* on a separate thread of execution. If you have a background in multithreading, you know that one of the most common reasons developers create secondary threads of execution is to invoke methods that require time to complete. Although the .NET base class libraries supply several namespaces devoted to multithreaded and parallel programming, delegates provide this functionality out of the box.

Now, how exactly does the compiler know how to define the `Invoke()`, `BeginInvoke()`, and `EndInvoke()` methods? To understand the process, here is the crux of the compiler-generated `BinaryOp` class type (bold italic marks the items specified by the defined delegate type):

```
sealed class BinaryOp : System.MulticastDelegate
{
  public int Invoke(int x, int y);
  public IAsyncResult BeginInvoke(int x, int y,
    AsyncCallback cb, object state);
  public int EndInvoke(IAsyncResult result);
}
```

First, notice that the parameters and return type defined for the `Invoke()` method exactly match the definition of the `BinaryOp` delegate. The initial parameters to `BeginInvoke()` members (two integers, in this case) are also based on the `BinaryOp` delegate; however, `BeginInvoke()` will always provide two final parameters (of type `AsyncCallback` and `object`) that are used to facilitate asynchronous method invocations. Finally, the return type of `EndInvoke()` is identical to the original delegate declaration and will always take as a sole parameter an object implementing the `IAsyncResult` interface.

Let's see another example. Assume you have defined a delegate type that can point to any method returning a string and receiving three System.Boolean input parameters.

```
public delegate string MyDelegate (bool a, bool b, bool c);
```

This time, the compiler-generated class breaks down as follows:

```
sealed class MyDelegate : System.MulticastDelegate
{
  public string Invoke(bool a, bool b, bool c);
  public IAsyncResult BeginInvoke(bool a, bool b, bool c,
    AsyncCallback cb, object state);
  public string EndInvoke(IAsyncResult result);
}
```

Delegates can also "point to" methods that contain any number of out or ref parameters (as well as array parameters marked with the params keyword). For example, assume the following delegate type:

```
public delegate string MyOtherDelegate(out bool a, ref bool b, int c);
```

The signatures of the Invoke() and BeginInvoke() methods look as you would expect; however, check out the following EndInvoke() method, which now includes the set of all out/ref arguments defined by the delegate type:

```
public sealed class MyOtherDelegate : System.MulticastDelegate
{
  public string Invoke(out bool a, ref bool b, int c);
  public IAsyncResult BeginInvoke(out bool a, ref bool b, int c,
    AsyncCallback cb, object state);
  public string EndInvoke(out bool a, ref bool b, IAsyncResult result);
}
```

To summarize, a C# delegate type definition results in a sealed class with three compiler-generated methods whose parameter and return types are based on the delegate's declaration. The following pseudocode approximates the basic pattern:

```
// This is only pseudo-code!
public sealed class DelegateName : System.MulticastDelegate
{
  public delegateReturnValue Invoke(allDelegateInputRefAndOutParams);

  public IAsyncResult BeginInvoke(allDelegateInputRefAndOutParams,
    AsyncCallback cb, object state);

  public delegateReturnValue EndInvoke(allDelegateRefAndOutParams,
    IAsyncResult result);
}
```

The System.MulticastDelegate and System.Delegate Base Classes

So, when you build a type using the C# delegate keyword, you are indirectly declaring a class type that derives from System.MulticastDelegate. This class provides descendants with access to a list that contains the addresses of the methods maintained by the delegate object, as well as several additional methods (and a few overloaded operators) to interact with the invocation list. Here are some select members of System.MulticastDelegate:

```
public abstract class MulticastDelegate : Delegate
{
  // Returns the list of methods "pointed to."
  public sealed override Delegate[] GetInvocationList();

  // Overloaded operators.
  public static bool operator ==(MulticastDelegate d1, MulticastDelegate d2);
  public static bool operator !=(MulticastDelegate d1, MulticastDelegate d2);

  // Used internally to manage the list of methods maintained by the delegate.
  private IntPtr _invocationCount;
  private object _invocationList;
}
```

System.MulticastDelegate obtains additional functionality from its parent class, System.Delegate. Here is a partial snapshot of the class definition:

```
public abstract class Delegate : ICloneable, ISerializable
{
  // Methods to interact with the list of functions.
  public static Delegate Combine(params Delegate[] delegates);
  public static Delegate Combine(Delegate a, Delegate b);
  public static Delegate Remove(Delegate source, Delegate value);
  public static Delegate RemoveAll(Delegate source, Delegate value);

  // Overloaded operators.
  public static bool operator ==(Delegate d1, Delegate d2);
  public static bool operator !=(Delegate d1, Delegate d2);

  // Properties that expose the delegate target.
  public MethodInfo Method { get; }
  public object Target { get; }
}
```

Now, understand that you can never directly derive from these base classes in your code (it is a compiler error to do so). Nevertheless, when you use the delegate keyword, you have indirectly created a class that "is-a" MulticastDelegate. Table 10-1 documents the core members common to all delegate types.

Table 10-1. *Select Members of* System.MulticastDelegate/System.Delegate

Member	Meaning in Life
Method	This property returns a System.Reflection.MethodInfo object that represents details of a static method maintained by the delegate.
Target	If the method to be called is defined at the object level (rather than a static method), Target returns an object that represents the method maintained by the delegate. If the value returned from Target equals null, the method to be called is a static member.
Combine()	This static method adds a method to the list maintained by the delegate. In C#, you trigger this method using the overloaded += operator as a shorthand notation.
GetInvocationList()	This method returns an array of System.Delegate objects, each representing a particular method that may be invoked.
Remove() RemoveAll()	These static methods remove a method (or all methods) from the delegate's invocation list. In C#, the Remove() method can be called indirectly using the overloaded -= operator.

The Simplest Possible Delegate Example

To be sure, delegates can cause some confusion when encountered for the first time. Thus, to get the ball rolling, let's take a look at a simple console application program (named SimpleDelegate) that makes use of the BinaryOp delegate type you've seen previously. Here is the complete code, with analysis to follow:

```
namespace SimpleDelegate
{
  // This delegate can point to any method,
  // taking two integers and returning an integer.
  public delegate int BinaryOp(int x, int y);

  // This class contains methods BinaryOp will
  // point to.
  public class SimpleMath
  {
    public static int Add(int x, int y) => x + y;
    public static int Subtract(int x, int y) => x - y;
  }

  class Program
  {
    static void Main(string[] args)
    {
      Console.WriteLine("***** Simple Delegate Example *****\n");

      // Create a BinaryOp delegate object that
      // "points to" SimpleMath.Add().
      BinaryOp b = new BinaryOp(SimpleMath.Add);
```

```
    // Invoke Add() method indirectly using delegate object.
    Console.WriteLine("10 + 10 is {0}", b(10, 10));
    Console.ReadLine();
  }
 }
}
```

Again, notice the format of the BinaryOp delegate type declaration; it specifies that BinaryOp delegate objects can point to any method taking two integers and returning an integer (the actual name of the method pointed to is irrelevant). Here, you have created a class named SimpleMath, which defines two static methods that match the pattern defined by the BinaryOp delegate.

When you want to assign the target method to a given delegate object, simply pass in the name of the method to the delegate's constructor.

```
// Create a BinaryOp delegate object that
// "points to" SimpleMath.Add().
BinaryOp b = new BinaryOp(SimpleMath.Add);
```

At this point, you are able to invoke the member pointed to using a syntax that looks like a direct function invocation.

```
// Invoke() is really called here!
Console.WriteLine("10 + 10 is {0}", b(10, 10));
```

Under the hood, the runtime actually calls the compiler-generated Invoke() method on your MulticastDelegate-derived class. You can verify this for yourself if you open your assembly in ildasm.exe and examine the CIL code within the Main() method.

```
.method private hidebysig static void Main(string[] args) cil managed
{
...
  callvirt instance int32 SimpleDelegate.BinaryOp::Invoke(int32, int32)
}
```

C# does not require you to explicitly call Invoke() within your codebase. Because BinaryOp can point to methods that take two arguments, the following code statement is also permissible:

```
Console.WriteLine("10 + 10 is {0}", b.Invoke(10, 10));
```

Recall that .NET delegates are *type-safe*. Therefore, if you attempt to create a delegate object pointing to a method that does not match the pattern, you receive a compile-time error. To illustrate, assume the SimpleMath class now defines an additional method named SquareNumber(), which takes a single integer as input.

```
public class SimpleMath
{
  public static int SquareNumber(int a) => a * a;
}
```

Given that the `BinaryOp` delegate can point *only* to methods that take two integers and return an integer, the following code is illegal and will not compile:

```
// Compiler error! Method does not match delegate pattern!
BinaryOp b2 = new BinaryOp(SimpleMath.SquareNumber);
```

Investigating a Delegate Object

Let's spice up the current example by creating a static method (named `DisplayDelegateInfo()`) within the `Program` class. This method will print out the names of the methods maintained by a delegate object, as well as the name of the class defining the method. To do this, you will iterate over the `System.Delegate` array returned by `GetInvocationList()`, invoking each object's `Target` and `Method` properties.

```
static void DisplayDelegateInfo(Delegate delObj)
{
  // Print the names of each member in the
  // delegate's invocation list.
  foreach (Delegate d in delObj.GetInvocationList())
  {
    Console.WriteLine("Method Name: {0}", d.Method);
    Console.WriteLine("Type Name: {0}", d.Target);
  }
}
```

Assuming you have updated your `Main()` method to actually call this new helper method, as shown here:

```
BinaryOp b = new BinaryOp(SimpleMath.Add);
DisplayDelegateInfo(b);
```

you would find the output shown next:

```
***** Simple Delegate Example *****

Method Name: Int32 Add(Int32, Int32)
Type Name:
10 + 10 is 20
```

Notice that the name of the target class (`SimpleMath`) is currently *not* displayed when calling the `Target` property. The reason has to do with the fact that your `BinaryOp` delegate is pointing to a *static method* and, therefore, there is no object to reference! However, if you update the `Add()` and `Subtract()` methods to be nonstatic (simply by deleting the `static` keywords), you could create an instance of the `SimpleMath` class and specify the methods to invoke using the object reference.

```
static void Main(string[] args)
{
  Console.WriteLine("***** Simple Delegate Example *****\n");

  // .NET delegates can also point to instance methods as well.
  SimpleMath m = new SimpleMath();
  BinaryOp b = new BinaryOp(m.Add);
```

```
    // Show information about this object.
    DisplayDelegateInfo(b);

    Console.WriteLine("10 + 10 is {0}", b(10, 10));
    Console.ReadLine();
}
```

In this case, you would find the output shown here:

```
***** Simple Delegate Example *****

Method Name: Int32 Add(Int32, Int32)
Type Name: SimpleDelegate.SimpleMath
10 + 10 is 20
```

■ **Source Code**   You can find the SimpleDelegate project in the Chapter 10 subdirectory.

Sending Object State Notifications Using Delegates

Clearly, the previous SimpleDelegate example was intended to be purely illustrative in nature, given that there would be no compelling reason to define a delegate simply to add two numbers. To provide a more realistic use of delegate types, let's use delegates to define a Car class that has the ability to inform external entities about its current engine state. To do so, you will take the following steps:

1. Define a new delegate type that will be used to send notifications to the caller.

2. Declare a member variable of this delegate in the Car class.

3. Create a helper function on the Car that allows the caller to specify the method to call back on.

4. Implement the Accelerate() method to invoke the delegate's invocation list under the correct circumstances.

To begin, create a new Console Application project named CarDelegate. Now, define a new Car class that looks initially like this:

```
public class Car
{
    // Internal state data.
    public int CurrentSpeed { get; set; }
    public int MaxSpeed { get; set; } = 100;
    public string PetName { get; set; }

    // Is the car alive or dead?
    private bool carIsDead;

    // Class constructors.
    public Car() {}
```

```
  public Car(string name, int maxSp, int currSp)
  {
    CurrentSpeed = currSp;
    MaxSpeed = maxSp;
    PetName = name;
  }
}
```

Now, consider the following updates, which address the first three points:

```
public class Car
{
  ...
  // 1) Define a delegate type.
  public delegate void CarEngineHandler(string msgForCaller);

  // 2) Define a member variable of this delegate.
  private CarEngineHandler listOfHandlers;

  // 3) Add registration function for the caller.
  public void RegisterWithCarEngine(CarEngineHandler methodToCall)
  {
    listOfHandlers = methodToCall;
  }
}
```

Notice in this example that you define the delegate types directly within the scope of the Car class, which is certainly not necessary but does help enforce the idea that the delegate works naturally with this particular class. The delegate type, CarEngineHandler, can point to any method taking a single string as input and void as a return value.

Next, note that you declare a private member variable of your delegate type (named listOfHandlers) and a helper function (named RegisterWithCarEngine()) that allows the caller to assign a method to the delegate's invocation list.

■ **Note**   Strictly speaking, you could have defined your delegate member variable as public, therefore avoiding the need to create additional registration methods. However, by defining the delegate member variable as private, you are enforcing encapsulation services and providing a more type-safe solution. You'll revisit the risk of public delegate member variables later in this chapter when you look at the C# event keyword.

At this point, you need to create the Accelerate() method. Recall, the point here is to allow a Car object to send engine-related messages to any subscribed listener. Here is the update:

```
// 4) Implement the Accelerate() method to invoke the delegate's
//    invocation list under the correct circumstances.
public void Accelerate(int delta)
{
  // If this car is "dead," send dead message.
  if (carIsDead)
```

```
  {
    if (listOfHandlers != null)
      listOfHandlers("Sorry, this car is dead...");
  }
  else
  {
    CurrentSpeed += delta;

    // Is this car "almost dead"?
    if (10 == (MaxSpeed - CurrentSpeed) && listOfHandlers != null)
    {
      listOfHandlers("Careful buddy! Gonna blow!");
    }
    if (CurrentSpeed >= MaxSpeed)
      carIsDead = true;
    else
      Console.WriteLine("CurrentSpeed = {0}", CurrentSpeed);
  }
}
```

Notice that before you invoke the methods maintained by the listOfHandlers member variable, you are checking it against a null value. The reason is that it will be the job of the caller to allocate these objects by calling the RegisterWithCarEngine() helper method. If the caller does not call this method and you attempt to invoke the delegate's invocation list, you will trigger a NullReferenceException at runtime. Now that you have the delegate infrastructure in place, observe the updates to the Program class:

```
class Program
{
  static void Main(string[] args)
  {
    Console.WriteLine("***** Delegates as event enablers *****\n");

    // First, make a Car object.
    Car c1 = new Car("SlugBug", 100, 10);

    // Now, tell the car which method to call
    // when it wants to send us messages.
    c1.RegisterWithCarEngine(new Car.CarEngineHandler(OnCarEngineEvent));

    // Speed up (this will trigger the events).
    Console.WriteLine("***** Speeding up *****");
    for (int i = 0; i < 6; i++)
      c1.Accelerate(20);
    Console.ReadLine();
  }
```

```
// This is the target for incoming events.
public static void OnCarEngineEvent(string msg)
{
  Console.WriteLine("\n***** Message From Car Object *****");
  Console.WriteLine("=> {0}", msg);
  Console.WriteLine("*********************************\n");
  }
}
```

The Main() method begins by simply making a new Car object. Since you are interested in hearing about the engine events, the next step is to call your custom registration function, RegisterWithCarEngine(). Recall that this method expects to be passed an instance of the nested CarEngineHandler delegate, and as with any delegate, you specify a "method to point to" as a constructor parameter. The trick in this example is that the method in question is located back in the Program class! Again, notice that the OnCarEngineEvent() method is a dead-on match to the related delegate in that it takes a string as input and returns void. Consider the output of the current example:

```
***** Delegates as event enablers *****
***** Speeding up *****
CurrentSpeed = 30
CurrentSpeed = 50
CurrentSpeed = 70

***** Message From Car Object *****
=> Careful buddy! Gonna blow!
*********************************
CurrentSpeed = 90
***** Message From Car Object *****
=> Sorry, this car is dead...
*********************************
```

Enabling Multicasting

Recall that .NET delegates have the built-in ability to *multicast*. In other words, a delegate object can maintain a list of methods to call, rather than just a single method. When you want to add multiple methods to a delegate object, you simply use the overloaded += operator, rather than a direct assignment. To enable multicasting on the Car class, you could update the RegisterWithCarEngine()method, like so:

```
public class Car
{
  // Now with multicasting support!
  // Note we are now using the += operator, not
  // the assignment operator (=).
  public void RegisterWithCarEngine(CarEngineHandler methodToCall)
  {
    listOfHandlers += methodToCall;
  }
...
}
```

When you use the += operator on a delegate object, the compiler resolves this to a call on the static Delegate.Combine() method. In fact, you could call Delegate.Combine() directly; however, the += operator offers a simpler alternative. There is no need to modify your current RegisterWithCarEngine() method, but here is an example if using Delegate.Combine() rather than the += operator:

```
public void RegisterWithCarEngine( CarEngineHandler methodToCall )
{
  if (listOfHandlers == null)
    listOfHandlers = methodToCall;
  else
    listOfHandlers = Delegate.Combine(listOfHandlers, methodToCall) as CarEngineHandler;
}
```

In any case, the caller can now register multiple targets for the same callback notification. Here, the second handler prints the incoming message in uppercase, just for display purposes:

```
class Program
{
  static void Main(string[] args)
  {
    Console.WriteLine("***** Delegates as event enablers *****\n");

    // First, make a Car object.
    Car c1 = new Car("SlugBug", 100, 10);

    // Register multiple targets for the notifications.
    c1.RegisterWithCarEngine(new Car.CarEngineHandler(OnCarEngineEvent));
    c1.RegisterWithCarEngine(new Car.CarEngineHandler(OnCarEngineEvent2));

    // Speed up (this will trigger the events).
    Console.WriteLine("***** Speeding up *****");
    for (int i = 0; i < 6; i++)
      c1.Accelerate(20);
    Console.ReadLine();
  }
  // We now have TWO methods that will be called by the Car
  // when sending notifications.
  public static void OnCarEngineEvent(string msg)
  {
    Console.WriteLine("\n***** Message From Car Object *****");
    Console.WriteLine("=> {0}", msg);
    Console.WriteLine("*********************************\n");
  }

  public static void OnCarEngineEvent2(string msg)
  {
    Console.WriteLine("=> {0}", msg.ToUpper());
  }
}
```

Removing Targets from a Delegate's Invocation List

The Delegate class also defines a static Remove() method that allows a caller to dynamically remove a method from a delegate object's invocation list. This makes it simple to allow the caller to "unsubscribe" from a given notification at runtime. While you could call Delegate.Remove() directly in code, C# developers can use the -= operator as a convenient shorthand notation. Let's add a new method to the Car class that allows a caller to remove a method from the invocation list.

```
public class Car
{
...
  public void UnRegisterWithCarEngine(CarEngineHandler methodToCall)
  {
    listOfHandlers -= methodToCall;
  }
}
```

With the current updates to the Car class, you could stop receiving the engine notification on the second handler by updating Main() as follows:

```
static void Main(string[] args)
{
  Console.WriteLine("***** Delegates as event enablers *****\n");

  // First, make a Car object.
  Car c1 = new Car("SlugBug", 100, 10);
  c1.RegisterWithCarEngine(new Car.CarEngineHandler(OnCarEngineEvent));

  // This time, hold onto the delegate object,
  // so we can unregister later.
  Car.CarEngineHandler handler2 = new Car.CarEngineHandler(OnCarEngineEvent2);
  c1.RegisterWithCarEngine(handler2);

  // Speed up (this will trigger the events).
  Console.WriteLine("***** Speeding up *****");
  for (int i = 0; i < 6; i++)
    c1.Accelerate(20);

  // Unregister from the second handler.
  c1.UnRegisterWithCarEngine(handler2);

  // We won't see the "uppercase" message anymore!
  Console.WriteLine("***** Speeding up *****");
  for (int i = 0; i < 6; i++)
    c1.Accelerate(20);

  Console.ReadLine();
}
```

378

One difference in Main() is that this time you are creating a Car.CarEngineHandler object and storing it in a local variable so you can use this object to unregister with the notification later. Thus, the second time you speed up the Car object, you no longer see the uppercase version of the incoming message data, as you have removed this target from the delegate's invocation list.

■ **Source Code**   You can find the CarDelegate project in the Chapter 10 subdirectory.

Method Group Conversion Syntax

In the previous CarDelegate example, you explicitly created instances of the Car.CarEngineHandler delegate object to register and unregister with the engine notifications.

```
static void Main(string[] args)
{
  Console.WriteLine("***** Delegates as event enablers *****\n");

  Car c1 = new Car("SlugBug", 100, 10);
  c1.RegisterWithCarEngine(new Car.CarEngineHandler(OnCarEngineEvent));

  Car.CarEngineHandler handler2 =
    new Car.CarEngineHandler(OnCarEngineEvent2);
  c1.RegisterWithCarEngine(handler2);
...
}
```

To be sure, if you need to call any of the inherited members of MulticastDelegate or Delegate, manually creating a delegate variable is the most straightforward way of doing so. However, in most cases, you don't really need to hang onto the delegate object. Rather, you typically need to use the delegate object only to pass in the method name as a constructor parameter.

As a simplification, C# provides a shortcut termed *method group conversion*. This feature allows you to supply a direct method name, rather than a delegate object, when calling methods that take delegates as arguments.

■ **Note**   As you will see later in this chapter, you can also use method group conversion syntax to simplify how you register with a C# event.

To illustrate, create a new Console Application project named CarDelegateMethodGroupConversion and insert the file containing the Car class you defined in the CarDelegate project (and update the namespace name in the Car.cs file to match your new namespace name). Now, consider the following Program class, which uses method group conversion to register and unregister from the engine notifications:

```
class Program
{
  static void Main(string[] args)
  {
    Console.WriteLine("***** Method Group Conversion *****\n");
    Car c1 = new Car();
```

```
  // Register the simple method name.
  c1.RegisterWithCarEngine(CallMeHere);

  Console.WriteLine("***** Speeding up *****");
  for (int i = 0; i < 6; i++)
    c1.Accelerate(20);

  // Unregister the simple method name.
  c1.UnRegisterWithCarEngine(CallMeHere);

  // No more notifications!
  for (int i = 0; i < 6; i++)
    c1.Accelerate(20);

  Console.ReadLine();
}

static void CallMeHere(string msg)
{
  Console.WriteLine("=> Message from Car: {0}", msg);
}
}
```

Notice that you are not directly allocating the associated delegate object but rather simply specifying a method that matches the delegate's expected signature (a method returning void and taking a single string, in this case). Understand that the C# compiler is still ensuring type safety. Thus, if the CallMeHere() method did not take a string and return void, you would be issued a compiler error.

■ **Source Code**   You can find the CarDelegateMethodGroupConversion project in the Chapter 10 subdirectory.

Understanding Generic Delegates

In the previous chapter, I mentioned that C# allows you to define generic delegate types. For example, assume you want to define a delegate type that can call any method returning void and receiving a single parameter. If the argument in question may differ, you could model this using a type parameter. To illustrate, consider the following code within a new Console Application project named GenericDelegate:

```
namespace GenericDelegate
{
  // This generic delegate can represnet any method
  // returning void and taking a single parameter of type T.
  public delegate void MyGenericDelegate<T>(T arg);

  class Program
  {
    static void Main(string[] args)
```

```
  {
    Console.WriteLine("***** Generic Delegates *****\n");

    // Register targets.
    MyGenericDelegate<string> strTarget = new MyGenericDelegate<string>(StringTarget);
    strTarget("Some string data");

    MyGenericDelegate<int> intTarget = new MyGenericDelegate<int>(IntTarget);
    intTarget(9);
    Console.ReadLine();
  }

  static void StringTarget(string arg)
  {
    Console.WriteLine("arg in uppercase is: {0}", arg.ToUpper());
  }

  static void IntTarget(int arg)
  {
    Console.WriteLine("++arg is: {0}", ++arg);
  }
  }
}
```

Notice that MyGenericDelegate<T> defines a single type parameter that represents the argument to pass to the delegate target. When creating an instance of this type, you are required to specify the value of the type parameter, as well as the name of the method the delegate will invoke. Thus, if you specified a string type, you send a string value to the target method.

```
// Create an instance of MyGenericDelegate<T>
// with string as the type parameter.
MyGenericDelegate<string> strTarget = new MyGenericDelegate<string>(StringTarget);
strTarget("Some string data");
```

Given the format of the strTarget object, the StringTarget() method must now take a single string as a parameter.

```
static void StringTarget(string arg)
{
  Console.WriteLine("arg in uppercase is: {0}", arg.ToUpper());
}
```

■ **Source Code**   You can find the GenericDelegate project in the Chapter 10 subdirectory.

The Generic Action<> and Func<> Delegates

Over the course of this chapter, you have seen that when you want to use delegates to enable callbacks in your applications, you typically follow the steps shown here:

1. Define a custom delegate that matches the format of the method being pointed to.

2. Create an instance of your custom delegate, passing in a method name as a constructor argument.

3. Invoke the method indirectly, via a call to Invoke() on the delegate object.

When you take this approach, you typically end up with a number of custom delegates that might never be used beyond the current task at hand (e.g., MyGenericDelegate<T>, CarEngineHandler, and so forth). While it may certainly be the case that you do indeed need to have a custom, uniquely named delegate type for your project, other times the exact *name* of the delegate type is irrelevant. In many cases, you simply want "some delegate" that takes a set of arguments and possibly has a return value other than void. In these cases, you can use the framework's built-in Action<> and Func<> delegate types. To illustrate their usefulness, create a new Console Application project named ActionAndFuncDelegates.

The generic Action<> delegate is defined in the System namespaces of the mscorlib.dll and System.Core.dll assemblies. You can use this generic delegate to "point to" a method that takes up to *16 arguments* (that ought to be enough!) and returns void. Now recall, because Action<> is a generic delegate, you will need to specify the underlying types of each parameter as well.

Update your Program class to define a new static method that takes three (or so) unique parameters. Here's an example:

```
// This is a target for the Action<> delegate.
static void DisplayMessage(string msg, ConsoleColor txtColor, int printCount)
{
  // Set color of console text.
  ConsoleColor previous = Console.ForegroundColor;
  Console.ForegroundColor = txtColor;

  for (int i = 0; i < printCount; i++)
  {
    Console.WriteLine(msg);
  }

  // Restore color.
  Console.ForegroundColor = previous;
}
```

Now, rather than building a custom delegate manually to pass the program's flow to the DisplayMessage() method, you can use the out-of-the-box Action<> delegate, as so:

```
static void Main(string[] args)
{
  Console.WriteLine("***** Fun with Action and Func *****");
```

```
// Use the Action<> delegate to point to DisplayMessage.
Action<string, ConsoleColor, int> actionTarget = new Action<string, ConsoleColor,
int>(DisplayMessage);
actionTarget("Action Message!", ConsoleColor.Yellow, 5);

    Console.ReadLine();
}
```

As you can see, using the Action<> delegate saves you the bother of defining a custom delegate type. However, recall that the Action<> delegate type can point only to methods that take a void return value. If you want to point to a method that does have a return value (and don't want to bother writing the custom delegate yourself), you can use Func<>.

The generic Func<> delegate can point to methods that (like Action<>) take up to 16 parameters and a custom return value. To illustrate, add the following new method to the Program class:

```
// Target for the Func<> delegate.
static int Add(int x, int y)
{
    return x + y;
}
```

Earlier in the chapter, I had you build a custom BinaryOp delegate to "point to" addition and subtraction methods. However, you can simplify your efforts using a version of Func<> that takes a total of three type parameters. Be aware that the *final* type parameter of Func<> is *always* the return value of the method. Just to solidify that point, assume the Program class also defines the following method:

```
static string SumToString(int x, int y)
{
  return (x + y).ToString();
}
```

Now, the Main() method can call each of these methods, as so:

```
Func<int, int, int> funcTarget = new Func<int, int, int>(Add);
int result = funcTarget.Invoke(40, 40);
Console.WriteLine("40 + 40 = {0}", result);

Func<int, int, string> funcTarget2 = new Func<int, int, string>(SumToString);
string sum = funcTarget2(90, 300);
Console.WriteLine(sum);
```

Also recall that method group conversion syntax would allow you to simplify the previous code to the following:

```
Func<int, int, int> funcTarget = Add;
int result = funcTarget.Invoke(40, 40);
Console.WriteLine("40 + 40 = {0}", result);

Func<int, int, string> funcTarget2 = SumToString;
string sum = funcTarget2(90, 300);
Console.WriteLine(sum);
```

In any case, given that Action<> and Func<> can save you the step of manually defining a custom delegate, you might be wondering if you should use them all the time. The answer, like so many aspects of programming, is "it depends." In many cases, Action<> and Func<> will be the preferred course of action (no pun intended). However, if you need a delegate that has a custom name that you feel helps better capture your problem domain, building a custom delegate is as simple as a single code statement. You'll see both approaches as you work over the remainder of this text.

■ **Note**   Many important .NET APIs make considerable use of Action<> and Func<> delegates, including the parallel programming framework and LINQ (among others).

That wraps up our initial look at the .NET delegate type. You will look at some additional details of working with delegates at the conclusion of this chapter and again in Chapter 19 during your examination of multithreading and asynchronous calls. Next, let's move on to the related topic of the C# event keyword.

■ **Source Code**   You can find the ActionAndFuncDelegates project in the Chapter 10 subdirectory.

Understanding C# Events

Delegates are fairly interesting constructs in that they enable objects in memory to engage in a two-way conversation. However, working with delegates in the raw can entail the creation of some boilerplate code (defining the delegate, declaring necessary member variables, and creating custom registration and unregistration methods to preserve encapsulation, etc.).

Moreover, when you use delegates in the raw as your application's callback mechanism, if you do not define a class's delegate member variables as private, the caller will have direct access to the delegate objects. In this case, the caller could reassign the variable to a new delegate object (effectively deleting the current list of functions to call), and, worse yet, the caller would be able to directly invoke the delegate's invocation list. To illustrate this problem, consider the following reworking (and simplification) of the Car class from the previous CarDelegate example:

```
public class Car
{
  public delegate void CarEngineHandler(string msgForCaller);

  // Now a public member!
  public CarEngineHandler listOfHandlers;

  // Just fire out the Exploded notification.
  public void Accelerate(int delta)
  {
    if (listOfHandlers != null)
      listOfHandlers("Sorry, this car is dead...");
  }
}
```

Notice that you no longer have private delegate member variables encapsulated with custom registration methods. Because these members are indeed public, the caller can directly access the listOfHandlers member variable and reassign this type to new CarEngineHandler objects and invoke the delegate whenever it so chooses.

```
class Program
{
  static void Main(string[] args)
  {
    Console.WriteLine("***** Agh! No Encapsulation! *****\n");
    // Make a Car.
    Car myCar = new Car();
    // We have direct access to the delegate!
    myCar.listOfHandlers = new Car.CarEngineHandler(CallWhenExploded);
    myCar.Accelerate(10);

    // We can now assign to a whole new object...
    // confusing at best.
    myCar.listOfHandlers = new Car.CarEngineHandler(CallHereToo);
    myCar.Accelerate(10);

    // The caller can also directly invoke the delegate!
    myCar.listOfHandlers.Invoke("hee, hee, hee...");
    Console.ReadLine();
  }

  static void CallWhenExploded(string msg)
  { Console.WriteLine(msg); }

  static void CallHereToo(string msg)
  { Console.WriteLine(msg); }
}
```

Exposing public delegate members breaks encapsulation, which not only can lead to code that is hard to maintain (and debug) but could also open your application to possible security risks! Here is the output of the current example:

```
***** Agh! No Encapsulation! *****

Sorry, this car is dead...
Sorry, this car is dead...
hee, hee, hee...
```

Obviously, you would not want to give other applications the power to change what a delegate is pointing to or to invoke the members without your permission. Given this, it is common practice to declare private delegate member variables.

■ **Source Code**   You can find the PublicDelegateProblem project in the Chapter 10 subdirectory.

The C# event Keyword

As a shortcut, so you don't have to build custom methods to add or remove methods to a delegate's invocation list, C# provides the event keyword. When the compiler processes the event keyword, you are automatically provided with registration and unregistration methods, as well as any necessary member variables for your delegate types. These delegate member variables are *always* declared private, and, therefore, they are not directly exposed from the object firing the event. To be sure, the event keyword can be used to simplify how a custom class sends out notifications to external objects.

Defining an event is a two-step process. First, you need to define a delegate type (or reuse an existing one) that will hold the list of methods to be called when the event is fired. Next, you declare an event (using the C# event keyword) in terms of the related delegate type.

To illustrate the event keyword, create a new console application named CarEvents. In this iteration of the Car class, you will define two events named AboutToBlow and Exploded. These events are associated to a single delegate type named CarEngineHandler. Here are the initial updates to the Car class:

```
public class Car
{
  // This delegate works in conjunction with the
  // Car's events.
  public delegate void CarEngineHandler(string msg);

  // This car can send these events.
  public event CarEngineHandler Exploded;
  public event CarEngineHandler AboutToBlow;
  ...
}
```

Sending an event to the caller is as simple as specifying the event by name, along with any required parameters as defined by the associated delegate. To ensure that the caller has indeed registered with the event, you will want to check the event against a null value before invoking the delegate's method set. With these points in mind, here is the new iteration of the Car's Accelerate() method:

```
public void Accelerate(int delta)
{
  // If the car is dead, fire Exploded event.
  if (carIsDead)
  {
    if (Exploded != null)
      Exploded("Sorry, this car is dead...");
  }
  else
  {
    CurrentSpeed += delta;

    // Almost dead?
    if (10 == MaxSpeed - CurrentSpeed
      && AboutToBlow != null)
    {
      AboutToBlow("Careful buddy! Gonna blow!");
    }
```

```
  // Still OK!
  if (CurrentSpeed >= MaxSpeed)
    carIsDead = true;
  else
    Console.WriteLine("CurrentSpeed = {0}", CurrentSpeed);
  }
}
```

With this, you have configured the car to send two custom events without having to define custom registration functions or declare delegate member variables. You will see the usage of this new automobile in just a moment, but first let's check the event architecture in a bit more detail.

Events Under the Hood

When the compiler processes the C# event keyword, it generates two hidden methods, one having an add_ prefix and the other having a remove_ prefix. Each prefix is followed by the name of the C# event. For example, the Exploded event results in two hidden methods named add_Exploded() and remove_Exploded(). If you were to check out the CIL instructions behind add_AboutToBlow(), you would find a call to the Delegate.Combine() method. Consider the partial CIL code:

```
.method public hidebysig specialname instance void
add_AboutToBlow(class CarEvents.Car/CarEngineHandler 'value') cil managed
{
...
  call class [mscorlib]System.Delegate
  [mscorlib]System.Delegate::Combine(
    class [mscorlib]System.Delegate, class [mscorlib]System.Delegate)
...
}
```

As you would expect, remove_AboutToBlow() will call Delegate.Remove() on your behalf.

```
.method public hidebysig specialname instance void
  remove_AboutToBlow(class CarEvents.Car/CarEngineHandler 'value')
  cil managed
{
...
  call class [mscorlib]System.Delegate
    [mscorlib]System.Delegate::Remove(
      class [mscorlib]System.Delegate, class [mscorlib]System.Delegate)
...
}
```

Finally, the CIL code representing the event itself makes use of the .addon and .removeon directives to map the names of the correct add_XXX() and remove_XXX() methods to invoke.

```
.event CarEvents.Car/EngineHandler AboutToBlow
{
  .addon instance void CarEvents.Car::add_AboutToBlow
    (class CarEvents.Car/CarEngineHandler)

  .removeon instance void CarEvents.Car::remove_AboutToBlow
    (class CarEvents.Car/CarEngineHandler)
}
```

Now that you understand how to build a class that can send C# events (and are aware that events are little more than a typing time-saver), the next big question is how to listen to the incoming events on the caller's side.

Listening to Incoming Events

C# events also simplify the act of registering the caller-side event handlers. Rather than having to specify custom helper methods, the caller simply uses the += and -= operators directly (which triggers the correct add_XXX() or remove_XXX() method in the background). When you want to register with an event, follow the pattern shown here:

```
// NameOfObject.NameOfEvent += new RelatedDelegate(functionToCall);
//
Car.CarEngineHandler d = new Car.CarEngineHandler(CarExplodedEventHandler);
myCar.Exploded += d;
```

When you want to detach from a source of events, use the -= operator, using the following pattern:

```
// NameOfObject.NameOfEvent -= new RelatedDelegate(functionToCall);
//
myCar.Exploded -= d;
```

Given these very predictable patterns, here is the refactored Main() method, now using the C# event registration syntax:

```
class Program
{
  static void Main(string[] args)
  {
    Console.WriteLine("***** Fun with Events *****\n");
    Car c1 = new Car("SlugBug", 100, 10);

    // Register event handlers.
    c1.AboutToBlow += new Car.CarEngineHandler(CarIsAlmostDoomed);
    c1.AboutToBlow += new Car.CarEngineHandler(CarAboutToBlow);

    Car.CarEngineHandler d = new Car.CarEngineHandler(CarExploded);
    c1.Exploded += d;

    Console.WriteLine("***** Speeding up *****");
    for (int i = 0; i < 6; i++)
      c1.Accelerate(20);
```

```
    // Remove CarExploded method
    // from invocation list.
    c1.Exploded -= d;

    Console.WriteLine("\n***** Speeding up *****");
    for (int i = 0; i < 6; i++)
      c1.Accelerate(20);
    Console.ReadLine();
  }

  public static void CarAboutToBlow(string msg)
  { Console.WriteLine(msg); }

  public static void CarIsAlmostDoomed(string msg)
  { Console.WriteLine("=> Critical Message from Car: {0}", msg); }

  public static void CarExploded(string msg)
  { Console.WriteLine(msg); }
}
```

To even further simplify event registration, you can use method group conversion. Consider the following iteration of Main():

```
static void Main(string[] args)
{
  Console.WriteLine("***** Fun with Events *****\n");
  Car c1 = new Car("SlugBug", 100, 10);
  // Register event handlers.
  c1.AboutToBlow += CarIsAlmostDoomed;
  c1.AboutToBlow += CarAboutToBlow;
  c1.Exploded += CarExploded;

  Console.WriteLine("***** Speeding up *****");
  for (int i = 0; i < 6; i++)
    c1.Accelerate(20);

  c1.Exploded -= CarExploded;

  Console.WriteLine("\n***** Speeding up *****");
  for (int i = 0; i < 6; i++)
    c1.Accelerate(20);

  Console.ReadLine();
}
```

Simplifying Event Registration Using Visual Studio

Visual Studio offers assistance with the process of registering event handlers. When you apply the += syntax during event registration, you will find an IntelliSense window displayed, inviting you to hit the Tab key to autocomplete the associated delegate instance (see Figure 10-2), which is captured using *method group conversion syntax*.

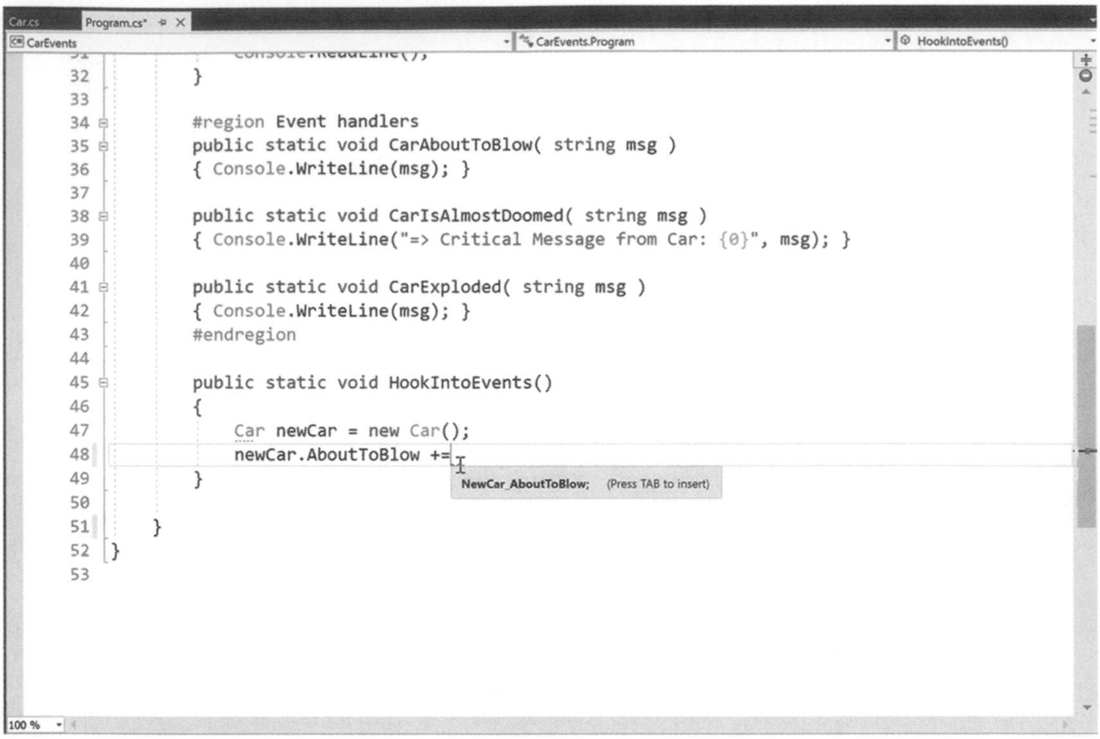

Figure 10-2. *Delegate selection IntelliSense*

After you hit the Tab key, the IDE will generate the new method automatically, as shown in Figure 10-3.

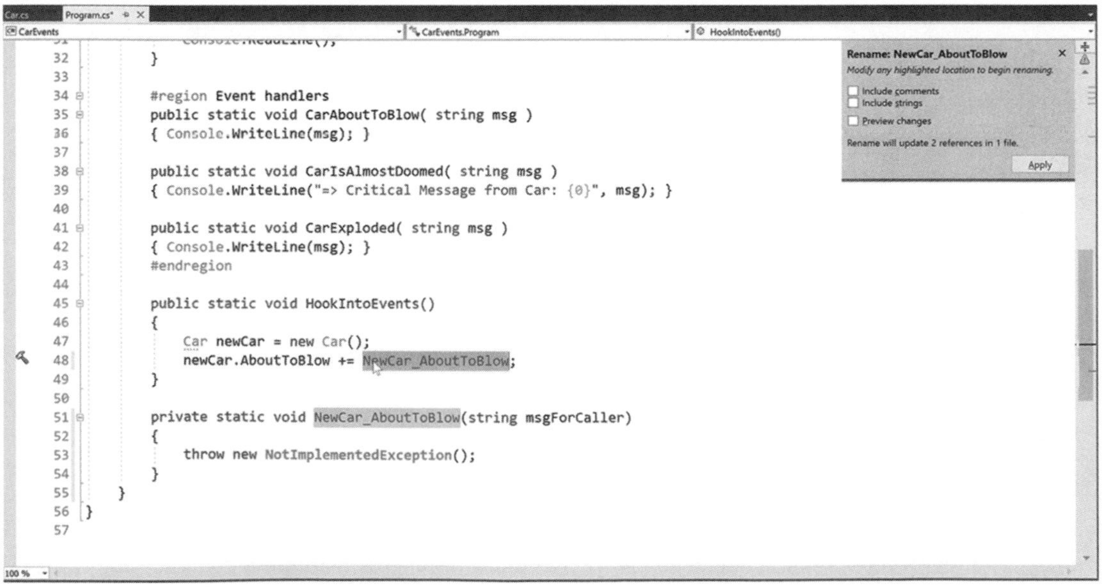

Figure 10-3. *Delegate target format IntelliSense*

Note the stub code is in the correct format of the delegate target (note that this method has been declared static because the event was registered within a static method).

```
static void NewCar_AboutToBlow(string msg)
{
  // Delete the following line and add your code!
  throw new NotImplementedException();
}
```

IntelliSense is available to all .NET events in the base class libraries. This IDE feature is a massive time-saver, given that it saves you from having to search the .NET help system to figure out both the correct delegate to use with a particular event and the format of the delegate target method.

Cleaning Up Event Invocation Using the C# 6.0 Null-Conditional Operator

In the current example, you most likely noticed that before you fired an event to any listener, you made sure to check for null. This is important given that if nobody is listening for your event but you fire it anyway, you will receive a null reference exception at runtime. While important, you might agree it is a bit clunky to make numerous conditional checks against null.

Thankfully, ever since the release of C# 6, you can leverage the null conditional operator (?), which essentially performs this sort of check automatically. Be aware, when using this new simplified syntax, you must manually call the Invoke() method of the underlying delegate. For example, rather than saying this:

```
// If the car is dead, fire Exploded event.
if (carIsDead)
{
    if (Exploded != null)
        Exploded("Sorry, this car is dead...");
}
```

you can now simply say the following:

```
// If the car is dead, fire Exploded event.
if (carIsDead)
{
    Exploded?.Invoke("Sorry, this car is dead...");
}
```

You could also update the code that fires the AboutToBlow event in a similar manner (note here I moved the check for null out of the original if statement):

```
// Almost dead?
if (10 == MaxSpeed - CurrentSpeed)
{
    AboutToBlow?.Invoke("Careful buddy!  Gonna blow!");
}
```

Because of the simplified syntax, you are likely to favor the null conditional operator when firing events. However, it is still perfectly acceptable to manually check for null when necessary.

■ **Source Code**   You can find the CarEvents project in the Chapter 10 subdirectory.

Creating Custom Event Arguments

Truth be told, there is one final enhancement you could make to the current iteration of the Car class that mirrors Microsoft's recommended event pattern. As you begin to explore the events sent by a given type in the base class libraries, you will find that the first parameter of the underlying delegate is a System.Object, while the second parameter is a descendant of System.EventArgs.

The System.Object argument represents a reference to the object that sent the event (such as the Car), while the second parameter represents information regarding the event at hand. The System.EventArgs base class represents an event that is not sending any custom information.

```
public class EventArgs
{
  public static readonly EventArgs Empty;
  public EventArgs();
}
```

For simple events, you can pass an instance of EventArgs directly. However, when you want to pass along custom data, you should build a suitable class deriving from EventArgs. For this example, assume you have a class named CarEventArgs, which maintains a string representing the message sent to the receiver.

```
public class CarEventArgs : EventArgs
{
  public readonly string msg;
  public CarEventArgs(string message)
  {
    msg = message;
  }
}
```

With this, you would now update the CarEngineHandler delegate type definition as follows (the events would be unchanged):

```
public class Car
{
  public delegate void CarEngineHandler(object sender, CarEventArgs e);
...
}
```

Here, when firing the events from within the Accelerate() method, you would now need to supply a reference to the current Car (via the this keyword) and an instance of the CarEventArgs type. For example, consider the following partial update:

```
public void Accelerate(int delta)
{
  // If the car is dead, fire Exploded event.
  if (carIsDead)
```

```
  {
    Exploded?.Invoke(this, new CarEventArgs("Sorry, this car is dead..."));
  }
  ...
}
```

On the caller's side, all you would need to do is update your event handlers to receive the incoming parameters and obtain the message via the read-only field. Here's an example:

```
public static void CarAboutToBlow(object sender, CarEventArgs e)
{
  Console.WriteLine("{0} says: {1}", sender, e.msg);
}
```

If the receiver wants to interact with the object that sent the event, you can explicitly cast the System. Object. From this reference, you can make use of any public member of the object that sent the event notification.

```
public static void CarAboutToBlow(object sender, CarEventArgs e)
{
  // Just to be safe, perform a
  // runtime check before casting.
  if (sender is Car c)
  {
    Console.WriteLine("Critical Message from {0}: {1}", c.PetName, e.msg);
  }
}
```

■ **Source Code**   You can find the CarEventArgs project in the Chapter 10 subdirectory.

The Generic EventHandler<T> Delegate

Given that so many custom delegates take an object as the first parameter and an EventArgs descendant as the second, you could further streamline the previous example by using the generic EventHandler<T> type, where T is your custom EventArgs type. Consider the following update to the Car type (notice how you no longer need to define a custom delegate type at all):

```
public class Car
{
  public event EventHandler<CarEventArgs> Exploded;
  public event EventHandler<CarEventArgs> AboutToBlow;
}
```

The Main() method could then use EventHandler<CarEventArgs> anywhere you previously specified CarEventHandler (or, once again, use method group conversion).

```
static void Main(string[] args)
{
  Console.WriteLine("***** Prim and Proper Events *****\n");

  // Make a car as usual.
  Car c1 = new Car("SlugBug", 100, 10);

  // Register event handlers.
  c1.AboutToBlow += CarIsAlmostDoomed;
  c1.AboutToBlow += CarAboutToBlow;

  EventHandler<CarEventArgs> d = new EventHandler<CarEventArgs>(CarExploded);
  c1.Exploded += d;
...
}
```

Great! At this point, you have seen the core aspects of working with delegates and events in the C# language. While you could use this information for just about all your callback needs, you will wrap up this chapter with a look at some final simplifications, specifically anonymous methods and lambda expressions.

■ **Source Code**   You can find the GenericCarEventArgs project in the Chapter 10 subdirectory.

Understanding C# Anonymous Methods

As you have seen, when a caller wants to listen to incoming events, it must define a custom method in a class (or structure) that matches the signature of the associated delegate. Here's an example:

```
class Program
{
  static void Main(string[] args)
  {
    SomeType t = new SomeType();

    // Assume "SomeDelegate" can point to methods taking no
    // args and returning void.
    t.SomeEvent += new SomeDelegate(MyEventHandler);
  }

  // Typically only called by the SomeDelegate object.
  public static void MyEventHandler()
  {
    // Do something when event is fired.
  }
}
```

When you think about it, however, methods such as MyEventHandler() are seldom intended to be called by any part of the program other than the invoking delegate. As far as productivity is concerned, it is a bit of a bother (though in no way a showstopper) to manually define a separate method to be called by the delegate object.

To address this point, it is possible to associate an event directly to a block of code statements at the time of event registration. Formally, such code is termed an *anonymous method*. To illustrate the syntax, check out the following Main() method, which handles the events sent from the Car class using anonymous methods, rather than specifically named event handlers:

```
class Program
{
  static void Main(string[] args)
  {
    Console.WriteLine("***** Anonymous Methods *****\n");
    Car c1 = new Car("SlugBug", 100, 10);

    // Register event handlers as anonymous methods.
    c1.AboutToBlow += delegate
    {
      Console.WriteLine("Eek! Going too fast!");
    };

    c1.AboutToBlow += delegate(object sender, CarEventArgs e)
    {
      Console.WriteLine("Message from Car: {0}", e.msg);
    };

    c1.Exploded += delegate(object sender, CarEventArgs e)
    {
      Console.WriteLine("Fatal Message from Car: {0}", e.msg);
    };

    // This will eventually trigger the events.
    for (int i = 0; i < 6; i++)
      c1.Accelerate(20);

    Console.ReadLine();
  }
}
```

■ **Note** The final curly bracket of an anonymous method must be terminated by a semicolon. If you fail to do so, you are issued a compilation error.

Again, notice that the Program type no longer defines specific static event handlers such as CarAboutToBlow() or CarExploded(). Rather, the unnamed (aka anonymous) methods are defined inline at the time the caller is handling the event using the += syntax. The basic syntax of an anonymous method matches the following pseudocode:

```
class Program
{
  static void Main(string[] args)
  {
    SomeType t = new SomeType();
    t.SomeEvent += delegate (optionallySpecifiedDelegateArgs)
    { /* statements */ };
  }
}
```

When handling the first AboutToBlow event within the previous Main() method, notice that you are not specifying the arguments passed from the delegate.

```
c1.AboutToBlow += delegate
{
  Console.WriteLine("Eek! Going too fast!");
};
```

Strictly speaking, you are not required to receive the incoming arguments sent by a specific event. However, if you want to make use of the possible incoming arguments, you will need to specify the parameters prototyped by the delegate type (as shown in the second handling of the AboutToBlow and Exploded events). Here's an example:

```
c1.AboutToBlow += delegate(object sender, CarEventArgs e)
{
  Console.WriteLine("Critical Message from Car: {0}", e.msg);
};
```

Accessing Local Variables

Anonymous methods are interesting in that they are able to access the local variables of the method that defines them. Formally speaking, such variables are termed *outer variables* of the anonymous method. A few important points about the interaction between an anonymous method scope and the scope of the defining method should be mentioned.

- An anonymous method cannot access ref or out parameters of the defining method.

- An anonymous method cannot have a local variable with the same name as a local variable in the outer method.

- An anonymous method can access instance variables (or static variables, as appropriate) in the outer class scope.

- An anonymous method can declare local variables with the same name as outer class member variables (the local variables have a distinct scope and hide the outer class member variables).

Assume your `Main()` method defined a local integer named `aboutToBlowCounter`. Within the anonymous methods that handle the `AboutToBlow` event, you will increment this counter by one and print out the tally before `Main()` completes.

```
static void Main(string[] args)
{
  Console.WriteLine("***** Anonymous Methods *****\n");
  int aboutToBlowCounter = 0;

  // Make a car as usual.
  Car c1 = new Car("SlugBug", 100, 10);

  // Register event handlers as anonymous methods.
  c1.AboutToBlow += delegate
  {
    aboutToBlowCounter++;
    Console.WriteLine("Eek! Going too fast!");
  };

  c1.AboutToBlow += delegate(object sender, CarEventArgs e)
  {
    aboutToBlowCounter++;
    Console.WriteLine("Critical Message from Car: {0}", e.msg);
  };

  // This will eventually trigger the events.
  for (int i = 0; i < 6; i++)
    c1.Accelerate(20);

  Console.WriteLine("AboutToBlow event was fired {0} times.",
    aboutToBlowCounter);
  Console.ReadLine();
}
```

After you run this updated `Main()` method, you will find the final `Console.WriteLine()` reports the `AboutToBlow` event was fired twice.

■ **Source Code**   You can find the AnonymousMethods project in the `Chapter 10` subdirectory.

Understanding Lambda Expressions

To conclude your look at the .NET event architecture, you will examine C# *lambda expressions*. As just explained, C# supports the ability to handle events "inline" by assigning a block of code statements directly to an event using anonymous methods, rather than building a stand-alone method to be called by the underlying delegate. Lambda expressions are nothing more than a concise way to author anonymous methods and ultimately simplify how you work with the .NET delegate type.

To set the stage for your examination of lambda expressions, create a new Console Application project named SimpleLambdaExpressions. To begin, consider the FindAll() method of the generic List<T> class. This method can be called when you need to extract a subset of items from the collection and is prototyped like so:

```
// Method of the System.Collections.Generic.List<T> class.
public List<T> FindAll(Predicate<T> match)
```

As you can see, this method returns a new List<T> that represents the subset of data. Also notice that the sole parameter to FindAll() is a generic delegate of type System.Predicate<T>. This delegate type can point to any method returning a bool and takes a single type parameter as the only input parameter.

```
// This delegate is used by FindAll() method
// to extract out the subset.
public delegate bool Predicate<T>(T obj);
```

When you call FindAll(), each item in the List<T> is passed to the method pointed to by the Predicate<T> object. The implementation of said method will perform some calculations to see whether the incoming data matches the necessary criteria and will return true or false. If this method returns true, the item will be added to the new List<T> that represents the subset (got all that?).

Before you see how lambda expressions can simplify working with FindAll(), let's work the problem out in longhand notation, using the delegate objects directly. Add a method (named TraditionalDelegateSyntax()) within your Program type that interacts with the System.Predicate<T> type to discover the even numbers in a List<T> of integers.

```
class Program
{
  static void Main(string[] args)
  {
    Console.WriteLine("***** Fun with Lambdas *****\n");
    TraditionalDelegateSyntax();
    Console.ReadLine();
  }

  static void TraditionalDelegateSyntax()
  {
    // Make a list of integers.
    List<int> list = new List<int>();
    list.AddRange(new int[] { 20, 1, 4, 8, 9, 44 });

    // Call FindAll() using traditional delegate syntax.
    Predicate<int> callback = IsEvenNumber;
    List<int> evenNumbers = list.FindAll(callback);

    Console.WriteLine("Here are your even numbers:");
    foreach (int evenNumber in evenNumbers)
    {
      Console.Write("{0}\t", evenNumber);
    }
    Console.WriteLine();
  }
```

```csharp
// Target for the Predicate<> delegate.
static bool IsEvenNumber(int i)
{
  // Is it an even number?
  return (i % 2) == 0;
}
}
```

Here, you have a method (IsEvenNumber()) that is in charge of testing the incoming integer parameter to see whether it is even or odd via the C# modulo operator, %. If you execute your application, you will find the numbers 20, 4, 8, and 44 print to the console.

While this traditional approach to working with delegates behaves as expected, the IsEvenNumber() method is invoked only in limited circumstances—specifically when you call FindAll(), which leaves you with the baggage of a full method definition. If you were to instead use an anonymous method, your code would clean up considerably. Consider the following new method of the Program class:

```csharp
static void AnonymousMethodSyntax()
{
  // Make a list of integers.
  List<int> list = new List<int>();
  list.AddRange(new int[] { 20, 1, 4, 8, 9, 44 });

  // Now, use an anonymous method.
  List<int> evenNumbers = list.FindAll(delegate(int i)
    { return (i % 2) == 0; } );

  Console.WriteLine("Here are your even numbers:");
  foreach (int evenNumber in evenNumbers)
  {
    Console.Write("{0}\t", evenNumber);
  }
  Console.WriteLine();
}
```

In this case, rather than directly creating a Predicate<T> delegate object and then authoring a standalone method, you are able to inline a method anonymously. While this is a step in the right direction, you are still required to use the delegate keyword (or a strongly typed Predicate<T>), and you must ensure that the parameter list is a dead-on match.

```csharp
List<int> evenNumbers = list.FindAll(
  delegate(int i)
  {
    return (i % 2) == 0;
  }
);
```

Lambda expressions can be used to simplify the call to FindAll() even more. When you use lambda syntax, there is no trace of the underlying delegate object whatsoever. Consider the following new method to the Program class:

```
static void LambdaExpressionSyntax()
{
  // Make a list of integers.
  List<int> list = new List<int>();
  list.AddRange(new int[] { 20, 1, 4, 8, 9, 44 });

  // Now, use a C# lambda expression.
  List<int> evenNumbers = list.FindAll(i => (i % 2) == 0);

  Console.WriteLine("Here are your even numbers:");
  foreach (int evenNumber in evenNumbers)
  {
    Console.Write("{0}\t", evenNumber);
  }
  Console.WriteLine();
}
```

In this case, notice the rather strange statement of code passed into the FindAll() method, which is in fact a lambda expression. In this iteration of the example, there is no trace whatsoever of the Predicate<T> delegate (or the delegate keyword, for that matter). All you have specified is the lambda expression.

```
i => (i % 2) == 0
```

Before I break this syntax down, first understand that lambda expressions can be used anywhere you would have used an anonymous method or a strongly typed delegate (typically with far fewer keystrokes). Under the hood, the C# compiler translates the expression into a standard anonymous method making use of the Predicate<T> delegate type (which can be verified using ildasm.exe or reflector.exe). Specifically, the following code statement:

```
// This lambda expression...
List<int> evenNumbers = list.FindAll(i => (i % 2) == 0);
```

is compiled into the following approximate C# code:

```
// ...becomes this anonymous method.
List<int> evenNumbers = list.FindAll(delegate (int i)
{
  return (i % 2) == 0;
});
```

Dissecting a Lambda Expression

A lambda expression is written by first defining a parameter list, followed by the => token (C#'s token for the lambda operator found in the *lambda calculus*), followed by a set of statements (or a single statement) that will process these arguments. From a high level, a lambda expression can be understood as follows:

```
ArgumentsToProcess => StatementsToProcessThem
```

Within the `LambdaExpressionSyntax()` method, things break down like so:

```
// "i" is our parameter list.
// "(i % 2) == 0" is our statement set to process "i".
List<int> evenNumbers = list.FindAll(i => (i % 2) == 0);
```

The parameters of a lambda expression can be explicitly or implicitly typed. Currently, the underlying data type representing the i parameter (an integer) is determined implicitly. The compiler is able to figure out that i is an integer based on the context of the overall lambda expression and the underlying delegate. However, it is also possible to explicitly define the type of each parameter in the expression by wrapping the data type and variable name in a pair of parentheses, as follows:

```
// Now, explicitly state the parameter type.
List<int> evenNumbers = list.FindAll((int i) => (i % 2) == 0);
```

As you have seen, if a lambda expression has a single, implicitly typed parameter, the parentheses may be omitted from the parameter list. If you want to be consistent regarding your use of lambda parameters, you can *always* wrap the parameter list within parentheses, leaving you with this expression:

```
List<int> evenNumbers = list.FindAll((i) => (i % 2) == 0);
```

Finally, notice that currently the expression has not been wrapped in parentheses (you have of course wrapped the modulo statement to ensure it is executed first before the test for equality). Lambda expressions do allow for the statement to be wrapped as follows:

```
// Now, wrap the expression as well.
List<int> evenNumbers = list.FindAll((i) => ((i % 2) == 0));
```

Now that you have seen the various ways to build a lambda expression, how can you read this lambda statement in human-friendly terms? Leaving the raw mathematics behind, the following explanation fits the bill:

```
// My list of parameters (in this case, a single integer named i)
// will be processed by the expression (i % 2) == 0.
List<int> evenNumbers = list.FindAll((i) => ((i % 2) == 0));
```

Processing Arguments Within Multiple Statements

The first lambda expression was a single statement that ultimately evaluated to a Boolean. However, as you know, many delegate targets must perform a number of code statements. For this reason, C# allows you to build lambda expressions using multiple statement blocks. When your expression must process the parameters using multiple lines of code, you can do so by denoting a scope for these statements using the expected curly brackets. Consider the following example update to the `LambdaExpressionSyntax()` method:

```
static void LambdaExpressionSyntax()
{
  // Make a list of integers.
  List<int> list = new List<int>();
  list.AddRange(new int[] { 20, 1, 4, 8, 9, 44 });
```

```
  // Now process each argument within a group of
  // code statements.
  List<int> evenNumbers = list.FindAll((i) =>
  {
    Console.WriteLine("value of i is currently: {0}", i);
    bool isEven = ((i % 2) == 0);
    return isEven;
  });

  Console.WriteLine("Here are your even numbers:");
  foreach (int evenNumber in evenNumbers)
  {
    Console.Write("{0}\t", evenNumber);
  }
  Console.WriteLine();
}
```

In this case, the parameter list (again, a single integer named i) is being processed by a set of code statements. Beyond the calls to Console.WriteLine(), the modulo statement has been broken into two code statements for increased readability. Assuming each of the methods you've looked at in this section are called from within Main():

```
static void Main(string[] args)
{
  Console.WriteLine("***** Fun with Lambdas *****\n");
  TraditionalDelegateSyntax();
  AnonymousMethodSyntax();
  Console.WriteLine();
  LambdaExpressionSyntax();
  Console.ReadLine();
}
```

you will find the following output:

```
***** Fun with Lambdas *****
Here are your even numbers:
20      4       8       44
Here are your even numbers:
20      4       8       44
value of i is currently: 20
value of i is currently: 1
value of i is currently: 4
value of i is currently: 8
value of i is currently: 9
value of i is currently: 44
Here are your even numbers:
20      4       8       44
```

■ **Source Code**   You can find the SimpleLambdaExpressions project in the Chapter 10 subdirectory.

Lambda Expressions with Multiple (or Zero) Parameters

The lambda expressions you have seen in this chapter so far processed a single parameter. This is not a requirement, however, as a lambda expression may process multiple arguments (or none). To illustrate the first scenario, create a Console Application project named LambdaExpressionsMultipleParams. Next, assume the following incarnation of the SimpleMath type:

```
public class SimpleMath
{
  public delegate void MathMessage(string msg, int result);
  private MathMessage mmDelegate;

  public void SetMathHandler(MathMessage target)
  {mmDelegate = target; }

  public void Add(int x, int y)
  {
    mmDelegate?.Invoke("Adding has completed!", x + y);
  }
}
```

Notice that the MathMessage delegate type is expecting two parameters. To represent them as a lambda expression, the Main() method might be written as follows:

```
static void Main(string[] args)
{
  // Register with delegate as a lambda expression.
  SimpleMath m = new SimpleMath();
  m.SetMathHandler((msg, result) =>
    {Console.WriteLine("Message: {0}, Result: {1}", msg, result);});

  // This will execute the lambda expression.
  m.Add(10, 10);
  Console.ReadLine();
}
```

Here, you are leveraging type inference, as the two parameters have not been strongly typed for simplicity. However, you could call SetMathHandler(), as follows:

```
m.SetMathHandler((string msg, int result) =>
  {Console.WriteLine("Message: {0}, Result: {1}", msg, result);});
```

Finally, if you are using a lambda expression to interact with a delegate taking no parameters at all, you may do so by supplying a pair of empty parentheses as the parameter. Thus, assuming you have defined the following delegate type:

```
public delegate string VerySimpleDelegate();
```

you could handle the result of the invocation as follows:

```
// Prints "Enjoy your string!" to the console.
VerySimpleDelegate d = new VerySimpleDelegate( () => {return "Enjoy your string!";} );
Console.WriteLine(d());
```

■ **Source Code**   You can find the LambdaExpressionsMultipleParams project in the Chapter 10 subdirectory.

Retrofitting the CarEvents Example Using Lambda Expressions

Given that the whole reason for lambda expressions is to provide a clean, concise manner to define an anonymous method (and therefore indirectly a manner to simplify working with delegates), let's retrofit the CarEventArgs project created earlier in this chapter. Here is a simplified version of that project's Program class, which makes use of lambda expression syntax (rather than the raw delegates) to hook into each event sent from the Car object:

```
static void Main(string[] args)
{
  Console.WriteLine("***** More Fun with Lambdas *****\n");

  // Make a car as usual.
  Car c1 = new Car("SlugBug", 100, 10);

  // Hook into events with lambdas!
  c1.AboutToBlow += (sender, e) => { Console.WriteLine(e.msg);};
  c1.Exploded += (sender, e) => { Console.WriteLine(e.msg); };

  // Speed up (this will generate the events).
  Console.WriteLine("\n***** Speeding up *****");
  for (int i = 0; i < 6; i++)
    c1.Accelerate(20);

  Console.ReadLine();
}
```

Lambdas and Expression-Bodied Members (Updated)

Now that you understand lambda expressions and how they work, it should be much clearer how expression-bodied members work under the covers. As mentioned in Chapter 4, as of C# 6, it is permissible to use the => operator to simplify some (but not all) member implementations. Specifically, if you have a method or property (in addition to a custom operator or conversion routine; see Chapter 11) that consists of exactly a single line of code in the implementation, you are not required to define a scope via curly bracket. You can instead leverage the lambda operator and write an expression-bodied member. In C# 7, you can also use this syntax for class constructors, finalizers (covered in Chapter 13), and get and set accessors on property members.

Consider the previous code example where you wired in code to handle the AboutToBlow and Exploded events. Note how you defined a curly-bracket scope to capture the Console.WriteLine() method calls. If you like, you could now simply write the following:

```
c1.AboutToBlow += (sender, e) => Console.WriteLine(e.msg);
c1.Exploded += (sender, e) => Console.WriteLine(e.msg);
```

Be aware, however, this new shortened syntax can be used anywhere at all, even when your code has nothing to do with delegates or events. So for example, if you were to build a trivial class to add two numbers, you might write the following:

```
class SimpleMath
{
  public int Add(int x, int y)
  {
    return x + y;
  }

  public void PrintSum(int x, int y)
  {
    Console.WriteLine(x + y);
  }
}
```

Alternatively, you could now write code like the following:

```
class SimpleMath
{
  public int Add(int x, int y) =>  x + y;
  public void PrintSum(int x, int y) => Console.WriteLine(x + y);
}
```

Ideally, at this point you can see the overall role of lambda expressions and understand how they provide a "functional manner" to work with anonymous methods and delegate types. Although the lambda operator (=>) might take a bit to get used to, always remember a lambda expression can be broken down to the following simple equation:

```
ArgumentsToProcess => StatementsToProcessThem
```

Or, if using the => operator to implement a single-line type member, it would be like this:

```
TypeMember => SingleCodeStatement
```

It is worth pointing out that the LINQ programming model also makes substantial use of lambda expressions to help simplify your coding efforts. You will examine LINQ beginning in Chapter 12.

■ **Source Code** You can use the CarEventsWithLambdas project in the Chapter 10 subdirectory.

Summary

In this chapter, you examined a number of ways in which multiple objects can partake in a bidirectional conversation. First, you looked at the C# delegate keyword, which is used to indirectly construct a class derived from System.MulticastDelegate. As you saw, a delegate object maintains a list of methods to call when told to do so. These invocations may be made synchronously (using the Invoke() method) or asynchronously (via the BeginInvoke() and EndInvoke() methods). Again, the asynchronous nature of .NET delegate types will be examined in Chapter 19.

You then examined the C# event keyword, which, when used in conjunction with a delegate type, can simplify the process of sending your event notifications to waiting callers. As shown via the resulting CIL, the .NET event model maps to hidden calls on the System.Delegate/System.MulticastDelegate types. In this light, the C# event keyword is purely optional in that it simply saves you some typing time. As well, you have seen that the C# 6.0 null conditional operator simplifies how you safely fire events to any interested party.

This chapter also explored a C# language feature termed *anonymous methods*. Using this syntactic construct, you are able to directly associate a block of code statements to a given event. As you have seen, anonymous methods are free to ignore the parameters sent by the event and have access to the "outer variables" of the defining method. You also examined a simplified way to register events using *method group conversion*.

Finally, you wrapped things up by looking at the C# *lambda operator*, =>. As shown, this syntax is a great shorthand notation for authoring anonymous methods, where a stack of arguments can be passed into a group of statements for processing. Any method in the .NET platform that takes a delegate object as an argument can be substituted with a related lambda expression, which will typically simplify your codebase quite a bit.

CHAPTER 11

■ ■ ■

Advanced C# Language Features

In this chapter, you'll deepen your understanding of the C# programming language by examining a number of more advanced topics. To begin, you'll learn how to implement and use an *indexer method*. This C# mechanism enables you to build custom types that provide access to internal subitems using an array-like syntax. After you learn how to build an indexer method, you'll see how to overload various operators (+, -, <, >, and so forth) and how to create custom explicit and implicit conversion routines for your types (and you'll learn why you might want to do this).

Next, you'll examine topics that are particularly useful when working with LINQ-centric APIs (though you can use them outside of the context of LINQ)—specifically extension methods and anonymous types.

To wrap things up, you'll learn how to create an "unsafe" code context to directly manipulate unmanaged pointers. While it is certainly true that using pointers in C# applications is a fairly infrequent activity, understanding how to do so can be helpful in some circumstances that involve complex interoperability scenarios.

Understanding Indexer Methods

As a programmer, you are certainly familiar with the process of accessing individual items contained within a simple array using the index operator ([ ]). Here's an example:

```
static void Main(string[] args)
{
  // Loop over incoming command-line arguments
  // using index operator.
  for(int i = 0; i < args.Length; i++)
    Console.WriteLine("Args: {0}", args[i]);

  // Declare an array of local integers.
  int[] myInts = { 10, 9, 100, 432, 9874};

  // Use the index operator to access each element.
  for(int j = 0; j < myInts.Length; j++)
    Console.WriteLine("Index {0}  = {1} ", j,  myInts[j]);
  Console.ReadLine();
}
```

This code is by no means a major news flash. However, the C# language provides the capability to design custom classes and structures that may be indexed just like a standard array, by defining an *indexer method*. This particular feature is most useful when you are creating custom collection classes (generic or nongeneric).

© Andrew Troelsen and Philip Japikse 2017
A. Troelsen and P. Japikse, *Pro C# 7*, https://doi.org/10.1007/978-1-4842-3018-3_11

Before examining how to implement a custom indexer, let's begin by seeing one in action. Assume you have added support for an indexer method to the custom PersonCollection type developed in Chapter 9 (specifically, the IssuesWithNonGenericCollections project). While you have not yet added the indexer, observe the following usage within a new Console Application project named SimpleIndexer:

```
// Indexers allow you to access items in an array-like fashion.
class Program
{
  static void Main(string[] args)
  {
    Console.WriteLine("***** Fun with Indexers *****\n");

    PersonCollection myPeople = new PersonCollection();

    // Add objects with indexer syntax.
    myPeople[0] = new Person("Homer", "Simpson", 40);
    myPeople[1] = new Person("Marge", "Simpson", 38);
    myPeople[2] = new Person("Lisa", "Simpson", 9);
    myPeople[3] = new Person("Bart", "Simpson", 7);
    myPeople[4] = new Person("Maggie", "Simpson", 2);

    // Now obtain and display each item using indexer.
    for (int i = 0; i < myPeople.Count; i++)
    {
      Console.WriteLine("Person number: {0}", i);
      Console.WriteLine("Name: {0} {1}",
        myPeople[i].FirstName, myPeople[i].LastName);
      Console.WriteLine("Age: {0}", myPeople[i].Age);
      Console.WriteLine();
    }
  }
}
```

As you can see, indexers allow you to manipulate the internal collection of subobjects just like a standard array. Now for the big question: how do you configure the PersonCollection class (or any custom class or structure) to support this functionality? An indexer is represented as a slightly modified C# property definition. In its simplest form, an indexer is created using the this[] syntax. Here is the required update for the PersonCollection class:

```
// Add the indexer to the existing class definition.
public class PersonCollection : IEnumerable
{
  private ArrayList arPeople = new ArrayList();

  // Custom indexer for this class.
  public Person this[int index]
  {
    get => (Person)arPeople[index];
    set => arPeople.Insert(index, value);
  }
}
```

■ **Note** The get and set accessors are using the C# 7 addition to expression-bodied members, introduced in Chapter 4 and explained in detail in Chapter 10.

Apart from using the this keyword, the indexer looks just like any other C# property declaration. For example, the role of the get scope is to return the correct object to the caller. Here, you are doing so by delegating the request to the indexer of the ArrayList object, as this class also supports an indexer. The set scope is in charge of adding new Person objects; this is achieved by calling the Insert() method of the ArrayList.

Indexers are yet another form of syntactic sugar, given that this functionality can also be achieved using "normal" public methods such as AddPerson() or GetPerson(). Nevertheless, when you support indexer methods on your custom collection types, they integrate well into the fabric of the .NET base class libraries.

While creating indexer methods is quite commonplace when you are building custom collections, do remember that generic types give you this functionality out of the box. Consider the following method, which uses a generic List<T> of Person objects. Note that you can simply use the indexer of List<T> directly. Here's an example:

```
static void UseGenericListOfPeople()
{
  List<Person> myPeople = new List<Person>();
  myPeople.Add(new Person("Lisa", "Simpson", 9));
  myPeople.Add(new Person("Bart", "Simpson", 7));

  // Change first person with indexer.
  myPeople[0] = new Person("Maggie", "Simpson", 2);

  // Now obtain and display each item using indexer.
  for (int i = 0; i < myPeople.Count; i++)
  {
    Console.WriteLine("Person number: {0}", i);
    Console.WriteLine("Name: {0} {1}", myPeople[i].FirstName, myPeople[i].LastName);
    Console.WriteLine("Age: {0}", myPeople[i].Age);
    Console.WriteLine();
  }
}
```

■ **Source Code** You can find the SimpleIndexer project in the Chapter 11 subdirectory.

Indexing Data Using String Values

The current PersonCollection class defined an indexer that allowed the caller to identify subitems using a numerical value. Understand, however, that this is not a requirement of an indexer method. Suppose you'd prefer to contain the Person objects using a System.Collections.Generic.Dictionary<TKey, TValue>

rather than an ArrayList. Given that Dictionary types allow access to the contained types using a key (such as a person's first name), you could define an indexer as follows:

```
public class PersonCollection : IEnumerable
{
  private Dictionary<string, Person> listPeople = new Dictionary<string, Person>();

  // This indexer returns a person based on a string index.
  public Person this[string name]
  {
    get => (Person)listPeople[name];
    set => listPeople[name] = value;
  }
  public void ClearPeople()
  { listPeople.Clear(); }

  public int Count => listPeople.Count;

  IEnumerator IEnumcrable.GetEnumeralur() => listPeople.GetEnumerator();
}
```

The caller would now be able to interact with the contained Person objects, as shown here:

```
static void Main(string[] args)
{
  Console.WriteLine("***** Fun with Indexers *****\n");

  PersonCollection myPeople = new PersonCollection();

  myPeople["Homer"] = new Person("Homer", "Simpson", 40);
  myPeople["Marge"] = new Person("Marge", "Simpson", 38);

  // Get "Homer" and print data.
  Person homer = myPeople["Homer"];
  Console.WriteLine(homer.ToString());

  Console.ReadLine();
}
```

Again, if you were to use the gencric Dictionary<TKey, TValue> type directly, you'd gain the indexer method functionality out of the box, without building a custom, nongeneric class supporting a string indexer. Nevertheless, do understand that the data type of any indexer will be based on how the supporting collection type allows the caller to retrieve subitems.

■ **Source Code**   You can find the StringIndexer project in the Chapter 11 subdirectory.

Overloading Indexer Methods

Understand that indexer methods may be overloaded on a single class or structure. Thus, if it makes sense to allow the caller to access subitems using a numerical index *or* a string value, you might define multiple indexers for a single type. By way of example, in ADO.NET (.NET's native database-access API), the DataSet class supports a property named Tables, which returns to you a strongly typed DataTableCollection type. As it turns out, DataTableCollection defines *three* indexers to get and set DataTable objects—one by ordinal position and the others by a friendly string moniker and optional containing namespace, as shown here:

```
public sealed class DataTableCollection : InternalDataCollectionBase
{
...
  // Overloaded indexers!
  public DataTable this[int index] { get; }
  public DataTable this[string name] { get; }
  public DataTable this[string name, string tableNamespace] { get; }
}
```

It is common for types in the base class libraries to support indexer methods. So be aware, even if your current project does not require you to build custom indexers for your classes and structures, that many types already support this syntax.

Indexers with Multiple Dimensions

You can also create an indexer method that takes multiple parameters. Assume you have a custom collection that stores subitems in a 2D array. If this is the case, you may define an indexer method as follows:

```
public class SomeContainer
{
  private int[,] my2DintArray = new int[10, 10];

  public int this[int row, int column]
  {  /* get or set value from 2D array */  }
}
```

Again, unless you are building a highly stylized custom collection class, you won't have much need to build a multidimensional indexer. Still, once again ADO.NET showcases how useful this construct can be. The ADO.NET DataTable is essentially a collection of rows and columns, much like a piece of graph paper or the general structure of a Microsoft Excel spreadsheet.

While DataTable objects are typically populated on your behalf using a related "data adapter," the following code illustrates how to manually create an in-memory DataTable containing three columns (for the first name, last name, and age of each record). Notice how once you have added a single row to the DataTable, you use a multidimensional indexer to drill into each column of the first (and only) row. (If you are following along, you'll need to import the System.Data namespace into your code file.)

```
static void MultiIndexerWithDataTable()
{
  // Make a simple DataTable with 3 columns.
  DataTable myTable = new DataTable();
  myTable.Columns.Add(new DataColumn("FirstName"));
  myTable.Columns.Add(new DataColumn("LastName"));
  myTable.Columns.Add(new DataColumn("Age"));
```

411

```
  // Now add a row to the table.
  myTable.Rows.Add("Mel", "Appleby", 60);

  // Use multidimension indexer to get details of first row.
  Console.WriteLine("First Name: {0}", myTable.Rows[0][0]);
  Console.WriteLine("Last Name: {0}", myTable.Rows[0][1]);
  Console.WriteLine("Age : {0}", myTable.Rows[0][2]);
}
```

Do be aware that you'll take a rather deep dive into ADO.NET beginning with Chapter 21, so if some of the previous code seems unfamiliar, fear not. The main point of this example is that indexer methods can support multiple dimensions and, if used correctly, can simplify the way you interact with contained subobjects in custom collections.

Indexer Definitions on Interface Types

Indexers can be defined on a given .NET interface type to allow supporting types to provide a custom implementation. Here is a simple example of an interface that defines a protocol for obtaining string objects using a numerical indexer:

```
public interface IStringContainer
{
  string this[int index] { get; set; }
}
```

With this interface definition, any class or structure that implements this interface must now support a read-write indexer that manipulates subitems using a numerical value. Here is a partial implementation of such as class:

```
class SomeClass : IStringContainer
{
  private List<string> myStrings = new List<string>();

  public string this[int index]
  {
    get => myStrings[index];
    set => myStrings.Insert(index, value);
  }
}
```

That wraps up the first major topic of this chapter. Now let's examine a language feature that lets you build custom classes or structures that respond uniquely to the intrinsic operators of C#. Next, allow me to introduce the concept of *operator overloading*.

Understanding Operator Overloading

C#, like any programming language, has a canned set of tokens that are used to perform basic operations on intrinsic types. For example, you know that the + operator can be applied to two integers to yield a larger integer.

```
// The + operator with ints.
int a = 100;
int b = 240;
int c = a + b; // c is now 340
```

Once again, this is no major news flash, but have you ever stopped and noticed how the same + operator can be applied to most intrinsic C# data types? For example, consider this code:

```
// + operator with strings.
string s1 = "Hello";
string s2 = " world!";
string s3 = s1 + s2;  // s3 is now "Hello World!"
```

In essence, the + operator functions in specific ways based on the supplied data types (strings or integers, in this case). When the + operator is applied to numerical types, the result is the summation of the operands. However, when the + operator is applied to string types, the result is string concatenation.

The C# language gives you the capability to build custom classes and structures that also respond uniquely to the same set of basic tokens (such as the + operator). While not every possible C# operator can be overloaded, many can, as shown in Table 11-1.

Table 11-1. *Overloadability of C# Operators*

C# Operator	Overloadability
+, -,!, ~, ++, --, true, false	These unary operators can be overloaded.
+, -, *, /, %, &, |, ^, <<, >>	These binary operators can be overloaded.
==,!=, <, >, <=, >=	These comparison operators can be overloaded. C# demands that "like" operators (i.e., < and >, <= and >=, == and !=) are overloaded together.
[]	The [ ] operator cannot be overloaded. As you saw earlier in this chapter, however, the indexer construct provides the same functionality.
()	The ( ) operator cannot be overloaded. As you will see later in this chapter, however, custom conversion methods provide the same functionality.
+=, -=, *=, /=, %=, &=, |=, ^=, <<=, >>=	Shorthand assignment operators cannot be overloaded; however, you receive them as a freebie when you overload the related binary operator.

Overloading Binary Operators

To illustrate the process of overloading binary operators, assume the following simple Point class is defined in a new Console Application project named OverloadedOps:

```
// Just a simple, everyday C# class.
public class Point
{
  public int X {get; set;}
  public int Y {get; set;}
```

```
  public Point(int xPos, int yPos)
  {
    X = xPos;
    Y = yPos;
  }
  public override string ToString() => $"[{this.X}, {this.Y}]";
}
```

Now, logically speaking, it makes sense to "add" Points together. For example, if you added together two Point variables, you should receive a new Point that is the summation of the X and Y values. Of course, it might also be helpful to subtract one Point from another. Ideally, you would like to be able to author the following code:

```
// Adding and subtracting two points?
static void Main(string[] args)
{
  Console.WriteLine("***** Fun with Overloaded Operators *****\n");

  // Make two points.
  Point ptOne = new Point(100, 100);
  Point ptTwo = new Point(40, 40);
  Console.WriteLine("ptOne = {0}", ptOne);
  Console.WriteLine("ptTwo = {0}", ptTwo);

  // Add the points to make a bigger point?
  Console.WriteLine("ptOne + ptTwo: {0} ", ptOne + ptTwo);

  // Subtract the points to make a smaller point?
  Console.WriteLine("ptOne - ptTwo: {0} ", ptOne - ptTwo);
  Console.ReadLine();
}
```

However, as your Point now stands, you will receive compile-time errors, as the Point type does not know how to respond to the + or - operators. To equip a custom type to respond uniquely to intrinsic operators, C# provides the operator keyword, which you can use only in conjunction with the static keyword. When you overload a binary operator (such as + and -), you will most often pass in two arguments that are the same type as the defining class (a Point in this example), as illustrated in the following code update:

```
// A more intelligent Point type.
public class Point
{
...
  // Overloaded operator +.
  public static Point operator + (Point p1, Point p2) => new Point(p1.X + p2.X, p1.Y + p2.Y);

  // Overloaded operator -.
  public static Point operator - (Point p1, Point p2) => new Point(p1.X - p2.X, p1.Y - p2.Y);
}
```

The logic behind operator + is simply to return a new Point object based on the summation of the fields of the incoming Point parameters. Thus, when you write pt1 + pt2, under the hood you can envision the following hidden call to the static operator + method:

```
// Pseudo-code: Point p3 = Point.operator+ (p1, p2)
Point p3 = p1 + p2;
```

Likewise, p1 – p2 maps to the following:

```
// Pseudo-code: Point p4 = Point.operator- (p1, p2)
Point p4 = p1 - p2;
```

With this update, your program now compiles, and you find you are able to add and subtract Point objects, as shown in the following output:

```
ptOne = [100, 100]
ptTwo = [40, 40]
ptOne + ptTwo: [140, 140]
ptOne - ptTwo: [60, 60]
```

When you are overloading a binary operator, you are not required to pass in two parameters of the same type. If it makes sense to do so, one of the arguments can differ. For example, here is an overloaded operator + that allows the caller to obtain a new Point that is based on a numerical adjustment:

```
public class Point
{
...
  public static Point operator + (Point p1, int change) => new Point(p1.X + change,
  p1.Y + change);

  public static Point operator + (int change, Point p1) => new Point(p1.X + change,
  p1.Y + change);
}
```

Notice that you need *both* versions of the method if you want the arguments to be passed in either order (i.e., you can't just define one of the methods and expect the compiler to automatically support the other one). You are now able to use these new versions of operator + as follows:

```
// Prints [110, 110].
Point biggerPoint = ptOne + 10;
Console.WriteLine("ptOne + 10 = {0}", biggerPoint);

// Prints [120, 120].
Console.WriteLine("10 + biggerPoint = {0}", 10 + biggerPoint);
Console.WriteLine();
```

And What of the += and –= Operators?

If you are coming to C# from a C++ background, you might lament the loss of overloading the shorthand assignment operators (+=, -=, and so forth). Don't despair. In terms of C#, the shorthand assignment operators are automatically simulated if a type overloads the related binary operator. Thus, given that the Point structure has already overloaded the + and - operators, you can write the following:

```
// Overloading binary operators results in a freebie shorthand operator.
static void Main(string[] args)
{
...
  // Freebie +=
  Point ptThree = new Point(90, 5);
  Console.WriteLine("ptThree = {0}", ptThree);
  Console.WriteLine("ptThree += ptTwo: {0}", ptThree += ptTwo);

  // Freebie -=
  Point ptFour = new Point(0, 500);
  Console.WriteLine("ptFour = {0}", ptFour);
  Console.WriteLine("ptFour -= ptThree: {0}", ptFour -= ptThree);
  Console.ReadLine();
}
```

Overloading Unary Operators

C# also allows you to overload various unary operators, such as ++ and --. When you overload a unary operator, you also must use the `static` keyword with the `operator` keyword; however, in this case you simply pass in a single parameter that is the same type as the defining class/structure. For example, if you were to update the Point with the following overloaded operators:

```
public class Point
{
...
  // Add 1 to the X/Y values for the incoming Point.
  public static Point operator ++(Point p1) => new Point(p1.X+1, p1.Y+1);

  // Subtract 1 from the X/Y values for the incoming Point.
  public static Point operator --(Point p1) => new Point(p1.X-1, p1.Y-1);
}
```

you could increment and decrement Point's x and y values like this:

```
static void Main(string[] args)
{
...
  // Applying the ++ and -- unary operators to a Point.
  Point ptFive = new Point(1, 1);
  Console.WriteLine("++ptFive = {0}", ++ptFive);  // [2, 2]
  Console.WriteLine("--ptFive = {0}", --ptFive);  // [1, 1]
```

```
  // Apply same operators as postincrement/decrement.
  Point ptSix = new Point(20, 20);
  Console.WriteLine("ptSix++ = {0}", ptSix++);  // [20, 20]
  Console.WriteLine("ptSix-- = {0}", ptSix--);  // [21, 21]
  Console.ReadLine();
}
```

Notice in the preceding code example you are applying the custom ++ and -- operators in two different manners. In C++, it is possible to overload pre- and post-increment/decrement operators separately. This is not possible in C#. However, the return value of the increment/decrement is automatically handled "correctly" free of charge (i.e., for an overloaded ++ operator, pt++ has the value of the unmodified object as its value within an expression, while ++pt has the new value applied before use in the expression).

Overloading Equality Operators

As you might recall from Chapter 6, System.Object.Equals() can be overridden to perform value-based (rather than referenced-based) comparisons between reference types. If you choose to override Equals() (and the often related System.Object.GetHashCode() method), it is trivial to overload the equality operators (== and !=). To illustrate, here is the updated Point type:

```
// This incarnation of Point also overloads the == and != operators.
public class Point
{
...
  public override bool Equals(object o) => o.ToString() == this.ToString();

  public override int GetHashCode() => this.ToString().GetHashCode();

  // Now let's overload the == and != operators.
  public static bool operator ==(Point p1, Point p2) => p1.Equals(p2);

  public static bool operator !=(Point p1, Point p2) => !p1.Equals(p2);
}
```

Notice how the implementation of operator == and operator != simply makes a call to the overridden Equals() method to get the bulk of the work done. Given this, you can now exercise your Point class as follows:

```
// Make use of the overloaded equality operators.
static void Main(string[] args)
{
...
  Console.WriteLine("ptOne == ptTwo : {0}", ptOne == ptTwo);
  Console.WriteLine("ptOne != ptTwo : {0}", ptOne != ptTwo);
  Console.ReadLine();
}
```

As you can see, it is quite intuitive to compare two objects using the well-known == and != operators, rather than making a call to Object. Equals(). If you do overload the equality operators for a given class, keep in mind that C# demands that if you override the == operator, you *must* also override the != operator (if you forget, the compiler will let you know).

Overloading Comparison Operators

In Chapter 8, you learned how to implement the IComparable interface to compare the relationship between two like objects. You can, in fact, also overload the comparison operators (<, >, <=, and >=) for the same class. As with the equality operators, C# demands that if you overload <, you must also overload >. The same holds true for the <= and >= operators. If the Point type overloaded these comparison operators, the object user could now compare Points, as follows:

```
// Using the overloaded < and > operators.
static void Main(string[] args)
{
...
  Console.WriteLine("ptOne < ptTwo : {0}", ptOne < ptTwo);
  Console.WriteLine("ptOne > ptTwo : {0}", ptOne > ptTwo);
  Console.ReadLine();
}
```

Assuming you have implemented the IComparable interface (or better yet, the generic equivalent), overloading the comparison operators is trivial. Here is the updated class definition:

```
// Point is also comparable using the comparison operators.
public class Point : IComparable<Point>
{
...
  public int CompareTo(Point other)
  {
    if (this.X > other.X && this.Y > other.Y)
      return 1;
    if (this.X < other.X && this.Y < other.Y)
      return -1;
    else
      return 0;
  }

  public static bool operator <(Point p1, Point p2) => p1.CompareTo(p2) < 0;

  public static bool operator >(Point p1, Point p2) => p1.CompareTo(p2) > 0;

  public static bool operator <=(Point p1, Point p2) => p1.CompareTo(p2) <= 0;

  public static bool operator >=(Point p1, Point p2) => p1.CompareTo(p2) >= 0;
}
```

Final Thoughts Regarding Operator Overloading

As you have seen, C# provides the capability to build types that can respond uniquely to various intrinsic, well-known operators. Now, before you go and retrofit all your classes to support such behavior, you must be sure that the operators you are about to overload make some sort of logical sense in the world at large.

For example, let's say you overloaded the multiplication operator for the MiniVan class. What exactly would it mean to multiply two MiniVan objects? Not much. In fact, it would be confusing for teammates to see the following use of MiniVan objects:

```
// Huh?! This is far from intuitive...
MiniVan newVan = myVan * yourVan;
```

Overloading operators is generally useful only when you're building atomic data types. Text, points, rectangles, fractions, and hexagons make good candidates for operator overloading. People, managers, cars, database connections, and web pages do not. As a rule of thumb, if an overloaded operator makes it *harder* for the user to understand a type's functionality, don't do it. Use this feature wisely.

■ **Source Code**   You can find the OverloadedOps project in the Chapter 11 subdirectory.

Understanding Custom Type Conversions

Let's now examine a topic closely related to operator overloading: custom type conversions. To set the stage for the discussion, let's quickly review the notion of explicit and implicit conversions between numerical data and related class types.

Recall: Numerical Conversions

In terms of the intrinsic numerical types (sbyte, int, float, etc.), an *explicit conversion* is required when you attempt to store a larger value in a smaller container, as this could result in a loss of data. Basically, this is your way to tell the compiler, "Leave me alone, I know what I am trying to do." Conversely, an *implicit conversion* happens automatically when you attempt to place a smaller type in a destination type that will not result in a loss of data.

```
static void Main()
{
  int a = 123;
  long b = a;      // Implicit conversion from int to long.
  int c = (int) b; // Explicit conversion from long to int.
}
```

Recall: Conversions Among Related Class Types

As shown in Chapter 6, class types may be related by classical inheritance (the "is-a" relationship). In this case, the C# conversion process allows you to cast up and down the class hierarchy. For example, a derived class can always be implicitly cast to a base type. However, if you want to store a base class type in a derived variable, you must perform an explicit cast, like so:

```
// Two related class types.
class Base{}
class Derived : Base{}
```

```
class Program
{
  static void Main(string[] args)
  {
    // Implicit cast between derived to base.
    Base myBaseType;
    myBaseType = new Derived();

    // Must explicitly cast to store base reference
    // in derived type.
    Derived myDerivedType = (Derived)myBaseType;
  }
}
```

This explicit cast works because the Base and Derived classes are related by classical inheritance. However, what if you have two class types in *different hierarchies* with no common parent (other than System.Object) that require conversions? Given that they are not related by classical inheritance, typical casting operations offer no help (and you would get a compiler error to boot!).

On a related note, consider value types (structures). Assume you have two .NET structures named Square and Rectangle. Given that structures cannot leverage classic inheritance (as they are always sealed), you have no natural way to cast between these seemingly related types.

While you could create helper methods in the structures (such as Rectangle.ToSquare()), C# lets you build custom conversion routines that allow your types to respond to the ( ) casting operator. Therefore, if you configured the structures correctly, you would be able to use the following syntax to explicitly convert between them as follows:

```
// Convert a Rectangle to a Square!
Rectangle rect = new Rectangle
{
  Width = 3;
  Height = 10;
}
Square sq = (Square)rect;
```

Creating Custom Conversion Routines

Begin by creating a new Console Application project named CustomConversions. C# provides two keywords, explicit and implicit, that you can use to control how your types respond during an attempted conversion. Assume you have the following structure definitions:

```
public struct Rectangle
{
  public int Width {get; set;}
  public int Height {get; set;}

  public Rectangle(int w, int h) : this()
  {
    Width = w;
    Height = h;
  }
```

```csharp
  public void Draw()
  {
    for (int i = 0; i < Height; i++)
    {
      for (int j = 0; j < Width; j++)
      {
        Console.Write("*");
      }
      Console.WriteLine();
    }
  }

  public override string ToString() => $"[Width = {Width}; Height = {Height}]";
}

public struct Square
{
  public int Length {get; set;}
  public Square(int l) : this()
  {
    Length = l;
  }

  public void Draw()
  {
    for (int i = 0; i < Length; i++)
    {
      for (int j = 0; j < Length; j++)
      {
        Console.Write("*");
      }
      Console.WriteLine();
    }
  }

  public override string ToString() => $"[Length = {Length}]", Length);

  // Rectangles can be explicitly converted into Squares.
  public static explicit operator Square(Rectangle r)
  {
    Square s = new Square {Length = r.Height};
    return s;
  }
}
```

■ **Note**   You'll notice in the `Square` and `Rectangle` constructors, I am explicitly chaining to the default constructor. The reason is that if you have a structure, which makes use of automatic property syntax (as you do here), the default constructor must be explicitly called (from all custom constructors) to initialize the private backing fields (for example, if the structures had any additional fields/properties, this default constructor would initialize these fields to default values). Yes, this is a quirky rule of C#, but after all, this is an advanced topics chapter.

Notice that this iteration of the Square type defines an explicit conversion operator. Like the process of overloading an operator, conversion routines make use of the C# operator keyword, in conjunction with the explicit or implicit keyword, and must be defined as static. The incoming parameter is the entity you are converting *from*, while the operator type is the entity you are converting *to*.

In this case, the assumption is that a square (being a geometric pattern in which all sides are of equal length) can be obtained from the height of a rectangle. Thus, you are free to convert a Rectangle into a Square, as follows:

```
static void Main(string[] args)
{
  Console.WriteLine("***** Fun with Conversions *****\n");
  // Make a Rectangle.
  Rectangle r = new Rectangle(15, 4);
  Console.WriteLine(r.ToString());
  r.Draw();

  Console.WriteLine();

  // Convert r into a Square,
  // based on the height of the Rectangle.
  Square s = (Square)r;
  Console.WriteLine(s.ToString());
  s.Draw();
  Console.ReadLine();
}
```

You can see the output here:

```
***** Fun with Conversions *****

[Width = 15; Height = 4]

***************
***************
***************
***************

[Length = 4]
****
****
****
****
```

While it may not be all that helpful to convert a Rectangle into a Square within the same scope, assume you have a function that has been designed to take Square parameters.

```
// This method requires a Square type.
static void DrawSquare(Square sq)
{
  Console.WriteLine(sq.ToString());
  sq.Draw();
}
```

Using your explicit conversion operation on the Square type, you can now pass in Rectangle types for processing using an explicit cast, like so:

```
static void Main(string[] args)
{
...
  // Convert Rectangle to Square to invoke method.
  Rectangle rect = new Rectangle(10, 5);
  DrawSquare((Square)rect);
  Console.ReadLine();
}
```

Additional Explicit Conversions for the Square Type

Now that you can explicitly convert Rectangles into Squares, let's examine a few additional explicit conversions. Given that a square is symmetrical on all sides, it might be helpful to provide an explicit conversion routine that allows the caller to cast from an integer type into a Square (which, of course, will have a side length equal to the incoming integer). Likewise, what if you were to update Square such that the caller can cast *from* a Square into an int? Here is the calling logic:

```
static void Main(string[] args)
{
...
  // Converting an int to a Square.
  Square sq2 = (Square)90;
  Console.WriteLine("sq2 = {0}", sq2);

  // Converting a Square to an int.
  int side = (int)sq2;
  Console.WriteLine("Side length of sq2 = {0}", side);
  Console.ReadLine();
}
```

and here is the update to the Square class:

```
public struct Square
{
...
  public static explicit operator Square(int sideLength)
```

```
  {
    Square newSq = new Square {Length = sideLength};
    return newSq;
  }

  public static explicit operator int (Square s) => s.Length;
}
```

To be honest, converting from a Square into an integer may not be the most intuitive (or useful) operation (after all, chances are you could just pass such values to a constructor). However, it does point out an important fact regarding custom conversion routines: the compiler does not care what you convert to or from, as long as you have written syntactically correct code.

Thus, as with overloading operators, just because you *can* create an explicit cast operation for a given type does not mean you *should*. Typically, this technique will be most helpful when you're creating .NET structure types, given that they are unable to participate in classical inheritance (where casting comes for free).

Defining Implicit Conversion Routines

So far, you have created various custom *explicit* conversion operations. However, what about the following *implicit* conversion?

```
static void Main(string[] args)
{
...
  Square s3 = new Square {Length = 83};

  // Attempt to make an implicit cast?
  Rectangle rect2 = s3;

  Console.ReadLine();
}
```

This code will not compile, given that you have not provided an implicit conversion routine for the Rectangle type. Now here is the catch: it is illegal to define explicit and implicit conversion functions on the same type if they do not differ by their return type or parameter set. This might seem like a limitation; however, the second catch is that when a type defines an *implicit* conversion routine, it is legal for the caller to make use of the *explicit* cast syntax!

Confused? To clear things up, let's add an implicit conversion routine to the Rectangle structure using the C# implicit keyword (note that the following code assumes the width of the resulting Rectangle is computed by multiplying the side of the Square by 2):

```
public struct Rectangle
{
...
  public static implicit operator Rectangle(Square s)
  {
    Rectangle r = new Rectangle
    {
      Height = s.Length,
      Width = s.Length * 2 // Assume the length of the new Rectangle with (Length x 2).
    };
```

```
    return r;
  }
}
```

With this update, you are now able to convert between types, as follows:

```
static void Main(string[] args)
{
...
  // Implicit cast OK!
  Square s3 = new Square { Length= 7};

  Rectangle rect2 = s3;
  Console.WriteLine("rect2 = {0}", rect2);

  // Explicit cast syntax still OK!
  Square s4 = new Square {Length = 3};
  Rectangle rect3 = (Rectangle)s4;

  Console.WriteLine("rect3 = {0}", rect3);
  Console.ReadLine();
}
```

That wraps up your look at defining custom conversion routines. As with overloaded operators, remember that this bit of syntax is simply a shorthand notation for "normal" member functions, and in this light it is always optional. When used correctly, however, custom structures can be used more naturally, as they can be treated as true class types related by inheritance.

■ **Source Code**   You can find the CustomConversions project in the Chapter 11 subdirectory.

Understanding Extension Methods

.NET 3.5 introduced the concept of *extension methods*, which allow you to add new methods or properties to a class or structure, without modifying the original type in any direct manner. So, where might this be helpful? Consider the following possibilities.

First, say you have a given class that is in production. It becomes clear over time that this class should support a handful of new members. If you modify the current class definition directly, you risk the possibility of breaking backward compatibility with older codebases making use of it, as they might not have been compiled with the latest and greatest class definition. One way to ensure backward compatibility is to create a new derived class from the existing parent; however, now you have two classes to maintain. As we all know, code maintenance is the least glamorous part of a software engineer's job description.

Now consider this situation. Let's say you have a structure (or maybe a sealed class) and want to add new members so that it behaves polymorphically in your system. Since structures and sealed classes cannot be extended, your only choice is to add the members to the type, once again risking backward compatibility!

Using extension methods, you are able to modify types without subclassing and without modifying the type directly. The catch is that the new functionality is offered to a type only if the extension methods have been referenced for use in your current project.

Defining Extension Methods

When you define extension methods, the first restriction is that they must be defined within a static class (see Chapter 5); therefore, each extension method must be declared with the static keyword. The second point is that all extension methods are marked as such by using the this keyword as a modifier on the first (and only the first) parameter of the method in question. The "this qualified" parameter represents the item being extended.

To illustrate, create a new Console Application project named ExtensionMethods. Now, assume you are authoring a class named MyExtensions that defines two extension methods. The first method allows any object to use a new method named DisplayDefiningAssembly() that makes use of types in the System. Reflection namespace to display the name of the assembly containing the type in question.

■ **Note**   You will formally examine the reflection API in Chapter 15. If you are new to the topic, simply understand that reflection allows you to discover the structure of assemblies, types, and type members at runtime.

The second extension method, named ReverseDigits(), allows any int to obtain a new version of itself where the value is reversed digit by digit. For example, if an integer with the value 1234 called ReverseDigits(), the integer returned is set to the value 4321. Consider the following class implementation (be sure to import the System.Reflection namespace if you are following along):

```
static class MyExtensions
{
  // This method allows any object to display the assembly
  // it is defined in.
  public static void DisplayDefiningAssembly(this object obj)
  {
    Console.WriteLine("{0} lives here: => {1}\n", obj.GetType().Name,
      Assembly.GetAssembly(obj.GetType()).GetName().Name);
  }

  // This method allows any integer to reverse its digits.
  // For example, 56 would return 65.
  public static int ReverseDigits(this int i)
  {
    // Translate int into a string, and then
    // get all the characters.
    char[] digits = i.ToString().ToCharArray();

    // Now reverse items in the array.
    Array.Reverse(digits);

    // Put back into string.
    string newDigits = new string(digits);
```

```
    // Finally, return the modified string back as an int.
    return int.Parse(newDigits);
  }
}
```

Again, note how the first parameter of each extension method has been qualified with the `this` keyword, before defining the parameter type. It is always the case that the first parameter of an extension method represents the type being extended. Given that `DisplayDefiningAssembly()` has been prototyped to extend `System.Object`, every type now has this new member, as `Object` is the parent to all types in the .NET platform. However, `ReverseDigits()` has been prototyped to extend only integer types; therefore, if anything other than an integer attempts to invoke this method, you will receive a compile-time error.

■ **Note**   Understand that a given extension method can have multiple parameters, but *only* the first parameter can be qualified with `this`. The additional parameters would be treated as normal incoming parameters for use by the method.

Invoking Extension Methods

Now that you have these extension methods in place, consider the following `Main()` method that applies the extension method to various types in the base class libraries:

```
static void Main(string[] args)
{
  Console.WriteLine("***** Fun with Extension Methods *****\n");

  // The int has assumed a new identity!
  int myInt = 12345678;
  myInt.DisplayDefiningAssembly();

  // So has the DataSet!
  System.Data.DataSet d = new System.Data.DataSet();
  d.DisplayDefiningAssembly();

  // And the SoundPlayer!
  System.Media.SoundPlayer sp = new System.Media.SoundPlayer();
  sp.DisplayDefiningAssembly();

  // Use new integer functionality.
  Console.WriteLine("Value of myInt: {0}", myInt);
  Console.WriteLine("Reversed digits of myInt: {0}", myInt.ReverseDigits());

  Console.ReadLine();
}
```

Here is the output:

```
***** Fun with Extension Methods *****

Int32 lives here: => mscorlib

DataSet lives here: => System.Data

SoundPlayer lives here: => System

Value of myInt: 12345678
Reversed digits of myInt: 87654321
```

Importing Extension Methods

When you define a class containing extension methods, it will no doubt be defined within a .NET namespace. If this namespace is different from the namespace using the extension methods, you will need to make use of the expected C# using keyword. When you do, your code file has access to all extension methods for the type being extended. This is important to remember because if you do not explicitly import the correct namespace, the extension methods are not available for that C# code file.

In effect, although it can appear on the surface that extension methods are global in nature, they are in fact limited to the namespaces that define them or the namespaces that import them. Thus, if you wrap the MyExtensions class into a namespace named MyExtensionMethods, as follows:

```
namespace MyExtensionMethods
{
  static class MyExtensions
  {
    ...
  }
}
```

other namespaces in the project would need to explicitly import the MyExtensionMethods namespace to gain the extension methods defined by your class.

■ **Note**   It is common practice to not only isolate extension methods into a dedicated .NET namespace but to isolate them into a dedicated class library. In this way, new applications can "opt in" to extensions by explicitly referencing the correct library and importing the namespace. Chapter 14 will examine the details of building and using custom .NET class libraries.

The IntelliSense of Extension Methods

Given that extension methods are not literally defined on the type being extended, it is certainly possible to become confused when examining an existing codebase. For example, assume you have imported a namespace that defined some number of extension methods authored by a teammate. As you are authoring your code, you might create a variable of the extended type, apply the dot operator, and find dozens of new methods that are not members of the original class definition!

Thankfully, Visual Studio's IntelliSense mechanism marks all extension methods, as shown in Figure 11-1.

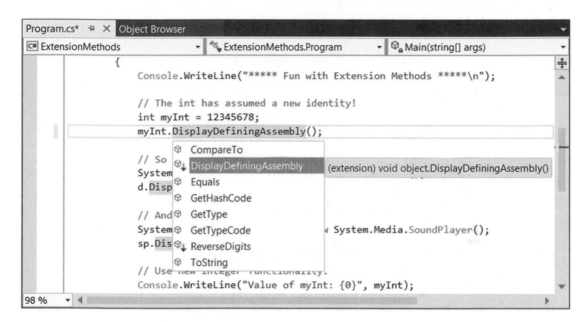

Figure 11-1. *The IntelliSense of extension methods*

Any method marked as such is a friendly reminder that the method is defined outside of the original class definition via an extension method.

■ **Source Code**   You can find the ExtensionMethods project in the Chapter 11 subdirectory.

Extending Types Implementing Specific Interfaces

At this point, you have seen how to extend classes (and, indirectly, structures that follow the same syntax) with new functionality via extension methods. It is also possible to define an extension method that can only extend a class or structure that implements the correct interface. For example, you could say something to the effect of "If a class or structure implements IEnumerable<T>, then that type gets the following new members." Of course, it is possible to demand that a type support any interface at all, including your own custom interfaces.

To illustrate, create a new Console Application project named InterfaceExtensions. The goal here is to add a new method to any type that implements IEnumerable, which would include any array and many nongeneric collection classes (recall from Chapter 8 that the generic IEnumerable<T> interface extends the nongeneric IEnumerable interface). Add the following extension class to your new project:

```
static class AnnoyingExtensions
{
  public static void PrintDataAndBeep(this System.Collections.IEnumerable iterator)
  {
    foreach (var item in iterator)
    {
      Console.WriteLine(item);
      Console.Beep();
    }
  }
}
```

Given that the PrintDataAndBeep() method can be used by any class or structure that implements IEnumerable, you could test via the following Main() method:

```
static void Main( string[] args )
{
  Console.WriteLine("***** Extending Interface Compatible Types *****\n");

  // System.Array implements IEnumerable!
  string[] data = { "Wow", "this", "is", "sort", "of", "annoying",
                    "but", "in", "a", "weird", "way", "fun!"};
  data.PrintDataAndBeep();

  Console.WriteLine();

  // List<T> implements IEnumerable!
  List<int> myInts = new List<int>() {10, 15, 20};
  myInts.PrintDataAndBeep();

  Console.ReadLine();
}
```

That wraps up your examination of C# extension methods. Remember that this particular language feature can be useful whenever you want to extend the functionality of a type but do not want to subclass (or cannot subclass if the type is sealed), for the purposes of polymorphism. As you will see later in the text, extension methods play a key role for LINQ APIs. In fact, you will see that under the LINQ APIs, one of the most common items being extended is a class or structure implementing (surprise!) the generic version of IEnumerable.

■ **Source Code** You can find the InterfaceExtensions project in the Chapter 11 subdirectory.

Understanding Anonymous Types

As an object-oriented programmer, you know the benefits of defining classes to represent the state and functionality of a given item you are attempting to model. To be sure, whenever you need to define a class that is intended to be reused across projects and that provides numerous bits of functionality through a set of methods, events, properties, and custom constructors, creating a new C# class is common practice.

However, there are other times when you would like to define a class simply to model a set of encapsulated (and somehow related) data points without any associated methods, events, or other specialized functionality. Furthermore, what if this type is to be used only by a handful of methods in your program? It would be rather a bother to define a full class definition as shown next when you know full well this class will be used in only a handful of places. To accentuate this point, here is the rough outline of what you might need to do when you need to create a "simple" data type that follows typical value-based semantics:

```
class SomeClass
{
  // Define a set of private member variables...

  // Make a property for each member variable...

  // Override ToString() to account for key member variables...

  // Override GetHashCode() and Equals() to work with value-based equality...
}
```

As you can see, it is not necessarily so simple. Not only do you need to author a fair amount of code, but you have another class to maintain in your system. For temporary data such as this, it would be useful to whip up a custom data type on the fly. For example, let's say you need to build a custom method that receives a set of incoming parameters. You would like to take these parameters and use them to create a new data type for use in this method scope. Further, you would like to quickly print out this data using the typical ToString() method and perhaps use other members of System.Object. You can do this very thing using anonymous type syntax.

Defining an Anonymous Type

When you define an anonymous type, you do so by using the var keyword (see Chapter 3) in conjunction with object initialization syntax (see Chapter 5). You must use the var keyword because the compiler will automatically generate a new class definition at compile time (and you never see the name of this class in your C# code). The initialization syntax is used to tell the compiler to create private backing fields and (read-only) properties for the newly created type.

To illustrate, create a new Console Application project named AnonymousTypes. Now, add the following method to your Program class, which composes a new type, on the fly, using the incoming parameter data:

```
static void BuildAnonType( string make, string color, int currSp )
{
  // Build anon type using incoming args.
  var car = new { Make = make, Color = color, Speed = currSp };

  // Note you can now use this type to get the property data!
  Console.WriteLine("You have a {0} {1} going {2} MPH", car.Color, car.Make, car.Speed);
```

431

```
// Anon types have custom implementations of each virtual
// method of System.Object. For example:
Console.WriteLine("ToString() == {0}", car.ToString());
}
```

You can call this method from Main(), as expected. However, do note that an anonymous type can also be created using hard-coded values, as shown here:

```
static void Main(string[] args)
{
  Console.WriteLine("***** Fun with Anonymous Types *****\n");

  // Make an anonymous type representing a car.
  var myCar = new { Color = "Bright Pink", Make = "Saab", CurrentSpeed = 55 };

  // Now show the color and make.
  Console.WriteLine("My car is a {0} {1}.", myCar.Color, myCar.Make);

  // Now call our helper method to build anonymous type via args.
  BuildAnonType("BMW", "Black", 90);

  Console.ReadLine();
}
```

So, at this point, simply understand that anonymous types allow you to quickly model the "shape" of data with very little overhead. This technique is little more than a way to whip up a new data type on the fly, which supports bare-bones encapsulation via properties and acts according to value-based semantics. To understand that last point, let's see how the C# compiler builds out anonymous types at compile time and, specifically, how it overrides the members of System.Object.

The Internal Representation of Anonymous Types

All anonymous types are automatically derived from System.Object and, therefore, support each of the members provided by this base class. Given this, you could invoke ToString(), GetHashCode(), Equals(), or GetType() on the implicitly typed myCar object. Assume your Program class defines the following static helper function:

```
static void ReflectOverAnonymousType(object obj)
{
  Console.WriteLine("obj is an instance of: {0}", obj.GetType().Name);
  Console.WriteLine("Base class of {0} is {1}", obj.GetType().Name, obj.GetType().BaseType);
  Console.WriteLine("obj.ToString() == {0}", obj.ToString());
  Console.WriteLine("obj.GetHashCode() == {0}", obj.GetHashCode());
  Console.WriteLine();
}
```

Now assume you invoke this method from Main(), passing in the myCar object as the parameter, like so:

```
static void Main(string[] args)
{
  Console.WriteLine("***** Fun with Anonymous Types *****\n");

  // Make an anonymous type representing a car.
  var myCar = new {Color = "Bright Pink", Make = "Saab", CurrentSpeed = 55};

  // Reflect over what the compiler generated.
  ReflectOverAnonymousType(myCar);
...

  Console.ReadLine();
}
```

The output will look similar to the following:

```
***** Fun with Anonymous Types *****

obj is an instance of: <>f__AnonymousType0`3
Base class of <>f__AnonymousType0`3 is System.Object
obj.ToString() = { Color = Bright Pink, Make = Saab, CurrentSpeed = 55 }
obj.GetHashCode() = -439083487
```

First, notice that, in this example, the myCar object is of type <>f AnonymousType0`3 (your name may differ). Remember that the assigned type name is completely determined by the compiler and is not directly accessible in your C# codebase.

Perhaps most important, notice that each name-value pair defined using the object initialization syntax is mapped to an identically named read-only property and a corresponding private read-only backing field. The following C# code approximates the compiler-generated class used to represent the myCar object (which again can be verified using ildasm.exe):

```
internal sealed class <>f__AnonymousType0<<Color>j__TPar,
  <Make>j__TPar, <CurrentSpeed>j__TPar>
{
  // Read-only fields.
  private readonly <Color>j__TPar <Color>i__Field;
  private readonly <CurrentSpeed>j__TPar <CurrentSpeed>i__Field;
  private readonly <Make>j__TPar <Make>i__Field;

  // Default constructor.
  public <>f__AnonymousType0(<Color>j__TPar Color,
    <Make>j__TPar Make, <CurrentSpeed>j__TPar CurrentSpeed);
  // Overridden methods.
  public override bool Equals(object value);
  public override int GetHashCode();
  public override string ToString();
```

```
  // Read-only properties.
  public <Color>j__TPar Color { get; }
  public <CurrentSpeed>j__TPar CurrentSpeed { get; }
  public <Make>j__TPar Make { get; }
}
```

The Implementation of ToString() and GetHashCode()

All anonymous types automatically derive from System.Object and are provided with an overridden version of Equals(), GetHashCode(), and ToString(). The ToString() implementation simply builds a string from each name-value pair. Here's an example:

```
public override string ToString()
{
  StringBuilder builder = new StringBuilder();
  builder.Append("{ Color = ");
  builder.Append(this.<Color>i__Field);
  builder.Append(", Make = ");
  builder.Append(this.<Make>i__Field);
  builder.Append(", CurrentSpeed = ");
  builder.Append(this.<CurrentSpeed>i__Field);
  builder.Append(" }");
  return builder.ToString();
}
```

The GetHashCode() implementation computes a hash value using each anonymous type's member variables as input to the System.Collections.Generic.EqualityComparer<T> type. Using this implementation of GetHashCode(), two anonymous types will yield the same hash value if (and only if) they have the same set of properties that have been assigned the same values. Given this implementation, anonymous types are well-suited to be contained within a Hashtable container.

The Semantics of Equality for Anonymous Types

While the implementation of the overridden ToString() and GetHashCode() methods is fairly straightforward, you might be wondering how the Equals() method has been implemented. For example, if you were to define two "anonymous cars" variables that specify the same name-value pairs, would these two variables be considered equal? To see the results firsthand, update your Program type with the following new method:

```
static void EqualityTest()
{
  // Make 2 anonymous classes with identical name/value pairs.
  var firstCar = new { Color = "Bright Pink", Make = "Saab", CurrentSpeed = 55 };
  var secondCar = new { Color = "Bright Pink", Make = "Saab", CurrentSpeed = 55 };

  // Are they considered equal when using Equals()?
  if (firstCar.Equals(secondCar))
    Console.WriteLine("Same anonymous object!");
  else
    Console.WriteLine("Not the same anonymous object!");
```

```
  // Are they considered equal when using ==?
  if (firstCar == secondCar)
    Console.WriteLine("Same anonymous object!");
  else
    Console.WriteLine("Not the same anonymous object!");

  // Are these objects the same underlying type?
  if (firstCar.GetType().Name == secondCar.GetType().Name)
    Console.WriteLine("We are both the same type!");
  else
    Console.WriteLine("We are different types!");

  // Show all the details.
  Console.WriteLine();
  ReflectOverAnonymousType(firstCar);
  ReflectOverAnonymousType(secondCar);
}
```

Assuming you have called this method from within Main(), here is the (somewhat surprising) output:

```
My car is a Bright Pink Saab.
You have a Black BMW going 90 MPH
ToString() == { Make = BMW, Color = Black, Speed = 90 }

Same anonymous object!
Not the same anonymous object!
We are both the same type!

obj is an instance of: <>f__AnonymousType0`3
Base class of <>f__AnonymousType0`3 is System.Object
obj.ToString() == { Color = Bright Pink, Make = Saab, CurrentSpeed = 55 }
obj.GetHashCode() == -439083487

obj is an instance of: <>f__AnonymousType0`3
Base class of <>f__AnonymousType0`3 is System.Object
obj.ToString() == { Color = Bright Pink, Make = Saab, CurrentSpeed = 55 }
obj.GetHashCode() == -439083487
```

When you run this test code, you will see that the first conditional test where you call Equals() returns true and, therefore, the message "Same anonymous object!" prints out to the screen. This is because the compiler-generated Equals() method uses value-based semantics when testing for equality (e.g., checking the value of each field of the objects being compared).

However, the second conditional test, which makes use of the C# equality operator (==), prints out "Not the same anonymous object!" This might seem at first glance to be a bit counterintuitive. This result is because anonymous types do *not* receive overloaded versions of the C# equality operators (== and !=). Given this, when you test for equality of anonymous types using the C# equality operators (rather than the Equals() method), the *references*, not the values maintained by the objects, are being tested for equality.

Last but not least, in the final conditional test (where you examine the underlying type name), you find that the anonymous types are instances of the same compiler-generated class type (in this example, <>f AnonymousType0`3) because firstCar and secondCar have the same properties (Color, Make, and CurrentSpeed).

435

This illustrates an important but subtle point: the compiler will generate a new class definition only when an anonymous type contains *unique* names of the anonymous type. Thus, if you declare identical anonymous types (again, meaning the same names) within the same assembly, the compiler generates only a single anonymous type definition.

Anonymous Types Containing Anonymous Types

It is possible to create an anonymous type that is composed of other anonymous types. For example, assume you want to model a purchase order that consists of a timestamp, a price point, and the automobile purchased. Here is a new (slightly more sophisticated) anonymous type representing such an entity:

```
// Make an anonymous type that is composed of another.
var purchaseItem = new {
  TimeBought = DateTime.Now,
  ItemBought = new {Color = "Red", Make = "Saab", CurrentSpeed = 55},
  Price = 34.000};

ReflectOverAnonymousType(purchaseItem);
```

At this point, you should understand the syntax used to define anonymous types, but you might still be wondering exactly where (and when) to use this new language feature. To be blunt, anonymous type declarations should be used sparingly, typically only when making use of the LINQ technology set (see Chapter 12). You would never want to abandon the use of strongly typed classes/structures simply for the sake of doing so, given anonymous types' numerous limitations, which include the following:

- You don't control the name of the anonymous type.

- Anonymous types always extend System.Object.

- The fields and properties of an anonymous type are always read-only.

- Anonymous types cannot support events, custom methods, custom operators, or custom overrides.

- Anonymous types are always implicitly sealed.

- Anonymous types are always created using the default constructor.

However, when programming with the LINQ technology set, you will find that in many cases this syntax can be helpful when you want to quickly model the overall *shape* of an entity rather than its functionality.

■ **Source Code**   You can find the AnonymousTypes project in the Chapter 11 subdirectory.

Working with Pointer Types

And now for the final topic of the chapter, which most likely will be the least used of all C# features for the vast majority of your .NET projects.

■ **Note**   In the examples that follow, I'm assuming you have some background in C++ pointer manipulation. If this is not true, feel free to skip this topic entirely. Using pointers will not be a common task for the vast majority of C# applications.

In Chapter 4, you learned that the .NET platform defines two major categories of data: value types and reference types. Truth be told, however, there is a third category: *pointer types*. To work with pointer types, you get specific operators and keywords that allow you to bypass the CLR's memory-management scheme and take matters into your own hands (see Table 11-2).

Table 11-2. *Pointer-Centric C# Operators and Keywords*

Operator/Keyword	Meaning in Life
*	This operator is used to create a pointer variable (i.e., a variable that represents a direct location in memory). As in C++, this same operator is used for pointer indirection.
&	This operator is used to obtain the address of a variable in memory.
->	This operator is used to access fields of a type that is represented by a pointer (the unsafe version of the C# dot operator).
[]	This operator (in an unsafe context) allows you to index the slot pointed to by a pointer variable (if you're a C++ programmer, you will recall the interplay between a pointer variable and the [] operator).
++, --	In an unsafe context, the increment and decrement operators can be applied to pointer types.
+, -	In an unsafe context, the addition and subtraction operators can be applied to pointer types.
==,!=, <, >, <=, =>	In an unsafe context, the comparison and equality operators can be applied to pointer types.
stackalloc	In an unsafe context, the stackalloc keyword can be used to allocate C# arrays directly on the stack.
fixed	In an unsafe context, the fixed keyword can be used to temporarily fix a variable so that its address can be found.

Now, before digging into the details, let me again point out that you will *seldom if ever* need to make use of pointer types. Although C# does allow you to drop down to the level of pointer manipulations, understand that the .NET runtime has absolutely no clue of your intentions. Thus, if you mismanage a pointer, you are the one in charge of dealing with the consequences. Given these warnings, when exactly would you need to work with pointer types? There are two common situations:

- You are looking to optimize select parts of your application by directly manipulating memory outside the management of the CLR.

- You are calling methods of a C-based .dll or COM server that demand pointer types as parameters. Even in this case, you can often bypass pointer types in favor of the System.IntPtr type and members of the System.Runtime.InteropServices. Marshal type.

In the event that you do decide to make use of this C# language feature, you are required to inform the C# compiler (`csc.exe`) of your intentions by enabling your project to support "unsafe code." To do so at the command line, simply supply the following /unsafe flag as an argument:

```
csc /unsafe *.cs
```

From Visual Studio, you will need to access your project's Properties page and select the Allow Unsafe Code box on the Build tab (see Figure 11-2). To experiment with pointer types, create a new Console Application project named UnsafeCode, and make sure you enable the Allow unsafe code setting.

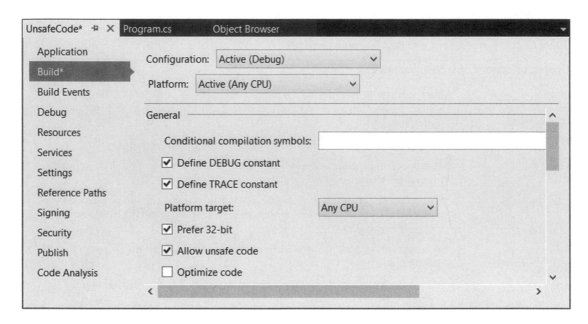

Figure 11-2. *Enabling unsafe code using Visual Studio*

The unsafe Keyword

When you want to work with pointers in C#, you must specifically declare a block of "unsafe code" using the unsafe keyword (any code that is not marked with the unsafe keyword is considered "safe" automatically). For example, the following Program class declares a scope of unsafe code within the safe Main() method:

```
class Program
{
  static void Main(string[] args)
  {
    unsafe
    {
      // Work with pointer types here!
    }

    // Can't work with pointers here!
  }
}
```

In addition to declaring a scope of unsafe code within a method, you can build structures, classes, type members, and parameters that are "unsafe." Here are a few examples to gnaw on (no need to define the Node or Node2 types in your current project):

```
// This entire structure is "unsafe" and can
// be used only in an unsafe context.
unsafe struct Node
{
  public int Value;
  public Node* Left;
  public Node* Right;
}


// This struct is safe, but the Node2* members
// are not. Technically, you may access "Value" from
// outside an unsafe context, but not "Left" and "Right".
public struct Node2
{
  public int Value;

  // These can be accessed only in an unsafe context!
  public unsafe Node2* Left;
  public unsafe Node2* Right;
}
```

Methods (static or instance level) may be marked as unsafe as well. For example, assume you know that a particular static method will make use of pointer logic. To ensure that this method can be called only from an unsafe context, you could define the method as follows:

```
static unsafe void SquareIntPointer(int* myIntPointer)
{
  // Square the value just for a test.
  *myIntPointer *= *myIntPointer;
}
```

The configuration of your method demands that the caller invoke SquareIntPointer() as follows:

```
static void Main(string[] args)
{
  unsafe
  {
    int myInt = 10;

    // OK, because we are in an unsafe context.
    SquareIntPointer(&myInt);
    Console.WriteLine("myInt: {0}", myInt);
  }

  int myInt2 = 5;
```

```
// Compiler error! Must be in unsafe context!
  SquareIntPointer(&myInt2);
  Console.WriteLine("myInt: {0}", myInt2);
}
```

If you would rather not force the caller to wrap the invocation within an unsafe context, you could update Main() with the unsafe keyword. In this case, the following code would compile:

```
static unsafe void Main(string[] args)
{
  int myInt2 = 5;
  SquareIntPointer(&myInt2);
  Console.WriteLine("myInt: {0}", myInt2);
}
```

If you run this Main() method, you will see the following output:

```
myInt: 25
```

Working with the * and & Operators

After you have established an unsafe context, you are then free to build pointers to data types using the * operator and obtain the address of what is being pointed to using the & operator. Unlike in C or C++, in C# the * operator is applied to the underlying type only, not as a prefix to each pointer variable name. For example, consider the following code, which illustrates both the correct and incorrect ways to declare pointers to integer variables:

```
// No! This is incorrect under C#!
int *pi, *pj;

// Yes! This is the way of C#.
int* pi, pj;
```

Consider the following unsafe method:

```
static unsafe void PrintValueAndAddress()
{
  int myInt;

  // Define an int pointer, and
  // assign it the address of myInt.
  int* ptrToMyInt = &myInt;

  // Assign value of myInt using pointer indirection.
  *ptrToMyInt = 123;

  // Print some stats.
  Console.WriteLine("Value of myInt {0}", myInt);
  Console.WriteLine("Address of myInt {0:X}", (int)&ptrToMyInt);
}
```

440

An Unsafe (and Safe) Swap Function

Of course, declaring pointers to local variables simply to assign their value (as in the previous example) is never required and not altogether useful. To illustrate a more practical example of unsafe code, assume you want to build a swap function using pointer arithmetic.

```
public unsafe static void UnsafeSwap(int* i, int* j)
{
  int temp = *i;
  *i = *j;
  *j = temp;
}
```

Very C-like, don't you think? However, given your work previously, you should be aware that you could write the following safe version of your swap algorithm using the C# ref keyword:

```
public static void SafeSwap(ref int i, ref int j)
{
  int temp = i;
  i = j;
  j = temp;
}
```

The functionality of each method is identical, thus reinforcing the point that direct pointer manipulation is not a mandatory task under C#. Here is the calling logic using a safe Main(), with an unsafe context:

```
static void Main(string[] args)
{
  Console.WriteLine("***** Calling method with unsafe code *****");

  // Values for swap.
  int i = 10, j = 20;

  // Swap values "safely."
  Console.WriteLine("\n***** Safe swap *****");
  Console.WriteLine("Values before safe swap: i = {0}, j = {1}", i, j);
  SafeSwap(ref i, ref j);
  Console.WriteLine("Values after safe swap: i = {0}, j = {1}", i, j);

  // Swap values "unsafely."
  Console.WriteLine("\n***** Unsafe swap *****");
  Console.WriteLine("Values before unsafe swap: i = {0}, j = {1}", i, j);
  unsafe { UnsafeSwap(&i, &j); }

  Console.WriteLine("Values after unsafe swap: i = {0}, j = {1}", i, j);
  Console.ReadLine();
}
```

Field Access via Pointers (the -> Operator)

Now assume you have defined a simple, safe Point structure, as follows:

```
struct Point
{
  public int x;
  public int y;

  public override string ToString() => $"({x}, {y})";
}
```

If you declare a pointer to a Point type, you will need to make use of the pointer field-access operator (represented by ->) to access its public members. As shown in Table 11-2, this is the unsafe version of the standard (safe) dot operator (.). In fact, using the pointer indirection operator (*), it is possible to dereference a pointer to (once again) apply the dot operator notation. Check out the unsafe method:

```
static unsafe void UsePointerToPoint()
{
  // Access members via pointer.
  Point point;
  Point* p = &point;
  p->x = 100;
  p->y = 200;
  Console.WriteLine(p->ToString());

  // Access members via pointer indirection.
  Point point2;
  Point* p2 = &point2;
  (*p2).x = 100;
  (*p2).y = 200;
  Console.WriteLine((*p2).ToString());
}
```

The stackalloc Keyword

In an unsafe context, you may need to declare a local variable that allocates memory directly from the call stack (and is, therefore, not subject to .NET garbage collection). To do so, C# provides the stackalloc keyword, which is the C# equivalent to the _alloca function of the C runtime library. Here is a simple example:

```
static unsafe void UnsafeStackAlloc()
{
  char* p = stackalloc char[256];
  for (int k = 0; k < 256; k++)
    p[k] = (char)k;
}
```

Pinning a Type via the fixed Keyword

As you saw in the previous example, allocating a chunk of memory within an unsafe context may be facilitated via the stackalloc keyword. By the very nature of this operation, the allocated memory is cleaned up as soon as the allocating method has returned (as the memory is acquired from the stack). However, assume a more complex example. During our examination of the -> operator, you created a value type named Point. Like all value types, the allocated memory is popped off the stack once the executing scope has terminated. For the sake of argument, assume Point was instead defined as a *reference* type, like so:

```
class PointRef // <= Renamed and retyped.
{
  public int x;
  public int y;
  public override string ToString() => $"({x}, {y})";
}
```

As you are aware, if the caller declares a variable of type Point, the memory is allocated on the garbage-collected heap. The burning question then becomes, "What if an unsafe context wants to interact with this object (or any object on the heap)?" Given that garbage collection can occur at any moment, imagine the problems encountered when accessing the members of Point at the very point in time such a sweep of the heap is underway. Theoretically, it is possible that the unsafe context is attempting to interact with a member that is no longer accessible or has been repositioned on the heap after surviving a generational sweep (which is an obvious problem).

To lock a reference type variable in memory from an unsafe context, C# provides the fixed keyword. The fixed statement sets a pointer to a managed type and "pins" that variable during the execution of the code. Without fixed, pointers to managed variables would be of little use, since garbage collection could relocate the variables unpredictably. (In fact, the C# compiler will not allow you to set a pointer to a managed variable except in a fixed statement.)

Thus, if you create a PointRef object and want to interact with its members, you must write the following code (or receive a compiler error):

```
public unsafe static void UseAndPinPoint()
{
  PointRef pt = new PointRef
  {
    x = 5,
    y = 6
  };

  // Pin pt in place so it will not
  // be moved or GC-ed.
  fixed (int* p = &pt.x)
  {
    // Use int* variable here!
  }

  // pt is now unpinned, and ready to be GC-ed once
  // the method completes.
  Console.WriteLine ("Point is: {0}", pt);
}
```

In a nutshell, the fixed keyword allows you to build a statement that locks a reference variable in memory, such that its address remains constant for the duration of the statement (or scope block). Any time you interact with a reference type from within the context of unsafe code, pinning the reference is a must.

The sizeof Keyword

The final unsafe-centric C# keyword to consider is sizeof. As in C++, the C# sizeof keyword is used to obtain the size in bytes of an *intrinsic data type*, but not a custom type, unless within an unsafe context. For example, the following method does not need to be declared "unsafe" as all arguments to the sizeof keyword are intrinsic types:

```
static void UseSizeOfOperator()
{
  Console.WriteLine("The size of short is {0}.", sizeof(short));
  Console.WriteLine("The size of int is {0}.", sizeof(int));
  Console.WriteLine("The size of long is {0}.", sizeof(long));
}
```

However, if you want to get the size of your custom Point structure, you need to update this method as so (note the unsafe keyword has been added):

```
unsafe static void UseSizeOfOperator()
{
...
  Console.WriteLine("The size of Point is {0}.", sizeof(Point));
}
```

■ **Source Code**   You can find the UnsafeCode project in the Chapter 11 subdirectory.

That wraps up the look at some of the more advanced features of the C# programming language. To make sure we are all on the same page here, I again must say that a majority of your .NET projects might never need to directly use these features (especially pointers). Nevertheless, as you will see in later chapters, some topics are quite useful, if not required, when working with the LINQ APIs, most notably extension methods and anonymous types.

Summary

The purpose of this chapter was to deepen your understanding of the C# programming language. First, you investigated various advanced type construction techniques (indexer methods, overloaded operators, and custom conversion routines).

Next, you examined the role of extension methods and anonymous types. As you'll see in some detail in the next chapter, these features are useful when working with LINQ-centric APIs (though you can use them anywhere in your code, should they be useful). Recall that anonymous methods allow you to quickly model the "shape" of a type, while extension methods allow you to tack on new functionality to types, without the need to subclass.

You spent the remainder of this chapter examining a small set of lesser-known keywords (sizeof, unsafe, and so forth) and during the process learned how to work with raw pointer types. As stated throughout the examination of pointer types, the vast majority of your C# applications will never need to use them.

CHAPTER 12

■ ■ ■

LINQ to Objects

Regardless of the type of application you are creating using the .NET platform, your program will certainly need to access some form of data as it executes. To be sure, data can be found in numerous locations, including XML files, relational databases, in-memory collections, and primitive arrays. Historically speaking, based on the location of said data, programmers needed to make use of different and unrelated APIs. The Language Integrated Query (LINQ) technology set, introduced initially in .NET 3.5, provides a concise, symmetrical, and strongly typed manner to access a wide variety of data stores. In this chapter, you will begin your investigation of LINQ by focusing on LINQ to Objects.

Before you dive into LINQ to Objects proper, the first part of this chapter quickly reviews the key C# programming constructs that enable LINQ. As you work through this chapter, you will find that implicitly typed local variables, object initialization syntax, lambda expressions, extension methods, and anonymous types will be quite useful (if not occasionally mandatory).

After this supporting infrastructure is reviewed, the remainder of the chapter will introduce you to the LINQ programming model and its role in the .NET platform. Here, you will come to learn the role of query operators and query expressions, which allow you to define statements that will interrogate a data source to yield the requested result set. Along the way, you will build numerous LINQ examples that interact with data contained within arrays as well as various collection types (both generic and nongeneric) and understand the assemblies, namespaces, and types that represent the LINQ to Objects API.

■ **Note** The information in this chapter is the foundation for future sections and chapters of this book, including Parallel LINQ (Chapter 19), Entity Framework (Chapter 22), and Entity Framework Core (Chapter 30).

LINQ-Specific Programming Constructs

From a high level, LINQ can be understood as a strongly typed query language, embedded directly into the grammar of C#. Using LINQ, you can build any number of expressions that have a look and feel similar to that of a database SQL query. However, a LINQ query can be applied to any number of data stores, including stores that have nothing to do with a literal relational database.

■ **Note** Although LINQ queries look similar to SQL queries, the syntax is *not* identical. In fact, many LINQ queries seem to be the exact opposite format of a similar database query! If you attempt to map LINQ directly to SQL, you will surely become frustrated. To keep your sanity, I recommend you try your best to regard LINQ queries as unique statements, which just "happen to look" similar to SQL.

© Andrew Troelsen and Philip Japikse 2017
A. Troelsen and P. Japikse, *Pro C# 7*, https://doi.org/10.1007/978-1-4842-3018-3_12

When LINQ was first introduced to the .NET platform in version 3.5, the C# and VB languages were each expanded with a large number of new programming constructs used to support the LINQ technology set. Specifically, the C# language uses the following core LINQ-centric features:

- Implicitly typed local variables
- Object/collection initialization syntax
- Lambda expressions
- Extension methods
- Anonymous types

These features have already been explored in detail within various chapters of the text. However, to get the ball rolling, let's quickly review each feature in turn, just to make sure we are all in the proper mind-set.

■ **Note**   Because the following sections are reviews of material covered elsewhere in the book, I have not included a C# code project for this content.

Implicit Typing of Local Variables

In Chapter 3, you learned about the var keyword of C#. This keyword allows you to define a local variable without explicitly specifying the underlying data type. The variable, however, is strongly typed, as the compiler will determine the correct data type based on the initial assignment. Recall this code example from Chapter 3:

```
static void DeclareImplicitVars()
{
  // Implicitly typed local variables.
  var myInt = 0;
  var myBool = true;
  var myString = "Time, marches on...";

  // Print out the underlying type.
  Console.WriteLine("myInt is a: {0}", myInt.GetType().Name);
  Console.WriteLine("myBool is a: {0}", myBool.GetType().Name);
  Console.WriteLine("myString is a: {0}", myString.GetType().Name);
}
```

This language feature is helpful, and often mandatory, when using LINQ. As you will see during this chapter, many LINQ queries will return a sequence of data types, which are not known until compile time. Given that the underlying data type is not known until the application is compiled, you obviously can't declare a variable explicitly!

Object and Collection Initialization Syntax

Chapter 5 explored the role of object initialization syntax, which allows you to create a class or structure variable and to set any number of its public properties in one fell swoop. The end result is a compact (yet still easy on the eyes) syntax that can be used to get your objects ready for use. Also recall from Chapter 9, the C# language allows you to use a similar syntax to initialize collections of objects. Consider the following code snippet, which uses collection initialization syntax to fill a List<T> of Rectangle objects, each of which maintains two Point objects to represent an (x,y) position:

```
List<Rectangle> myListOfRects = new List<Rectangle>
{
  new Rectangle {TopLeft = new Point { X = 10, Y = 10 },
                 BottomRight = new Point { X = 200, Y = 200}},
  new Rectangle {TopLeft = new Point { X = 2, Y = 2 },
                 BottomRight = new Point { X = 100, Y = 100}},
  new Rectangle {TopLeft = new Point { X = 5, Y = 5 },
                 BottomRight = new Point { X = 90, Y = 75}}
};
```

While you are never required to use collection/object initialization syntax, doing so results in a more compact codebase. Furthermore, this syntax, when combined with implicit typing of local variables, allows you to declare an anonymous type, which is useful when creating a LINQ projection. You'll learn about LINQ projections later in this chapter.

Lambda Expressions

The C# lambda operator (=>)was fully explored in Chapter 10. Recall that this operator allows you to build a lambda expression, which can be used any time you invoke a method that requires a strongly typed delegate as an argument. Lambdas greatly simplify how you work with .NET delegates, in that they reduce the amount of code you have to author by hand. Recall that a lambda expression can be broken down into the following usage:

```
( ArgumentsToProcess ) => { StatementsToProcessThem }
```

In Chapter 10, I walked you through how to interact with the FindAll() method of the generic List<T> class using three different approaches. After working with the raw Predicate<T> delegate and a C# anonymous method, you eventually arrived with the following (extremely concise) iteration that used the following lambda expression:

```
static void LambdaExpressionSyntax()
{
  // Make a list of integers.
  List<int> list = new List<int>();
  list.AddRange(new int[] { 20, 1, 4, 8, 9, 44 });

  // C# lambda expression.
  List<int> evenNumbers = list.FindAll(i => (i % 2) == 0);

  Console.WriteLine("Here are your even numbers:");
  foreach (int evenNumber in evenNumbers)
  {
    Console.Write("{0}\t", evenNumber);
  }
  Console.WriteLine();
}
```

Lambdas will be useful when working with the underlying object model of LINQ. As you will soon find out, the C# LINQ query operators are simply a shorthand notation for calling true-blue methods on a class named System.Linq.Enumerable. These methods typically always require delegates (the Func<> delegate in particular) as parameters, which are used to process your data to yield the correct result set. Using lambdas, you can streamline your code and allow the compiler to infer the underlying delegate.

Extension Methods

C# extension methods allow you to tack on new functionality to existing classes without the need to subclass. As well, extension methods allow you to add new functionality to sealed classes and structures, which could never be subclassed in the first place. Recall from Chapter 11, when you author an extension method, the first parameter is qualified with the this keyword and marks the type being extended. Also recall that extension methods must always be defined within a static class and must, therefore, also be declared using the static keyword. Here's an example:

```
namespace MyExtensions
{
  static class ObjectExtensions
  {
    // Define an extension method to System.Object.
    public static void DisplayDefiningAssembly(this object obj)
    {
      Console.WriteLine("{0} lives here:\n\t->{1}\n", obj.GetType().Name,
        Assembly.GetAssembly(obj.GetType()));
    }
  }
}
```

To use this extension, an application must import the namespace defining the extension (and possibly add a reference to the external assembly). At this point, simply import the defining namespace and code away.

```
static void Main(string[] args)
{
  // Since everything extends System.Object, all classes and structures
  // can use this extension.
  int myInt = 12345678;
  myInt.DisplayDefiningAssembly();

  System.Data.DataSet d = new System.Data.DataSet();
  d.DisplayDefiningAssembly();
  Console.ReadLine();
}
```

When you are working with LINQ, you will seldom, if ever, be required to manually build your own extension methods. However, as you create LINQ query expressions, you will actually be making use of numerous extension methods already defined by Microsoft. In fact, each C# LINQ query operator is a shorthand notation for making a manual call on an underlying extension method, typically defined by the System.Linq.Enumerable utility class.

Anonymous Types

The final C# language feature I'd like to quickly review is that of anonymous types, which was explored in Chapter 11. This feature can be used to quickly model the "shape" of data by allowing the compiler to generate a new class definition at compile time, based on a supplied set of name-value pairs. Recall that this type will be composed using value-based semantics, and each virtual method of System.Object will be overridden accordingly. To define an anonymous type, declare an implicitly typed variable and specify the data's shape using object initialization syntax.

```
// Make an anonymous type that is composed of another.
var purchaseItem = new {
  TimeBought = DateTime.Now,
  ItemBought = new {Color = "Red", Make = "Saab", CurrentSpeed = 55},
  Price = 34.000};
```

LINQ makes frequent use of anonymous types when you want to project new forms of data on the fly. For example, assume you have a collection of Person objects and want to use LINQ to obtain information on the age and Social Security number of each. Using a LINQ projection, you can allow the compiler to generate a new anonymous type that contains your information.

Understanding the Role of LINQ

That wraps up the quick review of the C# language features that allow LINQ to work its magic. However, why have LINQ in the first place? Well, as software developers, it is hard to deny that the vast majority of our programming time is spent obtaining and manipulating data. When speaking of "data," it is easy to immediately envision information contained within relational databases. However, another popular location for data is within XML documents or simple text files.

Data can be found in numerous places beyond these two common homes for information. For instance, say you have an array or generic List<T> type containing 300 integers and you want to obtain a subset that meets a given criterion (e.g., only the odd or even members in the container, only prime numbers, only nonrepeating numbers greater than 50). Or perhaps you are making use of the reflection APIs and need to obtain only metadata descriptions for each class deriving from a particular parent class within an array of Types. Indeed, data is *everywhere*.

Prior to .NET 3.5, interacting with a particular flavor of data required programmers to use very diverse APIs. Consider, for example, Table 12-1, which illustrates several common APIs used to access various types of data (I'm sure you can think of many other examples).

Table 12-1. *Ways to Manipulate Various Types of Data*

The Data You Want	How to Obtain It
Relational data	System.Data.dll, System.Data.SqlClient.dll, and so on
XML document data	System.Xml.dll
Metadata tables	The System.Reflection namespace
Collections of objects	System.Array and the System.Collections/System.Collections.Generic namespaces

Of course, nothing is wrong with these approaches to data manipulation. In fact, you can (and will) certainly make direct use of ADO.NET, the XML namespaces, reflection services, and the various collection types. However, the basic problem is that each of these APIs is an island unto itself, which offers little in the way of integration. True, it is possible (for example) to save an ADO.NET DataSet as XML and then manipulate it via the System.Xml namespaces, but nonetheless, data manipulation remains rather asymmetrical.

The LINQ API is an attempt to provide a consistent, symmetrical manner in which programmers can obtain and manipulate "data" in the broad sense of the term. Using LINQ, you are able to create directly within the C# programming language constructs called *query expressions*. These query expressions are based on numerous query operators that have been intentionally designed to look and feel similar (but not quite identical) to a SQL expression.

The twist, however, is that a query expression can be used to interact with numerous types of data—even data that has nothing to do with a relational database. Strictly speaking, "LINQ" is the term used to describe this overall approach to data access. However, based on where you are applying your LINQ queries, you will encounter various terms, such as the following:

- *LINQ to Objects*: This term refers to the act of applying LINQ queries to arrays and collections.

- *LINQ to XML*: This term refers to the act of using LINQ to manipulate and query XML documents.

- *LINQ to DataSet*: This term refers to the act of applying LINQ queries to ADO.NET DataSet objects.

- *LINQ to Entities*: This aspect of LINQ allows you to make use of LINQ queries within the ADO.NET Entity Framework (EF) API.

- *Parallel LINQ (aka PLINQ)*: This allows for parallel processing of data returned from a LINQ query.

Today, LINQ is an integral part of the .NET base class libraries, managed languages, and Visual Studio itself.

LINQ Expressions Are Strongly Typed

It is also important to point out that a LINQ query expression (unlike a traditional SQL statement) is *strongly typed*. Therefore, the C# compiler will keep you honest and make sure that these expressions are syntactically well-formed. Tools such as Visual Studio can use metadata for useful features such as IntelliSense, autocompletion, and so forth.

The Core LINQ Assemblies

As mentioned in Chapter 2, the New Project dialog of Visual Studio has the option of selecting which version of the .NET platform you want to compile against. When you opt to compile against .NET 3.5 or higher, each of the project templates will automatically reference the key LINQ assemblies, which can be viewed using Solution Explorer. Table 12-2 documents the role of the key LINQ assemblies. However, you will encounter additional LINQ libraries over the remainder of this book.

Table 12-2. *Core LINQ-Centric Assemblies*

Assembly	Meaning in Life
System.Core.dll	Defines the types that represent the core LINQ API. This is the one assembly you must have access to if you want to use any LINQ API, including LINQ to Objects.
System.Data.DataSetExtensions.dll	Defines a handful of types to integrate ADO.NET types into the LINQ programming paradigm (LINQ to DataSet).
System.Xml.Linq.dll	Provides functionality for using LINQ with XML document data (LINQ to XML).

To work with LINQ to Objects, you must make sure that every C# code file that contains LINQ queries imports the System.Linq namespace (primarily defined within System.Core.dll). If you do not do so, you will run into a number of problems. As a good rule of thumb, if you see a compiler error looking similar to this:

```
Error 1 Could not find an implementation of the query pattern for source type 'int[]'.
'Where' not found. Are you missing a reference to 'System.Core.dll' or a using directive
for 'System.Linq'?
```

the chances are extremely good that your C# file does not have the following using directive:

```
using System.Linq;
```

Applying LINQ Queries to Primitive Arrays

To begin examining LINQ to Objects, let's build an application that will apply LINQ queries to various array objects. Create a Console Application project named LinqOverArray, and define a static helper method within the Program class named QueryOverStrings().In this method, create a string array containing six or so items of your liking (here I listed a batch of video games in my library). Make sure to have at least two entries that contain numerical values and a few that have embedded spaces.

```
static void QueryOverStrings()
{
  // Assume we have an array of strings.
  string[] currentVideoGames = {"Morrowind", "Uncharted 2", "Fallout 3", "Daxter",
  "System Shock 2"};
}
```

Now, update Main() to invoke QueryOverStrings().

```
static void Main(string[] args)
{
  Console.WriteLine("***** Fun with LINQ to Objects *****\n");
  QueryOverStrings();
  Console.ReadLinc();
}
```

When you have any array of data, it is common to extract a subset of items based on a given requirement. Maybe you want to obtain only the subitems that contain a number (e.g., System Shock 2, Uncharted 2, and Fallout 3), have more or less than some number of characters, or don't contain embedded spaces (e.g., Morrowind or Daxter). While you could certainly perform such tasks using members of the System.Array type and a bit of elbow grease, LINQ query expressions can greatly simplify the process.

Going on the assumption that you want to obtain from the array only items that contain an embedded blank space and you want these items listed in alphabetical order, you could build the following LINQ query expression:

```
static void QueryOverStrings()
{
  // Assume we have an array of strings.
  string[] currentVideoGames = {"Morrowind", "Uncharted 2", "Fallout 3", "Daxter",
  "System Shock 2"};

  // Build a query expression to find the items in the array
  // that have an embedded space.
  IEnumerable<string> subset = from g in currentVideoGames where g.Contains(" ") orderby g
  select g;

  // Print out the results.
  foreach (string s in subset)
    Console.WriteLine("Item: {0}", s);
}
```

Notice that the query expression created here makes use of the from, in, where, orderby, and select LINQ query operators. You will dig into the formalities of query expression syntax later in this chapter. However, even now you should be able to read this statement roughly as "Give me the items inside of currentVideoGames that contain a space, ordered alphabetically."

Here, each item that matches the search criteria has been given the name g (as in "game"); however, any valid C# variable name would do:

```
IEnumerable<string> subset = from game in currentVideoGames
                             where game.Contains(" ") orderby
                             game select game;
```

Notice that the returned sequence is held in a variable named subset, typed as a type that implements the generic version of IEnumerable<T>, where T is of type System.String (after all, you are querying an array of strings). After you obtain the result set, you then simply print out each item using a standard foreach construct. If you run your application, you will find the following output:

```
***** Fun with LINQ to Objects *****
Item: Fallout 3
Item: System Shock 2
Item: Uncharted 2
```

Once Again, Using Extension Methods

The LINQ syntax used earlier (and the rest of this chapter) is referred to as LINQ *query expressions*, which is a format that is similar to SQL but (somewhat annoying) different. There is another syntax that uses extension methods. Most LINQ statements can be written using either format; however, some of the more complex queries will require using query expressions.

Create a new method named QueryOverStringsWithExtensionMethods() and enter the following code:

```
static void QueryOverStringsWithExtensionMethods()
{
  // Assume we have an array of strings.
  string[] currentVideoGames = {"Morrowind", "Uncharted 2", "Fallout 3", "Daxter",
  "System Shock 2"};

  // Build a query expression to find the items in the array
  // that have an embedded space.
  IEnumerable<string> subset =
    currentVideoGames.Where(g => g.Contains(" ")).OrderBy(g => g).Select(g => g);

  // Print out the results.
  foreach (string s in subset)
    Console.WriteLine("Item: {0}", s);
}
```

Everything is the same as the previos method, except for the line in bold. This is using the extension method syntax. This syntax uses lambda expressions within each method to define the operation. For example, the lambda in the Where() method defines the condition (where a value contains a space). Just as in the query expression syntax, the letter used to indicate the value being evaluated in the lambda is random; I could have used v for video games.

While the results are the same (running this method produces the same output as the previous method using the query expression), you will see soon that the *type* of the result set is slightly different. For most (if not practically all) scenarios, this difference doesn't cause any issues, and the formats can be used interchangeably.

Once Again, Without LINQ

To be sure, LINQ is never mandatory. If you so choose, you could have found the same result set by forgoing LINQ altogether and making use of programming primitives such as if statements and for loops. Here is a method that yields the same result as the QueryOverStrings() method but in a much more verbose manner:

```
static void QueryOverStringsLongHand()
{
  // Assume we have an array of strings.
  string[] currentVideoGames = {"Morrowind", "Uncharted 2", "Fallout 3", "Daxter",
  "System Shock 2"};

  string[] gamesWithSpaces = new string[5];
```

```
  for (int i = 0; i < currentVideoGames.Length; i++)
  {
    if (currentVideoGames[i].Contains(" "))
      gamesWithSpaces[i] = currentVideoGames[i];
  }

  // Now sort them.
  Array.Sort(gamesWithSpaces);

  // Print out the results.
  foreach (string s in gamesWithSpaces)
  {
    if( s != null)
      Console.WriteLine("Item: {0}", s);
  }
  Console.WriteLine();
}
```

While I am sure you can think of ways to tweak the previous method, the fact remains that LINQ queries can be used to radically simplify the process of extracting new subsets of data from a source. Rather than building nested loops, complex if/else logic, temporary data types, and so on, the C# compiler will perform the dirty work on your behalf, once you create a fitting LINQ query.

Reflecting Over a LINQ Result Set

Now, assume the Program class defines an additional helper function named ReflectOverQueryResults() that will print out various details of the LINQ result set (note the parameter is a System.Object to account for multiple types of result sets).

```
static void ReflectOverQueryResults(object resultSet, string queryType = "Query
Expressions")
{
  Console.WriteLine($"***** Info about your query using {queryType} *****");
  Console.WriteLine("resultSet is of type: {0}", resultSet.GetType().Name);
  Console.WriteLine("resultSet location: {0}", resultSet.GetType().Assembly.GetName().Name);
}
```

Update the core of QueryOverStrings() method to the following:

```
// Build a query expression to find the items in the array
// that have an embedded space.
IEnumerable<string> subset = from g in currentVideoGames where g.Contains(" ") orderby g
select g;
```

ReflectOverQueryResults(subset);

```
// Print out the results.
foreach (string s in subset)
  Console.WriteLine("Item: {0}", s);
```

When you run the application, you will see the subset variable is really an instance of the generic OrderedEnumerable<TElement, TKey> type (represented in terms of CIL code as OrderedEnumerable`2), which is an internal abstract type residing in the System.Core.dll assembly.

```
***** Info about your query using Query Expressions*****
resultSet is of type: OrderedEnumerable`2
resultSet location: System.Core
```

Make the same change to the QueryOverStringsWithExtensionMethods() method, with the exception of adding "Extension Methods" for the second parameter:

```
// Build a query expression to find the items in the array
// that have an embedded space.
IEnumerable<string> subset = currentVideoGames.Where(g => g.Contains(" ")).OrderBy(g =>
g).Select(g => g);
ReflectOverQueryResults(subset,"Extension Methods");

// Print out the results.
foreach (string s in subset)
  Console.WriteLine("Item: {0}", s);
```

When you run the application, you will see the subset variable is an instance of type System.Linq. Enumerable+WhereSelectEnumerableIterator. If you remove Select(g=>g) from the query, you will be back to having an instance of type OrderedEnumerable<TElement, TKey>. What does this all mean? For the overwhelming majority of developers, not much (if anything). They both derive from IEnumerable<T>, both can be iterated over in the same manner, and both can create a list or an array from their values.

```
***** Info about your query using Extension Methods *****
resultSet is of type: WhereSelectEnumerableIterator`2
resultSet location: System.Core
```

■ **Note**   Many of the types that represent a LINQ result are hidden by the Visual Studio Object Browser. These are low-level types not intended for direct use in your applications.

LINQ and Implicitly Typed Local Variables

While the current sample program makes it relatively easy to determine that the result set can be captured as an enumeration of the string object (e.g., IEnumerable<string>), I would guess that it is *not* clear that subset is really of type OrderedEnumerable<TElement, TKey>.

Given that LINQ result sets can be represented using a good number of types in various LINQ-centric namespaces, it would be tedious to define the proper type to hold a result set, because in many cases the underlying type may not be obvious or even directly accessible from your codebase (and as you will see, in some cases the type is generated at compile time).

To further accentuate this point, consider the following additional helper method defined within the Program class (which I assume you will invoke from within the Main() method):

```
static void QueryOverInts()
{
  int[] numbers = {10, 20, 30, 40, 1, 2, 3, 8};

  // Print only items less than 10.
  IEnumerable<int> subset = from i in numbers where i < 10 select i;

  foreach (int i in subset)
    Console.WriteLine("Item: {0}", i);
  ReflectOverQueryResults(subset);
}
```

In this case, the subset variable is a completely different underlying type. This time, the type implementing the IEnumerable<int> interface is a low-level class named WhereArrayIterator<T>.

```
Item: 1
Item: 2
Item: 3
Item: 8

***** Info about your query *****
resultSet is of type: WhereArrayIterator`1
resultSet location: System.Core
```

Given that the exact underlying type of a LINQ query is certainly not obvious, these first examples have represented the query results as an IEnumerable<T> variable, where T is the type of data in the returned sequence (string, int, etc.). However, this is still rather cumbersome. To add insult to injury, given that IEnumerable<T> extends the nongeneric IEnumerable interface, it would also be permissible to capture the result of a LINQ query as follows:

```
System.Collections.IEnumerable subset = from i in numbers where i < 10 select i;
```

Thankfully, implicit typing cleans things up considerably when working with LINQ queries.

```
static void QueryOverInts()
{
  int[] numbers = {10, 20, 30, 40, 1, 2, 3, 8};

  // Use implicit typing here...
  var subset = from i in numbers where i < 10 select i;

  // ...and here.
  foreach (var i in subset)
    Console.WriteLine("Item: {0} ", i);
  ReflectOverQueryResults(subset);
}
```

As a rule of thumb, you will always want to make use of implicit typing when capturing the results of a LINQ query. Just remember, however, that (in a vast majority of cases) the *real* return value is a type implementing the generic IEnumerable<T> interface.

Exactly what this type is under the covers (OrderedEnumerable<TElement, TKey>, WhereArrayIterator<T>, etc.) is irrelevant and not necessary to discover. As shown in the previous code example, you can simply use the var keyword within a foreach construct to iterate over the fetched data.

LINQ and Extension Methods

Although the current example does not have you author any extension methods directly, you are in fact using them seamlessly in the background. LINQ query expressions can be used to iterate over data containers that implement the generic IEnumerable<T> interface. However, the .NET System.Array class type (used to represent the array of strings and array of integers) does *not* implement this contract.

```
// The System.Array type does not seem to implement the correct
// infrastructure for query expressions!
public abstract class Array : ICloneable, IList, ICollection,
  IEnumerable, IStructuralComparable, IStructuralEquatable
{
  ...
}
```

While System.Array does not directly implement the IEnumerable<T> interface, it indirectly gains the required functionality of this type (as well as many other LINQ-centric members) via the static System.Linq.Enumerable class type.

This utility class defines a good number of generic extension methods (such as Aggregate<T>(), First<T>(), Max<T>(), etc.), which System.Array (and other types) acquires in the background. Thus, if you apply the dot operator on the currentVideoGames local variable, you will find a good number of members *not* found within the formal definition of System.Array (see Figure 12-1).

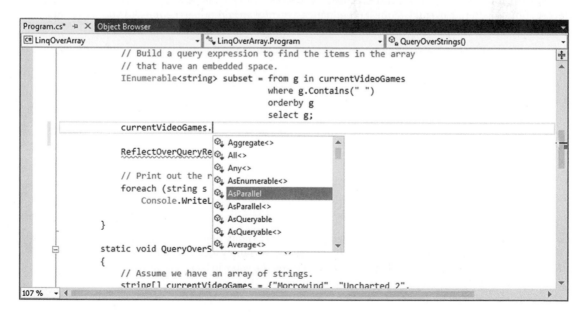

Figure 12-1. *The System.Array type has been extended with members of System.Linq.Enumerable*

The Role of Deferred Execution

Another important point regarding LINQ query expressions is that they are not actually evaluated until you iterate over the sequence. Formally speaking, this is termed *deferred execution*. The benefit of this approach is that you are able to apply the same LINQ query multiple times to the same container and rest assured you are obtaining the latest and greatest results. Consider the following update to the QueryOverInts() method:

```
static void QueryOverInts()
{
  int[] numbers = { 10, 20, 30, 40, 1, 2, 3, 8 };

  // Get numbers less than ten.
  var subset = from i in numbers where i < 10 select i;

  // LINQ statement evaluated here!
  foreach (var i in subset)
    Console.WriteLine("{0} < 10", i);
  Console.WriteLine();
  // Change some data in the array.
  numbers[0] = 4;

  // Evaluated again!
  foreach (var j in subset)
    Console.WriteLine("{0} < 10", j);

  Console.WriteLine();
  ReflectOverQueryResults(subset);
}
```

If you were to execute the program yet again, you would find the following output. Notice that the second time you iterate over the requested sequence, you find an additional member, as you set the first item in the array to be a value less than ten.

```
1 < 10
2 < 10
3 < 10
8 < 10

4 < 10
1 < 10
2 < 10
3 < 10
8 < 10
```

One useful aspect of Visual Studio is that if you set a breakpoint before the evaluation of a LINQ query, you are able to view the contents during a debugging session. Simply locate your mouse cursor over the LINQ result set variable (subset in Figure 12-2). When you do, you will be given the option of evaluating the query at that time by expanding the Results View option.

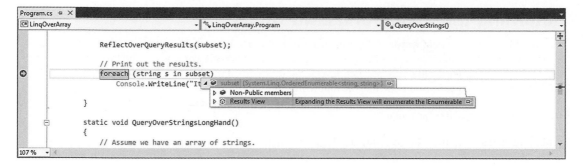

Figure 12-2. *Debugging LINQ expressions*

The Role of Immediate Execution

When you need to evaluate a LINQ expression from outside the confines of foreach logic, you are able to call any number of extension methods defined by the Enumerable type such as ToArray<T>(), ToDictionary<TSource,TKey>(), and ToList<T>(). These methods will cause a LINQ query to execute at the exact moment you call them to obtain a snapshot of the data. After you have done so, the snapshot of data may be independently manipulated.

```
static void ImmediateExecution()
{
  int[] numbers = { 10, 20, 30, 40, 1, 2, 3, 8 };

  // Get data RIGHT NOW as int[].
  int[] subsetAsIntArray = (from i in numbers where i < 10 select i).ToArray<int>();

  // Get data RIGHT NOW as List<int>.
  List<int> subsetAsListOfInts = (from i in numbers where i < 10 select i).ToList<int>();
}
```

Notice that the entire LINQ expression is wrapped within parentheses to cast it into the correct underlying type (whatever that might be) in order to call the extension methods of Enumerable.

Also recall from Chapter 9 that when the C# compiler can unambiguously determine the type parameter of a generic, you are not required to specify the type parameter. Thus, you could also call ToArray<T>() (or ToList<T>() for that matter) as follows:

```
int[] subsetAsIntArray = (from i in numbers where i < 10 select i).ToArray();
```

The usefulness of immediate execution is obvious when you need to return the results of a LINQ query to an external caller. And, as luck would have it, this happens to be the next topic of this chapter.

■ **Source Code**   You can find the LinqOverArray project in the Chapter 12 subdirectory.

Returning the Result of a LINQ Query

It is possible to define a field within a class (or structure) whose value is the result of a LINQ query. To do so, however, you cannot make use of implicit typing (as the var keyword cannot be used for fields), and the target of the LINQ query cannot be instance-level data; therefore, it must be static. Given these limitations, you will seldom need to author code like the following:

```
class LINQBasedFieldsAreClunky
{
  private static string[] currentVideoGames = {"Morrowind", "Uncharted 2",
    "Fallout 3", "Daxter", "System Shock 2"};

  // Can't use implicit typing here! Must know type of subset!
  private IEnumerable<string> subset = from g in currentVideoGames where g.Contains(" ")
  orderby g select g;

  public void PrintGames()
  {
    foreach (var item in subset)
    {
      Console.WriteLine(item);
    }
  }
}
```

More often than not, LINQ queries are defined within the scope of a method or property. Moreover, to simplify your programming, the variable used to hold the result set will be stored in an implicitly typed local variable using the var keyword. Now, recall from Chapter 3 that implicitly typed variables cannot be used to define parameters, return values, or fields of a class or structure.

Given this point, you might wonder exactly how you could return a query result to an external caller. The answer is, it depends. If you have a result set consisting of strongly typed data, such as an array of strings or a List<T> of Cars, you could abandon the use of the var keyword and use a proper IEnumerable<T> or IEnumerable type (again, as IEnumerable<T> extends IEnumerable). Consider the following example for a new console application named LinqRetValues:

```
class Program
{
  static void Main(string[] args)
  {
    Console.WriteLine("***** LINQ Return Values *****\n");
    IEnumerable<string> subset = GetStringSubset();

    foreach (string item in subset)
    {
      Console.WriteLine(item);
    }

    Console.ReadLine();
  }
```

```
static IEnumerable<string> GetStringSubset()
{
  string[] colors = {"Light Red", "Green", "Yellow", "Dark Red", "Red", "Purple"};

  // Note subset is an IEnumerable<string>-compatible object.
  IEnumerable<string> theRedColors = from c in colors where c.Contains("Red") select c;

  return theRedColors;
  }
}
```

The results are as expected.

```
Light Red
Dark Red
Red
```

Returning LINQ Results via Immediate Execution

This example works as expected, only because the return value of GetStringSubset() and the LINQ query within this method has been strongly typed. If you used the var keyword to define the subset variable, it would be permissible to return the value *only* if the method is still prototyped to return IEnumerable<string> (and if the implicitly typed local variable is in fact compatible with the specified return type).

Because it is a bit inconvenient to operate on IEnumerable<T>, you could make use of immediate execution. For example, rather than returning IEnumerable<string>, you could simply return a string[], provided that you transform the sequence to a strongly typed array. Consider this new method of the Program class, which does this very thing:

```
static string[] GetStringSubsetAsArray()
{
  string[] colors = {"Light Red", "Green", "Yellow", "Dark Red", "Red", "Purple"};

  var theRedColors = from c in colors where c.Contains("Red") select c;

  // Map results into an array.
  return theRedColors.ToArray();
}
```

With this, the caller can be blissfully unaware that their result came from a LINQ query and simply work with the array of strings as expected. Here's an example:

```
foreach (string item in GetStringSubsetAsArray())
{
    Console.WriteLine(item);
}
```

Immediate execution is also critical when attempting to return to the caller the results of a LINQ projection. You'll examine this topic a bit later in the chapter. Next up, let's look at how to apply LINQ queries to generic and nongeneric collection objects.

■ **Source Code**   You can find the LinqRetValues project in the Chapter 12 subdirectory.

Applying LINQ Queries to Collection Objects

Beyond pulling results from a simple array of data, LINQ query expressions can also manipulate data within members of the System.Collections.Generic namespace, such as the List<T> type. Create a new Console Application project named LinqOverCollections, and define a basic Car class that maintains a current speed, color, make, and pet name, as shown in the following code:

```
class Car
{
  public string PetName {get; set;} = "";
  public string Color {get; set;} = "";
  public int Speed {get; set;}
  public string Make {get; set;} = "";
}
```

Now, within your Main() method, define a local List<T> variable of type Car, and make use of object initialization syntax to fill the list with a handful of new Car objects.

```
static void Main(string[] args)
{
  Console.WriteLine("***** LINQ over Generic Collections *****\n");

  // Make a List<> of Car objects.
  List<Car> myCars = new List<Car>() {
    new Car{ PetName = "Henry", Color = "Silver", Speed = 100, Make = "BMW"},
    new Car{ PetName = "Daisy", Color = "Tan", Speed = 90, Make = "BMW"},
    new Car{ PetName = "Mary", Color = "Black", Speed = 55, Make = "VW"},
    new Car{ PetName = "Clunker", Color = "Rust", Speed = 5, Make = "Yugo"},
    new Car{ PetName = "Melvin", Color = "White", Speed = 43, Make = "Ford"}
  };

  Console.ReadLine();
}
```

Accessing Contained Subobjects

Applying a LINQ query to a generic container is no different from doing so with a simple array, as LINQ to Objects can be used on any type implementing IEnumerable<T>. This time, your goal is to build a query expression to select only the Car objects within the myCars list, where the speed is greater than 55.

After you get the subset, you will print out the name of each Car object by calling the PetName property. Assume you have the following helper method (taking a List<Car> parameter), which is called from within Main():

```
static void GetFastCars(List<Car> myCars)
{
  // Find all Car objects in the List<>, where the Speed is
  // greater than 55.
  var fastCars = from c in myCars where c.Speed > 55 select c;

  foreach (var car in fastCars)
  {
    Console.WriteLine("{0} is going too fast!", car.PetName);
  }
}
```

Notice that your query expression is grabbing only those items from the List<T> where the Speed property is greater than 55. If you run the application, you will find that Henry and Daisy are the only two items that match the search criteria.

If you want to build a more complex query, you might want to find only the BMWs that have a Speed value greater than 90. To do so, simply build a compound Boolean statement using the C# && operator.

```
static void GetFastBMWs(List<Car> myCars)
  {
  // Find the fast BMWs!
  var fastCars = from c in myCars where c.Speed > 90 && c.Make == "BMW" select c;
  foreach (var car in fastCars)
  {
    Console.WriteLine("{0} is going too fast!", car.PetName);
  }
}
```

In this case, the only pet name printed out is Henry.

Applying LINQ Queries to Nongeneric Collections

Recall that the query operators of LINQ are designed to work with any type implementing IEnumerable<T> (either directly or via extension methods). Given that System.Array has been provided with such necessary infrastructure, it might surprise you that the legacy (nongeneric) containers within System.Collections have not. Thankfully, it is still possible to iterate over data contained within nongeneric collections using the generic Enumerable.OfType<T>() extension method.

When calling OfType<T>() from a nongeneric collection object (such as the ArrayList), simply specify the type of item within the container to extract a compatible IEnumerable<T> object. In code, you can store this data point using an implicitly typed variable.

Consider the following new method, which fills an ArrayList with a set of Car objects (be sure to import the System.Collections namespace into your Program.cs file):

```
static void LINQOverArrayList()
{
  Console.WriteLine("***** LINQ over ArrayList *****");

  // Here is a nongeneric collection of cars.
  ArrayList myCars = new ArrayList() {
    new Car{ PetName = "Henry", Color = "Silver", Speed = 100, Make = "BMW"},
    new Car{ PetName = "Daisy", Color = "Tan", Speed = 90, Make = "BMW"},
    new Car{ PetName = "Mary", Color = "Black", Speed = 55, Make = "VW"},
    new Car{ PetName = "Clunker", Color = "Rust", Speed = 5, Make = "Yugo"},
    new Car{ PetName = "Melvin", Color = "White", Speed = 43, Make = "Ford"}
  };

  // Transform ArrayList into an IEnumerable<T>-compatible type.
  var myCarsEnum = myCars.OfType<Car>();

  // Create a query expression targeting the compatible type.
  var fastCars = from c in myCarsEnum where c.Speed > 55 select c;

  foreach (var car in fastCars)
  {
    Console.WriteLine("{0} is going too fast!", car.PetName);
  }
}
```

Similar to the previous examples, this method, when called from Main(), will display only the names Henry and Daisy, based on the format of the LINQ query.

Filtering Data Using OfType<T>( )

As you know, nongeneric types are capable of containing any combination of items, as the members of these containers (again, such as the ArrayList) are prototyped to receive System.Objects. For example, assume an ArrayList contains a variety of items, only a subset of which are numerical. If you want to obtain a subset that contains only numerical data, you can do so using OfType<T>( ) since it filters out each element whose type is different from the given type during the iterations.

```
static void OfTypeAsFilter()
{
  // Extract the ints from the ArrayList.
  ArrayList myStuff = new ArrayList();
  myStuff.AddRange(new object[] { 10, 400, 8, false, new Car(), "string data" });
  var myInts = myStuff.OfType<int>();

  // Prints out 10, 400, and 8.
  foreach (int i in myInts)
  {
    Console.WriteLine("Int value: {0}", i);
  }
}
```

At this point, you have had a chance to apply LINQ queries to arrays, generic collections, and nongeneric collections. These containers held both C# primitive types (integers, string data) as well as custom classes. The next task is to learn about many additional LINQ operators that can be used to build more complex and useful queries.

■ **Source Code**   You can find the LinqOverCollections project in the Chapter 12 subdirectory.

Investigating the C# LINQ Query Operators

C# defines a good number of query operators out of the box. Table 12-3 documents some of the more commonly used query operators.

■ **Note**   The .NET Framework SDK documentation provides full details regarding each of the C# LINQ operators. Look up the topic "LINQ General Programming Guide" for more information.

In addition to the partial list of operators shown in Table 12-3, the System.Linq.Enumerable class provides a set of methods that do not have a direct C# query operator shorthand notation but are instead exposed as extension methods. These generic methods can be called to transform a result set in various manners (Reverse<>(), ToArray<>(), ToList<>(), etc.). Some are used to extract singletons from a result set, others perform various set operations (Distinct<>(), Union<>(), Intersect<>(), ctc.), and still others aggregate results (Count<>(), Sum<>(), Min<>(), Max<>(), etc.).

Table 12-3. *Common LINQ Query Operators*

Query Operators	Meaning in Life
from, in	Used to define the backbone for any LINQ expression, which allows you to extract a subset of data from a fitting container.
Where	Used to define a restriction for which items to extract from a container.
Select	Used to select a sequence from the container.
join, on, equals, into	Performs joins based on specified key. Remember, these "joins" do not need to have anything to do with data in a relational database.
orderby, ascending, descending	Allows the resulting subset to be ordered in ascending or descending order.
group, by	Yields a subset with data grouped by a specified value.

To begin digging into more intricate LINQ queries, create a new Console Application project named FunWithLinqExpressions. Next, you need to define an array or collection of some sample data. For this project, you will make an array of `ProductInfo` objects, defined in the following code:

```
class ProductInfo
{
  public string Name {get; set;} = "";
  public string Description {get; set;} = "";
  public int NumberInStock {get; set;} = 0;

  public override string ToString()
    => $"Name={Name}, Description={Description}, Number in Stock={NumberInStock}";
}
```

Now populate an array with a batch of `ProductInfo` objects within your `Main()` method.

```
static void Main(string[] args)
{
  Console.WriteLine("***** Fun with Query Expressions *****\n");

  // This array will be the basis of our testing...
  ProductInfo[] itemsInStock = new[] {
    new ProductInfo{ Name = "Mac's Coffee", Description = "Coffee with TEETH",
    NumberInStock = 24},
    new ProductInfo{ Name = "Milk Maid Milk", Description = "Milk cow's love",
    NumberInStock = 100},
    new ProductInfo{ Name = "Pure Silk Tofu", Description = "Bland as Possible",
    NumberInStock = 120},
    new ProductInfo{ Name = "Crunchy Pops", Description = "Cheezy, peppery goodness",
    NumberInStock = 2},
    new ProductInfo{ Name = "RipOff Water", Description = "From the tap to your wallet",
    NumberInStock = 100},
    new ProductInfo{ Name = "Classic Valpo Pizza", Description = "Everyone loves
    pizza!",  NumberInStock = 73}
    };

  // We will call various methods here!
  Console.ReadLine();
}
```

Basic Selection Syntax

Because the syntactical correctness of a LINQ query expression is validated at compile time, you need to remember that the ordering of these operators is critical. In the simplest terms, every LINQ query expression is built using the from, in, and select operators. Here is the general template to follow:

```
var result = from matchingItem in container select matchingItem;
```

The item after the from operator represents an item that matches the LINQ query criteria, which can be named anything you choose. The item after the in operator represents the data container to search (an array, collection, XML document, etc.).

Here is a simple query, doing nothing more than selecting every item in the container (similar in behavior to a database Select * SQL statement). Consider the following:

```
static void SelectEverything(ProductInfo[] products)
{
  // Get everything!
  Console.WriteLine("All product details:");
  var allProducts = from p in products select p;

  foreach (var prod in allProducts)
  {
    Console.WriteLine(prod.ToString());
  }
}
```

To be honest, this query expression is not entirely useful, given that your subset is identical to that of the data in the incoming parameter. If you want, you could extract only the Name values of each car using the following selection syntax:

```
static void ListProductNames(ProductInfo[] products)
{
  // Now get only the names of the products.
  Console.WriteLine("Only product names:");
  var names = from p in products select p.Name;

  foreach (var n in names)
  {
    Console.WriteLine("Name: {0}", n);
  }
}
```

Obtaining Subsets of Data

To obtain a specific subset from a container, you can use the where operator. When doing so, the general template now becomes the following code:

```
var result = from item in container where BooleanExpression select item;
```

Notice that the where operator expects an expression that resolves to a Boolean. For example, to extract from the ProductInfo[] argument only the items that have more than 25 items on hand, you could author the following code:

```
static void GetOverstock(ProductInfo[] products)
{
  Console.WriteLine("The overstock items!");

  // Get only the items where we have more than
  // 25 in stock.
  var overstock = from p in products where p.NumberInStock > 25 select p;
```

```
foreach (ProductInfo c in overstock)
{
  Console.WriteLine(c.ToString());
}
}
```

As shown earlier in this chapter, when you are building a where clause, it is permissible to make use of any valid C# operators to build complex expressions. For example, recall this query that extracts out only the BMWs going at least 100 mph:

```
// Get BMWs going at least 100 mph.
var onlyFastBMWs = from c in myCars where c.Make == "BMW" && c.Speed >= 100 select c;
foreach (Car c in onlyFastBMWs)
{
  Console.WriteLine("{0} is going {1} MPH", c.PetName, c.Speed);
}
```

Projecting New Data Types

It is also possible to project new forms of data from an existing data source. Let's assume you want to take the incoming ProductInfo[] parameter and obtain a result set that accounts only for the name and description of each item. To do so, you can define a select statement that dynamically yields a new anonymous type.

```
static void GetNamesAndDescriptions(ProductInfo[] products)
{
  Console.WriteLine("Names and Descriptions:");
  var nameDesc = from p in products select new { p.Name, p.Description };

  foreach (var item in nameDesc)
  {
    // Could also use Name and Description properties directly.
    Console.WriteLine(item.ToString());
  }
}
```

Always remember that when you have a LINQ query that makes use of a projection, you have no way of knowing the underlying data type, as this is determined at compile time. In these cases, the var keyword is mandatory. As well, recall that you cannot create methods with implicitly typed return values. Therefore, the following method would not compile:

```
static var GetProjectedSubset(ProductInfo[] products)
{
    var nameDesc = from p in products select new { p.Name, p.Description };
    return nameDesc; // Nope!
}
```

CHAPTER 12 ■ LINQ TO OBJECTS

When you need to return projected data to a caller, one approach is to transform the query result into a .NET System.Array object using the ToArray() extension method. Thus, if you were to update your query expression as follows:

```
// Return value is now an Array.
static Array GetProjectedSubset(ProductInfo[] products)
{
  var nameDesc = from p in products select new { p.Name, p.Description };

  // Map set of anonymous objects to an Array object.
  return nameDesc.ToArray();
}
```

you could invoke and process the data from Main() as follows:

```
Array objs = GetProjectedSubset(itemsInStock);
foreach (object o in objs)
{
  Console.WriteLine(o); // Calls ToString() on each anonymous object.
}
```

Note that you must use a literal System.Array object and cannot make use of the C# array declaration syntax, given that you don't know the underlying type of type because you are operating on a compiler-generated anonymous class! Also note that you are not specifying the type parameter to the generic ToArray<T>() method, as you once again don't know the underlying data type until compile time, which is too late for your purposes.

The obvious problem is that you lose any strong typing, as each item in the Array object is assumed to be of type Object. Nevertheless, when you need to return a LINQ result set that is the result of a projection operation, transforming the data into an Array type (or another suitable container via other members of the Enumerable type) is mandatory.

Obtaining Counts Using Enumerable

When you are projecting new batches of data, you may need to discover exactly how many items have been returned into the sequence. Any time you need to determine the number of items returned from a LINQ query expression, simply use the Count() extension method of the Enumerable class. For example, the following method will find all string objects in a local array that have a length greater than six characters:

```
static void GetCountFromQuery()
{
  string[] currentVideoGames = {"Morrowind", "Uncharted 2", "Fallout 3", "Daxter",
  "System Shock 2"};

  // Get count from the query.
  int numb =  (from g in currentVideoGames where g.Length > 6 select g).Count();

  // Print out the number of items.
  Console.WriteLine("{0} items honor the LINQ query.", numb);
}
```

Reversing Result Sets

You can reverse the items within a result set quite simply using the Reverse<>() extension method of the Enumerable class. For example, the following method selects all items from the incoming ProductInfo[] parameter, in reverse:

```
static void ReverseEverything(ProductInfo[] products)
{
  Console.WriteLine("Product in reverse:");
  var allProducts = from p in products select p;
  foreach (var prod in allProducts.Reverse())
  {
    Console.WriteLine(prod.ToString());
  }
}
```

Sorting Expressions

As you have seen over this chapter's initial examples, a query expression can take an orderby operator to sort items in the subset by a specific value. By default, the order will be ascending; thus, ordering by a string would be alphabetical, ordering by numerical data would be lowest to highest, and so forth. If you need to view the results in a descending order, simply include the descending operator. Ponder the following method:

```
static void AlphabetizeProductNames(ProductInfo[] products)
{
  // Get names of products, alphabetized.
  var subset = from p in products orderby p.Name select p;

  Console.WriteLine("Ordered by Name:");
  foreach (var p in subset)
  {
    Console.WriteLine(p.ToString());
  }
}
```

Although ascending order is the default, you are able to make your intentions clear by using the ascending operator.

```
var subset = from p in products orderby p.Name ascending select p;
```

If you want to get the items in descending order, you can do so via the descending operator.

```
var subset = from p in products orderby p.Name descending select p;
```

LINQ As a Better Venn Diagramming Tool

The Enumerable class supports a set of extension methods that allows you to use two (or more) LINQ queries as the basis to find unions, differences, concatenations, and intersections of data. First, consider the Except() extension method, which will return a LINQ result set that contains the differences between two containers, which, in this case, is the value Yugo:

```
static void DisplayDiff()
{
  List<string> myCars = new List<String> {"Yugo", "Aztec", "BMW"};
  List<string> yourCars = new List<String>{"BMW", "Saab", "Aztec" };

  var carDiff = (from c in myCars select c).Except(from c2 in yourCars select c2);

  Console.WriteLine("Here is what you don't have, but I do:");
  foreach (string s in carDiff)
    Console.WriteLine(s); // Prints Yugo.
}
```

The Intersect() method will return a result set that contains the common data items in a set of containers. For example, the following method returns the sequence Aztec and BMW:

```
static void DisplayIntersection()
{
  List<string> myCars = new List<String> { "Yugo", "Aztec", "BMW" };
  List<string> yourCars = new List<String> { "BMW", "Saab", "Aztec" };

  // Get the common members.
  var carIntersect = (from c in myCars select c).Intersect(from c2 in yourCars select c2);

  Console.WriteLine("Here is what we have in common:");
  foreach (string s in carIntersect)
    Console.WriteLine(s); // Prints Aztec and BMW.
}
```

The Union() method, as you would guess, returns a result set that includes all members of a batch of LINQ queries. Like any proper union, you will not find repeating values if a common member appears more than once. Therefore, the following method will print out the values Yugo, Aztec, BMW, and Saab:

```
static void DisplayUnion()
{
  List<string> myCars = new List<String> { "Yugo", "Aztec", "BMW" };
  List<string> yourCars = new List<String> { "BMW", "Saab", "Aztec" };

  // Get the union of these containers.
  var carUnion = (from c in myCars select c).Union(from c2 in yourCars select c2);

  Console.WriteLine("Here is everything:");
  foreach (string s in carUnion)
    Console.WriteLine(s); // Prints all common members.
}
```

Finally, the Concat() extension method returns a result set that is a direct concatenation of LINQ result sets. For example, the following method prints out the results Yugo, Aztec, BMW, BMW, Saab, and Aztec:

```
static void DisplayConcat()
{
  List<string> myCars = new List<String> { "Yugo", "Aztec", "BMW" };
  List<string> yourCars = new List<String> { "BMW", "Saab", "Aztec" };

  var carConcat = (from c in myCars select c).Concat(from c2 in yourCars select c2);

  // Prints:
  // Yugo Aztec BMW BMW Saab Aztec.
  foreach (string s in carConcat)
    Console.WriteLine(s);
}
```

Removing Duplicates

When you call the Concat() extension method, you could very well end up with redundant entries in the fetched result, which could be exactly what you want in some cases. However, in other cases, you might want to remove duplicate entries in your data. To do so, simply call the Distinct() extension method, as shown here:

```
static void DisplayConcatNoDups()
{
  List<string> myCars = new List<String> { "Yugo", "Aztec", "BMW" };
  List<string> yourCars = new List<String> { "BMW", "Saab", "Aztec" };

  var carConcat = (from c in myCars select c).Concat(from c2 in yourCars select c2);

  // Prints:
  // Yugo Aztec BMW Saab.
  foreach (string s in carConcat.Distinct())
    Console.WriteLine(s);
}
```

LINQ Aggregation Operations

LINQ queries can also be designed to perform various aggregation operations on the result set. The Count() extension method is one such aggregation example. Other possibilities include obtaining an average, maximum, minimum, or sum of values using the Max(), Min(), Average(), or Sum() members of the Enumerable class. Here is a simple example:

```
static void AggregateOps()
{
  double[] winterTemps = { 2.0, -21.3, 8, -4, 0, 8.2 };

  // Various aggregation examples.
  Console.WriteLine("Max temp: {0}", (from t in winterTemps select t).Max());
```

```
Console.WriteLine("Min temp: {0}", (from t in winterTemps select t).Min());

Console.WriteLine("Average temp: {0}", (from t in winterTemps select t).Average());

Console.WriteLine("Sum of all temps: {0}", (from t in winterTemps select t).Sum());
}
```

These examples should give you enough knowledge to feel comfortable with the process of building LINQ query expressions. While there are additional operators you have not yet examined, you will see further examples later in this text when you learn about related LINQ technologies. To wrap up your first look at LINQ, the remainder of this chapter will dive into the details between the C# LINQ query operators and the underlying object model.

■ **Source Code**   You can find the FunWithLinqExpressions project in the Chapter 12 subdirectory.

The Internal Representation of LINQ Query Statements

At this point, you have been introduced to the process of building query expressions using various C# query operators (such as from, in, where, orderby, and select). Also, you discovered that some functionality of the LINQ to Objects API can be accessed only when calling extension methods of the Enumerable class. The truth of the matter, however, is that when compiled, the C# compiler actually translates all C# LINQ operators into calls on methods of the Enumerable class.

A great many of the methods of Enumerable have been prototyped to take delegates as arguments. In particular, many methods require a generic delegate named Func<>, which was introduced to you during your examination of generic delegates in Chapter 9. Consider the Where() method of Enumerable, which is called on your behalf when you use the C# where LINQ query operator.

```
// Overloaded versions of the Enumerable.Where<T>() method.
// Note the second parameter is of type System.Func<>.
public static IEnumerable<TSource> Where<TSource>(this IEnumerable<TSource> source,
    System.Func<TSource,int,bool> predicate)

public static IEnumerable<TSource> Where<TSource>(this IEnumerable<TSource> source,
    System.Func<TSource,bool> predicate)
```

The Func<> delegate (as the name implies) represents a pattern for a given function with a set of up to 16 arguments and a return value. If you were to examine this type using the Visual Studio object browser, you would notice various forms of the Func<> delegate. Here's an example:

```
// The various formats of the Func<> delegate.
public delegate TResult Func<T1,T2,T3,T4,TResult>(T1 arg1, T2 arg2, T3 arg3, T4 arg4)

public delegate TResult Func<T1,T2,T3,TResult>(T1 arg1, T2 arg2, T3 arg3)

public delegate TResult Func<T1,T2,TResult>(T1 arg1, T2 arg2)

public delegate TResult Func<T1,TResult>(T1 arg1)

public delegate TResult Func<TResult>()
```

Given that many members of System.Linq.Enumerable demand a delegate as input, when invoking them, you can either manually create a new delegate type and author the necessary target methods, make use of a C# anonymous method, or define a proper lambda expression. Regardless of which approach you take, the end result is identical.

While it is true that making use of C# LINQ query operators is far and away the simplest way to build a LINQ query expression, let's walk through each of these possible approaches, just so you can see the connection between the C# query operators and the underlying Enumerable type.

Building Query Expressions with Query Operators (Revisited)

To begin, create a new Console Application project named LinqUsingEnumerable. The Program class will define a series of static helper methods (each of which is called within the Main() method) to illustrate the various manners in which you can build LINQ query expressions.

The first method, QueryStringsWithOperators(), offers the most straightforward way to build a query expression and is identical to the code shown in the LinqOverArray example earlier in this chapter.

```
static void QueryStringWithOperators()
{
  Console.WriteLine("***** Using Query Operators *****");

  string[] currentVideoGames = {"Morrowind", "Uncharted 2", "Fallout 3", "Daxter",
  "System Shock 2"};

  var subset = from game in currentVideoGames where game.Contains(" ") orderby game
  select game;

  foreach (string s in subset)
    Console.WriteLine("Item: {0}", s);
}
```

The obvious benefit of using C# query operators to build query expressions is that the Func<> delegates and calls on the Enumerable type are out of sight and out of mind, as it is the job of the C# compiler to perform this translation. To be sure, building LINQ expressions using various query operators (from, in, where, or orderby) is the most common and straightforward approach.

Building Query Expressions Using the Enumerable Type and Lambda Expressions

Keep in mind that the LINQ query operators used here are simply shorthand versions for calling various extension methods defined by the Enumerable type. Consider the following QueryStringsWithEnumerableAndLambdas() method, which is processing the local string array now making direct use of the Enumerable extension methods:

```
static void QueryStringsWithEnumerableAndLambdas()
{
  Console.WriteLine("***** Using Enumerable / Lambda Expressions *****");

  string[] currentVideoGames = {"Morrowind", "Uncharted 2", "Fallout 3", "Daxter",
  "System Shock 2"};
```

```
// Build a query expression using extension methods
// granted to the Array via the Enumerable type.
var subset = currentVideoGames.Where(game => game.Contains(" "))
  .OrderBy(game => game).Select(game => game);

  // Print out the results.
  foreach (var game in subset)
    Console.WriteLine("Item: {0}", game);
Console.WriteLine();
}
```

Here, you begin by calling the Where() extension method on the currentVideoGames string array. Recall that the Array class receives this via an extension method granted by Enumerable. The Enumerable.Where() method requires a System.Func<T1, TResult> delegate parameter. The first type parameter of this delegate represents the IEnumerable<T> compatible data to process (an array of strings in this case), while the second type parameter represents the method result data, which is obtained from a single statement fed into the lambda expression.

The return value of the Where() method is hidden from view in this code example, but under the covers you are operating on an OrderedEnumerable type. From this object, you call the generic OrderBy() method, which also requires a Func<> delegate parameter. This time, you are simply passing each item in turn via a fitting lambda expression. The end result of calling OrderBy() is a new ordered sequence of the initial data.

Last but not least, you call the Select() method off the sequence returned from OrderBy(), which results in the final set of data that is stored in an implicitly typed variable named subset.

To be sure, this "longhand" LINQ query is a bit more complex to tease apart than the previous C# LINQ query operator example. Part of the complexity is, no doubt, due to the chaining together of calls using the dot operator. Here is the same query, with each step broken into discrete chunks (as you might guess, you could break down the overall query in various manners):

```
static void QueryStringsWithEnumerableAndLambdas2()
{
  Console.WriteLine("***** Using Enumerable / Lambda Expressions *****");

  string[] currentVideoGames = {"Morrowind", "Uncharted 2", "Fallout 3", "Daxter",
  "System Shock 2"};

  // Break it down!
  var gamesWithSpaces = currentVideoGames.Where(game => game.Contains(" "));
  var orderedGames = gamesWithSpaces.OrderBy(game => game);
  var subset = orderedGames.Select(game => game);

  foreach (var game in subset)
    Console.WriteLine("Item: {0}", game);
  Console.WriteLine();
}
```

As you might agree, building a LINQ query expression using the methods of the Enumerable class directly is much more verbose than making use of the C# query operators. As well, given that the methods of Enumerable require delegates as parameters, you will typically need to author lambda expressions to allow the input data to be processed by the underlying delegate target.

Building Query Expressions Using the Enumerable Type and Anonymous Methods

Given that C# lambda expressions are simply shorthand notations for working with anonymous methods, consider the third query expression created within the QueryStringsWithAnonymousMethods() helper function, shown here:

```
static void QueryStringsWithAnonymousMethods()
{
  Console.WriteLine("***** Using Anonymous Methods *****");

  string[] currentVideoGames = {"Morrowind", "Uncharted 2", "Fallout 3", "Daxter",
  "System Shock 2"};

  // Build the necessary Func<> delegates using anonymous methods.
  Func<string, bool> searchFilter = delegate(string game) { return game.Contains(" "); };
  Func<string, string> itemToProcess = delegate(string s) { return s; };

  // Pass the delegates into the methods of Enumerable.
  var subset = currentVideoGames.Where(searchFilter).OrderBy(itemToProcess).
  Select(itemToProcess);

  // Print out the results.
  foreach (var game in subset)
    Console.WriteLine("Item: {0}", game);
  Console.WriteLine();
}
```

This iteration of the query expression is even more verbose, because you are manually creating the Func<> delegates used by the Where(), OrderBy(), and Select() methods of the Enumerable class. On the plus side, the anonymous method syntax does keep all the delegate processing contained within a single method definition. Nevertheless, this method is functionally equivalent to the QueryStringsWithEnumerableAndLambdas() and QueryStringsWithOperators() methods created in the previous sections.

Building Query Expressions Using the Enumerable Type and Raw Delegates

Finally, if you want to build a query expression using the *really verbose approach*, you could avoid the use of lambdas/anonymous method syntax and directly create delegate targets for each Func<> type. Here is the final iteration of your query expression, modeled within a new class type named VeryComplexQueryExpression:

```
class VeryComplexQueryExpression
{
  public static void QueryStringsWithRawDelegates()
  {
    Console.WriteLine("***** Using Raw Delegates *****");

    string[] currentVideoGames = {"Morrowind", "Uncharted 2", "Fallout 3", "Daxter",
    "System Shock 2"};
```

```
  // Build the necessary Func<> delegates.
  Func<string, bool> searchFilter = new Func<string, bool>(Filter);
  Func<string, string> itemToProcess = new Func<string,string>(ProcessItem);

  // Pass the delegates into the methods of Enumerable.
  var subset = currentVideoGames.Where(searchFilter).OrderBy(itemToProcess).
               Select(itemToProcess);

  // Print out the results.
  foreach (var game in subset)
    Console.WriteLine("Item: {0}", game);
  Console.WriteLine();
}

// Delegate targets.
public static bool Filter(string game) {return game.Contains(" ");}
public static string ProcessItem(string game) { return game; }
}
```

You can test this iteration of your string-processing logic by calling this method within the `Main()` method of the `Program` class, as follows:

```
VeryComplexQueryExpression.QueryStringsWithRawDelegates();
```

If you were to now run the application to test each possible approach, it should not be too surprising that the output is identical, regardless of the path taken. Keep the following points in mind regarding how LINQ query expressions are represented under the covers:

- Query expressions are created using various C# query operators.

- Query operators are simply shorthand notations for invoking extension methods defined by the `System.Linq.Enumerable` type.

- Many methods of `Enumerable` require delegates (`Func<>` in particular) as parameters.

- Any method requiring a delegate parameter can instead be passed a lambda expression.

- Lambda expressions are simply anonymous methods in disguise (which greatly improve readability).

- Anonymous methods are shorthand notations for allocating a raw delegate and manually building a delegate target method.

Whew! That might have been a bit deeper under the hood than you wanted to have gone, but I hope this discussion has helped you understand what the user-friendly C# query operators are actually doing behind the scenes.

■ **Note**   You can find the LinqUsingEnumerable project in the `Chapter 12` subdirectory.

Summary

LINQ is a set of related technologies that attempts to provide a single, symmetrical manner to interact with diverse forms of data. As explained over the course of this chapter, LINQ can interact with any type implementing the IEnumerable<T> interface, including simple arrays as well as generic and nongeneric collections of data.

As you have seen, working with LINQ technologies is accomplished using several C# language features. For example, given that LINQ query expressions can return any number of result sets, it is common to make use of the var keyword to represent the underlying data type. As well, lambda expressions, object initialization syntax, and anonymous types can all be used to build functional and compact LINQ queries.

More importantly, you have seen how the C# LINQ query operators are simply shorthand notations for making calls on static members of the System.Linq.Enumerable type. As shown, most members of Enumerable operate on Func<T> delegate types, which can take literal method addresses, anonymous methods, or lambda expressions as input to evaluate the query.

CHAPTER 13

■ ■ ■

Understanding Object Lifetime

At this point in the book, you have learned a great deal about how to build custom class types using C#. Now you will see how the CLR manages allocated class instances (aka objects) via *garbage collection*. C# programmers never directly deallocate a managed object from memory (recall there is no `delete` keyword in the C# language). Rather, .NET objects are allocated to a region of memory termed the *managed heap*, where they will be automatically destroyed by the garbage collector "sometime in the future."

After you have looked at the core details of the collection process, you'll learn how to programmatically interact with the garbage collector using the `System.GC` class type (which is something you will typically not be required to do for a majority of your .NET projects). Next, you'll examine how the virtual `System.Object.Finalize()` method and `IDisposable` interface can be used to build classes that release internal *unmanaged resources* in a predictable and timely manner.

You will also delve into some functionality of the garbage collector introduced in .NET 4.0, including background garbage collections and lazy instantiation using the generic `System.Lazy<>` class. By the time you have completed this chapter, you will have a solid understanding of how .NET objects are managed by the CLR.

Classes, Objects, and References

To frame the topics covered in this chapter, it is important to further clarify the distinction between classes, objects, and reference variables. Recall that a class is nothing more than a blueprint that describes how an instance of this type will look and feel in memory. Classes, of course, are defined within a code file (which in C# takes a `*.cs` extension by convention). Consider the following simple `Car` class defined within a new C# Console Application project named SimpleGC:

```
// Car.cs
public class Car
{
  public int CurrentSpeed {get; set;}
  public string PetName {get; set;}

  public Car(){}
  public Car(string name, int speed)
  {
    PetName = name;
    CurrentSpeed = speed;
  }
  public override string ToString() => $"{PetName} is going {CurrentSpeed} MPH";
  }
}
```

© Andrew Troelsen and Philip Japikse 2017
A. Troelsen and P. Japikse, *Pro C# 7*, https://doi.org/10.1007/978-1-4842-3018-3_13

After a class has been defined, you may allocate any number of objects using the C# new keyword. Understand, however, that the new keyword returns a *reference* to the object on the heap, not the actual object. If you declare the reference variable as a local variable in a method scope, it is stored on the stack for further use in your application. When you want to invoke members on the object, apply the C# dot operator to the stored reference, like so:

```
class Program
{
  static void Main(string[] args)
  {
    Console.WriteLine("***** GC Basics *****");

    // Create a new Car object on the managed heap. We are returned a reference to this
object ("refToMyCar").
    Car refToMyCar = new Car("Zippy", 50);

    // The C# dot operator (.) is used to invoke members on the object using our reference
variable.
    Console.WriteLine(refToMyCar.ToString());
    Console.ReadLine();
  }
}
```

Figure 13-1 illustrates the class, object, and reference relationship.

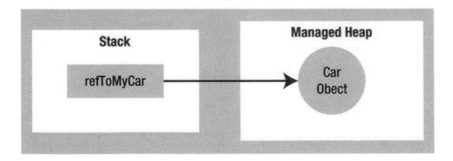

Figure 13-1. *References to objects on the managed heap*

■ **Note**   Recall from Chapter 4 that structures are *value types* that are always allocated directly on the stack and are never placed on the .NET managed heap. Heap allocation occurs only when you are creating instances of classes.

The Basics of Object Lifetime

When you are building your C# applications, you are correct to assume that the .NET runtime environment (aka the CLR) will take care of the managed heap without your direct intervention. In fact, the golden rule of .NET memory management is simple.

■ **Rule**   Allocate a class instance onto the managed heap using the new keyword and forget about it.

Once instantiated, the garbage collector will destroy an object when it is no longer needed. The next obvious question, of course, is, "How does the garbage collector determine when an object is no longer needed?" The short (i.e., incomplete) answer is that the garbage collector removes an object from the heap only if it is *unreachable* by any part of your codebase. Assume you have a method in your Program class that allocates a local Car object as follows:

```
static void MakeACar()
{
  // If myCar is the only reference to the Car object, it *may* be destroyed when this
  method returns.
  Car myCar = new Car();
}
```

Notice that this Car reference (myCar) has been created directly within the MakeACar() method and has not been passed outside of the defining scope (via a return value or ref/out parameters). Thus, once this method call completes, the myCar reference is no longer reachable, and the associated Car object is now a candidate for garbage collection. Understand, however, that you can't guarantee that this object will be reclaimed from memory immediately after MakeACar() has completed. All you can assume at this point is that when the CLR performs the next garbage collection, the myCar object could be safely destroyed.

As you will most certainly discover, programming in a garbage-collected environment greatly simplifies your application development. In stark contrast, C++ programmers are painfully aware that if they fail to manually delete heap-allocated objects, memory leaks are never far behind. In fact, tracking down memory leaks is one of the most time-consuming (and tedious) aspects of programming in unmanaged environments. By allowing the garbage collector to take charge of destroying objects, the burden of memory management has been lifted from your shoulders and placed onto those of the CLR.

The CIL of new

When the C# compiler encounters the new keyword, it emits a CIL newobj instruction into the method implementation. If you compile the current example code and investigate the resulting assembly using ildasm.exe, you'd find the following CIL statements within the MakeACar() method:

```
.method private hidebysig static void MakeACar() cil managed
{
  // Code size 8 (0x8)
  .maxstack 1
  .locals init ([0] class SimpleGC.Car myCar)
  IL_0000: nop
  IL_0001: newobj instance void SimpleGC.Car::.ctor()
  IL_0006: stloc.0
  IL_0007: ret
} // end of method Program::MakeACar
```

Before you examine the exact rules that determine when an object is removed from the managed heap, let's check out the role of the CIL newobj instruction in a bit more detail. First, understand that the managed heap is more than just a random chunk of memory accessed by the CLR. The .NET garbage collector is quite a tidy housekeeper of the heap, given that it will compact empty blocks of memory (when necessary) for the purposes of optimization.

To aid in this endeavor, the managed heap maintains a pointer (commonly referred to as the *next object pointer* or *new object pointer*) that identifies exactly where the next object will be located. That said, the newobj instruction tells the CLR to perform the following core operations:

1. Calculate the total amount of memory required for the object to be allocated (including the memory required by the data members and the base classes).

2. Examine the managed heap to ensure that there is indeed enough room to host the object to be allocated. If there is, the specified constructor is called, and the caller is ultimately returned a reference to the new object in memory, whose address just happens to be identical to the last position of the next object pointer.

3. Finally, before returning the reference to the caller, advance the next object pointer to point to the next available slot on the managed heap.

Figure 13-2 illustrates the basic process.

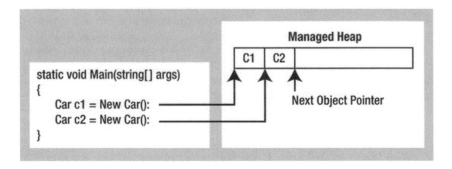

Figure 13-2. *The details of allocating objects onto the managed heap*

As your application is busy allocating objects, the space on the managed heap may eventually become full. When processing the newobj instruction, if the CLR determines that the managed heap does not have sufficient memory to allocate the requested type, it will perform a garbage collection in an attempt to free up memory. Thus, the next rule of garbage collection is also quite simple.

■ **Rule**   If the managed heap does not have sufficient memory to allocate a requested object, a garbage collection will occur.

Exactly *how* this garbage collection occurs, however, depends on which version of the .NET platform your application is running under. You'll look at the differences a bit later in this chapter.

Setting Object References to null

C/C++ programmers often set pointer variables to null to ensure they are no longer referencing unmanaged memory. Given this, you might wonder what the end result is of assigning object references to null under C#. For example, assume the MakeACar() subroutine has now been updated as follows:

```
static void MakeACar()
{
  Car myCar = new Car();
  myCar = null;
}
```

When you assign object references to null, the compiler generates CIL code that ensures the reference (myCar, in this example) no longer points to any object. If you once again made use of ildasm.exe to view the CIL code of the modified MakeACar(), you would find the ldnull opcode (which pushes a null value on the virtual execution stack) followed by a stloc.0 opcode (which sets the null reference on the variable).

```
.method private hidebysig static void MakeACar() cil managed
{
  // Code size 10 (0xa)
  .maxstack 1
  .locals init ([0] class SimpleGC.Car myCar)
  IL_0000:  nop
  IL_0001:  newobj instance void SimpleGC.Car::.ctor()
  IL_0006:  stloc.0
  IL_0007:  ldnull
  IL_0008:  stloc.0
  IL_0009:  ret
} // end of method Program::MakeACar
```

What you must understand, however, is that assigning a reference to null does not in any way force the garbage collector to fire up at that exact moment and remove the object from the heap. The only thing you have accomplished is explicitly clipping the connection between the reference and the object it previously pointed to. Given this point, setting references to null under C# is far less consequential than doing so in other C-based languages; however, doing so will certainly not cause any harm.

The Role of Application Roots

Now, back to the topic of how the garbage collector determines when an object is no longer needed. To understand the details, you need to be aware of the notion of *application roots*. Simply put, a *root* is a storage location containing a reference to an object on the managed heap. Strictly speaking, a root can fall into any of the following categories:

- References to global objects (though these are not allowed in C#, CIL code does permit allocation of global objects)

- References to any static objects/static fields

- References to local objects within an application's codebase

- References to object parameters passed into a method

- References to objects waiting to be *finalized* (described later in this chapter)

- Any CPU register that references an object

During a garbage collection process, the runtime will investigate objects on the managed heap to determine whether they are still reachable (i.e., rooted) by the application. To do so, the CLR will build an *object graph*, which represents each reachable object on the heap. Object graphs are explained in some detail during the discussion of object serialization in Chapter 20. For now, just understand that object graphs are used to document all reachable objects. As well, be aware that the garbage collector will never graph the same object twice, thus avoiding the nasty circular reference count found in COM programming.

Assume the managed heap contains a set of objects named A, B, C, D, E, F, and G. During garbage collection, these objects (as well as any internal object references they may contain) are examined for active roots. After the graph has been constructed, unreachable objects (which you can assume are objects C and F) are marked as garbage. Figure 13-3 diagrams a possible object graph for the scenario just described (you can read the directional arrows using the phrase *depends on* or *requires*; for example, E depends on G and B, A depends on nothing, and so on).

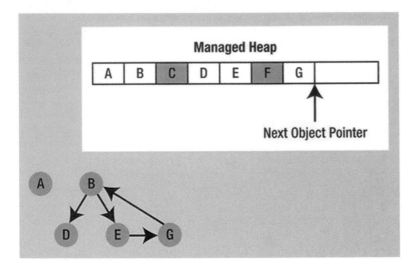

Figure 13-3. *Object graphs are constructed to determine which objects are reachable by application roots*

After objects have been marked for termination (C and F in this case—as they are not accounted for in the object graph), they are swept from memory. At this point, the remaining space on the heap is compacted, which in turn causes the CLR to modify the set of active application roots (and the underlying pointers) to refer to the correct memory location (this is done automatically and transparently). Last but not least, the next object pointer is readjusted to point to the next available slot. Figure 13-4 illustrates the resulting readjustment.

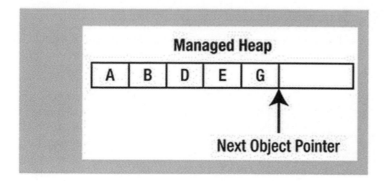

Figure 13-4. *A clean and compacted heap*

■ **Note** Strictly speaking, the garbage collector uses two distinct heaps, one of which is specifically used to store large objects. This heap is less frequently consulted during the collection cycle, given possible performance penalties involved with relocating large objects. Regardless, it is safe to consider the managed heap as a single region of memory.

Understanding Object Generations

When the CLR is attempting to locate unreachable objects, it does not literally examine every object placed on the managed heap. Doing so, obviously, would involve considerable time, especially in larger (i.e., real-world) applications.

To help optimize the process, each object on the heap is assigned to a specific "generation." The idea behind generations is simple: the longer an object has existed on the heap, the more likely it is to stay there. For example, the class that defined the main window of a desktop application will be in memory until the program terminates. Conversely, objects that have only recently been placed on the heap (such as an object allocated within a method scope) are likely to be unreachable rather quickly. Given these assumptions, each object on the heap belongs to one of the following generations:

- *Generation 0*: Identifies a newly allocated object that has never been marked for collection

- *Generation 1*: Identifies an object that has survived a garbage collection (i.e., it was marked for collection but was not removed because the sufficient heap space was acquired)

- *Generation 2*: Identifies an object that has survived more than one sweep of the garbage collector

---

■ **Note** Generations 0 and 1 are termed *ephemeral generations.* As explained in the next section, you will see that the garbage collection process does treat ephemeral generations differently.

The garbage collector will investigate all generation 0 objects first. If marking and sweeping (or said more plainly, getting rid of) these objects results in the required amount of free memory, any surviving objects are promoted to generation 1. To see how an object's generation affects the collection process, ponder Figure 13-5, which diagrams how a set of surviving generation 0 objects (A, B, and E) are promoted once the required memory has been reclaimed.

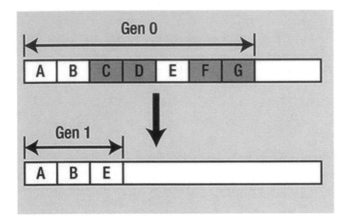

Figure 13-5. *Generation 0 objects that survive a garbage collection are promoted to generation 1*

If all generation 0 objects have been evaluated but additional memory is still required, generation 1 objects are then investigated for reachability and collected accordingly. Surviving generation 1 objects are then promoted to generation 2. If the garbage collector *still* requires additional memory, generation 2 objects are evaluated. At this point, if a generation 2 object survives a garbage collection, it remains a generation 2 object, given the predefined upper limit of object generations.

The bottom line is that by assigning a generational value to objects on the heap, newer objects (such as local variables) will be removed quickly, while older objects (such as a program's main window) are not "bothered" as often.

Concurrent Garbage Collection Prior to .NET 4.0

Prior to .NET 4.0, the runtime would clean up unused objects using a technique termed *concurrent garbage collection*. Under this model, when a collection takes place for any generation 0 or generation 1 objects (recall these are *ephemeral generations*), the garbage collector temporarily suspends all active *threads* within the current process to ensure that the application does not access the managed heap during the collection process.

You will examine the topic of threads in Chapter 19; for the time being, simply regard a thread as a path of execution within a running executable. After the garbage collection cycle has completed, the suspended threads are permitted to carry on their work. Thankfully, the .NET 3.5 (and earlier) garbage collector was highly optimized; I seldom (if ever) noticed this brief interruption in an application.

As an optimization, concurrent garbage collection allowed objects that were not located in one of the ephemeral generations to be cleaned up on a dedicated thread. This decreased (but didn't eliminate) the need for the .NET runtime to suspect active threads. Moreover, concurrent garbage collection allowed a program to continue allocating objects on the heap during the collection of nonephemeral generations.

Background Garbage Collection Under .NET 4.0 and Beyond

Beginning with .NET 4.0, the garbage collector is able to deal with thread suspension when it cleans up objects on the managed heap, using *background garbage collection*. Despite its name, this does not mean that all garbage collection now takes place on additional background threads of execution. Rather, if a background garbage collection is taking place for objects living in a nonephemeral generation, the .NET runtime is now able to collect objects on the ephemeral generations using a dedicated background thread.

On a related note, the .NET 4.0 and higher garbage collection has been improved to further reduce the amount of time a given thread involved with garbage collection details must be suspended. The end result of these changes is that the process of cleaning up unused objects living in generation 0 or generation 1 has been optimized and can result in better runtime performance of your programs (which is really important for real-time systems that require small, and predictable, GC stop time).

Do understand, however, that the introduction of this new garbage collection model has no effect on how you build your .NET applications. For all practical purposes, you can simply allow the .NET garbage collector to perform its work without your direct intervention (and be happy that the folks at Microsoft are improving the collection process in a transparent manner).

The System.GC Type

The mscorlib.dll assembly provides a class type named System.GC that allows you to programmatically interact with the garbage collector using a set of static members. Now, do be aware that you will seldom (if ever) need to make use of this class directly in your code. Typically, the only time you will use the members of System.GC is when you are creating classes that make internal use of *unmanaged resources*. This could be the case if you are building a class that makes calls into the Windows C-based API using the .NET platform invocation protocol or perhaps because of some very low-level and complicated COM interop logic. Table 13-1 provides a rundown of some of the more interesting members (consult the .NET Framework SDK documentation for complete details).

Table 13-1. *Select Members of the System.GC Type*

System.GC Member	Description
AddMemoryPressure() RemoveMemoryPressure()	Allows you to specify a numerical value that represents the calling object's "urgency level" regarding the garbage collection process. Be aware that these methods should alter pressure *in tandem* and, thus, never remove more pressure than the total amount you have added.
Collect()	Forces the GC to perform a garbage collection. This method has been overloaded to specify a generation to collect, as well as the mode of collection (via the GCCollectionMode enumeration).
CollectionCount()	Returns a numerical value representing how many times a given generation has been swept.
GetGeneration()	Returns the generation to which an object currently belongs.

(continued)

Table 13-1. (*continued*)

System.GC Member	Description
GetTotalMemory()	Returns the estimated amount of memory (in bytes) currently allocated on the managed heap. A Boolean parameter specifies whether the call should wait for garbage collection to occur before returning.
MaxGeneration	Returns the maximum number of generations supported on the target system. Under Microsoft's .NET 4.0, there are three possible generations: 0, 1, and 2.
SuppressFinalize()	Sets a flag indicating that the specified object should not have its Finalize() method called.
WaitForPending Finalizers()	Suspends the current thread until all finalizable objects have been finalized. This method is typically called directly after invoking GC.Collect().

To illustrate how the System.GC type can be used to obtain various garbage collection–centric details, consider the following Main() method, which makes use of several members of GC:

```
static void Main(string[] args)
{
  Console.WriteLine("***** Fun with System.GC *****");

  // Print out estimated number of bytes on heap.
  Console.WriteLine("Estimated bytes on heap: {0}", GC.GetTotalMemory(false));

  // MaxGeneration is zero based, so add 1 for display purposes.
  Console.WriteLine("This OS has {0} object generations.\n", (GC.MaxGeneration + 1));

  Car refToMyCar = new Car("Zippy", 100);
  Console.WriteLine(refToMyCar.ToString());

  // Print out generation of refToMyCar object.
  Console.WriteLine("Generation of refToMyCar is: {0}", GC.GetGeneration(refToMyCar));
  Console.ReadLine();
}
```

Forcing a Garbage Collection

Again, the whole purpose of the .NET garbage collector is to manage memory on your behalf. However, in some rare circumstances, it may be beneficial to programmatically force a garbage collection using GC.Collect(). Here are two common situations where you might consider interacting with the collection process:

- Your application is about to enter into a block of code that you don't want interrupted by a possible garbage collection.

- Your application has just finished allocating an extremely large number of objects and you want to remove as much of the acquired memory as soon as possible.

If you determine it could be beneficial to have the garbage collector check for unreachable objects, you could explicitly trigger a garbage collection, as follows:

```
static void Main(string[] args)
{
...
  // Force a garbage collection and wait for
  // each object to be finalized.
  GC.Collect();
  GC.WaitForPendingFinalizers();
...
}
```

When you manually force a garbage collection, you should always make a call to GC.WaitForPendingFinalizers(). With this approach, you can rest assured that all *finalizable objects* (described in the next section) have had a chance to perform any necessary cleanup before your program continues. Under the hood, GC.WaitForPendingFinalizers() will suspend the calling thread during the collection process. This is a good thing, as it ensures your code does not invoke methods on an object currently being destroyed!

The GC.Collect() method can also be supplied a numerical value that identifies the oldest generation on which a garbage collection will be performed. For example, to instruct the CLR to investigate only generation 0 objects, you would write the following:

```
static void Main(string[] args)
{
...
  // Only investigate generation 0 objects.
  GC.Collect(0);
  GC.WaitForPendingFinalizers();
...
}
```

As well, the Collect() method can also be passed in a value of the GCCollectionMode enumeration as a second parameter, to fine-tune exactly how the runtime should force the garbage collection. This enum defines the following values:

```
public enum GCCollectionMode
{
  Default,  // Forced is the current default.
  Forced,   // Tells the runtime to collect immediately!
  Optimized // Allows the runtime to determine whether the current time is optimal to
  reclaim objects.
}
```

As with any garbage collection, calling GC.Collect() promotes surviving generations. To illustrate, assume that your Main() method has been updated as follows:

```
static void Main(string[] args)
{
  Console.WriteLine("***** Fun with System.GC *****");

  // Print out estimated number of bytes on heap.
  Console.WriteLine("Estimated bytes on heap: {0}", GC.GetTotalMemory(false));

  // MaxGeneration is zero based.
  Console.WriteLine("This OS has {0} object generations.\n", (GC.MaxGeneration + 1));
  Car refToMyCar = new Car("Zippy", 100);
  Console.WriteLine(refToMyCar.ToString());

  // Print out generation of refToMyCar.
  Console.WriteLine("\nGeneration of refToMyCar is: {0}", GC.GetGeneration(refToMyCar));

  // Make a ton of objects for testing purposes.
  object[] tonsOfObjects = new object[50000];
  for (int i = 0; i < 50000; i++)
    tonsOfObjects[i] = new object();

  // Collect only gen 0 objects.
  GC.Collect(0, GCCollectionMode.Forced);
  GC.WaitForPendingFinalizers();

  // Print out generation of refToMyCar.
  Console.WriteLine("Generation of refToMyCar is: {0}",
  GC.GetGeneration(refToMyCar));

  // See if tonsOfObjects[9000] is still alive.
  if (tonsOfObjects[9000] != null)
  {
    Console.WriteLine("Generation of tonsOfObjects[9000] is: {0}", GC.GetGeneration(tonsOfO
bjects[9000]));
  }
  else
    Console.WriteLine("tonsOfObjects[9000] is no longer alive.");

  // Print out how many times a generation has been swept.
  Console.WriteLine("\nGen 0 has been swept {0} times", GC.CollectionCount(0));
  Console.WriteLine("Gen 1 has been swept {0} times", GC.CollectionCount(1));
  Console.WriteLine("Gen 2 has been swept {0} times", GC.CollectionCount(2));
  Console.ReadLine();
}
```

Here, I have purposely created a large array of `object` types (50,000 to be exact) for testing purposes. As you can see from the output that follows, even though this `Main()` method made only one explicit request for a garbage collection (via the `GC.Collect()` method), the CLR performed a number of them in the background.

```
***** Fun with System.GC *****
Estimated bytes on heap: 70240
This OS has 3 object generations.

Zippy is going 100 MPH

Generation of refToMyCar is: 0
Generation of refToMyCar is: 1
Generation of tonsOfObjects[9000] is: 1

Gen 0 has been swept 1 times
Gen 1 has been swept 0 times
Gen 2 has been swept 0 times
```

At this point, I hope you feel more comfortable regarding the details of object lifetime. In the next section, you'll examine the garbage collection process a bit further by addressing how you can build *finalizable objects,* as well as *disposable objects.* Be aware that the following techniques are typically necessary only if you are building C# classes that maintain internal unmanaged resources.

■ **Source Code**   You can find the SimpleGC project in the Chapter 13 subdirectory.

Building Finalizable Objects

In Chapter 6, you learned that the supreme base class of .NET, `System.Object`, defines a virtual method named `Finalize()`. The default implementation of this method does nothing whatsoever.

```
// System.Object
public class Object
{
  ...
  protected virtual void Finalize() {}
}
```

When you override `Finalize()` for your custom classes, you establish a specific location to perform any necessary cleanup logic for your type. Given that this member is defined as protected, it is not possible to directly call an object's `Finalize()` method from a class instance via the dot operator. Rather, the *garbage collector* will call an object's `Finalize()` method (if supported) before removing the object from memory.

■ **Note**   It is illegal to override `Finalize()` on structure types. This makes perfect sense given that structures are value types, which are never allocated on the heap to begin with and, therefore, are not garbage collected! However, if you create a structure that contains unmanaged resources that need to be cleaned up, you can implement the `IDisposable` interface (described shortly).

Of course, a call to `Finalize()` will (eventually) occur during a "natural" garbage collection or possibly when you programmatically force a collection via `GC.Collect()`. In addition, a type's finalizer method will automatically be called when the application domain hosting your application is unloaded from memory. Depending on your background in .NET, you may know that application domains (or simply AppDomains) are used to host an executable assembly and any necessary external code libraries. If you are not familiar with this .NET concept, you will be by the time you've finished Chapter 17. For now, note that when your AppDomain is unloaded from memory, the CLR automatically invokes finalizers for every finalizable object created during its lifetime.

Now, despite what your developer instincts may tell you, the vast majority of your C# classes will not require any explicit cleanup logic or a custom finalizer. The reason is simple: if your classes are just making use of other managed objects, everything will eventually be garbage-collected. The only time you would need to design a class that can clean up after itself is when you are using *unmanaged* resources (such as raw OS file handles, raw unmanaged database connections, chunks of unmanaged memory, or other unmanaged resources). Under the .NET platform, unmanaged resources are obtained by directly calling into the API of the operating system using Platform Invocation Services (PInvoke) or as a result of some elaborate COM interoperability scenarios. Given this, consider the next rule of garbage collection.

■ **Rule**   The only compelling reason to override `Finalize()` is if your C# class is using unmanaged resources via PInvoke or complex COM interoperability tasks (typically via various members defined by the `System.Runtime.InteropServices.Marshal` type). The reason is that under these scenarios you are manipulating memory that the CLR cannot manage.

Overriding System.Object.Finalize()

In the rare case that you do build a C# class that uses unmanaged resources, you will obviously want to ensure that the underlying memory is released in a predictable manner. Suppose you have created a new C# Console Application project named SimpleFinalize and inserted a class named `MyResourceWrapper` that uses an unmanaged resource (whatever that might be) and you want to override `Finalize()`. The odd thing about doing so in C# is that you can't do it using the expected `override` keyword.

```
class MyResourceWrapper
{
  // Compile-time error!
  protected override void Finalize(){ }
}
```

Rather, when you want to configure your custom C# class types to override the `Finalize()` method, you make use of a (C++-like) destructor syntax to achieve the same effect. The reason for this alternative form of overriding a virtual method is that when the C# compiler processes the finalizer syntax, it automatically adds a good deal of required infrastructure within the implicitly overridden Finalize() method (shown in just a moment).

C# finalizers look similar to constructors in that they are named identically to the class they are defined within. In addition, finalizers are prefixed with a tilde symbol (~). Unlike a constructor, however, a finalizer never takes an access modifier (they are implicitly protected), never takes parameters, and can't be overloaded (only one finalizer per class).

The following is a custom finalizer for MyResourceWrapper that will issue a system beep when invoked. Obviously, this example is only for instructional purposes. A real-world finalizer would do nothing more than free any unmanaged resources and would *not* interact with other managed objects, even those referenced by the current object, as you can't assume they are still alive at the point the garbage collector invokes your Finalize() method.

```
// Override System.Object.Finalize() via finalizer syntax.
class MyResourceWrapper
{
    // Clean up unmanaged resources here.
    // Beep when destroyed (testing purposes only!)
    ~MyResourceWrapper() => Console.Beep();
}
```

If you were to examine this C# destructor using ildasm.exe, you would see that the compiler inserts some necessary error-checking code. First, the code statements within the scope of your Finalize() method are placed within a try block (see Chapter 7). The related finally block ensures that your base classes' Finalize() method will always execute, regardless of any exceptions encountered within the try scope.

```
.method family hidebysig virtual instance void
  Finalize() cil managed
{
  // Code size        13 (0xd)
  .maxstack  1
  .try
  {
    IL_0000:  ldc.i4 0x4e20
    IL_0005:  ldc.i4 0x3e8
    IL_000a:  call
    void [mscorlib]System.Console::Beep(int32, int32)
    IL_000f:  nop
    IL_0010:  nop
    IL_0011:  leave.s IL_001b
  }  // end .try
  finally
  {
    IL_0013:  ldarg.0
    IL_0014:
      call instance void [mscorlib]System.Object::Finalize()
    IL_0019:  nop
    IL_001a:  endfinally
  } // end handler
  IL_001b:  nop
  IL_001c:  ret
} // end of method MyResourceWrapper::Finalize
```

If you then tested the MyResourceWrapper type, you would find that a system beep occurs when the application terminates, given that the CLR will automatically invoke finalizers upon AppDomain shutdown.

```
static void Main(string[] args)
{
  Console.WriteLine("***** Fun with Finalizers *****\n");
  Console.WriteLine("Hit the return key to shut down this app");
  Console.WriteLine("and force the GC to invoke Finalize()");
  Console.WriteLine("for finalizable objects created in this AppDomain.");
  Console.ReadLine();
  MyResourceWrapper rw = new MyResourceWrapper();
}
```

■ **Source Code**   You can find the SimpleFinalize project in the Chapter 13 subdirectory.

Detailing the Finalization Process

Not to beat a dead horse, but always remember that the role of the Finalize() method is to ensure that a .NET object can clean up unmanaged resources when it is garbage-collected. Thus, if you are building a class that does not make use of unmanaged memory (by far the most common case), finalization is of little use. In fact, if at all possible, you should design your types to avoid supporting a Finalize() method for the simple reason that finalization takes time.

When you allocate an object onto the managed heap, the runtime automatically determines whether your object supports a custom Finalize() method. If so, the object is marked as *finalizable*, and a pointer to this object is stored on an internal queue named the *finalization queue*. The finalization queue is a table maintained by the garbage collector that points to every object that must be finalized before it is removed from the heap.

When the garbage collector determines it is time to free an object from memory, it examines each entry on the finalization queue and copies the object off the heap to yet another managed structure termed the *finalization reachable table* (often abbreviated as *freachable* and pronounced "eff- reachable"). At this point, a separate thread is spawned to invoke the Finalize() method for each object on the freachable table *at the next garbage collection*. Given this, it will take, at the least, two garbage collections to truly finalize an object.

The bottom line is that while finalization of an object does ensure an object can clean up unmanaged resources, it is still nondeterministic in nature and, because of the extra behind-the-curtains processing, considerably slower.

Building Disposable Objects

As you have seen, finalizers can be used to release unmanaged resources when the garbage collector kicks in. However, given that many unmanaged objects are "precious items" (such as raw database or file handles), it could be valuable to release them as soon as possible instead of relying on a garbage collection to occur. As an alternative to overriding Finalize(), your class could implement the IDisposable interface, which defines a single method named Dispose() as follows:

```
public interface IDisposable
{
  void Dispose();
}
```

When you do implement the IDisposable interface, the assumption is that when the *object user* is finished using the object, the object user manually calls Dispose() before allowing the object reference to drop out of scope. In this way, an object can perform any necessary cleanup of unmanaged resources without incurring the hit of being placed on the finalization queue and without waiting for the garbage collector to trigger the class's finalization logic.

■ **Note**   Structures and class types can both implement IDisposable (unlike overriding Finalize(), which is reserved for class types), as the object user (not the garbage collector) invokes the Dispose() method.

To illustrate the use of this interface, create a new C# Console Application project named SimpleDispose. Here is an updated MyResourceWrapper class that now implements IDisposable, rather than overriding System.Object.Finalize():

```
// Implementing IDisposable.
class MyResourceWrapper : IDisposable
{
  // The object user should call this method
  // when they finish with the object.
  public void Dispose()
  {
    // Clean up unmanaged resources...
    // Dispose other contained disposable objects...
    // Just for a test.
    Console.WriteLine("***** In Dispose! *****");
  }
}
```

Notice that a Dispose() method not only is responsible for releasing the type's unmanaged resources but can also call Dispose() on any other contained disposable methods. Unlike with Finalize(), it is perfectly safe to communicate with other managed objects within a Dispose() method. The reason is simple: the garbage collector has no clue about the IDisposable interface and will never call Dispose(). Therefore, when the object user calls this method, the object is still living a productive life on the managed heap and has access to all other heap-allocated objects. The calling logic, shown here, is straightforward:

```
class Program
{
  static void Main(string[] args)
  {
    Console.WriteLine("***** Fun with Dispose *****\n");
    // Create a disposable object and call Dispose()
    // to free any internal resources.
    MyResourceWrapper rw = new MyResourceWrapper();
    rw.Dispose();
    Console.ReadLine();
  }
}
```

Of course, before you attempt to call Dispose() on an object, you will want to ensure the type supports the IDisposable interface. While you will typically know which base class library types implement IDisposable by consulting the .NET Framework 4.7 SDK documentation, a programmatic check can be accomplished using the is or as keywords discussed in Chapter 6.

```
class Program
{
  static void Main(string[] args)
  {
    Console.WriteLine("***** Fun with Dispose *****\n");
    MyResourceWrapper rw = new MyResourceWrapper();
    if (rw is IDisposable)
      rw.Dispose();
    Console.ReadLine();
  }
}
```

This example exposes yet another rule regarding memory management.

■ **Rule**   It is a good idea to call Dispose() on any object you directly create if the object supports IDisposable. The assumption you should make is that if the class designer chose to support the Dispose() method, the type has some cleanup to perform. If you forget, memory will eventually be cleaned up (so don't panic), but it could take longer than necessary.

There is one caveat to the previous rule. A number of types in the base class libraries that do implement the IDisposable interface provide a (somewhat confusing) alias to the Dispose() method, in an attempt to make the disposal-centric method sound more natural for the defining type. By way of an example, while the System.IO.FileStream class implements IDisposable (and therefore supports a Dispose() method), it also defines the following Close() method that is used for the same purpose:

```
// Assume you have imported
// the System.IO namespace...
static void DisposeFileStream()
{
  FileStream fs = new FileStream("myFile.txt", FileMode.OpenOrCreate);

  // Confusing, to say the least!
  // These method calls do the same thing!
  fs.Close();
  fs.Dispose();
}
```

While it does feel more natural to "close" a file rather than "dispose" of one, this doubling up of cleanup methods can be confusing. For the few types that do provide an alias, just remember that if a type implements IDisposable, calling Dispose() is always a safe course of action.

Reusing the C# using Keyword

When you are handling a managed object that implements IDisposable, it is quite common to make use of structured exception handling to ensure the type's Dispose() method is called in the event of a runtime exception, like so:

```
static void Main(string[] args)
{
  Console.WriteLine("***** Fun with Dispose *****\n");
  MyResourceWrapper rw = new MyResourceWrapper ();
  try
  {
    // Use the members of rw.
  }
  finally
  {
    // Always call Dispose(), error or not.
    rw.Dispose();
  }
}
```

While this is a fine example of defensive programming, the truth of the matter is that few developers are thrilled by the prospects of wrapping every disposable type within a try/finally block just to ensure the Dispose() method is called. To achieve the same result in a much less obtrusive manner, C# supports a special bit of syntax that looks like this:

```
static void Main(string[] args)
{
  Console.WriteLine("***** Fun with Dispose *****\n");
  // Dispose() is called automatically when the using scope exits.
  using(MyResourceWrapper rw = new MyResourceWrapper())
  {
    // Use rw object.
  }
}
```

If you looked at the following CIL code of the Main() method using ildasm.exe, you would find the using syntax does indeed expand to try/finally logic, with the expected call to Dispose():

```
.method private hidebysig static void Main(string[] args) cil managed
{
...
  .try
  {
    ...
  } // end .try
  finally
```

```
  {
...
  IL_0012: callvirt instance void
    SimpleFinalize.MyResourceWrapper::Dispose()
  } // end handler
...
} // end of method Program::Main
```

■ **Note**   If you attempt to "use" an object that does not implement IDisposable, you will receive a compiler error.

While this syntax does remove the need to manually wrap disposable objects within try/finally logic, the C# using keyword unfortunately now has a double meaning (importing namespaces and invoking a Dispose() method). Nevertheless, when you are working with .NET types that support the IDisposable interface, this syntactical construct will ensure that the object "being used" will automatically have its Dispose() method called once the using block has exited.

Also, be aware that it is possible to declare multiple objects *of the same type* within a using scope. As you would expect, the compiler will inject code to call Dispose() on each declared object.

```
static void Main(string[] args)
{
  Console.WriteLine("***** Fun with Dispose *****\n");

  // Use a comma-delimited list to declare multiple objects to dispose.
  using(MyResourceWrapper rw = new MyResourceWrapper(), rw2 = new MyResourceWrapper())
  {
    // Use rw and rw2 objects.
  }
}
```

■ **Source Code**   You can find the SimpleDispose project in the Chapter 13 subdirectory.

Building Finalizable and Disposable Types

At this point, you have seen two different approaches to constructing a class that cleans up internal unmanaged resources. On the one hand, you can use a finalizer. Using this technique, you have the peace of mind that comes with knowing the object cleans itself up when garbage-collected (whenever that may be) without the need for user interaction. On the other hand, you can implement IDisposable to provide a way for the object user to clean up the object as soon as it is finished. However, if the caller forgets to call Dispose(), the unmanaged resources may be held in memory indefinitely.

As you might suspect, it is possible to blend both techniques into a single class definition. By doing so, you gain the best of both models. If the object user does remember to call Dispose(), you can inform the garbage collector to bypass the finalization process by calling GC.SuppressFinalize(). If the object user forgets to call Dispose(), the object will eventually be finalized and have a chance to free up the internal resources. The good news is that the object's internal unmanaged resources will be freed one way or another.

Here is the next iteration of MyResourceWrapper, which is now finalizable and disposable, defined in a C# Console Application project named FinalizableDisposableClass:

```
// A sophisticated resource wrapper.
public class MyResourceWrapper : IDisposable
{
  // The garbage collector will call this method if the object user forgets to call
  Dispose().
  ~MyResourceWrapper()
  {
    // Clean up any internal unmanaged resources.
    // Do **not** call Dispose() on any managed objects.
  }
  // The object user will call this method to clean up resources ASAP.
  public void Dispose()
  {
    // Clean up unmanaged resources here.
    // Call Dispose() on other contained disposable objects.
    // No need to finalize if user called Dispose(), so suppress finalization.
    GC.SuppressFinalize(this);
  }
}
```

Notice that this Dispose() method has been updated to call GC.SuppressFinalize(), which informs the CLR that it is no longer necessary to call the destructor when this object is garbage-collected, given that the unmanaged resources have already been freed via the Dispose() logic.

A Formalized Disposal Pattern

The current implementation of MyResourceWrapper does work fairly well; however, you are left with a few minor drawbacks. First, the Finalize() and Dispose() methods each have to clean up the same unmanaged resources. This could result in duplicate code, which can easily become a nightmare to maintain. Ideally, you would define a private helper function that is called by either method.

Next, you'd like to make sure that the Finalize() method does not attempt to dispose of any managed objects, while the Dispose() method should do so. Finally, you'd also like to be certain the object user can safely call Dispose() multiple times without error. Currently, the Dispose() method has no such safeguards.

To address these design issues, Microsoft defined a formal, prim-and-proper disposal pattern that strikes a balance between robustness, maintainability, and performance. Here is the final (and annotated) version of MyResourceWrapper, which makes use of this official pattern:

```
class MyResourceWrapper : IDisposable
{
  // Used to determine if Dispose() has already been called.
  private bool disposed = false;

  public void Dispose()
  {
    // Call our helper method.
    // Specifying "true" signifies that the object user triggered the cleanup.
    CleanUp(true);
```

```
    // Now suppress finalization.
    GC.SuppressFinalize(this);
  }

  private void CleanUp(bool disposing)
  {
    // Be sure we have not already been disposed!
    if (!this.disposed)
    {

      // If disposing equals true, dispose all managed resources.
      if (disposing)
      {
        // Dispose managed resources.
      }
      // Clean up unmanaged resources here.
    }
    disposed = true;
  }
  ~MyResourceWrapper()
  {
    // Call our helper method.
    // Specifying "false" signifies that the GC triggered the cleanup.
    CleanUp(false);
  }
}
```

Notice that MyResourceWrapper now defines a private helper method named CleanUp(). By specifying true as an argument, you indicate that the object user has initiated the cleanup, so you should clean up all managed *and* unmanaged resources. However, when the garbage collector initiates the cleanup, you specify false when calling CleanUp() to ensure that internal disposable objects are *not* disposed (as you can't assume they are still in memory!). Last but not least, the bool member variable (disposed) is set to true before exiting CleanUp() to ensure that Dispose() can be called numerous times without error.

■ **Note**   After an object has been "disposed," it's still possible for the client to invoke members on it, as it is still in memory. Therefore, a robust resource wrapper class would also need to update each member of the class with additional coding logic that says, in effect, "If I am disposed, do nothing and return from the member."

To test the final iteration of MyResourceWrapper, add a call to Console.Beep() within the scope of your finalizer, like so:

```
~MyResourceWrapper()
{
  Console.Beep();
  // Call our helper method.
  // Specifying "false" signifies that the GC triggered the cleanup.
  CleanUp(false);
}
```

Next, update Main() as follows:

```
static void Main(string[] args)
{
  Console.WriteLine("***** Dispose() / Destructor Combo Platter *****");

  // Call Dispose() manually. This will not call the finalizer.
  MyResourceWrapper rw = new MyResourceWrapper();
  rw.Dispose();

  // Don't call Dispose(). This will trigger the finalizer and cause a beep.
  MyResourceWrapper rw2 = new MyResourceWrapper();
}
```

Notice that you are explicitly calling Dispose() on the rw object, so the destructor call is suppressed. However, you have "forgotten" to call Dispose() on the rw2 object; therefore, when the application terminates, you hear a single beep. If you were to comment out the call to Dispose() on the rw object, you would hear two beeps.

■ **Source Code**   You can find the FinalizableDisposableClass project in the Chapter 13 subdirectory.

That concludes your investigation of how the CLR manages your objects via garbage collection. While there are additional (somewhat esoteric) details regarding the collection process I haven't covered here (such as weak references and object resurrection), you are now in a perfect position for further exploration on your own. To wrap this chapter up, you will examine a programming feature called *lazy instantiation* of objects.

Understanding Lazy Object Instantiation

When you are creating classes, you might occasionally need to account for a particular member variable in code, which might never actually be needed, in that the object user might not call the method (or property) that makes use of it. Fair enough. However, this can be problematic if the member variable in question requires a large amount of memory to be instantiated.

For example, assume you are writing a class that encapsulates the operations of a digital music player. In addition to the expected methods, such as Play(), Pause(), and Stop(), you also want to provide the ability to return a collection of Song objects (via a class named AllTracks), which represents every single digital music file on the device.

If you'd like to follow along, create a new Console Application project named LazyObjectInstantiation, and define the following class types:

```
// Represents a single song.
class Song
{
  public string Artist { get; set; }
  public string TrackName { get; set; }
  public double TrackLength { get; set; }
}
```

```
// Represents all songs on a player.
class AllTracks
{
  // Our media player can have a maximum
  // of 10,000 songs.
  private Song[] allSongs = new Song[10000];

  public AllTracks()
  {
    // Assume we fill up the array
    // of Song objects here.
    Console.WriteLine("Filling up the songs!");
  }
}

// The MediaPlayer has-an AllTracks object.
class MediaPlayer
{
  // Assume these methods do something useful.
  public void Play() { /* Play a song */ }
  public void Pause() { /* Pause the song */ }
  public void Stop() { /* Stop playback */ }
  private AllTracks allSongs = new AllTracks();

  public AllTracks GetAllTracks()
  {
    // Return all of the songs.
    return allSongs;
  }
}
```

The current implementation of MediaPlayer assumes that the object user will want to obtain a list of songs via the GetAllTracks() method. Well, what if the object user does *not* need to obtain this list? In the current implementation, the AllTracks member variable will still be allocated, thereby creating 10,000 Song objects in memory, as follows:

```
static void Main(string[] args)
{
  Console.WriteLine("***** Fun with Lazy Instantiation *****\n");

  // This caller does not care about getting all songs,
  // but indirectly created 10,000 objects!
  MediaPlayer myPlayer = new MediaPlayer();
  myPlayer.Play();

  Console.ReadLine();
}
```

Clearly, you would rather not create 10,000 objects that nobody will use, as that will add a good deal of stress to the .NET garbage collector. While you could manually add some code to ensure the allSongs object is created only if used (perhaps using the factory method design pattern), there is an easier way.

The base class libraries provide a useful generic class named Lazy<>, defined in the System namespace of mscorlib.dll. This class allows you to define data that will *not* be created unless your codebase actually uses it. As this is a generic class, you must specify the type of item to be created on first use, which can be any type with the .NET base class libraries or a custom type you have authored yourself. To enable lazy instantiation of the AllTracks member variable, you can simply replace this:

```
// The MediaPlayer has-an AllTracks object.
class MediaPlayer
{
...
  private AllTracks allSongs = new AllTracks();

  public AllTracks GetAllTracks()
  {
    // Return all of the songs.
    return allSongs;
  }
}
```

with this:

```
// The MediaPlayer has-an Lazy<AllTracks> object.
class MediaPlayer
{
...
  private Lazy<AllTracks> allSongs = new Lazy<AllTracks>();
  public AllTracks GetAllTracks()
  {
    // Return all of the songs.
    return allSongs.Value;
  }
}
```

Beyond the fact that you are now representing the AllTracks member variable as a Lazy<> type, notice that the implementation of the previous GetAllTracks() method has also been updated. Specifically, you must use the read-only Value property of the Lazy<> class to obtain the actual stored data (in this case, the AllTracks object that is maintaining the 10,000 Song objects).

With this simple update, notice how the following updated Main() method will indirectly allocate the Song objects only if GetAllTracks() is indeed called:

```
static void Main(string[] args)
{
  Console.WriteLine("***** Fun with Lazy Instantiation *****\n");

  // No allocation of AllTracks object here!
  MediaPlayer myPlayer = new MediaPlayer();
  myPlayer.Play();
```

```
// Allocation of AllTracks happens when you call GetAllTracks().
MediaPlayer yourPlayer = new MediaPlayer();
AllTracks yourMusic = yourPlayer.GetAllTracks();

Console.ReadLine();
}
```

■ **Note**   Lazy object instantiation is useful not only to decrease allocation of unnecessary objects. You can also use this technique if a given member has expensive creation code, such as invoking a remote method, communication with a relational database, or whatnot.

Customizing the Creation of the Lazy Data

When you declare a Lazy<> variable, the actual internal data type is created using the default constructor, like so:

```
// Default constructor of AllTracks is called when the Lazy<>
// variable is used.
private Lazy<AllTracks> allSongs = new Lazy<AllTracks>();
```

While this might be fine in some cases, what if the AllTracks class had some additional constructors and you want to ensure the correct one is called? Furthermore, what if you have some extra work to do (beyond simply creating the AllTracks object) when the Lazy<> variable is made? As luck would have it, the Lazy<> class allows you to specify a generic delegate as an optional parameter, which will specify a method to call during the creation of the wrapped type.

The generic delegate in question is of type System.Func<>, which can point to a method that returns the same data type being created by the related Lazy<> variable and can take up to 16 arguments (which are typed using generic type parameters). In most cases, you will not need to specify any parameters to pass to the method pointed to by Func<>. Furthermore, to greatly simplify the use of the required Func<>, I recommend using a lambda expression (see Chapter 10 to review the delegate/lambda relationship).

With this in mind, the following is a final version of MediaPlayer that adds a bit of custom code when the wrapped AllTracks object is created. Remember, this method must return a new instance of the type wrapped by Lazy<> before exiting, and you can use any constructor you choose (here, you are still invoking the default constructor of AllTracks).

```
class MediaPlayer
{
...
  // Use a lambda expression to add additional code
  // when the AllTracks object is made.
  private Lazy<AllTracks> allSongs = new Lazy<AllTracks>( () =>
    {
      Console.WriteLine("Creating AllTracks object!");
      return new AllTracks();
    }
  );
```

```
public AllTracks GetAllTracks()
{
  // Return all of the songs.
  return allSongs.Value;
}
}
```

Sweet! I hope you can see the usefulness of the Lazy<> class. Essentially, this generic class allows you to ensure expensive objects are allocated only when the object user requires them. If you find this topic useful for your projects, you might also want to look up the System.Lazy<> class in the .NET Framework 4.5 SDK documentation for further examples of how to program for lazy instantiation.

■ **Source Code**   You can find the LazyObjectInstantiation project in the Chapter 13 subdirectory.

Summary

The point of this chapter was to demystify the garbage collection process. As you saw, the garbage collector will run only when it is unable to acquire the necessary memory from the managed heap (or when a given AppDomain unloads from memory). When a collection does occur, you can rest assured that Microsoft's collection algorithm has been optimized by the use of object generations, secondary threads for the purpose of object finalization, and a managed heap dedicated to hosting large objects.

This chapter also illustrated how to programmatically interact with the garbage collector using the System.GC class type. As mentioned, the only time you will really need to do so is when you are building finalizable or disposable class types that operate on unmanaged resources.

Recall that finalizable types are classes that have provided a destructor (effectively overriding the Finalize() method) to clean up unmanaged resources at the time of garbage collection. Disposable objects, on the other hand, are classes (or structures) that implement the IDisposable interface, which should be called by the object user when it is finished using said objects. Finally, you learned about an official "disposal" pattern that blends both approaches.

This chapter wrapped up with a look at a generic class named Lazy<>. As you saw, you can use this class to delay the creation of an expensive (in terms of memory consumption) object until the caller actually requires it. By doing so, you can help reduce the number of objects stored on the managed heap and also ensure expensive objects are created only when actually required by the caller.

PART V

Programming with .NET Assemblies

■ ■ ■

CHAPTER 14

Building and Configuring Class Libraries

During the first four parts of this book, you have created a number of "stand-alone" executable applications, in which all the programming logic was packaged within a single executable file (*.exe). These executable assemblies were using little more than the primary .NET class library, mscorlib.dll. While some simple .NET programs may be constructed using nothing more than the .NET base class libraries, chances are it will be commonplace for you (or your teammates) to isolate reusable programming logic into *custom* class libraries (*.dll files) that can be shared among applications.

In this chapter, you will learn about various ways to package your types into custom libraries of code. To begin, you'll learn the details of partitioning types into .NET namespaces. After this, you will examine the class library project templates of Visual Studio and learn the distinction between private and shared assemblies.

Next, you'll explore exactly how the .NET runtime resolves the location of an assembly, and you'll come to understand the global assembly cache, XML application configuration files (*.config files), publisher policy assemblies, and the System.Configuration namespace.

Defining Custom Namespaces

Before diving into the aspects of library deployment and configuration, the first task is to learn the details of packaging your custom types into .NET namespaces. Up to this point in the text, you've been building small test programs that leverage existing namespaces in the .NET universe (System, in particular). However, when you build larger applications with many types, it can be helpful to group your related types into custom namespaces. In C#, this is accomplished using the namespace keyword. Explicitly defining custom namespaces is even more important when creating .NET *.dll assemblies, as other developers will need to reference the library and import your custom namespaces to use your types.

To investigate the issues firsthand, begin by creating a new Console Application project named CustomNamespaces. Now, assume you are developing a collection of geometric classes named Square, Circle, and Hexagon. Given their similarities, you would like to group them together into a unique namespace called MyShapes within the CustomNamespaces.exe assembly. You have two basic approaches. First, you can choose to define all classes in a single C# file (ShapesLib.cs) as follows:

```
// ShapesLib.cs
using System;

namespace MyShapes
{
  // Circle class
  public class Circle { /* Interesting members... */ }
```

```
  // Hexagon class
  public class Hexagon { /* More interesting members... */ }

  // Square class
  public class Square { /* Even more interesting members... */ }
}
```

While the C# compiler has no problems with a single C# code file containing multiple types, this could be cumbersome when you want to reuse class definitions in new projects. For example, say you are building a new project and only need to use the Circle class. If all types are defined in a single code file, you are more or less stuck with the entire set. Therefore, as an alternative, you can split a single namespace across multiple C# files. To ensure each type is packaged into the same logical group, simply wrap the given class definitions in the same namespace scope, like so:

// Circle.cs
```
using System;

namespace MyShapes
{
  // Circle class
  public class Circle { /* Interesting methods... */ }
}
```

// Hexagon.cs
```
using System;

namespace MyShapes
{
  // Hexagon class
  public class Hexagon { /* More interesting methods... */ }
}
```

// Square.cs
```
using System;

namespace MyShapes
{
  // Square class
  public class Square { /* Even more interesting methods... */ }
}
```

In both cases, notice how the MyShapes namespace acts as the conceptual "container" of these classes. When another namespace (such as CustomNamespaces) wants to use types in a separate namespace, you use the using keyword, just as you would when using namespaces of the .NET base class libraries, as follows:

```
// Bring in a namespace from the base class libraries.
using System;

// Make use of types defined the MyShapes namespace.
using MyShapes;
```

```
namespace CustomNamespaces
{
  public class Program
  {
    static void Main(string[] args)
    {
      Hexagon h = new Hexagon();
      Circle c = new Circle();
      Square s = new Square();
    }
  }
}
```

For this particular example, the assumption is that the C# file (or files) that defines the MyShapes namespace is part of the same Console Application project that contains the file defining the CustomNamespaces namespace; in other words, all the files are used to compile a single .NET executable assembly. If you defined the MyShapes namespace within an external assembly, you would also need to add a reference to that library before you could compile successfully. You'll learn all the details of building applications that use external libraries during the course of this chapter.

Resolving Name Clashes with Fully Qualified Names

Technically speaking, you are not required to use the C# using keyword when referring to types defined in external namespaces. You could use the *fully qualified name* of the type, which, as you may recall from Chapter 1, is the type's name prefixed with the defining namespace. Here's an example:

```
// Note we are not importing MyShapes anymore!
using System;

namespace CustomNamespaces
{
  public class Program
  {
    static void Main(string[] args)
    {
      MyShapes.Hexagon h = new MyShapes.Hexagon();
      MyShapes.Circle c = new MyShapes.Circle();
      MyShapes.Square s = new MyShapes.Square();
    }
  }
}
```

Typically, there is no need to use a fully qualified name. Not only does it require a greater number of keystrokes, it also makes no difference whatsoever in terms of code size or execution speed. In fact, in CIL code, types are *always* defined with the fully qualified name. In this light, the C# using keyword is simply a typing time-saver.

However, fully qualified names can be helpful (and sometimes necessary) to avoid potential name clashes when using multiple namespaces that contain identically named types. Assume you have a new namespace termed My3DShapes, which defines the following three classes, capable of rendering a shape in stunning 3D:

```
// Another shape-centric namespace.
using System;
namespace My3DShapes
{
  // 3D Circle class.
  public class Circle { }

  // 3D Hexagon class.
  public class Hexagon { }

  // 3D Square class.
  public class Square { }
}
```

If you update the Program class as shown next, you are issued a number of compile-time errors, because both namespaces define identically named classes:

```
// Ambiguities abound!
using System;
using MyShapes;
using My3DShapes;

namespace CustomNamespaces
{
  public class Program
  {
    static void Main(string[] args)
    {
      // Which namespace do I reference?
      Hexagon h = new Hexagon(); // Compiler error!
      Circle c = new Circle();   // Compiler error!
      Square s = new Square();   // Compiler error!
    }
  }
}
```

The ambiguity can be resolved using the type's fully qualified name, like so:

```
// We have now resolved the ambiguity.
static void Main(string[] args)
{
  My3DShapes.Hexagon h = new My3DShapes.Hexagon();
  My3DShapes.Circle c = new My3DShapes.Circle();
  MyShapes.Square s = new MyShapes.Square();
}
```

Resolving Name Clashes with Aliases

The C# using keyword also lets you create an alias for a type's fully qualified name. When you do so, you define a token that is substituted for the type's full name at compile time. Defining aliases provides a second way to resolve name clashes. Here's an example:

```
using System;
using MyShapes;
using My3DShapes;

// Resolve the ambiguity using a custom alias.
using The3DHexagon = My3DShapes.Hexagon;

namespace CustomNamespaces
{
  class Program
  {
    static void Main(string[] args)
    {
      // This is really creating a My3DShapes.Hexagon class.
      The3DHexagon h2 = new The3DHexagon();
...
    }
  }
}
```

This alternative using syntax also lets you create an alias for a lengthy namespace. One of the longer namespaces in the base class library is System.Runtime.Serialization.Formatters.Binary, which contains a member named BinaryFormatter. If you want, you can create an instance of the BinaryFormatter as follows:

```
using bfHome = System.Runtime.Serialization.Formatters.Binary;

namespace MyApp
{
  class ShapeTester
  {
    static void Main(string[] args)
    {
      bfHome.BinaryFormatter b = new bfHome.BinaryFormatter();
      ...
    }
  }
}
```

as well as with a traditional using directive:

```
using System.Runtime.Serialization.Formatters.Binary;

namespace MyApp
{
  class ShapeTester
  {
    static void Main(string[] args)
    {
      BinaryFormatter b = new BinaryFormatter();
      ...
    }
  }
}
```

At this point in the game, there is no need to concern yourself with what the BinaryFormatter class is used for (you'll examine this class in Chapter 20). For now, simply remember that the C# using keyword can be used to define aliases for lengthy fully qualified names or, more commonly, to resolve name clashes that can arise when importing multiple namespaces that define identically named types.

■ **Note**   Be aware that overuse of C# aliases can result in a confusing codebase. If other programmers on your team are unaware of your custom aliases, they could assume the aliases refer to types in the .NET base class libraries and become quite confused when they can't find these tokens in the .NET Framework SDK documentation!

Creating Nested Namespaces

When organizing your types, you are free to define namespaces within other namespaces. The .NET base class libraries do so in numerous places to provide deeper levels of type organization. For example, the IO namespace is nested within System to yield System.IO. If you want to create a root namespace containing the existing My3DShapes namespace, you can update your code as follows:

```
// Nesting a namespace.
namespace Chapter14
{
  namespace My3DShapes
  {
    // 3D Circle class.
    public class Circle{ }

    // 3D Hexagon class.
    public class Hexagon{ }

    // 3D Square class.
    public class Square{ }
  }
}
```

In many cases, the role of a root namespace is simply to provide a further level of scope; therefore, it may not define any types directly within its scope (as in the case of the Chapter14 namespace). If this is the case, a nested namespace can be defined using the following compact form:

```
// Nesting a namespace (take two).
namespace Chapter14.My3DShapes
{
  // 3D Circle class.
  public class Circle{ }

  // 3D Hexagon class.
  public class Hexagon{ }

  // 3D Square class.
  public class Square{ }
}
```

Given that you have now nested the My3DShapes namespace within the Chapter14 root namespace, you need to update any existing using directives and type aliases, like so:

```
using Chapter14.My3DShapes;
using The3DHexagon = Chapter14.My3DShapes.Hexagon;
```

The Default Namespace of Visual Studio

On a final namespace-related note, it is worth pointing out that, by default, when you create a new C# project using Visual Studio, the name of your application's default namespace will be identical to the project name. From this point on, when you insert new code files using the Project ➤ Add New Item menu selection, types will automatically be wrapped within the default namespace. If you want to change the name of the default namespace, simply access the "Default namespace" option using the Application tab of the project's properties window (see Figure 14-1).

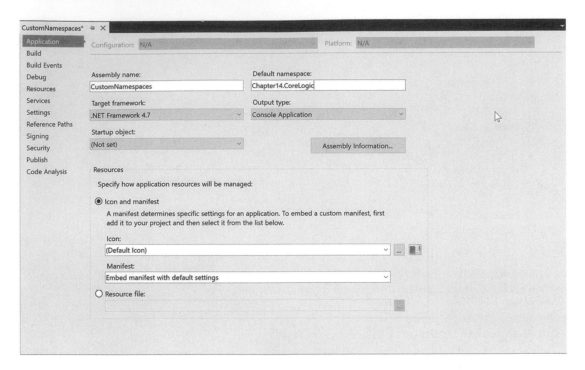

Figure 14-1. *Configuring the default namespace*

With this update, any new item inserted into the project will be wrapped within the Chapter14.
CoreLogic namespace (and, obviously, if another namespace wants to use these types, the correct using directive must be applied).

So far, so good. Now that you have seen some details regarding how to package your custom types into well-organized namespaces, let's quickly review the benefits and format of the .NET assembly. After this, you will delve into the details of creating, deploying, and configuring your custom class libraries.

■ **Source Code**   You can find the CustomNamespaces project in the Chapter 14 subdirectory.

The Role of .NET Assemblies

.NET applications are constructed by piecing together any number of *assemblies*. Simply put, an assembly is a versioned, self-describing binary file hosted by the CLR. Now, despite that .NET assemblies have the same file extensions (*.exe or *.dll) as previous Windows binaries, they have little in common with those files under the hood. Thus, to set the stage for the information to come, let's consider some of the benefits provided by the assembly format.

Assemblies Promote Code Reuse

As you have built your Console Application projects over the previous chapters, it might have seemed that *all* the applications' functionality was contained within the executable assembly you were constructing. In reality, your applications were leveraging numerous types contained within the always-accessible .NET code library, mscorlib.dll (recall that the C# compiler references mscorlib.dll automatically), and in the case of some examples System.Core.dll.

As you might know, a *code library* (also termed a *class library*) is a *.dll that contains types intended to be used by external applications. When you are creating executable assemblies, you will no doubt be leveraging numerous system-supplied and custom code libraries as you create your application. Do be aware, however, that a code library need not take a *.dll file extension. It is perfectly possible (although certainly not common) for an executable assembly to use types defined within an external executable file. In this light, a referenced *.exe can also be considered a code library.

Regardless of how a code library is packaged, the .NET platform allows you to reuse types in a language-independent manner. For example, you could create a code library in C# and reuse that library in any other .NET programming language. It is possible not only to allocate types across languages but also to derive from them. A base class defined in C# could be extended by a class authored in Visual Basic. Interfaces defined in F# can be implemented by structures defined in C#, and so forth. The point is that when you begin to break apart a single monolithic executable into numerous .NET assemblies, you achieve a *language-neutral* form of code reuse.

Assemblies Establish a Type Boundary

Recall that a type's *fully qualified name* is composed by prefixing the type's namespace (e.g., System) to its name (e.g., Console). Strictly speaking, however, the assembly in which a type resides further establishes a type's identity. For example, if you have two uniquely named assemblies (say, MyCars.dll and YourCars.dll) that both define a namespace (CarLibrary) containing a class named SportsCar, they are considered unique types in the .NET universe.

Assemblies Are Versionable Units

.NET assemblies are assigned a four-part numerical version number of the form *<major>.<minor>.<build>.<revision>*. (If you do not explicitly provide a version number, the assembly is automatically assigned a version of 1.0.0.0, given the default Visual Studio project settings.) This number, in conjunction with an optional *public key value*, allows multiple versions of the same assembly to coexist in harmony on a single machine. Formally speaking, assemblies that provide public key information are termed *strongly named*. As you will see in this chapter, by using a strong name, the CLR is able to ensure that the correct version of an assembly is loaded on behalf of the calling client.

Assemblies Are Self-Describing

Assemblies are regarded as *self-describing*, in part because they record every external assembly they must have access to in order to function correctly. Thus, if your assembly requires System.Windows.Forms.dll and System.Core.dll, this will be documented in the assembly's *manifest*. Recall from Chapter 1 that a manifest is a blob of metadata that describes the assembly itself (name, version, required external assemblies, etc.).

In addition to manifest data, an assembly contains metadata that describes the composition (member names, implemented interfaces, base classes, constructors, and so forth) of every contained type. Because an assembly is documented in such detail, the CLR does *not* consult the Windows system registry to resolve its location (quite the radical departure from Microsoft's legacy COM programming model). As you will discover during this chapter, the CLR makes use of an entirely new scheme to resolve the location of external code libraries.

Assemblies Are Configurable

Assemblies can be deployed as "private" or "shared." Private assemblies reside in the same directory (or possibly a subdirectory) as the client application that uses them. Shared assemblies, on the other hand, are libraries intended to be consumed by numerous applications on a single machine and are deployed to a specific directory termed the *global assembly cache*, or *GAC*.

Regardless of how you deploy your assemblies, you are free to author XML-based configuration files. Using these configuration files, you can instruct the CLR to "probe" for assemblies at a specific location, load a specific version of a referenced assembly for a particular client, or consult an arbitrary directory on your local machine, your network location, or a web-based URL. You'll learn a good deal more about XML configuration files throughout this chapter.

Understanding the Format of a .NET Assembly

Now that you've learned about several benefits provided by the .NET assembly, let's shift gears and get a better idea of how an assembly is composed under the hood. Structurally speaking, a .NET assembly (*.dll or *.exe) consists of the following elements:

- A Windows file header
- A CLR file header
- CIL code
- Type metadata
- An assembly manifest
- Optional embedded resources

While the first two elements (the Windows and CLR headers) are blocks of data you can typically always ignore, they do deserve some brief consideration. Here's an overview of each element.

The Windows File Header

The Windows file header establishes the fact that the assembly can be loaded and manipulated by the Windows family of operating systems. This header data also identifies the kind of application (console-based, GUI-based, or *.dll code library) to be hosted by Windows. If you open a .NET assembly using the dumpbin.exe utility (via a Windows command prompt) and specify the /headers flag as so:

```
dumpbin /headers CarLibrary.dll
```

you can view an assembly's Windows header information. Here is the (partial) Windows header information for the CarLibrary.dll assembly you will build a bit later in this chapter (if you would like to run dumpbin. exe yourself right now, you can specify the name of any *.dll or *.exe you wrote during this book in place of CarLibrary.dll):

```
Dump of file CarLibrary.dll

PE signature found
File Type: DLL

FILE HEADER VALUES
             14C machine (x86)
               3 number of sections
        4B37DCD8 time date stamp Sun Dec 27 16:16:56 2011
               0 file pointer to symbol table
               0 number of symbols
              E0 size of optional header
            2102 characteristics
                   Executable
                   32 bit word machine
                   DLL

OPTIONAL HEADER VALUES
             10B magic # (PE32)
            8.00 linker version
             E00 size of code
             600 size of initialized data
               0 size of uninitialized data
            2CDE entry point (00402CDE)
            2000 base of code
            4000 base of data
          400000 image base (00400000 to 00407FFF)
            2000 section alignment
             200 file alignment
            4.00 operating system version
            0.00 image version
            4.00 subsystem version
               0 Win32 version
            8000 size of image
             200 size of headers
               0 checksum
               3 subsystem (Windows CUI)
...
```

Now, remember that the vast majority of .NET programmers will never need to concern themselves with the format of the header data embedded in a .NET assembly. Unless you happen to be building a new .NET language compiler (where you *would* care about such information), you are free to remain blissfully unaware of the grimy details of the header data. Do be aware, however, that this information is used under the covers when Windows loads the binary image into memory.

The CLR File Header

The CLR header is a block of data that all .NET assemblies must support (and do support, courtesy of the C# compiler) to be hosted by the CLR. In a nutshell, this header defines numerous flags that enable the runtime to understand the layout of the managed file. For example, flags exist that identify the location of the metadata and resources within the file, the version of the runtime the assembly was built against, the value of the (optional) public key, and so forth. If you supply the /clrheader flag to dumpbin.exe like so:

```
dumpbin /clrheader CarLibrary.dll
```

you are presented with the internal CLR header information for a given .NET assembly, as shown here:

```
Dump of file CarLibrary.dll

File Type: DLL

  clr Header:

            48 cb
          2.05 runtime version
          2164 [      A74] RVA [size] of MetaData Directory
             1 flags
               IL Only
             0 entry point token
             0 [        0] RVA [size] of Resources Directory
             0 [        0] RVA [size] of StrongNameSignature Directory
             0 [        0] RVA [size] of CodeManagerTable Directory
             0 [        0] RVA [size] of VTableFixups Directory
             0 [        0] RVA [size] of ExportAddressTableJumps Directory
             0 [        0] RVA [size] of ManagedNativeHeader Directory
  Summary
          2000 .reloc
          2000 .rsrc
          2000 .text
```

Again, as a .NET developer, you will not need to concern yourself with the gory details of an assembly's CLR header information. Just understand that every .NET assembly contains this data, which is used behind the scenes by the .NET runtime as the image data loads into memory. Now turn your attention to some information that is much more useful in your day-to-day programming tasks.

CIL Code, Type Metadata, and the Assembly Manifest

At its core, an assembly contains CIL code, which, as you recall, is a platform- and CPU-agnostic intermediate language. At runtime, the internal CIL is compiled on the fly using a just-in-time (JIT) compiler, according to platform- and CPU-specific instructions. Given this design, .NET assemblies can indeed execute on a variety of architectures, devices, and operating systems. (Although you can live a happy and productive life without understanding the details of the CIL programming language, Chapter 18 offers an introduction to the syntax and semantics of CIL.)

An assembly also contains metadata that completely describes the format of the contained types, as well as the format of external types referenced by this assembly. The .NET runtime uses this metadata to resolve the location of types (and their members) within the binary, lay out types in memory, and facilitate remote method invocations. You'll check out the details of the .NET metadata format in Chapter 15 during your examination of reflection services.

An assembly must also contain an associated *manifest* (also referred to as *assembly metadata*). The manifest documents each *module* within the assembly, establishes the version of the assembly, and also documents any *external* assemblies referenced by the current assembly. As you will see over the course of this chapter, the CLR makes extensive use of an assembly's manifest during the process of locating external assembly references.

Optional Assembly Resources

Finally, a .NET assembly may contain any number of embedded resources, such as application icons, image files, sound clips, or string tables. In fact, the .NET platform supports *satellite assemblies* that contain nothing but localized resources. This can be useful if you want to partition your resources based on a specific culture (English, German, etc.) for the purposes of building international software. The topic of building satellite assemblies is outside the scope of this text; consult the .NET 4.7 Framework documentation for information on satellite assemblies if you are interested.

Building and Consuming Custom Class Library

To begin exploring the world of .NET class libraries, you'll first create a *.dll assembly (named CarLibrary) that contains a small set of public types. To build a code library using Visual Studio, select the Class Library project workspace via the File ➤ New Project menu option (see Figure 14-2). After creating the project, delete the autogenerated file Class1.cs.

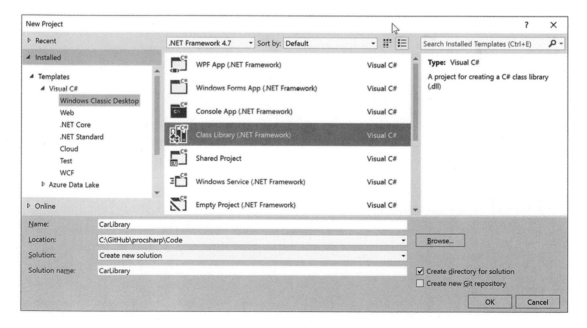

Figure 14-2. *Creating a C# class library*

The design of your automobile library begins with an abstract base class named Car that defines various state data via automatic property syntax. This class also has a single abstract method named TurboBoost(), which uses a custom enumeration (EngineState) representing the current condition of the car's engine. Insert a new C# class file into your project, named Car.cs, which contains the following code:

```csharp
using System;
using System.Collections.Generic;
using System.Linq;
using System.Text;
using System.Threading.Tasks;

namespace CarLibrary
{
  // Represents the state of the engine.
  public enum EngineState
  { engineAlive, engineDead }

  // The abstract base class in the hierarchy.
  public abstract class Car
  {
    public string PetName {get; set;}
    public int CurrentSpeed {get; set;}
    public int MaxSpeed {get; set;}

    protected EngineState egnState = EngineState.engineAlive;
    public EngineState EngineState => egnState;
    public abstract void TurboBoost();

    public Car(){}
    public Car(string name, int maxSp, int currSp)
    {
      PetName = name; MaxSpeed = maxSp; CurrentSpeed = currSp;
    }
  }
}
```

Now assume you have two direct descendants of the Car type named MiniVan and SportsCar. Each overrides the abstract TurboBoost() method by displaying an appropriate message via a Windows Forms message box. Insert a new C# class file into your project, named DerivedCars.cs, which contains the following code:

```csharp
using System;
using System.Collections.Generic;
using System.Linq;
using System.Text;
using System.Threading.Tasks;

// Keep reading! This won't compile until you reference a .NET library.
using System.Windows.Forms;
```

```
namespace CarLibrary
{
  public class SportsCar : Car
  {
    public SportsCar(){ }
    public SportsCar(string name, int maxSp, int currSp) : base (name, maxSp, currSp){ }

    public override void TurboBoost()
    {
      MessageBox.Show("Ramming speed!", "Faster is better...");
    }
  }

  public class MiniVan : Car
  {
    public MiniVan(){ }
    public MiniVan(string name, int maxSp, int currSp) : base (name, maxSp, currSp){ }

    public override void TurboBoost()
    {
      // Minivans have poor turbo capabilities!
      egnState = EngineState.engineDead;
      MessageBox.Show("Eek!", "Your engine block exploded!");
    }
  }
}
```

Notice how each subclass implements TurboBoost() using the Windows Form's MessageBox class, which is defined in the System.Windows.Forms.dll assembly. For your assembly to use the types defined within this external assembly, the CarLibrary project must add a reference to this assembly via the Add Reference dialog box (see Figure 14-3), which you can access through the Visual Studio Project ➤ Add Reference menu selection.

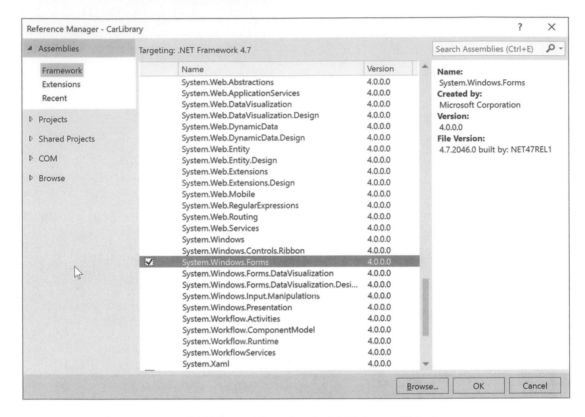

Figure 14-3. *Referencing external .NET assemblies using the Add Reference dialog box*

It is *really* important to understand that the assemblies displayed in the Framework area of the Add Reference dialog box do not represent every assembly on your machine. The Add Reference dialog box will *not* display your custom libraries, and it does *not* display all libraries located in the GAC (more details later in the chapter). Rather, this dialog box simply presents a list of common assemblies that Visual Studio is preprogrammed to display. When you are building applications that require the use of an assembly not listed within the Add Reference dialog box, you need to click the Browse node to manually navigate to the *.dll or *.exe in question.

■ **Note** Be aware that the Recent section of the Add Reference dialog box keeps a running list of previously referenced assemblies. This can be handy, as many .NET projects tend to use the same core set of external libraries.

Exploring the Manifest

Before using CarLibrary.dll from a client application, let's check out how the code library is composed under the hood. Assuming you have compiled this project, load CarLibrary.dll into ildasm.exe via the File ➤ Open menu, and navigate to the \bin\Debug subdirectory of your CarLibrary project. When you are done, you should see your library displayed in the IL disassembler tool (see Figure 14-4).

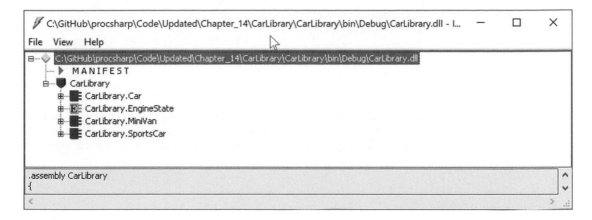

Figure 14-4. *CarLibrary.dll loaded into ildasm.exe*

Now, open the manifest of CarLibrary.dll by double-clicking the MANIFEST icon. The first code block in a manifest specifics all external assemblies required by the current assembly to function correctly. As you recall, CarLibrary.dll made use of types within mscorlib.dll and System.Windows.Forms.dll, both of which are listed in the manifest using the .assembly extern token, as shown here:

```
.assembly extern mscorlib
{
  .publickeytoken = (B7 7A 5C 56 19 34 E0 89 )
  .ver 4:0:0:0
}
.assembly extern System.Windows.Forms
{
  .publickeytoken = (B7 7A 5C 56 19 34 E0 89 )
  .ver 4:0:0:0
}
```

Here, each .assembly extern block is qualified by the .publickeytoken and .ver directives. The .publickeytoken instruction is present only if the assembly has been configured with a *strong name* (more details on strong names in the section "Understanding Strong Names" later in this chapter). The .ver token defines (of course) the numerical version identifier of the referenced assembly.

After the external references, you will find a number of .custom tokens that identify assembly-level attributes (copyright information, company name, assembly version, etc.). Here is a (very) partial listing of this particular chunk of manifest data:

```
.assembly CarLibrary
{
  .custom instance void ...AssemblyDescriptionAttribute...
  .custom instance void ...AssemblyConfigurationAttribute...
  .custom instance void ...RuntimeCompatibilityAttribute...
  .custom instance void ...TargetFrameworkAttribute...
  .custom instance void ...AssemblyTitleAttribute...
  .custom instance void ...AssemblyTrademarkAttribute...
  .custom instance void ...AssemblyCompanyAttribute...
```

```
  .custom instance void ...AssemblyProductAttribute...
  .custom instance void ...AssemblyCopyrightAttribute...
...
  .ver 1:0:0:0
}
.module CarLibrary.dll
```

Typically, these settings are established visually using the Properties window of your current project. Now, switching back to Visual Studio, if you click the Properties icon within Solution Explorer, you can click the Assembly Information button located on the (automatically selected) Application tab. This will bring up the dialog window shown in Figure 14-5.

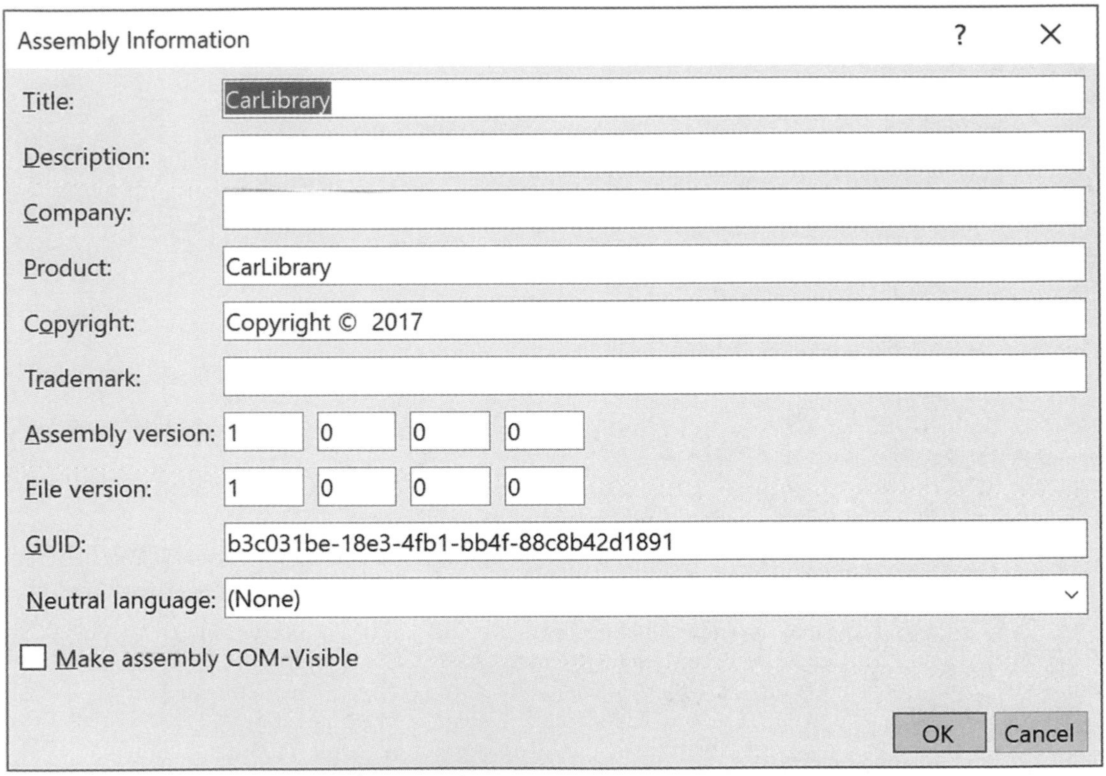

Figure 14-5. Editing assembly information using Visual Studio's Properties window

When you save your changes, the GUI editor updates your project's AssemblyInfo.cs file, which is maintained by Visual Studio and can be viewed by expanding the Properties node of Solution Explorer (see Figure 14-6).

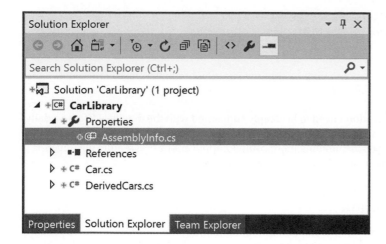

Figure 14-6. *The* `AssemblyInfo.cs` *file is updated as you use the Properties window*

If you view the contents of this C# file, you'll see a number of .NET *attributes* sandwiched between square brackets. Here's an example:

```
[assembly: AssemblyTitle("CarLibrary")]
[assembly: AssemblyDescription("")]
[assembly: AssemblyConfiguration("")]
[assembly: AssemblyCompany("")]
[assembly: AssemblyProduct("CarLibrary")]
[assembly: AssemblyCopyright("Copyright ©  2017")]
[assembly: AssemblyTrademark("")]
[assembly: AssemblyCulture("")]
```

Chapter 15 examines the role of attributes in depth, so don't sweat the details at this point. For now, just be aware that a majority of the attributes in `AssemblyInfo.cs` will be used to update the `.custom` token values within an assembly manifest.

Exploring the CIL

Recall that an assembly does not contain platform-specific instructions; rather, it contains platform-agnostic Common Intermediate Language (CIL) instructions. When the .NET runtime loads an assembly into memory, the underlying CIL is compiled (using the JIT compiler) into instructions that can be understood by the target platform. For example, back in `ildasm.exe`, if you double-click the `TurboBoost()` method of the `SportsCar` class, `ildasm.exe` will open a new window showing the CIL tokens that implement this method.

```
.method public hidebysig virtual instance void
  TurboBoost() cil managed
{
  // Code size       18 (0x12)
  .maxstack 8
  IL_0000: nop
  IL_0001: ldstr    "Ramming speed!"
```

```
IL_0006: ldstr  "Faster is better..."
IL_000b: call  valuetype [System.Windows.Forms]System.Windows.Forms.DialogResult
  [System.Windows.Forms]System.Windows.Forms.MessageBox::Show(string, string)
IL_0010: pop
IL_0011: ret
} // end of method SportsCar::TurboBoost
```

Again, while most .NET developers don't need to be deeply concerned with the details of CIL on a daily basis, Chapter 18 provides more details on its syntax and semantics. Believe it or not, understanding the grammar of CIL can be helpful when you are building more complex applications that require advanced services, such as runtime construction of assemblies (again, see Chapter 18).

Exploring the Type Metadata

Before you build some applications that use your custom .NET library, if you press the Ctrl+M keystroke combination in ildasm.exe, you can see the metadata for each type within the CarLibrary.dll assembly (see Figure 14-7).

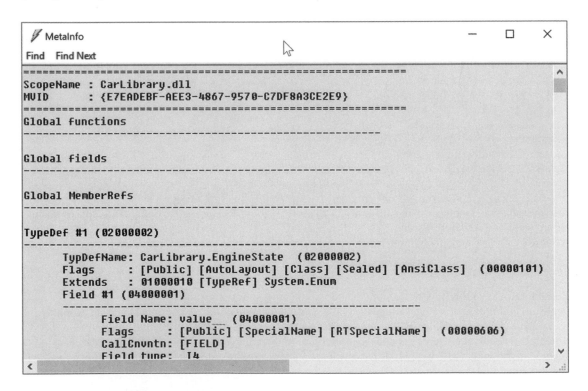

Figure 14-7. *Type metadata for the types within CarLibrary.dll*

As explained in the next chapter, an assembly's metadata is an important element of the .NET platform and serves as the backbone for numerous technologies (object serialization, late binding, extendable applications, etc.). In any case, now that you have looked inside the CarLibrary.dll assembly, you can build some client applications that use your types.

■ **Source Code**   You can find the CarLibrary project in the Chapter 14 subdirectory.

Building a C# Client Application

Because each of the CarLibrary types has been declared using the public keyword, other .NET applications are able to use them as well. Recall that you may also define types using the C# internal keyword (in fact, this is the default C# access mode). Internal types can be used only by the assembly in which they are defined. External clients can neither see nor create types marked with the internal keyword.

To use your library's functionality, create a new C# Console Application project named CSharpCarClient. After you have done so, set a reference to CarLibrary.dll using the Browse node of the Add Reference dialog box (if you compiled CarLibrary.dll using Visual Studio, your assembly is located in the \bin\Debug subdirectory of the CarLibrary project folder). At this point, you can build your client application to use the external types. Update your initial C# file as follows:

```
using System;
using System.Collections.Generic;
using System.Linq;
using System.Text;
using System.Threading.Tasks;

// Don't forget to import the CarLibrary namespace!
using CarLibrary;

namespace CSharpCarClient
{
  public class Program
  {
    static void Main(string[] args)
    {
      Console.WriteLine("***** C# CarLibrary Client App *****");
      // Make a sports car.
      SportsCar viper = new SportsCar("Viper", 240, 40);
      viper.TurboBoost();

      // Make a minivan.
      MiniVan mv = new MiniVan();
      mv.TurboBoost();

      Console.WriteLine("Done. Press any key to terminate");
      Console.ReadLine();
    }
  }
}
```

This code looks just like the code of the other applications developed thus far in the book. The only point of interest is that the C# client application is now using types defined within a separate custom library. Run your program and verify that you see the display of various message boxes.

You might be wondering exactly what happened when you referenced `CarLibrary.dll` using the Add Reference dialog box. If you click the Show All Files button of Solution Explorer, you will notice that Visual Studio added a copy of the original `CarLibrary.dll` into the `\bin\Debug` folder of the `CSharpCarClient` project folder (see Figure 14-8).

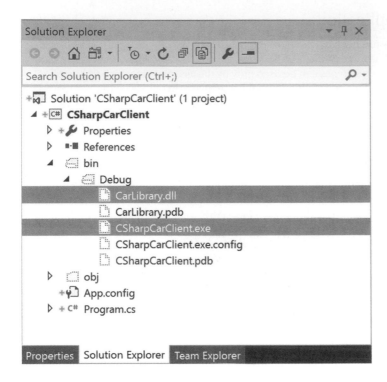

Figure 14-8. *Visual Studio copies private assemblies to the client's directory*

As explained shortly, `CarLibrary.dll` has been configured as a "private" assembly (which is the automatic behavior for all Visual Studio Class Library projects). When you reference private assemblies in new applications (such as `CSharpCarClient.exe`), the IDE responds by placing a copy of the library in the client application's output directory.

■ **Source Code**   You can find the CSharpCarClient project in the Chapter 14 subdirectory.

Building a Visual Basic Client Application

Recall that the .NET platform allows developers to share compiled code across programming languages. To illustrate the language-agnostic attitude of the .NET platform, let's create another Console Application project (VisualBasicCarClient), this time using Visual Basic (see Figure 14-9). Once you have created the project, set a reference to `CarLibrary.dll` using the Add Reference dialog box, which can be activated by the Project ➤ Add Reference menu option. Visual Studio remembers files that you have browsed for, and `CarLibary.dll` should be in your Recent list under the Browse tab.

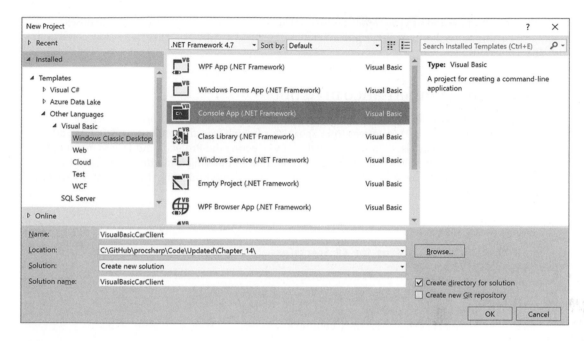

Figure 14-9. *Creating a Visual Basic Console Application project*

Like C#, Visual Basic allows you to list each namespace used within the current file. However, Visual Basic offers the Imports keyword rather than the C# using keyword, so add the following Imports statement within the Module1.vb code file:

```
Imports CarLibrary

Module Module1
  Sub Main()
  End Sub
End Module
```

Notice that the Main() method is defined within a Visual Basic module type. In a nutshell, modules are a Visual Basic notation for defining a class that can contain only static methods (much like a C# static class). In any case, to exercise the MiniVan and SportsCar types using the syntax of Visual Basic, update your Main() method as follows:

```
Sub Main()
  Console.WriteLine("***** VB CarLibrary Client App *****")
  ' Local variables are declared using the Dim keyword.
  Dim myMiniVan As New MiniVan()
  myMiniVan.TurboBoost()

  Dim mySportsCar As New SportsCar()
  mySportsCar.TurboBoost()
  Console.ReadLine()
End Sub
```

When you compile and run your application, you will once again find a series of message boxes displayed. Furthermore, this new client application has its own local copy of CarLibrary.dll located under the bin\Debug folder.

Cross-Language Inheritance in Action

An enticing aspect of .NET development is the notion of *cross-language inheritance*. To illustrate, let's create a new Visual Basic class that derives from SportsCar (which was authored using C#). First, add a new class file to your current Visual Basic application (by selecting the Project ➤ Add Class menu option) named PerformanceCar.vb. Update the initial class definition by deriving from the SportsCar type using the Inherits keyword. Then, override the abstract TurboBoost() method using the Overrides keyword, like so:

```
Imports CarLibrary

' This VB class is deriving from the C# SportsCar.
Public Class PerformanceCar
  Inherits SportsCar

  Public Overrides Sub TurboBoost()
    Console.WriteLine("Zero to 60 in a cool 4.8 seconds...")
  End Sub
End Class
```

To test this new class type, update the module's Main() method as follows:

```
Sub Main()
...
  Dim dreamCar As New PerformanceCar()

  ' Use Inherited property.
  dreamCar.PetName = "Hank"
  dreamCar.TurboBoost()
  Console.ReadLine()
End Sub
```

Notice that the dreamCar object is able to invoke any public member (such as the PetName property) found up the chain of inheritance, regardless of the fact that the base class was defined in a completely different language and in a completely different assembly! The ability to extend classes across assembly boundaries in a language-independent manner is a natural aspect of the .NET development cycle. This makes it easy to use compiled code written by individuals who would rather not build their shared code with C#.

■ **Source Code**   You can find the VisualBasicCarClient project in the Chapter 14 subdirectory.

Understanding Private Assemblies

Technically speaking, the class libraries you've created thus far in this chapter have been deployed as *private assemblies*. Private assemblies must be located within the same directory as the client application that's using them (the *application directory*) or a subdirectory thereof. Recall that when you add a reference to `CarLibrary.dll` while building the `CSharpCarClient.exe` and `VisualBasicCarClient.exe` applications, Visual Studio responded by placing a copy of `CarLibrary.dll` within the client's application directory (at least, after the first compilation).

When a client program uses the types defined within this external assembly, the CLR simply loads the local copy of `CarLibrary.dll`. Because the .NET runtime does not consult the system registry when searching for referenced assemblies, you can relocate the `CSharpCarClient.exe` (or `VisualBasicCarClient.exe`) and `CarLibrary.dll` assemblies to a new location on your machine and run the application (this is often termed *Xcopy deployment*).

Uninstalling (or replicating) an application that makes exclusive use of private assemblies is a no-brainer: simply delete (or copy) the application folder. More important, you do not need to worry that the removal of private assemblies will break any other applications on the machine.

The Identity of a Private Assembly

The full identity of a private assembly consists of the friendly name and numerical version, both of which are recorded in the assembly manifest. The *friendly name* is simply the name of the module that contains the assembly's manifest minus the file extension. For example, if you examine the manifest of the `CarLibrary.dll` assembly, you find the following:

```
.assembly CarLibrary
{
...
  .ver 1:0:0:0
}
```

Given the isolated nature of a private assembly, it should make sense that the CLR does not bother to use the version number when resolving its location. The assumption is that private assemblies do not need to have any elaborate version checking, as the client application is the only entity that "knows" of its existence. Because of this, it is possible for a single machine to have multiple copies of the same private assembly in various application directories.

Understanding the Probing Process

The .NET runtime resolves the location of a private assembly using a technique called *probing*, which is much less invasive than it sounds. Probing is the process of mapping an external assembly request to the location of the requested binary file. Strictly speaking, a request to load an assembly may be either *implicit* or *explicit*. An implicit load request occurs when the CLR consults the manifest to resolve the location of an assembly defined using the `.assembly extern` tokens. Here's an example:

```
// An implicit load request.
.assembly extern CarLibrary
{ ... }
```

An explicit load request occurs programmatically using the Load() or LoadFrom() method of the System.Reflection.Assembly class type, typically for the purposes of late binding and dynamic invocation of type members. You'll examine these topics further in Chapter 15, but for now you can see an example of an explicit load request in the following code:

```
// An explicit load request based on a friendly name.
Assembly asm = Assembly.Load("CarLibrary");
```

In either case, the CLR extracts the friendly name of the assembly and begins probing the client's application directory for a file named CarLibrary.dll. If this file cannot be located, an attempt is made to locate an executable assembly based on the same friendly name (for example, CarLibrary.exe). If neither file can be located in the application directory, the runtime gives up and throws a FileNotFoundException exception at runtime.

■ **Note**   Technically speaking, if a copy of the requested assembly cannot be found within the client's application directory, the CLR will also attempt to locate a client subdirectory with the same name as the assembly's friendly name (e.g., C:\MyClient\CarLibrary). If the requested assembly resides within this subdirectory, the CLR will load the assembly into memory.

Configuring Private Assemblies

While it is possible to deploy a .NET application by simply copying all required assemblies to a single folder on the user's hard drive, you will most likely want to define a number of subdirectories to group related content. For example, assume you have an application directory named C:\MyApp that contains CSharpCarClient.exe. Under this folder might be a subfolder named MyLibraries that contains CarLibrary.dll.

Regardless of the intended relationship between these two directories, the CLR will *not* probe the MyLibraries subdirectory unless you supply a configuration file. Configuration files contain various XML elements that allow you to influence the probing process. Configuration files must have the same name as the launching application and take a *.config file extension, and they must be deployed in the client's application directory. Thus, if you want to create a configuration file for CSharpCarClient.exe, it must be named CSharpCarClient.exe.config and be located (for this example) in the C:\MyApp directory.

To illustrate the process, create a new directory on your C: drive named MyApp using Windows Explorer. Next, copy CSharpCarClient.exe and CarLibrary.dll to this new folder, and run the program by double-clicking the executable. Your program should run successfully at this point.

Now, create a new subdirectory in C:\MyApp named MyLibraries (see Figure 14-10) and move CarLibrary.dll to this location.

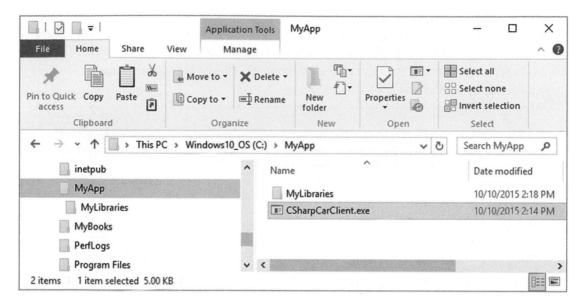

Figure 14-10. *CarLibrary.dll now resides under the MyLibraries subdirectory*

Try to run your client program again by double-clicking the executable. Because the CLR could not locate an assembly named CarLibrary directly within the application directory, you are presented with a rather nasty unhandled FileNotFoundException exception.

To instruct the CLR to probe under the MyLibraries subdirectory, create a new configuration file named CSharpCarClient.exe.config using any text editor, and save the file in the folder containing the CSharpCarClient.exe application, which in this example is C:\MyApp. Open this file and enter the following content exactly as shown (be aware that XML is case sensitive!):

```
<configuration>
  <runtime>
    <assemblyBinding xmlns="urn:schemas-microsoft-com:asm.v1">
      <probing privatePath="MyLibraries"/>
    </assemblyBinding>
  </runtime>
</configuration>
```

.NET *.config files always open with a root element named <configuration>. The nested <runtime> element may specify an <assemblyBinding> element, which nests a further element named <probing>. The privatePath attribute is the key point in this example, as it is used to specify the subdirectories relative to the application directory where the CLR should probe.

Once you've finished creating CSharpCarClient.exe.config, run the client by double-clicking the executable in Windows Explorer. You should find that CSharpCarClient.exe executes without a hitch (if this is not the case, double-check your *.config file for typos).

Do note that the <probing> element does not specify *which* assembly is located under a given subdirectory. In other words, you cannot say, "CarLibrary is located under the MyLibraries subdirectory, but MathLibrary is located under the OtherStuff subdirectory." The <probing> element simply instructs the CLR to investigate all specified subdirectories for the requested assembly until the first match is encountered.

■ **Note**   Be aware that the `privatePath` attribute cannot be used to specify an absolute (`C:\SomeFolder\`
`SomeSubFolder`) or relative (`..\SomeFolder\AnotherFolder`) path! If you need to specify a directory outside
the client's application directory, you will need to use a completely different XML element named `<codeBase>`
(more details on this element later in the chapter).

Multiple subdirectories can be assigned to the `privatePath` attribute using a semicolon-delimited
list. You have no need to do so at this time, but here is an example that informs the CLR to consult the
`MyLibraries` and `MyLibraries\Tests` client subdirectories:

```
<probing privatePath="MyLibraries;MyLibraries\Tests"/>
```

Next, for testing purposes, change the name of your configuration file (in one way or another) and
attempt to run the program once again. The client application should now fail. Remember that `*.config`
files must be prefixed with the same name as the related client application. By way of a final test, open your
configuration file for editing and capitalize any of the XML elements. Once the file is saved, your client
should fail to run once again (as XML is case sensitive).

■ **Note**   Understand that the CLR will load the first assembly it finds during the probing process. For example,
if the `C:\MyApp` folder did contain a copy of `CarLibrary.dll`, it will be loaded into memory, while the copy in
`MyLibraries` is effectively ignored.

The Role of the App.Config File

While you are always able to create XML configuration files by hand using your text editor of choice, Visual
Studio allows you to create a configuration file during the development of the client program. By default a
new Visual Studio project will contain a configuration file for editing. If you ever need to add one manually,
you may do so via the Project ➤ Add New Item menu option. Notice in Figure 14-11, you have left the name
of this file as the suggested `App.config`.

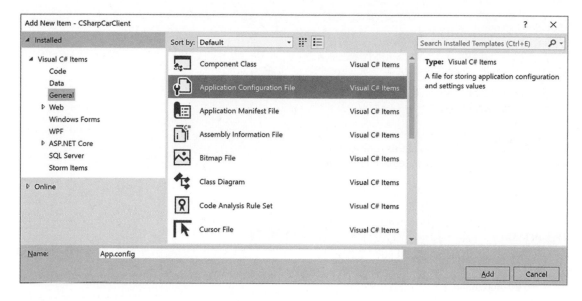

Figure 14-11. *Inserting a new XML configuration file*

If you open this file for viewing, you'll see a minimal set of instructions, to which you will add additional elements.

```
<?xml version="1.0" encoding="utf-8" ?>
<configuration>
  <startup>
    <supportedRuntime version="v4.0" sku=".NETFramework,Version=v4.7" />
  </startup>
</configuration>
```

Now, here is the cool thing. Each time you compile your project, Visual Studio will automatically copy the data in App.config to a new file in the \bin\Debug directory using the proper naming convention (such as CSharpCarClient.exe.config). However, this behavior will happen only if your configuration file is indeed named App.config; see Figure 14-12.

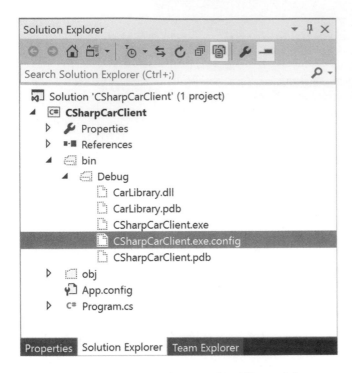

Figure 14-12. *The contents of App.config will be copied to a correctly named *.config in your output directory*

Using this approach, all you need to do is maintain `App.config`, and Visual Studio will ensure your application directory contains the latest and greatest configuration data (even if you happen to rename your project).

Understanding Shared Assemblies

Now that you understand how to deploy and configure a private assembly, you can begin to examine the role of a *shared assembly*. Like a private assembly, a shared assembly is a collection of types intended for reuse among projects. The most obvious difference between shared and private assemblies is that a single copy of a shared assembly can be used by several applications on the same machine.

Consider the fact that all the applications created in this text required access to `mscorlib.dll`. If you were to look in the application directory of each of these clients, you would *not* find a private copy of this .NET assembly. The reason is that `mscorlib.dll` has been deployed as a shared assembly. Clearly, if you need to create a machine-wide class library, this is the way to go.

■ **Note**   Deciding whether a code library should be deployed as a private or shared library is yet another design issue to contend with, and this will be based on many project-specific details. As a rule of thumb, when you are building libraries that need to be used by a wide variety of applications, shared assemblies can be quite helpful in that they can be updated to new versions easily (as you will see).

The Global Assembly Cache

As suggested in the previous paragraph, a shared assembly is not deployed within the same directory as the application that uses it. Rather, shared assemblies are installed into the GAC. However, the exact location of the GAC will depend on which versions of the .NET platform you installed on the target computer.

Machines that have not installed .NET 4.0 or higher will find the GAC is located in a subdirectory of your Windows directory named assembly (e.g., C:\Windows\assembly). These days, you might consider this the "historical GAC," as it can only contain .NET libraries compiled on versions 1.0, 2.0, 3.0, or 3.5. See Figure 14-13.

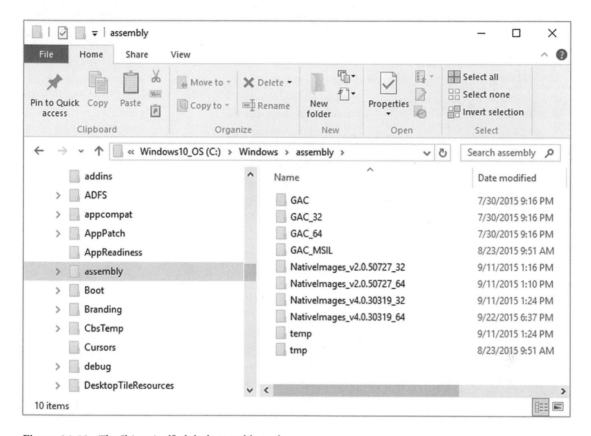

Figure 14-13. *The "historical" global assembly cache*

■ Note You cannot install executable assemblies (*.exe) into the GAC. Only assemblies that take the *.dll file extension can be deployed as a shared assembly.

With the release of .NET 4.0, Microsoft decided to isolate .NET 4.0 and higher libraries to a separate location, specifically, C:\Windows\Microsoft.NET\assembly\GAC_MSIL (Figure 14-14).

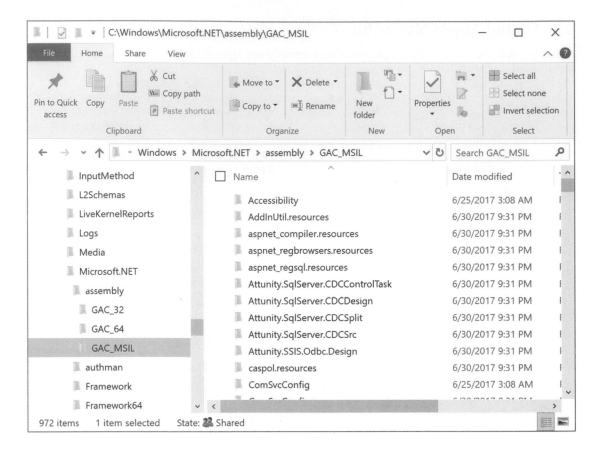

Figure 14-14. *The .NET 4.0 and higher global assembly cache*

Under this new folder, you will find a set of subdirectories, each of which is named identically to the friendly name of a particular code library (for example, \System.Windows.Forms, \System.Core, and so on). Beneath a given friendly name folder, you'll find yet another subdirectory that always takes the following naming convention:

```
v4.0_major.minor.build.revision_publicKeyTokenValue
```

The v4.0 prefix denotes that the library compiled under .NET version 4.0 or higher. That prefix is followed by a single underscore and then the version of the library in question (for example, 1.0.0.0). After a pair of underscores, you'll see another number termed the *public key token value*. As you will see in the next section, the public key value is part of the assembly's "strong name." Finally, under this folder, you will find a copy of the *.dll in question.

In this book, I am assuming you are building applications using .NET 4.7; therefore, if you install a library to the GAC, it will be installed under C:\Windows\Microsoft.NET\assembly\GAC_MSIL. However, be aware that if you were to configure a Class Library project to be compiled using version 3.5 or earlier, you would find shared libraries installed under C:\Windows\assembly.

Understanding Strong Names

Before you can deploy an assembly to the GAC, you must assign it a *strong name*, which is used to uniquely identify the publisher of a given .NET binary. Understand that a "publisher" can be an individual programmer (such as yourself), a department within a given company, or an entire company itself.

In some ways, a strong name is the modern-day .NET equivalent of the COM globally unique identifier (GUID) identification scheme. If you have a COM background, you might recall that AppIDs are GUIDs that identify a particular COM application. Unlike COM GUID values (which are nothing more than 128-bit numbers), strong names are based (in part) on two cryptographically related keys (*public keys* and *private keys*), which are much more unique and resistant to tampering than a simple GUID.

Formally, a strong name is composed of a set of related data, much of which is specified using the following assembly-level attributes:

- The friendly name of the assembly (which, you recall, is the name of the assembly minus the file extension)

- The version number of the assembly (assigned using the [AssemblyVersion] attribute)

- The public key value (assigned using the [AssemblyKeyFile] attribute)

- An optional culture identity value for localization purposes (assigned using the [AssemblyCulture] attribute)

- An embedded *digital signature*, created using a hash of the assembly's contents and the private key value

To provide a strong name for an assembly, your first step is to generate public/private key data using the .NET Framework sn.exe utility (which you'll do in a moment). The sn.exe utility generates a file (typically ending with the *.snk [Strong Name Key] file extension) that contains data for two distinct but mathematically related keys, the public key and the private key. Once the C# compiler is made aware of the location of your *.snk file, it will record the full public key value in the assembly manifest using the .publickey token at the time of compilation.

The C# compiler will also generate a hash code based on the contents of the entire assembly (CIL code, metadata, and so forth). As you recall from Chapter 6, a *hash code* is a numerical value that is statistically unique for a fixed input. Thus, if you modify any aspect of a .NET assembly (even a single character in a string literal), the compiler yields a different hash code. This hash code is combined with the private key data within the *.snk file to yield a digital signature embedded within the assembly's CLR header data. Figure 14-15 illustrates the process of strongly naming an assembly.

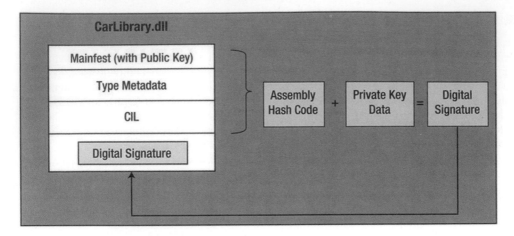

Figure 14-15. *At compile time, a digital signature is generated and embedded into the assembly based, in part, on public and private key data*

Understand that the actual `private` key data is not listed anywhere within the manifest but is used only to digitally sign the contents of the assembly (in conjunction with the generated hash code). Again, the whole idea of using public/private key data is to ensure that no two companies, departments, or individuals have the same identity in the .NET universe. In any case, once the process of assigning a strong name is complete, the assembly may be installed into the GAC.

■ **Note**   Strong names also provide a level of protection against potential evildoers tampering with your assembly's contents. Given this point, it is considered a .NET best practice to strongly name every assembly (including `*.exe` assemblies), regardless of whether it is deployed to the GAC.

Generating Strong Names at the Command Line

Let's walk through the process of assigning a strong name to the `CarLibrary` assembly created earlier in this chapter. These days, you will most likely generate the required `*.snk` file using Visual Studio. However, in the bad old days (circa 2003), the only option for strongly signing an assembly was to do so at the command line. Let's see how to do this.

The first order of business is to generate the required key data using the `sn.exe` utility. Although this tool has numerous command-line options, all you need to concern yourself with for the moment is the `-k` flag, which instructs the tool to generate a new file containing the public/private key information.

Create a new folder on your `C:` drive named `MyTestKeyPair` and change to that directory using the developer command prompt. Next, issue the following command to generate a file named `MyTestKeyPair.snk`:

```
sn -k MyTestKeyPair.snk
```

Now that you have your key data, you need to inform the C# compiler exactly where `MyTestKeyPair.snk` is located. Recall from earlier in this chapter, when you create any new C# project workspace using Visual Studio, one of the initial project files (located under the Properties node of Solution Explorer) is named `AssemblyInfo.cs`. This file contains a number of attributes that describe the assembly itself. The `[AssemblyKeyFile]` assembly-level attribute can be added to your `AssemblyInfo.cs` file to inform the compiler of the location of a valid *.snk file. Simply specify the path as a string parameter. Here's an example:

```
[assembly: AssemblyKeyFile(@"C:\MyTestKeyPair\MyTestKeyPair.snk")]
```

■ **Note** When you manually specify the [AssemblyKeyFile] attribute, Visual Studio will generate a warning informing you to use the /keyfile option of csc.exe or to establish the key file via the Visual Studio Properties window. You'll use the IDE to do so in just a moment (so feel free to ignore the generated warning).

Because the version of a shared assembly is one aspect of a strong name, selecting a version number for CarLibrary.dll is a necessary detail. In the AssemblyInfo.cs file, you will find another attribute named [AssemblyVersion]. Initially, the value is set to 1.0.0.0.

```
[assembly: AssemblyVersion("1.0.0.0")]
```

A .NET version number is composed of the four parts (*<major>.<minor>.<build>.<revision>*). While specifying a version number is entirely up to you, you can instruct Visual Studio to automatically increment the build and revision numbers as part of each compilation using the wildcard token, rather than with a specific build and revision value. You have no need to do so for this example; however, consider the following:

```
// Format: <Major number>.<Minor number>.<Build number>.<Revision number>
// Valid values for each part of the version number are between 0 and 65535.
[assembly: AssemblyVersion("1.0.*")]
```

At this point, the C# compiler has all the information needed to generate strong name data (as you are not specifying a unique culture value via the [AssemblyCulture] attribute, you "inherit" the culture of your current machine, which in my case would be U.S. English).

Compile your CarLibrary.dll code library, open your assembly into ildasm.exe, and check the manifest. You will now see that a new .publickey tag is used to document the full public key information, while the .ver token records the version specified via the [AssemblyVersion] attribute (see Figure 14-16).

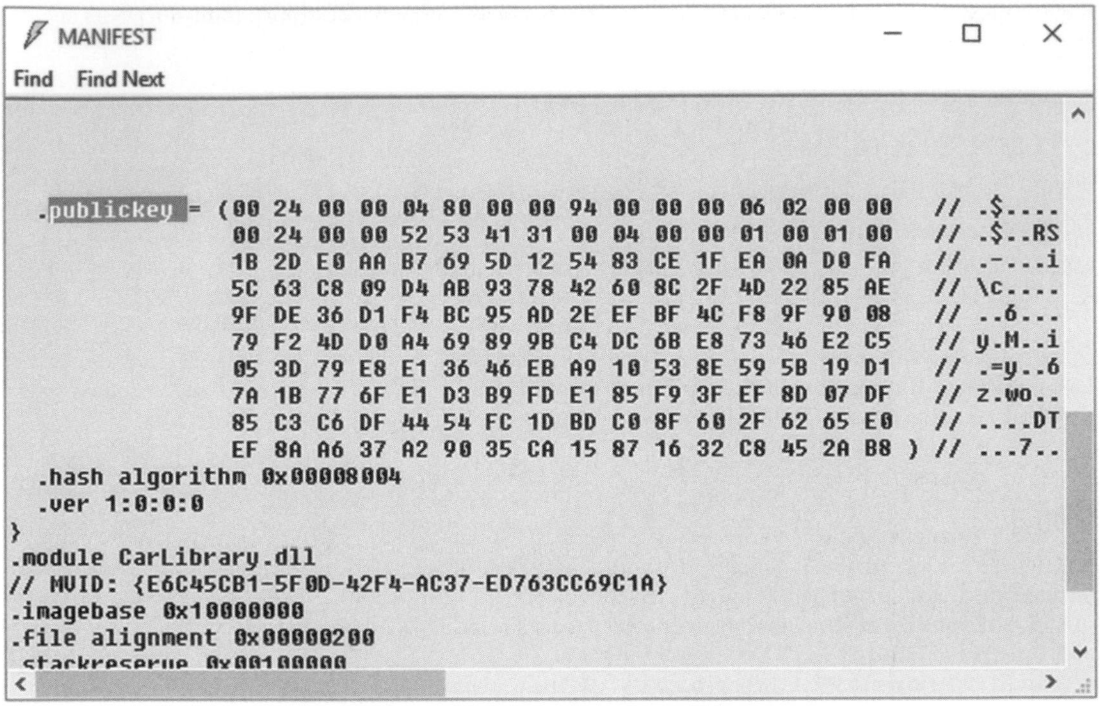

Figure 14-16. *A strongly named assembly records the public key in the manifest*

Great! At this point, you could deploy your shared CarLibrary.dll assembly to the GAC. However, remember that these days .NET developers can use Visual Studio to create strongly named assemblies using a friendly user interface rather than the cryptic sn.exe command-line tool. Before seeing how to do so, be sure you delete (or comment out) the following line of code from your AssemblyInfo.cs file (assuming you manually added this line during this section of the text):

```
// [assembly: AssemblyKeyFile(@"C:\MyTestKeyPair\MyTestKeyPair.snk")]
```

Generating Strong Names Using Visual Studio

Visual Studio allows you to specify the location of an existing *.snk file using the project's Properties window as well as generate a new *.snk file. To make a new *.snk file for the CarLibrary project, first double-click the Properties icon of the Solution Explorer and select the Signing tab. Next, select the "Sign the assembly" check box, and choose the <New...> option from the drop-down list (see Figure 14-17).

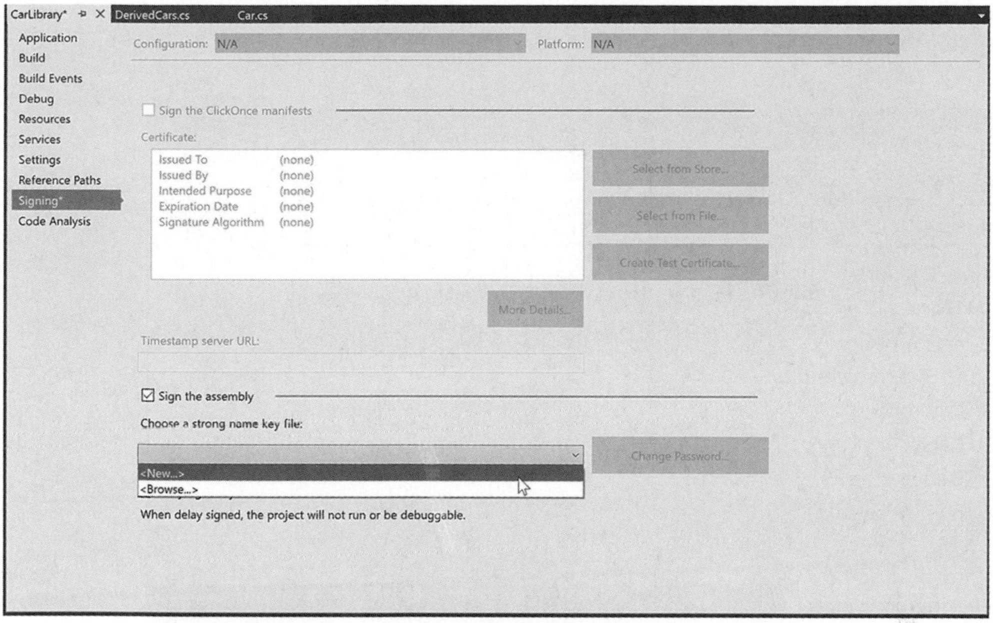

Figure 14-17. *Creating a new* `*.snk` *file using Visual Studio*

After you have done so, you will be asked to provide a name for your new `*.snk` file (such as `myKeyPair.snk`), and you'll have the option to password-protect your file (which is not required for this example); see Figure 14-18.

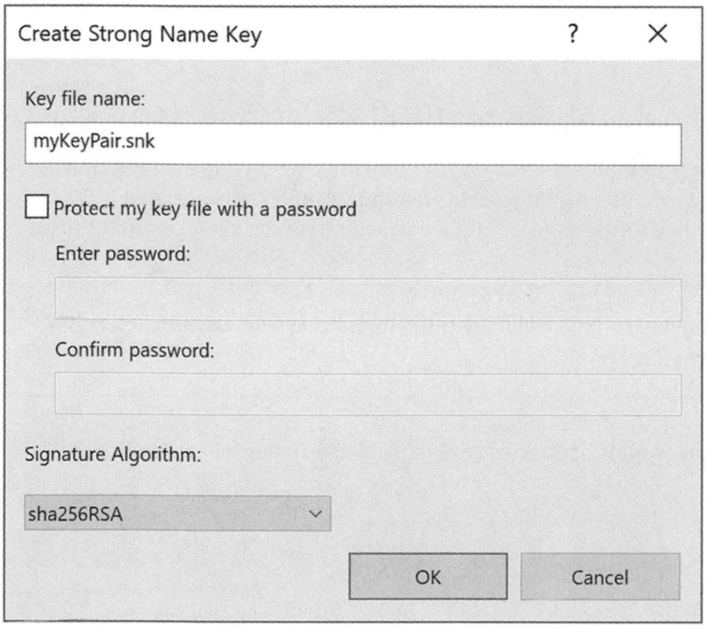

Figure 14-18. *Naming the new* `*.snk` *file using Visual Studio*

At this point, you will see your *.snk file within Solution Explorer (Figure 14-19). Every time you build your application, this data will be used to assign a proper strong name to the assembly.

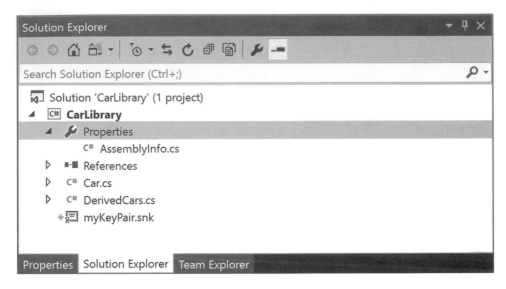

Figure 14-19. *Visual Studio will now strongly sign your assembly with each compilation*

■ **Note**   Recall that the Application tab of the Properties window provides a button named Assembly Information. When clicked, the button displays a dialog box that allows you to establish numerous assembly-level attributes, including the version number, copyright information, and so forth.

Installing Strongly Named Assemblies to the GAC

The final step is to install the (now strongly named) CarLibrary.dll into the GAC. While the preferred way to deploy assemblies to the GAC in a production setting is to create an installer package, the .NET Framework SDK ships with a command-line tool named gacutil.exe, which can be useful for quick tests.

■ **Note**   You must have administrator rights to interact with the GAC on your machine. Be sure to run your command window using the As Administrator option.

Table 14-1 documents some relevant options of gacutil.exe (specify the /? flag when you run the program to see each option).

Table 14-1. *Various Options of gacutil.exe*

Option	Meaning in Life
-i	Installs a strongly named assembly into the GAC
-u	Uninstalls an assembly from the GAC
-l	Displays the assemblies (or a specific assembly) in the GAC

To install a strongly named assembly using gacutil.exe, first open a command prompt and then change to the directory containing CarLibrary.dll. Here's an example (your path may differ):

```
cd C:\MyCode\CarLibrary\bin\Debug
```

Next, install the library using the -i command, like so:

```
gacutil /i CarLibrary.dll
```

After you have done so, you can verify that the library has been deployed by specifying the -l command as follows (note that you omit the file extension when using the -l command):

```
gacutil /l CarLibrary
```

If all is well, you should see the following output to the Console window (you will find a unique PublicKeyToken value, as expected):

```
The Global Assembly Cache contains the following assemblies:

CarLibrary, Version=1.0.0.0, Culture=neutral, PublicKeyToken=33a2bc294331e8b9,
processorArchitecture=MSIL

Number of items = 1
```

Furthermore, if you were to navigate to C:\Windows\Microsoft.NET\assembly\GAC_MSIL, you would find a new CarLibrary folder with the correct subdirectory structure (see Figure 14-20).

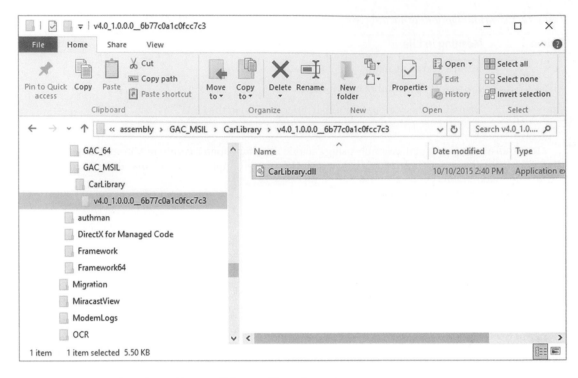

Figure 14-20. *The shared* `CarLibrary.dll` *assembly in the GAC*

Consuming a Shared Assembly

When you are building applications that use a shared assembly, the only difference from consuming a private assembly is in how you reference the library using Visual Studio. In reality, there is no difference as far as the tool is concerned—you still use the Add Reference dialog box.

When you need to reference a private assembly, you could use the Browse button to navigate to the correct subdirectory of the GAC. However, you can also simply navigate to the location of the strongly named assembly (such as the `/bin/debug` folder of a Class Library project) and reference the copy. Figure 14-21 shows the referenced library.

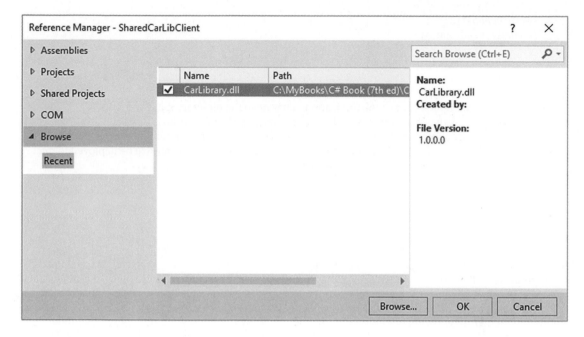

Figure 14-21. *Referencing the strongly named, shared CarLibrary (version 1.0.0.0) using Visual Studio*

Even though Visual Studio finds a strongly named library, by default it will still copy the library to the output folder of the client application. To change this behavior, right-click the icon for the referenced file in the Reference folder, select Properties, and change Copy Local to False.

To illustrate, create a new C# Console Application project named SharedCarLibClient and reference your CarLibrary.dll assembly as just described. As you would hope, you can now see an icon in your Solution Explorer's Reference folder. Select this icon and then view the Properties window (accessible from the Visual Studio View menu), and change the Copy Local property of the selected CarLibrary to False. Author the following test code in your new client application:

```
using System;
using System.Collections.Generic;
using System.Linq;
using System.Text;
using System.Threading.Tasks;

using CarLibrary;

namespace SharedCarLibClient
{
  class Program
  {
    static void Main(string[] args)
    {
      Console.WriteLine("***** Shared Assembly Client *****");
      SportsCar c = new SportsCar();
```

```
        c.TurboBoost();
        Console.ReadLine();
      }
    }
}
```

After you have compiled your client application, navigate to the directory that contains SharedCarLibClient.exe using Windows Explorer and notice that Visual Studio has *not* copied CarLibrary.dll to the client's application directory. When you reference an assembly whose manifest contains a .publickey value, Visual Studio assumes the strongly named assembly will be deployed to the GAC and, therefore, does not bother to copy the binary.

Exploring the Manifest of SharedCarLibClient

Recall that when you generate a strong name for an assembly, the entire public key is recorded in the assembly manifest. On a related note, when a client references a strongly named assembly, its manifest records a condensed hash value of the full public key, denoted by the .publickeytoken tag. If you open the manifest of SharedCarLibClient.exe using ildasm.exe, you would find the following (your public key token value will of course differ, as it is computed based on the public key value):

```
.assembly extern CarLibrary
{
  .publickeytoken = (33 A2 BC 29 43 31 E8 B9 )
  .ver 1:0:0:0
}
```

If you compare the value of the public key token recorded in the client manifest with the public key token value shown in the GAC, you will find a dead-on match. Recall that a public key represents one aspect of the strongly named assembly's identity. Given this, the CLR will load only version 1.0.0.0 of an assembly named CarLibrary that has a public key that can be hashed down to the value 33A2BC294331E8B9. If the CLR does not find an assembly meeting this description in the GAC (and did not find a private assembly named CarLibrary in the client's directory), a FileNotFoundException exception is thrown.

■ **Source Code**   You can find the SharedCarLibClient application in the Chapter 14 subdirectory.

Configuring Shared Assemblies

Like private assemblies, shared assemblies can be configured using a client *.config file. Of course, because shared assemblies are deployed to a well-known location (the GAC), you don't use the <privatePath> element as you did for private assemblies (although if the client is using both shared and private assemblies, the <privatePath> element may still exist in the *.config file).

You can use application configuration files in conjunction with shared assemblies whenever you want to instruct the CLR to bind to a *different* version of a specific assembly, effectively bypassing the value recorded in the client's manifest. This can be useful for a number of reasons. For example, imagine that you have shipped version 1.0.0.0 of an assembly and later discover a major bug. One corrective action would be to rebuild the client application to reference the correct version of the bug-free assembly (say, 1.1.0.0) and redistribute the updated client and new library to every target machine.

Another option is to ship the new code library and a *.config file that automatically instructs the runtime to bind to the new (bug-free) version. As long as the new version has been installed into the GAC, the original client runs without recompilation, redistribution, or fear of having to update your resume.

Here's another example: you have shipped the first version of a bug-free assembly (1.0.0.0), and after a month or two, you add new functionality to the assembly to yield version 2.0.0.0. Obviously, existing client applications that were compiled against version 1.0.0.0 have no clue about these new types, given that their code base makes no reference to them.

New client applications, however, want to make reference to the new functionality in version 2.0.0.0. Under .NET, you are free to ship version 2.0.0.0 to the target machines and have version 2.0.0.0 run alongside the older version 1.0.0.0. If necessary, existing clients can be dynamically redirected to load version 2.0.0.0 (to gain access to the implementation refinements), using an application configuration file without needing to recompile and redeploy the client application.

Freezing the Current Shared Assembly

To illustrate how to dynamically bind to a specific version of a shared assembly, open Windows Explorer and copy the current version of the compiled CarLibrary.dll assembly (1.0.0.0) into a distinct subdirectory (I called mine CarLibrary Version 1.0.0.0) to symbolize the freezing of this version (see Figure 14-22).

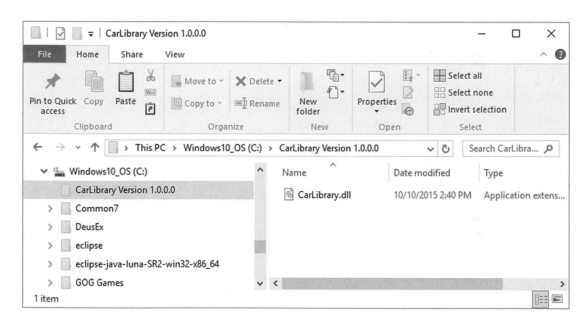

Figure 14-22. *Freezing the current version of CarLibrary.dll*

Building a Shared Assembly Version 2.0.0.0

Now, open your existing CarLibrary project and update your code base with a new enum type named MusicMedia that defines the following four possible musical devices:

```
// Which type of music player does this car have?
public enum MusicMedia
{
  musicCd,
  musicTape,
  musicRadio,
  musicMp3
}
```

As well, add a new public method to the Car type that allows the caller to turn on one of the given media players (be sure to import the System.Windows.Forms namespace if necessary), like so:

```
public abstract class Car
{
  public void TurnOnRadio(bool musicOn, MusicMedia mm)
    => MessageBox.Show(musicOn ? $"Jamming {mm}" : "Quiet time...");
}
```

Update the constructors of the Car class to display a MessageBox that verifies you are indeed using CarLibrary 2.0.0.0, as follows:

```
public abstract class Car
{
...
  public Car() => MessageBox.Show("CarLibrary Version 2.0!");
  public Car(string name, int maxSp, int currSp)
  {
    MessageBox.Show("CarLibrary Version 2.0!");
    PetName = name; MaxSpeed = maxSp; CurrentSpeed = currSp;
  }
...
}
```

Last but not least, before you recompile your new library, update the version to be 2.0.0.0. Recall you can do so in a visual manner by double-clicking the Properties icon of the Solution Explorer and clicking the Assembly Information button on the Application tab. After you do, simply update the Assembly Version number (see Figure 14-23).

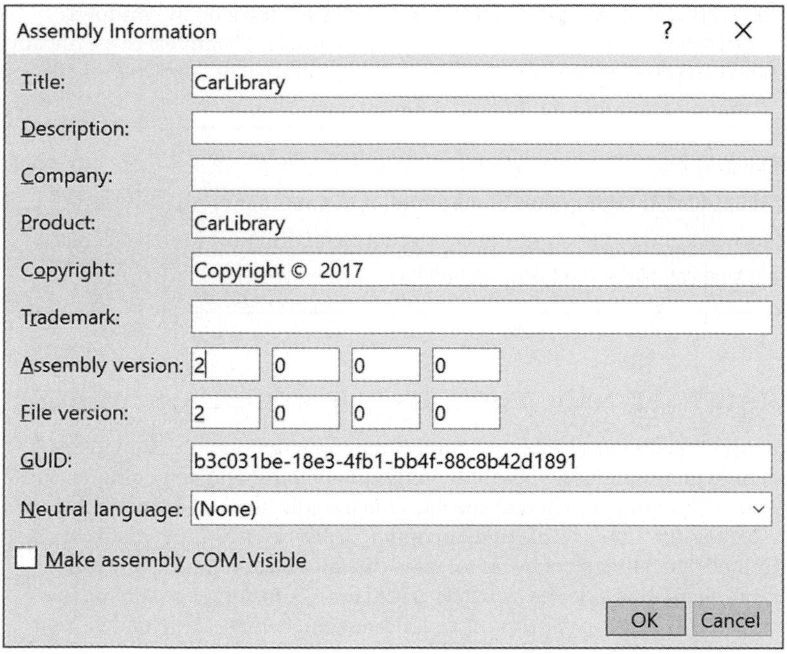

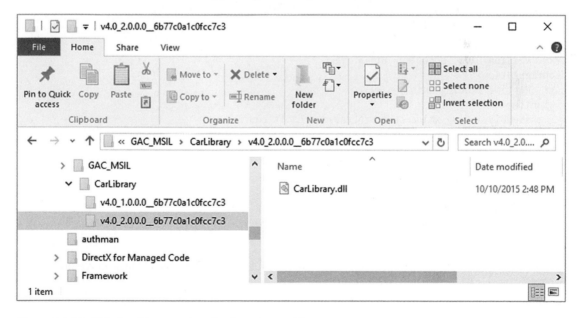

Figure 14-23. *Setting the version number of* `CarLibrary.dll` *to 2.0.0.0*

If you look in your project's \bin\Debug folder, you'll see that you have a new version of this assembly (2.0.0.0), while version 1.0.0.0 is safe in storage in the `CarLibrary Version 1.0.0.0` directory. Install this new assembly into the 4.0 GAC using `gacutil.exe`, as described earlier in this chapter. Notice that you now have two versions of the same assembly (see Figure 14-24).

Figure 14-24. *Side-by-side execution of a shared assembly*

If you run the current SharedCarLibClient.exe program by double-clicking the icon in Windows Explorer, you should *not* see the "CarLibrary Version 2.0!" message box appear, as the manifest is specifically requesting version 1.0.0.0. How then can you instruct the CLR to bind to version 2.0.0.0? Glad you asked!

■ **Note**   Visual Studio will automatically reset references when you compile your applications! Therefore, if you run your SharedCarLibClient.exe application within Visual Studio, it will grab CarLibrary.dll version 2.0.0.0! If you accidentally ran your application in this way, simply delete the current CarLibrary.dll reference and select version 1.0.0.0 (which I suggested you place in a folder named CarLibrary Version 1.0.0.0).

Dynamically Redirecting to Specific Versions of a Shared Assembly

When you want to tell the CLR to load a version of a shared assembly other than the version listed in the manifest, you can build a *.config file that contains a <dependentAssembly> element. When doing so, you will need to create an <assemblyIdentity> subelement that specifies the friendly name of the assembly listed in the client manifest (CarLibrary, for this example) and an optional culture attribute (which can be assigned an empty string or omitted altogether if you want to use the default culture for the machine). Moreover, the <dependentAssembly> element will define a <bindingRedirect> subelement to define the version *currently* in the manifest (via the oldVersion attribute) and the version in the GAC to load instead (via the newVersion attribute).

Update the current configuration file in the application directory of SharedCarLibClient named SharedCarLibClient.exe.config that contains the following XML data.

■ **Note**   The value of your public key token will be different from what you see in the following markup. To find your public key token value, recall you can open the client into ildasm.exe, double-click the MANIFEST icon, and copy the value to your clipboard (just be sure to remove the blank spaces!).

```
<?xml version="1.0" encoding="utf-8" ?>
<configuration>
  <!--Runtime binding info -->
  <runtime>
    <assemblyBinding xmlns="urn:schemas-microsoft-com:asm.v1">
      <dependentAssembly>
        <assemblyIdentity name="CarLibrary" publicKeyToken="64ee9364749d8328"
culture="neutral"/>
        <bindingRedirect oldVersion= "1.0.0.0" newVersion= "2.0.0.0"/>
      </dependentAssembly>
    </assemblyBinding>
  </runtime>
</configuration>
```

Now run the SharedCarLibClient.exe program by double-clicking the executable from Windows Explorer. You should see the message that version 2.0.0.0 has loaded.

Multiple <dependentAssembly> elements can appear within a client's configuration file. Although there's no need for this example, assume that the manifest of SharedCarLibClient.exe also references version 2.5.0.0 of an assembly named MathLibrary. If you wanted to redirect to version 3.0.0.0 of MathLibrary (in addition to version 2.0.0.0 of CarLibrary), the SharedCarLibClient.exe.config file would look like the following:

```
<configuration>
  <runtime>
    <assemblyBinding xmlns="urn:schemas-microsoft-com:asm.v1">
      <!-- Controls Binding to CarLibrary -->
      <dependentAssembly>
        <assemblyIdentity name="CarLibrary" publicKeyToken="64ee9364749d8328" culture=""/>
        <bindingRedirect oldVersion= "1.0.0.0" newVersion= "2.0.0.0"/>
      </dependentAssembly>

      <!-- Controls Binding to MathLibrary -->
      <dependentAssembly>
        <assemblyIdentity name="MathLibrary" publicKeyToken="64ee9364749d8328" culture=""/>
        <bindingRedirect oldVersion= "2.5.0.0" newVersion= "3.0.0.0"/>
      </dependentAssembly>
    </assemblyBinding>
  </runtime>
</configuration>
```

■ **Note** It is possible to specify a range of old version numbers via the oldVersion attribute; for example, <bindingRedirect oldVersion="1.0.0.0-1.2.0.0" newVersion="2.0.0.0"/> informs the CLR to use version 2.0.0.0 for any older version within the range of 1.0.0.0 to 1.2.0.0.

Understanding Publisher Policy Assemblies

The next configuration issue you'll examine is the role of *publisher policy assemblies*. As you've just seen, *.config files can be constructed to bind to a specific version of a shared assembly, thereby bypassing the version recorded in the client manifest. While this is all well and good, imagine you're an administrator who now needs to reconfigure *all* client applications on a given machine to rebind to version 2.0.0.0 of the CarLibrary.dll assembly. Given the strict naming convention of a configuration file, you would need to duplicate the same XML content in numerous locations (assuming you are, in fact, aware of the locations of the executables using CarLibrary!). Clearly this would be a maintenance nightmare.

Publisher policy allows the publisher of a given assembly (you, your department, your company, or what have you) to ship a binary version of a *.config file that is installed into the GAC along with the newest version of the associated assembly. The benefit of this approach is that client application directories do *not* need to contain specific *.config files. Rather, the CLR will read the current manifest and attempt to find the requested version in the GAC. However, if the CLR finds a publisher policy assembly, it will read the embedded XML data and perform the requested redirection *at the level of the GAC*.

Publisher policy assemblies are created at the command line using a .NET utility named al.exe (the assembly linker). Though this tool provides many options, building a publisher policy assembly requires passing in only the following input parameters:

- The location of the *.config or *.xml file containing the redirecting instructions

- The name of the resulting publisher policy assembly

- The location of the *.snk file used to sign the publisher policy assembly

- The version numbers to assign the publisher policy assembly being constructed

If you wanted to build a publisher policy assembly that controls CarLibrary.dll, the command set would be as follows (which must be entered on a single line within the command window):

```
al /link:CarLibraryPolicy.xml /out:policy.1.0.CarLibrary.dll /keyf:C:\MyKey\myKey.snk
/v:1.0.0.0
```

Here, the XML content is contained within a file named CarLibraryPolicy.xml. The name of the output file (which must be in the format policy.<major>.<minor>.assemblyToConfigure) is specified using the obvious /out flag. In addition, note that the name of the file containing the public/private key pair will also need to be supplied via the /keyf option. Remember, publisher policy files are shared and, therefore, must have strong names!

Once the al.exe tool has executed, the result is a new assembly that can be placed into the GAC to force all clients to bind to version 2.0.0.0 of CarLibrary.dll, without the use of a specific client application configuration file. Using this technique, you can design a machine-wide redirection for all applications using a specific version (or range of versions) of an existing assembly.

Disabling Publisher Policy

Now, assume you (as a system administrator) have deployed a publisher policy assembly (and the latest version of the related assembly) to the GAC of a client machine. As luck would have it, nine of the ten affected applications rebind to version 2.0.0.0 without error. However, the remaining client application (for whatever reason) blows up when accessing CarLibrary.dll 2.0.0.0. (As we all know, it is next to impossible to build backward-compatible software that works 100 percent of the time.)

In such a case, it is possible to build a configuration file for a specific troubled client that instructs the CLR to *ignore* the presence of any publisher policy files installed in the GAC. The remaining client applications that are happy to consume the newest .NET assembly will simply be redirected via the installed publisher policy assembly. To disable publisher policy on a client-by-client basis, author a (properly named) *.config file that uses the <publisherPolicy> element and set the apply attribute to no. When you do so, the CLR will load the version of the assembly originally listed in the client's manifest.

```
<configuration>
  <runtime>
    <assemblyBinding xmlns="urn:schemas-microsoft-com:asm.v1">
      <publisherPolicy apply="no" />
    </assemblyBinding>
  </runtime>
</configuration>
```

Understanding the <codeBase> Element

Application configuration files can also specify *codebases*. The <codeBase> element can be used to instruct the CLR to probe for dependent assemblies located at arbitrary locations (such as network endpoints or an arbitrary machine path outside a client's application directory).

If the value assigned to a <codeBase> element is located on a remote machine, the assembly will be downloaded on demand to a specific directory in the GAC termed the *download cache*. Given what you have learned about deploying assemblies to the GAC, it should make sense that assemblies loaded from a <codeBase> element will need to be assigned a strong name (after all, how else could the CLR install remote assemblies to the GAC?). If you are interested, you can view the content of your machine's download cache by supplying the /ldl option to gacutil.exe, like so:

```
gacutil /ldl
```

■ **Note**   Technically speaking, the <codeBase> element can be used to probe for assemblies that do not have strong names. However, the assembly's location must be relative to the client's application directory (and, thus, is little more than an alternative to the <privatePath> element).

To see the <codeBase> element in action, create a Console Application project named CodeBaseClient, set a reference to CarLibrary.dll version 2.0.0.0, and update the initial file as follows:

```csharp
using System;
using System.Collections.Generic;
using System.Linq;
using System.Text;
using System.Threading.Tasks;

using CarLibrary;

namespace CodeBaseClient
{
  class Program
  {
    static void Main(string[] args)
    {
      Console.WriteLine("***** Fun with CodeBases *****");
      SportsCar c = new SportsCar();
      Console.WriteLine("Sports car has been allocated.");
      Console.ReadLine();
    }
  }
}
```

Given that CarLibrary.dll has been deployed to the GAC, you are able to run the program as is. However, to illustrate the use of the <codeBase> element, create a new folder under your C: drive (perhaps C:\MyAsms) and place a copy of CarLibrary.dll version 2.0.0.0 into this directory.

Now, add an App.config file (or edit an existing App.config) to the CodeBaseClient project (as explained earlier in this chapter) and author the following XML content (remember that your .publickeytoken value will differ; consult your GAC as required):

```
<configuration>
...
  <runtime>
    <assemblyBinding xmlns="urn:schemas-microsoft-com:asm.v1">
      <dependentAssembly>
        <assemblyIdentity name="CarLibrary" publicKeyToken="33A2BC294331E8B9"
        culture="neutral"/>
        <codeBase version="2.0.0.0" href="file:///C:/MyAsms/CarLibrary.dll" />
      </dependentAssembly>
    </assemblyBinding>
  </runtime>
</configuration>
```

As you can see, the <codeBase> element is nested within the <assemblyIdentity> element, which makes use of the name and publicKeyToken attributes to specify the friendly name and associated publicKeyToken values. The <codeBase> element itself specifies the version and location (via the href property) of the assembly to load. If you were to delete version 2.0.0.0 of CarLibrary.dll from the GAC, this client would still run successfully, as the CLR is able to locate the external assembly under C:\MyAsms.

■ **Note** If you place assemblies at random locations on your development machine, you are in effect re-creating the system registry (and the related DLL hell), given that if you move or rename the folder containing your binaries, the current bind will fail. With that in mind, use <codeBase> with caution.

The <codeBase> element can also be helpful when referencing assemblies located on a remote networked machine. Assume you have permission to access a folder located at http://www.MySite.com. To download the remote *.dll to the GAC's download cache on your local machine, you could update the <codeBase> element as follows:

```
<codeBase version="2.0.0.0"
  href="http://www.MySite.com/Assemblies/CarLibrary.dll" />
```

■ **Source Code** You can find the CodeBaseClient application in the Chapter 14 subdirectory.

The System.Configuration Namespace

Currently, all of the *.config files shown in this chapter have made use of well-known XML elements that are read by the CLR to resolve the location of external assemblies. In addition to these recognized elements, it is perfectly permissible for a client configuration file to contain application-specific data that has nothing to do with binding heuristics. Given this, it should come as no surprise that the .NET Framework provides a namespace that allows you to programmatically read the data within a client configuration file.

The System.Configuration namespace provides a small set of types you can use to read custom data from a client's *.config file. These custom settings must be contained within the scope of an <appSettings>

element. The <appSettings> element contains any number of <add> elements that define key-value pairs to be obtained programmatically.

For example, assume you have an App.config file for a Console Application project named AppConfigReaderApp that defines two application-specific values, listed like so:

```xml
<?xml version="1.0" encoding="utf-8" ?>
<configuration>
  <startup>
    <supportedRuntime version="v4.0" sku=".NETFramework,Version=v4.7" />
  </startup>
  <!-- Custom App settings -->
  <appSettings>
    <add key="TextColor" value="Green" />
    <add key="RepeatCount" value="8" />
  </appSettings>
</configuration>
```

Reading these values for use by the client application is as simple as calling the instance-level GetValue() method of the System.Configuration.AppSettingsReader type. As shown in the following code, the first parameter to GetValue() is the name of the key in the *.config file, whereas the second parameter is the underlying type of the key (obtained via the C# typeof operator):

```csharp
using System;
using System.Collections.Generic;
using System.Linq;
using System.Text;
using System.Threading.Tasks;

using System.Configuration;

namespace AppConfigReaderApp
{
  class Program
  {
    static void Main(string[] args)
    {
      Console.WriteLine("***** Reading <appSettings> Data *****\n");

      // Get our custom data from the *.config file.
      AppSettingsReader ar = new AppSettingsReader();
      int numbOfTimes = (int)ar.GetValue("RepeatCount", typeof(int));
      string textColor = (string)ar.GetValue("TextColor", typeof(string));

      Console.ForegroundColor =  (ConsoleColor)Enum.Parse(typeof(ConsoleColor), textColor);

      // Now print a message correctly.
      for (int i = 0; i < numbOfTimes; i++)
        Console.WriteLine("Howdy!");
      Console.ReadLine();
    }
  }
}
```

■ **Source Code**   You can find the AppConfigReaderApp application in the `Chapter 14` subdirectory.

The Configuration File Schema Documentation

In this chapter, you were introduced to the role of XML configuration files. Here, you focused on a few settings you can add to the `<runtime>` element that control how the CLR will attempt to locate externally required libraries. As you work on upcoming chapters of this book (and as you move beyond this book and begin to build larger-scale software), you will quickly notice that use of XML configuration files is commonplace.

To be sure, the .NET platform uses `*.config` files in numerous APIs. For example, in Chapter 23, you will see that Windows Communication Foundation (WCF) uses configuration files to establish complex network settings. Later in this text when you examine web development via ASP.NET, you'll quickly note that the `web.config` file contains the same type of instructions as a desktop `App.config` file.

Because a given .NET configuration file can contain a large number of instructions, you should be aware that the entire schema of this XML file is documented online. Either search for *Configuration File Schema for the .NET Framework* or navigate to `https://docs.microsoft.com/en-us/dotnet/framework/configure-apps/file-schema/`.

Summary

This chapter examined the role of .NET class libraries (aka .NET `*.dlls`). As you have seen, class libraries are .NET binaries that contain logic intended to be reused across a variety of projects. Recall that libraries can be deployed in two primary ways, specifically privately or shared. Private assemblies are deployed to the client folder or a subdirectory thereof, provided you have a proper XML configuration file. Shared assemblies are libraries that can be used by any application on the machine and can also be influenced by the settings in a client-side configuration file.

You learned how shared assemblies are marked with a "strong name," which essentially establishes a unique identify for a library in the eyes of the CLR. As well, you learned about various command-line tools (`sn.exe` and `gacutil.exe`) that are used during the development and deployment of shared libraries.

The chapter wrapped up by examining the role of publisher policies and the process of storing and retrieving custom settings using the `System.Configuration` namespace.

CHAPTER 15

■ ■ ■

Type Reflection, Late Binding, and Attribute-Based Programming

As shown in Chapter 14, assemblies are the basic unit of deployment in the .NET universe. Using the integrated Object Browser of Visual Studio (and numerous other IDEs), you are able to examine the types within a project's referenced set of assemblies. Furthermore, external tools such as ildasm.exe allow you to peek into the underlying CIL code, type metadata, and assembly manifest for a given .NET binary. In addition to this design-time investigation of .NET assemblies, you are also able to *programmatically* obtain this same information using the System.Reflection namespace. To this end, the first task of this chapter is to define the role of reflection and the necessity of .NET metadata.

The remainder of the chapter examines a number of closely related topics, all of which hinge upon reflection services. For example, you'll learn how a .NET client may employ dynamic loading and late binding to activate types it has no compile-time knowledge of. You'll also learn how to insert custom metadata into your .NET assemblies through the use of system-supplied and custom attributes. To put all of these (seemingly esoteric) topics into perspective, the chapter closes by demonstrating how to build several "snap-in objects" that you can plug into an extendable desktop GUI application.

The Necessity of Type Metadata

The ability to fully describe types (classes, interfaces, structures, enumerations, and delegates) using metadata is a key element of the .NET platform. Numerous .NET technologies, such as Windows Communication Foundation (WCF), and object serialization require the ability to discover the format of types at runtime. Furthermore, cross-language interoperability, numerous compiler services, and an IDE's IntelliSense capabilities all rely on a concrete description of *type*.

Recall that the ildasm.exe utility allows you to view an assembly's type metadata using the Ctrl+M keyboard option (see Chapter 1). Thus, if you were to open any of the *.dll or *.exe assemblies created over the course of this book (such as the CarLibrary.dll created in the Chapter 14) using ildasm.exe and press Ctrl+M, you would find the relevant type metadata (see Figure 15-1).

© Andrew Troelsen and Philip Japikse 2017
A. Troelsen and P. Japikse, *Pro C# 7*, https://doi.org/10.1007/978-1-4842-3018-3_15

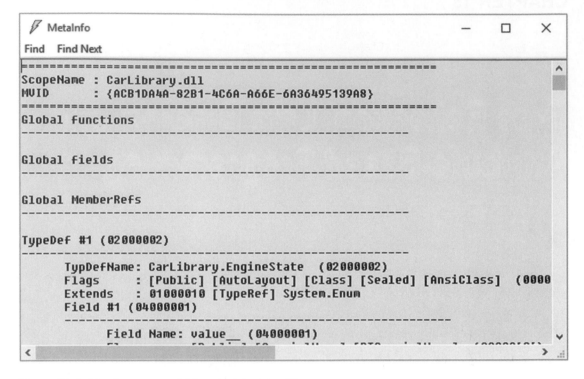

Figure 15-1. *Viewing an assembly's metadata using ildasm.exe*

As you can see, `ildasm.exe`'s display of .NET type metadata is verbose (the actual binary format is much more compact). In fact, if I were to list the entire metadata description representing the `CarLibrary.dll` assembly, it would span several pages. Given that this act would be a woeful waste of paper, let's just glimpse into some key metadata descriptions of the `CarLibrary.dll` assembly.

■ **Note**   Don't be too concerned with the exact syntax of every piece of .NET metadata in the next few sections. The bigger point to absorb is that .NET metadata is very descriptive and lists each internally defined (and externally referenced) type found within a given code base.

Viewing (Partial) Metadata for the EngineState Enumeration

Each type defined within the current assembly is documented using a `TypeDef` #n token (where `TypeDef` is short for *type definition*). If the type being described uses a type defined within a separate .NET assembly, the referenced type is documented using a `TypeRef` #n token (where `TypeRef` is short for *type reference*). A `TypeRef` token is a pointer (if you will) to the referenced type's full metadata definition in an external assembly. In a nutshell, .NET metadata is a set of tables that clearly mark all type definitions (`TypeDefs`) and referenced types (`TypeRefs`), all of which can be viewed using `ildasm.exe`'s metadata window.

As far as `CarLibrary.dll` goes, one `TypeDef` is the metadata description of the `CarLibrary.EngineState` enumeration (your number may differ; `TypeDef` numbering is based on the order in which the C# compiler processes the file).

```
TypeDef #2 (02000003)
--------------------------------------------------------
  TypDefName: CarLibrary.EngineState (02000003)
  Flags     : [Public] [AutoLayout] [Class] [Sealed] [AnsiClass] (00000101)
  Extends   : 01000001 [TypeRef] System.Enum
  Field #1 (04000006)
--------------------------------------------------------
    Field Name: value__  (04000006)
    Flags     : [Public] [SpecialName] [RTSpecialName] (00000606)
    CallCnvntn: [FIELD]
    Field type: I4

  Field #2 (04000007)
--------------------------------------------------------
  Field Name: engincAlive (04000007)
  Flags     : [Public] [Static] [Literal] [HasDefault] (00008056)
  DefltValue: (I4) 0
  CallCnvntn: [FIELD]
  Field type: ValueClass CarLibrary.EngineState
...
```

Here, the TypDefName token is used to establish the name of the given type, which in this case is the custom CarLibrary.EngineState enum. The Extends metadata token is used to document the base type of a given .NET type (in this case, the referenced type, System.Enum). Each field of an enumeration is marked using the Field #n token. For brevity, I have simply listed the metadata for CarLibrary.EngineState.engineAlive.

Viewing (Partial) Metadata for the Car Type

Here is a partial dump of the Car class that illustrates the following:

- How fields are defined in terms of .NET metadata
- How methods are documented via .NET metadata
- How an automatic property is represented in .NET metadata

```
TypeDef #3 (02000004)
--------------------------------------------------------
  TypDefName: CarLibrary.Car (02000004)
  Flags : [Public] [AutoLayout] [Class] [Abstract]
          [AnsiClass] [BeforeFieldInit] (00100081)
  Extends : 01000002 [TypeRef] System.Object
...

  Field #2 (0400000a)
--------------------------------------------------------
  Field Name: <PetName>k__BackingField (0400000A)
  Flags     : [Private] (00000001)
  CallCnvntn: [FIELD]
  Field type: String

...
```

```
Method #1 (06000001)
-------------------------------------------------------
    MethodName: get_PetName (06000001)
    Flags      : [Public] [HideBySig] [ReuseSlot] [SpecialName] (00000886)
    RVA        : 0x000020d0
    ImplFlags  : [IL] [Managed] (00000000)
    CallCnvntn: [DEFAULT]
    hasThis
    ReturnType: String
    No arguments.

...


Method #2 (06000002)
-------------------------------------------------------
  MethodName: set_PetName (06000002)
  Flags      : [Public] [HideBySig] [ReuseSlot] [SpecialName] (00000886)
  RVA        : 0x000020e7
  ImplFlags : [IL] [Managed] (00000000)
  CallCnvntn: [DEFAULT]
  hasThis
  ReturnType: Void
  1 Arguments
    Argument #1: String
  1 Parameters
    (1) ParamToken : (08000001) Name : value flags: [none] (00000000)
...


Property #1 (17000001)
-------------------------------------------------------
    Prop.Name : PetName (17000001)
    Flags      : [none] (00000000)
    CallCnvntn: [PROPERTY]
    hasThis
    ReturnType: String
    No arguments.
    DefltValue:
    Setter : (06000002) set_PetName
    Getter : (06000001) get_PetName
    0 Others
...
```

First, note that the Car class metadata marks the type's base class (System.Object) and includes various flags that describe how this type was constructed (e.g., [Public], [Abstract], and whatnot). Methods (such as the Car's constructor) are described in regard to their parameters, return value, and name.

Note how an automatic property results in a compiler-generated private backing field (which was named <PetName>k BackingField) and two compiler-generated methods (in the case of a read-write property) named, in this example, get_PetName() and set_PetName(). Finally, the actual property is mapped to the internal get/set methods using the .NET metadata Getter/Setter tokens.

Examining a TypeRef

Recall that an assembly's metadata will describe not only the set of internal types (Car, EngineState, etc.) but also any external types the internal types reference. For example, given that CarLibrary.dll has defined two enumerations, you find a TypeRef block for the System.Enum type, as follows:

```
TypeRef #1 (01000001)
-------------------------------------------------------
Token:              0x01000001
ResolutionScope:    0x23000001
TypeRefName:        System.Enum
```

Documenting the Defining Assembly

The ildasm.exe metadata window also allows you to view the .NET metadata that describes the assembly itself using the Assembly token. As you can see from the following (partial) listing, information documented within the Assembly table is (surprise, surprise!) the same information that can be viewable via the MANIFEST icon. The following is a partial dump of the manifest of CarLibrary.dll (version 2.0.0.0):

```
Assembly
-------------------------------------------------------
  Token: 0x20000001
  Name : CarLibrary
  Public Key    : 00 24 00 00 04 80 00 00 // Etc...

  Hash Algorithm : 0x00008004
  Major Version: 0x00000002
  Minor Version: 0x00000000
  Build Number: 0x00000000
  Revision Number: 0x00000000
  Locale: <null>
  Flags : [PublicKey] ...
```

Documenting Referenced Assemblies

In addition to the Assembly token and the set of TypeDef and TypeRef blocks, .NET metadata also makes use of AssemblyRef #n tokens to document each external assembly. Given that the CarLibrary.dll assembly makes use of the System.Windows.Forms.MessageBox class, you find an AssemblyRef for the System.Windows.Forms assembly, as shown in the following code:

```
AssemblyRef #2 (23000002)
-------------------------------------------------------
  Token: 0x23000002
  Public Key or Token: b7 7a 5c 56 19 34 e0 89
  Name: System.Windows.Forms
  Version: 4.0.0.0
  Major Version: 0x00000004
  Minor Version: 0x00000000
```

```
Build Number: 0x00000000
Revision Number: 0x00000000
Locale: <null>
HashValue Blob:
Flags: [none] (00000000)
```

Documenting String Literals

The final point of interest regarding .NET metadata is the fact that every string literal in your codebase is documented under the User Strings token.

```
User Strings
-------------------------------------------------------
70000001 : (11) L"Jamming {0}"
70000019 : (13) L"Quiet time..."
70000035 : (23) L"CarLibrary Version 2.0!"
70000065 : (14) L"Ramming speed!"
70000083 : (19) L"Faster is better..."
700000ab : ( 4) L"Eek!"
700000cd : (27) L"Your engine block exploded!"
```

■ **Note**   As illustrated in this last metadata listing, always be aware that all strings are clearly documented in the assembly metadata. This could have huge security consequences if you were to use string literals to capture passwords, credit card numbers, or other sensitive information.

The next question on your mind may be (in the best-case scenario) "How can I leverage this information in my applications?" or (in the worst-case scenario) "Why should I care about metadata?" To address both points of view, allow me to introduce .NET reflection services. Be aware that the usefulness of the topics presented over the pages that follow may be a bit of a head-scratcher until this chapter's endgame. So hang tight.

■ **Note**   You will also find a number of CustomAttribute tokens displayed by the MetaInfo window, which documents the attributes applied within the codebase. You'll learn about the role of .NET attributes later in this chapter.

Understanding Reflection

In the .NET universe, *reflection* is the process of runtime type discovery. Using reflection services, you are able to programmatically obtain the same metadata information displayed by ildasm.exe using a friendly object model. For example, through reflection, you can obtain a list of all types contained within a given *.dll or *.exe assembly, including the methods, fields, properties, and events defined by a given type. You can also dynamically discover the set of interfaces supported by a given type, the parameters of a method, and other related details (base classes, namespace information, manifest data, and so forth).

Like any namespace, System.Reflection (which is defined in mscorlib.dll) contains a number of related types. Table 15-1 lists some of the core items you should be familiar with.

Table 15-1. *A Sampling of Members of the* `System.Reflection` *Namespace*

Type	Meaning in Life
`Assembly`	This abstract class contains a number of members that allow you to load, investigate, and manipulate an assembly.
`AssemblyName`	This class allows you to discover numerous details behind an assembly's identity (version information, culture information, and so forth).
`EventInfo`	This abstract class holds information for a given event.
`FieldInfo`	This abstract class holds information for a given field.
`MemberInfo`	This is the abstract base class that defines common behaviors for the `EventInfo`, `FieldInfo`, `MethodInfo`, and `PropertyInfo` types.
`MethodInfo`	This abstract class contains information for a given method.
`Module`	This abstract class allows you to access a given module within a multifile assembly.
`ParameterInfo`	This class holds information for a given parameter.
`PropertyInfo`	This abstract class holds information for a given property.

To understand how to leverage the `System.Reflection` namespace to programmatically read .NET metadata, you need to first come to terms with the `System.Type` class.

The System.Type Class

The `System.Type` class defines a number of members that can be used to examine a type's metadata, a great number of which return types from the `System.Reflection` namespace. For example, `Type.GetMethods()` returns an array of `MethodInfo` objects, `Type.GetFields()` returns an array of `FieldInfo` objects, and so on. The complete set of members exposed by `System.Type` is quite expansive; however, Table 15-2 offers a partial snapshot of the members supported by `System.Type` (see the .NET Framework 4.7 SDK documentation for full details).

Table 15-2. *Select Members of* `System.Type`

Member	Meaning in Life

`IsAbstract`
`IsArray`
`IsClass`
`IsCOMObject`
`IsEnum`
`IsGenericTypeDefinition`
`IsGenericParameter`
`IsInterface`
`IsPrimitive`
`IsNestedPrivate`
`IsNestedPublic`
`IsSealed`
`IsValueType`
	These properties (among others) allow you to discover a number of basic traits about the `Type` you are referring to (e.g., if it is an abstract entity, an array, a nested class, and so forth).

(continued)

Table 15-2. (*continued*)

Member	Meaning in Life
GetConstructors() GetEvents() GetFields() GetInterfaces() GetMembers() GetMethods() GetNestedTypes() GetProperties()	These methods (among others) allow you to obtain an array representing the items (interface, method, property, etc.) you are interested in. Each method returns a related array (e.g., GetFields() returns a FieldInfo array, GetMethods() returns a MethodInfo array, etc.). Be aware that each of these methods has a singular form (e.g., GetMethod(), GetProperty(), etc.) that allows you to retrieve a specific item by name, rather than an array of all related items.
FindMembers()	This method returns a MemberInfo array based on search criteria.
GetType()	This static method returns a Type instance given a string name.
InvokeMember()	This method allows "late binding" for a given item. You'll learn about late binding later in this chapter.

Obtaining a Type Reference Using System.Object.GetType()

You can obtain an instance of the Type class in a variety of ways. However, the one thing you cannot do is directly create a Type object using the new keyword, as Type is an abstract class. Regarding your first choice, recall that System.Object defines a method named GetType(), which returns an instance of the Type class that represents the metadata for the current object.

```
// Obtain type information using a SportsCar instance.
SportsCar sc = new SportsCar();
Type t = sc.GetType();
```

Obviously, this approach will work only if you have compile-time knowledge of the type you want to reflect over (SportsCar in this case) and currently have an instance of the type in memory. Given this restriction, it should make sense that tools such as ildasm.exe do not obtain type information by directly calling System.Object.GetType() for each type, given that ildasm.exe was not compiled against your custom assemblies.

Obtaining a Type Reference Using typeof()

The next way to obtain type information is using the C# typeof operator, like so:

```
// Get the type using typeof.
Type t = typeof(SportsCar);
```

Unlike System.Object.GetType(), the typeof operator is helpful in that you do not need to first create an object instance to extract type information. However, your codebase must still have compile-time knowledge of the type you are interested in examining, as typeof expects the strongly typed name of the type.

Obtaining a Type Reference Using System.Type.GetType()

To obtain type information in a more flexible manner, you may call the static `GetType()` member of the `System.Type` class and specify the fully qualified string name of the type you are interested in examining. Using this approach, you do *not* need to have compile-time knowledge of the type you are extracting metadata from, given that `Type.GetType()` takes an instance of the omnipresent `System.String`.

■ **Note**　When I say you do not need compile-time knowledge when calling `Type.GetType()`, I am referring to the fact that this method can take any string value whatsoever (rather than a strongly typed variable). Of course, you would still need to know the name of the type in a "stringified" format!

The `Type.GetType()` method has been overloaded to allow you to specify two Boolean parameters, one of which controls whether an exception should be thrown if the type cannot be found, and the other of which establishes the case sensitivity of the string. To illustrate, ponder the following:

```
// Obtain type information using the static Type.GetType() method
// (don't throw an exception if SportsCar cannot be found and ignore case).
Type t = Type.GetType("CarLibrary.SportsCar", false, true);
```

In the previous example, notice that the string you are passing into `GetType()` makes no mention of the assembly containing the type. In this case, the assumption is that the type is defined within the currently executing assembly. However, when you want to obtain metadata for a type within an external private assembly, the string parameter is formatted using the type's fully qualified name, followed by a comma, followed by the friendly name of the assembly containing the type, like so:

```
// Obtain type information for a type within an external assembly.
Type t = Type.GetType("CarLibrary.SportsCar, CarLibrary");
```

As well, do know that the string passed into `Type.GetType()` may specify a plus token (+) to denote a *nested type*. Assume you want to obtain type information for an enumeration (`SpyOptions`) nested within a class named `JamesBondCar`. To do so, you would write the following:

```
// Obtain type information for a nested enumeration
// within the current assembly.
Type t = Type.GetType("CarLibrary.JamesBondCar+SpyOptions");
```

Building a Custom Metadata Viewer

To illustrate the basic process of reflection (and the usefulness of `System.Type`), let's create a Console Application project named MyTypeViewer. This program will display details of the methods, properties, fields, and supported interfaces (in addition to some other points of interest) for any type within `mscorlib.dll` (recall all .NET applications have automatic access to this core framework class library) or a type within MyTypeViewer itself. Once the application has been created, be sure to import the `System.Reflection` namespace.

```
// Need to import this namespace to do any reflection!
using System.Reflection;
```

Reflecting on Methods

The Program class will be updated to define a number of static methods, each of which takes a single System.Type parameter and returns void. First you have ListMethods(), which (as you might guess) prints the name of each method defined by the incoming type. Notice how Type.GetMethods() returns an array of System.Reflection. MethodInfo objects, which can be enumerated over using a standard foreach loop, as follows:

```
// Display method names of type.
static void ListMethods(Type t)
{
  Console.WriteLine("***** Methods *****");
  MethodInfo[] mi = t.GetMethods();
  foreach(MethodInfo m in mi)
    Console.WriteLine("->{0}", m.Name);
  Console.WriteLine();
}
```

Here, you are simply printing the name of the method using the MethodInfo.Name property. As you might guess, MethodInfo has many additional members that allow you to determine whether the method is static, virtual, generic, or abstract. As well, the MethodInfo type allows you to obtain the method's return value and parameter set. You'll spruce up the implementation of ListMethods() in just a bit.

If you wanted, you could also build a fitting LINQ query to enumerate the names of each method. Recall from Chapter 12, LINQ to Objects allows you to build strongly typed queries that can be applied to in-memory object collections. As a good rule of thumb, whenever you find blocks of looping or decision programming logic, you could make use of a related LINQ query. For example, you could rewrite the previous method as so:

```
static void ListMethods(Type t)
{
  Console.WriteLine("***** Methods *****");
  var methodNames = from n in t.GetMethods() select n.Name;
  foreach (var name in methodNames)
    Console.WriteLine("->{0}", name);
  Console.WriteLine();
}
```

Reflecting on Fields and Properties

The implementation of ListFields() is similar. The only notable difference is the call to Type.GetFields() and the resulting FieldInfo array. Again, to keep things simple, you are printing out only the name of each field using a LINQ query.

```
// Display field names of type.
static void ListFields(Type t)
{
  Console.WriteLine("***** Fields *****");
  var fieldNames = from f in t.GetFields() select f.Name;
  foreach (var name in fieldNames)
    Console.WriteLine("->{0}", name);
  Console.WriteLine();
}
```

The logic to display a type's properties is similar.

```
// Display property names of type.
static void ListProps(Type t)
{
  Console.WriteLine("***** Properties *****");
  var propNames = from p in t.GetProperties() select p.Name;
  foreach (var name in propNames)
    Console.WriteLine("->{0}", name);
  Console.WriteLine();
}
```

Reflecting on Implemented Interfaces

Next, you will author a method named ListInterfaces() that will print the names of any interfaces supported on the incoming type. The only point of interest here is that the call to GetInterfaces() returns an array of System.Types! This should make sense given that interfaces are, indeed, types.

```
// Display implemented interfaces.
static void ListInterfaces(Type t)
{
  Console.WriteLine("***** Interfaces *****");
  var ifaces = from i in t.GetInterfaces() select i;
  foreach(Type i in ifaces)
    Console.WriteLine("->{0}", i.Name);
}
```

■ **Note** Be aware that a majority of the "get" methods of System.Type (GetMethods(), GetInterfaces(), etc.) have been overloaded to allow you to specify values from the BindingFlags enumeration. This provides a greater level of control on exactly what should be searched for (e.g., only static members, only public members, include private members, etc.). Consult the .NET Framework 4.7 SDK documentation for details.

Displaying Various Odds and Ends

Last but not least, you have one final helper method that will simply display various statistics (indicating whether the type is generic, what the base class is, whether the type is sealed, and so forth) regarding the incoming type.

```
// Just for good measure.
static void ListVariousStats(Type t)
{
  Console.WriteLine("***** Various Statistics *****");
  Console.WriteLine("Base class is: {0}", t.BaseType);
  Console.WriteLine("Is type abstract? {0}", t.IsAbstract);
  Console.WriteLine("Is type sealed? {0}", t.IsSealed);
  Console.WriteLine("Is type generic? {0}", t.IsGenericTypeDefinition);
  Console.WriteLine("Is type a class type? {0}", t.IsClass);
  Console.WriteLine();
}
```

Implementing Main()

The Main() method of the Program class prompts the user for the fully qualified name of a type. Once you obtain this string data, you pass it into the Type.GetType() method and send the extracted System.Type into each of your helper methods. This process repeats until the user presses Q to terminate the application.

```
static void Main(string[] args)
{
  Console.WriteLine("***** Welcome to MyTypeViewer *****");
  string typeName = "";

  do
  {
    Console.WriteLine("\nEnter a type name to evaluate");
    Console.Write("or enter Q to quit: ");

    // Get name of type.
    typeName = Console.ReadLine();

    // Does user want to quit?
    if (typeName.Equals("Q",StringComparison.OrdinalIgnoreCase))
    {
      break;
    }

    // Try to display type.
    try
    {
      Type t = Type.GetType(typeName);
      Console.WriteLine("");
      ListVariousStats(t);
      ListFields(t);
      ListProps(t);
      ListMethods(t);
      ListInterfaces(t);
    }
    catch
    {
      Console.WriteLine("Sorry, can't find type");
    }
  } while (true);
}
```

At this point, MyTypeViewer.exe is ready to take a test-drive. For example, run your application and enter the following fully qualified names (be aware that the manner in which you invoked Type.GetType() requires case-sensitive string names):

- System.Int32

- System.Collections.ArrayList

- System.Threading.Thread

- System.Void
- System.IO.BinaryWriter
- System.Math
- System.Console
- MyTypeViewer.Program

For example, here is some partial output when specifying System.Math:

```
***** Welcome to MyTypeViewer *****

Enter a type name to evaluate
or enter Q to quit: System.Math

***** Various Statistics *****
Base class is: System.Object
Is type abstract? True
Is type sealed? True
Is type generic? False
Is type a class type? True

***** Fields *****
->PI
->E

***** Properties *****

***** Methods *****
->Acos
->Asin
->Atan
->Atan2
->Ceiling
->Ceiling
->Cos
...
```

Reflecting on Generic Types

When you call Type.GetType() to obtain metadata descriptions of generic types, you must make use of a special syntax involving a "backtick" character (`) followed by a numerical value that represents the number of type parameters the type supports. For example, if you want to print out the metadata description of System.Collections.Generic.List<T>, you would need to pass the following string into your application:

System.Collections.Generic.List`1

Here, you are using the numerical value of 1, given that List<T> has only one type parameter. However, if you want to reflect over Dictionary<TKey, TValue>, you would supply the value 2, like so:

```
System.Collections.Generic.Dictionary`2
```

Reflecting on Method Parameters and Return Values

So far, so good! Let's make a minor enhancement to the current application. Specifically, you will update the ListMethods() helper function to list not only the name of a given method but also the return type and incoming parameter types. The MethodInfo type provides the ReturnType property and GetParameters() method for these tasks. In the following modified code, notice that you are building a string that contains the type and name of each parameter using a nested foreach loop (without the use of LINQ):

```
static void ListMethods(Type t)
{
  Console.WriteLine("***** Methods *****");
  MethodInfo[] mi = t.GetMethods();
  foreach (MethodInfo m in mi)
  {
    // Get return type.
    string retVal = m.ReturnType.FullName;
    string paramInfo = "( ";
    // Get params.
    foreach (ParameterInfo pi in m.GetParameters())
    {
      paramInfo += string.Format("{0} {1} ", pi.ParameterType, pi.Name);
    }
    paramInfo += " )";

    // Now display the basic method sig.
    Console.WriteLine("->{0} {1} {2}", retVal, m.Name, paramInfo);
  }
  Console.WriteLine();
}
```

If you now run this updated application, you will find that the methods of a given type are much more detailed. If you enter your good friend System.Object as input to the program, the following methods will display:

```
***** Methods *****
->System.String ToString ( )
->System.Boolean Equals ( System.Object obj )
->System.Boolean Equals ( System.Object objA System.Object objB )
->System.Boolean ReferenceEquals ( System.Object objA System.Object objB )
->System.Int32 GetHashCode ( )
->System.Type GetType ( )
```

The current implementation of ListMethods() is helpful, in that you can directly investigate each parameter and method return type using the System.Reflection object model. As an extreme shortcut, be aware that all of the XXXInfo types (MethodInfo, PropertyInfo, EventInfo, etc.) have overridden

ToString() to display the signature of the item requested. Thus, you could also implement ListMethods() as follows (once again using LINQ, where you simply select all MethodInfo objects, rather than only the Name values):

```
static void ListMethods(Type t)
{
  Console.WriteLine("***** Methods *****");
  var methodNames = from n in t.GetMethods() select n;
  foreach (var name in methodNames)
    Console.WriteLine("->{0}", name);
  Console.WriteLine();
}
```

Interesting stuff, huh? Clearly the System.Reflection namespace and System.Type class allow you to reflect over many other aspects of a type beyond what MyTypeViewer is currently displaying. As you would hope, you can obtain a type's events, get the list of any generic parameters for a given member, and glean dozens of other details.

Nevertheless, at this point you have created a (somewhat capable) object browser. The major limitation, of course, is that you have no way to reflect beyond the current assembly (MyTypeViewer) or the always-accessible mscorlib.dll. This begs the question, "How can I build applications that can load (and reflect over) assemblies not referenced at compile time?" Glad you asked.

■ **Source Code**   You can find the MyTypeViewer project in the Chapter 15 subdirectory.

Dynamically Loading Assemblies

In Chapter 14, you learned all about how the CLR consults the assembly manifest when probing for an externally referenced assembly. However, there will be many times when you need to load assemblies on the fly programmatically, even if there is no record of said assembly in the manifest. Formally speaking, the act of loading external assemblies on demand is known as a *dynamic load*.

System.Reflection defines a class named Assembly. Using this class, you are able to dynamically load an assembly, as well as discover properties about the assembly itself. Using the Assembly type, you are able to dynamically load private or shared assemblies, as well as load an assembly located at an arbitrary location. In essence, the Assembly class provides methods (Load() and LoadFrom(), in particular) that allow you to programmatically supply the same sort of information found in a client-side *.config file.

To illustrate dynamic loading, create a new Console Application project named ExternalAssemblyReflector. Your task is to construct a Main() method that prompts for the friendly name of an assembly to load dynamically. You will pass the Assembly reference into a helper method named DisplayTypes(), which will simply print the names of each class, interface, structure, enumeration, and delegate it contains. The code is refreshingly simple.

```
using System;
using System.Collections.Generic;
using System.Linq;
using System.Text;

using System.Reflection;
using System.IO; // For FileNotFoundException definition.
```

```csharp
namespace ExternalAssemblyReflector
{
  class Program
  {
    static void DisplayTypesInAsm(Assembly asm)
    {
      Console.WriteLine("\n***** Types in Assembly *****");
      Console.WriteLine("->{0}", asm.FullName);
      Type[] types = asm.GetTypes();
      foreach (Type t in types)
        Console.WriteLine("Type: {0}", t);
      Console.WriteLine("");
    }

    static void Main(string[] args)
    {
      Console.WriteLine("***** External Assembly Viewer *****");

      string asmName = "";
      Assembly asm = null;

      do
      {
        Console.WriteLine("\nEnter an assembly to evaluate");
        Console.Write("or enter Q to quit: ");

        // Get name of assembly.
        asmName = Console.ReadLine();

        // Does user want to quit?
        if (asmName.Equals("Q",StringComparison.OrdicalIgnoreCase))
        {
          break;
        }

        // Try to load assembly.
        try
        {
          asm = Assembly.Load(asmName);
          DisplayTypesInAsm(asm);
        }
        catch
        {
          Console.WriteLine("Sorry, can't find assembly.");
        }
      } while (true);
    }
  }
}
```

Notice that the static Assembly.Load() method has been passed only the friendly name of the assembly you are interested in loading into memory. Thus, if you want to reflect over CarLibrary.dll, you will need to copy the CarLibrary.dll binary to the \bin\Debug directory of the ExternalAssemblyReflector application to run this program. Once you do, you will find output similar to the following:

```
***** External Assembly Viewer *****

Enter an assembly to evaluate
or enter Q to quit: CarLibrary

***** Types in Assembly *****
->CarLibrary, Version=2.0.0.0, Culture=neutral, PublicKeyToken=33a2bc294331e8b9
Type: CarLibrary.MusicMedia
Type: CarLibrary.EngineState
Type: CarLibrary.Car
Type: CarLibrary.SportsCar
Type: CarLibrary.MiniVan
```

If you want to make ExternalAssemblyReflector more flexible, you can update your code to load the external assembly using Assembly.LoadFrom() rather than Assembly.Load(), like so:

```
try
{
  asm = Assembly.LoadFrom(asmName);
  DisplayTypesInAsm(asm);
}
```

By doing so, you can enter an absolute path to the assembly you want to view (e.g., C:\MyApp\MyAsm.dll). Essentially, Assembly.LoadFrom() allows you to programmatically supply a <codeBase> value. With this adjustment, you can now pass in a full path to your Console Application project. Thus, if CarLibrary.dll was located under C:\MyCode, you could enter the following:

```
***** External Assembly Viewer *****

Enter an assembly to evaluate
or enter Q to quit: C:\MyCode\CarLibrary.dll

***** Types in Assembly *****
->CarLibrary, Version=2.0.0.0, Culture=neutral, PublicKeyToken=33a2bc294331e8b9
Type: CarLibrary.EngineState
Type: CarLibrary.Car
Type: CarLibrary.SportsCar
Type: CarLibrary.MiniVan
```

■ **Source Code**   You can find the ExternalAssemblyReflector project in the Chapter 15 subdirectory.

Reflecting on Shared Assemblies

The Assembly.Load() method has been overloaded a number of times. One variation allows you to specify a culture value (for localized assemblies), as well as a version number and public key token value (for shared assemblies). Collectively speaking, the set of items identifying an assembly is termed the *display name*. The format of a display name is a comma-delimited string of name-value pairs that begins with the friendly name of the assembly, followed by optional qualifiers (that may appear in any order). Here is the template to follow (optional items appear in parentheses):

```
Name (,Version = major.minor.build.revision) (,Culture = culture token)
(,PublicKeyToken= public key token)
```

When you're crafting a display name, the convention PublicKeyToken=null indicates that binding and matching against a nonstrongly named assembly is required. Additionally, Culture="" indicates matching against the default culture of the target machine. Here's an example:

```
// Load version 1.0.0.0 of CarLibrary using the default culture.
Assembly a =
  Assembly.Load(@"CarLibrary, Version=1.0.0.0, PublicKeyToken=null, Culture=""");
```

Also be aware that the System.Reflection namespace supplies the AssemblyName type, which allows you to represent the preceding string information in a handy object variable. Typically, this class is used in conjunction with System.Version, which is an OO wrapper around an assembly's version number. Once you have established the display name, it can then be passed into the overloaded Assembly.Load() method, like so:

```
// Make use of AssemblyName to define the display name.
AssemblyName asmName;
asmName = new AssemblyName();
asmName.Name = "CarLibrary";
Version v = new Version("1.0.0.0");
asmName.Version = v;
Assembly a = Assembly.Load(asmName);
```

To load a shared assembly from the GAC, the Assembly.Load() parameter must specify a PublicKeyToken value. For example, assume you have a new Console Application project named SharedAsmReflector and want to load version 4.0.0.0 of the System.Windows.Forms.dll assembly provided by the .NET base class libraries. Given that the number of types in this assembly is quite large, the following application prints out only the names of public enums, using a simple LINQ query:

```
using System;
using System.Collections.Generic;
using System.Linq;
using System.Text;

using System.Reflection;
using System.IO;
```

```
namespace SharedAsmReflector
{
  public class SharedAsmReflector
  {
    private static void DisplayInfo(Assembly a)
    {
      Console.WriteLine("***** Info about Assembly *****");
      Console.WriteLine("Loaded from GAC? {0}", a.GlobalAssemblyCache);
      Console.WriteLine("Asm Name: {0}", a.GetName().Name);
      Console.WriteLine("Asm Version: {0}", a.GetName().Version);
      Console.WriteLine("Asm Culture: {0}",
        a.GetName().CultureInfo.DisplayName);
      Console.WriteLine("\nHere are the public enums:");

      // Use a LINQ query to find the public enums.
      Type[] types = a.GetTypes();
      var publicEnums = from pe in types where pe.IsEnum &&
                     pe.IsPublic select pe;

      foreach (var pe in publicEnums)
      {
        Console.WriteLine(pe);
      }
    }

    static void Main(string[] args)
    {
      Console.WriteLine("***** The Shared Asm Reflector App *****\n");

      // Load System.Windows.Forms.dll from GAC.
      string displayName = null;
      displayName = "System.Windows.Forms," +
        "Version=4.0.0.0," +
        "PublicKeyToken=b77a5c561934e089," +
        @"Culture=""""";
      Assembly asm = Assembly.Load(displayName);
      DisplayInfo(asm);
      Console.WriteLine("Done!");
      Console.ReadLine();
    }
  }
}
```

■ **Source Code**   You can find the SharedAsmReflector project in the Chapter 15 subdirectory.

At this point, you should understand how to use some of the core members of the System.Reflection namespace to discover metadata at runtime. Of course, I realize despite the "cool factor," you likely will not need to build custom object browsers at your place of employment too often. Do recall, however, that reflection services are the foundation for a number of common programming activities, including late binding.

Understanding Late Binding

Simply put, *late binding* is a technique in which you are able to create an instance of a given type and invoke its members at runtime without having hard-coded compile-time knowledge of its existence. When you are building an application that binds late to a type in an external assembly, you have no reason to set a reference to the assembly; therefore, the caller's manifest has no direct listing of the assembly.

At first glance, it is not easy to see the value of late binding. It is true that if you can "bind early" to an object (e.g., add an assembly reference and allocate the type using the C# new keyword), you should opt to do so. For one reason, early binding allows you to determine errors at compile time, rather than at runtime. Nevertheless, late binding does have a critical role in any extendable application you may be building. You will have a chance to build such an "extendable" program at the end of this chapter, in the section "Building an Extendable Application." Until then, let's examine the role of the Activator class.

The System.Activator Class

The System.Activator class (defined in mscorlib.dll) is the key to the .NET late-binding process. For the current example, you are interested only in the Activator.CreateInstance() method, which is used to create an instance of a type à la late binding. This method has been overloaded numerous times to provide a good deal of flexibility. The simplest variation of the CreateInstance() member takes a valid Type object that describes the entity you want to allocate into memory on the fly.

Create a new Console Application project named LateBindingApp and import the System.IO and System.Reflection namespaces via the C# using keyword. Now, update the Program class as follows:

```
// This program will load an external library,
// and create an object using late binding.
public class Program
{
  static void Main(string[] args)
  {
    Console.WriteLine("***** Fun with Late Binding *****");
    // Try to load a local copy of CarLibrary.
    Assembly a = null;
    try
    {
      a = Assembly.Load("CarLibrary");
    }
    catch(FileNotFoundException ex)
    {
      Console.WriteLine(ex.Message);
      return;
    }
    if(a != null)
      CreateUsingLateBinding(a);

    Console.ReadLine();
  }
```

```
static void CreateUsingLateBinding(Assembly asm)
{
  try
  {
    // Get metadata for the Minivan type.
    Type miniVan = asm.GetType("CarLibrary.MiniVan");

    // Create a Minivan instance on the fly.
    object obj = Activator.CreateInstance(miniVan);
    Console.WriteLine("Created a {0} using late binding!", obj);
  }
  catch(Exception ex)
  {
    Console.WriteLine(ex.Message);
  }
}
```

Now, before you run this application, you will need to manually place a copy of `CarLibrary.dll` into the bin\Debug folder of this new application using Windows Explorer. The reason is that you are calling `Assembly.Load()`; therefore, the CLR will probe only in the client folder. (If you want, you could enter a path to the assembly using `Assembly.LoadFrom()`; however, there is no need to do so.)

■ **Note**   Don't add a reference to `CarLibrary.dll` using Visual Studio for this example! That will record this library in the client's manifest. The whole point of late binding is that you are trying to create an object that is not known at compile time.

Notice that the `Activator.CreateInstance()` method returns a `System.Object` rather than a strongly typed `MiniVan`. Therefore, if you apply the dot operator on the `obj` variable, you will fail to see any members of the `MiniVan` class. At first glance, you might assume you can remedy this problem with an explicit cast, like so:

```
// Cast to get access to the members of MiniVan?
// Nope! Compiler error!
object obj = (MiniVan)Activator.CreateInstance(minivan);
```

However, because your program has not added a reference to `CarLibrary.dll`, you cannot use the C# using keyword to import the `CarLibrary` namespace, and therefore, you can't use a `MiniVan` during the casting operation! Remember that the whole point of late binding is to create instances of objects for which there is no compile-time knowledge. Given this, how can you invoke the underlying methods of the `MiniVan` object stored in the `System.Object` reference? The answer, of course, is by using reflection.

Invoking Methods with No Parameters

Assume you want to invoke the `TurboBoost()` method of the `MiniVan`. As you recall, this method will set the state of the engine to "dead" and display an informational message box. The first step is to obtain a `MethodInfo` object for the `TurboBoost()` method using `Type.GetMethod()`. From the resulting `MethodInfo`, you are then able to call `MiniVan.TurboBoost` using `Invoke()`. `MethodInfo.Invoke()` requires you to send in all parameters that are to be given to the method represented by `MethodInfo`. These parameters are represented by an array of `System.Object` types (as the parameters for a given method could be any number of various entities).

581

Given that TurboBoost() does not require any parameters, you can simply pass null (meaning "this method has no parameters"). Update your CreateUsingLateBinding() method as follows:

```
static void CreateUsingLateBinding(Assembly asm)
{
  try
  {
    // Get metadata for the Minivan type.
    Type miniVan = asm.GetType("CarLibrary.MiniVan");

    // Create the Minivan on the fly.
    object obj = Activator.CreateInstance(miniVan);
    Console.WriteLine("Created a {0} using late binding!", obj);
    // Get info for TurboBoost.
    MethodInfo mi = miniVan.GetMethod("TurboBoost");

    // Invoke method ('null' for no parameters).
    mi.Invoke(obj, null);
  }
  catch(Exception ex)
  {
    Console.WriteLine(ex.Message);
  }
}
```

At this point, you will see the message box shown in Figure 15-2 once the TurboBoost() method is invoked.

Figure 15-2. *Late-bound method invocation*

Invoking Methods with Parameters

When you want to use late binding to invoke a method requiring parameters, you should package up the arguments as a loosely typed array of objects. Recall that version 2.0.0.0 of CarLibrary.dll defined the following method in the Car class:

```
public void TurnOnRadio(bool musicOn, MusicMedia mm)
{
  public void TurnOnRadio(bool musicOn, MusicMedia mm)
      => MessageBox.Show(musicOn ? $"Jamming {mm}" : "Quiet time...");
}
```

582

This method takes two parameters: a Boolean representing if the automobile's music system should be turned on or off and an enum representing the type of music player. Recall this enum was structured as so:

```
public enum MusicMedia
{
  musicCd,    // 0
  musicTape,  // 1
  musicRadio, // 2
  musicMp3    // 3
}
```

Here is a new method of the `Program` class, which invokes `TurnOnRadio()`. Notice that you are using the underlying numerical values of the `MusicMedia` enumeration to specify a "radio" media player.

```
static void InvokeMethodWithArgsUsingLateBinding(Assembly asm)
{
  try
  {
    // First, get a metadata description of the sports car.
    Type sport = asm.GetType("CarLibrary.SportsCar");

    // Now, create the sports car.
    object obj = Activator.CreateInstance(sport);
    // Invoke TurnOnRadio() with arguments.
    MethodInfo mi = sport.GetMethod("TurnOnRadio");
    mi.Invoke(obj, new object[] { true, 2 });
  }
  catch (Exception ex)
  {
    Console.WriteLine(ex.Message);
  }
}
```

Ideally, at this point, you can see the relationships among reflection, dynamic loading, and late binding. To be sure, the reflection API provides many additional features beyond what has been covered here, but you should be in good shape to dig into more details if you are interested.

Again, you still might wonder exactly *when* you should use these techniques in your own applications. The conclusion of this chapter should shed light on this issue; however, the next topic under investigation is the role of .NET attributes.

■ **Source Code**   You can find the LateBindingApp project in the `Chapter 15` subdirectory.

Understanding the Role of .NET Attributes

As illustrated at beginning of this chapter, one role of a .NET compiler is to generate metadata descriptions for all defined and referenced types. In addition to this standard metadata contained within any assembly, the .NET platform provides a way for programmers to embed additional metadata into an assembly using *attributes*. In a nutshell, attributes are nothing more than code annotations that can be applied to a given type (class, interface, structure, etc.), member (property, method, etc.), assembly, or module.

.NET attributes are class types that extend the abstract System.Attribute base class. As you explore the .NET namespaces, you will find many predefined attributes that you are able to use in your applications. Furthermore, you are free to build custom attributes to further qualify the behavior of your types by creating a new type deriving from Attribute.

The .NET base class library provides a number of attributes in various namespaces. Table 15-3 gives a snapshot of some—but by *absolutely* no means all—predefined attributes.

Table 15-3. *A Tiny Sampling of Predefined Attributes*

Attribute	Meaning in Life
[CLSCompliant]	Enforces the annotated item to conform to the rules of the Common Language Specification (CLS). Recall that CLS-compliant types are guaranteed to be used seamlessly across all .NET programming languages.
[DllImport]	Allows .NET code to make calls to any unmanaged C- or C++-based code library, including the API of the underlying operating system. Do note that [DllImport] is not used when communicating with COM-based software.
[Obsolete]	Marks a deprecated type or member. If other programmers attempt to use such an item, they will receive a compiler warning describing the error of their ways.
[Serializable]	Marks a class or structure as being "serializable," meaning it is able to persist its current state into a stream.
[NonSerialized]	Specifies that a given field in a class or structure should not be persisted during the serialization process.
[ServiceContract]	Marks a method as a contract implemented by a WCF service.

Understand that when you apply attributes in your code, the embedded metadata is essentially useless until another piece of software explicitly reflects over the information. If this is not the case, the blurb of metadata embedded within the assembly is ignored and completely harmless.

Attribute Consumers

As you would guess, the .NET 4.7 Framework SDK ships with numerous utilities that are indeed on the lookout for various attributes. The C# compiler (csc.exe) itself has been preprogrammed to discover the presence of various attributes during the compilation cycle. For example, if the C# compiler encounters the [CLSCompliant] attribute, it will automatically check the attributed item to ensure it is exposing only CLS-compliant constructs. By way of another example, if the C# compiler discovers an item attributed with the [Obsolete] attribute, it will display a compiler warning in the Visual Studio Error List window.

In addition to development tools, numerous methods in the .NET base class libraries are preprogrammed to reflect over specific attributes. For example, if you want to persist the state of an object to file, all you are required to do is annotate your class or structure with the [Serializable] attribute. If the Serialize() method of the BinaryFormatter class encounters this attribute, the object is automatically persisted to file in a compact binary format.

Finally, you are free to build applications that are programmed to reflect over your own custom attributes, as well as any attribute in the .NET base class libraries. By doing so, you are essentially able to create a set of "keywords" that are understood by a specific set of assemblies.

Applying Attributes in C#

To illustrate the process of applying attributes in C#, create a new Console Application project named ApplyingAttributes. Assume you want to build a class named Motorcycle that can be persisted in a binary format. To do so, simply apply the [Serializable] attribute to the class definition. If you have a field that should not be persisted, you may apply the [NonSerialized] attribute.

```
// This class can be saved to disk.
[Serializable]
public class Motorcycle
{
  // However, this field will not be persisted.
  [NonSerialized]
  float weightOfCurrentPassengers;
  // These fields are still serializable.
  bool hasRadioSystem;
  bool hasHeadSet;
  bool hasSissyBar;
}
```

■ **Note**   An attribute applies to the "very next" item. For example, the only nonserialized field of the Motorcycle class is weightOfCurrentPassengers. The remaining fields are serializable given that the entire class has been annotated with [Serializable].

At this point, don't concern yourself with the actual process of object serialization (Chapter 20 examines the details). Just notice that when you want to apply an attribute, the name of the attribute is sandwiched between square brackets.

Once this class has been compiled, you can view the extra metadata using ildasm.exe. Notice that these attributes are recorded using the serializable token (see the red triangle immediately inside the Motorcycle class) and the notserialized token (on the weightOfCurrentPassengers field; see Figure 15-3).

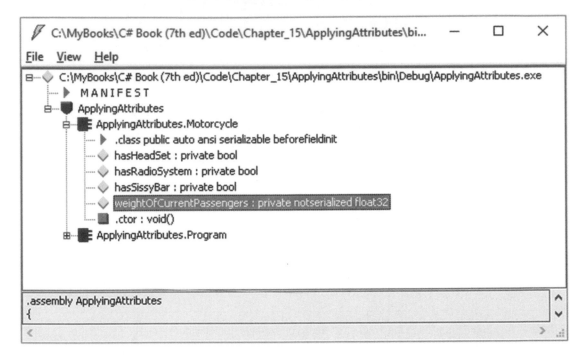

Figure 15-3. *Attributes shown in* ildasm.exe

As you might guess, a single item can be attributed with multiple attributes. Assume you have a legacy C# class type (HorseAndBuggy) that was marked as serializable but is now considered obsolete for current development. Rather than deleting the class definition from your codebase (and risk breaking existing software), you can mark the class with the [Obsolete] attribute. To apply multiple attributes to a single item, simply use a comma-delimited list, like so:

```
[Serializable, Obsolete("Use another vehicle!")]
public class HorseAndBuggy
{
  // ...
}
```

As an alternative, you can also apply multiple attributes on a single item by stacking each attribute as follows (the end result is identical):

```
[Serializable]
[Obsolete("Use another vehicle!")]
public class HorseAndBuggy
{
  // ...
}
```

C# Attribute Shorthand Notation

If you were consulting the .NET Framework 4.7 SDK documentation, you might have noticed that the actual class name of the [Obsolete] attribute is ObsoleteAttribute, not Obsolete. As a naming convention, all .NET attributes (including custom attributes you may create yourself) are suffixed with the Attribute token. However, to simplify the process of applying attributes, the C# language does not require you to type in the Attribute suffix. Given this, the following iteration of the HorseAndBuggy type is identical to the previous (it just involves a few more keystrokes):

```
[SerializableAttribute]
[ObsoleteAttribute("Use another vehicle!")]
public class HorseAndBuggy
{
  // ...
}
```

Be aware that this is a courtesy provided by C#. Not all .NET-enabled languages support this shorthand attribute syntax.

Specifying Constructor Parameters for Attributes

Notice that the [Obsolete] attribute is able to accept what appears to be a constructor parameter. If you view the formal definition of the [Obsolete] attribute by right-clicking the item in the code editor and selecting the Go To Definition menu option, you will find that this class indeed provides a constructor receiving a System.String.

```
public sealed class ObsoleteAttribute : Attribute
{
  public ObsoleteAttribute(string message, bool error);
  public ObsoleteAttribute(string message);
  public ObsoleteAttribute();
  public bool IsError { get; }
  public string Message { get; }
}
```

Understand that when you supply constructor parameters to an attribute, the attribute is *not* allocated into memory until the parameters are reflected upon by another type or an external tool. The string data defined at the attribute level is simply stored within the assembly as a blurb of metadata.

The Obsolete Attribute in Action

Now that HorseAndBuggy has been marked as obsolete, if you were to allocate an instance of this type:

```
static void Main(string[] args)
{
  HorseAndBuggy mule = new HorseAndBuggy();
}
```

you would find that the supplied string data is extracted and displayed within the Error List window of Visual Studio, as well as on the offending line of code when you hover your mouse cursor above the obsolete type (see Figure 15-4).

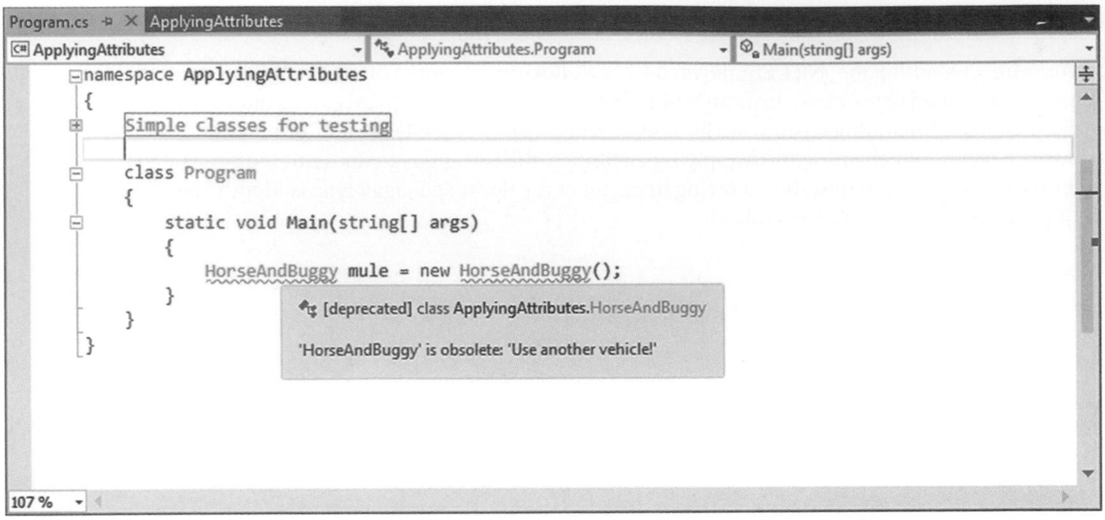

```
namespace ApplyingAttributes
{
    Simple classes for testing

    class Program
    {
        static void Main(string[] args)
        {
            HorseAndBuggy mule = new HorseAndBuggy();
        }              ╔═══════════════════════════════════════════╗
    }                  ║ ⚡ [deprecated] class ApplyingAttributes.HorseAndBuggy ║
}                      ║                                           ║
                       ║ 'HorseAndBuggy' is obsolete: 'Use another vehicle!' ║
                       ╚═══════════════════════════════════════════╝
```

Figure 15-4. *Attributes in action*

In this case, the "other piece of software" that is reflecting on the [Obsolete] attribute is the C# compiler. Ideally, at this point, you should understand the following key points regarding .NET attributes:

- Attributes are classes that derive from System.Attribute.

- Attributes result in embedded metadata.

- Attributes are basically useless until another agent reflects upon them.

- Attributes are applied in C# using square brackets.

Next up, let's examine how you can build your own custom attributes and a piece of custom software that reflects over the embedded metadata.

■ **Source Code**   You can find the ApplyingAttributes project in the Chapter 15 subdirectory.

Building Custom Attributes

The first step in building a custom attribute is to create a new class deriving from System.Attribute. Keeping in step with the automobile theme used throughout this book, assume you have created a new C# Class Library project named AttributedCarLibrary. This assembly will define a handful of vehicles, each of which is described using a custom attribute named VehicleDescriptionAttribute, as follows:

```
// A custom attribute.
public sealed class VehicleDescriptionAttribute : System.Attribute
{
  public string Description { get; set; }
```

```
    public VehicleDescriptionAttribute(string vehicalDescription) => Description =
    vehicalDescription;
    public VehicleDescriptionAttribute(){ }
}
```

As you can see, VehicleDescriptionAttribute maintains a piece of string data manipulated using an automatic property (Description). Beyond the fact that this class derived from System.Attribute, there is nothing unique to this class definition.

■ **Note** For security reasons, it is considered a .NET best practice to design all custom attributes as sealed. In fact, Visual Studio provides a code snippet named Attribute that will dump out a new System.Attribute-derived class into your code window. See Chapter 2 for full explication of using code snippets; however, recall you can expand any snippet by typing its name and pressing the Tab key twice.

Applying Custom Attributes

Given that VehicleDescriptionAttribute is derived from System.Attribute, you are now able to annotate your vehicles as you see fit. For testing purposes, add the following class definitions to your new class library:

```
// Assign description using a "named property."
[Serializable]
[VehicleDescription(Description = "My rocking Harley")]
public class Motorcycle
{
}

[Serializable]
[Obsolete ("Use another vehicle!")]
[VehicleDescription("The old gray mare, she ain't what she used to be...")]
public class HorseAndBuggy
{
}

[VehicleDescription("A very long, slow, but feature-rich auto")]
public class Winnebago
{
}
```

Named Property Syntax

Notice that the description of the Motorcycle is assigned a description using a new bit of attribute- centric syntax termed a *named property*. In the constructor of the first [VehicleDescription] attribute, you set the underlying string data by using the Description property. If this attribute is reflected upon by an external agent, the value is fed into the Description property (named property syntax is legal only if the attribute supplies a writable .NET property).

In contrast, the HorseAndBuggy and Winnebago types are not using named property syntax and are simply passing the string data via the custom constructor. In any case, once you compile the AttributedCarLibrary assembly, you can use ildasm.exe to view the injected metadata descriptions for your type. For example, Figure 15-5 shows an embedded description of the Winnebago class, specifically the data within the beforefieldinit item in ildasm.exe.

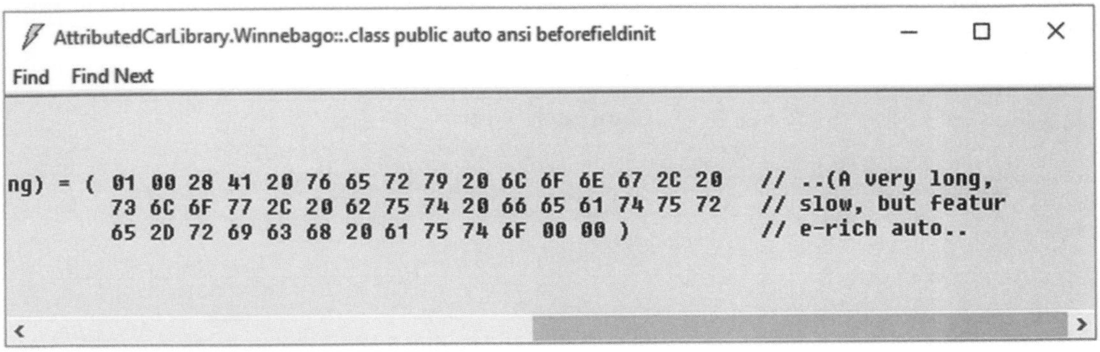

Figure 15-5. *Embedded vehicle description data*

Restricting Attribute Usage

By default, custom attributes can be applied to just about any aspect of your code (methods, classes, properties, and so on). Thus, if it made sense to do so, you could use VehicleDescription to qualify methods, properties, or fields (among other things).

```
[VehicleDescription("A very long, slow, but feature-rich auto")]
public class Winnebago
{
  [VehicleDescription("My rocking CD player")]
  public void PlayMusic(bool On)
  {
    ...
  }
}
```

In some cases, this is exactly the behavior you require. Other times, however, you may want to build a custom attribute that can be applied only to select code elements. If you want to constrain the scope of a custom attribute, you will need to apply the [AttributeUsage] attribute on the definition of your custom attribute. The [AttributeUsage] attribute allows you to supply any combination of values (via an OR operation) from the AttributeTargets enumeration, like so:

```
// This enumeration defines the possible targets of an attribute.
public enum AttributeTargets
{
  All, Assembly, Class, Constructor,
  Delegate, Enum, Event, Field, GenericParameter,
  Interface, Method, Module, Parameter,
  Property, ReturnValue, Struct
}
```

Furthermore, [AttributeUsage] also allows you to optionally set a named property (AllowMultiple) that specifies whether the attribute can be applied more than once on the same item (the default is false). As well, [AttributeUsage] allows you to establish whether the attribute should be inherited by derived classes using the Inherited named property (the default is true).

To establish that the [VehicleDescription] attribute can be applied only once on a class or structure, you can update the VehicleDescriptionAttribute definition as follows:

```
// This time, we are using the AttributeUsage attribute
// to annotate our custom attribute.
[AttributeUsage(AttributeTargets.Class | AttributeTargets.Struct, Inherited = false)]
public sealed class VehicleDescriptionAttribute : System.Attribute
{
...
}
```

With this, if a developer attempted to apply the [VehicleDescription] attribute on anything other than a class or structure, he or she is issued a compile-time error.

Assembly-Level Attributes

It is also possible to apply attributes on all types within a given assembly using the [assembly:] tag. For example, assume you want to ensure that every public member of every public type defined within your assembly is CLS compliant.

■ **Note** Chapter 1 mentioned the role of CLS-compliant assemblies. Recall that a CLS-compliant assembly can be used by all .NET programming languages out of the box. If you create public members of public types, which expose non-CLS-compliant programming constructs (such as unsigned data or pointer parameters), other .NET languages may not be able to use your functionality. Therefore, if you are building C# code libraries that need to be used by a wide variety of .NET languages, checking for CLS compliance is a must.

To do so, simply add the following assembly-level attribute at the top of any C# source code file. Be aware that all assembly- or module-level attributes must be listed outside the scope of any namespace scope! If you add assembly- or module-level attributes to your project, here is a recommended file layout to follow:

```
// List "using" statements first.
using System;
using System.Collections.Generic;
using System.Linq;
using System.Text;

// Now list any assembly- or module-level attributes.
// Enforce CLS compliance for all public types in this assembly.
[assembly: CLSCompliant(true)]
```

```
// Now, your namespace(s) and types.
namespace AttributedCarLibrary
{
  // Types...
}
```

If you now add a bit of code that falls outside the CLS specification (such as an exposed point of unsigned data):

```
// Ulong types don't jibe with the CLS.
public class Winnebago
{
  public ulong notCompliant;
}
```

you are issued a compiler warning.

The Visual Studio AssemblyInfo.cs File

By default, Visual Studio projects receive a file named `AssemblyInfo.cs`, which can be viewed by expanding the Properties icon of Solution Explorer (see Figure 15-6).

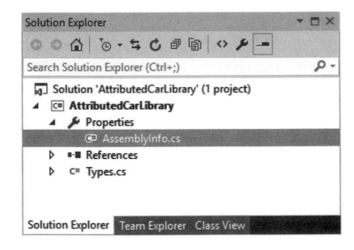

Figure 15-6. *The `AssemblyInfo.cs` file*

This file is a handy place to put attributes that are to be applied at the assembly level. You might recall from Chapter 14, during the examination of .NET assemblies, that the manifest contains assembly- level metadata, much of which comes from the assembly-level attributes shown in Table 15-4.

Table 15-4. *Select Assembly-Level Attributes*

Attribute	Meaning in Life
[AssemblyCompany]	Holds basic company information
[AssemblyCopyright]	Holds any copyright information for the product or assembly
[AssemblyCulture]	Provides information on what cultures or languages the assembly supports
[AssemblyDescription]	Holds a friendly description of the product or modules that make up the assembly
[AssemblyKeyFile]	Specifies the name of the file containing the key pair used to sign the assembly (i.e., establish a strong name)
[AssemblyProduct]	Provides product information
[AssemblyTrademark]	Provides trademark information
[AssemblyVersion]	Specifies the assembly's version information, in the format <major.minor. build.revision>

■ **Source Code**   You can find the AttributedCarLibrary project in the Chapter 15 subdirectory.

Reflecting on Attributes Using Early Binding

Remember that an attribute is quite useless until another piece of software reflects over its values. Once a given attribute has been discovered, that piece of software can take whatever course of action necessary. Now, like any application, this "other piece of software" could discover the presence of a custom attribute using either early binding or late binding. If you want to make use of early binding, you'll require the client application to have a compile-time definition of the attribute in question (VehicleDescriptionAttribute, in this case). Given that the AttributedCarLibrary assembly has defined this custom attribute as a public class, early binding is the best option.

To illustrate the process of reflecting on custom attributes, create a new C# Console Application project named VehicleDescriptionAttributeReader. Next, add a reference to the AttributedCarLibrary assembly. Finally, update your initial *.cs file with the following code:

```
// Reflecting on attributes using early binding.
using System;
using System.Collections.Generic;
using System.Linq;
using System.Text;

using AttributedCarLibrary;

namespace VehicleDescriptionAttributeReader
{
  class Program
  {
    static void Main(string[] args)
```

```
  {
    Console.WriteLine("***** Value of VehicleDescriptionAttribute *****\n");
    ReflectOnAttributesUsingEarlyBinding();
    Console.ReadLine();
  }

  private static void ReflectOnAttributesUsingEarlyBinding()
  {
    // Get a Type representing the Winnebago.
    Type t = typeof(Winnebago);

    // Get all attributes on the Winnebago.
    object[] customAtts = t.GetCustomAttributes(false);

    // Print the description.
    foreach (VehicleDescriptionAttribute v in customAtts)
      Console.WriteLine("-> {0}\n", v.Description);
  }
 }
}
```

The Type.GetCustomAttributes() method returns an object array that represents all the attributes applied to the member represented by the Type (the Boolean parameter controls whether the search should extend up the inheritance chain). Once you have obtained the list of attributes, iterate over each VehicleDescriptionAttribute class and print out the value obtained by the Description property.

■ **Source Code**   You can find the VehicleDescriptionAttributeReader project in the Chapter 15 subdirectory.

Reflecting on Attributes Using Late Binding

The previous example used early binding to print out the vehicle description data for the Winnebago type. This was possible because the VehicleDescriptionAttribute class type was defined as a public member in the AttributedCarLibrary assembly. It is also possible to make use of dynamic loading and late binding to reflect over attributes.

Create a new project called VehicleDescriptionAttributeReaderLateBinding and copy AttributedCarLibrary.dll to the project's \bin\Debug directory. Now, update your Program class as follows:

```
using System;
using System.Collections.Generic;
using System.Linq;
using System.Text;

using System.Reflection;
```

```
namespace VehicleDescriptionAttributeReaderLateBinding
{
  class Program
  {
    static void Main(string[] args)
    {
      Console.WriteLine("***** Value of VehicleDescriptionAttribute *****\n");
      ReflectAttributesUsingLateBinding();
      Console.ReadLine();
    }

    private static void ReflectAttributesUsingLateBinding()
    {
      try
      {
        // Load the local copy of AttributedCarLibrary.
        Assembly asm = Assembly.Load("AttributedCarLibrary");

        // Get type info of VehicleDescriptionAttribute.
        Type vehicleDesc = asm.GetType("AttributedCarLibrary.VehicleDescriptionAttribute");

        // Get type info of the Description property.
        PropertyInfo propDesc = vehicleDesc.GetProperty("Description");

        // Get all types in the assembly.
        Type[] types = asm.GetTypes();

        // Iterate over each type and obtain any VehicleDescriptionAttributes.
        foreach (Type t in types)
        {
          object[] objs = t.GetCustomAttributes(vehicleDesc, false);

          // Iterate over each VehicleDescriptionAttribute and print
          // the description using late binding.
          foreach (object o in objs)
          {
            Console.WriteLine("-> {0}: {1}\n", t.Name, propDesc.GetValue(o, null));
          }
        }
      }
      catch (Exception ex)
      {
        Console.WriteLine(ex.Message);
      }
    }
  }
}
```

If you were able to follow along with the examples in this chapter, this code should be (more or less) self-explanatory. The only point of interest is the use of the `PropertyInfo.GetValue()` method, which is used to trigger the property's accessor. Here is the output of the current example:

```
***** Value of VehicleDescriptionAttribute *****

-> Motorcycle: My rocking Harley

-> HorseAndBuggy: The old gray mare, she ain't what she used to be...

-> Winnebago: A very long, slow, but feature-rich auto
```

■ **Source Code**   You can find the VehicleDescriptionAttributeReaderLateBinding project in the Chapter 15 subdirectory.

Putting Reflection, Late Binding, and Custom Attributes in Perspective

Even though you have seen numerous examples of these techniques in action, you may still be wondering when to make use of reflection, dynamic loading, late binding, and custom attributes in your programs. To be sure, these topics can seem a bit on the academic side of programming (which may or may not be a bad thing, depending on your point of view). To help map these topics to a real-world situation, you need a solid example. Assume for the moment that you are on a programming team that is building an application with the following requirement:

- The product must be extendable by the use of additional third-party tools.

What exactly is meant by *extendable*? Well, consider the Visual Studio IDE. When this application was developed, various "hooks" were inserted into the codebase to allow other software vendors to "snap" (or plug in) custom modules into the IDE. Obviously, the Visual Studio development team had no way to set references to external .NET assemblies it had not developed yet (thus, no early binding), so how exactly would an application provide the required hooks? Here is one possible way to solve this problem:

1. First, an extendable application must provide some input mechanism to allow the user to specify the module to plug in (such as a dialog box or command-line flag). This requires *dynamic loading*.

2. Second, an extendable application must be able to determine whether the module supports the correct functionality (such as a set of required interfaces) to be plugged into the environment. This requires *reflection*.

3. Finally, an extendable application must obtain a reference to the required infrastructure (such as a set of interface types) and invoke the members to trigger the underlying functionality. This may require *late binding*.

Simply put, if the extendable application has been preprogrammed to query for specific interfaces, it is able to determine at runtime whether the type can be activated. Once this verification test has been passed, the type in question may support additional interfaces that provide a polymorphic fabric to their functionality. This is the exact approach taken by the Visual Studio team and, despite what you might be thinking, is not at all difficult!

Building an Extendable Application

In the sections that follow, I will take you through an example that illustrates the process of building an application that can be augmented by the functionality of external assemblies. To serve as a road map, the extendable application entails the following assemblies:

- CommonSnappableTypes.dll: This assembly contains type definitions that will be used by each snap-in object and will be directly referenced by the Windows Forms application.

- CSharpSnapIn.dll: A snap-in written in C#, which leverages the types of CommonSnappableTypes.dll.

- VbSnapIn.dll: A snap-in written in Visual Basic, which leverages the types of CommonSnappableTypes.dll.

- MyExtendableApp.exe: A console application that may be extended by the functionality of each snap-in.

This application will use dynamic loading, reflection, and late binding to dynamically gain the functionality of assemblies it has no prior knowledge of.

■ **Note**   You might be thinking to yourself, "My boss has never asked me to build a console application," and you are probably correct! The overwhelming majority of user-facing applications built with C# are either smart client (WinForms or WPF) or web (ASP.NET Web Forms or ASP.NET MVC). We are using console applications to allow you, the reader, to focus on the specific concepts of the example, in this case dynamic loading, reflection, and late binding. Later in this book you will explore "real" user-facing applications using WPF and ASP.NET MVC.

Building the Multiproject ExtendableApp Solution

Up to this point in this book, each application has been a stand-alone project. This was done to keep the examples simple and focused. However, in real-world development, more often than not you will be working with multiple projects together. Visual Studio was designed for that, and this example will show you how to do that. All of the projects that you have created so far also include a solution that wraps the project. By default, the solution name is the same as the first project name, but it doesn't have to be (and most of the time won't be).

To create the ExtendableApp solution, start by selecting File ➤ New Project to load the New Project dialog. Select Class Library, and enter the name **CommonSnappableTypes**. Before you click OK, enter the solution name **ExtendableApp**, as shown in Figure 15-7.

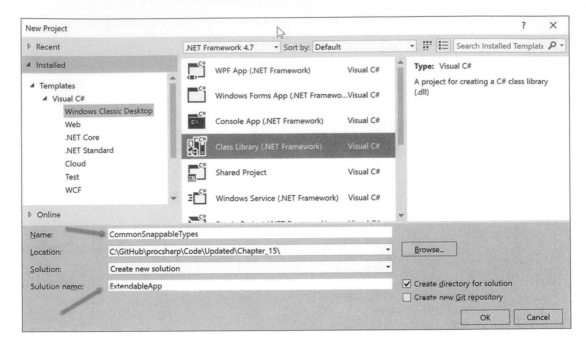

Figure 15-7. *Creating the CommonSnappableTypes project and the ExtendableApp solution*

Throughout the rest of this example, you will add the additional projects into the ExtendableApp solution, learn how to add project references, set build actions, and define the solution's startup project.

Building CommonSnappableTypes.dll

Delete the default `Class1.cs` file and add a new file named `SnappableTypes.cs`. The CommonSnappableTypes Class Library project defines two types, as shown here:

```
namespace CommonSnappableTypes
{
  public interface IAppFunctionality
  {
    void DoIt();
  }
  [AttributeUsage(AttributeTargets.Class)]
  public sealed class CompanyInfoAttribute : System.Attribute
  {
    public string CompanyName { get; set; }
    public string CompanyUrl { get; set; }
  }
}
```

The `IAppFunctionality` interface provides a polymorphic interface for all snap-ins that can be consumed by the extendable application. Given that this example is purely illustrative, you supply a single method named `DoIt()`. A more realistic interface (or a set of interfaces) might allow the object to generate scripting code, render an image onto the application's toolbox, or integrate into the main menu of the hosting application.

The CompanyInfoAttribute type is a custom attribute that can be applied on any class type that wants to be snapped into the container. As you can tell by the definition of this class, [CompanyInfo] allows the developer of the snap-in to provide some basic details about the component's point of origin.

Adding Projects to the Solution

Next up, you need to create a type that implements the IAppFunctionality interface. To add another project into the solution, right-click the ExtendableApp name in Solution Explorer (or click File ➤ Add ➤ New Project) and select Add ➤ New Project, as shown in Figure 15-8.

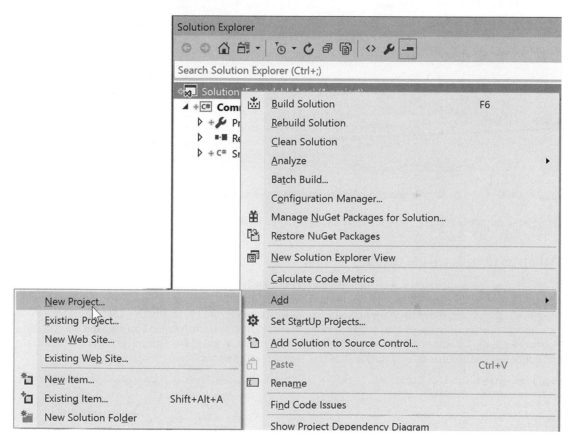

Figure 15-8. *Adding another project to the solution*

The resulting Add New Project dialog box is a little different now; as you can see, the solution options are no longer there, as illustrated in Figure 15-9.

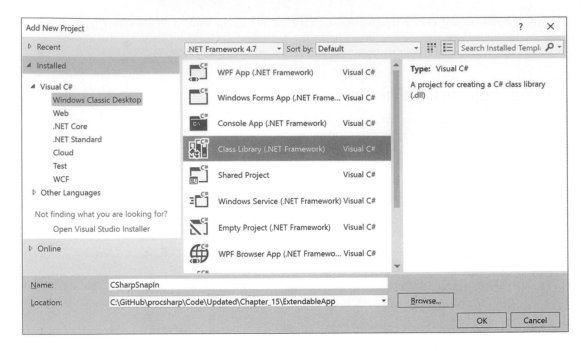

Figure 15-9. *The Add New Project dialog when adding a project into an existing solution*

Name the Class Library project CSharpSnapIn and click OK.

Adding Project References

This class library defines a class type named `CSharpModule`. Given that this class must make use of the types defined in `CommonSnappableTypes`, you need to add a reference to the CommonSnappableTypes project (not the assembly). The actual reference *does* point to the compiled assembly, but Visual Studio takes care of that for you.

To add a project reference, start by right-clicking the References node in Solution Explorer and selecting Add Reference. On the left side of the Reference Manager, select Projects ➤ Solutions. This will list all of the projects in the solution (there is currently only one) as shown in Figure 15-10. Select this as a reference and click OK.

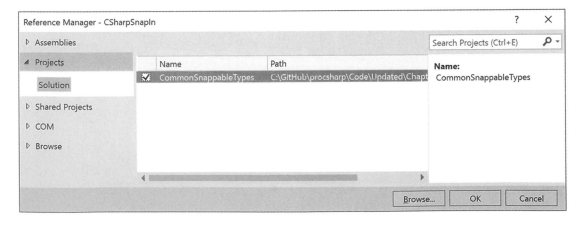

Figure 15-10. *Adding a project reference*

Building the C# Snap-In

Now that you have the reference in place, delete the `Class1.cs` file in the project, add a new file named `CSharpModule.cs`, and update the code to match the following (make sure to add the using statement for `CommonSnappableTypes`):

```csharp
using System;
using System.Collections.Generic;
using System.Linq;
using System.Text;

using CommonSnappableTypes;

namespace CSharpSnapIn
{
  [CompanyInfo(CompanyName = "FooBar", CompanyUrl = "www.FooBar.com")]
  public class CSharpModule : IAppFunctionality
  {
    void IAppFunctionality.DoIt()
    {
      Console.WriteLine("You have just used the C# snap-in!");
    }
  }
}
```

Notice that I chose to make use of explicit interface implementation (see Chapter 9) when supporting the `IAppFunctionality` interface. This is not required; however, the idea is that the only part of the system that needs to directly interact with this interface type is the hosting application. By explicitly implementing this interface, the `DoIt()` method is not directly exposed from the `CSharpModule` type.

Building the Visual Basic Snap-In

Now, to simulate the role of a third-party vendor that prefers Visual Basic over C#, add a new Visual Basic class library (VbSnapIn) that references the CommonSnappableTypes project, just like the previous CSharpSnapIn project. Delete the `Class1.vb` file and add a new one named `VbSnapIn.vb`.

The code is (again) intentionally simple.

```vbnet
Imports CommonSnappableTypes

<CompanyInfo(CompanyName:="Chucky's Software", CompanyUrl:="www.ChuckySoft.com")>
Public Class VbSnapIn
  Implements IAppFunctionality

  Public Sub DoIt() Implements CommonSnappableTypes.IAppFunctionality.DoIt
    Console.WriteLine("You have just used the VB snap in!")
  End Sub
End Class
```

Notice that applying attributes in the syntax of Visual Basic requires angle brackets (< >) rather than square brackets ([ ]). Also notice that the `Implements` keyword is used to implement interface types on a given class or structure.

Setting the Startup Project

The final project to add is a new C# console application (MyExtendableApp). When there is more than one project in a solution, Visual Studio needs to be informed about which project (or projects; multiproject starts will be covered later in this book) should be run when you click Run. By default, it's the first project added to your solution. You need the MyExtendableApp project to be first.

Setting the startup project is simple. Right-click the MyExtendableApp project in Solution Explorer and select Set as StartUp Project, as shown in Figure 15-11.

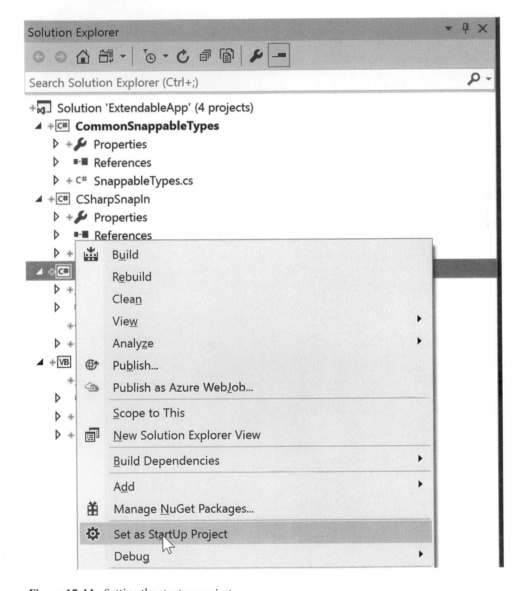

Figure 15-11. *Setting the startup project*

■ **Note**   If you right-click the ExtendableApp solution instead of one of the projects, the context menu option displayed is Set StartUp Projects. In addition to having just one project execute when you click Run, you can set up multiple projects to execute. This can be helpful if your solution contains a Web API RESTful service project and a web application that consumes the service. To run the web application, the RESTful service must be started as well. This will be demonstrated in later chapters.

Setting the Project Build Order

After adding the MyExtendableApp console application to the solution and setting it as the startup project, add a reference to the CommonSnappableTypes project and a reference to the System.Windows.Forms library, but *not* the CSharpSnapIn.dll or VbSnapIn.dll project.

When Visual Studio is given the command to run a solution, the startup projects and all referenced projects are built if any changes are detected; however, any unreferenced projects are *not* built. This can be changed by setting project dependencies under the Project Build Order context menu. This is accessed by right-clicking the solution, as shown in Figure 15-12.

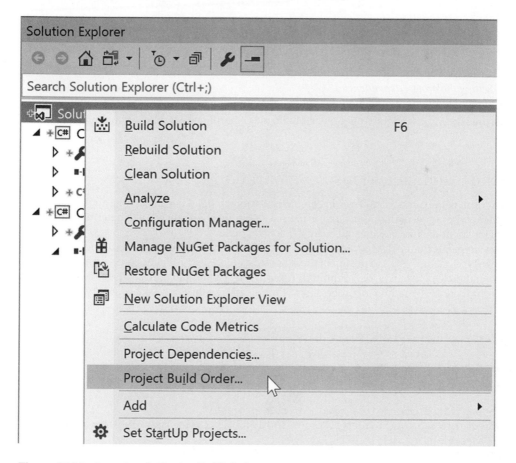

Figure 15-12. *Accessing the Project Build Order context menu*

Click the Dependencies tab and select MyExtendableApp in the drop-down. Notice that the CommonSnappableTypes project is already selected and the check box is disabled. This is because it is referenced directly. Select the CSharpSnapIn and VbSnapIn project check boxes as well, as shown in Figure 15-13.

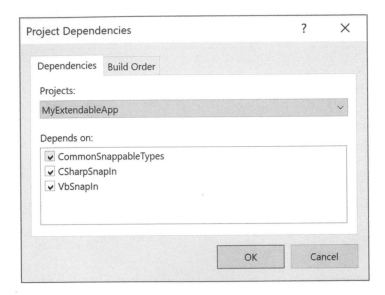

Figure 15-13. *Setting the project dependencies*

Now, each time the MyExtendableApp project is built, the CSharpSnapIn and VbSnapIn projects build as well.

Building the Extendable Console Application

Now that you have all of the infrastructure setup complete, it's time to build the extendable application. Remember that the whole goal of this application is to use late binding and reflection to determine the "snapability" of independent binaries created by third-party vendors.

Add using statements for the System.Reflection, System.Windows.Forms, System.IO, and CommonSnappableTypes namespaces to the top of the Program.cs file. Next, add the LoadSnapin() method. This method creates the Open File dialog, prompts the user to select a file, and then sends the selected file to the LoadExternalModule() method for processing (assuming it's not the CommonSnappableTypes.dll assembly).

```
static void LoadSnapin()
{
  // Allow user to select an assembly to load.
  OpenFileDialog dlg = new OpenFileDialog
  {
    //set the initial directory to the path of this project
    InitialDirectory = Path.GetDirectoryName(Assembly.GetExecutingAssembly().Location),
    Filter = "assemblies (*.dll)|*.dll|All files (*.*)|*.*",
    FilterIndex = 1
  };
```

```
  if (dlg.ShowDialog() != DialogResult.OK)
  {
    Console.WriteLine("User cancelled out of the open file dialog.");
    return;
  }
  if (dlg.FileName.Contains("CommonSnappableTypes"))
    Console.WriteLine("CommonSnappableTypes has no snap-ins!");
  else if (!LoadExternalModule(dlg.FileName))
    Console.WriteLine("Nothing implements IAppFunctionality!");
}
```

The LoadExternalModule() method performs the following tasks:

- Dynamically loads the selected assembly into memory

- Determines whether the assembly contains any types implementing IAppFunctionality

- Creates the type using late binding

If a type implementing IAppFunctionality is found, the DoIt() method is called and then sent to the DisplayCompanyData() method to output additional information from the reflected type.

```
private static bool LoadExternalModule(string path)
{
  bool foundSnapIn = false;
  Assembly theSnapInAsm = null;

  try
  {
    // Dynamically load the selected assembly.
    theSnapInAsm = Assembly.LoadFrom(path);
  }
  catch (Exception ex)
  {
    Console.WriteLine($"An error occurred loading the snapin: {ex.Message}");
    return foundSnapIn;
  }

  // Get all IAppFunctionality compatible classes in assembly.
  var theClassTypes = from t in theSnapInAsm.GetTypes()
    where t.IsClass && (t.GetInterface("IAppFunctionality") != null)
    select t;

  // Now, create the object and call DoIt() method.
  foreach (Type t in theClassTypes)
  {
    foundSnapIn = true;
    // Use late binding to create the type.
    IAppFunctionality itfApp = (IAppFunctionality) theSnapInAsm.CreateInstance(t.FullName,
    true);
    itfApp?.DoIt();
    //lstLoadedSnapIns.Items.Add(t.FullName);
```

```
    // Show company info.
    DisplayCompanyData(t);
  }
  return foundSnapIn;
}
```

The final task is to display the metadata provided by the [CompanyInfo] attribute. Create the DisplayCompanyData() method as follows. Notice this method takes a single System.Type parameter.

```
private static void DisplayCompanyData(Type t)
{
  // Get [CompanyInfo] data.
  var compInfo = from ci in t.GetCustomAttributes(false) where (ci is CompanyInfoAttribute)
select ci;

  // Show data.
  foreach (CompanyInfoAttribute c in compInfo)
  {
    Console.WriteLine($"More info about {c.CompanyName} can be found at {c.CompanyUrl}");
  }
}
```

Finally, update the Main() method to the following (note the attribute added at the top of the method):

```
[STAThread]
static void Main(string[] args)
{
  Console.WriteLine("***** Welcome to MyTypeViewer *****");
  do
  {
    Console.WriteLine("\nWould you like to load a snapin? [Y,N]");
    // Get name of type.
    string answer = Console.ReadLine();
    // Does user want to quit?
    if (!answer.Equals("Y", StringComparison.OrdinalIgnoreCase))
    {
      break;
    }
    // Try to display type.
    try
    {
      LoadSnapin();
    }
    catch (Exception ex)
    {
      Console.WriteLine("Sorry, can't find snapin");
    }
  }
  while (true);
}
```

The STAThread attribute is required for the Open File dialog; all Windows GUI applications are single-threaded (for the user interface). This will be discussed in the following chapters. Just know for now that to use the Open File dialog, the launching process must be marked as STA.

Excellent! That wraps up the example application. I hope you can see that the topics presented in this chapter can be quite helpful in the real world and are not limited to the tool builders of the world.

■ **Source Code** You can find the ExtendableApp solution in the Chapter 15 subdirectory.

Summary

Reflection is an interesting aspect of a robust OO environment. In the world of .NET, the keys to reflection services revolve around the System.Type class and the System.Reflection namespace. As you have seen, reflection is the process of placing a type under the magnifying glass at runtime to understand the who, what, where, when, why, and how of a given item.

Late binding is the process of creating an instance of a type and invoking its members without prior knowledge of the specific names of said members. Late binding is often a direct result of *dynamic loading*, which allows you to load a .NET assembly into memory programmatically. As shown during this chapter's extendable application example, this is a powerful technique used by tool builders as well as tool consumers.

This chapter also examined the role of attribute-based programming. When you adorn your types with attributes, the result is the augmentation of the underlying assembly metadata.

CHAPTER 16

■ ■ ■

Dynamic Types and the Dynamic Language Runtime

NET 4.0 introduced a new keyword to the C# language, specifically, `dynamic`. This keyword allows you to incorporate scripting-like behaviors into the strongly typed world of type safety, semicolons, and curly brackets. Using this loose typing, you can greatly simplify some complex coding tasks and also gain the ability to interoperate with a number of dynamic languages which are .NET savvy.

In this chapter, you will be introduced to the C# `dynamic` keyword and understand how loosely typed calls are mapped to the correct in-memory object using the Dynamic Language Runtime (DLR). After you understand the services provided by the DLR, you will see examples of using dynamic types to streamline how you can perform late-bound method calls (via reflection services) and to easily communicate with legacy COM libraries.

■ **Note** Don't confuse the C# `dynamic` keyword with the concept of a *dynamic assembly* (see Chapter 18). While you could use the `dynamic` keyword when building a dynamic assembly, these are ultimately two independent concepts.

The Role of the C# dynamic Keyword

In Chapter 3, you learned about the `var` keyword, which allows you to define local variables in such a way that the underlying date type is determined at compile time, based on the initial assignment (recall that this is termed *implicit typing*). Once this initial assignment has been made, you have a strongly typed variable, and any attempt to assign an incompatible value will result in a compiler error.

To begin your investigation into the C# `dynamic` keyword, create a new Console Application project named DynamicKeyword. Now, author the following method in your `Program` class, and verify that the final code statement will indeed trigger a compile time error if uncommented:

```
static void ImplicitlyTypedVariable()
{
  // a is of type List<int>.
  var a = new List<int> {90};
  // This would be a compile-time error!
  // a = "Hello";
}
```

© Andrew Troelsen and Philip Japikse 2017
A. Troelsen and P. Japikse, *Pro C# 7*, https://doi.org/10.1007/978-1-4842-3018-3_16

Using implicit typing simply for the sake of doing so is considered by some to be bad style (if you know you need a List<int>, just declare a List<int>). However, as you saw in Chapter 12, implicit typing is useful with LINQ, as many LINQ queries return enumerations of anonymous classes (via projections) that you cannot directly declare in your C# code. However, even in such cases, the implicitly typed variable is, in fact, strongly typed.

On a related note, as you learned in Chapter 6, System.Object is the topmost parent class in the .NET Framework and can represent anything at all. Again, if you declare a variable of type object, you have a strongly typed piece of data; however, what it points to in memory can differ based on your assignment of the reference. To gain access to the members the object reference is pointing to in memory, you need to perform an explicit cast.

Assume you have a simple class named Person that defines two automatic properties (FirstName and LastName) both encapsulating a string. Now, observe the following code:

```
static void UseObjectVariable()
{
    // Assume we have a class named Person.
    object o = new Person() { FirstName = "Mike", LastName = "Larson" };

    // Must cast object as Person to gain access
    // to the Person properties.
    Console.WriteLine("Person's first name is {0}", ((Person)o).FirstName);
}
```

Since the release of .NET 4.0, the C# language introduced a keyword named dynamic. From a high level, you can consider the dynamic keyword a specialized form of System.Object, in that any value can be assigned to a dynamic data type. At first glance, this can appear horribly confusing, as it appears you now have three ways to define data whose underlying type is not directly indicated in your codebase. For example, this method:

```
static void PrintThreeStrings()
{
    var s1 = "Greetings";
    object s2 = "From";
    dynamic s3 = "Minneapolis";

    Console.WriteLine("s1 is of type: {0}", s1.GetType());
    Console.WriteLine("s2 is of type: {0}", s2.GetType());
    Console.WriteLine("s3 is of type: {0}", s3.GetType());
}
```

would print out the following if invoked from Main():

```
s1 is of type: System.String
s2 is of type: System.String
s3 is of type: System.String
```

What makes a dynamic variable much (much) different from a variable declared implicitly or via a System.Object reference is that it is *not strongly typed*. Said another way, dynamic data is not *statically typed*. As far as the C# compiler is concerned, a data point declared with the dynamic keyword can be assigned any initial value at all and can be reassigned to any new (and possibly unrelated) value during its lifetime. Consider the following method and the resulting output:

```
static void ChangeDynamicDataType()
{
  // Declare a single dynamic data point
  // named "t".
  dynamic t = "Hello!";
  Console.WriteLine("t is of type: {0}", t.GetType());

  t = false;
  Console.WriteLine("t is of type: {0}", t.GetType());

  t = new List<int>();
  Console.WriteLine("t is of type: {0}", t.GetType());
}
```

```
t is of type: System.String
t is of type: System.Boolean
t is of type: System.Collections.Generic.List`1[System.Int32]
```

At this point in your investigation, do be aware that the previous code would compile and execute identically if you were to declare the t variable as a System.Object. However, as you will soon see, the dynamic keyword offers many additional features.

Calling Members on Dynamically Declared Data

Given that a dynamic variable can take on the identity of any type on the fly (just like a variable of type System.Object), the next question on your mind might be about calling members on the dynamic variable (properties, methods, indexers, register with events, etc.). Well, syntactically speaking, it will again look no different. Just apply the dot operator to the dynamic data variable, specify a public member, and supply any arguments (if required).

However (and this is a very big "however"), the validity of the members you specify will not be checked by the compiler! Remember, unlike a variable defined as a System.Object, dynamic data is not statically typed. It is not until runtime that you will know whether the dynamic data you invoked supports a specified member, whether you passed in the correct parameters, whether you spelled the member correctly, and so on. Thus, as strange as it might seem, the following method compiles perfectly:

```
static void InvokeMembersOnDynamicData()
{
  dynamic textData1 = "Hello";
  Console.WriteLine(textData1.ToUpper());

  // You would expect compiler errors here!
  // But they compile just fine.
  Console.WriteLine(textData1.toupper());
  Console.WriteLine(textData1.Foo(10, "ee", DateTime.Now));
}
```

Notice the second call to WriteLine() attempts to call a method named toupper() on the dynamic data point (note the incorrect casing—it should be ToUpper()). As you can see, textData1 is of type string, and therefore, you know it does not have a method of this name in all lowercase letters. Furthermore, string certainly does not have a method named Foo() that takes an int, string, and DataTime object!

Nevertheless, the C# compiler is satisfied. However, if you invoke this method from within Main(), you will get runtime errors similar to the following output:

```
Unhandled Exception: Microsoft.CSharp.RuntimeBinder.RuntimeBinderException:
'string' does not contain a definition for 'toupper'
```

Another obvious distinction between calling members on dynamic data and strongly typed data is that when you apply the dot operator to a piece of dynamic data, you will *not* see the expected Visual Studio IntelliSense. The IDE will allow you to enter any member name you could dream up.

It should make sense that IntelliSense is not possible with dynamic data. However, remember that this means you need to be extremely careful when you are typing C# code on such data points. Any misspelling or incorrect capitalization of a member will throw a runtime error, specifically an instance of the RuntimeBinderException class.

The Role of the Microsoft.CSharp.dll Assembly

When you create a new Visual Studio C# project, you will automatically have a reference set to an assembly named Microsoft.CSharp.dll (you can see this for yourself by looking in the References folder of the Solution Explorer). This library is small and defines only a single namespace (Microsoft.CSharp. RuntimeBinder) with two classes (see Figure 16-1).

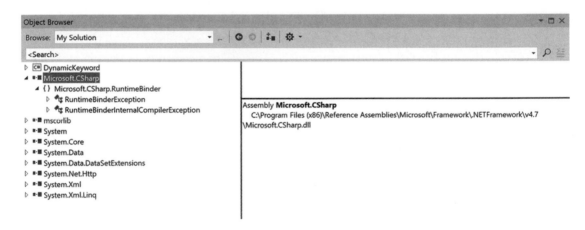

Figure 16-1. *The Microsoft.CSharp.dll assembly*

As you can tell by their names, both of these classes are strongly typed exceptions. The most common class, RuntimeBinderException, represents an error that will be thrown if you attempt to invoke a member on a dynamic data type, which does not actually exist (as in the case of the toupper() and Foo() methods). This same error will be raised if you specify the wrong parameter data to a member that does exist.

Because dynamic data is so volatile, whenever you are invoking members on a variable declared with the C# dynamic keyword, you could wrap the calls within a proper try/catch block and handle the error in a graceful manner, like so:

```
static void InvokeMembersOnDynamicData()
{
  dynamic textData1 = "Hello";

  try
  {
    Console.WriteLine(textData1.ToUpper());
    Console.WriteLine(textData1.toupper());
    Console.WriteLine(textData1.Foo(10, "ee", DateTime.Now));
  }
  catch (Microsoft.CSharp.RuntimeBinder.RuntimeBinderException ex)
  {
    Console.WriteLine(ex.Message);
  }
}
```

If you call this method again, you will find the call to ToUpper() (note the capital *T* and *U*) works correctly; however, you then find the error data displayed to the console.

```
HELLO
'string' does not contain a definition for 'toupper'
```

Of course, the process of wrapping all dynamic method invocations in a try/catch block is rather tedious. As long as you watch your spelling and parameter passing, this is not required. However, catching exceptions is handy when you might not know in advance if a member will be present on the target type.

The Scope of the dynamic Keyword

Recall that implicitly typed data (declared with the var keyword) is possible only for local variables in a member scope. The var keyword can never be used as a return value, a parameter, or a member of a class/structure. This is not the case with the dynamic keyword, however. Consider the following class definition:

```
class VeryDynamicClass
{
  // A dynamic field.
  private static dynamic myDynamicField;

  // A dynamic property.
  public dynamic DynamicProperty { get; set; }

  // A dynamic return type and a dynamic parameter type.
  public dynamic DynamicMethod(dynamic dynamicParam)
```

```
  {
    // A dynamic local variable.
    dynamic dynamicLocalVar = "Local variable";

    int myInt = 10;

    if (dynamicParam is int)
    {
      return dynamicLocalVar;
    }
    else
    {
      return myInt;
    }
  }
}
```

You could now invoke the public members as expected; however, as you are operating on dynamic methods and properties, you cannot be completely sure what the data type will be! To be sure, the VeryDynamicClass definition might not be useful in a real-world application, but it does illustrate the scope of where you can apply this C# keyword.

Limitations of the dynamic Keyword

While a great many things can be defined using the dynamic keyword, there are some limitations regarding its usage. While they are not showstoppers, do know that a dynamic data item cannot make use of lambda expressions or C# anonymous methods when calling a method. For example, the following code will always result in errors, even if the target method does indeed take a delegate parameter that takes a string value and returns void:

```
dynamic a = GetDynamicObject();

// Error! Methods on dynamic data can't use lambdas!
a.Method(arg => Console.WriteLine(arg));
```

To circumvent this restriction, you will need to work with the underlying delegate directly, using the techniques described in Chapter 10. Another limitation is that a dynamic point of data cannot understand any extension methods (see Chapter 11). Unfortunately, this would also include any of the extension methods that come from the LINQ APIs. Therefore, a variable declared with the dynamic keyword has limited use within LINQ to Objects and other LINQ technologies.

```
dynamic a = GetDynamicObject();

// Error! Dynamic data can't find the Select() extension method!
var data = from d in a select d;
```

Practical Uses of the dynamic Keyword

Given that dynamic data is not strongly typed, not checked at compile time, has no ability to trigger IntelliSense, and cannot be the target of a LINQ query, you are absolutely correct to assume that using the dynamic keyword just for the sake of doing so is a poor programming practice.

However, in a few circumstances, the dynamic keyword can radically reduce the amount of code you need to author by hand. Specifically, if you are building a .NET application that makes heavy use of late binding (via reflection), the dynamic keyword can save you typing time. As well, if you are building a .NET application that needs to communicate with legacy COM libraries (such as Microsoft Office products), you can greatly simplify your codebase via the dynamic keyword. By way of a final example, web sites built using the MVC design pattern frequently use the ViewBag type, which can also be accessed in a simplified manner using the dynamic keyword.

Like any "shortcut," you need to weigh the pros and cons. The use of the dynamic keyword is a trade-off between brevity of code and type safety. While C# is a strongly typed language at its core, you can opt in (or opt out) of dynamic behaviors on a call-by-call basis. Always remember that you never need to use the dynamic keyword. You could always get to the same end result by authoring alternative code by hand (and typically much more of it).

■ **Source Code**   You can find the DynamicKeyword project in the Chapter 16 subdirectory.

The Role of the Dynamic Language Runtime

Now that you better understand what "dynamic data" is all about, let's learn how it is processed. Since the release of .NET 4.0, the Common Language Runtime (CLR) was supplemented with a complementary runtime environment named the Dynamic Language Runtime. The concept of a "dynamic runtime" is certainly not new. In fact, many programming languages such as JavaScript, LISP, Ruby, and Python have used it for years. In a nutshell, a dynamic runtime allows a dynamic language the ability to discover types completely at runtime with no compile-time checks.

If you have a background in strongly typed languages (including C#, without dynamic types), the notion of such a runtime might seem undesirable. After all, you typically want to receive compile-time errors, not runtime errors, wherever possible. Nevertheless, dynamic languages/runtimes do provide some interesting features, including the following:

- An extremely flexible codebase. You can refactor code without making numerous changes to data types.

- A simple way to interoperate with diverse object types built in different platforms and programming languages.

- A way to add or remove members to a type, in memory, at runtime.

One role of the DLR is to enable various dynamic languages to run with the .NET runtime and give them a way to interoperate with other .NET code. These languages live in a dynamic universe, where type is discovered solely at runtime. And yet, these languages have access to the richness of the .NET base class libraries. Even better, their codebases can interoperate with C# (or vice versa), thanks to the inclusion of the dynamic keyword.

■ **Note**   This chapter will not address how the DLR can be used to integrate with dynamic languages.

The Role of Expression Trees

The DLR makes use of *expression trees* to capture the meaning of a dynamic call in neutral terms. For example, when the DLR encounters some C# code, such as the following:

```
dynamic d = GetSomeData();
d.SuperMethod(12);
```

it will automatically build an expression tree that says, in effect, "Call the method named SuperMethod on object d, passing in the number 12 as an argument." This information (formally termed the *payload*) is then passed to the correct runtime binder, which again could be the C# dynamic binder, the IronPython dynamic binder, or even (as explained shortly) legacy COM objects.

From here, the request is mapped into the required call structure for the target object. The nice thing about these expression trees (beyond that you don't need to manually create them) is that this allows you to write a fixed C# code statement and not worry about what the underlying target actually is (COM object, IronPython, IronRuby codebase, etc.). Figure 16-2 illustrates the concept of expression trees from a high level.

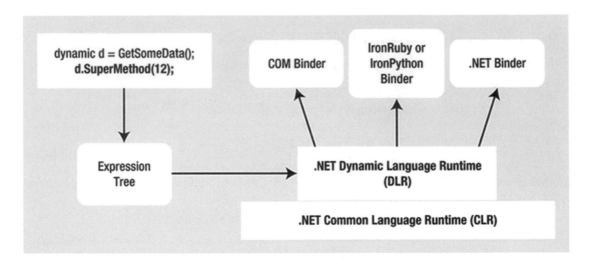

Figure 16-2. *Expression trees capture dynamic calls in neutral terms and are processed by binders*

The Role of the System.Dynamic Namespace

The System.Core.dll assembly includes a namespace named System.Dynamic. Truth be told, the chances are quite high that you will never need to use the types located here. However, if you were a language vendor who wanted to enable your dynamic languages to interact with the DLR, you could make use of the System.Dynamic namespace to build a custom runtime binder.

Again, you won't need to directly dig into the types of System.Dynamic in this book; however, feel free to check it out using the .NET Framework 4.7 SDK documentation if you are interested. For practical purposes, simply know that this namespace provides the necessary infrastructure to make a dynamic language ".NET aware."

Dynamic Runtime Lookup of Expression Trees

As explained, the DLR will pass the expression trees to a target object; however, this dispatching will be influenced by a few factors. If the dynamic data type is pointing in memory to a COM object, the expression tree is sent to a low-level COM interface named IDispatch. As you might know, this interface was COM's way of incorporating its own set of dynamic services. COM objects, however, can be used in a .NET application without the use of the DLR or C# dynamic keyword. Doing so, however (as you will see), tends to result in much more complex C# coding.

If the dynamic data is not pointing to a COM object, the expression tree may be passed to an object implementing the IDynamicObject interface. This interface is used behind the scenes to allow a language, such as IronRuby, to take a DLR expression tree and map it to Ruby specifics.

Finally, if the dynamic data is pointing to an object that is *not* a COM object and does *not* implement IDynamicObject, the object is a normal, everyday .NET object. In this case, the expression tree is dispatched to the C# runtime binder for processing. The process of mapping the expression tree to .NET specifics involves reflection services.

After the expression tree has been processed by a given binder, the dynamic data will be resolved to the real in-memory data type, after which the correct method is called with any necessary parameters. Now, let's see a few practical uses of the DLR, beginning with the simplification of late-bound .NET calls.

Simplifying Late-Bound Calls Using Dynamic Types

One instance where you might decide to use the dynamic keyword is when you are working with reflection services, specifically when making late-bound method calls. In Chapter 15, you saw a few examples of when this type of method call can be useful, most commonly when you are building some type of extensible application. At that time, you learned how to use the Activator.CreateInstance() method to create an object, for which you have no compile-time knowledge of (beyond its display name). You can then make use of the types of the System.Reflection namespace to invoke members via late binding. Recall the following example from Chapter 15:

```
static void CreateUsingLateBinding(Assembly asm)
{
  try
  {
    // Get metadata for the Minivan type.
    Type miniVan = asm.GetType("CarLibrary.MiniVan");

    // Create the Minivan on the fly.
    object obj = Activator.CreateInstance(miniVan);

    // Get info for TurboBoost.
    MethodInfo mi = miniVan.GetMethod("TurboBoost");

    // Invoke method ("null" for no parameters).
    mi.Invoke(obj, null);
  }
  catch (Exception ex)
  {
    Console.WriteLine(ex.Message);
  }
}
```

While this is code works as expected, you might agree it is a bit clunky. Here, you have to manually make use of the MethodInfo class, manually query the metadata, and so forth. The following is a version of this same method, now using the C# dynamic keyword and the DLR:

```
static void InvokeMethodWithDynamicKeyword(Assembly asm)
{
  try
  {
    // Get metadata for the Minivan type.
    Type miniVan = asm.GetType("CarLibrary.MiniVan");

    // Create the Minivan on the fly and call method!
    dynamic obj = Activator.CreateInstance(miniVan);
    obj.TurboBoost();
  }
  catch (Exception ex)
  {
    Console.WriteLine(ex.Message);
  }
}
```

By declaring the obj variable using the dynamic keyword, the heavy lifting of reflection is done on your behalf, courtesy of the DRL.

Leveraging the dynamic Keyword to Pass Arguments

The usefulness of the DLR becomes even more obvious when you need to make late-bound calls on methods that take parameters. When you use "longhand" reflection calls, arguments need to be packaged up as an array of objects, which are passed to the Invoke() method of MethodInfo.

To illustrate using a fresh example, begin by creating a new C# Console Application project named LateBindingWithDynamic. Next, add a Class Library project to the current solution (using the File ➤ Add ➤ New Project menu option) named MathLibrary (make sure LateBindingWithDynamic is still the StartUp project). Rename the initial Class1.cs file of the MathLibrary project to SimpleMath.cs, and implement the class like so:

```
public class SimpleMath
{
  public int Add(int x, int y)
  {
    return x + y;
  }
}
```

After you have compiled your MathLibrary.dll assembly, place a copy of this library in the \bin\ Debug folder of the LateBindingWithDynamic project. (If you click the Show All Files button for each project of Solution Explorer, you can simply drag and drop the file between projects.) At this point, your Solution Explorer should look something like Figure 16-3.

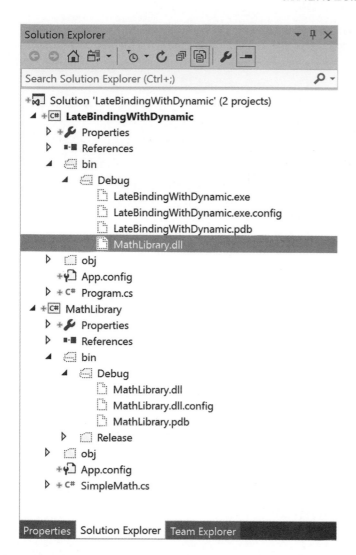

Figure 16-3. *The LateBindingWithDynamic project has a private copy of* `MathLibrary.dll`

■ **Note** Remember, the whole point of late binding is to allow an application to create an object for which it has no record in the manifest. This is why you manually copied `MathLibrary.dll` into the output folder of the C# Console Application, rather than reference the project using Visual Studio.

Now, import the System.Reflection namespace into the Program.cs file of your Console Application project. Next, add the following method to the Program class, which invokes the Add() method using typical reflection API calls:

```
private static void AddWithReflection()
{
  Assembly asm = Assembly.Load("MathLibrary");
  try
  {
    // Get metadata for the SimpleMath type.
    Type math = asm.GetType("MathLibrary.SimpleMath");

    // Create a SimpleMath on the fly.
    object obj = Activator.CreateInstance(math);

    // Get info for Add.
    MethodInfo mi = math.GetMethod("Add");

    // Invoke method (with parameters).
    object[] args = { 10, 70 };
    Console.WriteLine("Result is: {0}", mi.Invoke(obj, args));
  }
  catch (Exception ex)
  {
    Console.WriteLine(ex.Message);
  }
}
```

Now, consider the simplification of the previous logic with the dynamic keyword, via the following new method:

```
private static void AddWithDynamic()
{
  Assembly asm = Assembly.Load("MathLibrary");

  try
  {
    // Get metadata for the SimpleMath type.
    Type math = asm.GetType("MathLibrary.SimpleMath");

    // Create a SimpleMath on the fly.
    dynamic obj = Activator.CreateInstance(math);

    // Note how easily we can now call Add().
    Console.WriteLine("Result is: {0}", obj.Add(10, 70));
  }
  catch (Microsoft.CSharp.RuntimeBinder.RuntimeBinderException ex)
  {
    Console.WriteLine(ex.Message);
  }
}
```

Not too shabby! If you call both methods from the `Main()` method, you'll see identical output. However, when using the `dynamic` keyword, you saved yourself quite a bit of work. With dynamically defined data, you no longer need to manually package up arguments as an array of objects, query the assembly metadata, or other such details. If you are building an application that makes heavy use of dynamic loading/late binding, I am sure you can see how these code savings would add up over time.

■ **Source Code**   You can find the LateBindingWithDynamic solution in the Chapter 16 subdirectory.

Simplifying COM Interoperability Using Dynamic Data

Let's see another useful case for the `dynamic` keyword within the context of a COM interoperability project. Now, if you don't have much background in COM development, do be aware for this next example that a compiled COM library contains metadata, just like a .NET library; however, the format is completely different. Because of this, if a .NET program needs to communicate with a COM object, the first order of business is to generate what is known as an *interop assembly* (described in the following paragraphs). Doing so is quite straightforward. First create a new console application named ExportDataToOfficeApp, activate the Add Reference dialog box, select the COM tab, and find the COM library you want to use (see Figure 16-4).

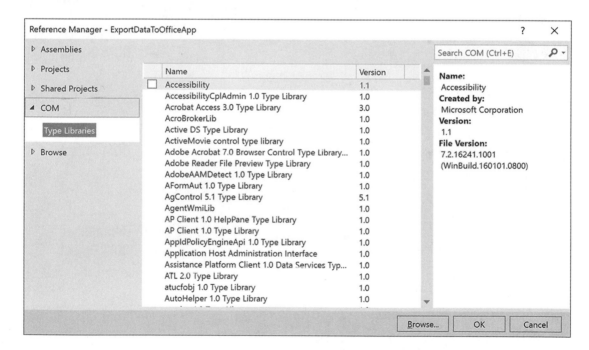

Figure 16-4. *The COM tab of the Add Reference dialog box will show you all registered COM libraries on your machine*

■ **Note**   Be aware that several important Microsoft object models (including Office products) are currently accessible only through COM interoperability. Thus, even if you do not have direct experience building COM applications, you might need to consume them from a .NET program.

Once you select a COM library, the IDE will respond by generating a new assembly that contains .NET descriptions of COM metadata. Formally speaking, these are termed *interoperability assemblies* (or simply, *interop assemblies*). Interop assemblies do not contain any implementation code, except for a small amount that helps translate COM events to .NET events. However, these interop assemblies are useful in that they shield your .NET codebase from the complex underbelly of COM internals.

In your C# code, you can directly program against the interop assembly, allowing the CLR (and if you use the dynamic keyword, the DLR) to automatically map .NET data types into COM types, and vice versa. Behind the scenes, data is marshaled between the .NET and COM applications using a Runtime Callable Wrapper (RCW), which is basically a dynamically generated proxy. This RCW proxy will marshal and transform .NET data types into COM types and map any COM return values into .NET equivalents.

Figure 16-5 shows the big picture of .NET to COM interoperability.

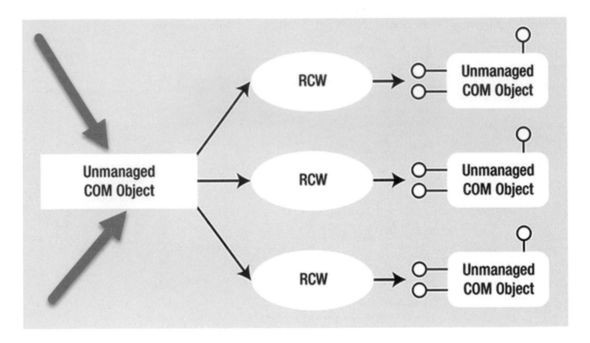

Figure 16-5. *.NET programs communicate with COM objects using a proxy termed the RCW*

The Role of Primary Interop Assemblies

Many COM libraries created by COM library vendors (such as the Microsoft COM libraries that allow access to the object model of Microsoft Office products) provide an "official" interoperability assembly termed a *primary interop assembly* (PIA). PIAs are optimized interop assemblies, which clean up (and possibly extend) the code typically generated when referencing a COM library using the Add Reference dialog box.

PIAs are typically listed in the Assemblies section of the Add Reference dialog box (under the Extensions subarea). In fact, if you reference a COM library from the COM tab of the Add Reference dialog box, Visual Studio will not generate a new interoperability library as it would normally do but would use the provided PIA instead. Figure 16-6 shows the PIA of the Microsoft Office Excel object model, which you will be using in the next example.

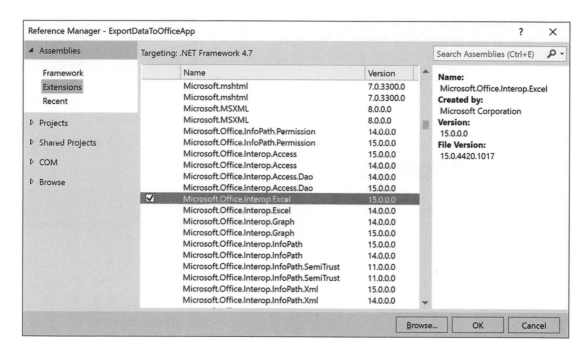

Figure 16-6. *PIAs are listed on the .NET tab of the Add Reference dialog box*

■ **Note**   If you did not install the Visual Studio Tools For Office (VSTO) individual component or "Office/SharePoint development" workload, you will need to do so to complete this section. You can rerun the installer to select the missing component, or you can use the Visual Studio Quick Launch (Ctrl+Q). Type **Visual Studio Tools for Office** in the Quick Launch, and select the Install option.

Embedding Interop Metadata

Before the release of .NET 4.0, when a C# application made use of a COM library (PIA or not), you needed to ensure the client machine had a copy of the interop assembly on their computer. Not only did this increase the size of your application installer package, but the install script had to check that the PIA assemblies were indeed present and, if not, install a copy to the GAC.

However, with .NET 4.0 and higher, you can now elect to embed the interoperability data directly within your compiled .NET application. When you do so, you are no longer required to ship a copy of the interoperability assembly along with your .NET application, as the necessary interoperability metadata is hard-coded in the .NET program.

By default, when you select a COM library (PIA or not) using the Add References dialog, the IDE will automatically set the Embed Interop Types property of the library to True. You can see this setting first hand by selecting a referenced interop library in the References folder of Solution Explorer and then investigating the Properties window (see Figure 16-7).

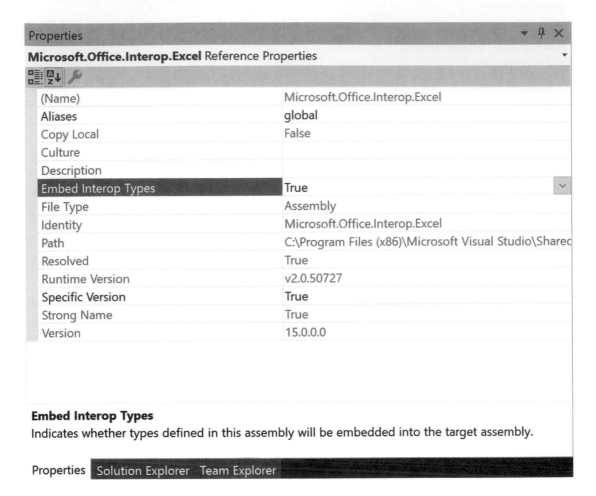

Figure 16-7. *Interop assembly logic can be embedded directly into your .NET application*

The C# compiler will include only the parts of the interop library you are actually using. Thus, if the real interop library has .NET descriptions of hundreds of COM objects, you will bring in only the definitions of the subset you are really using in your C# code. Beyond reducing the size of the application you need to ship to the client, you also have an easier installation path, as you don't need to install any missing PIAs on the target machine.

Common COM Interop Pain Points

Let's cover one more preliminary topic before the next example. Before the release of the DLR, when you authored C# code that used a COM library (via the interop assembly), you were sure to face a number of challenges. For example, many COM libraries defined methods that took optional arguments, which were not supported in C# until .NET 3.5. This required you to specify the value Type.Missing for every occurrence of the optional argument. For example, if a COM method took five arguments, all of which were optional, you would need to write the following C# code in order to accept the default values:

```
myComObj.SomeMethod(Type.Missing, Type.Missing, Type.Missing, Type.Missing, Type.Missing);
```

Thankfully, you are now able to author the following simplified code, given that the Type.Missing values will be inserted at compile time if you don't specify a specific value:

```
myComObj.SomeMethod();
```

On a related note, many COM methods provided support for named arguments, which, as you recall from Chapter 4, allows you to pass values to members in any order you require. Given that C# supports this same feature, it is simply to "skip" over a set of optional arguments you don't care about and set only the few you do.

Another common COM interop pain point has to do with the fact that many COM methods were designed to take and return a particular data type, termed the Variant. Much like the C# dynamic keyword, a Variant data type could be assigned to any type of COM data on the fly (strings, interface references, numerical values, etc.). Before you had the dynamic keyword, passing or receiving Variant data points required some hoop jumping, typically by way of numerous casting operations.

When you set the Embed Interop Types property to True, all COM Variant types are automatically mapped to dynamic data. This will not only reduce the need to extraneous casting operations when working with underlying COM Variant data types but will also further hide some COM complexities, such as working with COM indexers.

To showcase how C# optional arguments, named arguments, and the dynamic keyword all work together to simplify COM interop, you will now build an application that uses the Microsoft Office object model. As you work through the example, you will get a chance to use the new features, as well as forgo them, and then compare and contrast the workload.

COM Interop Using C# Dynamic Data

Now, back to creating the application. Add a new class name Car.cs that contains the following code:

```
namespace ExportDataToOfficeApp
{
  public class Car
  {
    public string Make { get; set; }
    public string Color { get; set; }
    public string PetName { get; set; }
  }
}
```

Next, create a list of Car records in the Main() method of Program.cs, as follows:

```
List<Car> carsInStock = new List<Car>
{
  new Car {Color="Green", Make="VW", PetName="Mary"},
  new Car {Color="Red", Make="Saab", PetName="Mel"},
  new Car {Color="Black", Make="Ford", PetName="Hank"},
  new Car {Color="Yellow", Make="BMW", PetName="Davie"}
};
```

Add the following namespace alias to the form's primary code file. Be aware that this is not mandatory to define an alias when interacting with COM libraries. However, by doing so, you have a handy qualifier for all the imported COM objects, which is handy if some of these COM objects have names that would clash with your .NET types.

```
// Create an alias to the Excel object model.
using Excel = Microsoft.Office.Interop.Excel;
```

Because you imported the COM library using Visual Studio, the PIA has been automatically configured so that the used metadata will be embedded into the .NET application (recall the role of the Embed Interop Types property). Therefore, all COM Variant data types are realized as dynamic data types. Furthermore, you can use C# optional arguments and named arguments. This being said, consider the following implementation of ExportToExcel():

```
static void ExportToExcel(List<Car> carsInStock)
{
  // Load up Excel, then make a new empty workbook.
  Excel.Application excelApp = new Excel.Application();
  excelApp.Workbooks.Add();

  // This example uses a single workSheet.
  Excel._Worksheet workSheet = excelApp.ActiveSheet;

  // Establish column headings in cells.
  workSheet.Cells[1, "A"] = "Make";
  workSheet.Cells[1, "B"] = "Color";
  workSheet.Cells[1, "C"] = "Pet Name";

  // Now, map all data in List<Car> to the cells of the spreadsheet.
  int row = 1;
  foreach (Car c in carsInStock)
  {
    row++;
    workSheet.Cells[row, "A"] = c.Make;
    workSheet.Cells[row, "B"] = c.Color;
    workSheet.Cells[row, "C"] = c.PetName;
  }

  // Give our table data a nice look and feel.
  workSheet.Range["A1"].AutoFormat(Excel.XlRangeAutoFormat.xlRangeAutoFormatClassic2);

  // Save the file, quit Excel, and display message to user.
  workSheet.SaveAs($@"{Environment.CurrentDirectory}\Inventory.xlsx");
  excelApp.Quit();
  Console.WriteLine("The Inventory.xslx file has been saved to your app folder");
}
```

This method begins by loading Excel into memory; however, you won't see it visible on your computer desktop. For this application, you are interested only in using the internal Excel object model. However, if you do want to actually display the UI of Excel, update your method with this additional line of code:

```
static void ExportToExcel(List<Car> carsInStock)
{
  // Load up Excel, then make a new empty workbook.
  Excel.Application excelApp = new Excel.Application();

  // Go ahead and make Excel visible on the computer.
  excelApp.Visible = true;
...
}
```

After you create an empty worksheet, you add three columns that are named similar to the properties of the Car class. Then, you fill the cells with the data of the List<Car> and save your file under the (hard-coded) name Inventory.xlsx.

At this point, if you run your application, add a few new records, and export your data to Excel, you will then be able to open the Inventory.xlsx file, which will be saved to the \bin\Debug folder of your Windows Forms application. Figure 16-8 shows a possible export.

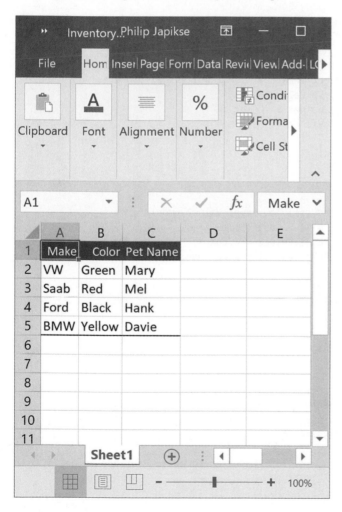

Figure 16-8. *Exporting your data to an Excel file*

COM interop Without C# Dynamic Data

Now, if you were to select the `Microsoft.Office.Interop.Excel.dll` assembly (in Solution Explorer) and set its Embed Interop Type property to False, you would have new compiler errors, as the COM `Variant` data is no longer realized as dynamic data but as `System.Object` variables. This will require you to update `ExportToExcel()` with a number of explicit casting operations.

As well, if this project were compiled under .NET 3.5 or earlier, you would no longer have the benefit of optional/named parameters and would have to explicitly mark all missing arguments. Here is a version of the `ExportToExcel()` method that would be required in earlier versions of C# (do note the increased complexity in code):

```
static void ExportToExcelManual(List<Car> carsInStock)
{
  Excel.Application excelApp = new Excel.Application();

  // Must mark missing params!
  excelApp.Workbooks.Add(Type.Missing);

  // Must cast Object as _Worksheet!
  Excel._Worksheet workSheet = (Excel._Worksheet)excelApp.ActiveSheet;

  // Must cast each Object as Range object then call low-level Value2 property!
  ((Excel.Range)excelApp.Cells[1, "A"]).Value2 = "Make";
  ((Excel.Range)excelApp.Cells[1, "B"]).Value2 = "Color";
  ((Excel.Range)excelApp.Cells[1, "C"]).Value2 = "Pet Name";

  int row = 1;
  foreach (Car c in carsInStock)
  {
    row++;
    // Must cast each Object as Range and call low-level Value2 prop!
    ((Excel.Range)workSheet.Cells[row, "A"]).Value2 = c.Make;
    ((Excel.Range)workSheet.Cells[row, "B"]).Value2 = c.Color;
    ((Excel.Range)workSheet.Cells[row, "C"]).Value2 = c.PetName;
  }

  // Must call get_Range method and then specify all missing args!
  excelApp.get_Range("A1", Type.Missing).AutoFormat(
    Excel.XlRangeAutoFormat.xlRangeAutoFormatClassic2,
    Type.Missing, Type.Missing, Type.Missing,
    Type.Missing, Type.Missing, Type.Missing);

  // Must specify all missing optional args!
  workSheet.SaveAs($@"{Environment.CurrentDirectory}\InventoryManual.xlsx",
    Type.Missing, Type.Missing, Type.Missing, Type.Missing, Type.Missing, Type.Missing,
    Type.Missing, Type.Missing, Type.Missing);
  excelApp.Quit();
  Console.WriteLine("The InventoryManual.xslx file has been saved to your app folder");
}
```

Although the end result of running this program is identical, this version of the method is much more verbose, as I am sure you agree. That wraps up your look at the C# dynamic keyword and the DLR. I hope you can see how these features can simplify complex programming tasks and (perhaps more importantly) understand the trade-offs. When you opt into dynamic data, you do lose a good amount of type safety, and your codebase is prone to many more runtime errors.

While there is certainly more to say about the DLR, this chapter has tried to focus on topics that are practical and useful in your day-to-day programming. If you want to learn more about advanced features of the Dynamic Language Runtime, such as integrating with scripting languages, be sure to consult the .NET Framework 4.7 SDK documentation (look up the topic "Dynamic Language Runtime Overview" to get started).

■ **Source Code**   You can find the ExportDataToOfficeApp project in the Chapter 16 subdirectory.

Summary

The dynamic keyword introduced in C# 4.0 allows you to define data whose true identity is not known until runtime. When processed by the new Dynamic Language Runtime, the automatically created "expression tree" will be passed to the correct dynamic language binder, where the payload will be unpackaged and sent to the correct object member.

Using dynamic data and the DLR, a number of complex C# programming tasks can be radically simplified, especially the act of incorporating COM libraries into your .NET applications. As you saw in this chapter, .NET 4.0 and higher provides a number of further simplifications to COM interop (which have nothing to do with dynamic data), such as embedding COM interop data into your applications, optional arguments, and named arguments.

While these features can certainly simplify your code, always remember that dynamic data makes your C# code much less type-safe and open to runtime errors. Be sure you weigh the pros and cons of using dynamic data in your C# projects, and test accordingly!

CHAPTER 17

■ ■ ■

Processes, AppDomains, and Object Contexts

In Chapters 14 and 15, you examined the steps taken by the CLR to resolve the location of a referenced external assembly, as well as the role of .NET metadata. In this chapter, you'll drill deeper into the details of how an assembly is hosted by the CLR and come to understand the relationship between processes, application domains, and object contexts.

In a nutshell, *application domains* (or simply *AppDomains*) are logical subdivisions within a given process that host a set of related .NET assemblies. As you will see, an AppDomain is further subdivided into *contextual boundaries*, which are used to group like-minded .NET objects. Using the notion of context, the CLR is able to ensure that objects with special runtime requirements are handled appropriately.

While it is true that many of your day-to-day programming tasks might not involve directly working with processes, AppDomains, or object contexts, understanding these topics is important when working with numerous .NET APIs, including Windows Communication Foundation (WCF), multithreading and parallel processing, and object serialization.

The Role of a Windows Process

The concept of a "process" existed within Windows-based operating systems well before the release of the .NET platform. In simple terms, a *process* is a running program. However, formally speaking, a process is an operating system–level concept used to describe a set of resources (such as external code libraries and the primary thread) and the necessary memory allocations used by a running application. For each *.exe loaded into memory, the OS creates a separate and isolated process for use during its lifetime.

Using this approach to application isolation, the result is a much more robust and stable runtime environment, given that the failure of one process does not affect the functioning of another. Furthermore, data in one process cannot be directly accessed by another process, unless you make use of a distributed computing programming API such as Windows Communication Foundation. Given these points, you can regard the process as a fixed, safe boundary for a running application.

Now, every Windows process is assigned a unique process identifier (PID) and may be independently loaded and unloaded by the OS as necessary (as well as programmatically). As you might be aware, the Processes tab of the Windows Task Manager utility (activated via the Ctrl+Shift+Esc keystroke combination) allows you to view various statistics regarding the processes running on a given machine. The Details tab allows you to view the assigned PID and image name (see Figure 17-1).

© Andrew Troelsen and Philip Japikse 2017
A. Troelsen and P. Japikse, *Pro C# 7*, https://doi.org/10.1007/978-1-4842-3018-3_17

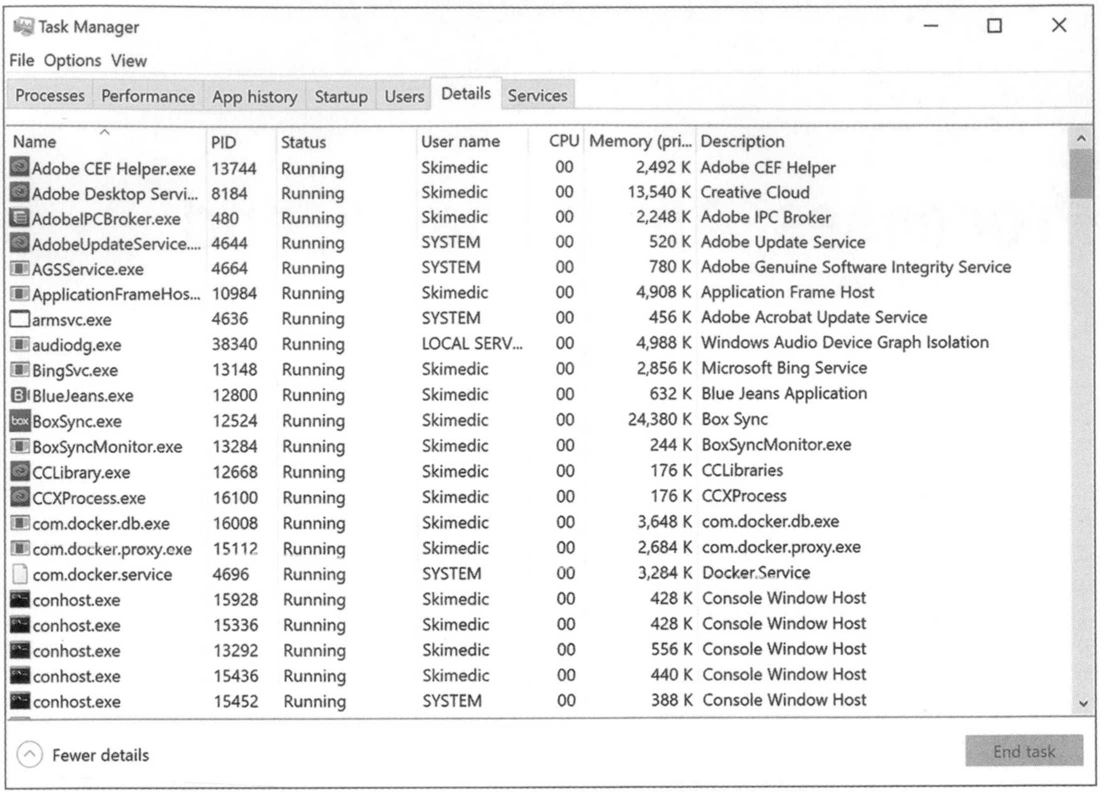

Figure 17-1. *The Windows Task Manager*

The Role of Threads

Every Windows process contains an initial "thread" that functions as the entry point for the application. Chapter 19 examines the details of building multithreaded applications under the .NET platform; however, to facilitate the topics presented here, you need a few working definitions. First, a *thread* is a path of execution within a process. Formally speaking, the first thread created by a process's entry point is termed the *primary thread*. Any .NET executable program (console application, Windows service, WPF application, etc.) marks its entry point with the Main() method. When this method is invoked, the primary thread is created automatically.

Processes that contain a single primary thread of execution are intrinsically *thread-safe*, given the fact that there is only one thread that can access the data in the application at a given time. However, a single-threaded process (especially one that is GUI-based) will often appear a bit unresponsive to the user if this single thread is performing a complex operation (such as printing out a lengthy text file, performing a mathematically intensive calculation, or attempting to connect to a remote server located thousands of miles away).

Given this potential drawback of single-threaded applications, the Windows API (as well as the .NET platform) makes it possible for the primary thread to spawn additional secondary threads (also termed *worker threads*) using a handful of Windows API functions such as CreateThread(). Each thread (primary or secondary) becomes a unique path of execution in the process and has concurrent access to all shared points of data within the process.

As you might have guessed, developers typically create additional threads to help improve the program's overall responsiveness. Multithreaded processes provide the illusion that numerous activities are happening at more or less the same time. For example, an application may spawn a worker thread to perform a labor-intensive unit of work (again, such as printing a large text file). As this secondary thread is churning away, the main thread is still responsive to user input, which gives the entire process the potential of delivering greater performance. However, this may not actually be the case: using too many threads in a single process can actually *degrade* performance, as the CPU must switch between the active threads in the process (which takes time).

On some machines, multithreading is most commonly an illusion provided by the OS. Machines that host a single (non-hyperthreaded) CPU do not have the ability to literally handle multiple threads at the same time. Rather, a single CPU will execute one thread for a unit of time (called a *time slice*) based in part on the thread's priority level. When a thread's time slice is up, the existing thread is suspended to allow another thread to perform its business. For a thread to remember what was happening before it was kicked out of the way, each thread is given the ability to write to Thread Local Storage (TLS) and is provided with a separate call stack, as illustrated in Figure 17-2.

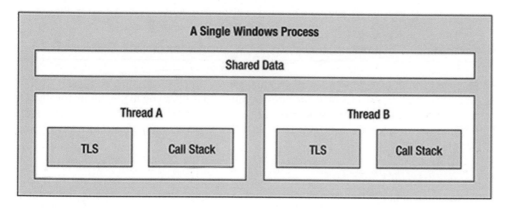

Figure 17-2. *The Windows process/thread relationship*

If the subject of threads is new to you, don't sweat the details. At this point, just remember that a thread is a unique path of execution within a Windows process. Every process has a primary thread (created via the executable's entry point) and may contain additional threads that have been programmatically created.

Interacting with Processes Under the .NET Platform

Although processes and threads are nothing new, the manner in which you interact with these primitives under the .NET platform has changed quite a bit (for the better). To pave the way to understanding the world of building multithreaded assemblies (see Chapter 19), let's begin by checking out how to interact with processes using the .NET base class libraries.

The System.Diagnostics namespace defines a number of types that allow you to programmatically interact with processes and various diagnostic-related types such as the system event log and performance counters. In this chapter, you are concerned with only the process-centric types defined in Table 17-1.

Table 17-1. *Select Members of the* System.Diagnostics *Namespace*

Process-Centric Types of the System.Diagnostics Namespace	Meaning in Life
Process	The Process class provides access to local and remote processes and also allows you to programmatically start and stop processes.
ProcessModule	This type represents a module (*.dll or *.exe) that is loaded into a particular process. Understand that the ProcessModule type can represent *any* module—COM-based, .NET-based, or traditional C-based binaries.
ProcessModuleCollection	This provides a strongly typed collection of ProcessModule objects.
ProcessStartInfo	This specifies a set of values used when starting a process via the Process.Start() method.
ProcessThread	This type represents a thread within a given process. Be aware that ProcessThread is a type used to diagnose a process's thread set and is not used to spawn new threads of execution within a process.
ProcessThreadCollection	This provides a strongly typed collection of ProcessThread objects.

The System.Diagnostics.Process class allows you to analyze the processes running on a given machine (local or remote). The Process class also provides members that allow you to programmatically start and terminate processes, view (or modify) a process's priority level, and obtain a list of active threads and/or loaded modules within a given process. Table 17-2 lists some of the key properties of System.Diagnostics.Process.

Table 17-2. *Select Properties of the Process Type*

Property	Meaning in Life
ExitTime	This property gets the timestamp associated with the process that has terminated (represented with a DateTime type).
Handle	This property returns the handle (represented by an IntPtr) associated to the process by the OS. This can be useful when building .NET applications that need to communicate with unmanaged code.
Id	This property gets the PID for the associated process.
MachineName	This property gets the name of the computer the associated process is running on.
MainWindowTitle	MainWindowTitle gets the caption of the main window of the process (if the process does not have a main window, you receive an empty string).
Modules	This property provides access to the strongly typed ProcessModuleCollection type, which represents the set of modules (*.dll or *.exe) loaded within the current process.
ProcessName	This property gets the name of the process (which, as you would assume, is the name of the application itself).
Responding	This property gets a value indicating whether the user interface of the process is responding to user input (or is currently "hung").
StartTime	This property gets the time that the associated process was started (via a DateTime type).
Threads	This property gets the set of threads that are running in the associated process (represented via a collection of ProcessThread objects).

In addition to the properties just examined, `System.Diagnostics.Process` also defines a few useful methods (see Table 17-3).

Table 17-3. *Select Methods of the Process Type*

Method	Meaning in Life
CloseMainWindow()	This method closes a process that has a user interface by sending a close message to its main window.
GetCurrentProcess()	This static method returns a new Process object that represents the currently active process.
GetProcesses()	This static method returns an array of new Process objects running on a given machine.
Kill()	This method immediately stops the associated process.
Start()	This method starts a process.

Enumerating Running Processes

To illustrate the process of manipulating Process objects (pardon the redundancy), create a C# Console Application project named ProcessManipulator that defines the following static helper method within the Program class (be sure you import the System.Diagnostics namespace in your code file):

```
static void ListAllRunningProcesses()
{
  // Get all the processes on the local machine, ordered by
  // PID.
  var runningProcs = from proc in Process.GetProcesses(".") orderby proc.Id select proc;

  // Print out PID and name of each process.
  foreach(var p in runningProcs)
  {
    string info = $"-> PID: {p.Id}\tName: {p.ProcessName}",
    Console.WriteLine(info);
  }
  Console.WriteLine("***********************************\n");
}
```

The static `Process.GetProcesses()` method returns an array of Process objects that represent the running processes on the target machine (the dot notation shown here represents the local computer). After you have obtained the array of Process objects, you are able to invoke any of the members listed in Tables 17-2 and 17-3. Here, you are simply displaying the PID and the name of each process, ordered by PID. Assuming the Main() method has been updated to call ListAllRunningProcesses() as follows:

```
static void Main(string[] args)
{
  Console.WriteLine("***** Fun with Processes *****\n");
  ListAllRunningProcesses();
  Console.ReadLine();
}
```

you will see the names and PIDs for all processes on your local computer. Here is some partial output from my current machine (your output will most likely be different):

```
***** Fun with Processes *****

-> PID: 0       Name: Idle
-> PID: 4       Name: System
-> PID: 108     Name: iexplore
-> PID: 268     Name: smss
-> PID: 432     Name: csrss
-> PID: 448     Name: svchost
-> PID: 472     Name: wininit
-> PID: 504     Name: csrss
-> PID: 536     Name: winlogon
-> PID: 560     Name: services
-> PID: 584     Name: lsass
-> PID: 592     Name: lsm
-> PID: 660     Name: devenv
-> PID: 684     Name: svchost
-> PID: 760     Name: svchost
-> PID: 832     Name: svchost
-> PID: 844     Name: svchost
-> PID: 856     Name: svchost
-> PID: 900     Name: svchost
-> PID: 924     Name: svchost
-> PID: 956     Name: VMwareService
-> PID: 1116    Name: spoolsv
-> PID: 1136    Name: ProcessManipulator.vshost
************************************
```

Investigating a Specific Process

In addition to obtaining a complete list of all running processes on a given machine, the static `Process.GetProcessById()` method allows you to obtain a single `Process` object via the associated PID. If you request access to a nonexistent PID, an `ArgumentException` exception is thrown. For example, if you were interested in obtaining a `Process` object representing a process with the PID of 987, you could write the following code:

```
// If there is no process with the PID of 987, a runtime exception will be thrown.
static void GetSpecificProcess()
{
  Process theProc = null;
  try
  {
    theProc = Process.GetProcessById(987);
  }
  catch(ArgumentException ex)
  {
    Console.WriteLine(ex.Message);
  }
}
```

At this point, you have learned how to get a list of all processes, as well as a specific process on a machine via a PID lookup. While it is somewhat useful to discover PIDs and process names, the Process class also allows you to discover the set of current threads and libraries used within a given process. Let's see how to do so.

Investigating a Process's Thread Set

The set of threads is represented by the strongly typed ProcessThreadCollection collection, which contains some number of individual ProcessThread objects. To illustrate, assume the following additional static helper function has been added to your current application:

```
static void EnumThreadsForPid(int pID)
{
  Process theProc = null;
  try
  {
    theProc = Process.GetProcessById(pID);
  }
  catch(ArgumentException ex)
  {
    Console.WriteLine(ex.Message);
    return;
  }

  // List out stats for each thread in the specified process.
  Console.WriteLine("Here are the threads used by: {0}", theProc.ProcessName);
  ProcessThreadCollection theThreads = theProc.Threads;

  foreach(ProcessThread pt in theThreads)
  {
    string info =
        $"-> Thread ID: {pt.Id}\tStart Time: {pt.StartTime.ToShortTimeString()}\tPriority:
{pt.PriorityLevel}";
    Console.WriteLine(info);
  }
  Console.WriteLine("***********************************\n");
}
```

As you can see, the Threads property of the System.Diagnostics.Process type provides access to the ProcessThreadCollection class. Here, you are printing the assigned thread ID, start time, and priority level of each thread in the process specified by the client. Now, update your program's Main() method to prompt the user for a PID to investigate, as follows:

```
static void Main(string[] args)
{
...
  // Prompt user for a PID and print out the set of active threads.
  Console.WriteLine("***** Enter PID of process to investigate *****");
  Console.Write("PID: ");
  string pID = Console.ReadLine();
  int theProcID = int.Parse(pID);
```

```
  EnumThreadsForPid(theProcID);
  Console.ReadLine();
}
```

When you run your program, you can now enter the PID of any process on your machine and see the threads used in the process. The following output shows the threads used by PID 22952 on my machine, which happens to be hosting Firefox:

```
***** Enter PID of process to investigate *****
PID: 22952
Here are the threads used by: firefox
-> Thread ID: 680      Start Time: 9:05 AM      Priority: Normal
-> Thread ID: 2040     Start Time: 9:05 AM      Priority: Normal
-> Thread ID: 880      Start Time: 9:05 AM      Priority: Normal
-> Thread ID: 3380     Start Time: 9:05 AM      Priority: Normal
-> Thread ID: 3376     Start Time: 9:05 AM      Priority: Normal
-> Thread ID: 3448     Start Time: 9:05 AM      Priority: Normal
-> Thread ID: 3476     Start Time: 9:05 AM      Priority: Normal
-> Thread ID: 2264     Start Time: 9:05 AM      Priority: Normal
-> Thread ID: 2380     Start Time: 9:05 AM      Priority: Normal
-> Thread ID: 2384     Start Time: 9:05 AM      Priority: Normal
-> Thread ID: 2308     Start Time: 9:05 AM      Priority: Normal
-> Thread ID: 3096     Start Time: 9:07 AM      Priority: Highest
-> Thread ID: 3600     Start Time: 9:45 AM      Priority: Normal
-> Thread ID: 1412     Start Time: 10:02 AM     Priority: Normal
```

The ProcessThread type has additional members of interest beyond Id, StartTime, and PriorityLevel. Table 17-4 documents some members of interest.

Table 17-4. *Select Members of the ProcessThread Type*

Member	Meaning in Life
CurrentPriority	Gets the current priority of the thread
Id	Gets the unique identifier of the thread
IdealProcessor	Sets the preferred processor for this thread to run on
PriorityLevel	Gets or sets the priority level of the thread
ProcessorAffinity	Sets the processors on which the associated thread can run
StartAddress	Gets the memory address of the function that the operating system called that started this thread
StartTime	Gets the time that the operating system started the thread
ThreadState	Gets the current state of this thread
TotalProcessorTime	Gets the total amount of time that this thread has spent using the processor
WaitReason	Gets the reason that the thread is waiting

Before you read any further, be aware that the ProcessThread type is *not* the entity used to create, suspend, or kill threads under the .NET platform. Rather, ProcessThread is a vehicle used to obtain diagnostic information for the active Windows threads within a running process. Again, you will investigate how to build multithreaded applications using the System.Threading namespace in Chapter 19.

Investigating a Process's Module Set

Next up, let's check out how to iterate over the number of loaded modules that are hosted within a given process. When talking about processes, a *module* is a general term used to describe a given *.dll (or the *.exe itself) that is hosted by a specific process. When you access the ProcessModuleCollection via the Process.Modules property, you are able to enumerate over *all modules* hosted within a process: .NET-based, COM-based, or traditional C-based libraries. Ponder the following additional helper function that will enumerate the modules in a specific process based on the PID:

```
static void EnumModsForPid(int pID)
{
  Process theProc = null;
  try
  {
    theProc = Process.GetProcessById(pID);
  }
  catch(ArgumentException ex)
  {
    Console.WriteLine(ex.Message);
    return;
  }

  Console.WriteLine("Here are the loaded modules for: {0}", theProc.ProcessName);
  ProcessModuleCollection theMods = theProc.Modules;
  foreach(ProcessModule pm in theMods)
  {
    string info = $"-> Mod Name: {pm.ModuleName}";
    Console.WriteLine(info);
  }
  Console.WriteLine("************************************\n");
}
```

To see some possible output, let's check out the loaded modules for the process hosting the current example program (ProcessManipulator). To do so, run the application, identify the PID assigned to ProcessManipulator.exe (via the Task Manager), and pass this value to the EnumModsForPid() method (be sure to update your Main() method accordingly). Once you do, you might be surprised to see the list of

*.dlls used for a simple Console Application project (GDI32.dll, USER32.dll, ole32.dll, and so forth). Consider the following output:

```
Here are the loaded modules for: ProcessManipulator
-> Mod Name: ProcessManipulator.exe
-> Mod Name: ntdll.dll
-> Mod Name: MSCOREE.DLL
-> Mod Name: KERNEL32.dll
-> Mod Name: KERNELBASE.dll
-> Mod Name: ADVAPI32.dll
-> Mod Name: msvcrt.dll
-> Mod Name: sechost.dll
-> Mod Name: RPCRT4.dll
-> Mod Name: SspiCli.dll
-> Mod Name: CRYPTBASE.dll
-> Mod Name: mscoreei.dll
-> Mod Name: SHLWAPI.dll
-> Mod Name: GDI32.dll
-> Mod Name: USER32.dll
-> Mod Name: LPK.dll
-> Mod Name: USP10.dll
-> Mod Name: IMM32.DLL
-> Mod Name: MSCTF.dll
-> Mod Name: clr.dll
-> Mod Name: MSVCR100_CLR0400.dll
-> Mod Name: mscorlib.ni.dll
-> Mod Name: nlssorting.dll
-> Mod Name: ole32.dll
-> Mod Name: clrjit.dll
-> Mod Name: System.ni.dll
-> Mod Name: System.Core.ni.dll
-> Mod Name: psapi.dll
-> Mod Name: shfolder.dll
-> Mod Name: SHELL32.dll
************************************
```

Starting and Stopping Processes Programmatically

The final aspects of the System.Diagnostics.Process class examined here are the Start() and Kill() methods. As you can gather by their names, these members provide a way to programmatically launch and terminate a process, respectively. For example, consider the following static StartAndKillProcess() helper method:

■ **Note** You must be running Visual Studio with Administrator rights to start new processes. If this is not the case, you will receive a runtime error.

```
static void StartAndKillProcess()
{
  Process ffProc = null;

  // Launch Firefox, and go to Facebook!
  try
  {
    ffProc = Process.Start("FireFox.exe", "www.facebook.com");
  }
  catch (InvalidOperationException ex)
  {
    Console.WriteLine(ex.Message);
  }

  Console.Write("--> Hit enter to kill {0}...", ffProc.ProcessName);
  Console.ReadLine();

  // Kill the iexplore.exe process.
  try
  {
    ffProc.Kill();
  }
  catch (InvalidOperationException ex)
  {
    Console.WriteLine(ex.Message);
  }
}
```

The static `Process.Start()` method has been overloaded a few times. At a minimum, you will need to specify the friendly name of the process you want to launch (such as Microsoft Internet Explorer, `iexplore.exe`). This example uses a variation of the `Start()` method that allows you to specify any additional arguments to pass into the program's entry point (i.e., the `Main()` method).

After you call the `Start()` method, you are returned a reference to the newly activated process. When you want to terminate the process, simply call the instance-level `Kill()` method. Here, you are wrapping the calls to `Start()` and `Kill()` within a `try/catch` block and handling any `InvalidOperationException` errors. This is especially important when calling the `Kill()` method, as this error will be raised if the process has already been terminated prior to calling `Kill()`.

Controlling Process Startup Using the ProcessStartInfo Class

The `Start()` method also allows you to pass in a `System.Diagnostics.ProcessStartInfo` type to specify additional bits of information regarding how a given process should come to life. Here is a partial definition of `ProcessStartInfo` (see the .NET Framework 4.5 SDK documentation for full details):

```
public sealed class ProcessStartInfo : object
{
  public ProcessStartInfo();
  public ProcessStartInfo(string fileName);
  public ProcessStartInfo(string fileName, string arguments);
  public string Arguments { get; set; }
  public bool CreateNoWindow { get; set; }
```

```
  public StringDictionary EnvironmentVariables { get; }
  public bool ErrorDialog { get; set; }
  public IntPtr ErrorDialogParentHandle { get; set; }
  public string FileName { get; set; }
  public bool LoadUserProfile { get; set; }
  public SecureString Password { get; set; }
  public bool RedirectStandardError { get; set; }
  public bool RedirectStandardInput { get; set; }
  public bool RedirectStandardOutput { get; set; }
  public Encoding StandardErrorEncoding { get; set; }
  public Encoding StandardOutputEncoding { get; set; }
  public bool UseShellExecute { get; set; }
  public string Verb { get; set; }
  public string[] Verbs { get; }
  public ProcessWindowStyle WindowStyle { get; set; }
  public string WorkingDirectory { get; set; }
}
```

To illustrate how to fine-tune your process startup, here is a modified version of StartAndKillProcess(), which will load Firefox, navigate to www.facebook.com, and show the window in a maximized state:

```
static void StartAndKillProcess()
{
  Process ffProc = null;

  // Launch Firefox, and go to Facebook, with maximized window.
  try
  {
    ProcessStartInfo startInfo = new
      ProcessStartInfo("FireFox.exe", "www.facebook.com");
    startInfo.WindowStyle = ProcessWindowStyle.Maximized;

    ffProc = Process.Start(startInfo);
  }
  catch (InvalidOperationException ex)
  {
    Console.WriteLine(ex.Message);
  }
...
}
```

Great! Now that you understand the role of Windows processes and how to interact with them from C# code, you are ready to investigate the concept of a .NET application domain.

■ **Source Code**   You can find the ProcessManipulator project in the Chapter 17 subdirectory.

Understanding .NET Application Domains

Under the .NET platform, executables are not hosted directly within a Windows process, as is the case in traditional unmanaged applications. Rather, a .NET executable is hosted by a logical partition within a process called an *application domain*. As you will see, a single process may contain multiple application domains, each of which is hosting a .NET executable. This additional subdivision of a traditional Windows process offers several benefits, some of which are as follows:

- AppDomains are a key aspect of the OS-neutral nature of the .NET platform, given that this logical division abstracts away the differences in how an underlying OS represents a loaded executable.

- AppDomains are far less expensive in terms of processing power and memory than a full-blown process. Thus, the CLR is able to load and unload application domains much quicker than a formal process and can drastically improve scalability of server applications.

- AppDomains provide a deeper level of isolation for hosting a loaded application. If one AppDomain within a process fails, the remaining AppDomains remain functional.

As mentioned, a single process can host any number of AppDomains, each of which is fully and completely isolated from other AppDomains within this process (or any other process). Given this fact, be aware that an application running in one AppDomain is unable to obtain data of any kind (global variables or static fields) within another AppDomain, unless they use a distributed programming protocol (such as Windows Communication Foundation).

While a single process *may* host multiple AppDomains, this is not typically the case. At the least, an OS process will host what is termed the *default application domain*. This specific application domain is automatically created by the CLR at the time the process launches. After this point, the CLR creates additional application domains on an as-needed basis.

The System.AppDomain Class

The .NET platform allows you to programmatically monitor AppDomains, create new AppDomains (or unload them) at runtime, load assemblies into AppDomains, and perform a whole slew of additional tasks, using the AppDomain class in the System namespace of mscorlib.dll. Table 17-5 documents some useful methods of the AppDomain class (consult the .NET Framework 4.7 SDK documentation for full details).

Table 17-5. *Select Methods of AppDomain*

Method	Meaning in Life
CreateDomain()	This static method allows you to create a new AppDomain in the current process.
CreateInstance()	This creates an instance of a type in an external assembly, after loading said assembly into the calling application domain.
ExecuteAssembly()	This method executes an *.exe assembly within an application domain, given its file name.
GetAssemblies()	This method gets the set of .NET assemblies that have been loaded into this application domain (COM-based or C-based binaries are ignored).
GetCurrentThreadId()	This static method returns the ID of the active thread in the current application domain.
Load()	This method is used to dynamically load an assembly into the current application domain.
Unload()	This is another static method that allows you to unload a specified AppDomain within a given process.

■ **Note** The .NET platform does not allow you to unload a specific assembly from memory. The only way to programmatically unload libraries is to tear down the hosting application domain via the Unload() method.

In addition, the AppDomain class defines a set of properties that can be useful when you want to monitor activity of a given application domain. Table 17-6 documents some core properties of interest.

Table 17-6. *Select Properties of AppDomain*

Property	Meaning in Life
BaseDirectory	This gets the directory path that the assembly resolver uses to probe for assemblies.
CurrentDomain	This static property gets the application domain for the currently executing thread.
FriendlyName	This gets the friendly name of the current application domain.
MonitoringIsEnabled	This gets or sets a value that indicates whether CPU and memory monitoring of application domains is enabled for the current process. Once monitoring is enabled for a process, it cannot be disabled.
SetupInformation	This gets the configuration details for a given application domain, represented by an AppDomainSetup object.

Last but not least, the AppDomain class supports a set of events that correspond to various aspects of an application domain's life cycle. Table 17-7 shows some of the more useful events you can hook into.

Table 17-7. *Select Events of the AppDomain Type*

Event	Meaning in Life
AssemblyLoad	This occurs when an assembly is loaded into memory.
AssemblyResolve	This event will fire when the assembly resolver cannot find the location of a required assembly.
DomainUnload	This occurs when an AppDomain is about to be unloaded from the hosting process.
FirstChanceException	This event allows you to be notified that an exception has been thrown from the application domain, before the CLR will begin looking for a fitting catch statement.
ProcessExit	This occurs on the default application domain when the default application domain's parent process exits.
UnhandledException	This occurs when an exception is not caught by an exception handler.

Interacting with the Default Application Domain

Recall that when a .NET executable starts, the CLR will automatically place it into the default AppDomain of the hosting process. This is done automatically and transparently, and you never have to author any specific code to do so. However, it is possible for your application to gain access to this default application domain using the static AppDomain.CurrentDomain property. After you have this access point, you are able to hook into any events of interest or use the methods and properties of AppDomain to perform some runtime diagnostics.

To learn how to interact with the default application domain, begin by creating a new Console Application project named DefaultAppDomainApp. Now, update your Program class with the following logic, which will simply display some details about the default application domain, using a number of members of the AppDomain class:

```
class Program
{
  static void Main(string[] args)
  {
    Console.WriteLine("***** Fun with the default AppDomain *****\n");
    DisplayDADStats();
    Console.ReadLine();
  }

  private static void DisplayDADStats()
  {
    // Get access to the AppDomain for the current thread.
    AppDomain defaultAD = AppDomain.CurrentDomain;

    // Print out various stats about this domain.
    Console.WriteLine("Name of this domain: {0}", defaultAD.FriendlyName);
    Console.WriteLine("ID of domain in this process: {0}", defaultAD.Id);
    Console.WriteLine("Is this the default domain?: {0}", defaultAD.IsDefaultAppDomain());
    Console.WriteLine("Base directory of this domain: {0}", defaultAD.BaseDirectory);
  }
}
```

The output of this example is shown here:

```
***** Fun with the default AppDomain *****

Name of this domain: DefaultAppDomainApp.exe
ID of domain in this process: 1
Is this the default domain?: True
Base directory of this domain: E:\MyCode\DefaultAppDomainApp\bin\Debug\
```

Notice that the name of the default application domain will be identical to the name of the executable that is contained within it (DefaultAppDomainApp.exe, in this example). Also notice that the base directory value, which will be used to probe for externally required private assemblies, maps to the current location of the deployed executable.

Enumerating Loaded Assemblies

It is also possible to discover all the loaded .NET assemblies within a given application domain using the instance-level GetAssemblies() method. This method will return to you an array of Assembly objects, which, as you recall from the Chapter 15, is a member of the System.Reflection namespace (so don't forget to import this namespace into your C# code file).

To illustrate, define a new method named ListAllAssembliesInAppDomain() within the Program class. This helper method will obtain all loaded assemblies and print the friendly name and version of each.

```
static void ListAllAssembliesInAppDomain()
{
  // Get access to the AppDomain for the current thread.
  AppDomain defaultAD = AppDomain.CurrentDomain;

  // Now get all loaded assemblies in the default AppDomain.
  Assembly[] loadedAssemblies = defaultAD.GetAssemblies();
  Console.WriteLine("***** Here are the assemblies loaded in {0} *****\n",
    defaultAD.FriendlyName);
  foreach(Assembly a in loadedAssemblies)
  {
    Console.WriteLine("-> Name: {0}", a.GetName().Name);
    Console.WriteLine("-> Version: {0}\n", a.GetName().Version);
  }
}
```

Assuming you have updated your Main() method to call this new member, you will see that the application domain hosting your executable is currently making use of the following .NET libraries:

```
***** Here are the assemblies loaded in DefaultAppDomainApp.exe *****

-> Name: mscorlib
-> Version: 4.0.0.0

-> Name: DefaultAppDomainApp
-> Version: 1.0.0.0
```

Now understand that the list of loaded assemblies can change at any time as you author new C# code. For example, assume you have updated your ListAllAssembliesInAppDomain() method to make use of a LINQ query, which will order the loaded assemblies by name, as follows:

```
static void ListAllAssembliesInAppDomain()
{
  // Get access to the AppDomain for the current thread.
  AppDomain defaultAD = AppDomain.CurrentDomain;

  // Now get all loaded assemblies in the default AppDomain.
  var loadedAssemblies = from a in defaultAD.GetAssemblies()
    orderby a.GetName().Name select a;

  Console.WriteLine("***** Here are the assemblies loaded in {0} *****\n",
      defaultAD.FriendlyName);
  foreach (var a in loadedAssemblies)
  {
    Console.WriteLine("-> Name: {0}", a.GetName().Name);
    Console.WriteLine("-> Version: {0}\n", a.GetName().Version);
  }
}
```

If you were to run the program once again, you would see that System.Core.dll and System.dll have also been loaded into memory, as they are required for the LINQ to Objects API.

```
***** Here are the assemblies loaded in DefaultAppDomainApp.exe *****

-> Name: DefaultAppDomainApp
-> Version: 1.0.0.0

-> Name: mscorlib
-> Version: 4.0.0.0

-> Name: System
-> Version: 4.0.0.0

-> Name: System.Core
-> Version: 4.0.0.0
```

Receiving Assembly Load Notifications

If you want to be informed by the CLR when a new assembly has been loaded into a given application domain, you may handle the AssemblyLoad event. This event is typed against the AssemblyLoadEventHandler delegate, which can point to any method taking a System.Object as the first parameter and an AssemblyLoadEventArgs as the second.

Let's add one final method to the current Program class called InitDAD(). As the name suggests, this method will initialize the default application domain, specifically by handling the AssemblyLoad event via a fitting lambda expression.

```
private static void InitDAD()
{
  // This logic will print out the name of any assembly
  // loaded into the applicaion domain, after it has been
  // created.
  AppDomain defaultAD = AppDomain.CurrentDomain;
  defaultAD.AssemblyLoad += (o, s) =>
    {
      Console.WriteLine("{0} has been loaded!", s.LoadedAssembly.GetName().Name);
    };
}
```

As you would expect, when you run the modified application, you will be notified when a new assembly has been loaded. Here, you are simply printing the friendly name of the assembly using the `LoadedAssembly` property of the incoming `AssemblyLoadedEventArgs` parameter.

■ **Source Code** You can find the DefaultAppDomainApp project in the `Chapter 17` subdirectory.

Creating New Application Domains

Recall that a single process is capable of hosting multiple application domains via the static `AppDomain.CreateDomain()` method. While creating new AppDomains on the fly is a rather infrequent task for most .NET applications, it is important to understand the basics of doing so. For example, as you will see later in this text, when you build *dynamic assemblies* (see Chapter 18), you will need to install them into a custom AppDomain. As well, several .NET security APIs require you to understand how to construct new AppDomains to isolate assemblies based on supplied security credentials.

To investigate how to create new application domains on the fly (and how to load new assemblies into these custom homes), create a new Console Application project named CustomAppDomains. The `AppDomain.CreateDomain()` method has been overloaded a number of times. At minimum, you will specify the friendly name of the new application domain to be constructed. Update your `Program` class with the following code. Here, you are leveraging the `ListAllAssembliesInAppDomain()` method from the previous example; however, this time you are passing in the `AppDomain` object to analyze as an incoming argument.

```
class Program
{
  static void Main(string[] args)
  {
    Console.WriteLine("***** Fun with Custom AppDomains *****\n");

    // Show all loaded assemblies in default AppDomain.
    AppDomain defaultAD = AppDomain.CurrentDomain;
    ListAllAssembliesInAppDomain(defaultAD);
    // Make a new AppDomain.
    MakeNewAppDomain();
    Console.ReadLine();
  }
```

```
private static void MakeNewAppDomain()
{
  // Make a new AppDomain in the current process and
  // list loaded assemblies.
  AppDomain newAD = AppDomain.CreateDomain("SecondAppDomain");
  ListAllAssembliesInAppDomain(newAD);
}

static void ListAllAssembliesInAppDomain(AppDomain ad)
{
  // Now get all loaded assemblies in the default AppDomain.
  var loadedAssemblies = from a in ad.GetAssemblies()
                         orderby a.GetName().Name select a;

  Console.WriteLine("***** Here arc the assemblies loaded in {0} *****\n",
    ad.FriendlyName);
  foreach (var a in loadedAssemblies)
  {
    Console.WriteLine("-> Name: {0}", a.GetName().Name);
    Console.WriteLine("-> Version: {0}\n", a.GetName().Version);
  }
}
}
```

If you run the current example, you will see that the default application domain (CustomAppDomains.
exe) has loaded mscorlib.dll, System.dll, System.Core.dll, and CustomAppDomains.exe, given the C#
codebase of the current project. However, the new application domain contains only mscorlib.dll, which,
as you recall, is the one .NET assembly that is always loaded by the CLR for every application domain.

```
***** Fun with Custom AppDomains *****

***** Here are the assemblies loaded in CustomAppDomains.exe *****

-> Name: CustomAppDomains
-> Version: 1.0.0.0

-> Name: mscorlib
-> Version: 4.0.0.0

-> Name: System
-> Version: 4.0.0.0

-> Name: System.Core
-> Version: 4.0.0.0

***** Here are the assemblies loaded in SecondAppDomain *****

-> Name: mscorlib
-> Version: 4.0.0.0
```

■ **Note**   If you debug this project (via F5), you will find many additional assemblies are loaded into each AppDomain, which are used by the Visual Studio debugging process. Running this project (via Ctrl+F5) will display only the assemblies directly within each AppDomain.

This might seem counterintuitive if you have a background in traditional Windows. (As you might suspect, both application domains have access to the same assembly set.) Recall, however, that an assembly loads into an *application domain*, not directly into the process itself.

Loading Assemblies into Custom Application Domains

The CLR will always load assemblies into the default application domain when required. However, if you do ever manually create new AppDomains, you can load assemblies into said AppDomain using the AppDomain.Load() method. Also, be aware that the AppDomain.ExecuteAssembly() method can be called to load an *.exe assembly and execute the Main() method.

Assume that you want to load CarLibrary.dll into your new secondary AppDomain. Provided you have copied this library to the \bin\Debug folder of the current application, you could update the MakeNewAppDomain() method as so (be sure to import the System.IO namespace to gain access to the FileNotFoundException class):

```
private static void MakeNewAppDomain()
{
  // Make a new AppDomain in the current process.
  AppDomain newAD = AppDomain.CreateDomain("SecondAppDomain");

  try
  {
    // Now load CarLibrary.dll into this new domain.
    newAD.Load("CarLibrary");
  }
  catch (FileNotFoundException ex)
  {
    Console.WriteLine(ex.Message);
  }

  // List all assemblies.
  ListAllAssembliesInAppDomain(newAD);
}
```

This time, the output of the program would appear as so (note the presence of CarLibrary.dll):

```
***** Fun with Custom AppDomains *****

***** Here are the assemblies loaded in CustomAppDomains.exe *****

-> Name: CustomAppDomains
-> Version: 1.0.0.0
```

```
-> Name: mscorlib
-> Version: 4.0.0.0

-> Name: System
-> Version: 4.0.0.0

-> Name: System.Core
-> Version: 4.0.0.0

***** Here are the assemblies loaded in SecondAppDomain *****

-> Name: CarLibrary
-> Version: 2.0.0.0

-> Name: mscorlib
-> Version: 4.0.0.0
```

■ **Note**   Remember, if you debug this application, you will see many additional libraries loaded into each application domain.

Programmatically Unloading AppDomains

It is important to point out that the CLR does not permit unloading individual .NET assemblies. However, using the AppDomain.Unload() method, you are able to selectively unload a given application domain from its hosting process. When you do so, the application domain will unload each assembly in turn.

Recall that the AppDomain type defines the DomainUnload event, which is fired when a custom application domain is unloaded from the containing process. Another event of interest is the ProcessExit event, which is fired when the default application domain is unloaded from the process (which obviously entails the termination of the process itself).

If you want to programmatically unload newAD from the hosting process and be notified when the associated application domain is torn down, you could update MakeNewAppDomain() with the following additional logic:

```
private static void MakeNewAppDomain()
{
  // Make a new AppDomain in the current process.
  AppDomain newAD = AppDomain.CreateDomain("SecondAppDomain");
  newAD.DomainUnload += (o, s) =>
  {
    Console.WriteLine("The second AppDomain has been unloaded!");
  };

  try
  {
    // Now load CarLibrary.dll into this new domain.
    newAD.Load("CarLibrary");
  }
```

```
  catch (FileNotFoundException ex)
  {
    Console.WriteLine(ex.Message);
  }

  // List all assemblies.
  ListAllAssembliesInAppDomain(newAD);

  // Now tear down this AppDomain.
  AppDomain.Unload(newAD);
}
```

If you want to be notified when the default application domain is unloaded, modify your `Main()` method to handle the `ProcessEvent` event of the default application domain, like so:

```
static void Main(string[] args)
{
  Console.WriteLine("***** Fun with Custom AppDomains *****\n");

  // Show all loaded assemblies in default AppDomain.
  AppDomain defaultAD = AppDomain.CurrentDomain;
  defaultAD.ProcessExit += (o, s) =>
  {
    Console.WriteLine("Default AD unloaded!");
  };

  ListAllAssembliesInAppDomain(defaultAD);

  MakeNewAppDomain();
  Console.ReadLine();
}
```

That wraps up your look at the .NET application domain. To conclude this chapter, let's look at one further level of partitioning, which is used to group objects into contextual boundaries.

■ **Source Code**   You can find the CustomAppDomains project in the `Chapter 17` subdirectory.

Understanding Object Context Boundaries

As you have just seen, AppDomains are logical partitions within a process used to host .NET assemblies. On a related note, a given application domain may be further subdivided into numerous context boundaries. In a nutshell, a .NET context provides a way for a single AppDomain to establish a "specific home" for a given object.

■ **Note**   While understanding processes and application domains is quite important, most .NET applications will never demand that you work with object contexts. I've included this overview material just to paint a more complete picture.

Using context, the CLR is able to ensure that objects that have special runtime requirements are handled in an appropriate and consistent manner by intercepting method invocations into and out of a given context. This layer of interception allows the CLR to adjust the current method invocation to conform to the contextual settings of a given object. For example, if you define a C# class type that requires automatic thread safety (using the [Synchronization] attribute), the CLR will create a "synchronized context" during allocation.

Just as a process defines a default AppDomain, every application domain has a default context. This default context (sometimes referred to as *context 0*, given that it is always the first context created within an application domain) is used to group together .NET objects that have no specific or unique contextual needs. As you might expect, a vast majority of .NET objects are loaded into context 0. If the CLR determines a newly created object has special needs, a new context boundary is created within the hosting application domain. Figure 17-3 illustrates the process/AppDomain/context relationship.

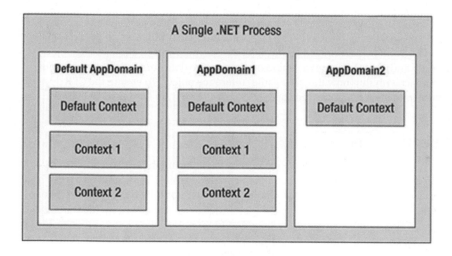

Figure 17-3. *Processes, application domains, and context boundaries*

Context-Agile and Context-Bound Types

.NET objects that do not demand any special contextual treatment are termed *context-agile objects*. These objects can be accessed from anywhere within the hosting AppDomain without interfering with the object's runtime requirements. Building context-agile objects is easy, given that you simply do nothing (specifically, you do not adorn the type with any contextual attributes and do not derive from the System. ContextBoundObject base class). Here's an example:

```
// A context-agile object is loaded into context zero.
class SportsCar{}
```

On the other hand, objects that do demand contextual allocation are termed *context-bound objects*, and they *must* derive from the System.ContextBoundObject base class. This base class solidifies the fact that the object in question can function appropriately only within the context in which it was created. Given the role of .NET context, it should stand to reason that if a context-bound object were to somehow end up in an incompatible context, bad things would be guaranteed to occur at the most inopportune times.

In addition to deriving from System.ContextBoundObject, a context-sensitive type will also be adorned by a special category of .NET attributes termed (not surprisingly) *context attributes*. All context attributes derive from the ContextAttribute base class. Let's see an example.

Defining a Context-Bound Object

Assume that you want to define a class (SportsCarTS) that is automatically thread safe in nature, even though you have not hard-coded thread synchronization logic within the member implementations. To do so, derive from ContextBoundObject and apply the [Synchronization] attribute as follows:

```
using System.Runtime.Remoting.Contexts;

// This context-bound type will only be loaded into a
// synchronized (hence thread-safe) context.
[Synchronization]
class SportsCarTS : ContextBoundObject
{}
```

Types that are attributed with the [Synchronization] attribute are loaded into a thread-safe context. Given the special contextual needs of the SportsCarTS class type, imagine the problems that would occur if an allocated object were moved from a synchronized context into a nonsynchronized context. The object is suddenly no longer thread-safe and, thus, becomes a candidate for massive data corruption, as numerous threads are attempting to interact with the (now thread-volatile) reference object. To ensure the CLR does not move SportsCarTS objects outside a synchronized context, simply derive from ContextBoundObject.

Inspecting an Object's Context

Although few of the applications you will write will need to programmatically interact with context, here is an illustrative example. Create a new Console Application project named ObjectContextApp. This application defines one context-agile class (SportsCar) and a single context-bound type (SportsCarTS) as follows:

```
using System;
using System.Runtime.Remoting.Contexts; // For Context type.
using System.Threading;  // For Thread type.

// SportsCar has no special contextual
// needs and will be loaded into the
// default context of the AppDomain.
class SportsCar
{
  public SportsCar()
  {
    // Get context information and print out context ID.
    Context ctx = Thread.CurrentContext;
    Console.WriteLine("{0} object in context {1}",
      this.ToString(), ctx.ContextID);
    foreach(IContextProperty itfCtxProp in ctx.ContextProperties)
      Console.WriteLine("-> Ctx Prop: {0}", itfCtxProp.Name);
  }
}

// SportsCarTS demands to be loaded in
// a synchronization context.
[Synchronization]
```

```
class SportsCarTS : ContextBoundObject
{
  public SportsCarTS()
  {
    // Get context information and print out context ID.
    Context ctx = Thread.CurrentContext;
    Console.WriteLine("{0} object in context {1}",
      this.ToString(), ctx.ContextID);
    foreach(IContextProperty itfCtxProp in ctx.ContextProperties)
      Console.WriteLine("-> Ctx Prop: {0}", itfCtxProp.Name);
  }
}
```

Notice that each constructor obtains a Context object from the current thread of execution, via the static Thread.CurrentContext property. Using the Context object, you are able to print statistics about the contextual boundary, such as its assigned ID, as well as a set of descriptors obtained via Context. ContextProperties. This property returns an array of objects implementing the IContextProperty interface, which exposes each descriptor through the Name property. Now, update Main() to allocate an instance of each class type, like so:

```
static void Main(string[] args)
{
  Console.WriteLine("***** Fun with Object Context *****\n");

  // Objects will display contextual info upon creation.
  SportsCar sport = new SportsCar();
  Console.WriteLine();

  SportsCar sport2 = new SportsCar();
  Console.WriteLine();

  SportsCarTS synchroSport = new SportsCarTS();
  Console.ReadLine();
}
```

As the objects come to life, the class constructors will dump out various bits of context-centric information (the "lease life time service property" printout is a low-level aspect of the .NET remoting layer and can be ignored).

```
***** Fun with Object Context *****

ObjectContextApp.SportsCar object in context 0
-> Ctx Prop: LeaseLifeTimeServiceProperty

ObjectContextApp.SportsCar object in context 0
-> Ctx Prop: LeaseLifeTimeServiceProperty

ObjectContextApp.SportsCarTS object in context 1
-> Ctx Prop: LeaseLifeTimeServiceProperty
-> Ctx Prop: Synchronization
```

Given that the SportsCar class has not been qualified with a context attribute, the CLR has allocated sport and sport2 into context 0 (i.e., the default context). However, the SportsCarTS object is loaded into a unique contextual boundary (which has been assigned a context ID of 1), given that this context-bound type was adorned with the [Synchronization] attribute.

■ **Source Code**   You can find the ObjectContextApp project in the Chapter 17 subdirectory.

Summarizing Processes, AppDomains, and Context

At this point, you should have a much better idea about how a .NET assembly is hosted by the CLR. These are the key points:

- A .NET process hosts one to many application domains. Each AppDomain is able to host any number of related .NET assemblies. AppDomains may be independently loaded and unloaded by the CLR (or programmatically via the System.AppDomain type).

- A given AppDomain consists of one to many contexts. Using a context, the CLR is able to place a "special needs" object into a logical container to ensure that its runtime requirements are honored.

If the previous pages have seemed to be a bit too low level for your liking, fear not. For the most part, the CLR automatically deals with the details of processes, application domains, and contexts on your behalf. The good news, however, is that this information provides a solid foundation for understanding multithreaded programming under the .NET platform.

Summary

The point of this chapter was to examine exactly how a .NET-executable image is hosted by the .NET platform. As you have seen, the long-standing notion of a Windows process has been altered under the hood to accommodate the needs of the CLR. A single process (which can be programmatically manipulated via the System.Diagnostics.Process type) is now composed of one or more application domains, which represent isolated and independent boundaries within a process.

As you have seen, a single process can host multiple application domains, each of which is capable of hosting and executing any number of related assemblies. Furthermore, a single application domain can contain any number of contextual boundaries. Using this additional level of type isolation, the CLR can ensure that special-need objects are handled correctly.

■ ■ ■

CHAPTER 18

Understanding CIL and the Role of Dynamic Assemblies

When you are building a full-scale .NET application, you will most certainly use C# (or a similar managed language such as Visual Basic), given its inherent productivity and ease of use. However, as you learned in the first chapter, the role of a managed compiler is to translate *.cs code files into terms of CIL code, type metadata, and an assembly manifest. As it turns out, CIL is a full-fledged .NET programming language, with its own syntax, semantics, and compiler (ilasm.exe).

In this chapter, you will be given a tour of .NET's mother tongue. Here you will understand the distinction between a CIL *directive*, CIL *attribute*, and CIL *opcode*. You will then learn about the role of round-trip engineering of a .NET assembly and various CIL programming tools. The remainder of the chapter will then walk you through the basics of defining namespaces, types, and members using the grammar of CIL. The chapter will wrap up with an examination of the role of the System.Reflection.Emit namespace and explain how it is possible to construct an assembly (with CIL instructions) dynamically at runtime.

Of course, few programmers will ever need to work with raw CIL code on a day-to-day basis. Therefore, I will start this chapter by examining a few reasons why getting to know the syntax and semantics of this low-level .NET language might be worth your while.

Motivations for Learning the Grammar of CIL

CIL is the true mother tongue of the .NET platform. When you build a .NET assembly using your managed language of choice (C#, VB, F#, etc.), the associated compiler translates your source code into terms of CIL. Like any programming language, CIL provides numerous structural and implementation-centric tokens. Given that CIL is just another .NET programming language, it should come as no surprise that it is possible to build your .NET assemblies directly using CIL and the CIL compiler (ilasm.exe) that ships with the .NET Framework SDK.

Now while it is true that few (if any!) programmers would choose to build an entire .NET application directly with CIL, CIL is still an extremely interesting intellectual pursuit. Simply put, the more you understand the grammar of CIL, the better able you are to move into the realm of advanced .NET development. By way of some concrete examples, individuals who possess an understanding of CIL are capable of the following:

- Disassembling an existing .NET assembly, editing the CIL code, and recompiling the updated code base into a modified .NET binary. For example, there are some scenarios where you might need to modify CIL to interoperate with some advanced COM features.

© Andrew Troelsen and Philip Japikse 2017
A. Troelsen and P. Japikse, *Pro C# 7*, https://doi.org/10.1007/978-1-4842-3018-3_18

- Building dynamic assemblies using the System.Reflection.Emit namespace. This API allows you to generate an in-memory .NET assembly, which can optionally be persisted to disk. This is a useful technique for the tool builders of the world who need to generate assemblies on the fly.

- Understanding aspects of the CTS that are not supported by higher-level managed languages but do exist at the level of CIL. To be sure, CIL is the only .NET language that allows you to access every aspect of the CTS. For example, using raw CIL, you are able to define global-level members and fields (which are not permissible in C#).

Again, to be perfectly clear, if you choose *not* to concern yourself with the details of CIL code, you are still absolutely able to gain mastery of C# and the .NET base class libraries. In many ways, knowledge of CIL is analogous to a C (and C++) programmer's understanding of assembly language. Those who know the ins and outs of the low-level "goo" are able to create rather advanced solutions for the task at hand and gain a deeper understanding of the underlying programming (and runtime) environment. So, if you are up for the challenge, let's begin to examine the details of CIL.

■ **Note**   Understand that this chapter is not intended to be a comprehensive treatment of the syntax and semantics of CIL. If you require a full examination of the topic, I recommend downloading the official ECMA specification (ecma-335.pdf) from the ECMA International web site (www.ecma-international.org).

Examining CIL Directives, Attributes, and Opcodes

When you begin to investigate low-level languages such as CIL, you are guaranteed to find new (and often intimidating-sounding) names for familiar concepts. For example, at this point in the text, if you were shown the following set of items

```
{new, public, this, base, get, set, explicit, unsafe, enum, operator, partial}
```

you would most certainly understand them to be keywords of the C# language (which is correct). However, if you look more closely at the members of this set, you might be able to see that while each item is indeed a C# keyword, it has radically different semantics. For example, the enum keyword defines a System.Enum-derived type, while the this and base keywords allow you to reference the current object or the object's parent class, respectively. The unsafe keyword is used to establish a block of code that cannot be directly monitored by the CLR, while the operator keyword allows you to build a hidden (specially named) method that will be called when you apply a specific C# operator (such as the plus sign).

In stark contrast to a higher-level language such as C#, CIL does not just simply define a general set of keywords per se. Rather, the token set understood by the CIL compiler is subdivided into the following three broad categories based on semantics:

- CIL directives

- CIL attributes

- CIL operation codes (opcodes)

Each category of CIL token is expressed using a particular syntax, and the tokens are combined to build a valid .NET assembly.

The Role of CIL Directives

First up, there is a set of well-known CIL tokens that are used to describe the overall structure of a .NET assembly. These tokens are called *directives*. CIL directives are used to inform the CIL compiler how to define the namespaces(s), type(s), and member(s) that will populate an assembly.

Directives are represented syntactically using a single dot (.) prefix (e.g., .namespace, .class, .publickeytoken, .method, .assembly, etc.). Thus, if your *.il file (the conventional extension for a file containing CIL code) has a single .namespace directive and three .class directives, the CIL compiler will generate an assembly that defines a single .NET namespace containing three .NET class types.

The Role of CIL Attributes

In many cases, CIL directives in and of themselves are not descriptive enough to fully express the definition of a given .NET type or type member. Given this fact, many CIL directives can be further specified with various CIL *attributes* to qualify how a directive should be processed. For example, the .class directive can be adorned with the public attribute (to establish the type visibility), the extends attribute (to explicitly specify the type's base class), and the implements attribute (to list the set of interfaces supported by the type).

■ **Note**   Don't confuse a .NET attribute (see Chapter 15) with that of a CIL attribute, which are two very different concepts.

The Role of CIL Opcodes

Once a .NET assembly, namespace, and type set have been defined in terms of CIL using various directives and related attributes, the final remaining task is to provide the type's implementation logic. This is a job for *operation codes*, or simply *opcodes*. In the tradition of other low-level languages, many CIL opcodes tend to be cryptic and completely unpronounceable by us mere humans. For example, if you need to load a string variable into memory, you don't use a friendly opcode named LoadString but rather ldstr.

Now, to be fair, some CIL opcodes do map quite naturally to their C# counterparts (e.g., box, unbox, throw, and sizeof). As you will see, the opcodes of CIL are always used within the scope of a member's implementation, and unlike CIL directives, they are never written with a dot prefix.

The CIL Opcode/CIL Mnemonic Distinction

As just explained, opcodes such as ldstr are used to implement the members of a given type. In reality, however, tokens such as ldstr are *CIL mnemonics* for the actual *binary CIL opcodes*. To clarify the distinction, assume you have authored the following method in C#:

```
static int Add(int x, int y)
{
  return x + y;
}
```

The act of adding two numbers is expressed in terms of the CIL opcode 0X58. In a similar vein, subtracting two numbers is expressed using the opcode 0X59, and the act of allocating a new object on the managed heap is achieved using the 0X73 opcode. Given this reality, understand that the "CIL code" processed by a JIT compiler is actually nothing more than blobs of binary data.

Thankfully, for each binary opcode of CIL, there is a corresponding mnemonic. For example, the add mnemonic can be used rather than 0X58, sub rather than 0X59, and newobj rather than 0X73. Given this opcode/mnemonic distinction, realize that CIL decompilers such as ildasm.exe translate an assembly's binary opcodes into their corresponding CIL mnemonics. For example, here would be the CIL presented by ildasm.exe for the previous C# Add() method (your exact output may differ based on your version of .NET):

```
.method private hidebysig static int32 Add(int32 x,
  int32 y) cil managed
{
  // Code size 9 (0x9)
  .maxstack 2
  .locals init ([0] int32 CS$1$0000)
  IL_0000: nop
  IL_0001: ldarg.0
  IL_0002: ldarg.1
  IL_0003: add
  IL_0004: stloc.0
  IL_0005: br.s IL_0007
  IL_0007: ldloc.0
  IL_0008: ret
}
```

Unless you're building some extremely low-level .NET software (such as a custom managed compiler), you'll never need to concern yourself with the literal numeric binary opcodes of CIL. For all practical purposes, when .NET programmers speak about "CIL opcodes," they're referring to the set of friendly string token mnemonics (as I've done within this text and will do for the remainder of this chapter) rather than the underlying numerical values.

Pushing and Popping: The Stack-Based Nature of CIL

Higher-level .NET languages (such as C#) attempt to hide low-level CIL grunge from view as much as possible. One aspect of .NET development that is particularly well hidden is that CIL is a stack-based programming language. Recall from the examination of the collection namespaces (see Chapter 9) that the Stack<T> class can be used to push a value onto a stack as well as pop the topmost value off of the stack for use. Of course, CIL developers do not use an object of type Stack<T> to load and unload the values to be evaluated; however, the same pushing and popping mind-set still applies.

Formally speaking, the entity used to hold a set of values to be evaluated is termed the *virtual execution stack*. As you will see, CIL provides a number of opcodes that are used to push a value onto the stack; this process is termed *loading*. As well, CIL defines a number of additional opcodes that transfer the topmost value on the stack into memory (such as a local variable) using a process termed *storing*.

In the world of CIL, it is impossible to access a point of data directly, including locally defined variables, incoming method arguments, or field data of a type. Rather, you are required to explicitly load the item onto the stack, only to then pop it off for later use (keep this point in mind, as it will help explain why a given block of CIL code can look a bit redundant).

■ **Note**   Recall that CIL is not directly executed but compiled on demand. During the compilation of CIL code, many of these implementation redundancies are optimized away. Furthermore, if you enable the code optimization option for your current project (using the Build tab of the Visual Studio Project Properties window), the compiler will also remove various CIL redundancies.

To understand how CIL leverages a stack-based processing model, consider a simple C# method, `PrintMessage()`, which takes no arguments and returns void. Within the implementation of this method, you will simply print the value of a local string variable to the standard output stream, like so:

```
public void PrintMessage()
{
  string myMessage = "Hello.";
  Console.WriteLine(myMessage);
}
```

If you were to examine how the C# compiler translates this method in terms of CIL, you would first find that the `PrintMessage()` method defines a storage slot for a local variable using the `.locals` directive. The local string is then loaded and stored in this local variable using the `ldstr` (load string) and `stloc.0` opcodes (which can be read as "store the current value in a local variable at storage slot zero").

The value (again, at index 0) is then loaded into memory using the `ldloc.0` ("load the local argument at index 0") opcode for use by the `System.Console.WriteLine()` method invocation (specified using the `call` opcode). Finally, the function returns via the `ret` opcode. Here is the (annotated) CIL code for the `PrintMessage()` method (note that I've removed the `nop` opcodes from this listing, for brevity):

```
.method public hidebysig instance void PrintMessage() cil managed
{
  .maxstack 1
  // Define a local string variable (at index 0).
  .locals init ([0] string myMessage)

  // Load a string onto the stack with the value "Hello."
  ldstr " Hello."

  // Store string value on the stack in the local variable.
  stloc.0

  // Load the value at index 0.
  ldloc.0

  // Call method with current value.
  call void [mscorlib]System.Console::WriteLine(string)
  ret
}
```

■ **Note**   As you can see, CIL supports code comments using the double-slash syntax (as well as the `/*...*/` syntax, for that matter). As in C#, code comments are completely ignored by the CIL compiler.

Now that you have the basics of CIL directives, attributes, and opcodes, let's see a practical use of CIL programming, beginning with the topic of round-trip engineering.

Understanding Round-Trip Engineering

You are aware of how to use `ildasm.exe` to view the CIL code generated by the C# compiler (see Chapter 1). What you might not know, however, is that `ildasm.exe` allows you to dump the CIL contained within an assembly loaded into `ildasm.exe` to an external file. Once you have the CIL code at your disposal, you are free to edit and recompile the codebase using the CIL compiler, `ilasm.exe`.

Formally speaking, this technique is termed *round-trip engineering*, and it can be useful under select circumstances, such as the following:

- You need to modify an assembly for which you no longer have the source code.

- You are working with a less-than-perfect .NET language compiler that has emitted ineffective (or flat-out incorrect) CIL code, and you want to modify the codebase.

- You are constructing a COM interoperability library and want to account for some COM IDL attributes that have been lost during the conversion process (such as the COM [`helpstring`] attribute).

To illustrate the process of round-tripping, begin by creating a new C# code file (`HelloProgram.cs`) using a simple text editor such as Notepad, and define the following class type. (You are free to create a new Console Application project using Visual Studio if you want. However, be sure to delete the `AssemblyInfo.cs` file to decrease the amount of generated CIL code.)

```
// A simple C# console app.
using System;

// Note that we are not wrapping our class in a namespace,
// to help simplify the generated CIL code.
class Program
{
  static void Main(string[] args)
  {
    Console.WriteLine("Hello CIL code!");
    Console.ReadLine();
  }
}
```

Save your file to a convenient location (for example, `C:\RoundTrip`) and compile your program using `csc.exe`, like so:

```
csc HelloProgram.cs
```

Now, open `HelloProgram.exe` with `ildasm.exe` and, using the File ➤ Dump menu option, save the raw CIL code to a new `*.il` file (`HelloProgram.il`) in the same folder containing your compiled assembly (all the default values of the resulting dialog box are fine as is).

■ **Note**   `ildasm.exe` will also generate a `*.res` file when dumping the contents of an assembly to file. These resource files can be ignored (and deleted) throughout this chapter, as you will not be using them. This file contains some low-level CLR security information (among other things).

Now you are able to view HelloProgram.il using your text editor of choice. Here is the (slightly reformatted and annotated) result:

```
// Referenced assemblies.
.assembly extern mscorlib
{
  .publickeytoken = (B7 7A 5C 56 19 34 E0 89 )
  .ver 4:0:0:0
}

// Our assembly.
.assembly HelloProgram
{
  /**** TargetFrameworkAttribute data removed for clarity! ****/

  .hash algorithm 0x00008004
  .ver 0:0:0:0
}
.module HelloProgram.exe
.imagebase 0x00400000
.file alignment 0x00000200
.stackreserve 0x00100000
.subsystem 0x0003
.corflags 0x00000003

// Definition of Program class.
.class private auto ansi beforefieldinit Program
  extends [mscorlib]System.Object
{
  .method private hidebysig static void Main(string[] args) cil managed
  {
    // Marks this method as the entry point of the
    // executable.
    .entrypoint
    .maxstack 8
    IL_0000: nop
    IL_0001: ldstr "Hello CIL code!"
    IL_0006: call void [mscorlib]System.Console::WriteLine(string)
    IL_000b: nop
    IL_000c: call string [mscorlib]System.Console::ReadLine()
    IL_0011: pop
    IL_0012: ret
  }

  // The default constructor.
  .method public hidebysig specialname rtspecialname
    instance void .ctor() cil managed
  {
    .maxstack 8
    IL_0000: ldarg.0
    IL_0001: call instance void [mscorlib]System.Object::.ctor()
    IL_0006: ret
  }
}
```

First, notice that the *.il file opens by declaring each externally referenced assembly the current assembly is compiled against. Here, you can see a single .assembly extern token set for the always present mscorlib.dll. Of course, if your class library used types within other referenced assemblies, you would find additional .assembly extern directives.

Next, you find the formal definition of your HelloProgram.exe assembly, which has been assigned a default version of 0.0.0.0 (given that you did not specify a value using the [AssemblyVersion] attribute). The assembly is further described using various CIL directives (such as .module, .imagebase, and so forth).

After documenting the externally referenced assemblies and defining the current assembly, you find a definition of the Program type. Note that the .class directive has various attributes (many of which are actually optional) such as extends, shown here, which marks the base class of the type:

```
.class private auto ansi beforefieldinit Program
    extends [mscorlib]System.Object
{ ... }
```

The bulk of the CIL code represents the implementation of the class's default constructor and the Main() method, both of which are defined (in part) with the .method directive. Once the members have been defined using the correct directives and attributes, they are implemented using various opcodes.

It is critical to understand that when interacting with .NET types (such as System.Console) in CIL, you will *always* need to use the type's fully qualified name. Furthermore, the type's fully qualified name must *always* be prefixed with the friendly name of the defining assembly (in square brackets). Consider the following CIL implementation of Main():

```
.method private hidebysig static void Main(string[] args) cil managed
{
    .entrypoint
    .maxstack 8
    IL_0000: nop
    IL_0001: ldstr "Hello CIL code!"
    IL_0006: call void [mscorlib]System.Console::WriteLine(string)
    IL_000b: nop
    IL_000c: call string [mscorlib]System.Console::ReadLine()
    IL_0011: pop
    IL_0012: ret
}
```

The implementation of the default constructor in terms of CIL code makes use of yet another "load-centric" instruction (ldarg.0). In this case, the value loaded onto the stack is not a custom variable specified by you but the current object reference (more details on this later). Also note that the default constructor explicitly makes a call to the base class constructor, as follows (which, in this case, is your good friend System.Object):

```
.method public hidebysig specialname rtspecialname
    instance void .ctor() cil managed
{
    .maxstack 8
    IL_0000: ldarg.0
    IL_0001: call instance void [mscorlib]System.Object::.ctor()
    IL_0006: ret
}
```

The Role of CIL Code Labels

One thing you certainly have noticed is that each line of implementation code is prefixed with a token of the form IL_XXX: (e.g., IL_0000:, IL_0001:, and so on). These tokens are called *code labels* and may be named in any manner you choose (provided they are not duplicated within the same member scope). When you dump an assembly to file using ildasm.exe, it will automatically generate code labels that follow an IL_XXX: naming convention. However, you may change them to reflect a more descriptive marker. Here's an example:

```
.method private hidebysig static void Main(string[] args) cil managed
{
  .entrypoint
  .maxstack 8
  Nothing_1: nop
  Load_String: ldstr "Hello CIL code!"
  PrintToConsole: call void [mscorlib]System.Console::WriteLine(string)
  Nothing_2: nop
  WaitFor_KeyPress: call string [mscorlib]System.Console::ReadLine()
  RemoveValueFromStack: pop
  Leave_Function: ret
}
```

The truth of the matter is that most code labels are completely optional. The only time code labels are truly mandatory is when you are authoring CIL code that makes use of various branching or looping constructs, as you can specify where to direct the flow of logic via these code labels. For the current example, you can remove these autogenerated labels altogether with no ill effect, like so:

```
.method private hidebysig static void Main(string[] args) cil managed
{
  .entrypoint
  .maxstack 8
  nop
  ldstr "Hello CIL code!"
  call void [mscorlib]System.Console::WriteLine(string)
  nop
  call string [mscorlib]System.Console::ReadLine()
  pop
  ret
}
```

Interacting with CIL: Modifying an *.il File

Now that you have a better understanding of how a basic CIL file is composed, let's complete the round-tripping experiment. The goal here is to update the CIL within the existing *.il file as follows:

1. Add a reference to the System.Windows.Forms.dll assembly.

2. Load a local string within Main().

3. Call the System.Windows.Forms.MessageBox.Show() method using the local string variable as an argument.

The first step is to add a new .assembly directive (qualified with the extern attribute) that specifies your assembly requires the System.Windows.Forms.dll assembly. To do so, update the *.il file with the following logic after the external reference to mscorlib:

```
.assembly extern System.Windows.Forms
{
  .publickeytoken = (B7 7A 5C 56 19 34 E0 89)
  .ver 4:0:0:0
}
```

Be aware that the value assigned to the .ver directive may differ depending on which version of the .NET platform you have installed on your development machine. Here, you see that System.Windows.Forms. dll version 4.0.0.0 is used and has the public key token of B77A5C561934E089. If you open the GAC (see Chapter 14) and locate your version of the System.Windows.Forms.dll assembly, you can simply copy the correct version and public key token value.

Next, you need to alter the current implementation of the Main() method. Locate this method within the *.il file and remove the current implementation code (the .maxstack and .entrypoint directives should remain intact), like so:

```
.method private hidebysig static void Main(string[] args) cil managed
{
  .entrypoint
  .maxstack 8
  // ToDo: Write new CIL code!
}
```

Again, the goal here is to push a new string onto the stack and call the MessageBox.Show() method (rather than the Console.WriteLine() method). Recall that when you specify the name of an external type, you must use the type's fully qualified name (in conjunction with the friendly name of the assembly). Also notice that in terms of CIL, every method call documents the fully qualified return type. Keeping these things in mind, update the Main() method as follows:

```
.method private hidebysig static void Main(string[] args) cil managed
{
  .entrypoint
  .maxstack 8

  ldstr "CIL is way cool"
  call valuetype [System.Windows.Forms]
    System.Windows.Forms.DialogResult
    [System.Windows.Forms]
  System.Windows.Forms.MessageBox::Show(string)
  pop
  ret
}
```

In effect, you have just updated the CIL code to correspond to the following C# class definition:

```
class Program
{
  static void Main(string[] args)
  {
    System.Windows.Forms.MessageBox.Show("CIL is way cool");
  }
}
```

Compiling CIL Code Using ilasm.exe

Assuming you have saved this modified *.il file, you can compile a new .NET assembly using the ilasm.exe (CIL compiler) utility. While the CIL compiler has numerous command-line options (all of which can be seen by specifying the -? option), Table 18-1 shows the core flags of interest.

Table 18-1. *Common ilasm.exe Command-Line Flags*

Flag	Meaning in Life
/debug	Includes debug information (such as local variable and argument names, as well as line numbers).
/dll	Produces a *.dll file as output.
/exe	Produces an *.exe file as output. This is the default setting and may be omitted.
/key	Compiles the assembly with a strong name using a given *.snk file.
/output	Specifies the output file name and extension. If you do not use the /output flag, the resulting file name (minus the file extension) is the same as the name of the first source file.

To compile your updated HelloProgram.il file into a new .NET *.exe, you can issue the following command within a Developer Command prompt:

```
ilasm /exe HelloProgram.il /output=NewAssembly.exe
```

Assuming things have worked successfully, you will see the report shown here:

```
Microsoft (R) .NET Framework IL Assembler. Version 4.7.2528.0
Copyright (c) Microsoft Corporation. All rights reserved.
Assembling 'HelloProgram.il' to EXE --> 'NewAssembly.exe'
Source file is UTF-8

Assembled method Program::Main
Assembled method Program::.ctor
Creating PE file

Emitting classes:
Class 1: Program
```

```
Emitting fields and methods:
Global
Class 1 Methods: 2;

Emitting events and properties:
Global
Class 1
Writing PE file
Operation completed successfully
```

At this point, you can run your new application. Sure enough, rather than showing a message within the console window, you will now see a message box displaying your message. While the output of this simple example is not all that spectacular, it does illustrate one practical use of programming in CIL round-tripping.

The Role of peverify.exe

When you are building or modifying assemblies using CIL code, it is always advisable to verify that the compiled binary image is a well-formed .NET image using the peverify.exe command-line tool, like so:

```
peverify NewAssembly.exe
```

This tool will examine all opcodes within the specified assembly for valid CIL code. For example, in terms of CIL code, the evaluation stack must always be empty before exiting a function. If you forget to pop off any remaining values, the ilasm.exe compiler will still generate a compiled assembly (given that compilers are concerned only with *syntax*). peverify.exe, on the other hand, is concerned with *semantics*. If you did forget to clear the stack before exiting a given function, peverify.exe will let you know before you try running your code base.

■ **Source Code**   You can find the RoundTrip example in the Chapter 18 subdirectory.

Understanding CIL Directives and Attributes

Now that you have seen how ildasm.exe and ilasm.exe can be used to perform a round-trip, you can get down to the business of checking out the syntax and semantics of CIL itself. The next sections will walk you through the process of authoring a custom namespace containing a set of types. However, to keep things simple, these types will not contain any implementation logic for their members (yet). After you understand how to create empty types, you can then turn your attention to the process of defining "real" members using CIL opcodes.

Specifying Externally Referenced Assemblies in CIL

Create a new file named CILTypes.il using your editor of choice. The first task a CIL project will require is to list the set of external assemblies used by the current assembly. For this example, you will only use types found within mscorlib.dll. To do so, the .assembly directive will be qualified using the external attribute. When you are referencing a strongly named assembly, such as mscorlib.dll, you'll want to specify the .publickeytoken and .ver directives as well, like so:

```
.assembly extern mscorlib
{
  .publickeytoken = (B7 7A 5C 56 19 34 E0 89 )
  .ver 4:0:0:0
}
```

■ **Note**   Strictly speaking, you are not required to explicitly reference `mscorlib.dll` as an external reference, as `ilasm.exe` will do so automatically. However, for each external .NET library your CIL project requires, you will need to author a similar `.assembly extern` directive.

Defining the Current Assembly in CIL

The next order of business is to define the assembly you are interested in building using the `.assembly` directive. At the simplest level, an assembly can be defined by specifying the friendly name of the binary, like so:

```
// Our assembly.
.assembly CILTypes { }
```

While this indeed defines a new .NET assembly, you will typically place additional directives within the scope of the assembly declaration. For this example, update your assembly definition to include a version number of 1.0.0.0 using the `.ver` directive (note that each numerical identifier is separated by *colons*, not the C#-centric dot notation), as follows:

```
// Our assembly.
.assembly CILTypes
{
  .ver 1:0:0:0
}
```

Given that the CILTypes assembly is a single-file assembly (see Chapter 14), you will finish up the assembly definition using the following single `.module` directive, which marks the official name of your .NET binary, `CILTypes.dll`:

```
.assembly CILTypes
{
  .ver 1:0:0:0
}
// The module of our single-file assembly.
.module CILTypes.dll
```

In addition to `.assembly` and `.module` are CIL directives that further qualify the overall structure of the .NET binary you are composing. Table 18-2 lists a few of the more common assembly-level directives.

Table 18-2. Additional Assembly-Centric Directives

Directive	Meaning in Life
.mresources	If your assembly uses internal resources (such as bitmaps or string tables), this directive is used to identify the name of the file that contains the resources to be embedded.
.subsystem	This CIL directive is used to establish the preferred UI that the assembly wants to execute within. For example, a value of 2 signifies that the assembly should run within a GUI application, whereas a value of 3 denotes a console executable.

Defining Namespaces in CIL

Now that you have defined the look and feel of your assembly (and the required external references), you can create a .NET namespace (MyNamespace) using the `.namespace` directive, like so:

```
// Our assembly has a single namespace.
.namespace MyNamespace {}
```

Like C#, CIL namespace definitions can be nested within further namespaces. There is no need to define a root namespace here; however, for the sake of argument, assume you want to create the following root namespace named MyCompany:

```
.namespace MyCompany
{
  .namespace MyNamespace {}
}
```

Like C#, CIL allows you to define a nested namespace as follows:

```
// Defining a nested namespace.
.namespace MyCompany.MyNamespace {}
```

Defining Class Types in CIL

Empty namespaces are not very interesting, so let's now check out the process of defining a class type using CIL. Not surprisingly, the `.class` directive is used to define a new class. However, this simple directive can be adorned with numerous additional attributes, to further qualify the nature of the type. To illustrate, add a public class to your namespace named MyBaseClass. As in C#, if you do not specify an explicit base class, your type will automatically be derived from System.Object.

```
.namespace MyNamespace
{
  // System.Object base class assumed.
  .class public MyBaseClass {}
}
```

When you are building a class type that derives from any class other than System.Object, you use the extends attribute. Whenever you need to reference a type defined within the same assembly, CIL demands that you also use the fully qualified name (however, if the base type is within the same assembly, you can omit the assembly's friendly name prefix). Therefore, the following attempt to extend MyBaseClass results in a compiler error:

```
// This will not compile!
.namespace MyNamespace
{
  .class public MyBaseClass {}

  .class public MyDerivedClass
    extends MyBaseClass {}
}
```

To correctly define the parent class of MyDerivedClass, you must specify the full name of MyBaseClass as follows:

```
// Better!
.namespace MyNamespace
{
  .class public MyBaseClass {}

  .class public MyDerivedClass
    extends MyNamespace.MyBaseClass {}
}
```

In addition to the public and extends attributes, a CIL class definition may take numerous additional qualifiers that control the type's visibility, field layout, and so on. Table 18-3 illustrates some (but not all) of the attributes that may be used in conjunction with the .class directive.

Table 18-3. *Various Attributes Used in Conjunction with the* .class *Directive*

Attributes	Meaning in Life
public, private, nested assembly, nested famandassem, nested family, nested famorassem, nested public, nested private	CIL defines various attributes that are used to specify the visibility of a given type. As you can see, raw CIL offers numerous possibilities other than those offered by C#. Refer to ECMA 335 for details if you are interested.
abstract, sealed	These two attributes may be tacked onto a .class directive to define an abstract class or sealed class, respectively.
auto, sequential, explicit	These attributes are used to instruct the CLR how to lay out field data in memory. For class types, the default layout flag (auto) is appropriate. Changing this default can be helpful if you need to use P/Invoke to call into unmanaged C code.
extends, implements	These attributes allow you to define the base class of a type (via extends) or implement an interface on a type (via implements).

Defining and Implementing Interfaces in CIL

As odd as it might seem, interface types are defined in CIL using the .class directive. However, when the .class directive is adorned with the interface attribute, the type is realized as a CTS interface type. Once an interface has been defined, it may be bound to a class or structure type using the CIL implements attribute, like so:

```
.namespace MyNamespace
{
  // An interface definition.
  .class public interface IMyInterface {}

  // A simple base class.
  .class public MyBaseClass {}

  // MyDerivedClass now implements IMyInterface,
  // and extends MyBaseClass.
  .class public MyDerivedClass
    extends MyNamespace.MyBaseClass
    implements MyNamespace.IMyInterface {}
}
```

■ **Note** The extends clause must precede the implements clause. As well, the implements clause can incorporate a comma-separated list of interfaces.

As you recall from Chapter 9, interfaces can function as the base interface to other interface types in order to build interface hierarchies. However, contrary to what you might be thinking, the extends attribute cannot be used to derive interface A from interface B. The extends attribute is used only to qualify a type's base class. When you want to extend an interface, you will use the implements attribute yet again. Here's an example:

```
// Extending interfaces in terms of CIL.
.class public interface IMyInterface {}

.class public interface IMyOtherInterface
  implements MyNamespace.IMyInterface {}
```

Defining Structures in CIL

The .class directive can be used to define a CTS structure if the type extends System.ValueType. As well, the .class directive must be qualified with the sealed attribute (given that structures can never be a base structure to other value types). If you attempt to do otherwise, ilasm.exe will issue a compiler error.

```
// A structure definition is always sealed.
.class public sealed MyStruct
  extends [mscorlib]System.ValueType{}
```

Do be aware that CIL provides a shorthand notation to define a structure type. If you use the `value` attribute, the new type will derive the type from `[mscorlib]System.ValueType` automatically. Therefore, you could define `MyStruct` as follows:

```
// Shorthand notation for declaring a structure.
.class public sealed value MyStruct{}
```

Defining Enums in CIL

.NET enumerations (as you recall) derive from `System.Enum`, which is a `System.ValueType` (and therefore must also be sealed). When you want to define an enum in terms of CIL, simply extend `[mscorlib]System.Enum`, like so:

```
// An enum.
.class public sealed MyEnum
  extends [mscorlib]System.Enum{}
```

Like a structure definition, enumerations can be defined with a shorthand notation using the enum attribute. Here's an example:

```
// Enum shorthand.
.class public sealed enum MyEnum{}
```

You'll see how to specify the name-value pairs of an enumeration in just a moment.

■ **Note** The other fundamental .NET type, the delegate, also has a specific CIL representation. See Chapter 10 for details.

Defining Generics in CIL

Generic types also have a specific representation in the syntax of CIL. Recall from Chapter 9 that a given generic type or generic member may have one or more type parameters. For example, the `List<T>` type has a single type parameter, while `Dictionary<TKey, TValue>` has two. In terms of CIL, the number of type parameters is specified using a backward-leaning single tick (`` ` ``), followed by a numerical value representing the number of type parameters. Like C#, the actual value of the type parameters is encased within angled brackets.

■ **Note** On most keyboards, you can find the `` ` `` character on the key above the Tab key (and to the left of the 1 key).

For example, assume you want to create a `List<T>` variable, where T is of type `System.Int32`. In C#, you would type the following:

```
void SomeMethod()
{
  List<int> myInts = new List<int>();
}
```

In CIL, you would author the following (which could appear in any CIL method scope):

```
// In C#: List<int> myInts = new List<int>();
newobj instance void class [mscorlib]
  System.Collections.Generic.List`1<int32>::.ctor()
```

Notice that this generic class is defined as List`1<int32>, as List<T> has a single type parameter. However, if you needed to define a Dictionary<string, int> type, you would do so as follows:

```
// In C#: Dictionary<string, int> d = new Dictionary<string, int>();
newobj instance void class [mscorlib]
  System.Collections.Generic.Dictionary`2<string,int32>::.ctor()
```

As another example, if you have a generic type that uses another generic type as a type parameter, you would author CIL code such as the following:

```
// In C#: List<List<int>> myInts = new List<List<int>>();
newobj instance void class [mscorlib]
  System.Collections.Generic.List`1<class
    [mscorlib]System.Collections.Generic.List`1<int32>>::.ctor()
```

Compiling the CILTypes.il File

Even though you have not yet added any members or implementation code to the types you have defined, you are able to compile this *.il file into a .NET DLL assembly (which you must do, as you have not specified a Main() method). Open a command prompt and enter the following command to ilasm.exe:

```
ilasm /dll CilTypes.il
```

After you have done so, can now open your compiled assembly into ildasm.exe to verify the creation of each type. After you have confirmed the contents of your assembly, run peverify.exe against it, like so:

```
peverify CilTypes.dll
```

Notice that you are issued errors, given that all your types are completely empty. Here is some partial output:

```
Microsoft (R) .NET Framework PE Verifier. Version 4.0.30319.33440
Copyright (c) Microsoft Corporation. All rights reserved.

[MD]: Error: Value class has neither fields nor size parameter. [token:0x02000005]
[MD]: Error: Enum has no instance field. [token:0x02000006]
...
```

To understand how to populate a type with content, you first need to examine the fundamental data types of CIL.

.NET Base Class Library, C#, and CIL Data Type Mappings

Table 18-4 illustrates how a .NET base class type maps to the corresponding C# keyword and how each C# keyword maps into raw CIL. As well, Table 18-4 documents the shorthand constant notations used for each CIL type. As you will see in just a moment, these constants are often referenced by numerous CIL opcodes.

Table 18-4. *Mapping .NET Base Class Types to C# Keywords, and C# Keywords to CIL*

.NET Base Class Type	C# Keyword	CIL Representation	CIL Constant Notation
System.SByte	sbyte	int8	I1
System.Byte	byte	unsigned int8	U1
System.Int16	short	int16	I2
System.UInt16	ushort	unsigned int16	U2
System.Int32	int	int32	I4
System.UInt32	uint	unsigned int32	U4
System.Int64	long	int64	I8
System.UInt64	ulong	unsigned int64	U8
System.Char	char	char	CHAR
System.Single	float	float32	R4
System.Double	double	float64	R8
System.Boolean	bool	bool	BOOLEAN
System.String	string	string	N/A
System.Object	object	object	N/A
System.Void	void	void	VOID

■ **Note**　The System.IntPtr and System.UIntPtr types map to native int and native unsigned int (this is good to know, as many of COM interoperability and P/Invoke scenarios use these extensively).

Defining Type Members in CIL

As you are already aware, .NET types may support various members. Enumerations have some set of name-value pairs. Structures and classes may have constructors, fields, methods, properties, static members, and so on. Over the course of this book's first 17 chapters, you have already seen partial CIL definitions for the items previously mentioned, but nevertheless, here is a quick recap of how various members map to CIL primitives.

Defining Field Data in CIL

Enumerations, structures, and classes can all support field data. In each case, the .field directive will be used. For example, let's breathe some life into the skeleton MyEnum enumeration and define the following three name-value pairs (note the values are specified within parentheses):

```
.class public sealed enum MyEnum
{
  .field public static literal valuetype
  MyNamespace.MyEnum A = int32(0)
  .field public static literal valuetype
  MyNamespace.MyEnum B = int32(1)
  .field public static literal valuetype
  MyNamespace.MyEnum C = int32(2)
}
```

Fields that reside within the scope of a .NET System.Enum-derived type are qualified using the static and literal attributes. As you would guess, these attributes set up the field data to be a fixed value accessible from the type itself (e.g., MyEnum.A).

■ **Note**   The values assigned to an enum value may also be in hexadecimal with a 0x prefix.

Of course, when you want to define a point of field data within a class or structure, you are not limited to a point of public static literal data. For example, you could update MyBaseClass to support two points of private, instance-level field data, set to default values:

```
.class public MyBaseClass
{
  .field private string stringField = "hello!"
  .field private int32 intField = int32(42)
}
```

As in C#, class field data will automatically be initialized to an appropriate default value. If you want to allow the object user to supply custom values at the time of creation for each of these points of private field data, you (of course) need to create custom constructors.

Defining Type Constructors in CIL

The CTS supports both instance-level and class-level (static) constructors. In terms of CIL, instance-level constructors are represented using the .ctor token, while a static-level constructor is expressed via .cctor (class constructor). Both of these CIL tokens must be qualified using the rtspecialname (return type special name) and specialname attributes. Simply put, these attributes are used to identify a specific CIL token that can be treated in unique ways by a given .NET language. For example, in C#, constructors do not define a return type; however, in terms of CIL, the return value of a constructor is indeed void.

```
.class public MyBaseClass
{
  .field private string stringField
  .field private int32 intField
```

```
.method public hidebysig specialname rtspecialname
  instance void .ctor(string s, int32 i) cil managed
{
  // TODO: Add implementation code...
}
}
```

Note that the .ctor directive has been qualified with the instance attribute (as it is not a static constructor). The cil managed attributes denote that the scope of this method contains CIL code, rather than unmanaged code, which may be used during platform invocation requests.

Defining Properties in CIL

Properties and methods also have specific CIL representations. By way of an example, if MyBaseClass were updated to support a public property named TheString, you would author the following CIL (note again the use of the specialname attribute):

```
.class public MyBaseClass
{
...
  .method public hidebysig specialname
    instance string get_TheString() cil managed
  {
    // TODO: Add implementation code...
  }

  .method public hidebysig specialname
    instance void set_TheString(string 'value') cil managed
  {
    // TODO: Add implementation code...
  }

  .property instance string TheString()
  {
    .get instance string
      MyNamespace.MyBaseClass::get_TheString()
    .set instance void
      MyNamespace.MyBaseClass::set_TheString(string)
  }
}
```

In terms of CIL, a property maps to a pair of methods that take get_ and set_ prefixes. The .property directive makes use of the related .get and .set directives to map property syntax to the correct "specially named" methods.

■ **Note**   Notice that the incoming parameter to the set method of a property is placed in single quotation marks, which represents the name of the token to use on the right side of the assignment operator within the method scope.

Defining Member Parameters

In a nutshell, specifying arguments in CIL is (more or less) identical to doing so in C#. For example, each argument is defined by specifying its data type, followed by the parameter name. Furthermore, like C#, CIL provides a way to define input, output, and pass-by-reference parameters. As well, CIL allows you to define a parameter array argument (aka the C# params keyword), as well as optional parameters.

To illustrate the process of defining parameters in raw CIL, assume you want to build a method that takes an int32 (by value), an int32 (by reference), a [mscorlib]System.Collection.ArrayList, and a single output parameter (of type int32). In terms of C#, this method would look something like the following:

```
public static void MyMethod(int inputInt,
  ref int refInt, ArrayList ar, out int outputInt)
{
  outputInt = 0; // Just to satisfy the C# compiler...
}
```

If you were to map this method into CIL terms, you would find that C# reference parameters are marked with an ampersand (&) suffixed to the parameter's underlying data type (int32&).

Output parameters also use the & suffix, but they are further qualified using the CIL [out] token. Also notice that if the parameter is a reference type (in this case, the [mscorlib]System.Collections.ArrayList type), the class token is prefixed to the data type (not to be confused with the .class directive!).

```
.method public hidebysig static void MyMethod(int32 inputInt,
  int32& refInt,
  class [mscorlib]System.Collections.ArrayList ar,
  [out] int32& outputInt) cil managed
{
  ...
}
```

Examining CIL Opcodes

The final aspect of CIL code you'll examine in this chapter has to do with the role of various operational codes (opcodes). Recall that an opcode is simply a CIL token used to build the implementation logic for a given member. The complete set of CIL opcodes (which is fairly large) can be grouped into the following broad categories:

- Opcodes that control program flow

- Opcodes that evaluate expressions

- Opcodes that access values in memory (via parameters, local variables, etc.)

To provide some insight to the world of member implementation via CIL, Table 18-5 defines some of the more useful opcodes that are directly related to member implementation logic, grouped by related functionality.

Table 18-5. *Various Implementation-Specific CIL Opcodes*

Opcodes	Meaning in Life
add, sub, mul, div, rem	These CIL opcodes allow you to add, subtract, multiply, and divide two values (rem returns the remainder of a division operation).
and, or, not, xor	These CIL opcodes allow you to perform bit-wise operations on two values.
ceq, cgt, clt	These CIL opcodes allow you to compare two values on the stack in various manners. Here are some examples: ceq: Compare for equality cgt: Compare for greater than clt: Compare for less than
box, unbox	These CIL opcodes are used to convert between reference types and value types.
ret	This CIL opcode is used to exit a method and return a value to the caller (if necessary).
beq, bgt, ble, blt, switch	These CIL opcodes (in addition to many other related opcodes) are used to control branching logic within a method. Here are some examples: beq: Break to code label if equal bgt: Break to code label if greater than ble: Break to code label if less than or equal to blt: Break to code label if less than All the branch-centric opcodes require that you specify a CIL code label to jump to if the result of the test is true.
call	This CIL opcode is used to call a member on a given type.
newarr, newobj	These CIL opcodes allow you to allocate a new array or new object type into memory (respectively).

The next broad category of CIL opcodes (a subset of which is shown in Table 18-6) is used to load (push) arguments onto the virtual execution stack. Note how these load-specific opcodes take an ld (load) prefix.

Table 18-6. *The Primary Stack-Centric Opcodes of CIL*

Opcode	Meaning in Life
ldarg (with numerous variations)	Loads a method's argument onto the stack. In addition to the general ldarg (which works in conjunction with a given index that identifies the argument), there are numerous other variations.
	For example, ldarg opcodes that have a numerical suffix (ldarg_0) hard-code which argument to load. As well, variations of the ldarg opcode allow you to hard-code the data type using the CIL constant notation shown in Table 18-4 (ldarg_I4, for an int32), as well as the data type and value (ldarg_I4_5, to load an int32 with the value of 5).
ldc (with numerous variations)	Loads a constant value onto the stack.
ldfld (with numerous variations)	Loads the value of an instance-level field onto the stack.
ldloc (with numerous variations)	Loads the value of a local variable onto the stack.
ldobj	Obtains all the values gathered by a heap-based object and places them on the stack.
ldstr	Loads a string value onto the stack.

In addition to the set of load-specific opcodes, CIL provides numerous opcodes that *explicitly* pop the topmost value off the stack. As shown over the first few examples in this chapter, popping a value off the stack typically involves storing the value into temporary local storage for further use (such as a parameter for an upcoming method invocation). Given this, note how many opcodes that pop the current value off the virtual execution stack take an st (store) prefix. Table 18-7 hits the highlights.

Table 18-7. *Various Pop-Centric Opcodes*

Opcode	Meaning in Life
pop	Removes the value currently on top of the evaluation stack but does not bother to store the value
starg	Stores the value on top of the stack into the method argument at a specified index
stloc (with numerous variations)	Pops the current value from the top of the evaluation stack and stores it in a local variable list at a specified index
stobj	Copies a value of a specified type from the evaluation stack into a supplied memory address
stsfld	Replaces the value of a static field with a value from the evaluation stack

Do be aware that various CIL opcodes will *implicitly* pop values off the stack to perform the task at hand. For example, if you are attempting to subtract two numbers using the sub opcode, it should be clear that sub will have to pop off the next two available values before it can perform the calculation. Once the calculation is complete, the result of the value (surprise, surprise) is pushed onto the stack once again.

The .maxstack Directive

When you write method implementations using raw CIL, you need to be mindful of a special directive named .maxstack. As its name suggests, .maxstack establishes the maximum number of variables that may be pushed onto the stack at any given time during the execution of the method. The good news is that the .maxstack directive has a default value (8), which should be safe for a vast majority of methods you might be authoring. However, if you want to be explicit, you are able to manually calculate the number of local variables on the stack and define this value explicitly, like so:

```
.method public hidebysig instance void
  Speak() cil managed
{
  // During the scope of this method, exactly
  // 1 value (the string literal) is on the stack.
  .maxstack 1
  ldstr "Hello there..."
  call void [mscorlib]System.Console::WriteLine(string)
  ret
}
```

Declaring Local Variables in CIL

Let's first check out how to declare a local variable. Assume you want to build a method in CIL named MyLocalVariables() that takes no arguments and returns void. Within the method, you want to define three local variables of types System.String, System.Int32, and System.Object. In C#, this member would appear as follows (recall that locally scoped variables do not receive a default value and should be set to an initial state before further use):

```
public static void MyLocalVariables()
{
  string myStr = "CIL code is fun!";
  int myInt = 33;
  object myObj = new object();
}
```

If you were to construct MyLocalVariables() directly in CIL, you could author the following:

```
.method public hidebysig static void
  MyLocalVariables() cil managed
{
  .maxstack 8
  // Define three local variables.
  .locals init ([0] string myStr, [1] int32 myInt, [2] object myObj)
  // Load a string onto the virtual execution stack.
  ldstr "CIL code is fun!"
  // Pop off current value and store in local variable [0].
  stloc.0

  // Load a constant of type "i4"
  // (shorthand for int32) set to the value 33.
  ldc.i4 33
```

```
// Pop off current value and store in local variable [1].
stloc.1

// Create a new object and place on stack.
newobj instance void [mscorlib]System.Object::.ctor()
// Pop off current value and store in local variable [2].
stloc.2
ret
}
```

As you can see, the first step taken to allocate local variables in raw CIL is to use the `.locals` directive, which is paired with the `init` attribute. Within the scope of the related parentheses, your goal is to associate a given numerical index to each variable (shown here as [0], [1], and [2]). As you can see, each index is identified by its data type and an optional variable name. After the local variables have been defined, you load a value onto the stack (using the various load-centric opcodes) and store the value within the local variable (using the various storage-centric opcodes).

Mapping Parameters to Local Variables in CIL

You have already seen how to declare local variables in raw CIL using the `.locals init` directive; however, you have yet to see exactly how to map incoming parameters to local methods. Consider the following static C# method:

```
public static int Add(int a, int b)
{
  return a + b;
}
```

This innocent-looking method has a lot to say in terms of CIL. First, the incoming arguments (a and b) must be pushed onto the virtual execution stack using the `ldarg` (load argument) opcode. Next, the `add` opcode will be used to pop the next two values off the stack and find the summation and store the value on the stack yet again. Finally, this sum is popped off the stack and returned to the caller via the `ret` opcode. If you were to disassemble this C# method using `ildasm.exe`, you would find numerous additional tokens injected by `csc.exe`, but the crux of the CIL code is quite simple.

```
.method public hidebysig static int32 Add(int32 a,
  int32 b) cil managed
{
  .maxstack 2
  ldarg.0 // Load "a" onto the stack.
  ldarg.1 // Load "b" onto the stack.
  add     // Add both values.
  ret
}
```

The Hidden this Reference

Notice that the two incoming arguments (a and b) are referenced within the CIL code using their indexed position (index 0 and index 1), given that the virtual execution stack begins indexing at position 0.

CHAPTER 18 ■ UNDERSTANDING CIL AND THE ROLE OF DYNAMIC ASSEMBLIES

One thing to be mindful of when you are examining or authoring CIL code is that every nonstatic method that takes incoming arguments automatically receives an implicit additional parameter, which is a reference to the current object (think the C# this keyword). Given this, if the Add() method were defined as *nonstatic*, like so:

```
// No longer static!
public int Add(int a, int b)
{
  return a + b;
}
```

the incoming a and b arguments are loaded using ldarg.1 and ldarg.2 (rather than the expected ldarg.0 and ldarg.1 opcodes). Again, the reason is that slot 0 actually contains the implicit this reference. Consider the following pseudocode:

```
// This is JUST pseudo-code!
.method public hidebysig static int32 AddTwoIntParams(
  MyClass_HiddenThisPointer this, int32 a, int32 b) cil managed
{
  ldarg.0 // Load MyClass_HiddenThisPointer onto the stack.
  ldarg.1 // Load "a" onto the stack.
  ldarg.2 // Load "b" onto the stack.
...
}
```

Representing Iteration Constructs in CIL

Iteration constructs in the C# programming language are represented using the for, foreach, while, and do keywords, each of which has a specific representation in CIL. Consider the following classic for loop:

```
public static void CountToTen()
{
  for(int i = 0; i < 10; i++)
    ;
}
```

Now, as you may recall, the br opcodes (br, blt, and so on) are used to control a break in flow when some condition has been met. In this example, you have set up a condition in which the for loop should break out of its cycle when the local variable i is equal to or greater than the value of 10. With each pass, the value of 1 is added to i, at which point the test condition is yet again evaluated.

Also recall that when you use any of the CIL branching opcodes, you will need to define a specific code label (or two) that marks the location to jump to when the condition is indeed true. Given these points, ponder the following (augmented) CIL code generated via ildasm.exe (including the autogenerated code labels):

```
.method public hidebysig static void CountToTen() cil managed
{
  .maxstack 2
  .locals init ([0] int32 i) // Init the local integer "i".
  IL_0000: ldc.i4.0       // Load this value onto the stack.
  IL_0001: stloc.0        // Store this value at index "0".
  IL_0002: br.s IL_0008    // Jump to IL_0008.
```

```
  IL_0004: ldloc.0          // Load value of variable at index 0.
  IL_0005: ldc.i4.1         // Load the value "1" on the stack.
  IL_0006: add              // Add current value on the stack at index 0.
  IL_0007: stloc.0
  IL_0008: ldloc.0          // Load value at index "0".
  IL_0009: ldc.i4.s 10      // Load value of "10" onto the stack.
  IL_000b: blt.s IL_0004    // Less than? If so, jump back to IL_0004
  IL_000d: ret
}
```

In a nutshell, this CIL code begins by defining the local int32 and loading it onto the stack. At this point, you jump back and forth between code labels IL_0008 and IL_0004, each time bumping the value of i by 1 and testing to see whether i is still less than the value 10. If so, you exit the method.

■ **Source Code**   You can find the CilTypes example in the Chapter 18 subdirectory.

Building a .NET Assembly with CIL

Now that you've taken a tour of the syntax and semantics of raw CIL, it's time to solidify your current understanding by building a .NET application using nothing but ilasm.exe and your text editor of choice. Specifically, your application will consist of a privately deployed, single-file *.dll that contains two class type definitions, and a console-based *.exe that interacts with these types.

Building CILCars.dll

The first order of business is to build the *.dll to be consumed by the client. Open a text editor and create a new *.il file named CILCars.il. This single-file assembly will use two external .NET assemblies. Begin by updating your code file as follows:

```
// Reference mscorlib.dll and
// System.Windows.Forms.dll.
.assembly extern mscorlib
{
  .publickeytoken = (B7 7A 5C 56 19 34 E0 89 )
  .ver 4:0:0:0
}
.assembly extern System.Windows.Forms
{
  .publickeytoken = (B7 7A 5C 56 19 34 E0 89 )
  .ver 4:0:0:0
}

// Define the single-file assembly.
.assembly CILCars
{
  .hash algorithm 0x00008004
  .ver 1:0:0:0
}
.module CILCars.dll
```

This assembly will contain two class types. The first type, CILCar, defines two points of field data (public for simplicity in this example) and a custom constructor. The second type, CILCarInfo, defines a single static method named Display(), which takes CILCar as a parameter and returns void. Both types are in the CILCars namespace. In terms of CIL, CILCar can be implemented as follows:

```
// Implementation of CILCars.CILCar type.
.namespace CILCars
{
  .class public auto ansi beforefieldinit CILCar
    extends [mscorlib]System.Object
  {
    // The field data of the CILCar.
    .field public string petName
    .field public int32 currSpeed

    // The custom constructor simply allows the caller
    // to assign the field data.
    .method public hidebysig specialname rtspecialname
    instance void .ctor(int32 c, string p) cil managed
    {
    .maxstack 8

    // Load first arg onto the stack and call base class ctor.
    ldarg.0 // "this" object, not the int32!
    call instance void [mscorlib]System.Object::.ctor()

    // Now load first and second args onto the stack.
    ldarg.0 // "this" object
    ldarg.1 // int32 arg

    // Store topmost stack (int 32) member in currSpeed field.
    stfld int32 CILCars.CILCar::currSpeed

    // Load string arg and store in petName field.
    ldarg.0 // "this" object
    ldarg.2 // string arg
    stfld string CILCars.CILCar::petName
    ret
  }
 }
}
```

Keeping in mind that the real first argument for any nonstatic member is the current object reference, the first block of CIL simply loads the object reference and calls the base class constructor. Next, you push the incoming constructor arguments onto the stack and store them into the type's field data using the stfld (store in field) opcode.

Now let's implement the second type in this namespace: CILCarInfo. The meat of the type is found within the static Display() method. In a nutshell, the role of this method is to take the incoming CILCar parameter, extract the values of its field data, and display it in a Windows Forms message box. Here is the complete implementation of CILCarInfo (which should be defined within the CILCars namespace) with analysis to follow:

```
.class public auto ansi beforefieldinit CILCarInfo
  extends [mscorlib]System.Object
{
  .method public hidebysig static void
    Display(class CILCars.CILCar c) cil managed
  {
    .maxstack 8

    // We need a local string variable.
    .locals init ([0] string caption)

    // Load string and the incoming CILCar onto the stack.
    ldstr "{0}'s speed is:"
    ldarg.0

    // Now place the value of the CILCar's petName on the
    // stack and call the static String.Format() method.
    ldfld string CILCars.CILCar::petName
    call string [mscorlib]System.String::Format(string, object)
    stloc.0

    // Now load the value of the currSpeed field and get its string
    // representation (note call to ToString()).
    ldarg.0
    ldflda int32 CILCars.CILCar::currSpeed
    call instance string [mscorlib]System.Int32::ToString()
    ldloc.0

    // Now call the MessageBox.Show() method with loaded values.
    call valuetype [System.Windows.Forms]
        System.Windows.Forms.DialogResult
        [System.Windows.Forms]
        System.Windows.Forms.MessageBox::Show(string, string)
    pop
    ret
  }
}
```

Although the amount of CIL code is a bit more than you see in the implementation of CILCar, things are still rather straightforward. First, given that you are defining a static method, you don't have to be concerned with the hidden object reference (thus, the ldarg.0 opcode really does load the incoming CILCar argument).

The method begins by loading a string ("{0}'s speed is") onto the stack, followed by the CILCar argument. After these two values are in place, you load the value of the petName field and call the static System.String.Format() method to substitute the curly bracket placeholder with the CILCar's pet name.

The same general procedure takes place when processing the currSpeed field, but note that you use the ldflda opcode, which loads the argument address onto the stack. At this point, you call System.Int32.ToString() to transform the value at said address into a string type. Finally, after both strings have been formatted as necessary, you call the MessageBox.Show() method.

At this point, you are able to compile your new *.dll using ilasm.exe with the following command:

```
ilasm /dll CILCars.il
```

and verify the contained CIL using peverify.exe, as follows:

```
peverify CILCars.dll
```

Building CILCarClient.exe

Now you can build a simple *.exe assembly with a Main() method that will do the following:

- Make a CILCar object
- Pass the object into the static CILCarInfo.Display() method

Create a new file named CarClient.il and define external references to mscorlib.dll and CILCars. dll (don't forget to place a copy of this .NET assembly in the client's application directory!). Next, define a single type (Program) that manipulates the CILCars.dll assembly. Here's the complete code:

```
// External assembly refs.
.assembly extern mscorlib
{
  .publickeytoken = (B7 7A 5C 56 19 34 E0 89)
  .ver 4:0:0:0
}
.assembly extern CILCars
{
  .ver 1:0:0:0
}

// Our executable assembly.
.assembly CarClient
{
  .hash algorithm 0x00008004
  .ver 1:0:0:0
}
.module CarClient.exe

// Implementation of Program type.
.namespace CarClient
{
  .class private auto ansi beforefieldinit Program
  extends [mscorlib]System.Object
  {
    .method private hidebysig static void
    Main(string[] args) cil managed
    {
      // Marks the entry point of the *.exe.
      .entrypoint
      .maxstack 8
```

```
// Declare a local CILCar variable and push
// values onto the stack for ctor call.
.locals init ([0] class
[CILCars]CILCars.CILCar myCilCar)
ldc.i4 55
ldstr "Junior"

// Make new CilCar; store and load reference.
newobj instance void
  [CILCars]CILCars.CILCar::.ctor(int32, string)
stloc.0
ldloc.0

// Call Display() and pass in topmost value on stack.
call void [CILCars]
  CILCars.CILCarInfo::Display(
      class [CILCars]CILCars.CILCar)
ret
  }
 }
}
```

The one opcode that is important to point out is `.entrypoint`. Recall from the discussion earlier in this chapter that this opcode is used to mark which method of an `*.exe` functions as the entry point of the module. In fact, given that `.entrypoint` is how the CLR identifies the initial method to execute, this method can be called anything, although here you are using the standard method name of `Main()`. The remainder of the CIL code found in the `Main()` method is your basic pushing and popping of stack-based values.

Do note, however, that the creation of a `CILCar` object involves the use of the `newobj` opcode. On a related note, recall that when you want to invoke a member of a type using raw CIL, you use the double-colon syntax and, as always, use the fully qualified name of the type. With this, you can compile your new file with `ilasm.exe`, verify your assembly with `peverify.exe`, and execute your program. Issue the following commands within your command prompt:

```
ilasm CarClient.il
peverify CarClient.exe
CarClient.exe
```

■ **Source Code**   You can find the CilCars example in the Chapter 18 subdirectory.

Understanding Dynamic Assemblies

To be sure, the process of building a complex .NET application in CIL would be quite the labor of love. On the one hand, CIL is an extremely expressive programming language that allows you to interact with all the programming constructs allowed by the CTS. On the other hand, authoring raw CIL is tedious, error-prone, and painful. While it is true that knowledge is power, you might indeed wonder just how important it is to commit the laws of CIL syntax to memory. The answer is, "It depends." To be sure, most of your .NET programming endeavors will not require you to view, edit, or author CIL code. However, with the CIL primer behind you, you are now ready to investigate the world of dynamic assemblies (as opposed to static assemblies) and the role of the `System.Reflection.Emit` namespace.

The first question you may have is, "What exactly is the difference between static and dynamic assemblies?" By definition, *static assemblies* are .NET binaries loaded directly from disk storage, meaning they are located somewhere on your hard drive in a physical file (or possibly a set of files in the case of a multifile assembly) at the time the CLR requests them. As you might guess, every time you compile your C# source code, you end up with a static assembly.

A *dynamic assembly*, on the other hand, is created in memory, on the fly, using the types provided by the System.Reflection.Emit namespace. The System.Reflection.Emit namespace makes it possible to create an assembly and its modules, type definitions, and CIL implementation logic at *runtime*. After you have done so, you are then free to save your in-memory binary to disk. This, of course, results in a new static assembly. To be sure, the process of building a dynamic assembly using the System.Reflection.Emit namespace does require some level of understanding regarding the nature of CIL opcodes.

Although creating dynamic assemblies is a fairly advanced (and uncommon) programming task, they can be useful under various circumstances. Here's an example:

- You are building a .NET programming tool that needs to generate assemblies on demand based on user input.

- You are building a program that needs to generate proxies to remote types on the fly, based on the obtained metadata.

- You want to load a static assembly and dynamically insert new types into the binary image.

This being said, let's check out the types within System.Reflection.Emit.

Exploring the System.Reflection.Emit Namespace

Creating a dynamic assembly requires you to have some familiarity with CIL opcodes, but the types of the System.Reflection.Emit namespace hide the complexity of CIL as much as possible. For example, rather than directly specifying the necessary CIL directives and attributes to define a class type, you can simply use the TypeBuilder class. Likewise, if you want to define a new instance-level constructor, you have no need to emit the specialname, rtspecialname, or .ctor token; rather, you can use the ConstructorBuilder. Table 18-8 documents the key members of the System.Reflection.Emit namespace.

Table 18-8. *Select Members of the* System.Reflection.Emit *Namespace*

Members	Meaning in Life
AssemblyBuilder	Used to create an assembly (*.dll or *.exe) at runtime. *.exes must call the ModuleBuilder.SetEntryPoint() method to set the method that is the entry point to the module. If no entry point is specified, a *.dll will be generated.
ModuleBuilder	Used to define the set of modules within the current assembly.
EnumBuilder	Used to create a .NET enumeration type.
TypeBuilder	May be used to create classes, interfaces, structures, and delegates within a module at runtime.
MethodBuilder LocalBuilder PropertyBuilder FieldBuilder ConstructorBuilder CustomAttributeBuilder ParameterBuilder EventBuilder	Used to create type members (such as methods, local variables, properties, constructors, and attributes) at runtime.
ILGenerator	Emits CIL opcodes into a given type member.
OpCodes	Provides numerous fields that map to CIL opcodes. This type is used in conjunction with the various members of System.Reflection.Emit.ILGenerator.

In general, the types of the System.Reflection.Emit namespace allow you to represent raw CIL tokens programmatically during the construction of your dynamic assembly. You will see many of these members in the example that follows; however, the ILGenerator type is worth checking out straightaway.

The Role of the System.Reflection.Emit.ILGenerator

As its name implies, the ILGenerator type's role is to inject CIL opcodes into a given type member. However, you cannot directly create ILGenerator objects, as this type has no public constructors; rather, you receive an ILGenerator type by calling specific methods of the builder-centric types (such as the MethodBuilder and ConstructorBuilder types). Here's an example:

```
// Obtain an ILGenerator from a ConstructorBuilder
// object named "myCtorBuilder".
ConstructorBuilder myCtorBuilder =
  new ConstructorBuilder(/* ...various args... */);

ILGenerator myCILGen = myCtorBuilder.GetILGenerator();
```

Once you have an ILGenerator in your hands, you are then able to emit the raw CIL opcodes using any number of methods. Table 18-9 documents some (but not all) methods of ILGenerator.

Table 18-9. *Various Methods of* `ILGenerator`

Method	Meaning in Life
`BeginCatchBlock()`	Begins a catch block
`BeginExceptionBlock()`	Begins an exception scope for an exception
`BeginFinallyBlock()`	Begins a finally block
`BeginScope()`	Begins a lexical scope
`DeclareLocal()`	Declares a local variable
`DefineLabel()`	Declares a new label
`Emit()`	Is overloaded numerous times to allow you to emit CIL opcodes
`EmitCall()`	Pushes a `call` or `callvirt` opcode into the CIL stream
`EmitWriteLine()`	Emits a call to `Console.WriteLine()` with different types of values
`EndExceptionBlock()`	Ends an exception block
`EndScope()`	Ends a lexical scope
`ThrowException()`	Emits an instruction to throw an exception
`UsingNamespace()`	Specifies the namespace to be used in evaluating locals and watches for the current active lexical scope

The key method of `ILGenerator` is `Emit()`, which works in conjunction with the `System.Reflection.Emit.OpCodes` class type. As mentioned earlier in this chapter, this type exposes a good number of read-only fields that map to raw CIL opcodes. The full set of these members are all documented within online help, and you will see various examples in the pages that follow.

Emitting a Dynamic Assembly

To illustrate the process of defining a .NET assembly at runtime, let's walk through the process of creating a single-file dynamic assembly named `MyAssembly.dll`. Within this module is a class named `HelloWorld`. The `HelloWorld` class supports a default constructor and a custom constructor that is used to assign the value of a private member variable (`theMessage`) of type `string`. In addition, `HelloWorld` supports a public instance method named `SayHello()`, which prints a greeting to the standard I/O stream, and another instance method named `GetMsg()`, which returns the internal private string. In effect, you are going to programmatically generate the following class type:

```
// This class will be created at runtime
// using System.Reflection.Emit.
public class HelloWorld
{
  private string theMessage;
  HelloWorld() {}
  HelloWorld(string s) {theMessage = s;}

  public string GetMsg() {return theMessage;}
  public void SayHello()
  {
    System.Console.WriteLine("Hello from the HelloWorld class!");
  }
}
```

Assume you have created a new Visual Studio Console Application project named DynamicAsmBuilder and you import the `System.Reflection`, `System.Reflection.Emit`, and `System.Threading` namespaces. Define a static method named `CreateMyAsm()` in the `Program` class. This single method is in charge of the following:

- Defining the characteristics of the dynamic assembly (name, version, etc.)

- Implementing the `HelloClass` type

- Saving the in-memory assembly to a physical file

Also note that the `CreateMyAsm()` method takes as a single parameter a `System.AppDomain` type, which will be used to obtain access to the `AssemblyBuilder` type associated with the current application domain (see Chapter 17 for a discussion of .NET application domains). Here is the complete code, with analysis to follow:

```
// The caller sends in an AppDomain type.
public static void CreateMyAsm(AppDomain curAppDomain)
{
  // Establish general assembly characteristics.
  AssemblyName assemblyName = new AssemblyName();
  assemblyName.Name = "MyAssembly";
  assemblyName.Version = new Version("1.0.0.0");

  // Create new assembly within the current AppDomain.
  AssemblyBuilder assembly =
    curAppDomain.DefineDynamicAssembly(assemblyName, AssemblyBuilderAccess.Save);

  // Given that we are building a single-file
  // assembly, the name of the module is the same as the assembly.
  ModuleBuilder module =
    assembly.DefineDynamicModule("MyAssembly", "MyAssembly.dll");

  // Define a public class named "HelloWorld".
  TypeBuilder helloWorldClass = module.DefineType("MyAssembly.HelloWorld", TypeAttributes.
Public);

  // Define a private String member variable named "theMessage".
  FieldBuilder msgField =
    helloWorldClass.DefineField("theMessage", Type.GetType("System.String"),
FieldAttributes.Private);

  // Create the custom ctor.
  Type[] constructorArgs = new Type[1];
  constructorArgs[0] = typeof(string);
  ConstructorBuilder constructor =
    helloWorldClass.DefineConstructor(MethodAttributes.Public,
    CallingConventions.Standard,
    constructorArgs);
  ILGenerator constructorIL = constructor.GetILGenerator();
  constructorIL.Emit(OpCodes.Ldarg_0);
  Type objectClass = typeof(object);
```

```
ConstructorInfo superConstructor = objectClass.GetConstructor(new Type[0]);
constructorIL.Emit(OpCodes.Call, superConstructor);
constructorIL.Emit(OpCodes.Ldarg_0);
constructorIL.Emit(OpCodes.Ldarg_1);
constructorIL.Emit(OpCodes.Stfld, msgField);
constructorIL.Emit(OpCodes.Ret);

// Create the default ctor.
helloWorldClass.DefineDefaultConstructor(MethodAttributes.Public);
// Now create the GetMsg() method.
MethodBuilder getMsgMethod =
  helloWorldClass.DefineMethod("GetMsg", MethodAttributes.Public,
  typeof(string), null);
ILGenerator methodIL = getMsgMethod.GetILGenerator();
methodIL.Emit(OpCodes.Ldarg_0);
methodIL.Emit(OpCodes.Ldfld, msgField);
methodIL.Emit(OpCodes.Ret);

// Create the SayHello method.
MethodBuilder sayHiMethod =
  helloWorldClass.DefineMethod("SayHello",
  MethodAttributes.Public, null, null);
methodIL = sayHiMethod.GetILGenerator();
methodIL.EmitWriteLine("Hello from the HelloWorld class!");
methodIL.Emit(OpCodes.Ret);

// "Bake" the class HelloWorld.
// (Baking is the formal term for emitting the type.)
helloWorldClass.CreateType();

// (Optionally) save the assembly to file.
assembly.Save("MyAssembly.dll");
}
```

Emitting the Assembly and Module Set

The method body begins by establishing the minimal set of characteristics about your assembly, using the
AssemblyName and Version types (defined in the System.Reflection namespace). Next, you obtain an
AssemblyBuilder type via the instance-level AppDomain.DefineDynamicAssembly() method (recall the
caller will pass an AppDomain reference into the CreateMyAsm() method), like so:

```
// Establish general assembly characteristics
// and gain access to the AssemblyBuilder type.
public static void CreateMyAsm(AppDomain curAppDomain)
{
  AssemblyName assemblyName = new AssemblyName();
  assemblyName.Name = "MyAssembly";
  assemblyName.Version = new Version("1.0.0.0");
```

```
// Create new assembly within the current AppDomain.
AssemblyBuilder assembly =
  curAppDomain.DefineDynamicAssembly(assemblyName,
  AssemblyBuilderAccess.Save);
...
}
```

As you can see, when calling AppDomain.DefineDynamicAssembly(), you must specify the access mode of the assembly you want to define, the most common values of which are shown in Table 18-10.

Table 18-10. *Common Values of the AssemblyBuilderAccess Enumeration*

Value	Meaning in Life
ReflectionOnly	Represents that a dynamic assembly can only be reflected over
Run	Represents that a dynamic assembly can be executed in memory but not saved to disk
RunAndSave	Represents that a dynamic assembly can be executed in memory and saved to disk
Save	Represents that a dynamic assembly can be saved to disk but not executed in memory

The next task is to define the module set for your new assembly. Given that the assembly is a single-file unit, you need to define only a single module. If you were to build a multifile assembly using the DefineDynamicModule() method, you would specify an optional second parameter that represents the name of a given module (e.g., myMod.dotnetmodule). However, when creating a single-file assembly, the name of the module will be identical to the name of the assembly itself. In any case, once the DefineDynamicModule() method has returned, you are provided with a reference to a valid ModuleBuilder type.

```
// The single-file assembly.
ModuleBuilder module =
  assembly.DefineDynamicModule("MyAssembly", "MyAssembly.dll");
```

The Role of the ModuleBuilder Type

ModuleBuilder is the key type used during the development of dynamic assemblies. As you would expect, ModuleBuilder supports a number of members that allow you to define the set of types contained within a given module (classes, interfaces, structures, etc.) as well as the set of embedded resources (string tables, images, etc.) contained within. Table 18-11 describes a few of the creation-centric methods. (Do note that each method will return to you a related type that represents the type you want to construct.)

Table 18-11. *Select Members of the ModuleBuilder Type*

Method	Meaning in Life
DefineEnum()	Used to emit a .NET enum definition
DefineResource()	Defines a managed embedded resource to be stored in this module
DefineType()	Constructs a TypeBuilder, which allows you to define value types, interfaces, and class types (including delegates)

The key member of the ModuleBuilder class to be aware of is DefineType(). In addition to specifying the name of the type (via a simple string), you will also use the System.Reflection.TypeAttributes enum to describe the format of the type itself. Table 18-12 lists some (but not all) of the key members of the TypeAttributes enumeration.

Table 18-12. *Select Members of the TypeAttributes Enumeration*

Member	Meaning in Life
Abstract	Specifies that the type is abstract
Class	Specifies that the type is a class
Interface	Specifies that the type is an interface
NestedAssembly	Specifies that the class is nested with assembly visibility and is thus accessible only by methods within its assembly
NestedFamANDAssem	Specifies that the class is nested with assembly and family visibility and is thus accessible only by methods lying in the intersection of its family and assembly
NestedFamily	Specifies that the class is nested with family visibility and is thus accessible only by methods within its own type and any subtypes
NestedFamORAssem	Specifies that the class is nested with family or assembly visibility and is thus accessible only by methods lying in the union of its family and assembly
NestedPrivate	Specifies that the class is nested with private visibility
NestedPublic	Specifies that the class is nested with public visibility
NotPublic	Specifies that the class is not public
Public	Specifies that the class is public
Sealed	Specifies that the class is concrete and cannot be extended
Serializable	Specifies that the class can be serialized

Emitting the HelloClass Type and the String Member Variable

Now that you have a better understanding of the role of the ModuleBuilder.CreateType() method, let's examine how you can emit the public HelloWorld class type and the private string variable.

```
// Define a public class named "MyAssembly.HelloWorld".
TypeBuilder helloWorldClass = module.DefineType("MyAssembly.HelloWorld",
  TypeAttributes.Public);
```

```
// Define a private String member variable named "theMessage".
FieldBuilder msgField =
  helloWorldClass.DefineField("theMessage",
  Type.GetType("System.String"),
  FieldAttributes.Private);
```

Notice how the TypeBuilder.DefineField() method provides access to a FieldBuilder type. The TypeBuilder class also defines other methods that provide access to other "builder" types. For example, DefineConstructor() returns a ConstructorBuilder, DefineProperty() returns a PropertyBuilder, and so forth.

Emitting the Constructors

As mentioned earlier, the TypeBuilder.DefineConstructor() method can be used to define a constructor for the current type. However, when it comes to implementing the constructor of HelloClass, you need to inject raw CIL code into the constructor body, which is responsible for assigning the incoming parameter to the internal private string. To obtain an ILGenerator type, you call the GetILGenerator() method from the respective "builder" type you have reference to (in this case, the ConstructorBuilder type).

The Emit() method of the ILGenerator class is the entity in charge of placing CIL into a member implementation. Emit() itself makes frequent use of the OpCodes class type, which exposes the opcode set of CIL using read-only fields. For example, OpCodes.Ret signals the return of a method call, OpCodes.Stfld makes an assignment to a member variable, and OpCodes.Call is used to call a given method (in this case, the base class constructor). That said, ponder the following constructor logic:

```
// Create the custom constructor taking
// a single System.String argument.
Type[] constructorArgs = new Type[1];
constructorArgs[0] = typeof(string);
ConstructorBuilder constructor =
  helloWorldClass.DefineConstructor(MethodAttributes.Public,
  CallingConventions.Standard, constructorArgs);

// Now emit the necessary CIL into the ctor.
ILGenerator constructorIL = constructor.GetILGenerator();
constructorIL.Emit(OpCodes.Ldarg_0);
Type objectClass = typeof(object);
ConstructorInfo superConstructor = objectClass.GetConstructor(new Type[0]);
constructorIL.Emit(OpCodes.Call, superConstructor); // Call base class ctor.

// Load the object's "this" pointer on the stack.
constructorIL.Emit(OpCodes.Ldarg_0);

// Load incoming argument on virtual stack and store in msgField.
constructorIL.Emit(OpCodes.Ldarg_1);
constructorIL.Emit(OpCodes.Stfld, msgField); // Assign msgField.
constructorIL.Emit(OpCodes.Ret);             // Return.
```

Now, as you are well aware, as soon as you define a custom constructor for a type, the default constructor is silently removed. To redefine the no-argument constructor, simply call the DefineDefaultConstructor() method of the TypeBuilder type as follows:

```
// Reinsert the default ctor.
helloWorldClass.DefineDefaultConstructor(MethodAttributes.Public);
```

This single call emits the standard CIL code used to define a default constructor.

```
.method public hidebysig specialname rtspecialname
  instance void .ctor() cil managed
{
  .maxstack 1
  ldarg.0
  call instance void [mscorlib]System.Object::.ctor()
  ret
}
```

Emitting the SayHello() Method

Last but not least, let's examine the process of emitting the SayHello() method. The first task is to obtain a MethodBuilder type from the helloWorldClass variable. After you do this, you define the method and obtain the underlying ILGenerator to inject the CIL instructions, like so:

```
// Create the SayHello method.
MethodBuilder sayHiMethod =
  helloWorldClass.DefineMethod("SayHello",
  MethodAttributes.Public, null, null);
methodIL = sayHiMethod.GetILGenerator();

// Write a line to the Console.
methodIL.EmitWriteLine("Hello from the HelloWorld class!");
methodIL.Emit(OpCodes.Ret);
```

Here you have established a public method (MethodAttributes.Public) that takes no parameters and returns nothing (marked by the null entries contained in the DefineMethod() call). Also note the EmitWriteLine() call. This helper member of the ILGenerator class automatically writes a line to the standard output with minimal fuss and bother.

Using the Dynamically Generated Assembly

Now that you have the logic in place to create and save your assembly, all that's needed is a class to trigger the logic. To come full circle, assume your current project defines a second class named AsmReader. The logic in Main() obtains the current AppDomain via the Thread.GetDomain() method that will be used to host the assembly you will dynamically create. Once you have a reference, you are able to call the CreateMyAsm() method.

To make things a bit more interesting, after the call to CreateMyAsm() returns, you will exercise some late binding (see Chapter 15) to load your newly created assembly into memory and interact with the members of the HelloWorld class. Update your Main() method as follows:

```
static void Main(string[] args)
{
  Console.WriteLine("***** The Amazing Dynamic Assembly Builder App *****");
  // Get the application domain for the current thread.
  AppDomain curAppDomain = Thread.GetDomain();

  // Create the dynamic assembly using our helper f(x).
  CreateMyAsm(curAppDomain);
  Console.WriteLine("-> Finished creating MyAssembly.dll.");

  // Now load the new assembly from file.
  Console.WriteLine("-> Loading MyAssembly.dll from file.");
  Assembly a = Assembly.Load("MyAssembly");

  // Get the HelloWorld type.
  Type hello = a.GetType("MyAssembly.HelloWorld");

  // Create HelloWorld object and call the correct ctor.
  Console.Write("-> Enter message to pass HelloWorld class: ");
```

```
    string msg = Console.ReadLine();
    object[] ctorArgs = new object[1];
    ctorArgs[0] = msg;
    object obj = Activator.CreateInstance(hello, ctorArgs);

    // Call SayHello and show returned string.
    Console.WriteLine("-> Calling SayHello() via late binding.");
    MethodInfo mi = hello.GetMethod("SayHello");
    mi.Invoke(obj, null);

    // Invoke method.
    mi = hello.GetMethod("GetMsg");
    Console.WriteLine(mi.Invoke(obj, null));
}
```

In effect, you have just created a .NET assembly that is able to create and execute .NET assemblies at runtime! That wraps up the examination of CIL and the role of dynamic assemblies. I hope this chapter has deepened your understanding of the .NET type system, the syntax and semantics of CIL, and how the C# compiler processes your code at compile time.

■ **Source Code**   You can find the DynamicAsmBuilder project in the Chapter 18 subdirectory.

Summary

This chapter provided an overview of the syntax and semantics of CIL. Unlike higher-level managed languages such as C#, CIL does not simply define a set of keywords but provides directives (used to define the structure of an assembly and its types), attributes (which further qualify a given directive), and opcodes (which are used to implement type members).

You were introduced to a few CIL-centric programming tools and learned how to alter the contents of a .NET assembly with new CIL instructions using round-trip engineering. After this point, you spent time learning how to establish the current (and referenced) assembly, namespaces, types, and members. I wrapped up with a simple example of building a .NET code library and executable using little more than CIL, command-line tools, and a bit of elbow grease.

Finally, you took an introductory look at the process of creating a *dynamic assembly*. Using the System. Reflection.Emit namespace, it is possible to define a .NET assembly in memory at runtime. As you have seen firsthand, using this particular API requires you to know the semantics of CIL code in some detail. While the need to build dynamic assemblies is certainly not a common task for most .NET applications, it can be useful for those of you who need to build support tools and other programming utilities.

■ ■ ■

PART VI

Introducing the .NET Base Class Libraries

CHAPTER 19

■ ■ ■

Multithreaded, Parallel, and Async Programming

Nobody enjoys working with an application that is sluggish during its execution. Moreover, nobody enjoys starting a task in an application (perhaps initiated by clicking a toolbar item) that prevents other parts of the program from being as responsive as possible. Before the release of .NET, building applications that had the ability to perform multiple tasks typically required authoring complex C++ code that used the Windows threading APIs. Thankfully, the .NET platform provides a number of ways for you to build software that can perform complex operations on unique paths of execution, with far fewer pain points.

This chapter begins by defining the overall nature of a "multithreaded application." Next, you will revisit the .NET delegate type to investigate its intrinsic support for *asynchronous method invocations*. As you'll see, this technique allows you to invoke a method on a secondary thread of execution without needing to manually create or configure the thread itself.

Next, you'll be introduced to the original threading namespace that has shipped since .NET 1.0, specifically System.Threading. Here you'll examine numerous types (Thread, ThreadStart, etc.) that allow you to explicitly create additional threads of execution and synchronize your shared resources, which helps ensure that multiple threads can share data in a nonvolatile manner.

The remaining parts of this chapter will examine three more recent techniques .NET developers can use to build multithreaded software, specifically the Task Parallel Library (TPL), Parallel LINQ (PLINQ), and the new (as of C# 6) intrinsic asynchronous keywords of C# (async and await). As you will see, these features can dramatically simplify how you can build responsive multithreaded software applications.

The Process/AppDomain/Context/Thread Relationship

In Chapter 17, a *thread* was defined as a path of execution within an executable application. While many .NET applications can live happy and productive single-threaded lives, an assembly's primary thread (spawned by the CLR when Main() executes) may create secondary threads of execution at any time to perform additional units of work. By creating additional threads, you can build more responsive (but not necessarily faster executing on single-core machines) applications.

The System.Threading namespace was released with .NET 1.0 and offers one approach to build multithreaded applications. The Thread class is perhaps the core type, as it represents a given thread. If you want to programmatically obtain a reference to the thread currently executing a given member, simply call the static Thread.CurrentThread property, like so:

```
static void ExtractExecutingThread()
{
  // Get the thread currently
  // executing this method.
  Thread currThread = Thread.CurrentThread;
}
```

Under the .NET platform, there is *not* a direct one-to-one correspondence between application domains and threads. In fact, a given AppDomain can have numerous threads executing within it at any given time. Furthermore, a particular thread is not confined to a single application domain during its lifetime. Threads are free to cross application domain boundaries as the Windows OS thread scheduler and the .NET CLR see fit.

Although active threads can be moved between AppDomain boundaries, a given thread can execute within only a single application domain at any point in time (in other words, it is impossible for a single thread to be doing work in more than one AppDomain at once). When you want to programmatically gain access to the AppDomain that is hosting the current thread, call the static Thread.GetDomain() method, like so:

```
static void ExtractAppDomainHostingThread()
{
  // Obtain the AppDomain hosting the current thread.
  AppDomain ad = Thread.GetDomain();
}
```

A single thread may also be moved into a particular context at any given time, and it may be relocated within a new context at the whim of the CLR. When you want to obtain the current context a thread happens to be executing in, use the static Thread.CurrentContext property (which returns a System.Runtime.Remoting.Contexts.Context object), like so:

```
static void ExtractCurrentThreadContext()
{
  // Obtain the context under which the
  // current thread is operating.
  Context ctx = Thread.CurrentContext;
}
```

Again, the CLR is the entity that is in charge of moving threads into (and out of) application domains and contexts. As a .NET developer, you can usually remain blissfully unaware where a given thread ends up (or exactly when it is placed into its new boundary). Nevertheless, you should be aware of the various ways of obtaining the underlying primitives.

The Problem of Concurrency

One of the many "joys" (read: painful aspects) of multithreaded programming is that you have little control over how the underlying operating system or the CLR uses its threads. For example, if you craft a block of code that creates a new thread of execution, you cannot guarantee that the thread executes immediately. Rather, such code only instructs the OS/CLR to execute the thread as soon as possible (which is typically when the thread scheduler gets around to it).

Furthermore, given that threads can be moved between application and contextual boundaries as required by the CLR, you must be mindful of which aspects of your application are *thread-volatile* (e.g., subject to multithreaded access) and which operations are *atomic* (thread-volatile operations are the dangerous ones!).

To illustrate the problem, assume a thread is invoking a method of a specific object. Now assume that this thread is instructed by the thread scheduler to suspend its activity to allow another thread to access the same method of the same object.

If the original thread was not completely finished with its operation, the second incoming thread may be viewing an object in a partially modified state. At this point, the second thread is basically reading bogus data, which is sure to give way to extremely odd (and hard to find) bugs, which are even harder to replicate and debug.

Atomic operations, on the other hand, are always safe in a multithreaded environment. Sadly, there are few operations in the .NET base class libraries that are guaranteed to be atomic. Even the act of assigning a value to a member variable is not atomic! Unless the .NET Framework 4.7 SDK documentation specifically says an operation is atomic, you must assume it is thread-volatile and take precautions.

The Role of Thread Synchronization

At this point, it should be clear that multithreaded programs are in themselves quite volatile, as numerous threads can operate on the shared resources at (more or less) the same time. To protect an application's resources from possible corruption, .NET developers must use any number of threading primitives (such as locks, monitors, and the [Synchronization] attribute or language keyword support) to control access among the executing threads.

Although the .NET platform cannot make the difficulties of building robust multithreaded applications completely disappear, the process has been simplified considerably. Using types defined within the System.Threading namespace, the Task Parallel Library (TPL), and the C# async and await language keywords, you are able to work with multiple threads with minimal fuss and bother.

Before diving into the System.Threading namespace, the TPL, and the C# async and await keywords, you will begin by examining how the .NET delegate type can be used to invoke a method in an asynchronous manner. While it is most certainly true that since .NET 4.6, the new C# async and await keywords offer a simpler alternative to asynchronous delegates, it is still important that you know how to interact with code using this approach (trust me; there is a ton of code in production that uses asynchronous delegates).

A Brief Review of the .NET Delegate

Recall that a .NET delegate is essentially a type-safe, object-oriented, function pointer. When you define a .NET delegate type, the C# compiler responds by building a sealed class that derives from System.MulticastDelegate (which in turn derives from System.Delegate). These base classes provide every delegate with the ability to maintain a list of method addresses, all of which may be invoked at a later time. Consider the following BinaryOp delegate, first defined in Chapter 10:

```
// A C# delegate type.
public delegate int BinaryOp(int x, int y);
```

Based on its definition, BinaryOp can point to any method taking two integers (by value) as arguments and returning an integer. Once compiled, the defining assembly now contains a full-blown class definition that is dynamically generated when you build your project, based on the delegate declaration. In the case of BinaryOp, this class looks more or less like the following (shown in pseudocode):

```
public sealed class BinaryOp : System.MulticastDelegate
{
  public BinaryOp(object target, uint functionAddress);
  public int Invoke(int x, int y);
  public IAsyncResult BeginInvoke(int x, int y,
    AsyncCallback cb, object state);
  public int EndInvoke(IAsyncResult result);
}
```

Recall that the generated Invoke() method is used to invoke the methods maintained by a delegate object in a *synchronous manner*. Therefore, the calling thread (such as the primary thread of the application) is forced to wait until the delegate invocation completes. Also recall that in C# the Invoke() method does not need to be directly called in code but can be triggered indirectly, under the hood, when applying "normal" method invocation syntax.

Consider the following Console Application program (SyncDelegateReview), which invokes the static Add() method in a synchronous (aka blocking) manner (be sure to import the System.Threading namespace into your C# code file, as you will be calling the Thread.Sleep() method):

```
namespace SyncDelegateReview
{
  public delegate int BinaryOp(int x, int y);

  class Program
  {
    static void Main(string[] args)
    {
      Console.WriteLine("***** Synch Delegate Review *****");

      // Print out the ID of the executing thread.
      Console.WriteLine("Main() invoked on thread {0}.",
        Thread.CurrentThread.ManagedThreadId);

      // Invoke Add() in a synchronous manner.
      BinaryOp b = new BinaryOp(Add);

      // Could also write b.Invoke(10, 10);
      int answer = b(10, 10);

      // These lines will not execute until
      // the Add() method has completed.
      Console.WriteLine("Doing more work in Main()!");
      Console.WriteLine("10 + 10 is {0}.", answer);
      Console.ReadLine();
    }
```

```
static int Add(int x, int y)
{
  // Print out the ID of the executing thread.
  Console.WriteLine("Add() invoked on thread {0}.",
    Thread.CurrentThread.ManagedThreadId);

  // Pause to simulate a lengthy operation.
  Thread.Sleep(5000);
  return x + y;
}
}
}
```

Within the Add() method, you are invoking the static Thread.Sleep() method to suspend the calling thread for approximately five seconds to simulate a lengthy task. Given that you are invoking the Add() method in a *synchronous* manner, the Main() method will not print out the result of the operation until the Add() method has completed.

Next, note that the Main() method is obtaining access to the current thread (via Thread. CurrentThread) and printing the ID of the thread via the ManagedThreadId property. This same logic is repeated in the static Add() method. As you might suspect, given that all the work in this application is performed exclusively by the primary thread, you find the same ID value displayed to the console.

```
***** Synch Delegate Review *****
Main() invoked on thread 1.
Add() invoked on thread 1.
Doing more work in Main()!
10 + 10 is 20.

Press any key to continue . . .
```

When you run this program, you should notice that a five-second delay takes place before you see the final Console.WriteLine() logic in Main() execute. Although many (if not most) methods may be called synchronously without ill effect, .NET delegates can be instructed to call their methods asynchronously if necessary.

■ **Source Code**   You can find the SyncDelegateReview project in the Chapter 19 subdirectory.

The Asynchronous Nature of Delegates

If you are new to the topic of multithreading, you might wonder what exactly an *asynchronous* method invocation is all about. As you are no doubt fully aware, some programming operations take time. Although the previous Add() was purely illustrative in nature, imagine that you built a single-threaded application that is invoking a method on a remote web service operation, calling a method performing a long-running database query, downloading a large document, or writing 500 lines of text to an external file. While performing these operations, the application could appear to hang for some amount of time. Until the task at hand has been processed, all other aspects of this program (such as menu activation, toolbar clicking, or console output) are suspended (which can aggravate users).

Therefore, the question is, how can you tell a delegate to invoke a method on a separate thread of execution to simulate numerous tasks performing "at the same time"? The good news is that every .NET delegate type is automatically equipped with this capability. The even better news is that you are *not* required to directly dive into the details of the System.Threading namespace to do so (although these entities can quite naturally work hand in hand).

The BeginInvoke() and EndInvoke() Methods

When the C# compiler processes the delegate keyword, the dynamically generated class defines two methods named BeginInvoke() and EndInvoke(). Given the definition of the BinaryOp delegate, these methods are prototyped as follows:

```
public sealed class BinaryOp : System.MulticastDelegate
{
...
  // Used to invoke a method asynchronously.
  public IAsyncResult BeginInvoke(int x, int y,
    AsyncCallback ch, object state);

  // Used to fetch the return value
  // of the invoked method.
  public int EndInvoke(IAsyncResult result);
}
```

The first set of parameters passed into BeginInvoke() will be based on the format of the C# delegate (two integers, in the case of BinaryOp). The final two arguments will always be System.AsyncCallback and System.Object. You'll examine the role of these parameters shortly; for the time being, though, I'll supply null for each. Also note that the return value of EndInvoke() is an integer, based on the return type of BinaryOp, while the single parameter of this method is always of type IAsyncResult.

The System.IAsyncResult Interface

The BeginInvoke() method always returns an object implementing the IAsyncResult interface, while EndInvoke() requires an IAsyncResult-compatible type as its sole parameter. The IAsyncResult-compatible object returned from BeginInvoke() is basically a coupling mechanism that allows the calling thread to obtain the result of the asynchronous method invocation at a later time via EndInvoke(). The IAsyncResult interface (defined in the System namespace) is defined as follows:

```
public interface IAsyncResult
{
  object AsyncState { get; }
  WaitHandle AsyncWaitHandle { get; }
  bool CompletedSynchronously { get; }
  bool IsCompleted { get; }
}
```

In the simplest case, you are able to avoid directly invoking these members. All you have to do is cache the IAsyncResult-compatible object returned by BeginInvoke() and pass it to EndInvoke() when you are ready to obtain the result of the method invocation. As you will see, you are able to invoke the members of an IAsyncResult-compatible object when you want to become "more involved" with the process of fetching the method's return value.

> ■ **Note** If you asynchronously invoke a method that provides a `void` return value, you can simply "fire and forget." In such cases, you will never need to cache the `IAsyncResult`-compatible object or call `EndInvoke()` in the first place (as there is no return value to retrieve).

Invoking a Method Asynchronously

To instruct the `BinaryOp` delegate to invoke `Add()` asynchronously, you will modify the logic in the previous project (feel free to add code to the existing project; however, in your lab downloads, you will find a new Console Application project named AsyncDelegate). Update the previous `Main()` method as follows:

```
static void Main(string[] args)
{
  Console.WriteLine("***** Async Delegate Invocation *****");

  // Print out the ID of the executing thread.
  Console.WriteLine("Main() invoked on thread {0}.",
    Thread.CurrentThread.ManagedThreadId);

  // Invoke Add() on a secondary thread.
  BinaryOp b = new BinaryOp(Add);
  IAsyncResult ar = b.BeginInvoke(10, 10, null, null);

  // Do other work on primary thread...
  Console.WriteLine("Doing more work in Main()!");

  // Obtain the result of the Add()
  // method when ready.
  int answer = b.EndInvoke(ar);
  Console.WriteLine("10 + 10 is {0}.", answer);
  Console.ReadLine();
}
```

If you run this application, you will find that two unique thread IDs are displayed, given that there are in fact multiple threads working within the current AppDomain.

```
***** Async Delegate Invocation *****
Main() invoked on thread 1.
Doing more work in Main()!
Add() invoked on thread 3.
10 + 10 is 20.
```

In addition to the unique ID values, you will also notice upon running the application that the `Doing more work in Main()!` message displays immediately, while the secondary thread is occupied attending to its business.

707

Synchronizing the Calling Thread

If you think carefully about the current implementation of Main(), you might realize that the time span between calling BeginInvoke() and EndInvoke() is clearly less than five seconds. Therefore, once Doing more work in Main()! prints to the console, the calling thread is now blocked and waiting for the secondary thread to complete before being able to obtain the result of the Add() method. Therefore, you are effectively making yet another *synchronous call*.

```
static void Main(string[] args)
{
...
  BinaryOp b = new BinaryOp(Add);

  // Once the next statement is processed,
  // the calling thread is now blocked until
  // BeginInvoke() completes.
  IAsyncResult ar = b.BeginInvoke(10, 10, null, null);

  // This call takes far less than five seconds!
  Console.WriteLine("Doing more work in Main()!");

  // Now we are waiting again for other thread to complete!
  int answer = b.EndInvoke(ar);
...
}
```

Obviously, asynchronous delegates would lose their appeal if the calling thread had the potential of being blocked under various circumstances. To allow the calling thread to discover whether the asynchronously invoked method has completed its work, the IAsyncResult interface provides the IsCompleted property. Using this member, the calling thread is able to determine whether the asynchronous call has indeed completed before calling EndInvoke().

If the method has not completed, IsCompleted returns false, and the calling thread is free to carry on its work. If IsCompleted returns true, the calling thread is able to obtain the result in the "least blocking manner" possible. Ponder the following update to the Main() method:

```
static void Main(string[] args)
{
...
  BinaryOp b = new BinaryOp(Add);
  IAsyncResult ar - b.BeginInvoke(10, 10, null, null);

  // This message will keep printing until
  // the Add() method is finished.
  while(!ar.IsCompleted)
  {
    Console.WriteLine("Doing more work in Main()!");
    Thread.Sleep(1000);
  }
  // Now we know the Add() method is complete.
  int answer = b.EndInvoke(ar);
...
}
```

Here, you enter a loop that will continue processing the `Console.WriteLine()` statement until the secondary thread has completed. After this has occurred, you can obtain the result of the `Add()` method, knowing full well the method has indeed completed. The call to `Thread.Sleep(1000)` is not necessary for this particular application to function correctly; however, by forcing the primary thread to wait for approximately one second during each iteration, it prevents the same message from printing hundreds of times. Here is the output (your output might differ slightly, based on the speed of your machine and when threads come to life):

```
***** Async Delegate Invocation *****
Main() invoked on thread 1.
Doing more work in Main()!
Add() invoked on thread 3.
Doing more work in Main()!
Doing more work in Main()!
Doing more work in Main()!
Doing more work in Main()!
Doing more work in Main()!
10 + 10 is 20.
```

In addition to the `IsCompleted` property, the `IAsyncResult` interface provides the `AsyncWaitHandle` property for more flexible waiting logic. This property returns an instance of the `WaitHandle` type, which exposes a method named `WaitOne()`. The benefit of `WaitHandle.WaitOne()` is that you can specify the maximum wait time. If the specified amount of time is exceeded, `WaitOne()` returns `false`. Ponder the following updated `while` loop, which no longer uses a call to `Thread.Sleep()`:

```
while (!ar.AsyncWaitHandle.WaitOne(1000, true))
{
  Console.WriteLine("Doing more work in Main()!");
}
```

While these properties of `IAsyncResult` do provide a way to synchronize the calling thread, they are not the most efficient approach. In many ways, the `IsCompleted` property is much like a really annoying manager (or classmate) who is constantly asking, "Are you done yet?" Thankfully, delegates provide a number of additional (and more elegant) techniques to obtain the result of a method that has been called asynchronously.

■ **Source Code** You can find the AsyncDelegate project in the `Chapter 19` subdirectory.

The Role of the AsyncCallback Delegate

Rather than polling a delegate to determine whether an asynchronously invoked method has completed, it would be more efficient to have the secondary thread inform the calling thread when the task is finished. When you want to enable this behavior, you will need to supply an instance of the `System.AsyncCallback` delegate as a parameter to `BeginInvoke()`, which up until this point has been null. However, when you do supply an `AsyncCallback` object, the delegate will call the specified method automatically when the asynchronous call has completed.

■ **Note** The callback method will be called on the secondary thread, not the primary thread. This has important implications when using threads within a graphical user interface (WPF or Windows Forms) as controls have thread-affinity, meaning they can be manipulated only by the thread that created them. You'll see some examples of working the threads from a GUI later in this chapter, during the examination of the Task Parallel Library (TPL) and the C# `async` and `await` keywords.

Like any delegate, AsyncCallback can invoke methods that match only a specific pattern, which in this case is a method taking IAsyncResult as the sole parameter and returning nothing.

```
// Targets of AsyncCallback must match the following pattern.
void MyAsyncCallbackMethod(IAsyncResult iar)
```

Assume you have another Console Application project (AsyncCallbackDelegate) making use of the BinaryOp delegate. This time, however, you will not poll the delegate to determine whether the Add() method has completed. Rather, you will define a static method named AddComplete() to receive the notification that the asynchronous invocation is finished. Also, this example uses a class-level static bool field, which will be used to keep the primary thread in Main() running a task until the secondary thread is finished.

■ **Note** The use of this Boolean variable in this example is, strictly speaking, not thread-safe, as there are two different threads that have access to its value. This will be permissible for the current example; however, as a *very* good rule of thumb, you must ensure data that can be shared among multiple threads is locked down. You'll see how to do so later in this chapter.

```
namespace AsyncCallbackDelegate
{
  public delegate int BinaryOp(int x, int y);

  class Program
  {
    private static bool isDone = false;

    static void Main(string[] args)
    {
      Console.WriteLine("***** AsyncCallbackDelegate Example *****");
      Console.WriteLine("Main() invoked on thread {0}.",
        Thread.CurrentThread.ManagedThreadId);

      BinaryOp b = new BinaryOp(Add);
      IAsyncResult ar = b.BeginInvoke(10, 10,
        new AsyncCallback(AddComplete), null);

      // Assume other work is performed here...
      while (!isDone)
      {
        Console.WriteLine("Working....");
```

```
        Thread.Sleep(1000);
      }
      Console.ReadLine();
    }

  static int Add(int x, int y)
  {
    Console.WriteLine("Add() invoked on thread {0}.",Thread.CurrentThread.ManagedThreadId);
    Thread.Sleep(5000);
    return x + y;
  }

  static void AddComplete(IAsyncResult iar)
  {
    Console.WriteLine("AddComplete() invoked on thread {0}.",Thread.CurrentThread.
    ManagedThreadId);
    Console.WriteLine("Your addition is complete");
    isDone = true;
  }
 }
}
```

Again, the static AddComplete() method will be invoked by the AsyncCallback delegate when the Add() method has completed. If you run this program, you can confirm that the secondary thread is the thread invoking the AddComplete() callback.

```
***** AsyncCallbackDelegate Example *****
Main() invoked on thread 1.
Add() invoked on thread 3.
Working....
Working....
Working....
Working....
Working....
AddComplete() invoked on thread 3.
Your addition is complete
```

Like other examples in this chapter, your output might be slightly different. In fact, you might see one final Working... printout occur after the addition is complete. This is just a by-product of the forced one-second delay in Main().

The Role of the AsyncResult Class

Currently, the AddComplete() method is not printing the actual result of the operation (adding two numbers). The reason is that the target of the AsyncCallback delegate (AddComplete(), in this example) does not have access to the original BinaryOp delegate created in the scope of Main(); therefore, you can't call EndInvoke() from within AddComplete()!

While you could simply declare the BinaryOp variable as a static member variable in the class to allow both methods to access the same object, a more elegant solution is to use the incoming IAsyncResult parameter.

The incoming IAsyncResult parameter passed into the target of the AsyncCallback delegate is actually an instance of the AsyncResult class (note the lack of an I prefix) defined in the System.Runtime.Remoting. Messaging namespace. The AsyncDelegate property returns a reference to the original asynchronous delegate that was created elsewhere.

Therefore, if you want to obtain a reference to the BinaryOp delegate object allocated within Main(), simply cast the System.Object returned by the AsyncDelegate property into type BinaryOp. At this point, you can trigger EndInvoke() as expected.

```
// Don't forget to import
// System.Runtime.Remoting.Messaging!
static void AddComplete(IAsyncResult iar)
{
  Console.WriteLine("AddComplete() invoked on thread {0}.", Thread.CurrentThread.
  ManagedThreadId);
  Console.WriteLine("Your addition is complete");

  // Now get the result.
  AsyncResult ar = (AsyncResult)iar;
  BinaryOp b = (BinaryOp)ar.AsyncDelegate;
  Console.WriteLine("10 + 10 is {0}.", b.EndInvoke(iar));
  isDone = true;
}
```

Passing and Receiving Custom State Data

The final aspect of asynchronous delegates you need to address is the final argument to the BeginInvoke() method (which has been null up to this point). This parameter allows you to pass additional state information to the callback method from the primary thread. Because this argument is prototyped as a System.Object, you can pass in any type of data whatsoever, as long as the callback method knows what to expect. Assume for the sake of demonstration that the primary thread wants to pass in a custom text message to the AddComplete() method, like so:

```
static void Main(string[] args)
{
...
  IAsyncResult ar = b.BeginInvoke(10, 10, new AsyncCallback(AddComplete),
    "Main() thanks you for adding these numbers.");
...
}
```

To obtain this data within the scope of AddComplete(), use the AsyncState property of the incoming IAsyncResult parameter. Notice that an explicit cast will be required; therefore, the primary and secondary threads must agree on the underlying type returned from AsyncState.

```
static void AddComplete(IAsyncResult iar)
{
...
  // Retrieve the informational object and cast it to string.
  string msg = (string)iar.AsyncState;
  Console.WriteLine(msg);
  isDone = true;
}
```

Here is the output of the final iteration:

```
***** AsyncCallbackDelegate Example *****
Main() invoked on thread 1.
Add() invoked on thread 3.
Working....
Working....
Working....
Working....
Working....
AddComplete() invoked on thread 3.
Your addition is complete
10 + 10 is 20.
Main() thanks you for adding these numbers.
```

Now that you understand how a .NET delegate can be used to automatically spin off a secondary thread of execution to handle an asynchronous method invocation, you can turn your attention to directly interacting with threads using the System.Threading namespace. Recall that this namespace was the original .NET threading API that shipped since version 1.0.

■ **Source Code**   You can find the AsyncCallbackDelegate project in the Chapter 19 subdirectory.

The System.Threading Namespace

Under the .NET platform, the System.Threading namespace provides a number of types that enable the direct construction of multithreaded applications. In addition to providing types that allow you to interact with a particular CLR thread, this namespace defines types that allow access to the CLR- maintained thread pool, a simple (non-GUI-based) Timer class, and numerous types used to provide synchronized access to shared resources. Table 19-1 lists some of the important members of this namespace. (Be sure to consult the .NET Framework 4.7 SDK documentation for full details.)

Table 19-1. *Core Types of the System.Threading Namespace*

Type	Meaning in Life
Interlocked	This type provides atomic operations for variables that are shared by multiple threads.
Monitor	This type provides the synchronization of threading objects using locks and wait/signals. The C# lock keyword uses a Monitor object under the hood.
Mutex	This synchronization primitive can be used for synchronization between application domain boundaries.
ParameterizedThreadStart	This delegate allows a thread to call methods that take any number of arguments.
Semaphore	This type allows you to limit the number of threads that can access a resource, or a particular type of resource, concurrently.
Thread	This type represents a thread that executes within the CLR. Using this type, you are able to spawn additional threads in the originating AppDomain.
ThreadPool	This type allows you to interact with the CLR-maintained thread pool within a given process.
ThreadPriority	This enum represents a thread's priority level (Highest, Normal, etc.).
ThreadStart	This delegate is used to specify the method to call for a given thread. Unlike the ParameterizedThreadStart delegate, targets of ThreadStart must always have the same prototype.
ThreadState	This enum specifies the valid states a thread may take (Running, Aborted, etc.).
Timer	This type provides a mechanism for executing a method at specified intervals.
TimerCallback	This delegate type is used in conjunction with Timer types.

The System.Threading.Thread Class

The most primitive of all types in the System.Threading namespace is Thread. This class represents an object-oriented wrapper around a given path of execution within a particular AppDomain. This type also defines a number of methods (both static and instance level) that allow you to create new threads within the current AppDomain, as well as to suspend, stop, and destroy a particular thread. Consider the list of core static members in Table 19-2.

Table 19-2. *Key Static Members of the Thread Type*

Static Member	Meaning in Life
CurrentContext	This read-only property returns the context in which the thread is currently running.
CurrentThread	This read-only property returns a reference to the currently running thread.
GetDomain() GetDomainID()	These methods return a reference to the current AppDomain or the ID of the domain in which the current thread is running.
Sleep()	This method suspends the current thread for a specified time.

The Thread class also supports several instance-level members, some of which are shown in Table 19-3.

Table 19-3. *Select Instance-Level Members of the Thread Type*

Instance-Level Member	Meaning in Life
IsAlive	Returns a Boolean that indicates whether this thread has been started (and has not yet terminated or aborted).
IsBackground	Gets or sets a value indicating whether this thread is a "background thread" (more details in just a moment).
Name	Allows you to establish a friendly text name of the thread.
Priority	Gets or sets the priority of a thread, which may be assigned a value from the ThreadPriority enumeration.
ThreadState	Gets the state of this thread, which may be assigned a value from the ThreadState enumeration.
Abort()	Instructs the CLR to terminate the thread as soon as possible.
Interrupt()	Interrupts (e.g., wakes) the current thread from a suitable wait period.
Join()	Blocks the calling thread until the specified thread (the one on which Join() is called) exits.
Resume()	Resumes a thread that has been previously suspended.
Start()	Instructs the CLR to execute the thread ASAP.
Suspend()	Suspends the thread. If the thread is already suspended, a call to Suspend() has no effect.

■ **Note** Aborting or suspending an active thread is generally considered a bad idea. When you do so, there is a chance (however small) that a thread could "leak" its workload when disturbed or terminated.

Obtaining Statistics About the Current Thread of Execution

Recall that the entry point of an executable assembly (i.e., the Main() method) runs on the primary thread of execution. To illustrate the basic use of the Thread type, assume you have a new Console Application project named ThreadStats. As you know, the static Thread.CurrentThread property retrieves a Thread object that represents the currently executing thread. Once you have obtained the current thread, you are able to print out various statistics, like so:

```
// Be sure to import the System.Threading namespace.
static void Main(string[] args)
{
  Console.WriteLine("***** Primary Thread stats *****\n");

  // Obtain and name the current thread.
  Thread primaryThread = Thread.CurrentThread;
  primaryThread.Name = "ThePrimaryThread";
```

715

```
  // Show details of hosting AppDomain/Context.
  Console.WriteLine("Name of current AppDomain: {0}",
    Thread.GetDomain().FriendlyName);
  Console.WriteLine("ID of current Context: {0}",
    Thread.CurrentContext.ContextID);

  // Print out some stats about this thread.
  Console.WriteLine("Thread Name: {0}",
    primaryThread.Name);
  Console.WriteLine("Has thread started?: {0}",
    primaryThread.IsAlive);
  Console.WriteLine("Priority Level: {0}",
    primaryThread.Priority);
  Console.WriteLine("Thread State: {0}",
    primaryThread.ThreadState);
  Console.ReadLine();
}
```

Here is the current output:

```
***** Primary Thread stats *****
Name of current AppDomain: ThreadStats.exe
ID of current Context: 0
Thread Name: ThePrimaryThread
Has thread started?: True
Priority Level: Normal
Thread State: Running
```

The Name Property

While this code is more or less self-explanatory, do notice that the Thread class supports a property called Name. If you do not set this value, Name will return an empty string. However, once you assign a friendly string moniker to a given Thread object, you can greatly simplify your debugging endeavors. If you are using Visual Studio, you may access the Threads window during a debugging session (select Debug ➤ Windows ➤ Threads when the program is running). As you can see from Figure 19-1, you can quickly identify the thread you want to diagnose.

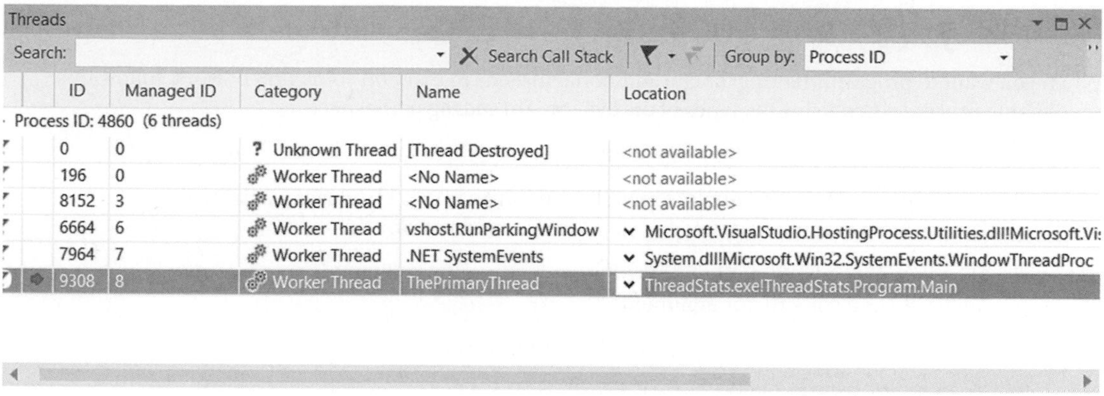

	ID	Managed ID	Category	Name	Location
Threads					▾ □ ×
Search:			▾ ✕ Search Call Stack ▼ ▾ ⬚ Group by: Process ID ▾		''
· Process ID: 4860 (6 threads)					
▸	0	0	? Unknown Thread	[Thread Destroyed]	<not available>
▸	196	0	⚙ Worker Thread	<No Name>	<not available>
▸	8152	3	⚙ Worker Thread	<No Name>	<not available>
▸	6664	6	⚙ Worker Thread	vshost.RunParkingWindow	⌄ Microsoft.VisualStudio.HostingProcess.Utilities.dll!Microsoft.Vi:
▸	7964	7	⚙ Worker Thread	.NET SystemEvents	⌄ System.dll!Microsoft.Win32.SystemEvents.WindowThreadProc
⬧	9308	8	⚙ Worker Thread	ThePrimaryThread	⌄ ThreadStats.exe!ThreadStats.Program.Main

◂ ▸

Figure 19-1. *Debugging a thread with Visual Studio*

The Priority Property

Next, notice that the Thread type defines a property named Priority. By default, all threads have a priority level of Normal. However, you can change this at any point in the thread's lifetime using the ThreadPriority property and the related System.Threading.ThreadPriority enumeration, like so:

```
public enum ThreadPriority
{
  Lowest,
  BelowNormal,
  Normal, // Default value.
  AboveNormal,
  Highest
}
```

If you were to assign a thread's priority level to a value other than the default (ThreadPriority.Normal), understand that you would have no direct control over when the thread scheduler switches between threads. In reality, a thread's priority level offers a hint to the CLR regarding the importance of the thread's activity. Thus, a thread with the value ThreadPriority.Highest is not necessarily guaranteed to be given the highest precedence.

Again, if the thread scheduler is preoccupied with a given task (e.g., synchronizing an object, switching threads, or moving threads), the priority level will most likely be altered accordingly. However, all things being equal, the CLR will read these values and instruct the thread scheduler how to best allocate time slices. Threads with an identical thread priority should each receive the same amount of time to perform their work.

In most cases, you will seldom (if ever) need to directly alter a thread's priority level. In theory, it is possible to jack up the priority level on a set of threads, thereby preventing lower-priority threads from executing at their required levels (so use caution).

■ **Source Code**   You can find the ThreadStats project in the Chapter 19 subdirectory.

Manually Creating Secondary Threads

When you want to programmatically create additional threads to carry on some unit of work, follow this predictable process when using the types of the System.Threading namespace:

1. Create a method to be the entry point for the new thread.

2. Create a new ParameterizedThreadStart (or ThreadStart) delegate, passing the address of the method defined in step 1 to the constructor.

3. Create a Thread object, passing the ParameterizedThreadStart/ThreadStart delegate as a constructor argument.

4. Establish any initial thread characteristics (name, priority, etc.).

5. Call the Thread.Start() method. This starts the thread at the method referenced by the delegate created in step 2 as soon as possible.

As stated in step 2, you may use two distinct delegate types to "point to" the method that the secondary thread will execute. The ThreadStart delegate can point to any method that takes no arguments and returns nothing. This delegate can be helpful when the method is designed to simply run in the background without further interaction.

The obvious limitation of ThreadStart is that you are unable to pass in parameters for processing. However, the ParameterizedThreadStart delegate type allows a single parameter of type System.Object. Given that anything can be represented as a System.Object, you can pass in any number of parameters via a custom class or structure. Do note, however, that the ParameterizedThreadStart delegate can only point to methods that return void.

Working with the ThreadStart Delegate

To illustrate the process of building a multithreaded application (as well as to demonstrate the usefulness of doing so), assume you have a Console Application project (SimpleMultiThreadApp) that allows the end user to choose whether the application will perform its duties using the single primary thread or whether it will split its workload using two separate threads of execution.

Assuming you have imported the System.Threading namespace, your first step is to define a method to perform the work of the (possible) secondary thread. To keep focused on the mechanics of building multithreaded programs, this method will simply print out a sequence of numbers to the console window, pausing for approximately two seconds with each pass. Here is the full definition of the Printer class:

```
public class Printer
{
  public void PrintNumbers()
  {
    // Display Thread info.
    Console.WriteLine("-> {0} is executing PrintNumbers()",
      Thread.CurrentThread.Name);

    // Print out numbers.
    Console.Write("Your numbers: ");
    for(int i = 0; i < 10; i++)
    {
      Console.Write("{0}, ", i);
      Thread.Sleep(2000);
    }
```

```
    Console.WriteLine();
  }
}
```

Now, within `Main()`, you will first prompt the user to determine whether one or two threads will be used to perform the application's work. If the user requests a single thread, you will simply invoke the `PrintNumbers()` method within the primary thread. However, if the user specifies two threads, you will create a `ThreadStart` delegate that points to `PrintNumbers()`, pass this delegate object into the constructor of a new `Thread` object, and call `Start()` to inform the CLR this thread is ready for processing.

To begin, set a reference to the `System.Windows.Forms.dll` assembly (and import the `System.Windows.Forms` namespace) and display a message within `Main()` using `MessageBox.Show()` (you'll see the point of doing so after you run the program). Here is the complete implementation of `Main()`:

```
static void Main(string[] args)
{
  Console.WriteLine("***** The Amazing Thread App *****\n");
  Console.Write("Do you want [1] or [2] threads? ");
  string threadCount = Console.ReadLine();

  // Name the current thread.
  Thread primaryThread = Thread.CurrentThread;
  primaryThread.Name = "Primary";

  // Display Thread info.
  Console.WriteLine("-> {0} is executing Main()",
  Thread.CurrentThread.Name);

  // Make worker class.
  Printer p = new Printer();

  switch(threadCount)
  {
    case "2":
      // Now make the thread.
      Thread backgroundThread =
        new Thread(new ThreadStart(p.PrintNumbers));
      backgroundThread.Name = "Secondary";
      backgroundThread.Start();
    break;
    case "1":
      p.PrintNumbers();
    break;
    default:
      Console.WriteLine("I don't know what you want...you get 1 thread.");
      goto case "1";
  }
  // Do some additional work.
  MessageBox.Show("I'm busy!", "Work on main thread...");
  Console.ReadLine();
}
```

Now, if you run this program with a single thread, you will find that the final message box will not display the message until the entire sequence of numbers has printed to the console. As you are explicitly pausing for approximately two seconds after each number is printed, this will result in a less-than-stellar end-user experience. However, if you select two threads, the message box displays instantly, given that a unique Thread object is responsible for printing the numbers to the console.

■ **Source Code**   You can find the SimpleMultiThreadApp project in the Chapter 19 subdirectory.

Working with the ParameterizedThreadStart Delegate

Recall that the ThreadStart delegate can point only to methods that return void and take no arguments. While this might fit the bill in some cases, if you want to pass data to the method executing on the secondary thread, you will need to use the ParameterizedThreadStart delegate type. To illustrate, let's re-create the logic of the AsyncCallbackDelegate project created earlier in this chapter, this time using the ParameterizedThreadStart delegate type.

To begin, create a new Console Application project named AddWithThreads and import the System. Threading namespace. Now, given that ParameterizedThreadStart can point to any method taking a System.Object parameter, you will create a custom type containing the numbers to be added, like so:

```
class AddParams
{
  public int a, b;

  public AddParams(int numb1, int numb2)
  {
    a = numb1;
    b = numb2;
  }
}
```

Next, create a static method in the Program class that will take an AddParams parameter and print the sum of the two numbers involved, as follows:

```
static void Add(object data)
{
  if (data is AddParams)
  {
    Console.WriteLine("ID of thread in Add(): {0}",
      Thread.CurrentThread.ManagedThreadId);

    AddParams ap = (AddParams)data;
    Console.WriteLine("{0} + {1} is {2}",
      ap.a, ap.b, ap.a + ap.b);
  }
}
```

The code within Main() is straightforward. Simply use ParameterizedThreadStart rather than ThreadStart, like so:

```
static void Main(string[] args)
{
  Console.WriteLine("***** Adding with Thread objects *****");
  Console.WriteLine("ID of thread in Main(): {0}",
    Thread.CurrentThread.ManagedThreadId);

  // Make an AddParams object to pass to the secondary thread.
  AddParams ap = new AddParams(10, 10);
  Thread t = new Thread(new ParameterizedThreadStart(Add));
  t.Start(ap);

  // Force a wait to let other thread finish.
  Thread.Sleep(5);

  Console.ReadLine();
}
```

The AutoResetEvent Class

In these first few examples, you have used a few crude ways to inform the primary thread to wait until the secondary thread has completed. During your examination of asynchronous delegates, you used a simple bool variable as a toggle; however, this is not a recommended solution, as both threads can access the same point of data, and this can lead to data corruption. A safer but still undesirable alternative is to call Thread. Sleep() for a fixed amount of time. The problem here is that you don't want to wait longer than necessary.

One simple, and thread-safe, way to force a thread to wait until another is completed is to use the AutoResetEvent class. In the thread that needs to wait (such as a Main() method), create an instance of this class and pass in false to the constructor to signify you have not yet been notified. Then, at the point at which you are willing to wait, call the WaitOne() method. Here is the update to the Program class, which will do this very thing using a static-level AutoResetEvent member variable:

```
class Program
{
  private static AutoResetEvent waitHandle = new AutoResetEvent(false);

  static void Main(string[] args)
  {
    Console.WriteLine("***** Adding with Thread objects *****");
    Console.WriteLine("ID of thread in Main(): {0}",
      Thread.CurrentThread.ManagedThreadId);
    AddParams ap = new AddParams(10, 10);
    Thread t = new Thread(new ParameterizedThreadStart(Add));
    t.Start(ap);

    // Wait here until you are notified!
    waitHandle.WaitOne();
    Console.WriteLine("Other thread is done!");
```

```
    Console.ReadLine();
  }
...
}
```

When the other thread is completed with its workload, it will call the Set() method on the same instance of the AutoResetEvent type.

```
static void Add(object data)
{
  if (data is AddParams)
  {
    Console.WriteLine("ID of thread in Add(): {0}",
      Thread.CurrentThread.ManagedThreadId);

    AddParams ap = (AddParams)data;
    Console.WriteLine("{0} + {1} is {2}",
      ap.a, ap.b, ap.a + ap.b);

    // Tell other thread we are done.
    waitHandle.Set();
  }
}
```

■ **Source Code**   You can find the AddWithThreads project in the Chapter 19 subdirectory.

Foreground Threads and Background Threads

Now that you have seen how to programmatically create new threads of execution using the System.Threading namespace, let's formalize the distinction between foreground threads and background threads.

- *Foreground threads* have the ability to prevent the current application from terminating. The CLR will not shut down an application (which is to say, unload the hosting AppDomain) until all foreground threads have ended.

- *Background threads* (sometimes called *daemon threads*) are viewed by the CLR as expendable paths of execution that can be ignored at any point in time (even if they are currently laboring over some unit of work). Thus, if all foreground threads have terminated, any and all background threads are automatically killed when the application domain unloads.

It is important to note that foreground and background threads are *not* synonymous with primary and worker threads. By default, every thread you create via the Thread.Start() method is automatically a foreground thread. Again, this means that the AppDomain will not unload until all threads of execution have completed their units of work. In most cases, this is exactly the behavior you require.

For the sake of argument, however, assume that you want to invoke Printer.PrintNumbers() on a secondary thread that should behave as a background thread. Again, this means that the method pointed to by the Thread type (via the ThreadStart or ParameterizedThreadStart delegate) should be able to halt safely as soon as all foreground threads are done with their work. Configuring such a thread is as simple as setting the IsBackground property to true, like so:

```
static void Main(string[] args)
{
  Console.WriteLine("***** Background Threads *****\n");
  Printer p = new Printer();
  Thread bgroundThread =
    new Thread(new ThreadStart(p.PrintNumbers));

  // This is now a background thread.
  bgroundThread.IsBackground = true;
  bgroundThread.Start();
}
```

Notice that this Main() method is *not* making a call to Console.ReadLine() to force the console to remain visible until you press the Enter key. Thus, when you run the application, it will shut down immediately because the Thread object has been configured as a background thread. Given that the Main() method triggers the creation of the primary *foreground* thread, as soon as the logic in Main() completes, the AppDomain unloads before the secondary thread is able to complete its work.

However, if you comment out the line that sets the IsBackground property, you will find that each number prints to the console, as all foreground threads must finish their work before the AppDomain is unloaded from the hosting process.

For the most part, configuring a thread to run as a background type can be helpful when the worker thread in question is performing a noncritical task that is no longer needed when the main task of the program is finished. For example, you could build an application that pings an e-mail server every few minutes for new e-mails, updates current weather conditions, or performs some other noncritical task.

The Issue of Concurrency

When you build multithreaded applications, your program needs to ensure that any piece of shared data is protected against the possibility of numerous threads changing its value. Given that all threads in an AppDomain have concurrent access to the shared data of the application, imagine what might happen if multiple threads were accessing the same point of data. As the thread scheduler will force threads to suspend their work at random, what if thread A is kicked out of the way before it has fully completed its work? Thread B is now reading unstable data.

To illustrate the problem of concurrency, let's build another Console Application project named MultiThreadedPrinting. This application will once again use the Printer class created previously, but this time the PrintNumbers() method will force the current thread to pause for a randomly generated amount of time.

```
public class Printer
{
  public void PrintNumbers()
  {
...
    for (int i = 0; i < 10; i++)
    {
      // Put thread to sleep for a random amount of time.
      Random r = new Random();
```

```
      Thread.Sleep(1000 * r.Next(5));
      Console.Write("{0}, ", i);
    }
    Console.WriteLine();
  }
}
```

The `Main()` method is responsible for creating an array of ten (uniquely named) Thread objects, each of which is making calls on the *same instance* of the Printer object as follows:

```
class Program
{
  static void Main(string[] args)
  {
    Console.WriteLine("*****Synchronizing Threads *****\n");

    Printer p = new Printer();

    // Make 10 threads that are all pointing to the same
    // method on the same object.
    Thread[] threads = new Thread[10];
    for (int i = 0; i < 10; i++)
    {
      threads[i] = new Thread(new ThreadStart(p.PrintNumbers))
      {
        Name = $"Worker thread #{i}"
      };
    }
    // Now start each one.
    foreach (Thread t in threads)
      t.Start();
    Console.ReadLine();
  }
}
```

Before looking at some test runs, let's recap the problem. The primary thread within this AppDomain begins life by spawning ten secondary worker threads. Each worker thread is told to make calls on the PrintNumbers() method on the *same* Printer instance. Given that you have taken no precautions to lock down this object's shared resources (the console), there is a good chance that the current thread will be kicked out of the way before the PrintNumbers() method is able to print the complete results. Because you don't know exactly when (or if) this might happen, you are bound to get unpredictable results. For example, you might find the output shown here:

```
*****Synchronizing Threads *****

-> Worker thread #1 is executing PrintNumbers()
Your numbers: -> Worker thread #0 is executing PrintNumbers()
-> Worker thread #2 is executing PrintNumbers()
Your numbers: -> Worker thread #3 is executing PrintNumbers()
Your numbers: -> Worker thread #4 is executing PrintNumbers()
Your numbers: -> Worker thread #6 is executing PrintNumbers()
```

```
Your numbers: -> Worker thread #7 is executing PrintNumbers()
Your numbers: -> Worker thread #8 is executing PrintNumbers()
Your numbers: -> Worker thread #9 is executing PrintNumbers()
Your numbers: Your numbers: -> Worker thread #5 is executing PrintNumbers()
Your numbers: 0, 0, 0, 0, 1, 0, 0, 1, 1, 1, 2, 2, 2, 3, 3, 3, 2, 1, 0, 0, 4, 3,
4, 1, 2, 4, 5, 5, 5, 6, 6, 6, 2, 7, 7, 7, 3, 4, 0, 8, 4, 5, 1, 5, 8, 8, 9,
2, 6, 1, 0, 9, 1,
6, 2, 7, 9,
2, 1, 7, 8, 3, 2, 3, 3, 9,
8, 4, 4, 5, 9,
4, 3, 5, 5, 6, 3, 6, 7, 4, 7, 6, 8, 7, 4, 8, 5, 5, 6, 6, 8, 7, 7, 9,
8, 9,
8, 9,
9,
9,
```

Now run the application a few more times. Here is another possibility (your results will certainly differ):

```
*****Synchronizing Threads *****

-> Worker thread #0 is executing PrintNumbers()
-> Worker thread #1 is executing PrintNumbers()
-> Worker thread #2 is executing PrintNumbers()
Your numbers: -> Worker thread #4 is executing PrintNumbers()
Your numbers: -> Worker thread #5 is executing PrintNumbers()
Your numbers: Your numbers: -> Worker thread #6 is executing PrintNumbers()
Your numbers: -> Worker thread #7 is executing PrintNumbers()
Your numbers: Your numbers: -> Worker thread #8 is executing PrintNumbers()
Your numbers: -> Worker thread #9 is executing PrintNumbers()
Your numbers: -> Worker thread #3 is executing PrintNumbers()
Your numbers: 0, 0, 0, 0, 0, 0, 0, 0, 0, 0, 1, 1, 1, 1, 1, 1, 1, 1, 1, 1, 2, 2,
2, 2, 2, 2, 2, 2, 2, 2, 3, 3, 3, 3, 3, 3, 3, 3, 3, 3, 4, 4, 4, 4, 4, 4, 4, 4, 4,
 4, 5, 5, 5, 5, 5, 5, 5, 5, 5, 5, 6, 6, 6, 6, 6, 6, 6, 6, 6, 6, 7, 7, 7, 7, 7, 7
, 7, 7, 7, 7, 8, 8, 8, 8, 8, 8, 8, 8, 8, 8, 9,
9,
9,
9,
9,
9,
9,
9,
9,
9,
```

■ **Note** If you are unable to generate unpredictable outputs, increase the number of threads from 10 to 100 (for example) or introduce another call to Thread.Sleep() within your program. Eventually, you will encounter the concurrency issue.

There are clearly some problems here. As each thread is telling the Printer to print the numerical data, the thread scheduler is happily swapping threads in the background. The result is inconsistent output. What you need is a way to programmatically enforce synchronized access to the shared resources. As you would guess, the System.Threading namespace provides a number of synchronization-centric types. The C# programming language also provides a particular keyword for the very task of synchronizing shared data in multithreaded applications.

Synchronization Using the C# lock Keyword

The first technique you can use to synchronize access to shared resources is the C# lock keyword. This keyword allows you to define a scope of statements that must be synchronized between threads. By doing so, incoming threads cannot interrupt the current thread, thus preventing it from finishing its work. The lock keyword requires you to specify a *token* (an object reference) that must be acquired by a thread to enter within the lock scope. When you are attempting to lock down a *private* instance-level method, you can simply pass in a reference to the current type, as follows:

```
private void SomePrivateMethod()
{
  // Use the current object as the thread token.
  lock(this)
  {
    // All code within this scope is thread safe.
  }
}
```

However, if you are locking down a region of code within a *public* member, it is safer (and a best practice) to declare a private object member variable to serve as the lock token, like so:

```
public class Printer
{
  // Lock token.
  private object threadLock = new object();

  public void PrintNumbers()
  {
    // Use the lock token.
    lock (threadLock)
    {
      ...
    }
  }
}
```

In any case, if you examine the PrintNumbers() method, you can see that the shared resource the threads are competing to gain access to is the console window. Therefore, if you scope all interactions with the Console type within a lock scope, as follows:

```
public void PrintNumbers()
{
  // Use the private object lock token.
  lock (threadLock)
```

```
{
  // Display Thread info.
  Console.WriteLine("-> {0} is executing PrintNumbers()",
    Thread.CurrentThread.Name);
  // Print out numbers.
  Console.Write("Your numbers: ");
  for (int i = 0; i < 10; i++)
  {
    Random r = new Random();
    Thread.Sleep(1000 * r.Next(5));
    Console.Write("{0}, ", i);
  }
  Console.WriteLine();
  }
}
```

you have effectively designed a method that will allow the current thread to complete its task. Once a thread enters into a lock scope, the lock token (in this case, a reference to the current object) is inaccessible by other threads until the lock is released after the lock scope has exited. Thus, if thread A has obtained the lock token, other threads are unable to enter *any scope* that uses the same lock token until thread A relinquishes the lock token.

■ **Note**　If you are attempting to lock down code in a static method, simply declare a private static object member variable to serve as the lock token.

If you now run the application, you can see that each thread has ample opportunity to finish its business.

```
*****Synchronizing Threads *****
-> Worker thread #0 is executing PrintNumbers()
Your numbers: 0, 1, 2, 3, 4, 5, 6, 7, 8, 9,
-> Worker thread #1 is executing PrintNumbers()
Your numbers: 0, 1, 2, 3, 4, 5, 6, 7, 8, 9,
-> Worker thread #3 is executing PrintNumbers()
Your numbers: 0, 1, 2, 3, 4, 5, 6, 7, 8, 9,
-> Worker thread #2 is executing PrintNumbers()
Your numbers: 0, 1, 2, 3, 4, 5, 6, 7, 8, 9,
-> Worker thread #4 is executing PrintNumbers()
Your numbers: 0, 1, 2, 3, 4, 5, 6, 7, 8, 9,
-> Worker thread #5 is executing PrintNumbers()
Your numbers: 0, 1, 2, 3, 4, 5, 6, 7, 8, 9,
-> Worker thread #7 is executing PrintNumbers()
Your numbers: 0, 1, 2, 3, 4, 5, 6, 7, 8, 9,
-> Worker thread #6 is executing PrintNumbers()
Your numbers: 0, 1, 2, 3, 4, 5, 6, 7, 8, 9,
-> Worker thread #8 is executing PrintNumbers()
Your numbers: 0, 1, 2, 3, 4, 5, 6, 7, 8, 9,
-> Worker thread #9 is executing PrintNumbers()
Your numbers: 0, 1, 2, 3, 4, 5, 6, 7, 8, 9,
```

■ **Source Code**   You can find the MultiThreadedPrinting project in the Chapter 19 subdirectory.

Synchronization Using the System.Threading.Monitor Type

The C# lock statement is really just a shorthand notation for working with the System.Threading.Monitor class. Once processed by the C# compiler, a lock scope actually resolves to the following (which you can verify using ildasm.exe):

```
public void PrintNumbers()
{
  Monitor.Enter(threadLock);
  try
  {
    // Display Thread info.
    Console.WriteLine("-> {0} is executing PrintNumbers()",
      Thread.CurrentThread.Name);

    // Print out numbers.
    Console.Write("Your numbers: ");
    for (int i = 0; i < 10; i++)
    {
      Random r = new Random();
      Thread.Sleep(1000 * r.Next(5));
      Console.Write("{0}, ", i);
    }
    Console.WriteLine();
  }
  finally
  {
    Monitor.Exit(threadLock);
  }
}
```

First, notice that the Monitor.Enter() method is the ultimate recipient of the thread token you specified as the argument to the lock keyword. Next, all code within a lock scope is wrapped within a try block. The corresponding finally clause ensures that the thread token is released (via the Monitor.Exit() method), regardless of any possible runtime exception. If you were to modify the MultiThreadPrinting program to make direct use of the Monitor type (as just shown), you would find the output is identical.

Now, given that the lock keyword seems to require less code than making explicit use of the System.Threading.Monitor type, you might wonder about the benefits of using the Monitor type directly. The short answer is control. If you use the Monitor type, you are able to instruct the active thread to wait for some duration of time (via the static Monitor.Wait() method), inform waiting threads when the current thread is completed (via the static Monitor.Pulse() and Monitor.PulseAll() methods), and so on.

As you would expect, in a great number of cases, the C# lock keyword will fit the bill. However, if you are interested in checking out additional members of the Monitor class, consult the .NET Framework 4.7 SDK documentation.

Synchronization Using the System.Threading.Interlocked Type

Although it always is hard to believe until you look at the underlying CIL code, assignments and simple arithmetic operations are *not atomic*. For this reason, the System.Threading namespace provides a type that allows you to operate on a single point of data atomically with less overhead than with the Monitor type. The Interlocked class defines the key static members shown in Table 19-4.

Table 19-4. *Select Static Members of the System.Threading.Interlocked Type*

Member	Meaning in Life
CompareExchange()	Safely tests two values for equality and, if equal, exchanges one of the values with a third
Decrement()	Safely decrements a value by 1
Exchange()	Safely swaps two values
Increment()	Safely increments a value by 1

Although it might not seem like it from the onset, the process of atomically altering a single value is quite common in a multithreaded environment. Assume you have a method named AddOne() that increments an integer member variable named intVal. Rather than writing synchronization code such as the following:

```
public void AddOne()
{
  lock(myLockToken)
  {
    intVal++;
  }
}
```

you can simplify your code via the static Interlocked.Increment() method. Simply pass in the variable to increment by reference. Do note that the Increment() method not only adjusts the value of the incoming parameter but also returns the new value.

```
public void AddOne()
{
  int newVal = Interlocked.Increment(ref intVal);
}
```

In addition to Increment() and Decrement(), the Interlocked type allows you to atomically assign numerical and object data. For example, if you want to assign the value of a member variable to the value 83, you can avoid the need to use an explicit lock statement (or explicit Monitor logic) and use the Interlocked.Exchange() method, like so:

```
public void SafeAssignment()
{
  Interlocked.Exchange(ref myInt, 83);
}
```

Finally, if you want to test two values for equality and change the point of comparison in a thread- safe manner, you are able to leverage the `Interlocked.CompareExchange()` method as follows:

```
public void CompareAndExchange()
{
  // If the value of i is currently 83, change i to 99.
  Interlocked.CompareExchange(ref i, 99, 83);
}
```

Synchronization Using the [Synchronization] Attribute

The final synchronization primitive examined here is the [Synchronization] attribute, which is a member of the System.Runtime.Remoting.Contexts namespace. In essence, this class-level attribute effectively locks down *all* instance member code of the object for thread safety. When the CLR allocates objects attributed with [Synchronization], it will place the object within a synchronized context. As you might recall from Chapter 17, objects that should not be removed from a contextual boundary should derive from ContextBoundObject. Therefore, if you want to make the Printer class type thread-safe (without explicitly writing thread-safe code within the class members), you could update the definition as follows:

```
using System.Runtime.Remoting.Contexts;
...

// All methods of Printer are now thread safe!
[Synchronization]
public class Printer : ContextBoundObject
{
  public void PrintNumbers()
  {
    ...
  }
}
```

In some ways, this approach can be seen as the lazy way to write thread-safe code, given that you are not required to dive into the details about which aspects of the type arc truly manipulating thread- sensitive data. The major downfall of this approach, however, is that even if a given method is not making use of thread-sensitive data, the CLR will *still* lock invocations to the method. Obviously, this could degrade the overall functionality of the type, so use this technique with care.

Programming with Timer Callbacks

Many applications have the need to call a specific method during regular intervals of time. For example, you might have an application that needs to display the current time on a status bar via a given helper function. As another example, you might want to have your application call a helper function every so often to perform noncritical background tasks such as checking for new e-mail messages. For situations such as these, you can use the System.Threading.Timer type in conjunction with a related delegate named TimerCallback.

To illustrate, assume you have a Console Application project (TimerApp) that will print the current time every second until the user presses a key to terminate the application. The first obvious step is to write the method that will be called by the Timer type (be sure to import System.Threading into your code file).

```
class Program
{
  static void PrintTime(object state)
  {
    Console.WriteLine("Time is: {0}",
      DateTime.Now.ToLongTimeString());
  }

  static void Main(string[] args)
  {
  }
}
```

Notice the PrintTime() method has a single parameter of type System.Object and returns void. This is not optional, given that the TimerCallback delegate can only call methods that match this signature. The value passed into the target of your TimerCallback delegate can be any type of object (in the case of the e-mail example, this parameter might represent the name of the Microsoft Exchange server to interact with during the process). Also note that given that this parameter is indeed a System.Object, you are able to pass in multiple arguments using a System.Array or custom class/structure.

The next step is to configure an instance of the TimerCallback delegate and pass it into the Timer object. In addition to configuring a TimerCallback delegate, the Timer constructor allows you to specify the optional parameter information to pass into the delegate target (defined as a System.Object), the interval to poll the method, and the amount of time to wait (in milliseconds) before making the first call. Here's an example:

```
static void Main(string[] args)
{
  Console.WriteLine("***** Working with Timer type *****\n");

  // Create the delegate for the Timer type.
  TimerCallback timeCB = new TimerCallback(PrintTime);

  // Establish timer settings.
  Timer t = new Timer(
    timeCB,     // The TimerCallback delegate object.
    null,       // Any info to pass into the called method (null for no info).
    0,          // Amount of time to wait before starting (in milliseconds).
    1000);      // Interval of time between calls (in milliseconds).

  Console.WriteLine("Hit Enter key to terminate...");
  Console.ReadLine();
}
```

In this case, the `PrintTime()` method will be called roughly every second and will pass in no additional information to said method. Here is the output:

```
***** Working with Timer type *****

Hit key to terminate...
Time is: 6:51:48 PM
Time is: 6:51:49 PM
Time is: 6:51:50 PM
Time is: 6:51:51 PM
Time is: 6:51:52 PM
Press any key to continue . . .
```

If you did want to send in some information for use by the delegate target, simply substitute the `null` value of the second constructor parameter with the appropriate information, like so:

```
// Establish timer settings.
Timer t = new Timer(timeCB, "Hello From Main", 0, 1000);
```

You can then obtain the incoming data as follows:

```
static void PrintTime(object state)
{
  Console.WriteLine("Time is: {0}, Param is: {1}",
    DateTime.Now.ToLongTimeString(), state.ToString());
}
```

Using a Stand-Alone Discard

In the previous example, the Timer variable isn't used in any execution path, so it can be replaced with a discard, as follows:

```
var _ = new Timer(
  timeCB,     // The TimerCallback delegate object.
  null,       // Any info to pass into the called method (null for no info).
  0,          // Amount of time to wait before starting (in milliseconds).
  1000);      // Interval of time between calls (in milliseconds).
```

■ **Source Code** You can find the TimerApp project in the Chapter 19 subdirectory.

Understanding the CLR ThreadPool

The next thread-centric topic you will examine in this chapter is the role of the CLR thread pool. When you invoke a method asynchronously using delegate types (via the `BeginInvoke()` method), the CLR does not literally create a new thread. For purposes of efficiency, a delegate's `BeginInvoke()` method leverages a pool of worker threads that is maintained by the runtime. To allow you to interact with this pool of waiting threads, the `System.Threading` namespace provides the `ThreadPool` class type.

If you want to queue a method call for processing by a worker thread in the pool, you can use the ThreadPool.QueueUserWorkItem() method. This method has been overloaded to allow you to specify an optional System.Object for custom state data in addition to an instance of the WaitCallback delegate.

```
public static class ThreadPool
{
  ...
  public static bool QueueUserWorkItem(WaitCallback callBack);
  public static bool QueueUserWorkItem(WaitCallback callBack,
                                        object state);
}
```

The WaitCallback delegate can point to any method that takes a System.Object as its sole parameter (which represents the optional state data) and returns nothing. Do note that if you do not provide a System.Object when calling QueueUserWorkItem(), the CLR automatically passes a null value. To illustrate queuing methods for use by the CLR thread pool, ponder the following program, which uses the Printer type once again. In this case, however, you are not manually creating an array of Thread objects; rather, you are assigning members of the pool to the PrintNumbers() method.

```
class Program
{
  static void Main(string[] args)
  {
    Console.WriteLine("***** Fun with the CLR Thread Pool *****\n");

    Console.WriteLine("Main thread started. ThreadID = {0}",
      Thread.CurrentThread.ManagedThreadId);

    Printer p = new Printer();

    WaitCallback workItem = new WaitCallback(PrintTheNumbers);

    // Queue the method ten times.
    for (int i = 0; i < 10; i++)
    {
      ThreadPool.QueueUserWorkItem(workItem, p);
    }
    Console.WriteLine("All tasks queued");
    Console.ReadLine();
  }
  static void PrintTheNumbers(object state)
  {
    Printer task = (Printer)state;
    task.PrintNumbers();
  }
}
```

At this point, you might be wondering if it would be advantageous to use the CLR-maintained thread pool rather than explicitly creating Thread objects. Consider these benefits of leveraging the thread pool:

- The thread pool manages threads efficiently by minimizing the number of threads that must be created, started, and stopped.

- By using the thread pool, you can focus on your business problem rather than the application's threading infrastructure.

However, using manual thread management is preferred in some cases. Here's an example:

- If you require foreground threads or must set the thread priority. Pooled threads are *always* background threads with default priority (ThreadPriority.Normal).

- If you require a thread with a fixed identity in order to abort it, suspend it, or discover it by name.

■ **Source Code**   You can find the ThreadPoolApp project in the Chapter 19 subdirectory.

That wraps up your investigation of the System.Threading namespace. To be sure, understanding the topics presented thus far in the chapter (especially during your examination of concurrency issues) will be extremely valuable when creating a multithreaded application. Given this foundation, you will now turn your attention to a number of new thread-centric topics that are available only with .NET 4.0 and higher. To begin, you will examine the role of an alternative threading model, termed the TPL.

Parallel Programming Using the Task Parallel Library

At this point in the chapter, you have examined two programming techniques (using asynchronous delegates and via the members of System.Threading) that allow you to build multithreaded software. Recall that both of these approaches will work under any version of the .NET platform.

Beginning with the release of .NET 4.0, Microsoft introduced a new approach to multithreaded application development using a parallel programming library termed the *Task Parallel Library* (TPL). Using the types of System.Threading.Tasks, you can build fine-grained, scalable parallel code without having to work directly with threads or the thread pool.

This is not to say, however, that you will not use the types of System.Threading when you use the TPL. In reality, these two threading toolkits can work together quite naturally. This is especially true in that the System.Threading namespace still provides a majority of the synchronization primitives you examined previously (Monitor, Interlocked, and so forth). This being said, you will quite likely find that you will favor working with the TPL rather than the original System.Threading namespace, given that the same set of tasks can be performed in a more straightforward manner.

■ **Note**   On a related note, be aware that the C# async and await keywords use various members of the System.Threading.Tasks namespace.

The System.Threading.Tasks Namespace

Collectively speaking, the types of System.Threading.Tasks are referred to as the *Task Parallel Library*. The TPL will automatically distribute your application's workload across available CPUs dynamically, using the CLR thread pool. The TPL handles the partitioning of the work, thread scheduling, state management, and other low-level details. The end result is that you can maximize the performance of your .NET applications, while being shielded from many of complexities of directly working with threads (see Figure 19-2).

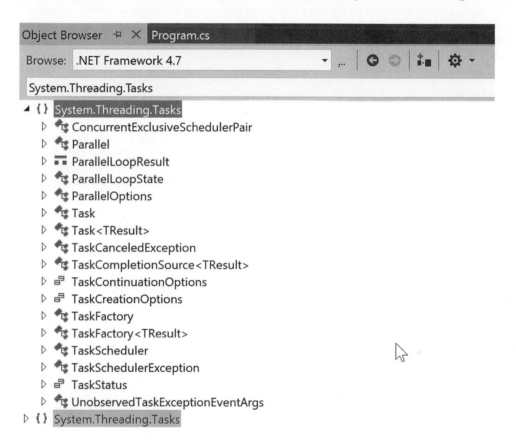

Figure 19-2. Members of the System.Threading.Tasks namespace

The Role of the Parallel Class

A key class of the TPL is System.Threading.Tasks.Parallel. This class supports a number of methods that allow you to iterate over a collection of data (specifically, an object implementing IEnumerable<T>) in a parallel fashion. If you were to look up the Parallel class in the .NET Framework 4.7 SDK documentation, you would see that this class supports two primary static methods, Parallel.For() and Parallel.ForEach(), each of which defines numerous overloaded versions.

These methods allow you to author a body of code statements that will be processed in a parallel manner. In concept, these statements are the same sort of logic you would write in a normal looping construct (via the for or foreach C# keywords). The benefit is that the Parallel class will pluck threads from the thread pool (and manage concurrency) on your behalf.

735

Both of these methods require you to specify an `IEnumerable`- or `IEnumerable<T>`-compatible container that holds the data you need to process in a parallel manner. The container could be a simple array, a nongeneric collection (such as `ArrayList`), a generic collection (such as `List<T>`), or the results of a LINQ query.

In addition, you will need to use the `System.Func<T>` and `System.Action<T>` delegates to specify the target method that will be called to process the data. You've already encountered the `Func<T>` delegate in Chapter 12, during your investigation of LINQ to Objects. Recall that `Func<T>` represents a method that can have a given return value and a varied number of arguments. The `Action<T>` delegate is similar to `Func<T>`, in that it allows you to point to a method taking some number of parameters. However, `Action<T>` specifies a method that can only return `void`.

While you could call the `Parallel.For()` and `Parallel.ForEach()` methods and pass a strongly typed `Func<T>` or `Action<T>` delegate object, you can simplify your programming by using a fitting C# anonymous method or lambda expression.

Data Parallelism with the Parallel Class

The first way to use the TPL is to perform *data parallelism*. Simply put, this term refers to the task of iterating over an array or collection in a parallel manner using the `Parallel.For()` or `Parallel.ForEach()` method. Assume you need to perform some labor-intensive file I/O operations. Specifically, you need to load a large number of `*.jpg` files into memory, flip them upside down, and save the modified image data to a new location.

The .NET Framework 4.7 SDK documentation provides a console-based example of this very situation; however, you will see how to perform the same overall task using a graphical user interface so you can examine the use of "anonymous delegates" to allow secondary threads to update the primary user interface thread (aka the UI thread).

■ **Note** When you are building a multithreaded graphical user interface (GUI) application, secondary threads can never directly access user interface controls. The reason is that controls (buttons, text boxes, labels, progress bars, etc.) have thread affinity with the thread that created them. In the following example, I'll illustrate one way to allow secondary threads to access UI items in a thread-safe manner. You'll see a more simplified approach when you examine the C# `async` and `await` keywords.

To illustrate, create a new Windows Presentation Foundation application (the template is abbreviated to WPF App (.NET Framework)) named DataParallelismWithForEach.

■ **Note** Windows Presentation Foundation (WPF) will be covered in detail in Chapters 24 to 26. If you haven't worked with WPF, everything you need for this example is listed here. If you would rather just follow along with a completed solution, you can find DataParallismWithForEach in the `Chapter 19` folder.

Double-click the `MainWindow.xaml` file in Solution Explorer, and replace all of the XAML with the following:

```
<Window x:Class="DataParallelismWithForEach.MainWindow"
        xmlns="http://schemas.microsoft.com/winfx/2006/xaml/presentation"
        xmlns:x="http://schemas.microsoft.com/winfx/2006/xaml"
        xmlns:d="http://schemas.microsoft.com/expression/blend/2008"
        xmlns:mc="http://schemas.openxmlformats.org/markup-compatibility/2006"
        xmlns:local="clr-namespace:DataParallelismWithForEach"
```

```
          mc:Ignorable="d"
          Title="Fun with TPL" Height="200" Width="400">
  <Grid>
    <Grid.RowDefinitions>
      <RowDefinition Height="Auto"/>
      <RowDefinition Height="*"/>
      <RowDefinition Height="Auto"/>
    </Grid.RowDefinitions>
    <Label Grid.Row="0" Grid.Column="0">
      Feel free to type here while the images are processed...
    </Label>
    <TextBox Grid.Row="1" Grid.Column="0"  Margin="10,10,10,10"/>
    <Grid Grid.Row="2" Grid.Column="0">
      <Grid.ColumnDefinitions>
        <ColumnDefinition Width="Auto"/>
        <ColumnDefinition Width="*"/>
        <ColumnDefinition Width="Auto"/>
      </Grid.ColumnDefinitions>
            <Button Name="cmdCancel" Grid.Row="0" Grid.Column="0" Margin="10,10,0,10"
                        Click="cmdCancel_Click">
                Cancel
            </Button>
            <Button Name="cmdProcess" Grid.Row="0" Grid.Column="2" Margin="0,10,10,10"
                        Click="cmdProcess_Click">
                Click to Flip Your Images!
            </Button>
    </Grid>
  </Grid>
</Window>
```

Again, don't worry about what the markup means or how it works; you will spend plenty of time with WPF shortly. The GUI of the application consists of a multiline TextBox and a single Button (named cmdProcess). The purpose of the text area is to allow you to enter data while the work is being performed in the background, thus illustrating the nonblocking nature of the parallel task.

Double-click the MainWindow.xaml.cs file (you might have to expand the node by MainWindow.xaml), and add the following using statements to the top of the file:

```
// Be sure you have these namespaces!
Using System.Drawing;
using System.Threading.Tasks;
using System.Threading;
using System.IO;
```

■ **Note**   You should update the string passed into the following Directory.GetFiles() method call to point to a path on your computer that has some image files (such as a personal folder of family pictures). I've included some sample images (that ship with the Windows operating system) in the Solution directory for your convenience. Alternatively, you can copy the TestPictures directory into the bin\Debug directory under this project and leave the strings as they are.

```
public partial class MainWindow : Window
{
  public MainWindow()
  {
    InitializeComponent();
  }

  private void cmdCancel_Click(object sender, EventArgs e)
  {
    // This will be updated shortly
  }

  private void cmdProcess_Click(object sender, EventArgs e)
  {
    ProcessFiles();
  }

  private void ProcessFiles()
  {
    // Load up all *.jpg files, and make a new folder for the modified data.
    string[] files = Directory.GetFiles(@".\TestPictures", "*.jpg", SearchOption.
      AllDirectories);
    string newDir = @".\ModifiedPictures";
    Directory.CreateDirectory(newDir);

    // Process the image data in a blocking manner.
    foreach (string currentFile in files)
    {
      string filename = Path.GetFileName(currentFile);

      using (Bitmap bitmap = new Bitmap(currentFile))
      {
        bitmap.RotateFlip(RotateFlipType.Rotate180FlipNone);
        bitmap.Save(Path.Combine(newDir, filename));

        // Print out the ID of the thread processing the current image.
        this.Title = $"Processing {fielname} on thread {Thread.CurrentThread.
                ManagedThreadId}";
      }
    }
  }
}
```

Notice that the ProcessFiles() method will rotate each *.jpg file under the specified directory, which currently contains ten files (again, be sure to update the path sent into Directory.GetFiles() as necessary). Currently, all the work is happening on the primary thread of the executable. Therefore, if the button is clicked, the program will appear to hang. Furthermore, the caption of the window will also report that the same primary thread is processing the file, as we have only a single thread of execution.

To process the files on as many CPUs as possible, you can rewrite the current foreach loop to use Parallel.ForEach(). Recall that this method has been overloaded numerous times; however, in the simplest form, you must specify the IEnumerable<T>-compatible object that contains the items to process (that would be the files string array) and an Action<T> delegate that points to the method that will perform the work.

Here is the relevant update, using the C# lambda operator in place of a literal `Action<T>` delegate object. Notice that you are currently *commenting out* the line of code that displayed the ID of the thread executing the current image file. See the next section to find out the reason why.

```
// Process the image data in a parallel manner!
Parallel.ForEach(files, currentFile =>
  {
    string filename = Path.GetFileName(currentFile);

    using (Bitmap bitmap = new Bitmap(currentFile))
    {
      bitmap.RotateFlip(RotateFlipType.Rotate180FlipNone);
      bitmap.Save(Path.Combine(newDir, filename));

      // This code statement is now a problem! See next section.
      // this.Title = $"Processing {filename} on thread {Thread.CurrentThread.ManagedThreadId}"
      // Thread.CurrentThread.ManagedThreadId);
    }
  }
);
```

Accessing UI Elements on Secondary Threads

You'll notice that I've commented out the previous line of code that updated the caption of the main window with the ID of the currently executing thread. As noted previously, GUI controls have "thread affinity" with the thread that created them. If secondary threads attempt to access a control they did not directly create, you are bound to run into runtime errors when debugging your software. On the flip side, if you were to *run* the application (via Ctrl+F5), you might not ever find any problems whatsoever with the original code.

■ **Note**   Let me reiterate the previous point: when you debug (F5) a multithreaded application, Visual Studio is often able to catch errors that arise when a secondary thread is "touching" a control created on the primary thread. However, oftentimes when you run (Ctrl+F5) the application, the application could appear to run correctly (or it might error straightaway). Until you take precautions (examined next), your application has the potential of raising a runtime error under such circumstances.

One approach that you can use to allow these secondary threads to access the controls in a thread-safe manner is yet another delegate-centric technique, specifically an *anonymous delegate*. The `Control` parent class in WPF defines a `Dispatcher` object, which manages the work items for a thread. This object has a method named `Invoke()`, which takes a `System.Delegate` as input. You can call this method when you are in a coding context involving secondary threads to provide a thread-safe manner to update the UI of the given control. Now, while you could write all of the required delegate code directly, most developers use anonymous delegates as a simple alternative. Here is the relevant update to the content with the previously commented-out code statement:

```
using (Bitmap bitmap = new Bitmap(currentFile))
{
  bitmap.RotateFlip(RotateFlipType.Rotate180FlipNone);
  bitmap.Save(Path.Combine(newDir, filename));
```

```
// Eek! This will not work anymore!
//this.Title = $"Processing {filename} on thread {Thread.CurrentThread.ManagedThreadId}";

// Invoke on the Form object, to allow secondary threads to access controls
// in a thread-safe manner.
this.Dispatcher.Invoke((Action)delegate
  {
    this.Title = $"Processing {filename} on thread {Thread.CurrentThread.ManagedThreadId}";
  }
);
}
```

Now, if you run program, the TPL will indeed distribute the workload to multiple threads from the thread pool, using as many CPUs as possible. However, you will not see the window's caption display the name of each unique thread, and you won't see anything if you type in the text box until all the images have been processed! The reason is that the primary UI thread is still blocked, waiting for all the other threads to finish up their business.

The Task Class

The Task class allows you to easily invoke a method on a secondary thread and can be used as a simple alternative to working with asynchronous delegates. Update the Click handler of your Button control as so:

```
private void cmdProcess_Click(object sender, EventArgs e)
{
  // Start a new "task" to process the files.
  Task.Factory.StartNew(() => ProcessFiles());
}
```

The Factory property of Task returns a TaskFactory object. When you call its StartNew() method, you pass in an Action<T> delegate (here, hidden away with a fitting lambda expression) that points to the method to invoke in an asynchronous manner. With this small update, you will now find that the window's title will show which thread from the thread pool is processing a given file, and better yet, the text area is able to receive input, as the UI thread is no longer blocked.

Handling Cancellation Request

One improvement you can make to the current example is to provide a way for the user to stop the processing of the image data, via a second (aptly named) Cancel button. Thankfully, the Parallel.For() and Parallel.ForEach() methods both support cancellation through the use of *cancellation tokens*. When you invoke methods on Parallel, you can pass in a ParallelOptions object, which in turn contains a CancellationTokenSource object.

First, define the following new private member variable in your Form-derived class of type CancellationTokenSource named cancelToken:

```
public partial class MainWindow :Window
{
  // New Window-level variable.
  private CancellationTokenSource cancelToken = new CancellationTokenSource();
...
}
```

Update the Click event to the following code:

```
private void cmdCancel_Click(object sender, EventArgs e)
{
  // This will be used to tell all the worker threads to stop!
  cancelToken.Cancel();
}
```

Now, the real modifications need to occur within the ProcessFiles() method. Consider the final implementation:

```
private void ProcessFiles()
{
  // Use ParallelOptions instance to store the CancellationToken.
  ParallelOptions parOpts = new ParallelOptions();
  parOpts.CancellationToken = cancelToken.Token;
  parOpts.MaxDegreeOfParallelism = System.Environment.ProcessorCount;

  // Load up all *.jpg files, and make a new folder for the modified data.
  string[] files = Directory.GetFiles(@".\TestPictures", "*.jpg", SearchOption.
  AllDirectories);
  string newDir = @".\ModifiedPictures";
  Directory.CreateDirectory(newDir);

  try
  {
    // Process the image data in a parallel manner!
    Parallel.ForEach(files, parOpts, currentFile =>
    {
      parOpts.CancellationToken.ThrowIfCancellationRequested();

      string filename = Path.GetFileName(currentFile);
      using (Bitmap bitmap = new Bitmap(currentFile))
      {
        bitmap.RotateFlip(RotateFlipType.Rotate180FlipNone);
        bitmap.Save(Path.Combine(newDir, filename));
        this.Invoke((Action)delegate
          {
            this.Title = $"Processing {filename} on thread {Thread.CurrentThread.
                      ManagedThreadId}";
          }
        );
      }
    }
    );
    this.Invoke((Action)delegate
    {
      this.Title = "Done!";
    });
  }
```

```
  catch (OperationCanceledException ex)
  {
    this.Invoke((Action)delegate
    {
      this.Title = ex.Message;
    });
  }
}
```

Notice that you begin the method by configuring a ParallelOptions object, setting the CancellationToken property to use the CancellationTokenSource token. Also note that when you call the Parallel.ForEach() method, you pass in the ParallelOptions object as the second parameter.

Within the scope of the looping logic, you make a call to ThrowIfCancellationRequested() on the token, which will ensure if the user clicks the Cancel button, all threads will stop, and you will be notified via a runtime exception. When you catch the OperationCanceledException error, you will set the text of the main window to the error message.

■ **Source Code**   You can find the DataParallelismWithForEach project in the Chapter 19 subdirectory.

Task Parallelism Using the Parallel Class

In addition to data parallelism, the TPL can also be used to easily fire off any number of asynchronous tasks using the Parallel.Invoke() method. This approach is a bit more straightforward than using delegates or members from System.Threading; however, if you require more control over the way tasks are executed, you could forgo use of Parallel.Invoke() and use the Task class directly, as you did in the previous example.

To illustrate task parallelism, create a new console application called MyEBookReader and be sure the System.Threading, System.Threading.Tasks, and System.Net namespaces are imported at the top of Program.cs (this example is a modification of a useful example in the .NET Framework SDK documentation). Here, you will fetch a publicly available e-book from Project Gutenberg (www.gutenberg.org) and then perform a set of lengthy tasks in parallel.

The book is downloaded in the GetBook() method, shown here:

```
static void GetBook()
{
  WebClient wc = new WebClient();
  wc.DownloadStringCompleted += (s, eArgs) =>
  {
    theEBook = eArgs.Result;
    Console.WriteLine("Download complete.");
    GetStats();
  };

  // The Project Gutenberg EBook of A Tale of Two Cities, by Charles Dickens
  // You might have to run it twice if you've never visited the site before, since the first
  // time you visit there is a message box that pops up, and breaks this code.
  wc.DownloadStringAsync(new Uri("http://www.gutenberg.org/files/98/98-8.txt"));
}
```

The WebClient class is a member of System.Net. This class provides a number of methods for sending data to and receiving data from a resource identified by a URI. As it turns out, many of these methods have an asynchronous version, such as DownloadStringAsync(). This method will spin up a new thread from the CLR thread pool automatically. When the WebClient is done obtaining the data, it will fire the DownloadStringCompleted event, which you are handling here using a C# lambda expression. If you were to call the synchronous version of this method (DownloadString()), the "Downloading" message wouldn't show until the download was complete.

Next, the GetStats() method is implemented to extract the individual words contained in the theEBook variable and then pass the string array to a few helper functions for processing as follows:

```
static void GetStats()
{
  // Get the words from the e-book.
  string[] words = theEBook.Split(new char[]
    { ' ', '\u000A', ',', '.', ';', ':', '-', '?', '/' },
    StringSplitOptions.RemoveEmptyEntries);

  // Now, find the ten most common words.
  string[] tenMostCommon = FindTenMostCommon(words);

  // Get the longest word.
  string longestWord = FindLongestWord(words);

  // Now that all tasks are complete, build a string to show all stats.
  StringBuilder bookStats = new StringBuilder("Ten Most Common Words are:\n");
  foreach (string s in tenMostCommon)
  {
    bookStats.AppendLine(s);
  }

  bookStats.AppendFormat("Longest word is: {0}", longestWord);
  bookStats.AppendLine();
  Console.WriteLine(bookStats.ToString(), "Book info");
}
```

The FindTenMostCommon() method uses a LINQ query to obtain a list of string objects that occur most often in the string array, while FindLongestWord() locates, well, the longest word.

```
private string[] FindTenMostCommon(string[] words)
{
    var frequencyOrder = from word in words
                         where word.Length > 6
                         group word by word into g
                         orderby g.Count() descending
                         select g.Key;
    string[] commonWords = (frequencyOrder.Take(10)).ToArray();
    return commonWords;
}
private string FindLongestWord(string[] words)
{
    return (from w in words orderby w.Length descending select w).FirstOrDefault();
}
```

If you were to run this project, the amount of time to perform all tasks could take a goodly amount of time, based on the CPU count of your machine and overall processor speed. Eventually, you should see the output shown in Figure 19-3.

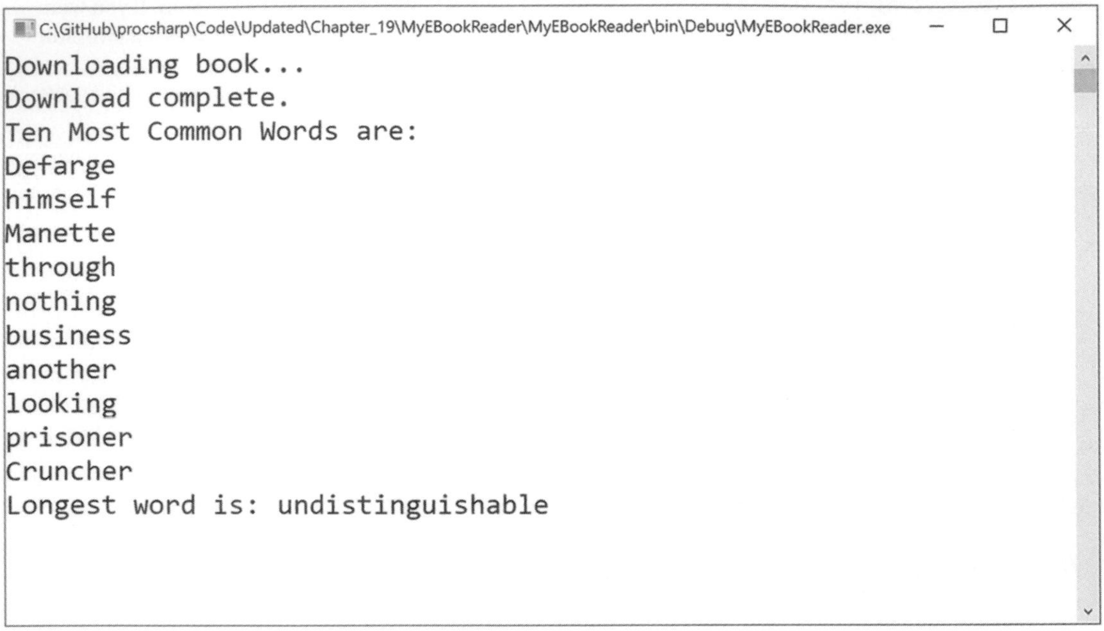

C:\GitHub\procsharp\Code\Updated\Chapter_19\MyEBookReader\MyEBookReader\bin\Debug\MyEBookReader.exe

```
Downloading book...
Download complete.
Ten Most Common Words are:
Defarge
himself
Manette
through
nothing
business
another
looking
prisoner
Cruncher
Longest word is: undistinguishable
```

Figure 19-3. *Stats about the downloaded e-book*

You can help ensure that your application uses all available CPUs on the host machine by invoking the FindTenMostCommon() and FindLongestWord() methods in parallel. To do so, modify your GetStats() method as so:

```
static void GetStats()
{
  // Get the words from the e-book.
  string[] words = theEBook.Split(
    new char[] { ' ', '\u000A', ',', '.', ';', ':', '-', '?', '/' },
    StringSplitOptions.RemoveEmptyEntries);
  string[] tenMostCommon = null;
  string longestWord = string.Empty;

  Parallel.Invoke(
    () =>
    {
      // Now, find the ten most common words.
      tenMostCommon = FindTenMostCommon(words);
    },
    () =>
```

```
  {
    // Get the longest word.
    longestWord = FindLongestWord(words);
  });

  // Now that all tasks are complete, build a string to show all stats.
  ...
}
```

The `Parallel.Invoke()` method expects a parameter array of `Action<>` delegates, which you have supplied indirectly using lambda expressions. Again, while the output is identical, the benefit is that the TPL will now use all possible processors on the machine to invoke each method in parallel if possible.

■ **Source Code**   You can find the MyEBookReader project in the `Chapter 19` subdirectory.

Parallel LINQ Queries (PLINQ)

To wrap up your look at the TPL, be aware that there is another way you can incorporate parallel tasks into your .NET applications. If you choose, you can use a set of extension methods that allow you to construct a LINQ query that will perform its workload in parallel (if possible). Fittingly, LINQ queries that are designed to run in parallel are termed *PLINQ queries*.

Like parallel code authored using the `Parallel` class, PLINQ has the option of ignoring your request to process the collection in parallel if need be. The PLINQ framework has been optimized in numerous ways, which includes determining whether a query would, in fact, perform faster in a synchronous manner.

At runtime, PLINQ analyzes the overall structure of the query, and if the query is likely to benefit from parallelization, it will run concurrently. However, if parallelizing a query would hurt performance, PLINQ just runs the query sequentially. If PLINQ has a choice between a potentially expensive parallel algorithm or an inexpensive sequential algorithm, it chooses the sequential algorithm by default.

The necessary extension methods are found within the `ParallelEnumerable` class of the `System.Linq` namespace. Table 19-5 documents some useful PLINQ extensions.

Table 19-5. *Select Members of the `ParallelEnumerable` Class*

Member	Meaning in Life
`AsParallel()`	Specifies that the rest of the query should be parallelized, if possible
`WithCancellation()`	Specifies that PLINQ should periodically monitor the state of the provided cancellation token and cancel execution if it is requested
`WithDegreeOfParallelism()`	Specifies the maximum number of processors that PLINQ should use to parallelize the query
`ForAll()`	Enables results to be processed in parallel without first merging back to the consumer thread, as would be the case when enumerating a LINQ result using the `foreach` keyword

To see PLINQ in action, create a console application named PLINQDataProcessingWithCancellation and import the System.Threading and System.Threading.Tasks namespaces (if not already there). When processing starts, the program will fire off a new Task, which executes a LINQ query that investigates a large array of integers, looking for only the items where x % 3 == 0 is true. Here is a *nonparallel* version of the query:

```
class Program
{
  static void Main(string[] args)
  {
    Console.WriteLine("Start any key to start processing");
    Console.ReadKey();

    Console.WriteLine("Processing");
    Task.Factory.StartNew(() => ProcessIntData());
    Console.ReadLine();
  }

  static void ProcessIntData()
  {
    // Get a very large array of integers.
    int[] source = Enumerable.Range(1, 10_000_000).ToArray();
    // Find the numbers where num % 3 == 0 is true, returned
    // in descending order.
    int[] modThreeIsZero = (from num in source where num % 3 == 0
        orderby num descending select num).ToArray();
    Console.WriteLine($"Found { modThreeIsZero.Count()} numbers that match query!");
  }
}
```

Opting in to a PLINQ Query

If you want to inform the TPL to execute this query in parallel (if possible), you will want to use the AsParallel() extension method as so:

```
int[] modThreeIsZero = (from num in source.AsParallel() where num % 3 == 0
                        orderby num descending select num).ToArray();
```

Notice how the overall format of the LINQ query is identical to what you saw in previous chapters. However, by including a call to AsParallel(), the TPL will attempt to pass the workload off to an available CPU.

Cancelling a PLINQ Query

It is also possible to use a CancellationTokenSource object to inform a PLINQ query to stop processing under the correct conditions (typically because of user intervention). Declare a class-level CancellationTokenSource object named cancelToken and update the Main() method to take input from the user. Here is the relevant code update:

```
class Program
{
  static CancellationTokenSource cancelToken = new CancellationTokenSource();

  static void Main(string[] args)
  {
    do
    {
      Console.WriteLine("Start any key to start processing");
      Console.ReadKey();
      Console.WriteLine("Processing");
      Task.Factory.StartNew(() => ProcessIntData());
      Console.Write("Enter Q to quit: ");
      string answer = Console.ReadLine();
      // Does user want to quit?
      if (answer.Equals("Q", StringComparison.OrdinalIgnoreCase))
      {
        cancelToken.Cancel();
        break;
      }
    } while (true);
    Console.ReadLine();
  }
```

Now, inform the PLINQ query that it should be on the lookout for an incoming cancellation request by chaining on the WithCancellation() extension method and passing in the token. In addition, you will want to wrap this PLINQ query in a proper try/catch scope and deal with the possible exception. Here is the final version of the ProcessIntData() method:

```
static void ProcessIntData()
{
  // Get a very large array of integers.
  int[] source = Enumerable.Range(1, 10_000_000).ToArray();
  // Find the numbers where num % 3 == 0 is true, returned
  // in descending order.
  int[] modThreeIsZero = null;
  try
  {
    modThreeIsZero = (from num in source.AsParallel().WithCancellation(cancelToken.Token)
            where num % 3 == 0
            orderby num descending
            select num).ToArray();
    Console.WriteLine();
    Console.WriteLine($"Found {modThreeIsZero.Count()} numbers that match query!");
  }
  catch (OperationCanceledException ex)
  {
    Console.WriteLine(ex.Message);
  }
}
```

When running this, you will want to hit Q and enter pretty quickly to actually see the message from the cancellation token. On my development machine, I had about 1 (one) second to quit before it finished on its own.

■ **Source Code**   You can find the PLINQDataProcessingWithCancellation project in the Chapter 19 subdirectory.

Asynchronous Calls with the async Keyword

I have covered a lot of terse material in this (rather lengthy) chapter. To be sure, building, debugging, and understanding complex multithreaded applications are challenging in any framework. While the TPL, PLINQ, and the delegate type can simplify matters to some extent (especially when compared to other platforms and languages), developers are still required to be fairly savvy with the ins and outs of various advanced techniques.

Since the release of .NET 4.5, the C# programming language (and for that matter, the VB programming language) has been updated with two new keywords that further simplify the process of authoring asynchronous code. In contrast to all the examples in this chapter, when you use the new async and await keywords, the compiler will generate a good deal of threading code on your behalf, using numerous members of the System.Threading and System.Threading.Tasks namespaces.

A First Look at the C# async and await Keywords

The async keyword of C# is used to qualify that a method, lambda expression, or anonymous method should be called in an asynchronous manner *automatically*. Yes, it's true. Simply by marking a method with the async modifier, the CLR will create a new thread of execution to handle the task at hand. Furthermore, when you are calling an async method, the await keyword will *automatically* pause the current thread from any further activity until the task is complete, leaving the calling thread free to continue on its merry way.

To illustrate, create a console application named FunWithCSharpAsync and import the System.Threading and System.Threading.Tasks namespaces into Program.cs. Add a method named DoWork(), which forces the calling thread to wait for five seconds. Also, change the Main() method to async with a return type of Task (these will be explained shortly). Here is the story thus far:

```
class Program
{
  static async Task Main(string[] args)
  {
    Console.WriteLine(" Fun With Async ===>");
    //This is to prompt Visual Studio to upgrade project to C# 7.1
    List<int> l = default;
    Console.WriteLine(DoWork());
    Console.WriteLine("Completed");
    Console.ReadLine();
  }
  static string DoWork()
  {
    Thread.Sleep(5_000);
    return "Done with work!";
  }
}
```

■ **Note**   For this to work, your project must be configured for C# 7.1. However, at the time of this writing, Visual Studio doesn't pick up this change as valid, so you must either configure you project manually or add another 7.1 feature into the code so Visual Studio will make the change.

First, notice that the Main() method has been marked with the async keyword. This marks the method as a member to be called in a nonblocking manner. You'll learn more about this shortly.

Now, given your work in this chapter, you know that if you were to run the program, you would need to wait five seconds before anything else can happen. If this was a graphical application, the entire screen would be locked until the work was completed.

If you were to use any of the previous techniques shown in this chapter to make your program more responsive, you would have a good deal of work ahead of you. However, since .NET 4.5, you can author the following C# codebase:

```
static async Task Main(string[] args)
{
  //ommitted for brevity
  string message = await DoWorkAsync();
  Console.WriteLine(message);
  //ommitted for brevity
}

static string DoWork()
{
  Thread.Sleep(5_000);
  return "Done with work!";
}
static async Task<string> DoWorkAsync()
{
  return await Task.Run(() =>
  {
    Thread.Sleep(5_000);
    return "Done with work!";
  });
}
```

Notice the await keyword *before* naming the method that will be called in an asynchronous manner. This is important: if you decorate a method with the async keyword but do not have at least one internal await-centric method call, you have essentially built a synchronous method call (in fact, you will be given a compiler warning to this effect).

Now, notice that you are required to use the Task class from the System.Threading.Tasks namespace to refactor your DoWork() method into the DoWorkAsync() method. Basically, rather than returning a specific return value straightaway (a string object in the current example), you return a Task<T> object, where the generic type parameter T is the underlying, actual return value (with me so far?).

The implementation of DoWorkAsync() now directly returns a Task<T> object, which is the return value of Task.Run(). The Run() method takes a Func<> or Action<> delegate, and as you know by this point in the text, you can simplify your life by using a lambda expression. Basically, your new version of DoWorkAsync() is essentially saying the following:

> *When you call me, I will run a new task. This task will cause the calling thread to sleep for five seconds, and when it is done, it gives me a string return value. I'll put this string in a new Task<string> object and return it to the caller.*

Having translated this new implementation of DoWorkAsync() into more natural (poetic) language, you gain some insight into the real role of the await token. This keyword will always modify a method that returns a Task object. When the flow of logic reaches the await token, the calling thread is suspended in this method until the call completes. If you were to run this version of the application, you would find that the Completed message shows before the Done with work! message. If this were a graphical application, the user could continue to use the UI while the DoWorkAsync() method executes.

Naming Conventions for Asynchronous Methods

Of course, you noticed the name change from DoWork() to DoWorkAsync(), but why the change? Let's say that the new version of the method was still named DoWork(); however, the calling code has been implemented as so:

```
//Oops! No await keyword here!
string message = DoWork();
```

Notice you did indeed mark the method with the async keyword, but you neglected to use the await keyword as a decorator before the DoWork() method call. At this point, you will have compiler errors, as the return value of DoWork() is a Task object, which you are attempting to assign directly to a string variable. Remember, the await token is in charge of extracting the internal return value contained in the Task object. Since you have not used this token, you have a type mismatch.

■ **Note** An "awaitable" method is simply a method that returns a Task<T>.

Given that methods that return Task objects can now be called in a nonblocking manner via the async and await tokens, Microsoft recommends (as a best practice) that any method returning a Task be marked with an Async suffix. In this way, developers who know the naming convention receive a visual reminder that the await keyword is required, if they intend to invoke the method within an asynchronous context.

■ **Note** Event handlers for GUI controls (such as a button Click handler) that use the async /await keywords do not follow this naming convention (by convention—pardon the redundancy!).

Async Methods Returning Void

Currently, your DoWorkAsync() method is returning a Task, which contains "real data" for the caller that will be obtained transparently via the await keyword. However, what if you want to build an asynchronous method that returns void? In this case, you use the nongeneric Task class and omit any return statement, like so:

```
static async Task MethodReturningVoidAsync()
{
  await Task.Run(() => { /* Do some work here... */
                         Thread.Sleep(4_000);
                       });
  Console.WriteLine("Void method completed");

}
```

The caller of this method would then use the await and async keywords as so:

```
await MethodReturningVoidAsync();
Console.WriteLine("Void method complete");
```

Async Methods with Multiple Awaits

It is completely permissible for a single async method to have multiple await contexts within its implementation. The following is perfectly acceptable code:

```
static async Task MultiAwaits()
{
    await Task.Run(() => { Thread.Sleep(2_000); });
    Console.WriteLine("Done with first task!");

    await Task.Run(() => { Thread.Sleep(2_000); });
    Console.WriteLine("Done with second task!");

    await Task.Run(() => { Thread.Sleep(2_000); });
    Console.WriteLine("Done with third task!");
}
```

Again, here each task is not doing much more than suspending the current thread for a spell; however, any unit of work could be represented by these tasks (calling a web service, reading a database, or what have you).

Calling Async Methods from Non-async Methods

Each of the previous examples used the async keyword to return the thread to calling code while the async method executes. In review, you can only use the await keyword in a method marked async. What if you can't (or don't want to) mark a method async?

Fortunately, there are other ways to call async methods. If you just don't use await keyword, code in that method continues past the async method without returning to the caller. If you needed to actually wait for your async method to complete (which is what happens when you use the await keyword), you can call Result on the method. This is a property of the Task object; it waits for execution to complete and then returns the underlying data of the Task. For example, you could call the DoWorkAsync() method like this:

```
Console.WriteLine(DoWorkAsync().Result);
```

To halt execution until an async method returns with a void return type, simply call Wait() on the Task, like this:

```
MethodReturningVoidAsync().Wait();
```

Await in catch and finally Blocks

C# 6 introduced the ability to place await calls in catch and finally blocks. The method itself must be async to do this. The following code example demonstrates the capability:

```
static async Task<string> MethodWithTryCatch()
{
  try
  {
    //Do some work
    return "Hello";
  }
  catch (Exception ex)
  {
    await LogTheErrors();
    throw;
  }
  finally
  {
    await DoMagicCleanUp();
  }
}
```

Generalized Async Return Types (New)

Prior to C# 7, the only return options for async methods were Task, Task<T>, and void. C# 7 enables additional return types, as long as they follow the async pattern. One concrete example is ValueTask, available in the System.Threading.Tasks.Extensions NuGet package. To install the package, open Package Manager Console (from View ➤ Other Windows) and enter the following:

```
install-package System.Threading.Tasks.Extensions
```

Once that package is installed, you can create code like this:

```
static async ValueTask<int> ReturnAnInt()
{
  await Task.Delay(1_000);
  return 5;
}
```

All of the same rules apply; it's just a Task for value types instead of forcing allocation of an object on the heap.

Local Functions (New)

Local functions were introduced in Chapter 4 and used in Chapter 8 with iterators. They can also be beneficial for async methods. To demonstrate the benefit, you need to first see the problem. Add a new method named MethodWithProblems() and add the following code:

```
static async Task MethodWithProblems(int firstParam, int secondParam)
{
  Console.WriteLine("Enter");
  await Task.Run(() =>
  {
    //Call long running method
    Thread.Sleep(4_000);
    Console.WriteLine("First Complete");
    //Call another long running method that fails because
    //the second parameter is out of range
    Console.WriteLine("Something bad happened");
  });
}
```

The scenario is that the second long-running task fails because of invalid input data. You can (and should) add checks to the beginning of the method, but since the entire method is asynchronous, there's no guarantee when the checks will be executed. It would be better for the checks to happen right away before the calling code moves on. In the following update, the checks are done in a synchronous manner, and then the private function is executed asynchronously.

```
static async Task MethodWithProblemsFixed(int firstParam, int secondParam)
{
  Console.WriteLine("Enter");
  if (secondParam < 0)
  {
    Console.WriteLine("Bad data");
    return;
  }

  actualImplementation();

  async Task actualImplementation()
  {
    await Task.Run(() =>
    {
      //Call long running method
      Thread.Sleep(4_000);
      Console.WriteLine("First Complete");
      //Call another long running method that fails because
      //the second parameter is out of range
      Console.WriteLine("Something bad happened");
    });
  }
}
```

Wrapping Up async and await

This section contained a lot of examples; here are the key points of this section:

- Methods (as well as lambda expressions or anonymous methods) can be marked with the async keyword to enable the method to do work in a nonblocking manner.

- Methods (as well as lambda expressions or anonymous methods) marked with the async keyword will run synchronously until the await keyword is encountered.

- A single async method can have multiple await contexts.

- When the await expression is encountered, the calling thread is suspended until the awaited task is complete. In the meantime, control is returned to the caller of the method.

- The await keyword will hide the returned Task object from view, appearing to directly return the underlying return value. Methods with no return value simply return void.

- Parameter checking and other error handling should be done in the main section of the method, with the actual async portion moved to a private function.

- For stack variables, the ValueTask is more efficient than the Task object, which might cause boxing and unboxing.

- As a naming convention, methods that are to be called asynchronously should be marked with the Async suffix.

■ **Source Code**   You can find the FunWithCSharpAsync project the Chapter 19 subdirectory.

Summary

This chapter began by examining how .NET delegate types can be configured to execute a method in an asynchronous manner. As you have seen, the BeginInvoke() and EndInvoke() methods allow you to indirectly manipulate a secondary thread with minimum fuss and bother. During this discussion, you were also introduced to the IAsyncResult interface and AsyncResult class type. As you learned, these types provide various ways to synchronize the calling thread and obtain possible method return values.

The next part of this chapter examined the role of the System.Threading namespace. As you learned, when an application creates additional threads of execution, the result is that the program in question is able to carry out numerous tasks at (what appears to be) the same time. You also examined several manners in which you can protect thread-sensitive blocks of code to ensure that shared resources do not become unusable units of bogus data.

This chapter then examined some new models for working with multithreaded development introduced with .NET 4.0, specifically the Task Parallel Library and PLINQ. I wrapped things up by covering the role of the async and await keywords. As you have seen, these keywords are using many types of the TPL framework in the background; however, the compiler does a majority of the work to create the complex threading and synchronization code on your behalf.

■ ■ ■

CHAPTER 20

File I/O and Object Serialization

When you create desktop applications, the ability to save information between user sessions is commonplace. This chapter examines a number of I/O-related topics as seen through the eyes of the .NET Framework. The first order of business is to explore the core types defined in the System.IO namespace and learn how to modify a machine's directory and file structure programmatically. The next task is to explore various ways to read from and write to character-based, binary-based, string-based, and memory-based data stores.

After you learn how to manipulate files and directories using the core I/O types, you will examine the related topic of *object serialization*. You can use object serialization to persist and retrieve the state of an object to (or from) any System.IO.Stream-derived type. The ability to serialize objects is critical when you want to copy an object to a remote machine using various remoting technologies such as Windows Communication Foundation. However, serialization is quite useful in its own right and will likely play a role in many of your .NET applications (distributed or not).

■ **Note**   To ensure you can run each of the examples in this chapter, start Visual Studio with administrative rights (just right-click the Visual Studio icon and select Run as Administrator. If you do not do so, you may encounter runtime security exceptions when accessing the computer file system.

Exploring the System.IO Namespace

In the framework of .NET, the System.IO namespace is the region of the base class libraries devoted to file-based (and memory-based) input and output (I/O) services. Like any namespace, System.IO defines a set of classes, interfaces, enumerations, structures, and delegates, most of which you can find in mscorlib.dll. In addition to the types contained within mscorlib.dll, the System.dll assembly defines additional members of the System.IO namespace. Note that all Visual Studio projects automatically set a reference to both assemblies.

Many of the types within the System.IO namespace focus on the programmatic manipulation of physical directories and files. However, additional types provide support to read data from and write data to string buffers, as well as raw memory locations. Table 20-1 outlines the core (nonabstract) classes, providing a road map of the functionality in System.IO.

Table 20-1. *Key Members of the System.IO Namespace*

Nonabstract I/O Class Type	Meaning in Life
BinaryReader BinaryWriter	These classes allow you to store and retrieve primitive data types (integers, Booleans, strings, and whatnot) as a binary value.
BufferedStream	This class provides temporary storage for a stream of bytes that you can commit to storage at a later time.
Directory DirectoryInfo	You use these classes to manipulate a machine's directory structure. The Directory type exposes functionality using *static members*, while the DirectoryInfo type exposes similar functionality from a valid *object reference*.
DriveInfo	This class provides detailed information regarding the drives that a given machine uses.
File FileInfo	You use these classes to manipulate a machine's set of files. The File type exposes functionality using *static members*, while the FileInfo type exposes similar functionality from a valid *object reference*.
FileStream	This class gives you random file access (e.g., seeking capabilities) with data represented as a stream of bytes.
FileSystemWatcher	This class allows you to monitor the modification of external files in a specified directory.
MemoryStream	This class provides random access to streamed data stored in memory rather than in a physical file.
Path	This class performs operations on System.String types that contain file or directory path information in a platform-neutral manner.
StreamWriter StreamReader	You use these classes to store (and retrieve) textual information to (or from) a file. These types do not support random file access.
StringWriter StringReader	Like the StreamReader/StreamWriter classes, these classes also work with textual information. However, the underlying storage is a string buffer rather than a physical file.

In addition to these concrete class types, System.IO defines a number of enumerations, as well as a set of abstract classes (e.g., Stream, TextReader, and TextWriter), that define a shared polymorphic interface to all descendants. You will read about many of these types in this chapter.

The Directory(Info) and File(Info) Types

System.IO provides four classes that allow you to manipulate individual files, as well as interact with a machine's directory structure. The first two types, Directory and File, expose creation, deletion, copying, and moving operations using various static members. The closely related FileInfo and DirectoryInfo types expose similar functionality as instance-level methods (therefore, you must allocate them with the new keyword). In Figure 20-1, the Directory and File classes directly extend System.Object, while DirectoryInfo and FileInfo derive from the abstract FileSystemInfo type.

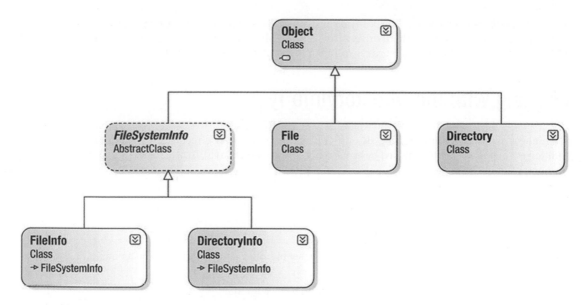

Figure 20-1. *The File- and Directory-centric types*

FileInfo and DirectoryInfo typically serve as better choices for obtaining full details of a file or directory (e.g., time created or read/write capabilities) because their members tend to return strongly typed objects. In contrast, the Directory and File class members tend to return simple string values rather than strongly typed objects. This is only a guideline, however; in many cases, you can get the same work done using File/FileInfo or Directory/DirectoryInfo.

The Abstract FileSystemInfo Base Class

The DirectoryInfo and FileInfo types receive many behaviors from the abstract FileSystemInfo base class. For the most part, you use the members of the FileSystemInfo class to discover general characteristics (such as time of creation, various attributes, and so forth) about a given file or directory. Table 20-2 lists some core properties of interest.

Table 20-2. *FileSystemInfo Properties*

Property	Meaning in Life
Attributes	Gets or sets the attributes associated with the current file that are represented by the FileAttributes enumeration (e.g., is the file or directory read-only, encrypted, hidden, or compressed?)
CreationTime	Gets or sets the time of creation for the current file or directory
Exists	Determines whether a given file or directory exists
Extension	Retrieves a file's extension
FullName	Gets the full path of the directory or file
LastAccessTime	Gets or sets the time the current file or directory was last accessed
LastWriteTime	Gets or sets the time when the current file or directory was last written to
Name	Obtains the name of the current file or directory

FileSystemInfo also defines the Delete() method. This is implemented by derived types to delete a given file or directory from the hard drive. Also, you can call Refresh() prior to obtaining attribute information to ensure that the statistics regarding the current file (or directory) are not outdated.

Working with the DirectoryInfo Type

The first creatable I/O-centric type you will examine is the DirectoryInfo class. This class contains a set of members used for creating, moving, deleting, and enumerating over directories and subdirectories. In addition to the functionality provided by its base class (FileSystemInfo), DirectoryInfo offers the key members detailed in Table 20-3.

Table 20-3. *Key Members of the DirectoryInfo Type*

Member	Meaning in Life
Create() CreateSubdirectory()	Creates a directory (or set of subdirectories) when given a path name
Delete()	Deletes a directory and all its contents
GetDirectories()	Returns an array of DirectoryInfo objects that represent all subdirectories in the current directory
GetFiles()	Retrieves an array of FileInfo objects that represent a set of files in the given directory
MoveTo()	Moves a directory and its contents to a new path
Parent	Retrieves the parent directory of this directory
Root	Gets the root portion of a path

You begin working with the DirectoryInfo type by specifying a particular directory path as a constructor parameter. Use the dot (.) notation if you want to obtain access to the current working directory (the directory of the executing application). Here are some examples:

```
// Bind to the current working directory.
DirectoryInfo dir1 = new DirectoryInfo(".");
// Bind to C:\Windows,
// using a verbatim string.
DirectoryInfo dir2 = new DirectoryInfo(@"C:\Windows");
```

In the second example, you assume that the path passed into the constructor (C:\Windows) already exists on the physical machine. However, if you attempt to interact with a nonexistent directory, a System.IO.DirectoryNotFoundException is thrown. Thus, if you specify a directory that is not yet created, you need to call the Create() method before proceeding, like so:

```
// Bind to a nonexistent directory, then create it.
DirectoryInfo dir3 = new DirectoryInfo(@"C:\MyCode\Testing");
dir3.Create();
```

After you create a `DirectoryInfo` object, you can investigate the underlying directory contents using any of the properties inherited from `FileSystemInfo`. To see this in action, create a new Console Application project named DirectoryApp and update your C# file to import `System.IO`. Update your `Program` class with the following new static method that creates a new `DirectoryInfo` object mapped to `C:\Windows` (adjust your path if need be), which displays a number of interesting statistics:

```
class Program
{
  static void Main(string[] args)
  {
    Console.WriteLine("***** Fun with Directory(Info) *****\n");
    ShowWindowsDirectoryInfo();
    Console.ReadLine();
  }

  static void ShowWindowsDirectoryInfo()
  {
    // Dump directory information.
    DirectoryInfo dir = new DirectoryInfo(@"C:\Windows");
    Console.WriteLine("***** Directory Info *****");
    Console.WriteLine("FullName: {0}", dir.FullName);
    Console.WriteLine("Name: {0}", dir.Name);
    Console.WriteLine("Parent: {0}", dir.Parent);
    Console.WriteLine("Creation: {0}", dir.CreationTime);
    Console.WriteLine("Attributes: {0}", dir.Attributes);
    Console.WriteLine("Root: {0}", dir.Root);
    Console.WriteLine("*************************\n");
  }
}
```

While your output might differ, you should see something similar to the following:

```
***** Fun with Directory(Info) *****

***** Directory Info *****
FullName: C:\Windows
Name: Windows
Parent:
Creation: 7/9/2017 8:52:58 AM
Attributes: Directory
Root: C:\
*************************
```

Enumerating Files with the DirectoryInfo Type

In addition to obtaining basic details of an existing directory, you can extend the current example to use some methods of the `DirectoryInfo` type. First, you can leverage the `GetFiles()` method to obtain information about all `*.jpg` files located in the `C:\Windows\Web\Wallpaper` directory.

CHAPTER 20 ■ FILE I/O AND OBJECT SERIALIZATION

■ **Note** If your machine does not have a `C:\Windows\Web\Wallpaper` directory, retrofit this code to read files of a directory on your machine (e.g., to read all `*.bmp` files from the `C:\Windows` directory).

The `GetFiles()` method returns an array of `FileInfo` objects, each of which exposes details of a particular file (you will learn the full details of the `FileInfo` type later in this chapter). Assume that you have the following static method of the `Program` class, which you call from `Main()`:

```
static void DisplayImageFiles()
{
  DirectoryInfo dir = new DirectoryInfo(@"C:\Windows\Web\Wallpaper");
  // Get all files with a *.jpg extension.
  FileInfo[] imageFiles = dir.GetFiles("*.jpg", SearchOption.AllDirectories);

  // How many were found?
  Console.WriteLine("Found {0} *.jpg files\n", imageFiles.Length);

  // Now print out info for each file.
  foreach (FileInfo f in imageFiles)
  {
    Console.WriteLine("***************************");
    Console.WriteLine("File name: {0}", f.Name);
    Console.WriteLine("File size: {0}", f.Length);
    Console.WriteLine("Creation: {0}", f.CreationTime);
    Console.WriteLine("Attributes: {0}", f.Attributes);
    Console.WriteLine("***************************\n");
  }
}
```

Notice that you specify a search option when you call `GetFiles()`; you do this to look within all subdirectories of the root. After you run the application, you will see a listing of all files that match the search pattern.

Creating Subdirectories with the DirectoryInfo Type

You can programmatically extend a directory structure using the `DirectoryInfo.CreateSubdirectory()` method. This method can create a single subdirectory, as well as multiple nested subdirectories, in a single function call. This method illustrates how to do so, extending the directory structure of the `C:` drive with some custom subdirectories:

```
static void ModifyAppDirectory()
{
  DirectoryInfo dir = new DirectoryInfo(@"C:\");

  // Create \MyFolder off application directory.
  dir.CreateSubdirectory("MyFolder");

  // Create \MyFolder2\Data off application directory.
  dir.CreateSubdirectory(@"MyFolder2\Data");
}
```

760

You are not required to capture the return value of the CreateSubdirectory() method, but you should be aware that a DirectoryInfo object representing the newly created item is passed back on successful execution. Consider the following update to the previous method. Note the dot notation in the constructor of DirectoryInfo, which gives you access to the application's installation point.

```
static void ModifyAppDirectory()
{
  DirectoryInfo dir = new DirectoryInfo(".");

  // Create \MyFolder off initial directory.
  dir.CreateSubdirectory("MyFolder");

  // Capture returned DirectoryInfo object.
  DirectoryInfo myDataFolder = dir.CreateSubdirectory(@"MyFolder2\Data");

  // Prints path to ..\MyFolder2\Data.
  Console.WriteLine("New Folder is: {0}", myDataFolder);
}
```

If you call this method from within Main() and examine your Windows directory using Windows Explorer, you will see that the new subdirectories are present and accounted for.

Working with the Directory Type

You have seen the DirectoryInfo type in action; now you're ready to learn about the Directory type. For the most part, the static members of Directory mimic the functionality provided by the instance-level members defined by DirectoryInfo. Recall, however, that the members of Directory typically return string data rather than strongly typed FileInfo/DirectoryInfo objects.

Now let's look at some functionality of the Directory type; this final helper function displays the names of all drives mapped to the current computer (using the Directory.GetLogicalDrives() method) and uses the static Directory.Delete() method to remove the \MyFolder and \MyFolder2\Data subdirectories created previously.

```
static void FunWithDirectoryType()
{
  // List all drives on current computer.
  string[] drives = Directory.GetLogicalDrives();
  Console.WriteLine("Here are your drives:");
  foreach (string s in drives)
    Console.WriteLine("--> {0} ", s);

  // Delete what was created.
  Console.WriteLine("Press Enter to delete directories");
  Console.ReadLine();
  try
  {
    Directory.Delete(@"C:\MyFolder");
```

```
  // The second parameter specifies whether you
  // wish to destroy any subdirectories.
  Directory.Delete(@"C:\MyFolder2", true);
}
catch (IOException e)
{
  Console.WriteLine(e.Message);
}
}
```

■ **Source Code**   You can find the DirectoryApp project in the Chapter 20 subdirectory.

Working with the DriveInfo Class Type

The System.IO namespace provides a class named DriveInfo. Like Directory.GetLogicalDrives(), the static DriveInfo.GetDrives() method allows you to discover the names of a machine's drives. Unlike Directory.GetLogicalDrives(), however, DriveInfo provides numerous other details (e.g., the drive type, available free space, and volume label). Consider the following Program class defined within a new Console Application project named DriveInfoApp (don't forget to import System.IO):

```
class Program
{
  static void Main(string[] args)
  {
    Console.WriteLine("***** Fun with DriveInfo *****\n");

    // Get info regarding all drives.
    DriveInfo[] myDrives = DriveInfo.GetDrives();
    // Now print drive stats.
    foreach(DriveInfo d in myDrives)
    {
      Console.WriteLine("Name: {0}", d.Name);
      Console.WriteLine("Type: {0}", d.DriveType);

      // Check to see whether the drive is mounted.
      if(d.IsReady)
      {
        Console.WriteLine("Free space: {0}", d.TotalFreeSpace);
        Console.WriteLine("Format: {0}", d.DriveFormat);
        Console.WriteLine("Label: {0}", d.VolumeLabel);
      }
      Console.WriteLine();
    }
    Console.ReadLine();
  }
}
```

Here is some possible output:

```
***** Fun with DriveInfo *****

Name: C:\
Type: Fixed
Free space: 791699763200
Format: NTFS
Label: Windows10_OS

Name: D:\
Type: Fixed
Free space: 23804067840
Format: NTFS
Label: LENOVO

Press any key to continue . . .
```

At this point, you have investigated some core behaviors of the Directory, DirectoryInfo, and DriveInfo classes. Next, you'll learn how to create, open, close, and destroy the files that populate a given directory.

■ **Source Code** You can find the DriveInfoApp project in the Chapter 20 subdirectory.

Working with the FileInfo Class

As shown in the previous DirectoryApp example, the FileInfo class allows you to obtain details regarding existing files on your hard drive (e.g., time created, size, and file attributes) and aids in the creation, copying, moving, and destruction of files. In addition to the set of functionality inherited by FileSystemInfo, you can find some core members unique to the FileInfo class, which you can see described in Table 20-4.

Table 20-4. FileInfo Core Members

Member	Meaning in Life
AppendText()	Creates a StreamWriter object (described later) that appends text to a file
CopyTo()	Copies an existing file to a new file
Create()	Creates a new file and returns a FileStream object (described later) to interact with the newly created file
CreateText()	Creates a StreamWriter object that writes a new text file
Delete()	Deletes the file to which a FileInfo instance is bound
Directory	Gets an instance of the parent directory
DirectoryName	Gets the full path to the parent directory

(*continued*)

Table 20-4. (continued)

Member	Meaning in Life
Length	Gets the size of the current file
MoveTo()	Moves a specified file to a new location, providing the option to specify a new file name
Name	Gets the name of the file
Open()	Opens a file with various read/write and sharing privileges
OpenRead()	Creates a read-only FileStream object
OpenText()	Creates a StreamReader object (described later) that reads from an existing text file
OpenWrite()	Creates a write-only FileStream object

Note that a majority of the methods of the FileInfo class return a specific I/O-centric object (e.g., FileStream and StreamWriter) that allows you to begin reading and writing data to (or reading from) the associated file in a variety of formats. You will check out these types in just a moment; however, before you see a working example, you'll find it helpful to examine various ways to obtain a file handle using the FileInfo class type.

The FileInfo.Create() Method

One way you can create a file handle is to use the FileInfo.Create() method, like so:

```
static void Main(string[] args)
{
  // Make a new file on the C drive.
  FileInfo f = new FileInfo(@"C:\Test.dat");
  FileStream fs = f.Create();

  // Use the FileStream object...

  // Close down file stream.
  fs.Close();
}
```

Notice that the FileInfo.Create() method returns a FileStream object, which exposes synchronous and asynchronous write/read operations to/from the underlying file (more details in a moment). Be aware that the FileStream object returned by FileInfo.Create() grants full read/write access to all users.

Also notice that after you finish with the current FileStream object, you must ensure you close down the handle to release the underlying unmanaged stream resources. Given that FileStream implements IDisposable, you can use the C# using scope to allow the compiler to generate the teardown logic (see Chapter 8 for details), like so:

```
static void Main(string[] args)
{
  // Defining a using scope for file I/O
  // types is ideal.
```

```
  FileInfo f = new FileInfo(@"C:\Test.dat");
  using (FileStream fs = f.Create())
  {
    // Use the FileStream object...
  }
}
```

The FileInfo.Open() Method

You can use the FileInfo.Open() method to open existing files, as well as to create new files with far more precision than you can with FileInfo.Create(). This works because Open() typically takes several parameters to qualify exactly how to iterate the file you want to manipulate. Once the call to Open() completes, you are returned a FileStream object. Consider the following logic:

```
static void Main(string[] args)
{
  // Make a new file via FileInfo.Open().
  FileInfo f2 = new FileInfo(@"C:\Test2.dat");
  using(FileStream fs2 = f2.Open(FileMode.OpenOrCreate,
    FileAccess.ReadWrite, FileShare.None))
  {
    // Use the FileStream object...
  }
}
```

This version of the overloaded Open() method requires three parameters. The first parameter of the Open() method specifies the general flavor of the I/O request (e.g., make a new file, open an existing file, and append to a file), which you specify using the FileMode enumeration (see Table 20-5 for details), like so:

```
public enum FileMode
{
  CreateNew,
  Create,
  Open,
  OpenOrCreate,
  Truncate,
  Append
}
```

Table 20-5. *Members of the FileMode Enumeration*

Member	Meaning in Life
CreateNew	Informs the OS to make a new file. If it already exists, an IOException is thrown.
Create	Informs the OS to make a new file. If it already exists, it will be overwritten.
Open	Opens an existing file. If the file does not exist, a FileNotFoundException is thrown.
OpenOrCreate	Opens the file if it exists; otherwise, a new file is created.
Truncate	Opens an existing file and truncates the file to 0 bytes in size.
Append	Opens a file, moves to the end of the file, and begins write operations (you can use this flag only with a write-only stream). If the file does not exist, a new file is created.

You use the second parameter of the Open() method, a value from the FileAccess enumeration, to determine the read/write behavior of the underlying stream, as follows:

```
public enum FileAccess
{
  Read,
  Write,
  ReadWrite
}
```

Finally, the third parameter of the Open() method, FileShare, specifies how to share the file among other file handlers. Here are the core names:

```
public enum FileShare
{
  Delete,
  Inheritable,
  None,
  Read,
  ReadWrite,
  Write
}
```

The FileInfo.OpenRead() and FileInfo.OpenWrite() Methods

The FileInfo.Open() method allows you to obtain a file handle in a flexible manner, but the FileInfo class also provides members named OpenRead() and OpenWrite(). As you might imagine, these methods return a properly configured read-only or write-only FileStream object, without the need to supply various enumeration values. Like FileInfo.Create() and FileInfo.Open(), OpenRead() and OpenWrite() return a FileStream object (note that the following code assumes you have files named Test3.dat and Test4.dat on your C: drive):

```
static void Main(string[] args)
{
  // Get a FileStream object with read-only permissions.
  FileInfo f3 = new FileInfo(@"C:\Test3.dat");
  using(FileStream readOnlyStream = f3.OpenRead())
  {
    // Use the FileStream object...
  }

  // Now get a FileStream object with write-only permissions.
  FileInfo f4 = new FileInfo(@"C:\Test4.dat");
  using(FileStream writeOnlyStream = f4.OpenWrite())
  {
    // Use the FileStream object...
  }
}
```

The FileInfo.OpenText() Method

Another open-centric member of the FileInfo type is OpenText(). Unlike Create(), Open(), OpenRead(), or OpenWrite(), the OpenText() method returns an instance of the StreamReader type, rather than a FileStream type. Assuming you have a file named boot.ini on your C: drive, the following snippet gives you access to its contents:

```
static void Main(string[] args)
{
  // Get a StreamReader object.
  FileInfo f5 = new FileInfo(@"C:\boot.ini");
  using(StreamReader sreader = f5.OpenText())
  {
    // Use the StreamReader object...
  }
}
```

As you will see shortly, the StreamReader type provides a way to read character data from the underlying file.

The FileInfo.CreateText() and FileInfo.AppendText() Methods

The final two FileInfo methods of interest at this point are CreateText() and AppendText(). Both return a StreamWriter object, as shown here:

```
static void Main(string[] args)
{
  FileInfo f6 = new FileInfo(@"C:\Test6.txt");
  using(StreamWriter swriter = f6.CreateText())
  {
    // Use the StreamWriter object...
  }

  FileInfo f7 = new FileInfo(@"C:\FinalTest.txt");
  using(StreamWriter swriterAppend = f7.AppendText())
  {
    // Use the StreamWriter object...
  }
}
```

As you might guess, the StreamWriter type provides a way to write character data to the underlying file.

Working with the File Type

The File type uses several static members to provide functionality almost identical to that of the FileInfo type. Like FileInfo, File supplies AppendText(), Create(), CreateText(), Open(), OpenRead(), OpenWrite(), and OpenText() methods. In many cases, you can use the File and FileInfo types interchangeably. To see this in action, you can simplify each of the previous FileStream examples by using the File type instead, like so:

```
static void Main(string[] args)
{
  // Obtain FileStream object via File.Create().
  using(FileStream fs = File.Create(@"C:\Test.dat"))
  {}

  // Obtain FileStream object via File.Open().
  using(FileStream fs2 = File.Open(@"C:\Test2.dat",
    FileMode.OpenOrCreate,
    FileAccess.ReadWrite, FileShare.None))
  {}

  // Get a FileStream object with read-only permissions.
  using(FileStream readOnlyStream = File.OpenRead(@"Test3.dat"))
  {}

  // Get a FileStream object with write-only permissions.
  using(FileStream writeOnlyStream = File.OpenWrite(@"Test4.dat"))
  {}

  // Get a StreamReader object.
  using(StreamReader sreader = File.OpenText(@"C:\boot.ini"))
  {}

  // Get some StreamWriters.
  using(StreamWriter swriter = File.CreateText(@"C:\Test6.txt"))
  {}

  using(StreamWriter swriterAppend = File.AppendText(@"C:\FinalTest.txt"))
  {}
}
```

Additional File-Centric Members

The File type also supports a few members, shown in Table 20-6, which can greatly simplify the processes of reading and writing textual data.

Table 20-6. *Methods of the File Type*

Method	Meaning in Life
ReadAllBytes()	Opens the specified file, returns the binary data as an array of bytes, and then closes the file
ReadAllLines()	Opens a specified file, returns the character data as an array of strings, and then closes the file
ReadAllText()	Opens a specified file, returns the character data as a System.String, and then closes the file
WriteAllBytes()	Opens the specified file, writes out the byte array, and then closes the file
WriteAllLines()	Opens a specified file, writes out an array of strings, and then closes the file
WriteAllText()	Opens a specified file, writes the character data from a specified string, and then closes the file

You can use these methods of the File type to read and write batches of data in only a few lines of code. Even better, each of these members automatically closes down the underlying file handle. For example, the following console program (named SimpleFileIO) persists the string data into a new file on the C: drive (and reads it into memory) with minimal fuss (this example assumes you have imported System.IO):

```
class Program
{
  static void Main(string[] args)
  {
    Console.WriteLine("***** Simple I/O with the File Type *****\n");
    string[] myTasks = {
      "Fix bathroom sink", "Call Dave",
      "Call Mom and Dad", "Play Xbox One"};

    // Write out all data to file on C drive.
    File.WriteAllLines(@"tasks.txt", myTasks);

    // Read it all back and print out.
    foreach (string task in File.ReadAllLines(@"tasks.txt"))
    {
      Console.WriteLine("TODO: {0}", task);
    }
    Console.ReadLine();
  }
}
```

The lesson here is that when you want to obtain a file handle quickly, the File type will save you some keystrokes. However, one benefit of creating a FileInfo object first is that you can investigate the file using the members of the abstract FileSystemInfo base class.

■ **Source Code**   You can find the SimpleFileIO project in the Chapter 20 subdirectory.

The Abstract Stream Class

At this point, you have seen many ways to obtain FileStream, StreamReader, and StreamWriter objects, but you have yet to read data from or write data to a file using these types. To understand how to do this, you'll need to familiarize yourself with the concept of a *stream*. In the world of I/O manipulation, a *stream* represents a chunk of data flowing between a source and a destination. Streams provide a common way to interact with a *sequence of bytes*, regardless of what kind of device (e.g., file, network connection, or printer) stores or displays the bytes in question.

The abstract System.IO.Stream class defines several members that provide support for synchronous and asynchronous interactions with the storage medium (e.g., an underlying file or memory location).

■ **Note**   The concept of a stream is not limited to file I/O. To be sure, the .NET libraries provide stream access to networks, memory locations, and other stream-centric abstractions.

Again, Stream descendants represent data as a raw stream of bytes; therefore, working directly with raw streams can be quite cryptic. Some Stream-derived types support *seeking*, which refers to the process of obtaining and adjusting the current position in the stream. Table 20-7 helps you understand the functionality provided by the Stream class by describing its core members.

Table 20-7. *Abstract Stream Members*

Member	Meaning in Life
CanRead CanWrite CanSeek	Determines whether the current stream supports reading, seeking, and/or writing.
Close()	Closes the current stream and releases any resources (such as sockets and file handles) associated with the current stream. Internally, this method is aliased to the Dispose() method; therefore, *closing a stream* is functionally equivalent to *disposing a stream*.
Flush()	Updates the underlying data source or repository with the current state of the buffer and then clears the buffer. If a stream does not implement a buffer, this method does nothing.
Length	Returns the length of the stream in bytes.
Position	Determines the position in the current stream.
Read() ReadByte() ReadAsync()	Reads a sequence of bytes (or a single byte) from the current stream and advances the current position in the stream by the number of bytes read.
Seek()	Sets the position in the current stream.
SetLength()	Sets the length of the current stream.
Write() WriteByte() WrriteAsync()	Writes a sequence of bytes (or a single byte) to the current stream and advances the current position in this stream by the number of bytes written.

Working with FileStreams

The FileStream class provides an implementation for the abstract Stream members in a manner appropriate for file-based streaming. It is a fairly primitive stream; it can read or write only a single byte or an array of bytes. However, you will not often need to interact directly with the members of the FileStream type. Instead, you will probably use various *stream wrappers*, which make it easier to work with textual data or .NET types. Nevertheless, you will find it helpful to experiment with the synchronous read/write capabilities of the FileStream type.

Assume you have a new Console Application project named FileStreamApp (and verify that System.IO and System.Text are imported into your initial C# code file). Your goal is to write a simple text message to a new file named myMessage.dat. However, given that FileStream can operate only on raw bytes, you will be required to encode the System.String type into a corresponding byte array. Fortunately, the System.Text namespace defines a type named Encoding that provides members that encode and decode strings to (or from) an array of bytes (check out the .NET Framework SDK documentation for more details about the Encoding type).

Once encoded, the byte array is persisted to file with the FileStream.Write() method. To read the bytes back into memory, you must reset the internal position of the stream (using the Position property) and call the ReadByte() method. Finally, you display the raw byte array and the decoded string to the console. Here is the complete Main() method:

```
// Don't forget to import the System.Text and System.IO namespaces.
static void Main(string[] args)
{
  Console.WriteLine("***** Fun with FileStreams *****\n");

  // Obtain a FileStream object.
  using(FileStream fStream = File.Open(@"myMessage.dat",
    FileMode.Create))
  {
    // Encode a string as an array of bytes.
    string msg = "Hello!";
    byte[] msgAsByteArray = Encoding.Default.GetBytes(msg);

    // Write byte[] to file.
    fStream.Write(msgAsByteArray, 0, msgAsByteArray.Length);

    // Reset internal position of stream.
    fStream.Position = 0;

    // Read the types from file and display to console.
    Console.Write("Your message as an array of bytes: ");
    byte[] bytesFromFile = new byte[msgAsByteArray.Length];
    for (int i = 0; i < msgAsByteArray.Length; i++)
    {
      bytesFromFile[i] = (byte)fStream.ReadByte();
      Console.Write(bytesFromFile[i]);
    }
```

```
  // Display decoded messages.
  Console.Write("\nDecoded Message: ");
  Console.WriteLine(Encoding.Default.GetString(bytesFromFile));
  }
  Console.ReadLine();
}
```

This example populates the file with data, but it also punctuates the major downfall of working directly with the FileStream type: it demands to operate on raw bytes. Other Stream-derived types operate in a similar manner. For example, if you want to write a sequence of bytes to a region of memory, you can allocate a MemoryStream. Likewise, if you want to push an array of bytes through a network connection, you can use the NetworkStream class (in the System.Net.Sockets namespace).

As mentioned previously, the System.IO namespace provides several *reader* and *writer* types that encapsulate the details of working with Stream-derived types.

■ **Source Code**   You can find the FileStreamApp project in the Chapter 20 subdirectory.

Working with StreamWriters and StreamReaders

The StreamWriter and StreamReader classes are useful whenever you need to read or write character-based data (e.g., strings). Both of these types work by default with Unicode characters; however, you can change this by supplying a properly configured System.Text.Encoding object reference. To keep things simple, assume that the default Unicode encoding fits the bill.

StreamReader derives from an abstract type named TextReader, as does the related StringReader type (discussed later in this chapter). The TextReader base class provides a limited set of functionality to each of these descendants; specifically, it provides the ability to read and peek into a character stream.

The StreamWriter type (as well as StringWriter, which you will examine later in this chapter) derives from an abstract base class named TextWriter. This class defines members that allow derived types to write textual data to a given character stream.

To aid in your understanding of the core writing capabilities of the StreamWriter and StringWriter classes, Table 20-8 describes the core members of the abstract TextWriter base class.

Table 20-8. *Core Members of TextWriter*

Member	Meaning in Life
Close()	This method closes the writer and frees any associated resources. In the process, the buffer is automatically flushed (again, this member is functionally equivalent to calling the Dispose() method).
Flush()	This method clears all buffers for the current writer and causes any buffered data to be written to the underlying device; however, it does not close the writer.
NewLine	This property indicates the newline constant for the derived writer class. The default line terminator for the Windows OS is a carriage return, followed by a line feed (\r\n).
Write() WriteAsync()	This overloaded method writes data to the text stream without a newline constant.
WriteLine() WriteLineAsync()	This overloaded method writes data to the text stream with a newline constant.

■ **Note** The last two members of the TextWriter class probably look familiar to you. If you recall, the System.Console type has Write() and WriteLine() members that push textual data to the standard output device. In fact, the Console.In property wraps a TextReader, and the Console.Out property wraps a TextWriter.

The derived StreamWriter class provides an appropriate implementation for the Write(), Close(), and Flush() methods, and it defines the additional AutoFlush property. When set to true, this property forces StreamWriter to flush all data every time you perform a write operation. Be aware that you can gain better performance by setting AutoFlush to false, provided you always call Close() when you finish writing with a StreamWriter.

Writing to a Text File

To see the StreamWriter type in action, create a new Console Application project named StreamWriterReaderApp and import System.IO. The following Main() method creates a new file named reminders.txt in the current execution folder, using the File.CreateText() method. Using the obtained StreamWriter object, you can add some textual data to the new file.

```
static void Main(string[] args)
{
  Console.WriteLine("***** Fun with StreamWriter / StreamReader *****\n");

  // Get a StreamWriter and write string data.
  using(StreamWriter writer = File.CreateText("reminders.txt"))
  {
    writer.WriteLine("Don't forget Mother's Day this year...");
    writer.WriteLine("Don't forget Father's Day this year...");
    writer.WriteLine("Don't forget these numbers:");
    for(int i = 0; i < 10; i++)
      writer.Write(i + " ");

    // Insert a new line.
    writer.Write(writer.NewLine);
  }

  Console.WriteLine("Created file and wrote some thoughts...");
  Console.ReadLine();
}
```

After you run this program, you can examine the contents of this new file (see Figure 20-2). You will find this file under the bin\Debug folder of your current application because you did not specify an absolute path at the time you called CreateText().

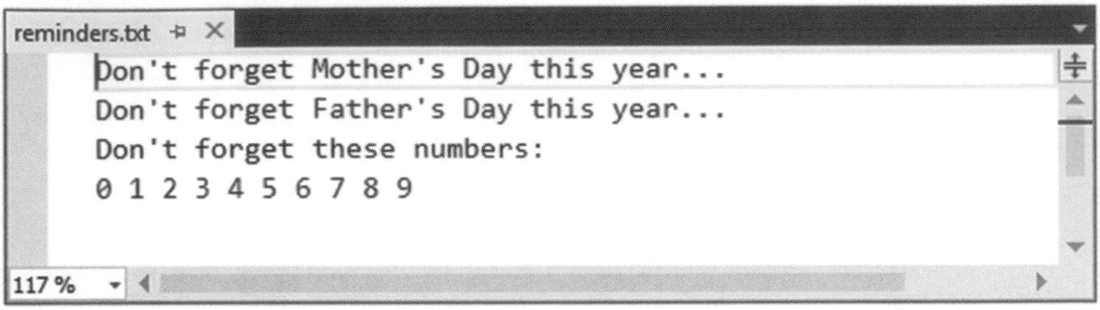

```
reminders.txt  ⏸ ✕
      Don't forget Mother's Day this year...
      Don't forget Father's Day this year...
      Don't forget these numbers:
      0 1 2 3 4 5 6 7 8 9


117 %  ▾ ◀
```

Figure 20-2. *The contents of your* `*.txt` *file*

Reading from a Text File

Next, you will learn to read data from a file programmatically by using the corresponding `StreamReader` type. Recall that this class derives from the abstract `TextReader`, which offers the functionality described in Table 20-9.

Table 20-9. *TextReader Core Members*

Member	Meaning in Life
`Peek()`	Returns the next available character (expressed as an integer) without actually changing the position of the reader. A value of `-1` indicates you are at the end of the stream.
`Read()` `ReadAsync()`	Reads data from an input stream.
`ReadBlock()` `ReadBlockAsync()`	Reads a specified maximum number of characters from the current stream and writes the data to a buffer, beginning at a specified index.
`ReadLine()` `ReadLineAsync()`	Reads a line of characters from the current stream and returns the data as a string (a `null` string indicates EOF).
`ReadToEnd()` `ReadToEndAsync()`	Reads all characters from the current position to the end of the stream and returns them as a single string.

If you now extend the current sample application to use a `StreamReader`, you can read in the textual data from the `reminders.txt` file, as shown here:

```
static void Main(string[] args)
{
  Console.WriteLine("***** Fun with StreamWriter / StreamReader *****\n");
...
  // Now read data from file.
  Console.WriteLine("Here are your thoughts:\n");
  using(StreamReader sr = File.OpenText("reminders.txt"))
  {
    string input = null;
    while ((input = sr.ReadLine()) != null)
```

```
  {
    Console.WriteLine (input);
  }
}
Console.ReadLine();
}
```

After you run the program, you will see the character data in `reminders.txt` displayed to the console.

Directly Creating StreamWriter/StreamReader Types

One of the confusing aspects of working with the types within `System.IO` is that you can often achieve an identical result using different approaches. For example, you have already seen that you can use the `CreateText()` method to obtain a `StreamWriter` with the `File` or `FileInfo` type. It so happens that you can work with `StreamWriters` and `StreamReaders` another way: by creating them directly. For example, you could retrofit the current application as follows:

```
static void Main(string[] args)
{
  Console.WriteLine("***** Fun with StreamWriter / StreamReader *****\n");

  // Get a StreamWriter and write string data.
  using(StreamWriter writer = new StreamWriter("reminders.txt"))
  {
    ...
  }

  // Now read data from file.
  using(StreamReader sr = new StreamReader("reminders.txt"))
  {
    ...
  }
}
```

Although it can be a bit confusing to see so many seemingly identical approaches to file I/O, keep in mind that the end result is greater flexibility. In any case, you are now ready to examine the role of the `StringWriter` and `StringReader` classes, given that you have seen how to move character data to and from a given file using the `StreamWriter` and `StreamReader` types.

■ **Source Code**   You can find the StreamWriterReaderApp project in the `Chapter 20` subdirectory.

Working with StringWriters and StringReaders

You can use the `StringWriter` and `StringReader` types to treat textual information as a stream of in-memory characters. This can prove helpful when you would like to append character-based information to an underlying buffer. The following Console Application project (named StringReaderWriterApp) illustrates this by writing a block of string data to a StringWriter object, rather than to a file on the local hard drive (don't forget to import System.IO):

```
static void Main(string[] args)
{
  Console.WriteLine("***** Fun with StringWriter / StringReader *****\n");

  // Create a StringWriter and emit character data to memory.
  using(StringWriter strWriter = new StringWriter())
  {
    strWriter.WriteLine("Don't forget Mother's Day this year...");
    // Get a copy of the contents (stored in a string) and dump
    // to console.
    Console.WriteLine("Contents of StringWriter:\n{0}", strWriter);
  }
  Console.ReadLine();
}
```

StringWriter and StreamWriter both derive from the same base class (TextWriter), so the writing logic is more or less identical. However, given the nature of StringWriter, you should also be aware that this class allows you to use the following GetStringBuilder() method to extract a System.Text.StringBuilder object:

```
using (StringWriter strWriter = new StringWriter())
{
  strWriter.WriteLine("Don't forget Mother's Day this year...");
  Console.WriteLine("Contents of StringWriter:\n{0}", strWriter);

  // Get the internal StringBuilder.
  StringBuilder sb = strWriter.GetStringBuilder();
  sb.Insert(0, "Hey!! ");
  Console.WriteLine("-> {0}", sb.ToString());
  sb.Remove(0, "Hey!! ".Length);
  Console.WriteLine("-> {0}", sb.ToString());
}
```

When you want to read from a stream of character data, you can use the corresponding StringReader type, which (as you would expect) functions identically to the related StreamReader class. In fact, the StringReader class does nothing more than override the inherited members to read from a block of character data, rather than from a file, as shown here:

```
using (StringWriter strWriter = new StringWriter())
{
  strWriter.WriteLine("Don't forget Mother's Day this year...");
  Console.WriteLine("Contents of StringWriter:\n{0}", strWriter);

  // Read data from the StringWriter.
  using (StringReader strReader = new StringReader(strWriter.ToString()))
  {
    string input = null;
    while ((input = strReader.ReadLine()) != null)
```

```
  {
    Console.WriteLine(input);
  }
 }
}
```

■ **Source Code**   You can find StringReaderWriterApp in the Chapter 20 subdirectory.

Working with BinaryWriters and BinaryReaders

The final writer/reader sets you will examine in this section are BinaryReader and BinaryWriter. Both derive directly from System.Object. These types allow you to read and write discrete data types to an underlying stream in a compact binary format. The BinaryWriter class defines a highly overloaded Write() method to place a data type in the underlying stream. In addition to the Write() member, BinaryWriter provides additional members that allow you to get or set the Stream-derived type; it also offers support for random access to the data (see Table 20-10).

Table 20-10. *BinaryWriter Core Members*

Member	Meaning in Life
BaseStream	This read-only property provides access to the underlying stream used with the BinaryWriter object.
Close()	This method closes the binary stream.
Flush()	This method flushes the binary stream.
Seek()	This method sets the position in the current stream.
Write()	This method writes a value to the current stream.

The BinaryReader class complements the functionality offered by BinaryWriter with the members described in Table 20-11.

Table 20-11. *BinaryReader Core Members*

Member	Meaning in Life
BaseStream	This read-only property provides access to the underlying stream used with the BinaryReader object.
Close()	This method closes the binary reader.
PeekChar()	This method returns the next available character without advancing the position in the stream.
Read()	This method reads a given set of bytes or characters and stores them in the incoming array.
ReadXXXX()	The BinaryReader class defines numerous read methods that grab the next type from the stream (e.g., ReadBoolean(), ReadByte(), and ReadInt32()).

The following example (a Console Application project named BinaryWriterReader) writes a number of data types to a new *.dat file:

```
static void Main(string[] args)
{
  Console.WriteLine("***** Fun with Binary Writers / Readers *****\n");

  // Open a binary writer for a file.
  FileInfo f = new FileInfo("BinFile.dat");
  using(BinaryWriter bw = new BinaryWriter(f.OpenWrite()))
  {
    // Print out the type of BaseStream.
    // (System.IO.FileStream in this case).
    Console.WriteLine("Base stream is: {0}", bw.BaseStream);

    // Create some data to save in the file.
    double aDouble = 1234.67;
    int anInt = 34567;
    string aString = "A, B, C";

    // Write the data.
    bw.Write(aDouble);
    bw.Write(anInt);
    bw.Write(aString);
  }
  Console.WriteLine("Done!");
  Console.ReadLine();
}
```

Notice how the FileStream object returned from FileInfo.OpenWrite() is passed to the constructor of the BinaryWriter type. Using this technique makes it easy to *layer in* a stream before writing out the data. Note that the constructor of BinaryWriter takes any Stream-derived type (e.g., FileStream, MemoryStream, or BufferedStream). Thus, writing binary data to memory instead is as simple as supplying a valid MemoryStream object.

To read the data out of the BinFile.dat file, the BinaryReader type provides a number of options. Here, you call various read-centric members to pluck each chunk of data from the file stream:

```
static void Main(string[] args)
{
...
  FileInfo f = new FileInfo("BinFile.dat");
...
  // Read the binary data from the stream.
  using(BinaryReader br = new BinaryReader(f.OpenRead()))
  {
    Console.WriteLine(br.ReadDouble());
    Console.WriteLine(br.ReadInt32());
    Console.WriteLine(br.ReadString());
  }
  Console.ReadLine();
}
```

■ **Source Code**   You can find the BinaryWriterReader application in the Chapter 20 subdirectory.

Watching Files Programmatically

Now that you have a better handle on the use of various readers and writers, you'll look at the role of the FileSystemWatcher class. This type can be quite helpful when you want to monitor (or "watch") files on your system programmatically. Specifically, you can instruct the FileSystemWatcher type to monitor files for any of the actions specified by the System.IO.NotifyFilters enumeration (many of these members are self-explanatory, but you should still check the .NET Framework 4.7 SDK documentation for more details).

```
public enum NotifyFilters
{
  Attributes, CreationTime,
  DirectoryName, FileName,
  LastAccess, LastWrite,
  Security, Size
}
```

To begin working with the FileSystemWatcher type, you need to set the Path property to specify the name (and location) of the directory that contains the files you want to monitor, as well as the Filter property that defines the file extensions of the files you want to monitor.

At this point, you may choose to handle the Changed, Created, and Deleted events, all of which work in conjunction with the FileSystemEventHandler delegate. This delegate can call any method matching the following pattern:

```
// The FileSystemEventHandler delegate must point
// to methods matching the following signature.
void MyNotificationHandler(object source, FileSystemEventArgs e)
```

You can also handle the Renamed event using the RenamedEventHandler delegate type, which can call methods that match the following signature:

```
// The RenamedEventHandler delegate must point
// to methods matching the following signature.
void MyRenamedHandler(object source, RenamedEventArgs e)
```

While you could use the traditional delegate/event syntax to handle each event, you can certainly make use of lambda expression syntax as well (the downloadable code for this project uses lambda syntax, if you are interested).

Next, let's look at the process of watching a file. Assume you have created a new directory on your C: drive named MyFolder that contains various *.txt files (named whatever you like). The following Console Application project (named MyDirectoryWatcher) monitors the *.txt files in the MyFolder directory and prints messages when files are created, deleted, modified, or renamed:

```
static void Main(string[] args)
{
  Console.WriteLine("***** The Amazing File Watcher App *****\n");
  // Establish the path to the directory to watch.
  FileSystemWatcher watcher = new FileSystemWatcher();
```

779

```
  try
  {
    watcher.Path = @"C:\MyFolder";
  }
  catch(ArgumentException ex)
  {
    Console.WriteLine(ex.Message);
    return;
  }
  // Set up the things to be on the lookout for.
  watcher.NotifyFilter = NotifyFilters.LastAccess
    | NotifyFilters.LastWrite
    | NotifyFilters.FileName
    | NotifyFilters.DirectoryName;

  // Only watch text files.
  watcher.Filter = "*.txt";

  // Add event handlers.
  watcher.Changed += new FileSystemEventHandler(OnChanged);
  watcher.Created += new FileSystemEventHandler(OnChanged);
  watcher.Deleted += new FileSystemEventHandler(OnChanged);
  watcher.Renamed += new RenamedEventHandler(OnRenamed);

  // Begin watching the directory.
  watcher.EnableRaisingEvents = true;

  // Wait for the user to quit the program.
  Console.WriteLine(@"Press 'q' to quit app.");
  while(Console.Read()!='q')
    ;
}
```

The following two event handlers simply print the current file modification:

```
static void OnChanged(object source, FileSystemEventArgs e)
{
  // Specify what is done when a file is changed, created, or deleted.
  Console.WriteLine("File: {0} {1}!", e.FullPath, e.ChangeType);
}

static void OnRenamed(object source, RenamedEventArgs e)
{
  // Specify what is done when a file is renamed.
  Console.WriteLine("File: {0} renamed to {1}", e.OldFullPath, e.FullPath);
}
```

To test this program, run the application and open Windows Explorer. Try renaming your files, creating a *.txt file, deleting a *.txt file, and so forth. You will see various bits of information generated about the state of the text files within your MyFolder, as in this example:

```
***** The Amazing File Watcher App *****

Press 'q' to quit app.
File: C:\MyFolder\New Text Document.txt Created!
File: C:\MyFolder\New Text Document.txt renamed to C:\MyFolder\Hello.txt
File: C:\MyFolder\Hello.txt Changed!
File: C:\MyFolder\Hello.txt Changed!
File: C:\MyFolder\Hello.txt Deleted!
```

■ **Source Code**   You can find the MyDirectoryWatcher application in the Chapter 20 subdirectory.

That wraps up this chapter's look at fundamental I/O operations within the .NET platform. While you will certainly use these techniques in many of your applications, you might also find that *object serialization* services can greatly simplify how you persist large amounts of data.

Understanding Object Serialization

The term *serialization* describes the process of persisting (and possibly transferring) the state of an object into a stream (e.g., file stream and memory stream). The persisted data sequence contains all the necessary information you need to reconstruct (or *deserialize*) the state of the object for use later. Using this technology makes it trivial to save vast amounts of data (in various formats). In many cases, saving application data using serialization services results in less code than using the readers/writers you find in the System.IO namespace.

For example, assume you want to create a GUI-based desktop application that provides a way for end users to save their preferences (e.g., window color and font size). To do this, you might define a class named UserPrefs that encapsulates 20 or so pieces of field data. Now, if you were to use a System.IO.BinaryWriter type, you would need to save each field of the UserPrefs object *manually*. Likewise, if you were to load the data from a file back into memory, you would need to use a System.IO.BinaryReader and (once again) *manually* read in each value to reconfigure a new UserPrefs object.

This is all doable, but you can save yourself a good amount of time by marking the UserPrefs class with the [Serializable] attribute, like so:

```
[Serializable]
public class UserPrefs
{
  public string WindowColor;
  public int FontSize;
}
```

Doing this means that you can persist the entire state of the object with only a few lines of code. Without getting hung up on the details for the time being, consider the following `Main()` method:

```
static void Main(string[] args)
{
  UserPrefs userData= new UserPrefs();
  userData.WindowColor = "Yellow";
  userData.FontSize = 50;

  // The BinaryFormatter persists state data in a binary format.
  // You would need to import System.Runtime.Serialization.Formatters.Binary
  // to gain access to BinaryFormatter.
  BinaryFormatter binFormat = new BinaryFormatter();

  // Store object in a local file.
  using(Stream fStream = new FileStream("user.dat",
    FileMode.Create, FileAccess.Write, FileShare.None))
  {
    binFormat.Serialize(fStream, userData);
  }
  Console.ReadLine();
}
```

.NET object serialization makes it easy to persist objects; however, the processes used behind the scenes are quite sophisticated. For example, when an object is persisted to a stream, all associated data (e.g., base class data and contained objects) is automatically serialized, as well. Therefore, if you attempt to persist a derived class, all data up the chain of inheritance comes along for the ride. As you will see, you use an object graph to represent a set of interrelated objects.

.NET serialization services also allow you to persist an object graph in a variety of formats. The previous code example uses the `BinaryFormatter` type; therefore, the state of the `UserPrefs` object is persisted as a compact binary format. You can also persist an object graph into SOAP or XML format using other types. These formats can be quite helpful when you need to ensure that your persisted objects travel well across operating systems, languages, and architectures.

■ **Note** WCF prefers a slightly different mechanism for serializing objects to/from WCF service operations; it uses the `[DataContract]` and `[DataMember]` attributes. You'll learn more about this in Chapter 23.

Finally, understand that you can persist an object graph into *any* `System.IO.Stream`-derived type. In the previous example, you used the `FileStream` type to persist a `UserPrefs` object into a local file. However, if you would rather store an object to a specific region of memory, you could use a `MemoryStream` type instead. All that matters is that the sequence of data correctly represents the state of objects within the graph.

The Role of Object Graphs

As mentioned previously, the CLR will account for all related objects to ensure that data is persisted correctly when an object is serialized. This set of related objects is referred to as an *object graph*. Object graphs provide a simple way to document how a set of items refer to each other. Be aware that object graphs are *not* denoting OOP *is-a* or *has-a* relationships. Rather, you can read the arrows in an object diagram as "requires" or "depends on."

Each object in an object graph is assigned a unique numerical value. Keep in mind that the numbers assigned to the members in an object graph are arbitrary and have no real meaning to the outside world.

Once you assign all objects a numerical value, the object graph can record each object's set of dependencies.

For example, assume you have created a set of classes that model some automobiles (of course). You have a base class named Car, which *has-a* Radio. Another class named JamesBondCar extends the Car base type. Figure 20-3 shows a possible object graph that models these relationships.

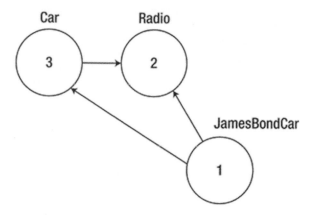

Figure 20-3. *A simple object graph*

When reading object graphs, you can use the phrase *depends on* or *refers to* when connecting the arrows. Thus, in Figure 20-3, you can see that the Car refers to the Radio class (given the *has-a* relationship). JamesBondCar refers to Car (given the *is-a* relationship), as well as to Radio (it inherits this protected member variable).

Of course, the CLR does not paint pictures in memory to represent a graph of related objects. Rather, the relationship documented in Figure 20-4 is represented by a mathematical formula that looks something like this:

```
[Car 3, ref 2], [Radio 2], [JamesBondCar 1, ref 3, ref 2]
```

If you parse this formula, you can see that object 3 (the Car) has a dependency on object 2 (the Radio). Object 2, the Radio, is a lone wolf and requires nobody. Finally, object 1 (the JamesBondCar) has a dependency on object 3, as well as object 2. In any case, when you serialize or deserialize an instance of JamesBondCar, the object graph ensures that the Radio and Car types also participate in the process.

The beautiful thing about the serialization process is that the graph representing the relationships among your objects is established automatically behind the scenes. As you will see later in this chapter, however, you can become more involved in the construction of a given object graph by customizing the serialization process using attributes and interfaces.

■ **Note** Strictly speaking, the XmlSerializer type (described later in this chapter) does not persist state using object graphs; however, this type still serializes and deserializes related objects in a predictable manner.

Configuring Objects for Serialization

To make an object available to .NET serialization services, all you need to do is decorate each related class (or structure) with the [Serializable] attribute. If you determine that a given type has some member data that should not (or perhaps cannot) participate in the serialization scheme, you can mark such fields with the [NonSerialized] attribute. This can be helpful if you want to reduce the size of the persisted data and you have member variables in a serializable class that do not need to be remembered (e.g., fixed values, random values, and transient data).

Defining Serializable Types

To get the ball rolling, create a new Console Application project named SimpleSerialize. Insert a new class named Radio, which has been marked [Serializable], excluding a single member variable (radioID) that has been marked [NonSerialized] and will, therefore, not be persisted into the specified data stream.

```
[Serializable]
public class Radio
{
  public bool hasTweeters;
  public bool hasSubWoofers;
  public double[] stationPresets;

  [NonSerialized]
  public string radioID = "XF-552RR6";
}
```

Next, insert two additional class types to represent the JamesBondCar and Car classes, both of which are also marked [Serializable] and define the following pieces of field data:

```
[Serializable]
public class Car
{
  public Radio theRadio = new Radio();
  public bool isHatchBack;
}

[Serializable]
public class JamesBondCar : Car
{
  public bool canFly;
  public bool canSubmerge;
}
```

Be aware that you cannot inherit the [Serializable] attribute from a parent class. Therefore, if you derive a class from a type marked [Serializable], the child class must be marked [Serializable] as well, or it cannot be persisted. In fact, all objects in an object graph must be marked with the [Serializable] attribute. If you attempt to serialize a nonserializable object using the BinaryFormatter or SoapFormatter, you will receive a SerializationException at runtime.

Public Fields, Private Fields, and Public Properties

Notice that in each of these classes you define the field data as public; this helps keep the example simple. Of course, private data exposed using public properties would be preferable from an OO point of view. Also, for the sake of simplicity, this example does not define any custom constructors on these types; therefore, all unassigned field data will receive the expected default values.

OO design principles aside, you might wonder how the various formatters expect a type's field data to be defined in order to be serialized into a stream. The answer is that it depends. If you persist an object's state using the BinaryFormatter or SoapFormatter, it makes absolutely no difference. These types are programmed to serialize *all* serializable fields of a type, regardless of whether they are public fields, private fields, or private fields exposed through public properties. Recall, however, that if you have points of data that you do not want to be persisted into the object graph, you can selectively mark public or private fields as [NonSerialized], as you do with the string field of the Radio type.

The situation is quite different if you use the XmlSerializer type, however. This type will *only* serialize public data fields or private data exposed by public properties. Private data not exposed from properties will be ignored. For example, consider the following serializable Person type:

```
[Serializable]
public class Person
{
  // A public field.
  public bool isAlive = true;

  // A private field.
  private int personAge = 21;

  // Public property/private data.
  private string fName = string.Empty;
  public string FirstName
  {
    get { return fName; }
    set { fName = value; }
  }
}
```

If you processed the preceding with BinaryFormatter or SoapFormatter, you would find that the isAlive, personAge, and fName fields are saved into the selected stream. However, the XmlSerializer would *not* save the value of personAge because this piece of private data is not encapsulated by a public type property. If you wanted to persist the age of the person with the XmlSerializer, you would need to define the field publicly or encapsulate the private member using a public property.

Choosing a Serialization Formatter

After you configure your types to participate in the .NET serialization scheme by applying the necessary attributes, your next step is to choose which format (binary, SOAP, or XML) you should use when persisting your object's state. Each possibility is represented by the following classes:

- BinaryFormatter
- SoapFormatter
- XmlSerializer

■ **Note** You might be wondering why JSON isn't on this list. JSON is covered in Chapter 27.

The BinaryFormatter type serializes your object's state to a stream using a compact binary format. This type is defined within the System.Runtime.Serialization.Formatters.Binary namespace that is part of mscorlib.dll. If you want to gain access to this type, you can specify the following C# using directive:

```
// Gain access to the BinaryFormatter in mscorlib.dll.
using System.Runtime.Serialization.Formatters.Binary;
```

The SoapFormatter type persists an object's state as a SOAP message (the standard XML format for passing messages to/from a SOAP-based web service). This type is defined within the System.Runtime. Serialization.Formatters.Soap namespace, which is defined in a *separate assembly*. Thus, to format your object graph into a SOAP message, you must first set a reference to System.Runtime.Serialization. Formatters.Soap.dll using the Visual Studio Add Reference dialog box and then specify the following C# using directive:

```
// Must reference System.Runtime.Serialization.Formatters.Soap.dll.
using System.Runtime.Serialization.Formatters.Soap;
```

Finally, if you want to persist a tree of objects as an XML document, you can use the XmlSerializer type. To use this type, you need to specify that you are using the System.Xml.Serialization namespace and set a reference to the assembly System.Xml.dll. As luck would have it, all Visual Studio project templates automatically reference System.Xml.dll; therefore, all you need to do is use the following namespace:

```
// Defined within System.Xml.dll.
using System.Xml.Serialization;
```

The IFormatter and IRemotingFormatter Interfaces

Regardless of which formatter you choose to use, be aware that all of them derive directly from System.Object, so they do *not* share a common set of members from a serialization-centric base class. However, the BinaryFormatter and SoapFormatter types do support common members through the implementation of the IFormatter and IRemotingFormatter interfaces (strange as it might seem, the XmlSerializer implements neither).

System.Runtime.Serialization.IFormatter defines the core Serialize() and Deserialize() methods, which do the grunt work to move your object graphs into and out of a specific stream. Beyond these members, IFormatter defines the following few properties that the implementing type uses behind the scenes:

```
public interface IFormatter
{
  SerializationBinder Binder { get; set; }
  StreamingContext Context { get; set; }
  ISurrogateSelector SurrogateSelector { get; set; }
  object Deserialize(Stream serializationStream);
  void Serialize(Stream serializationStream, object graph);
}
```

The `System.Runtime.Remoting.Messaging.IRemotingFormatter` interface (which is leveraged internally by the .NET remoting layer) overloads the `Serialize()` and `Deserialize()` members into a manner more appropriate for distributed persistence. Note that `IRemotingFormatter` derives from the more general `IFormatter` interface.

```
public interface IRemotingFormatter : IFormatter
{
  object Deserialize(Stream serializationStream, HeaderHandler handler);
  void Serialize(Stream serializationStream, object graph, Header[] headers);
}
```

Although you might not need to interact directly with these interfaces for most of your serialization endeavors, recall that interface-based polymorphism allows you to hold an instance of `BinaryFormatter` or `SoapFormatter` using an `IFormatter` reference. Therefore, if you want to build a method that can serialize an object graph using either of these classes, you could write the following:

```
static void SerializeObjectGraph(IFormatter itfFormat, Stream destStream, object graph)
{
  itfFormat.Serialize(destStream, graph);
}
```

Type Fidelity Among the Formatters

The most obvious difference among the three formatters is how the object graph is persisted to the stream (binary, SOAP, or XML). You should also be aware of a few more subtle points of distinction, specifically, how the formatters contend with *type fidelity*. When you use the `BinaryFormatter` type, it will persist not only the field data of the objects in the object graph but also each type's fully qualified name and the full name of the defining assembly (name, version, public key token, and culture). These extra points of data make the `BinaryFormatter` an ideal choice when you want to transport objects by value (e.g., as a full copy) across machine boundaries for .NET-centric applications.

The `SoapFormatter` persists traces of the assembly of origin through the use of an XML namespace. For example, recall the `Person` type earlier in this chapter. If this type were persisted as a SOAP message, you would find that the opening element of `Person` is qualified by the generated `xmlns`. Consider this partial definition, paying special attention to the a1 XML namespace:

```
<a1:Person id="ref-1" xmlns:a1=
  "http://schemas.microsoft.com/clr/nsassem/SimpleSerialize/MyApp%2C%20
  Version%3D1.0.0.0%2C%20Culture%3Dneutral%2C%20PublicKeyToken%3Dnull">
  <isAlive>true</isAlive>
  <personAge>21</personAge>
  <fName id="ref-3">Mel</fName>
</a1:Person>
```

However, the `XmlSerializer` does *not* attempt to preserve full type fidelity; therefore, it does not record the type's fully qualified name or assembly of origin. This might seem like a limitation at first glance, but XML serialization is used by classic .NET web services, which can be called from clients on any platform (not just .NET). This means that there is no point serializing full .NET type metadata. Here is a possible XML representation of the Person type:

```
<?xml version="1.0"?>
<Person xmlns:xsi="http://www.w3.org/2001/XMLSchema-instance"
        xmlns:xsd="http://www.w3.org/2001/XMLSchema">
  <isAlive>true</isAlive>
  <PersonAge>21</PersonAge>
  <FirstName>Frank</FirstName>
</Person>
```

If you want to persist an object's state in a manner that can be used by any operating system (e.g., Windows, macOS, and various Linux distributions), application framework (e.g., .NET, Java Enterprise Edition, and COM), or programming language, you do not want to maintain full type fidelity because you cannot assume all possible recipients can understand .NET-specific data types. Given this, SoapFormatter and XmlSerializer are ideal choices when you need to ensure as broad a reach as possible for the persisted tree of objects.

Serializing Objects Using the BinaryFormatter

You can use the BinaryFormatter type to illustrate how easy it is to persist an instance of the JamesBondCar to a physical file. Again, the two key methods of the BinaryFormatter type to be aware of are Serialize() and Deserialize().

- Serialize(): Persists an object graph to a specified stream as a sequence of bytes

- Deserialize(): Converts a persisted sequence of bytes to an object graph

Assume you have created an instance of JamesBondCar, modified some state data, and want to persist your spy mobile into a *.dat file. Begin by creating the *.dat file itself. You can achieve this by creating an instance of the System.IO.FileStream type. At this point, you can create an instance of the BinaryFormatter and pass in the FileStream and object graph to persist. Consider the following Main() method:

```
// Be sure to import the System.Runtime.Serialization.Formatters.Binary
// and System.IO namespaces.
static void Main(string[] args)
{
  Console.WriteLine("***** Fun with Object Serialization *****\n");

  // Make a JamesBondCar and set state.
  JamesBondCar jbc = new JamesBondCar();
  jbc.canFly = true;
  jbc.canSubmerge = false;
  jbc.theRadio.stationPresets = new double[]{89.3, 105.1, 97.1};
  jbc.theRadio.hasTweeters = true;

  // Now save the car to a specific file in a binary format.
  SaveAsBinaryFormat(jbc, "CarData.dat");
  Console.ReadLine();
}
```

You implement the SaveAsBinaryFormat() method like this:

```
static void SaveAsBinaryFormat(object objGraph, string fileName)
{
  // Save object to a file named CarData.dat in binary.
  BinaryFormatter binFormat = new BinaryFormatter();

  using(Stream fStream = new FileStream(fileName,
        FileMode.Create, FileAccess.Write, FileShare.None))
  {
    binFormat.Serialize(fStream, objGraph);
  }
  Console.WriteLine("=> Saved car in binary format!");
}
```

The BinaryFormatter.Serialize() method is the member responsible for composing the object graph and moving the byte sequence to some Stream-derived type. In this case, the stream happens to be a physical file. You could also serialize your object types to any Stream-derived type, such as a memory location or network stream.

After you run your program, you can view the contents of the CarData.dat file that represents this instance of the JamesBondCar by navigating to the \bin\Debug folder of the current project. Figure 20-4 shows this file opened within Visual Studio.

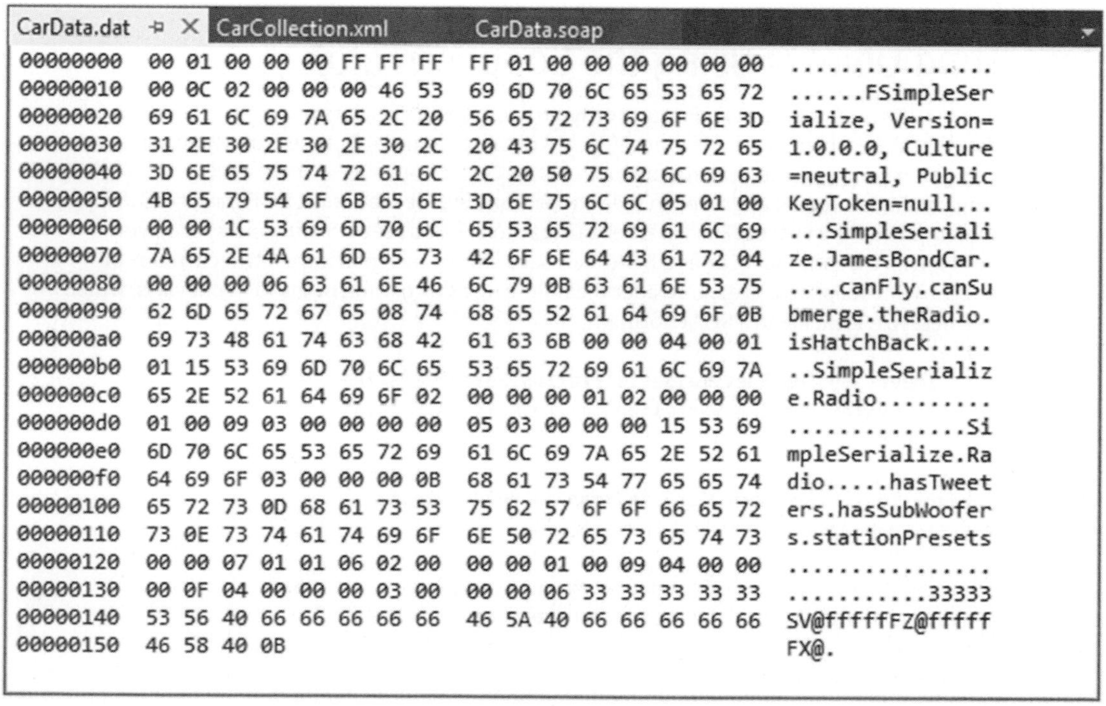

Figure 20-4. JamesBondCar serialized using a BinaryFormatter

Deserializing Objects Using the BinaryFormatter

Now suppose you want to read the persisted JamesBondCar from the binary file back into an object variable. After you open CarData.dat programmatically (with the File.OpenRead() method), you can call the Deserialize() method of the BinaryFormatter. Be aware that Deserialize() returns a general System.Object type, so you need to impose an explicit cast, as shown here:

```
static void LoadFromBinaryFile(string fileName)
{
  BinaryFormatter binFormat = new BinaryFormatter();

  // Read the JamesBondCar from the binary file.
  using(Stream fStream = File.OpenRead(fileName))
  {
    JamesBondCar carFromDisk =
      (JamesBondCar)binFormat.Deserialize(fStream);
    Console.WriteLine("Can this car fly? : {0}", carFromDisk.canFly);
  }
}
```

Notice that when you call Deserialize(), you pass the Stream-derived type that represents the location of the persisted object graph. Once you cast the object back into the correct type, you will find the state data has been retained from the point at which you saved the object.

Serializing Objects Using the SoapFormatter

Your next choice of formatter is the SoapFormatter type, which serializes data in a proper SOAP envelope. In a nutshell, the Simple Object Access Protocol (SOAP) defines a standard process in which you can invoke methods in a platform- and OS-neutral manner.

Assuming you have added a reference to the System.Runtime.Serialization.Formatters.Soap.dll assembly (and imported the System.Runtime.Serialization.Formatters.Soap namespace), you can persist and retrieve a JamesBondCar as a SOAP message simply by replacing each occurrence of BinaryFormatter with SoapFormatter. Consider the following new method of the Program class, which serializes an object to a local file in a SOAP format:

```
// Be sure to import System.Runtime.Serialization.Formatters.Soap
// and reference System.Runtime.Serialization.Formatters.Soap.dll.
static void SaveAsSoapFormat (object objGraph, string fileName)
{
  // Save object to a file named CarData.soap in SOAP format.
  SoapFormatter soapFormat = new SoapFormatter();

  using(Stream fStream = new FileStream(fileName,
    FileMode.Create, FileAccess.Write, FileShare.None))
  {
    soapFormat.Serialize(fStream, objGraph);
  }
  Console.WriteLine("=> Saved car in SOAP format!");
}
```

As before, you use `Serialize()` and `Deserialize()` to move the object graph into and out of the stream. If you call this method from `Main()` and run the application, you can open the resulting *.soap file. Here you can locate the XML elements that mark the stateful values of the current `JamesBondCar`, as well as the relationship between the objects in the graph by using the `#ref` tokens (see Figure 20-5).

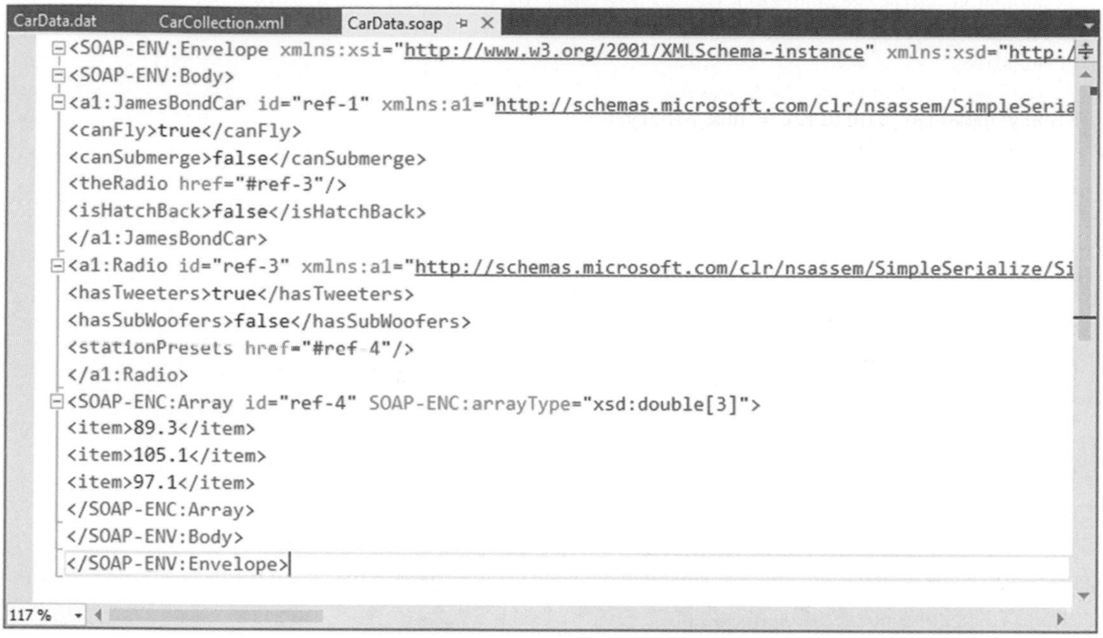

```
CarData.dat        CarCollection.xml      CarData.soap  ⊞  ×
  ⊟<SOAP-ENV:Envelope xmlns:xsi="http://www.w3.org/2001/XMLSchema-instance" xmlns:xsd="http://
  ⊟<SOAP-ENV:Body>
  ⊟<a1:JamesBondCar id="ref-1" xmlns:a1="http://schemas.microsoft.com/clr/nsassem/SimpleSeria
    <canFly>true</canFly>
    <canSubmerge>false</canSubmerge>
    <theRadio href="#ref-3"/>
    <isHatchBack>false</isHatchBack>
  </a1:JamesBondCar>
  ⊟<a1:Radio id="ref-3" xmlns:a1="http://schemas.microsoft.com/clr/nsassem/SimpleSerialize/Si
    <hasTweeters>true</hasTweeters>
    <hasSubWoofers>false</hasSubWoofers>
    <stationPresets href="#ref-4"/>
  </a1:Radio>
  ⊟<SOAP-ENC:Array id="ref-4" SOAP-ENC:arrayType="xsd:double[3]">
    <item>89.3</item>
    <item>105.1</item>
    <item>97.1</item>
  </SOAP-ENC:Array>
  </SOAP-ENV:Body>
  </SOAP-ENV:Envelope>|
117 %   ▾  ◀
```

Figure 20-5. *JamesBondCar serialized using a SoapFormatter*

Serializing Objects Using the XmlSerializer

In addition to the SOAP and binary formatters, the `System.Xml.dll` assembly provides a third formatter, `System.Xml.Serialization.XmlSerializer`. You can use this formatter to persist the *public* state of a given object as pure XML, as opposed to XML data wrapped within a SOAP message. Working with this type is a bit different from working with the `SoapFormatter` or `BinaryFormatter` type. Consider the following code, which assumes you have imported the `System.Xml.Serialization` namespace:

```
static void SaveAsXmlFormat(object objGraph, string fileName)
{
  // Save object to a file named CarData.xml in XML format.
  XmlSerializer xmlFormat = new XmlSerializer(typeof(JamesBondCar));

  using(Stream fStream = new FileStream(fileName,
    FileMode.Create, FileAccess.Write, FileShare.None))
  {
    xmlFormat.Serialize(fStream, objGraph);
  }
  Console.WriteLine("=> Saved car in XML format!");
}
```

791

The key difference is that the XmlSerializer type requires you to specify type information that represents the class you want to serialize. If you were to look within the newly generated XML file (assuming you call this new method from within Main()), you would find the XML data shown here:

```
<?xml version="1.0"?>
<JamesBondCar xmlns:xsi="http://www.w3.org/2001/XMLSchema-instance"
xmlns:xsd="http://www.w3.org/2001/XMLSchema">
  <theRadio>
    <hasTweeters>true</hasTweeters>
    <hasSubWoofers>false</hasSubWoofers>
    <stationPresets>
      <double>89.3</double>
      <double>105.1</double>
      <double>97.1</double>
    </stationPresets>
    <radioID>XF-552RR6</radioID>
  </theRadio>
  <isHatchBack>false</isHatchBack>
  <canFly>true</canFly>
  <canSubmerge>false</canSubmerge>
</JamesBondCar>
```

■ **Note**   The XmlSerializer demands that all serialized types in the object graph support a default constructor (so be sure to add it back if you define custom constructors). If this is not the case, you will receive an InvalidOperationException at runtime.

Controlling the Generated XML Data

If you have a background in XML technologies, you know that it is often critical to ensure the data within an XML document conforms to a set of rules that establish the *validity* of the data. Understand that a *valid* XML document does not have anything to do with the syntactic well-being of the XML elements (e.g., all opening elements must have a closing element). Rather, valid documents conform to agreed- upon formatting rules (e.g., field X must be expressed as an attribute and not a subelement), which are typically defined by an XML schema or document-type definition (DTD) file.

By default, XmlSerializer serializes all public fields/properties as XML elements, rather than as XML attributes. If you want to control how the XmlSerializer generates the resulting XML document, you can decorate types with any number of additional .NET attributes from the System.Xml.Serialization namespace. Table 20-12 documents some (but not all) of the .NET attributes that influence how XML data is encoded to a stream.

Table 20-12. *Select Attributes of the* System.Xml.Serialization *Namespace*

.NET Attribute	Meaning in Life
[XmlAttribute]	You can use this .NET attribute on a public field or property in a class to tell XmlSerializer to serialize the data as an XML attribute (rather than as a subelement).
[XmlElement]	The field or property will be serialized as an XML element named as you so choose.
[XmlEnum]	This attribute provides the element name of an enumeration member.
[XmlRoot]	This attribute controls how the root element will be constructed (namespace and element name).
[XmlText]	The property or field will be serialized as XML text (i.e., the content between the start tag and the end tag of the root element).
[XmlType]	This attribute provides the name and namespace of the XML type.

This simple example illustrates how the field data of JamesBondCar is currently persisted as XML:

```
<?xml version="1.0" encoding="utf-8"?>
<JamesBondCar xmlns:xsi="http://www.w3.org/2001/XMLSchema-instance"
              xmlns:xsd="http://www.w3.org/2001/XMLSchema">
...
  <canFly>true</canFly>
  <canSubmerge>false</canSubmerge>
</JamesBondCar>
```

If you want to specify a custom XML namespace that qualifies the JamesBondCar and encodes the canFly and canSubmerge values as XML attributes, you can do so by modifying the C# definition of JamesBondCar, like so:

```
[Serializable, XmlRoot(Namespace = "http://www.MyCompany.com")]
public class JamesBondCar : Car
{
  [XmlAttribute]
  public bool canFly;
  [XmlAttribute]
  public bool canSubmerge;
}
```

This yields the following XML document (note the opening <JamesBondCar> element):

```
<?xml version="1.0"""?>
<JamesBondCar xmlns:xsi="http://www.w3.org/2001/XMLSchema-instance"
              xmlns:xsd="http://www.w3.org/2001/XMLSchema"
  canFly="true" canSubmerge="false"
  xmlns="http://www.MyCompany.com">
...
</JamesBondCar>
```

Of course, you can use many other .NET attributes to control how the XmlSerializer generates the resulting XML document. For full details, look up the System.Xml.Serialization namespace in the .NET Framework 4.7 SDK documentation.

Serializing Collections of Objects

Now that you have seen how to persist a single object to a stream, you're ready to examine how to save a set of objects. As you might have noticed, the Serialize() method of the IFormatter interface does not provide a way to specify an arbitrary number of objects as input (only a single System.Object). On a related note, the return value of Deserialize() is, again, a single System.Object (the same basic limitation holds true for XmlSerializer).

```
public interface IFormatter
{
...
  object Deserialize(Stream serializationStream);
  void Serialize(Stream serializationStream, object graph);
}
```

Recall that the System.Object represents a complete tree of objects. Given this, if you pass in an object that has been marked as [Serializable] and contains other [Serializable] objects, the entire set of objects is persisted in a single method call. As luck would have it, most of the types you find in the System. Collections and System.Collections.Generic namespaces have already been marked as [Serializable]. Therefore, if you would like to persist a set of objects, simply add the desired set to the container (such as a normal array, an ArrayList, or a List<T>) and serialize the object to your stream of choice.

Now assume that you want to update the JamesBondCar class with a two-argument constructor so you can set a few pieces of state data (note that you add back the default constructor as required by the XmlSerializer).

```
[Serializable,
 XmlRoot(Namespace = "http://www.MyCompany.com")]
public class JamesBondCar : Car
{
  public JamesBondCar(bool skyWorthy, bool seaWorthy)
  {
    canFly = skyWorthy;
    canSubmerge = seaWorthy;
  }
  // The XmlSerializer demands a default constructor!
  public JamesBondCar(){}
...
}
```

With this, you can now persist any number of JamesBondCars.

```
static void SaveListOfCars()
{
  // Now persist a List<T> of JamesBondCars.
  List<JamesBondCar> myCars = new List<JamesBondCar>();
  myCars.Add(new JamesBondCar(true, true));
```

```
  myCars.Add(new JamesBondCar(true, false));
  myCars.Add(new JamesBondCar(false, true));
  myCars.Add(new JamesBondCar(false, false));

  using(Stream fStream = new FileStream("CarCollection.xml",
    FileMode.Create, FileAccess.Write, FileShare.None))
  {
    XmlSerializer xmlFormat = new XmlSerializer(typeof(List<JamesBondCar>));
    xmlFormat.Serialize(fStream, myCars);
  }
  Console.WriteLine("=> Saved list of cars!");
}
```

You use XmlSerializer here, so you are required to specify type information for each of the subobjects within the root object (List<JamesBondCar>, in this case). However, the logic would be even more straightforward if you were to use the BinaryFormatter or SoapFormatter type instead, as shown here:

```
static void SaveListOfCarsAsBinary()
{
  // Save ArrayList object (myCars) as binary.
  List<JamesBondCar> myCars = new List<JamesBondCar>();

  BinaryFormatter binFormat = new BinaryFormatter();
  using(Stream fStream = new FileStream("AllMyCars.dat",
    FileMode.Create, FileAccess.Write, FileShare.None))
  {
    binFormat.Serialize(fStream, myCars);
  }
  Console.WriteLine("=> Saved list of cars in binary!");
}
```

■ **Source Code**   You can find the SimpleSerialize application in the Chapter 20 subdirectory.

Customizing the Soap/Binary Serialization Process

In a majority of cases, the default serialization scheme provided by the .NET platform will be exactly what you require. Simply apply the [Serializable] attribute to your related types and pass the tree of objects to your formatter of choice for processing. In some cases, however, you might want to become more involved with how a tree is constructed and handled during the serialization process. For example, perhaps you have a business rule that says all field data must be persisted using a particular format, or perhaps you need to add additional bits of data to the stream that do not map directly to fields in the object being persisted (e.g., timestamps and unique identifiers).

When you want to become more involved with the process of object serialization, the System.Runtime.Serialization namespace provides several types that allow you to do so. Table 20-13 describes some of the core types you should be aware of.

Table 20-13. *System.Runtime.Serialization Namespace Core Types*

Type	Meaning in Life
ISerializable	You can implement this interface on a [Serializable] type to control its serialization and deserialization.
ObjectIDGenerator	This type generates IDs for members in an object graph.
[OnDeserialized]	This attribute allows you to specify a method that will be called immediately after the object has been deserialized.
[OnDeserializing]	This attribute allows you to specify a method that will be called before the deserialization process.
[OnSerialized]	This attribute allows you to specify a method that will be called immediately after the object has been serialized.
[OnSerializing]	This attribute allows you to specify a method that will be called before the serialization process.
[OptionalField]	This attribute allows you to define a field on a type that can be missing from the specified stream.
[SerializationInfo]	In essence, this class is a *property bag* that maintains name-value pairs representing the state of an object during the serialization process.

A Deeper Look at Object Serialization

Before you examine various ways that you can customize the serialization process, you will find it helpful to take a deeper look at what takes place behind the scenes. When the BinaryFormatter serializes an object graph, it is in charge of transmitting the following information into the specified stream:

- The fully qualified name of the objects in the graph (e.g., MyApp.JamesBondCar)

- The name of the assembly defining the object graph (e.g., MyApp.exe)

- An instance of the SerializationInfo class that contains all stateful data maintained by the members in the object graph

During the deserialization process, the BinaryFormatter uses this same information to build an identical copy of the object, using the information extracted from the underlying stream. SoapFormatter uses a quite similar process.

■ **Note**   Recall that the XmlSerializer does not persist a type's fully qualified name or the name of the defining assembly; this behavior helps keep the state of the object as mobile as possible. This type is concerned only with persisting exposed public data.

Beyond moving the required data into and out of a stream, formatters also analyze the members in the object graph for the following pieces of infrastructure:

- A check is made to determine whether the object is marked with the [Serializable] attribute. If the object is not, a SerializationException is thrown.

- If the object is marked [Serializable], a check is made to determine whether the object implements the ISerializable interface. If this is the case, GetObjectData() is called on the object.

- If the object does not implement ISerializable, the default serialization process is used, serializing all fields not marked as [NonSerialized].

In addition to determining whether the type supports ISerializable, formatters are also responsible for discovering whether the types in question support members that have been adorned with the [OnSerializing], [OnSerialized], [OnDeserializing], or [OnDeserialized] attributes. You'll examine the role of these attributes in momentarily, but first you need to look at the role of ISerializable.

Customizing Serialization Using ISerializable

Objects that are marked [Serializable] have the option of implementing the ISerializable interface. Doing so lets you get "involved" with the serialization process and perform any pre- or post-data formatting.

The ISerializable interface is quite simple, given that it defines only a single method, GetObjectData().

```
// When you wish to tweak the serialization process,
// implement ISerializable.
public interface ISerializable
{
  void GetObjectData(SerializationInfo info,
    StreamingContext context);
}
```

The GetObjectData() method is called automatically by a given formatter during the serialization process. The implementation of this method populates the incoming SerializationInfo parameter with a series of name-value pairs that (typically) map to the field data of the object being persisted. SerializationInfo defines numerous variations on the overloaded AddValue() method, as well as a small set of properties that allow the type to get and set the type's name, defining assembly, and member count. Here is a partial snapshot:

```
public sealed class SerializationInfo
{
  public SerializationInfo(Type type, IFormatterConverter converter);
  public string AssemblyName { get; set; }
  public string FullTypeName { get; set; }
  public int MemberCount { get; }
  public void AddValue(string name, short value);
  public void AddValue(string name, ushort value);
  public void AddValue(string name, int value);
...
}
```

Types that implement the ISerializable interface must also define a special constructor that takes the following signature:

```
// You must supply a custom constructor with this signature
// to allow the runtime engine to set the state of your object.
[Serializable]
class SomeClass : ISerializable
{
  protected SomeClass (SerializationInfo si, StreamingContext ctx) {...}
  ...
}
```

Notice that the visibility of this constructor is set as *protected*. This is permissible because the formatter will have access to this member, regardless of its visibility. These special constructors tend to be marked as protected (or private for that matter) to ensure that the casual object user can never create an object in this manner. The first parameter of this constructor is an instance of the SerializationInfo type (which you've seen previously).

The second parameter of this special constructor is a StreamingContext type, which contains information regarding the source of the bits. The most informative member of StreamingContext is the State property, which represents a value from the StreamingContextStates enumeration. The values of this enumeration represent the basic composition of the current stream.

Unless you intend to implement some low-level custom remoting services, you will seldom need to deal with this enumeration directly. Nevertheless, here are the possible names of the StreamingContextStates enum (consult the .NET Framework 4.7 SDK documentation for full details):

```
public enum StreamingContextStates
{
  CrossProcess,
  CrossMachine,
  File,
  Persistence,
  Remoting,
  Other,
  Clone,
  CrossAppDomain,
  All
}
```

Now let's look at how to customize the serialization process using ISerializable. Assume you have a new Console Application project (named CustomSerialization) that defines a class type containing two points of string data. Also assume that you must ensure that the string objects are serialized to the stream in all uppercase and deserialized from the stream in lowercase. To account for such rules, you could implement ISerializable like this (be sure to import the System.Runtime.Serialization namespace):

```
[Serializable]
class StringData : ISerializable
{
  private string dataItemOne = "First data block";
  private string dataItemTwo= "More data";

  public StringData(){}
```

```
protected StringData(SerializationInfo si, StreamingContext ctx)
{
  // Rehydrate member variables from stream.
  dataItemOne = si.GetString("First_Item").ToLower();
  dataItemTwo = si.GetString("dataItemTwo").ToLower();
}

void ISerializable.GetObjectData(SerializationInfo info, StreamingContext ctx)
{
  // Fill up the SerializationInfo object with the formatted data.
  info.AddValue("First_Item", dataItemOne.ToUpper());
  info.AddValue("dataItemTwo", dataItemTwo.ToUpper());
}
}
```

Notice that when you fill the SerializationInfo type with the GetObjectData() method, you are *not* required to name the data points identically to the type's internal member variables. This can obviously be helpful if you need to further decouple the type's data from the persisted format. Be aware, however, that you will need to obtain the values from the special, protected constructor using the same names assigned within GetObjectData().

To test your customization, assume that you want to persist an instance of MyStringData using a SoapFormatter (so update your assembly references and imports accordingly), as follows:

```
static void Main(string[] args)
{
  Console.WriteLine("***** Fun with Custom Serialization *****");

  // Recall that this type implements ISerializable.
  StringData myData = new StringData();

  // Save to a local file in SOAP format.
  SoapFormatter soapFormat = new SoapFormatter();
  using(Stream fStream = new FileStream("MyData.soap",
    FileMode.Create, FileAccess.Write, FileShare.None))
  {
    soapFormat.Serialize(fStream, myData);
  }
  Console.ReadLine();
}
```

When you view the resulting *.soap file, you will see that the string fields have been persisted in uppercase, as so:

```
<SOAP-ENV:Envelope xmlns:xsi="http://www.w3.org/2001/XMLSchema-instance"
  xmlns:xsd="http://www.w3.org/2001/XMLSchema"
  xmlns:SOAP-ENC="http://schemas.xmlsoap.org/soap/encoding/"
  xmlns:SOAP-ENV="http://schemas.xmlsoap.org/soap/envelope/"
  xmlns:clr="http://schemas.microsoft.com/soap/encoding/clr/1.0"
  SOAP-ENV:encodingStyle="http://schemas.xmlsoap.org/soap/encoding/">
<SOAP-ENV:Body>
```

```
<a1:StringData id="ref-1" ...>
  <First_Item id="ref-3">FIRST DATA BLOCK</First_Item>
  <dataItemTwo id="ref-4">MORE DATA</dataItemTwo>
</a1:StringData>
</SOAP-ENV:Body>

</SOAP-ENV:Envelope>
```

Customizing Serialization Using Attributes

Although implementing the ISerializable interface is one way to customize the serialization process, the preferred way to customize the serialization process is to define methods that are attributed with any of the new serialization-centric attributes: [OnSerializing], [OnSerialized], [OnDeserializing], or [OnDeserialized]. Using these attributes is less cumbersome than implementing ISerializable because you do not need to interact manually with an incoming SerializationInfo parameter. Instead, you can modify your state data directly, while the formatter operates on the type.

■ **Note**   You can find these serialization attributes defined in the System.Runtime.Serialization namespace.

When you define methods decorated with these attributes, you must define the methods so they receive a StreamingContext parameter and return nothing (otherwise, you will receive a runtime exception). Note that you are not required to account for each of the serialization-centric attributes, and you can simply contend with the stages of serialization you want to intercept. The following snippet illustrates this. Here, a new [Serializable] type has the same requirements as StringData, but this time you account for using the [OnSerializing] and [OnDeserialized] attributes:

```
[Serializable]
class MoreData
{
  private string dataItemOne = "First data block";
  private string dataItemTwo= "More data";

  [OnSerializing]
  private void OnSerializing(StreamingContext context)
  {
    // Called during the serialization process.
    dataItemOne = dataItemOne.ToUpper();
    dataItemTwo = dataItemTwo.ToUpper();
  }

  [OnDeserialized]
  private void OnDeserialized(StreamingContext context)
  {
    // Called when the deserialization process is complete.
    dataItemOne = dataItemOne.ToLower();
    dataItemTwo = dataItemTwo.ToLower();
  }
}
```

If you were to serialize this new type, you would again find that the data has been persisted as uppercase and deserialized as lowercase.

■ **Source Code**   You can find the CustomSerialization project in the Chapter 20 subdirectory.

With this example behind you, your exploration of the core details of object serialization services, including various ways to customize the process, is complete. As you have seen, the serialization and deserialization process makes it easy to persist large amounts of data, and it can be less labor-intensive than working with the various reader/writer classes of the System.IO namespace.

Summary

You began this chapter by examining the use of the Directory(Info) and File(Info) types. As you learned, these classes allow you to manipulate a physical file or directory on your hard drive. Next, you examined a number of classes derived from the abstract Stream class. Given that Stream-derived types operate on a raw stream of bytes, the System.IO namespace provides numerous reader/writer types (e.g., StreamWriter, StringWriter, and BinaryWriter) that simplify the process. Along the way, you also checked out the functionality provided by DriveType, learned how to monitor files using the FileSystemWatcher type, and saw how to interact with streams in an asynchronous manner.

This chapter also introduced you to the topic of object serialization services. As you have seen, the .NET platform uses an object graph to account for the full set of related objects that you want to persist to a stream. As long as each member in the object graph has been marked with the [Serializable] attribute, the data is persisted using your format of choice (binary or SOAP).

You also learned that it is possible to customize the out-of-the-box serialization process using two possible approaches. First, you learned how to implement the ISerializable interface (and support a special private constructor), which enables you to become more involved with how formatters persist the supplied data. Second, you learned about a set of .NET attributes that simplify the process of custom serialization. All you need to do is apply the [OnSerializing], [OnSerialized], [OnDeserializing], or [OnDeserialized] attribute on members that take a StreamingContext parameter, and the formatters will invoke them accordingly.

CHAPTER 21

■ ■ ■

Data Access with ADO.NET

The .NET platform defines a number of namespaces that allow you to interact with relational database systems. Collectively speaking, these namespaces are known as ADO.NET. In this chapter, you'll learn about the overall role of ADO.NET and the core types and namespaces, and then you'll move on to the topic of ADO.NET data providers. The .NET platform supports numerous data providers (both provided as part of the .NET Framework and available from third-party sources), each of which is optimized to communicate with a specific database management system (e.g., Microsoft SQL Server, Oracle, and MySQL).

After you understand the common functionality provided by various data providers, you will then look at the data provider factory pattern. As you will see, using types within the System.Data.Common namespace (and related App.config file), you can build a single codebase that can dynamically pick and choose the underlying data provider without the need to recompile or redeploy the application's codebase.

Next, you will learn how to work directly with the SQL Server database provider, creating and opening connections to retrieve data, and then move on to inserting, updating, and deleting data, followed by examining the topic of database transactions. Finally, you will execute SQL Server's bulk copy feature using ADO.NET to load a list of records into the database.

■ **Note**   This chapter focuses on the raw ADO.NET. Chapter 22 covers the Entity Framework (EF), Microsoft's object-relational mapping (ORM) framework. ORMs, like the Entity Framework, make it much simpler (and faster) to create data access code. But they still rely on ADO.NET for data access under the covers. A solid understanding of how ADO.NET works is vital when troubleshooting an issue with your data access, especially when it was created by a framework and not written by you. Also, you will encounter scenarios that aren't solved by EF (such as executing a SQL bulk copy), and you will need to know ADO.NET to solve those issues.

A High-Level Definition of ADO.NET

If you have a background in Microsoft's previous COM-based data access model (Active Data Objects [ADO]) and are just starting to work with the .NET platform, you need to understand that ADO.NET has little to do with ADO beyond the letters *A*, *D*, and *O*. While it is true that there is some relationship between the two systems (e.g., each has the concept of connection and command objects), some familiar ADO types (e.g., the Recordset) no longer exist. Furthermore, you can find many new ADO.NET types that have no direct equivalent under classic ADO (e.g., the data adapter).

■ **Note** Prior editions of this book contained a chapter on ADO.NET data sets, data tables, and their related technologies. This chapter is still available as Appendix A.

From a programmatic point of view, the bulk of ADO.NET is represented by a core assembly named `System.Data.dll`. Within this binary, you can find a good number of namespaces (see Figure 21-1), many of which represent the types of a particular ADO.NET data provider (defined momentarily).

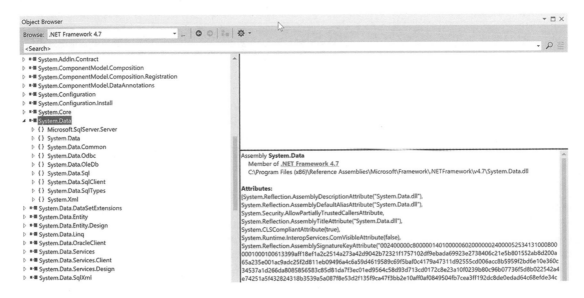

Figure 21-1. `System.Data.dll` is the core ADO.NET assembly

It turns out most Visual Studio project templates automatically reference this key data access assembly. You should also understand that there are other ADO.NET-centric assemblies beyond `System.Data.dll`, which you might need to reference manually in your current project using the Add Reference dialog box.

The Three Faces of ADO.NET

You can use the ADO.NET libraries in three conceptually unique manners: connected, disconnected, or through an ORM such as the Entity Framework. When you use the *connected layer* (the subject of this chapter), your codebase explicitly connects to and disconnects from the underlying data store. When you use ADO.NET in this manner, you typically interact with the data store using connection objects, command objects, and data reader objects.

The *disconnected layer* (covered in Appendix A) allows you to manipulate a set of `DataTable` objects (contained within a `DataSet`) that functions as a client-side copy of the external data. After a caller receives a `DataSet`, it is able to traverse and manipulate the contents. If the caller wants to submit the changes back to the data store, the data adapter (in conjunction with a set of SQL statements) is used to update the data source.

The third method (covered in Chapter 22) is to use an object-relational mapper, such as NHibernate or the Entity Framework. Object-relational mappers use C# objects represent the data in an application-centric manner and abstract much of the data access code away from the developer. EF also allows you to interact with relational databases using strongly typed LINQ queries that dynamically create database-specific queries.

Understanding ADO.NET Data Providers

ADO.NET does not provide a single set of objects that communicate with multiple database management systems (DBMSs). Rather, ADO.NET supports multiple *data providers*, each of which is optimized to interact with a specific DBMS. The first benefit of this approach is that you can program a specific data provider to access any unique features of a particular DBMS. The second benefit is that a specific data provider can connect directly to the underlying engine of the DBMS in question without an intermediate mapping layer standing between the tiers.

Simply put, a data provider is a set of types defined in a given namespace that understand how to communicate with a specific type of data source. Regardless of which data provider you use, each defines a set of class types that provide core functionality. Table 21-1 documents some of the core common types, their base class (all defined in the System.Data.Common namespace), and the key interfaces (each is defined in the System.Data namespace) they implement.

Table 21-1. *The Core Objects of an ADO.NET Data Provider*

Type of Object	Base Class	Relevant Interfaces	Meaning in Life
Connection	DbConnection	IDbConnection	Provides the ability to connect to and disconnect from the data store. Connection objects also provide access to a related transaction object.
Command	DbCommand	IDbCommand	Represents a SQL query or a stored procedure. Command objects also provide access to the provider's data reader object.
DataReader	DbDataReader	IDataReader, IDataRecord	Provides forward-only, read-only access to data using a server-side cursor.
DataAdapter	DbDataAdapter	IDataAdapter, IDbDataAdapter	Transfers DataSets between the caller and the data store. Data adapters contain a connection and a set of four internal command objects used to select, insert, update, and delete information from the data store.
Parameter	DbParameter	IDataParameter, IDbDataParameter	Represents a named parameter within a parameterized query.
Transaction	DbTransaction	IDbTransaction	Encapsulates a database transaction.

Although the specific names of these core classes will differ among data providers (e.g., SqlConnection versus OdbcConnection), each class derives from the same base class (DbConnection, in the case of connection objects) that implements identical interfaces (e.g., IDbConnection). Given this, you would be correct to assume that after you learn how to work with one data provider, the remaining providers prove quite straightforward.

■ **Note**   When you refer to a connection object under ADO.NET, you're actually referring to a specific DbConnection-derived type; there is no class literally named *Connection.* The same idea holds true for a *command object*, *data adapter object*, and so forth. As a naming convention, the objects in a specific data provider are prefixed with the name of the related DBMS (e.g., SqlConnection, SqlConnection, and SqlDataReader).

Figure 21-2 shows the big picture behind ADO.NET data providers. Note how the diagram illustrates that the client assembly can be any type of .NET application: console program, Windows Forms application, WPF application, ASP.NET web page, WCF service, Web API service, .NET code library, and so on.

A data provider will supply you with other types beyond the objects shown in Figure 21-2; however, these core objects define a common baseline across all data providers.

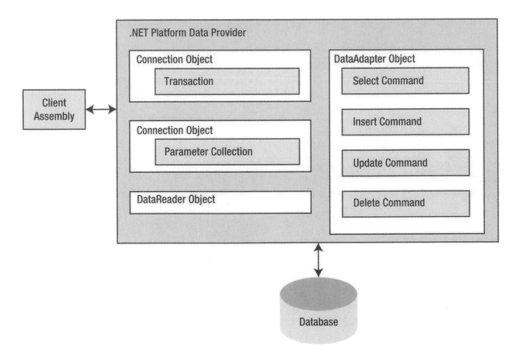

Figure 21-2. *ADO.NET data providers provide access to a given DBMS*

The Microsoft-Supplied ADO.NET Data Providers

Microsoft's .NET distribution ships with numerous data providers, including a provider for SQL Server and OLE DB/ODBC-style connectivity. Table 21-2 documents the namespace and containing assembly for each Microsoft ADO.NET data provider.

Table 21-2. *Microsoft ADO.NET Data Providers*

Data Provider	Namespace	Assembly
OLE DB	System.Data.OleDb	System.Data.dll
Microsoft SQL Server LocalDb	System.Data.SqlClient	System.Data.dll
ODBC	System.Data.Odbc	System.Data.dll

■ **Note**   If you need to connect to an Oracle database, you will need to use the Oracle-supplied Oracle Developer Tools for Visual Studio. If you open Server Explorer and select New Connection and then Oracle Database, Visual Studio will provide a link where they can be downloaded. The current location for the tools is www.oracle.com/technetwork/topics/dotnet/whatsnew/vs2012welcome-1835382.html.

There is no specific data provider that maps directly to the Jet engine (used by Microsoft Access). If you want to interact with an Access data file, you need to use the OLE DB or ODBC data provider.

The OLE DB data provider, which is composed of the types defined in the System.Data.OleDb namespace, allows you to access data located in any data store that supports the classic COM-based OLE DB protocol. You can use this provider to communicate with any OLE DB–compliant database simply by tweaking the Provider segment of your connection string.

However, the OLE DB provider interacts with various COM objects behind the scenes, which can affect the performance of your application. By and large, the OLE DB data provider is useful only if you interact with a DBMS that does not define a specific .NET data provider. However, given that these days any DBMS worth its salt should have a custom ADO.NET data provider for download, you should consider System.Data.OleDb to be a legacy namespace that has little use in the .NET 4.7 world. (This is even more the case with the advent of the data provider factory model introduced under .NET 2.0, which you will learn about shortly).

■ **Note**   There is one case in which using the types of System.Data.OleDb is necessary: when you need to communicate with Microsoft SQL Server version 6.5 or earlier. The System.Data.SqlClient namespace can communicate only with Microsoft SQL Server version 7.0 or higher.

The Microsoft SQL Server data provider offers direct access to Microsoft SQL Server data stores— and *only* SQL Server data stores (version 7.0 and greater). The System.Data.SqlClient namespace contains the types used by the SQL Server provider and offers the same basic functionality as the OLE DB provider. The key difference is that the SQL Server provider bypasses the OLE DB layer and gives numerous performance benefits. The Microsoft SQL Server data provider also allows you to gain access to the unique features of this particular DBMS.

The remaining Microsoft-supplied provider (System.Data.Odbc) provides access to ODBC connections. The ODBC types defined within the System.Data.Odbc namespace are typically useful only if you need to communicate with a given DBMS for which there is no custom .NET data provider. This is true because ODBC is a widespread model that provides access to a number of data stores.

Obtaining Third-Party ADO.NET Data Providers

In addition to the data providers that ship from Microsoft (as well as Oracle's custom .NET library), numerous third-party data providers exist for various open source and commercial databases. While you will most likely be able to obtain an ADO.NET data provider directly from the database vendor, you should be aware of the following site:

https://docs.microsoft.com/en-us/dotnet/framework/data/adonet/ado-net-overview

This web site is one of many sites that documents each known ADO.NET data provider and provides links for more information and downloads. Here, you will find numerous ADO.NET providers, including SQLite, IBM DB2, MySQL, Postgres, Sybase, and many others.

Given the large number of ADO.NET data providers, the examples in this book will use the Microsoft SQL Server data provider (`System.Data.SqlClient.dll`). Recall that this provider allows you to communicate with Microsoft SQL Server version 7.0 and higher, including SQL Server Express and LocalDb. If you intend to use ADO.NET to interact with another DBMS, you should have no problem doing so once you understand the material presented in the pages that follow.

Additional ADO.NET Namespaces

In addition to the .NET namespaces that define the types of a specific data provider, the .NET base class libraries provide a number of additional ADO.NET-centric namespaces, some of which you can see in Table 21-3.

Table 21-3. *Select Additional ADO.NET-Centric Namespaces*

Namespace	Meaning in Life
`Microsoft.SqlServer.Server`	This namespace provides types that facilitate CLR and SQL Server 2005 and later integration services.
`System.Data`	This namespace defines the core ADO.NET types used by all data providers, including common interfaces and numerous types that represent the disconnected layer (e.g., `DataSet` and `DataTable`).
`System.Data.Common`	This namespace contains types shared between all ADO.NET data providers, including the common abstract base classes.
`System.Data.Sql`	This namespace contains types that allow you to discover Microsoft SQL Server instances installed on the current local network.
`System.Data.SqlTypes`	This namespace contains native data types used by Microsoft SQL Server. You can always use the corresponding CLR data types, but the types in the `SqlTypes` namespace are optimized to work with SQL Server (e.g., if your SQL Server database contains an integer value, you can represent it using either `int` or `SqlTypes.SqlInt32`).

Note that this chapter does not examine every type within every ADO.NET namespace (that task would require a large book all by itself); however, it is quite important that you understand the types within the `System.Data` namespace.

The Types of the System.Data Namespace

Of all the ADO.NET namespaces, `System.Data` is the lowest common denominator. You cannot build ADO.NET applications without specifying this namespace in your data access applications. This namespace contains types that are shared among all ADO.NET data providers, regardless of the underlying data store. In addition to a number of database-centric exceptions (e.g., `NoNullAllowedException`, `RowNotInTableException`, and `MissingPrimaryKeyException`), `System.Data` contains types that represent various database primitives (e.g., tables, rows, columns, and constraints), as well as the common interfaces implemented by data provider objects. Table 21-4 lists some of the core types you should be aware of.

Table 21-4. *Core Members of the* System.Data *Namespace*

Type	Meaning in Life
Constraint	Represents a constraint for a given DataColumn object
DataColumn	Represents a single column within a DataTable object
DataRelation	Represents a parent-child relationship between two DataTable objects
DataRow	Represents a single row within a DataTable object
DataSet	Represents an in-memory cache of data consisting of any number of interrelated DataTable objects
DataTable	Represents a tabular block of in-memory data
DataTableReader	Allows you to treat a DataTable as a fire-hose cursor (forward only, read-only data access)
DataView	Represents a customized view of a DataTable for sorting, filtering, searching, editing, and navigation
IDataAdapter	Defines the core behavior of a data adapter object
IDataParameter	Defines the core behavior of a parameter object
IDataReader	Defines the core behavior of a data reader object
IDbCommand	Defines the core behavior of a command object
IDbDataAdapter	Extends IDataAdapter to provide additional functionality of a data adapter object
IDbTransaction	Defines the core behavior of a transaction object

Your next task is to examine the core interfaces of System.Data at a high level; this can help you understand the common functionality offered by any data provider. You will also learn specific details throughout this chapter; however, for now it's best to focus on the overall behavior of each interface type.

The Role of the IDbConnection Interface

The IDbConnection type is implemented by a data provider's *connection object*. This interface defines a set of members used to configure a connection to a specific data store. It also allows you to obtain the data provider's transaction object. Here is the formal definition of IDbConnection:

```
public interface IDbConnection : IDisposable
{
  string ConnectionString { get; set; }
  int ConnectionTimeout { get; }
  string Database { get; }
  ConnectionState State { get; }

  IDbTransaction BeginTransaction();
  IDbTransaction BeginTransaction(IsolationLevel il);
  void ChangeDatabase(string databaseName);
  void Close();
  IDbCommand CreateCommand();
  void Open();
}
```

■ **Note**   Like many other types in the .NET base class libraries, the Close() method is functionally equivalent to calling the Dispose() method directly or indirectly within C# by using scope (see Chapter 13).

The Role of the IDbTransaction Interface

The overloaded BeginTransaction() method defined by IDbConnection provides access to the provider's *transaction object*. You can use the members defined by IDbTransaction to interact programmatically with a transactional session and the underlying data store.

```
public interface IDbTransaction : IDisposable
{
  IDbConnection Connection { get; }
  IsolationLevel IsolationLevel { get; }

  void Commit();
  void Rollback();
}
```

The Role of the IDbCommand Interface

Next up is the IDbCommand interface, which will be implemented by a data provider's *command object*. Like other data access object models, command objects allow programmatic manipulation of SQL statements, stored procedures, and parameterized queries. Command objects also provide access to the data provider's data reader type through the overloaded ExecuteReader() method.

```
public interface IDbCommand : IDisposable
{
  IDbConnection Connection { get; set; }
  IDbTransaction Transaction { get; set; }
  string CommandText { get; set; }
  int CommandTimeout { get; set; }
  CommandType CommandType { get; set; }
  IDataParameterCollection Parameters { get; }
  UpdateRowSource UpdatedRowSource { get; set; }

  void Prepare();
  void Cancel();
  IDbDataParameter CreateParameter();
  int ExecuteNonQuery();
  IDataReader ExecuteReader();
  IDataReader ExecuteReader(CommandBehavior behavior);
  object ExecuteScalar();
}
```

The Role of the IDbDataParameter and IDataParameter Interfaces

Notice that the Parameters property of IDbCommand returns a strongly typed collection that implements IDataParameterCollection. This interface provides access to a set of IDbDataParameter-compliant class types (e.g., parameter objects).

810

```
public interface IDbDataParameter : IDataParameter
{
  byte Precision { get; set; }
  byte Scale { get; set; }
  int Size { get; set; }
}
```

IDbDataParameter extends the IDataParameter interface to obtain the following additional behaviors:

```
public interface IDataParameter
{
  DbType DbType { get; set; }
  ParameterDirection Direction { get; set; }
  bool IsNullable { get; }
  string ParameterName { get; set; }
  string SourceColumn { get; set; }
  DataRowVersion SourceVersion { get; set; }
  object Value { get; set; }
}
```

As you will see, the functionality of the IDbDataParameter and IDataParameter interfaces allows you to represent parameters within a SQL command (including stored procedures) through specific ADO.NET parameter objects, rather than through hard-coded string literals.

The Role of the IDbDataAdapter and IDataAdapter Interfaces

You use *data adapters* to push and pull DataSets to and from a given data store. The IDbDataAdapter interface defines the following set of properties that you can use to maintain the SQL statements for the related select, insert, update, and delete operations:

```
public interface IDbDataAdapter : IDataAdapter
{
  IDbCommand SelectCommand { get; set; }
  IDbCommand InsertCommand { get; set; }
  IDbCommand UpdateCommand { get; set; }
  IDbCommand DeleteCommand { get; set; }
}
```

In addition to these four properties, an ADO.NET data adapter picks up the behavior defined in the base interface, IDataAdapter. This interface defines the key function of a data adapter type: the ability to transfer DataSets between the caller and underlying data store using the Fill() and Update() methods. The IDataAdapter interface also allows you to map database column names to more user-friendly display names with the TableMappings property.

```
public interface IDataAdapter
{
  MissingMappingAction MissingMappingAction { get; set; }
  MissingSchemaAction MissingSchemaAction { get; set; }
  ITableMappingCollection TableMappings { get; }
```

```
  DataTable[] FillSchema(DataSet dataSet, SchemaType schemaType);
  int Fill(DataSet dataSet);
  IDataParameter[] GetFillParameters();
  int Update(DataSet dataSet);
}
```

The Role of the IDataReader and IDataRecord Interfaces

The next key interface to be aware of is IDataReader, which represents the common behaviors supported by a given data reader object. When you obtain an IDataReader-compatible type from an ADO.NET data provider, you can iterate over the result set in a forward-only, read-only manner.

```
public interface IDataReader : IDisposable, IDataRecord
{
  int Depth { get; }
  bool IsClosed { get; }
  int RecordsAffected { get; }

  void Close();
  DataTable GetSchemaTable();
  bool NextResult();
  bool Read();
}
```

Finally, IDataReader extends IDataRecord, which defines many members that allow you to extract a strongly typed value from the stream, rather than casting the generic System.Object retrieved from the data reader's overloaded indexer method. Here is the IDataRecord interface definition:

```
public interface IDataRecord
{
  int FieldCount { get; }
  object this[ int i ] { get; }
  object this[ string name ] { get; }
  string GetName(int i);
  string GetDataTypeName(int i);
  Type GetFieldType(int i);
  object GetValue(int i);
  int GetValues(object[] values);
  int GetOrdinal(string name);
  bool GetBoolean(int i);
  byte GetByte(int i);
  long GetBytes(int i, long fieldOffset, byte[] buffer, int bufferoffset, int length);
  char GetChar(int i);
  long GetChars(int i, long fieldoffset, char[] buffer, int bufferoffset, int length);
  Guid GetGuid(int i);
  short GetInt16(int i);
  int GetInt32(int i);
  long GetInt64(int i);
  float GetFloat(int i);
  double GetDouble(int i);
  string GetString(int i);
```

```
  Decimal GetDecimal(int i);
  DateTime GetDateTime(int i);
  IDataReader GetData(int i);
  bool IsDBNull(int i);
}
```

■ **Note**   You can use the IDataReader.IsDBNull() method to discover programmatically whether a specified field is set to null before obtaining a value from the data reader (to avoid triggering a runtime exception). Also recall that C# supports nullable data types (see Chapter 4), which are ideal for interacting with data columns that could be null in the database table.

Abstracting Data Providers Using Interfaces

At this point, you should have a better idea of the common functionality found among all .NET data providers. Recall that even though the exact names of the implementing types will differ among data providers, you can program against these types in a similar manner—that's the beauty of interface- based polymorphism. For example, if you define a method that takes an IDbConnection parameter, you can pass in any ADO.NET connection object, like so:

```
public static void OpenConnection(IDbConnection cn)
{
  // Open the incoming connection for the caller.
  connection.Open();
}
```

■ **Note**   Interfaces are not strictly required; you can achieve the same level of abstraction using abstract base classes (such as DbConnection) as parameters or return values.

The same holds true for member return values. For example, consider the following simple C# console application (named MyConnectionFactory), which allows you to obtain a specific connection object based on the value of a custom enumeration. For diagnostic purposes, you simply print the underlying connection object using reflection services and then enter the following code:

```
using System;
using static System.Console;
// Need these to get definitions of common interfaces,
// and various connection objects for our test.
using System.Data;
using System.Data.SqlClient;
using System.Data.Odbc;
using System.Data.OleDb;

namespace MyConnectionFactory
{
  // A list of possible providers.
  enum DataProvider
  { SqlServer, OleDb, Odbc, None }
```

```
class Program
{

  static void Main(string[] args)
  {
    WriteLine("**** Very Simple Connection Factory *****\n");
    // Get a specific connection.
    IDbConnection myConnection = GetConnection(DataProvider.SqlServer);
    WriteLine($"Your connection is a {myConnection.GetType().Name}");
    // Open, use and close connection...
    ReadLine();
  }

  // This method returns a specific connection object
  // based on the value of a DataProvider enum.
  static IDbConnection GetConnection(DataProvider dataProvider)
  {
    IDbConnection connection = null;
    switch (dataProvider)
    {
      case DataProvider.SqlServer:
        connection = new SqlConnection();
        break;
      case DataProvider.OleDb:
        connection = new OleDbConnection();
        break;
      case DataProvider.Odbc:
        connection = new OdbcConnection();
        break;
    }
    return connection;
  }
 }
}
```

■ **Note**   Visual Studio 2015 introduces use static. By adding use static System.Console; to your other using statements, you can simply write WriteLine("some text") instead of Console.WriteLine("some text"). For all the console projects in this and subsequent chapters, I will be using the shorter version by adding using static System.Console; to the top of my files.

The benefit of working with the general interfaces of System.Data (or, for that matter, the abstract base classes of System.Data.Common) is that you have a much better chance of building a flexible codebase that can evolve over time. For example, today you might be building an application that targets Microsoft SQL Server; however, it's possible your company could switch to a different database months down the road. If you build a solution that hard-codes the Microsoft SQL Server–specific types of System.Data.SqlClient, you would obviously need to edit, recompile, and redeploy the assembly should the back-end database management system change.

Increasing Flexibility Using Application Configuration Files

To increase the flexibility of your ADO.NET applications, you could incorporate a client-side *.config file that uses custom key-value pairs within the <appSettings> element. Recall from Chapter 14 that you can obtain the custom data stored within a *.config file programmatically by using types within the System. Configuration namespace. For example, assume you have specified a data provider value within a configuration file, as in this example:

```
<configuration>
  <appSettings>
    <!-- This key value maps to one of our enum values. -->
    <add key="provider" value="SqlServer"/>
  </appSettings>
  <startup>
    <supportedRuntime version="v4.0" sku=".NETFramework,Version=v4.7"/>
  </startup>
</configuration>
```

With this, you could update Main() to obtain the underlying data provider programmatically. Doing this essentially builds a *connection object factory* that allows you to change the provider but without requiring you to recompile your codebase (you simply change the *.config file). Here are the relevant updates to Main():

```
static void Main(string[] args)
{
  WriteLine("**** Very Simple Connection Factory *****\n");
  // Read the provider key.
  string dataProviderString = ConfigurationManager.AppSettings["provider"];
  // Transform string to enum.
  DataProvider dataProvider = DataProvider.None;
  if (Enum.IsDefined(typeof (DataProvider), dataProviderString))
  {
    dataProvider = (DataProvider) Enum.Parse(typeof (DataProvider), dataProviderString);
  }
  else
  {
    WriteLine("Sorry, no provider exists!");
    ReadLine();
    return;
  }
  // Get a specific connection.
  IDbConnection myConnection = GetConnection(dataProvider);
  WriteLine($"Your connection is a {myConnection?.GetType().Name ?? "unrecognized type"}");
  // Open, use and close connection...
  ReadLine();
}
```

■ **Note**   To use the ConfigurationManager type, be sure to set a reference to the System.Configuration. dll assembly and import the System.Configuration namespace.

At this point, you have authored some ADO.NET code that allows you to specify the underlying connection dynamically. One obvious problem, however, is that this abstraction is used only within the MyConnectionFactory.exe application. If you were to rework this example within a .NET code library (e.g., MyConnectionFactory.dll), you would be able to build any number of clients that could obtain various connection objects using layers of abstraction.

However, obtaining a connection object is only one aspect of working with ADO.NET. To make a worthwhile data provider factory library, you would also have to account for command objects, data readers, transaction objects, and other data-centric types. Building such a code library would not necessarily be difficult, but it would require a considerable amount of code and time.

Since the release of .NET 2.0, the kind folks in Redmond have built this exact functionality directly into the .NET base class libraries. You will examine this formal API in just a moment; however, first you need to create a custom database to use throughout this chapter (and for many chapters to come).

■ **Source Code**   You can find the MyConnectionFactory project in the Chapter 21 subdirectory.

Creating the AutoLot Database

As you work through this chapter, you will execute queries against a simple SQL Server test database named AutoLot. In keeping with the automotive theme used throughout this book, this database will contain three interrelated tables (Inventory, Orders, and Customers) that contain various bits of data representing order information for a fictional automobile sales company.

■ **Note**   Prior editions of the book used Visual Studio to design and create tables and stored procedures, along with other database interactions. While that still works, it's more efficient to use the free SQL Server Management Studio (SSMS), so this edition forward will use SSMS instead of Visual Studio.

Installing SQL Server 2016 and SQL Server Management Studio

The assumption in this book is that you have a copy of Microsoft SQL Server 2016 (any edition) installed. A special instance named (localdb)\mssqllocaldb is installed with Visual Studio 2017 and will be used throughout this book. If you have another edition (Express, for example), you can use that instance with this book as well; you will just need to change your connection screen appropriately. I also recommend you download and install SQL Server Management Studio (SSMS) 17 (or higher), which can be downloaded from here:

https://docs.microsoft.com/en-us/sql/ssms/download-sql-server-management-studio-ssms

Microsoft SQL Server Express 2016 is free for use to follow along with this book, and if you want to download a copy, you can do that from here:

https://www.microsoft.com/en-us/sql-server/sql-server-editions-express

---

■ **SQL Backup**   You can find a SQL Server backup (autolot.bak) in the Chapter 21 folder of the downloadable code.

Creating the Inventory Table

To begin building your testing database, launch SQL Server Management Studio. You will be prompted to enter a server name. Enter **(localdb)\msslqlocaldb** (or your connection string) and click Connect, as shown in Figure 21-3.

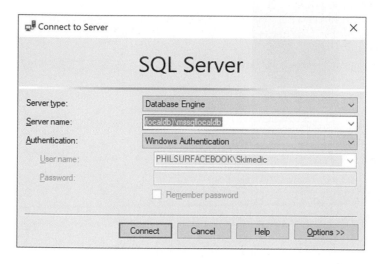

Figure 21-3. *Connecting to SQL Server with SQL Server Management Studio 2017*

Once SSMS opens, right-click the Databases node in Object Explorer and select New Database from the context menu. In the resulting dialog, enter **AutoLot** for the database name and leave all the other settings at their defaults, as shown in Figure 21-4. Click OK to create the database.

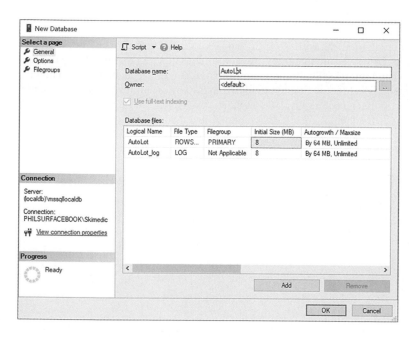

Figure 21-4. *Creating a new SQL Server Express instance*

At this point, the AutoLot database is empty of any database objects (e.g., tables, stored procedures, and so on). To insert a new database table, expand the Databases node and then expand the AutoLot node. Right-click the Tables node and select Table (see Figure 21-5).

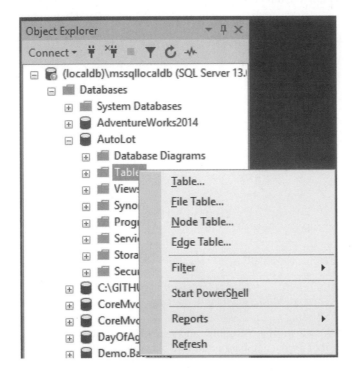

Figure 21-5. *Adding the Inventory table*

Use the table editor to add four columns (CarId, Make, Color, and PetName). Set CarId as type int and the other properties as type nvarchar(50). Ensure that the CarId column has been set to the primary key (do this by right-clicking the CarId row and selecting Set Primary Key) and as an identity specification (changed on the Properties tab by using CarId in the Identity Column field in the Properties window. Update the name of the table to Inventory. Also, notice that all columns but CarId can be assigned null values. As a final step, click the Save icon to save the table to the database. Figure 21-6 shows the final table settings.

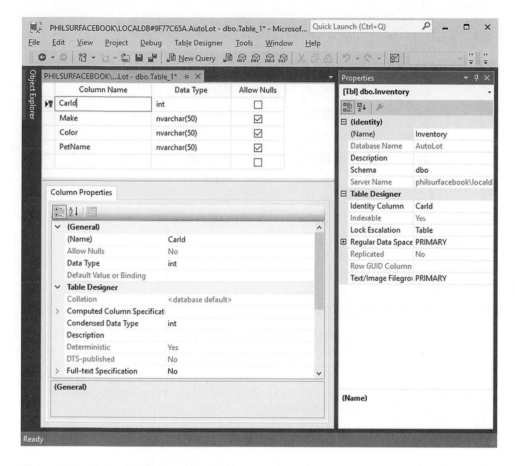

Figure 21-6. *Designing the Inventory table*

Adding Test Records to the Inventory Table

To add records to your first table, expand the Tables node, right-click the Inventory table, and select Edit Top 200 Rows. If you don't see the Inventory table, click Refresh in the Object Explorer. Enter a handful of new automobiles of your choosing (to make it interesting, be sure to include some cars that have identical colors and makes). Remember that the CarId field is an identity column, so the database takes care of creating a unique value for you. Figure 21-7 shows one possible list of inventory records.

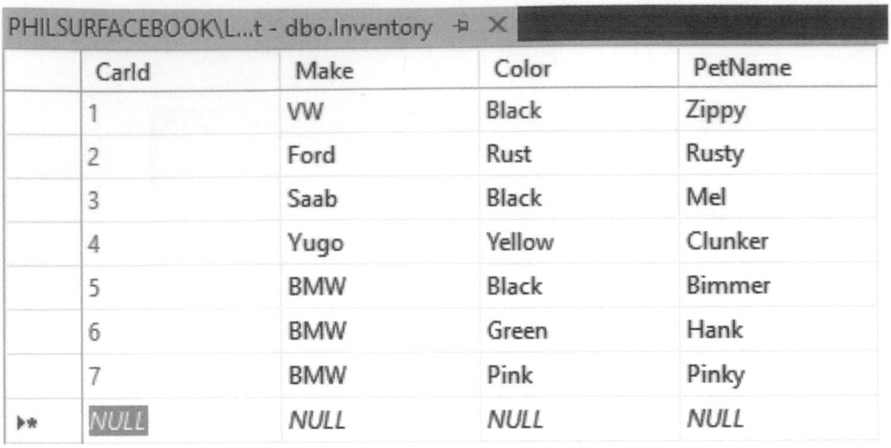

	CarId	Make	Color	PetName
	1	VW	Black	Zippy
	2	Ford	Rust	Rusty
	3	Saab	Black	Mel
	4	Yugo	Yellow	Clunker
	5	BMW	Black	Bimmer
	6	BMW	Green	Hank
	7	BMW	Pink	Pinky
▶*	NULL	NULL	NULL	NULL

Figure 21-7. *Populating the Inventory table*

Authoring the GetPetName() Stored Procedure

Later in this chapter, you will learn how to use ADO.NET to invoke stored procedures. As you might already know, stored procedures are code routines stored within a database that do something. Like C# methods, stored procedures can return data or just operate on data without returning anything. You will add a single stored procedure that will return an automobile's pet name, based on the supplied CarId value. To do so, expand the Programmability node in the AutoLot database, right-click the Stored Procedures node, and select Stored Procedure. Clear out the template that is loaded, and enter the following:

```
CREATE PROCEDURE GetPetName
@carID int,
@petName char(10) output
AS
SELECT @petName = PetName from Inventory where CarId = @carID
```

■ **Note**   Stored procedures do not have to return data using output parameters, as shown here; however, doing things this way sets the stage for material covered later in this chapter.

Click Execute (or press F5) to create the stored procedure.

Creating the Customers and Orders Tables

The AutoLot database needs two additional tables: Customers and Orders. The Customers table (as the name suggests) will contain a list of customers and will be represented by three columns: CustId (the primary key), FirstName, and LastName. You can create the Customers table by following the same steps you used to create the Inventory table, or you can create the table using T-SQL (the "programming" language of SQL Server). To do that, create a new query by clicking the New Query button. Make sure the database is set to AutoLot, as shown in Figure 21-8.

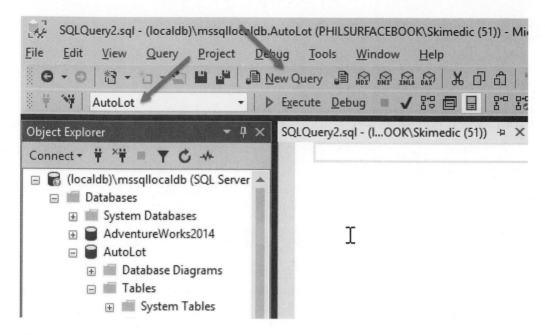

Figure 21-8. *Creating a new query window to create the* Customers *table*

Enter the following text and click Execute to create the table:

```
CREATE TABLE [dbo].[Customers]
    (
        [CustID] INT IDENTITY(1, 1) NOT NULL ,
        [FirstName] NVARCHAR(50) NULL ,
        [LastName] NVARCHAR(50) NULL ,
        PRIMARY KEY CLUSTERED ( [CustID] ASC )
    );
```

After you create your table, add a handful of customer records (see Figure 21-9).

	CustID	FirstName	LastName
▶	1	Dave	Brenner
	2	Matt	Walton
	3	Steve	Hagen
	4	Pat	Walton
*	NULL	NULL	NULL

PHILSURFACEBOOK\...t - dbo.Customers

Figure 21-9. *Populating the* Customers *table*

You will use your final table, Orders, to represent the automobile a given customer purchased. Create a new query, enter the following code, and click Execute:

```
CREATE TABLE [dbo].[Orders]
(
[OrderId] INT NOT NULL PRIMARY KEY IDENTITY,
[CustId] INT NOT NULL,
[CarId] INT NOT NULL
)
```

Now add data to your Orders table. You haven't created any table relationships yet, so you will have to manually make sure you enter values that exist in each table. Select a unique CarId for each CustId value (see Figure 21-10 for entries based on the previously shown sample data).

	OrderId	CustId	CarId
▶	1	1	5
	2	2	1
	3	3	4
	4	4	7
*	NULL	NULL	NULL

PHILSURFACEBOOK\...oLot - dbo.Orders

Figure 21-10. Populating the Orders table

For example, the entries used in this text indicate that Dave Brenner (CustId = 1) is interested in the black BMW (CarId = 5), while Pat Walton (CustId = 4) has her eye on the pink BMW (CarId = 7).

Creating the Table Relationships

The easiest way to create table relationships is by creating a database diagram. Double-click the Database Diagrams node; you will be prompted to add the required support objects, as shown in Figure 21-11.

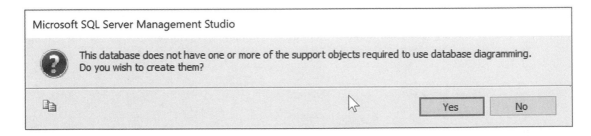

Figure 21-11. Adding the support objects for database diagramming

Right-click the Database Diagrams node and select New Database Diagram. In the Add Table dialog, select all of the tables and click Add, as shown in Figure 21-12.

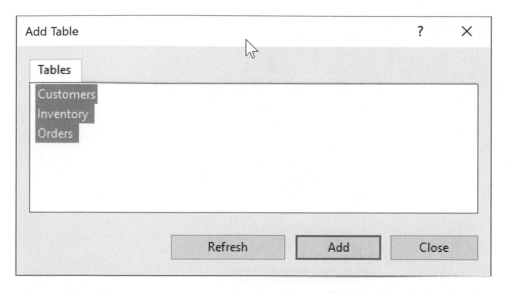

Figure 21-12. *Adding the tables to the database diagram*

To create a foreign key, click the `CarId` column in the `Inventory` table and drag it to the `Orders` table. When you do this, SSMS will match up the CarId columns in both tables and present a dialog to confirm the selections, as shown in Figure 21-13. Click OK to accept the default selections.

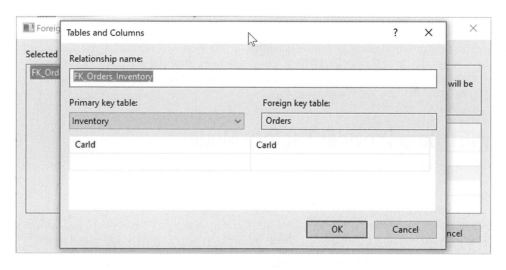

Figure 21-13. *Matching fields in the related tables*

On the next screen, click OK to complete the process.

Next, drag the `CustId` from the `Customers` table to the `CustId` of the `Orders` table. Make sure the fields match (`CustId` from `Customers` and `CustId` from `Orders`). On the next screen, expand the INSERT And UPDATE Specification node, and set the Delete Rule and Update Rule settings to Cascade, as shown in Figure 21-14.

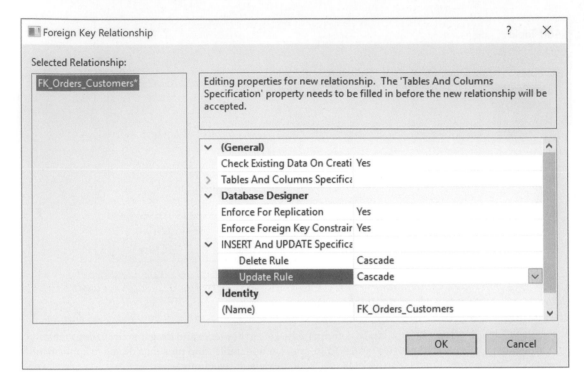

Figure 21-14. *Setting the Delete and Update rules to Cascade*

Click the Save button, and choose a name for the diagram (such as AutoLotDiagram).

With this, the `AutoLot` database is complete! Of course, this is a far cry from a real-world corporate database, but it will serve your needs for this chapter. Now that you have a database to test with, you can dive into the details of the ADO.NET data provider factory model.

The ADO.NET Data Provider Factory Model

The .NET data provider factory pattern allows you to build a single codebase using generalized data access types. Furthermore, using application configuration files (and the `<connectionStrings>` subelement), you can obtain providers and connection strings declaratively, without the need to recompile or redeploy the assembly that uses the ADO.NET APIs.

To understand the data provider factory implementation, recall from Table 21-1 that the classes within a data provider all derive from the same base classes defined within the `System.Data.Common` namespace.

- `DbCommand`: The abstract base class for all command classes

- `DbConnection`: The abstract base class for all connection classes

- `DbDataAdapter`: The abstract base class for all data adapter classes

- `DbDataReader`: The abstract base class for all data reader classes

- `DbParameter`: The abstract base class for all parameter classes

- `DbTransaction`: The abstract base class for all transaction classes

Each of the Microsoft-supplied data providers contains a class type that derives from System.Data. Common.DbProviderFactory. This base class defines several methods that retrieve provider-specific data objects. Here are the members of DbProviderFactory:

```
public abstract class DbProviderFactory
{
..public virtual bool CanCreateDataSourceEnumerator { get;};
  public virtual DbCommand CreateCommand();
  public virtual DbCommandBuilder CreateCommandBuilder();
  public virtual DbConnection CreateConnection();
  public virtual DbConnectionStringBuilder CreateConnectionStringBuilder();
  public virtual DbDataAdapter CreateDataAdapter();
  public virtual DbParameter CreateParameter();
  public virtual CodeAccessPermission CreatePermission(PermissionState state);
  public virtual DbDataSourceEnumerator CreateDataSourceEnumerator();
}
```

To obtain the DbProviderFactory-derived type for your data provider, the System.Data.Common namespace provides a class type named DbProviderFactories (note the plural in this type's name). You can use the static GetFactory() method to obtain the specific DbProviderFactory object of the specified data provider; do this by specifying a string name that represents the .NET namespace containing the provider's functionality, like so:

```
static void Main(string[] args)
{
  // Get the factory for the SQL data provider.
  DbProviderFactory sqlFactory =
    DbProviderFactories.GetFactory("System.Data.SqlClient");
...
}
```

Of course, rather than obtaining a factory using a hard-coded string literal, you could instead read in this information from a client-side *.config file (much like the earlier MyConnectionFactory example). You will learn how to do this shortly; for the moment, you can obtain the associated provider-specific data objects (e.g., connections, commands, and data readers) once you have obtained the factory for your data provider.

■ **Note**   For all practical purposes, you can regard the argument sent to DbProviderFactories. GetFactory() as the name of the data provider's .NET namespace. In reality, the machine.config value uses this string value to load the correct library dynamically from the global assembly cache.

A Complete Data Provider Factory Example

For a complete example, you can create a new C# Console Application project (named DataProviderFactory) that prints out the automobile inventory of the AutoLot database. For this initial example, you will hard-code the data access logic directly within the DataProviderFactory.exe assembly (to keep things simple). As you progress through this chapter (and the next covering the Entity Framework), you will see better ways to do this.

Begin by adding a reference to the System.Configuration.dll assembly and importing the System. Configuration namespace. Next, update the App.config file to include the <appSettings> element with the following elements (make sure to change the connection string to your specific installation):

```xml
<?xml version="1.0" encoding="utf-8" ?>
<configuration>
 <appSettings>
  <!-- Which provider? -->
  <add key="provider" value="System.Data.SqlClient" />

  <!-- Which connection string? -->
  <add key="connectionString" value= "Data Source=(localdb)\mssqllocaldb;
          Initial Catalog=AutoLot;Integrated Security=True"/>
 </appSettings>
 <startup>
  <supportedRuntime version="v4.0" sku=".NETFramework,Version=v4.7"/>
 </startup>
</configuration>
```

Now that you have a proper *.config file, you can read in the provider and connectionString values using the ConfigurationManager.AppSettings indexer. The provider value will be passed to the DbProviderFactories.GetFactory() method to obtain the data provider–specific factory type. You will use the connectionString value to set the ConnectionString property of the DbConnection-derived type.

Assuming you have imported the System.Data, System.Data.Common, and static System.Console namespaces, you can update your Main() method like this:

```
static void Main(string[] args)
{
  WriteLine("***** Fun with Data Provider Factories *****\n");
  // Get Connection string/provider from *.config.
  string dataProvider =
    ConfigurationManager.AppSettings["provider"];
  string connectionString =
    ConfigurationManager.AppSettings["connectionString"];

  // Get the factory provider.
  DbProviderFactory factory = DbProviderFactories.GetFactory(dataProvider);

  // Now get the connection object.
  using (DbConnection connection = factory.CreateConnection())
  {
    if (connection == null)
    {
      ShowError("Connection");
      return;
    }
    WriteLine($"Your connection object is a: {connection.GetType().Name}");
    connection.ConnectionString = connectionString;
    connection.Open();

    // Make command object.
    DbCommand command = factory.CreateCommand();
```

```
    if (command == null)
    {
      ShowError("Command");
      return;
    }
    WriteLine($"Your command object is a: {command.GetType().Name}");
    command.Connection = connection;
    command.CommandText = "Select * From Inventory";

    // Print out data with data reader.
    using (DbDataReader dataReader = command.ExecuteReader())
    {
      WriteLine($"Your data reader object is a: {dataReader.GetType().Name}");

      WriteLine("\n***** Current Inventory *****");
      while (dataReader.Read())
        WriteLine($"-> Car #{dataReader["CarId"]} is a {dataReader["Make"]}.");
    }
  }
  ReadLine();
}

private static void ShowError(string objectName)
{
  WriteLine($"There was an issue creating the {objectName}");
    ReadLine();
}
```

Notice that, for diagnostic purposes, you use reflection services to print the name of the underlying connection, command, and data reader. If you run this application, you will find the following current data in the Inventory table of the AutoLot database printed to the console:

```
***** Fun with Data Provider Factories *****

Your connection object is a: SqlConnection
Your command object is a: SqlCommand
Your data reader object is a: SqlDataReader

***** Current Inventory *****
-> Car #1 is a VW.
-> Car #2 is a Ford.
-> Car #3 is a Saab.
-> Car #4 is a Yugo.
-> Car #5 is a BMW.
-> Car #6 is a BMW.
-> Car #7 is a BMW.
```

Now change the *.config file to specify System.Data.OleDb as the data provider, update your connection string with Provider=SQLNCLI11, and change the Integrated Security value from true to SSPI, like so:

```
<configuration>
 <appSettings>
  <!-- Which provider? -->
```

827

```
<add key="provider" value="System.Data.OleDb" />
<!-- Which connection string? -->
<add key="connectionString" value=
"Provider=SQLNCLI11;Data Source=(localdb)\mssqllocaldb;
  Integrated Security=SSPI;Initial Catalog=AutoLot"/>
</appSettings>
<startup>
  <supportedRuntime version="v4.0" sku=".NETFramework,Version=v4.7"/>
</startup>
</configuration>
```

Doing this indicates that the System.Data.OleDb types are used behind the scenes and gives the following output:

```
***** Fun with Data Provider Factories *****

Your connection object is a: OleDbConnection
Your command object is a: OleDbCommand
Your data reader object is a: OleDbDataReader

***** Current Inventory *****
-> Car #1 is a VW.
-> Car #2 is a Ford.
-> Car #3 is a Saab.
-> Car #4 is a Yugo.
-> Car #5 is a BMW.
-> Car #6 is a BMW.
-> Car #7 is a BMW.
```

Of course, based on your experience with ADO.NET, you might be a bit unsure exactly what the connection, command, and data reader objects actually *do*. Don't sweat the details for the time being (quite a few pages remain in this chapter, after all!). At this point, it's enough to know that you can use the ADO.NET data provider factory model to build a single codebase that can consume various data providers in a declarative manner.

A Potential Drawback with the Data Provider Factory Model

Although this is a powerful model, you must make sure that the codebase uses only types and methods common to all providers through the members of the abstract base classes. Therefore, when authoring your codebase, you are limited to the members exposed by DbConnection, DbCommand, and the other types of the System.Data.Common namespace.

Given this, you might find that this generalized approach prevents you from directly accessing some of the bells and whistles of a particular DBMS. If you must be able to invoke specific members of the underlying provider (e.g., SqlConnection), you can do so using an explicit cast, as in this example:

```
using (DbConnection connection = factory.CreateConnection())
{
  if (connection == null)
  {
    ShowError("Connection");
```

```
      return;
   }
   WriteLine($"Your connection object is a: {connection.GetType().Name}");
   connection.ConnectionString = connectionString;
   connection.Open();

   var sqlConnection = connection as SqlConnection;
   if (sqlConnection != null)
   {
     // Print out which version of SQL Server is used.
     WriteLine(sqlConnection.ServerVersion);
   }
   //Remainder removed for brevity
}
```

When doing this, however, your codebase becomes a bit harder to maintain (and less flexible) because you must add a number of runtime checks. Nevertheless, if you need to build data access libraries in the most flexible way possible, the data provider factory model provides a great mechanism for doing so.

The <connectionStrings> Element

Currently, your connection string data is in the <appSettings> element of your *.config file. Application configuration files can define an element named <connectionStrings>. Within this element, you can define any number of name-value pairs that can be programmatically read into memory using the ConfigurationManager.ConnectionStrings indexer. One advantage of this approach (as opposed to using the <appSettings> element and the ConfigurationManager.AppSettings indexer) is that you can define multiple connection strings for a single application in a consistent manner.

To see this in action, update your current App.config file as follows (note that each connection string is documented using the name and connectionString attributes rather than the key and value attributes you find in <appSettings>):

```xml
<configuration>
 <appSettings>
  <!-- Which provider? -->
  <add key="provider" value="System.Data.SqlClient" />
 </appSettings>

  <!-- Here are the connection strings. -->
  <connectionStrings>
    <add name ="AutoLotSqlProvider" connectionString =
        "Data Source=(localdb)\mssqllocaldb;
        Integrated Security=true;Initial Catalog=AutoLot"/>

    <add name ="AutoLotOleDbProvider" connectionString =
        "Provider=SQLNCLI11;Data Source=(localdb)\mssqllocaldb;
        Integrated Security=SSPI;Initial Catalog=AutoLot"/>
 </connectionStrings>
 <startup>
    <supportedRuntime version="v4.0" sku=".NETFramework,Version=v4.7"/>
 </startup>
</configuration>
```

You can now update your Main() method as follows:

```
static void Main(string[] args)
{
  WriteLine("***** Fun with Data Provider Factories *****\n");
  string dataProvider =
    ConfigurationManager.AppSettings["provider"];
  string connectionString =
    ConfigurationManager.ConnectionStrings["AutoLotSqlProvider"].ConnectionString;
...
}
```

At this point, you have an application that can display the results of the Inventory table of the AutoLot database using a neutral codebase. Offloading the provider name and connection string to an external *.config file means that the data provider factory model can dynamically load the correct provider in the background. With this first example behind you, you can now dive into the details of working with ADO.NET. The rest of the chapter (and book) will focus specifically on the System.Data.SqlClient namespace, which makes sense since the back-end database is SQL Server.

■ **Source Code**   You can find the DataProviderFactory project in the Chapter 21 subdirectory.

Understanding the Connected Layer of ADO.NET

Recall that the *connected layer* of ADO.NET allows you to interact with a database using the connection, command, and data reader objects of your data provider. You have already used these objects in the previous DataProviderFactory application, and now you'll walk through the process again, this time using an expanded example. You need to perform the following steps when you want to connect to a database and read the records using a data reader object:

1. Allocate, configure, and open your connection object.

2. Allocate and configure a command object, specifying the connection object as a constructor argument or with the Connection property.

3. Call ExecuteReader() on the configured command class.

4. Process each record using the Read() method of the data reader.

To get the ball rolling, create a new Console Application project named AutoLotDataReader and import the System.Data and System.Data.SqlClient namespaces. Here is the complete code within Main() (analysis will follow):

```
class Program
{
  static void Main(string[] args)
  {
    WriteLine("***** Fun with Data Readers *****\n");

    // Create and open a connection.
    using (SqlConnection connection = new SqlConnection())
    {
```

```
      connection.ConnectionString =
        @"Data Source=(localdb)\mssqllocaldb;Integrated Security=true;Initial Catalog=AutoLot";
        connection.Open();

      // Create a SQL command object.
      string sql = "Select * From Inventory";
      SqlCommand myCommand = new SqlCommand(sql, connection);

      // Obtain a data reader a la ExecuteReader().
      using (SqlDataReader myDataReader = myCommand.ExecuteReader())
      {
        // Loop over the results.
        while (myDataReader.Read())
        {
          WriteLine($"-> Make: {myDataReader["Make"]}, PetName: {myDataReader["PetName"]},
            Color: {myDataReader["Color"]}.");
        }
      }
    }
    ReadLine();
  }
}
```

Working with Connection Objects

The first step to take when working with a data provider is to establish a session with the data source using the connection object (which, as you recall, derives from DbConnection). .NET connection objects are provided with a formatted *connection string*; this string contains a number of name-value pairs, separated by semicolons. You use this information to identify the name of the machine you want to connect to, the required security settings, the name of the database on that machine, and other data provider–specific information.

As you can infer from the preceding code, the Initial Catalog name refers to the database you want to establish a session with. The Data Source name identifies the name of the machine that maintains the database. I am using (localdb)\mssqllocaldb, which refers to the version of SQL Server Express that is installed with Visual Studio 2017. If you were using a different instance, you define the property as machinename\instance. For example, MYSERVER\SQLSERVER2016 means MYSERVER is the name of the server and SQLSERVER2016 is the name of the instance. If the machine is local to the development, you can use a period (.) or the token (local) for the server name. If the SQL Server instance is the default instance, the instance name is left off. For example, if you created AutoLot on a Microsoft SQL Server installation set up as the default instance on your local computer, you would use Data Source=(local).

Beyond this, you can supply any number of tokens that represent security credentials. You set the Integrated Security to true, which uses the current Windows account credentials for user authentication.

■ **Note**   Look up the ConnectionString property of your data provider's connection object in the .NET Framework 4.7 SDK documentation to learn more about each name-value pair for your specific DBMS.

After you establish your connection string, you can use a call to Open() to establish a connection with the DBMS. In addition to the ConnectionString, Open(), and Close() members, a connection object provides a number of members that let you configure additional settings regarding your connection, such as timeout settings and transactional information. Table 21-5 lists some (but not all) members of the DbConnection base class.

Table 21-5. *Members of the DbConnection Type*

Member	Meaning in Life
BeginTransaction()	You use this method to begin a database transaction.
ChangeDatabase()	You use this method to change the database on an open connection.
ConnectionTimeout	This read-only property returns the amount of time to wait while establishing a connection before terminating and generating an error (the default value is 15 seconds). If you would like to change the default, specify a Connect Timeout segment in the connection string (e.g., Connect Timeout=30).
Database	This read-only property gets the name of the database maintained by the connection object.
DataSource	This read-only property gets the location of the database maintained by the connection object.
GetSchema()	This method returns a DataTable object that contains schema information from the data source.
State	This read-only property gets the current state of the connection, which is represented by the ConnectionState enumeration.

The properties of the DbConnection type are typically read-only in nature and are useful only when you want to obtain the characteristics of a connection at runtime. When you need to override default settings, you must alter the construction string itself. For example, the following connection string sets the connection timeout setting from 15 seconds to 30 seconds:

```
static void Main(string[] args)
{
  WriteLine("***** Fun with Data Readers *****\n");

  using(SqlConnection connection = new SqlConnection())
  {
    connection.ConnectionString =
      @"Data Source=(localdb)\mssqllocaldb;" +
      "Integrated Security=SSPI;Initial Catalog=AutoLot;Connect Timeout=30";
    connection.Open();

    // New helper function (see below).
    ShowConnectionStatus(connection);
...
}
```

In the preceding code, you pass your connection object as a parameter to a new static helper method in the Program class named ShowConnectionStatus(), which you implement as follows:

```
static void ShowConnectionStatus(SqlConnection connection)
{
  // Show various stats about current connection object.
  WriteLine("***** Info about your connection *****");
  WriteLine($"Database location: {connection.DataSource}");
  WriteLine($"Database name: {connection.Database}");
```

```
  WriteLine($"Timeout: {connection.ConnectionTimeout}");
  WriteLine($"Connection state: {connection.State}\n");
}
```

While most of these properties are self-explanatory, the State property is worth a special mention. You can assign this property any value of the ConnectionState enumeration, as shown here:

```
public enum ConnectionState
{
  Broken,
  Closed,
  Connecting,
  Executing,
  Fetching,
  Open
}
```

However, the only valid ConnectionState values are ConnectionState.Open, ConnectionState. Connecting, and ConnectionState.Closed (the remaining members of this enum are reserved for future use). Also, it is always safe to close a connection, even if the connection state is currently ConnectionState. Closed.

Working with ConnectionStringBuilder Objects

Working with connection strings programmatically can be cumbersome because they are often represented as string literals, which are difficult to maintain and error-prone at best. The Microsoft- supplied ADO.NET data providers support *connection string builder objects*, which allow you to establish the name-value pairs using strongly typed properties. Consider the following update to the current Main() method:

```
static void Main(string[] args)
{
  WriteLine("***** Fun with Data Readers *****\n");

  // Create a connection string via the builder object.
  var cnStringBuilder = new SqlConnectionStringBuilder
  {
    InitialCatalog = "AutoLot",
    DataSource = @"(localdb)\mssqllocaldb",
    ConnectTimeout = 30,
    IntegratedSecurity = true
  };

  using(SqlConnection connection = new SqlConnection())
  {
    connection.ConnectionString = cnStringBuilder.ConnectionString;
    connection.Open();
    ShowConnectionStatus(connection);
...
  }
  ReadLine();
}
```

In this iteration, you create an instance of SqlConnectionStringBuilder, set the properties accordingly, and obtain the internal string using the ConnectionString property. Also note that you use the default constructor of the type. If you so choose, you can also create an instance of your data provider's connection string builder object by passing in an existing connection string as a starting point (this can be helpful when you read these values dynamically from an App.config file). Once you have hydrated the object with the initial string data, you can change specific name-value pairs using the related properties, as in this example:

```
static void Main(string[] args)
{
  WriteLine("***** Fun with Data Readers *****\n");

  // Assume you really obtained the connectionString value from a *.config file.
  string connectionString = @"Data Source=(localdb)\mssqllocaldb;" +
                "Integrated Security=true;Initial Catalog=AutoLot";

  SqlConnectionStringBuilder cnStringBuilder =
    new SqlConnectionStringBuilder(connectionString);

  // Change timeout value.
  cnStringBuilder.ConnectTimeout = 5;
...
}
```

Working with Command Objects

Now that you understand better the role of the connection object, the next order of business is to check out how to submit SQL queries to the database in question. The SqlCommand type (which derives from DbCommand) is an OO representation of a SQL query, table name, or stored procedure. You specify the type of command using the CommandType property, which can take any value from the CommandType enum, as shown here:

```
public enum CommandType
{
  StoredProcedure,
  TableDirect,
  Text // Default value.
}
```

When you create a command object, you can establish the SQL query as a constructor parameter or directly by using the CommandText property. Also when you create a command object, you need to specify the connection you want to use. Again, you can do so as a constructor parameter or by using the Connection property. Consider this code snippet:

```
// Create command object via ctor args.
string sql = "Select * From Inventory";
SqlCommand myCommand = new SqlCommand(sql, connection);
// Create another command object via properties.
SqlCommand testCommand = new SqlCommand();
testCommand.Connection = connection;
testCommand.CommandText = sql;
```

Realize that, at this point, you have not literally submitted the SQL query to the AutoLot database but instead prepared the state of the command object for future use. Table 21-6 highlights some additional members of the DbCommand type.

Table 21-6. *Members of the DbCommand Type*

Member	Meaning in Life
CommandTimeout	Gets or sets the time to wait while executing the command before terminating the attempt and generating an error. The default is 30 seconds.
Connection	Gets or sets the DbConnection used by this instance of the DbCommand.
Parameters	Gets the collection of DbParameter objects used for a parameterized query.
Cancel()	Cancels the execution of a command.
ExecuteReader()	Executes a SQL query and returns the data provider's DbDataReader object, which provides forward-only, read-only access for the result of the query.
ExecuteNonQuery()	Executes a SQL nonquery (e.g., an insert, update, delete, or create table).
ExecuteScalar()	A lightweight version of the ExecuteReader() method that was designed specifically for singleton queries (e.g., obtaining a record count).
Prepare()	Creates a prepared (or compiled) version of the command on the data source. As you might know, a *prepared query* executes slightly faster and is useful when you need to execute the same query multiple times (typically with different parameters each time).

Working with Data Readers

After you establish the active connection and SQL command, the next step is to submit the query to the data source. As you might guess, you have a number of ways to do this. The DbDataReader type (which implements IDataReader) is the simplest and fastest way to obtain information from a data store. Recall that data readers represent a read-only, forward-only stream of data returned one record at a time. Given this, data readers are useful only when submitting SQL selection statements to the underlying data store.

Data readers are useful when you need to iterate over large amounts of data quickly and you do not need to maintain an in-memory representation. For example, if you request 20,000 records from a table to store in a text file, it would be rather memory-intensive to hold this information in a DataSet (because a DataSet holds the entire result of the query in memory at the same time).

A better approach is to create a data reader that spins over each record as rapidly as possible. Be aware, however, that data reader objects (unlike data adapter objects, which you'll examine later) maintain an open connection to their data source until you explicitly close the connection.

You obtain data reader objects from the command object using a call to ExecuteReader(). The data reader represents the current record it has read from the database. The data reader has an indexer method (e.g., [ ] syntax in C#) that allows you to access a column in the current record. You can access the column either by name or by zero-based integer.

The following use of the data reader leverages the Read() method to determine when you have reached the end of your records (using a false return value). For each incoming record that you read from the database, you use the type indexer to print out the make, pet name, and color of each automobile. Also note that you call Close() as soon as you finish processing the records, which frees up the connection object.

```
static void Main(string[] args)
{
...
```

```
// Obtain a data reader via ExecuteReader().
using(SqlDataReader myDataReader = myCommand.ExecuteReader())
{
  // Loop over the results.
  while (myDataReader.Read())
  {
    WriteLine($"-> Make: { myDataReader["Make"]}, PetName: { myDataReader["PetName"]},
    Color: { myDataReader["Color"]}.");
  }
}
ReadLine();
}
```

In the preceding snippet, you overload the indexer of a data reader object to take either a string (representing the name of the column) or an int (representing the column's ordinal position). Thus, you can clean up the current reader logic (and avoid hard-coded string names) with the following update (note the use of the FieldCount property):

```
while (myDataReader.Read())
{
  WriteLine("***** Record *****");
  for (int i = 0; i < myDataReader.FieldCount; i++)
  {
    WriteLine($"{myDataReader.GetName(i)} = { myDataReader.GetValue(i)} ");
  }
  WriteLine();
}
```

If you compile and run your project at this point, you should see a list of all automobiles in the Inventory table of the AutoLot database. The following output shows the initial few records from my own version of AutoLot:

```
***** Fun with Data Readers *****

***** Info about your connection *****
Database location: (localdb)\mssqllocaldb
Database name: AutoLot
Timeout: 30
Connection state: Open

***** Record *****
CarId = 1
Make = VW
Color = Black
PetName = Zippy

***** Record *****
CarId = 2
Make = Ford
Color = Rust
PetName = Rusty
```

Obtaining Multiple Result Sets Using a Data Reader

Data reader objects can obtain multiple result sets using a single command object. For example, if you want to obtain all rows from the Inventory table, as well as all rows from the Customers table, you can specify both SQL Select statements using a semicolon delimiter, like so:

```
string sql = "Select * From Inventory;Select * from Customers";
```

After you obtain the data reader, you can iterate over each result set using the NextResult() method. Note that you are always returned the first result set automatically. Thus, if you want to read over the rows of each table, you can build the following iteration construct:

```
do
{
  while (myDataReader.Read())
  {
    WriteLine("***** Record *****");
    for (int i = 0; i < myDataReader.FieldCount; i++)
    {
      WriteLine($"{myDataReader.GetName(i)} = {myDataReader.GetValue(i)}");
    }
    WriteLine();
  }
} while (myDataReader.NextResult());
```

At this point, you should be more aware of the functionality data reader objects bring to the table. Always remember that a data reader can process only SQL Select statements; you cannot use them to modify an existing database table using Insert, Update, or Delete requests. Modifying an existing database requires additional investigation of command objects.

■ **Source Code**   You can find the AutoLotDataReader project in the Chapter 21 subdirectory.

Working with Create, Update, and Delete Queries

The ExecuteReader() method extracts a data reader object that allows you to examine the results of a SQL Select statement using a forward-only, read-only flow of information. However, when you want to submit SQL statements that result in the modification of a given table (or any other nonquery SQL statement, such as creating tables or granting permissions), you call the ExecuteNonQuery() method of your command object. This single method performs inserts, updates, and deletes based on the format of your command text.

■ **Note**   Technically speaking, a *nonquery* is a SQL statement that does not return a result set. Thus, Select statements are queries, while Insert, Update, and Delete statements are not. Given this, ExecuteNonQuery() returns an int that represents the number of rows affected, not a new set of records.

All of the database interactions examples in this chapter so far have only opened connections and used them to retrieve data. This is just one part of working with a database; a data access framework would not be of much use unless it also fully supported create, read, update, and delete (CRUD) functionality. Next, you will learn how to do this using calls to ExecuteNonQuery().

Begin by creating a new C# Class Library project named AutoLotDAL (short for *AutoLot Data Access Layer*) and delete the default class file. Add a new folder using the Project ➤ New Folder menu option (make sure you have the project selected in Solution Explorer) and name this folder DataOperations. In this new folder, add a new class named InventoryDAL.cs and change the class to public. This class will define various members to interact with the Inventory table of the AutoLot database. Finally, import the following .NET namespaces:

```
// You will use the SQL server
// provider; however, it would also be
// permissible to use the ADO.NET
// factory pattern for greater flexibility.
using System.Data;
using System.Data.SqlClient;
```

■ **Note**   You might recall from Chapter 13 that when objects use types that manage raw resources (e.g., a database connection), it is a good practice to implement IDisposable and author a proper finalizer. In a production environment, classes such as InventoryDAL would do the same; however, you won't do that here so you can stay focused on the particulars of ADO.NET.

Adding the Constructors

Create a constructor that takes a string parameter (connectionString) and assigns the value to a class-level variable. Next, create a default constructor that passes a default connection string to the other constructor. This enables the calling code to change the connection string if necessary from the default. The relevant code is as follows:

```
private readonly string _connectionString;
public InventoryDAL() : this(@"Data Source = (localdb)\mssqllocaldb;Integrated
Security=true;Initial Catalog=AutoLot")
{
}
public InventoryDAL(string connectionString)
  => _connectionString = connectionString;
```

Opening and Closing the Connection

Next, add a class-level variable to hold a connection that will be used by the data access code. Also, add two methods, one to open the connection (OpenConnection()) and the other to close the connection (CloseConnection()). In the CloseConnection() method, check the state of the connection, and if it's not closed, then call Close() on the connection. The code listing follows:

```
private SqlConnection _sqlConnection = null;
private void OpenConnection()
{
  _sqlConnection = new SqlConnection { ConnectionString = _connectionString };
  _sqlConnection.Open();
}
private void CloseConnection()
```

```
{
  if (_sqlConnection?.State != ConnectionState.Closed)
  {
    _sqlConnection?.Close();
  }
}
```

For the sake of brevity, most of the methods in the InventoryDAL class will not test for possible exceptions, nor will it throw custom exceptions to report various issues with the execution (e.g., a malformed connection string). If you were to build an industrial-strength data access library, you would absolutely want to use structured exception handling techniques (as covered in Chapter 7) to account for any runtime anomalies.

Create the Car Model

Modern data access libraries use classes (commonly called *models*) that are used to represent and transport the data from the database. You will see in the next chapter that the concept is a foundation of ORMs like the Entity Framework, but now, you are just going to create one model to represent a row in the Inventory table. Add a new folder to your project named Models, and add a new public class named Car. Update the code to the following:

```
public class Car
{
  public int CarId { get; set; }
  public string Color { get; set; }
  public string Make { get; set; }
  public string PetName { get; set; }
}
```

Adding the Selection Methods

You start by combining what you already know about Command objects, DataReaders, and generic collections to get all of the records from the Inventory table. As you saw earlier in this chapter, a data provider's data reader object allows for a selection of records using a read-only, forward-only, server-side cursor using the Read() method. The CommandBehavior property on the DataReader is set to automatically close the connection when the reader is closed. The GetAllInventory() method returns a List<Car> to represent all the data in the Inventory table:

```
using AutoLotDAL.Models;
public List<Car> GetAllInventory()
{
  OpenConnection();
  // This will hold the records.
  List<Car> inventory = new List<Car>();

  // Prep command object.
  string sql = "Select * From Inventory";
  using (SqlCommand command = new SqlCommand(sql, _sqlConnection))
  {
    command.CommandType = CommandType.Text;
    SqlDataReader dataReader = command.ExecuteReader(CommandBehavior.CloseConnection);
```

```
    while (dataReader.Read())
    {
      inventory.Add(new Car
      {
        CarId = (int)dataReader["CarId"],
        Color = (string)dataReader["Color"],
        Make = (string)dataReader["Make"],
        PetName = (string)dataReader["PetName"]
      });
    }
    dataReader.Close();
  }
  return inventory;
}
```

The next selection method gets a single car based on the CarId:

```
public Car GetCar(int id)
{
  OpenConnection();
  Car car = null;
  string sql = $"Select * From Inventory where CarId = {id}";
  using (SqlCommand command = new SqlCommand(sql, _sqlConnection))
  {
    command.CommandType = CommandType.Text;
    SqlDataReader dataReader = command.ExecuteReader(CommandBehavior.CloseConnection);
    while (dataReader.Read())
    {
      car = new Car
      {
        CarId = (int)dataReader["CarId"],
        Color = (string)dataReader["Color"],
        Make = (string)dataReader["Make"],
        PetName = (string)dataReader["PetName"]
      };
    }
    dataReader.Close();
  }
  return car;
}
```

Inserting a New Car

Inserting a new record into the Inventory table is as simple as formatting the SQL Insert statement (based on user input), opening the connection, calling the ExecuteNonQuery() using your command object, and closing the connection. You can see this in action by adding a public method to your InventoryDAL type named InsertAuto() that takes four parameters that map to the four columns of the Inventory table (CarId, Color, Make, and PetName). You use these arguments to format a string type to insert the new record. Finally, use your SqlConnection object to execute the SQL statement.

```
public void InsertAuto(string color, string make, string petName)
{
  OpenConnection();
  // Format and execute SQL statement.
  string sql = $"Insert Into Inventory (Make, Color, PetName) Values ('{make}', '{color}',
  '{petName}')";
  // Execute using our connection.
  using (SqlCommand command = new SqlCommand(sql, _sqlConnection))
  {
    command.CommandType = CommandType.Text;
    command.ExecuteNonQuery();
  }
  CloseConnection();
}
```

This previous method takes three string values and works as long as the calling code passes the strings in the correct order. A better method uses the Car model to make a strongly typed method, ensuring all the properties are passed into the method in the correct order.

Create the Strongly Type InsertCar() Method

Add another InsertAuto() method that takes a Car model as a parameter to your InventoryDAL class. Also add a using for AutoLotDAL.Models to the top of the class, as shown here:

```
public void InsertAuto(Car car)
{
  OpenConnection();
  // Format and execute SQL statement.
  string sql = "Insert Into Inventory (Make, Color, PetName) Values " +
    $"('{car.Make}', '{car.Color}', '{car.PetName}')";

  // Execute using our connection.
  using (SqlCommand command = new SqlCommand(sql, _sqlConnection))
  {
    command.CommandType = CommandType.Text;
    command.ExecuteNonQuery();
  }
  CloseConnection();
}
```

Defining classes that represent records in a relational database is a common way to build a data access library and is the core of the Entity Framework, as you will see in the next chapter.

■ **Note** Building a SQL statement using string concatenation can be risky from a security point of view (think: SQL injection attacks). The preferred way to build command text is to use a parameterized query, which you will learn about later in this chapter.

Adding the Deletion Logic

Deleting an existing record is as simple as inserting a new record. Unlike when you created the code for InsertAuto(), this time you will learn about an important try/catch scope that handles the possibility of attempting to delete a car that is currently on order for an individual in the Customers table. The default INSERT and UPDATE options for foreign keys default to preventing the deletion of related records in link tables. When this happens, a SqlException is thrown. A real program would handle that error intelligently; however, in this sample, you are just throwing a new exception. Add the following method to the InventoryDAL class type:

```
public void DeleteCar(int id)
{
  OpenConnection();
  // Get ID of car to delete, then do so.
  string sql = $"Delete from Inventory where CarId = '{id}'";
  using (SqlCommand command = new SqlCommand(sql, _sqlConnection))
  {
    try
    {
      command.CommandType = CommandType.Text;
      command.ExecuteNonQuery();
    }
    catch (SqlException ex)
    {
      Exception error = new Exception("Sorry! That car is on order!", ex);
      throw error;
    }
  }
  CloseConnection();
}
```

Adding the Update Logic

When it comes to the act of updating an existing record in the Inventory table, the first thing you must decide is what you want to allow the caller to change, whether it's the car's color, the pet name, the make, or all of the above. One way to give the caller complete flexibility is to define a method that takes a string type to represent any sort of SQL statement, but that is risky at best.

Ideally, you want to have a set of methods that allow the caller to update a record in a variety of ways. However, for this simple data access library, you will define a single method that allows the caller to update the pet name of a given automobile, like so:

```
public void UpdateCarPetName(int id, string newPetName)
{
  OpenConnection();
  // Get ID of car to modify the pet name.
  string sql = $"Update Inventory Set PetName = '{newPetName}' Where CarId = '{id}'";
  using (SqlCommand command = new SqlCommand(sql, _sqlConnection))
  {
    command.ExecuteNonQuery();
  }
  CloseConnection();
}
```

Working with Parameterized Command Objects

Currently, the insert, update, and delete logic for the InventoryDAL type uses hard-coded string literals for each SQL query. With *parameterized queries*, SQL parameters are objects, rather than simple blobs of text. Treating SQL queries in a more object-oriented manner helps reduce the number of typos (given strongly typed properties); plus, parameterized queries typically execute much faster than a literal SQL string because they are parsed exactly once (rather than each time the SQL string is assigned to the CommandText property). Parameterized queries also help protect against SQL injection attacks (a well-known data access security issue).

To support parameterized queries, ADO.NET command objects maintain a collection of individual parameter objects. By default, this collection is empty, but you can insert any number of parameter objects that map to a *placeholder parameter* in the SQL query. When you want to associate a parameter within a SQL query to a member in the command object's parameters collection, you can prefix the SQL text parameter with the @ symbol (at least when using Microsoft SQL Server; not all DBMSs support this notation).

Specifying Parameters Using the DbParameter Type

Before you build a parameterized query, you need to familiarize yourself with the DbParameter type (which is the base class to a provider's specific parameter object). This class maintains a number of properties that allow you to configure the name, size, and data type of the parameter, as well as other characteristics, including the parameter's direction of travel. Table 21-7 describes some key properties of the DbParameter type.

Table 21-7. *Key Members of the DbParameter Type*

Property	Meaning in Life
DbType	Gets or sets the native data type of the parameter, represented as a CLR data type
Direction	Gets or sets whether the parameter is input-only, output-only, bidirectional, or a return value parameter
IsNullable	Gets or sets whether the parameter accepts null values
ParameterName	Gets or sets the name of the DbParameter
Size	Gets or sets the maximum parameter size of the data in bytes; this is useful only for textual data
Value	Gets or sets the value of the parameter

Now let's look at how to populate a command object's collection of DBParameter-compatible objects by reworking the following version of the InsertAuto() method to leverage parameter objects (you could perform a similar reworking for your remaining methods; however, that's not necessary for this example):

```
public void InsertAuto(Car car)
{
  OpenConnection();
  // Note the "placeholders" in the SQL query.
  string sql = "Insert Into Inventory" +
    "(Make, Color, PetName) Values" +
    "(@Make, @Color, @PetName)";
```

```
  // This command will have internal parameters.
  using (SqlCommand command = new SqlCommand(sql, _sqlConnection))
  {
    // Fill params collection.
    SqlParameter parameter = new SqlParameter
    {
      ParameterName = "@Make",
      Value = car.Make,
      SqlDbType = SqlDbType.Char,
      Size = 10
    };
    command.Parameters.Add(parameter);

    parameter = new SqlParameter
    {
      ParameterName = "@Color",
      Value = car.Color,
      SqlDbType = SqlDbType.Char,
      Size = 10
    };
    command.Parameters.Add(parameter);

    parameter = new SqlParameter
    {
      ParameterName = "@PetName",
      Value = car.PetName,
      SqlDbType = SqlDbType.Char,
      Size = 10
    };
    command.Parameters.Add(parameter);

    command.ExecuteNonQuery();
    CloseConnection();
  }
}
```

Again, notice that your SQL query consists of four embedded placeholder symbols, each of which is prefixed with the @ token. You can use the SqlParameter type to map each placeholder using the ParameterName property and specify various details (e.g., its value, data type, and size) in a strongly typed matter. After each parameter object is hydrated, it is added to the command object's collection through a call to Add().

■ **Note** This example uses various properties to establish a parameter object. Note, however, that parameter objects support a number of overloaded constructors that allow you to set the values of various properties (which will result in a more compact codebase).

While building a parameterized query often requires more code, the end result is a more convenient way to tweak SQL statements programmatically, as well as to achieve better overall performance. They also are extremely helpful when you want to trigger a stored procedure.

Executing a Stored Procedure

Recall that a *stored procedure* is a named block of SQL code stored in the database. You can construct stored procedures so they return a set of rows or scalar data types or do anything else that makes sense (e.g., insert, update, or delete records); you can also have them take any number of optional parameters. The end result is a unit of work that behaves like a typical method, except that it is located on a data store rather than a binary business object. Currently, your AutoLot database defines a single stored procedure named GetPetName.

Now consider the following final method of the InventoryDAL type, which invokes your stored procedure:

```
public string LookUpPetName(int carId)
{
  OpenConnection();
  string carPetName;

  // Establish name of stored proc.
  using (SqlCommand command = new SqlCommand("GetPetName", _sqlConnection))
  {
    command.CommandType = CommandType.StoredProcedure;

    // Input param.
    SqlParameter param = new SqlParameter
    {
      ParameterName = "@carId",
      SqlDbType = SqlDbType.Int,
      Value = carId,
      Direction = ParameterDirection.Input
    };
    command.Parameters.Add(param);

    // Output param.
    param = new SqlParameter
    {
      ParameterName = "@petName",
      SqlDbType = SqlDbType.Char,
      Size = 10,
      Direction = ParameterDirection.Output
    };
    command.Parameters.Add(param);

    // Execute the stored proc.
    command.ExecuteNonQuery();

    // Return output param.
    carPetName = (string)command.Parameters["@petName"].Value;
    CloseConnection();
  }
  return carPetName;
}
```

One important aspect of invoking a stored procedure is to keep in mind that a command object can represent a SQL statement (the default) or the name of a stored procedure. When you want to inform a command object that it will be invoking a stored procedure, you pass in the name of the procedure

845

(as a constructor argument or by using the `CommandText` property) and must set the `CommandType` property to the value `CommandType.StoredProcedure`. (If you fail to do this, you will receive a runtime exception because the command object is expecting a SQL statement by default.)

```
SqlCommand command = new SqlCommand("GetPetName", _sqlConnection);
command.CommandType = CommandType.StoredProcedure;
```

Next, notice that the `Direction` property of a parameter object allows you to specify the direction of travel for each parameter passed to the stored procedure (e.g., input parameter, output parameter, in/out parameter, or return value). As before, you add each parameter object to the command object's parameters collection.

```
// Input param.
SqlParameter param = new SqlParameter
{
  ParameterName = "@carID",
  SqlDbType = SqlDbType.Int,
  Value = car.CarID,
  Direction = ParameterDirection.Input
};
command.Parameters.Add(param);
```

After the stored procedure completes with a call to `ExecuteNonQuery()`, you can obtain the value of the output parameter by investigating the command object's parameter collection and casting accordingly.

```
// Return output param.
carPetName = (string)command.Parameters["@petName"].Value;
```

At this point, you have an extremely simple data access library that you can use to build a client to display and edit your data (e.g., console-based, desktop GUI, or an HTML-based web application). You have not yet examined how to build graphical user interfaces, so next you will test your data library from a new console application.

Creating a Console-Based Client Application

Add a new console application (named AutoLotClient) to the AutoLotDAL solution. Set the new project as the startup project (by right-clicking the project in Solution Explorer and selecting Set as StartUp Project) and add a reference to the AutoLotDAL project. Add the following `using` statements to the top of `Program.cs`:

```
using AutoLotDAL.DataOperations;
using AutoLotDAL.Models;
```

Replace the `Main()` method with the following code to exercise `AutoLotDAL`:

```
class Program
{
  static void Main(string[] args)
  {
    InventoryDAL dal = new InventoryDAL();
    var list = dal.GetAllInventory();
    Console.WriteLine(" ************** All Cars ************** ");
```

```
    Console.WriteLine("CarId\tMake\tColor\tPet Name");
    foreach (var itm in list)
    {
      Console.WriteLine($"{itm.CarId}\t{itm.Make}\t{itm.Color}\t{itm.PetName}");
    }
    Console.WriteLine();
    var car = dal.GetCar(list.OrderBy(x=>x.Color).Select(x => x.CarId).First());
    Console.WriteLine(" ************* First Car By Color ************* ");
    Console.WriteLine("CarId\tMake\tColor\tPet Name");
    Console.WriteLine($"{car.CarId}\t{car.Make}\t{car.Color}\t{car.PetName}");

    try
    {
      dal.DeleteCar(5);
      Console.WriteLine("Car deleted.");
    }
    catch (Exception ex)
    {
      Console.WriteLine($"An exception occurred: {ex.Message}");
    }
    dal.InsertAuto(new Car {Color="Blue",Make="Pilot",PetName = "TowMonster"});
    list = dal.GetAllInventory();
    var newCar = list.First(x => x.PetName == "TowMonster");
    Console.WriteLine(" ************* New Car ************* ");
    Console.WriteLine("CarId\tMake\tColor\tPet Name");
    Console.WriteLine($"{newCar.CarId}\t{newCar.Make}\t{newCar.Color}\t{newCar.PetName}");
    dal.DeleteCar(newCar.CarId);
    var petName = dal.LookUpPetName(car.CarId);
    Console.WriteLine(" ************* New Car ************* ");
    Console.WriteLine($"Car pet name: {petName}");
    Console.Write("Press enter to continue...");
    Console.ReadLine();
  }
}
```

Understanding Database Transactions

Let's wrap up this examination of ADO.NET by taking a look at the concept of a database transaction. Simply put, a *transaction* is a set of database operations that must either *all* succeed or *all* fail as a collective unit. As you might imagine, transactions are quite important to ensure that table data is safe, valid, and consistent.

Transactions are important when a database operation involves interacting with multiple tables or multiple stored procedures (or a combination of database atoms). The classic transaction example involves the process of transferring monetary funds between two bank accounts. For example, if you were to transfer $500 from your savings account into your checking account, the following steps should occur in a transactional manner:

1. The bank should remove $500 from your savings account.

2. The bank should add $500 to your checking account.

It would be an extremely bad thing if the money were removed from the savings account but not transferred to the checking account (because of some error on the bank's part) because then you would be out $500! However, if these steps are wrapped up into a database transaction, the DBMS ensures that all related steps occur as a single unit. If any part of the transaction fails, the entire operation is *rolled back* to the original state. On the other hand, if all steps succeed, the transaction is *committed*.

■ **Note** You might be familiar with the acronym ACID from looking at transactional literature. This represents the four key properties of a prim-and-proper transaction: *atomic* (all or nothing), *consistent* (data remains stable throughout the transaction), *isolated* (transactions do not step on each other's feet), and *durable* (transactions are saved and logged).

It turns out that the .NET platform supports transactions in a variety of ways. This chapter will look at the transaction object of your ADO.NET data provider (`SqlTransaction`, in the case of `System.Data.SqlClient`). The .NET base class libraries also provide transactional support within numerous APIs, including the following:

- `System.EnterpriseServices`: This namespace (located in the `System.EnterpriseServices.dll` assembly) provides types that allow you to integrate with the COM+ runtime layer, including its support for distributed transactions.

- `System.Transactions`: This namespace (located in the `System.Transactions.dll` assembly) contains classes that allow you to write your own transactional applications and resource managers for a variety of services (e.g., MSMQ, ADO.NET, and COM+).

- *Windows Communication Foundation*: The WCF API provides services to facilitate transactions with various distributed binding classes.

In addition to the baked-in transactional support within the .NET base class libraries, it is possible to use the SQL language of your database management system. For example, you could author a stored procedure that uses the `BEGIN TRANSACTION`, `ROLLBACK`, and `COMMIT` statements.

Key Members of an ADO.NET Transaction Object

While transactional-aware types exist throughout the base class libraries, you will focus on transaction objects found within an ADO.NET data provider, all of which derive from `DBTransaction` and implement the `IDbTransaction` interface. Recall from the beginning of this chapter that `IDbTransaction` defines a handful of members as follows:

```
public interface IDbTransaction : IDisposable
{
  IDbConnection Connection { get; }
  IsolationLevel IsolationLevel { get; }

  void Commit();
  void Rollback();
}
```

Notice the `Connection` property, which returns a reference to the connection object that initiated the current transaction (as you'll see, you obtain a transaction object from a given connection object). You call the `Commit()` method when each of your database operations have succeeded. Doing this causes each of the pending changes to be persisted in the data store. Conversely, you can call the `Rollback()` method in the event of a runtime exception, which informs the DMBS to disregard any pending changes, leaving the original data intact.

■ **Note** The IsolationLevel property of a transaction object allows you to specify how aggressively a transaction should be guarded against the activities of other parallel transactions. By default, transactions are isolated completely until committed. Consult the .NET Framework 4.7 SDK documentation for full details regarding the values of the IsolationLevel enumeration.

Beyond the members defined by the IDbTransaction interface, the SqlTransaction type defines an additional member named Save(), which allows you to define *save points*. This concept allows you to roll back a failed transaction up until a named point, rather than rolling back the entire transaction. Essentially, when you call Save() using a SqlTransaction object, you can specify a friendly string moniker. When you call Rollback(), you can specify this same moniker as an argument to perform an effective *partial rollback*. Calling Rollback() with no arguments causes all the pending changes to be rolled back.

Adding a CreditRisks Table to the AutoLot Database

Now let's look at how you use ADO.NET transactions. Begin by using the SQL Server Management Studio to add a new table named CreditRisks to the AutoLot database, which has the same columns as the Customers table you created earlier in this chapter: CustId, which is the primary key; FirstName; and LastName. As its name suggests, CreditRisks is where you banish the undesirable customers who fail a credit check. The SQL to create the table is shown here:

```
CREATE TABLE [dbo].[CreditRisks](
    [CustID] [INT] IDENTITY(1,1) NOT NULL,
    [FirstName] [NVARCHAR](50) NULL,
    [LastName] [NVARCHAR](50) NULL,
PRIMARY KEY CLUSTERED ( [CustID] ASC )
)
```

Like the earlier savings-to-checking money transfer example, this example, where you move a risky customer from the Customers table into the CreditRisks table, should occur under the watchful eye of a transactional scope (after all, you will want to remember the names of those who are not creditworthy). Specifically, you need to ensure *either* that you successfully delete the current credit risks from the Customers table and add them to the CreditRisks table or that neither of these database operations occurs.

■ **Note** From a database design perspective, you do not need to build a whole new database table to capture high-risk customers; instead, you could add a Boolean column named IsCreditRisk to the existing Customers table. However, this new table lets you play with a simple transaction.

Adding a Transaction Method to InventoryDAL

Now let's look at how you work with ADO.NET transactions programmatically. Begin by opening the AutoLotDAL code library project you created earlier and add a new public method named ProcessCreditRisk() to the InventoryDAL class to deal with perceived credit risks. (Note that this example avoids using a parameterized query to keep the implementation simple; however, you'd want to use such a query for a production-level method).

```csharp
public void ProcessCreditRisk(bool throwEx, int custId)
{
  OpenConnection();
  // First, look up current name based on customer ID.
  string fName;
  string lName;
  var cmdSelect = new SqlCommand($"Select * from Customers where CustId = {custId}",
          _sqlConnection);
  using (var dataReader = cmdSelect.ExecuteReader())
  {
    if (dataReader.HasRows)
    {
      dataReader.Read();
      fName = (string)dataReader["FirstName"];
      lName = (string)dataReader["LastName"];
    }
    else
    {
      CloseConnection();
      return;
    }
  }

  // Create command objects that represent each step of the operation.
  var cmdRemove =
    new SqlCommand($"Delete from Customers where CustId = {custId}",
      _sqlConnection);

  var cmdInsert =
    new SqlCommand("Insert Into CreditRisks" +
      $"(FirstName, LastName) Values('{fName}', '{lName}')",
      _sqlConnection);

  // We will get this from the connection object.
  SqlTransaction tx = null;
  try
  {
    tx = _sqlConnection.BeginTransaction();

    // Enlist the commands into this transaction.
    cmdInsert.Transaction = tx;
    cmdRemove.Transaction = tx;

    // Execute the commands.
    cmdInsert.ExecuteNonQuery();
    cmdRemove.ExecuteNonQuery();

    // Simulate error.
    if (throwEx)
    {
      throw new Exception("Sorry!  Database error! Tx failed...");
    }
```

```
    // Commit it!
    tx.Commit();
  }
  catch (Exception ex)
  {
    Console.WriteLine(ex.Message);
    // Any error will roll back transaction.  Using the new conditional access operator to
    check for null.
    tx?.Rollback();
  }
  finally
  {
    CloseConnection();
  }
}
```

Here, you use an incoming bool parameter to represent whether you will throw an arbitrary exception when you attempt to process the offending customer. This allows you to simulate an unforeseen circumstance that will cause the database transaction to fail. Obviously, you do this here only for illustrative purposes; a true database transaction method would not want to allow the caller to force the logic to fail on a whim!

Note that you use two SqlCommand objects to represent each step in the transaction you will kick off. After you obtain the customer's first and last names based on the incoming custID parameter, you can obtain a valid SqlTransaction object from the connection object using BeginTransaction(). Next, and most importantly, you must *enlist each command object* by assigning the Transaction property to the transaction object you have just obtained. If you fail to do so, the Insert/Delete logic will not be under a transactional context.

After you call ExecuteNonQuery() on each command, you throw an exception if (and only if) the value of the bool parameter is true. In this case, all pending database operations are rolled back. If you do not throw an exception, both steps will be committed to the database tables once you call Commit(). Now compile your modified AutoLotDAL project to ensure you do not have any typos.

Testing Your Database Transaction

In SSMS, select one of the customers, and take notice of the CustId. In my copy of the data, I am going to use Dave Benner, with a CustID of 1. Next, add a new method to Program.cs in the AutoLotClient project named MoveCustomer().

```
public static void MoveCustomer()
{
  Console.WriteLine("***** Simple Transaction Example *****\n");

  // A simple way to allow the tx to succeed or not.
  bool throwEx = true;

  Console.Write("Do you want to throw an exception (Y or N): ");
  var userAnswer = Console.ReadLine();
  if (userAnswer?.ToLower() == "n")
  {
    throwEx = false;
  }

  var dal = new InventoryDAL();
```

```
// Process customer 1 - enter the id for the customer to move.
dal.ProcessCreditRisk(throwEx, 1);
Console.WriteLine("Check CreditRisk table for results");
Console.ReadLine();
}
```

If you were to run your program and elect to throw an exception, you would find that the customer is *not* removed from the Customers table because the entire transaction has been rolled back. However, if you did not throw an exception, you would find that the customer is no longer in the Customers table and has been placed in the CreditRisks table instead.

Executing Bulk Copies with ADO.NET

In cases where you need to load lots of records into the database, the methods shown so far would be rather inefficient. SQL Server has a feature called *bulk copy* that is designed specifically for this scenario, and it's wrapped up in ADO.NET with the SqlBulkCopy class. This section of the chapter shows how to do this with ADO.NET.

Exploring the SqlBulkCopy Class

The SqlBulkCopy class has one method, WriteToServer() (and the async version WriteToServerAsync()), that processes a list of records and writes the data to the database more efficiently than writing a series of insert statements and running them with a Command object. The WriteToServer overloads take a DataTable, a DataReader, or an array of DataRows, as shown in Figure 21-15.

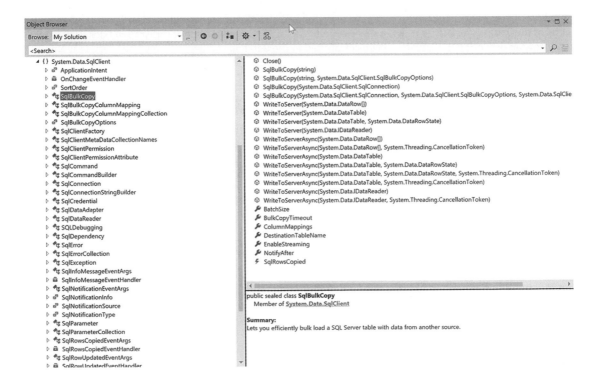

Figure 21-15. *Exploring the SqlBulkCopy class*

To keep with the theme of this chapter, you are going use the `DataReader` version. For that, you need to create a custom data reader.

Creating a Custom Data Reader

You want your custom data reader to be generic and hold a list of the models that you want to import. Begin by creating a new folder in the `AutoLotDAL` project named `BulkImport`, and in the folder, create a new generic interface named `IMyDataReader` that implements `IDataReader`, like this:

```
public interface IMyDataReader<T> : IDataReader
{
  List<T> Records { get; set; }
}
```

Next comes the task of implementing the custom data reader. As you have already seen, data readers have lots of moving parts. The good news for you is that, for `SqlBulkCopy`, you have to implement only a handful of them. Create a new generic class named `MyDataReader` and have it implement `IMyDataReader`. Also, update the `using` statements to the following:

```
using System;
using System.Collections.Generic;
using System.Data;
using System.Linq;
using System.Reflection;
```

I have Visual Studio implement all the methods for you, and you will have your starting point for the custom data reader. The only methods that need to be implemented for this scenario are detailed in Table 21-8.

Table 21-8. *Key Methods of* `IDataReader` *for* `SqlBulkCopy`

Method	Meaning in Life
Read	Gets the next record; returns `true` if there is another record or returns `false` if at the end of the list
FieldCount	Gets the total number of fields in the data source
GetName	Gets the name of a field based on the ordinal position
GetOrdinal	Gets the ordinal position of the field based on the name of a field
GetValue	Gets the value of a field based on the ordinal position

Starting with the `Read()` method, return `false` if the reader is at the end of the list, and return `true` (and increment a class-level counter) if the reader is not at the end of the list. Add a class-level variable to hold the current index of the `List<T>` and update the `Read()` method like this:

```
public class MyDataReader<T> : IMyDataReader<T>
{
  private int _currentIndex = -1;
  public bool Read()
  {
    if ((_currentIndex + 1) >= Records.Count) return false;
    _currentIndex++;
```

```
        return true;
    }
}
```

Each of the get methods and the `FieldCount` methods requires an intimate knowledge of the specific model to be loaded. You could certainly hard-code the details for each type, but that would be a lot of work. An example of the `GetName()` method (using the `Car` model) would be as follows:

```
public object GetValue(int i)
{
    Car currentRecord = Records[_currentIndex] as Car;
    switch (i)
    {
        case 0: return currentRecord.CarId;
        case 1: return currentRecord.Color;
        case 2: return currentRecord.Make;
        case 3: return currentRecord.PetName;
        default: return string.Empty;
    }
}
```

The database has only four tables, but that means you still have four variations of the data reader. Imagine if you had a real production database with many more tables! You can do better than this using reflection (covered in Chapter 15) and LINQ to Objects (covered in Chapter 12). Create a default constructor that will get all the properties of the generic type as well as create a `Dictionary` from the reflected properties that ties the name of each property to its index. Also add two class-level variables to hold the values gathered in the constructor. The added code is as follows:

```
private readonly PropertyInfo[] _propertyInfos;
private readonly Dictionary<string, int> _nameDictionary;

public MyDataReader()
{
    _propertyInfos = typeof(T).GetProperties();
    _nameDictionary = _propertyInfos
        .Select((x, index) => new { x.Name, index })
        .ToDictionary(pair => pair.Name, pair => pair.index);
}
```

Now, the following methods can be implemented generically, using the reflected information. The updated methods are shown here:

```
public int FieldCount => _propertyInfos.Length;

public string GetName(int i)
    => i >= 0 && i < FieldCount ? _propertyInfos[i].Name : string.Empty;

public int GetOrdinal(string name)
    => _nameDictionary.ContainsKey(name) ? _nameDictionary[name] : -1;

public object GetValue(int i)
    => _propertyInfos[i].GetValue(Records[_currentIndex]);
```

Executing the Bulk Copy

Add a new public static class named ProcessBulkImport.cs to the BulkImport folder. Add the code to handle opening and closing connections (similar to the code in the InventoryDAL class), as follows:

```
private static SqlConnection _sqlConnection = null;
private static readonly string _connectionString =
    @"Data Source = (localdb)\mssqllocaldb;Integrated Security=true;Initial
    Catalog=AutoLot";

private static void OpenConnection()
{
  _sqlConnection = new SqlConnection {ConnectionString = _connectionString};
  _sqlConnection.Open();
}
private static void CloseConnection()
{
  if (_sqlConnection?.State != ConnectionState.Closed)
  {
    _sqlConnection?.Close();
  }
}
```

The SqlBulkCopy class requires the name (and schema, if different than dbo) to process the records. After creating a new SqlBulkCopy instance (passing in the connection object), set the DestinationTableName property. Then, create a new instance of the custom data reader holding the list to be bulk copied, and call WriteToServer. The ExecuteBulkImport method is shown here:

```
public static void ExecuteBulkImport<T>(IEnumerable<T> records, string tableName)
{
  OpenConnection();
  using (SqlConnection conn = _sqlConnection)
  {
    SqlBulkCopy bc = new SqlBulkCopy(conn)
    {
      DestinationTableName = tableName
    };
    var dataReader = new MyDataReader<T>(records.ToList());
    try
    {
      bc.WriteToServer(dataReader);
    }
    catch (Exception ex)
    {
      //Should do something here
    }
    finally
    {
      CloseConnection();
    }
  }
}
```

Testing the Bulk Copy

Add a new method to `Program.cs` named `DoBulkCopy.cs`. Create a list of `Car` objects, and pass that (and the name of the table) into the `ExecuteBulkImport` method. The rest of the code displays the results of the bulk copy:

```
public static void DoBulkCopy()
{
  Console.WriteLine(" ************* Do Bulk Copy ************* ");
  var cars = new List<Car>
  {
    new Car() {Color = "Blue", Make = "Honda", PetName = "MyCar1"},
    new Car() {Color = "Red", Make = "Volvo", PetName = "MyCar2"},
    new Car() {Color = "White", Make = "VW", PetName = "MyCar3"},
    new Car() {Color = "Yellow", Make = "Toyota", PetName = "MyCar4"}
  };
  ProcessBulkImport.ExecuteBulkImport(cars, "Inventory");
  InventoryDAL dal = new InventoryDAL();
  var list = dal.GetAllInventory();
  Console.WriteLine(" ************* All Cars ************* ");
  Console.WriteLine("CarId\tMake\tColor\tPet Name");
  foreach (var itm in list)
  {
    Console.WriteLine($"{itm.CarId}\t{itm.Make}\t{itm.Color}\t{itm.PetName}");
  }
  Console.WriteLine();
}
```

While adding four new cars doesn't show the merits of the work involved in using the `SqlBulkCopy` class, imagine trying to load *thousands* of records. I have done this with customers, and the load time has been mere seconds, where looping through each record took hours! As with everything in .NET, this is just another tool to keep in your toolbox to use when it makes the most sense.

■ **Source Code**   You can find the AutoLotDAL solution in the `Chapter 21` subdirectory.

Summary

ADO.NET is the native data access technology of the .NET platform, and you can use it in three distinct manners: connected, disconnected, or through ORMs, such as the Entity Framework. In this chapter, you began by learning the role of data providers, which are essentially concrete implementations of several abstract base classes (in the `System.Data.Common` namespace) and interface types (in the `System.Data` namespace). You also saw that it is possible to build a provider-neutral codebase using the ADO.NET data provider factory model.

You also learned that you can use connection objects, transaction objects, command objects, and data reader objects of the connected layer to select, update, insert, and delete records. Also, recall that command objects support an internal parameter collection, which you can use to add some type safety to your SQL queries; these also prove quite helpful when triggering stored procedures.

Next, you learned how to safeguard your data manipulation code with transactions and wrapped up the chapter with a look at using the `SqlBulkCopy` class to load large amounts of data into SQL Server using .NET.

CHAPTER 22

■ ■ ■

Introducing Entity Framework 6

The previous chapter examined the fundamentals of ADO.NET. ADO.NET has enabled .NET programmers to work with relational data (in a relatively straightforward manner) since the initial release of the .NET platform. However, Microsoft introduced a new component of the ADO.NET API called the *Entity Framework* (or simply, *EF*) in .NET 3.5 Service Pack 1.

■ **Note**   While this first version of EF was widely criticized, the EF team at Microsoft has been hard at work releasing new versions. The current version of EF for the full .NET Framework is currently (at the time of this writing) 6.1.3, which is packed full of features and performance enhancements over earlier versions. Entity Framework Core (formerly called EF 7) is also available and is covered in Part IX along with .NET Core.

The overarching goal of EF is to allow you to interact with data from relational databases using an object model that maps directly to the business objects (or domain objects) in your application. For example, rather than treating a batch of data as a collection of rows and columns, you can operate on a collection of strongly typed objects termed *entities*. These entities are also natively LINQ aware, and you can query against them using the same LINQ grammar you learned about in Chapter 12. The EF runtime engine translates your LINQ queries into proper SQL queries on your behalf.

This chapter will introduce you to data access using the Entity Framework. You will learn about creating a domain model, mapping model classes to the database, and the role of the DbContext class. You will also learn about navigation properties, transactions, and concurrency checking.

By the time you complete this chapter, you will have the final version of AutoLotDAL.dll. You will use this version of AutoLotDAL.dll for the rest of the book (until you rebuild it using EF .NET Core later in this book).

■ **Note**   All the versions of the Entity Framework (up to and including EF 6.*x*) support using an entity designer to create an entity data model XML (EDMX) file. Starting with version 4.1, EF added support for plain old CLR objects (POCO) using a technique referred to as Code First. EF Core will support only the Code First paradigm, dropping all EDMX support. For this reason (and a host of other issues with the EDMX paradigm), this chapter uses only the Code First paradigm. The Code First name is actually terrible, since it gives the impression that you can't use it with an existing database. I prefer the term Code Centric, but Microsoft didn't ask my opinion!

© Andrew Troelsen and Philip Japikse 2017

A. Troelsen and P. Japikse, *Pro C# 7*, https://doi.org/10.1007/978-1-4842-3018-3_22

Understanding the Role of the Entity Framework

ADO.NET provides you with a fabric that lets you select, insert, update, and delete data with connections, commands, and data readers. While this is all well and good, these aspects of ADO.NET force you to treat the fetched data in a manner that is tightly coupled to the physical database schema. Recall, for example, that when you use the connected layer, you typically iterate over each record by specifying column names to a data reader.

When you use ADO.NET, you must always be mindful of the physical structure of the back-end database. You must know the schema of each data table, author potentially complex SQL queries to interact with said data table(s), and so forth. This can force you to author some fairly verbose C# code because C# itself does not speak the language of the database schema directly.

To make matters worse, the way in which a physical database is usually constructed is squarely focused on database constructs such as foreign keys, views, stored procedures, and data normalization, not object-oriented programming.

The Entity Framework lessens the gap between the goals and optimization of the database and the goals and optimization of object-oriented programming. Using EF, you can interact with a relational database without ever seeing a line of SQL code (if you so choose). Rather, when you apply LINQ queries to your strongly typed classes, the EF runtime generates proper SQL statements on your behalf.

■ **Note**   *LINQ to Entities* is the term that describes the act of applying LINQ queries to ADO.NET EF entity objects.

EF is simply another approach to the data-access APIs and is not necessarily intended to completely replace using ADO.NET directly from C# code. However, once you spend some time working with EF, you will quickly find yourself preferring this rich object model over creating all of your data access code from scratch. EF is another tool in your toolbox, and only you can decide what approach works best for your project.

■ **Note**   You might recall a database programming API introduced with .NET 3.5 called LINQ to SQL. This API is close in concept (and fairly close in terms of programming constructs) to EF. LINQ to SQL is in maintenance mode, meaning it will receive only critical bug fixes. If you have an application using LINQ to SQL, know that Microsoft's official policy is to support all software for at least ten years after its "end of life." So while it won't be removed from your machine by the software guardians, the official word from those kind folks in Redmond is that you should put your efforts into EF, not LINQ to SQL. They certainly are focusing on EF.

The Role of Entities

The strongly typed classes mentioned previously (and demonstrated with the Car class in the previous chapter) are officially called *entities*. Entities are a conceptual model of a physical database that maps to your business domain. Formally speaking, this model is termed an *entity data model* (EDM). The EDM is a client-side set of classes that are mapped to a physical database by Entity Framework convention and configuration. You should understand that the entities need not map directly to the database schema, and typically they don't. You are free to structure your entity classes to fit your application needs and then map your unique entities to your database schema.

■ **Note**   In the Code First world, most people refer to the POCO classes as *models* and the collection of these classes as the *object graph*. When the model classes are instantiated with data from the data store, they are then referred to as *entities*. In reality, the terms are pretty much used interchangeably, and both will be used throughout this text.

For example, take the simple `Inventory` table in the `AutoLot` database and the `Car` model class from the previous chapter. Through model configuration, you inform EF that the `Car` model represents the `Inventory` table. This loose coupling means you can shape the entities so they closely model your business domain.

■ **Note**   In many cases, the model classes will be identically named to the related database tables. However, remember that you can always reshape the model to match your business situation.

You will build a full example with EF in just a bit. However, for the time being, consider the following `Program` class, which uses the `Car` model class and a related context class (covered soon) named `AutoLotEntities` to add a new row to the `Inventory` table of `AutoLot`.

```
class Program
{
  static void Main(string[] args)
  {
    // Connection string automatically read from config file.
    using (AutoLotEntities context = new AutoLotEntities())
    {
        // Add a new record to Inventory table, using our model.
      context.Cars.Add(new Car() { Color = "Black",
                                   Make = "Pinto",
                                   PetName = "Pete" });
      context.SaveChanges();
    }
  }
}
```

EF examines the configuration of your models and your context class to take the client-side representation of the `Inventory` table (here, a class named `Car`) and map it back to the correct columns of the `Inventory` table. Notice that you see no trace of any sort of SQL INSERT statement. You simply add a new `Car` object to the collection maintained by the aptly named `Cars` property of the context object and then save your changes.

There is no magic in the preceding example. Under the covers, a connection to the database is made and opened, a proper SQL statement is generated and executed, and the connection is released and closed. These details are handled on your behalf by the framework. Now let's look at the core services of EF that make this possible.

The Building Blocks of the Entity Framework

EF (at its core) uses the ADO.NET infrastructure you have already examined in the previous chapter. Like any ADO.NET interaction, EF uses an ADO.NET data provider to communicate with the data store. However, the data provider must be updated so it supports a new set of services before it can interact with the EF API. As you might expect, the Microsoft SQL Server data provider has been updated with the necessary infrastructure, which is accounted for when using the `System.Data.Entity.dll` assembly.

■ **Note**   Many third-party databases (e.g., Oracle and MySQL) provide EF-aware data providers. If you are not using SQL Server, consult your database vendor for details or navigate to `https://docs.microsoft.com/en-us/dotnet/framework/data/adonet/ado-net-overview` for a list of known ADO.NET data providers.

In addition to adding the necessary bits to the Microsoft SQL Server data provider, the `System.Data.Entity.dll` assembly contains various namespaces that account for the EF services themselves. The first key piece of the EF API to concentrate on is the `DbContext` class. You will create a derived, model-specific context when you use EF for your data access libraries.

The Role of the DbContext Class

The `DbContext` class represents a combination of the Unit of Work and Repository patterns that can be used to query from a database and group together changes that will be written back as a single unit of work. `DbContext` provides a number of core services to child classes, including the ability to save all changes (which results in a database update), tweak the connection string, delete objects, call stored procedures, and handle other fundamental details. Table 22-1 shows some of the more commonly used members of the `DbContext`.

Table 22-1. *Common Members of* `DbContext`

Member of **DbContext**	Meaning in Life
DbContext	Constructor used by default in the derived context class. The string parameter is either the database name or the connection string stored in the `*.config` file.
Entry Entry<TEntity>	Retrieves the `System.Data.Entity.Infrastructure.DbEntityEntry` object providing access to information and the ability to perform actions on the entity.
GetValidationErrors	Validates tracked entries and returns a collection of `System.Data.Entity.Validation.DbEntityValidationResults`.
SaveChanges SaveChangesAsync	Saves all changes made in this context to the database. Returns the number of affected entities.
Configuration	Provides access to the configuration properties of the context.
Database	Provides a mechanism for creation/deletion/existence checks for the underlying database, executes stored procedures and raw SQL statements against the underlying data store, and exposes transaction functionality.

`DbContext` also implements `IObjectContextAdapter`, so any of the functionality available in the `ObjectContext` class is also available. While `DbContext` takes care of most of your needs, there are two events that can be extremely helpful, as you will see later in the chapter. Table 22-2 lists the events.

Table 22-2. *Events in* `DbContext`

Events of **DbContext**	Meaning in Life
ObjectMaterialized	Fires when a new entity object is created from the data store as part of a query or load operation
SavingChanges	Occurs when changes are being saved to the data store but prior to the data being persisted

The Role of the Derived Context Class

As mentioned, the DbContext class provides the core functionality when working with EF Code First. In your projects, you will create a class that derives from DbContext for your specific domain. In the constructor, you need to pass the name of the connection string for this context class to the base class, as shown here:

```
public class AutoLotEntities : DbContext
{
  public AutoLotEntities() : base("name=AutoLotConnection")
  {
  }
  protected override void Dispose(bool disposing)
  {
  }
}
```

The Role of DbSet<T>

To add tables into your context, you add a DbSet<T> for each table in your object model. To enable lazy loading, the properties in the context need to be virtual, like this:

```
public virtual DbSet<CreditRisk> CreditRisks { get; set; }
public virtual DbSet<Customer> Customers { get; set; }
public virtual DbSet<Inventory> Inventory { get; set; }
public virtual DbSet<Order> Orders { get; set; }
```

Each DbSet<T> provides a number of core services to each collection, such as creating, deleting, and finding records in the represented table. Table 22-3 describes some of the core members of the DbSet<T> class.

Table 22-3. *Common Members of* DbSet<T>

Member of **DbSet<T>**	**Meaning in Life**
Add AddRange	Allows you to insert a new object (or range of objects) into the collection. They will be marked with the Added state and will be inserted into the database when SaveChanges (or SaveChangesAsync) is called on the DbContext.
Attach	Associates an object with the DbContext. This is commonly used in disconnected applications like ASP.NET/MVC.
Create Create<T>	Creates a new instance of the specified entity type.
Find FindAsync	Finds a data row by the primary key and returns an object representing that row.
Remove RemoveRange	Marks an object (or range of objects) for deletion.
SqlQuery	Creates a raw SQL query that will return entities in this set.

Once you drill into the correct property of the object context, you can call any member of DbSet<T>. Consider again the sample code shown in the first few pages of this chapter:

```
using (AutoLotEntities context = new AutoLotEntities())
{
  // Add a new record to Inventory table, using our entity.
  context.Cars.Add(new Car() { ColorOfCar = "Black",
                               MakeOfCar = "Pinto",
                               NicknameOfCar = "Pete" });
  context.SaveChanges();
}
```

Here, AutoLotEntities *is-a* derived DbContext. The Cars property gives you access to the DbSet<Car> variable. You use this reference to insert a new Car entity object and tell the DbContext to save all changes to the database.

DbSet<T> is typically the target of LINQ to Entity queries; as such, DbSet<T> supports the same extension methods you learned about in Chapter 12, such as ForEach(), Select(), and All(). Moreover, DbSet<T> gains a good deal of functionality from its direct parent class, DbQuery<T>, which is a class that represents a strongly typed LINQ (or Entity SQL) query.

Code First Explained

As mentioned in a previous note, Code First doesn't mean you can't use EF with an existing database. It really just means no EDMX model. I prefer the term Code Centric, since that's what it really means. You can use Code First from an existing database or create a new database from the entities using EF migrations.

Transaction Support

All versions of EF wrap each call to SaveChanges/SaveChangesAsync in a transaction. The isolation level of these automatic transactions is the same as the default isolation level for the database (which is READ COMMITTED for SQL Server). You can add more control to the transactional support in EF if you need it. For more information, see https://msdn.microsoft.com/en-us/data/dn456843.aspx?f=255&MSPPErr or=-2147217396.

■ **Note** Although not covered in this book, executing SQL statements using ExecuteSqlCommand() from the DbContext database object is now wrapped in an implicit transaction. This is new in EF version 6.

Entity State and Change Tracking

The DbChangeTracker automatically tracks the state for any object loaded into a DbSet<T> within a DbContext. In the previous examples, while inside the using statement, any changes to the data will be tracked and saved when SaveChanges is called on the AutoLotEntities class. Table 22-4 lists the possible values for the state of an object.

Table 22-4. *Entity State Enumeration Values*

Value	Meaning in Life
Detached	The object exists but is not being tracked. An entity is in this state immediately after it has been created and before it is added to the object context.
Unchanged	The object has not been modified since it was attached to the context or since the last time that the SaveChanges() method was called.
Added	The object is new and has been added to the object context, and the SaveChanges() method has not been called.
Deleted	The object has been deleted from the object context but not yet removed from the data store.
Modified	One of the scalar properties on the object was modified, and the SaveChanges() method has not been called.

If you need to check the state of an object, use the following code:

```
EntityState state = context.Entry(entity).State;
```

You usually don't need to worry about the state of your objects. However, in the case of deleting an object, you can set the state of an object to `EntityState.Deleted` and save a round-trip to the database. You will do this later in the chapter.

Entity Framework Data Annotations

Data annotations are C# attributes that are used to shape your entities. Table 22-5 lists some of the most commonly used data annotations for defining how your entity classes and properties map to database tables and fields. There are many more annotations that you can use to refine your model and add validations, as you will see throughout the rest of this chapter and book.

Table 22-5. *Data Annotations Supported by the Entity Framework*

Data Annotation	Meaning in Life
Key	Defines the primary key for the model. This is not necessary if the key property is named Id or combines the class name with Id, such as OrderId. If the key is a composite, you must add the Column attribute with an Order, such as Column[Order=1] and Column[Order=2]. Key fields are implicitly also [Required].
Required	Declares the property as not nullable.
ForeignKey	Declares a property that is used as the foreign key for a navigation property.
StringLength	Specifies the min and max lengths for a string property.
NotMapped	Declares a property that is not mapped to a database field.
ConcurrencyCheck	Flags a field to be used in concurrency checking when the database server does updates, inserts, or deletes.
TimeStamp	Declares a type as a row version or timestamp (depending on the database provider).

(*continued*)

Table 22-5. *(continued)*

Data Annotation	Meaning in Life
Table Column	Allows you to name your model classes and fields differently than how they are declared in the database. The Table attribute allows specification of the schema as well (as long as the data store supports schemas).
DatabaseGenerated	Specifies if the field is database generated. This takes one of Computed, Identity, or None.
NotMapped	Specifies that EF needs to ignore this property in regard to database fields.
Index	Specifies that a column should have an index created for it. You can specify clustered, unique, name, and order.

Code First from an Existing Database

Now that you have a better understanding of what the ADO.NET Entity Framework is and how it works from a high level, it's time to look at your first full example. You will build a simple console app that uses Code First from an existing database to create the model classes representing the existing AutoLot database you built in Chapter 21.

Generating the Model

Begin by creating a new Console Application project named AutoLotConsoleApp. Add a folder to the project through the Project ➤ New Folder menu option and name it EF. Select the new EF folder and then select Project ➤ Add New Item (be sure to highlight the Data node) to insert a new ADO.NET Entity Data Model item named AutoLotEntities (as in Figure 22-1).

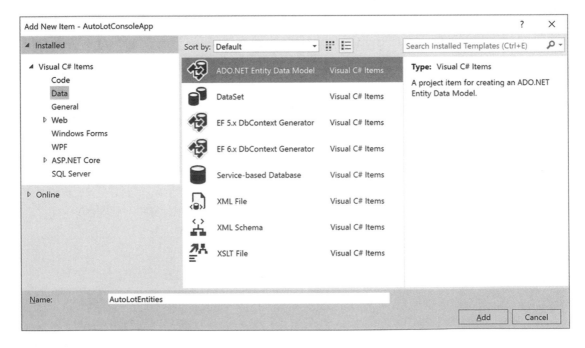

Figure 22-1. *Inserting a new ADO.NET EDM project item*

Clicking the Add button launches the Entity Model Data Wizard. The wizard's first step allows you to select the option to generate an EDM using the Entity Framework Designer (from an existing database or by creating an empty designer) or using Code First (from an existing database or by creating an empty DbContext). Select the "Code First from database" option and click the Next button (see Figure 22-2).

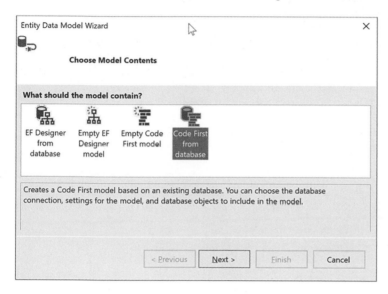

Figure 22-2. *Generating an EDM from an existing database*

The Choose Your Database Connection screen will autopopulate with any connection strings stored in Visual Studio. If you already have a connection to your database within the Visual Studio Server Explorer, you will see it listed in the drop-down combo box (as shown in Figure 22-5). If this is not the case, click the New Connection button.

This loads the Choose Data Source screen. Select Microsoft SQL Server and click Continue, as shown in Figure 22-3.

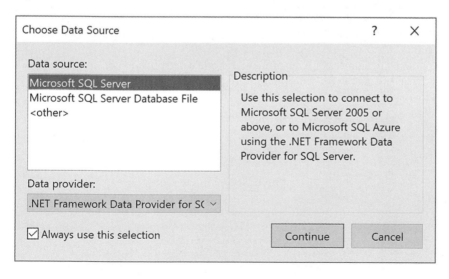

Figure 22-3. *Select SQL Server for the new connection string*

On the next screen, select (localdb)\mssqllocaldb for the server and then select AutoLot for the database, as shown in Figure 22-4.

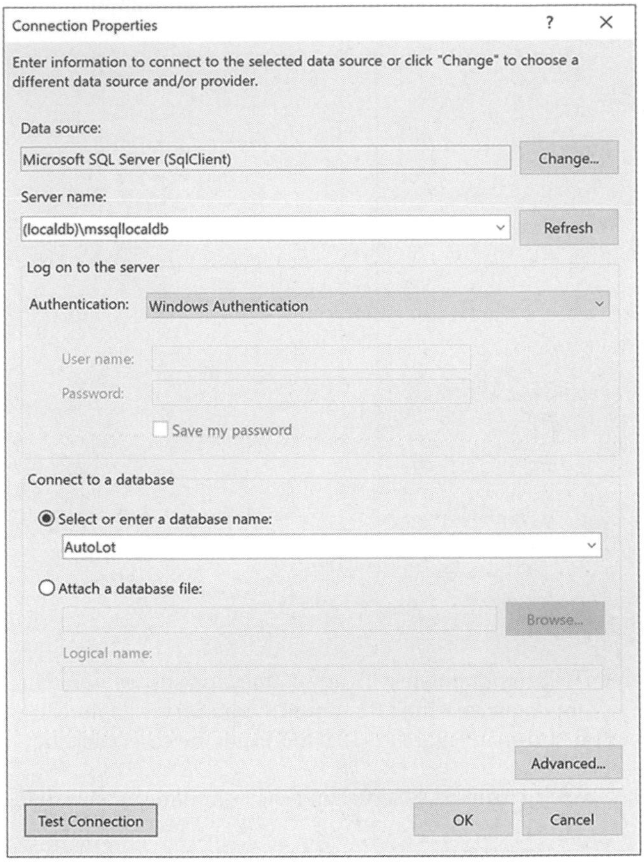

Figure 22-4. *Creating the connection string to AutoLot*

After clicking OK, your new connection string will be created and selected on the Choose Your Data Connection screen. Make sure the box to save the connection string is selected and set the App.config setting to AutoLotConnection, as shown in Figure 22-5.

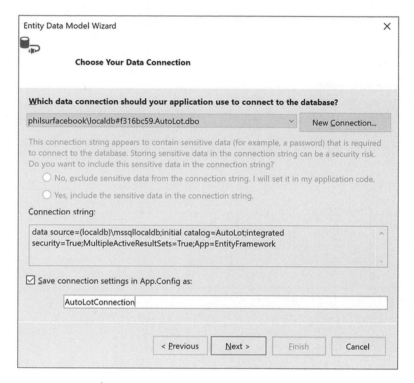

Figure 22-5. *Selecting the database used to generate the model*

Before you click the Next button, take a moment to examine the format of your connection string.

```
Data source= (localdb)\mssqllocaldb;Initial Catalog=AutoLot;Integrated Security=True;
MultipleActiveResultSets=true;App=EntityFramework
```

This is similar to what you used in Chapter 21, with the addition of the `App=EntityFramework` name-value pair. App is short for application name, which can be used when troubleshooting SQL Server issues.

In the wizard's final step, you select the items from the database you want generated into the EDM. Select all the application tables, making sure you don't select `sysdiagrams` (if it exists in your database), as shown in Figure 22-6. Click the Finish button to generate your models and the derived `DbContext`.

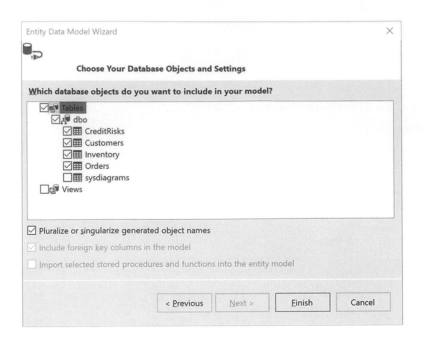

Figure 22-6. *Selecting the database items*

What Did That Do?

After you complete the wizard, you will see several new classes in your project: one for each table that you selected in the wizard and another one named `AutoLotEntities` (the same name you entered in the first step of the wizard). By default, the names of your entity classes and properties will match the original database object names. Using the data annotations listed in Table 21-5, you can change the entity names, as well as property names, to something else if needed (or wanted). Later in this chapter you will use data annotations to make some modifications to your entity classes.

■ **Note**   The Fluent API is another way to configure your model classes and properties to map them to the database. Everything you can do with data annotations, you can also do with code through the Fluent API. Because of space and time constraints, I focus on covering data annotations in this chapter with only a brief mention of the Fluent API.

Open the `Inventory` class and examine the attributes on the class and the properties. At the class level, the `Table` attribute specifies what database table the class maps to. At the property level, there are two attributes in use. The first you see is the `Key` attribute, which specifies the primary key for the table. The other attribute is `StringLength`, which specifies the string length for the database field.

■ **Note**   There are also two `SuppressMessage` attributes. This instructs static analyzers such as FXCop and the new Roslyn code analyzers to turn off the specific rules listed in the constructor. These are not covered in this chapter, and for clarity, I've removed them from the sample code.

```
[Table("Inventory")]
public partial class Inventory
{
  public Inventory()
  {
    Orders = new HashSet<Order>();
  }

  [Key]
  public int CarId { get; set; }

  [StringLength(50)]
  public string Make { get; set; }

  [StringLength(50)]
  public string Color { get; set; }

  [StringLength(50)]
  public string PetName { get; set; }

  public virtual ICollection<Order> Orders { get; set; }
}
```

You can also see that the Inventory class has a collection of Order objects and that the Order class contains a Car property. These are navigation properties and will be covered shortly.

```
public partial class Order
{
  public int OrderId { get; set; }

  public int CustId { get; set; }

  public int CarId { get; set; }

  public virtual Customer Customer { get; set; }

  public virtual Inventory Inventory { get; set; }
}
```

Next, open the AutoLotEntities class. This class derives from the DbContext class and contains a DbSet<TEntity> property for each table that you specified in the wizard. It also overrides OnModelCreating() to use FluentAPI to define the relationships between the Orders and Inventory tables.

```
public partial class AutoLotEntities : DbContext
{
  public AutoLotEntities()
    : base("name=AutoLotConnection")
  {
  }

  public virtual DbSet<CreditRisk> CreditRisks { get; set; }
  public virtual DbSet<Customer> Customers { get; set; }
  public virtual DbSet<Inventory> Inventories { get; set; }
  public virtual DbSet<Order> Orders { get; set; }
```

```
protected override void OnModelCreating(DbModelBuilder modelBuilder)
{
    modelBuilder.Entity<Inventory>()
        .HasMany(e => e.Orders)
        .WithRequired(e => e.Inventory)
        .WillCascadeOnDelete(false);
}
}
```

Finally, open the App.config file. You will see a new configSection (named entityFramework), as well as the connection string generated by the wizard. Most of this you can ignore, but if you change the database location, you will need to modify the connection string to the new database.

```
<configuration>
  <configSections>
    <!-- For more information on Entity Framework configuration, visit http://go.microsoft.
    com/fwlink/?LinkID=237468 -->
    <section name="entityFramework" type="System.Data.Entity.Internal.ConfigFile.
    EntityFrameworkSection, EntityFramework, Version=6.0.0.0, Culture=neutral, PublicKeyToke
    n=b77a5c561934e089" requirePermission="false" />
  </configSections>
  <startup>
    <supportedRuntime version="v4.0" sku=".NETFramework,Version=v4.6" />
  </startup>
  <entityFramework>
    <defaultConnectionFactory type="System.Data.Entity.Infrastructure.SqlConnectionFactory,
    EntityFramework" />
    <providers>
      <provider invariantName="System.Data.SqlClient" type="System.Data.Entity.SqlServer.
      SqlProviderServices, EntityFramework.SqlServer" />
    </providers>
  </entityFramework>
  <connectionStrings>
    <add name="AutoLotConnection" connectionString="data source=(localdb)\mssqllocaldb;
    initial catalog=AutoLot;integrated security=True;MultipleActiveResultSets=True;
    App=EntityFramework" providerName="System.Data.SqlClient" />
  </connectionStrings>
</configuration>
```

Changing the Default Mappings

The [Table("Inventory")] class-level data annotation maps the class to the Inventory table in the database, regardless of what the actual name of the class. Change the file name and class name (and the constructor) to Car. The [Column("PetName")] attribute maps the decorated C# property to the PetName field on the table, allowing you to change the C# property name to anything you want, for example to the name CarNickName. The updated class looks like this:

```
[Table("Inventory")]
public partial class Car
{
    public Car()
    {
```

```
      Orders = new HashSet<Order>();
  }

  [StringLength(50), Column("PetName")]
  public string CarNickName { get; set; }

  //remainder of the class not shown for brevity
}
```

Note that you will also have to change the type of the `Inventory` property to `Car` in the `Order` class. You can also change the property name, as shown here:

```
public partial class Order
{
  public virtual Car Car { get; set; }

  //remainder of the class not shown for brevity
}
```

The final change to make is to the `AutoLotEntities` class. Open the file and change the two occurrences of `Inventory` to `Car` and `DbSet<Car>` to `Cars`. The updated code is shown here:

```
public partial class AutoLotEntities : DbContext
{
  public AutoLotEntities()
    : base("name=AutoLotConnection")
  {
  }

  // Additional code removed for brevity

  public virtual DbSet<Car> Cars { get; set; }

  protected override void OnModelCreating(DbModelBuilder modelBuilder)
  {
    modelBuilder.Entity<Car>()
      .HasMany(e => e.Orders)
      .WithRequired(e => e.Car)
      .WillCascadeOnDelete(false);

    // Additional code removed for brevity
  }
}
```

Adding Features to the Generated Model Classes

All the designer-generated classes have been declared with the `partial` keyword. This is especially useful when working with the EF programming model because you can add additional methods to your entity classes that help you model your business domain better.

For example, you can override the `ToString()` method of the `Car` entity class to return the state of the entity with a well-formatted `string`. If you add this to the generated class, you risk losing that custom code

871

each time you regenerate your model classes. Instead, define the following partial class declaration in a new file named CarPartial.cs. The new class is listed here:

```
public partial class Car
{
  public override string ToString()
  {
    // Since the PetName column could be empty, supply
    // the default name of **No Name**.
    return $"{this.CarNickName ?? "**No Name**"} is a {this.Color} {this.Make} with ID
{this.CarId}.";
  }
}
```

Using the Model Classes in Code

Now that you have your model classes, you can author some code that interacts with them and therefore the database. Begin by adding the following using statements to your Program class:

```
using AutoLotConsoleApp.EF;
using AutoLotConsoleApp.Models;
using static System.Console;
```

Inserting Data

Once the entity classes and properties are mapped to the database tables and fields, when changes to the data in the DbSet<T> collections need to be persisted, EF will generate the SQL to make the changes. Adding new records is as simple as adding records to the DbSet<T> and calling SaveChanges(). You can either add one record at a time or add a range of records.

Inserting a Record

To add a new record, create a new instance of the model class, add it to the appropriate DbSet<T> property from the AutoLotEntities context class, and then call SaveChanges(). Add a helper method to the Program. cs class named AddNewRecord() with the following code:

```
  private static int AddNewRecord()
  {
    // Add record to the Inventory table of the AutoLot database.
    using (var context = new AutoLotEntities())
    {
      try
      {
        // Hard-code data for a new record, for testing.
        var car = new Car() { Make = "Yugo", Color = "Brown", CarNickName="Brownie"};
        context.Cars.Add(car);
        context.SaveChanges();
        // On a successful save, EF populates the database generated identity field.
        return car.CarId;
      }
```

```
    catch(Exception ex)
    {
      WriteLine(ex.InnerException?.Message);
      return 0;
    }
  }
}
```

This code uses the Add() method on the DbSet<Car> class. The Add() method takes an object of type Car and adds it to the Cars collection on the AutoLotEntities context class. When an object is added to a DbSet<T>, the DbChangeTracker marks the state of the new object as EntityState.Added. When SaveChanges is called on the DbContext, SQL statements are generated for all pending changes tracked in the DbChangeTracker (in this case an insert statement) and executed against the database. If there was more than one change, they would be executed within a transaction. If no errors occur, then the changes are persisted to the database, and any database-generated properties (in this case the CarId property) get updated with the values from the database.

To see this in action, update the Main() method like this:

```
static void Main(string[] args)
{
  WriteLine("***** Fun with ADO.NET EF *****\n");
  int carId = AddNewRecord();
  WriteLine(carId);
  ReadLine();
}
```

The output to the console is indeed the CarId of the new record. When new records are added (or existing records are updated), EF executes a SELECT statement for the values of database-computed columns on your behalf to get the value and populate your entity's properties.

Inserting Multiple Records

In addition to adding a single record at a time, you add multiple records in one call with the AddRange() method. This method takes an IEnumerable<T> and adds all the items in the list to the DbSet<T>.

```
private static void AddNewRecords(IEnumerable<Car> carsToAdd)
{
  using (var context = new AutoLotEntities())
  {
    context.Cars.AddRange(carsToAdd);
    context.SaveChanges();
  }
}
```

Even though all the records are now in the DbSet<T>, just like when adding one record, nothing happens to the database until SaveChanges() is called. Consider AddRange() as a convenience method. You could iterate through the collection, calling Add() for each item in the collection, and then call SaveChanges(), which ends in the same result as calling AddRange() and then SaveChanges().

Selecting Records

There are several ways to get records out of the database using EF. The simplest way to get the data from the database is to iterate over a DbSet<Car>. This is equivalent to executing the following SQL command:

```
Select * from Inventory
```

To see this in action, add a new method named PrintAllInventory() and loop through the Cars property of the DbContext, printing each car (using the overridden ToString() method), as follows:

```
private static void PrintAllInventory()
{
    // Select all items from the Inventory table of AutoLot,
    // and print out the data using our custom ToString() of the Car entity class.
    using (var context = new AutoLotEntities())
    {
    foreach (Car c in context.Cars)
      {
        WriteLine(c);
      }
    }
}
```

Behind the scenes, EF retrieves all the Inventory records from the database and, using a DataReader, creates a new instance of the Car class for each row returned from the database.

Querying with SQL from DbSet<T>

You can also use inline SQL or stored procedures to retrieve entities from the database. The caveat is that the query fields must match the properties of the class being populated. To test this, update the PrintInventory() method to the following:

```
private static void PrintAllInventory()
{
  using (var context = new AutoLotEntities())
  {
    foreach (Car c in context.Cars.SqlQuery("Select CarId,Make,Color,PetName as CarNickName
from Inventory where Make=@p0", "BMW"))
    {
      WriteLine(c);
    }
  }
}
```

The good news is that when called on a DbSet<T>, this method fills the list with tracked entities, which means that any changes or deletions will get propagated to the database when SaveChanges is called. The bad news (as you can see from the SQL text) is that SqlQuery doesn't understand the mapping changes that you made earlier. Not only do you have to use the database table and field names, but any field name changes (such as the change to PetName) must be aliased from the database field name to the model property name.

Querying with SQL from DbContext.Database

The Database property of the DbContext also has a SqlQuery method that can be used to populate DbSet<T> entities as well as objects that are not part of your model (such as a view model). Suppose you have another class (named ShortCar) that is defined as follows:

```
public class ShortCar
{
  public int CarId { get; set; }
  public string Make { get; set; }
  public override string ToString() => $"{this.Make} with ID {this.CarId}.";
}
```

You can create and populate a list of ShortCar objects with the following code:

```
foreach (ShortCar c in context.Database.SqlQuery(typeof(ShortCar),"Select CarId,Make from
Inventory"))
{
  WriteLine(c);
}
```

It's important to understand that when calling SqlQuery on the Database object, the returned classes are *never* tracked, even if the objects are defined as a DbSet<T> on your context.

Querying with LINQ

EF becomes much more powerful when you incorporate LINQ queries. Consider this update to the PrintInventory() method that uses LINQ to get the records from the database:

```
private static void PrintAllInventory()
{
    foreach (Car c in context.Cars.Where(c => c.Make == "BMW"))
    {
      WriteLine(c);
    }
}
```

The LINQ statement is translated into a SQL query similar to the following:

```
Select * from Inventory where Make = 'BMW';
```

Given that you have already worked with many LINQ expressions in Chapter 13, a few more examples will suffice for the time being.

```
private static void FunWithLinqQueries()
{
  using (var context = new AutoLotEntities())
  {
    // Get a projection of new data.
    var colorsMakes = from item in context.Cars select new { item.Color, item.Make };
    foreach (var item in colorsMakes)
```

```
    {
      WriteLine(item);
    }

    // Get only items where Color == "Black"
    var blackCars = from item in context.Cars where item.Color == "Black" select item;
    foreach (var item in blackCars)
    {
      WriteLine(item);
    }
  }
}
```

Searching with Find()

Find() is a special LINQ method, in that it first looks in the DbChangeTracker for the entity being requested and, if found, returns that instance to the calling method. If it isn't found, EF does a database call to create the requested instance.

Find() only searches by primary key (simple or complex), so you must keep that in mind when using it. An example of Find() in action looks like this:

```
WriteLine(context.Cars.Find(5));
```

The Timing of EF Query Execution

Each of the previous methods returns data from the database. It's important to understand *when* the queries execute. One of the beauties of EF is that select queries don't execute until the resulting collection is iterated over. The query will also execute once ToList() or ToArray() is called on the query. This enables chaining of calls and building up a query as well as controlling exactly when the first database call is made. However, with lazy loading, you give up control over when the queries are made on navigation properties that weren't loaded with the initial call.

Take the following updated version of the FunWithLinqQueries() method. The first two lines are setting up the query. Not until the collection is iterated over with the foreach is the database call made.

```
private static void ChainingLinqQueries()
{
  using (var context = new AutoLotEntities())
  {
    //Not executed
    DbSet<Car> allData = context.Cars;

    //Not Executed.
    var colorsMakes = from item in allData select new { item.Color, item.Make };

    //Now it's executed
    foreach (var item in colorsMakes)
    {
      WriteLine(item);
    }
  }
}
```

The Role of Navigation Properties

As the name suggests, *navigation properties* allow you to find related data in other entities without having to author complex JOIN queries. In SQL Server, navigation properties are represented by foreign key relationships. To account for these foreign key relationships in EF, each class in your model contains virtual properties that connect your classes together. For example, in the Inventory.cs class, the Orders property is defined as virtual ICollection<Order>.

```
public virtual ICollection<Order> Orders { get; set; }
```

This tells EF that each Inventory database record (renamed to the Car class in the examples) can have zero to many Order records.

On the other side of the equation, the Order model has a one-to-one relationship with the Inventory (Car) record. The Order model navigates back to the Inventory model through another virtual property of type Inventory.

```
public virtual Car Car { get; set; }
```

In SQL Server, foreign keys are properties that tie tables together. In this example, the Orders table has a foreign key named CarId. In the Orders model, this is represented by the following property:

```
public int CarId { get; set; }
```

■ **Note**   If the CarId foreign key were a nullable int, then it would have a zero-to-one relationship.

By convention, if EF finds a property named <Class>Id, then it will be used as the foreign key for a navigation property of type <Class>. As with any other name of classes and properties, this can be changed. For example, if you wanted to name the property Foo, you would update the class to this:

```
public partial class Order
{
  [Column("CarId")]
  public int Foo { get; set; }
  [ForeignKey(nameof(Foo))]
//rest of the class omitted for brevity
}
```

Lazy, Eager, and Explicit Loading

Loading data from the database into entity classes can happen three different ways: lazy, eager, and explicit. Lazy and eager loading are based on settings on the context, and the third, explicit, is developer controlled.

Lazy Loading

Lazy loading means that EF loads the direct object(s) requested but replaces any navigation properties with proxies. The virtual modifier allows the proxy assignment to the navigation properties. If any of the properties on a navigation property are requested in code, EF creates a new database call, executes it, and populates the object's details. For example, if you had the following code, EF would call one query to get all the Cars and then for each Car execute another query to get all the Orders for each car:

877

```
using (var context = new AutoLotEntities())
{
  foreach (Car c in context.Cars)
  {
    foreach (Order o in c.Orders)
    {
      WriteLine(o.OrderId);
    }
  }
}
```

While it is a plus to only load the data you need, you can see from the previous example that it might become a performance nightmare if you aren't careful about how lazy loading is utilized. You can turn off lazy loading by setting the LazyLoadingEnabled property on the DbContext configuration, like this:

```
context.Configuration.LazyLoadingEnabled = false;
```

If you know that you need to orders for each car, then you should consider using eager loading, covered next.

Eager Loading

When you know you want to load related records for an object, writing multiple queries against a relational database is inefficient. The prudent database developer would write one query utilizing SQL joins to get the related data. Eager loading does just that for C# developers using EF. For example, if you knew you needed all Cars and all of their related Orders, you would change the previous code to this:

```
using (var context = new AutoLotEntities())
{
  foreach (Car c in context.Cars.Include(c=>c.Orders))
  {
    foreach (Order o in c.Orders)
    {
      WriteLine(o.OrderId);
    }
  }
}
```

The Include() LINQ method informs EF to create a SQL statement that joins the tables together, just as you would if you were writing the SQL yourself. The resulting query executed against the database now resembles this:

```
SELECT
    [Project1].[CarId] AS [CarId],
    [Project1].[Make] AS [Make],
    [Project1].[Color] AS [Color],
    [Project1].[PetName] AS [PetName],
    [Project1].[C1] AS [C1],
    [Project1].[OrderId] AS [OrderId],
    [Project1].[CustId] AS [CustId],
    [Project1].[CarId1] AS [CarId1]
    FROM ( SELECT
```

```
      [Extent1].[CarId] AS [CarId],
      [Extent1].[Make] AS [Make],
      [Extent1].[Color] AS [Color],
      [Extent1].[PetName] AS [PetName],
      [Extent2].[OrderId] AS [OrderId],
      [Extent2].[CustId] AS [CustId],
      [Extent2].[CarId] AS [CarId1],
      CASE WHEN ([Extent2].[OrderId] IS NULL) THEN CAST(NULL AS int) ELSE 1 END AS [C1]
      FROM  [dbo].[Inventory] AS [Extent1]
      LEFT OUTER JOIN [dbo].[Orders] AS [Extent2] ON [Extent1].[CarId] = [Extent2].[CarId]
   )  AS [Project1]
   ORDER BY [Project1].[CarId] ASC, [Project1].[C1] ASC
```

The exact syntax of the query doesn't really matter; I've shown it to demonstrate that all Cars and their related Orders are getting retrieved in one call to the database.

Explicit Loading

The final way to load records is through explicit loading. Explicit loading allows you to explicitly load a collection or class at the end of a navigation property. To get the related object(s), you use the Collection() (for collections) or Reference() (for single objects) methods of context to choose what to load and then call Load(). The following code shows both methods in action:

```
context.Configuration.LazyLoadingEnabled = false;
foreach (Car c in context.Cars)
{
    context.Entry(c).Collection(x => x.Orders).Load();
    foreach (Order o in c.Orders)
    {
        WriteLine(o.OrderId);
    }
}
foreach (Order o in context.Orders)
{
  context.Entry(o).Reference(x => x.Car).Load();
}
```

Which data access model you use depends on the needs of your project. If you leave lazy loading enabled (the default setting), then you have to be careful that your application doesn't become too chatty. If you turn it off, you need to make sure you load related data before trying to use it.

Deleting Data

Deleting records from the database can be done using the DbSet<T> (conceptually the same as adding records) but can also be done using EntityState. You will see both of these approaches in action in the next sections.

Deleting a Single Record

One way to delete a single record is to locate the correct item in the DbSet<T> and then call DbSet<T>. Remove(), passing in that instance. Calling the Remove method removes the item from the collection and sets the EntityState to EntityState.Deleted. Even though it's removed from the DbSet<T>, it's not removed from the context (or the database) until SaveChanges() is called.

One catch in this process is that the instance to be removed must already be tracked (in other words, loaded into the DbSet<T>). One common pattern is used in MVC (covered later in this book), where the primary key of the item to be deleted is passed into the Delete action. This item is retrieved using Find(), then removed from the DbSet<T> with Remove(), and then persisted to the database with SaveChanges(), as in the following example:

```
private static void RemoveRecord(int carId)
{
  // Find a car to delete by primary key.
  using (var context = new AutoLotEntities())
  {
    // See if we have it.
    Car carToDelete = context.Cars.Find(carId);
    if (carToDelete != null)
    {
      context.Cars.Remove(carToDelete);
      //This code is purely demonstrative to show the entity state changed to Deleted
      if (context.Entry(carToDelete).State != EntityState.Deleted)
      {
        throw new Exception("Unable to delete the record");
      }
      context.SaveChanges();
    }
  }
}
```

■ **Note** Calling Find() before deleting a record requires an extra round-trip to the database. First you pull the record back and then delete it. Deleting data can also be accomplished by changing the EntityState, which will be covered shortly.

Deleting Multiple Records

You can also remove multiple records at once by using RemoveRange() on the DbSet<T>. Just like the Remove() method, the items to be removed must be tracked.

The RemoveRange() method takes an IEnumerable<T> as a parameter, as shown in the following example:

```
private static void RemoveMultipleRecords(IEnumerable<Car> carsToRemove)
{
  using (var context = new AutoLotEntities())
  {
    //Each record must be loaded in the DbChangeTracker
    context.Cars.RemoveRange(carsToRemove);
    context.SaveChanges();
  }
}
```

Remember, though, that nothing happens to the database until SaveChanges() is called.

Deleting a Record Using EntityState

The final way to delete a record is by using EntityState. You start by creating a new instance of the item to be deleted, assigning the primary key to the new instance, and setting the EntityState to EntityState. Deleted. This adds the item to the DbChangeTracker for you, so when SaveChanges() is called, the record is deleted. Note that the record didn't have to be queried from the database first. The following code demonstrates this:

```
private static void RemoveRecordUsingEntityState(int carId)
{
  using (var context = new AutoLotEntities())
  {
    Car carToDelete = new Car() { CarId = carId };
    context.Entry(carToDelete).State = EntityState.Deleted;
    try
    {
      context.SaveChanges();
    }
    catch (DbUpdateConcurrencyException ex)
    {
      WriteLine(ex);
    }
  }
}
```

You gain performance (since you are not making an extra call to the database), but you lose the validation that the object exists in the database (if that matters to your scenario). If the CarId does not exist in the database, EF will throw a DbUpdateConcurrencyException in the System.Data.Entity. Infrastructure namespace. The DbUpdateConcurrencyException is covered in detail later in this chapter.

■ **Note**   If an instance with the same primary key is already being tracked, this method will fail, since you can't have two of the same entities with the same primary key being tracked by the DbChangeTracker.

Updating a Record

Updating a record pretty much follows the same pattern. Locate the object you want to change, set new property values on the returned entity, and save the changes, like so:

```
private static void UpdateRecord(int carId)
{
  // Find a car to delete by primary key.
  using (var context = new AutoLotEntities())
  {
    // Grab the car, change it, save!
    Car carToUpdate = context.Cars.Find(carId);
    if (carToUpdate != null)
    {
      WriteLine(context.Entry(carToUpdate).State);
      carToUpdate.Color = "Blue";
      WriteLine(context.Entry(carToUpdate).State);
```

```
      context.SaveChanges();
    }
  }
}
```

Handling Database Changes

In this section, you created an EF solution that started with an existing database. This works great, for example, when your organization has dedicated DBAs and you are provided with a database that you don't control. As your database changes over time, all you need to do is run the wizard again and re-create your `AutoLotEntities` class; the model classes will be rebuilt for you as well. Make sure that any additions to the model classes are done using partial classes; otherwise, you will lose your work when you rerun the wizard.

This initial example should go a long way toward helping you understand the nuts and bolts of working with the Entity Framework.

■ **Source Code**   You can find the AutoLotConsoleApp example in the `Chapter 22` subdirectory.

Creating the AutoLot Data Access Layer

In the previous section, you used a wizard to create the entities and context from an existing database. EF can also create your database for you based on your model classes and derived `DbContext` class. In addition to creating the initial database, EF enables you to use migrations to update your database to match any model changes. Even better, you can use the wizard to create your initial models and context and then switch to a C#-centric approach and use migrations to keep your database in sync.

■ **Note**   This is the version of `AutoLotDAL.dll` that will carry forward for the rest of the book.

To get started, create a new Class Library project named AutoLotDAL. Delete the default class that was created and add two folders, named `EF` and `Models`. Add the Entity Framework to the project using NuGet. Right-click the project name and click Manage NuGet Packages. You didn't need to explicitly add EF to the previous example because the wizard took care of that for you. Once the NuGet Package Manager loads, enter **EntityFramework** in the search box, select the EntityFramework package, and click Install, as shown in Figure 22-7.

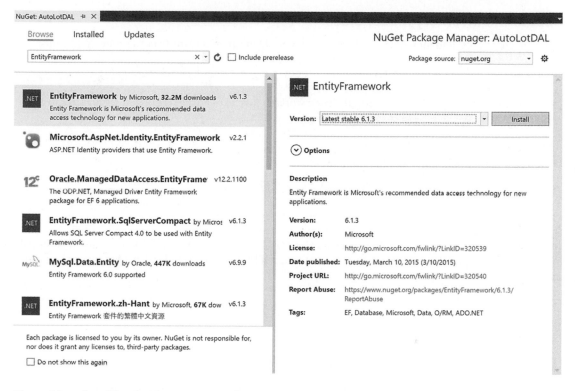

Figure 22-7. *Installing the Entity Framework into the project*

Accept the changes and the license agreement, and the Entity Framework (version 6.1.3 at the time of this writing) will be installed into your project.

Adding the Model Classes

Start by copying the models (Car.cs, CarPartial.cs, CreditRisk.cs, Customer.cs, and Order.cs) from the AutoLotConsoleApp project into the Models folder of the new app. Correct all of the namespaces (by changing them to AutoLotDAL.Models) and revert the changes from the last section:

- Change the Car class, constructor, and file names back to Inventory.

- Change the CarPartial file name to InventoryPartial, and name the class name Inventory.

- Change the Car type to Inventory in the Order class.

- Return the Inventory.CarNickName property name to PetName.

- Update the ToString() method in the Inventory partial class to use PetName.

- Change Foo back to CarId in the Order class.

Update the Inventory Model Class

Open Inventory.cs, and move the initialization of the HashSet<Order> to the Orders property, like this:

```
public virtual ICollection<Order> Orders { get; set; } = new HashSet<Order>();
```

This doesn't change anything in how the code works; it just takes advantage of new C# features to clean up the code.

Update the InventoryPartial Class

Import the following namespace into the InventoryPartial.cs file:

```
using System.ComponentModel.DataAnnotations.Schema;
```

Add a calculated field that combines the Make and Color of the car. This is a field that is not to be stored in the database or populated when an object is materialized from the data reader. The [NotMapped] attribute informs EF that this is a .NET-only property.

```
[NotMapped]
public string MakeColor => $"{Make} + ({Color})";
```

Update the Customer Model Class

Open the Customer.cs class and move the creation of the new HashSet<Order> to the property like this:

```
public virtual ICollection<Order> Orders { get; set; } = new HashSet<Order>();
```

Next, add a .NET-only field to return the FullName of the Customer, like this:

```
[NotMapped]
public string FullName => FirstName + " " + LastName;
```

Update the DbContext

Copy the AutoLotEntities class from the previous project into the EF folder of the current project. Update the namespace and change DbSet<Car> to DbSet<Inventory>. Also, change Car to Inventory in the OnModelCreating method.

Update the App.config File

Open the App.config file and look at the changes that were made by NuGet when you installed the EntityFramework package. Most of them should look familiar to you. What's missing is the connection string, so add that into the App.Config file like this:

```
<connectionStrings>
  <add name="AutoLotConnection" connectionString="data source=(LocalDb)\MSSQLLocalDB;
  initial catalog=AutoLot;integrated security=True;MultipleActiveResultSets=True;
  App=EntityFramework" providerName="System.Data.SqlClient" />
</connectionStrings>
```

■ **Note**   You might be wondering what you just did since you were just re-creating what the reverse engineering of the database created in the previous section. What you did was save a lot of typing and printed pages. The situation you are replicating is one where the database does not yet exist, so everything is created in C# code first and then (as you will soon see) migrated to the database. I just happened to have good code lying around that saves me time and space in an already long chapter.

Initializing the Database

A powerful EF feature is the ability to make sure the database matches the model as well as initializes the database with data. This is especially handy during development and testing since the process can restore the database to a known state before each run of your code. There are two classes that you can derive from to turn this feature on: DropCreateDatabaseIfModelChanges<TContext> and DropCreateDatabaseAlways<TContext>

Start by creating a new class in the EF directory named MyDataInitializer. Make the class public and inherit DropCreateDatabaseAlways<AutoLotEntities>. Add the following using statement:

```
using AutoLotDAL.Models;
```

Next, add an override for the Seed() method, like this:

```
public class MyDataInitializer : DropCreateDatabaseAlways<AutoLotEntities>
{
  protected override void Seed(AutoLotEntities context)
  {
    base.See(context);
  }
}
```

The DropCreateDatabaseAlways class is a generic class that gets typed for a DbContext class, in this case, the AutoLotEntities class. As the name implies, it will drop and re-create the database every time the initializer is executed. There is also a DropCreateDatabaseIfModelChanges<TContext> class that drops and re-creates the database when there are changes in the model.

Executing an Upsert

Upsert is a term that is a combination of *update* and *insert* and is supported by EF with the AddOrUpdate() method on the DbSet<T>. The method takes a lambda expression to specify what defines the uniqueness of each record and then the list of objects to upsert. If the record exists (based on the uniqueness key) in the database, it will be updated. If it doesn't exist, it will be inserted. Here is an example of an upsert for the Inventory class that checks for the Main and Color of each car before inserting the records:

```
context.Cars.AddOrUpdate(x=>new {x.Make,x.Color},car);
```

Seeding the Database

The Seed() method in both of the initialization classes is used to populate the database. By using the AddOrUpdate() method, you can make sure that your database is restored to the same state without duplicating data.

Here is an example of how to seed the database with the same records you used in the previous chapter:

```
protected override void Seed(AutoLotEntities context)
{
  var customers = new List<Customer>
  {
    new Customer {FirstName = "Dave", LastName = "Brenner"},
    new Customer {FirstName = "Matt", LastName = "Walton"},
    new Customer {FirstName = "Steve", LastName = "Hagen"},
    new Customer {FirstName = "Pat", LastName = "Walton"},
    new Customer {FirstName = "Bad", LastName = "Customer"},
  };
  customers.ForEach(x => context.Customers.AddOrUpdate(
    c=>new {c.FirstName, c.LastName},x));
  var cars = new List<Inventory>
  {
    new Inventory {Make = "VW", Color = "Black", PetName = "Zippy"},
    new Inventory {Make = "Ford", Color = "Rust", PetName = "Rusty"},
    new Inventory {Make = "Saab", Color = "Black", PetName = "Mel"},
    new Inventory {Make = "Yugo", Color = "Yellow", PetName = "Clunker"},
    new Inventory {Make = "BMW", Color = "Black", PetName = "Bimmer"},
    new Inventory {Make = "BMW", Color = "Green", PetName = "Hank"},
    new Inventory {Make = "BMW", Color = "Pink", PetName = "Pinky"},
    new Inventory {Make = "Pinto", Color = "Black", PetName = "Pete"},
    new Inventory {Make = "Yugo", Color = "Brown", PetName = "Brownie"},
  };
  context.Inventory.AddOrUpdate(x=>new {x.Make,x.Color},cars.ToArray());
  var orders = new List<Order>
  {
    new Order {Inventory= cars[0], Customer = customers[0]},
    new Order {Inventory= cars[1], Customer = customers[1]},
    new Order {Inventory= cars[2], Customer = customers[2]},
    new Order {Inventory= cars[3], Customer = customers[3]},
  };
  orders.ForEach(x => context.Orders.AddOrUpdate(c=>new{c.CarId,c.CustId},x));
  context.CreditRisks.AddOrUpdate(x=>new {x.FirstName,x.LastName},
    new CreditRisk
      {
        CustID = customers[4].CustID,
        FirstName = customers[4].FirstName,
        LastName = customers[4].LastName,
      });
}
```

The last step is to set the initializer, with the following code (which you will add in the next section):

```
Database.SetInitializer(new MyDataInitializer());
```

Test-Driving AutoLotDAL

The test-drive code is similar to what you did in the prior version of AutoLotDal.dll. Later in the chapter you will update this to use custom repositories, but for now, you need to test the data initialization and seed code. Start by adding a new Console Application project named AutoLotTestDrive to the solution and set this project as the startup project. Add EF to the project through NuGet, and update connectionStrings in App.config to the following:

```
<connectionStrings>
  <add name="AutoLotConnection" connectionString="data source=(localdb)\mssqllocadb;
  initial catalog=AutoLot;integrated security=True;MultipleActiveResultSets=True;
  App=EntityFramework" providerName="System.Data.SqlClient" />
</connectionStrings>
```

Add a reference to the AutoLotDAL project. Open Program.cs and add the following using statements:

```
using AutoLotDAL.EF;
using AutoLotDAL.Models;
```

Now, add the following code to the Main() method:

```
static void Main(string[] args)
{
  Database.SetInitializer(new MyDataInitializer());
  Console.WriteLine("***** Fun with ADO.NET EF Code First *****\n");

  using (var context = new AutoLotEntities())
  {
    foreach (Inventory c in context.Inventory)
    {
      Console.WriteLine(c);
    }
  }
  Console.ReadLine();
}
```

The SetInitializer() method drops and re-creates the database and then runs the Seed() method to populate the database. While this is pretty much what you accomplished in the previous section, the real power comes with EF migrations, covered next.

Entity Framework Migrations

Once you deploy your app to production, you can't keep dropping the database every time your users run the app. If your model changes, you need to keep your database in sync. This is where EF migrations come into play. Before creating your first migration, you are going to make some changes to illustrate the problem. Start by opening Program.cs and comment out the following line:

```
Database.SetInitializer(new MyDataInitializer());
```

■ **Note** As discussed earlier, the data initializer drops and re-creates the database, either each time the app runs or when the model changes. If you don't comment out the SetInitializer line, this next section won't work for you.

Create the Initial Migration

Each time a context is created and used to do database operations, it checks for the existence of the __MigrationHistory table. If the table exists, the context checks for the most recent record in the table and compares a hash of the current EF model to the most recent hash stored in the table. If the values are different, then EF will throw an exception.

■ **Note** When you create your model from an existing database, the __MigrationHistory table does *not* get created. Why does it matter? When your DbContext class is instantiated and before the first call to the database from your custom code, EF checks the migration history. Since this table doesn't exist, there are a series of exceptions generated and swallowed by the framework. As you well know, exceptions can be expensive operations, and this can potentially cause a performance issue. Even if you don't ever plan on using migrations, you should enable migrations as covered in the next section.

Enable Migrations

Start by deleting the AutoLot database by using the Object Explorer in SSMS. Next, enable migrations for your project. To do this, open the Package Manager Console (the command-line tool for managing NuGet packages) by selecting View ➤ Other Windows ➤ Package Manager Console. Make sure Default Project is set to AutoLotDAL and enter enable-migrations, as shown in Figure 22-8.

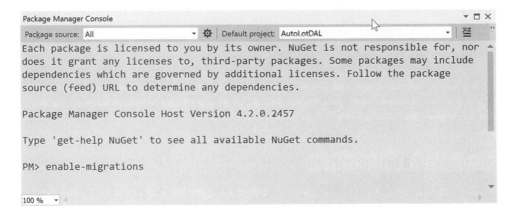

Figure 22-8. *Enabling migrations on AutoLotDAL*

You will see a message that states "Checking if the context targets an existing database...." You will see that a Migrations folder is created with one class named Configuration.cs.

Examine the `Configuration.cs` class. The code in the constructor instructs EF to disable automatic migrations (which is the setting you will use most of the time since you want to have control over how migrations work). The `Seed()` method enables you to add data to the database just like the `Seed()` method in the database initializer.

```
internal sealed class Configuration : DbMigrationsConfiguration<AutoLotDAL.
EF.AutoLotEntities>
{
  public Configuration()
  {
    AutomaticMigrationsEnabled = false;
  }

  protected override void Seed(AutoLotDAL.EF.AutoLotEntities context)
  {
  }
}
```

Create the Initial Migration

In the Package Manager Console, enter the following:

```
Add-migration Initial
```

This creates an additional file in the `Migrations` folder named similar to `201707262033409_Initial.cs`. The name of the file starts with the date and CPU time, which is followed by the name of the migration. This naming format enables EF to run migrations in the correct chronological order (if more than one exists).

Open the `201707262033409_Initial.cs` class. Take note of the two methods, one named `Up()` and the other `Down()`. The `Up()` method is for applying the changes to the database, and the `Down()` method is used to roll back the changes. When you apply a migration, any earlier migrations that have not been applied get applied by running the `Up()` methods, and any later migrations are rolled back automatically using the `Down()` methods.

Update the Database

To update the database, enter the following in the Package Manager Console:

```
update-database
```

This creates the database and the tables, as well as the `__MIgrationHistory` table. It adds a row for the migration just applied.

MigrationId	ContextKey	Model	ProductVersion
201707262033409_Initial	AutoLotDAL.Migrations.Configuration	0x1F8B08000000...	6.1.3-40302

Now that the database and the model are in sync, you can safely start updating the model.

Update the Model

There are several changes that you want to make to the model. Once those are complete, you will create another migration to sync up the database.

Adding EntityBase

Your models are not consistent with the names of their primary keys, and that is something you want to change. You are going to change all of the primary key fields to the name of Id and push the Id fields into a base class. Start by creating a new folder named Base in the Models folder. Add a new class named EntityBase.cs. Update the code to the following (note the using statements):

```
using System.ComponentModel.DataAnnotations;

namespace AutoLotDAL.Models.Base
{
  public class EntityBase
  {
    [Key]
    public int Id { get; set; }
  }
}
```

Update all the model classes to inherit from EntityBase, remove the primary key fields, and update the foreign key names in the Order class. I've also updated the navigation properties on the Order class using the ForeignKey data annotation. Here is the updated Order class:

```
public partial class Order : EntityBase
{
  public int CustomerId { get; set; }
  public int CarId { get; set; }
  [ForeignKey(nameof(CustomerId))]
  public virtual Customer Customer { get; set; }
  [ForeignKey(nameof(CarId))]
  public virtual Inventory Car { get; set; }
}
```

You will also need to fix the build errors in MyDataInitializer.

Adding a TimeStamp Property

Another change to make is to add concurrency checking to the database. To do this, you will add a Timestamp property to all your tables using the Timestamp data annotation. Update the EntityBase class to the following:

```
public class EntityBase
{
  [Key]
  public int Id { get; set; }
  [Timestamp]
  public byte[] Timestamp { get; set; }
}
```

The Timestamp data annotation maps the field to the SQL Server RowVersion data type, which in C# is represented as a byte[]. This field will now participate in concurrency checking, covered shortly.

Update the Credit Risk Class

Finally, you are going to create a unique index on the FirstName and LastName properties using data annotations. Since this is a complex key, you also need to specify a name for the index and the order for each column in the index. In this example, the index name is IDX_CreditRisk_Name, and the column order for the index is LastName and then FirstName, and the index is created as unique. Add the following using statement:

```
using System.ComponentModel.DataAnnotations.Schema;
```

Finally, update the class to the following:

```
public partial class CreditRisk : EntityBase
{
  [StringLength(50)]
  [Index("IDX_CreditRisk_Name",IsUnique = true,Order=2)]
  public string FirstName { get; set; }
  [StringLength(50)]
  [Index("IDX_CreditRisk_Name", IsUnique = true, Order = 1)]
  public string LastName { get; set; }
}
```

Create the Final Migration

Now that the model is updated, it's time to create the final migration for the example. In the Package Manager Console, enter the following:

```
Add-migration Final
```

This creates an additional file in the Migrations folder named 201707262025040_Final.cs.
If you run the migration now, you will encounter some errors. After all, the process is not perfect! You need to make a slight modification to the Up() method. Move the last four lines up to the location in bold.

```
public override void Up()
{
  DropForeignKey("dbo.Orders", "CarId", "dbo.Inventory");
  DropForeignKey("dbo.Orders", "CustId", "dbo.Customers");
  RenameColumn(table: "dbo.Orders", name: "CustId", newName: "CustomerId");
  RenameIndex(table: "dbo.Orders", name: "IX_CustId", newName: "IX_CustomerId");
  DropPrimaryKey("dbo.Inventory");
  DropPrimaryKey("dbo.Orders");
  DropPrimaryKey("dbo.Customers");
  DropPrimaryKey("dbo.CreditRisks");
  DropColumn("dbo.Inventory", "CarId");
  DropColumn("dbo.Orders", "OrderId");
  DropColumn("dbo.Customers", "CustID");
  DropColumn("dbo.CreditRisks", "CustID");
  AddColumn("dbo.Inventory", "Id", c => c.Int(nullable: false, identity: true));
  AddColumn("dbo.Orders", "Id", c => c.Int(nullable: false, identity: true));
  AddColumn("dbo.Customers", "Id", c => c.Int(nullable: false, identity: true));
  AddColumn("dbo.CreditRisks", "Id", c => c.Int(nullable: false, identity: true));
  AddPrimaryKey("dbo.Inventory", "Id");
```

```
        AddPrimaryKey("dbo.Orders", "Id");
        AddPrimaryKey("dbo.Customers", "Id");
        AddPrimaryKey("dbo.CreditRisks", "Id");
        CreateIndex("dbo.CreditRisks", new[] { "LastName", "FirstName" }, unique: true, name:
        "IDX_CreditRisk_Name");
        AddForeignKey("dbo.Orders", "CarId", "dbo.Inventory", "Id");
        AddForeignKey("dbo.Orders", "CustomerId", "dbo.Customers", "Id", cascadeDelete: true);
        //DropColumn("dbo.Inventory", "CarId");
        //DropColumn("dbo.Orders", "OrderId");
        //DropColumn("dbo.Customers", "CustID");
        //DropColumn("dbo.CreditRisks", "CustID");
    }
```

You will also have to update the Down() method, as follows:

```
public override void Down()
{
    DropForeignKey("dbo.Orders", "CustomerId", "dbo.Customers");
    DropForeignKey("dbo.Orders", "CarId", "dbo.Inventory");
    DropPrimaryKey("dbo.CreditRisks");
    DropPrimaryKey("dbo.Customers");
    DropPrimaryKey("dbo.Orders");
    DropPrimaryKey("dbo.Inventory");
    DropColumn("dbo.CreditRisks", "Id");
    DropColumn("dbo.Customers", "Id");
    DropColumn("dbo.Orders", "Id");
    DropColumn("dbo.Inventory", "Id");
    AddColumn("dbo.CreditRisks", "CustID", c => c.Int(nullable: false, identity: true));
    AddColumn("dbo.Customers", "CustID", c => c.Int(nullable: false, identity: true));
    AddColumn("dbo.Orders", "OrderId", c => c.Int(nullable: false, identity: true));
    AddColumn("dbo.Inventory", "CarId", c => c.Int(nullable: false, identity: true));
    //DropForeignKey("dbo.Orders", "CustomerId", "dbo.Customers");
    //DropForeignKey("dbo.Orders", "CarId", "dbo.Inventory");
    DropIndex("dbo.CreditRisks", "IDX_CreditRisk_Name");
    //DropPrimaryKey("dbo.CreditRisks");
    //DropPrimaryKey("dbo.Customers");
    //DropPrimaryKey("dbo.Orders");
    //DropPrimaryKey("dbo.Inventory");
    //DropColumn("dbo.CreditRisks", "Id");
    //DropColumn("dbo.Customers", "Id");
    //DropColumn("dbo.Orders", "Id");
    //DropColumn("dbo.Inventory", "Id");
    AddPrimaryKey("dbo.CreditRisks", "CustID");
    AddPrimaryKey("dbo.Customers", "CustID");
    AddPrimaryKey("dbo.Orders", "OrderId");
    AddPrimaryKey("dbo.Inventory", "CarId");
    RenameIndex(table: "dbo.Orders", name: "IX_CustomerId", newName: "IX_CustId");
    RenameColumn(table: "dbo.Orders", name: "CustomerId", newName: "CustId");
    AddForeignKey("dbo.Orders", "CustId", "dbo.Customers", "CustID", cascadeDelete: true);
    AddForeignKey("dbo.Orders", "CarId", "dbo.Inventory", "CarId");
}
```

Update the database again using the Package Manager Console. The final task is to update the database. Type update-database in the Package Manager Console, and you will get a message that the migration has been applied.

Seeding the Database

Copy the Seed() code from MyDataInitializer into the Seed() method of the Configure.cs class. Use the Package Manager Console to update the database again, and the Seed() method executes, populating the database with data.

Adding Repositories for Code Reuse

A common design pattern for data access is the Repository pattern. As described by Martin Fowler, the core of this pattern is to mediate between the domain and data mapping layers.

■ **Note**   This next section is not meant to be (nor does it pretend to be) a literal interpretation of Mr. Fowler's design pattern. If you are interested in the original pattern that motivated my code, you can find more information on the repository pattern on Martin Fowler's web site at www.martinfowler.com/eaaCatalog/ repository.html.

Adding the IRepo Interface

My version of the pattern starts with an interface that exposes the vast majority of the standard methods you will use in a data access library. Start by adding a new folder in the AutoLotDAL project named Repos. Add a new interface into the Repos folder named IRepo. Update the using statements to the following:

```
using System.Collections.Generic;
```

The full interface is listed here:

```
public interface IRepo<T>
{
    int Add(T entity);
    int AddRange(IList<T> entities);
    int Save(T entity);
    int Delete(int id, byte[] timeStamp)
    int Delete(T entity);
    T GetOne(int? id);
    List<T> GetAll();

    List<T> ExecuteQuery(string sql);
    List<T> ExecuteQuery(string sql, object[] sqlParametersObjects);
}
```

Adding the BaseRepo

Next, add another class to the Repos directory named BaseRepo. This class will implement the IRepo interface and provide the core functionality for type-specific repos (coming next). Update the using statements to the following:

```
using System;
using System.Collections.Generic;
using System.Data.Entity;
using System.Data.Entity.Infrastructure;
using System.Linq;
using AutoLotDAL.EF;
using AutoLotDAL.Models.Base;
```

Make the class public and implement IRepo and IDisposable. In the constructor, create a new instance of AutoLotEntities and set it to a class-level variable. The Set<T> method points to the property on the context that is of the same type as T, such as the Cars property, and is accessible via Set<Inventory>. Also add a protected property to expose the context to derived classes. The code is shown here:

```
public class BaseRepo<T> : IDisposable,IRepo<T> where T:EntityBase, new()
{
    private readonly DbSet<T> _table;
    private readonly AutoLotEntities _db;
    public BaseRepo()
    {
        _db = new AutoLotEntities();
        _table = _db.Set<T>();
    }
    protected AutoLotEntities Context => _db;

    public void Dispose()
    {
        _db?.Dispose();
    }
}
```

Implement the SaveChanges() Helper Methods

Next, add a method to wrap the context's SaveChanges() method. There is typically a significant amount of code and error handling code associated with calling these methods, and it is best to write that code only once and place it in the base class. The exception handlers for the SaveChanges() method on the DbContext are stubbed out. In a production application, you would need to handle any exceptions accordingly.

```
internal int SaveChanges()
{
  try
  {
    return _db.SaveChanges();
  }
  catch (DbUpdateConcurrencyException ex)
  {
```

```
    //Thrown when there is a concurrency error
    //for now, just rethrow the exception
    throw;
  }
  catch (DbUpdateException ex)
  {
    //Thrown when database update fails
    //Examine the inner exception(s) for additional
    //details and affected objects
    //for now, just rethrow the exception
    throw;
  }
  catch (CommitFailedException ex)
  {
    //handle transaction failures here
    //for now, just rethrow the exception
    throw;
  }
  catch (Exception ex)
  {
    //some other exception happened and should be handled
    throw;
  }
}
```

■ **Note**   Creating a new instance of the DbContext can be an expensive process from a performance perspective. This is sample code that creates a new instance of AutoLotEntities with every instance of a repository. If this isn't performing as well as you like (or need), then consider using just one context class and sharing it among repositories. There isn't one absolute way to code this because every situation is different and must be customized to your particular application.

Retrieve Records

The GetOne() method wraps the Find() method of the DbSet<T>. Similarly, the GetAll() method wraps the ToList() method. The code is listed here:

```
public T GetOne(int? id) => _table.Find(id);
public virtual List<T> GetAll() => _table.ToList();
```

Retrieve Records with SQL

The last four methods of the interface to implement are the SQL string methods. They pass through the string and parameters to the DbSet<T> and are shown here:

```
public List<T> ExecuteQuery(string sql) => _table.SqlQuery(sql).ToList();
public List<T> ExecuteQuery(string sql, object[] sqlParametersObjects)
  => _table.SqlQuery(sql, sqlParametersObjects).ToList();
```

■ **Note**   You should be extremely careful running raw SQL strings against a data store, especially if the string accepts input from a user. Doing so makes your application ripe for SQL injection attacks. This book doesn't cover security, but I do want to point out the dangers of running raw SQL statements.

Add Records

The Add() methods are wrappers for the related Add() methods on the context. The advantage is encapsulating the SaveChanges() method and related error handling.

```
public int Add(T entity)
{
  _table.Add(entity);
  return SaveChanges();
}
public int AddRange(IList<T> entities)
{
  _table.AddRange(entities);
  return SaveChanges();
}
```

■ **Note**   The example code persists the changes to the database every time they are executed. You can certainly modify this code to batch up the changes.

Updating Records

For the Save() method, first set the EntityState of the entity to EntityState.Modified and then call SaveChanges(). Setting the state ensures that the context will propagate the changes to the server. The code is listed here:

```
public int Save(T entity)
{
  _db.Entry(entity).State = EntityState.Modified;
  return SaveChanges();
}
```

Deleting Records

You will add similar code for the Delete() method. If the calling code passes in an object, the generic methods in the BaseRepo set the state to EntityState.Deleted and then call SaveChanges(). If the calling code passes in a key value and a timestamp, a new object is created, the EntityState is changed to Deleted, and then SaveChanges() is called. The code is listed here:

```
public int Delete(int id, byte[] timeStamp)
{
  _db.Entry(new T() {Id = id, Timestamp = timeStamp}).State = EntityState.Deleted;
  return SaveChanges();
}
```

```
public int Delete(T entity)
{
  _db.Entry(entity).State = EntityState.Deleted;
  return SaveChanges();
}
```

Entity-Specific Repos

This design allows for entity-specific repos that provide additional functionality, such as sorted searches or eager fetching. You currently don't need any, but you will create them for future use. They all follow the same pattern: inherit from BaseRepo<T> and add custom data access methods. Here is the InventoryRepo with a customized GetAll() method as an example:

```
public class InventoryRepo : BaseRepo<Inventory>
{
  public override List<Inventory> GetAll() => Context.Inventory.OrderBy(x=>x.PetName).
ToList();
}
```

Test-Driving AutoLotDAL Take 2

Now that you have the data access layer completed, it's time to return to the AutoLotTestDrive project and write some more code.

Printing Inventory Records

Add the following code to the Main() function in Program.cs:

```
Console.WriteLine("***** Using a Repository *****\n");
using (var repo = new InventoryRepo())
{
  foreach (Inventory c in repo.GetAll())
  {
    Console.WriteLine(c);
  }
}
```

You will see the list of cars, sorted by PetName.

Adding Inventory Records

Adding new records shows the simplicity of calling EF using a repository. Add a new method, create a new Inventory record, and call Add() on the repo.

```
private static void AddNewRecord(Inventory car)
{
  // Add record to the Inventory table of the AutoLot
  // database.
```

```
  using (var repo = new InventoryRepo())
  {
    repo.Add(car);
  }
}
```

Editing Records

Saving changes to records is just as simple. Get an Inventory object, make some changes, and call Save() on the InventoryRepo class. The code is shown here:

```
private static void UpdateRecord(int carId)
{
  using (var repo = new InventoryRepo())
  {
    // Grab the car, change it, save!
    var carToUpdate = repo.GetOne(carId);
    if (carToUpdate == null) return;
    carToUpdate.Color = "Blue";
    repo.Save(carToUpdate);
  }
}
```

Deleting Records

Deleting records can be done with an entity or with the key properties of an entity, in this case the Id and Timestamp. Concurrency is covered shortly; just understand at this point that the Timestamp is required to uniquely identify a record.

```
private static void RemoveRecordByCar(Inventory carToDelete)
{
  using (var repo = new InventoryRepo())
  {
    repo.Delete(carToDelete);
  }
}
private static void RemoveRecordById(int carId, byte[] timeStamp)
{
  using (var repo = new InventoryRepo())
  {
    repo.Delete(carId, timeStamp);
  }
}
```

Concurrency

A common problem in multiuser applications is concurrency issues. Unless you program with concurrency in mind, if two users update the same record, the last one in wins. This might be perfectly fine for your application, but if not, EF and SQL Server provide a convenient mechanism for checking for concurrency clashes.

The Timestamp data annotation triggers SQL Server to create a RowVersion column. The value in this column is maintained by SQL Server and is updated any time a record is added or updated. It also changes how EF builds and runs queries that update or delete data from the database. For example, a call to delete no longer just looks for the primary key but also includes the Timestamp field in the where clause. For example, if deleting an Inventory record, the generated SQL is updated to something like this:

```
Execute NonQuery "DELETE [dbo].[Inventory] WHERE (([CarId] = @0) AND ([Timestamp] = @1))"
```

If two users retrieve the same record, update that record, and then attempt to save, the first user will successfully update since the Timestamp in their object matches the Rowversion of the record (presuming no other action happened on that record). When the second user tries to save the record, nothing will happen because the where clause fails to locate a record. This triggers a DbUpdateConcurrencyException since the number of records to be modified (or deleted) in the DbChangetracker (in this example, one record) doesn't match the number of records actually affected (in this example, zero).

DbUpdateConcurrencyException exposes an Entries collection that holds all of the entities that failed to be processed. Each entry exposes the original properties, the current properties, and (via a database call) the current database properties. The following code demonstrates this. The two instances of the InventoryRepo make sure a concurrency exception is raised.

```
private static void TestConcurrency()
{
    var repo1 = new InventoryRepo();
    //Use a second repo to make sure using a different context
    var repo2 = new InventoryRepo();
    var car1 = repo1.GetOne(1);
    var car2 = repo2.GetOne(1);
    car1.PetName = "NewName";
    repo1.Save(car1);
    car2.PetName = "OtherName";
    try
    {
        repo2.Save(car2);
    }
    catch (DbUpdateConcurrencyException ex)
    {
        var entry = ex.Entries.Single();
        var currentValues = entry.CurrentValues;
        var originalValues = entry.OriginalValues;
        var dbValues = entry.GetDatabaseValues();
        Console.WriteLine(" ******** Concurrency ***********");
        Console.WriteLine("Type\tPetName");
        Console.WriteLine($"Current:\t{currentValues[nameof(Inventory.PetName)]}");
        Console.WriteLine($"Orig:\t{originalValues[nameof(Inventory.PetName)]}");
        Console.WriteLine($"db:\t{dbValues[nameof(Inventory.PetName)]}");
    }
}
```

```
***** Concurrency *****
Type:        PetName
Current:     OtherName
Orig:        Zippy
Db:          NewName
```

What you do with this information is up to the needs of your application. EF and SQL Server provide the tools needed to detect concurrency conflicts.

Interception

The final topic in this chapter regarding EF covers interception. As you have seen in the previous examples, a lot of "magic" happens behind the scenes for the data to move from the data store into your object model, and vice versa. Interception is the process of running code at different phases of the process.

The IDbCommandInterceptor Interface

It all starts with the IDbCommandInterceptor interface, listed here:

```
public interface IDbCommandInterceptor : IDbInterceptor
{
  void NonQueryExecuted(DbCommand command, DbCommandInterceptionContext<int>
  interceptionContext);
  void NonQueryExecuting(DbCommand command, DbCommandInterceptionContext<int>
  interceptionContext);
  void ReaderExecuted(DbCommand command,
    DbCommandInterceptionContext<DbDataReader> interceptionContext);
  void ReaderExecuting(DbCommand command,
    DbCommandInterceptionContext<DbDataReader> interceptionContext);
  void ScalarExecuted(DbCommand command, DbCommandInterceptionContext<object>
  interceptionContext);
  void ScalarExecuting(DbCommand command, DbCommandInterceptionContext<object>
  interceptionContext);
}
```

As you can probably infer from the names, this interface contains methods that are called by EF just prior and just after certain events. For example, the ReaderExecuting() method is called just *before* a reader is executed, and ReaderExecuted() is called just *after* a reader is executed. For this example, you will simply write to the console in each of these methods. In a production system, the logic will be more appropriate to your requirements.

Adding Interception to AutoLotDAL

Add a new folder named Interception to the AutoLotDAL project and a new class to the folder named ConsoleWriterInterceptor. Make the class public, add System.Data.Entity.Infrastructure. Interception as a using statement, and inherit from IDbCommandInterceptor. After you implement the missing members, you code should look like this:

```
public class ConsoleWriterInterceptor : IDbCommandInterceptor
{
  public void NonQueryExecuting(DbCommand command,
    DbCommandInterceptionContext<int> interceptionContext)
  {
  }
}
```

```
    public void NonQueryExecuted(DbCommand command,
        DbCommandInterceptionContext<int> interceptionContext)
    {
    }

    public void ReaderExecuting(DbCommand command,
        DbCommandInterceptionContext<DbDataReader> interceptionContext)
    {
    }

    public void ReaderExecuted(DbCommand command,
        DbCommandInterceptionContext<DbDataReader> interceptionContext)
    {
    }

    public void ScalarExecuting(DbCommand command,
        DbCommandInterceptionContext<object> interceptionContext)
    {
    }

    public void ScalarExecuted(DbCommand command,
        DbCommandInterceptionContext<object> interceptionContext)
    {
    }
}
```

To keep the example simple, you are just going to write to the console whether the call is asynchronous and the text of the command. Add a using for static System.Console and add a private method named WriteInfo() that takes a bool and a string. The code is listed here:

```
private void WriteInfo(bool isAsync, string commandText)
{
    WriteLine($"IsAsync: {isAsync}, Command Text: {commandText}");
}
```

In each of the methods from the interface, add a call to the WriteInfo() method like this:

```
WriteInfo(interceptionContext.IsAsync,command.CommandText);
```

Registering the Interceptor

Interceptors can be registered through code or in the application configuration file. Registering them in code isolates them from changes to the configuration file and therefore ensures that they are always registered. If you need more flexibility, the configuration file might be the better choice. For this example, you are going to register the interceptor in code.

Open the AutoLotEntities.cs class and add the following using statements:

```
using System.Data.Entity.Infrastructure.Interception;
```

Next, in the constructor, add the following line of code:

```
DbInterception.Add(new ConsoleWriterInterceptor());
```

Execute one of the test methods from earlier in this chapter, and you will see the additional output from the logger written to the console. This is a simple example but illustrates the capabilities of the interceptor class.

■ **Note**   The DbCommandInterceptionContext<T> contains much more than you have explored here. Please consult the .NET Framework 4.7 SDK documentation for more information.

Adding the DatabaseLogger Interceptor

EF now ships with a built-in logging interceptor if all you want to do is simple logging. To add this capability, start by opening the AutoLotEntities.cs class and comment out your console logger. Add a static read-only member of type DatabaseLogger (in the System.Data.Entity.Infrastructure.Interception namespace). The constructor takes two parameters; the first is the file name for the log file, and the second is optional and indicates whether the log should be appended to (the default is false). In the constructor, call StartLogging() on the interceptor and add the instance to the list of interceptors. The updated code is shown here:

```
static readonly DatabaseLogger DatabaseLogger =
  new DatabaseLogger("sqllog.txt", true);
public AutoLotEntities() : base("name=AutoLotConnection")
{
  //DbInterception.Add(new ConsoleWriterInterceptor());
  DatabaseLogger.StartLogging();
  DbInterception.Add(DatabaseLogger);
}
```

The last change is to leverage the DbContext implementation of the IDisposable pattern to stop logging and remove the interceptor. The code is shown here:

```
protected override void Dispose(bool disposing)
{
  DbInterception.Remove(DatabaseLogger);
  DatabaseLogger.StopLogging();
  base.Dispose(disposing);
}
```

ObjectMaterialized and SavingChanges Events

Creating a custom interceptor can provide a significant amount of functionality but can also involve a lot of work. Two of the most common scenarios are handled by two of the events on the ObjectContext class, ObjectMaterialized and SavingChanges. The ObjectMaterialized event fires when an object is reconstituted from the data store, just before the instance is returned to the calling code, and the SavingChanges event occurs when the object's data is about to be propagated to the data store, just after the SaveChanges() method is called on the context.

Accessing the Object Context

The DbContext doesn't expose the Object context directly, but it does implement the IObjectContextAdapter interface, which grants access to the ObjectContext. To get to the ObjectContext, you need to cast AutoLotEntities to IObjectContextAdapter. Update the using statements to the following:

```
using System;
using System.Data.Entity;
using System.Data.Entity.Core.Objects;
using System.Data.Entity.Infrastructure;
using System.Data.Entity.Infrastructure.Interception;
using AutoLotDAL.Interception;
using AutoLotDAL.Models;
```

Next, update the constructor and add the two event handlers, like this:

```
public AutoLotEntities(): base("name=AutoLotConnection")
{
  //Interceptor code
  var context = (this as IObjectContextAdapter).ObjectContext;
  context.ObjectMaterialized += OnObjectMaterialized;
  context.SavingChanges += OnSavingChanges;
}

private void OnSavingChanges(object sender, EventArgs eventArgs)
{
}

private void OnObjectMaterialized(object sender,
System.Data.Entity.Core.Objects.ObjectMaterializedEventArgs e)
{
}
```

ObjectMaterialized

The ObjectMaterialized event's arguments provide access to the entity being reconstituted. This event fires immediately after a model's properties are populated by EF and just before the context serves it up to the calling code. While you won't use this event in this chapter, it is invaluable when working with WPF, as you will see in Chapter 28.

SavingChanges

As mentioned, the SavingChanges event fires just after the SaveChanges() method is called (on the DbContext) but before the database is updated. By accessing the ObjectContext passed into the event handler, all the entities in the transaction are accessible through the ObjectStateEntry property on the DbContext. Table 22-6 shows some of the key properties.

Table 22-6. *Key Members of* `ObjectStateEntry`

Member of DbContext	Meaning in Life
CurrentValues	The current values of the entity's properties
OriginalValues	The original values of the entity's properties
Entity	The entity represented by the `ObjectStateEntry` object
State	The current state of the entity (e.g., Modified, Added, Deleted)

The `ObjectStateEntry` also exposes a set of methods that can be used on the entity. Some of these are listed in Table 22-7.

Table 22-7. *Key Methods of* `ObjectStateEntry`

Member of DbContext	Meaning in Life
AcceptChanges	Accepts the current values as the original values
ApplyCurrentValues	Sets the current values to match those of a supplied object
ApplyOriginalValues	Sets the original values to match those of a supplied object
ChangeState	Updates the state of the entity
GetModifiedProperties	Returns the names of all changed properties
IsPropertyChanges	Checks a specific property for changes
RejectPropertyChanges	The current state of the entity (e.g. Modified, Added, Deleted)

This permits you to write code that rejects any changes to a vehicle's color if the color is red, like this:

```
private void OnSavingChanges(object sender, EventArgs eventArgs)
{
  //Sender is of type ObjectContext.  Can get current and original values, and
  //cancel/modify the save operation as desired.
  var context = sender as ObjectContext;
  if (context == null) return;
  foreach (ObjectStateEntry item in
    context.ObjectStateManager.GetObjectStateEntries(
      EntityState.Modified | EntityState.Added))
  {
    //Do something important here
    if ((item.Entity as Inventory)!=null)
    {
      var entity = (Inventory) item.Entity;
      if (entity.Color == "Red")
      {
        item.RejectPropertyChanges(nameof(entity.Color));
      }
    }
  }
}
```

Splitting the Models from the Data Access Layer

Currently, the data access layer is all in one project, with all the EF code and the models grouped together. While that is sufficient for many applications, sometimes (as you will see with WPF MMVM in Chapter 28 and ASP.NET in Chapters 29 to 30), it is better to split out the models from the EF code.

Fortunately, this is extremely simple. Add a new class library project named AutoLotDAL.Models to your solution and delete the generated Class1.cs class. Add a reference to System.ComponentModel. DataAnnotations and then use NuGet Package Manager to add EntityFramework to the project. Move all the files and folders from the Models directory of the AutoLotDAL project into the new project and adjust the namespaces. Add a reference from AutoLotDAL to AutoLotDAL.Models and add a reference from AutoLotTestDrive to AutoLotDAL.Models.

■ **Source Code**   You can find the updated AutoLotDAL example in the Chapter 22 subdirectory.

Deploying to SQL Server Express

SQL Server's LocalDb is great for development and local testing, but at some point, you will need to move your database to another instance. In this example, you will deploy your database to SQL Server Express, which is useful for development but can also be used by more than one person and supports local services (such as IIS and WCF). There are two easy ways to do this, and you will explore them both next.

■ **Note**   If you have not already installed SQL Server Express 2016, you can download the installer from here: https://www.microsoft.com/en-us/sql-server/sql-server-editions-express.

Deploying to SQL Server Express Using Migrations

Once you have your database ready to deploy to another instance of SQL Server, the first mechanism (if you have access to the instance that you are deploying to) is as simple as changing the connection string and executing update-database! Open the App.config file in AutoLotDAL and update the connection string to point to SQL Server Express. The exact string will depend on how you installed SQL Server Express, but it should look something like this:

```
<connectionStrings>
  <add name="AutoLotConnection" connectionString="data source=.\SQLEXPRESS2016;initial
catalog=AutoLot;integrated security=True;MultipleActiveResultSets=True;App=EntityFramework"
providerName="System.Data.SqlClient" />
</connectionStrings>
```

When you run update-database, you will see the updates getting applied.

You can also specify a different connection string in the update-database command. Instead of changing the connection string in the App.config file, you could run the following command in the Package Manager Console:

```
Update-Database -ProjectName AutolotDAL -ConnectionString "data source=.\SQLEXPRESS2016;
initial catalog=AutoLot;integrated security=True;MultipleActiveResultSets=True;
App=EntityFramework" -ConnectionProviderName "System.Data.SqlClient"
```

■ **Note**   There are many more options available for `update-database`. To get the full list of them (and any other EF commands), use `get-help update-database`.

Creating a Migration Script

Changing the connection string is certainly simple, but what if you don't have access to the database and everything must go through a DBA? EF has you covered for that as well. The `update-database` command can also create a SQL script to do all of the changes for you. Adding the `-script` parameter will examine the target database and create a script to any migrations that have not yet been applied. Enter the following command into the Package Manager Console (note I changed the catalog name so that a file will be produced):

```
Update-Database -ProjectName AutolotDAL -ConnectionString "data source=.\SQLEXPRESS2016;
initial catalog=AutoLot2;integrated security=True;MultipleActiveResultSets=True;
App=EntityFramework" -ConnectionProviderName "System.Data.SqlClient" -script
```

This will create a script that you can send off to your DBA to execute for you. The one downside is that when you create a script like this, the `Seed()` method of the `Configuration` class is not executed or included in the SQL script. You will have to seed the database with initial data in some other manner.

Summary

Over the past two chapters, you went on a tour of data manipulation using ADO.NET, specifically the connected layer and the Entity Framework. The Entity Framework (and other ORMS) provides value in getting projects to market faster, but it is still vital to understand the inner workings on ADO.NET. To be sure, you have only scratched the surface of all the topics found within the ADO.NET technology set. To dive deeper into any of the topics presented in this book (as well to examine a number of related items), I recommend consulting the .NET Framework 4.7 SDK documentation.

This chapter wrapped up your formal investigation of database programming using ADO.NET by examining the role of the Entity Framework. EF allows you to program against a conceptual model that closcly maps to your business domain. While you can reshape your entities in any way you choose, the EF runtime ensures that the changed data is mapped to the correct physical table data.

Along the way you learned about data annotations, which is one way to describe the mapping between your domain model and the database model. You learned about how EF handles transactions; creating, saving, and deleting data; and how entity state fits in.

You then used database migrations to keep the changes to your model in sync with the database, checked for concurrency errors, and added logging and interception.

CHAPTER 23

Introducing Windows Communication Foundation

Windows Communication Foundation (WCF) is the name of the API designed specifically for the process of building distributed systems. Unlike other specific distributed APIs you might have used in the past (e.g., DCOM, .NET remoting, XML web services, message queuing), WCF provides a single, unified, and extendable programming object model that you can use to interact with a number of previously diverse distributed technologies.

This chapter begins by framing the need for WCF and examining the problems it intends to solve. After you look at the services provided by WCF, you'll turn your attention to examining the key .NET assemblies, namespaces, and types that represent this programming model. Over the remainder of this chapter, you'll build several WCF services, hosts, and clients using various WCF development tools.

■ **Note**   In this chapter, you will author code that will require that you launch Visual Studio with administrative privileges (furthermore, you must have administrative privileges). To launch Visual Studio with the correct admin rights, right-click the Visual Studio icon and select Run As Administrator.

Choosing a Distributed API

The Windows operating system has historically provided many APIs for building distributed systems. While it is true that most people consider a *distributed system* to involve at least two networked computers, this term in the broader sense can refer to two executables that need to exchange data, even if they happen to be running on the same physical machine. Using this definition, selecting a distributed API for your current programming task typically involves asking the following pivotal question:

> *Will this system be used exclusively in house, or will external users require access to the application's functionality?*

If you build a distributed system for in-house use, you have a far greater chance of ensuring that each connected computer is running the same operating system and using the same programming framework (e.g., .NET, COM, or the Java platform). Running in-house systems also means that you can leverage your existing security system for purposes of authentication, authorization, and so forth. In this situation, you might be willing to select a particular distributed API that will tie you to a specific operating system/ programming framework for the purposes of performance.

© Andrew Troelsen and Philip Japikse 2017
A. Troelsen and P. Japikse, *Pro C# 7*, https://doi.org/10.1007/978-1-4842-3018-3_23

In contrast, if you build a system that others must reach from outside of your walls, you have a whole other set of issues to contend with. First, you will most likely *not* be able to dictate to external users which operating system(s) they can use, which programming framework(s) they can use, or how they configure their security settings.

Second, if you happen to work for a larger company or in a university setting that uses numerous operating systems and programming technologies, an in-house application suddenly faces the same challenges as an outward-facing application. In either of these cases, you need to limit yourself to a more flexible distributed API to ensure the furthest reach of your application.

Based on your answer to this key distributed computing question, the next task is to pinpoint exactly which API (or set of APIs) to use. This chapter covers WCF. Another popular choice is ASP.NET Web API (covered in Chapter 27).

■ **Note** WCF (and the technologies it encompasses) has nothing to do with building an HTML-based web site. While it is true that web applications can be considered distributed because two machines are typically involved in the exchange, WCF is about establishing connections between machines to share the functionality of remote components—not for displaying HTML in a web browser. Chapter 28 will examine building web sites with the .NET platform.

The Role of WCF

The wide array of distributed technologies makes it difficult to pick the right tool for the job. This is further complicated by the fact that several of these technologies overlap in the services they provide (most notably in the areas of transactions and security).

Even when a .NET developer has selected what appear to be the correct technologies for the task at hand, building, maintaining, and configuring such an application are complex tasks, at best. Each API has its own programming model, its own unique set of configuration tools, and so forth. Prior to WCF, this meant that it was difficult to plug and play distributed APIs without authoring a considerable amount of custom infrastructure. For example, if you build your system using the .NET remoting APIs and you later decide that XML web services are a more appropriate solution, you need to reengineer your codebase.

WCF is a distributed computing toolkit that integrates these previously independent distributed technologies into a streamlined API represented primarily by the System.ServiceModel namespace. Using WCF, you can expose services to callers using a wide variety of techniques. For example, if you build an in-house application where all connected machines are Windows-based, you can use various TCP protocols to ensure the fastest possible performance. You can also expose this same service with HTTP and SOAP to allow external callers to leverage its functionality, regardless of the programming language or operating system.

Given that WCF allows you to pick the correct protocol for the job (using a common programming model), you will find that it becomes quite easy to plug and play the underlying plumbing of your distributed application. In most cases, you can do so without having to recompile or redeploy the client/service software because the grungy details are often relegated to application configuration files.

An Overview of WCF Features

Interoperability and integration of diverse APIs are only two (important) aspects of WCF. WCF also provides a rich software fabric that complements the remoting technologies it exposes. Consider the following list of major WCF features:

- Support for strongly typed *as well as* untyped messages. This approach allows .NET applications to share custom types efficiently, while software created using other platforms (such as Java) can consume streams of loosely typed XML.

- Support for several *bindings* (e.g., raw HTTP, TCP, MSMQ, WebSockets, named pipes, and so on) allows you to choose the most appropriate plumbing to transport message data.

- Support for the latest-and-greatest web service specifications (WS-*).

- A fully integrated security model encompassing both native Windows/.NET security protocols and numerous neutral-security techniques built on web service standards.

- Support for session-like state management techniques, as well as support for one-way or stateless messages.

As impressive as this list of features might be, it only scratches the surface of the functionality WCF provides. WCF also offers tracing and logging facilities, performance counters, a publish-and-subscribe event model, and transactional support, among other features.

An Overview of Service-Oriented Architecture

Yet another benefit of WCF is that it is based on the design principles established by *service-oriented architecture* (SOA). To be sure, SOA is a major buzzword in the industry; and like most buzzwords, SOA can be defined in numerous ways. Simply put, SOA is a way to design a distributed system where several autonomous *services* work in conjunction by passing *messages* across boundaries (either networked machines or two processes on the same machine) using well-defined *interfaces*.

In the world of WCF, you typically create these well-defined interfaces using CLR interface types (see Chapter 9). In a more general sense, however, the interface of a service simply describes the set of members that might be invoked by external callers.

The team that designed WCF observed the four tenets of SOA design principles. While these tenets are typically honored automatically simply by building a WCF application, understanding these four cardinal design rules of SOA can help you understand WCF better. The sections that follow provide a brief overview of each tenet.

Tenet 1: Boundaries Are Explicit

This tenet reiterates that the functionality of a WCF service is expressed using well-defined interfaces (e.g., descriptions of each member, its parameters, and its return values). The only way that an external caller can communicate with a WCF service is through the interface, and the external caller remains blissfully unaware of the underlying implementation details.

Tenet 2: Services Are Autonomous

The term *autonomous entities* refers to the fact that a given WCF service is (as much as possible) an island unto itself. An autonomous service should be independent with regard to version, deployment, and installation issues. To help promote this tenet, you can fall back on a key aspect of interface-based programming. Once an interface is in production, it should never be changed (or you will risk breaking existing clients). When you need to extend the functionality of your WCF service, you author new interfaces that model the desired functionality.

Tenet 3: Services Communicate via Contract, Not Implementation

The third tenet is yet another by-product of interface-based programming. The implementation details of a WCF service (e.g., the language it was written in, how it accomplishes its work, etc.) are of no concern to the external caller. WCF clients interact with services solely through their exposed public interfaces.

Tenet 4: Service Compatibility Is Based on Policy

Because CLR interfaces provide strongly typed contracts for all WCF clients (and can also be used to generate a related Web Services Description Language [WSDL] document based on your choice of binding), it is important to realize that interfaces and WSDL alone are not expressive enough to detail aspects of what the service is capable of doing. Given this, SOA allows you to define *policies* that further qualify the semantics of the service (e.g., the expected security requirements used to talk to the service). Using these policies, you can basically separate the low-level syntactic description of your service (the exposed interfaces) from the semantic details of how they work and how they need to be invoked.

WCF: The Bottom Line

WCF is the recommended API when you want to build an in-house application using TCP protocols or move data between programs on the same machine using named pipes. WCF can also be used to expose data to the world at large using HTTP-based protocols, although ASP.NET Web API (Chapter 30) is also a popular platform for RESTful services.

This is not to say you cannot use the original .NET distributed-centric namespaces (e.g., `System. Runtime.Remoting`, `System.Messaging`, `System.EnterpriseServices`, and `System.Web.Services`) in new development efforts. In some cases (e.g., if you need to build COM+ objects), you must do so. In any case, if you have used these APIs in previous projects, you will find learning WCF straightforward. Like the technologies that preceded it, WCF makes considerable use of XML-based configuration files, .NET attributes, and proxy generation utilities.

With this introductory foundation behind you, you can concentrate on the topic of building WCF applications. Again, you should understand that full coverage of WCF would require an entire book because each of the supported services (e.g., MSMQ, COM+, P2P, and named pipes) could be a chapter unto itself. Here, you will learn the overall process of building WCF programs using both TCP- and HTTP-based (e.g., web service) protocols. This should put you in a good position to study these topics further, as you see fit.

Investigating the Core WCF Assemblies

As you might expect, the programming fabric of WCF is represented by a set of .NET assemblies installed into the GAC. Table 23-1 describes the overall role of the core WCF assemblies you need to use in just about any WCF application.

Table 23-1. *Core WCF Assemblies*

Assembly	Meaning in Life
System.Runtime.Serialization.dll	This core assembly defines namespaces and types that you can use for serializing and deserializing objects in the WCF framework.
System.ServiceModel.dll	This core assembly contains the types used to build any sort of WCF application.

The two assemblies listed in Table 23-1 define many new namespaces and types. You should consult the .NET Framework 4.7 SDK documentation for complete details; however, Table 23-2 documents the roles of some of the important namespaces.

Table 23-2. *Core WCF Namespaces*

Namespace	Meaning in Life
System.Runtime.Serialization	This defines many types you use to control how data is serialized and deserialized within the WCF framework.
System.ServiceModel	This primary WCF namespace defines binding and hosting types, as well as basic security and transactional types.
System.ServiceModel.Configuration	This defines numerous types that provide programmatic access to WCF configuration files.
System.ServiceModel.Description	This defines types that provide an object model to the addresses, bindings, and contracts defined within WCF configuration files.
System.ServiceModel.MsmqIntegration	This contains types to integrate with the MSMQ service.
System.ServiceModel.Security	This defines numerous types to control aspects of the WCF security layers.

The Visual Studio WCF Project Templates

As will be explained in more detail later in this chapter, a WCF application is typically represented by three interrelated assemblies, one of which is a *.dll that contains the types that external callers can communicate with (in other words, the WCF service itself). When you want to build a WCF service, it is perfectly permissible to select a standard Class Library project template (see Chapter 14) as a starting point and manually reference the WCF assemblies.

Alternatively, you can create a new WCF service by selecting the WCF Service Library project template of Visual Studio (see Figure 23-1). This project type automatically sets references to the required WCF assemblies; however, it also generates a good deal of starter code, which you will likely often delete.

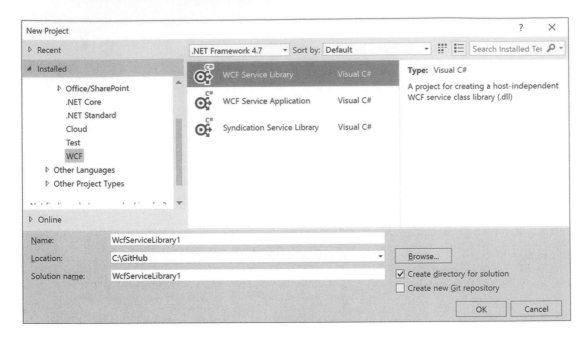

Figure 23-1. *The Visual Studio WCF Service Library project template*

One benefit of selecting the WCF Service Library project template is that it also supplies you with an App.config file, which might seem strange because you are building a .NET *.dll, not a .NET *.exe. However, this file is useful because when you debug or run your WCF Service Library project, the Visual Studio IDE will automatically launch the WCF Test Client application. This program (WcfTestClient.exe) will look up the settings in the App.config file so it can host your service for testing purposes. You'll learn more about the WCF Test Client later in this chapter.

■ **Note**   The App.config file of the WCF Service Library project is also useful because it shows you the bare-bones settings used to configure a WCF host application. In fact, you can copy and paste much of this code into the configuration file of your production services.

The WCF Service Web Site Project Template

You can find yet another Visual Studio WCF-centric project template in the New Web Site dialog box, which you activate using the File ➤ New ➤ Web Site menu option (see Figure 23-2).

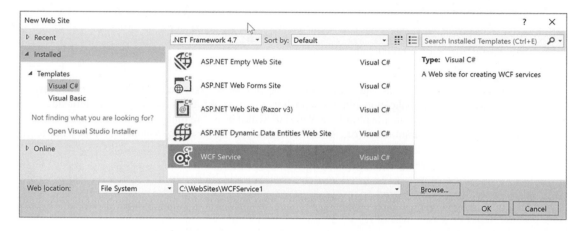

Figure 23-2. *The Visual Studio web-based WCF Service project template*

This WCF Service project template is useful when you know from the outset that your WCF service will use HTTP-based protocols rather than, for example, TCP or named pipes. This option can automatically create a new Internet Information Services (IIS) virtual directory to contain your WCF program files, create a proper `Web.config` file to expose the service through HTTP, and author the necessary `*.svc` file (you'll learn more about `*.svc` files later in this chapter). Thus, the web-based WCF Service project is a time-saver because the IDE automatically sets up the required IIS infrastructure.

In contrast, if you build a new WCF service using the WCF Service Library option, you have the ability to host the service in a variety of ways (e.g., custom host, Windows service, or manually built IIS virtual directory). This option is more appropriate when you need to build a custom host for your WCF service that can work with any number of WCF bindings.

The Basic Composition of a WCF Application

When you build a WCF distributed system, you will typically do so by creating the following three interrelated assemblies:

- *The WCF Service assembly*: This `*.dll` contains the classes and interfaces that represent the overall functionality you want to expose to external callers.

- *The WCF Service host*: This software module is the entity that hosts your WCF service assembly.

- *The WCF client*: This is the application that accesses the service's functionality through an intervening proxy.

As mentioned previously, the WCF Service assembly is a .NET class library that contains a number of WCF contracts and their implementations. The key difference is that the interface contracts are adorned with various attributes that control data type representation, how the WCF runtime interacts with the exposed types, and so forth.

The second assembly, the WCF Service host, can be literally any .NET executable. As you will see later in this chapter, WCF was set up so that you can expose services easily from any type of application (e.g., Windows Forms, a Windows service, and WPF applications). When you build a custom host, you use the `ServiceHost` type and possibly a related `*.config` file. The latter contains details regarding the server-side plumbing you want to use. However, if you use IIS as the host for your WCF service, you don't need to build a custom host programmatically because IIS will use the `ServiceHost` type behind the scenes.

■ **Note**   It is also possible to host a WCF service using the Windows Activation Service (WAS); you can consult the .NET Framework 4.7 SDK documentation for details.

The final assembly represents the client that makes calls into the WCF service. As you might expect, this client can be any type of .NET application. Similar to the host, client applications typically use a client-side `*.config` file that defines the client-side plumbing. You should also be aware that you can easily have a client application written in another framework (e.g., Java) if you build your WCF service using HTTP-based bindings.

Figure 23-3 illustrates the relationship between these three interrelated WCF assemblies (from a high level). Behind the scenes, several lower-level details are used to represent the required plumbing (e.g., factories, channels, and listeners). These low-level details are usually hidden from view; however, they can be extended or customized if required. In most cases, the default plumbing fits the bill sufficiently.

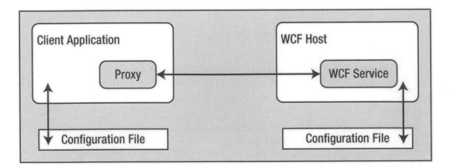

Figure 23-3. *A high-level look at a typical WCF application*

It is also worth pointing out that using a server-side or client-side `*.config` file is technically optional. If you want, you can hard-code the host (as well as the client) to specify the necessary plumbing (e.g., endpoints, binding, and addresses). The obvious problem with this approach is that if you need to change the plumbing details, you will need to recode, recompile, and redeploy a number of assemblies. Using a `*.config` file keeps your codebase much more flexible because changing the plumbing is as simple as updating the file's content and restarting the application. On the other hand, programmatic configuration allows an application more dynamic flexibility—it can choose how to configure the plumbing based on *if-tests*, for example.

The ABCs of WCF

Hosts and clients communicate with each other by agreeing on the ABCs, a friendly mnemonic for remembering the core building blocks of a WCF application *address*, *binding*, and *contract*, defined as follows:

- *Address*: This describes the location of the service. In code, you represent this with a `System.Uri` type; however, you typically store the value in `*.config` files.

- *Binding*: WCF ships with a many different bindings that specify network protocols, encoding mechanisms, and the transport layer.

- *Contract*: This provides a description of each method exposed from the WCF service.

You should realize that the ABC abbreviation does not imply that a developer must define the address first, followed by binding, and ending with the contract. In many cases, a WCF developer begins by defining a contract for the service, followed by establishing an address and bindings (any order will do, as long as each aspect is accounted for). Before you move on to building your first WCF application, let's take a more detailed look at the ABCs.

Understanding WCF Contracts

Understanding the notion of a *contract* is the key to building a WCF service. While not mandatory, the vast majority of your WCF applications will begin by defining a set of .NET interface types that are used to represent the set of members a given WCF service will support. Specifically, interfaces that represent a WCF contract are called *service contracts*. The classes (or structures) that implement them are called *service types*.

WCF service contracts are adorned with various attributes, the most common of which are defined in the System.ServiceModel namespace. When the members of a service contract (the methods in the interface) contain only simple data types (e.g., numerical data, Booleans, and string data), you can build a complete WCF service using nothing more than the [ServiceContract] and [OperationContract] attributes.

However, if your members expose custom types, you will likely use various types in the System.Runtime. Serialization namespace (see Figure 23-4) of the System.Runtime.Serialization.dll assembly. Here you will find additional attributes (e.g., [DataMember] and [DataContract]) to fine-tune the process of defining how your composite types are serialized to and from XML when they are passed to and from service operations.

Figure 23-4. System.Runtime.Serialization *defines a number of attributes used when building WCF data contracts*

Strictly speaking, you are not required to use CLR interfaces to define a WCF contract. Many of these same attributes can be applied on public members of a public class (or structure). However, given the many benefits of interface-based programming (e.g., polymorphism and elegant versioning), it is safe to consider that using CLR interfaces to describe a WCF contract is a best practice.

Understanding WCF Bindings

Once you define and implement a contract (or a set of contracts) in your service library, the next logical step is to build a hosting agent for the WCF service itself. As mentioned previously, you have a variety of possible hosts to choose from, all of which must specify the *bindings* used by remote callers to gain access to the service type's functionality.

WCF ships with many binding choices, each of which is tailored to a specific need. If none of the out-of-the-box bindings fits the bill, you can create your own by extending the CustomBinding type (something you will not do in this chapter). A WCF binding can specify the following characteristics:

- The transport layer used to move data (HTTP, MSMQ, named pipes, REST, WebSockets, and TCP)

- The channels used by the transport (one-way, request-reply, and duplex)

- The encoding mechanism used to deal with the data itself such as XML or binary

- Any supported web service protocols (if permitted by the binding), such as WS-Security, WS-Transactions, WS-Reliability, and so on

Let's take a look at your basic choices.

HTTP-Based Bindings

The BasicHttpBinding, WSHttpBinding, WSDualHttpBinding, and WSFederationHttpBinding options are geared toward exposing contract types through HTTP/SOAP protocols. If you require the furthest reach possible for your service (e.g., multiple operating systems and multiple programming architectures), you want to focus on these bindings because all of these binding types encode data based on XML representation and use HTTP on the wire.

Table 23-3 shows how you can represent a WCF binding in code (using class types within the System.ServiceModel namespace) or as XML attributes defined within *.config files.

Table 23-3. *The HTTP-Centric WCF Bindings*

Binding Class	Binding Element	Meaning in Life
BasicHttpBinding	<basicHttpBinding>	You use this to build a WS-Basic Profile–conformant (WS-I Basic Profile 1.1) WCF service. This binding uses HTTP as the transport and Text/XML as the default message encoding.
WSHttpBinding	<wsHttpBinding>	This is similar to BasicHttpBinding but provides more web service features. This binding adds support for transactions, reliable messaging, and WS-Addressing.

(continued)

Table 23-3. *(continued)*

Binding Class	Binding Element	Meaning in Life
WSDualHttpBinding	`<wsDualHttpBinding>`	This is similar to `WSHttpBinding` but intended for use with duplex contracts (e.g., the service and client can send messages back and forth). This binding supports only SOAP security and requires reliable messaging.
WSFederationHttpBinding	`<wsFederationHttpBinding>`	This is a secure and interoperable binding that supports the WS-Federation protocol, enabling organizations that are in a federation to authenticate and authorize users efficiently.

As its name suggests, `BasicHttpBinding` is the simplest of all web service–centric protocols. Specifically, this binding ensures that your WCF service conforms to a specification named WS-I Basic Profile 1.1 (defined by WS-I). The main reason to use this binding is for maintaining backward compatibility with applications that were previously built to communicate with ASP.NET web services (which have been part of the .NET libraries since version 1.0).

The `WSHttpBinding` protocol not only incorporates support for a subset of the WS-* specification (transactions, security, and reliable sessions) but also supports the ability to handle binary data encoding using Message Transmission Optimization Mechanism (MTOM).

The main benefit of `WSDualHttpBinding` is that it adds the ability to allow the caller and sender to communicate using *duplex messaging*, which is a fancy way of saying they can engage in a two-way conversation. When selecting `WSDualHttpBinding`, you can hook into the WCF publish/subscribe event model.

Finally, `WSFederationHttpBinding` is the web service–based protocol you might want to consider when security among a group of organizations is of the utmost importance. This binding supports the WS-Trust, WS-Security, and WS-SecureConversation specifications, which are represented by the WCF CardSpace APIs.

TCP-Based Bindings

If you build a distributed application involving machines that are configured with the .NET 4.5 libraries (in other words, all machines are running the Windows operating system), you can gain performance benefits by bypassing web service bindings and opting for a TCP binding, which ensures that all data is encoded in a compact binary format, rather than XML. Again, when you use the bindings shown in Table 23-4, the client and host must be .NET applications.

Table 23-4. *The TCP-Centric WCF Bindings*

Binding Class	Binding Element	Meaning in Life
NetNamedPipeBinding	`<netNamedPipeBinding>`	Serves as a secure, reliable, optimized binding for on-the-same-machine communication between .NET applications
NetPeerTcpBinding	`<netPeerTcpBinding>`	Provides a secure binding for P2P network applications
NetTcpBinding	`<netTcpBinding>`	Serves as a secure and optimized binding suitable for cross-machine communication between .NET applications

The NetTcpBinding class uses TCP to move binary data between the client and WCF service. As mentioned previously, this will result in higher performance than the web service protocols but limits you to an in-house Windows solution. On the plus side, NetTcpBinding supports transactions, reliable sessions, and secure communications.

Like NetTcpBinding, NetNamedPipeBinding supports transactions, reliable sessions, and secure communications; however, it has no ability to make cross-machine calls. If you want to find the fastest way to push data between WCF applications on the same machine (e.g., cross-application domain communications), NetNamedPipeBinding is the binding choice of champions. For more information on NetPeerTcpBinding, consult the .NET Framework 4.7 SDK documentation for details regarding P2P networking.

MSMQ-Based Bindings

Finally, the NetMsmqBinding and MsmqIntegrationBinding bindings are of immediate interest if you want to integrate with a Microsoft MSMQ server. This chapter will not examine the details of using MSMQ bindings, but Table 23-5 documents the basic role of each.

Table 23-5. *The MSMQ-Centric WCF Bindings*

Binding Class	Binding Element	Meaning in Life
MsmqIntegrationBinding	<msmqIntegrationBinding>	You can use this binding to enable WCF applications to send and receive messages to and from existing MSMQ applications that use COM, native C++, or the types defined in the System.Messaging namespace.
NetMsmqBinding	<netMsmqBinding>	You can use this queued binding for cross-machine communication between .NET applications. This is the preferred approach among the MSMQ-centric bindings.

Understanding WCF Addresses

Once you establish the contracts and bindings, the final piece of the puzzle is to specify an *address* for the WCF service. This is important because remote callers will be unable to communicate with the remote types if they cannot locate them! Like most aspects of WCF, an address can be hard-coded in an assembly (using the System.Uri type) or offloaded to a *.config file.

In either case, the exact format of the WCF address will differ based on your choice of binding (HTTP based, named pipes, TCP based, or MSMQ based). From a high level, WCF addresses can specify the following bits of information:

- Scheme: This is the transport protocol (e.g., HTTP).

- MachineName: This is the fully qualified domain of the machine.

- Port: This is optional in many cases; for example, the default for HTTP bindings is port 80.

- Path: This is the path to the WCF service.

This information can be represented by the following generalized template (the `Port` value is optional because some bindings don't use them):

```
scheme://<MachineName>[:Port]/Path
```

When you use an HTTP-based binding (e.g., `basicHttpBinding`, `wsHttpBinding`, `wsDualHttpBinding`, or `wsFederationHttpBinding`), the address breaks down like this (recall that HTTP-based protocols default to port 80 if you do not specify a port number):

```
http://localhost:8080/MyWCFService
```

If you use TCP-centric bindings (e.g., `NetTcpBinding` or `NetPeerTcpBinding`), the URI takes the following format:

```
net.tcp://localhost:8080/MyWCFService
```

The MSMQ-centric bindings (`NetMsmqBinding` and `MsmqIntegrationBinding`) are unique in their URI format because MSMQ can use public or private queues, which are available only on the local machine, and port numbers have no meaning in an MSMQ-centric URI. Consider the following URI, which describes a private queue named `MyPrivateQ`:

```
net.msmq://localhost/private$/MyPrivateQ
```

Last but not least, the address format used for the named-pipe binding, `NetNamedPipeBinding`, breaks down like this (recall that named pipes allow for interprocess communication for applications on the same physical machine):

```
net.pipe://localhost/MyWCFService
```

While a single WCF service might expose only a single address (based on a single binding), it is possible to configure a collection of unique addresses (with different bindings). You can do this in a `*.config` file by defining multiple `<endpoint>` elements. Here, you can specify any number of ABCs for the same service. This approach can be helpful when you want to allow callers to select which protocol they would like to use when communicating with the service.

Building a WCF Service

Now that you have a better understanding about the building blocks of a WCF application, it's time to create your first sample application and see how the ABCs are accounted for in code and configuration. This first example avoids using the Visual Studio WCF project templates so you can focus on the specific steps involved in making a WCF service.

Begin by creating a new C# Class Library project named MagicEightBallServiceLib and name the solution MagicEightBallServiceHTTP. Next, rename your initial file from `Class1.cs` to `MagicEightBallService.cs` and then add a reference to the `System.ServiceModel.dll` assembly. In the initial code file, specify that you are using the `System.ServiceModel` namespace. At this point, your C# file should look like this (note you have a public class at this point):

```csharp
// The key WCF namespace.
using System.ServiceModel;

namespace MagicEightBallServiceLib
{
```

```
public class MagicEightBallService
{
}
}
```

Your class type implements a single WCF service contract represented by a strongly typed CLR interface named IEightBall. As you most likely know, the Magic 8 Ball is a toy that allows you to view one of a handful of fixed answers to a question you might ask. Your interface here will define a single method that allows the caller to pose a question to the Magic 8 Ball to obtain a random answer.

WCF service interfaces are adorned with the [ServiceContract] attribute, while each interface member is decorated with the [OperationContract] attribute (you'll learn more details regarding these two attributes in just a moment). Create a new file named IEightBall.cs, and add the following code:

```
[ServiceContract]
public interface IEightBall
{
    // Ask a question, receive an answer!
    [OperationContract]
    string ObtainAnswerToQuestion(string userQuestion);
}
```

■ **Note**   It is permissible to define a service contract interface that contains methods not adorned with the [OperationContract] attribute; however, such members will not be exposed through the WCF runtime.

As you know from your study of the interface type (see Chapter 8), interfaces are quite useless until they are implemented by a class or structure that fleshes out their functionality. Like a real Magic 8 Ball, the implementation of your service type (MagicEightBallService) will randomly return a canned answer from an array of strings. Also, your default constructor will display an information message that will be (eventually) displayed within the host's console window (for diagnostic purposes).

```
public class MagicEightBallService : IEightBall
{
    // Just for display purposes on the host.
    public MagicEightBallService()
    {
        Console.WriteLine("The 8-Ball awaits your question...");
    }

    public string ObtainAnswerToQuestion(string userQuestion)
    {
        string[] answers = { "Future Uncertain", "Yes", "No",
            "Hazy", "Ask again later", "Definitely" };

        // Return a random response.
        Random r = new Random();
        return answers[r.Next(answers.Length)];
    }
}
```

At this point, your WCF Service library is complete. However, before you construct a host for this service, you need to examine some additional details of the [ServiceContract] and [OperationContract] attributes.

The [ServiceContract] Attribute

For a CLR interface to participate in the services provided by WCF, it must be adorned with the [ServiceContract] attribute. Like many other .NET attributes, the ServiceContractAttribute type supports many properties that further qualify its intended purpose. You can set two properties, Name and Namespace, to control the name of the service type and the name of the XML namespace that defines the service type. If you use an HTTP-specific binding, you use these values to define the <portType> elements of the related WSDL document.

Here, you do not bother to assign a Name value because the default name of the service type is directly based on the C# class name. However, the default name for the underlying XML namespace is simply http://tempuri.org (you should change this for all your WCF services).

When you build a WCF service that will send and receive custom data types (which you are not currently doing), it is important that you establish a meaningful value to the underlying XML namespace because this ensures that your custom types are unique. As you might know from your experience building XML web services, XML namespaces provide a way to wrap your custom types in a unique container to ensure that your types do not clash with types in another organization.

For this reason, you can update your interface definition with a more fitting definition, which, much like the process of defining an XML namespace in a .NET Web Service project, is typically the URI of the service's point of origin, as in the following example:

```
[ServiceContract(Namespace = "http://MyCompany.com")]
public interface IEightBall
{
  ...
}
```

Beyond Namespace and Name, the [ServiceContract] attribute can be configured with the additional properties shown in Table 23-6. Be aware that some of these settings will be ignored, depending on your binding selection.

Table 23-6. *Various Named Properties of the* [ServiceContract] *Attribute*

Property	Meaning in Life
CallbackContract	Establishes whether this service contract requires callback functionality for two-way message exchange (e.g., duplex bindings).
ConfigurationName	Locates the service element in an application configuration file. The default is the name of the service implementation class.
ProtectionLevel	Allows you to specify the degree to which the contract binding requires encryption, digital signatures, or both for endpoints that expose the contract.
SessionMode	Establishes whether sessions are allowed, not allowed, or required by this service contract.

The [OperationContract] Attribute

Methods that you intend to use within the WCF framework must be attributed with the [OperationContract] attribute, which can also be configured with various named properties. You can use the properties shown in Table 23-7 to declare that a given method is intended to be one-way in nature, supports asynchronous invocation, requires encrypted message data, and so forth (again, many of these values might be ignored based on your binding selection).

921

Table 23-7. *Various Named Properties of the* [OperationContract] *Attribute*

Property	Meaning in Life
AsyncPattern	Indicates whether the operation is implemented asynchronously using a Begin/End method pair on the service. This allows the service to offload processing to another server-side thread; this has nothing to do with the client calling the method asynchronously!
IsInitiating	Specifies whether this operation can be the initial operation in a session.
IsOneWay	Indicates whether the operation consists of only a single input message (and no associated output).
IsTerminating	Specifies whether the WCF runtime should attempt to terminate the current session after the operation completes.

For the initial example, you don't need to configure the ObtainAnswerToQuestion() method with additional traits; this means you can use the [OperationContract] attribute as currently defined.

Service Types As Operational Contracts

Finally, recall that the use of interfaces is not required when building WCF service types. In fact, it is possible to apply the [ServiceContract] and [OperationContract] attributes directly to the service type itself, like so:

```
// This is only for illustrative purposes
// and not used for the current example.
[ServiceContract(Namespace = "http://MyCompany.com")]
public class ServiceTypeAsContract
{
  [OperationContract]
  void SomeMethod() { }

  [OperationContract]
  void AnotherMethod() { }
}
```

You can take this approach; however, you receive many benefits if you explicitly define an interface type to represent the service contract. The most obvious benefit is that you can apply a given interface to multiple service types (authored in a variety of languages and architectures) to achieve a high degree of polymorphism. Another benefit is that you can use a service contract interface as the basis of new contracts (using interface inheritance), without having to carry any implementation baggage.

In any case, your first WCF Service library is now complete. Compile your project to ensure you do not have any typos.

Hosting the WCF Service

You are now ready to define a host. Although you would host a production-level service from a Windows service or an IIS virtual directory, you will make your first host a simple console named MagicEightBallServiceHost.

Add a new Console application named MagicEightBallServiceHost to the solution and set it as the startup project. Add a reference to the System.ServiceModel.dll assembly and MagicEightBallServiceLib project and then update your initial code file by importing the System.ServiceModel and MagicEightBallServiceLib namespaces, like so:

```
using System;
...

using System.ServiceModel;
using MagicEightBallServiceLib;

namespace MagicEightBallServiceHost
{
  class Program
  {
    static void Main(string[] args)
    {
      Console.WriteLine("***** Console Based WCF Host *****");
      Console.ReadLine();
    }
  }
}
```

The first step you must take when building a host for a WCF service type is to decide whether you want to define the necessary hosting logic completely in code or to relegate several low-level details to an application configuration file. As mentioned previously, the benefit of *.config files is that the host can change the underlying plumbing without requiring you to recompile and redeploy the executable. However, always remember this is strictly optional because you can hard-code the hosting logic using the types within the System.ServiceModel.dll assembly.

This console-based host will use an application configuration file, so insert this new file (if your project does not currently have one) into your current project by using the Project ➤ Add New Item menu option and then choosing Application Configuration File.

Establishing the ABCs Within an App.config File

When you build a host for a WCF service type, you follow a predictable set of steps—some that rely on configuration and some that rely on code. These steps are as follows:

- Define the *endpoint* for the WCF service being hosted within the host's configuration file.

- Programmatically use the ServiceHost type to expose the service types available from this endpoint.

- Ensure the host remains running to service incoming client requests. Obviously, this step is not required if you host your service types using a Windows service or IIS.

In the world of WCF, the term *endpoint* represents the address, binding, and contract rolled together in a nice, tidy package. In XML, an endpoint is expressed using the <endpoint> element and the address, binding, and contract elements. Update your *.config file to specify a single endpoint (reachable through port 8080) exposed by this host, like so:

```xml
<?xml version = "1.0" encoding = "utf-8" ?>
<configuration>
  <system.serviceModel>
    <services>
      <service name = "MagicEightBallServiceLib.MagicEightBallService">
        <endpoint address = "http://localhost:8080/MagicEightBallService"
                  binding = "basicHttpBinding"
                  contract = "MagicEightBallServiceLib.IEightBall"/>
      </service>
    </services>
  </system.serviceModel>
  <startup>
    <supportedRuntime version="v4.0" sku=".NETFramework,Version=v4.7" />
  </startup>
</configuration>
```

Notice that the <system.serviceModel> element is the root for all of a host's WCF settings. Each service exposed by the host is represented by a <service> element that is wrapped by the <services> base element. Here, your single <service> element uses the (optional) name attribute to specify the friendly name of the service type.

The nested <endpoint> element handles the task of defining the address, the binding model (basicHttpBinding, in this example), and the fully qualified name of the interface type defining the WCF service contract (IEightBall). Because you are using an HTTP-based binding, you use the http:// scheme, specifying an arbitrary port ID.

Coding Against the ServiceHost Type

With the current configuration file in place, the actual programming logic required to complete the host is simple. When your executable starts up, you will create an instance of the ServiceHost class and inform it which WCF service it is responsible for hosting. At runtime, this object will automatically read the data within the scope of the <system.serviceModel> element of the host's *.config file to determine the correct address, binding, and contract. It will then create the necessary plumbing.

```csharp
static void Main(string[] args)
{
  Console.WriteLine("***** Console Based WCF Host *****");
  using (ServiceHost serviceHost = new ServiceHost(typeof(MagicEightBallService)))
  {
    // Open the host and start listening for incoming messages.
    serviceHost.Open();

    // Keep the service running until the Enter key is pressed.
    Console.WriteLine("The service is ready.");
    Console.WriteLine("Press the Enter key to terminate service.");
    Console.ReadLine();
  }
}
```

If you run this application now, you will find that the host is alive in memory, ready to take incoming requests from remote clients.

■ **Note**   Recall that you must launch Visual Studio with administrative privileges to run many WCF project types!

Specifying Base Addresses

Currently, you create your ServiceHost using a constructor that requires only the service's type information. However, it is also possible to pass in an array of System.Uri types as a constructor argument to represent the collection of addresses this service is accessible from. Currently, you find the address using the *.config file. However, assume that you were to update the using scope like this:

```
using (ServiceHost serviceHost = new
  ServiceHost(typeof(MagicEightBallService),
  new Uri[]{new Uri("http://localhost:8080/MagicEightBallService")}))
{
  ...
}
```

If you did, you could now define your endpoint like this:

```
<endpoint address = ""
          binding = "basicHttpBinding"
          contract = "MagicEightBallServiceLib.IEightBall"/>
```

Of course, too much hard-coding within a host's code base decreases flexibility. Therefore, the current host example assumes you create the service host simply by supplying the following type information, as you did before:

```
using (ServiceHost serviceHost = new ServiceHost(typeof(MagicEightBallService)))
{
  ...
}
```

One of the (slightly frustrating) aspects of authoring host *.config files is that you have several ways to construct the XML descriptors, based on the amount of hard-coding you have in the codebase (as you have just seen in the case of the optional Uri array). Here's a reworking that shows yet another way to author *.config files:

```
<?xml version = "1.0" encoding = "utf-8" ?>
<configuration>
  <system.serviceModel>
    <services>
      <service name = "MagicEightBallServiceLib.MagicEightBallService">

        <!-- Address obtained from <baseAddresses> -->
        <endpoint address = ""
                  binding = "basicHttpBinding"
                  contract = "MagicEightBallServiceLib.IEightBall"/>

        <!-- List all of the base addresses in a dedicated section -->
        <host>
          <baseAddresses>
```

```
            <add baseAddress = "http://localhost:8080/MagicEightBallService"/>
          </baseAddresses>
        </host>
      </service>
    </services>
  </system.serviceModel>
  <startup>
    <supportedRuntime version="v4.0" sku=".NETFramework,Version=v4.7" />
  </startup>
</configuration>
```

In this case, the address attribute of the <endpoint> element is still empty; regardless of the fact that you do not specify an array of Uri objects in code when creating the ServiceHost, the application runs as before because the value is pulled from the baseAddresses scope. The benefit of storing the base address in a <host>'s <baseAddresses> region is that other parts of a *.config file also need to know the address of the service's endpoint. Thus, rather than having to copy and paste address values within a single *.config file, you can isolate the single value, as shown in the preceding snippet.

■ **Note**   In a later example, you'll be introduced to a graphical configuration tool that allows you to author configuration files in a less tedious manner.

In any case, you have a bit more work to do before you build a client application to communicate with your service. Specifically, you will dig a bit deeper into the role of the ServiceHost class type and <service. serviceModel> element, as well as the role of metadata exchange (MEX) services.

Details of the ServiceHost Type

You use the ServiceHost class type to configure and expose a WCF service from the hosting executable. However, be aware that you will use this type directly only when building a custom *.exe to host your services. If you use IIS to expose a service, the ServiceHost object is created automatically on your behalf.

As you have seen, this type requires a complete service description, which is obtained dynamically through the configuration settings of the host's *.config file. While this happens automatically when you create a ServiceHost object, it is possible to configure the state of your ServiceHost object manually using a number of members. In addition to Open() and Close() (which communicate with your service in a synchronous manner), Table 23-8 illustrates some further members of interest.

Table 23-8. *Select Members of the ServiceHost Type*

Members	Meaning in Life
Authorization	This property gets the authorization level for the service being hosted.
AddDefaultEndpoints()	This method is used to configure a WCF Service host programmatically so it uses any number of prebuilt endpoints supplied by the framework.
AddServiceEndpoint()	This method allows you to register an endpoint to the host programmatically.
BaseAddresses	This property obtains the list of registered base addresses for the current service.
BeginOpen() BeginClose()	These methods allow you to open and close a ServiceHost object asynchronously, using the standard asynchronous .NET delegate syntax.

(continued)

Table 23-8. *(continued)*

Members	Meaning in Life
CloseTimeout	This property allows you to set and get the time allowed for the service to close down.
Credentials	This property obtains the security credentials used by the current service.
EndOpen() EndClose()	These methods are the asynchronous counterparts to BeginOpen() and BeginClose().
OpenTimeout	This property allows you to set and get the time allowed for the service to start up.
State	This property gets a value that indicates the current state of the communication object, which is represented by the CommunicationState enum (e.g., opened, closed, and created).

You can see some additional aspects of ServiceHost in action by updating your Program class as follows, with a new static method that prints out the ABCs of each endpoint used by the host:

```
static void DisplayHostInfo(ServiceHost host)
{
  Console.WriteLine();
  Console.WriteLine("***** Host Info *****");

  foreach (System.ServiceModel.Description.ServiceEndpoint se
    in host.Description.Endpoints)
  {
    Console.WriteLine("Address: {0}", se.Address);
    Console.WriteLine("Binding: {0}", se.Binding.Name);
    Console.WriteLine("Contract: {0}", se.Contract.Name);
  }
  Console.WriteLine("*********************");
}
```

Now, assuming that you call this new method from within Main() after opening your host:

```
using (ServiceHost serviceHost = new ServiceHost(typeof(MagicEightBallService)))
{
  // Open the host and start listening for incoming messages.
  serviceHost.Open();
  DisplayHostInfo(serviceHost);
...
}
```

the following statistics will be shown as output:

```
***** Console Based WCF Host *****

***** Host Info *****
Address: http://localhost:8080/MagicEightBallService
Binding: BasicHttpBinding
Contract: IEightBall
```

```
*********************
The service is ready.
Press the Enter key to terminate service.
```

■ **Note** When running a host (or client) in this chapter, be sure to truly "run" the program from within Visual Studio (Ctrl+F5) and not debug (F5) the program to ensure your host and client processes can run independently.

Details of the <system.serviceModel> Element

Like any XML element, `<system.serviceModel>` can define a set of subelements, each of which can be qualified using various attributes. While you should consult the .NET Framework 4.7 SDK documentation for full details regarding the set of possible attributes, here is a skeleton that lists some (but not all) useful subelements:

```
<system.serviceModel>
  <behaviors>
  </behaviors>
  <client>
  </client>
  <commonBehaviors>
  </commonBehaviors>
  <diagnostics>
  </diagnostics>
  <comContracts>
  </comContracts>
  <services>
  </services>
  <bindings>
  </bindings>
</system.serviceModel>
```

You'll see more exotic configuration files as you move through the chapter; however, you can see the crux of each subelement in Table 23-9.

Table 23-9. *Select Subelements of* `<service.serviceModel>`

Subelement	Meaning in Life
behaviors	WCF supports various endpoint and service behaviors. In a nutshell, a *behavior* allows you to qualify further the functionality of a host, service, or client.
bindings	This element allows you to fine-tune each of the WCF-supplied bindings (e.g., basicHttpBinding and netMsmqBinding), as well as to specify any custom bindings used by the host.
Client	This element contains a list of endpoints a client uses to connect to a service. Obviously, this is not particularly useful in a host's *.config file.
comContracts	This element defines COM contracts enabled for WCF and COM interoperability.

(continued)

Table 23-9. *(continued)*

Subelement	Meaning in Life
commonBehaviors	This element can be set only within a machine.config file. You can use it to define all of the behaviors used by each WCF service on a given machine.
Diagnostics	This element contains settings for the diagnostic features of WCF. The user can enable/ disable tracing, performance counters, and the WMI provider; the user can also add custom message filters.
services	This element contains a collection of WCF services exposed by the host.

Enabling Metadata Exchange

Recall that WCF client applications communicate with the WCF service through an intervening proxy type. While you could author the proxy code completely by hand, doing so would be tedious and error-prone. Ideally, you could use a tool to generate the necessary grunge code (including the client-side *.config file). Thankfully, the .NET Framework 4.7 SDK provides a command-line tool (svcutil.exe) for this purpose. Also, Visual Studio provides similar functionality through its Project ➤ Add Service Reference menu option.

For these tools to generate the necessary proxy code/*.config file, however, they must be able to discover the format of the WCF service interfaces and any defined data contracts (e.g., the method names and type of parameters).

Metadata exchange (MEX) is a WCF *service behavior* that you can use to fine-tune how the WCF runtime handles your service. Simply put, each <behavior> element can define a set of activities a given service can subscribe to. WCF provides numerous behaviors out of the box, and it is possible to build your own.

The MEX behavior (which is disabled by default) will intercept any metadata requests sent through HTTP GET. You must enable MEX if you want to allow svcutil.exe or Visual Studio to automate the creation of the required client-side proxy *.config file.

Enabling MEX is a matter of tweaking the host's *.config file with the proper settings (or authoring the corresponding C# code). First, you must add a new <endpoint> just for MEX. Second, you need to define a WCF behavior to allow HTTP GET access. Third, you need to associate this behavior by name to your service using the behaviorConfiguration attribute on the opening <service> element. Finally, you need to add a <host> element to define the base address of this service (MEX will look here to figure out the locations of the types to describe).

■ **Note**   You can bypass this final step if you pass in a System.Uri object to represent the base address as a parameter to the ServiceHost constructor.

Consider the following updated host *.config file, which creates a custom <behavior> element (named EightBallServiceMEXBehavior) that is associated to your service through the behaviorConfiguration attribute within the <service> definition:

```
<?xml version = "1.0" encoding = "utf-8" ?>
<configuration>
  <system.serviceModel>
    <services>
      <service name = "MagicEightBallServiceLib.MagicEightBallService"
              behaviorConfiguration="EightBallServiceMEXBehavior">
        <endpoint address = ""
```

```
              binding = "basicHttpBinding"
              contract = "MagicEightBallServiceLib.IEightBall"/>

      <!-- Enable the MEX endpoint -->
      <endpoint address = "mex"
                binding = "mexHttpBinding"
                contract = "IMetadataExchange" />

      <!-- Need to add this so MEX knows the address of our service -->
      <host>
        <baseAddresses>
          <add baseAddress = "http://localhost:8080/MagicEightBallService"/>
        </baseAddresses>
      </host>
    </service>
  </services>

  <!-- A behavior definition for MEX -->
  <behaviors>
    <serviceBehaviors>
      <behavior name = "EightBallServiceMEXBehavior" >
        <serviceMetadata httpGetEnabled = "true" />
      </behavior>
    </serviceBehaviors>
  </behaviors>
  </system.serviceModel>
</configuration>
```

You can now rerun your service host application and view its metadata description using the web browser of your choice. To do so, enter the address as the URL while the host is still running, like so:

```
http://localhost:8080/MagicEightBallService
```

Once you are at the home page for your WCF service (see Figure 23-5), you are provided with basic details regarding how to interact with this service programmatically, as well as a way to view the WSDL contract by clicking the hyperlink at the top of the page. Recall that Web Service Description Language (WSDL) is a grammar that describes the structure of web services at a given endpoint.

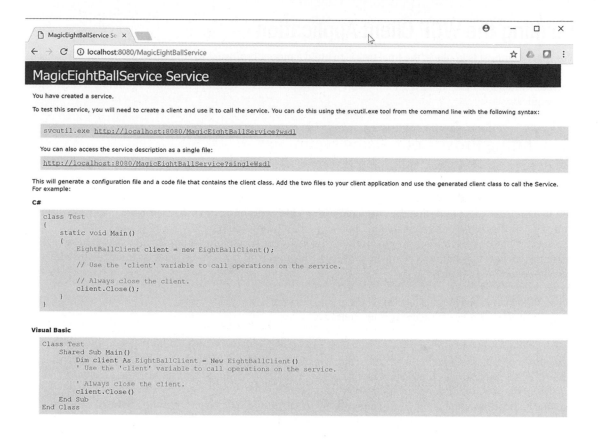

Figure 23-5. *Ready-to-view metadata using MEX*

Your host now exposes two different endpoints (one for the service and one for MEX), so your host's console output will appear like this:

```
***** Console Based WCF Host *****

***** Host Info *****
Address: http://localhost:8080/MagicEightBallService
Binding: BasicHttpBinding
Contract: IEightBall

Address: http://localhost:8080/MagicEightBallService/mex
Binding: MetadataExchangeHttpBinding
Contract: IMetadataExchange
*********************

The service is ready.
```

Building the WCF Client Application

Now that your host is in place, the final task is to build a piece of software to communicate with this WCF service type. While you could take the long road and build the necessary infrastructure by hand (a feasible but labor-intensive task), the .NET Framework 4.7 SDK provides several approaches to generate a client-side proxy quickly.

Generating Proxy Code Using svcutil.exe

The first way you can build a client-side proxy is to use the svcutil.exe command-line tool. Using svcutil.exe, you can generate a new C# language file that represents the proxy code itself, as well as a client-side configuration file. You can do this by specifying the service's endpoint as the first parameter. You use the /out: flag to define the name of the *.cs file containing the proxy, and you use the /config: option to specify the name of the generated client-side *.config file.

Assuming your service is currently running, the following command set passed into svcutil.exe will generate two new files in the working directory (which should, of course, be entered as a single line within a developer command prompt):

```
svcutil http://localhost:8080/MagicEightBallService
        /out:myProxy.cs /config:app.config
```

If you open the myProxy.cs file, you will find a client-side representation of the IEightBall interface, as well as a new class named EightBallClient, which is the proxy class itself. This class derives from the generic class, System.ServiceModel.ClientBase<T>, where T is the registered service interface.

In addition to a number of custom constructors, each method of the proxy (which is based on the original interface methods) will be implemented to use the inherited Channel property to invoke the correct service method. Here is a partial snapshot of the proxy type:

```
[System.Diagnostics.DebuggerStepThroughAttribute()]
[System.CodeDom.Compiler.GeneratedCodeAttribute("System.ServiceModel",
  "4.0.0.0")]
public partial class EightBallClient :
  System.ServiceModel.ClientBase<IEightBall>, IEightBall
{
...
  public string ObtainAnswerToQuestion(string userQuestion)
  {
    return base.Channel.ObtainAnswerToQuestion(userQuestion);
  }
}
```

When you create an instance of the proxy type in your client application, the base class will establish a connection to the endpoint using the settings specified in the client-side application configuration file. Much like the server-side configuration file, the generated client-side App.config file contains an <endpoint> element and details about the basicHttpBinding used to communicate with the service.

You will also find the following <client> element, which (again) establishes the ABCs from the client's perspective:

```
<client>
  <endpoint
  address = "http://localhost:8080/MagicEightBallService"
  binding = "basicHttpBinding" bindingConfiguration = "BasicHttpBinding_IEightBall"
  contract = "IEightBall" name = "BasicHttpBinding_IEightBall" />
</client>
```

At this point, you could include these two files into a client project (and reference the System.
ServiceModel.dll assembly) and then use the proxy type to communicate with the remote WCF service.
However, you'll take a different approach here, looking at how Visual Studio can help you further automate
the creation of client-side proxy files.

Generating Proxy Code Using Visual Studio

Like any good command-line tool, svcutil.exe provides a great number of options that you can use to
control how the client proxy is generated. If you do not require these advanced options, you can generate
the same two files using the Visual Studio IDE. For the client project, add a new Console Application project
named MagicEightBallServiceClient to the solution and run (not debug) the application, While the service is
running, select the Add Service Reference option from the Project menu.

After you activate this menu option, select MagicEightBallService from the drop-down and click the Go
button to see the service description (see Figure 23-6).

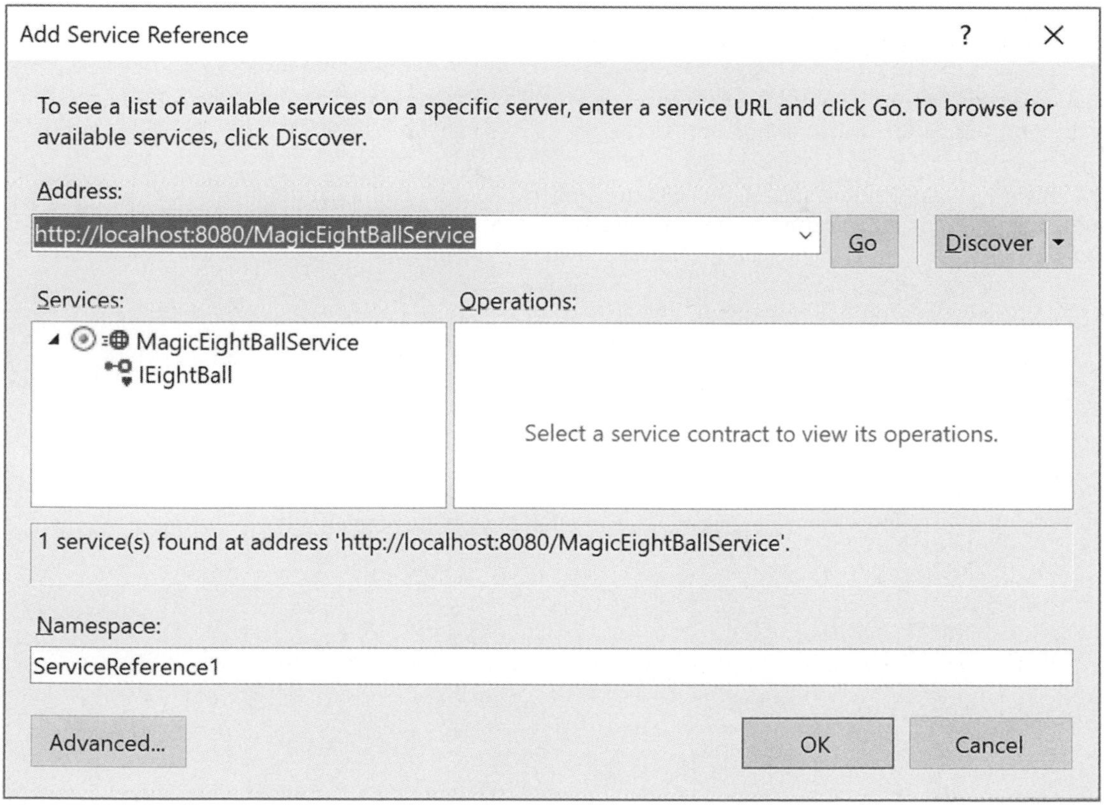

Figure 23-6. *Generating the proxy files using Visual Studio*

Beyond creating and inserting the proxy files into your current project, this tool is kind enough to reference the WCF assemblies automatically on your behalf. In accordance with a naming convention, the proxy class is defined within a namespace called ServiceReference1, which is nested in the client's namespace (to avoid possible name clashes). Here is the complete client code:

```
// Location of the proxy.
using MagicEightBallServiceClient.ServiceReference1;

namespace MagicEightBallServiceClient
{
  class Program
  {
    static void Main(string[] args)
    {
      Console.WriteLine("***** Ask the Magic 8 Ball *****\n");

      using (EightBallClient ball = new EightBallClient())
      {
        Console.Write("Your question: ");
        string question = Console.ReadLine();
        string answer =
          ball.ObtainAnswerToQuestion(question);
        Console.WriteLine("8-Ball says: {0}", answer);
      }
      Console.ReadLine();
    }
  }
}
```

Right-click the solution and select Set Startup Projects. Select "Multiple startup projects," move MagicEightBallServiceHost to the top of the list, and set the MagicEightBallServiceHost and MagicEightBallServiceClient projects to Start, as shown in Figure 23-7.

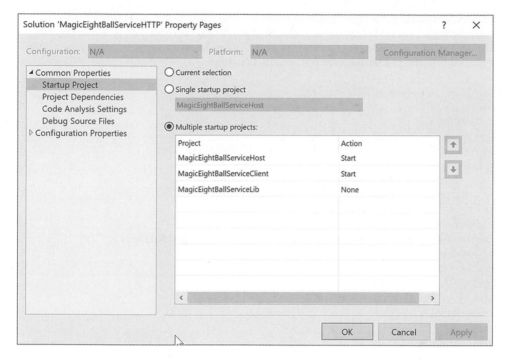

Figure 23-7. *Refreshing the proxy and client-side *.config file*

Now when you click Start (and give the service a minute to start up), you can ask a question in the client window and get a random answer in the client console window. Here is one possible output:

```
***** Ask the Magic 8 Ball *****

Your question: Will I ever finish Fallout 4?
8-Ball says: No

Press any key to continue . . .
```

■ **Source Code**   You can find the MagicEightBallServiceHTTP solution in the Chapter 23 folder.

Configuring a TCP-Based Binding

At this point, the host and client applications are both configured to use the simplest of the HTTP-based bindings, basicHttpBinding. Recall that the benefit of offloading settings to configuration files is that you can change the underlying plumbing in a declarative manner and expose multiple bindings for the same service.

To illustrate this, you can try a little experiment. Create a new folder on your C: drive (or wherever you happen to be saving your code) named EightBallTCP; in this new folder, create two subdirectories named Host and Client.

Next, use Windows Explorer to navigate to the \bin\Debug folder of the host project (from earlier in this chapter) and copy `MagicEightBallServiceHost.exe`, `MagicEightBallServiceHost.exe.config`, and `MagicEightBallServiceLib.dll` to the `C:\EightBallTCP\Host` folder. Now use a simple text editor to open the `*.config` file for editing and modify the existing contents as follows:

```xml
<?xml version = "1.0" encoding = "utf-8" ?>
<configuration>
  <system.serviceModel>
    <services>
      <service name = "MagicEightBallServiceLib.MagicEightBallService">
        <endpoint address = ""
                  binding = "netTcpBinding"
                  contract = "MagicEightBallServiceLib.IEightBall"/>
        <host>
          <baseAddresses>
            <add baseAddress = "net.tcp://localhost:8090/MagicEightBallService"/>
          </baseAddresses>
        </host>
      </service>
    </services>
  </system.serviceModel>
</configuration>
```

Essentially, this host's `*.config` file strips out all the MEX settings (because you already built the proxy) and establishes that it is using the `netTcpBinding` binding type through a unique port. Now run the application by double-clicking the `*.exe`. If all is well, you should see the host output shown here:

```
***** Console Based WCF Host *****

***** Host Info *****
Address: net.tcp://localhost:8090/MagicEightBallService
Binding: NetTcpBinding
Contract: IEightBall

*********************
The service is ready.
Press the Enter key to terminate service.
```

To complete the test, copy the `MagicEightBallServiceClient.exe` and `MagicEightBallServiceClient.exe.config` files from the \bin\Debug folder of the client application (from earlier in this chapter) into the `C:\EightBallTCP\Client` folder. Update the client configuration file like this:

```xml
<?xml version = "1.0" encoding = "utf-8" ?>
<configuration>
  <system.serviceModel>
    <client>
      <endpoint address = "net.tcp://localhost:8090/MagicEightBallService"
                binding = "netTcpBinding"
                contract = "ServiceReference1.IEightBall"
                name = "netTcpBinding_IEightBall" />
```

```
      </client>
    </system.serviceModel>
</configuration>
```

This client-side configuration file is a massive simplification compared to what the Visual Studio proxy generator authored. Notice how you have completely removed the existing `<bindings>` element. Originally, the `*.config` file contained a `<bindings>` element with a `<basicHttpBinding>` subelement that supplied numerous details of the client's binding settings (e.g., timeouts).

The truth is you never needed that detail for this example because you automatically obtain the default values of the underlying `BasicHttpBinding` object. If you needed, you could of course update the existing `<bindings>` element to define details of the `<netTcpBinding>` subelement; however, doing so is not required if you are happy with the default values of the `NetTcpBinding` object.

In any case, you should now be able to run your client application. Assuming the host is still running in the background, you will be able to move data between your assemblies using TCP.

■ **Source Code**   You can find the MagicEightBallTCP config files in the `Chapter 23` subdirectory.

Simplifying Configuration Settings

As you were working through the first example of the chapter, you might have noticed that the hosting configuration logic is quite verbose. For example, your host's `*.config` file (for the original basic HTTP binding) needed to define an `<endpoint>` element for the service, a second `<endpoint>` element for MEX, a `<baseAddresses>` element (technically optional) to reduce redundant URIs, and then a `<behaviors>` section to define the runtime nature of metadata exchange.

To be sure, learning how to author hosting `*.config` files can be a major hurdle when building WCF services. To make matters more frustrating, a good number of WCF services tend to require the same basic settings in a host configuration file. For example, if you were to make a new WCF service and a new host and you wanted to expose this service using `<basicHttpBinding>` with MEX support, the required `*.config` file would look almost identical to the one you previously authored.

Thankfully, since the release of .NET 4.0, the Windows Communication Foundation API ships with a number of simplifications, including default settings (and other shortcuts) that make the process of building host configuration files much easier.

Leveraging Default Endpoints

Before support for default endpoints, if you called `Open()` on the `ServiceHost` object and you had not yet specified at least one `<endpoint>` element in your configuration file, the runtime would throw an exception. And you would get a similar result if you called `AddServiceEndpoint()` in code to specify an endpoint. However, since the release of .NET 4.5, every WCF service is automatically provided with *default endpoints* that capture commonplace configuration details for each supported protocol.

If you were to open the `machine.config` file for .NET 4.5, you would find a new element named `<protocolMapping>`. This element documents which WCF bindings to use by default, if you do not specify any.

```
<system.serviceModel>
...
  <protocolMapping>
    <add scheme = "http" binding="basicHttpBinding"/>
```

```
    <add scheme = "net.tcp" binding="netTcpBinding"/>
    <add scheme = "net.pipe" binding="netNamedPipeBinding"/>
    <add scheme = "net.msmq" binding="netMsmqBinding"/>
  </protocolMapping>
  ...
</system.serviceModel>
```

To use these default bindings, all you need to do is specify base addresses in your host configuration file. To see this in action, open the HTTP-based MagicEightBallServiceHost project in Visual Studio. Now update your hosting *.config file by completely removing the <endpoint> element for your WCF service and all MEX-specific data. Your configuration file should now look like this:

```
<configuration>
  <system.serviceModel>
    <services>
      <service name = "MagicEightBallServiceLib.MagicEightBallService" >
        <host>
          <baseAddresses>
            <add baseAddress = "http://localhost:8080/MagicEightBallService"/>
          </baseAddresses>
        </host>
      </service>
    </services>
  </system.serviceModel>
</configuration>
```

Because you specified a valid HTTP <baseAddress>, your host will automatically use basicHttpBinding. If you run your host again, you will see the same listing of ABC data.

```
***** Console Based WCF Host *****

***** Host Info *****
Address: http://localhost:8080/MagicEightBallService
Binding: BasicHttpBinding
Contract: IEightBall
*********************
The service is ready.
Press the Enter key to terminate service.
```

You have not yet enabled MEX, but you will do so in a moment using another simplification known as *default behavior configurations*. First, however, you will learn how to expose a single WCF service using multiple bindings.

Exposing a Single WCF Service Using Multiple Bindings

Since its first release, WCF has had the ability to allow a single host to expose a WCF service using multiple endpoints. For example, you could expose the MagicEightBallService using HTTP, TCP, and named pipe bindings simply by adding new endpoints to your configuration file. Once you restart the host, all the necessary plumbing is created automatically.

This is a huge benefit for many reasons. Before WCF, it was difficult to expose a single service using multiple bindings because each type of binding (e.g., HTTP and TCP) had its own programming model.

Nevertheless, the ability to allow a caller to pick the most appropriate binding is extremely useful. In-house callers might like to use TCP bindings, an outwardly facing client (outside of your company firewall) would need to use HTTP to access, while clients on the same machine might opt to use a named pipe.

To do this before .NET 4.5, your hosting configuration file would need to define multiple <endpoint> elements manually. It would also have to define multiple <baseAddress> elements for each protocol. However, today you can simply author the following configuration file:

```
<configuration>
  <system.serviceModel>
    <services>
      <service name = "MagicEightBallServiceLib.MagicEightBallService" >
        <host>
          <baseAddresses>
            <add baseAddress = "http://localhost:8080/MagicEightBallService"/>
            <add baseAddress =
                "net.tcp://localhost:8099/MagicEightBallService"/>
          </baseAddresses>
        </host>
      </service>
    </services>
  </system.serviceModel>
</configuration>
```

If you compile your project (to refresh the deployed *.config file) and restart the host, you will now see the following endpoint data:

```
***** Console Based WCF Host *****

***** Host Info *****
Address: http://localhost:8080/MagicEightBallService
Binding: BasicHttpBinding
Contract: IEightBall
Address: net.tcp://localhost:8099/MagicEightBallService
Binding: NetTcpBinding
Contract: IEightBall
*********************
The service is ready.
Press the Enter key to terminate service.
```

Now that your WCF service can be reachable from two unique endpoints, you might wonder how the caller is able to select between them. When you generate a client-side proxy, the Add Service reference tool will give each exposed endpoint a string name in the client-side *.config file. In code, you can pass in the correct string name to the proxy's constructor, and sure enough, the correct binding will be used. Before you can do this, however, you need to reestablish MEX for this modified hosting configuration file and learn how to tweak the settings of a default binding.

Changing Settings for a WCF Binding

If you specify the ABCs of a service in C# code (which you will do later in this chapter), it becomes obvious how you change the default settings of a WCF binding; you simply change the property values of the object! For example, if you want to use BasicHttpBinding but also want to change the timeout settings, you could do so as follows:

```
void ConfigureBindingInCode()
{
  BasicHttpBinding binding = new BasicHttpBinding();
  binding.OpenTimeout = TimeSpan.FromSeconds(30);
  ...
}
```

It has always been possible to configure settings for a binding in a declarative manner. For example, .NET 3.5 lets you build a host configuration file that changed the OpenTimeout property of BasicHttpBinding, like so:

```
<configuration>
  <system.serviceModel>

    <bindings>s
      <basicHttpBinding>
        <binding name = "myCustomHttpBinding"
                 openTimeout = "00:00:30" />
      </basicHttpBinding>
    </bindings>

    <services>
      <service name = "WcfMathService.MyCalc">
        <endpoint address = "http://localhost:8080/MyCalc"
                  binding = "basicHttpBinding"
                  bindingConfiguration = "myCustomHttpBinding"
                  contract = "WcfMathService.IBasicMath" />
      </service>
    </services>
  </system.serviceModel>
</configuration>
```

Here, you have a configuration file for a service named WcfMathService.MyCalc, which supports a single interface named IBasicMath. Note how the <bindings> section allows you to define a named <binding> element, which tweaks settings for a given binding. Within the <endpoint> of the service, you can connect your specific settings using the bindingConfiguration attribute.

This sort of hosting configuration still works as expected; however, if you leverage a default endpoint, you can't connect the <binding> to the <endpoint>! As luck would have it, you can control the settings of a default endpoint simply by omitting the name attribute of the <binding> element. For example, this snippet changes some properties of the default BasicHttpBinding and NetTcpBinding objects used in the background:

```
<configuration>
  <system.serviceModel>
    <services>
      <service name = "MagicEightBallServiceLib.MagicEightBallService" >
        <host>
```

```
      <baseAddresses>
        <add baseAddress = "http://localhost:8080/MagicEightBallService"/>
        <add baseAddress =
          "net.tcp://localhost:8099/MagicEightBallService"/>
        </baseAddresses>
      </host>
    </service>
  </services>

  <bindings>
    <basicHttpBinding>
      <binding openTimeout = "00:00:30" />
    </basicHttpBinding>
    <netTcpBinding>
      <binding closeTimeout = "00:00:15" />
    </netTcpBinding>
  </bindings>

  </system.serviceModel>
</configuration>
```

Leveraging the Default MEX Behavior Configuration

A proxy generation tool must discover the composition of a service at runtime before it can do its work. In WCF, you allow this runtime discovery to occur by enabling MEX. Again, most host configuration files need to enable MEX (at least during development); fortunately, the way you configure MEX seldom changes, so .NET 4.5 and above provides a few handy shortcuts.

The most useful shortcut is out-of-the-box MEX support. You don't need to add a MEX endpoint, define a named MEX service behavior, and then connect the named binding to the service (as you did in the HTTP version of the MagicEightBallServiceHost); instead, you can now simply add the following:

```
<configuration>
  <system.serviceModel>
    <services>
      <service name = "MagicEightBallServiceLib.MagicEightBallService" >
        <host>
          <baseAddresses>
            <add baseAddress = "http://localhost:8080/MagicEightBallService"/>
            <add baseAddress =
              "net.tcp://localhost:8099/MagicEightBallService"/>
          </baseAddresses>
        </host>
      </service>
    </services>

  <bindings>
    <basicHttpBinding>
      <binding openTimeout = "00:00:30" />
    </basicHttpBinding>
    <netTcpBinding>
      <binding closeTimeout = "00:00:15" />
    </netTcpBinding>
  </bindings>
```

```
    <behaviors>
      <serviceBehaviors>
        <behavior>
          <!-- To get default MEX,
               don't name your <serviceMetadata> element -->
          <serviceMetadata httpGetEnabled = "true"/>
        </behavior>
      </serviceBehaviors>
    </behaviors>
  </system.serviceModel>
</configuration>
```

The trick is that the `<serviceMetadata>` element no longer has a `name` attribute (also notice the `<service>` element no longer needs the `behaviorConfiguration` attribute). With this adjustment, you get free MEX support at runtime. To test this, you can run your host (after you compile to refresh the configuration file) and type in the following URL in a browser:

```
http://localhost:8080/MagicEightBallService
```

After you do this, you can click the `wsdl` link at the top of the web page to see the WSDL description of the service (refer to Figure 23-5 for a refresher). Note that you do not see the host's console window print data for the MEX endpoint because you have not explicitly defined an endpoint for `IMetadataExchange` in your configuration file. Nevertheless, MEX is enabled, and you can start to build client proxies.

Refreshing the Client Proxy and Selecting the Binding

Assuming your updated host has been compiled and is running in the background, you will now want to open the client application and refresh the current service reference. Begin by opening the Service References folder in Solution Explorer. Next, right-click the current ServiceReference1 and select the Update Service Reference menu option (see Figure 23-8).

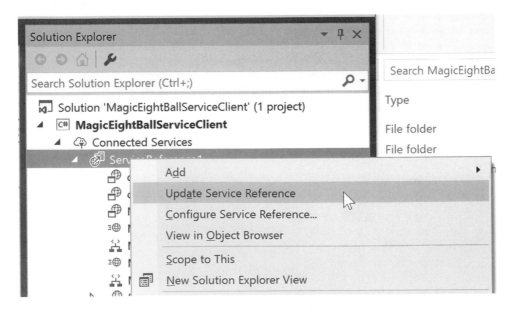

Figure 23-8. *Refreshing the proxy and client-side *.config file*

After you have done this, you will see that the client-side *.config file has two bindings to select from: one for HTTP and one for TCP. As you can see, you give each binding a fitting name. Here is a partial listing of the refreshed configuration file:

```
<configuration>
  <system.serviceModel>

    <bindings>
      <basicHttpBinding>
        <binding name = "BasicHttpBinding_IEightBall" ... />
      </basicHttpBinding>

      <netTcpBinding>
        <binding name = "NetTcpBinding_IEightBall" ... />
      </netTcpBinding>
    </bindings>
...
  </system.serviceModel>
</configuration>
```

The client can use these names when it creates the proxy object to select the binding it wants to use. Thus, if your client would like to use TCP, you could update the client side C# code as follows:

```
static void Main(string[] args)
{
  Console.WriteLine("***** Ask the Magic 8 Ball *****\n");

  using (EightBallClient ball = new EightBallClient("NetTcpBinding_IEightBall"))
  {
    ...
  }
  Console.ReadLine();
}
```

If a client would rather use the HTTP binding, you could write the following:

```
using (EightBallClient ball = new
      EightBallClient("BasicHttpBinding_IEightBall"))
{
...
}
```

That wraps up the current example, which showcased a number of useful shortcuts. These features simplify how you can author hosting configuration files. Next up, you will see how to use the WCF Service Library project template.

■ **Source Code**   You can find the MagicEightBallServiceClient project located in the Chapter 23 subdirectory.

Using the WCF Service Library Project Template

Before building a more exotic WCF service that communicates with the AutoLot data access layer you created in Chapter 22, the next example will illustrate a number of important topics, including the benefits of the WCF Service Library project template, the WCF Test Client, the WCF configuration editor, hosting WCF services within a Windows service, and asynchronous client calls. To stay focused on these new concepts, this WCF service will be kept intentionally simple.

Building a Simple Math Service

To begin, create a new WCF Service Library project named MathServiceLibrary. Now change the name of the initial IService1.cs file to IBasicMath.cs. After you do so, *delete* all the example code within the MathServiceLibrary namespace and replace it with the following code:

```
[ServiceContract(Namespace="http://MyCompany.com")]
public interface IBasicMath
{
  [OperationContract]
  int Add(int x, int y);
}
```

Next, change the name of the Service1.cs file to MathService.cs, delete all the example code within the MathServiceLibrary namespace (again), and implement your service contract as follows:

```
public class MathService : IBasicMath
{
  public int Add(int x, int y)
  {
    // To simulate a lengthy request.
    System.Threading.Thread.Sleep(5000);
    return x + y;
  }
}
```

Also take a moment to notice that this *.config file has already been enabled to support MEX; by default, your service endpoint uses the basicHttpBinding protocol.

Testing the WCF Service with WcfTestClient.exe

One benefit of using the WCF Service Library project is that when you debug or run your library, it will read the settings in the *.config file and use them to load the WCF Test Client application (WcfTestClient.exe). This GUI-based application allows you to test each member of your service interface as you build the WCF service; this means you don't have to build a host/client manually simply for testing purposes, as you did previously.

Figure 23-9 shows the testing environment for MathService. Notice that when you double-click an interface method, you can specify input parameters and invoke the member.

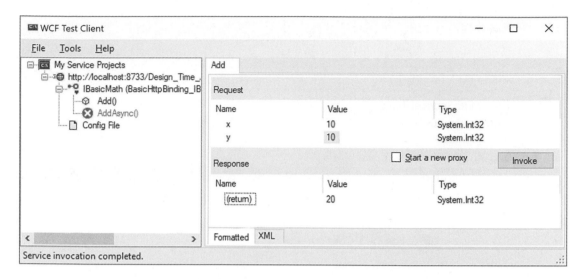

Figure 23-9. *Testing the WCF service using WcfTestClient.exe*

This utility works out of the box when you have created a WCF Service Library project; however, be aware that you can use this tool to test any WCF service when you start it at the command line by specifying a MEX endpoint. For example, if you were to start the `MagicEightBallServiceHost.exe` application, you could specify the following command at a developer command prompt:

```
wcftestclient http://localhost:8080/MagicEightBallService
```

After you do this, you can invoke `ObtainAnswerToQuestion()` in a similar manner.

Altering Configuration Files Using SvcConfigEditor.exe

Another benefit of using the WCF Service Library project is that you are able to right-click the `App.config` file within Solution Explorer to activate the GUI-based Service Configuration Editor, `SvcConfigEditor.exe` (see Figure 23-10). This same technique can be used from a client application that has referenced a WCF service.

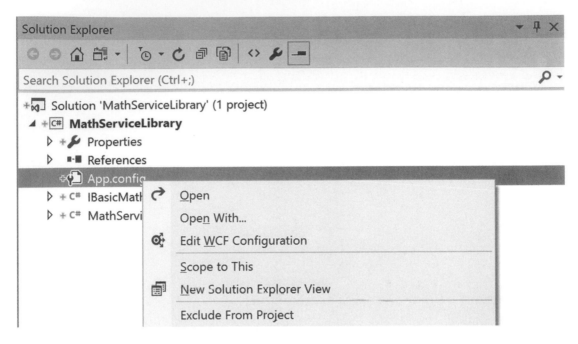

Figure 23-10. *GUI-based *.config file editing starts here*

After you activate this tool, you can change the XML-based data using a friendly user interface. Using a tool such as this to maintain your `*.config` files provides many benefits. First (and foremost), you can rest assured that the generated markup conforms to the expected format and is typo-free. Second, it is a great way to see the valid values that could be assigned to a given attribute. Finally, you no longer need to author tedious XML data manually.

Figure 23-11 shows the overall look and feel of the Service Configuration Editor. Truth be told, an entire chapter could be devoted to describing all the interesting options SvcConfigEditor.exe supports. Be sure to take time to investigate this tool; also be aware that you can access a fairly detailed help system by pressing F1.

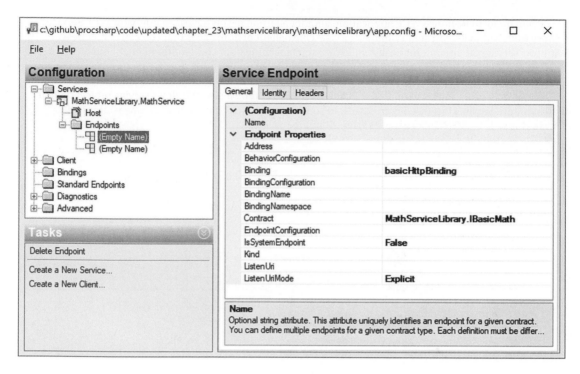

Figure 23-11. *Working with the WCF Service Configuration Editor*

■ **Note**   The SvcConfigEditor.exe utility can edit (or create) configuration files, even if you do not select an initial WCF Service Library project. Use a Developer Command window to launch the tool and then use the File Open menu option to load an existing *.config file for editing.

You have no need to further configure your WCF MathService; at this point, you can move on to the task of building a custom host.

Hosting the WCF Service Within a Windows Service

Hosting a WCF service from within a console application (or within a GUI desktop application, for that matter) is not an ideal choice for a production-level server, given that the host must remain running visibly in the background to service clients. Even if you were to minimize the hosting application to the Windows taskbar, it would still be far too easy to accidentally shut down the host, thereby terminating the connection with any client applications.

■ **Note**   While it is true that a desktop Windows application does not *have* to show a main window, a typical *.exe does require user interaction to load the executable. However, you can configure a Windows service (described next) to run even if no users are currently logged on to the workstation.

If you build an in-house WCF application, another alternative you have is to host your WCF Service Library from within a dedicated Windows service. One benefit of doing so is that you can configure a Windows service to start automatically when the target machine boots up. Another benefit is that Windows services run invisibly in the background (unlike your console application) and do not require user interactivity (and you don't need IIS installed on the host computer).

Next, you will learn how to build such a host. Begin by adding a new Windows service project named MathWindowsServiceHost (see Figure 23-12) to your solution. After you do this, rename your initial `Service1.cs` file to `MathWinService.cs` using Solution Explorer.

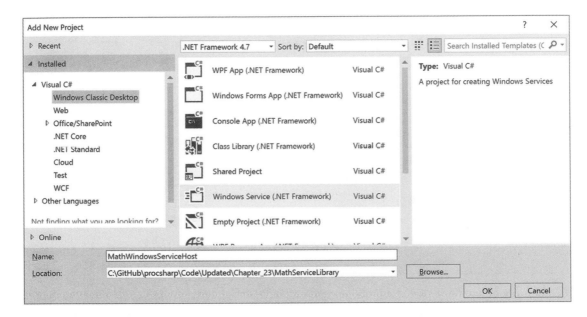

Figure 23-12. *Creating a Windows service to host your WCF service*

Specifying the ABCs in Code

Now assume you have set a reference to your `MathServiceLibrary.dll` and `System.ServiceModel.dll` assemblies. All you need to do is use the `ServiceHost` type in the `OnStart()` and `OnStop()` methods of your Windows service type. Open the code file for your service host class (by right-clicking the designer and selecting View Code) and add the following logic:

```
// Be sure to import these namespaces:
using MathServiceLibrary;
using System.ServiceModel;
using System.ServiceProcesses;

namespace MathWindowsServiceHost
{
  public partial class MathWinService: ServiceBase
  {
    // A member variable of type ServiceHost.
    private ServiceHost myHost;
```

```
    public MathWinService()
    {
      InitializeComponent();
    }

    protected override void OnStart(string[] args)
    {
      // Just to be really safe.
      myHost?.Close();
      // Create the host.
      myHost = new ServiceHost(typeof(MathService));
      // The ABCs in code!
      Uri address = new Uri("http://localhost:8080/MathServiceLibrary");
      WSHttpBinding binding = new WSHttpBinding();
      Type contract = typeof(IBasicMath);
      // Add this endpoint.
      myHost.AddServiceEndpoint(contract, binding, address);
      // Open the host.
      myHost.Open();
    }
    protected override void OnStop()
    {
      // Shut down the host.
      myHost?.Close();
    }
  }
}
```

While nothing prevents you from using a configuration file when building a Windows service host for a WCF service, here (for a change of pace) you establish the endpoint programmatically using the Uri, WSHttpBinding, and Type classes, rather than by using a *.config file. After you create each aspect of the ABCs, you inform the host programmatically by calling AddServiceEndpoint().

If you want to inform the runtime that you want to gain access to each of the default endpoint bindings stored in the .NET 4.5 machine.config file, you can simplify your programming logic by specifying base addresses when you invoke the constructor of ServiceHost. In this case, you do not need to specify the ABCs manually in code or call AddServiceEndpoint(); instead, you call AddDefaultEndpoints(). Consider the following update:

```
protected override void OnStart(string[] args)
{
  myHost?.Close();
  // Create the host and specify a URL for an HTTP binding.
  myHost = new ServiceHost(typeof(MathService), new Uri("http://localhost:8080/
MathServiceLibrary"));

  // Opt in for the default endpoints!
  myHost.AddDefaultEndpoints();

  // Open the host.
  myHost.Open();
}
```

Enabling MEX

While you could enable MEX programmatically as well, here you will opt for a configuration file. Modify the App.config file in your Windows service project so that it contains the following default MEX settings:

```
<?xml version = "1.0" encoding = "utf-8" ?>
<configuration>
  <system.serviceModel>
    <services>
      <service name = "MathServiceLibrary.MathService">
      </service>
    </services>

    <behaviors>
      <serviceBehaviors>
        <behavior>
          <serviceMetadata httpGetEnabled = "true"/>
        </behavior>
      </serviceBehaviors>
    </behaviors>

  </system.serviceModel>
</configuration>
```

Creating a Windows Service Installer

To register your Windows service with the operating system, you need to add an installer to your project that contains the necessary code to allow you to register the service. To do so, right-click the Windows service designer surface and select Add Installer (see Figure 23-13).

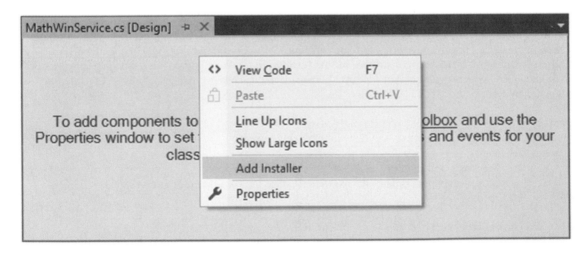

Figure 23-13. *Adding an installer for the Windows service*

Once you do this, you can see two components have been added to a new designer surface representing the installer. The first component (named serviceProcessInstaller1 by default) represents an item that can install a new Windows service on the target machine. Select this item on the designer and use the Properties window to set the Account property to LocalSystem (see Figure 23-14).

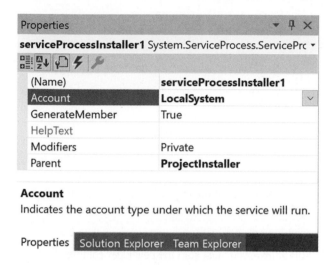

Figure 23-14. *Be sure to run the Windows service as a local system account*

The second component (named serviceInstaller1) represents a type that will install your particular Windows service. Again, use the Properties window to change the ServiceName property to MathService, set the StartType property to Automatic, and add a friendly description of your Windows service using the Description property (see Figure 23-15).

Properties	▾ 🔲 ✕
serviceInstaller1 System.ServiceProcess.ServiceInstaller ▾	
(Name)	**serviceInstaller1**
DelayedAutoStart	False
Description	This is the math service
DisplayName	
GenerateMember	True
HelpText	
Modifiers	Private
Parent	**ProjectInstaller**
ServiceName	**MathService**
⊞ ServicesDependedOn	String[] Array
StartType	**Automatic**

Description
Indicates the service's description (a brief comment that e...

Properties | Solution Explorer | Team Explorer

Figure 23-15. *Configuring installer details*

Open the `Program.cs` file in the `MathWindowsServiceHost` project, and update the `Main()` method to this:

```
static void Main()
{
  ServiceBase[] ServicesToRun;
  ServicesToRun = new ServiceBase[]
  {
    new MathWinService()
  };
  ServiceBase.Run(ServicesToRun);
}
```

At this point, you can compile your application.

Installing the Windows Service

A Windows service can be installed on the host machine using a traditional setup program (such as an *.msi installer) or via the `installutil.exe` command-line tool.

■ **Note** To install a Windows service using `installutil.exe`, you must start the developer command prompt under administrative privileges. To do so, right-click the Developer Command Prompt icon and select Run As Administrator.

Using a developer command prompt (running as administrator), change to the \bin\Debug folder of your MathWindowsServiceHost project. Now, enter the following command (be sure you are running as administrator!):

```
installutil MathWindowsServiceHost.exe
```

Assuming the installation succeeded, you can now open the Services applet located under the Administrative Tools folder of your Control Panel. You should see the friendly name of your Windows service listed alphabetically. After you locate it, make sure you start the service on your local machine using the Start link (see Figure 23-16).

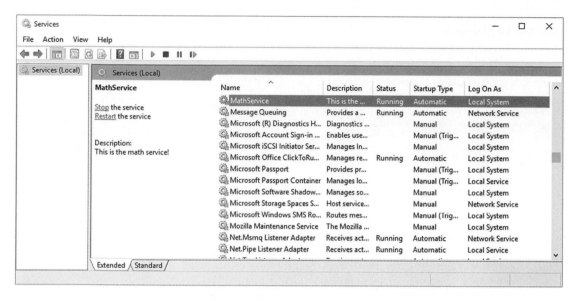

Figure 23-16. *Viewing your Windows service, which hosts your WCF service*

Now that the service is alive and kicking, the last step is to build a client application to consume its services.

Invoking a Service Asynchronously from the Client

Add a new Console Application project (named MathClient) to the solution and set it as the startup project. Next, set a service reference to your running WCF service (that is currently hosted by the Windows service running in the background) using the Add Service Reference option of Visual Studio (you'll need to type the URL in the Addresses box, which should be `http://localhost:8080/MathServiceLibrary`). Don't click the OK button yet, however! Notice that the Add Service Reference dialog box has an Advanced button in the lower-left corner (see Figure 23-17).

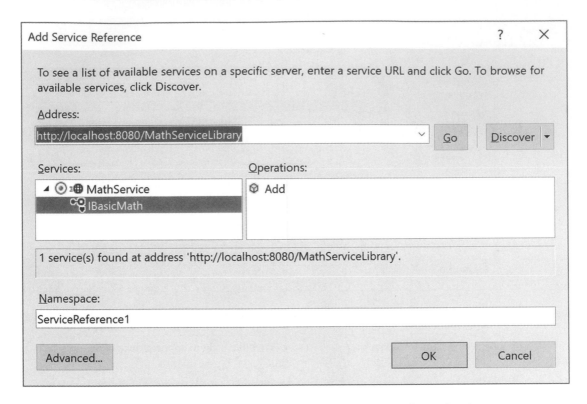

Figure 23-17. *Referencing your MathService and getting ready to configure advanced settings*

Click this button now to view the additional proxy configuration settings (see Figure 23-18). You can use this dialog box to generate code that allows you to call the remote methods in an asynchronous manner, provided you select the "Generate asynchronous operators" radio option. Go ahead and select this option for the time being.

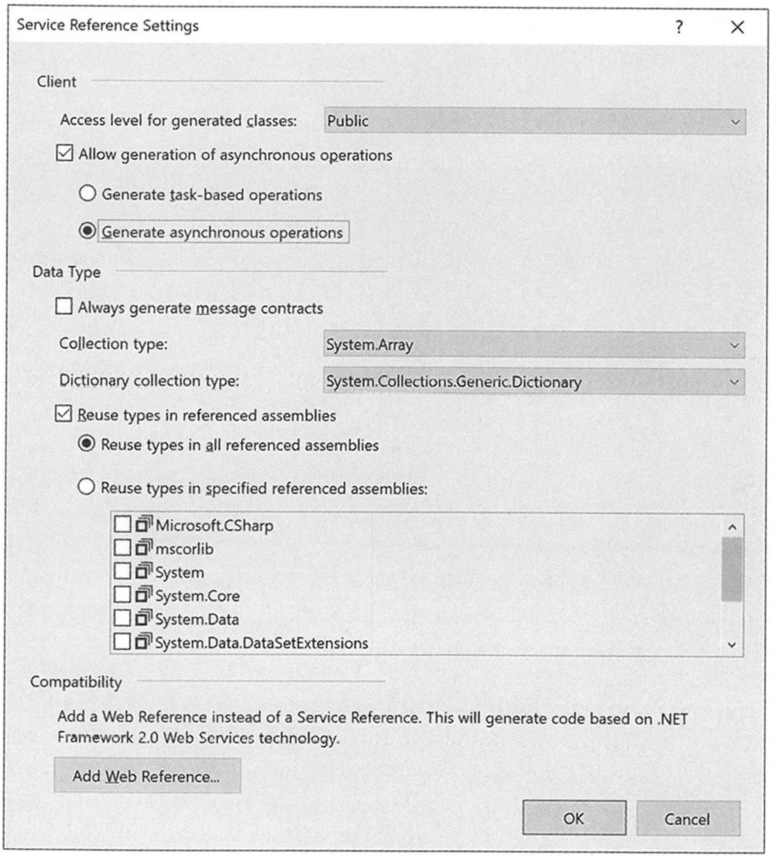

Figure 23-18. *Advanced client-side proxy configuration options*

At this point, the proxy code contains additional methods that allow you to invoke each member of the service contract using the expected Begin/End asynchronous invocation pattern described in Chapter 19. Here is a simple implementation that uses a lambda expression rather than a strongly typed AsyncCallback delegate:

```
using System;
using System.Threading;
using MathClient.ServiceReference1;
...

namespace MathClient
{
  class Program
  {
    static void Main(string[] args)
    {
      Console.WriteLine("***** The Async Math Client *****\n");
      using (BasicMathClient proxy = new BasicMathClient())
      {
```

```
        proxy.Open();
        // Add numbers in an async manner, using a lambda expression.
        IAsyncResult result = proxy.BeginAdd(2, 3,
          ar =>
          {
            Console.WriteLine("2 + 3 = {0}", proxy.EndAdd(ar));
          },
          null);
        while (!result.IsCompleted)
        {
          Thread.Sleep(200);
          Console.WriteLine("Client working...");
        }
      }
    }
    Console.ReadLine();
    }
  }
}
```

■ **Source Code**   You can find the MathServiceLibrary solution in the Chapter 23 subdirectory.

Designing WCF Data Contracts

This chapter's final example shows you how to construct WCF *data contracts*. The previous WCF services
defined simple methods that operate on primitive CLR data types. When you use of any of the HTTP binding
types (e.g., basicHttpBinding and wsHttpBinding), incoming and outgoing simple data types are automatically
formatted into XML elements. On a related note, if you use a TCP-based binding (such as netTcpBinding), the
parameters and return values of simple data types are transmitted using a compact binary format.

■ **Note**   The WCF runtime will also automatically encode any type marked with the [Serializable]
attribute; however, this is not the preferred way to define WCF contracts, and it is included only for backward
compatibility.

However, when you define service contracts that use custom classes as parameters or return values, it
is a best practice to model such data using WCF data contracts. Simply put, a data contract is a type adorned
with the [DataContract] attribute. Likewise, you must mark each field you expect to be used as part of the
proposed contract with the [DataMember] attribute.

■ **Note**   In earlier versions of the .NET platform, it was mandatory to use [DataContract] and [DataMember]
to ensure custom data types were correctly represented. Microsoft has since relaxed this requirement;
technically speaking, you are not required to use these attributes on custom data types; however, it is
considered a .NET best practice.

Using the Web-centric WCF Service Project Template

The next WCF service will allow external callers to interact with the AutoLot data access layer you created in Chapter 22. Moreover, this final WCF service will be created using the web-based WCF Service template and be hosted under IIS.

To begin, launch Visual Studio (with administrator rights) and access the File ➤ New ➤ Web Site menu option. Select the WCF Service project type and ensure the Web Location drop-down is set to HTTP (which will install the service under IIS). Expose the service from the following URI:

```
http://localhost/AutoLotWCFService
```

Figure 23-19 shows the configured project.

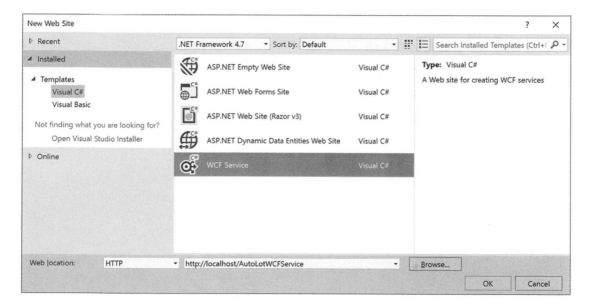

Figure 23-19. *Creating a web-centric WCF service*

After you have done this, right-click the solution (in Solution Explorer), select Add ➤ Existing Project, select the AutoLotDAL project from Chapter 22, and repeat for AutoLotDAL.Models. You could also just add a reference to AutoLotDAL.dll and AutoLotDAL.Models.dll, but adding the project enables debugging the data access later.

In the App_Code folder, rename the IService.cs file to IAutoLotService.cs and then define the initial service contract within your newly named file, like so:

```
[ServiceContract]
public interface IAutoLotService
{
  [OperationContract]
  void InsertCar(string make, string color, string petname);

  [OperationContract]
  void InsertCar(InventoryRecord car);
```

```
  [OperationContract]
  List<InventoryRecord> GetInventory();
}
```

This interface defines three methods, one of which returns a list of the (yet-to-be-created) InventoryRecord type. You might recall that the GetAll() method of the InventoryRepo returns a List<T> of Inventory records, and this might make you wonder why your service's GetInventory() method returns a List<T> of InventoryRecord, a different class.

WCF was built to honor the use of SOA principles, one of which is to program against contracts, not implementations. Therefore, you won't return the .NET-specific Inventory type to an external caller; instead, you will return a custom data contract (InventoryRecord) that will be correctly expressed in the contained WSDL document in an agnostic manner.

To create the custom data contract, add a new class under the App_Code folder named InventoryRecord.cs. Define the InventoryRecord data contract as follows:

```
using System.Runtime.Serialization;

[DataContract]
public class InventoryRecord
{
  [DataMember]
  public int ID;

  [DataMember]
  public string Make;

  [DataMember]
  public string Color;

  [DataMember]
  public string PetName;
}
```

If you were to implement the IAutoLotService interface as it now stands and then build a host and attempt to call these methods from a client, you might be surprised to see that you would get a runtime exception. The reason: one of the requirements of a WSDL description is that each method exposed from a given endpoint must be *uniquely named*. Thus, while method overloading works just fine as far as C# is concerned, the current web service specifications do not permit two identically named InsertCar() methods.

Fortunately, the [OperationContract] attribute supports a named property (Name) that allows you to specify how the C# method will be represented within a WSDL description. Given this, you can update the second version of InsertCar() as follows:

```
public interface IAutoLotService
{
...
  [OperationContract(Name = "InsertCarWithDetails")]
  void InsertCar(InventoryRecord car);
}
```

Update NuGet Packages and Install AutoMapper and EF

Before implementing the service contract, you need to add the AutoMapper Nuget package. This package specializes in converting one object into another object based on property names and values.

■ **Note**   AutoMapper is extremely powerful, and I am only scratching the surface of it in this chapter. You will use AutoMapper in several later chapters. For more information on what AutoMapper offers, please see the documentation at http://automapper.org/.

Right-click the AutoLotWCFService project and select Manage NuGet Packages. When the screen loads, you might see a message that states "Some NuGet packages are missing from this solution…." If you see this, click the Restore button at the end of the message.

Next, click Browse at the top, and if AutoMapper isn't already showing, enter **AutoMapper** in the Search box. Select it and click Install, as shown in Figure 23-20.

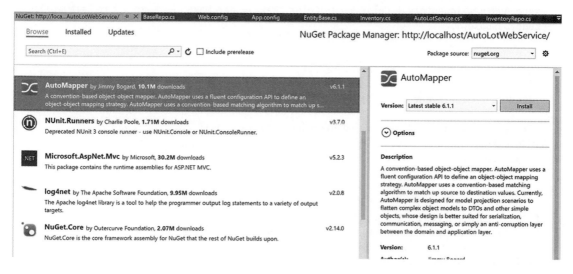

Figure 23-20. *Installing AutoMapper*

Finally, install the EntityFramework 6.1.3 NuGet package using NuGet Package Manager.

Implementing the Service Contract

Now rename Service.cs to AutoLotService.cs. The AutoLotService type implements the IAutoLotService interface as follows (be sure to import the AutoLotDAL.Models, AutoLotDAL.Repos, and AutoMapper namespaces into this code file):

```
using AutoLotDAL.Models;
using AutoLotDAL.Repos;
using AutoMapper;
```

```
public class AutoLotService : IAutoLotService
{
  public AutoLotService()
  {
    Mapper.Initialize(cfg => cfg.CreateMap<Inventory, InventoryRecord>());
  }

  public void InsertCar(string make, string color, string petname)
  {
    var repo = new InventoryRepo();
    repo.Add(new Inventory {Color = color, Make = make, PetName = petname});
    repo.Dispose();
  }

  public void InsertCar(InventoryRecord car)
  {
    var repo = new InventoryRepo();
    repo.Add(new Inventory { Color = car.Color, Make = car.Make, PetName = car.PetName});
    repo.Dispose();
  }

  public List<InventoryRecord> GetInventory()
  {
    var repo = new InventoryRepo();
    var records = repo.GetAll();
    var results = Mapper.Map<List<InventoryRecord>>(records);
    repo.Dispose();
    return results;
  }
}
```

In the constructor, you inform AutoMapper the types you will be converting by using the generic CreateMap() function and passing in the From and To types, as follows:

```
Mapper.Initialize(cfg => cfg.CreateMap<Inventory, InventoryRecord>());
```

When converting the List<T> of Inventory types to a List<T> of InventoryRecord types, you then call the Map() function, as follows:

```
var results = Mapper.Map<List<InventoryRecord>>(records);
```

The rest of the code is very straightforward, calling methods on the InventoryRepo.

The Role of the *.svc File

When you create a web-centric WCF service, you will find your project contains a specific file with an *.svc file extension. This particular file is required for any WCF service hosted by IIS; it describes the name and location of the service implementation within the install point. Because you have changed the names of your starter files and WCF types, you must now update the contents of the Service.svc file as follows:

```
<%@ ServiceHost Language="C#" Debug="true"
  Service="AutoLotService" CodeBehind="~/App_Code/AutoLotService.cs" %>
```

Examining the Web.config File

The Web.config file of a WCF service created under HTTP will use a number of the WCF simplifications examined earlier in this chapter. As will be described in more detail during your examination of ASP.NET later in this book, the Web.config file serves a similar purpose to an executable's *.config file; however, it also controls a number of web-specific settings. For this example, notice that MEX is enabled, and you do not have to specify a custom <endpoint> manually.

```
<configuration>

  <system.serviceModel>
    <behaviors>
      <serviceBehaviors>
        <behavior>
          <!-- To avoid disclosing metadata information, set the value below to false and
          remove the
              metadata endpoint above before deployment -->
          <serviceMetadata httpGetEnabled="true" httpsGetEnabled="true" />
          <!-- To receive exception details in faults for debugging purposes,  set the value
          below to true.
              Set to false before deployment to avoid disclosing exception information -->
          <serviceDebug includeExceptionDetailInFaults="false"/>
        </behavior>
      </serviceBehaviors>
    </behaviors>
    <serviceHostingEnvironment aspNetCompatibilityEnabled="true" multipleSiteBindingsEnabled
    ="true" />
  </system.serviceModel>

</configuration>
```

Add the Connection String to the Web.config File

The final change for Web.config is to add the connection string for the AutoLot database in SQL Server Express. This version needs to add the User Id and Password as well as remove the Integrated Security entry or change a series of settings in IIS and SQL Server. Your entry should look something like this:

```
<connectionStrings>
  <add name="AutoLotConnection" connectionString="data source=.\SQLEXPRESS2016;
  initial catalog=AutoLot;MultipleActiveResultSets=True;App=EntityFramework;
  User Id=myUser;Password=myPassword" providerName="System.Data.SqlClient" />
</connectionStrings>
```

■ **Note**   SQL Server must have "SQL Server and Windows Authentication mode" enabled for this example to work. If you are using the code from the download files, you will need to update the User Id and Password settings to match your configuration. As a final note, LocalDb and IIS do not play well together. While you *can* make them work together, it's better to use SQL Server Express or higher editions with WPF.

Testing the Service

Now you are free to build any sort of client to test your service, including passing in the endpoint of the `*.svc` file to the `WcfTestClient.exe` application.

```
WcfTestClient http://localhost/AutoLotWCFService/Service.svc
```

If you want to build a custom client application, you can use the Add Service Reference dialog box, as you did for the MagicEightBallServiceClient and MathClient project examples earlier in this chapter.

■ **Source Code**   You can find the AutoLotWCFService project in the Chapter 23 subdirectory.

That wraps up your look at the Windows Communication Foundation API. Of course, there is much more to WCF than could be covered in this introductory chapter; however, if you understand the materials presented here, you are in great shape to seek out more details as you see fit. Be sure to consult the .NET Framework 4.7 SDK documentation if you want to learn more about WCF.

Summary

This chapter introduced you to Windows Communication Foundation (WCF), which represents the core distributed programming API under the .NET platform. As explained in this chapter, the major motivation behind WCF was to provide a unified object model that exposes a number of (previously unrelated) distributed computing APIs under a single umbrella. Furthermore, a WCF service is represented by specified addresses, bindings, and contracts (which you can remember easily by the friendly abbreviation ABC).

You also learned that a typical WCF application involves the use of three interrelated assemblies. The first assembly defines the service contracts and service types that represent the service's functionality. This assembly is then hosted by a custom executable, an IIS virtual directory, or a Windows service. Finally, the client assembly uses a generated code file that defines a proxy type (and settings within the application configuration file) to communicate with the remote type.

The chapter also examined how to use a number of WCF programming tools, such as `SvcConfigEditor.exe` (which allows you to modify `*.config` files), the `WcfTestClient.exe` application (to test a WCF service quickly), and various Visual Studio WCF project templates. You also learned about a number of configuration simplifications, including default endpoints and behaviors.

PART VII

Windows Presentation Foundation

CHAPTER 24

■ ■ ■

Introducing Windows Presentation Foundation and XAML

When version 1.0 of the .NET platform was released, programmers who needed to build graphical desktop applications made use of two APIs named Windows Forms and GDI+, packaged up primarily in the `System.Windows.Forms.dll` and `System.Drawing.dll` assemblies. While Windows Forms/GDI+ are still viable APIs for building traditional desktop GUIs, Microsoft shipped an alternative GUI desktop API named Windows Presentation Foundation (WPF) beginning with the release of .NET 3.0.

This initial WPF chapter begins by examining the motivation behind this new GUI framework, which will help you see the differences between the Windows Forms/GDI+ and WPF programming models. Next, you will come to know the role of several important classes, including `Application`, `Window`, `ContentControl`, `Control`, `UIElement`, and `FrameworkElement`.

This chapter will then introduce you to an XML-based grammar named *Extensible Application Markup Language* (XAML; pronounced "zammel"). Here, you will learn the syntax and semantics of XAML (including attached property syntax and the role of type converters and markup extensions)

This chapter wraps up by investigating the integrated WPF designers of Visual Studio by building your first WPF application. During this time, you will learn to intercept keyboard and mouse activities, define application-wide data, and perform other common WPF tasks.

The Motivation Behind WPF

Over the years, Microsoft has created numerous graphical user interface toolkits (raw C/C++/Windows API development, VB6, MFC, etc.) to build desktop executables. Each of these APIs provided a codebase to represent the basic aspects of a GUI application, including main windows, dialog boxes, controls, menu systems, and other basic necessities. With the initial release of the .NET platform, the Windows Forms API quickly became the preferred model for UI development, given its simple yet very powerful object model.

While many full-featured desktop applications have been successfully created using Windows Forms, the fact of the matter is that this programming model is rather *asymmetrical*. Simply put, `System.Windows.Forms.dll` and `System.Drawing.dll` do not provide direct support for many additional technologies required to build a feature-rich desktop application. To illustrate this point, consider the ad hoc nature of GUI desktop development before the release of WPF (see Table 24-1).

© Andrew Troelsen and Philip Japikse 2017
A. Troelsen and P. Japikse, *Pro C# 7*, https://doi.org/10.1007/978-1-4842-3018-3_24

Table 24-1. *Pre-WPF Solutions to Desired Functionalities*

Desired Functionality	Technology
Building windows with controls	Windows Forms
2D graphics support	GDI+ (System.Drawing.dll)
3D graphics support	DirectX APIs
Support for streaming video	Windows Media Player APIs
Support for flow-style documents	Programmatic manipulation of PDF files

As you can see, a Windows Forms developer must pull in types from a number of unrelated APIs and object models. While it is true that making use of these diverse APIs might look similar syntactically (it is just C# code, after all), you might also agree that each technology requires a radically different mind-set. For example, the skills required to create a 3D rendered animation using DirectX are completely different from those used to bind data to a grid. To be sure, it is difficult for a Windows Forms programmer to master the diverse nature of each API.

Unifying Diverse APIs

WPF was purposely created to merge these previously unrelated programming tasks into a single unified object model. Thus, if you need to author a 3D animation, you have no need to manually program against the DirectX API (although you could) because 3D functionality is baked directly into WPF. To see how well things have cleaned up, consider Table 24-2, which illustrates the desktop development model ushered in as of .NET 3.0.

Table 24-2. *.NET 3.0 Solutions to Desired Functionalities*

Desired Functionality	Technology
Building forms with controls	WPF
2D graphics support	WPF
3D graphics support	WPF
Support for streaming video	WPF
Support for flow-style documents	WPF

The obvious benefit here is that .NET programmers now have a single, *symmetrical* API for all common GUI desktop programming needs. After you become comfortable with the functionality of the key WPF assemblies and the grammar of XAML, you'll be amazed how quickly you can create sophisticated UIs.

Providing a Separation of Concerns via XAML

Perhaps one of the most compelling benefits is that WPF provides a way to cleanly separate the look and feel of a GUI application from the programming logic that drives it. Using XAML, it is possible to define the UI of an application via XML *markup*. This markup (ideally generated using tools such as Microsoft Visual Studio or Microsoft Expression Blend) can then be connected to a related C# code file to provide the guts of the program's functionality.

■ **Note**   XAML is not limited to WPF applications. Any application can use XAML to describe a tree of .NET objects, even if they have nothing to do with a visible user interface.

As you dig into WPF, you might be surprised how much flexibility this "desktop markup" provides. XAML allows you to define not only simple UI elements (buttons, grids, list boxes, etc.) in markup but also interactive 2D and 3D graphics, animations, data binding logic, and multimedia functionality (such as video playback).

XAML also makes it easy to customize how a control should render out its visual appearance. For example, defining a circular button control that animates your company logo requires just a few lines of markup. As shown in Chapter 27, WPF controls can be modified through styles and templates, which allow you to change the overall look and feel of an application with minimum fuss and bother. Unlike Windows Forms development, the only compelling reason to build a custom WPF control from the ground up is if you need to change the *behaviors* of a control (e.g., add custom methods, properties, or events; subclass an existing control to override virtual members). If you simply need to change the *look and feel* of a control (again, such as a circular animated button), you can do so entirely through markup.

Providing an Optimized Rendering Model

GUI toolkits such as Windows Forms, MFC, or VB6 performed all graphical rendering requests (including the rendering of UI elements such as buttons and list boxes) using a low-level, C-based API (GDI), which has been part of the Windows OS for years. GDI provides adequate performance for typical business applications or simple graphical programs; however, if a UI application needed to tap into high-performance graphics, DirectX was required.

The WPF programming model is quite different in that GDI is *not* used when rendering graphical data. All rendering operations (e.g., 2D graphics, 3D graphics, animations, control rendering, etc.) now make use of the DirectX API. The first obvious benefit is that your WPF applications will automatically take advantage of hardware and software optimizations. As well, WPF applications can tap into very rich graphical services (blur effects, anti-aliasing, transparency, etc.) without the complexity of programming directly against the DirectX API.

■ **Note**   Although WPF does push all rendering requests to the DirectX layer, I don't want to suggest that a WPF application will perform as fast as building an application using unmanaged C++ and DirectX directly. Although significant advances have been made in WPF in .NET 4.7, if you are intending to build a desktop application that requires the fastest possible execution speed (such as a 3D video game), unmanaged C++ and DirectX are still the best approach.

Simplifying Complex UI Programming

To recap the story thus far, Windows Presentation Foundation (WPF) is an API for building desktop applications that integrates various desktop APIs into a single object model and provides a clean separation of concerns via XAML. In addition to these major points, WPF applications also benefit from a simple way to integrate services into your programs, which historically were quite complex to account for. The following is a quick rundown of the core WPF features:

- A number of layout managers (far more than Windows Forms) to provide extremely flexible control over the placement and repositioning of content.

- Use of an enhanced data-binding engine to bind content to UI elements in a variety of ways.

- A built-in style engine, which allows you to define "themes" for a WPF application.

- Use of vector graphics, which allows content to be automatically resized to fit the size and resolution of the screen hosting the application.

- Support for 2D and 3D graphics, animations, and video and audio playback.

- A rich typography API, such as support for XML Paper Specification (XPS) documents, fixed documents (WYSIWYG), flow documents, and document annotations (e.g., a Sticky Notes API).

- Support for interoperating with legacy GUI models (e.g., Windows Forms, ActiveX, and Win32 HWNDs). For example, you can incorporate custom Windows Forms controls into a WPF application, and vice versa.

Now that you have some idea of what WPF brings to the table, let's look at the various types of applications that can be created using this API. Many of these features will be explored in detail in the chapters to come.

Investigating the WPF Assemblies

WPF is ultimately little more than a collection of types bundled within .NET assemblies. Table 24-3 describes the key assemblies used to build WPF applications, each of which must be referenced when creating a new project. As you would hope, Visual Studio WPF projects reference these required assemblies automatically.

Table 24-3. *Core WPF Assemblies*

Assembly	Meaning in Life
PresentationCore.dll	This assembly defines numerous namespaces that constitute the foundation of the WPF GUI layer. For example, this assembly contains support for the WPF Ink API, animation primitives, and numerous graphical rendering types.
PresentationFramework.dll	This assembly contains a majority of the WPF controls, the Application and Window classes, support for interactive 2D graphics and numerous types used in data binding.
System.Xaml.dll	This assembly provides namespaces that allow you to program against a XAML document at runtime. By and large, this library is useful only if you are authoring WPF support tools or need absolute control over XAML at runtime.
WindowsBase.dll	This assembly defines types that constitute the infrastructure of the WPF API, including those representing WPF threading types, security types, various type converters, and support for *dependency properties* and *routed events* (described in Chapter 27).

Collectively, these four assemblies define a number of new namespaces and hundreds of new .NET classes, interfaces, structures, enumerations, and delegates. While you should consult the .NET Framework 4.7 SDK documentation for complete details, Table 24-4 describes the role of some (but certainly not all) of the important namespaces.

Table 24-4. *Core WPF Namespaces*

Namespace	Meaning in Life
System.Windows	This is the root namespace of WPF. Here, you will find core classes (such as Application and Window) that are required by any WPF desktop project.
System.Windows.Controls	This contains all of the expected WPF widgets, including types to build menu systems, tool tips, and numerous layout managers.
System.Windows.Data	This contains types to work with the WPF data-binding engine, as well as support for data-binding templates.
System.Windows.Documents	This contains types to work with the documents API, which allows you to integrate PDF-style functionality into your WPF applications, via the XML Paper Specification (XPS) protocol.
System.Windows.Ink	This provides support for the Ink API, which allows you to capture input from a stylus or mouse, respond to input gestures, and so forth. This is useful for Tablet PC programming; however, any WPF can make use of this API.
System.Windows.Markup	This namespace defines a number of types that allow XAML markup (and the equivalent binary format, BAML) to be parsed and processed programmatically.
System.Windows.Media	This is the root namespace to several media-centric namespaces. Within these namespaces you will find types to work with animations, 3D rendering, text rendering, and other multimedia primitives.
System.Windows.Navigation	This namespace provides types to account for the navigation logic employed by XAML browser applications (XBAPs) as well as standard desktop applications that require a navigational page model.
System.Windows.Shapes	This defines classes that allow you to render interactive 2D graphics that automatically respond to mouse input.

To begin your journey into the WPF programming model, you'll examine two members of the System. Windows namespace that are commonplace to any traditional desktop development effort: Application and Window.

■ **Note** If you have created desktop UIs using the Windows Forms API, be aware that the System.Windows. Forms.* and System.Drawing.* assemblies are not related to WPF. These libraries represent the original .NET GUI toolkit, Windows Forms/GDI+.

The Role of the Application Class

The System.Windows.Application class represents a global instance of a running WPF application. This class supplies a Run() method (to start the application), a series of events that you are able to handle in order to interact with the application's lifetime (such as Startup and Exit), and a number of events that are specific to XAML browser applications (such as events that fire as a user navigates between pages). Table 24-5 details some of the key properties.

Table 24-5. *Key Properties of the Application Type*

Property	Meaning in Life
Current	This static property allows you to gain access to the running Application object from anywhere in your code. This can be helpful when a window or dialog box needs to gain access to the Application object that created it, typically to access application-wide variables and functionality.
MainWindow	This property allows you to programmatically get or set the main window of the application.
Properties	This property allows you to establish and obtain data that is accessible throughout all aspects of a WPF application (windows, dialog boxes, etc.).
StartupUri	This property gets or sets a URI that specifies a window or page to open automatically when the application starts.
Windows	This property returns a WindowCollection type, which provides access to each window created from the thread that created the Application object. This can be helpful when you want to iterate over each open window of an application and alter its state (such as minimizing all windows).

Constructing an Application Class

Any WPF application will need to define a class that extends Application. Within this class, you will define your program's entry point (the Main() method), which creates an instance of this subclass and typically handles the Startup and Exit events (as necessary). Here is an example:

```
// Define the global application object
// for this WPF program.
class MyApp : Application
{
  [STAThread]
  static void Main(string[] args)
  {
    // Create the application object.
    MyApp app = new MyApp();

    // Register the Startup/Exit events.
    app.Startup += (s, e) => { /* Start up the app */ };
    app.Exit += (s, e) => { /* Exit the app */ };
  }
}
```

Within the Startup handler, you will most often process any incoming command-line arguments and launch the main window of the program. The Exit handler, as you would expect, is where you can author any necessary shutdown logic for the program (e.g., save user preferences, write to the Windows registry).

■ **Note** The Main() method of a WPF application must be attributed with the [STAThread] attribute, which ensures any legacy COM objects used by your application are thread-safe. If you do not annotate Main() in this way, you will encounter a runtime exception.

Enumerating the Windows Collection

Another interesting property exposed by Application is Windows, which provides access to a collection representing each window loaded into memory for the current WPF application. Recall that as you create new Window objects, they are automatically added into the Application.Windows collection. Here is an example method that will minimize each window of the application (perhaps in response to a given keyboard gesture or menu option triggered by the end user):

```
static void MinimizeAllWindows()
{
  foreach (Window wnd in Application.Current.Windows)
  {
    wnd.WindowState = WindowState.Minimized;
  }
}
```

You'll build some WPF applications shortly, but until then, let's check out the core functionality of the Window type and learn about a number of important WPF base classes in the process.

The Role of the Window Class

The System.Windows.Window class (located in the PresentationFramework.dll assembly) represents a single window owned by the Application-derived class, including any dialog boxes displayed by the main window. Not surprisingly, Window has a series of parent classes, each of which brings more functionality to the table. Consider Figure 24-1, which shows the inheritance chain (and implemented interfaces) for System.Windows.Window as seen through the Visual Studio Object Browser.

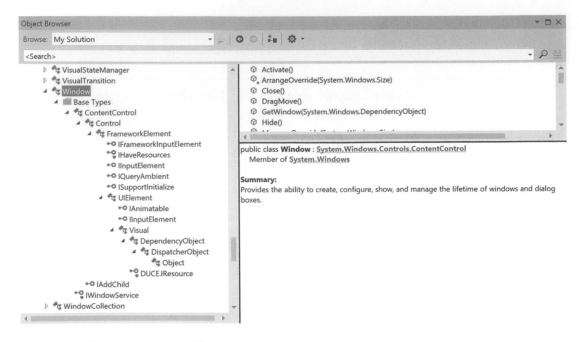

Figure 24-1. *The hierarchy of the Window class*

You'll come to understand the functionality provided by many of these base classes as you progress through this chapter and the chapters to come. However, to whet your appetite, the following sections present a breakdown of the functionality provided by each base class (consult the .NET Framework 4.7 SDK documentation for full details).

The Role of System.Windows.Controls.ContentControl

The direct parent of Window is ContentControl, which is quite possibly the most enticing of all WPF classes. This base class provides derived types with the ability to host a single piece of *content*, which, simply put, refers to the visual data placed within the interior of the control's surface area via the Content property. The WPF content model makes it very simple to customize the basic look and feel of a content control.

For example, when you think of a typical "button" control, you tend to assume that the content is a simple string literal (OK, Cancel, Abort, etc.). If you are using XAML to describe a WPF control and the value you want to assign to the Content property can be captured as a simple string, you may set the Content property within the element's opening definition as so (don't fret over the exact markup at this point):

```
<!-- Setting the Content value in the opening element -->
<Button Height="80" Width="100" Content="OK"/>
```

■ **Note** The Content property can also be set in C# code, which allows you to change the interior of a control at runtime.

However, content can be almost anything. For example, let's say you want to have a "button" that has something more interesting than a simple string, perhaps a custom graphic and a blurb of text. In other UI frameworks such as Windows Forms, you would be required to build a custom control, which could entail quite a bit of code and a whole new class to maintain. With the WPF content model, there is no need to do so.

When you want to assign the Content property to a value that cannot be captured as a simple array of characters, you can't assign it using an attribute in the control's opening definition. Rather, you must define the content data *implicitly*, within the element's scope. For example, the following <Button> contains a <StackPanel> as content, which itself contains some unique data (an <Ellipse> and <Label>, to be exact):

```
<!-- Implicitly setting the Content property with complex data -->
<Button Height="80" Width="100">
  <StackPanel>
    <Ellipse Fill="Red" Width="25" Height="25"/>
    <Label Content ="OK!"/>
  </StackPanel>
</Button>
```

You can also make use of XAML's *property-element syntax* to set complex content. Consider the following functionally equivalent <Button> definition, which sets the Content property explicitly using property-element syntax (again, you'll find more information on XAML later in this chapter, so don't sweat the details just yet):

```
<!-- Setting the Content property using property-element syntax -->
<Button Height="80" Width="100">
  <Button.Content>
    <StackPanel>
      <Ellipse Fill="Red" Width="25" Height="25"/>
      <Label Content ="OK!"/>
    </StackPanel>
  </Button.Content>
</Button>
```

Do be aware that not every WPF element derives from ContentControl and, therefore, not all controls support this unique content model (however, most do). As well, some WPF controls add a few refinements to the basic content model you have just examined. Chapter 25 will examine the role of WPF content in much more detail.

The Role of System.Windows.Controls.Control

Unlike ContentControl, all WPF controls share the Control base class as a common parent. This base class provides numerous core members that account for basic UI functionality. For example, Control defines properties to establish the control's size, opacity, tab order logic, the display cursor, background color, and so forth. Furthermore, this parent class provides support for *templating services*. As explained in Chapter 27, WPF controls can completely change the way they render their appearance using templates and styles. Table 24-6 documents some key members of the Control type, grouped by related functionality.

Table 24-6. *Key Members of the Control Type*

Members	Meaning in Life
Background, Foreground, BorderBrush, BorderThickness, Padding, HorizontalContentAlignment, VerticalContentAlignment	These properties allow you to set basic settings regarding how the control will be rendered and positioned.
FontFamily, FontSize, FontStretch, FontWeight	These properties control various font-centric settings.
IsTabStop, TabIndex	These properties are used to establish tab order among controls on a window.
MouseDoubleClick, PreviewMouseDoubleClick	These events handle the act of double-clicking a widget.
Template	This property allows you to get and set the control's template, which can be used to change the rendering output of the widget.

The Role of System.Windows.FrameworkElement

This base class provides a number of members that are used throughout the WPF framework, such as support for storyboarding (used within animations) and support for data binding, as well as the ability to name a member (via the Name property), obtain any resources defined by the derived type, and establish the overall dimensions of the derived type. Table 24-7 hits the highlights.

Table 24-7. *Key Members of the FrameworkElement Type*

Members	Meaning in Life
ActualHeight, ActualWidth, MaxHeight, MaxWidth, MinHeight, MinWidth, Height, Width	These properties control the size of the derived type.
ContextMenu	Gets or sets the pop-up menu associated with the derived type.
Cursor	Gets or sets the mouse cursor associated with the derived type.
HorizontalAlignment, VerticalAlignment	Gets or sets how the type is positioned within a container (such as a panel or list box).
Name	Allows to you assign a name to the type in order to access its functionality in a code file.
Resources	Provides access to any resources defined by the type (see Chapter 29 for an examination of the WPF resource system).
ToolTip	Gets or sets the tool tip associated with the derived type.

The Role of System.Windows.UIElement

Of all the types within a Window's inheritance chain, the UIElement base class provides the greatest amount of functionality. The key task of UIElement is to provide the derived type with numerous events to allow the derived type to receive focus and process input requests. For example, this class provides numerous events to account for drag-and-drop operations, mouse movement, keyboard input, and stylus input (for Pocket PCs and Tablet PCs).

Chapter 25 digs into the WPF event model in detail; however, many of the core events will look quite familiar (MouseMove, KeyUp, MouseDown, MouseEnter, MouseLeave, etc.). In addition to defining dozens of events, this parent class provides a number of properties to account for control focus, enabled state, visibility, and hit testing logic, as shown in Table 24-8.

Table 24-8. *Key Members of the* UIElement *Type*

Members	Meaning in Life
Focusable, IsFocused	These properties allow you to set focus on a given derived type.
IsEnabled	This property allows you to control whether a given derived type is enabled or disabled.
IsMouseDirectlyOver, IsMouseOver	These properties provide a simple way to perform hit-testing logic.
IsVisible, Visibility	These properties allow you to work with the visibility setting of a derived type.
RenderTransform	This property allows you to establish a transformation that will be used to render the derived type.

The Role of System.Windows.Media.Visual

The Visual class type provides core rendering support in WPF, which includes hit testing of graphical data, coordinate transformation, and bounding box calculations. In fact, the Visual class interacts with the underlying DirectX subsystem to actually draw data on the screen. As you will examine in Chapter 26, WPF provides three possible manners in which you can render graphical data, each of which differs in terms of functionality and performance. Use of the Visual type (and its children, such as DrawingVisual) provides the most lightweight way to render graphical data, but it also entails the greatest amount of manual code to account for all the required services. Again, more details to come in Chapter 28.

The Role of System.Windows.DependencyObject

WPF supports a particular flavor of .NET properties termed *dependency properties*. Simply put, this style of property provides extra code to allow the property to respond to several WPF technologies such as styles, data binding, animations, and so forth. For a type to support this new property scheme, it will need to derive from the DependencyObject base class. While dependency properties are a key aspect of WPF development, much of the time their details are hidden from view. Chapter 25 dives further into the details of dependency properties.

The Role of System.Windows.Threading.DispatcherObject

The final base class of the Window type (beyond System.Object, which I assume needs no further explanation at this point in the book) is DispatcherObject. This type provides one property of interest, Dispatcher, which returns the associated System.Windows.Threading.Dispatcher object. The Dispatcher class is the entry point to the event queue of the WPF application, and it provides the basic constructs for dealing with concurrency and threading.

Understanding the Syntax of WPF XAML

Production-level WPF applications will typically make use of dedicated tools to generate the necessary XAML. As helpful as these tools are, it is a good idea to have an understanding of the overall structure of XAML markup. To help in your learning process, allow me to introduce a popular (and free) tool that allows you to easily experiment with XAML.

Introducing Kaxaml

When you are first learning the grammar of XAML, it can be helpful to use a free tool named *Kaxaml*. You can obtain this popular XAML editor/parser from the Kaxaml directory in the downloadable files.

■ **Note** For many editions of this book, I've pointed users to `www.kaxaml.com`, but unfortunately, that site has been retired. I have a copy of the `.msi` package in the downloadable materials for this book, and I've also forked the repository to my personal GitHub account (`www.github.com/skimedic/kaxaml`) to make sure it will live on. Much respect and thanks to the developers of Kaxaml; it's a great tool and has helped countless developers learn XAML.

Kaxaml is helpful in that it has no clue about C# source code, event handlers, or implementation logic. It is a much more straightforward way to test XAML snippets than using a full-blown Visual Studio WPF project template. As well, Kaxaml has a number of integrated tools, such as a color chooser, a XAML snippet manager, and even an "XAML scrubber" option that will format your XAML based on your settings. When you first open Kaxaml, you will find simple markup for a <Page> control, as follows:

```
<Page
  xmlns="http://schemas.microsoft.com/winfx/2006/xaml/presentation"
  xmlns:x="http://schemas.microsoft.com/winfx/2006/xaml">
  <Grid>

  </Grid>
</Page>
```

Like a Window, a Page contains various layout managers and controls. However, unlike a Window, Page objects cannot run as stand-alone entities. Rather, they must be placed inside a suitable host such as a NavigationWindow or a Frame. The good news is that you can type identical markup within a <Page> or <Window> scope.

■ **Note** If you change the <Page> and </Page> elements in the Kaxaml markup window to <Window> and </Window>, you can press the F5 key to load a new window onto the screen.

As an initial test, enter the following markup into the XAML pane at the bottom of the tool:

```
<Page
  xmlns="http://schemas.microsoft.com/winfx/2006/xaml/presentation"
  xmlns:x="http://schemas.microsoft.com/winfx/2006/xaml">
```

```xaml
    <Grid>
      <!-- A button with custom content -->
      <Button Height="100" Width="100">
        <Ellipse Fill="Green" Height="50" Width="50"/>
      </Button>
    </Grid>
</Page>
```

You should now see your page render at the upper part of the Kaxaml editor (see Figure 24-2).

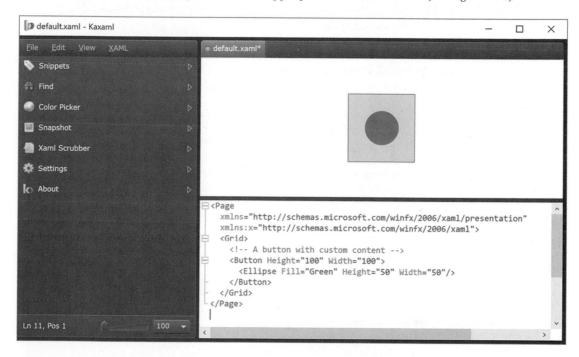

Figure 24-2. *Kaxaml is a helpful (and free) tool used to learn the grammar of XAML.*

As you work with Kaxaml, remember that this tool does not allow you to author any markup that entails code compilation (however, using x:Name is allowed). This includes defining an x:Class attribute (for specifying a code file), entering event handler names in markup, or using any XAML keywords that also entail code compilation (such as FieldModifier or ClassModifier). Any attempt to do so will result in a markup error.

XAML XML Namespaces and XAML "Keywords"

The root element of a WPF XAML document (such as a <Window>, <Page>, <UserControl>, or <Application> definition) will almost always make reference to the following two predefined XML namespaces:

```xaml
<Page
  xmlns="http://schemas.microsoft.com/winfx/2006/xaml/presentation"
  xmlns:x="http://schemas.microsoft.com/winfx/2006/xaml">
  <Grid>

  </Grid>
</Page>
```

The first XML namespace, http://schemas.microsoft.com/winfx/2006/xaml/presentation, maps a slew of WPF .NET namespaces for use by the current *.xaml file (System.Windows, System.Windows.Controls, System.Windows.Data, System.Windows.Ink, System.Windows.Media, System.Windows.Navigation, etc.).

This one-to-many mapping is actually hard-coded within the WPF assemblies (WindowsBase.dll, PresentationCore.dll, and PresentationFramework.dll) using the assembly-level [XmlnsDefinition] attribute. For example, if you open the Visual Studio object browser and select the PresentationCore.dll assembly, you will see listings such as the following, which essentially imports System.Windows:

```
[assembly: XmlnsDefinition("http://schemas.microsoft.com/winfx/2006/xaml/presentation",
                           "System.Windows")]
```

The second XML namespace, http://schemas.microsoft.com/winfx/2006/xaml, is used to include XAML-specific "keywords" (for lack of a better term) as well as the inclusion of the System.Windows.Markup namespace, as follows:

```
[assembly: XmlnsDefinition("http://schemas.microsoft.com/winfx/2006/xaml",
                           "System.Windows.Markup")]
```

One rule of any well-formed XML document (remember, XAML is an XML-based grammar) is that the opening root element designates one XML namespace as the *primary namespace*, which typically is the namespace that contains the most commonly used items. If a root element requires the inclusion of additional secondary namespaces (as seen here), they must be defined using a unique tag prefix (to resolve any possible name clashes). As a convention, the prefix is simply x; however, this can be any unique token you require, such as XamlSpecificStuff.

```
<Page
  xmlns="http://schemas.microsoft.com/winfx/2006/xaml/presentation"
  xmlns:XamlSpecificStuff="http://schemas.microsoft.com/winfx/2006/xaml">
  <Grid>
    <!-- A button with custom content -->
    <Button XamlSpecificStuff:Name="button1" Height="100" Width="100">
      <Ellipse Fill="Green" Height="50" Width="50"/>
    </Button>
  </Grid>
</Page>
```

The obvious downside of defining wordy XML namespace prefixes is you are required to type XamlSpecificStuff each time your XAML file needs to refer to one of the items defined within this XAML-centric XML namespace. Given that XamlSpecificStuff requires many additional keystrokes, just stick with x.

In any case, beyond the x:Name, x:Class, and x:Code keywords, the http://schemas.microsoft.com/winfx/2006/xaml XML namespace also provides access to additional XAML keywords, the most common of which are shown in Table 24-9.

Table 24-9. *XAML Keywords*

XAML Keyword	Meaning in Life
x:Array	Represents a .NET array type in XAML.
x:ClassModifier	Allows you to define the visibility of the C# class (internal or public) denoted by the Class keyword.
x:FieldModifier	Allows you to define the visibility of a type member (internal, public, private, or protected) for any named subelement of the root (e.g., a <Button> within a <Window> element). A *named element* is defined using the Name XAML keyword.
x:Key	Allows you to establish a key value for a XAML item that will be placed into a dictionary element.
x:Name	Allows you to specify the generated C# name of a given XAML element.
x:Null	Represents a null reference.
x:Static	Allows you to make reference to a static member of a type.
x:Type	The XAML equivalent of the C# typeof operator (it will yield a System.Type based on the supplied name).
x:TypeArguments	Allows you to establish an element as a generic type with a specific type parameter (e.g., List<int> vs. List<bool>).

In addition to these two necessary XML namespace declarations, it is possible, and sometimes necessary, to define additional tag prefixes in the opening element of a XAML document. You will typically do so whenever you need to describe in XAML a .NET class defined in an external assembly.

For example, say you have built a few custom WPF controls and packaged them in a library named MyControls.dll. Now, if you want to create a new Window that uses these controls, you can establish a custom XML namespace that maps to your library using the clr-namespace and assembly tokens. Here is some example markup that creates a tag prefix named myCtrls, which can be used to access controls in your library:

```
<Window x:Class="WpfApplication1.MainWindow"
  xmlns="http://schemas.microsoft.com/winfx/2006/xaml/presentation"
  xmlns:x="http://schemas.microsoft.com/winfx/2006/xaml"
  xmlns:myCtrls="clr-namespace:MyControls;assembly=MyControls"
  Title="MainWindow" Height="350" Width="525">
  <Grid>
    <myCtrls:MyCustomControl />
  </Grid>
</Window>
```

The clr-namespace token is assigned to the name of the .NET namespace in the assembly, while the assembly token is set to the friendly name of the external *.dll assembly. You can use this syntax for any external .NET library you would like to manipulate in markup. While there is no need to do so at the current time, future chapters will require you to define custom XML namespace declarations to describe types in markup.

■ **Note**   If you need to define a class in markup that is part of the current assembly but in a different .NET namespace, your xmlns tag prefix is defined without the assembly= attribute, like so:

```
xmlns:myCtrls="clr-namespace:SomeNamespaceInMyApp"
```

Controlling Class and Member Variable Visibility

You will see many of these keywords in action where required in the chapters to come; however, by way of a simple example, consider the following XAML <Window> definition that makes use of the ClassModifier and FieldModifier keywords, as well as x:Name and x:Class (remember that kaxaml.exe will not allow you to make use of any XAML keyword that entails code compilation, such as x:Code, x:FieldModifier, or x:ClassModifier):

```
<!-- This class will now be declared internal in the *.g.cs file -->
<Window x:Class="MyWPFApp.MainWindow" x:ClassModifier ="internal"
  xmlns="http://schemas.microsoft.com/winfx/2006/xaml/presentation"
  xmlns:x="http://schemas.microsoft.com/winfx/2006/xaml">

  <!-- This button will be public in the *.g.cs file -->
  <Button x:Name ="myButton" x:FieldModifier ="public" Content = "OK"/>
</Window>
```

By default, all C#/XAML type definitions are public, while members default to internal. However, based on your XAML definition, the resulting autogenerated file contains an internal class type with a public Button variable.

```
internal partial class MainWindow : System.Windows.Window,
  System.Windows.Markup.IComponentConnector
{
  public System.Windows.Controls.Button myButton;
...
}
```

XAML Elements, XAML Attributes, and Type Converters

After you have established your root element and any required XML namespaces, your next task is to populate the root with a *child element*. In a real-world WPF application, the child will be a layout manager (such as a Grid or StackPanel) that contains, in turn, any number of additional UI elements that describe the user interface. The next chapter examines these layout managers in detail, so for now just assume that your <Window> type will contain a single Button element.

As you have already seen over the course of this chapter, XAML *elements* map to a class or structure type within a given .NET namespace, while the *attributes* within the opening element tag map to properties or events of the type. To illustrate, enter the following <Button> definition into Kaxaml:

```
<Page
  xmlns="http://schemas.microsoft.com/winfx/2006/xaml/presentation"
  xmlns:x="http://schemas.microsoft.com/winfx/2006/xaml">
  <Grid>
    <!-- Configure the look and feel of a Button -->
    <Button Height="50" Width="100" Content="OK!"
            FontSize="20" Background="Green" Foreground="Yellow"/>
  </Grid>
</Page>
```

Notice that the values assigned to each property have been captured as a simple text value. This may seem like a complete mismatch of data types because if you were to make this Button in C# code, you would *not* assign string objects to these properties but would make use of specific data types. For example, here is the same button authored in code:

```
public void MakeAButton()
{
  Button myBtn = new Button();
  myBtn.Height = 50;
  myBtn.Width = 100;
  myBtn.FontSize = 20;
  myBtn.Content = "OK!";
  myBtn.Background = new SolidColorBrush(Colors.Green);
  myBtn.Foreground = new SolidColorBrush(Colors.Yellow);
}
```

As it turns out, WPF ships with a number of *type converter* classes, which will be used to transform simple text values into the correct underlying data type. This process happens transparently (and automatically).

While this is all well and good, there will be many times when you need to assign a much more complex value to a XAML attribute, which cannot be captured as a simple string. For example, let's say you want to build a custom brush to set the Background property of the Button. If you are building the brush in code, it is quite straightforward, as shown here:

```
public void MakeAButton()
{
...
  // A fancy brush for the background.
  LinearGradientBrush fancyBruch =
    new LinearGradientBrush(Colors.DarkGreen, Colors.LightGreen, 45);
  myBtn.Background = fancyBruch;
  myBtn.Foreground = new SolidColorBrush(Colors.Yellow);
}
```

How, can you represent your complex brush as a string? Well, you can't! Thankfully, XAML provides a special syntax that can be used whenever you need to assign a property value to a complex object, termed *property element syntax.*

Understanding XAML Property-Element Syntax

Property-element syntax allows you to assign complex objects to a property. Here is a XAML description for a Button that makes use of a LinearGradientBrush to set its Background property:

```
<Button Height="50" Width="100" Content="OK!"
        FontSize="20" Foreground="Yellow">
  <Button.Background>
    <LinearGradientBrush>
      <GradientStop Color="DarkGreen" Offset="0"/>
      <GradientStop Color="LightGreen" Offset="1"/>
    </LinearGradientBrush>
  </Button.Background>
</Button>
```

Notice that within the scope of the <Button> and </Button> tags, you have defined a subscope named <Button.Background>. Within this scope, you have defined a custom <LinearGradientBrush>. (Don't worry about the exact code for the brush; you'll learn about WPF graphics in Chapter 28).

Generally speaking, any property can be set using property-element syntax, which always breaks down to the following pattern:

```
<DefiningClass>
  <DefiningClass.PropertyOnDefiningClass>
    <!-- Value for Property here! -->
  </DefiningClass.PropertyOnDefiningClass>
</DefiningClass>
```

While any property *could* be set using this syntax, if you can capture a value as a simple string, you will save yourself typing time. For example, here is a much more verbose way to set the Width of your Button:

```
<Button Height="50" Content="OK!"
        FontSize="20" Foreground="Yellow">
...
  <Button.Width>
    100
  </Button.Width>
</Button>
```

Understanding XAML Attached Properties

In addition to property-element syntax, XAML defines a special syntax used to set a value to an *attached property*. Essentially, an attached property allows a child element to set the value for a property that is actually defined in a parent element. The general template to follow looks like this:

```
<ParentElement>
  <ChildElement ParentElement.PropertyOnParent = "Value">
</ParentElement>
```

The most common use of attached property syntax is to position UI elements within one of the WPF layout manager classes (Grid, DockPanel, etc.). The next chapter dives into these panels in some detail; for now, enter the following in Kaxaml:

```
<Page
  xmlns="http://schemas.microsoft.com/winfx/2006/xaml/presentation"
  xmlns:x="http://schemas.microsoft.com/winfx/2006/xaml">
  <Canvas Height="200" Width="200" Background="LightBlue">
    <Ellipse Canvas.Top="40" Canvas.Left="40" Height="20" Width="20" Fill="DarkBlue"/>
  </Canvas>
</Page>
```

Here, you have defined a Canvas layout manager that contains an Ellipse. Notice that the Ellipse is able to inform its parent (the Canvas) where to position its top/left position using attached property syntax.

There are a few items to be aware of regarding attached properties. First and foremost, this is not an all-purpose syntax that can be applied to *any* property of *any* parent. For example, the following XAML cannot be parsed without error:

```
<!-- Error! Set Background property on Canvas via attached property? -->
<Canvas Height="200" Width="200">
  <Ellipse Canvas.Background="LightBlue"
           Canvas.Top="40" Canvas.Left="90"
           Height="20" Width="20" Fill="DarkBlue"/>
</Canvas>
```

In reality, attached properties are a specialized form of a WPF-specific concept termed a *dependency property*. Unless a property was implemented in a specific manner, you cannot set its value using attached property syntax. You will explore dependency properties in a detail in Chapter 25.

■ **Note**   Kaxaml and Visual Studio both have IntelliSense, which will show you valid attached properties that can be set by a given element.

Understanding XAML Markup Extensions

As explained, property values are most often represented using a simple string or via property-element syntax. There is, however, another way to specify the value of a XAML attribute, using *markup extensions*. Markup extensions allow a XAML parser to obtain the value for a property from a dedicated, external class. This can be beneficial given that some property values require a number of code statements to execute to figure out the value.

Markup extensions provide a way to cleanly extend the grammar of XAML with new functionality. A markup extension is represented internally as a class that derives from MarkupExtension. Note that the chances of you ever needing to build a custom markup extension will be slim to none. However, a subset of XAML keywords (such as x:Array, x:Null, x:Static, and x:Type) are markup extensions in disguise!

A markup extension is sandwiched between curly brackets, like so:

```
<Element PropertyToSet = "{MarkUpExtension}"/>
```

To see some markup extensions in action, author the following into Kaxaml:

```
<Page
  xmlns="http://schemas.microsoft.com/winfx/2006/xaml/presentation"
  xmlns:x="http://schemas.microsoft.com/winfx/2006/xaml"
  xmlns:CorLib="clr-namespace:System;assembly=mscorlib">

  <StackPanel>
    <!-- The Static markup extension lets us obtain a value
         from a static member of a class -->
    <Label Content ="{x:Static CorLib:Environment.OSVersion}"/>
    <Label Content ="{x:Static CorLib:Environment.ProcessorCount}"/>

    <!-- The Type markup extension is a XAML version of
         the C# typeof operator -->
    <Label Content ="{x:Type Button}" />
    <Label Content ="{x:Type CorLib:Boolean}" />

    <!-- Fill a ListBox with an array of strings! -->
    <ListBox Width="200" Height="50">
```

```
    <ListBox.ItemsSource>
      <x:Array Type="CorLib:String">
        <CorLib:String>Sun Kil Moon</CorLib:String>
        <CorLib:String>Red House Painters</CorLib:String>
        <CorLib:String>Besnard Lakes</CorLib:String>
      </x:Array>
    </ListBox.ItemsSource>
  </ListBox>
  </StackPanel>
</Page>
```

First, notice that the <Page> definition has a new XML namespace declaration, which allows you to gain access to the System namespace of mscorlib.dll. With this XML namespace established, you first make use of the x:Static markup extension and grab values from OSVersion and ProcessorCount of the System. Environment class.

The x:Type markup extension allows you to gain access to the metadata description of the specified item. Here, you are simply assigning the fully qualified names of the WPF Button and System.Boolean types.

The most interesting part of this markup is the ListBox. Here, you are setting the ItemsSource property to an array of strings declared entirely in markup! Notice here how the x:Array markup extension allows you to specify a set of subitems within its scope:

```
<x:Array Type="CorLib:String">
  <CorLib:String>Sun Kil Moon</CorLib:String>
  <CorLib:String>Red House Painters</CorLib:String>
  <CorLib:String>Besnard Lakes</CorLib:String>
</x:Array>
```

■ **Note**   The previous XAML example is used only to illustrate a markup extension in action. As you will see in Chapter 25, there are much easier ways to populate ListBox controls!

Figure 24-3 shows the markup of this <Page> in Kaxaml.

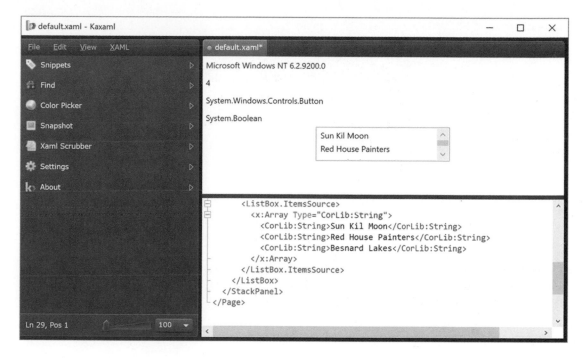

Figure 24-3. *Markup extensions allow you to set values via the functionality of a dedicated class*

You have now seen numerous examples that showcase each of the core aspects of the XAML syntax. As you might agree, XAML is interesting in that it allows you to describe a tree of .NET objects in a declarative manner. While this is extremely helpful when configuring graphical user interfaces, do remember that XAML can describe *any* type from *any* assembly, provided it is a nonabstract type containing a default constructor.

Building WPF Applications Using Visual Studio

Let's examine how Visual Studio can simplify the construction of WPF programs.

■ **Note**   Here, I will point out some key features of using Visual Studio to build WPF applications. Forthcoming chapters will illustrate additional aspects of the IDE where necessary.

The WPF Project Templates

The New Project dialog box of Visual Studio defines a set of WPF project workspaces, all of which are contained under the Window Classic Desktop node of the Visual C# root. Here, you can choose from several project types, including a WPF App, Windows Forms App, and many more. To begin, create a new WPF application named WpfTesterApp (see Figure 24-4).

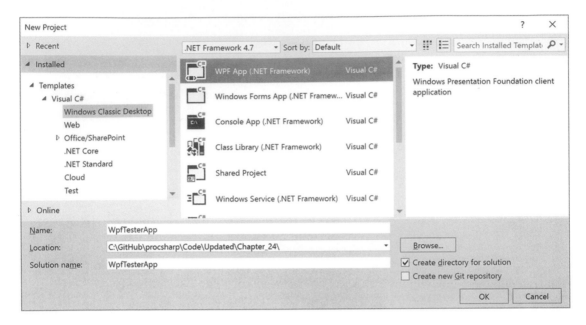

Figure 24-4. *The WPF project templates of Visual Studio can be found under the Windows Classic Desktop node*

Beyond setting references to each of the WPF assemblies (`PresentationCore.dll`, `PresentationFramework.dll`, `System.Xaml.dll`, and `WindowsBase.dll`), you will be provided with initial `Window` and `Application` derived classes, each represented using a XAML and C# code file.

The Toolbox and XAML Designer/Editor

Visual Studio provides a Toolbox (which you can open via the View menu) that contains numerous WPF controls. The top part of the panel holds the most commonly used controls, and the bottom contains all of the controls (see Figure 24-5).

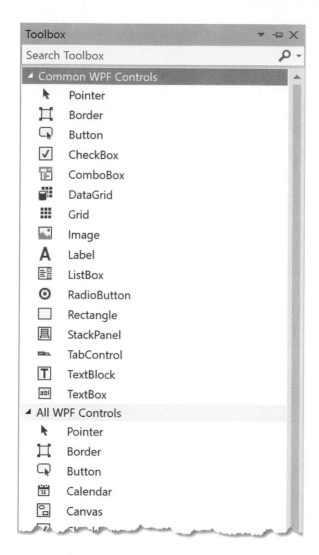

Figure 24-5. *The Toolbox contains the WPF controls that can be placed on the designer surface*

Using a standard drag-and-drop operation, you can place any of these controls onto the window's designer surface or drag the control into the XAML markup editor at the bottom of the designer. When you do, the initial XAML will be authored on your behalf. Use your mouse to drag a `Button` control and a `Calendar` control onto the designer surface. After you have done so, notice how you can relocate and resize your controls (and be sure to examine the resulting XAML generated based on your edits).

In addition to building the UI via the mouse and toolbox, you can manually enter your markup using the integrated XAML editor. As you can see in Figure 24-6, you do get IntelliSense support, which can help simplify the authoring of the markup. For example, try to add the `Background` property to the opening `<Window>` element.

Figure 24-6. *The WPF Window designer*

Take a few moments to add some property values directly in the XAML editor. Be sure you take the time to become comfortable using this aspect of the WPF designer.

Setting Properties Using the Properties Window

After you have placed some controls onto your designer (or manually defined them in the editor), you can then make use of the Properties window to set property values for the selected control, as well as rig up event handlers for the selected control. By way of a simple test, select your Button control on the designer. Now, use the Properties window to change the Background color of the Button using the integrated Brushes editor (see Figure 24-7; you will learn more about the Brushes editor in Chapter 26, during your examination of WPF graphics).

■ **Note**   The Properties window provides a Search text area at the top. Type in the name of a property you would like to set to quickly find the item in question.

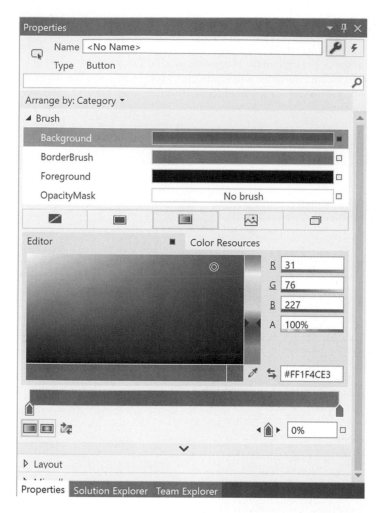

Figure 24-7. *The Properties window can be used to configure the UI of a WPF control*

After you have finished tinkering with the Brushes editor, check out the generated markup. It might look something like this:

```
<Button Content="Button" HorizontalAlignment="Left" Margin="10,10,0,0"
VerticalAlignment="Top" Width="75">
  <Button.Background>
    <LinearGradientBrush EndPoint="0.5,1" StartPoint="0.5,0">
      <GradientStop Color="Black" Offset="0"/>
      <GradientStop Color="#FFE90E0E" Offset="1"/>
      <GradientStop Color="#FF1F4CE3"/>
    </LinearGradientBrush>
  </Button.Background>
</Button>
```

Handling Events Using the Properties Window

If you want to handle events for a given control, you can also make use of the Properties window, but this time you need to click the Events button at the upper right of the Properties window (look for the lightning bolt icon). Ensure that the button is selected on your designer, and locate the `Click` event. Once you do, double-click directly on the `Click` event entry. This will cause Visual Studio to automatically build an event handler that takes the following general form:

`NameOfControl_NameOfEvent`

Since you did not rename your button, the Properties window shows that it generated an event handler named `Button_Click` (see Figure 24-8).

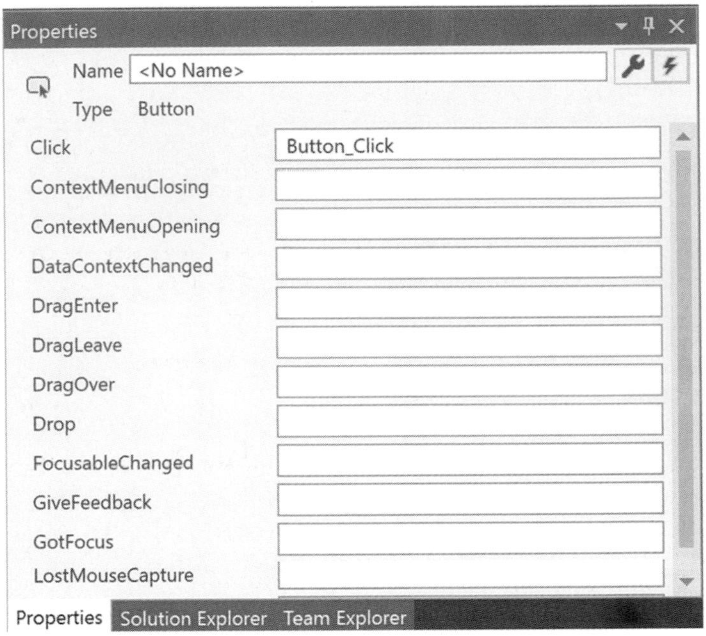

Figure 24-8. *Handling events using the Properties window*

As well, Visual Studio generated the corresponding C# event handler in your window's code file. Here, you can add any sort of code that must execute when the button is clicked. For a quick test, just enter the following code statement:

```
private void Button_Click(object sender, RoutedEventArgs e)
{
  MessageBox.Show("You clicked the button!");
}
```

Handling Events in the XAML Editor

You can also handle events directly in the XAML editor. By way of an example, place your mouse within the `<Window>` element and type in the `MouseMove` event, followed by the equal sign. Once you do, you will see that Visual Studio displays any compatible handlers in your code file (if they exist), as well as the `Create` method option (see Figure 24-9).

```
    1   ...<Window x.Class="WpfTesterApp.MainWindow"                         ▾  ⚡ MouseMove
    2            xmlns="http://schemas.microsoft.com/winfx/2006/xaml/presentation"
    3            xmlns:x="http://schemas.microsoft.com/winfx/2006/xaml"
    4            xmlns:d="http://schemas.microsoft.com/expression/blend/2008"
    5            xmlns:mc="http://schemas.openxmlformats.org/markup-compatibility/2006"
    6            xmlns:local="clr-namespace:WpfTesterApp"
    7            mc:Ignorable="d"
    8            Title="MainWindow" Height="350" Width="525" MouseMove="">
    9        <Grid>                                              ⚡ Create method MainWindow_OnMouseMove(object, MouseEve...)
   10            <Button Content="Button" HorizontalAlignment="Left" Mar⊕ Button_Click(object, RoutedEventArgs)
   11                    VerticalAlignment="Top" Width="75" Click="Butto⊕ OnContentChanged(object, object)
   12                <Button.Background>
   13                    <LinearGradientBrush EndPoint="0.5,1" StartPoint="0.5,0">
   14                        <GradientStop Color="Black" Offset="0"/>
   15                        <GradientStop Color="#FFE90E0E" Offset="1"/>
   16                        <GradientStop Color="#FF1F4CE3"/>
   17                    </LinearGradientBrush>
   18                </Button.Background>
   19                </Button>
```

Figure 24-9. *Handling events using the XAML editor*

Let the IDE create the MouseMove event handler, enter the following code, and then run the application to see the end result:

```
private void MainWindow_MouseMove (object sender, MouseEventArgs e)
{
  this.Title = e.GetPosition(this).ToString();
}
```

■ **Note**   Chapter 28 covers MVVM and the Command pattern, which is a much better way to handle click events in enterprise applications. But if you need only a simple app, handling click events with a straight event handler is perfectly acceptable.

The Document Outline Window

When you work with any XAML-based project, you will certainly make use of a healthy amount of markup to represent your UIs. When you begin to work with more complex XAML, it can be useful to visualize the markup in order to quickly select an item to edit on the Visual Studio designer.

Currently, your markup is quite tame because you have defined only a few controls within the initial <Grid>. Nevertheless, locate the Document Outline window in your IDE, mounted by default on the left side of Visual Studio (if you cannot locate it, simply activate it using the View ➤ Other Windows menu option). Now, make sure your XAML designer is the active window in the IDE (rather than the C# code file), and you will notice the Document Outline window displays the nested elements (see Figure 24-10).

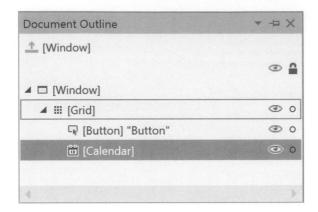

Figure 24-10. *Visualizing your XAML via the Document Outline window*

This tool also provides a way to temporarily hide a given item (or set of items) on the designer as well as lock items to prevent additional edits from taking place. In the next chapter, you will see how the Document Outline window also provides many other features to group selected items into new layout managers (among other features).

Enable or Disable the XAML Debugger

When you run the application, you will see the `MainWindow` on the screen. You will also see the interactive debugger, as shown in Figure 24-11.

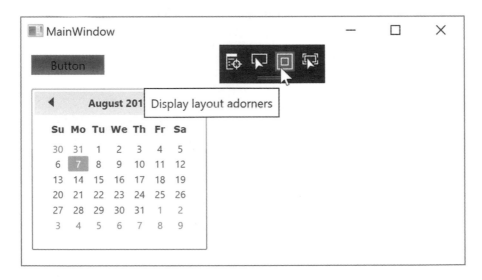

Figure 24-11. *XAML UI debugging*

If you want to turn this off, you will find the entries for XAML debugging under Tools ➤ Options ➤ Debugging ➤ General. Deselect the boxes to prevent the debugger window from overlaying your windows. Figure 24-12 shows the entries.

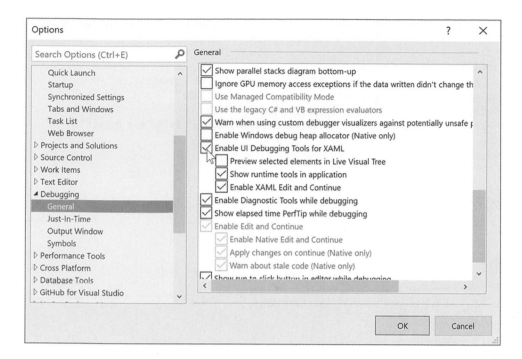

Figure 24-12. *XAML UI debugging*

Examining the App.xaml File

How did the project know what window to launch? Even more intriguing, if you examine the code files in your application, you will also see that there isn't a Main() method anywhere to be found. You've learned throughout this book that applications must have an entry point, so how does .NET know how to launch your app? Fortunately, both of these plumbing items are handled for you through the Visual Studio templates and the WPF framework.

To solve the riddle of which window to launch, the App.xaml file defines an application class through markup. In addition to the namespace definitions, it defines application properties such as the StartupUri, application-wide resources (covered in Chapter 27), and specific handlers for application events such as Startup and Exit. The StartupUri indicates which window to load on startup. Open the App.xaml file and examine the markup, shown here:

```
<Application x:Class="WpfTesterApp.App"
            xmlns="http://schemas.microsoft.com/winfx/2006/xaml/presentation"
            xmlns:x="http://schemas.microsoft.com/winfx/2006/xaml"
            xmlns:local="clr-namespace:WpfTesterApp"
            StartupUri="MainWindow.xaml">
    <Application.Resources>
    </Application.Resources>
</Application>
```

Using the XAML designer and using Visual Studio code completion, add handlers for the Startup and Exit events. Your updated XAML should look like this (notice the change in bold):

```
<Application x:Class="WpfTesterApp.App"
             xmlns="http://schemas.microsoft.com/winfx/2006/xaml/presentation"
             xmlns:x="http://schemas.microsoft.com/winfx/2006/xaml"
             xmlns:local="clr-namespace:WpfTesterApp"
             StartupUri="MainWindow.xaml" Startup="App_OnStartup" Exit="App_OnExit">
    <Application.Resources>
    </Application.Resources>
</Application>
```

If you look at the App.xaml.cs file, it should look like this:

```
public partial class App : Application
{
  private void App_OnStartup(object sender, StartupEventArgs e)
  {
  }
  private void App_OnExit(object sender, ExitEventArgs e)
  {
  }
}
```

Note that the class is marked as partial. In fact, all the code-behind windows for XAML files are marked partial. That is key to solving the riddle of where the Main() method lives. But first, you need to examine what happens when msbuild.exe processes XAML files.

Mapping the Window XAML Markup to C# Code

When msbuild.exe processed your *.csproj file, it produced three files for each XAML file in your project with the form of *.g.cs (where g denotes auto*generated*), *.g.i.cs (where *i* denotes IntelliSense), and *.baml (for Binary Application Markup Language). These are saved into the \obj\Debug directory (and can be viewed in Solution Explorer by clicking the Show All Files button). You might have to hit the Refresh button in Solution Explorer to see them since they are not part of the actual project, but build artifacts.

To make the most sense of the process, it's helpful to provide names for your controls. Go ahead and provide names for the Button and Calendar controls, as follows:

```
<Button Name="ClickMe" Content="Button" HorizontalAlignment="Left" Margin="10,10,0,0"
        VerticalAlignment="Top" Width="75" Click="Button_Click">
//omitted for brevity
</Button>
<Calendar Name="MyCalendar" HorizontalAlignment="Left" Margin="10,41,0,0"
VerticalAlignment="Top"/>
```

Now rebuild your solution (or project) and refresh the files in Solution Explorer. If you open the MainWindow.g.cs file into a text editor, you will find a class named MainWindow, which extends the Window base class. The name of this class is a direct result of the x:Class attribute in the <Window> start tag.

This class defines a private member variable of type bool (named _contentLoaded), which was not directly accounted for in the XAML markup. This data member is used to determine (and ensure) the content of the window is assigned only once. This class also contains a member variable of type System.Windows.

Controls.Button, named ClickMe. The name of the control is based on the x:Name (or the shorthand form Name) attribute value within the opening <Button> declaration. What you don't see is a variable for the Calendar control. This is because msbuild.exe creates a variable for each *named* control in your XAML that has related code in the code-behind. If there isn't any code, there isn't any need for a variable. To make matters more confusing, if you hadn't named the Button control, there wouldn't be a variable for it either. This is part of the magic of WPF and is tied into the IComponentConnector interface implementation.

The compiler-generated class also explicitly implements the WPF IComponentConnector interface defined in the System.Windows.Markup namespace. This interface defines a single method called Connect(), which has been implemented to prep each control defined in the markup and rig up the event logic as specified within the original MainWindow.xaml file. You can see the handler being set up for the ClickMe click event. Before the method completes, the _contentLoaded member variable is set to true. Here is the crux of the method:

```
void System.Windows.Markup.IComponentConnector.Connect(int connectionId, object target)
{
  switch (connectionId)
  {
    case 1:
    this.ClickMe = ((System.Windows.Controls.Button)(target));
    #line 11 "..\..\MainWindow.xaml"
    this.ClickMe.Click += new System.Windows.RoutedEventHandler(this.Button_Click);
    #line default
    #line hidden
    return;
  }
  this._contentLoaded = true;
}
```

To show the effects of unnamed controls with code, add an event handler for the SelectedDatesChanged event on the calendar. Rebuild the application, refresh the files, and reload the MainWindow.g.cs file. In the Connect() method, you now see the following code block:

```
#line 20 "..\..\MainWindow.xaml"
this.MyCalendar.SelectedDatesChanged += new
    System.EventHandler<System.Windows.Controls.SelectionChangedEventArgs>(
        this.MyCalendar_OnSelectedDatesChanged);
```

This tells the framework that the control on line 20 of the XAML file has SelectedDatesChanged event handler assigned, as shown in the preceding code.

Last but not least, the MainWindow class defines and implements a method named InitializeComponent(). You might expect that this method contains code that sets up the look and feel of each control by setting various properties (Height, Width, Content, etc.). However, this is not the case! How then do the controls take on the correct UI? The logic with InitializeComponent() resolves the location of an embedded assembly resource that is named identical to the original *.xaml file, like so:

```
public void InitializeComponent() {
  if (_contentLoaded) {
    return;
  }
  _contentLoaded = true;
  System.Uri resourceLocater = new System.Uri("/WpfTesterApp;component/mainwindow.xaml",
      System.UriKind.Relative);
```

```
#line 1 "..\..\MainWindow.xaml"
System.Windows.Application.LoadComponent(this, resourceLocater);
#line default
#line hidden
}
```

At this point, the question becomes, *what exactly is this embedded resource?*

The Role of BAML

As you might have guessed from the name, Binary Application Markup Language (BAML) is a compact, binary representation of the original XAML data. This *.baml file is embedded as a resource (via a generated *.g.resources file) into the compiled assembly. This BAML resource contains all the data needed to establish the look and feel of the UI widgets (again, such as the Height and Width properties).

The important takeaway here is to understand that a WPF application contains within itself a binary representation (the BAML) of the markup. At runtime, this BAML will be plucked out of the resource container and used to make sure all windows and controls are initialized to the correct look and feel.

Also, remember that the name of these binary resources are *identical* to the name of the stand-alone *.xaml files you authored. However, this does not imply in any way that you must distribute the loose *.xaml files with your compiled WPF program. Unless you build a WPF application that will dynamically load and parse *.xaml files at runtime, you will never need to ship the original markup.

Solving the Mystery of Main()

Now that you know how the MSBuild process works, open the App.g.cs file. Here you will find the autogenerated Main() method that initializes and runs your application object.

```
public static void Main() {
  WpfTesterApp.App app = new WpfTesterApp.App();
  app.InitializeComponent();
  app.Run();
}
```

The InitializeComponent() method configures the application properties, including the StartupUri and the event handlers for the Startup and Exit events.

```
public void InitializeComponent() {
    #line 5 "..\..\App.xaml"
    this.Startup += new System.Windows.StartupEventHandler(this.App_OnStartup);
    #line default
    #line hidden
    #line 5 "..\..\App.xaml"
    this.Exit += new System.Windows.ExitEventHandler(this.App_OnExit);
    #line default
    #line hidden
    #line 5 "..\..\App.xaml"
    this.StartupUri = new System.Uri("MainWindow.xaml", System.UriKind.Relative);
    #line default
    #line hidden
}
```

Interacting with Application-Level Data

Recall that the Application class defines a property named Properties, which allows you to define a collection of name-value pairs via a type indexer. Because this indexer has been defined to operate on type System.Object, you are able to store any sort of item within this collection (including your custom classes) to be retrieved at a later time using a friendly moniker. Using this approach, it is simple to share data across all windows in a WPF application.

To illustrate, you will update the current Startup event handler to check the incoming command-line arguments for a value named /GODMODE (a common cheat code for many PC video games). If you find this token, you will establish a bool value set to true within the properties collection of the same name (otherwise, you will set the value to false).

This sounds simple enough, but how are you going to pass the incoming command-line arguments (typically obtained from the Main() method) to your Startup event handler? One approach is to call the static Environment.GetCommandLineArgs() method. However, these same arguments are automatically added to the incoming StartupEventArgs parameter and can be accessed via the Args property. That being said, here is the first update to the current codebase:

```
private void App_OnStartup(object sender, StartupEventArgs e)
{
  Application.Current.Properties["GodMode"] = false;
  // Check the incoming command-line arguments and see if they
  // specified a flag for /GODMODE.
  foreach (string arg in e.Args)
  {
    if (arg.Equals("/godmode",StringComparison.OrdinalIgnoreCase))
    {
      Application.Current.Properties["GodMode"] = true;
      break;
    }
  }
}
```

Application-wide data can be accessed from anywhere within the WPF application. All you are required to do is obtain an access point to the global application object (via Application.Current) and investigate the collection. For example, you could update the Click event handler of the Button as so:

```
private void Button_Click(object sender, RoutedEventArgs e)
{
  // Did user enable /godmode?
  if ((bool)Application.Current.Properties["GodMode"])
  {
    MessageBox.Show("Cheater!");
  }
}
```

With this, if you enter the /godmode command-line argument into the Debug tab in the project properties and then run the program, you will be shamed and the program will exit. You can also run the program from a command line by entering the following command (open a command prompt and navigate to the bin/debug directory):

```
WpfAppAllCode.exe /godmode
```

997

You will see the shameful message box displayed when terminating the application.

■ **Note**   Recall that you can supply command-line arguments within Visual Studio. Simply double-click the Properties icon within Solution Explorer, click the Debug tab from the resulting editor, and enter /godmode within the "Command line arguments" editor.

Handling the Closing of a Window Object

End users can shut down a window by using numerous built-in system-level techniques (e.g., clicking the X close button on the window's frame) or by indirectly calling the Close() method in response to some user interaction element (e.g., File ➤ Exit). In either case, WPF provides two events that you can intercept to determine whether the user is *truly* ready to shut down the window and remove it from memory. The first event to fire is Closing, which works in conjunction with the CancelEventHandler delegate.

This delegate expects target methods to take System.ComponentModel.CancelEventArgs as the second parameter. CancelEventArgs provides the Cancel property, which when set to true will prevent the window from actually closing (this is handy when you have asked the user if he really wants to close the window or if perhaps he would like to save his work first).

If the user does indeed want to close the window, CancelEventArgs.Cancel can be set to false (which is the default setting). This will then cause the Closed event to fire (which works with the System. EventHandler delegate), making it the point at which the window is about to be closed for good.

Update the MainWindow class to handle these two events by adding these code statements to the current constructor, like so:

```
public MainWindow()
{
  InitializeComponent();
  this.Closed+=MainWindow_OnClosed;
  this.Closing += MainWindow_Closing;
}
```

Now, implement the corresponding event handlers as so:

```
private void MainWindow_Closing(object sender, System.ComponentModel.CancelEventArgs e)
{
  // See if the user really wants to shut down this window.
  string msg = "Do you want to close without saving?";
  MessageBoxResult result = MessageBox.Show(msg,
    "My App", MessageBoxButton.YesNo, MessageBoxImage.Warning);
  if (result == MessageBoxResult.No)
  {
    // If user doesn't want to close, cancel closure.
    e.Cancel = true;
  }
}

private void MainWindow_Closed(object sender, EventArgs e)
{
  MessageBox.Show("See ya!");
}
```

Now, run your program and attempt to close the window, either by clicking the X icon in the upper right of the window or by clicking the button control. You should see the confirmation dialog asking if you really want to leave. If you answer Yes, you will then see the farewell message. Clicking the No button will keep the window in memory.

Intercepting Mouse Events

The WPF API provides a number of events you can capture to interact with the mouse. Specifically, the UIElement base class defines a number of mouse-centric events such as MouseMove, MouseUp, MouseDown, MouseEnter, MouseLeave, and so forth.

Consider, for example, the act of handling the MouseMove event. This event works in conjunction with the System.Windows.Input.MouseEventHandler delegate, which expects its target to take a System.Windows.Input.MouseEventArgs type as the second parameter. Using MouseEventArgs, you are able to extract the (x, y) position of the mouse and other relevant details. Consider the following partial definition:

```
public class MouseEventArgs : InputEventArgs
{
...
  public Point GetPosition(IInputElement relativeTo);
  public MouseButtonState LeftButton { get; }
  public MouseButtonState MiddleButton { get; }
  public MouseDevice MouseDevice { get; }
  public MouseButtonState RightButton { get; }
  public StylusDevice StylusDevice { get; }
  public MouseButtonState XButton1 { get; }
  public MouseButtonState XButton2 { get; }
}
```

■ **Note**   The XButton1 and XButton2 properties allow you to interact with "extended mouse buttons" (such as the "next" and "previous" buttons found on some mouse controls). These are often used to interact with a browser's history list to navigate between visited pages.

The GetPosition() method allows you to get the (x, y) value relative to a UI element on the window. If you are interested in capturing the position relative to the activated window, simply pass in this. Handle the MouseMove event in the constructor of your MainWindow class, like so:

```
public MainWindow(string windowTitle, int height, int width)
{
...
  this.MouseMove += MainWindow_MouseMove;
}
```

Here is an event handler for MouseMove that will display the location of the mouse in the window's title area (notice you are translating the returned Point type into a text value via ToString()):

```
private void MainWindow_MouseMove(object sender,
  System.Windows.Input.MouseEventArgs e)
{
```

```
// Set the title of the window to the current (x,y) of the mouse.
this.Title = e.GetPosition(this).ToString();
}
```

Intercepting Keyboard Events

Processing keyboard input for the focused window is also straightforward. UIElement defines a number of events that you can capture to intercept keypresses from the keyboard on the active element (e.g., KeyUp, KeyDown). The KeyUp and KeyDown events both work with the System.Windows.Input.KeyEventHandler delegate, which expects the target's second event handler to be of type KeyEventArgs, which defines several public properties of interest, shown here:

```
public class KeyEventArgs : KeyboardEventArgs
{
...
  public bool IsDown { get; }
  public bool IsRepeat { get; }
  public bool IsToggled { get; }
  public bool IsUp { get; }
  public Key Key { get; }
  public KeyStates KeyStates { get; }
  public Key SystemKey { get; }
}
```

To illustrate handling the KeyDown event in the constructor of MainWindow (just like you did for the previous events), implement the following event handler that changes the content of the button with the currently pressed key:

```
private void MainWindow_KeyDown(object sender, System.Windows.Input.KeyEventArgs e)
{
  // Display key press on the button.
  ClickMe.Content = e.Key.ToString();
}
```

At this point in the chapter, WPF might look like nothing more than yet another GUI framework that is providing (more or less) the same services as Windows Forms, MFC, or VB6. If this were in fact the case, you might question the need for yet another UI toolkit. To truly see what makes WPF so unique, you require an understanding of the XML-based grammar, XAML.

■ **Source Code**   You can find the WpfTesterApp project in the Chapter 24 subdirectory.

Exploring the WPF Documentation

To close this chapter, I want to point out that the .NET 4.7 Framework SDK documentation provides an entire section devoted to the topic of WPF. As you explore this API and read the remaining WPF-centric chapters, you will do yourself a great service if you consult the help system early and often. Here, you will find a huge amount of sample XAML plus detailed tutorials on a wide variety of topics ranging from 3D graphics programing to complex data binding operations.

You can access the WPF documentation via the Docs ➤ .NET ➤ .NET Framework ➤ Windows Presentation Foundation menu; it's located at `https://docs.microsoft.com/en-us/dotnet/framework/wpf/index`.

Summary

Windows Presentation Foundation (WPF) is a user interface toolkit introduced with the release of .NET 3.0. The major goal of WPF is to integrate and unify a number of previously unrelated desktop technologies (2D graphics, 3D graphics, window and control development, etc.) into a single, unified programming model. Beyond this point, WPF programs typically make use of XAML, which allows you to declare the look and feel of your WPF elements via markup.

Recall that XAML allows you to describe trees of .NET objects using a declarative syntax. During this chapter's investigation of XAML, you were exposed to several new bits of syntax, including property-element syntax and attached properties, as well as the role of type converters and XAML markup extensions.

XAML is a key aspect for any production-level WPF application. The final example of this chapter gave you a chance to build a WPF application that showed many of the concepts discussed in this chapter. The next chapters will dive deeper into these concepts as well as introduce many more.

CHAPTER 25

■ ■ ■

WPF Controls, Layouts, Events, and Data Binding

Chapter 24 provided a foundation for the WPF programming model, including an examination of the `Window` and `Application` classes, the grammar of XAML, and the use of code files. Chapter 24 also introduced you to the process of building WPF applications using the designers of Visual Studio. In this chapter, you will dig into the construction of more sophisticated graphical user interfaces using several new controls and layout managers, learning about additional features of the WPF designers of Visual Studio along the way.

This chapter will also examine some important related WPF control topics such as the data-binding programming model and the use of control commands. You will also learn how to use the Ink and Documents APIs, which allow you to capture stylus (or mouse) input and build rich-text documents using the XML Paper Specification, respectively.

A Survey of the Core WPF Controls

Unless you are new to the concept of building graphical user interfaces (which is fine), the general purpose of the major WPF controls should not raise too many issues. Regardless of which GUI toolkit you might have used in the past (e.g., VB 6.0, MFC, Java AWT/Swing, Windows Forms, macOS, or GTK+/GTK# [among others]), the core WPF controls listed in Table 25-1 are likely to look familiar.

Table 25-1. *The Core WPF Controls*

WPF Control Category	Example Members	Meaning in Life
Core user input controls	`Button`, `RadioButton`, `ComboBox`, `CheckBox`, `Calendar`, `DatePicker`, `Expander`, `DataGrid`, `ListBox`, `ListView`, `ToggleButton`, `TreeView`, `ContextMenu`, `ScrollBar`, `Slider`, `TabControl`, `TextBlock`, `TextBox`, `RepeatButton`, `RichTextBox`, `Label`	WPF provides an entire family of controls you can use to build the crux of a user interface.
Window and control adornments	`Menu`, `ToolBar`, `StatusBar`, `ToolTip`, `ProgressBar`	You use these UI elements to decorate the frame of a `Window` object with input devices (such as the `Menu`) and user informational elements (e.g., `StatusBar` and `ToolTip`).

(continued)

© Andrew Troelsen and Philip Japikse 2017
A. Troelsen and P. Japikse, *Pro C# 7*, https://doi.org/10.1007/978-1-4842-3018-3_25

Table 25-1. *(continued)*

WPF Control Category	Example Members	Meaning in Life
Media controls	Image, MediaElement, SoundPlayerAction	These controls provide support for audio/video playback and image display.
Layout controls	Border, Canvas, DockPanel, Grid, GridView, GridSplitter, GroupBox, Panel, TabControl, StackPanel, Viewbox, WrapPanel	WPF provides numerous controls that allow you to group and organize other controls for the purpose of layout management.

The WPF Ink Controls

In addition to the common WPF controls listed in Table 25-1, WPF defines additional controls for working with the digital Ink API. This aspect of WPF development is useful during Tablet PC development because it lets you capture input from the stylus. However, this is not to say a standard desktop application cannot leverage the Ink API because the same controls can capture input using the mouse.

The System.Windows.Ink namespace of PresentationCore.dll contains various Ink API support types (e.g., Stroke and StrokeCollection); however, a majority of the Ink API controls (e.g., InkCanvas and InkPresenter) are packaged up with the common WPF controls under the System.Windows.Controls namespace in the PresentationFramework.dll assembly. You'll work with the Ink API later in this chapter.

The WPF Document Controls

WPF also provides controls for advanced document processing, allowing you to build applications that incorporate Adobe PDF–style functionality. Using the types within the System.Windows.Documents namespace (also in the PresentationFramework.dll assembly), you can create print-ready documents that support zooming, searching, user annotations (sticky notes), and other rich text services.

Under the covers, however, the document controls do not use Adobe PDF APIs; rather, they use the XML Paper Specification (XPS) API. To the end user, there will really appear to be no difference because PDF documents and XPS documents have an almost identical look-and-feel. In fact, you can find many free utilities that allow you to convert between the two file formats on the fly. Because of space limitation, these controls won't be covered in this edition.

WPF Common Dialog Boxes

WPF also provides you with a few common dialog boxes such as OpenFileDialog and SaveFileDialog. These dialog boxes are defined within the Microsoft.Win32 namespace of the PresentationFramework. dll assembly. Working with either of these dialog boxes is a matter of creating an object and invoking the ShowDialog() method, like so:

```
using Microsoft.Win32;
//omitted for brevity
private void btnShowDlg_Click(object sender, RoutedEventArgs e)
{
  // Show a file save dialog.
  SaveFileDialog saveDlg = new SaveFileDialog();
  saveDlg.ShowDialog();
}
```

As you would hope, these classes support various members that allow you to establish file filters and directory paths and gain access to user-selected files. You will put these file dialogs to use in later examples; you will also learn how to build custom dialog boxes to gather user input.

The Details Are in the Documentation

Despite what you might be thinking, the intent of this chapter is *not* to walk through each and every member of each and every WPF control. Rather, you will receive an overview of the various controls with an emphasis on the underlying programming model and key services common to most WPF controls.

To round out your understanding of the particular functionality of a given control, be sure to consult the .NET Framework 4.7 SDK documentation—specifically, the Control Library section of the help system, which you can find at https://docs.microsoft.com/en-us/dotnet/framework/wpf/controls/index.

Here you will find full details of each control, various code samples (in XAML, C#, as well as VB), and information regarding a control's inheritance chain, implemented interfaces, and applied attributes. Make sure you take time to look up the controls examined in this chapter for complete details.

A Brief Review of the Visual Studio WPF Designer

A majority of these standard WPF controls have been packaged up in the `System.Windows.Controls` namespace of the `PresentationFramework.dll` assembly. When you build a WPF application using Visual Studio, you will find most of these common controls contained in the toolbox, provided you have a WPF designer open as the active window.

Similar to other UI frameworks created with Visual Studio, you can drag these controls onto the WPF window designer and configure them using the Properties window (which you learned about in Chapter 24). While Visual Studio will generate a good amount of the XAML on your behalf, it is not uncommon to edit the markup yourself manually. Let's review the basics.

Working with WPF Controls Using Visual Studio

You might recall from Chapter 24 that when you place a WPF control onto the Visual Studio designer, you want to set the x:Name property through the Properties window (or through XAML directly) because this allows you to access the object in your related C# code file. You might also recall that you can use the Events tab of the Properties window to generate event handlers for a selected control. Thus, you could use Visual Studio to generate the following markup for a simple Button control:

```
<Button x:Name="btnMyButton" Content="Click Me!" Height="23" Width="140" Click="btnMyButton_
Click" />
```

Here, you set the Content property of the Button to a simple string with the value "Click Me!". However, thanks to the WPF control content model, you could fashion a Button that contains the following complex content:

```
<Button x:Name="btnMyButton" Height="121" Width="156" Click="btnMyButton_Click">
  <Button.Content>
    <StackPanel Height="95" Width="128" Orientation="Vertical">
      <Ellipse Fill="Red" Width="52" Height="45" Margin="5"/>
      <Label Width="59" FontSize="20" Content="Click!" Height="36" />
    </StackPanel>
  </Button.Content>
</Button>
```

You might also recall that the immediate child element of a ContentControl-derived class is the implied content; therefore, you do not need to define a Button.Content scope explicitly when specifying complex content. You could simply author the following:

```
<Button x:Name="btnMyButton" Height="121" Width="156" Click="btnMyButton_Click">
  <StackPanel Height="95" Width="128" Orientation="Vertical">
    <Ellipse Fill="Red" Width="52" Height="45" Margin="5"/>
    <Label Width="59" FontSize="20" Content="Click!" Height="36" />
  </StackPanel>
</Button>
```

In either case, you set the button's Content property to a StackPanel of related items. You can also author this sort of complex content using the Visual Studio designer. After you define the layout manager for a content control, you can select it on the designer to serve as a drop target for the internal controls. At this point, you can edit each using the Properties window. If you were to use the Properties window to handle the Click event for the Button control (as shown in the previous XAML declarations), the IDE would generate an empty event handler, to which you could add your own custom code, like so:

```
private void btnMyButton_Click(object sender, RoutedEventArgs e)
{
  MessageBox.Show("You clicked the button!");
}
```

Working with the Document Outline Editor

You should recall from the previous chapter that the Document Outline window of Visual Studio (which you can open using the View ➤ Other Windows menu) is useful when designing a WPF control that has complex content. The logical tree of XAML is displayed for the Window you are building, and if you click any of these nodes, it is automatically selected in the visual designer and the XAML editor for editing.

With the current edition of Visual Studio, the Document Outline window has a few additional features that you might find useful. To the right of any node you will find an icon that looks similar to an eyeball. When you toggle this button, you can opt to hide or show an item on the designer, which can be helpful when you want to focus in on a particular segment to edit (note that this will *not* hide the item at runtime; this is only hides items on the designer surface).

Right next to the "eyeball icon" is a second toggle that allows you to lock an item on the designer. As you might guess, this can be helpful when you want to make sure you (or your co-workers) do not accidently change the XAML for a given item. In effect, locking an item makes it read-only at design time (however, you can obviously change the object's state at runtime).

Controlling Content Layout Using Panels

A WPF application invariably contains a good number of UI elements (e.g., user input controls, graphical content, menu systems, and status bars) that need to be well organized within various windows. After you place the UI elements, you need to make sure they behave as intended when the end user resizes the window or possibly a portion of the window (as in the case of a splitter window). To ensure your WPF controls retain their position within the hosting window, you can take advantage of a good number of *panel types* (also known as *layout managers*).

By default, a new WPF Window created with Visual Studio will use a layout manager of type Grid (more details in just a bit). However, for now, assume a Window with no declared layout manager, like so:

```
<Window x:Class="MyWPFApp.MainWindow"
  xmlns="http://schemas.microsoft.com/winfx/2006/xaml/presentation"
  xmlns:x="http://schemas.microsoft.com/winfx/2006/xaml"
  Title="Fun with Panels!" Height="285" Width="325">

</Window>
```

When you declare a control directly inside a window that doesn't use panels, the control is positioned dead-center in the container. Consider the following simple window declaration, which contains a single Button control. Regardless of how you resize the window, the UI widget is always equidistant from all four sides of the client area. The Button's size is determined by the assigned Height and Width properties of the Button.

```
<!- This button is in the center of the window at all times ->
<Window x:Class="MyWPFApp.MainWindow"
  xmlns="http://schemas.microsoft.com/winfx/2006/xaml/presentation"
  xmlns:x="http://schemas.microsoft.com/winfx/2006/xaml"
  Title="Fun with Panels!" Height="285" Width="325">

  <Button x:Name="btnOK" Height = "100" Width="80" Content="OK"/>
</Window>
```

You might also recall that if you attempt to place multiple elements directly within the scope of a Window, you will receive markup and compile-time errors. The reason for these errors is that a window (or any descendant of ContentControl for that matter) can assign only a single object to its Content property. Therefore, the following XAML yields markup and compile-time errors:

```
<!- Error! Content property is implicitly set more than once! ->
<Window x:Class="MyWPFApp.MainWindow"
  xmlns="http://schemas.microsoft.com/winfx/2006/xaml/presentation"
  xmlns:x="http://schemas.microsoft.com/winfx/2006/xaml"
  Title="Fun with Panels!" Height="285" Width="325">
  <!- Error! Two direct child elements of the <Window>! ->
  <Label x:Name="lblInstructions" Width="328" Height="27" FontSize="15" Content="Enter
  Information"/>
  <Button x:Name="btnOK" Height = "100" Width="80" Content="OK"/>
</Window>
```

Obviously, a window that can contain only a single control is of little use. When a window needs to contain multiple elements, those elements must be arranged within any number of panels. The panel will contain all of the UI elements that represent the window, after which the panel itself is used as the single object assigned to the Content property.

The System.Windows.Controls namespace provides numerous panels, each of which controls how subelements are maintained. You can use panels to establish how the controls behave if the end user resizes the window, if the controls remain exactly where they were placed at design time, if the controls reflow horizontally from left to right or vertically from top to bottom, and so forth.

You can also intermix panel controls within other panels (e.g., a DockPanel that contains a StackPanel of other items) to provide a great deal of flexibility and control. Table 25-2 documents the role of some commonly used WPF panel controls.

Table 25-2. *Core WPF Panel Controls*

Panel Control	Meaning in Life
Canvas	Provides a classic mode of content placement. Items stay exactly where you put them at design time.
DockPanel	Locks content to a specified side of the panel (Top, Bottom, Left, or Right).
Grid	Arranges content within a series of cells, maintained within a tabular grid.
StackPanel	Stacks content in a vertical or horizontal manner, as dictated by the Orientation property.
WrapPanel	Positions content from left to right, breaking the content to the next line at the edge of the containing box. Subsequent ordering happens sequentially from top to bottom or from right to left, depending on the value of the Orientation property.

In the next few sections, you will learn how to use these commonly used panel types by copying some predefined XAML data into the kaxaml.exe application you installed in Chapter 24. You can find all these loose XAML files contained inside the PanelMarkup subfolder of your Chapter 25 code download folder. When working with Kaxaml, to simulate resizing a window, change the height or width of the Page element in the markup.

Positioning Content Within Canvas Panels

If you come from a WinForms background, you will probably feel most at home with the Canvas panel because it allows for absolute positioning of UI content. If the end user resizes the window to an area that is smaller than the layout maintained by the Canvas panel, the internal content will not be visible until the container is stretched to a size equal to or larger than the Canvas area.

To add content to a Canvas, you begin by defining the required controls within the scope of the opening and closing Canvas tags. Next, specify the upper-left corner for each control; this is where the rendering should begin using the Canvas.Top and Canvas.Left properties. You can specify the bottom-right area indirectly in each control by setting its Height and Width properties or directly by using the Canvas.Right and Canvas.Bottom properties.

To see Canvas in action, open the provided SimpleCanvas.xaml file using kaxaml.exe. You should see the following Canvas definition (if loading these examples into a WPF application, you will want to change the Page tag to a Window tag):

```
<Page
  xmlns="http://schemas.microsoft.com/winfx/2006/xaml/presentation"
  xmlns:x="http://schemas.microsoft.com/winfx/2006/xaml"
...
  Title="Fun with Panels!" Height="285" Width="325">
  <Canvas Background="LightSteelBlue">
    <Button x:Name="btnOK" Canvas.Left="212" Canvas.Top="203" Width="80" Content="OK"/>
    <Label x:Name="lblInstructions" Canvas.Left="17" Canvas.Top="14" Width="328" Height="27"
    FontSize="15"
          Content="Enter Car Information"/>
    <Label x:Name="lblMake" Canvas.Left="17" Canvas.Top="60" Content="Make"/>
    <TextBox x:Name="txtMake" Canvas.Left="94" Canvas.Top="60" Width="193" Height="25"/>
    <Label x:Name="lblColor" Canvas.Left="17" Canvas.Top="109" Content="Color"/>
    <TextBox x:Name="txtColor" Canvas.Left="94" Canvas.Top="107" Width="193" Height="25"/>
```

```
    <Label x:Name="lblPetName" Canvas.Left="17" Canvas.Top="155" Content="Pet Name"/>
    <TextBox x:Name="txtPetName" Canvas.Left="94" Canvas.Top="153" Width="193" Height="25"/>
  </Canvas>
</Page>
```

You should see the window shown in Figure 25-1 in the top half of the screen.

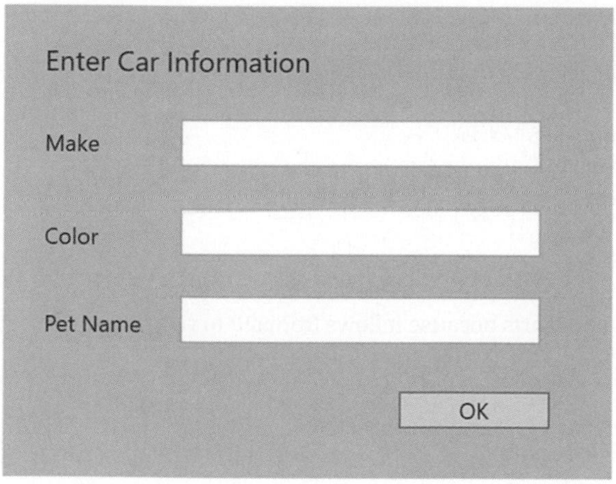

Figure 25-1. *The Canvas layout manager allows for absolute positioning of content*

Note that the order you declare content within a Canvas is not used to calculate placement; instead, placement is based on the control's size and the Canvas.Top, Canvas.Bottom, Canvas.Left, and Canvas. Right properties.

■ **Note** If subelements within a Canvas do not define a specific location using attached property syntax (e.g., Canvas.Left and Canvas.Top), they automatically attach to the extreme upper-left corner of Canvas.

Using the Canvas type might seem like the preferred way to arrange content (because it feels so familiar), but this approach does suffer from some limitations. First, items within a Canvas do not dynamically resize themselves when applying styles or templates (e.g., their font sizes are unaffected). Second, the Canvas will not attempt to keep elements visible when the end user resizes the window to a smaller surface.

Perhaps the best use of the Canvas type is for positioning *graphical content*. For example, if you were building a custom image using XAML, you certainly would want the lines, shapes, and text to remain in the same location, rather than see them dynamically repositioned as the user resizes the window! You'll revisit Canvas in Chapter 26 when you examine WPF's graphical rendering services.

Positioning Content Within WrapPanel Panels

A WrapPanel allows you to define content that will flow across the panel as the window is resized. When positioning elements in a WrapPanel, you do not specify top, bottom, left, and right docking values as you typically do with Canvas. However, each subelement is free to define a Height and Width value (among other property values) to control its overall size in the container.

Because content within a WrapPanel does not dock to a given side of the panel, the order in which you declare the elements is important (content is rendered from the first element to the last). If you were to load the XAML data found within the SimpleWrapPanel.xaml file, you would find it contains the following markup (enclosed within a Page definition):

```
<WrapPanel Background="LightSteelBlue">
  <Label x:Name="lblInstruction" Width="328" Height="27" FontSize="15" Content="Enter Car
  Information"/>
  <Label x:Name="lblMake" Content="Make"/>
  <TextBox x:Name="txtMake" Width="193" Height="25"/>
  <Label x:Name="lblColor" Content="Color"/>
  <TextBox x:Name="txtColor" Width="193" Height="25"/>
  <Label x:Name="lblPetName" Content="Pet Name"/>
  <TextBox x:Name="txtPetName" Width="193" Height="25"/>
  <Button x:Name="btnOK" Width="80" Content="OK"/>
</WrapPanel>
```

When you load this markup, the content looks out of sorts because it flows from left to right across the window (see Figure 25-2).

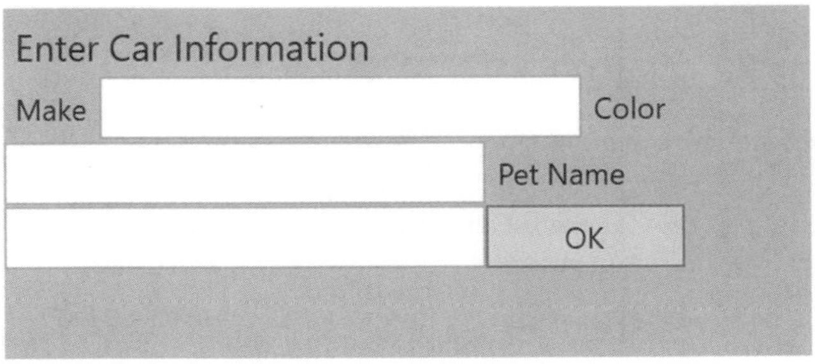

Figure 25-2. *Content in a WrapPanel behaves much like a traditional HTML page*

By default, content within a WrapPanel flows from left to right. However, if you change the value of the Orientation property to Vertical, you can have content wrap in a top-to-bottom manner.

```
<WrapPanel Background="LightSteelBlue" Orientation ="Vertical">
```

You can declare a WrapPanel (as well as some other panel types) by specifying ItemWidth and ItemHeight values, which control the default size of each item. If a subelement does provide its own Height and/or Width value, it will be positioned relative to the size established by the panel. Consider the following markup:

```
<Page
    xmlns="http://schemas.microsoft.com/winfx/2006/xaml/presentation"
    xmlns:x="http://schemas.microsoft.com/winfx/2006/xaml"
    Title="Fun with Panels!" Height="100" Width="650">
  <WrapPanel Background="LightSteelBlue" Orientation ="Horizontal" ItemWidth ="200"
  ItemHeight ="30">
    <Label x:Name="lblInstruction" FontSize="15" Content="Enter Car Information"/>
    <Label x:Name="lblMake" Content="Make"/>
```

```
    <TextBox x:Name="txtMake"/>
    <Label x:Name="lblColor" Content="Color"/>
    <TextBox x:Name="txtColor"/>
    <Label x:Name="lblPetName" Content="Pet Name"/>
    <TextBox x:Name="txtPetName"/>
    <Button x:Name="btnOK" Width ="80" Content="OK"/>
</WrapPanel>
</Page>
```

The rendered code looks like Figure 25-3 (notice the size and position of the Button control, which has a specified unique Width value).

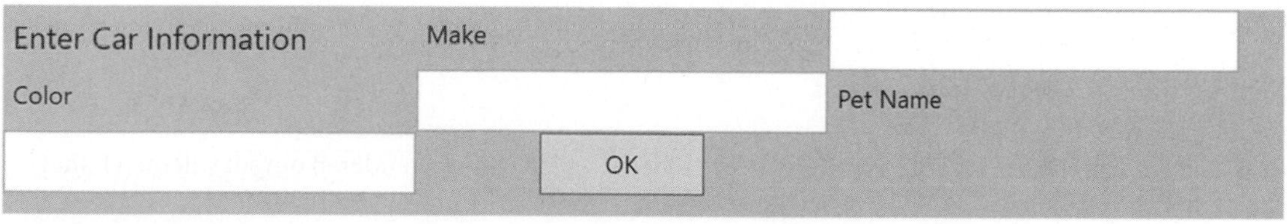

Figure 25-3. *A WrapPanel can establish the width and height of a given item*

As you might agree after looking at Figure 25-3, a WrapPanel is not typically the best choice for arranging content directly in a window because its elements can become scrambled as the user resizes the window. In most cases, a WrapPanel will be a subelement to another panel type, allowing a small area of the window to wrap its content when resized (e.g., a ToolBar control).

Positioning Content Within StackPanel Panels

Like a WrapPanel, a StackPanel control arranges content into a single line that can be oriented horizontally or vertically (the default), based on the value assigned to the Orientation property. The difference, however, is that the StackPanel will *not* attempt to wrap the content as the user resizes the window. Rather, the items in the StackPanel will simply stretch (based on their orientation) to accommodate the size of the StackPanel itself. For example, the SimpleStackPanel.xaml file contains the following markup, which results in the output shown in Figure 25-4:

```
<StackPanel Background="LightSteelBlue">
  <Label x:Name="lblInstruction"
        FontSize="15" Content="Enter Car Information"/>
  <Label x:Name="lblMake" Content="Make"/>
  <TextBox Name="txtMake"/>
  <Label x:Name="lblColor" Content="Color"/>
  <TextBox x:Name="txtColor"/>
  <Label x:Name="lblPetName" Content="Pet Name"/>
  <TextBox x:Name="txtPetName"/>
  <Button x:Name="btnOK" Width ="80" Content="OK"/>
</StackPanel>
```

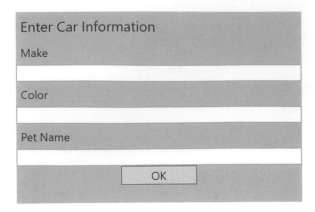

Figure 25-4. *Vertical stacking of content*

If you assign the Orientation property to Horizontal as follows, the rendered output will match that shown in Figure 25-5:

```
<StackPanel Background="LightSteelBlue" Orientation="Horizontal">
```

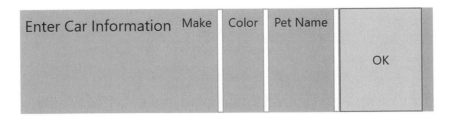

Figure 25-5. *Horizontal stacking of content*

Again, as is the case with the WrapPanel, you will seldom want to use a StackPanel to arrange content directly within a window. Instead, you should use StackPanel as a subpanel to a master panel.

Positioning Content Within Grid Panels

Of all the panels provided with the WPF APIs, Grid is far and away the most flexible. Like an HTML table, the Grid can be carved up into a set of cells, each one of which provides content. When defining a Grid, you perform three steps.

1. Define and configure each column.

2. Define and configure each row.

3. Assign content to each cell of the grid using attached property syntax.

■ **Note** If you do not define any rows or columns, the Grid defaults to a single cell that fills the entire surface of the window. Furthermore, if you do not assign a cell value (column and row) for a subelement within a Grid, it automatically attaches to column 0, row 0.

You achieve the first two steps (defining the columns and rows) by using the `Grid.ColumnDefinitions` and `Grid.RowDefinitions` elements, which contain a collection of `ColumnDefinition` and `RowDefinition` elements, respectively. Each cell within a grid is indeed a true .NET object, so you can configure the look and feel and behavior of each cell as you see fit.

Here is a `Grid` definition (that you can find in the `SimpleGrid.xaml` file) that arranges your UI content as shown in Figure 25-6:

```xml
<Grid ShowGridLines ="True" Background ="LightSteelBlue">
  <!- Define the rows/columns ->
  <Grid.ColumnDefinitions>
    <ColumnDefinition/>
    <ColumnDefinition/>
  </Grid.ColumnDefinitions>
  <Grid.RowDefinitions>
    <RowDefinition/>
    <RowDefinition/>
  </Grid.RowDefinitions>

  <!- Now add the elements to the grid's cells ->
  <Label x:Name="lblInstruction" Grid.Column ="0" Grid.Row ="0"
         FontSize="15" Content="Enter Car Information"/>
  <Button x:Name="btnOK" Height ="30" Grid.Column ="0"
          Grid.Row ="0" Content="OK"/>
  <Label x:Name="lblMake" Grid.Column ="1"
         Grid.Row ="0" Content="Make"/>
  <TextBox x:Name="txtMake" Grid.Column ="1"
           Grid.Row ="0" Width="193" Height="25"/>
  <Label x:Name="lblColor" Grid.Column ="0"
         Grid.Row ="1" Content="Color"/>
  <TextBox x:Name="txtColor" Width="193" Height="25"
           Grid.Column ="0" Grid.Row ="1" />

  <!- Just to keep things interesting, add some color to the pet name cell ->
  <Rectangle Fill ="LightGreen" Grid.Column ="1" Grid.Row ="1" />
  <Label x:Name="lblPetName" Grid.Column ="1" Grid.Row ="1" Content="Pet Name"/>
  <TextBox x:Name="txtPetName" Grid.Column ="1" Grid.Row ="1"
           Width="193" Height="25"/>
</Grid>
```

Notice that each element (including a light green Rectangle element thrown in for good measure) connects itself to a cell in the grid using the `Grid.Row` and `Grid.Column` attached properties. By default, the ordering of cells in a grid begins at the upper left, which you specify using `Grid.Column="0"` `Grid.Row="0"`. Given that your grid defines a total of four cells, you can identify the bottom-right cell using `Grid.Column="1"` `Grid.Row="1"`.

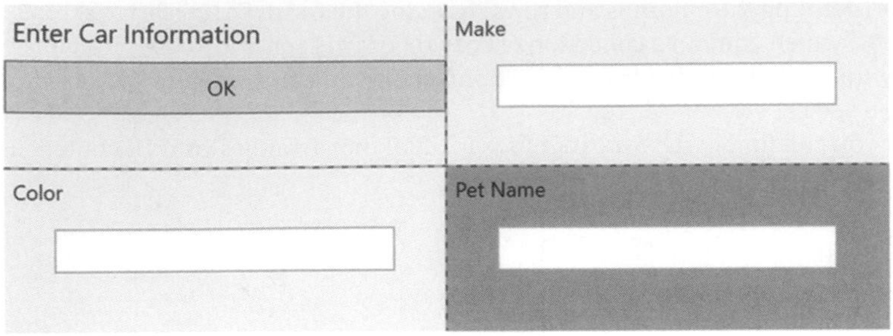

Figure 25-6. *The Grid panel in action*

Sizing Grid Columns and Rows

Columns and rows in a grid can be sized in one of three ways.

- Absolute sizing (e.g., 100).

- Autosizing

- Relative sizing (e.g., 3x)

Absolute sizing is exactly what you would expect; the column (or row) is sized to a specific number of device-independent units. Autosizing sizes each column or row based on the controls contained with the column or row. Relative sizing is pretty much equivalent to percentage sizing in CSS. The total count of the numbers in relatively sized columns or rows gets divided into the total amount of available space.

In the following example, the first row gets 25 percent of the space, and the second row gets 75 percent of the space:

```
<Grid.ColumnDefinitions>
  <ColumnDefinition Width="1*" />
  <ColumnDefinition Width="3*" />
</Grid.ColumnDefinitions>
```

Grids with GridSplitter Types

Grid objects can also support *splitters*. As you might know, splitters allow the end user to resize rows or columns of a grid type. As this is done, the content within each resizable cell will reshape itself based on how the items have been contained. Adding splitters to a Grid is easy to do; you simply define the GridSplitter control, using attached property syntax to establish which row or column it affects.

Be aware that you must assign a Width or Height value (depending on vertical or horizontal splitting) for the splitter to be visible on the screen. Consider the following simple Grid type with a splitter on the first column (Grid.Column = "0"). The contents of the provided GridWithSplitter.xaml file look like this:

```
<Grid Background ="LightSteelBlue">
  <!- Define columns ->
  <Grid.ColumnDefinitions>
    <ColumnDefinition Width ="Auto"/>
    <ColumnDefinition/>
  </Grid.ColumnDefinitions>
```

```
<!- Add this label to cell 0 ->
<Label x:Name="lblLeft" Background ="GreenYellow"
       Grid.Column="0" Content ="Left!"/>

<!- Define the splitter ->
<GridSplitter Grid.Column ="0" Width ="5"/>

<!- Add this label to cell 1 ->
<Label x:Name="lblRight" Grid.Column ="1" Content ="Right!"/>
</Grid>
```

First, notice that the column that will support the splitter has a Width property of Auto. Next, notice that the GridSplitter uses attached property syntax to establish which column it is working with. If you were to view this output, you would find a five-pixel splitter that allows you to resize each Label. Note that the content fills up the entire cell because you have not specified Height or Width properties for either Label (see Figure 25-7).

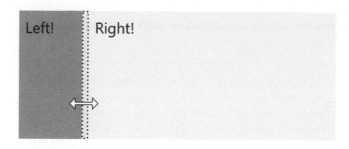

Figure 25-7. *Grid types containing splitters*

Positioning Content Within DockPanel Panels

DockPanel is typically used as a container that holds any number of additional panels for grouping related content. DockPanels use attached property syntax (as shown with the Canvas or Grid types) to control where each item docks itself within the DockPanel.

The SimpleDockPanel.xaml file defines the following simple DockPanel definition that results in the output shown in Figure 25-8:

```
<DockPanel LastChildFill ="True" Background="AliceBlue">
  <!-- Dock items to the panel -->
  <Label DockPanel.Dock ="Top" Name="lblInstruction" FontSize="15" Content="Enter Car
  Information"/>
  <Label DockPanel.Dock ="Left" Name="lblMake" Content="Make"/>
  <Label DockPanel.Dock ="Right" Name="lblColor" Content="Color"/>
  <Label DockPanel.Dock ="Bottom" Name="lblPetName" Content="Pet Name"/>
  <Button Name="btnOK" Content="OK"/>
</DockPanel>
```

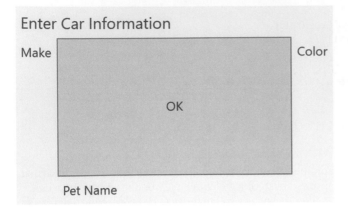

Figure 25-8. *A simple* `DockPanel`

■ **Note** If you add multiple elements to the same side of a `DockPanel`, they will stack along the specified edge in the order they are declared.

The benefit of using `DockPanel` types is that, as the user resizes the window, each element remains connected to the specified side of the panel (through `DockPanel.Dock`). Also notice that the opening `DockPanel` tag in this example sets the `LastChildFill` attribute to `true`. Given that the `Button` control is indeed the "last child" in the container, it will therefore be stretched within the remaining space.

Enabling Scrolling for Panel Types

It is worth pointing out that WPF supplies a `ScrollViewer` class, which provides automatic scrolling behaviors for data within panel objects. The `SimpleScrollViewer.xaml` file defines the following:

```
<ScrollViewer>
  <StackPanel>
    <Button Content ="First" Background = "Green" Height ="40"/>
    <Button Content ="Second" Background = "Red" Height ="40"/>
    <Button Content ="Third" Background = "Pink" Height ="40"/>
    <Button Content ="Fourth" Background = "Yellow" Height ="40"/>
    <Button Content ="Fifth" Background = "Blue" Height ="40"/>
  </StackPanel>
</ScrollViewer>
```

You can see the result of the previous XAML definition in Figure 25-9 (notice the scroll bar on the right since the window isn't sized to show all five buttons).

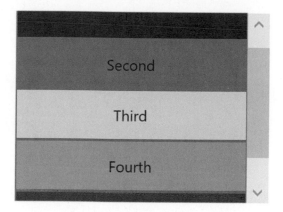

Figure 25-9. *Working with the* ScrollViewer *type*

As you would expect, each panel provides numerous members that allow you to fine-tune content placement. On a related note, many WPF controls support two properties of interest (Padding and Margin) that allow the control itself to inform the panel how it wishes to be treated. Specifically, the Padding property controls how much extra space should surround the interior control, while Margin controls the extra space around the exterior of a control.

This wraps up this chapter's look at the major panel types of WPF, as well as the various ways they position their content. Next, you'll learn how to use the Visual Studio designers to create layouts.

Configuring Panels Using the Visual Studio Designers

Now that you have been given a walk-through of the XAML used to define some common layout managers, you will be happy to know that Visual Studio has some very good design-time support for constructing your layouts. The key to doing so lies with the Document Outline window described earlier in this chapter. To illustrate some of the basics, create a new WPF application project named VisualLayoutTester.

Notice how your initial Window makes use of a Grid layout by default, as shown here:

```
<Window x:Class="VisualLayoutTester.MainWindow"
    xmlns="http://schemas.microsoft.com/winfx/2006/xaml/presentation"
    xmlns:x="http://schemas.microsoft.com/winfx/2006/xaml"
    xmlns:d="http://schemas.microsoft.com/expression/blend/2008"
    xmlns:mc="http://schemas.openxmlformats.org/markup-compatibility/2006"
    xmlns:local="clr-namespace:VisualLayoutTesterApp"
    mc:Ignorable="d"
        Title="MainWindow" Height="350" Width="525">
    <Grid>
    </Grid>
</Window>
```

If you are happy using the Grid layout system, notice in Figure 25-10 that you can easily carve out and resize the grid's cells using the visual layout. To do so, first select the Grid component in your Document Outline window and then click the grid's border to create new rows and columns.

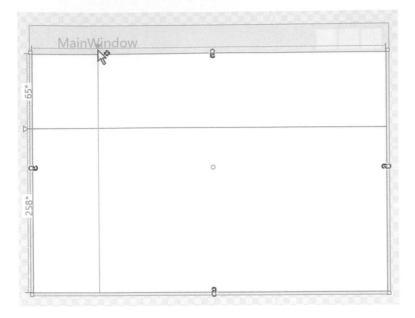

Figure 25-10. *The* Grid *control can be visually cut into cells using the IDE's designer*

Now, let's say you have defined a grid with some number of cells. You can then drag and drop controls into a given cell of the layout system, and the IDE will automatically set the Grid.Row and Grid.Column properties of the control in question. Here is some possible markup generated by the IDE after dragging a Button into a predefined cell:

```
<Button x:Name="button" Content="Button" Grid.Column="1" HorizontalAlignment="Left"
Margin="21,21.4,0,0" Grid.Row="1" VerticalAlignment="Top" Width="75"/>
```

Now, let's say you would rather not use a Grid at all. If you right-click any layout node in the Document Outline window, you will find a menu option that allows you to change the current container into another (see Figure 25-11). Be aware that when you do so, you will (most likely) radically change the positioning of the controls because the controls will conform to the rules of the new panel type.

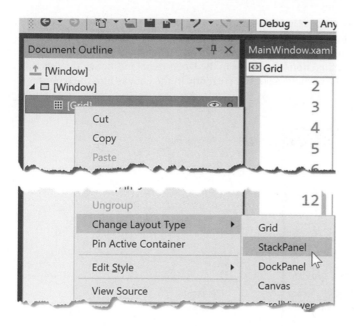

Figure 25-11. *The Document Outline window allows you to convert to new panel types*

Another handy trick is the ability to select a set of controls on the visual designer and group them into a new, nested layout manager. Assume you have a Canvas that defines a set of random objects (if you want to try, convert the initial Grid to a Canvas using the technique shown in Figure 25-11). Now, select a set of items on the designer by holding down the Ctrl key and clicking each item with the left mouse button. If you then right-click the selection, you can group the selected items into a new subpanel (see Figure 25-12).

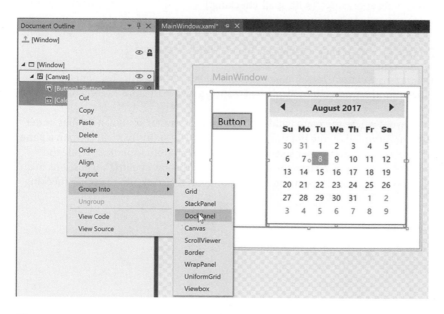

Figure 25-12. *Grouping items into a new subpanel*

After you have done so, examine the Document Outline window once again to verify the nested layout system. As you build full-featured WPF windows, you will most likely always need to make use of a nested layout system, rather than simply picking a single panel for all of the UI display (in fact, the remaining WPF examples in the text will typically do so). On a final note, the nodes in the Document Outline window are all drag and droppable. For example, if you wanted to move a control currently in the Canvas into the parent panel, you could do so as suggested in Figure 25-13.

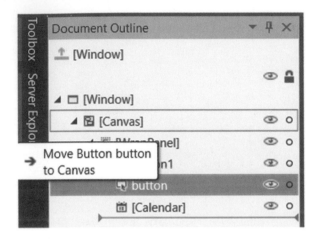

Figure 25-13. *Relocating items via the Document Outline window*

As you work through the remaining WPF chapters, I'll point out additional layout shortcuts where possible. However, it's definitely worth your time to experiment and test various features yourself. To keep you moving in the right direction, the next example in the chapter will illustrate how to build a nested layout manager for a custom text processing application (with spell-checking!).

Building a Window's Frame Using Nested Panels

As mentioned, a typical WPF window will not use a single panel control but instead will nest panels within other panels to gain the desired layout system. Begin by creating a new WPF application named MyWordPad.

Your goal is to construct a layout where the main window has a topmost menu system, a toolbar under the menu system, and a status bar mounted on the bottom of the window. The status bar will contain a pane to hold text prompts that are displayed when the user selects a menu item (or toolbar button), while the menu system and toolbar will offer UI triggers to close the application and display spelling suggestions in an Expander widget. Figure 25-14 shows the initial layout you are shooting for; it also shows the spell-checking capabilities within WPF.

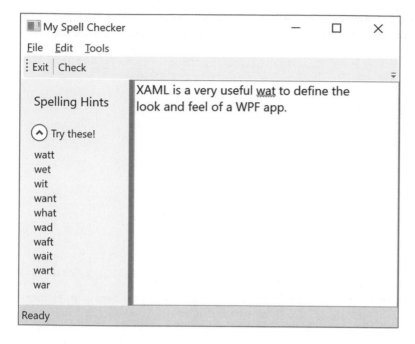

Figure 25-14. *Using nested panels to establish a window's UI*

To begin building this UI, update the initial XAML definition for your Window type so it uses a DockPanel child element, rather than the default Grid, as follows:

```
<Window x:Class="MyWordPad.MainWindow"
    xmlns="http://schemas.microsoft.com/winfx/2006/xaml/presentation"
    xmlns:x="http://schemas.microsoft.com/winfx/2006/xaml"
    xmlns:d="http://schemas.microsoft.com/expression/blend/2008"
    xmlns:mc="http://schemas.openxmlformats.org/markup-compatibility/2006"
    xmlns:local="clr-namespace:MyWordPad"
    mc:Ignorable="d"
    Title="My Spell Checker" Height="350" Width="525">
  <!- This panel establishes the content for the window ->
  <DockPanel>
  </DockPanel>
</Window>
```

Building the Menu System

Menu systems in WPF are represented by the Menu class, which maintains a collection of MenuItem objects. When building a menu system in XAML, you can have each MenuItem handle various events. The most notable of these events is Click, which occurs when the end user selects a subitem. In this example, you begin by building the two topmost menu items (File and Tools; you will build the Edit menu later in this example), which expose Exit and Spelling Hints subitems, respectively.

In addition to handling the Click event for each subitem, you also need to handle the MouseEnter and MouseExit events, which you will use to set the status bar text in a later step. Add the following markup within your DockPanel scope:

```
<!-- Dock menu system on the top -->
<Menu DockPanel.Dock ="Top"
      HorizontalAlignment="Left" Background="White" BorderBrush ="Black">
  <MenuItem Header="_File">
    <Separator/>
    <MenuItem Header ="_Exit" MouseEnter ="MouseEnterExitArea"
              MouseLeave ="MouseLeaveArea" Click ="FileExit_Click"/>
    </MenuItem>
    <MenuItem Header="_Tools">
      <MenuItem Header ="_Spelling Hints"
          MouseEnter ="MouseEnterToolsHintsArea"
          MouseLeave ="MouseLeaveArea" Click ="ToolsSpellingHints_Click"/>
  </MenuItem>
</Menu>
```

Notice that you dock the menu system to the top of the DockPanel. Also, you use the Separator element to insert a thin horizontal line in the menu system, directly before the Exit option. Also notice that the Header values for each MenuItem contain an embedded underscore token (e.g., _Exit). You use this token to establish which letter will be underlined when the end user presses the Alt key (for keyboard shortcuts). This is a change from the & character used in Windows Forms since XAML is based on XML, and the & character has meaning in XML.

So far you've implemented the complete the menu system definition; next, you need to implement the various event handlers. First, you have the File Exit handler, FileExit_Click(), which simply closes the window, which in turn terminates the application because this is your topmost window. The MouseEnter and MouseExit event handlers for each subitem will eventually update your status bar; however, for now, you will simply provide shells. Finally, the ToolsSpellingHints_Click() handler for the Tools Spelling Hints menu item will also remain a shell for the time being. Here are the current updates to your code-behind file (including adding using statements for Microsoft.Win32 and System.IO):

```
using Microsoft.Win32;
using System.IO;
public partial class MainWindow : Window
{
  public MainWindow()
  {
    InitializeComponent();
  }

  protected void FileExit_Click(object sender, RoutedEventArgs args)
  {
    // Close this window.
    this.Close();
  }

  protected void ToolsSpellingHints_Click(object sender, RoutedEventArgs args)
  {
  }
```

```
    protected void MouseEnterExitArea(object sender, RoutedEventArgs args)
    {
    }
    protected void MouseEnterToolsHintsArea(object sender, RoutedEventArgs args)
    {
    }
    protected void MouseLeaveArea(object sender, RoutedEventArgs args)
    {
    }
}
```

Building Menus Visually

While it is always good to know how to manually define items in XAML, it can be a tad on the tedious side. Visual Studio supports visual design support for menu systems, toolbars, status bars, and many other UI controls. If you right-click the Menu control, you will notice an Add MenuItem option. As the name suggests, this adds a new menu item to the Menu control. After you have added a set of topmost items, you can then add submenu items and separators, expand or collapse the menu itself, and perform other menu-centric operations via a second right-click.

As you see the reminder of the current MyWordPad example, I'll typically show you the final generated XAML; however, do take the time to experiment with the visual designers to simplify the task at hand.

Building the Toolbar

Toolbars (represented by the ToolBar class in WPF) typically provide an alternative manner for activating a menu option. Add the following markup directly after the closing scope of your Menu definition:

```
<!-- Put Toolbar under the Menu -->
<ToolBar DockPanel.Dock ="Top" >
  <Button Content ="Exit" MouseEnter ="MouseEnterExitArea"
          MouseLeave ="MouseLeaveArea" Click ="FileExit_Click"/>
  <Separator/>
  <Button Content ="Check" MouseEnter ="MouseEnterToolsHintsArea"
          MouseLeave ="MouseLeaveArea" Click ="ToolsSpellingHints_Click"
          Cursor="Help" />
</ToolBar>
```

Your ToolBar control consists of two Button controls, which just so happen to handle the same events and are handled by the same methods in your code file. Using this technique, you can double up your handlers to serve both menu items and toolbar buttons. Although this toolbar uses the typical push buttons, you should appreciate that the ToolBar type "is-a" ContentControl; therefore, you are free to embed any types into its surface (e.g., drop-down lists, images, and graphics). The only other point of interest here is that the Check button supports a custom mouse cursor through the Cursor property.

■ **Note**   You can optionally wrap the ToolBar element within a ToolBarTray element, which controls layout, docking, and drag-and-drop operations for a set of ToolBar objects. Consult the .NET Framework 4.7 SDK documentation for details.

Building the Status Bar

A StatusBar control will be docked to the lower portion of the DockPanel and contain a single TextBlock control, which you have not used prior to this point in the chapter. You can use a TextBlock to hold text that supports numerous textual annotations, such as bold text, underlined text, line breaks, and so forth. Add the following markup directly after the previous ToolBar definition:

```
<!-- Put a StatusBar at the bottom -->
<StatusBar DockPanel.Dock ="Bottom" Background="Beige" >
  <StatusBarItem>
    <TextBlock Name="statBarText" Text="Ready"/>
  </StatusBarItem>
</StatusBar>
```

Finalizing the UI Design

The final aspect of your UI design is to define a splittable Grid that defines two columns. On the left, place an Expander control that will display a list of spelling suggestions, wrapped within a StackPanel. On the right, place a TextBox control that supports multiple lines and scrollbars, and includes enabled spell-checking. You mount the entire Grid to the left of the parent DockPanel. Add the following XAML markup directly under the StatusBar markup to complete the definition of your window's UI:

```
<Grid DockPanel.Dock ="Left" Background ="AliceBlue">
  <!-- Define the rows and columns -->
  <Grid.ColumnDefinitions>
    <ColumnDefinition />
    <ColumnDefinition />
  </Grid.ColumnDefinitions>

  <GridSplitter Grid.Column ="0" Width ="5" Background ="Gray" />
  <StackPanel Grid.Column="0" VerticalAlignment ="Stretch" >
    <Label Name="lblSpellingInstructions" FontSize="14" Margin="10,10,0,0">
      Spelling Hints
    </Label>

    <Expander Name="expanderSpelling" Header ="Try these!"
            Margin="10,10,10,10">
      <!-- This will be filled programmatically -->
      <Label Name ="lblSpellingHints" FontSize ="12"/>
    </Expander>
  </StackPanel>

  <!-- This will be the area to type within -->
  <TextBox  Grid.Column ="1"
            SpellCheck.IsEnabled ="True"
            AcceptsReturn ="True"
            Name ="txtData" FontSize ="14"
            BorderBrush ="Blue"
            VerticalScrollBarVisibility="Auto"
            HorizontalScrollBarVisibility="Auto">
  </TextBox>
</Grid>
```

1024

Implementing the MouseEnter/MouseLeave Event Handlers

At this point, the UI of your window is complete. The only remaining tasks are to provide an implementation for the remaining event handlers. Begin by updating your C# code file so that each of the MouseEnter, MouseLeave, and MouseExit handlers set the text pane of the status bar with a fitting message to help the end user, like so:

```
public partial class MainWindow : System.Windows.Window
{
...
  protected void MouseEnterExitArea(object sender, RoutedEventArgs args)
  {
    statBarText.Text = "Exit the Application";
  }
  protected void MouseEnterToolsHintsArea(object sender, RoutedEventArgs args)
  {
    statBarText.Text = "Show Spelling Suggestions";
  }
  protected void MouseLeaveArea(object sender, RoutedEventArgs args)
  {
    statBarText.Text = "Ready";
  }
}
```

At this point, you can run your application. You should see your status bar change its text based on which menu item/toolbar button you hover your mouse over.

Implementing the Spell-Checking Logic

The WPF API ships with built-in spell-checker support, which is independent of Microsoft Office products. This means you don't need to use the COM interop layer to use the spell-checker of Microsoft Word; instead, you can easily add the same type of support with only a few lines of code.

You might recall that when you defined the TextBox control, you set the SpellCheck.IsEnabled property to true. When you do this, misspelled words are underlined with a red squiggle, just as they are in Microsoft Office. Even better, the underlying programming model gives you access to the spell-checker engine, which allows you to get a list of suggestions for misspelled words. Add the following code to your ToolsSpellingHints_Click() method:

```
protected void ToolsSpellingHints_Click(object sender, RoutedEventArgs args)
{
  string spellingHints = string.Empty;

  // Try to get a spelling error at the current caret location.
  SpellingError error = txtData.GetSpellingError(txtData.CaretIndex);
  if (error != null)
  {
    // Build a string of spelling suggestions.
    foreach (string s in error.Suggestions)
    {
      spellingHints += $"{s}\n";
    }
```

```
    // Show suggestions and expand the expander.
    lblSpellingHints.Content = spellingHints;
    expanderSpelling.IsExpanded = true;
  }
}
```

The preceding code is quite simple. You simply figure out the current location of the caret in the text box by using the CaretIndex property to extract a SpellingError object. If there is an error at said location (meaning the value is not null), you loop over the list of suggestions using the aptly named Suggestions property. After you have all the suggestions for the misspelled word, you connect the data to the Label in the Expander.

So there you have it! With only a few lines of procedural code (and a healthy dose of XAML), you have the beginnings of a functioning word processor. An understanding of *control commands* can help you add a bit more pizzazz.

Understanding WPF Commands

WPF provides support for what might be considered *control-agnostic events* via the *command architecture*. A typical .NET event is defined within a specific base class and can be used only by that class or a derivative thereof. Therefore, normal .NET events are tightly coupled to the class in which they are defined.

In contrast, WPF commands are event-like entities that are independent from a specific control and, in many cases, can be successfully applied to numerous (and seemingly unrelated) control types. By way of a few examples, WPF supports copy, paste, and cut commands, which you can apply to a wide variety of UI elements (e.g., menu items, toolbar buttons, and custom buttons), as well as keyboard shortcuts (e.g., Ctrl+C and Ctrl+V).

While other UI toolkits (such as Windows Forms) provided standard events for such purposes, using them typically left you with redundant and hard-to-maintain code. Under the WPF model, you can use commands as an alternative. The end result typically yields a smaller and more flexible codebase.

The Intrinsic Command Objects

WPF ships with numerous built-in control commands, all of which you can configure with associated keyboard shortcuts (or other input gestures). Programmatically speaking, a WPF command is any object that supports a property (often called Command) that returns an object implementing the ICommand interface, as shown here:

```
public interface ICommand
{
    // Occurs when changes occur that affect whether
    // or not the command should execute.
    event EventHandler CanExecuteChanged;

    // Defines the method that determines whether the command
    // can execute in its current state.
    bool CanExecute(object parameter);

    // Defines the method to be called when the command is invoked.
    void Execute(object parameter);
}
```

WPF provides various command classes, which expose close to 100 command objects, out of the box. These classes define numerous properties that expose specific command objects, each of which implements ICommand. Table 25-3 documents some of the standard command objects available (be sure to consult the .NET Framework 4.7 SDK documentation for complete details).

Table 25-3. *The Intrinsic WPF Control Command Objects*

WPF Class	Command Objects	Meaning in Life
ApplicationCommands	Close, Copy, Cut, Delete, Find, Open, Paste, Save, SaveAs, Redo, Undo	Various application-level commands
ComponentCommands	MoveDown, MoveFocusBack, MoveLeft, MoveRight, ScrollToEnd, ScrollToHome	Various commands common to UI components
MediaCommands	BoostBase, ChannelUp, ChannelDown, FastForward, NextTrack, Play, Rewind, Select, Stop	Various media-centric commands
NavigationCommands	BrowseBack, BrowseForward, Favorites, LastPage, NextPage, Zoom	Various commands relating to the WPF navigation model
EditingCommands	AlignCenter, CorrectSpellingError, DecreaseFontSize, EnterLineBreak, EnterParagraphBreak, MoveDownByLine, MoveRightByWord	Various commands relating to the WPF Documents API

Connecting Commands to the Command Property

If you want to connect any of the WPF command properties to a UI element that supports the Command property (such as a Button or MenuItem), you have very little work to do. You can see how to do this by updating the current menu system so it supports a new topmost menu item named Edit and three subitems to account for copying, pasting, and cutting of textual data, like so:

```xml
<Menu DockPanel.Dock ="Top" HorizontalAlignment="Left" Background="White" BorderBrush
="Black">
  <MenuItem Header="_File" Click ="FileExit_Click" >
    <MenuItem Header ="_Exit" MouseEnter ="MouseEnterExitArea" MouseLeave ="MouseLeaveArea"
        Click ="FileExit_Click"/>
  </MenuItem>

  <!-- New menu item with commands! -->
  <MenuItem Header="_Edit">
    <MenuItem Command ="ApplicationCommands.Copy"/>
    <MenuItem Command ="ApplicationCommands.Cut"/>
    <MenuItem Command ="ApplicationCommands.Paste"/>
  </MenuItem>

  <MenuItem Header="_Tools">
    <MenuItem Header ="_Spelling Hints"
            MouseEnter ="MouseEnterToolsHintsArea"
            MouseLeave ="MouseLeaveArea"
            Click ="ToolsSpellingHints_Click"/>
  </MenuItem>
</Menu>
```

Notice that each of the subitems on the Edit menu has a value assigned to the Command property. Doing this means that the menu items automatically receive the correct name and shortcut key (e.g., Ctrl+C for a cut operation) in the menu item UI; it also means that the application is now *copy, cut, and paste*–aware with no procedural code!

If you run the application and select some of text, you can use your new menu items out of the box. As a bonus, your application is also equipped to respond to a standard right-click operation to present the user with the same options.

Connecting Commands to Arbitrary Actions

If you want to connect a command object to an arbitrary (application-specific) event, you will need to drop down to procedural code. Doing so is not complex, but it does involve a bit more logic than you see in XAML. For example, assume that you want to have the entire window respond to the F1 key so that when the end user presses this key, he will activate an associated help system. Also, assume your code file for the main window defines a new method named SetF1CommandBinding(), which you call within the constructor after the call to InitializeComponent().

```
public MainWindow()
{
  InitializeComponent();
  SetF1CommandBinding();
}
```

This new method will programmatically create a new CommandBinding object, which you can use whenever you need to bind a command object to a given event handler in your application. Here, you configure your CommandBinding object to operate with the ApplicationCommands.Help command, which is automatically F1-aware:

```
private void SetF1CommandBinding()
{
  CommandBinding helpBinding = new CommandBinding(ApplicationCommands.Help);
  helpBinding.CanExecute += CanHelpExecute;
  helpBinding.Executed += HelpExecuted;
  CommandBindings.Add(helpBinding);
}
```

Most CommandBinding objects will want to handle the CanExecute event (which allows you to specify whether the command occurs based on the operation of your program) and the Executed event (which is where you can author the content that should occur once the command occurs). Add the following event handlers to your Window-derived type (note the format of each method, as required by the associated delegates):

```
private void CanHelpExecute(object sender, CanExecuteRoutedEventArgs e)
{
  // Here, you can set CanExecute to false if you want to prevent the command from
  executing.
  e.CanExecute = true;
}

private void HelpExecuted(object sender, ExecutedRoutedEventArgs e)
{
  MessageBox.Show("Look, it is not that difficult. Just type something!", "Help!");
}
```

In the preceding snippet, you implemented CanHelpExecute() so it always allows F1 help to launch; you do this by simply returning true. However, if you have certain situations where the help system should not display, you can account for this and return false when necessary. Your "help system" displayed within HelpExecuted() is little more than a message box. At this point, you can run your application. When you press the F1 key on your keyboard, you will see your message box appear.

Working with the Open and Save Commands

To complete the current example, you will add functionality to save your text data to an external file and open up *.txt files for editing. If you want to take the long road, you can manually add programming logic that enables or disables new menu items based on whether your TextBox has data inside it. Once again, however, you can use commands to decrease your burden.

Begin by updating the MenuItem element that represents your topmost File menu by adding the following two new submenus that use the Save and Open ApplicationCommands objects:

```
<MenuItem Header="_File">
  <MenuItem Command ="ApplicationCommands.Open"/>
  <MenuItem Command ="ApplicationCommands.Save"/>
  <Separator/>
  <MenuItem Header ="_Exit"
            MouseEnter ="MouseEnterExitArea"
            MouseLeave ="MouseLeaveArea" Click ="FileExit_Click"/>
</MenuItem>
```

Again, remember that all command objects implement the ICommand interface, which defines two events (CanExecute and Executed). Now you need to enable the entire window so it can check whether it is currently okay to fire these commands; if so, you can define an event handler to execute the custom code.

You do this by populating the CommandBindings collection maintained by the window. Doing so in XAML requires that you use property element syntax to define a Window.CommandBindings scope in which you place two CommandBinding definitions. Update your Window like this:

```
<Window x:Class="MyWordPad.MainWindow"
  xmlns="http://schemas.microsoft.com/winfx/2006/xaml/presentation"
  xmlns:x="http://schemas.microsoft.com/winfx/2006/xaml"
  Title="MySpellChecker" Height="331" Width="508"
  WindowStartupLocation ="CenterScreen" >

  <!-- This will inform the Window which handlers to call,
       when testing for the Open and Save commands. -->
  <Window.CommandBindings>
    <CommandBinding Command="ApplicationCommands.Open"
                    Executed="OpenCmdExecuted"
                    CanExecute="OpenCmdCanExecute"/>
    <CommandBinding Command="ApplicationCommands.Save"
                    Executed="SaveCmdExecuted"
                    CanExecute="SaveCmdCanExecute"/>
  </Window.CommandBindings>

  <!-- This panel establishes the content for the window -->
  <DockPanel>
  ...
  </DockPanel>
</Window>
```

1029

Now right-click each of the Executed and CanExecute attributes in your XAML editor and pick the Navigate to Event Handler menu option. As you might recall from Chapter 24, this will automatically generate stub code for the event itself. At this point, you should have four empty handlers in the C# code file for the window.

The implementation of CanExecute event handlers will tell the window that it is okay to fire the corresponding Executed events at any time by setting the CanExecute property of the incoming CanExecuteRoutedEventArgs object.

```
private void OpenCmdCanExecute(object sender, CanExecuteRoutedEventArgs e)
{
  e.CanExecute = true;
}

private void SaveCmdCanExecute(object sender, CanExecuteRoutedEventArgs e)
{
  e.CanExecute = true;
}
```

The corresponding Executed handlers perform the actual work of displaying the open and save dialog boxes; they also send the data in your TextBox to a file. Begin by making sure that you import the System.IO and Microsoft.Win32 namespaces into your code file. The following completed code is straightforward:

```
private void OpenCmdExecuted(object sender, ExecutedRoutedEventArgs e)
{
  // Create an open file dialog box and only show XAML files.
  var openDlg = new OpenFileDialog { Filter = "Text Files |*.txt"};

  // Did they click on the OK button?
  if (true == openDlg.ShowDialog())
  {
    // Load all text of selected file.
    string dataFromFile = File.ReadAllText(openDlg.FileName);

    // Show string in TextBox.
    txtData.Text = dataFromFile;
  }
}

private void SaveCmdExecuted(object sender, ExecutedRoutedEventArgs e)
{
  var saveDlg = new SaveFileDialog { Filter = "Text Files |*.txt"};

  // Did they click on the OK button?
  if (true == saveDlg.ShowDialog())
  {
    // Save data in the TextBox to the named file.
    File.WriteAllText(saveDlg.FileName, txtData.Text);
  }
}
```

■ **Note** Chapter 30 will take a much deeper look into the WPF command system. In it, you will create custom commands base on ICommand as well as RelayCommands.

That wraps up this example and your initial look at working with WPF controls. Here, you learned how to work with basic commands, menu systems, status bars, toolbars, nested panels, and a few basic UI controls, such as TextBox and Expander. The next example will work with some more exotic controls, while examining several important WPF services at the same time.

■ **Source Code** You can find the MyWordPad project in the Chapter 25 subdirectory.

Understanding Routed Events

You might have noticed the RoutedEventArgs parameter instead of EventArgs in the previous code example. The routed events model is a refinement of the standard CLR event model designed to ensure that events can be processed in a manner that is fitting for XAML's description of a tree of objects. Assume you have a new WPF application project named WPFRoutedEvents. Now, update the XAML description of the initial window by adding the following Button control, which defines some complex content:

```
<Button Name="btnClickMe" Height="75" Width = "250" Click ="btnClickMe_Clicked">
  <StackPanel Orientation ="Horizontal">
    <Label Height="50" FontSize ="20">Fancy Button!</Label>
    <Canvas Height ="50" Width ="100" >
      <Ellipse Name = "outerEllipse" Fill ="Green" Height ="25"
              Width ="50" Cursor="Hand" Canvas.Left="25" Canvas.Top="12"/>
      <Ellipse Name = "innerEllipse" Fill ="Yellow" Height = "15" Width ="36"
              Canvas.Top="17" Canvas.Left="32"/>
    </Canvas>
  </StackPanel>
</Button>
```

Notice in the Button's opening definition you have handled the Click event by specifying the name of a method to be called when the event is raised. The Click event works with the RoutedEventHandler delegate, which expects an event handler that takes an object as the first parameter and a System.Windows. RoutedEventArgs as the second. Implement this handler as so:

```
public void btnClickMe_Clicked(object sender, RoutedEventArgs e)
{
  // Do something when button is clicked.
  MessageBox.Show("Clicked the button");
}
```

If you run your application, you will see this message box display, regardless of which part of the button's content you click (the green Ellipse, the yellow Ellipse, the Label, or the Button's surface). This is a good thing. Imagine how tedious WPF event handling would be if you were forced to handle a Click event for every one of these subelements. Not only would the creation of separate event handlers for each aspect of the Button be labor intensive, you would end up with some mighty nasty code to maintain down the road.

Thankfully, WPF *routed events* take care of ensuring that your single Click event handler will be called regardless of which part of the button is clicked automatically. Simply put, the routed events model automatically propagates an event up (or down) a tree of objects, looking for an appropriate handler.

Specifically speaking, a routed event can make use of three *routing strategies*. If an event is moving from the point of origin up to other defining scopes within the object tree, the event is said to be a *bubbling event*. Conversely, if an event is moving from the outermost element (e.g., a Window) down to the point of origin, the event is said to be a *tunneling event*. Finally, if an event is raised and handled only by the originating element (which is what could be described as a normal CLR event), it is said to be a *direct event*.

The Role of Routed Bubbling Events

In the current example, if the user clicks the inner yellow oval, the Click event bubbles out to the next level of scope (the Canvas), then to the StackPanel, and finally to the Button where the Click event handler is handled. In a similar way, if the user clicks the Label, the event is bubbled to the StackPanel and then finally to the Button element.

Given this bubbling routed event pattern, you have no need to worry about registering specific Click event handlers for all members of a composite control. However, if you want to perform custom clicking logic for multiple elements within the same object tree, you can do so.

By way of illustration, assume you need to handle the clicking of the outerEllipse control in a unique manner. First, handle the MouseDown event for this subelement (graphically rendered types such as the Ellipse do not support a Click event; however, they can monitor mouse button activity via MouseDown, MouseUp, etc.).

```
<Button Name="btnClickMe" Height="75" Width = "250"
        Click ="btnClickMe_Clicked">
  <StackPanel Orientation ="Horizontal">
    <Label Height="50" FontSize ="20">Fancy Button!</Label>
    <Canvas Height ="50" Width ="100" >
      <Ellipse Name = "outerEllipse" Fill ="Green"
               Height ="25" MouseDown ="outerEllipse_MouseDown"
               Width ="50" Cursor="Hand" Canvas.Left="25" Canvas.Top="12"/>
      <Ellipse Name = "innerEllipse" Fill ="Yellow" Height = "15" Width ="36"
               Canvas.Top="17" Canvas.Left="32"/>
    </Canvas>
  </StackPanel>
</Button>
```

Then implement an appropriate event handler, which for illustrative purposes will simply change the Title property of the main window, like so:

```
public void outerEllipse_MouseDown(object sender, MouseButtonEventArgs e)
{
  // Change title of window.
  this.Title = "You clicked the outer ellipse!";
}
```

With this, you can now take different courses of action depending on where the end user has clicked (which boils down to the outer ellipse and everywhere else within the button's scope).

■ **Note** Routed bubbling events always move from the point of origin to the *next defining scope*. Thus, in this example, if you click the innerEllipse object, the event will be bubbled to the Canvas, *not* to the outerEllipse because they are both Ellipse types within the scope of Canvas.

Continuing or Halting Bubbling

Currently, if the user clicks the outerEllipse object, it will trigger the registered MouseDown event handler for this Ellipse object, at which point the event bubbles to the button's Click event. If you want to inform WPF to stop bubbling up the tree of objects, you can set the Handled property of the EventArgs parameter to true, as follows:

```
public void outerEllipse_MouseDown(object sender, MouseButtonEventArgs e)
{
  // Change title of window.
  this.Title = "You clicked the outer ellipse!";
  // Stop bubbling!
  e.Handled = true;
}
```

In this case, you would find that the title of the window is changed, but you will not see the MessageBox displayed by the Click event handler of the Button. In a nutshell, routed bubbling events make it possible to allow a complex group of content to act either as a single logical element (e.g., a Button) or as discrete items (e.g., an Ellipse within the Button).

The Role of Routed Tunneling Events

Strictly speaking, routed events can be *bubbling* (as just described) or *tunneling* in nature. Tunneling events (which all begin with the Preview suffix—e.g., PreviewMouseDown) drill down from the topmost element into the inner scopes of the object tree. By and large, each bubbling event in the WPF base class libraries is paired with a related tunneling event that fires *before* the bubbling counterpart. For example, before the bubbling MouseDown event fires, the tunneling PreviewMouseDown event fires first.

Handling a tunneling event looks just like the processing of handling any other events; simply assign the event handler name in XAML (or, if needed, use the corresponding C# event-handling syntax in your code file) and implement the handler in the code file. Just to illustrate the interplay of tunneling and bubbling events, begin by handling the PreviewMouseDown event for the outerEllipse object, like so:

```
<Ellipse Name = "outerEllipse" Fill ="Green" Height ="25"
        MouseDown ="outerEllipse_MouseDown"
        PreviewMouseDown ="outerEllipse_PreviewMouseDown"
        Width ="50" Cursor="Hand" Canvas.Left="25" Canvas.Top="12"/>
```

Next, retrofit the current C# class definition by updating each event handler (for all objects) to append data about the current event into a string member variable named mouseActivity, using the incoming event args object. This will allow you to observe the flow of events firing in the background.

```
public partial class MainWindow : Window
{
  string _mouseActivity = string.Empty;
  public MainWindow()
```

```
{
  InitializeComponent();
}
public void btnClickMe_Clicked(object sender, RoutedEventArgs e)
{
  AddEventInfo(sender, e);
  MessageBox.Show(_mouseActivity, "Your Event Info");
  // Clear string for next round.
  _mouseActivity = "";
}
private void AddEventInfo(object sender, RoutedEventArgs e)
{
  _mouseActivity += string.Format(
    "{0} sent a {1} event named {2}.\n", sender,
    e.RoutedEvent.RoutingStrategy,
    e.RoutedEvent.Name);
}
private void outerEllipse_MouseDown(object sender, MouseButtonEventArgs e)
{
  AddEventInfo(sender, e);
}
private void outerEllipse_PreviewMouseDown(object sender, MouseButtonEventArgs e)
{
  AddEventInfo(sender, e);
}
}
```

Notice that you are not halting the bubbling of an event for any event handler. If you run this application, you will see a unique message box display based on where you click the button. Figure 25-15 shows the result of clicking the outer Ellipse object.

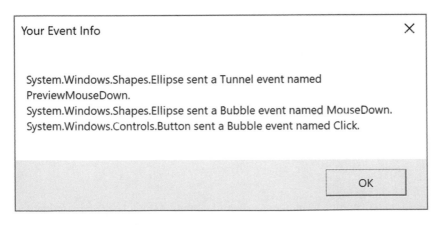

Figure 25-15. *Tunneling first, bubbling second*

So, why do WPF events typically tend to come in pairs (one tunneling and one bubbling)? The answer is that by previewing events, you have the power to perform any special logic (data validation, disable bubbling action, etc.) before the bubbling counterpart fires. By way of an example, assume you have a TextBox that should contain only numerical data. You could handle the PreviewKeyDown event, and if you see the user has entered non-numerical data, you could cancel the bubbling event by setting the Handled property to true.

As you would guess, when you are building a custom control that contains custom events, you could author the event in such a way that it can bubble (or tunnel) through a tree of XAML. For the purpose of this chapter, I will not be examining how to build custom routed events (however, the process is not that different from building a custom dependency property). If you are interested, check out the topic "Routed Events Overview" within the .NET Framework 4.7 SDK documentation. In it you will find a number of tutorials that will help you on your way.

■ **Source Code**   You can find the WPFRoutedEvents project in the Chapter 25 subdirectory.

A Deeper Look at WPF APIs and Controls

The remainder of this chapter will give you a chance to build a new WPF application using Visual Studio. The goal is to create a UI that consists of a TabControl widget containing a set of tabs. Each tab will illustrate some new WPF controls and interesting APIs you might want to make use of in your software projects. Along the way, you will also learn additional features of the Visual Studio WPF designers.

Working with the TabControl

To get started, create a new WPF application named WpfControlsAndAPIs. As mentioned, your initial window will contain a TabControl with three different tabs, each of which shows off a set of related controls and/or WPF APIs. Update the window's Width to 800 and Height to 350.

Locate the TabControl control in the Visual Studio toolbox, drop one onto your designer, and update the markup to the following:

```
<TabControl Name="MyTabControl" HorizontalAlignment="Stretch" VerticalAlignment="Stretch">
    <TabItem Header="TabItem">
        <Grid Background="#FFE5E5E5"/>
    </TabItem>
    <TabItem Header="TabItem">
        <Grid Background="#FFE5E5E5"/>
    </TabItem>
</TabControl>
```

You will notice that you are given two tab items automatically. To add additional tabs, you simply need to right-click the TabControl node in the Document Outline window and select the Add TabItem menu option (you can also right-click the TabControl on the designer to activate the same menu option) or just start typing in the XAML editor. Add one additional tab using either approach.

Now, update each TabItem control through the XAML editor and change the Header property for each tab, naming them Ink API, Data Binding, and DataGrid. At this point, your window designer should look like what you see in Figure 25-16.

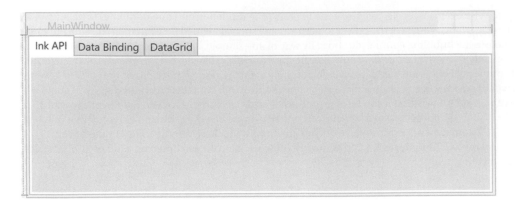

Figure 25-16. *The initial layout of the tab system*

Be aware that when you select a tab for editing, that tab becomes the active tab, and you can design that tab by dragging controls from the Toolbox window. Now that you have the core TabControl defined, you can work out the details tab by tab and learn more features of the WPF API along the way.

Building the Ink API Tab

The first tab will be used to show the overall role of WPF's digital Ink API, which allows you to incorporate painting functionality into a program easily. Of course, the application does not literally need to be a painting application; you can use this API for a wide variety of purposes, including capturing handwriting input.

■ **Note** For most of the rest of this chapter (and the next WPF chapters as well), I will be editing the XAML directly instead of using the various windows. While the dragging and dropping of controls works, more often than not the layout isn't what you want (Visual Studio adds in margins and padding based on where you drop the control), and you spend a significant amount of time cleaning up the XAML anyway.

Begin by changing the Grid tag under the Ink API TabItem to a StackPanel and add a closing tag (make sure to remove "/" from the opening tag). Your markup should look like this:

```
<TabItem Header="Ink API">
  <StackPanel Background="#FFE5E5E5">
  </StackPanel>
</TabItem>
```

Designing the Toolbar

Add a new ToolBar control (using the XAML editor) named InkToolbar with a height of 60.

```
<ToolBar Name="InkToolBar" Height="60">
</ToolBar>
```

Add three RadioButton controls inside a WrapPanel, inside a Border control, as follows:

```
<Border Margin="0,2,0,2.4" Width="280" VerticalAlignment="Center">
  <WrapPanel>
    <RadioButton x:Name="inkRadio" Margin="5,10" Content="Ink Mode!" IsChecked="True" />
    <RadioButton x:Name="eraseRadio" Margin="5,10" Content="Erase Mode!" />
    <RadioButton x:Name="selectRadio" Margin="5,10" Content="Select Mode!" />
  </WrapPanel>
</Border>
```

When a RadioButton control is not placed inside of a parent panel control, it will take on a UI identical to a Button control! That's why I wrapped the RadioButton controls in the WrapPanel.

Next, add a Separator and then a ComboBox with a Width of 175 and a Margin of 10,0,0,0. Add three ComboBoxItem tags with content of Red, Green, and Blue, and follow the entire ComboBox with another Separator control, as follows:

```
<Separator/>
<ComboBox x:Name="comboColors" Width="175" Margin-"10,0,0,0">
  <ComboBoxItem Content="Red"/>
  <ComboBoxItem Content="Green"/>
  <ComboBoxItem Content="Blue"/>
</ComboBox>
<Separator/>
```

The RadioButton Control

In this example, you want these three RadioButton controls to be mutually exclusive. In other GUI frameworks, ensuring that a group of related controls (such as radio buttons) were mutually exclusive required that you place them in the same group box. You don't need to do this under WPF. Instead, you can simply assign them all to the same *group name*. This is helpful because the related items do not need to be physically collected in the same area but can be anywhere in the window.

The RadioButton class includes an IsChecked property, which toggles between true and false when the end user clicks the UI element. Furthermore, RadioButton provides two events (Checked and Unchecked) that you can use to intercept this state change.

Add the Save, Load, and Delete Buttons

The final controls in the ToolBar control will be a Grid holding three Button controls. Add the following markup after the last Separator control:

```
<Grid>
  <Grid.ColumnDefinitions>
    <ColumnDefinition Width="Auto"/>
    <ColumnDefinition Width="Auto"/>
    <ColumnDefinition Width="Auto"/>
  </Grid.ColumnDefinitions>
  <Button Grid.Column="0" x:Name="btnSave" Margin="10,10" Width="70" Content="Save Data"/>
  <Button Grid.Column="1" x:Name="btnLoad" Margin="10,10" Width="70" Content="Load Data"/>
  <Button Grid.Column="2" x:Name="btnClear" Margin="10,10" Width="70" Content="Clear"/>
</Grid>
```

Add the InkCanvas Control

The final control for the TabControl is the InkCanvas control. Add the following markup after the closing ToolBar tag and before the closing StackPanel tag, as follows:

```
<InkCanvas x:Name="MyInkCanvas" Background="#FFB6F4F1" />
```

Preview the Window

At this point, you're ready to test the program, which you can do by pressing the F5 key. You should now see three mutually exclusive radio buttons, a combo box with three selections, and three buttons (see Figure 25-17).

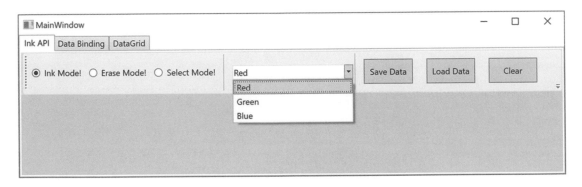

Figure 25-17. *The completed layout for the Ink API tab*

Handling Events for the Ink API Tab

The next step for the Ink API tab is to handle the Click event for each RadioButton control. As you have done in other WPF projects in this book, simply click the lightning bolt icon of the Visual Studio Properties editor to enter the names of event handlers. Using this approach, route the Click event for each button to the same handler, named RadioButtonClicked. After you handle all three Click events, handle the SelectionChanged event of the ComboBox using a handler named ColorChanged. When you finish, you should have the following C# code:

```
public partial class MainWindow : Window
{
  public MainWindow()
  {
    this.InitializeComponent();

    // Insert code required on object creation below this point.
  }
  private void RadioButtonClicked(object sender,RoutedEventArgs e)
  {
    // TODO: Add event handler implementation here.
  }
```

```
private void ColorChanged(object sender,SelectionChangedEventArgs e)
{
  // TODO: Add event handler implementation here.
}
}
```

You will implement these handlers in a later step, so leave them empty for the time being.

Add Controls to the Toolbox

You added an InkCanvas control by editing the XAML directly. If you wanted to use the UI to add it, the Visual Studio toolbox does *not* show you every possible WPF component by default. But you can update the items that are displayed in the toolbox.

To do so, right-click anywhere in the Toolbox area and select the Choose Items menu option. After a moment or two, you will see a list of possible components to add to the Toolbox. For your purposes, you are interested in adding the InkCanvas control (see Figure 25-18).

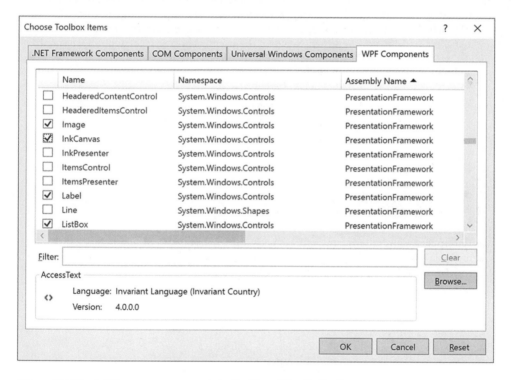

Figure 25-18. Adding new components to the Visual Studio Toolbox

The InkCanvas Control

Just adding the InkCanvas enables drawing in your window. You can use your mouse or, if you have a touch-enabled device, your finger or a digitizer pen. Run the application and draw into the box (see Figure 25-19).

Figure 25-19. *The InkCanvas in action*

The InkCanvas does more than draw mouse (or stylus) strokes; it also supports a number of unique editing modes, controlled by the EditingMode property. You can assign this property any value from the related InkCanvasEditingMode enumeration. For this example, you are interested in Ink mode, which is the default option you just witnessed; Select mode, which allows the user to select a region with the mouse to move or resize; and EraseByStoke, which will delete the previous mouse stroke.

■ **Note**　A *stroke* is the rendering that takes place during a single mouse down/mouse up operation. The InkCanvas stores all strokes in a StrokeCollection object, which you can access using the Strokes property.

Update your RadioButtonClicked() hander with the following logic, which places the InkCanvas in the correct mode, based on the selected RadioButton:

```
private void RadioButtonClicked(object sender,RoutedEventArgs e)
{
  // Based on which button sent the event, place the InkCanvas in a unique
  // mode of operation.
  switch((sender as RadioButton)?.Content.ToString())
  {
    // These strings must be the same as the Content values for each
    // RadioButton.
    case "Ink Mode!":
      this.MyInkCanvas.EditingMode = InkCanvasEditingMode.Ink;
    break;

    case "Erase Mode!":
      this.MyInkCanvas.EditingMode = InkCanvasEditingMode.EraseByStroke;
    break;

    case "Select Mode!":
      this.MyInkCanvas.EditingMode = InkCanvasEditingMode.Select;
    break;
  }
}
```

Also, set the mode to Ink by default in the window's constructor. And while you are at it, set a default selection for the ComboBox (more details on this control in the next section), as follows:

```
public MainWindow()
{
  this.InitializeComponent();

  // Be in Ink mode by default.
  this.MyInkCanvas.EditingMode = InkCanvasEditingMode.Ink;
  this.inkRadio.IsChecked = true;
  this.comboColors.SelectedIndex = 0;
}
```

Now run your program again by pressing F5. Enter Ink mode and draw some data. Next, enter Erase mode and remove the previous mouse stroke you entered (you'll notice the mouse icon automatically looks like an eraser). Finally, enter Select mode and select some strokes by using the mouse as a lasso.

After you circle the item, you can move it around the canvas and resize its dimensions. Figure 25-20 shows your edit modes at work.

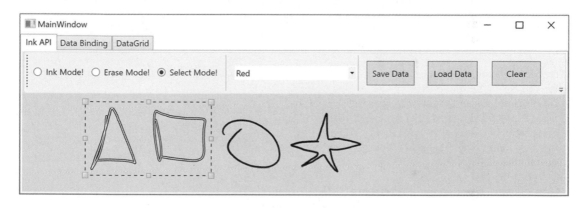

Figure 25-20. *The InkCanvas in action, with edit modes!*

The ComboBox Control

After you populate a ComboBox control (or a ListBox), you have three ways to determine the selected item. First, if you want to find the numerical index of the item selected, you can use the SelectedIndex property (which is zero-based; a value of -1 represents no selection). Second, if you want to obtain the object within the list that has been selected, the SelectedItem property fits the bill. Third, the SelectedValue allows you to obtain the value of the selected object (typically obtained using a call to ToString()).

You need to add the last bit of code for this tab to change the color of the strokes entered on the InkCanvas. The DefaultDrawingAttributes property of InkCanvas returns a DrawingAttributes object that allows you to configure numerous aspect of the pen nib, including its size and color (among other settings). Update your C# code with this implementation of the ColorChanged() method:

```
private void ColorChanged(object sender, SelectionChangedEventArgs e)
{
  // Get the selected value in the combo box.
  string colorToUse =
    (this.comboColors.SelectedItem as ComboBoxItem)?.Content.ToString();
```

```
// Change the color used to render the strokes.
this.MyInkCanvas.DefaultDrawingAttributes.Color =
    (Color)ColorConverter.ConvertFromString(colorToUse);
}
```

Now recall that the ComboBox has a collection of ComboBoxItems. If you view the generated XAML, you'll see the following definition:

```
<ComboBox x:Name="comboColors" Width="100" SelectionChanged="ColorChanged">
  <ComboBoxItem Content="Red"/>
  <ComboBoxItem Content="Green"/>
  <ComboBoxItem Content="Blue"/>
</ComboBox>
```

When you call SelectedItem, you grab the selected ComboBoxItem, which is stored as a general Object. After you cast the Object as a ComboBoxItem, you pluck out the value of the Content, which will be the string Red, Green, or Blue. This string is then converted to a Color object using the handy ColorConverter utility class. Now run your program again. You should be able to change between colors as you render your image.

Note that the ComboBox and ListBox controls can contain complex content as well, rather than a list of text data. You can get a sense of some of the things that are possible by opening the XAML editor for your window and changing the definition of your ComboBox so it contains a set of StackPanel elements, each of which contains an Ellipse and a Label (notice that the Width of the ComboBox is 175).

```
<ComboBox x:Name="comboColors" Width="175" Margin="10,0,0,0" SelectionChang
ed">
  <StackPanel Orientation ="Horizontal" Tag="Red">
    <Ellipse Fill ="Red" Height ="50" Width ="50"/>
    <Label FontSize ="20" HorizontalAlignment="Center"
           VerticalAlignment="Center" Content="Red"/>
  </StackPanel>

  <StackPanel Orientation ="Horizontal" Tag="Green">
    <Ellipse Fill ="Green" Height ="50" Width ="50"/>
    <Label FontSize ="20" HorizontalAlignment="Center"
           VerticalAlignment="Center" Content="Green"/>
  </StackPanel>

  <StackPanel Orientation ="Horizontal" Tag="Blue">
    <Ellipse Fill ="Blue" Height ="50" Width ="50"/>
    <Label FontSize ="20" HorizontalAlignment="Center"
           VerticalAlignment="Center" Content="Blue"/>
  </StackPanel>
</ComboBox>
```

Notice that each StackPanel assigns a value to its Tag property, which is a simple, fast, and convenient way to discover which stack of items has been selected by the user (there are better ways to do this, but this will do for now). With this adjustment, you need to change the implementation of your ColorChanged() method, like this:

```
private void ColorChanged(object sender, SelectionChangedEventArgs e)
{
  // Get the Tag of the selected StackPanel.
  string colorToUse = (this.comboColors.SelectedItem
     as StackPanel).Tag.ToString();
  ...
}
```

Now run your program again and take note of your unique ComboBox (see Figure 25-21).

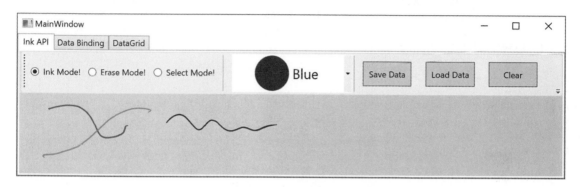

Figure 25-21. *A custom ComboBox, thanks to the WPF content model*

Saving, Loading, and Clearing InkCanvas Data

The last part of this tab will enable you to save and load your canvas data, as well as clear it of all content by adding event handlers for the buttons in the toolbar. Update the XAML for the buttons by adding markup for the click events, as follows:

```
<Button Grid.Column="0" x:Name="btnSave" Margin="10,10" Width="70" Content="Save Data"
Click="SaveData"/>
<Button Grid.Column="1" x:Name="btnLoad" Margin="10,10" Width="70" Content="Load Data"
Click="LoadData"/>
<Button Grid.Column="2" x:Name="btnClear" Margin="10,10" Width="70" Content="Clear"
Click="Clear"/>
```

Next, import the System.IO and System.Windows.Ink namespaces to your code file. Implement the handlers, like this:

```
private void SaveData(object sender, RoutedEventArgs e)
{
  // Save all data on the InkCanvas to a local file.
  using (FileStream fs = new FileStream("StrokeData.bin", FileMode.Create))
  {
    this.MyInkCanvas.Strokes.Save(fs);
    fs.Close();
  }
}
```

```
private void LoadData(object sender, RoutedEventArgs e)
{
  // Fill StrokeCollection from file.
  using(FileStream fs = new FileStream("StrokeData.bin", FileMode.Open, FileAccess.Read))
  {
    StrokeCollection strokes = new StrokeCollection(fs);
    this.MyInkCanvas.Strokes = strokes;
  }
}

  private void Clear(object sender, RoutedEventArgs e)
  {
    // Clear all strokes.
    this.MyInkCanvas.Strokes.Clear();
}
```

You should now be able to save your data to a file, load it from the file, and clear the InkCanvas of all data. That wraps up the first tab of the TabControl, as well as your examination of the WPF digital Ink API. To be sure, there is more to say about this technology; however, you should be in a good position to dig into the topic further if that interests you. Next, you will learn how to use WPF data binding.

Introducing the WPF Data-Binding Model

Controls are often the target of various data-binding operations. Simply put, *data binding* is the act of connecting control properties to data values that might change over the course of your application's lifetime. Doing so lets a user interface element display the state of a variable in your code. For example, you might use data binding to accomplish the following:

- Check a CheckBox control based on a Boolean property of a given object

- Display data in DataGrid objects from a relational database table

- Connect a Label to an integer that represents the number of files in a folder

When you use the intrinsic WPF data-binding engine, you must be aware of the distinction between the *source* and the *destination* of the binding operation. As you might expect, the source of a data-binding operation is the data itself (e.g., a Boolean property or relational data), while the destination (target) is the UI control property that uses the data content (e.g., a property on a CheckBox or TextBox control).

In addition to binding to traditional data, WPF enables element binding, as stated in the previous examples. This means you can bind (for example) the visibility of a property based on the checked property of a check box. You could certainly do this in WinForms, but it had to be done through code. The WPF framework provides a rich data-binding ecosystem that can be almost entirely handled in markup. This also enables you to ensure that the source and destination stay in sync if either of their values changes.

Building the Data Binding Tab

Using the Document Outline editor, change the Grid of your second tab to a StackPanel. Now, use the Toolbox and Properties editor of Visual Studio to build the following initial layout:

```
<TabItem x:Name="tabDataBinding" Header="Data Binding">
  <StackPanel Width="250">
    <Label Content="Move the scroll bar to see the current value"/>
```

```
<!-- The scrollbar's value is the source of this data bind. -->
<ScrollBar x:Name="mySB" Orientation="Horizontal" Height="30"
        Minimum = "1" Maximum = "100" LargeChange="1" SmallChange="1"/>

<!-- The label's content will be bound to the scroll bar! -->
<Label x:Name="labelSBThumb" Height="30" BorderBrush="Blue"
        BorderThickness="2" Content = "0"/>
  </StackPanel>
</TabItem>
```

Notice that the ScrollBar object (named mySB here) has been configured with a range between 1 and 100. The goal is to ensure that, as you reposition the thumb of the scrollbar (or click the left or right arrow), the Label will automatically update with the current value. Currently, the Content property of the Label control is set to the value "0"; however, you will change this via a data-binding operation.

Establishing Data Bindings

The glue that makes it possible to define a binding in XAML is the {Binding} markup extension. While you can define bindings through Visual Studio, it's just as easy to do it directly in the markup. Edit the Content property for the Label named labelSBThumb to the following:

```
<Label x:Name="labelSBThumb" Height="30" BorderBrush="Blue" BorderThickness="2"
        Content = "{Binding Path=Value, ElementName=mySB}"/>
```

Note the value assigned to the Label's Content property. The {Binding} statement denotes a data binding operation. The ElementName value represents the source of the data-binding operation (the ScrollBar object), while the Path indicates the property being bound to, in this case the Value of the scrollbar.

If you run your program again, you will find that the content of the label updates based on the scrollbar value as you move the thumb!

The DataContext Property

You can define a data-binding operation in XAML using an alternative format, where it is possible to break out the values specified by the {Binding} markup extension by explicitly setting the DataContext property to the source of the binding operation, as follows:

```
<!-- Breaking object/value apart via DataContext -->
<Label x:Name="labelSBThumb" Height="30" BorderBrush="Blue" BorderThickness="2"
        DataContext = "{Binding ElementName=mySB}" Content = "{Binding Path=Value}" />
```

In the current example, the output would be identical if you were to modify the markup in this way. Given this, you might wonder when you would want to set the DataContext property explicitly. Doing so can be helpful because subelements can inherit its value in a tree of markup.

In this way, you can easily set the same data source to a family of controls, rather than having to repeat a bunch of redundant "{Binding ElementName=X, Path=Y}" XAML values to multiple controls. For example, assume you have added the following new Button to the StackPanel of this tab (you'll see why it is so large in just a moment):

```
<Button Content="Click" Height="200"/>
```

You could use Visual Studio to generate data bindings for multiple controls, but instead try entering the modified markup manually using the XAML editor, like so:

```
<!-- Note the StackPanel sets the DataContext property. -->
<StackPanel Background="#FFE5E5E5" DataContext = "{Binding ElementName=mySB}">
  <Label Content="Move the scroll bar to see the current value"/>

  <ScrollBar Orientation="Horizontal" Height="30" Name="mySB"
             Maximum = "100" LargeChange="1" SmallChange="1"/>

  <!-- Now both UI elements use the scrollbar's value in unique ways. -->
  <Label x:Name="labelSBThumb" Height="30" BorderBrush="Blue" BorderThickness="2"
         Content = "{Binding Path=Value}"/>

  <Button Content="Click" Height="200" FontSize = "{Binding Path=Value}"/>
</StackPanel>
```

Here, you set the DataContext property on the StackPanel directly. Therefore, as you move the thumb, you see not only the current value on the Label but also the font size of the Button grow and shrink accordingly, based on the same value (Figure 25-22 shows one possible output).

Figure 25-22. *Binding the ScrollBar value to a Label and a Button*

Formatting the Bound Data

The ScrollBar type uses a double to represent the value of the thumb, rather than an expected whole number (e.g., an integer). Therefore, as you drag the thumb, you will find various floating-point numbers displayed within the Label (e.g., 61.0576923076923). The end user would find this rather unintuitive because he is most likely expecting to see whole numbers (e.g., 61, 62, and 63).

If you want to format the data, you can add a ContentStringFormat property, passing in a custom string and a .NET format specifier, as follows:

```
<Label x:Name="labelSBThumb" Height="30" BorderBrush="Blue"
  BorderThickness="2" Content = "{Binding Path=Value}" ContentStringFormat="The value is:
  {0:F0}"/>
```

If you don't have any text in the format specification, then you need to lead with an empty set of braces, which is the excape sequence for XAML. This lets the processor know that the next characters are literals and not a binding statement, for example. Here is the updated XAML:

```
<Label x:Name="labelSBThumb" Height="30" BorderBrush="Blue"
  BorderThickness="2" Content = "{Binding Path=Value}" ContentStringFormat="{}{0:F0}"/>
```

■ **Note**   If you are binding a Text property of a control, you can add a StringFormat name-value pair right in the binding statement. It only needs to be separate for Content properties.

Data Conversion Using IValueConverter

If you need to do more than just format the data, you can create a custom class that implements the IValueConverter interface of the System.Windows.Data namespace. This interface defines two members that allow you to perform the conversion to and from the target and destination (in the case of a two-way data binding). After you define this class, you can use it to qualify further the processing of your data-binding operation.

Instead of using the format property, you can use a value converter to display whole numbers within the Label control. To do this, add a new class (named MyDoubleConverter) to the project class. Next, add the following:

```
class MyDoubleConverter : IValueConverter
{
  public object Convert(object value, Type targetType, object parameter,  System.
Globalization.CultureInfo culture)
  {
    // Convert the double to an int.
    double v = (double)value;
    return (int)v;
  }

  public object ConvertBack(object value, Type targetType, object parameter,  System.
Globalization.CultureInfo culture)
  {
    // You won't worry about "two-way" bindings here, so just return the value.
    return value;
  }
}
```

The Convert() method is called when the value is transferred from the source (the ScrollBar) to the destination (the Text property of the TextBox). You will receive many incoming arguments, but you only need to manipulate the incoming object for this conversion, which is the value of the current double. You can use this type to cast the type into an integer and return the new number.

The ConvertBack() method will be called when the value is passed from the destination to the source (if you have enabled a two-way binding mode). Here, you simply return the value straightaway. Doing so lets you type a floating-point value into the TextBox (e.g., 99.9) and have it automatically convert to a whole-number value (e.g., 99) when the user tabs off the control. This "free" conversion happens because the Convert() method is called again, after a call to ConvertBack(). If you were simply to return null from ConvertBack(), your binding would appear to be out of sync because the text box would still be displaying a floating-point number.

To use this converter in markup, you first have to create a local resource representing the custom class you just built. Don't worry about the mechanics of adding resources; the next few chapters will dive deeper into this subject. Add the following just after the opening Window tag:

```
<Window.Resources>
  <local:MyDoubleConverter x:Key="DoubleConverter"/>
</Window.Resources>
```

Next, update the binding statement for the Label control to the following:

```
<Label x:Name="labelSBThumb" Height="30" BorderBrush="Blue"
     BorderThickness="2" Content = "{Binding Path=Value,Converter={StaticResource
DoubleConverter}}" />
```

Now when you run the app, you see only whole numbers.

Establishing Data Bindings in Code

You can also register your data conversion class in code. Begin by cleaning up the current definition of the Label control in your data binding tab so that it no longer uses the {Binding} markup extension.

```
<Label x:Name="labelSBThumb" Height="30" BorderBrush="Blue" BorderThickness="2" />
```

Make sure there is a using for System.Windows.Data; then in your window's constructor, call a new private helper function called SetBindings(). In this method, add the following code (and make sure to call it from the constructor):

```
private void SetBindings()
{
  // Create a Binding object.
  Binding b = new Binding();

  // Register the converter, source, and path.
  b.Converter = new MyDoubleConverter();
  b.Source = this.mySB;
  b.Path = new PropertyPath("Value");

  // Call the SetBinding method on the Label.
  this.labelSBThumb.SetBinding(Label.ContentProperty, b);
}
```

The only part of this function that probably looks a bit off is the call to SetBinding(). Notice that the first parameter calls a static, read-only field of the Label class named ContentProperty. As you will learn later in this chapter, you are specifying what is known as a *dependency property*. For the time being, just know that when you set bindings in code, the first argument will nearly always require you to specify the name of the class that wants the binding (the Label, in this case), followed by a call to the underlying property with the Property suffix. In any case, running the application illustrates that the Label prints out only whole numbers.

Building the DataGrid Tab

The previous data-binding example illustrated how to configure two (or more) controls to participate in a data-binding operation. While this is helpful, it is also possible to bind data from XML files, database data, and in-memory objects. To complete this example, you will design the final tab of your tab control so it displays data obtained from the Inventory table of the AutoLot database.

As with the other tabs, you begin by changing the current Grid to a StackPanel. Do this by directly updating the XAML using Visual Studio. Now define a DataGrid control in your new StackPanel named gridInventory, like so:

```
<TabItem x:Name="tabDataGrid" Header="DataGrid">
  <StackPanel>
    <DataGrid x:Name="gridInventory" Height="288"/>
  </StackPanel>
</TabItem>
```

Use the NuGet package manager to add Entity Framework to your project. Next, right-click the solution, select Add ➤ Existing Project, and add the AutoLotDAL project from Chapter 22. Add a reference to the AutoLotDAL project from the WpfControlsAndAPIs project. Add the connection string into the App.config file. Mine is as follows:

```
<connectionStrings>
    <add name="AutoLotConnection" connectionString="data source=(LocalDb)\
MSSQLLocalDB;initial catalog=AutoLot;integrated security=True;MultipleActiveResultSets=True;
App=EntityFramework" providerName="System.Data.SqlClient" />
</connectionStrings>
```

Open the code file for your window and add a final helper function called ConfigureGrid(); make sure you call this from your constructor. Assuming that you did import the AutoLotDAL namespace, all you need to do is add a few lines of code, like so:

```
using AutoLotDAL.Repos;
private void ConfigureGrid()
{
  using (var repo = new InventoryRepo())
  {
    // Build a LINQ query that gets back some data from the Inventory table.
    gridInventory.ItemsSource =
        repo.GetAll().Select(x -> new { x.Id, x.Make, x.Color, x.PetName });
  }
}
```

The LINQ query creates a new anonymous object that excludes the Timestamp property, since there isn't any value to the user to see that field. If you were to run the project, you see the data populating the grid. If you want to make the grid somewhat fancier, you can use the Visual Studio Properties window to edit grid to make it more appealing.

That wraps up the current example. You'll see some other controls in action during later chapters; at this point, however, you should feel comfortable with the process of building UIs in Visual Studio and manually using XAML and C# code.

■ **Source Code**   You can find the WpfControlsAndAPIs project in the Chapter 25 subdirectory.

Understanding the Role of Dependency Properties

Like any .NET API, WPF makes use of each member of the .NET type system (classes, structures, interfaces, delegates, enumerations) and each type member (properties, methods, events, constant data, read-only fields, etc.) within its implementation. However, WPF also supports a unique programming concept termed a *dependency property*.

Like a "normal" .NET property (often termed a *CLR property* in the WPF literature), dependency properties can be set declaratively using XAML or programmatically within a code file. Furthermore, dependency properties (like CLR properties) ultimately exist to encapsulate data fields of a class and can be configured as read-only, write-only, or read-write.

To make matters more interesting, in almost every case you will be blissfully unaware that you have actually set (or accessed) a dependency property as opposed to a CLR property! For example, the Height and Width properties that WPF controls inherit from FrameworkElement, as well as the Content member inherited from ControlContent, are all, in fact, dependency properties.

```
<!-- Set three dependency properties! -->
<Button x:Name = "btnMyButton" Height = "50" Width = "100" Content = "OK"/>
```

Given all of these similarities, why does WPF define a new term for such a familiar concept? The answer lies in how a dependency property is implemented within the class. You'll see a coding example in just a little bit; however, from a high level, all dependency properties are created in the following manner:

- First, the class that defined a dependency property must have DependencyObject in its inheritance chain.

- A single dependency property is represented as a public, static, read-only field in the class of type DependencyProperty. By convention, this field is named by suffixing the word Property to the name of the CLR wrapper (see final bullet point).

- The DependencyProperty variable is registered via a static call to DependencyProperty.Register(), which typically occurs in a static constructor or inline when the variable is declared.

- Finally, the class will define a XAML-friendly CLR property, which makes calls to methods provided by DependencyObject to get and set the value.

Once implemented, dependency properties provide a number of powerful features that are used by various WPF technologies including data binding, animation services, styles, templates, and so forth. In a nutshell, the motivation of dependency properties is to provide a way to compute the value of a property based on the value of other inputs. Here is a list of some of these key benefits, which go well beyond those of the simple data encapsulation found with a CLR property:

- Dependency properties can inherit their values from a parent element's XAML definition. For example, if you defined a value for the FontSize attribute in the opening tag of a Window, all controls in that Window would have the same font size by default.

- Dependency properties support the ability to have values set by elements contained within their XAML scope, such as a Button setting the Dock property of a DockPanel parent. (Recall that *attached properties* do this very thing because attached properties are a form of dependency properties.)

- Dependency properties allow WPF to compute a value based on multiple external values, which can be important for animation and data-binding services.

- Dependency properties provide infrastructure support for WPF triggers (also used quite often when working with animation and data binding).

1050

Now remember, in many cases you will interact with an existing dependency property in a manner identical to a normal CLR property (thanks to the XAML wrapper). In the previous section, which covered data binding, you saw that if you need to establish a data binding in code, you must call the SetBinding() method on the object that is the destination of the operation and specify the *dependency property* it will operate on, like so:

```
private void SetBindings()
{
  Binding b = new Binding();
  b.Converter = new MyDoubleConverter();
  b.Source = this.mySB;
  b.Path = new PropertyPath("Value");

  // Specify the dependency property!
  this.labelSBThumb.SetBinding(Label.ContentProperty, b);
}
```

You will see similar code when you examine how to start an animation in code in Chapter 27.

```
// Specify the dependency property!
rt.BeginAnimation(RotateTransform.AngleProperty, dblAnim);
```

The only time you need to build your own custom dependency property is when you are authoring a custom WPF control. For example, if you are building a UserControl that defines four custom properties and you want these properties to integrate well within the WPF API, you should author them using dependency property logic.

Specifically, if your properties need to be the target of a data-binding or animation operation, if the property must broadcast when it has changed, if it must be able to work as a Setter in a WPF style, or if it must be able to receive their values from a parent element, a normal CLR property will *not* be enough. If you were to use a normal CLR property, other programmers may indeed be able to get and set a value; however, if they attempt to use your properties within the context of a WPF service, things will not work as expected. Because you can never know how others might want to interact with the properties of your custom UserControl classes, you should get in the habit of *always* defining dependency properties when building custom controls.

Examining an Existing Dependency Property

Before you learn how to build a custom dependency property, let's take a look at how the Height property of the FrameworkElement class has been implemented internally. The relevant code is shown here (with my included comments):

```
// FrameworkElement is-a DependencyObject.
public class FrameworkElement : UIElement, IFrameworkInputElement,
  IInputElement, ISupportInitialize, IHaveResources, IQueryAmbient
{
...
  // A static read-only field of type DependencyProperty.
  public static readonly DependencyProperty HeightProperty;

  // The DependencyProperty field is often registered
  // in the static constructor of the class.
```

```
static FrameworkElement()
{
  ...
  HeightProperty = DependencyProperty.Register(
    "Height",
    typeof(double),
    typeof(FrameworkElement),
    new FrameworkPropertyMetadata((double) 1.0 / (double) 0.0,
      FrameworkPropertyMetadataOptions.AffectsMeasure,
      new PropertyChangedCallback(FrameworkElement.OnTransformDirty)),
    new ValidateValueCallback(FrameworkElement.IsWidthHeightValid));
  }

  // The CLR wrapper, which is implemented using
  // the inherited GetValue()/SetValue() methods.
  public double Height
  {
    get { return (double) base.GetValue(HeightProperty); }
    set { base.SetValue(HeightProperty, value); }
  }
}
```

As you can see, dependency properties require quite a bit of additional code from a normal CLR property! And in reality, a dependency can be even more complex than what you see here (thankfully, many implementations are simpler than Height).

First, remember that if a class wants to define a dependency property, it must have DependencyObject in the inheritance chain because this is the class that defines the GetValue() and SetValue() methods used in the CLR wrapper. Because FrameworkElement *is-a* DependencyObject, this requirement is satisfied.

Next, recall that the entity that will hold the actual value of the property (a double in the case of Height) is represented as a public, static, read-only field of type DependencyProperty. The name of this field should, by convention, always be named by suffixing the word Property to the name of the related CLR wrapper, like so:

```
public static readonly DependencyProperty HeightProperty;
```

Given that dependency properties are declared as static fields, they are typically created (and registered) within the static constructor of the class. The DependencyProperty object is created via a call to the static DependencyProperty.Register() method. This method has been overloaded many times; however, in the case of Height, DependencyProperty.Register() is invoked as follows:

```
HeightProperty = DependencyProperty.Register(
  "Height",
  typeof(double),
  typeof(FrameworkElement),
  new FrameworkPropertyMetadata((double)0.0,
    FrameworkPropertyMetadataOptions.AffectsMeasure,
    new PropertyChangedCallback(FrameworkElement.OnTransformDirty)),
  new ValidateValueCallback(FrameworkElement.IsWidthHeightValid));
```

The first argument to DependencyProperty.Register() is the name of the normal CLR property on the class (Height, in this case), while the second argument is the type information of the underlying data type it is encapsulating (a double). The third argument specifies the type information of the class that this property belongs to (FrameworkElement, in this case). While this might seem redundant (after all, the HeightProperty field is already defined within the FrameworkElement class), this is a very clever aspect of WPF in that it allows one class to register properties on another (even if the class definition has been sealed!).

The fourth argument passed to DependencyProperty.Register() in this example is what really gives dependency properties their own unique flavor. Here, a FrameworkPropertyMetadata object is passed that describes various details regarding how WPF should handle this property with respect to callback notifications (if the property needs to notify others when the value changes) and various options (represented by the FrameworkPropertyMetadataOptions enum) that control what is affected by the property in question. (Does it work with data binding? Can it be inherited?) In this case, the constructor arguments of FrameworkPropertyMetadata break down as so:

```
new FrameworkPropertyMetadata(
  // Default value of property.
  (double)0.0,

  // Metadata options.
  FrameworkPropertyMetadataOptions.AffectsMeasure,

  // Delegate pointing to method called when property changes.
  new PropertyChangedCallback(FrameworkElement.OnTransformDirty)
)
```

Because the final argument to the FrameworkPropertyMetadata constructor is a delegate, note that its constructor parameter is pointing to a static method on the FrameworkElement class named OnTransformDirty(). I won't bother to show the code behind this method, but be aware that any time you are building a custom dependency property, you can specify a PropertyChangedCallback delegate to point to a method that will be called when your property value has been changed.

This brings me to the final parameter passed to the DependencyProperty.Register() method, a second delegate of type ValidateValueCallback, which points to a method on the FrameworkElement class that is called to ensure the value assigned to the property is valid.

```
new ValidateValueCallback(FrameworkElement.IsWidthHeightValid)
```

This method contains logic you might normally expect to find in the set block of a property (more information on this point in the next section).

```
private static bool IsWidthHeightValid(object value)
{
  double num = (double) value;
  return ((!DoubleUtil.IsNaN(num) && (num >= 0.0))
    && !double.IsPositiveInfinity(num));
}
```

After the DependencyProperty object has been registered, the final task is to wrap the field within a normal CLR property (Height, in this case). Notice, however, that the get and set scopes do not simply return or set a class-level double-member variable but do so indirectly using the GetValue() and SetValue() methods from the System.Windows.DependencyObject base class, as follows:

```
public double Height
{
  get { return (double) base.GetValue(HeightProperty); }
  set { base.SetValue(HeightProperty, value); }
}
```

Important Notes Regarding CLR Property Wrappers

So, just to recap the story thus far, dependency properties look like normal everyday properties when you get or set their values in XAML or code, but behind the scenes they are implemented with much more elaborate coding techniques. Remember, the whole reason to go through this process is to build a custom control that has custom properties that need to integrate with WPF services that demand communication with a dependency property (e.g., animation, data binding, and styles).

Even though part of the implementation of a dependency property includes defining a CLR wrapper, *you should never put validation logic in the set block*. For that matter, the CLR wrapper of a dependency property *should never do anything other than call GetValue() or SetValue()*.

The reason is that the WPF runtime has been constructed in such a way that when you write XAML that seems to set a property, such as

```
<Button x:Name="myButton" Height="100" .../>
```

the runtime will completely bypass the set block of the Height property and *directly* call SetValue()! The reason for this odd behavior has to do with a simple optimization technique. If the WPF runtime were to call the set block of the Height property, it would have to perform runtime reflection to figure out where the DependencyProperty field (specified by the first argument to SetValue()) is located, reference it in memory, and so forth. The same story holds true if you were to write XAML that retrieves the value of the Height property—GetValue() would be called directly.

Since this is the case, why do you need to build this CLR wrapper at all? Well, WPF XAML does not allow you to call functions in markup, so the following markup would be an error:

```
<!-- Nope! Can't call methods in WPF XAML! -->
<Button x:Name="myButton" this.SetValue("100") .../>
```

In effect, when you set or get a value in markup using the CLR wrapper, think of it as a way to tell the WPF runtime, "Hey! Go call GetValue()/SetValue() for me since I can't directly do it in markup!" Now, what if you call the CLR wrapper in code like so:

```
Button b = new Button();
b.Height = 10;
```

In this case, if the set block of the Height property contained code other than a call to SetValue(), it *would* execute because the WPF XAML parser optimization is not involved.

The basic rule to remember is that when registering a dependency property, use a ValidateValueCallback delegate to point to a method that performs the data validation. This ensures that the correct behavior will occur, regardless of whether you use XAML or code to get/set a dependency property.

Building a Custom Dependency Property

If you have a slight headache at this point in the chapter, this is a perfectly normal response. Building dependency properties can take some time to get used to. However, for better or worse, it is part of the process of building many custom WPF controls, so let's take a look at how to build a dependency property.

Begin by creating a new WPF application named CustomDepProp. Now, using the Project menu, activate the Add User Control menu option, and create a control named ShowNumberControl.xaml.

■ **Note** You will learn more details about the WPF UserControl in Chapter 27, so just follow along as shown for now.

Just like a window, WPF UserControl types have a XAML file and a related code file. Update the XAML of your user control to define a single Label control in the Grid, like so:

```
<UserControl x:Class="CustomDepProp.ShowNumberControl"
    xmlns="http://schemas.microsoft.com/winfx/2006/xaml/presentation"
    xmlns:x="http://schemas.microsoft.com/winfx/2006/xaml"
    xmlns:mc="http://schemas.openxmlformats.org/markup-compatibility/2006"
    xmlns:d="http://schemas.microsoft.com/expression/blend/2008"
    xmlns:local="clr-namespace:CustomDepProp"
    mc:Ignorable="d"
    d:DesignHeight="300" d:DesignWidth="300">
  <Grid>
    <Label x:Name="numberDisplay" Height="50" Width="200" Background="LightBlue"/>
  </Grid>
</UserControl>
```

In the code file of this custom control, create a normal, everyday .NET property that wraps an int and sets the Content property of the Label with the new value, as follows:

```
public partial class ShowNumberControl : UserControl
{
  public ShowNumberControl()
  {
    InitializeComponent();
  }

  // A normal, everyday .NET property.
  private int _currNumber = 0;
  public int CurrentNumber
  {
    get => _currNumber;
    set
    {
      _currNumber = value;
      numberDisplay.Content = CurrentNumber.ToString();
    }
  }
}
```

Now, update the XAML definition of your window to declare an instance of your custom control within a StackPanel layout manger. Because your custom control is not part of the core WPF assembly stack, you will need to define a custom XML namespace that maps to your control. Here is the required markup:

```
<Window x:Class="CustomDepPropApp.MainWindow"
    xmlns="http://schemas.microsoft.com/winfx/2006/xaml/presentation"
    xmlns:x="http://schemas.microsoft.com/winfx/2006/xaml"
    xmlns:d="http://schemas.microsoft.com/expression/blend/2008"
    xmlns:mc="http://schemas.openxmlformats.org/markup-compatibility/2006"
    xmlns:myCtrls="clr-namespace:CustomDepProp"
    xmlns:local="clr-namespace:CustomDepProp"
    mc:Ignorable="d"
    Title="Simple Dependency Property App" Height="150" Width="250"
    WindowStartupLocation="CenterScreen">
```

```
  <StackPanel>
    <myCtrls:ShowNumberControl x:Name="myShowNumberCtrl" CurrentNumber="100"/>
  </StackPanel>
</Window>
```

As you can see, the Visual Studio designer appears to correctly display the value that you set in the CurrentNumber property (see Figure 25-23).

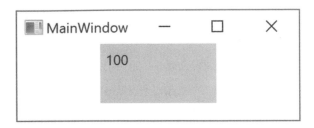

Figure 25-23. *It appears your property works as expected*

However, what if you want to apply an animation object to the CurrentNumber property so that the value changes from 100 to 200 over a period of 10 seconds? If you wanted to do so in markup, you might update your myCtrls:ShowNumberControl scope as so:

```
<myCtrls:ShowNumberControl x:Name="myShowNumberCtrl" CurrentNumber="100">
  <myCtrls:ShowNumberControl.Triggers>
    <EventTrigger RoutedEvent = "myCtrls:ShowNumberControl.Loaded">
      <EventTrigger.Actions>
        <BeginStoryboard>
          <Storyboard TargetProperty = "CurrentNumber">
            <Int32Animation From = "100" To = "200" Duration = "0:0:10"/>
          </Storyboard>
        </BeginStoryboard>
      </EventTrigger.Actions>
    </EventTrigger>
  </myCtrls:ShowNumberControl.Triggers>
</myCtrls:ShowNumberControl>
```

If you run your application, the animation object cannot find a proper target, so it is ignored. The reason is that the CurrentNumber property has not been registered as a dependency property! To fix matters, return to the code file of your custom control, and completely comment out the current property logic (including the private backing field). Now, position your mouse cursor within the scope of the class and type in the propdp code snippet. After you have typed propdp, press the Tab key twice. You will find the snippet expands to give you the basic skeleton of a dependency property as follows:

```
public int MyProperty
{
  get { return (int)GetValue(MyPropertyProperty); }
  set { SetValue(MyPropertyProperty, value); }
}
// Using a DependencyProperty as the backing store for MyProperty.  This enables animation,
styling, binding, etc...
```

```
public static readonly DependencyProperty MyPropertyProperty =
  DependencyProperty.Register("MyProperty", typeof(int), typeof(ownerclass), new
  PropertyMetadata(0));
```

Update the entered template to match the following code:

```
public int CurrentNumber
{
  get => (int)GetValue(CurrentNumberProperty);
  set => SetValue(CurrentNumberProperty, value);
}

public static readonly DependencyProperty CurrentNumberProperty =
  DependencyProperty.Register("CurrentNumber",
    typeof(int),
    typeof(ShowNumberControl),
    new UIPropertyMetadata(0));
```

This is similar to what you saw in the implementation of the Height property; however, the code snippet registers the property inline rather than within a static constructor (which is fine). Also notice that a UIPropertyMetadata object is used to define the default value of the integer (0) rather than the more complex FrameworkPropertyMetadata object. This is the simplest version of CurrentNumber as a dependency property.

Adding a Data Validation Routine

Although you now have a dependency property named CurrentNumber, you still won't see your animation take hold. The next adjustment you might want to make is to specify a function to call to perform some data validation logic. For this example, assume that you need to ensure that the value of CurrentNumber is between 0 and 500.

To do so, add a final argument to the DependencyProperty.Register() method of type ValidateValueCallback, which points to a method named ValidateCurrentNumber.

ValidateValueCallback is a delegate that can only point to methods returning bool and take an object as the only argument. This object represents the new value that is being assigned. Implement ValidateCurrentNumber to return true or false, if the incoming value is within the expected range.

```
public static readonly DependencyProperty CurrentNumberProperty =
  DependencyProperty.Register("CurrentNumber",
    typeof(int),
    typeof(ShowNumberControl),
    new UIPropertyMetadata(100),
    new ValidateValueCallback(ValidateCurrentNumber));

public static bool ValidateCurrentNumber(object value)
{
  // Just a simple business rule. Value must be between 0 and 500.
  return Convert.ToInt32(value) >= 0 && Convert.ToInt32(value) <= 500;
}
```

Responding to the Property Change

So, now you have a valid number but still no animation. The final change you need to make is to specify a second argument to the constructor of UIPropertyMetadata, which is a PropertyChangedCallback object. This delegate can point to any method that takes a DependencyObject as the first parameter and a DependencyPropertyChangedEventArgs as the second. First, update your code as so:

```
// Note the second param of UIPropertyMetadata construtor.
public static readonly DependencyProperty CurrentNumberProperty =
  DependencyProperty.Register("CurrentNumber", typeof(int), typeof(ShowNumberControl),
  new UIPropertyMetadata(100, new PropertyChangedCallback(CurrentNumberChanged)),
  new ValidateValueCallback(ValidateCurrentNumber));
```

Within the CurrentNumberChanged() method, your ultimate goal is to change the Content of the Label to the new value assigned by the CurrentNumber property. You have one big problem, however: the CurrentNumberChanged() method is static, as it must be to work with the static DependencyProperty object. So, how are you supposed to gain access to the Label for the current instance of ShowNumberControl? That reference is contained in the first DependencyObject parameter. You can find the new value using the incoming event arguments. Here is the necessary code that will change the Content property of the Label:

```
private static void CurrentNumberChanged(DependencyObject depObj,
    DependencyPropertyChangedEventArgs args)
{
  // Cast the DependencyObject into ShowNumberControl.
  ShowNumberControl c = (ShowNumberControl)depObj;
  // Get the Label control in the ShowNumberControl.
  Label theLabel = c.numberDisplay;
  // Set the Label with the new value.
  theLabel.Content = args.NewValue.ToString();
}
```

Whew! That was a long way to go just to change the output of a label. The benefit is that your CurrentNumber dependency property can now be the target of a WPF style, an animation object, the target of a data-binding operation, and so forth. If you run your application once again, you should now see the value change during execution.

That wraps up your look at WPF dependency properties. While I hope you have a much better idea about what these constructs allow you to do and have a better idea of how to make your own, please be aware that there are many details I have not covered here.

If you find yourself in a position where you are building a number of custom controls that support custom properties, please look up the topic "Properties" under the "WPF Fundamentals" node of the .NET Framework 4.7 SDK documentation. In it you will find many more examples of building dependency properties, attached properties, various ways to configure property metadata, and a slew of other details.

■ **Source Code**   You can find the CustomDepPropApp project in the Chapter 25 subdirectory.

Summary

This chapter examined several aspects of WPF controls, beginning with an overview of the control toolkit and the role of layout managers (panels). The first example gave you a chance to build a simple word processor application that illustrated the integrated spell-checking functionality of WPF, as well as how to build a main window with menu systems, status bars, and toolbars.

More importantly, you examined how to use WPF commands. Recall that you can attach these control-agnostic events to a UI element or an input gesture to inherit out-of-the-box services automatically (e.g., clipboard operations).

You also learned quite a bit about building complex UI's in XAML, and you learned about the WPF Ink API at the same time. You also received an introduction to WPF data-binding operations, including how to use the WPF DataGrid class to display data from your custom AutoLot database.

Finally, you investigated how WPF places a unique spin on traditional .NET programming primitives, specifically properties and events. As you have seen, a *dependency property* allows you to build a property that can integrate within the WPF set of services (animations, data bindings, styles, and so on). On a related note, *routed events* provide a way for an event to flow up or down a tree of markup.

CHAPTER 26

■ ■ ■

WPF Graphics Rendering Services

In this chapter, you'll examine the graphical rendering capabilities of WPF. As you'll see, WPF provides three separate ways to render graphical data: shapes, drawings, and visuals. After you understand the pros and cons of each approach, you will start learning about the world of interactive 2D graphics using the classes within System.Windows.Shapes. After this, you'll see how drawings and geometries allow you to render 2D data in a more lightweight manner. Last but not least, you'll learn how the visual layer gives you the greatest level of power and performance.

Along the way, you will explore a number of related topics, such as how to create custom brushes and pens, how to apply graphical transformations to your renderings, and how to perform hit-test operations. In particular, you'll see how the integrated tools of Visual Studio and an additional tool named Inkscape can simplify your graphical coding endeavors.

■ **Note**   Graphics are a key aspect of WPF development. Even if you are not building a graphics-heavy application (such as a video game or multimedia application), the topics in this chapter are critical when you work with services such as control templates, animations, and data-binding customization.

Understanding WPF's Graphical Rendering Services

WPF uses a particular flavor of graphical rendering that goes by the term *retained-mode graphics*. Simply put, this means that since you are using XAML or procedural code to generate graphical renderings, it is the responsibility of WPF to persist these visual items and ensure that they are correctly redrawn and refreshed in an optimal manner. Thus, when you render graphical data, it is always present, even when the end user hides the image by resizing or minimizing the window, by covering the window with another, and so forth.

In stark contrast, previous Microsoft graphical rendering APIs (including Windows Forms' GDI+) were *immediate-mode* graphical systems. In this model, it was up to the programmer to ensure that rendered visuals were correctly "remembered" and updated during the life of the application. For example, in a Windows Forms application, rendering a shape such as a rectangle involved handling the Paint event (or overriding the virtual OnPaint() method), obtaining a Graphics object to draw the rectangle, and, most important, adding the infrastructure to ensure that the image was persisted when the user resized the window (for example, creating member variables to represent the position of the rectangle and calling Invalidate() throughout your program).

The shift from immediate-mode to retained-mode graphics is indeed a good thing, as programmers have far less grungy graphics code to author and maintain. However, I'm not suggesting that the WPF graphics API is *completely* different from earlier rendering toolkits. For example, like GDI+, WPF supports various brush types and pen objects, techniques for hit-testing, clipping regions, graphical transformations,

© Andrew Troelsen and Philip Japikse 2017
A. Troelsen and P. Japikse, *Pro C# 7*, https://doi.org/10.1007/978-1-4842-3018-3_26

and so on. So, if you currently have a background in GDI+ (or C/C++-based GDI), you already know a good deal about how to perform basic renderings under WPF.

WPF Graphical Rendering Options

As with other aspects of WPF development, you have a number of choices regarding how to perform your graphical rendering, beyond the decision to do so via XAML or procedural C# code (or perhaps a combination of both). Specifically, WPF provides the following three distinct ways to render graphical data:

- *Shapes*: WPF provides the System.Windows.Shapes namespace, which defines a small number of classes for rendering 2D geometric objects (rectangles, ellipses, polygons, etc.). While these types are simple to use and powerful, they do come with a fair amount of memory overhead if used with reckless abandon.

- *Drawings and geometries*: The WPF API provides a second way to render graphical data, using descendants from the System.Windows.Media.Drawing abstract class. Using classes such as GeometryDrawing or ImageDrawing (in addition to various *geometry objects*), you can render graphical data in a more lightweight (but less feature-rich) manner.

- *Visuals*: The fastest and most lightweight way to render graphical data under WPF is using the visual layer, which is accessible only through C# code. Using descendants of System.Windows.Media.Visual, you can speak directly to the WPF graphical subsystem.

The reason for offering different ways to do the same thing (i.e., render graphical data) has to do with memory use and, ultimately, application performance. Because WPF is such a graphically intensive system, it is not unreasonable for an application to render hundreds or even thousands of different images on a window's surface, and the choice of implementation (shapes, drawings, or visuals) could have a huge impact.

Do understand that when you build a WPF application, chances are good you'll use all three options. As a rule of thumb, if you need a modest amount of *interactive* graphical data that can be manipulated by the user (receive mouse input, display tooltips, etc.), you'll want to use members in the System.Windows.Shapes namespace.

In contrast, drawings and geometries are more appropriate when you need to model complex, generally noninteractive, vector-based graphical data using XAML or C#. While drawings and geometries can still respond to mouse events, hit-testing, and drag-and-drop operations, you will typically need to author more code to do so.

Last but not least, if you require the fastest possible way to render massive amounts of graphical data, the visual layer is the way to go. For example, let's say you are using WPF to build a scientific application that can plot out thousands of points of data. Using the visual layer, you can render the plot points in the most optimal way possible. As you will see later in this chapter, the visual layer is accessible only via C# code and is not XAML-friendly.

No matter which approach you take (shapes, drawings and geometries, or visuals), you will make use of common graphical primitives such as brushes (which fill interiors), pens (which draw exteriors), and transformation objects (which, well, transform the data). To begin the journey, you will start working with the classes of System.Windows.Shapes.

■ **Note**   WPF also ships with a full-blown API that can be used to render and manipulate 3D graphics, which is not addressed in this edition of the text. Please consult the .NET Framework 4.7 SDK documentation if you are interested in incorporating 3D graphics into your applications.

Rendering Graphical Data Using Shapes

Members of the System.Windows.Shapes namespace provide the most straightforward, most interactive, yet most memory-intensive way to render a two-dimensional image. This namespace (defined in the PresentationFramework.dll assembly) is quite small and consists of only six sealed classes that extend the abstract Shape base class: Ellipse, Rectangle, Line, Polygon, Polyline, and Path.

The abstract Shape class inherits from FrameworkElement, which inherits from UIElement. These classes define members to deal with sizing, tooltips, mouse cursors, and whatnot. Given this inheritance chain, when you render graphical data using Shape-derived classes, the objects are just about as functional (as far as user interactivity is concerned) as a WPF control!

For example, determining whether the user has clicked your rendered image is no more complicated than handling the MouseDown event. By way of a simple example, if you authored this XAML of a Rectangle object in the Grid of your initial Window:

```
<Rectangle x:Name="myRect" Height="30" Width="30" Fill="Green" MouseDown="myRect_
MouseDown"/>
```

you could implement a C# event handler for the MouseDown event that changes the rectangle's background color when clicked, like so:

```
private void myRect_MouseDown(object sender, MouseButtonEventArgs e)
{
  // Change color of Rectangle when clicked.
  myRect.Fill = Brushes.Pink;
}
```

Unlike with other graphical toolkits you may have used, you do *not* need to author a ton of infrastructure code that manually maps mouse coordinates to the geometry, manually calculates hit-testing, renders to an off-screen buffer, and so forth. The members of System.Windows.Shapes simply respond to the events you register with, just like a typical WPF control (e.g., Button, etc.).

The downside of all this out-of-the-box functionality is that the shapes do take up a fair amount of memory. If you're building a scientific application that plots thousands of points on the screen, using shapes would be a poor choice (essentially, it would be about as memory-intensive as rendering thousands of Button objects!). However, when you need to generate an interactive 2D vector image, shapes are a wonderful choice.

Beyond the functionality inherited from the UIElement and FrameworkElement parent classes, Shape defines a number of members for each of the children; some of the more useful ones are shown in Table 26-1.

Table 26-1. *Key Properties of the Shape Base Class*

Properties	Meaning in Life
DefiningGeometry	Returns a Geometry object that represents the overall dimensions of the current shape. This object contains *only* the plot points that are used to render the data and has no trace of the functionality from UIElement or FrameworkElement.
Fill	Allows you to specify a brush object to fill the interior portion of a shape.
GeometryTransform	Allows you to apply transformations to a shape *before* it is rendered on the screen. The inherited RenderTransform property (from UIElement) applies the transformation *after* it has been rendered on the screen.
Stretch	Describes how to fill a shape within its allocated space, such as its position within a layout manager. This is controlled using the corresponding System.Windows.Media.Stretch enumeration.
Stroke	Defines a brush object or, in some cases, a pen object (which is really a brush in disguise) that is used to paint the border of a shape.
StrokeDashArray, StrokeEndLineCap, StrokeStartLineCap, StrokeThickness	These (and other) stroke-related properties control how lines are configured when drawing the border of a shape. In a majority of cases, these properties will configure the brush used to draw a border or line.

■ **Note**   If you forget to set the Fill and Stroke properties, WPF will give you "invisible" brushes and, therefore, the shape will not be visible on the screen!

Adding Rectangles, Ellipses, and Lines to a Canvas

You will build a WPF application that can render shapes using XAML and C# and, while doing so, learn a bit about the process of hit-testing. Create a new WPF application named RenderingWithShapes, and change the title of MainWindow.xaml to "Fun with Shapes!" Update the initial XAML of the <Window>, replacing the Grid with a <DockPanel> containing a (now empty) <ToolBar> and a <Canvas>. Note that each contained item has a fitting name via the Name property.

```
<DockPanel LastChildFill="True">
  <ToolBar DockPanel.Dock="Top" Name="mainToolBar" Height="50">
  </ToolBar>
  <Canvas Background="LightBlue" Name="canvasDrawingArea"/>
</DockPanel>
```

Now, populate the <ToolBar> with a set of <RadioButton> objects, each of which contains a specific Shape-derived class as content. Notice that each <RadioButton> is assigned to the same GroupName (to ensure mutual exclusivity) and is also given a fitting name.

```
<ToolBar DockPanel.Dock="Top" Name="mainToolBar" Height="50">
  <RadioButton Name="circleOption" GroupName="shapeSelection">
    <Ellipse Fill="Green" Height="35" Width="35" />
  </RadioButton>
```

```
<RadioButton Name="rectOption" GroupName="shapeSelection">
  <Rectangle Fill="Red" Height="35" Width="35" RadiusY="10" RadiusX="10" />
</RadioButton>
<RadioButton Name="lineOption" GroupName="shapeSelection">
  <Line Height="35" Width="35" StrokeThickness="10" Stroke="Blue"
        X1="10" Y1="10" Y2="25" X2="25"
        StrokeStartLineCap="Triangle" StrokeEndLineCap="Round" />
</RadioButton>
</ToolBar>
```

As you can see, declaring Rectangle, Ellipse, and Line objects in XAML is quite straightforward and requires little comment. Recall that the Fill property is used to specify a *brush* to paint the interior of a shape. When you require a solid-colored brush, just specify a hard-coded string of known values, and the underlying type converter will generate the correct object. One interesting feature of the Rectangle type is that it defines RadiusX and RadiusY properties to allow you to render curved corners.

Line represents its starting and ending points using the X1, X2, Y1, and Y2 properties (given that *height* and *width* make little sense when describing a line). Here you are setting up a few additional properties that control how to render the starting and ending points of the Line, as well as how to configure the stroke settings. Figure 26-1 shows the rendered toolbar, as seen through the Visual Studio WPF designer.

Figure 26-1. *Using Shapes as content for a set of RadioButtons*

Now, using the Properties window of Visual Studio, handle the MouseLeftButtonDown event for the Canvas, and handle the Click event for each RadioButton. In your C# file, your goal is to render the selected shape (a circle, square, or line) when the user clicks within the Canvas. First, define the following nested enum (and corresponding member variable) within your Window-derived class:

```
public partial class MainWindow : Window
{
  private enum SelectedShape
  { Circle, Rectangle, Line }
  private SelectedShape _currentShape;
}
```

Within each Click event handler, set the currentShape member variable to the correct SelectedShape value, as follows:

```
private void circleOption_Click(object sender, RoutedEventArgs e)
{
  _currentShape = SelectedShape.Circle;
}
```

```
private void rectOption_Click(object sender, RoutedEventArgs e)
{
  _currentShape = SelectedShape.Rectangle;
}

private void lineOption_Click(object sender, RoutedEventArgs e)
{
  _currentShape = SelectedShape.Line;
}
```

With the MouseLeftButtonDown event handler of the Canvas, you will render out the correct shape (of a predefined size), using the X,Y position of the mouse cursor as a starting point. Here is the complete implementation, with analysis to follow:

```
private void canvasDrawingArea_MouseLeftButtonDown(object sender, MouseButtonEventArgs e)
{
  Shape shapeToRender = null;
  // Configure the correct shape to draw.
  switch (_currentShape)
  {
    case SelectedShape.Circle:
      shapeToRender = new Ellipse() { Fill = Brushes.Green, Height = 35, Width = 35 };
      break;
    case SelectedShape.Rectangle:
      shapeToRender = new Rectangle()
        { Fill = Brushes.Red, Height = 35, Width = 35, RadiusX = 10, RadiusY = 10 };
      break;
    case SelectedShape.Line:
      shapeToRender = new Line()
      {
        Stroke = Brushes.Blue,
        StrokeThickness = 10,
        X1 = 0, X2 = 50, Y1 = 0, Y2 = 50,
        StrokeStartLineCap= PenLineCap.Triangle,
        StrokeEndLineCap = PenLineCap.Round
      };
      break;
    default:
      return;
  }
  // Set top/left position to draw in the canvas.
  Canvas.SetLeft(shapeToRender, e.GetPosition(canvasDrawingArea).X);
  Canvas.SetTop(shapeToRender, e.GetPosition(canvasDrawingArea).Y);
  // Draw shape!
  canvasDrawingArea.Children.Add(shapeToRender);
}
```

■ **Note** You might notice that the Ellipse, Rectangle, and Line objects being created in this method have the same property settings as the corresponding XAML definitions! As you might hope, you can streamline this code, but that requires an understanding of the WPF object resources, which you will examine in Chapter 27.

As you can see, you are testing the currentShape member variable to create the correct Shape-derived object. After this point, you set the top-left value within the Canvas using the incoming MouseButtonEventArgs. Last but not least, you add the new Shape-derived type to the collection of UIElement objects maintained by the Canvas. If you run your program now, you should be able to click anywhere in the canvas and see the selected shape rendered at the location of the left mouse-click.

Removing Rectangles, Ellipses, and Lines from a Canvas

With the Canvas maintaining a collection of objects, you might wonder how you can dynamically remove an item, perhaps in response to the user right-clicking a shape. You can certainly do this using a class in the System.Windows.Media namespace called the VisualTreeHelper. Chapter 27 will explain the roles of "visual trees" and "logical trees" in some detail. Until then, you can handle the MouseRightButtonDown event on your Canvas object and implement the corresponding event handler like so:

```
private void canvasDrawingArea_MouseRightButtonDown(object sender, MouseButtonEventArgs e)
{
  // First, get the X,Y location of where the user clicked.
  Point pt = e.GetPosition((Canvas)sender);
  // Use the HitTest() method of VisualTreeHelper to see if the user clicked
  // on an item in the canvas.
  HitTestResult result = VisualTreeHelper.HitTest(canvasDrawingArea, pt);
  // If the result is not null, they DID click on a shape!
  if (result != null)
  {
      // Get the underlying shape clicked on, and remove it from
      // the canvas.
      canvasDrawingArea.Children.Remove(result.VisualHit as Shape);
  }
}
```

This method begins by obtaining the exact X,Y location the user clicked in the Canvas and performs a hit-test operation via the static VisualTreeHelper.HitTest() method. The return value, a HitTestResult object, will be set to null if the user does not click a UIElement within the Canvas. If HitTestResult is *not* null, you can obtain the underlying UIElement that was clicked via the VisualHit property, which you are casting into a Shape-derived object (remember, a Canvas can hold any UIElement, not just shapes!). Again, you'll get more details on exactly what a "visual tree" is in the next chapter.

■ **Note**   By default, VisualTreeHelper.HitTest() returns the topmost UIElement clicked and does not provide information on other objects below that item (e.g., objects overlapping by Z-order).

With this modification, you should be able to add a shape to the canvas with a left mouse-click and delete an item from the canvas with a right mouse-click!

So far, so good. At this point, you have used Shape-derived objects to render content on RadioButtons using XAML and populated a Canvas using C#. You will add a bit more functionality to this example when you examine the role of brushes and graphical transformations. On a related note, a different example in this chapter will illustrate drag-and-drop techniques on UIElement objects. Until then, let's examine the remaining members of System.Windows.Shapes.

Working with Polylines and Polygons

The current example used only three of the Shape-derived classes. The remaining child classes (Polyline, Polygon, and Path) are extremely tedious to render correctly without tool support (such as Microsoft Blend, the companion tool for Visual Studio designed for WPF developers, or other tools that can create vector graphics) simply because they require a large number of plot points to represent their output. You'll learn about the role of Microsoft Blend in just a moment, but until then, here is an overview of the remaining Shapes types.

The Polyline type lets you define a collection of (x, y) coordinates (via the Points property) to draw a series of line segments that do not require connecting ends. The Polygon type is similar; however, it is programmed so that it will always close the starting and ending points and fill the interior with the specified brush. Assume you have authored the following <StackPanel> in the Kaxaml editor:

```
<!-- Polylines do not automatically connect the ends. -->
<Polyline Stroke ="Red" StrokeThickness ="20" StrokeLineJoin ="Round" Points ="10,10 40,40
10,90 300,50"/>
<!-- A Polygon always closes the end points. -->
<Polygon Fill ="AliceBlue" StrokeThickness ="5" Stroke ="Green" Points ="40,10 70,80 10,50"
/>
```

Figure 26-2 shows the rendered output in Kaxaml.

Figure 26-2. *Polygons and polylines*

Working with Paths

Using the Rectangle, Ellipse, Polygon, Polyline, and Line types alone to draw a detailed 2D vector image would be extremely complex, as these primitives do not allow you to easily capture graphical data such as curves, unions of overlapping data, and so forth. The final Shape-derived class, Path, provides the ability to define complex 2D graphical data represented as a collection of independent *geometries*. After you have defined a collection of such geometries, you can assign them to the Data property of the Path class, where this information will be used to render your complex 2D image.

The Data property takes a System.Windows.Media.Geometry-derived class, which contains the key members described in Table 26-2.

Table 26-2. *Select Members of the* System.Windows.Media.Geometry *Type*

Member	Meaning in Life
Bounds	Establishes the current bounding rectangle containing the geometry.
FillContains()	Determines whether a given Point (or other Geometry object) is within the bounds of a particular Geometry-derived class. This is useful for hit-testing calculations.
GetArea()	Returns the entire area that a Geometry-derived type occupies.
GetRenderBounds()	Returns a Rect that contains the smallest possible rectangle that could be used to render the Geometry-derived class.
Transform	Assigns a Transform object to the geometry to alter the rendering.

The classes that extend Geometry (see Table 26-3) look very much like their Shape-derived counterparts. For example, EllipseGeometry has similar members to Ellipse. The big distinction is that Geometry-derived classes *do not know* how to render themselves directly because they are not UIElements. Rather, Geometry-derived classes represent little more than a collection of plot-point data, which say in effect "If a Path uses my data, this is how I would render myself."

■ **Note** Path is not the only class in WPF that can use a collection of geometries. For example, DoubleAnimationUsingPath, DrawingGroup, GeometryDrawing, and even UIElement can all use geometries for rendering, using the PathGeometry, ClipGeometry, Geometry, and Clip properties, respectively.

Table 26-3. *Geometry-Derived Classes*

Geometry Class	Meaning in Life
LineGeometry	Represents a straight line
RectangleGeometry	Represents a rectangle
EllipseGeometry	Represents an ellipse
GeometryGroup	Allows you to group together several Geometry objects
CombinedGeometry	Allows you to merge two different Geometry objects into a single shape
PathGeometry	Represents a figure composed of lines and curves

The following is a Path that makes use of a few Geometry-derived types. Notice that you are setting the Data property of Path to a GeometryGroup object that contains other Geometry-derived objects such as EllipseGeometry, RectangleGeometry, and LineGeometry. Figure 26-3 shows the output.

```
<!-- A Path contains a set of geometry objects, set with the Data property. -->
<Path Fill = "Orange" Stroke = "Blue" StrokeThickness = "3">
  <Path.Data>
    <GeometryGroup>
      <EllipseGeometry Center = "75,70" RadiusX = "30" RadiusY = "30" />
    <RectangleGeometry Rect = "25,55 100 30" />
    <LineGeometry StartPoint="0,0" EndPoint="70,30" />
    <LineGeometry StartPoint="70,30" EndPoint="0,30" />
```

```
      </GeometryGroup>
    </Path.Data>
</Path>
```

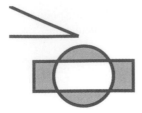

Figure 26-3. *A Path containing various Geometry objects*

The image in Figure 26-3 could have been rendered using the Line, Ellipse, and Rectangle classes shown earlier. However, this would have put various UIElement objects in memory. When you use geometries to model the plot points of what to draw and then place the geometry collection into a container that can render the data (Path, in this case), you reduce the memory overhead.

Now recall that Path has the same inheritance chain as any other member of System.Windows.Shapes and therefore has the ability to send the same event notifications as other UIElements. Thus, if you were to define this same <Path> element in a Visual Studio project, you could determine whether the user clicked anywhere in the sweeping line simply by handling a mouse event (remember, Kaxaml does not allow you to handle events for the markup you have authored).

The Path Modeling "Mini-Language"

Of all the classes listed in Table 26-3, PathGeometry is the most complex to configure in terms of XAML or code. This has to do with the fact that each *segment* of the PathGeometry is composed of objects that contain various segments and figures (for example, ArcSegment, BezierSegment, LineSegment, PolyBezierSegment, PolyLineSegment, PolyQuadraticBezierSegment, etc.). Here is an example of a Path object whose Data property has been set to a <PathGeometry> composed of various figures and segments:

```
<Path Stroke="Black" StrokeThickness="1" >
  <Path.Data>
    <PathGeometry>
      <PathGeometry.Figures>
        <PathFigure StartPoint="10,50">
          <PathFigure.Segments>
            <BezierSegment
              Point1="100,0"
              Point2="200,200"
              Point3="300,100"/>
            <LineSegment Point="400,100" />
            <ArcSegment
              Size="50,50" RotationAngle="45"
              IsLargeArc="True" SweepDirection="Clockwise"
              Point="200,100"/>
          </PathFigure.Segments>
        </PathFigure>
      </PathGeometry.Figures>
```

```
      </PathGeometry>
    </Path.Data>
</Path>
```

Now, to be perfectly honest, few programmers will ever need to manually build complex 2D images by directly describing Geometry- or PathSegment-derived classes. Later in this chapter, you will learn how to convert vector graphics into path statements that can be used in XAML.

Even with the assistance of these tools, the amount of XAML required to define a complex Path object would be ghastly, as the data consists of full descriptions of various Geometry- or PathSegment-derived classes. To produce more concise and compact markup, the Path class has been designed to understand a specialized "mini-language."

For example, rather than setting the Data property of Path to a collection of Geometry- and PathSegment-derived types, you can set the Data property to a single string literal containing a number of known symbols and various values that define the shape to be rendered. Here is a simple example, and the resulting output is shown in Figure 26-4:

```
<Path Stroke="Black" StrokeThickness="3" Data="M 10,75 C 70,15 250,270 300,175 H 240" />
```

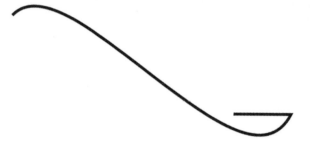

Figure 26-4. *The path mini-language allows you to compactly describe a Geometry/PathSegment object model.*

The M command (short for *move*) takes an X,Y position that represents the starting point of the drawing. The C command takes a series of plot points to render a *curve* (a cubic Bézier curve to be exact), while H draws a *horizontal* line.

Now, to be perfectly honest, the chances that you will ever need to manually build or parse a string literal containing path mini-language instructions are slim to none. However, at the least, you will no longer be surprised when you view XAML-generated dedicated tools. If you are interested in examining the details of this particular grammar, look up "Path Markup Syntax" in the .NET Framework 4.7 SDK documentation.

WPF Brushes and Pens

Each of the WPF graphical rendering options (shape, drawing and geometries, and visuals) makes extensive use of *brushes*, which allow you to control how the interior of a 2D surface is filled. WPF provides six different brush types, all of which extend System.Windows.Media.Brush. While Brush is abstract, the descendants described in Table 26-4 can be used to fill a region with just about any conceivable option.

Table 26-4. WPF Brush-Derived Types

Brush Type	Meaning in Life
DrawingBrush	Paints an area with a Drawing-derived object (GeometryDrawing, ImageDrawing, or VideoDrawing)
ImageBrush	Paints an area with an image (represented by an ImageSource object)
LinearGradientBrush	Paints an area with a linear gradient
RadialGradientBrush	Paints an area with a radial gradient
SolidColorBrush	Paints a single color, set with the Color property
VisualBrush	Paints an area with a Visual-derived object (DrawingVisual, Viewport3DVisual, and ContainerVisual)

The DrawingBrush and VisualBrush classes allow you to build a brush based on an existing Drawing- or Visual-derived class. These brush classes are used when you are working with the other two graphical options of WPF (drawings or visuals) and will be examined later in this chapter.

ImageBrush, as the name suggests, lets you build a brush that displays image data from an external file or embedded application resource, by setting the ImageSource property. The remaining brush types (LinearGradientBrush and RadialGradientBrush) are quite straightforward to use, though typing in the required XAML can be a tad verbose. Thankfully, Visual Studio supports integrated brush editors that make it simple to generate stylized brushes.

Configuring Brushes Using Visual Studio

Let's update your WPF drawing program, RenderingWithShapes, to use some more interesting brushes. The three shapes you've employed so far to render data on your toolbar use simple, solid colors, so you can capture their values using simple string literals. To spice things up a tad, you will now use the integrated brush editor. Ensure that the XAML editor of your initial window is the open window within the IDE, and select the Ellipse element. Now, in the Properties window, locate the Brush category and then click Fill property listed on the top (see Figure 26-5).

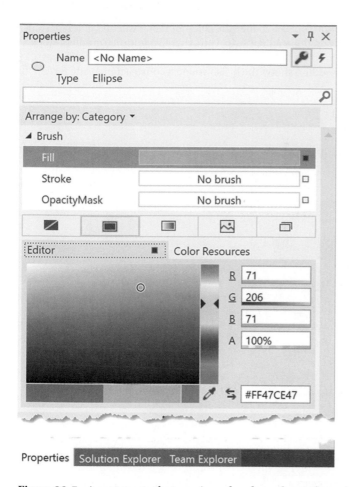

Figure 26-5. *Any property that requires a brush can be configured with the integrated brush editor*

At the top of the Brushes editor, you will see a set of properties that are all "brush compatible" for the selected item (i.e., Fill, Stroke, and OpacityMask). Below this, you will see a series of tabs that allow you to configure different types of brushes, including the current solid color brush. You can use the color selector tool, as well as the ARGB (alpha, red, green, and blue, where "alpha" controls transparency) editors to control the color of the current brush. Using these sliders and the related color selection area, you can create any sort of solid color. Use these tools to change the Fill color of your Ellipse and view the resulting XAML. You'll notice the color is stored as a hexadecimal value, as follows:

```
<Ellipse Fill="#FF47CE47" Height="35" Width="35" />
```

More interestingly, this same editor allows you to configure gradient brushes, which are used to define a series of colors and transition points. Recall that this Brushes editor provides you with a set of tabs, the first of which lets you set a *null brush* for no rendered output. The other four allow you to set up a solid color brush (what you just examined), gradient brush, tile brush, or image brush.

Click the gradient brush button and the editor will display a few new options (see Figure 26-6). The three buttons on the lower left allow you to pick a linear gradient, pick a radial gradient, or reverse the gradient stops. The bottommost strip will show you the current color of each gradient stop, each of which is marked by a "thumb" on the strip. As you drag these thumbs around the gradient strip, you can control the gradient offset. Furthermore, when you click a given thumb, you can change the color for that particular gradient stop via the color selector. Finally, if you click directly on the gradient strip, you can add additional gradient stops.

Take a few minutes to play around with this editor to build a radial gradient brush containing three gradient stops, set to your colors of choice. Figure 26-6 shows the brush you just constructed, using three different shades of green.

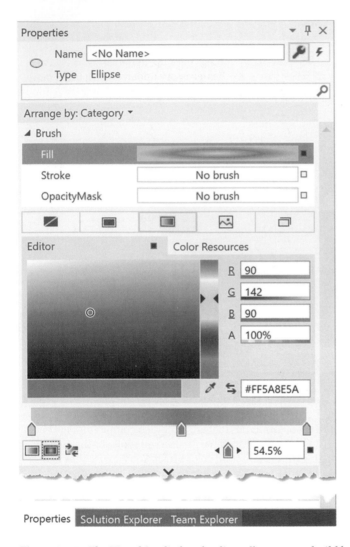

Figure 26-6. *The Visual Studio brush editor allows you to build basic gradient brushes*

When you are done, the IDE will update your XAML with a custom brush, set to a brush-compatible property (the Fill property of the Ellipse in this example) using property-element syntax, as follows:

```
<Ellipse Height="35" Width="35">
  <Ellipse.Fill>
    <RadialGradientBrush>
      <GradientStop Color="#FF77F177" Offset="0"/>
      <GradientStop Color="#FF11E611" Offset="1"/>
```

```
    <GradientStop Color="#FF5A8E5A" Offset="0.545"/>
  </RadialGradientBrush>
  </Ellipse.Fill>
</Ellipse>
```

Configuring Brushes in Code

Now that you have built a custom brush for the XAML definition of your Ellipse, the corresponding C# code is out-of-date, in that it will still render a solid green circle. To sync things back up, update the correct case statement to use the same brush you just created. The following is the necessary update, which looks more complex than you might expect, just because you are converting the hexadecimal value to a proper Color object via the System.Windows.Media.ColorConverter class (see Figure 26-7 for the modified output):

```
case SelectedShape.Circle:
  shapeToRender = new Ellipse() { Height = 35, Width = 35 };
  // Make a RadialGradientBrush in code!
  RadialGradientBrush brush = new RadialGradientBrush();
  brush.GradientStops.Add(new GradientStop(
    (Color)ColorConverter.ConvertFromString("#FF77F177"), 0));
  brush.GradientStops.Add(new GradientStop(
    (Color)ColorConverter.ConvertFromString("#FF11E611"), 1));
  brush.GradientStops.Add(new GradientStop(
    (Color)ColorConverter.ConvertFromString("#FF5A8E5A"), 0.545));
  shapeToRender.Fill = brush;
  break;
```

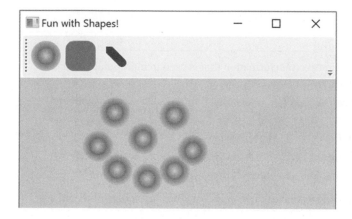

Figure 26-7. *Drawing circles with a bit more pizzazz!*

By the way, you can build GradientStop objects by specifying a simple color as the first constructor parameter using the Colors enumeration, which returns a configured Color object.

```
GradientStop g = new GradientStop(Colors.Aquamarine, 1);
```

Or, if you require even finer control, you can pass in a configured Color object, like so:

```
Color myColor = new Color() { R = 200, G = 100, B = 20, A = 40 };
GradientStop g = new GradientStop(myColor, 34);
```

Of course, the Colors enum and Color class are not limited to gradient brushes. You can use them anytime you need to represent a color value in code.

Configuring Pens

In comparison with brushes, a *pen* is an object for drawing borders of geometries or, in the case of the Line or PolyLine class, the line geometry itself. Specifically, the Pen class allows you to draw a specified thickness, represented by a double value. In addition, a Pen can be configured with the same sort of properties seen in the Shape class, such as starting and stopping pen caps, dot-dash patterns, and so forth. For example, you can add the following markup to a shape to define the pen attributes:

```
<Pen Thickness="10" LineJoin="Round" EndLineCap="Triangle" StartLineCap="Round" />
```

In many cases, you won't need to directly create a Pen object because this will be done indirectly when you assign a value to properties, such as StrokeThickness to a Shape-derived type (as well as other UIElements). However, building a custom Pen object is handy when working with Drawing-derived types (described later in the chapter). Visual Studio does not have a pen editor, *per se*, but it does allow you to configure all the stroke-centric properties of a selected item using the Properties window.

Applying Graphical Transformations

To wrap up the discussion of using shapes, let's address the topic of *transformations*. WPF ships with numerous classes that extend the System.Windows.Media.Transform abstract base class. Table 26-5 documents many of the key out-of-the-box Transform-derived classes.

Table 26-5. *Key Descendants of the* System.Windows.Media.Transform *Type*

Type	Meaning in Life
MatrixTransform	Creates an arbitrary matrix transformation that is used to manipulate objects or coordinate systems in a 2D plane
RotateTransform	Rotates an object clockwise about a specified point in a 2D (x, y) coordinate system
ScaleTransform	Scales an object in the 2D (x, y) coordinate system
SkewTransform	Skews an object in the 2D (x, y) coordinate system
TranslateTransform	Translates (moves) an object in the 2D (x, y) coordinate system
TransformGroup	Represents a composite Transform composed of other Transform objects

Transformations can be applied to any UIElement (e.g., descendants of Shape as well as controls such as Button controls, TextBox controls, and the like). Using these transformation classes, you can render graphical data at a given angle; skew the image across a surface; and expand, shrink, or flip the target item in a variety of ways.

■ **Note** While transformation objects can be used anywhere, you will find them most useful when working with WPF animations and custom control templates. As you will see later in the chapter, you can use WPF animations to incorporate visual cues to the end user for a custom control.

Transformations (or a whole set of them) can be assigned to a target object (e.g., Button, Path, etc.) using two common properties, LayoutTransform and RenderTransform.

The LayoutTransform property is helpful in that the transformation occurs *before* elements are rendered into a layout manager, and therefore the transformation will not affect z-ordering operations (in other words, the transformed image data will not overlap).

The RenderTransform property, on the other hand, occurs after the items are in their container, and therefore it is quite possible that elements can be transformed in such a way that they could overlap each other, based on how they were arranged in the container.

A First Look at Transformations

You will add some transformational logic to your RenderingWithShapes project in just a moment. However, to see transformation objects in action, open Kaxaml and define a simple StackPanel in the root Page or Window, and set the Orientation property to Horizontal. Now, add the following Rectangle, which will be drawn at a 45-degree angle using a RotateTransform object:

```
<!-- A Rectangle with a rotate transformation. -->
<Rectangle Height ="100" Width ="40" Fill ="Red">
  <Rectangle.LayoutTransform>
    <RotateTransform Angle ="45"/>
  </Rectangle.LayoutTransform>
</Rectangle>
```

Here is a <Button> that is skewed across the surface by 20 degrees, using a <SkewTransform>:

```
<!-- A Button with a skew transformation. -->
<Button Content ="Click Me!" Width="95" Height="40">
  <Button.LayoutTransform>
    <SkewTransform AngleX ="20" AngleY ="20"/>
  </Button.LayoutTransform>
</Button>
```

And for good measure, here is an Ellipse that is scaled by 20 degrees with a ScaleTransform (note the values set to the initial Height and Width), as well as a TextBox that has a group of transformation objects applied to it:

```
<!-- An Ellipse that has been scaled by 20%. -->
<Ellipse Fill ="Blue" Width="5" Height="5">
  <Ellipse.LayoutTransform>
    <ScaleTransform ScaleX ="20" ScaleY ="20"/>
  </Ellipse.LayoutTransform>
</Ellipse>
<!-- A TextBox that has been rotated and skewed. -->
<TextBox Text ="Me Too!" Width="50" Height="40">
  <TextBox.LayoutTransform>
    <TransformGroup>
      <RotateTransform Angle ="45"/>
      <SkewTransform AngleX ="5" AngleY ="20"/>
    </TransformGroup>
  </TextBox.LayoutTransform>
</TextBox>
```

Note that when a transformation is applied, you are not required to perform any manual calculations to correctly respond to hit-testing, input focus, or whatnot. The WPF graphics engine handles such tasks on your behalf. For example, in Figure 26-8, you can see that the TextBox is still responsive to keyboard input.

Figure 26-8. *The results of graphical transformation objects*

Transforming Your Canvas Data

Now, let's incorporate some transformational logic into your RenderingWithShapes example. In addition to applying a transformation object to a single item (e.g., Rectangle, TextBox, etc.), you can also apply transformation objects to a layout manager in order to transform all of the internal data. You could, for example, render the entire DockPanel of the main window at an angle.

```
<DockPanel LastChildFill="True">
  <DockPanel.LayoutTransform>
    <RotateTransform Angle="45"/>
  </DockPanel.LayoutTransform>
...
</DockPanel>
```

This is a bit extreme for this example, so let's add a final (less aggressive) feature that allows the user to flip the entire Canvas and all contained graphics. Begin by adding a final ToggleButton to your ToolBar, defined as follows:

```
<ToggleButton Name="flipCanvas" Click="flipCanvas_Click" Content="Flip Canvas!"/>
```

Within the Click event handler, create a RotateTransform object and connect it to the Canvas object via the LayoutTransform property if this new ToggleButton is clicked. If the ToggleButton is not clicked, remove the transformation by setting the same property to null.

```
private void flipCanvas_Click(object sender, RoutedEventArgs e)
{
  if (flipCanvas.IsChecked == truc)
  {
    RotateTransform rotate = new RotateTransform(-180);
    canvasDrawingArea.LayoutTransform = rotate;
  }
  else
  {
    canvasDrawingArea.LayoutTransform = null;
  }
}
```

Run your application and add a bunch of graphics throughout the canvas area, making sure to go edge to edge with them. If you click your new button, you will find that the shape data flows outside of the boundaries of the canvas! This is because you have not defined a clipping region (see Figure 26-9).

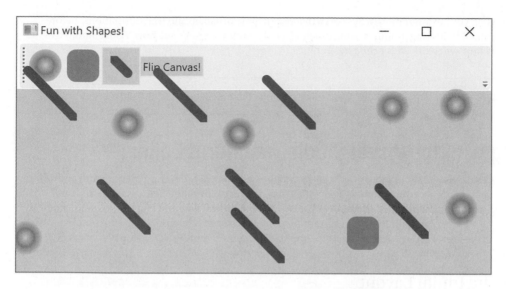

Figure 26-9. *Oops! Your data is flowing outside of the canvas after the transformation!*

Fixing this is trivial. Rather than manually authoring complex clipping-logic code, simply set the ClipToBounds property of the Canvas to true, which prevents child elements from being rendered outside the parent's boundaries. If you run your program again, you'll find the data will not bleed off the canvas boundary.

```
<Canvas ClipToBounds = "True" ... >
```

The last tiny modification to make has to do with the fact that when you flip the canvas by pressing your toggle button and then click the canvas to draw a new shape, the point at which you click is *not* the point where the graphical data is applied. Rather, the data is rendered above the mouse cursor.

To resolve this issue, apply the same transformation object to the shape being drawn before the rendering occurs (via RenderTransform). Here is the crux of the code:

```
private void canvasDrawingArea_MouseLeftButtonDown(object sender, MouseButtonEventArgs e)
{
  //omitted for brevity
  if (flipCanvas.IsChecked == true)
  {
    RotateTransform rotate = new RotateTransform(-180);
    shapeToRender.RenderTransform = rotate;
  }
  // Set top/left to draw in the canvas.
  Canvas.SetLeft(shapeToRender, e.GetPosition(canvasDrawingArea).X);
  Canvas.SetTop(shapeToRender, e.GetPosition(canvasDrawingArea).Y);

  // Draw shape!
  canvasDrawingArea.Children.Add(shapeToRender);
}
```

This wraps up your examination of System.Windows.Shapes, brushes, and transformations. Before looking at the role of rendering graphics using drawings and geometries, let's see how Visual Studio can be used to simplify how you work with primitive graphics.

■ **Source Code**   You can find the RenderingWithShapes project in the Chapter 26 subdirectory.

Working with the Visual Studio Transform Editor

In the previous example, you applied various transformations by manually entering markup and authoring some C# code. While this is certainly useful, you will be happy to know that the latest version of Visual Studio ships with an integrated transformation editor. Recall that any UI element can be the recipient of transformational services, including a layout system containing various UI elements. To illustrate the use of Visual Studio's transform editor, create a new WPF application named FunWithTransforms.

Building the Initial Layout

First, split your initial Grid into two columns using the integrated grid editor (the exact size does not matter). Now, locate the StackPanel control within your Toolbox and add it to take up the entire space of the first column of the Grid; then add three Button controls to the StackPanel, like so:

```
<Grid>
  <Grid.ColumnDefinitions>
    <ColumnDefinition Width="*"/>
    <ColumnDefinition Width="*"/>
  </Grid.ColumnDefinitions>
  <StackPanel Grid.Row="0" Grid.Column="0">
    <Button Name="btnSkew" Content="Skew" Click="Skew"/>
    <Button Name="btnRotate" Content="Rotate" Click="Rotate"/>
    <Button Name="btnFlip" Content="Flip" Click="Flip"/>
  </StackPanel>
</Grid>
```

Add the handlers for the buttons to the code page, like this:

```
private void Skew(object sender, RoutedEventArgs e)
{
}
private void Rotate(object sender, RoutedEventArgs e)
{
}
private void Flip(object sender, RoutedEventArgs e)
{
}
```

To finalize the UI, create a graphic of your choosing (using any of the techniques discussed in this chapter) defined in the second column of the Grid. The markup used in the sample is listed here:

```xml
<Canvas x:Name="myCanvas" Grid.Column="1" Grid.Row="0">
  <Ellipse HorizontalAlignment="Left" VerticalAlignment="Top"
      Height="186"  Width="92" Stroke="Black"
      Canvas.Left="20" Canvas.Top="31">
    <Ellipse.Fill>
      <RadialGradientBrush>
        <GradientStop Color="#FF951ED8" Offset="0.215"/>
        <GradientStop Color="#FF2FECB0" Offset="1"/>
      </RadialGradientBrush>
    </Ellipse.Fill>
  </Ellipse>
  <Ellipse HorizontalAlignment="Left" VerticalAlignment="Top"
      Height="101" Width="110" Stroke="Black"
      Canvas.Left="122" Canvas.Top-"126">
    <Ellipse.Fill>
      <LinearGradientBrush EndPoint="0.5,1" StartPoint="0.5,0">
        <GradientStop Color="#FFB91DDC" Offset="0.355"/>
        <GradientStop Color="#FFB0381D" Offset="1"/>
      </LinearGradientBrush>
    </Ellipse.Fill>
  </Ellipse>
</Canvas>
```

Figure 26-10 shows the final layout for the example.

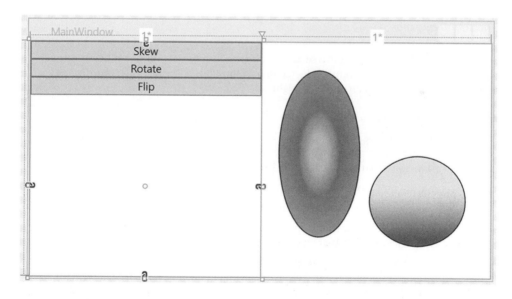

Figure 26-10. *The layout of your transformation example*

Applying Transformations at Design Time

As mentioned, Visual Studio provides an integrated Transform editor, which can be found in the Properties panel. Locate this area, and make sure you expand the Transform section to view the RenderTransform and LayoutTransform sections of the editor (see Figure 26-11).

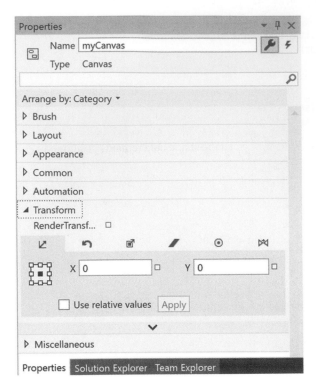

Figure 26-11. *The Transform editor*

Similar to the Brushes section, the Transform section provides a number of tabs to configure various types of graphical transformation to the currently selected item. Table 26-6 describes each transformation option, listed in the order of evaluating each tab left to right.

Table 26-6. *Blend Transformation Options*

Transformation Option	Meaning in Life
Translate	Allows you to offset the location of an item on an X, Y position.
Rotate	Allows you to rotate an item on a 360-degree angle.
Scale	Allows you to grow or shrink an item by a factor in the X and Y directions.
Skew	Allows you to skew the bounding box containing the selected item by a factor in the X and Y directions.
Center Point	When you rotate or flip an object, the item moves relative to a fixed point, called the object's center point. By default, an object's center point is located at the object's center; however, this transformation allows you to change an object's center point in order to rotate or flip the object around a different point.
Flip	Flips a selected item based on an X or Y center point.

I suggest you test each of these transformations using your custom shape as a target (just press Ctrl+Z to undo the previous operation). Like many other aspects of the Transform Properties panel, each transformation section has a unique set of configuration options, which should become fairly understandable as you tinker. For example, the Skew transform editor allows you to set the X and Y skew values, the Flip transform editor allows you to flip on the x- or y-axis, and so forth.

Transforming the Canvas in Code

The implementation of each Click event handler will be more or less the same. You will configure a transformation object and assign it to the myCanvas object. Then, when you run the application, you can click a button to see the result of the applied transformation. Here is the complete code for each event handler (notice that you are setting the LayoutTransform property so the shape data remains positioned relative to the parent container):

```
private void Flip(object sender, System.Windows.RoutedEventArgs e)
{
  myCanvas.LayoutTransform = new ScaleTransform(-1, 1);
}


private void Rotate(object sender, System.Windows.RoutedEventArgs e)
{
  myCanvas.LayoutTransform = new RotateTransform(180);
}


private void Skew(object sender, System.Windows.RoutedEventArgs e)
{
  myCanvas.LayoutTransform = new SkewTransform(40, -20);
}
```

■ **Source Code**   You can find the FunWithTransformations project in the Chapter 26 subdirectory.

Rendering Graphical Data Using Drawings and Geometries

While the Shape types allow you to generate any sort of interactive two-dimensional surface, they entail quite a bit of memory overhead due to their rich inheritance chain. And though the Path class can help remove some of this overhead using contained geometries (rather than a large collection of other shapes), WPF provides a sophisticated drawing and geometry programming interface that renders even more lightweight 2D vector images.

The entry point into this API is the abstract System.Windows.Media.Drawing class (in PresentationCore.dll), which on its own does little more than define a bounding rectangle to hold the rendering. The Drawing class is significantly more lightweight than Shape, given that neither UIElement nor FrameworkElement is in the inheritance chain.

WPF provides various classes that extend Drawing, each of which represents a particular way of drawing the content, as described in Table 26-7.

Table 26-7. *WPF Drawing-Derived Types*

Type	Meaning in Life
DrawingGroup	Used to combine a collection of separate Drawing-derived objects into a single composite rendering.
GeometryDrawing	Used to render 2D shapes in a very lightweight manner.
GlyphRunDrawing	Used to render textual data using WPF graphical rendering services.
ImageDrawing	Used to render an image file, or geometry set, into a bounding rectangle.
VideoDrawing	Used to play an audio file or video file. This type can only be fully exploited using procedural code. If you would like to play videos via XAML, the MediaPlayer type is a better choice.

Because they are more lightweight, Drawing-derived types do not have intrinsic support for handling input events, as they are not UIElements or FrameworkElements (although it is possible to programmatically perform hit-testing logic).

Another key difference between Drawing-derived types and Shape-derived types is that Drawing-derived types have no ability to render themselves, as they do not derive from UIElement! Rather, derived types must be placed within a hosting object (specifically, DrawingImage, DrawingBrush, or DrawingVisual) to display their content.

DrawingImage allows you to place drawing and geometries inside a WPF Image control, which typically is used to display data from an external file. DrawingBrush allows you to build a brush based on a drawing and its geometries in order to set a property that requires a brush. Finally, DrawingVisual is used only in the "visual" layer of graphical rendering, which is driven completely via C# code.

Although using drawings is a bit more complex than using simple shapes, this decoupling of graphical composition from graphical rendering makes the Drawing-derived types much more lightweight than the Shape-derived types, while still retaining key services.

Building a DrawingBrush Using Geometries

Earlier in this chapter, you filled a Path with a group of geometries, like so:

```
<Path Fill = "Orange" Stroke = "Blue" StrokeThickness = "3">
  <Path.Data>
    <GeometryGroup>
      <EllipseGeometry Center = "75,70" RadiusX = "30" RadiusY = "30" />
    <RectangleGeometry Rect = "25,55 100 30" />
    <LineGeometry StartPoint="0,0" EndPoint="70,30" />
    <LineGeometry StartPoint="70,30" EndPoint="0,30" />
  </GeometryGroup>
  </Path.Data>
</Path>
```

By doing this, you gain interactivity from Path but are still fairly lightweight given your geometries. However, if you want to render the same output and have no need for any (out-of-the-box) interactivity, you can place the same <GeometryGroup> inside a DrawingBrush, like this:

```
<DrawingBrush>
  <DrawingBrush.Drawing>
    <GeometryDrawing>
```

```
        <GeometryDrawing.Geometry>
          <GeometryGroup>
              <EllipseGeometry Center = "75,70" RadiusX = "30" RadiusY = "30" />
              <RectangleGeometry Rect = "25,55 100 30" />
              <LineGeometry StartPoint="0,0" EndPoint="70,30" />
              <LineGeometry StartPoint="70,30" EndPoint="0,30" />
            </GeometryGroup>
        </GeometryDrawing.Geometry>
        <!-- A custom pen to draw the borders. -->
        <GeometryDrawing.Pen>
            <Pen Brush="Blue" Thickness="3"/>
        </GeometryDrawing.Pen>
        <!-- A custom brush to fill the interior. -->
        <GeometryDrawing.Brush>
            <SolidColorBrush Color="Orange"/>
        </GeometryDrawing.Brush>
      </GeometryDrawing>
    </DrawingBrush.Drawing>
</DrawingBrush>
```

When you place a group of geometries into a DrawingBrush, you also need to establish the Pen object used to draw the boundaries because you no longer inherit a Stroke property from the Shape base class. Here, you created a <Pen> with the same settings used in the Stroke and StrokeThickness values of the previous Path example.

Furthermore, since you no longer inherit a Fill property from Shape, you also need to use property element syntax to define a brush object to use for the <DrawingGeometry>, which here is a solid colored orange brush, just like the previous Path settings.

Painting with the DrawingBrush

Now that you have a DrawingBrush, you can use it to set the value of any property requiring a brush object. For example, if you are authoring this markup in Kaxaml, you could use property-element syntax to paint your drawing over the entire surface of a Page, like so:

```
<Page
  xmlns="http://schemas.microsoft.com/winfx/2006/xaml/presentation"
  xmlns:x="http://schemas.microsoft.com/winfx/2006/xaml">
  <Page.Background>
    <DrawingBrush>
    <!-- Same DrawingBrush as seen above. -->
    </DrawingBrush>
  </Page.Background>
</Page>
```

Or, you can use this <DrawingBrush> to set a different brush-compatible property, such as the Background property of a Button.

```
<Page
  xmlns="http://schemas.microsoft.com/winfx/2006/xaml/presentation"
  xmlns:x="http://schemas.microsoft.com/winfx/2006/xaml">
  <Button Height="100" Width="100">
```

```
<Button.Background>
  <DrawingBrush>
  <!-- Same DrawingBrush as seen above. -->
  </DrawingBrush>
</Button.Background>
</Button>
</Page>
```

No matter which brush-compatible property you set with your custom `<DrawingBrush>`, the bottom line is you are rendering a 2D vector image with much less overhead than the same 2D image rendered with shapes.

Containing Drawing Types in a DrawingImage

The `DrawingImage` type allows you to plug your drawing geometry into a WPF `<Image>` control. Consider the following:

```
<Image>
  <Image.Source>
    <DrawingImage>
      <DrawingImage.Drawing>
        <!--Same GeometryDrawing from above -->
      </DrawingImage.Drawing>
    </DrawingImage>
  </Image.Source>
</Image>
```

In this case, your `<GeometryDrawing>` has been placed into a `<DrawingImage>`, rather than a `<DrawingBrush>`. Using this `<DrawingImage>`, you can set the `Source` property of the `Image` control.

Working with Vector Images

As you might agree, it would be quite challenging for a graphic artist to create a complex vector-based image using the tools and techniques provided by Visual Studio. Graphic artists have their own set of tools that can produce amazing vector graphics. Neither Visual Studio nor its companion Expression Blend for Visual Studio have that type of design power. Before you can import vector images into WPF application, they must be converted into Path expressions. At that point, you can program against the generated object model using Visual Studio.

■ **Note** You can find the image being used (`LaserSign.svg`) as well as the exported path (`LaserSign.xaml`) data in the `Chapter 26` folder of the download files. The image is originally from Wikipedia, located in this article: `https://en.wikipedia.org/wiki/Hazard_symbol`.

Converting a Sample Vector Graphic File into XAML

Before you can import complex graphical data (such as vector graphics) into a WPF application, you need to convert the graphics into path data. As an example of how to do this, start with a sample `.svg` image file, such as the laser sign referenced in the preceding note. Then download and install an open source tool called Inkscape (located at `www.inkscape.org`). Using Inkscape, open the `LaserSign.svg` file from the chapter download. You might be prompted to upgrade the format. Fill in the selections as shown in Figure 26-12.

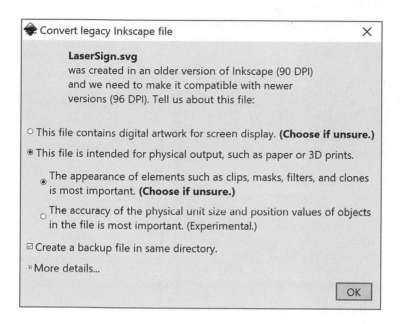

Figure 26-12. *Upgrading the SVG file to the latest format in InkScape*

The next steps will seem a bit odd at first, but once you get over the oddity, it is a simple way to convert vector images to the correct XAML. When you have the image the way you want it, select the File ➤ Print menu option. Next, select the Microsoft XPS Document Writer as the printer target and then click Print. On the next screen, enter a file name and select where the file should be saved; then click Save. Now you have a complete *.xps (or *.oxps) file.

■ **Note**   Depending on a number of variables with your system configuration, the generated file will have either the .xps or .oxps extension. Either way, the process works the same.

The *.xps and *.oxps formats are actually .zip files. Rename the extension of the file to .zip and you can open the file in File Explorer (or 7-zip, or your favorite archive tool). You will see that it contains the hierarchy shown in Figure 26-13.

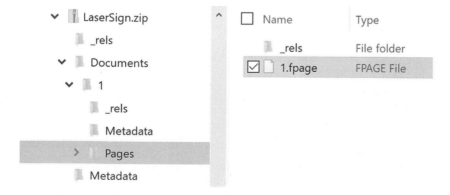

Figure 26-13. *The folder hierarchy of the printed XPS file*

The file that you need is in the Pages directory (Documents/1/Pages) and is named 1.fpage. Open the file with a text editor and copy everything except the <FixedPage> open and closing tags. The path data can then be copied into the Kaxaml and placed inside a Canvas in the main Window. Your image will show in the XAML window!

Importing the Graphical Data into a WPF Project

At this point, create a new WPF application named InteractiveLaserSign. Resize the Window to a Height of 625 and Width of 675, and replace the Grid with a Canvas:

```
<Window x:Class="InteractiveLaserSign.MainWindow"
        xmlns="http://schemas.microsoft.com/winfx/2006/xaml/presentation"
        xmlns:x="http://schemas.microsoft.com/winfx/2006/xaml"
        xmlns:d="http://schemas.microsoft.com/expression/blend/2008"
        xmlns:mc="http://schemas.openxmlformats.org/markup-compatibility/2006"
        xmlns:local="clr-namespace:InteractiveLaserSign"
        mc:Ignorable="d"
        Title="MainWindow" Height="625" Width="675">
    <Canvas>
    </Canvas>
</Window>
```

Copy the entire XAML from the 1.fpage file (excluding the outer FixedPage tag) and paste into the Canvas control. View the Window in design mode, and you will see the sign reproduced in your application.

If you view the Document Outline, you will see that each part of the image is represented as a XAML Path element. If you resize your Window, the image quality stays the same, regardless of how big you make the window. This is because images represented by Path elements are rendered using the drawing engine and math instead of flipping pixels.

Interacting with the Sign

Recall that routed event tunnel and bubble, so any Path clicked inside the Canvas can be handled by a click event handler on the canvas. Update the Canvas markup to the following:

```
<Canvas MouseLeftButtonDown="Canvas_MouseLeftButtonDown">
```

Add the event handler with the following code:

```
private void Canvas_MouseLeftButtonDown(object sender, MouseButtonEventArgs e)
{
  if (e.OriginalSource is Path p)
  {
    p.Fill = new SolidColorBrush(Colors.Red);
  }
}
```

Now, run your application. Click the lines to see the effects.

You now understand the process of generating Path data for complex graphics and how to interact with the graphical data in code. As you might agree, the ability for professional graphic artists to generate complex graphical data and export the data as XAML is extremely powerful. Once the graphical data has been generated, developers can import the markup and program against the object model.

■ **Source Code**   You can find the InteractiveLaserSign project in the Chapter 26 subdirectory.

Rendering Graphical Data Using the Visual Layer

The final option for rendering graphical data with WPF is termed the *visual layer*. As mentioned, you can gain access to this layer only through code (it is not XAML-friendly). While a vast majority of your WPF applications will work just fine using shapes, drawings, and geometries, the visual layer does provide the fastest possible way to render huge amounts of graphical data. This low-level graphical layer can also be useful when you need to render a single image over a large area. For example, if you need to fill the background of a window with a plain, static image, the visual layer is the fastest way to do so. It can also be useful if you need to change between window backgrounds quickly, based on user input or whatnot.

I won't spend too much time delving into the details of this aspect of WPF programming, but let's build a small sample program to illustrate the basics.

The Visual Base Class and Derived Child Classes

The abstract System.Windows.Media.Visual class type supplies a minimal set of services (rendering, hit-testing, transformations) to render graphics, but it does not provide support for additional nonvisual services, which can lead to code bloat (input events, layout services, styles, and data binding). The Visual class is an abstract base class. You need to use one of the derived types to perform actual rendering operations. WPF provides a handful of subclasses, including DrawingVisual, Viewport3DVisual, and ContainerVisual.

In this example, you will focus only on DrawingVisual, a lightweight drawing class that is used to render shapes, images, or text.

A First Look at Using the DrawingVisual Class

To render data onto a surface using DrawingVisual, you need to take the following basic steps:

1.   Obtain a DrawingContext object from the DrawingVisual class.

2.   Use the DrawingContext to render the graphical data.

These two steps represent the bare minimum necessary for rendering some data to a surface. However, if you want the graphical data you've rendered to be responsive to hit-testing calculations (which would be important for adding user interactivity), you will also need to perform these additional steps:

1.   Update the logical and visual trees maintained by the container upon which you are rendering.

2.   Override two virtual methods from the FrameworkElement class, allowing the container to obtain the visual data you have created.

You will examine these final two steps in a bit. First, to illustrate how you can use the DrawingVisual class to render 2D data, create a new WPF application named RenderingWithVisuals. Your first goal is to use a DrawingVisual to dynamically assign data to a WPF Image control. Begin by updating the XAML of your window to handle the Loaded event, like so:

```
<Window x:Class="RenderingWithVisuals.MainWindow"
        <!--omitted for brevity -->
        Title="Fun With Visual Layer" Height="350" Width="525"
        Loaded="MainWindow_Loaded">
```

Next, replace the Grid with a StackPanel and add an Image in the StackPanel, like this:

```
<StackPanel Background="AliceBlue" Name="myStackPanel">
  <Image Name="myImage" Height="80"/>
</StackPanel>
```

Your <Image> control does not yet have a Source value because that will happen at runtime. The Loaded event will do the work of building the in-memory graphical data, using a DrawingBrush object. Here is the implementation of the Loaded event handler:

```
private void MainWindow_Loaded(object sender, RoutedEventArgs e)
{
  const int TextFontSize = 30;
  // Make a System.Windows.Media.FormattedText object.
  FormattedText text = new FormattedText("Hello Visual Layer!",
    new System.Globalization.CultureInfo("en-us"),
    FlowDirection.LeftToRight,
    new Typeface(this.FontFamily, FontStyles.Italic, FontWeights.DemiBold, FontStretches.
    UltraExpanded),
    TextFontSize,
    Brushes.Green,
    null,
    VisualTreeHelper.GetDpi(this).PixelsPerDip);
  // Create a DrawingVisual, and obtain the DrawingContext.
  DrawingVisual drawingVisual = new DrawingVisual();
  using(DrawingContext drawingContext = drawingVisual.RenderOpen())
  {
    // Now, call any of the methods of DrawingContext to render data.
    drawingContext.DrawRoundedRectangle(Brushes.Yellow, new Pen(Brushes.Black, 5),
      new Rect(5, 5, 450, 100), 20, 20);
    drawingContext.DrawText(text, new Point(20, 20));
  }
  // Dynamically make a bitmap, using the data in the DrawingVisual.
  RenderTargetBitmap bmp = new RenderTargetBitmap(500, 100, 100, 90, PixelFormats.Pbgra32);
  bmp.Render(drawingVisual);
  // Set the source of the Image control!
  myImage.Source = bmp;
}
```

This code introduces a number of new WPF classes, which I will briefly comment on here (be sure to check the .NET Framework 4.7 SDK documentation for full details if you are interested). The method begins by creating a new FormattedText object that represents the textual portion of the in-memory image you are constructing. As you can see, the constructor allows you to specify numerous attributes such as font size, font family, foreground color, and the text itself.

Next, you obtain the necessary DrawingContext object via a call to RenderOpen() on the DrawingVisual instance. Here, you are rendering a colored, rounded rectangle into the DrawingVisual, followed by your formatted text. In both cases, you are placing the graphical data into the DrawingVisual using hard-coded values, which is not necessarily a great idea for production but is fine for this simple test.

The last few statements map the DrawingVisual into a RenderTargetBitmap object, which is a member of the System.Windows.Media.Imaging namespace. This class will take a visual object and transform it into an in-memory bitmap image. After this point, you set the Source property of the Image control, and sure enough, you will see the output in Figure 26-14.

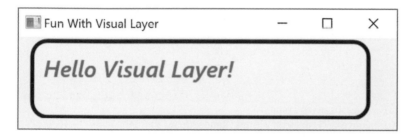

Figure 26-14. *Using the visual layer to render an in-memory bitmap*

Rendering Visual Data to a Custom Layout Manager

While it is interesting to use DrawingVisual to paint onto the background of a WPF control, it is perhaps more common to build a custom layout manager (Grid, StackPanel, Canvas, etc.) that uses the visual layer internally to render its content. After you have created such a custom layout manager, you can plug it into a normal Window (or Page or UserControl) and have a part of the UI using a highly optimized rendering agent while the noncritical aspects of the hosting Window are using shapes and drawings for the remainder of the graphical data.

If you don't require the extra functionality provided by a dedicated layout manager, you could opt to simply extend FrameworkElement, which does have the necessary infrastructure to also contain visual items. To illustrate how this could be done, insert a new class to your project named CustomVisualFrameworkElement. Extend this class from FrameworkElement and import the System.Windows, System.Windows.Input, and System.Windows.Media namespaces.

This class will maintain a member variable of type VisualCollection, which contains two fixed DrawingVisual objects (of course, you could add new members to this collection via a mouse operation, but this example will keep it simple). Update your class with the following new functionality:

```
public class CustomVisualFrameworkElement : FrameworkElement
{
    // A collection of all the visuals we are building.
    VisualCollection theVisuals;
    public CustomVisualFrameworkElement()
    {
```

```
  // Fill the VisualCollection with a few DrawingVisual objects.
  // The ctor arg represents the owner of the visuals.
  theVisuals = new VisualCollection(this) { AddRect(),AddCircle()};
}
private Visual AddCircle()
{
  DrawingVisual drawingVisual = new DrawingVisual();
  // Retrieve the DrawingContext in order to create new drawing content.
  using (DrawingContext drawingContext = drawingVisual.RenderOpen())
  {
    // Create a circle and draw it in the DrawingContext.
    Rect rect = new Rect(new Point(160, 100), new Size(320, 80));
    drawingContext.DrawEllipse(Brushes.DarkBlue, null, new Point(70, 90), 40, 50);
  }
    return drawingVisual;
}
private Visual AddRect()
{
  DrawingVisual drawingVisual = new DrawingVisual();
  using (DrawingContext drawingContext = drawingVisual.RenderOpen())
  {
    Rect rect = new Rect(new Point(160, 100), new Size(320, 80));
    drawingContext.DrawRectangle(Brushes.Tomato, null, rect);
  }
  return drawingVisual;
  }
}
```

Now, before you can use this custom FrameworkElement in your Window, you must override two key virtual methods mentioned previously, both of which are called internally by WPF during the rendering process. The GetVisualChild() method returns a child at the specified index from the collection of child elements. The read-only VisualChildrenCount property returns the number of visual child elements within this visual collection. Both methods are easy to implement because you can delegate the real work to the VisualCollection member variable.

```
protected override int VisualChildrenCount => theVisuals.Count;
protected override Visual GetVisualChild(int index)
{
  // Value must be greater than zero, so do a sanity check.
  if (index < 0 || index >= theVisuals.Count)
  {
    throw new ArgumentOutOfRangeException();
  }
return theVisuals[index];
}
```

You now have just enough functionality to test your custom class. Update the XAML description of the Window to add one of your CustomVisualFrameworkElement objects to the existing StackPanel. Doing so will require you to add a custom XML namespace that maps to your .NET namespace.

```
<Window x:Class="RenderingWithVisuals.MainWindow"
  xmlns="http://schemas.microsoft.com/winfx/2006/xaml/presentation"
  xmlns:x="http://schemas.microsoft.com/winfx/2006/xaml"
```

```
    xmlns:local="clr-namespace:RenderingWithVisuals"
    Title="Fun with the Visual Layer" Height="350" Width="525"
    Loaded="Window_Loaded" WindowStartupLocation="CenterScreen">
        <StackPanel Background="AliceBlue" Name="myStackPanel">
            <Image Name="myImage" Height="80"/>
            <local:CustomVisualFrameworkElement/>
        </StackPanel>
    </Window>
```

When you run the program, you will see the result shown in Figure 26-15.

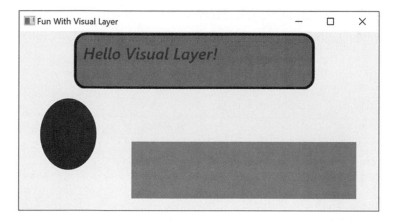

Figure 26-15. *Using the visual layer to render data to a custom* FrameworkElement

Responding to Hit-Test Operations

Because DrawingVisual does not have any of the infrastructure of UIElement or FrameworkElement, you will need to programmatically add in the ability to calculate hit-test operations. Thankfully, this is fairly easy to do in the visual layer because of the concept of *logical* and *visual* trees. As it turns out, when you author a blob of XAML, you are essentially building a logical tree of elements. However, behind every logical tree is a much richer description known as the visual tree, which contains lower-level rendering instructions.

Chapter 27 will delve into these trees in more detail, but for now, just understand that until you register your custom visuals with these data structures, you will not be able to perform hit-testing operations. Luckily, the VisualCollection container does this on your behalf (which explains why you needed to pass in a reference to the custom FrameworkElement as a constructor argument).

First, update the CustomVisualFrameworkElement class to handle the MouseDown event in the class constructor using standard C# syntax, like so:

```
this.MouseDown += CustomVisualFrameworkElement_MouseDown;
```

The implementation of this handler will call the VisualTreeHelper.HitTest() method to see whether the mouse is within the boundaries of one of the rendered visuals. To do this, you specify as a parameter to HitTest() a HitTestResultCallback delegate that will perform the calculations. If you click a visual, you will toggle between a skewed rendering of the visual and the original rendering. Add the following methods to your CustomVisualFrameworkElement class:

```
void CustomVisualFrameworkElement_MouseDown(object sender, MouseButtonEventArgs e)
{
    // Figure out where the user clicked.
    Point pt = e.GetPosition((UIElement)sender);
```

1093

```
// Call helper function via delegate to see if we clicked on a visual.
VisualTreeHelper.HitTest(this, null,
  new HitTestResultCallback(myCallback), new PointHitTestParameters(pt));
}

public HitTestResultBehavior myCallback(HitTestResult result)
{
    // Toggle between a skewed rendering and normal rendering,
    // if a visual was clicked.
    if (result.VisualHit.GetType() == typeof(DrawingVisual))
    {
      if (((DrawingVisual)result.VisualHit).Transform == null)
      {
        ((DrawingVisual)result.VisualHit).Transform = new SkewTransform(7, 7);
      }
      else
      {
        ((DrawingVisual)result.VisualHit).Transform = null;
      }
    }

    // Tell HitTest() to stop drilling into the visual tree.
    return HitTestResultBehavior.Stop;
}
```

Now, run your program once again. You should now be able to click either rendered visual and see the transformation in action! While this is just a simple example of working with the visual layer of WPF, remember that you make use of the same brushes, transformations, pens, and layout managers as you would when working with XAML. As a result, you already know quite a bit about working with this Visual-derived classes.

■ **Source Code**   You can find the RenderingWithVisuals project in the Chapter 26 subdirectory.

That wraps up your investigation of the graphical rendering services of Windows Presentation Foundation. While you learned a number of interesting topics, the reality is that you have only scratched the surface of WPF's graphical capabilities. I will leave it in your hands to dig deeper into the topics of shapes, drawings, brushes, transformations, and visuals (and, to be sure, you will see some additional details of these topics in the remaining WPF chapters).

Summary

Because Windows Presentation Foundation is such a graphically intensive GUI API, it comes as no surprise that we are given a number of ways to render graphical output. This chapter began by examining each of three ways a WPF application can do so (shapes, drawings, and visuals) and discussed various rendering primitives such as brushes, pens, and transformations.

Remember that when you need to build interactive 2D renderings, shapes make the process very simple. However, static, noninteractive renderings can be rendered in a more optimal manner by using drawings and geometries, while the visual layer (accessible only in code) gives you maximum control and performance.

■ ■ ■

CHAPTER 27

WPF Resources, Animations, Styles, and Templates

This chapter introduces you to three important (and interrelated) topics that will deepen your understanding of the Windows Presentation Foundation (WPF) API. The first order of business is to learn the role of *logical resources*. As you will see, the logical resource (also known as an *object resource*) system is a way to name and refer to commonly used objects within a WPF application. While logical resources are often authored in XAML, they can also be defined in procedural code.

Next, you will learn how to define, execute, and control an animation sequence. Despite what you might think, WPF animations are not limited to video game or multimedia applications. Under the WPF API, animations can be as subtle as making a button appear to glow when it receives focus or expanding the size of a selected row in a DataGrid. Understanding animations is a key aspect of building custom control templates (as you'll see in later in this chapter).

You'll then explore the role of WPF styles and templates. Much like a web page that uses CSS or the ASP.NET theme engine, a WPF application can define a common look and feel for a set of controls. You can define these styles in markup and store them as object resources for later use, and you can also apply them dynamically at runtime. The final example will teach you how to build custom control templates.

Understanding the WPF Resource System

Your first task is to examine the topic of embedding and accessing application resources. WPF supports two flavors of resources. The first is a *binary resource*, and this category typically includes items most programmers consider to be resources in the traditional sense (embedded image files or sound clips, icons used by the application, and so on).

The second flavor, termed *object resources* or *logical resources*, represents a named .NET object that can be packaged and reused throughout the application. While any .NET object can be packaged as an object resource, logical resources are particularly helpful when working with graphical data of any sort, given that you can define commonly used graphic primitives (brushes, pens, animations, etc.) and refer to them when required.

Working with Binary Resources

Before getting to the topic of object resources, let's quickly examine how to package up *binary resources* such as icons or image files (e.g., company logos or images for an animation) into your applications. If you'd like to follow along, create a new WPF application named BinaryResourcesApp. Update the markup for your initial window to handle the Window Loaded event and to use a DockPanel as the layout root, like so:

```
<Window x:Class="BinaryResourcesApp.MainWindow"
  <!-- Omitted for brevity -->
    Title="Fun with Binary Resources" Height="500" Width="649" Loaded="MainWindow_OnLoaded">
  <DockPanel LastChildFill="True">
  </DockPanel>
</Window>
```

Now, let's say your application needs to display one of three image files inside part of the window, based on user input. The WPF Image control can be used to display not only a typical image file (*.bmp, *.gif, *.ico, *.jpg, *.png, *.wdp, or *.tiff) but also data in a DrawingImage (as you saw in Chapter 26). You might build a UI for your window that supports a DockPanel containing a simple toolbar with Next and Previous buttons. Below this toolbar you can place an Image control, which currently does not have a value set to the Source property, like so:

```
<DockPanel LastChildFill="True">
  <ToolBar Height="60" Name="picturePickerToolbar" DockPanel.Dock="Top">
    <Button x:Name="btnPreviousImage" Height="40" Width="100" BorderBrush="Black"
            Margin="5" Content="Previous" Click="btnPreviousImage_Click"/>
    <Button x:Name="btnNextImage" Height="40" Width="100" BorderBrush="Black"
            Margin="5" Content="Next" Click="btnNextImage_Click"/>
  </ToolBar>

  <!-- We will fill this Image in code. -->
  <Border BorderThickness="2" BorderBrush="Green">
    <Image x:Name="imageHolder" Stretch="Fill" />
  </Border>
</DockPanel>
```

Next, add the following empty event handlers (unless you used Visual Studio to add the handlers, in which case they are already in your code file):

```
private void MainWindow_OnLoaded(object sender, RoutedEventArgs e)
{
}
private void btnPreviousImage_Click(object sender, RoutedEventArgs e)
{
}
private void btnNextImage_Click(object sender, RoutedEventArgs e)
{
}
```

When the window loads, images will be added to a collection that the Next and Previous buttons will cycle through. Now that the application framework is in place, let's examine the different options for implementing this.

Including Loose Resource Files in a Project

One option is to ship your image files as a set of loose files in a subdirectory of the application install path. Start by adding a new folder (named Images) to your project. Into this folder add some images by right-clicking and selecting Add ➤ Existing Item. Make sure to change the file filter in the Add Existing Item dialog to *.* so the image files show. You can add your own image files or use the three image files named Deer.jpg, Dogs.jpg, and Welcome.jpg from the downloadable code.

Configuring the Loose Resources

To copy the content of your \Images folder to the \bin\Debug folder when the project builds, begin by selecting all the images in Solution Explorer. Now, with these images still selected, right-click and select Properties to open the Properties window. Set the Build Action property to Content, and set the Copy to Output Directory property to Copy always (see Figure 27-1).

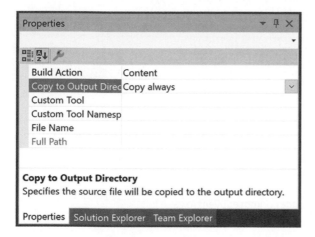

Figure 27-1. *Configuring the image data to be copied to your output directory*

■ **Note**   You could also select Copy if Newer, which will save you time if you're building large projects with a lot of content. For this example, Copy always works just fine.

If you build your project, you can now click the Show All Files button of Solution Explorer and view the copied Image folder under your \bin\Debug directory (you might need to click the Refresh button).

Programmatically Loading an Image

WPF provides a class named BitmapImage, which is part of the System.Windows.Media.Imaging namespace. This class allows you to load data from an image file whose location is represented by a System.Uri object. Add a List<BitmapImage> to hold all of the images, as well as an int to store the index of the currently displayed image.

```
// A List of BitmapImage files.
List<BitmapImage> _images = new List<BitmapImage>();
// Current position in the list.
private int _currImage = 0;
```

In the Loaded event of your window, fill the list of images and then set the Image control source to the first image in the list.

```
private void MainWindow_OnLoaded(object sender, RoutedEventArgs e)
{
  try
  {
    string path = Environment.CurrentDirectory;
    // Load these images from disk when the window loads.
    _images.Add(new BitmapImage(new Uri($@"{path}\Images\Deer.jpg")));
    _images.Add(new BitmapImage(new Uri($@"{path}\Images\Dogs.jpg")));
    _images.Add(new BitmapImage(new Uri($@"{path}\Images\Welcome.jpg")));
    // Show first image in the List.
    imageHolder.Source = _images[_currImage];
  }
  catch (Exception ex)
  {
    MessageBox.Show(ex.Message);
  }
}
```

Next, implement the previous and next handlers to loop through the images. If the user gets to the end of the list, start them back at the beginning, and vice versa.

```
private void btnPreviousImage_Click(object sender, RoutedEventArgs e)
{
  if (--_currImage < 0)
  {
    _currImage = _images.Count - 1;
  }
  imageHolder.Source = _images[_currImage];
}
private void btnNextImage_Click(object sender, RoutedEventArgs e)
{
  if (++_currImage >= _images.Count)
  {
    _currImage = 0;
  }
  imageHolder.Source = _images[_currImage];
}
```

At this point, you can run your program and flip through each picture.

Embedding Application Resources

If you'd rather configure your image files to be compiled directly into your .NET assembly as binary resources, select the image files in Solution Explorer (in the \Images folder, not in the \bin\Debug\Images folder). Change the Build Action property to Resource, and set the Copy to Output Directory property to Do not copy (see Figure 27-2).

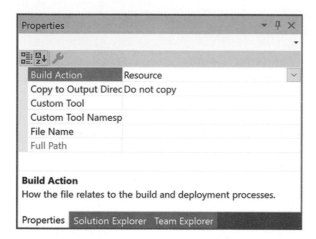

Figure 27-2. Configuring the images to be embedded resources

Now, using Visual Studio's Build menu, select the Clean Solution option to wipe out the current contents of \bin\Debug\Images and then rebuild your project. Refresh Solution Explorer, and observe the absence of data in your \bin\Debug\Images directory. With the current build options, your graphical data is no longer copied to the output folder and is now embedded within the assembly itself. This ensures that the resources exist but also increases the size of your compiled assembly.

You need to modify your code to load these images into your list by extracting them from the compiled assembly.

```
// Extract from the assembly and then load images
_images.Add(new BitmapImage(new Uri(@"/Images/Deer.jpg", UriKind.Relative)));
_images.Add(new BitmapImage(new Uri(@"/Images/Dogs.jpg", UriKind.Relative)));
_images.Add(new BitmapImage(new Uri(@"/Images/Welcome.jpg", UriKind.Relative)));
```

In this case, you no longer need to determine the installation path and can simply list the resources by name, which takes into account the name of the original subdirectory. Also notice, when you create your Uri objects, you specify a UriKind value of Relative. At this point, your executable is a stand-alone entity that can be run from any location on the machine because all the compiled data is within the binary.

■ **Source Code**   You can find BinaryResourcesApp in the Chapter 27 subdirectory.

Working with Object (Logical) Resources

When you are building a WPF application, it is common to define a blurb of XAML to use in multiple locations within a window, or perhaps across multiple windows or projects. For example, say you have created the *perfect* linear gradient brush, which consists of ten lines of markup. Now, you want to use that brush as the background color for every Button control in the project (which consists of eight windows) for a total of sixteen Button controls.

The worst thing you could do is to copy and paste the XAML to every control. Clearly, this would be a nightmare to maintain, as you would need to make numerous changes any time you wanted to tweak the look and feel of the brush.

Thankfully, *object resources* allow you to define a blob of XAML, give it a name, and store it in a fitting dictionary for later use. Like a binary resource, object resources are often compiled into the assembly that requires them. However, you don't need to tinker with the Build Action property to do so. As long as you place your XAML into the correct location, the compiler will take care of the rest.

Working with object resources is a big part of WPF development. As you will see, object resources can be far more complex than a custom brush. You can define a XAML-based animation, a 3D rendering, a custom control style, data template, control template, and more, and package each one as a reusable resource.

The Role of the Resources Property

As mentioned, object resources must be placed in a fitting dictionary object to be used across an application. As it stands, every descendant of FrameworkElement supports a Resources property. This property encapsulates a ResourceDictionary object that contains the defined object resources. The ResourceDictionary can hold any type of item because it operates on System.Object types and may be manipulated via XAML or procedural code.

In WPF, all controls, Windows, Pages (used when building navigation applications), and UserControls extend FrameworkElement, so just about all widgets provide access to a ResourceDictionary. Furthermore, the Application class, while not extending FrameworkElement, supports an identically named Resources property for the same purpose.

Defining Window-wide Resources

To begin exploring the role of object resources, create a new WPF application named ObjectResourcesApp and change the initial Grid to a horizontally aligned StackPanel layout manager. Into this StackPanel, define two Button controls like so (you really don't need much to illustrate the role of object resources, so this will do):

```
<StackPanel Orientation="Horizontal">
  <Button Margin="25" Height="200" Width="200" Content="OK" FontSize="20"/>
  <Button Margin="25" Height="200" Width="200" Content="Cancel" FontSize="20"/>
</StackPanel>
```

Now, select the OK button and set the Background color property to a custom brush type using the integrated Brushes editor (discussed in Chapter 26). After you've done so, notice how the brush is embedded within the scope of the <Button> and </Button> tags, as shown here:

```
<Button Margin="25" Height="200" Width="200" Content="OK" FontSize="20">
  <Button.Background>
    <RadialGradientBrush>
      <GradientStop Color="#FFC44EC4" Offset="0" />
      <GradientStop Color="#FF829CEB" Offset="1" />
      <GradientStop Color="#FF793879" Offset="0.669" />
    </RadialGradientBrush>
  </Button.Background>
</Button>
```

To allow the Cancel button to use this brush as well, you should promote the scope of your `<RadialGradientBrush>` to a parent element's resource dictionary. For example, if you move it to the `<StackPanel>`, both buttons can use the same brush because they are child elements of the layout manager. Even better, you could package the brush into the resource dictionary of the `Window` itself so all of the window's content can use it.

When you need to define a resource, you use the property element syntax to set the `Resources` property of the owner. You also give the resource item an `x:Key` value, which will be used by other parts of the window when they want to refer to the object resource. Be aware that `x:Key` and `x:Name` are not the same! The `x:Name` attribute allows you to gain access to the object as a member variable in your code file, while the `x:Key` attribute allows you to refer to an item in a resource dictionary.

Visual Studio allows you to promote a resource to a higher scope using its respective Properties window. To do so, first identify the property that has the complex object you want to package as a resource (the `Background` property, in this example). To the right of the property is a small square that, when clicked, will open a pop-up menu. From it, select the Convert to New Resource option (see Figure 27-3).

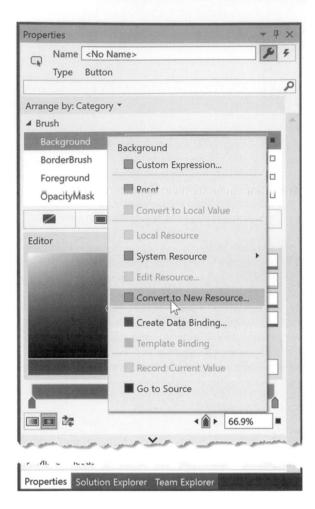

Figure 27-3. *Moving a complex object into a resource container*

You are asked to name your resource (myBrush) and specify where to place it. For this example, leave the default selection of the current document (see Figure 27-4).

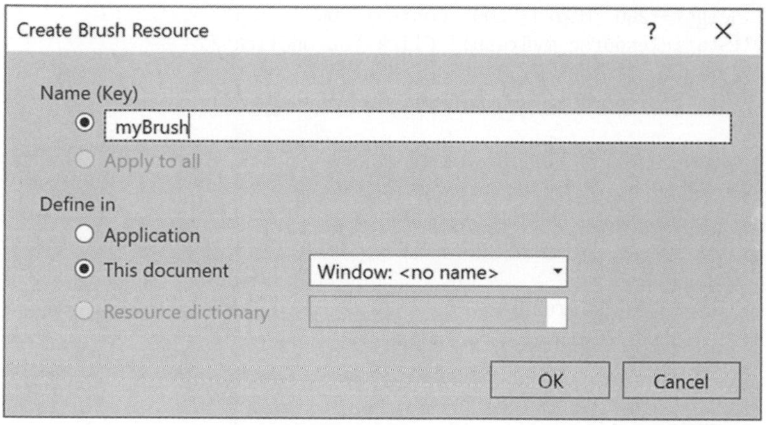

Create Brush Resource   ?   ✕

Name (Key)

○ | myBrush |

○ Apply to all

Define in

○ Application

◉ This document | Window: \<no name> ▾ |

○ Resource dictionary | |

[OK]   [Cancel]

Figure 27-4. *Naming the object resource*

When you're done, you will see the brush has been moved inside the `Window.Resources` tag.

```
<Window.Resources>
  <RadialGradientBrush x:Key="myBrush">
    <GradientStop Color="#FFC44EC4" Offset="0" />
    <GradientStop Color="#FF829CEB" Offset="1" />
    <GradientStop Color="#FF793879" Offset="0.669" />
  </RadialGradientBrush>
</Window.Resources>
```

And the Button control's Background has been updated to use a new resource.

```
<Button Margin="25" Height="200" Width="200" Content="OK"
        FontSize="20" Background="{DynamicResource myBrush}"/>
```

The Create Resource Wizard creates the new resource as a DynamicResource. You will learn about DynamicResources later in the text, but for now, change it to a StaticResource, like this:

```
<Button Margin="25" Height="200" Width="200" Content="OK"
    FontSize="20" Background="{StaticResource myBrush}"/>
```

To see the benefit, update the Cancel Button's Background property to the same StaticResource, and you can see the reuse in action.

```
<Button Margin="25" Height="200" Width="200" Content="Cancel"
    FontSize="20" Background="{StaticResource myBrush}"/>
```

The {StaticResource} Markup Extension

The {StaticResource} markup extension applies the resource only once (on initialization) and stays "connected" to the original object during the life of the application. Some properties (such as gradient stops) will update, but if you create a new Brush, for example, the control will not be updated. To see this in action, add a Name and Click event hander to each Button control, as follows:

1103

```
<Button Name="Ok" Margin="25" Height="200" Width="200" Content="OK"
    FontSize="20" Background="{StaticResource myBrush}" Click="Ok_OnClick"/>
<Button Name="Cancel" Margin="25" Height="200" Width="200" Content="Cancel"
    FontSize="20" Background="{StaticResource myBrush}" Click="Cancel_OnClick"/>
```

Next, add the following code to the Ok_OnClick() event handler:

```
private void Ok_OnClick(object sender, RoutedEventArgs e)
{
  // Get the brush and make a change.
  var b = (RadialGradientBrush)Resources["myBrush"];
  b.GradientStops[1] = new GradientStop(Colors.Black, 0.0);
}
```

■ **Note** You are using the Resources indexer to locate a resource by name here. Be aware, however, that this will throw a runtime exception if the resource can't be found. You could also use the TryFindResource() method, which will not throw a runtime error; it will simply return null if the specified resource can't be located.

When you run the program and click the OK Button, you see the gradients change appropriately. Now add the following code to the Cancel_OnClick() event handler:

```
private void Cancel_OnClick(object sender, RoutedEventArgs e)
{
  // Put a totally new brush into the myBrush slot.
  Resources["myBrush"] = new SolidColorBrush(Colors.Red);
}
```

Run the program again, click the Cancel Button, and nothing happens!

The {DynamicResource} Markup Extension

It is also possible for a property to use the DynamicResource markup extension. To see the difference, change the markup for the Cancel Button to the following:

```
<Button Name="Cancel" Margin="25" Height="200" Width="200" Content="Cancel"
                FontSize="20" Background="{DynamicResource myBrush}" Click="Cancel_OnClick"/>
```

This time, when you click the Cancel Button, the background for the Cancel Button changes, but the background for the OK Button remains the same. This is because the {DynamicResource} markup extension is able to detect whether the underlying keyed object has been replaced with a new object. As you might guess, this requires some extra runtime infrastructure, so you should typically stick to using {StaticResource} unless you know you have an object resource that will be swapped with a different object at runtime and you want all items using that resource to be informed.

Application-Level Resources

When you have object resources in a window's resource dictionary, all items in the window are free to make use of it, but other windows in the application cannot. The solution to share resources across your application is to define the object resource at the application level, rather than at the window level. There is no way to automate this within Visual Studio, so simply cut the current brush object out of the `<Windows.Resources>` scope, and place it in the `<Application.Resources>` scope in your `App.xaml` file.

Now any additional window or control in your application is free to use this same brush. If you want to set the `Background` property for a control, the application-level resources are available for selection, as shown in Figure 27-5.

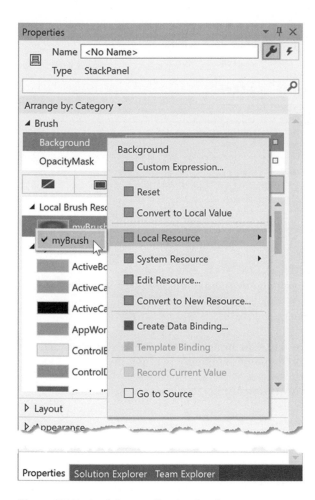

Figure 27-5. *Applying application-level resources*

Defining Merged Resource Dictionaries

Application-level resources are a quite often good enough, but they don't help reuse across projects. In this case, you want to define what is known as a *merged resource dictionary*. Think of it as a class library for WPF resources; it is nothing more than a `.xaml` file that contains a collection of resources. A single project can have as many of these files as required (one for brushes, one for animations, and so forth), each of which can be inserted using the Add New Item dialog box activated via the Project menu (see Figure 27-6).

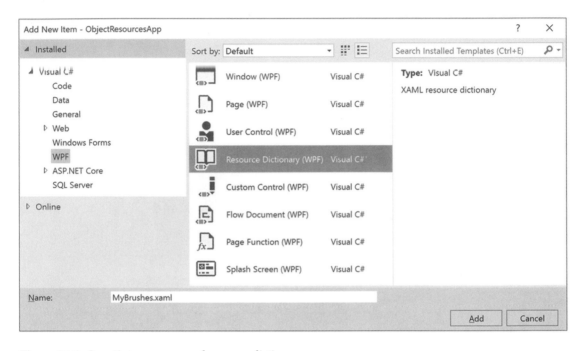

Figure 27-6. *Inserting a new merged resource dictionary*

In the new `MyBrushes.xaml` file, cut the current resources in the `Application.Resources` scope and move them into your dictionary, like so:

```
<ResourceDictionary xmlns=http://schemas.microsoft.com/winfx/2006/xaml/presentation
  xmlns:local="clr-namespace:ObjectResourcesApp"
  xmlns:x="http://schemas.microsoft.com/winfx/2006/xaml">
  <RadialGradientBrush x:Key="myBrush">
    <GradientStop Color="#FFC44EC4" Offset="0" />
    <GradientStop Color="#FF829CEB" Offset="1" />
    <GradientStop Color="#FF793879" Offset="0.669" />
  </RadialGradientBrush>
</ResourceDictionary>
```

Even though this resource dictionary is part of your project, all resource dictionaries must be merged (typically at the application level) into an existing resource dictionary in order to be used. To do this, use the following format in the `App.xaml` file (note that multiple resource dictionaries can be merged by adding multiple `<ResourceDictionary>` elements within the `<ResourceDictionary.MergedDictionaries>` scope):

```
<Application.Resources>
  <ResourceDictionary>
    <ResourceDictionary.MergedDictionaries>
      <ResourceDictionary Source = "MyBrushes.xaml"/>
    </ResourceDictionary.MergedDictionaries>
  </ResourceDictionary>
</Application.Resources>
```

The problem with this approach is that each resource file must be added to each project that needs the resources. A better approach for sharing resources is to define a .NET class library to share between projects, which you will do next.

Defining a Resource-Only Assembly

The easiest way to build a resource-only assembly is to actually begin with a WPF User Control Library project. Add such a project (named MyBrushesLibrary) to your current solution via the Add ➤ New Project menu option of Visual Studio (see Figure 27-7).

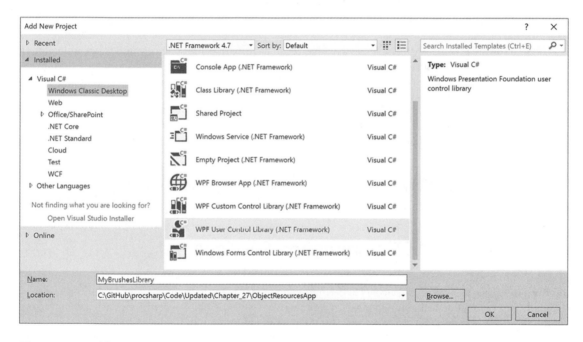

Figure 27-7. *Adding a user control library as a starting point for a resource-only library*

Now, delete the UserControl1.xaml file from the project. Next, drag and drop the MyBrushes.xaml file into your MyBrushesLibrary project and delete it from the ObjectResourcesApp project. Finally, open MyBrushes.xaml in the MyBrushesLibrary project and change the x:local namespace in the file to clr-namespace:MyBrushesLibrary. Your MyBrushes.xaml file should look like this:

```
<ResourceDictionary xmlns="http://schemas.microsoft.com/winfx/2006/xaml/presentation"
                    xmlns:x="http://schemas.microsoft.com/winfx/2006/xaml"
                    xmlns:local="clr-namespace:MyBrushesLibrary">
```

```
<RadialGradientBrush x:Key="myBrush">
    <GradientStop Color="#FFC44EC4" Offset="0" />
    <GradientStop Color="#FF829CEB" Offset="1" />
    <GradientStop Color="#FF793879" Offset="0.669" />
</RadialGradientBrush>
</ResourceDictionary>
```

Compile your User Control Library project. Next, reference this library from the ObjectResourcesApp project using the Add Reference dialog box. Now, merge these binary resources into the application-level resource dictionary of the ObjectResourcesApp project. Doing so, however, requires some rather funky syntax, shown here:

```
<Application.Resources>
  <ResourceDictionary>
    <ResourceDictionary.MergedDictionaries>
    <!-- The syntax is /NameOfAssembly;Component/NameOfXamlFileInAssembly.xaml -->
    <ResourceDictionary Source = "/MyBrushesLibrary;Component/MyBrushes.xaml"/>
    </ResourceDictionary.MergedDictionaries>
  </ResourceDictionary>
</Application.Resources>
```

First, be aware that this string is space-sensitive. If you have extra white space around your semicolon or forward slashes, you will generate errors. The first part of the string is the friendly name of the external library (no file extension). After the semicolon, type in the word Component followed by the name of the compiled binary resource, which will be identical to the original XAML resource dictionary.

That wraps up the examination of WPF's resource management system. You will make good use of these techniques for most (if not all) of your applications. Next up, let's investigate the integrated animation API of Windows Presentation Foundation.

■ **Source Code**   You can find the ObjectResourcesApp project in the Chapter 27 subdirectory.

Understanding WPF's Animation Services

In addition to the graphical rendering services you examined in Chapter 26, WPF supplies a programming interface to support animation services. The term *animation* may bring to mind visions of spinning company logos, a sequence of rotating image resources (to provide the illusion of movement), text bouncing across the screen, or specific types of programs such as video games or multimedia applications.

While WPF's animation APIs could certainly be used for such purposes, animation can be used any time you want to give an application additional flair. For example, you could build an animation for a button on a screen that magnifies slightly when the mouse cursor hovers within its boundaries (and shrinks back once the mouse cursor moves beyond the boundaries). Or you could animate a window so that it closes using a particular visual appearance, such as slowly fading into transparency. A more business application–centric use is to fade in error messages on an application screen to improve the user experience. In fact, WPF's animation support can be used within any sort of application (a business application, multimedia programs, video games, etc.) whenever you want to provide a more engaging user experience.

As with many other aspects of WPF, the notion of building animations is nothing new. What is new is that, unlike other APIs you might have used in the past (including Windows Forms), developers are not required to author the necessary infrastructure by hand. Under WPF, there's no need to create the background threads or timers used to advance the animation sequence, define custom types to represent the animation, erase and redraw images, or bother with tedious mathematical calculations. Like other aspects of WPF, you can build an animation entirely using XAML, entirely using C# code, or using a combination of the two.

■ **Note**   Visual Studio has no support for authoring animations using GUI animation tools. If you author an animation with Visual Studio, you will do so by typing in the XAML directly. However, Blend for Visual Studio (the companion product that ships with Visual Studio 2017) does indeed have a built-in animation editor that can simplify your life a good deal.

The Role of the Animation Class Types

To understand WPF's animation support, you must begin by examining the animation classes within the `System.Windows.Media.Animation` namespace of `PresentationCore.dll`. Here you will find more than 100 different class types that are named using the `Animation` token.

All of these classes can be placed into one of three broad categories. First, any class that follows the name convention *DataType*Animation (`ByteAnimation`, `ColorAnimation`, `DoubleAnimation`, `Int32Animation`, etc.) allows you to work with linear interpolation animations. This enables you to change a value smoothly over time from a start value to a final value.

Next, the classes that follow the naming convention *DataType*AnimationUsingKeyFrames (`StringAnimationUsingKeyFrames`, `DoubleAnimationUsingKeyFrames`, `PointAnimationUsingKeyFrames`, etc.) represent "key frame animations," which allow you to cycle through a set of defined values over a period of time. For example, you could use key frames to change the caption of a button by cycling through a series of individual characters.

Finally, classes that follow the *DataType*AnimationUsingPath naming convention (`DoubleAnimationUsingPath`, `PointAnimationUsingPath`, among others) are path-based animations that allow you to animate objects to move along a path you define. By way of an example, if you were building a GPS application, you could use a path-based animation to move an item along the quickest travel route to the user's destination.

Now, obviously, these classes are *not* used to somehow provide an animation sequence directly to a variable of a particular data type (after all, how exactly could you animate the value "9" using an `Int32Animation`?).

For example, consider the `Label` type's `Height` and `Width` properties, both of which are dependency properties wrapping a `double`. If you wanted to define an animation that would increase the height of a label over a time span, you could connect a `DoubleAnimation` object to the `Height` property and allow WPF to take care of the details of performing the actual animation itself. By way of another example, if you wanted to transition the color of a brush type from green to yellow over a period of five seconds, you could do so using the `ColorAnimation` type.

To be clear, these `Animation` classes can be connected to any *dependency property* of a given object that matches the underlying types. As explained in Chapter 25, dependency properties are a specialized form of property required by many WPF services including animation, data binding, and styles.

By convention, a dependency property is defined as a static, read-only field of the class and is named by suffixing the word `Property` to the normal property name. For example, the dependency property for the `Height` property of a `Button` would be accessed in code using `Button.HeightProperty`.

The To, From, and By Properties

All Animation classes define the following handful of key properties that control the starting and ending values used to perform the animation:

- To: This property represents the animation's ending value.

- From: This property represents the animation's starting value.

- By: This property represents the total amount by which the animation changes its starting value.

Despite that all Animation classes support the To, From, and By properties, they do not receive them via virtual members of a base class. The reason for this is that the underlying types wrapped by these properties vary greatly (integers, colors, Thickness objects, etc.), and representing all possibilities using a single base class would result in complex coding constructs.

On a related note, you might also wonder why .NET generics were not used to define a single generic animation class with a single type parameter (e.g., Animate<T>). Again, given that there are so many underlying data types (colors, vectors, ints, strings, etc.) used to animated dependency properties, it would not be as clean a solution as you might expect (not to mention XAML has only limited support for generic types).

The Role of the Timeline Base Class

Although a single base class was not used to define virtual To, From, and By properties, the Animation classes do share a common base class: System.Windows.Media.Animation.Timeline. This type provides a number of additional properties that control the pacing of the animation, as described in Table 27-1.

Table 27-1. *Key Members of the Timeline Base Class*

Properties	Meaning in Life
AccelerationRatio, DecelerationRatio, SpeedRatio	These properties can be used to control the overall pacing of the animation sequence.
AutoReverse	This property gets or sets a value that indicates whether the timeline plays in reverse after it completes a forward iteration (the default value is false).
BeginTime	This property gets or sets the time at which this timeline should begin. The default value is 0, which begins the animation immediately.
Duration	This property allows you to set a duration of time to play the timeline.
FillBehavior, RepeatBehavior	These properties are used to control what should happen once the timeline has completed (repeat the animation, do nothing, etc.).

Authoring an Animation in C# Code

Specifically, you will build a Window that contains a Button, which has the odd behavior of spinning in a circle (based on the upper-left corner) whenever the mouse enters its surface area. Begin by creating a new WPF application named SpinningButtonAnimationApp. Update the initial markup to the following (note you are handling the button's MouseEnter event):

```
<Button x:Name="btnSpinner" Height="50" Width="100" Content="I Spin!"
    MouseEnter="btnSpinner_MouseEnter" Click="btnSpinner_OnClick"/>
```

In the code-behind file, import the System.Windows.Media.Animation namespace and add the following code in the window's C# code file:

```
private bool _isSpinning = false;

private void btnSpinner_MouseEnter(object sender, MouseEventArgs e)
{
  if (!_isSpinning)
  {
    _isSpinning = true;
    // Make a double animation object, and register
    // with the Completed event.
    var dblAnim = new DoubleAnimation();
    dblAnim.Completed += (o, s) => { _isSpinning = false; };
    // Set the start value and end value.
    dblAnim.From = 0;
    dblAnim.To = 360;
    // Now, create a RotateTransform object, and set
    // it to the RenderTransform property of our
    // button.
    var rt = new RotateTransform();
    btnSpinner.RenderTransform = rt;
    // Now, animation the RotateTransform object.
    rt.BeginAnimation(RotateTransform.AngleProperty, dblAnim);
  }
}
private void btnSpinner_OnClick(object sender, RoutedEventArgs e)
{

}
```

The first major task of this method is to configure a DoubleAnimation object, which will start at the value 0 and end at the value 360. Notice that you are handling the Completed event on this object as well, to toggle a class-level bool variable that is used to ensure that if an animation is currently being performed, you don't "reset" it to start again.

Next, you create a RotateTransform object that is connected to the RenderTransform property of your Button control (btnSpinner). Last but not least, you inform the RenderTransform object to begin animating its Angle property using your DoubleAnimation object. When you are authoring animations in code, you typically do so by calling BeginAnimation() and then pass in the underlying *dependency property* you would like to animate (remember, by convention, this is a static field on the class), followed by a related animation object.

Let's add another animation to the program, which will cause the button to fade into invisibility when clicked. First, add the following code in the Click event handler:

```
private void btnSpinner_Click(object sender, RoutedEventArgs e)
{
  var dblAnim = new DoubleAnimation
  {
    From = 1.0,
    To = 0.0
  };
  btnSpinner.BeginAnimation(Button.OpacityProperty, dblAnim);
}
```

Here, you are changing the Opacity property value to fade the button out of view. Currently, however, this is hard to do, as the button is spinning very fast! How, then, can you control the pace of an animation? Glad you asked.

Controlling the Pace of an Animation

By default, an animation will take approximately one second to transition between the values assigned to the From and To properties. Therefore, your button has one second to spin around a full 360-degree angle, while the button will fade away to invisibility (when clicked) over the course of one second.

If you want to define a custom amount of time for an animation's transition, you may do so via the animation object's Duration property, which can be set to an instance of a Duration object. Typically, the time span is established by passing a TimeSpan object to the Duration's constructor. Consider the following update that will give the button a full four seconds to rotate:

```
private void btnSpinner_MouseEnter(object sender, MouseEventArgs e)
{
  if (!_isSpinning)
  {
    _isSpinning = true;

    // Make a double animation object, and register
    // with the Completed event.
    var dblAnim = new DoubleAnimation();
    dblAnim.Completed += (o, s) => { _isSpinning = false; };

    // Button has four seconds to finish the spin!
    dblAnim.Duration = new Duration(TimeSpan.FromSeconds(4));

...
  }
}
```

With this adjustment, you should have a fighting chance of clicking the button while it is spinning, at which point it will fade away.

■ **Note**   The BeginTime property of an Animation class also takes a TimeSpan object. Recall that this property can be set to establish a wait time before starting an animation sequence.

Reversing and Looping an Animation

You can also tell Animation objects to play an animation in reverse at the completion of the animation sequence by setting the AutoReverse property to true. For example, if you want to have the button come back into view after it has faded away, you could author the following:

```
private void btnSpinner_OnClick(object sender, RoutedEventArgs e)
{
  DoubleAnimation dblAnim = new DoubleAnimation
```

```
{
  From = 1.0,
  To = 0.0
};
// Reverse when done.
dblAnim.AutoReverse = true;
btnSpinner.BeginAnimation(Button.OpacityProperty, dblAnim);
}
```

If you'd like to have an animation repeat some number of times (or to never stop once activated), you can do so using the RepeatBehavior property, which is common to all Animation classes. If you pass in a simple numerical value to the constructor, you can specify a hard-coded number of times to repeat. On the other hand, if you pass in a TimeSpan object to the constructor, you can establish an amount of time the animation should repeat. Finally, if you want an animation to loop *ad infinitum*, you can simply specify RepeatBehavior.Forever. Consider the following ways you could change the repeat behaviors of either of the DoubleAnimation objects used in this example:

```
// Loop forever.
dblAnim.RepeatBehavior = RepeatBehavior.Forever;
```

```
// Loop three times.
dblAnim.RepeatBehavior = new RepeatBehavior(3);
```

```
// Loop for 30 seconds.
dblAnim.RepeatBehavior = new RepeatBehavior(TimeSpan.FromSeconds(30));
```

That wraps up your investigation about how to animate aspects of an object using C# code and the WPF animation API. Next, you will learn how to do the same using XAML.

■ **Source Code**   You can find the SpinningButtonAnimationApp project in the Chapter 27 subdirectory.

Authoring Animations in XAML

Authoring animations in markup is similar to authoring them in code, at least for simple, straightforward animation sequences. When you need to capture more complex animations, which may involve changing the values of numerous properties at once, the amount of markup can grow considerably. Even if you use a tool to generate XAML-based animations, it is important to know the basics of how an animation is represented in XAML because this will make it easier for you to modify and tweak tool-generated content.

■ **Note**   You will find a number of XAML files in the XamlAnimations folder of the downloadable source code. As you go through the next several pages, copy these markup files into your custom XAML editor or into the Kaxaml editor to see the results.

For the most part, creating an animation is similar to what you saw already. You still configure an Animation object and associate it to an object's property. One big difference, however, is that WPF is not function call–friendly. As a result, instead of calling BeginAnimation(), you use a *storyboard* as a layer of indirection.

Let's walk through a complete example of an animation defined in terms of XAML, followed by a detailed breakdown. The following XAML definition will display a window that contains a single label. As soon as the Label object loads into memory, it begins an animation sequence in which the font size increases from 12 points to 100 over a period of four seconds. The animation will repeat for as long as the Window object is loaded in memory. You can find this markup in the GrowLabelFont.xaml file, so copy it into Kaxaml (make sure to press F5 to show the window) and observe the behavior.

```
<Window
  xmlns="http://schemas.microsoft.com/winfx/2006/xaml/presentation"
  xmlns:x="http://schemas.microsoft.com/winfx/2006/xaml"
  Height="200" Width="600" WindowStartupLocation="CenterScreen" Title="Growing Label Font!">
  <StackPanel>
    <Label Content = "Interesting...">
      <Label.Triggers>
        <EventTrigger RoutedEvent = "Label.Loaded">
          <EventTrigger.Actions>
            <BeginStoryboard>
              <Storyboard TargetProperty = "FontSize">
                <DoubleAnimation From = "12" To = "100" Duration = "0:0:4"
                  RepeatBehavior = "Forever"/>
              </Storyboard>
            </BeginStoryboard>
          </EventTrigger.Actions>
        </EventTrigger>
      </Label.Triggers>
    </Label>
  </StackPanel>
</Window>
```

Now, let's break this example down, bit by bit.

The Role of Storyboards

Working from the innermost element outward, you first encounter the <DoubleAnimation> element, which makes use of the same properties you set in procedural code (From, To, Duration, and RepeatBehavior).

```
<DoubleAnimation From = "12" To = "100" Duration = "0:0:4"
                 RepeatBehavior = "Forever"/>
```

As mentioned, Animation elements are placed within a <Storyboard> element, which is used to map the animation object to a given property on the parent type via the TargetProperty property, which in this case is FontSize. A <Storyboard> is always wrapped in a parent element named <BeginStoryboard>.

```
<BeginStoryboard>
  <Storyboard TargetProperty = "FontSize">
    <DoubleAnimation From = "12" To = "100" Duration = "0:0:4"
                     RepeatBehavior = "Forever"/>
  </Storyboard>
</BeginStoryboard>
```

The Role of Event Triggers

After the `<BeginStoryboard>` element has been defined, you need to specify some sort of action that will cause the animation to begin executing. WPF has a few different ways to respond to runtime conditions in markup, one of which is termed a *trigger*. From a high level, you can consider a trigger a way of responding to an event condition in XAML, without the need for procedural code.

Typically, when you respond to an event in C#, you author custom code that will execute when the event occurs. A trigger, however, is just a way to be notified that some event condition has happened ("I'm loaded into memory!" or "The mouse is over me!" or "I have focus!").

Once you've been notified that an event condition has occurred, you can start the storyboard. In this example, you are responding to the `Label` being loaded into memory. Because it is the `Label`'s `Loaded` event you are interested in, the `<EventTrigger>` is placed in the `Label`'s trigger collection.

```
<Label Content = "Interesting...">
  <Label.Triggers>
    <EventTrigger RoutedEvent = "Label.Loaded">
      <EventTrigger.Actions>
        <BeginStoryboard>
          <Storyboard TargetProperty = "FontSize">
            <DoubleAnimation From = "12" To = "100" Duration = "0:0:4"
                             RepeatBehavior = "Forever"/>
          </Storyboard>
        </BeginStoryboard>
      </EventTrigger.Actions>
    </EventTrigger>
  </Label.Triggers>
</Label>
```

Let's see another example of defining an animation in XAML, this time using a *key frame* animation.

Animation Using Discrete Key Frames

Unlike the linear interpolation animation objects, which can only move between a starting point and an ending point, the *key frame* counterparts allow you to create a collection of specific values for an animation that should take place at specific times.

To illustrate the use of a discrete key frame type, assume you want to build a `Button` control that animates its content so that over the course of three seconds the value "OK!" appears, one character at a time. You'll find the following markup in the `AnimateString.xaml` file. Copy this markup into your `MyXamlPad.exe` program (or Kaxaml) and view the results:

```
<Window xmlns="http://schemas.microsoft.com/winfx/2006/xaml/presentation"
    xmlns:x="http://schemas.microsoft.com/winfx/2006/xaml"
    Height="100" Width="300"
    WindowStartupLocation="CenterScreen" Title="Animate String Data!">
    <StackPanel>
      <Button Name="myButton" Height="40"
              FontSize="16pt" FontFamily="Verdana" Width = "100">
        <Button.Triggers>
          <EventTrigger RoutedEvent="Button.Loaded">
            <BeginStoryboard>
              <Storyboard>
```

```
                    <StringAnimationUsingKeyFrames RepeatBehavior = "Forever"
                       Storyboard.TargetProperty="Content"
                       Duration="0:0:3">
                       <DiscreteStringKeyFrame Value="" KeyTime="0:0:0" />
                       <DiscreteStringKeyFrame Value="O" KeyTime="0:0:1" />
                       <DiscreteStringKeyFrame Value="OK" KeyTime="0:0:1.5" />
                       <DiscreteStringKeyFrame Value="OK!" KeyTime="0:0:2" />
                    </StringAnimationUsingKeyFrames>
                 </Storyboard>
               </BeginStoryboard>
             </EventTrigger>
          </Button.Triggers>
       </Button>
    </StackPanel>
</Window>
```

First, notice that you have defined an event trigger for your button to ensure that your storyboard executes when the button has loaded into memory. The StringAnimationUsingKeyFrames class is in charge of changing the content of the button, via the Storyboard.TargetProperty value.

Within the scope of the <StringAnimationUsingKeyFrames> element, you define four DiscreteStringKeyFrame elements, which change the button's Content property over the course of two seconds (note that the duration established by StringAnimationUsingKeyFrames is a total of three seconds, so you will see a slight pause between the final ! and looping O).

Now that you have a better feel for how to build animations in C# code and XAML, let's look at the role of WPF styles, which make heavy use of graphics, object resources, and animations.

■ **Source Code**   You can find these loose XAML files in the XamlAnimations subdirectory of Chapter 27.

Understanding the Role of WPF Styles

When you are building the UI of a WPF application, it is not uncommon for a family of controls to require a shared look and feel. For example, you might want all button types to have the same height, width, background color, and font size for their string content. Although you could handle this by setting each button's individual properties to identical values, such an approach makes it difficult to implement changes down the road because you would need to reset the same set of properties on multiple objects for every change.

Thankfully, WPF offers a simple way to constrain the look and feel of related controls using *styles*. Simply put, a WPF style is an object that maintains a collection of property-value pairs. Programmatically speaking, an individual style is represented using the System.Windows.Style class. This class has a property named Setters, which exposes a strongly typed collection of Setter objects. It is the Setter object that allows you to define the property-value pairs.

In addition to the Setters collection, the Style class also defines a few other important members that allow you to incorporate triggers, restrict where a style can be applied, and even create a new style based on an existing style (think of it as "style inheritance"). In particular, be aware of the following members of the Style class:

- Triggers: Exposes a collection of trigger objects, which allow you to capture various event conditions within a style

- BasedOn: Allows you to build a new style based on an existing style

- TargetType: Allows you to constrain where a style can be applied

Defining and Applying a Style

In almost every case, a `Style` object will be packaged as an object resource. Like any object resource, you can package it at the window or application level, as well as within a dedicated resource dictionary (this is great because it makes the `Style` object easily accessible throughout your application). Now recall that the goal is to define a `Style` object that fills (at minimum) the `Setters` collection with a set of property-value pairs.

Let's build a style that captures the basic font characteristics of a control in your application. Start by creating a new WPF application named `WpfStyles`. Open your `App.xaml` file and define the following named style:

```
<Application.Resources>
  <Style x:Key ="BasicControlStyle">
    <Setter Property = "Control.FontSize" Value ="14"/>
    <Setter Property = "Control.Height" Value = "40"/>
    <Setter Property = "Control.Cursor" Value = "Hand"/>
  </Style>
</Application.Resources>
```

Notice that your `BasicControlStyle` adds three `Setter` objects to the internal collection. Now, let's apply this style to a few controls in your main window. Because this style is an object resource, the controls that want to use it still need to use the `{StaticResource}` or `{DynamicResource}` markup extension to locate the style. When they find the style, they will set the resource item to the identically named `Style` property. Replace the default `Grid` control with the following markup:

```
<StackPanel>
  <Label x:Name="lblInfo" Content="This style is boring..."
        Style="{StaticResource BasicControlStyle}" Width="150"/>
  <Button x:Name="btnTestButton" Content="Yes, but we are reusing settings!"
        Style="{StaticResource BasicControlStyle}" Width="250"/>
</StackPanel>
```

If you view the `Window` in the Visual Studio designer (or run the application), you'll find that both controls support the same cursor, height, and font size.

Overriding Style Settings

While both of your controls have opted in to the style, if a control wants to apply a style and then change some of the defined settings, that's fine. For example, the `Button` will now use the `Help` cursor (rather than the `Hand` cursor defined in the style).

```
<Button x:Name="btnTestButton" Content="Yes, but we are reusing settings!"
        Cursor="Help" Style="{StaticResource BasicControlStyle}" Width="250" />
```

Styles are processed before the individual property settings of the control using the style; therefore, controls can "override" settings on a case-by-case basis.

The Effect of TargetType on Styles

Currently, your style is defined in such a way that any control can adopt it (and has to do so explicitly by setting the control's Style property), given that each property is qualified by the Control class. For a program that defines dozens of settings, this would entail a good amount of repeated code. One way to clean this style up a bit is to use the TargetType attribute. When you add this attribute to a Style's opening element, you can mark exactly once where it can be applied (in this example, in App.XAML).

```
<Style x:Key ="BasicControlStyle" TargetType="Control">
  <Setter Property = "FontSize" Value ="14"/>
  <Setter Property = "Height" Value = "40"/>
  <Setter Property = "Cursor" Value = "Hand"/>
</Style>
```

■ **Note** When you build a style that uses a base class type, you needn't be concerned if you assign a value to a dependency property not supported by derived types. If the derived type does not support a given dependency property, it is ignored.

This is somewhat helpful, but you still have a style that can apply to any control. The TargetType attribute is more useful when you want to define a style that can be applied to only a particular type of control. Add the following new style to the application's resource dictionary:

```
<Style x:Key ="BigGreenButton" TargetType="Button">
  <Setter Property = "FontSize" Value ="20"/>
  <Setter Property = "Height" Value = "100"/>
  <Setter Property = "Width" Value = "100"/>
  <Setter Property = "Background" Value = "DarkGreen"/>
  <Setter Property = "Foreground" Value = "Yellow"/>
</Style>
```

This style will work only on Button controls (or a subclass of Button). If you apply it to an incompatible element, you will get markup and compiler errors. Add a new Button that uses this new style, as follows:

```
<Button x:Name="btnAnotherButton" Content="OK!" Margin="0,10,0,0"
    Style="{StaticResource BigGreenButton}" Width="250" Cursor="Help"/>
```

You'll see output like that shown in Figure 27-8.

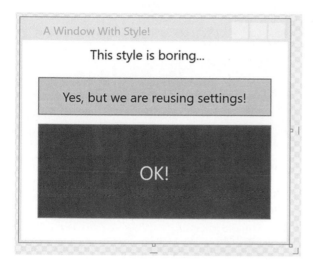

Figure 27-8. *Controls with different styles*

Another effect of TargetType is that the style will get applied to all elements of that type within the scope of the style definition as long as the x:Key property *doesn't* exist.

Here is another application-level style that will apply automatically to all TextBox controls in the current application:

```xml
<!-- The default style for all text boxes. -->
<Style TargetType="TextBox">
  <Setter Property = "FontSize" Value ="14"/>
  <Setter Property = "Width" Value = "100"/>
  <Setter Property = "Height" Value = "30"/>
  <Setter Property = "BorderThickness" Value = "5"/>
  <Setter Property = "BorderBrush" Value = "Red"/>
  <Setter Property = "FontStyle" Value = "Italic"/>
</Style>
```

You can now define any number of TextBox controls, and they will automatically get the defined look. If a given TextBox does not want this default look and feel, it can opt out by setting the Style property to {x:Null}. For example, txtTest will get the default unnamed style, while txtTest2 is doing things its own way.

```xml
<TextBox x:Name="txtTest"/>
<TextBox x:Name="txtTest2" Style="{x:Null}" BorderBrush="Black"
        BorderThickness="5" Height="60" Width="100" Text="Ha!"/>
```

Subclassing Existing Styles

You can also build new styles using an existing style, via the BasedOn property. The style you are extending must have been given a proper x:Key in the dictionary, as the derived style will reference it by name using the {StaticResource} or {DynamicResource} markup extension. Here is a new style based on BigGreenButton, which rotates the button element by 20 degrees:

```
<!-- This style is based on BigGreenButton. -->
<Style x:Key ="TiltButton" TargetType="Button" BasedOn = "{StaticResource BigGreenButton}">
  <Setter Property = "Foreground" Value = "White"/>
  <Setter Property = "RenderTransform">
    <Setter.Value>
      <RotateTransform Angle = "20"/>
    </Setter.Value>
  </Setter>
</Style>
```

To use this new style, update the markup for the button to this:

```
<Button x:Name="btnAnotherButton" Content="OK!" Margin="0,10,0,0"
    Style="{StaticResource TitlButton}" Width="250" Cursor="Help"/>
```

This changes the appearance to the image shown in Figure 27-9.

Figure 27-9. *Using a derived style*

Defining Styles with Triggers

WPF styles can also contain triggers by packaging up `Trigger` objects within the `Triggers` collection of the `Style` object. Using triggers in a style allows you to define certain `<Setter>` elements in such a way that they will be applied only if a given trigger condition is `true`. For example, perhaps you want to increase the size of a font when the mouse is over a button. Or maybe you want to make sure that the text box with the current focus is highlighted with a given color. Triggers are useful for these sorts of situations, in that they allow you to take specific actions when a property changes, without the need to author explicit C# code in a code-behind file.

Here is an update to the `TextBox` style that ensures that when a `TextBox` has the input focus, it will receive a yellow background:

```
<!-- The default style for all text boxes. -->
<Style TargetType="TextBox">
  <Setter Property = "FontSize" Value ="14"/>
  <Setter Property = "Width" Value = "100"/>
  <Setter Property = "Height" Value = "30"/>
  <Setter Property = "BorderThickness" Value = "5"/>
  <Setter Property = "BorderBrush" Value = "Red"/>
```

```
    <Setter Property = "FontStyle" Value = "Italic"/>
    <!-- The following setter will be applied only when the text box is in focus. -->
    <Style.Triggers>
      <Trigger Property = "IsFocused" Value = "True">
        <Setter Property = "Background" Value = "Yellow"/>
      </Trigger>
    </Style.Triggers>
</Style>
```

If you test this style, you'll find that as you tab between various TextBox objects, the currently selected TextBox has a bright yellow background (provided it has not opted out by assigning {x:Null} to the Style property).

Property triggers are also very smart, in that when the trigger's condition is *not true*, the property automatically receives the default assigned value. Therefore, as soon as a TextBox loses focus, it also automatically becomes the default color without any work on your part. In contrast, event triggers (examined when you looked at WPF animations) do not automatically revert to a previous condition.

Defining Styles with Multiple Triggers

Triggers can also be designed in such a way that the defined <Setter> elements will be applied when *multiple conditions* are true. Let's say you want to set the background of a TextBox to Yellow only if it has the active focus and the mouse is hovering within its boundaries. To do so, you can make use of the <MultiTrigger> element to define each condition, like so:

```
<!-- The default style for all text boxes. -->
<Style TargetType="TextBox">
  <Setter Property = "FontSize" Value ="14"/>
  <Setter Property = "Width" Value = "100"/>
  <Setter Property = "Height" Value = "30"/>
  <Setter Property = "BorderThickness" Value = "5"/>
  <Setter Property = "BorderBrush" Value = "Red"/>
  <Setter Property = "FontStyle" Value = "Italic"/>
  <!-- The following setter will be applied only when the text box is
  in focus AND the mouse is over the text box. -->
  <Style.Triggers>
    <MultiTrigger>
      <MultiTrigger.Conditions>
          <Condition Property = "IsFocused" Value = "True"/>
          <Condition Property = "IsMouseOver" Value = "True"/>
      </MultiTrigger.Conditions>
      <Setter Property = "Background" Value = "Yellow"/>
    </MultiTrigger>
  </Style.Triggers>
</Style>
```

Animated Styles

Styles can also incorporate triggers that kick off an animation sequence. Here is one final style that, when applied to Button controls, will cause the controls to grow and shrink in size when the mouse is inside the button's surface area:

```
<!-- The growing button style! -->
<Style x:Key = "GrowingButtonStyle" TargetType="Button">
  <Setter Property = "Height" Value = "40"/>
  <Setter Property = "Width" Value = "100"/>
  <Style.Triggers>
    <Trigger Property = "IsMouseOver" Value = "True">
      <Trigger.EnterActions>
        <BeginStoryboard>
          <Storyboard TargetProperty = "Height">
            <DoubleAnimation From = "40" To = "200"
                             Duration = "0:0:2" AutoReverse="True"/>
          </Storyboard>
        </BeginStoryboard>
      </Trigger.EnterActions>
    </Trigger>
  </Style.Triggers>
</Style>
```

Here, the Triggers collection is on the lookout for the IsMouseOver property to return true. When this occurs, you define a <Trigger.EnterActions> element to execute a simple storyboard that forces the button to grow to a Height value of 200 (and then return to a Height of 40) over two seconds. If you want to perform other property changes, you could also define a <Trigger.ExitActions> scope to define any custom actions to take when IsMouseOver changes to false.

Assigning Styles Programmatically

Recall that a style can be applied at runtime as well. This can be helpful if you want to let end users choose how their UI looks and feels or if you need to enforce a look and feel based on security settings (e.g., the DisableAllButton style) or what have you.

During this project, you have defined a number of styles, many of which can apply to Button controls. So, let's retool the UI of your main window to allow the user to pick from some of these styles by selecting names in a ListBox. Based on the user's selection, you will apply the appropriate style. Here is the new (and final) markup for the <Window> element:

```
<DockPanel >
  <StackPanel Orientation="Horizontal" DockPanel.Dock="Top" Margin="0,0,0,50">
    <Label Content="Please Pick a Style for this Button" Height="50"/>
    <ListBox x:Name ="lstStyles" Height ="80" Width ="150" Background="LightBlue"
             SelectionChanged ="comboStyles_Changed" />
  </StackPanel>
  <Button x:Name="btnStyle" Height="40" Width="100" Content="OK!"/>
</DockPanel>
```

The ListBox control (named lstStyles) will be filled dynamically within the window's constructor, like so:

```
public MainWindow()
{
  InitializeComponent();
  // Fill the list box with all the Button styles.
  lstStyles.Items.Add("GrowingButtonStyle");
  lstStyles.Items.Add("TiltButton");
  lstStyles.Items.Add("BigGreenButton");
  lstStyles.Items.Add("BasicControlStyle");}
}
```

The final task is to handle the SelectionChanged event in the related code file. Notice in the following code how you are able to extract the current resource by name, using the inherited TryFindResource() method:

```
private void comboStyles_Changed(object sender, SelectionChangedEventArgs e)
{
  // Get the selected style name from the list box.
  var currStyle = (Style)TryFindResource(lstStyles.SelectedValue);
  if (currStyle == null) return;
  // Set the style of the button type.
  this.btnStyle.Style = currStyle;
}
```

When you run this application, you can pick from one of these four button styles on the fly. Figure 27-10 shows your completed application.

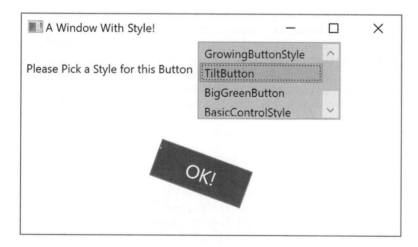

Figure 27-10. *Controls with different styles*

■ **Source Code**   You can find the WpfStyles project in the Chapter 27 subdirectory.

Logical Trees, Visual Trees, and Default Templates

Now that you understand styles and resources, there are a few more preparatory topics to investigate before you begin learning how to build custom controls. Specifically, you need to learn the distinction between a logical tree, a visual tree, and a default template. When you are typing XAML into Visual Studio or a tool such as kaxaml.exe, your markup is the *logical view* of the XAML document. As well, if you author C# code that adds new items to a layout control, you are inserting new items into the logical tree. Essentially, a logical view represents how your content will be positioned within the various layout managers for a main Window (or another root element, such as Page or NavigationWindow).

However, behind every logical tree is a much more verbose representation termed a *visual tree*, which is used internally by WPF to correctly render elements onto the screen. Within any visual tree, there will be full details of the templates and styles used to render each object, including any necessary drawings, shapes, visuals, and animations.

It is useful to understand the distinction between logical and visual trees because when you are building a custom control template, you are essentially replacing all or part of the default visual tree of a control and inserting your own. Therefore, if you want a Button control to be rendered as a star shape, you could define a new star template and plug it into the Button's visual tree. Logically, the Button is still of type Button, and it supports all of the properties, methods, and events as expected. But visually, it has taken on a whole new appearance. This fact alone makes WPF an extremely useful API, given that other toolkits would require you to build a new class to make a star-shaped button. With WPF, you simply need to define new markup.

■ **Note**   WPF controls are often described as *lookless*. This refers to the fact that the look and feel of a WPF control is completely independent (and customizable) from its behavior.

Programmatically Inspecting a Logical Tree

While analyzing a window's logical tree at runtime is not a tremendously common WPF programming activity, it is worth mentioning that the System.Windows namespace defines a class named LogicalTreeHelper, which allows you to inspect the structure of a logical tree at runtime. To illustrate the connection between logical trees, visual trees, and control templates, create a new WPF application named TreesAndTemplatesApp.

Replace the Grid with the following markup that contains two Button controls and a large read-only TextBox with scrollbars enabled. Make sure you use the IDE to handle the Click event of each button. The following XAML will do nicely:

```
<DockPanel LastChildFill="True">
  <Border Height="50" DockPanel.Dock="Top" BorderBrush="Blue">
    <StackPanel Orientation="Horizontal">
      <Button x:Name="btnShowLogicalTree" Content="Logical Tree of Window"
              Margin="4" BorderBrush="Blue" Height="40" Click="btnShowLogicalTree_Click"/>
      <Button x:Name="btnShowVisualTree" Content="Visual Tree of Window"
              BorderBrush="Blue" Height="40" Click="btnShowVisualTree_Click"/>
    </StackPanel>
  </Border>
  <TextBox x:Name="txtDisplayArea" Margin="10" Background="AliceBlue" IsReadOnly="True"
          BorderBrush="Red" VerticalScrollBarVisibility="Auto" HorizontalScrollBarVisibility
          ="Auto" />
</DockPanel>
```

Within your C# code file, define a `string` member variable named `_dataToShow`. Now, within the `Click` handler for the `btnShowLogicalTree` object, call a helper function that calls itself recursively in order to populate the string variable with the logical tree of the `Window`. To do so, you will call the static `GetChildren()` method of `LogicalTreeHelper`. Here is the code:

```csharp
private string _dataToShow = string.Empty;

private void btnShowLogicalTree_Click(object sender, RoutedEventArgs e)
{
  _dataToShow = "";
  BuildLogicalTree(0, this);
  txtDisplayArea.Text = _dataToShow;
}

void BuildLogicalTree(int depth, object obj)
{
  // Add the type name to the dataToShow member variable.
  _dataToShow += new string(' ', depth) + obj.GetType().Name + "\n";
  // If an item is not a DependencyObject, skip it.
  if (!(obj is DependencyObject))
    return;
  // Make a recursive call for each logical child.
  foreach (var child in LogicalTreeHelper.GetChildren((DependencyObject)obj))
  {
      BuildLogicalTree(depth + 5, child);
  }
}
```

If you run your application and click this first button, you will see a tree print in the text area, which is just about an exact replica of the original XAML (see Figure 27-11).

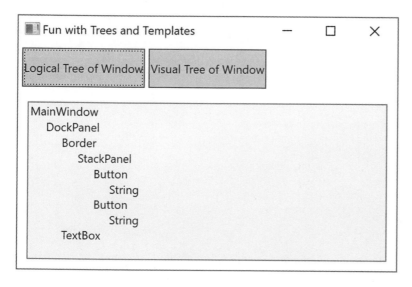

Figure 27-11. *Viewing a logical tree at runtime*

Programmatically Inspecting a Visual Tree

A Window's visual tree can also be inspected at runtime using the VisualTreeHelper class of System.Windows.Media. Here is a Click implementation of the second Button control (btnShowVisualTree), which performs similar recursive logic to build a textual representation of the visual tree:

```
using System.Windows.Media;

private void btnShowVisualTree_Click(object sender, RoutedEventArgs e)
{
  _dataToShow = "";
  BuildVisualTree(0, this);
  txtDisplayArea.Text = _dataToShow;
}
void BuildVisualTree(int depth, DependencyObject obj)
{
  // Add the type name to the dataToShow member variable.
  _dataToShow += new string(' ', depth) + obj.GetType().Name + "\n";
  // Make a recursive call for each visual child.
  for (int i = 0; i < VisualTreeHelper.GetChildrenCount(obj); i++)
  {
    BuildVisualTree(depth + 1, VisualTreeHelper.GetChild(obj, i));
  }
}
```

As you can see in Figure 27-12, the visual tree exposes a number of lower-level rendering agents such as ContentPresenter, AdornerDecorator, TextBoxLineDrawingVisual, and so forth.

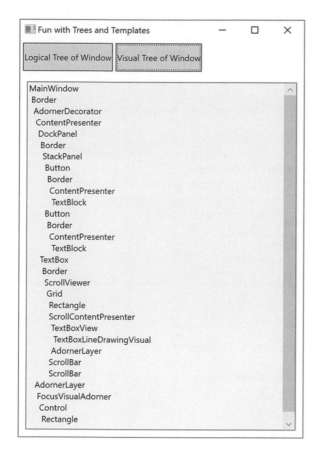

Figure 27-12. *Viewing a visual tree at runtime*

Programmatically Inspecting a Control's Default Template

Recall that a visual tree is used by WPF to understand how to render a Window and all contained elements. Every WPF control stores its own set of rendering commands within its default template. Programmatically speaking, any template can be represented as an instance of the ControlTemplate class. As well, you can obtain a control's default template by using the aptly named Template property, like so:

```
// Get the default template of the Button.
Button myBtn = new Button();
ControlTemplate template = myBtn.Template;
```

Likewise, you could create a new ControlTemplate object in code and plug it into a control's Template property as follows:

```
// Plug in a new template for the button to use.
Button myBtn = new Button();
ControlTemplate customTemplate = new ControlTemplate();

// Assume this method adds all the code for a star template.
MakeStarTemplate(customTemplate);
myBtn.Template = customTemplate;
```

1127

While you could build a new template in code, it is far more common to do so in XAML. However, before you start building your own templates, let's finish the current example and add the ability to view the default template of a WPF control at runtime. This can be a really useful way to take a look at the overall composition of a template. Update the markup of your window with a new StackPanel of controls docked to the left side of the master DockPanel, defined as so (placed just before the <TextBox> element):

```xml
<Border DockPanel.Dock="Left" Margin="10" BorderBrush="DarkGreen" BorderThickness="4"
Width="358">
  <StackPanel>
    <Label Content="Enter Full Name of WPF Control" Width="340" FontWeight="DemiBold" />
    <TextBox x:Name="txtFullName" Width="340" BorderBrush="Green"
            Background="BlanchedAlmond" Height="22" Text="System.Windows.Controls.Button" />
    <Button x:Name="btnTemplate" Content="See Template" BorderBrush="Green"
            Height="40" Width="100" Margin="5" Click="btnTemplate_Click"
            HorizontalAlignment="Left" />
    <Border BorderBrush="DarkGreen" BorderThickness="2" Height="260"
            Width="301" Margin="10" Background="LightGreen" >
      <StackPanel x:Name="stackTemplatePanel" />
    </Border>
  </StackPanel>
</Border>
```

Add an empty event handler function for the btnTemplate_Click event like this:

```csharp
private void btnTemplate_Click(object sender, RoutedEventArgs e)
{
}
```

The upper-left text area allows you to enter in the fully qualified name of a WPF control located in the PresentationFramework.dll assembly. Once the library is loaded, you will dynamically create an instance of the object and display it in the large square in the bottom left. Last but not least, the control's default template will be displayed in the right-hand text area. First, add a new member variable to your C# class of type Control, like so:

```csharp
private Control _ctrlToExamine = null;
```

Here is the remaining code, which will require you to import the System.Reflection, System.Xml, and System.Windows.Markup namespaces:

```csharp
private void btnTemplate_Click(object sender, RoutedEventArgs e)
{
  _dataToShow = "";
  ShowTemplate();
  txtDisplayArea.Text = _dataToShow;
}
```

```csharp
private void ShowTemplate()
{
  // Remove the control that is currently in the preview area.
  if (_ctrlToExamine != null)
    stackTemplatePanel.Children.Remove(_ctrlToExamine);
  try
  {
    // Load PresentationFramework, and create an instance of the
    // specified control. Give it a size for display purposes, then add to the
    // empty StackPanel.
    Assembly asm = Assembly.Load("PresentationFramework, Version=4.0.0.0," +
      "Culture=neutral, PublicKeyToken=31bf3856ad364e35");
    _ctrlToExamine = (Control)asm.CreateInstance(txtFullName.Text);
    _ctrlToExamine.Height = 200;
    _ctrlToExamine.Width = 200;
    _ctrlToExamine.Margin = new Thickness(5);
    stackTemplatePanel.Children.Add(_ctrlToExamine);
    // Define some XML settings to preserve indentation.
    var xmlSettings = new XmlWriterSettings{Indent = true};
    // Create a StringBuilder to hold the XAML.
    var strBuilder = new StringBuilder();
    // Create an XmlWriter based on our settings.
    var xWriter = XmlWriter.Create(strBuilder, xmlSettings);
    // Now save the XAML into the XmlWriter object based on the ControlTemplate.
    XamlWriter.Save(_ctrlToExamine.Template, xWriter);
    // Display XAML in the text box.
    _dataToShow = strBuilder.ToString();
  }
  catch (Exception ex)
  {
    _dataToShow = ex.Message;
  }
}
```

The bulk of the work is just tinkering with the compiled BAML resource to map it into a XAML `string`. Figure 27-13 shows your final application in action, displaying the default template of the `System.Windows.Controls.DatePicker` control. The image shows the `Calendar`, which is accessed by clicking the button on the right side of the control.

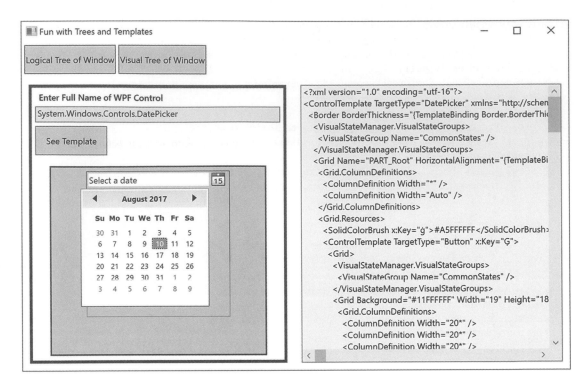

Figure 27-13. *Investigating a* `ControlTemplate` *at runtime*

Great! You should have a better idea about how logical trees, visual trees, and control default templates work together. Now you can spend the remainder of this chapter learning how to build custom templates and user controls.

■ **Source Code**   You can find the TreesAndTemplatesApp project in the `Chapter 27` subdirectory.

Building a Control Template with the Trigger Framework

When you build a custom template for a control, you could do so with nothing but C# code. Using this approach, you would add data to a `ControlTemplate` object and then assign it to a control's `Template` property. Most of the time, however, you will define the look and feel of a `ControlTemplate` using XAML and add bits of code (or possible quite a bit of code) to drive the runtime behavior.

In the remainder of this chapter, you will examine how to build custom templates using Visual Studio. Along the way, you will learn about the WPF trigger framework and the Visual State Manager (VSM), and you'll see how to use animations to incorporate visual cues for the end user. Using Visual Studio alone to build complex templates can entail a fair amount of typing and a bit of heavy lifting. To be sure, production-level templates will benefit from the use of Blend for Visual Studio, the (now) free companion application installed with Visual Studio. However, given that this edition of the text does not include coverage of Blend, it's time to roll up your sleeves and pound out some markup.

To begin, create a new WPF application named ButtonTemplate. For this project, you are more interested in the mechanics of creating and using templates, so replace the Grid with the following markup:

```
<StackPanel Orientation="Horizontal">
  <Button x:Name="myButton" Width="100" Height="100" Click="myButton_Click"/>
</StackPanel>
```

In the Click event handler, simply display a message box (via MessageBox.Show()) to show a message confirming the clicking of the control. Remember, when you build custom templates, the *behavior* of the control is constant, but the *look* may vary.

Currently, this Button is rendered using the default template, which, as the previous example illustrated, is a BAML resource within a given WPF assembly. When you want to define your own template, you essentially replace this default visual tree with your own creation. To begin, update the definition of the <Button> element to specify a new template using the property element syntax. This template will give the control a round appearance.

```
<Button x:Name="myButton" Width="100" Height="100" Click="myButton_Click">
  <Button.Template>
    <ControlTemplate>
      <Grid x:Name="controlLayout">
        <Ellipse x:Name="buttonSurface" Fill = "LightBlue"/>
        <Label x:Name="buttonCaption" VerticalAlignment = "Center"
               HorizontalAlignment = "Center"
               FontWeight = "Bold" FontSize = "20" Content = "OK!"/>
      </Grid>
    </ControlTemplate>
  </Button.Template>
</Button>
```

Here, you have defined a template that consists of a named Grid control containing a named Ellipse and a Label. Because your Grid has no defined rows or columns, each child stacks on top of the previous control, which centers the content. If you run your application now, you will notice that the Click event will fire *only* when the mouse cursor is within the bounds of the Ellipse! This is a great feature of the WPF template architecture: you do not need to recalculate hit-testing, bounds checking, or any other low-level detail. So, if your template used a Polygon object to render some oddball geometry, you can rest assured that the mouse hit-testing details are relative to the shape of the control, not the larger bounding rectangle.

Templates as Resources

Currently, your template is embedded to a specific Button control, which limits reuse. Ideally, you would place your template into a resource dictionary so you can reuse your round button template between projects or, at minimum, move it into the application resource container for reuse within this project. Let's move the local Button resource to the application level by cutting the template definition from the Button and pasting it into the Application.Resources tag in the App.xaml file. Add in a Key and a TargetType, as follows:

```
<Application.Resources>
  <ControlTemplate x:Key="RoundButtonTemplate" TargetType="{x:Type Button}">
    <Grid x:Name="controlLayout">
      <Ellipse x:Name="buttonSurface" Fill = "LightBlue"/>
```

```
        <Label x:Name="buttonCaption" VerticalAlignment = "Center" HorizontalAlignment
        = "Center"
                FontWeight = "Bold" FontSize = "20" Content = "OK!"/>
      </Grid>
    </ControlTemplate>
</Application.Resources>
```

Update the `Button` markup to the following:

```
<Button x:Name="myButton" Width="100" Height="100" Click="myButton_Click"
                Template="{StaticResource RoundButtonTemplate}">
</Button>
```

Now, because this resource is available for the entire application, you can define any number of round buttons just by simply applying the template. Create two additional `Button` controls that use this template for testing purposes (no need to handle the `Click` event for these new items).

```
<StackPanel>
    <Button x:Name="myButton" Width="100" Height="100"
            Click="myButton_Click"
            Template="{StaticResource RoundButtonTemplate}"></Button>
    <Button x:Name="myButton2" Width="100" Height="100"
            Template="{StaticResource RoundButtonTemplate}"></Button>
    <Button x:Name="myButton3" Width="100" Height="100"
            Template="{StaticResource RoundButtonTemplate}"></Button>
</StackPanel>
```

Incorporating Visual Cues Using Triggers

When you define a custom template, all of the visual cues of the default template are removed as well. For example, the default button template contains markup that informs the control how to look when certain UI events occur, such as when it receives focus, when it is clicked with the mouse, when it is enabled (or disabled), and so on. Users are quite accustomed to these sort of visual cues because it gives the control somewhat of a tactile response. However, your `RoundButtonTemplate` does not define any such markup, so the look of the control is identical regardless of the mouse activity. Ideally, your control should look slightly different when clicked (maybe via a color change or drop shadow) to let the user know the visual state has changed.

This can be done using triggers, as you have already learned. For simple operations, triggers work perfectly well. There are additional ways to do this that are beyond the scope of this book, but there is more information available at https://docs.microsoft.com/en-us/dotnet/framework/wpf/controls/customizing-the-appearance-of-an-existing-control.

By way of example, update your `RoundButtonTemplate` with the following markup, which adds two triggers. The first will change the color of the control to blue and the foreground color to yellow when the mouse is over the surface. The second shrinks the size of the `Grid` (and, therefore, all child elements) when the control is pressed via the mouse.

```
<ControlTemplate x:Key="RoundButtonTemplate" TargetType="Button" >
    <Grid x:Name="controlLayout">
        <Ellipse x:Name="buttonSurface" Fill="LightBlue" />
        <Label x:Name="buttonCaption" Content="OK!" FontSize="20" FontWeight="Bold"
                HorizontalAlignment="Center" VerticalAlignment="Center" />
    </Grid>
```

```
<ControlTemplate.Triggers>
  <Trigger Property = "IsMouseOver" Value = "True">
    <Setter TargetName = "buttonSurface" Property = "Fill" Value = "Blue"/>
    <Setter TargetName = "buttonCaption" Property = "Foreground" Value = "Yellow"/>
  </Trigger>
  <Trigger Property = "IsPressed" Value="True">
    <Setter TargetName="controlLayout" Property="RenderTransformOrigin" Value="0.5,0.5"/>
    <Setter TargetName="controlLayout" Property="RenderTransform">
      <Setter.Value>
        <ScaleTransform ScaleX="0.8" ScaleY="0.8"/>
      </Setter.Value>
    </Setter>
  </Trigger>
</ControlTemplate.Triggers>
</ControlTemplate>
```

The Role of the {TemplateBinding} Markup Extension

The problem with the control template is that each of the buttons look and say the same thing. Updating the markup to the following has no effect:

```
<Button x:Name="myButton" Width="100" Height="100"
  Background="Red" Content="Howdy!" Click="myButton_Click"
  Template="{StaticResource RoundButtonTemplate}" />
<Button x:Name="myButton2" Width="100" Height="100"
  Background="LightGreen" Content="Cancel!" Template="{StaticResource RoundButtonTemplate}" />
<Button x:Name="myButton3" Width="100" Height="100"
  Background="Yellow" Content="Format" Template="{StaticResource RoundButtonTemplate}" />
```

This is because the control's default properties (such as BackGround and Content) are overridden in the template. To enable them, they must be mapped to the related properties in the template. You can solve these issues by using the {TemplateBinding} markup extension when you build your template. This allows you to capture property settings defined by the control using your template and use them to set values in the template itself.

Here is a reworked version of RoundButtonTemplate, which now uses this markup extension to map the Background property of the Button to the Fill property of the Ellipse; it also makes sure the Content of the Button is indeed passed to the Content property of the Label:

```
<Ellipse x:Name="buttonSurface" Fill="{TemplateBinding Background}"/>
<Label x:Name="buttonCaption" Content="{TemplateBinding Content}"
     FontSize="20" FontWeight="Bold" HorizontalAlignment="Center"
     VerticalAlignment="Center" />
```

With this update, you can now create buttons of various colors and textual values (see Figure 27-14). Figure 27-14 shows the result of the updated XAML.

Figure 27-14. *Template bindings allow values to pass through to the internal controls*

The Role of ContentPresenter

When you designed your template, you used a Label to display the textual value of the control. Like the Button, the Label supports a Content property. Therefore, given your use of {TemplateBinding}, you could define a Button that contains complex content beyond that of a simple string.

However, what if you need to pass in complex content to a template member that does *not* have a Content property? When you want to define a generalized *content display area* in a template, you can use the ContentPresenter class as opposed to a specific type of control (Label or TextBlock). There is no need to do so for this example; however, here is some simple markup that illustrates how you could build a custom template that uses ContentPresenter to show the value of the Content property of the control using the template:

```
<!-- This button template will display whatever is set to the Content of the hosting button. -->
<ControlTemplate x:Key="NewRoundButtonTemplate" TargetType="Button">
  <Grid>
    <Ellipse Fill="{TemplateBinding Background}"/>
    <ContentPresenter HorizontalAlignment="Center" VerticalAlignment="Center"/>
  </Grid>
</ControlTemplate>
```

Incorporating Templates into Styles

Currently, your template simply defines a basic look and feel of the Button control. However, the process of establishing the basic properties of the control (content, font size, font weight, etc.) is the responsibility of the Button itself.

```
<!-- Currently the Button must set basic property values, not the template. -->
<Button x:Name ="myButton" Foreground ="Black" FontSize ="20" FontWeight ="Bold"
        Template ="{StaticResource RoundButtonTemplate}" Click ="myButton_Click"/>
```

If you want, you could establish these values *in the template*. By doing so, you can effectively create a default look and feel. As you might have already realized, this is a job for WPF styles. When you build a style (to account for basic property settings), you can define a template *within the style*! Here is your updated application resource in the application resources in App.xaml, which has been rekeyed as RoundButtonStyle:

```xml
<!-- A style containing a template. -->
<Style x:Key ="RoundButtonStyle" TargetType ="Button">
  <Setter Property ="Foreground" Value ="Black"/>
  <Setter Property ="FontSize" Value ="14"/>
  <Setter Property ="FontWeight" Value ="Bold"/>
  <Setter Property="Width" Value="100"/>
  <Setter Property="Height" Value="100"/>
  <!-- Here is the template! -->
  <Setter Property ="Template">
    <Setter.Value>
      <ControlTemplate TargetType ="Button">
          <!-- Control template from above example -->
      </ControlTemplate>
    </Setter.Value>
  </Setter>
</Style>
```

With this update, you can now create button controls by setting the Style property as so:

```xml
<Button x:Name="myButton" Background="Red" Content="Howdy!"
        Click="myButton_Click" Style="{StaticResource RoundButtonStyle}"/>
```

While the rendering and behavior of the button are identical, the benefit of nesting templates within styles is that you are able to provide a canned set of values for common properties. That wraps up your look at how to use Visual Studio and the trigger framework to build custom templates for a control. While there is still much more about the Windows Presentation Foundation API than has been examined here, you should be in a solid position for further study.

■ **Source Code**   You can find the ButtonTemplate project in the Chapter 27 subdirectory.

Summary

The first part of this chapter examined the resource management system of WPF. You began by looking at how to work with binary resources, and then you examined the role of object resources. As you learned, object resources are named blobs of XAML that can be stored at various locations in order to reuse content.

Next, you learned about WPF's animation framework. Here you had a chance to create some animations using C# code, as well as with XAML. You learned that if you define an animation in markup, you use <Storyboard> elements and triggers to control execution. You then looked at the WPF-style mechanism, which makes heavy use of graphics, object resources, and animations.

You examined the relationship between a *logical tree* and a *visual tree*. The logical tree is basically a one-to-one correspondence of the markup you author to describe a WPF root element. Behind this logical tree is a much deeper visual tree that contains detailed rendering instructions.

The role of a *default template* was then examined. Remember, when you are building custom templates, you are essentially ripping out all (or part) of a control's visual tree and replacing it with your own custom implementation.

CHAPTER 28

∎ ∎ ∎

WPF Notifications, Validations, Commands, and MVVM

This chapter will conclude your investigation of the WPF programming model by covering the capabilities that support the Model-View-ViewModel (MVVM) pattern. The first section covers the Model-View-ViewModel pattern. Next, you learn about the WPF notification system and its implementation of the Observable pattern through observable models and observable collections. Having the data in the UI accurately portray the current state of the data automatically improves the user experience significantly and reduces the manual coding required in older technologies (such as WinForms) to achieve the same result.

Building on the Observable pattern, you will examine the mechanisms to add validation into your application. Validation is a vital part of any application—not only letting the user know that something is wrong but also letting them know *what* is wrong. To inform the user what the error is, you will also learn how to incorporate validation into the view markup.

Next, you will take a deeper dive into the WPF command system and create custom commands to encapsulate program logic, much as you did in Chapter 25 with the built-in commands. There are several advantages to creating custom commands, including (but not limited to) enabling code reuse, logic encapsulation, and separation of concerns.

Finally, you will bring all of this together in a sample MVVM application.

Introducing Model-View-ViewModel

Before you dive into notifications, validations, and commands in WPF, it would be good to understand the end goal of this chapter, which is the Model-View-ViewModel pattern (MVVM). Derived from Martin Fowler's Presentation Model pattern, MVVM leverages XAML-specific capabilities, discussed in this chapter, to make your WPF development faster and cleaner. The name itself describes the main components of the pattern: model, view, view model.

The Model

The *model* is the object representation of your data. In MVVM, models are conceptually the same as the models from your Data Access layer (DAL). Sometimes they are the same physical class, but there is no requirement for this. As you read this chapter, you will learn how to decide whether you can use your DAL models or whether you need to create new ones.

Models typically take advantage of the built-in (or custom) validations through data annotations and the INotifyDataErrorInfo interface and are configured as observable to tie into the WPF notification system. You will see all of this later in this chapter.

© Andrew Troelsen and Philip Japikse 2017
A. Troelsen and P. Japikse, *Pro C# 7*, https://doi.org/10.1007/978-1-4842-3018-3_28

The View

The *view* is the UI of the application, and it is designed to be very lightweight. Think of the menu board at a drive-thru restaurant. The board displays menu items and prices, and it has a mechanism so the user can communicate with the back-end systems. However, there isn't any intelligence built into the board, unless it is specifically user interface logic, such as turning on the lights if it gets dark.

MVVM Views should be developed with the same goals in mind. Any intelligence should be built into the application elsewhere. The only code in the code-behind file (e.g., `MainWindow.xaml.cs`) should be directly related to manipulating the UI. It should not be based on business rules or anything that needs to be persisted for future use. While not a main goal of MVVM, well-developed MVVM applications typically have very little code in the code-behind.

The View Model

In WPF and other XAML technologies, the *view model* serves two purposes.

- The view model provides a single stop for all the data needed by the view. This doesn't mean the view model is responsible for getting the actual data; instead, it is merely a transport mechanism to move the data from the data store to the view. Usually, there is a one-to-one correlation between views and view models, but architectural differences exist, and your mileage may vary.

- The second job is to act as the controller for the view. Just like the menu board, the view model takes direction from the user and relays that call to the relevant code to make sure the proper actions are taken. Quite often this code is in the form of custom commands.

Anemic Models or Anemic View Models

In the early days of WPF, when developers were still working out how best to implement the MVVM pattern, there were significant (and sometimes heated) discussions about *where* to implement items like validation and the Observable pattern. One camp (the anemic model camp) argued that it all should be in the view model since adding those capabilities to the model broke separation of concerns. The other camp (the anemic view model camp) argued it should all be in the models since that reduced duplication of code.

The real answer is, of course, it depends. When `INotifyPropertyChanged`, `IDataErrorInfo`, and `INotifyDataErrorInfo` are implemented on the model classes, this ensures that the relevant code is close to the target of the code (as you will see in this chapter) and is implemented only once for each model. That being said, there are times when your `view model` classes will need to be developed as observables themselves. At the end of the day, you need to determine what makes the most sense for your application, without over-complicating your code or sacrificing the benefits of MVVM.

■ **Note**   There are multiple MVVM frameworks available for WPF, such as MVVMLite, Caliburn.Micro, and Prism (although Prism is much more than just an MVVM framework). This chapter discusses the MVVM pattern and the features in WPF that support implementing the pattern. I leave it to you, the reader, to examine the different frameworks and select the one that best matches your app's needs.

The WPF Binding Notification System

A significant shortcoming in the binding system for WinForms is a lack of notifications. If the data represented in the view is updated programmatically, the UI must also be refreshed programmatically to keep them in sync. This leads to a lot of calls to Refresh() on controls, typically more than are absolutely necessary in order to be safe. While usually not a significant performance issue to include too many calls to Refresh(), if you don't include enough, the experience for the user could be affected negatively.

The binding system built into XAML-based applications corrects this problem by enabling you to hook your data objects and collections into a notification system by developing them as observables. Whenever a property's value changes on an observable model or the collection changes (e.g., items are added, removed, or reordered) on an observable collection, an event is raised (either NotifyPropertyChanged or NotifyCollectionChanged). The binding framework automatically listens for those events to occur and updates the bound controls when they fire. Even better, as a developer, you have control over which properties raise the notifications. Sounds perfect, right? Well, it's not *quite* perfect. There can be a fair amount of code involved in setting this up for observable models if you are doing it all by hand. Fortunately, there is an open source framework that makes it much simpler, as you shall soon see.

Observable Models and Collections

In this section, you will create an application that uses observable models and collections. To get started, create a new WPF application named WpfNotifications. The application will be a master-detail form, allowing the user to select a specific car using a ComboBox, and then the details for that car will be displayed in the TextBox controls below. Update MainWindow.xaml to the following markup:

```
<Grid IsSharedSizeScope="True" Margin="5,0,5,5">
  <Grid.RowDefinitions>
    <RowDefinition Height="Auto"/>
    <RowDefinition Height="Auto"/>
  </Grid.RowDefinitions>
  <Grid Grid.Row="0">
    <Grid.ColumnDefinitions>
      <ColumnDefinition Width="Auto" SharedSizeGroup="CarLabels"/>
      <ColumnDefinition Width="*"/>
    </Grid.ColumnDefinitions>
    <Label Grid.Column="0" Content="Vehicle"/>
    <ComboBox Name="cboCars"  Grid.Column="1" DisplayMemberPath="PetName" />
</Grid>
<Grid Grid.Row="1" Name="DetailsGrid">
  <Grid.ColumnDefinitions>
    <ColumnDefinition Width="Auto" SharedSizeGroup="CarLabels"/>
    <ColumnDefinition Width="*"/>
  </Grid.ColumnDefinitions>
  <Grid.RowDefinitions>
    <RowDefinition Height="Auto"/>
    <RowDefinition Height="Auto"/>
    <RowDefinition Height="Auto"/>
    <RowDefinition Height="Auto"/>
  </Grid.RowDefinitions>
  <Label Grid.Column="0" Grid.Row="0" Content="Make"/>
  <TextBox Grid.Column="1" Grid.Row="0" />
```

```
<Label Grid.Column="0" Grid.Row="1" Content="Color"/>
<TextBox Grid.Column="1" Grid.Row="1" />
<Label Grid.Column="0" Grid.Row="2" Content="Pet Name"/>
<TextBox Grid.Column="1" Grid.Row="2" />
<StackPanel Grid.Column="0" Grid.ColumnSpan="2" Grid.Row="3"
    HorizontalAlignment="Right" Orientation="Horizontal" Margin="0,5,0,5">
  <Button x:Name="btnAddCar" Content="Add Car" Margin="5,0,5,0" Padding="4, 2" />
  <Button x:Name="btnChangeColor" Content="Change Color" Margin="5,0,5,0"
      Padding="4, 2"/>
</StackPanel>
</Grid>
</Grid>
```

Your window will resemble Figure 28-1.

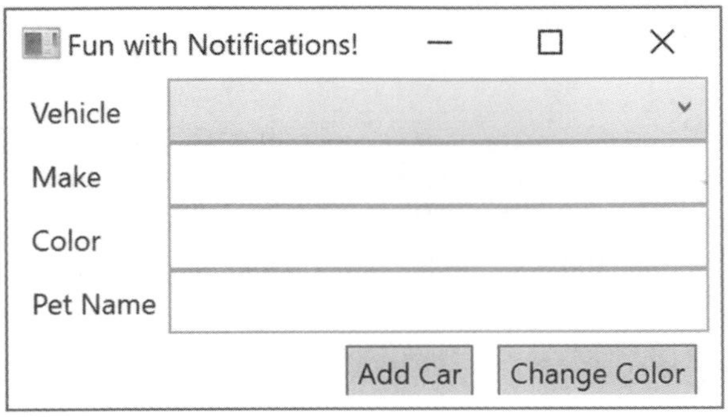

Figure 28-1. *Master-detail window displaying inventory details*

The IsSharedSizeScope tag on the Grid control sets up child grids to share dimensions. The ColumnDefinitions marked SharedSizeGroup will automatically be sized to the same width without any programming needed. In this example, if the Pet Name label was changed to something much longer, the Vehicle column (which is in a different Grid control) would be sized to match it, keeping the window's appearance nice and tidy.

Next, right-click the project name in Solution Explorer, select Add ➤ New Folder, and name the folder Models. In this new folder, create a class named Inventory. The initial class is listed here:

```
public class Inventory
{
  public int CarId { get; set; }
  public string Make { get; set; }
  public string Color { get; set; }
  public string PetName { get; set; }
}
```

Adding Bindings and Data

The next step is to add the binding statements for the controls. Remember that data-binding statements revolve around a data context, and this can be set on the control itself or on a parent control. Here, you are going to set the context on the DetailsGrid, so each control contained will inherit that data context.

Set the DataContext to the SelectedItem property of the ComboBox. Update the Grid that holds the detail controls to the following:

```
<Grid Grid.Row="1" Name="DetailsGrid" DataContext="{Binding ElementName=cboCars,
Path=SelectedItem}">
```

The text boxes in the DetailsGrid will show the individual properties of the select car. Add the appropriate text attributes and related bindings to the TextBox controls, like so:

```
<TextBox Grid.Column="1" Grid.Row="0" Text="{Binding Path=Make}" />
<TextBox Grid.Column="1" Grid.Row="1" Text="{Binding Path=Color}" />
<TextBox Grid.Column="1" Grid.Row="2" Text="{Binding Path=PetName}" />
```

Finally, add data to the ComboBox. In MainWindow.xaml.cs, create a new list of Inventory records, and set the ItemsSource for the ComboBox to the list. Also, add the using statement for the Notifications.Models namespace.

```
using WpfNotifications.Models;
//omitted for brevity
public partial class MainWindow : Window
{
  readonly IList<Inventory> _cars = new List<Inventory>();
  public MainWindow()
  {
    InitializeComponent();
    _cars.Add(new Inventory {CarId = 1, Color = "Blue", Make = "Chevy", PetName = "Kit"});
    _cars.Add(new Inventory {CarId = 2, Color = "Red", Make = "Ford", PetName = "Red Rider"});
    cboCars.ItemsSource = _cars;
    }
}
```

Run the app. You'll see that the vehicle selector has two cars to choose from. Choose one of them, and the text boxes will be automatically populated with the vehicle detail. Change the color of one of the vehicles, select the other vehicle, and then go back to the vehicle you edited. You will see the new color is indeed still attached to the vehicle. This isn't anything remarkable; you've seen the power of XAML data binding in previous examples.

Programmatically Changing the Vehicle Data

While the previous example works as expected, if the data is changed programmatically, the UI will *not* reflect the changes unless you program the app to refresh the data. To demonstrate this, add an event handler for the btnChangeColor Button, like so:

```
<Button x:Name="btnChangeColor" Content="Change Color" Margin="5,0,5,0"
    Padding="4, 2" Click="BtnChangeColor_OnClick"/>
```

In the `BtnChangeColor_Click()` event handler, use the `SelectedItem` property of the `ComboBox` to locate the selected record from the cars list, and change the color to `Pink`. The code is listed here:

```
private void BtnChangeColor_Click(object sender, RoutedEventArgs e)
{
  _cars.First(x => x.CarId == ((Inventory)cboCars.SelectedItem)?.CarId).Color = "Pink";
}
```

Run the app, select a vehicle, and click the Change Color button. Nothing changes visibly. Select the other vehicle and go back to your originally selected vehicle. Now you will see the updated value. This is not a very good experience for the user!

Now add an event handler to the `btnAddCar` button, like this:

```
<Button x:Name="btnAddCar" Content="Add Car" Margin="5,0,5,0" Padding="4, 2"
  Click="BtnAddCar_OnClick" />
```

In the `BtnAddCar_Click` event handler, add a new record to the `Inventory` list.

```
private void BtnAddCar_Click(object sender, RoutedEventArgs e)
{
  var maxCount = _cars?.Max(x => x.CarId) ?? 0;
  _cars?.Add(new Inventory { CarId=++maxCount,Color="Yellow",Make="VW",PetName="Birdie"});
}
```

Run the app, click the Add Car button, and examine the contents of the `ComboBox`. Even though you know there are three cars in the list, only two are displayed! To correct both of these problems, you will convert the `Inventory` class to an observable model and use an observable collection to hold all of the `Inventory` instances.

Observable Models

The problem of data changing on a property of your model and not being displayed in the UI is resolved by implementing the `INotifyPropertyChanged` interface on your `Inventory` model class. The `INotifyPropertyChanged` interface contains a single event: `PropertyChangedEvent`. The XAML binding engine listens for this event for each bound property on classes that implement the `INotifyPropertyChanged` interface. The interface is shown here:

```
public interface INotifyPropertyChanged
{
  event PropertyChangedEventHandler PropertyChanged;
}
```

Add the following `using` statements to the `Inventory.cs` class:

```
using System.ComponentModel;
using System.Runtime.CompilerServices;
```

Next, implement the INotifyPropertyChanged interface on the class, as follows:

```
public class Inventory : INotifyPropertyChanged
{
  //Omitted for brevity
  public event PropertyChangedEventHandler PropertyChanged;
}
```

The PropertyChanged event takes an object reference and a new instance of the PropertyChangedEventArgs class, like in this example:

```
PropertyChanged?.Invoke(this, new PropertyChangedEventArgs("Model"));
```

The first parameter is the object instance that is raising the event. The PropertyChangedEventArgs constructor takes a string that indicates the property that was changed and needs to be updated. When the event is raised, the binding engine looks for any controls bound to the named property on that instance. If you pass String.Empty into the PropertyChangedEventArgs, all of the bound properties of the instance are updated.

You control which properties are enlisted in the automatic updates. Only those properties that raise the PropertyChanged event in the setter will be automatically updated. This is usually all of the properties on your model classes, but you have the option of omitting certain properties based on your application's requirements. Instead of raising the event directly in the setter for each of the enlisted properties, a common pattern is to create a helper method (typically named OnPropertyChanged) that raises the event on behalf of the properties, usually in a base class for your models. Add the following method and code into the Inventory.cs class:

```
protected void OnPropertyChanged([CallerMemberName] string propertyName = "")
{
  PropertyChanged?.Invoke(this, new PropertyChangedEventArgs(propertyName));
}
```

In versions of .NET prior to 4.5, you had to pass the string name of the property into your helper method. If the property name of your class changed, you had to remember to update the string passed into helper method, or the update would not work. Starting in .NET 4.5, you can take advantage of the [CallerMemberName] attribute. This attribute assigns the name of the method that calls into the method to the parameter marked with the attribute, in this case, the propertyName parameter.

Next, update each of the automatic properties in the Inventory class to have a full getter and setter with a backing field. When the value is changed, call the OnPropertyChanged helper method. Here is the CarId property updated:

```
private int _carId;
public int CarId
{
  get => _carId;
  set
  {
    if (value == _carId) return;
    _carId = value;
    OnPropertyChanged();
  }
}
```

Make sure you do the same for all of the properties in the class and then run the app again. Select a vehicle and click the Change Color button. You will immediately see the change show up in the UI. First problem solved!

Using nameof

A feature added in C# 6 is the nameof operator, which provides the string name of the item passed into the nameof method. You can use this in the calls to OnPropertyChanged() in your setters, like this:

```
public string Color
{
  get { return _color; }
  set
  {
    if (value == _color) return;
    _color = value;
    OnPropertyChanged(nameof(Color));
  }
}
```

Note that you don't have to remove the CallerMemberName attribute from the OnPropertyChanged when you use the nameof method (although it becomes unnecessary). In the end, whether you use the nameof method or the CallerMemberName attribute comes down to a matter of personal choice.

Observable Collections

The next problem to resolve is updating the UI when the contents of a collection changes. This is done by implementing the INotifyCollectionChanged interface. Like the INotifyPropertyChanged interface, this interface exposes one event, the CollectionChanged event. Unlike the INotifyPropertyChanged event, implementing this interface by hand is more than just calling a method in the setter. You need to create a full List implementation and raise the CollectionChanged event any time your list changes.

Using the ObservableCollections Class

Fortunately, there is a much easier way than creating your own collection class. The ObservableCollection<T> class implements INotifyCollectionChanged, INotifyPropertyChanged, and Collection<T>, and it is part of the .NET Framework. No extra work! To see this, add a using statement for System.Collections.ObjectModel and then update the private field for _cars to the following:

```
private readonly IList<Inventory> _cars = new ObservableCollection<Inventory>();
```

Run the app again, and click the Add Car button. You will see the new records appear appropriately.

Implementing a Dirty Flag

Another advantage of observable models is the ability to track state changes. While some object-relational mapping (ORM) tools like Entity Framework provide some rudimentary state tracking, with observable models, dirty tracking (tracking when one or more of an object's values have changed) is trivial. Add a bool property named IsChanged to the Inventory class. Make sure to call OnPropertyChanged() just like the other properties in the Inventory class.

```
private bool _isChanged;
public bool IsChanged {
  get => _isChanged;
  set
  {
    if (value == _isChanged) return;
    _isChanged = value;
    OnPropertyChanged();
  }
}
```

You need to set the IsChanged property to true in the OnPropertyChanged() method. You also need to make sure you aren't setting IsChanged to true when IsChanged is updated, or you will hit a stack overflow exception! Update the OnPropertyChanged method to the following (which uses the nameof method discussed earlier):

```
protected virtual void OnPropertyChanged([CallerMemberName] string propertyName = "")
{
  if (propertyName != nameof(IsChanged))
  {
    IsChanged = true;
  }
  PropertyChanged?.Invoke(this, new PropertyChangedEventArgs(propertyName));
}
```

Open MainWindow.xaml, and add an additional RowDefinition to the DetailsGrid. Add the following to the end of the Grid, which contains a Label and a CheckBox, bound to the IsChanged property, as follows:

```
<Label Grid.Column="0" Grid.Row="4" Content="Is Changed"/>
<CheckBox Grid.Column="1" Grid.Row="4" VerticalAlignment="Center"
    Margin="10,0,0,0" IsEnabled="False" IsChecked="{Binding Path=IsChanged}" />
```

If you were run the app now, you would see that every single record shows up as changed, even though you haven't changed anything! This is because object creation sets property values, and setting any values calls OnPropertyChanged(). This sets the object's IsChanged property. To correct this, set the IsChanged property to false as the last property in the object initialization code. Open MainWindow.xaml.cs and change the code that creates the list to the following:

```
_cars.Add(
    new Inventory {CarId = 1, Color = "Blue", Make = "Chevy", PetName = "Kit",
    IsChanged = false});
_cars.Add(
    new Inventory {CarId = 2, Color = "Red", Make = "Ford", PetName = "Red Rider",
    IsChanged = false});
```

Run the app again, select a vehicle, and click the Change Color button. You will see the check box get selected along with the updated color.

Updating the Source Through UI Interaction

You might notice that if you type text into the UI, the Is Changed check box doesn't actually get selected until you tab out of the control being edited. This is because of the UpdateSourceTrigger property on the TextBox bindings. The UpdateSourceTrigger determines what event (such as changing the value, tabbing out, etc.) causes the UI to update the underlying data. There are four options, as shown in Table 28-1.

Table 28-1. *UpdateSourceTrigger Values*

Member	Meaning in Life
Default	Set to the default for the control (e.g., LostFocus for TextBox controls).
Explicit	Updates the source object only when the UpdateSource method is called.
LostFocus	Updates when the control loses focus. This is the default for TextBox controls.
PropertyChanged	Updates as soon as the property changes. This is the default for CheckBox controls.

The default source trigger for a TextBox is the LostFocus event. Change this to PropertyChanged by updating the binding for the Color TextBox to the following XAML:

```
<TextBox Grid.Column="1" Grid.Row="1" Text="{Binding Path=Color, UpdateSourceTrigger=
PropertyChanged}" />
```

Now, when you run the app and start typing into the Color text box, the check box is immediately selected. You might ask why the default is set to LostFocus for TextBox controls. Any validation (covered in a moment) for a model fires in conjunction with the UpdateSourceTrigger. For a TextBox, this would then potentially cause errors continually flashing until the user entered the correct values. For example, if the validation rules don't allow less than five characters in a TextBox, the error would show on each keystroke until the user got five or more entered. In those cases, it's best to wait for the user to tab out of the TextBox (after completing the change to the text) to update the source.

Use PropertyChanged.Fody to Implement Observable Models

You can imagine that if you have complex models, implementing INotifyPropertyChanged can be quite tedious. Fortunately, some smart minds have solved this predicament. There is an open source project called PropertyChanged.Fody that addresses this concern. This project is an extension of the Fody Project (https://github.com/Fody/Fody/), an open source tool for weaving .NET assemblies. *Weaving* is the process of manipulating the IL generated during the build process. PropertyChanged.Fody adds in all of the plumbing code for INotifyPropertyChanged for you, and if you have a property named IsChanged, it will be updated when another property changes, just as you did manually in the earlier example in this chapter.

■ **Note**   You can find more information about the PropertyChanged project at https://github.com/Fody/PropertyChanged.

To install the necessary packages, right-click your project name, select Manage NuGet Packages, and search for and install `propertychanged.fody`. Once that is done, rename your `Inventory` class to `InventoryManual`, and create a new `Inventory` class like this:

```
public class Inventory : INotifyPropertyChanged
{
  public bool IsChanged { get; set; }
  public int CarId { get; set; }
  public string Make { get; set; }
  public string Color { get; set; }
  public string PetName { get; set; }
  public event PropertyChangedEventHandler PropertyChanged;
}
```

When your project is compiled, any class that implements `INotifyPropertyChanged` will have all of the plumbing (including updating the setters, handling `IsChanged`, and adding on an `OnPropertyChanged()` method). Run the project again, and you will see all of the updates and `IsChanged` functionality works as expected!

Updating the Fody Package Can Break PropertyChanged.Fody

The PropertyChanged.Fody NuGet package has a dependency on the Fody NuGet package. The version of Fody specified in the PorpertyChange.Fody manifest is 2.0.0, however, the current version of Fody is 2.1.2. If you update the Fody package, to version 2.1.2, you will break the PropertyChanged.Fody package, at least at the time of this writing. This is because the Fody update overwrites the `FodyWeavers.xml` file and removes any added packages. Fortunately, it's easy to fix.

Open the `FodyWeavers.xml` file, and make sure it reads as follows:

```xml
<?xml version="1.0" encoding="utf-8" ?>
<Weavers>
    <PropertyChanged />
</Weavers>
```

This will add PropertyChanged.Fody back into your project.

Wrapping Up Notifications and Observables

Using `INotifyPropertyChanged` on your models and `ObservableCollections` classes for your lists improves the user experience by keeping the data and the UI in sync. While neither interface is complicated, they do require updates to your code. Fortunately, Microsoft has included the `ObservableCollection` class to handle all of the plumbing to create observable collections. Just as fortunate is the update to the Fody project to add `INotifyPropertyChanged` functionality automatically. With these two tools in hand, there isn't any reason to not implement observables in your WPF applications.

■ **Source Code**   You can find the WpfNotifications project in the `Chapter 28` subdirectory.

WPF Validations

Now that you've implemented `INotifyPropertyChanged` and are using an `ObservableCollection`, it's time to add validations to your application. Applications need to validate user input and provide feedback to the user when the data entered is incorrect. This section covers the most common validation mechanisms for modern WPF applications, but these are still just a portion of the capabilities built into WPF.

■ **Note**   For a full explanation of all of the validations methods in WPF, please see Matthew McDonald's *Pro WPF in C# 4.5*, available from Apress at `www.apress.com/9781430243656`.

Validation occurs when a data binding attempts to update the data source. In addition to built-in validations, such as exceptions in a property's setter, you can create custom validation rules. If *any* validation rule (built-in or custom) fails, the `Validation` class, discussed shortly, comes into play.

■ **Note**   For each of the sections in this chapter, you can continue working in the same project from the previous section, or you can create a copy of the project for each new section. For each section of this chapter, I have created a separate application, starting where the previous section ended. This is to enable you to see the progression through the chapter in different projects. Take note the project-specific namespaces in each section will refer to the new project I am using, so make sure you add the correct namespaces if you are following along with just one project.

Updating the Sample for the Validation Examples

I have copied the previous section's code into a new project called WpfValidations. If you are using the same project from the previous section, you just need to make note of the namespace changes in the following code examples. Update `MainWindow.xaml` to add an additional `RowDefinition` to the `DetailsGrid`, and in that row add a `Label` and a `TextBox` for the `CarId` property, as follows (you will need to increment all of the other `Grid.Row` properties by 1):

```
<Label Grid.Column="0" Grid.Row="0" Content="Id"/>
<TextBox Grid.Column="1" Grid.Row="0" Text="{Binding Path=CarId}" />
```

When you run the app and select a record, the `Id` text box is automatically populated with the primary key value (as expected). Now that you have updated the core application, it's time to explore validations in WPF.

The Validation Class

Before adding validations to your project, it's important to understand the `Validation` class. This class is part of the validation framework, and it provides methods and attached properties that can be used to display validation results. There are three main properties of the `Validation` class commonly used when handling validation errors (shown in Table 28-2). You will use each of these through the rest of this section.

Table 28-2. *Key Members of the Validation Class*

Member	Meaning in Life
HasError	Attached property indicating that a validation rule failed somewhere in the process
Errors	Collection of all active ValidationError objects
ErrorTemplate	Control template that becomes visible and adorns the bound element when HasError is set to true

Validation Options

As mentioned, XAML technologies have several mechanisms for incorporating validation logic into your application. You will examine three of the most commonly used validation choices in the next sections.

Notify on Exceptions

While exceptions should not be used to enforce business logic, exceptions can and do happen, and they should be handled appropriately. In case they aren't handled in code, the user should receive visual feedback of the problem. An important change from WinForms is that WPF binding exceptions are not, by default, propagated to the user as exceptions. They are, however, visually indicated, using an adorner (visual layer that resides on top of your controls).

To test this, run the app, select a record from the ComboBox, and clear out the Id value. Since the CarId property is defined as an int (not a nullable int), a numeric value is required. When you tab out of the Id field, an empty string is sent to the CarId property by the binding framework, and since an empty string can't be converted to an int, an exception in thrown in the setter. Normally, an unhandled exception would generate a message box to the user, but in this case, nothing like that happened. If you look in the Debug portion of the Output window, you will see the following:

```
System.Windows.Data Error: 7 : ConvertBack cannot convert value '' (type 'String').
BindingExpression:Path=CarId; DataItem='Inventory' (HashCode=24111608); target element is
'TextBox' (Name=''); target property is 'Text' (type 'String') FormatException:'System.
FormatException: Input string was not in a correct format.
```

Visual display of the exception is a thin red box around the control, as shown in Figure 28-2.

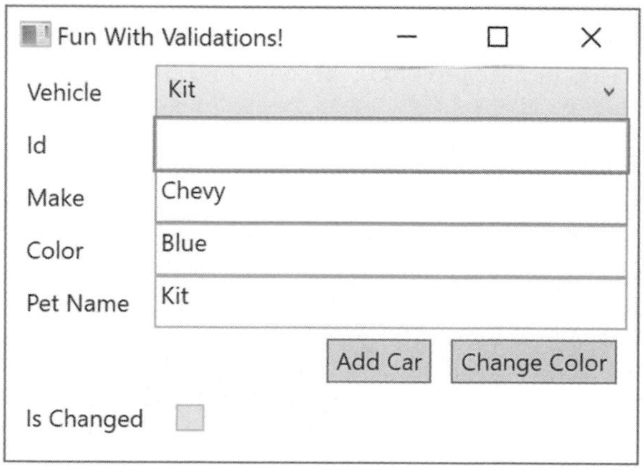

Figure 28-2. *The default error template*

The red box is the ErrorTemplate property of the Validation object and acts as an adorner for the bound control. While the default look and feel shows that there is indeed an error, there isn't any indication as to *what* is wrong. The good news is that the ErrorTemplate is completely customizable, as you will see later in this chapter.

IDataErrorInfo

The IDataErrorInfo interface provides a mechanism for you to add custom validations to your model classes. This interface is added directly to your model (or view model) classes, and the validation code is placed inside your model classes (preferably in partial classes). This centralizes validation code in your project, in direct contrast to WinForms projects, where validation was typically done in the UI itself.

The IDataErrorInfo interface, shown here, contains two properties: an indexer and a string property named Error. Note that the WPF binding engine doesn't use the Error property.

```
public interface IDataErrorInfo
{
  string this[string columnName] { get; }
  string Error { get; }
}
```

You will be adding the Inventory partial class shortly, but first you need to update the Inventory. cs class and mark it as partial. Next, add another file to the Models directory named InventoryPartial. cs. Rename this class Inventory, make sure the class is marked as partial, and add the IDataErrorInfo interface. Finally, implement the API for the interface. The initial code is listed here:

```
public partial class Inventory : IDataErrorInfo
{
  private string _error;
  public string this[string columnName]
  {
    get { return string.Empty; }
  }

  public string Error => _error;
}
```

For a bound control to opt in to the IDataErrorInfo interface, it must add ValidatesOnDataErrors to the binding expression. Update the binding expression for the Make text box to the following (and update the rest of the binding statements in the same way):

```
<TextBox Grid.Column="1" Grid.Row="1" Text="{Binding Path=Make, ValidatesOnDataErrors=True}" />
```

Once this update is made to the binding statements, the indexer on the model gets called each time the PropertyChanged event is raised. The property name from the event is used as the columnName parameter in the indexer. If the indexer returns string.Empty, the framework assumes that all validations passed, and no error condition exists. If the indexer returns anything but string.Empty, an error is presumed to exist on the property for that object instance, and each control that is bound to the property being validated on this specific instance of the class is considered to have an error, the HasError property of the Validation object is set to true, and the ErrorTemplate adorner is activated for the controls effected.

Next, you will add some simple validation logic to the indexer in InventoryPartial.cs. The validation rules are simple.

- If Make equals ModelT, set the error equal to "Too Old".

- If Make equals Chevy and Color equals Pink, set the error equal to $"{Make}'s don't come in {Color}".

Start by adding a switch statement for each of the properties. To avoid using magic strings in the case statements, you will again use the nameof method. If the code falls through the switch statement, return string.Empty. Next, add the validation rules. In the proper case statements, add a check of the property value based on the rules listed earlier. In the case statement for the Make property, first check to make sure the value isn't ModelT. If it is, return the error. If that passes, the next line will call into a helper method that returns an error if the second rule is violated, or it will return string.Empty if it is not. In the case statement for the Color property, also call the helper method. The code is as follows:

```
public string this[string columnName]
{
  get
  {
    switch (columnName)
    {
      case nameof(CarId):
        break;
      case nameof(Make):
        if (Make == "ModelT")
        {
          return "Too Old";
        }
        return CheckMakeAndColor();
      case nameof(Color):
        return CheckMakeAndColor();
      case nameof(PetName):
        break;
    }
    return string.Empty;
  }
}

internal string CheckMakeAndColor()
{
    if (Make == "Chevy" && Color == "Pink")
    {
        return $"{Make}'s don't come in {Color}";
    }
    return string.Empty;
}
```

Run the app, select the Red Rider vehicle (the Ford), and change the Make to ModelT. Once you tab out of the field, the red error decorator appears. Now select Kit (which is a Chevy) from the drop-down, and click the Change Color button to change the color to Pink. Immediately the red error adorner appears on the Color field but doesn't appear on the Make text box. Now, change Make to Ford, tab out of the text box, and note that the red adorner does *not* disappear!

This is because the indexer runs only when the PropertyChanged event is fired for a property. As discussed in the "WPP Binding Notification System", the PropertyChanged event fires when the source object's property changes, and this happens either through code (such as clicking the Change Color button) or through user interaction (the timing of this is controlled through the UpdateSourceTrigger). When you changed the color, the Make property did not change, so the event did not fire for the Make property. Since the event didn't fire, the indexer did not get called, so the validation for the Make property didn't run.

There are two ways to fix this. The first is to change PropertyChangedEventArgs to update every bound property by passing in string.Empty instead of a field name. As discussed, this causes the binding engine to update *every* property on that instance. Add an OnPropertyChanged method and code it like this:

```
protected virtual void OnPropertyChanged([CallerMemberName] string propertyName = "")
{
  if (propertyName != nameof(IsChanged))
  {
    IsChanged = true;
  }
  //PropertyChanged?.Invoke(this, new PropertyChangedEventArgs(propertyName));
  PropertyChanged?.Invoke(this, new PropertyChangedEventArgs(string.Empty));
}
```

■ **Note** The PropertyChanged.Fody package automatically adds an OnPropertyChanged() method, unless it finds one already in the class marked with INotifyPropertyChanged. Since you want to change the default implementation by updating all fields, you add the method yourself, and it will be used by the PropertyChanged. Fody package.

Now, when you run the same test, you see that both the Make and Color text boxes are adorned with the error template when one of them is updated. So, why not always raise the event in this manner? It's largely a matter of performance. It's *possible* that refreshing every property on an object could hamper performance. Of course, there's no way to know without testing, and your mileage may (and probably will) vary.

The other solution is to raise the PropertyChanged event for the other dependent field(s) when one changes. The downside to using this mechanism is that you (or other developers who support your app) must know that the Make and Color properties are related through the validation code.

INotifyDataErrorInfo

The INotifyDataErrorInfo interface introduced in .NET 4.5 builds on the IDataErrorInfo interface and adds additional capabilities for validation. Of course, with additional power comes additional work! In a drastic shift from prior validation techniques that you had to specifically opt into, the ValidatesOnNotifyDataErrors binding property defaults to true, so adding the property to your binding statements is optional.

The INotifyDataErrorInfo interface is extremely small but does take a fair amount of plumbing code to make it effective, as you will see shortly. The interface is shown here:

```
public interface INotifyDataErrorInfo
{
  bool HasErrors { get; }
  event EventHandler<DataErrorsChangedEventArgs> ErrorsChanged;
  IEnumerable GetErrors(string propertyName);
}
```

The HasErrors property is used by the binding engine to determine whether there are *any* errors on any of the instance's properties. If the GetErrors() method is called with a null or empty string for the propertyName parameter, it returns all errors that exist in the instance. If a propertyName is passed into the method, only the errors for that particular property are returned. The ErrorsChanged event (like the PropertyChanged and CollectionChanged events) notifies the binding engine to update the UI for the current list of errors.

Implement the Supporting Code

When implementing INotifyDataErrorInfo, most of the code is usually pushed into a base model class so it needs be written only once. Start by replacing IDataErrorInfo with INotifyDataErrorInfo to the InventoryPartial.cs class (you can leave the code from IDataErrorInfo in the class; it won't get in the way).

After adding the interface members, add a Dictionary<string,List<string>> that will hold any errors grouped by property name. You will also need to add a using statement for System.Collections.Generic. Both are shown here:

```
using System.Collections.Generic;
private readonly Dictionary<string,List<string>> _errors =   new Dictionary<string,
List<string>>();
```

The HasErrors property should return true if there are *any* errors in the dictionary. This is easily accomplished like this (you can delete the _hasErrors variable):

```
public bool HasErrors => _errors.Count != 0;
```

Next, create a helper method to raise the ErrorsChanged event (just like raising the PropertyChanged event) like this:

```
private void OnErrorsChanged(string propertyName)
{
  ErrorsChanged?.Invoke(this, new DataErrorsChangedEventArgs(propertyName));
}
```

As mentioned earlier, the GetErrors() method should return any and all errors in the dictionary if the parameter is empty or null. If a propertyName value is passed in, it will return any errors found for that property. If the parameter doesn't match (or there aren't any errors for a property), then the method will return null.

```
public IEnumerable GetErrors(string propertyName)
{
  if (string.IsNullOrEmpty(propertyName))
  {
    return _errors.Values;
  }
  return _errors.ContainsKey(propertyName) ? _errors[propertyName] : null;
}
```

The final set of helpers will add one or more errors for a property or clear all of the errors for a property or all properties. Any time the dictionary changes, remember to call the OnErrorsChanged() helper method.

```
private void AddError(string propertyName, string error)
{
    AddErrors(propertyName, new List<string> { error });
}
private void AddErrors(string propertyName, IList<string> errors)
{
    var changed = false;
    if (!_errors.ContainsKey(propertyName))
    {
        _errors.Add(propertyName, new List<string>());
        changed = true;
    }
    foreach (var err in errors)
    {
        if (_errors[propertyName].Contains(err)) continue;
        _errors[propertyName].Add(err);
        changed = true;
    }
    if (changed)
    {
        OnErrorsChanged(propertyName);
    }
}
protected void ClearErrors(string propertyName = "")
{
    if (String.IsNullOrEmpty(propertyName))
    {
        _errors.Clear();
    }
    else
    {
        _errors.Remove(propertyName);
    }
    OnErrorsChanged(propertyName);
}
```

Now the question is, how is this code activated? The binding engine listens for the ErrorsChanged event and will update the UI if there is a change in the errors collection for a binding statement. But the validation code still needs a trigger to execute. There are two mechanisms for this, and they will be discussed next.

Use INotifyDataErrorInfo for Validations

One place to check for errors is in the property setters, like the following example, simplified to just check for the ModelT validation:

```
public string Make
{
    get { return _make; }
    set
    {
        if (value == _make) return;
        _make = value;
```

```
        if (Make == "ModelT")
        {
            AddError(nameof(Make), "Too Old");
        }
        else
        {
            ClearErrors(nameof(Make));
        }
        OnPropertyChanged(nameof(Make));
        //OnPropertyChanged(nameof(Color));
    }
}
```

There are several issues with this approach. First, it doesn't work with your current approach of injecting the support for INotifyPropertyChanged using PropertyChanged.Fody. Second, you have to combine validation logic with property setters, making the code harder to read and support.

Combine IDataErrorInfo with INotifyDataErrorInfo for Validations

You saw in the previous section that IDataErrorInfo can be added to a partial class, which means you don't have to update your setters. You also saw that the indexer automatically gets called when PropertyChanged is raised on a property. Combining IDataErrorInfo and INotifyDataErrorInfo provides you with the additional features for validations from INotifyDataErrorInfo and with the separation from the setters provided by IDataErrorInfo.

Add the IDataErrorInfo interface back onto the Inventory class that is in InventoryPartial.cs.

```
public partial class Inventory : IDataErrorInfo, INotifyDataErrorInfo
```

The purpose of using IDataErrorInfo is not to run validations but to make sure your validation code that leverages INotifyDataErrorInfo gets called every time PropertyChanged is raised on your object. Since you aren't using IDataErrorInfo for validation, always return string.Empty. Update the indexer and the CheckMakeAndColor() helper method to the following code:

```
public string this[string columnName]
{
  get
  {
    bool hasError = false;
    switch (columnName)
    {
      case nameof(CarId):
        break;
      case nameof(Make):
        hasError = CheckMakeAndColor();
        if (Make == "ModelT")
        {
          AddError(nameof(Make), "Too Old");
          hasError = true;
        }
```

```
      if (!hasError)
      {
        //This is not perfect logic, just illustrative of the pattern
        ClearErrors(nameof(Make));
        ClearErrors(nameof(Color));
      }
      break;
    case nameof(Color):
      hasError = CheckMakeAndColor();
      if (!hasError)
      {
        ClearErrors(nameof(Make));
        ClearErrors(nameof(Color));
      }
      break;
    case nameof(PetName):
      break;
  }
  return string.Empty;
}
}
internal bool CheckMakeAndColor()
{
  if (Make == "Chevy" && Color == "Pink")
  {
    AddError(nameof(Make), $"{Make}'s don't come in {Color}");
    AddError(nameof(Color), $"{Make}'s don't come in {Color}");
    return true;
  }
  return false;
}
```

Run the app, select Chevy, and change the color to Pink. In addition to the red adorners around the Make and Model text boxes, you will also see a red box adorner around the entire grid that holds the Inventory details fields (shown in Figure 28-3).

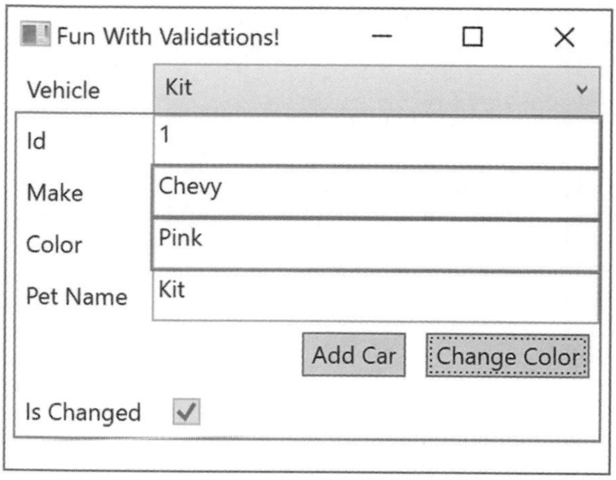

Figure 28-3. *The updated error adorner*

This is another advantage of using INotifyDataErrorInfo. In addition to the controls in error, the control defining the data context also gets adorned with the error template.

Show All Errors

The Errors property on the Validation class returns all the validation errors on a particular object in the form of ValidationError objects. Each ValidationError object has an ErrorContent property that contains the list of error messages for the property. This means the error messages you want to display are in this list within a list. To display them properly, you need to create a ListBox that holds a ListBox to display the data. It sounds a bit recursive, but it will make sense once you see it.

Start by adding another row to the DetailsGrid and increase the Height of the Window to at least 300. Add a ListBox in the last row, and bind the ItemsSource to the DetailsGrid, using Validation.Errors for the path, as follows:

```
<ListBox Grid.Row="6" Grid.Column="0" Grid.ColumnSpan="2"
    ItemsSource="{Binding ElementName=DetailsGrid, Path=(Validation.Errors)}">
</ListBox>
```

Add a DataTemplate to the ListBox, and in the DataTemplate, add a ListBox that is bound to the ErrorContent property. The data context for each ListBoxItem in this case is a ValidationError object, so you don't need to set the data context, just the path. Set the binding path to ErrorContent, like this:

```
<ListBox.ItemTemplate>
  <DataTemplate>
    <ListBox ItemsSource="{Binding Path=ErrorContent}"/>
  </DataTemplate>
</ListBox.ItemTemplate>
```

Run the app, select Chevy, and set the color to Pink. You will see the errors displayed in Figure 28-4.

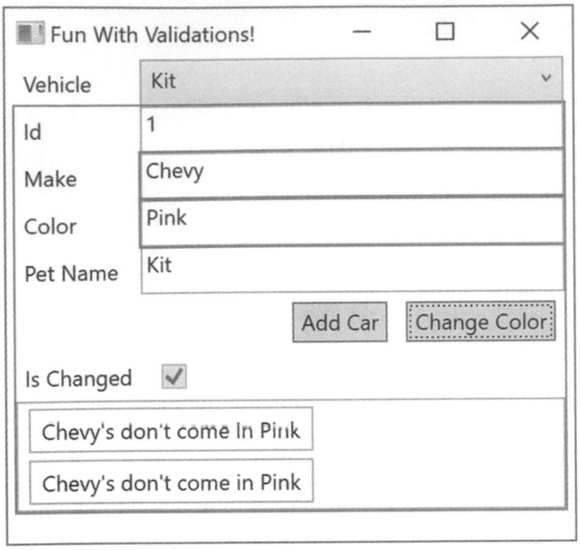

Figure 28-4. *Showing the errors collection*

This just scratches the surface of what you can do with validations and with displaying the errors generated, but it should have you well on your way to developing informative UIs that improve the user experience.

Move the Support Code to a Base Class

As you probably noticed, there is a lot of code now in the `InventoryPartial.cs` class. Since this example has only one model class, this isn't terrible. But, as you add models to a real application, you don't want to have to add all of that plumbing into each partial class for your models. The best thing to do is to push all of that supporting code down to a base class. You will do that now.

Add a new class file to the `Models` folder named `EntityBase.cs`. Add using statements for `System.Collections` and `System.ComponentModel`. Make the class public, and add the `INotifyDataErrorInfo` interface, like this:

```
using System;
using System.Collections;
using System.Collections.Generic;
using System.ComponentModel;
using System.Linq;

namespace Validations.Models
{
    public class EntityBase : INotifyDataErrorInfo
}
```

Move all of the code from InventoryPartial.cs that relates to INofityDataErrorInfo into the new base class. Any private methods need to be made protected. Next, remove the INotifyDataErrorInfo interface from the InventoryPartial.cs class, and add EntityBase as a base class, as follows:

```
public partial class Inventory : EntityBase, IDataErrorInfo
{
 //removed for brevity
}
```

Now, any additional model classes you create will inherit all of the INotifyDataErrorInfo plumbing code.

Leverage Data Annotations with WPF

WPF can leverage data annotations as well for UI validation. Let's add some data annotations to the Inventory model.

Add Data Annotations to the Model

Add a project reference to System.ComponentModel.DataAnnotations and then open up Inventory.cs and add a using statement for System.ComponentModel.DataAnnotations. Add the [Required] attribute to the CarId, Make, and Color properties, and add [StringLength(50)] to Make, Color, and PetName. The Required attribute adds a validation rule that the property must not be null (admittedly, this is redundant for the CarId property since it is not a nullable int). The StringLength(50) attribute adds a validation rule that the value of the property cannot be longer than 50 characters.

Check for Data Annotation–Based Validation Errors

Unlike ASP.NET (which can automatically check the model for validation errors based on data annotations), in WPF you have to programmatically check for data annotation-based validation errors. Two key classes for annotation-based validations are the ValidationContext and Validator classes. The ValidationContext class provides a context for checking a class for validation errors. The Validator class allows you to check an object for attribute-based errors within a ValidationContext.

Open EntityBase.cs, and add the following using statements:

```
using System.ComponentModel;
using System.ComponentModel.DataAnnotations;
```

Next, create a new method named GetErrorsFromAnnotations. This method is generic, takes a string property name and a value of type T as the parameters, and returns a string array. Make sure the method is marked as protected. The signature is listed here:

```
protected string[] GetErrorsFromAnnotations<T>(string propertyName, T value)
```

In the method, create a List<ValidationResult> variable that will hold the results of validation checks and create a ValidationContext scoped to the property name passed into the method. When you have those two items in place, call Validate.TryValidateProperty, which returns a bool. If everything passes (in regard to data annotation validations), it returns true. If not, it returns false and populates the List<ValidationResult> with the errors. The complete code is shown here:

```
protected string[] GetErrorsFromAnnotations<T>(string propertyName, T value)
{
  var results = new List<ValidationResult>();
  var vc = new ValidationContext(this, null, null) { MemberName = propertyName };
  var isValid = Validator.TryValidateProperty(value, vc, results);
  return (isValid)?null:Array.ConvertAll(results.ToArray(), o => o.ErrorMessage);
}
```

Now you can update the indexer method in InventoryPartial.cs to check for any errors based on data annotations. If any errors are found, add them to the errors collection supporting INotifyDataErrorInfo. The updated indexer code is shown here:

```
bool hasError = false;
switch (columnName)
{
  case nameof(CarId):
    AddErrors(nameof(CarId),GetErrorsFromAnnotations(nameof(CarId),CarId));
    break;
  case nameof(Make):
    hasError = CheckMakeAndColor();
    if (Make == "ModelT")
    {
      AddError(nameof(Make), "Too Old");
      hasError = true;
    }
    if (!hasError)
    {
      //This is not perfect logic, just illustrative of the pattern
      ClearErrors(nameof(Make));
      ClearErrors(nameof(Color));
    }
    AddErrors(nameof(Make), GetErrorsFromAnnotations(nameof(Make), Make));
    break;
  case nameof(Color):
    hasError = CheckMakeAndColor();
    if (!hasError)
    {
      ClearErrors(nameof(Make));
      ClearErrors(nameof(Color));
    }
    AddErrors(nameof(Color), GetErrorsFromAnnotations(nameof(Color), Color));
    break;
  case nameof(PetName):
    AddErrors(nameof(PetName), GetErrorsFromAnnotations(nameof(PetName), PetName));
    break;
}
return string.Empty;
```

You will also have to update the AddErrors() method to make sure that an empty list doesn't get added to the _errors dictionary.

```
protected void AddErrors(string propertyName, IList<string> errors)
{
  if (errors?.Count == 0)
  {
    return;
  }
  //omitted for brevity
}
```

Run the app, select one of the vehicles, and add text for the color that is longer than 50 characters. When you cross the 50-character threshold, the StringLength data annotation creates a validation error, and it is reported to the user, as shown in Figure 28-5.

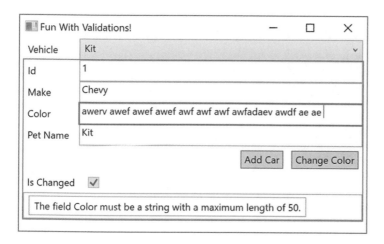

Figure 28-5. *Validating the required data annotation*

Customizing the ErrorTemplate

The final topic is to create a style that will be applied when a control is in error and also update the ErrorTemplate to display more meaningful error information. As you learned in Chapter 27, controls are customizable through styles and control templates.

Start by adding a new style in the Windows.Resources section of MainWindow.xaml with a target type of TextBox. Next, add a trigger on the style that sets properties when the Validation.HasError property is set to true. The properties and the values to set are Background (Pink), Foreground (Black), and Tooltip to the ErrorContent. The Background and Foreground setters are nothing new, but the syntax for setting the ToolTip needs some explanation. The binding points back to the control that this style is applied to, in this case, the TextBox. The path is the first ErrorContent value of the Validation.Errors collection. The markup is as follows:

```
<Window.Resources>
  <Style TargetType="{x:Type TextBox}">
    <Style.Triggers>
```

```xml
        <Trigger Property="Validation.HasError" Value="true">
          <Setter Property="Background" Value="Pink" />
          <Setter Property="Foreground" Value="Black" />
          <Setter Property="ToolTip"
              Value="{Binding RelativeSource={RelativeSource Self},
              Path=(Validation.Errors)[0].ErrorContent}"/>
        </Trigger>
      </Style.Triggers>
    </Style>
  </Window.Resources>
```

Run the app and create an error condition. The result will be similar to Figure 28-6, complete with tooltip showing the error message.

Figure 28-6. *Showing a custom ErrorTemplate*

The previous style changed the appearance of any TextBox that has an error condition. Next, you will create a custom control template to update the ErrorTemplate of the Validation class to show a red exclamation mark and set the tooltips for the exclamation mark. The ErrorTemplate is an *adorner*, which sits on top of the control. While the style just created updates the control itself, the ErrorTemplate will sit on top of the control.

Place a setter immediately after the Style.Triggers closing tag within the style you just created. You will be creating a control template that consists of a TextBlock (to show the exclamation mark) and a BorderBrush to surround the TextBox that contains the error(s). There is a special tag in XAML for the control that is being adorned with the ErrorTemplate named AdornedElementPlaceholder. By adding a name to this control, you can access the errors that are associated with the control. In this example, you want to access the Validation.Errors property so you can get the ErrorContent (just like you did in the Style.Trigger). Here is the full markup for the setter:

```
<Setter Property="Validation.ErrorTemplate">
  <Setter.Value>
    <ControlTemplate>
      <DockPanel LastChildFill="True">
        <TextBlock Foreground="Red" FontSize="20" Text="!"
          ToolTip="{Binding ElementName=controlWithError,
          Path=AdornedElement.(Validation.Errors)[0].ErrorContent}"/>
        <Border BorderBrush="Red" BorderThickness="1">
          <AdornedElementPlaceholder Name="controlWithError" />
        </Border>
      </DockPanel>
    </ControlTemplate>
  </Setter.Value>
</Setter>
```

Run the app and create an error condition. The result will be similar to Figure 28-7.

Figure 28-7. *Showing a custom ErrorTemplate*

Wrapping up Validations

This completes your look at validation methods within WPF. Of course, there is much more that you can do. For more information, consult the WPF documentation.

■ **Source Code**   You can find the WpfValidations project in the Chapter 28 subdirectory.

Creating Custom Commands

As with the validations sections, you can continue working in the same project or create a new one and copy all of the code over to it. I will create a new project named WpfCommands. If you are using the same project, be sure to pay attention to the namespaces in the code samples in this section and adjust them as needed.

As you learned in Chapter 25, commands are an integral part of WPF. Commands can be hooked up to WPF controls (such as Button and MenuItem controls) to handle user events, such as the Click event. Instead of creating an event handler directly and adding the code directly into the code-behind file, the Execute method of the command is executed when the click event fires. The CanExecute() method is used to enable or disable the control based on custom code. In addition to the built-in commands you used in Chapter 25, you can create your own custom commands by implementing the ICommand interface. By using commands instead of event handlers, you gain the benefit of encapsulating application code, as well as automatically enabling and disabling controls based on business logic.

Implementing the ICommand Interface

As a quick review from Chapter 25, the ICommand interface is listed here:

```
public interface ICommand
{
  event EventHandler CanExecuteChanged;
  bool CanExecute(object parameter);
  void Execute(object parameter);
}
```

Adding the ChangeColorCommand

The event handlers for your Button controls will be replaced with commands, starting with the Change Color button. Start by adding a new folder (named Cmds) in your project. Add a new class named ChangeColorCommand.cs. Make the class public, and implement the ICommand interface. Add the following using statements (the first one might vary depending on whether you created a new project for this sample):

```
using WpfCommands.Models;
using System.Windows.Input;
```

Your class should look like this:

```
public class ChangeColorCommand : ICommand
{
  public bool CanExecute(object parameter)
  {
    throw new NotImplementedException();
  }
  public void Execute(object parameter)
  {
    throw new NotImplementedException();
  }
  public event EventHandler CanExecuteChanged;
}
```

If the CanExecute() method returns true, any bound controls will be enabled, and if it returns false, they will be disabled. If a control is enabled (because CanExecute() returns true) and clicked, the Execute() method will fire. The parameter passed into both of these methods comes from the UI based on the CommandParameter property set on binding statements. The CanExecuteChanged event ties into the binding and notification system to inform the UI that the result of the CanExecute() method has changed (much like the PropertyChanged event).

In this example, the Change Color button should work only if the parameter is not null and of type Inventory. Update the CanExecute() method to the following:

```
public bool CanExecute(object parameter) => (parameter as Inventory) != null;
```

The value for the Execute() method parameter is the same as for the CanExecute() method. Since the Execute() method can execute only if the object is of type Inventory, then the argument must be cast to an Inventory type and have the color updated, as follows:

```
public void Execute(object parameter)
{
  ((Inventory)parameter).Color="Pink";
}
```

Attaching the Command to the CommandManager

The final update for the command class is to type the command into the command manager. The CanExecute() method fires when the Window first loads and then when the command manager instructs it to reexecute. Each command class has to opt in to the command manager. This is done by updating the code regarding the CanExecuteChanged event, as follows:

```
public event EventHandler CanExecuteChanged
{
  add => CommandManager.RequerySuggested += value;
  remove => CommandManager.RequerySuggested -= value;
}
```

Updating MainWindow.xaml.cs

The next change is to create an instance of this class that the Button can access. For now, you will place this in the code-behind file for the MainWindow (later in this chapter you will move this into a view model). Open MainWindow.xaml.cs and delete the Click event handler for the Change Color button. Add the following using statements to the top of the file (again, the namespace may vary based on whether you are still using the same project or started a new one):

```
using WpfCommands.Cmds;
using System.Windows.Input;
```

Next, add a public property named ChangeColorCmd of type ICommand with a backing field. In the expression body for the property, return the backing property (make sure to instantiate a new instance of the ChangeColorCommand if the backing field is null).

```
private ICommand _changeColorCommand = null;
public ICommand ChangeColorCmd => _changeColorCommand ?? (_changeColorCommand = new
ChangeColorCommand());
```

Updating MainWindow.xaml

As you saw in Chapter 25, clickable controls in WPF (like Button controls) have a Command property that allows you to assign a command object to the control. Start by connecting your command instantiated in the code-behind to the btnChangeColor button. Since the property for the command is on the MainWindow class, you use the RelativeSourceMode binding syntax to get to the Window that contains the Button, as follows:

```
Command="{Binding Path=ChangeColorCmd,
  RelativeSource={RelativeSource Mode=FindAncestor, AncestorType={x:Type Window}}}"
```

The Button still needs to send in an Inventory object as the parameter for the CanExecute() and Execute() methods. This is assigned through the CommandParameter property. You set this to the SelectedItem of the cboCars ComboBox, as follows:

```
CommandParameter="{Binding ElementName=cboCars, Path=SelectedItem}"
```

The complete markup for the button is shown here:

```
<Button x:Name="btnChangeColor" Content="Change Color" Margin="5,0,5,0"
    Padding="4, 2" Command="{Binding Path=ChangeColorCmd,
        RelativeSource={RelativeSource Mode=FindAncestor, AncestorType={x:Type Window}}}"
    CommandParameter="{Binding ElementName=cboCars, Path=SelectedItem}"/>
```

Testing the Application

Run the application. You will see that the Change Color command is *not* enabled, as shown in Figure 28-8, since there isn't a vehicle selected.

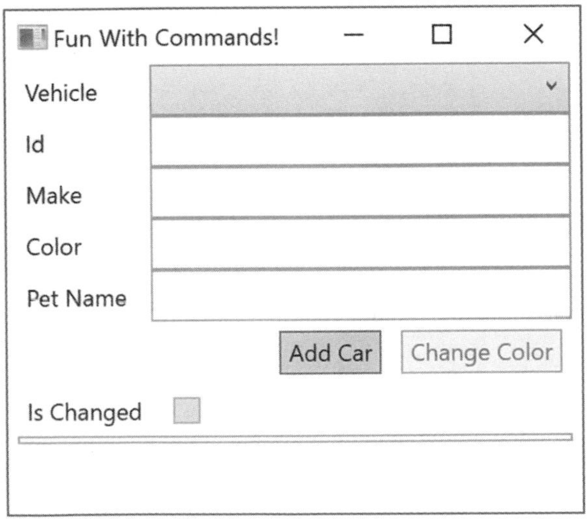

Figure 28-8. *A window with nothing selected*

Now, select a vehicle; the button will become enabled, and clicking it will change the color, as expected!

Creating the CommandBase Class

If you continued with this pattern for AddCarCommand.cs, there would be code that would be repeated between the classes. This is a good sign that a base class can help. Create a new class in the Cmds folder named CommandBase.cs and add a using for the System.Windows.Input namespace. Set the class to public and implement the ICommand interface. Change the class and the Execute() and CanExecute() methods to abstract. Finally, add in the update to the CanExecuteChanged event from the ChangeColorCommand class. The full implementation is listed here:

```
using System;
using System.Windows.Input;

namespace WpfCommands.Cmds
{
  public abstract class CommandBase : ICommand
  {
    public abstract bool CanExecute(object parameter);
    public abstract void Execute(object parameter);
    public event EventHandler CanExecuteChanged
    {
      add => CommandManager.RequerySuggested += value;
      remove => CommandManager.RequerySuggested -= value;
    }
  }
}
```

Adding the AddCarCommand Class

Add a new class named AddCarCommand.cs to the Cmds folder. Make the class public and add CommandBase as the base class. Add the following using statements to the top of the file:

```
using System.Collections.ObjectModel;
using System.Linq;
using WpfCommands.Models;
```

The parameter is expected to be an ObservableCollection<Inventory>, so check to make sure of this in the CanExecute() method. If it is, then the Execute() method should add an additional car, just like the Click event handler.

```
public class AddCarCommand :CommandBase
{
  public override bool CanExecute(object parameter)
  {
    return parameter != null && parameter is ObservableCollection<Inventory>;
  }
  public override void Execute(object parameter)
  {
    if (parameter is ObservableCollection<Inventory> cars)
```

```
    {
      var maxCount = cars?.Max(x => x.CarId) ?? 0;
      cars?.Add(new Inventory { CarId = ++maxCount, Color = "Yellow", Make = "VW",
      PetName = "Birdie" });
    }
  }
}
```

Updating MainWindow.xaml.cs

Add a public property named AddCarCmd of type ICommand with a backing field. In the expression body for the property, return the backing property (make sure to instantiate a new instance of the AddCarCommand if the backing field is null).

```
private ICommand _addCarCommand = null;
public ICommand AddCarCmd => _addCarCommand?? (_addCarCommand= new AddCarCommand());
```

Updating MainWindow.xaml

Update the XAML to remove the Click attribute and add the Command and CommandParameter attributes. The AddCarCommand will receive the list of cars from the cboCars combo box. The entire button's XAML is as follows:

```
<Button x:Name="btnAddCar" Content="Add Car" Margin="5,0,5,0" Padding="4, 2"
  Command="{Binding Path=AddCarCmd,
      RelativeSource={RelativeSource Mode=FindAncestor, AncestorType={x:Type Window}}}"
  CommandParameter="{Binding ElementName=cboCars, Path=ItemsSource}"/>
```

With this in place, you can now add cars and update the color of cars (I know, pretty limited functionality) using reusable code contained in stand-alone classes.

Updating ChangeColorCommand

The final step is to update the ChangeColorCommand to inherit from CommandBase. Change ICommand to CommandBase, add the override keyword to both methods, and delete the CanExecuteChanged code. It's really that simple! The new code is listed here:

```
public class ChangeColorCommand : CommandBase
{
  public override bool CanExecute(object parameter) => (parameter as Inventory) != null;
  public override void Execute(object parameter)
  {
    ((Inventory)parameter).Color = "Pink";
  }
}
```

RelayCommands

Another implementation of the command pattern in WPF is the RelayCommand. Instead of creating a new class for each command, this pattern uses delegates to implement the ICommand interface. It is a lightweight implementation, in that each command doesn't have its own class. RelayCommands are usually used when there isn't any reuse needed for the implementation of the command.

Creating the Base RelayCommand

RelayCommands are typically implemented in two classes. The base RelayCommand class is used when there aren't any parameters needed for the CanExecute() and Execute() methods, and RelayCommand<T> is used when a parameter is required. You will start with the base RelayCommand class, which leverages the CommandBase class. Add a new class named RelayCommand.cs to the Cmds folder. Make the class public and add CommandBase as the base class. Add two class-level variables to hold the Execute() and CanExecute() delegates.

```
private readonly Action _execute;
private readonly Func<bool> _canExecute;
```

Create three constructors. The first is the default constructor (needed by the RelayCommand<T> derived class), the second is a constructor that takes an Action parameter, and the third is a constructor that takes an Action parameter and a Func parameter, as follows:

```
public RelayCommand(){}
public RelayCommand(Action execute) : this(execute, null) { }
public RelayCommand(Action execute, Func<bool> canExecute)
{
  _execute = execute ?? throw new ArgumentNullException(nameof(execute));
  _canExecute = canExecute;
}
```

Finally, implement the CanExecute() and Execute() overrides. CanExecute() returns true if the Func is null; or if it is not null, it executes and returns true. Execute() executes the Action parameter.

```
public override bool CanExecute(object parameter)
    => _canExecute == null || _canExecute();
public override void Execute(object parameter) { _execute(); }
```

Creating RelayCommand<T>

Add a new class named RelayCommandT.cs to the Cmds folder. This class is almost a carbon copy of the base class, except that the delegates all take a parameter. Make the class public and generic, and add RelayCommand as the base class, as follows:

```
public class RelayCommand<T> : RelayCommand
```

Add two class-level variables to hold the Execute() and CanExecute() delegates:

```
private readonly Action<T> _execute;
private readonly Func<T, bool> _canExecute;
```

Create two constructors. The first takes an Action<T> parameter, and the second takes an Action<T> parameter and a Func<T,bool> parameter, as follows:

```
public RelayCommand(Action<T> execute) : this(execute, null) { }
public RelayCommand(Action<T> execute, Func<T, bool> canExecute)
{
  _execute = execute ?? throw new ArgumentNullException(nameof(execute));
  _canExecute = canExecute;
}
```

Finally, implement the CanExecute() and Execute() overrides. CanExecute() returns true of the Func is null; or, if it is not null, it executes and returns true. Execute() executes the Action parameter.

```
public override bool CanExecute(object parameter) => _canExecute == null ||
_canExecute((T)parameter);
public override void Execute(object parameter) { _execute((T)parameter); }
```

Updating MainWindow.xaml.cs

When you use RelayCommands, all of the methods for the delegates need to be specified when a new command is constructed. This doesn't mean that the code needs to live in the code-behind (as is shown here); it just has to be accessible from the code-behind. It could live in another class (or even another assembly), providing the code encapsulation benefits of creating a custom command class.

Add a new private variable of type RelayCommand<Inventory> and a public property named DeleteCarCmd, as shown here:

```
private RelayCommand<Inventory> _deleteCarCommand = null;
public RelayCommand<Inventory> DeleteCarCmd => _deleteCarCommand ??
      (_deleteCarCommand = new RelayCommand<Inventory>(DeleteCar,CanDeleteCar));
```

The DeleteCar() and CanDeleteCar() methods must be created as well, as follows:

```
private bool CanDeleteCar(Inventory car) => car != null;
private void DeleteCar(Inventory car)
{
  _cars.Remove(car);
}
```

Notice the strong typing in the methods—this is one of the benefits of using RelayCommand<T>.

Adding and Implementing the Delete Car Button

The final step to tie it all together is to add the button and assign the Command and CommandParameter bindings. Add the following markup:

```
<Button x:Name="btnDeleteCar" Content="Delete Car" Margin="5,0,5,0" Padding="4, 2"
  Command="{Binding Path=DeleteCarCmd,
      RelativeSource={RelativeSource Mode=FindAncestor, AncestorType={x:Type Window}}}"
  CommandParameter="{Binding ElementName=cboCars, Path=SelectedItem}"/>
```

Now when you run the application, you can test that the Delete Car button is enabled only if a car is selected in the drop-down and that clicking the button does indeed delete the car from the inventory list.

Wrapping Up Commands

The concludes your brief journey into WPF commands. By moving the event handling out of the code-behind file and into individual command classes, you gain the benefit of code encapsulating, reuse, and improved maintainability. If you don't need that much separation of concerns, you can use the lighter-weight `RelayCommand` implementation. The goal is to improve maintainability and code quality, so choose the method that works best for you.

■ **Source Code**   You can find the WpfCommands project in the Chapter 28 subdirectory.

Migrate Code and Data to a View Model

As in the "WPF Validations" section, you can continue working in the same project, or you can create a new one and copy all of the code over. I will create a new project named WpfViewModel. If you are using the same project, be sure to pay attention to the namespaces in the code samples in this section and adjust as needed.

Create a new folder named ViewModels in your project, and add a new class named MainWindowViewModel.cs into that folder. Add the following namespaces:

```
using System.Collections.ObjectModel;
using System.Windows.Input;
using WpfViewModel.Cmds;
using WpfViewModel.Models;
```

■ **Note**   A popular convention is to name the view models after the window they support. I typically follow that convention and will do so in this chapter. However, like any pattern or convention, this isn't a rule, and you will find a wide range of opinions on this.

Moving the MainWindow.xaml.cs Code

Almost all the code from the code-behind file will be moved to the view model. At the end, there will only be a few lines, including the call to `InitializeComponent()` and the code for setting the data context for the window to the view model.

Create a public property of type `IList<Inventory>` named Cars, like this:

```
public IList<Inventory> Cars { get; } = new ObservableCollection<Inventory>();
```

Create a default constructor and move all the inventory creation code from the MainWindow.xaml.cs file, updating the list variable name. You can also delete the _cars variable from MainWindow.xaml.cs. Here is the view model constructor:

```
public MainWindowViewModel()
{
  Cars.Add(
    new Inventory { CarId = 1, Color = "Blue", Make = "Chevy", PetName = "Kit",
    IsChanged = false });
  Cars.Add(
    new Inventory { CarId = 2, Color = "Red", Make = "Ford", PetName = "Red Rider",
    IsChanged = false });
}
```

Next, move all of the command-related code from the window code-behind file to the view model, updating the _cars variable reference to Cars. Here is just the changed code:

```
//rest omitted for brevity
private void DeleteCar(Inventory car)
{
  Cars.Remove(car);
}
```

Updating the MainWindow Code and Markup

Most of the code has been removed from the MainWindow.xaml.cs file. Remove the line that assigns the ItemsSource for the combo box, leaving only the call to InitializeComponent. It should now look like this:

```
public MainWindow()
{
    InitializeComponent();
}
```

Add the following using statement to the top of the file:

```
using WpfViewModel.ViewModels;
```

Next, create a strongly typed property to hold the instance of the view model:

```
public MainWindowViewModel ViewModel { get; set; } = new MainWindowViewModel();
```

Finally, add a DataContext property to the window's declaration in XAML:

```
DataContext="{Binding ViewModel, RelativeSource={RelativeSource Self}}"
```

Updating the Control Markup

Now that the DataContext for the Window is set to the view model, the XAML bindings for the controls need to be updated. Starting with the combo box, update the markup by adding an ItemsSource:

```
<ComboBox Name="cboCars" Grid.Column="1" DisplayMemberPath="PetName"
ItemsSource="{Binding Cars}" />
```

This works because the data context for the Window is the MainWindowViewModel, and Cars is a public property on the view model. Recall that binding calls walk up the element tree until a data context is located. Next, you need to update the bindings for the Button controls. This is straightforward; since the bindings are already set to the window level, you just need to update the binding statement to start with the DataContext property, as follows:

```
<Button x:Name="btnAddCar" Content="Add Car" Margin="5,0,5,0" Padding="4, 2"
    Command="{Binding Path=DataContext.AddCarCmd,
        RelativeSource={RelativeSource Mode=FindAncestor, AncestorType={x:Type Window}}}"
    CommandParameter="{Binding ElementName=cboCars, Path=ItemsSource}"/>
<Button x:Name="btnDeleteCar" Content="Delete Car" Margin="5,0,5,0" Padding="4, 2"
    Command="{Binding Path=DataContext.DeleteCarCmd,
        RelativeSource={RelativeSource Mode=FindAncestor, AncestorType={x:Type Window}}}"
    CommandParameter="{Binding ElementName=cboCars, Path=SelectedItem}" />
<Button x:Name="btnChangeColor" Content="Change Color" Margin="5,0,5,0" Padding="4, 2"
    Command="{Binding Path=DataContext.ChangeColorCmd,
        RelativeSource={RelativeSource Mode=FindAncestor, AncestorType={x:Type Window}}}"
    CommandParameter="{Binding ElementName=cboCars, Path=SelectedItem}"/>
```

Wrapping Up View Models

Believe it or not, you have just completed your first MVVM WPF application. You might be thinking—"This isn't a real application. What about data? The data in this example is hard-coded." And you would be correct. It's not a real app; it's demoware. However, that is the beauty of the MVVM pattern. The view doesn't know anything about where the data is coming from; it's just binding to a property on the view model. You can swap out view model implementations, perhaps using a version with hard-coded data for testing and one that hits the database for production.

There are a lot of additional points that could be discussed, including various open source frameworks, the View Model Locator pattern, and a host of differing opinions on how to best implement the pattern. That's the beauty of software design patterns—there are usually many correct ways to implement it, and you just need to find the best manner based on your business and technical requirements.

■ **Source Code**   You can find the WpfViewModel project in the Chapter 28 subdirectory.

Updating AutoLotDAL for MVVM

For this section, you are going to plug the data access layer from Chapter 22 into your WPF application. Start by creating a new WPF application named WpfMVVM. Copy (don't just reference) the AutoLotDAL and AutoLotDAL.Models projects from Chapter 22 and paste them next to your WPF application. This section won't make changes to all of the models in the data access library, just the changes for the Inventory model class. I'll leave it to you, the reader, to make the rest of the changes in case you want to expand the sample.

You need to make a few changes specifically for WPF. Add a reference from WpfMVVM to AutoLotDAL and AutoLotDAL.Models, and add a reference from AutoLotDAL to AutoLotDAL.Models (sometimes project references get dropped when copying projects).

Updating the EntityBase Class

The first thing that you need to do is update all the models with the validation code that you created to support IDataErrorInfo and INotifyDataErrorInfo. Move all of the code from your WpfMvvm.EntityBase class into the AutoLotDAL.Base.EntityBase class. Additionally, add the INotifyDataErrorInfo and INotifyPropoertyChanged interfaces. Add the PropertyChanged event (it's currently in the Inventory class in your WPF project). Finally, add a bool IsChanged, making sure to mark it as NotMapped so EF doesn't try to save it in the database.

```
public class EntityBase : INotifyDataErrorInfo, INotifyPropertyChanged
{
  [Key]
  public int Id { get; set; }
  [Timestamp]
  public byte[] Timestamp { get; set; }
  [NotMapped]
  public bool IsChanged { get; set; }
  public event PropertyChangedEventHandler PropertyChanged;
  //code from Wpf Entity Base class, omitted here for brevity
}
```

Updating the Inventory Partial Class

Copy all the code from the InventoryPartial.cs file in the WPF project, and paste it into the InventoryPartial.cs file in the AutoLotDAL.Models project, making sure to preserve any code already in the destination file. Add IDataErrorInfo as an interface to the partial class. Add the EntityBase and IDataErrorInfo interfaces to the partial class.

```
public partial class Inventory : EntityBase, IDataErrorInfo
```

Adding PropertyChanged.Fody to the Models Project

The PropertyChanged.Fody package must be installed to any project that needs the NotifyPropertyChanged code injected into classes, which for WPF is all of the models and, for you, the AutoLotDAL.Models project. Using the NuGet package manager, install the package into the AutoLotDAL.Models project.

Also, install the Entity Framework into the Models project. You don't need to update the App.config file since that connection string data will live in the WPF project.

Adding Entity Framework and Connection Strings to the WPF Project

Install the Entity Framework into the WPF application, and update App.config to include the connection string (adjusting as necessary for your development environment).

```
<connectionStrings>
  <add name="AutoLotConnection" connectionString="data source=(LocalDb)\MSSQLLocalDB;
  initial catalog=AutoLot;integrated security=True;MultipleActiveResultSets=True;
  App=EntityFramework" providerName="System.Data.SqlClient" />
</connectionStrings>
```

Updating the MainWindow XAML

The sample WPF code is using CarId as the primary key for the Inventory class, but the AutoLotDAL projects define the primary key for all tables as Id. Open MainWindow.XAML and change the binding from CarID to Id.

```
<TextBox Grid.Column="1" Grid.Row="0" Text="{Binding Path=Id}" />
```

Updating the View Model

Now it's time to take out the hard-coded data and use the data access layer for your application. Open MainWindowViewModel.cs and add the following using statements to the top of the file:

```
using AutoLotDAL.Models;
using AutoLotDAL.Repos;
```

Update the Cars property to the following:

```
public IList<Inventory> Cars { get; }
```

Next, delete the code from the constructor, and add the following call to InventoryRepo:

```
public MainWindowViewModel()
{
  Cars = new ObservableCollection<Inventory>(new InventoryRepo().GetAll());
}
```

Updating the AddCarCommand

The final change to the WPF application is to replace the references to CarId with Id in AddCarCommand.cs. The updated code should look like this:

```
public override void Execute(object parameter)
{
  if (parameter is ObservableCollection<Inventory> cars)
  {
    var maxCount = cars?.Max(x => x.Id) ?? 0;
    cars?.Add(new Inventory { Id = ++maxCount, Color = "Yellow", Make = "VW",
    PetName = "Birdie" });
  }
}
```

Using ObjectMaterialized with Entity Framework

If you run the project now, you will see that every car that is loaded is showing as changed. This is because EF calls the setters for the properties as objects are materialized from the data store. If you recall from Chapter 22, the ObjectMaterialized event fires every time EF is done reconstituting an object from the database, but just before the object is returned to the calling code. This will be used to resolve this problem.

Open AutoLotEntities.cs, and in the OnObjectMaterialized event handler, check to see whether the Entity property of the ObjectMaterializedEventArgs is of type EntityBase. If it is, then set the IsChanged property to false. The code will look like this:

```
private void OnObjectMaterialized(object sender, ObjectMaterializedEventArgs e)
{
  var model = (e.Entity as EntityBase);
  if (model != null)
  {
    model.IsChanged = false;
  }
}
```

Make sure the constructor hooks up the event with the context.

```
public AutoLotEntities(): base("name=AutoLotConnection")
{
  var context = (this as IObjectContextAdapter).ObjectContext;
  context.ObjectMaterialized += OnObjectMaterialized;
}
```

Run the app. Select a record from the drop-down, and you will see that the IsChanged flag is no longer set when the form first loads. If you edit a field, the IsChanged flag still gets set correctly.

Summary

This chapter examined the WPF topics that support the Model-View-ViewModel pattern. You started off learning how to tie model classes and collections into the notification system in the binding manager. You implemented INotifyPropertyChanged and used ObservableCollections classes to keep the UI in sync with the bound data. You also learned how to use PropertyChanged.Fody to do the work of implementing INotifyPropertyChanged automatically.

Next, you added validation code to the model using IDataErrorInfo and INotifyDataErrorInfo and checked for data annotation errors. You then displayed any validation errors in the UI so the user would know what the problem is and how to fix it, and you created a style and custom control template to render errors in a meaningful way.

Finally, you put it all together by adding a view model, and you cleaned up the UI markup and code-behind file to increase separation of concerns. You updated AutoLotDAL to add validation and notifications and used ObjectMaterialized to clean up the objects as they materialize.

PART VIII

ASP.NET

CHAPTER 29

■ ■ ■

Introducing ASP.NET MVC

This chapter introduces ASP.MVC, a .NET framework for creating web applications. ASP.NET MVC grew out of the user community (specifically the ALT.NET movement) asking for a framework that more closely adhered to the tenants of HTTP, was more testable, and adhered to separation of concerns.

■ **Note**   The previous edition of the book covered ASP.NET Web Forms in great detail. In this edition, the Web Forms chapters have been moved to the appendixes for your reference.

This chapter begins with a brief explanation of the MVC pattern and then dives right into creating an MVC project. After getting a solid understanding of MVC and the generated scaffolding, you will build the inventory pages for CarLotMVC.

Introducing the MVC Pattern

The Model-View-Controller (MVC) pattern has been around since the 1970s, originally created as a pattern for use in Smalltalk. The pattern has made a resurgence recently, with implementations in many different and varied languages, including Java (Spring Framework), Ruby (Ruby on Rails), and many JavaScript client frameworks such as Angular and EmberJS. For .NET developers, the pattern is implemented as a framework called ASP.NET MVC, first introduced in 2007.

The Model

The *model* is the data of your application. The data is typically represented by plain old CLR objects (POCOs), as used in the data access library created in the previous two chapters. View models are composed of one or more models and shaped specifically for the view that uses them. Think of models and view models as database tables and database views. This closely resembles the concepts from Chapter 28, which covered Model-View-ViewModel in the Windows Presentation Foundation.

Academically, models should be extremely clean and not contain validation or any other business rules. Pragmatically, whether or not models contain validation logic or other business rules entirely depends on the language and frameworks used, as well as specific application needs. For example, EF Core contains many data annotations that double as a mechanism for shaping the database tables and a means for validation in Core MVC. In this book, the examples focus on reducing duplication of code, which places data annotations and validations where they make the most sense.

The View

The *view* is the UI of the application. Views accept commands and render the results of those commands to the user. The view should be as lightweight as possible and not actually process any of the work; instead, it should hand off all work to the controller. This should also be familiar to you from Chapter 28.

The Controller

The controller is the brains of the operation. Controllers have two responsibilities; the first is taking commands/requests from the user (referred to as *actions*) and correctly marshaling them appropriately (such as to a repository), and the second is to send any changes to the view. Controllers (as well as models and views) should be lightweight and leverage other components to maintain separation of concerns. This all sounds simple, doesn't it? Before you dive into building an MVC application, there is that age-old question...

Why MVC?

By the time ASP.NET MVC was released in 2007, ASP.NET Web Forms had been in production for six years. Thousands of sites built on Web Forms were in production, with more and more coming online every day. So, why would Microsoft make a new framework from scratch? Before I answer that, a short look backward in time is appropriate.

When Microsoft first released ASP.NET Web Forms, web development wasn't as prolific as it is today. The stateless paradigm was a difficult one to grasp, especially for smart client developers (such as those making desktop apps with Visual Basic 6, MFC, and PowerBuilder). To bridge the knowledge gap and make it easier for developers to build web sites, Web Forms enabled many of the desktop concepts, such as state (through viewstate) and prebuilt controls.

The plan worked. Web Forms was generally well received, and many developers made the jump to web developers. A thriving third-party ecosystem supplying Web Forms controls (and many other .NET controls) grew up in lockstep with Web Forms and .NET. Everything was coming up roses!

At the same time, developers were learning more about (and becoming comfortable with) the statelessness of programming for the Web, the HTTP protocol, HMTL, and JavaScript. These developers needed the bridging technologies less and less and wanted more and more control of the rendered views.

With each new version of Web Forms, additional features and capabilities were added into the framework, each adding to the weight of the applications. The increasing complexity of web sites being developed meant items such as viewstate were growing seemingly out of control. Even worse, some early decisions made in the creation of Web Forms (such as *where* viewstate was placed in the rendered page) were causing issues such as performance degradation to rear their ugly heads. This was causing some high-profile "defections" from .NET to other languages, like Ruby (using Ruby on Rails).

But Microsoft couldn't (and wisely wouldn't) remove those bridging technologies and other code from the ASP.NET core without risking millions of lines of code. Something had to be done, and retooling Web Forms wasn't a realistic option, although significant work was put into ASP.NET Web Forms 4.5 to resolve (or at least mitigate) many of the issues. Microsoft had some hard decisions to make: how to keep the existing web developers (and the control ecosystem that grew up with Web Forms) happy and productive, while providing a platform for those developers who wanted to be closer to the metal of the Web.

Enter ASP.NET MVC

For all of aforementioned reasons, a new framework was born. ASP.NET MVC was created to be an alternative to ASP.NET Web Forms. There are some noticeable differences between ASP.NET Web Forms and ASP.NET MVC, such as removing code-behind files in views, control support, and viewstate. In addition to supporting testability, dependency injection, separation of control, and many other clean code concepts, the Razor view engine was created (starting with version 3 of ASP.NET MVC). All these improvements came with a catch: using ASP.NET MVC requires a deeper knowledge of HTML and JavaScript and the way HTTP actually works.

Convention over Configuration

One of the tenants of ASP.NET MVC is convention over configuration. This means that there are specific conventions (such as naming conventions and directory structure) for MVC projects that reduce the amount of configuration that is required for your application. While this reduction of manual (or templated) configuration is usually a good thing, it also means you need to know the conventions. As you progress through this chapter, you will see several of the conventions in action.

The ASP.NET MVC Application Template

Enough theory. It's time for code. Visual Studio ships with a rather complete project template for building ASP.NET MVC apps, and you will take full advantage of that when you build CarLotMVC.

The New Project Wizard

Start by launching Visual Studio and selecting File ➤ New ➤ Project. In the left sidebar, select Web under Visual C#, select ASP.NET Web Application (.NET Framework), and change Name to CarLotMVC, as shown in Figure 29-1.

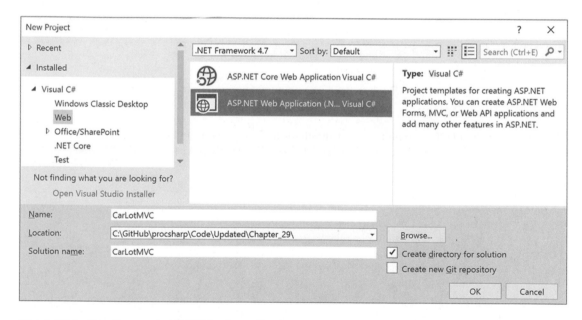

Figure 29-1. *Creating a new ASP.NET web application*

On the next screen, select the MVC template. Notice that the MVC check box is selected under "Add folders and core references for" and the others are not. If you wanted to create a hybrid application that supported MVC *and* Web Forms, you could select the Web Forms check box as well. For this example, just select MVC, as shown in Figure 29-2. Also notice the "Add unit tests" check box. If you select this option, another project will be created for you that provides a basic framework for unit testing your ASP.NET application. Because of space limitations, unit testing ASP.NET MVC is not covered in this book. Don't click OK yet, as you'll examine the authentication mechanisms for your project.

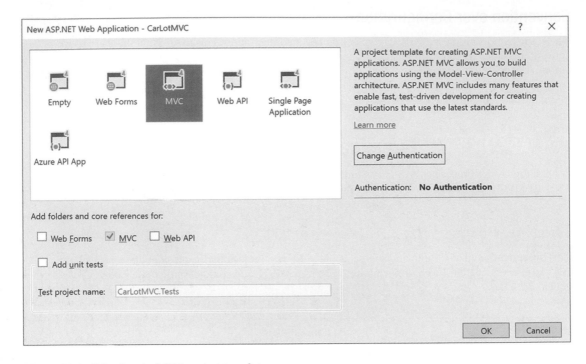

Figure 29-2. *Selecting the MVC project template*

Authentication Options

Click the Change Authentication button, and you will see the dialog shown in Figure 29-3. Leave the authentication set to No Authentication (the default), click OK, and click OK in the Select a Template dialog.

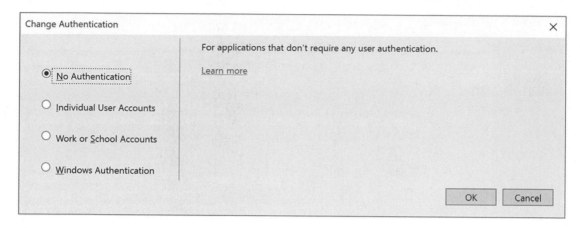

Figure 29-3. *Authentication options for ASP.NET projects*

Table 29-1 discusses the four authentication options available to MVC applications.

Table 29-1. *Authentication Choices*

Option	Meaning in Life
No Authentication	No mechanism for logging in, entity classes for membership, or a membership database.
Individual User Accounts	Uses ASP.NET Identity (formerly known as ASP.NET Membership) for user authentication.
Work and School Accounts	For applications that authenticate with Active Directory, Azure Active Directory, or Office 365.
Windows Authentication	Uses Windows Authentication. This is intended for intranet web sites.

■ **Note** I don't cover authentication in this book because of space limitations. For more information on authentication in MVC, please see Adam Freeman's book *Pro ASP.NET MVC 5* (www.apress.com/ 9781430265290?gtmf=s).

Once that's completed, you will see a *lot* of generated files and folders. You'll be examining these in the next sections.

Project Overview

Replacing the `Project_Readme.html` file from previous versions of the Visual Studio ASP.NET MVC templates is the Project Overview feature. When the project first loads (after initial creation), the Project Overview provides links to additional documentation and training, wiring up connected services, and publishing, as shown in Figure 29-4.

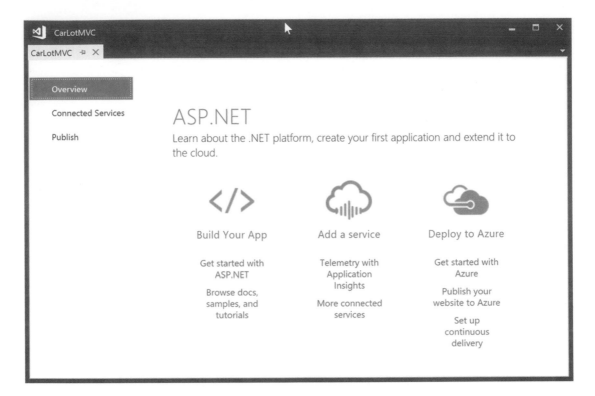

Figure 29-4. *The Project Overview*

To open the Project Overview again, right-click the project in Solution Explorer and select Overview.

Project Root Files

While most of the files in MVC projects have specific locations where they should be placed, there are a few files that are in the root of the project. Table 29-2 lists the files in the root of a default MVC site and whether or not they are deployed with the application.

Table 29-2. *Files in the Project Root*

File	Meaning in Life	Deployed?
favicon.ico	The icon that is displayed by browsers in the address bar next to the page name. Not having this can cause performance issues, as browsers will continually look for this.	Yes
Global.asax/ Global.asax.cs	The entry point into the application (like ASP.NET Web Forms).	Yes
packages.config	Configuration information for NuGet packages used in the project.	No
ApplicationInsights. config	Used to configure application insights (not covered in this book).	Yes
Startup.cs	Startup class for Open Web Interface for .NET (OWIN) – used by ASP.NET Identity.	Yes (Compiled)
Web.config	Project configuration file.	Yes

Global.asax.cs

The Global.asax.cs file is where you hook into the ASP.NET pipeline. The default project template uses only the Application_Start event handler, but there are many more events that can be hooked into if you need them. Table 29-3 lists the most commonly used events.

Table 29-3. *Commonly Used Global.asax.cs Events*

Event	Meaning in Life
Application_Start	Raised on the first request for the application
Application_End	Raised when the application ends
Application_Error	Raised when an unhandled error occurs
Session_Start	Raised on the first request for a new session
Session_End	Raised when a session ends (or times out)
Application_BeginRequest	Raised when a request is made to the server
Application_EndRequest	Raised as the last event in the HTTP pipeline chain of execution when ASP.NET responds to a request

The Models Folder

This is exactly what it sounds like; it's the place to put model classes. In larger applications, you should use a data access library to hold your data access models. The Models folder is most commonly used for view-specific models, such as the model classes generated by Visual Studio for ASP.NET Identity.

The Controllers Folder

Again, just as the name implies, the Controllers folder is where the controllers in your application live. I will cover controllers in great detail later in this chapter.

The Views Folder

The Views folder is where the MVC views are stored (as the name suggests). There is a convention for the directory structure contained in the Views folder. Each controller gets its own folder under the main Views folder. Controllers look for their views in a folder of the same name as the controller (minus the word *Controller*). For example, the Views/Home folder holds all the views for the HomeController controller class.

In the root of the Views folder there is a Web.config file and a file named _ViewStart.cshtml. The Web.config file is specific for the views in this folder hierarchy, defines the base page type (e.g., System.Web.Mvc.WebViewPage), and, in Razor-based projects, adds all the references and using statements for Razor.

The _ViewStart.cshtml file executes before any views are rendered to the user. Currently, this file only specifies the default layout view to use for views without one specifically assigned. The layout view is analogous to the master page in Web Forms and will be covered in more detail later in this chapter.

The Shared Folder

A special folder under Views is named Shared. This folder is accessible to all views. This folder contains two files; the first is the _Layout.cshtml file, and the second is Error.cshtml. The _Layout.cshtml file is the default layout specified in _ViewStart.cshtml. The Error.cshtml file is the default error template for the application.

■ **Note**   Why the leading underscore for _ViewStart.html (and _Layout.cshtml)? The Razor view engine was originally created for WebMatrix, which would allow any file that did *not* start with an underscore to be rendered, so core files (such as layout and configuration) all have names that begin with an underscore. You will also see this naming convention used for partial views. However, this is not a convention that MVC cares about since MVC doesn't have the same issue as WebMatrix, but the underscore legacy lives on anyway.

The ASP.NET Folders

There are also folders reserved for ASP.NET. An example of this is the App_Data folder that is included in the default MVC template. This folder is a special folder designed to store any file-based data needed by the site. There are also folders for storing code, resources, and themes. The ASP.NET folders can be added by right-clicking the project, selecting Add ➤ Add New ASP.NET Web Folder, and selecting one from the resulting dialog. The ASP.NET folders are not viewable from the web site, even if folder navigation is enabled. Table 29-4 lists the available ASP.NET web folders.

Table 29-4. *ASP.NET Web Folders*

Folder	Meaning in Life
App_Code	Code files contained in this folder are dynamically compiled.
App_GlobalResources	Holds resource files available to the entire application. Typically used for localization.
App_LocalResources	Contains resources available to a specific page. Typically used for localization.
App_Data	Contains file-based data used by the application.
App_Browsers	Place to hold browser capability files.
App_Themes	Holds themes for the site.

The App_Start Folder

Early versions of MVC contained all the site configuration code (such as routing and security) in the Global.asax.cs class. As the amount of configuration grew, the developers on the MVC team wisely split the code into separate classes to better follow single responsibility. Out of this refactoring, the App_Start folder and its contained classes were born (details in Table 29-5). Any code in the App_Start folder gets automatically compiled into the site.

Table 29-5. *Files in App_Start*

File	Meaning in Life
BundleConfig.cs	Creates the file bundles for JavaScript and CSS files. Additional bundles can (and should) be created in this class.
FilterConfig.cs	Registers action filters (such as authentication or authorization) at a global scope.
IdentityConfig.cs	Contains support classes for ASP.NET Identity.
RouteConfig.cs	Class where the routing table is configured.
Startup.Auth.cs	Entry point for configuration of ASP.NET Identity.

BundleConfig

This class sets up the bundles and minification settings for CSS and JavaScript files. By default, when using ScriptBundle, the files are bundled and minified (see the next section for an explanation of bundling and minification) for production and not bundled or minified for debug mode. This can be controlled through Web.config or in the class itself. To turn off bundling and minification, enter the following into the system. web section of your top-level Web.config (if it doesn't already exist):

```
<system.web>
    <compilation debug="true" targetFramework="4.7" />
</system.web>
```

Or add BundleTable.EnableOptimizations = false in the RegisterBundles method in BundleConfig.cs, as follows:

```
public static void RegisterBundles(BundleCollection bundles)
{
  bundles.Add(new ScriptBundle("~/bundles/jquery").Include("~/Scripts/jquery-{version}.js"));
  // Code removed for clarity.
  BundleTable.EnableOptimizations = false;
}
```

Bundling

Bundling is the process of combining multiple files into one. This is done for a couple of reasons; the main reason is to speed up your site. Browsers have a limit of how many files they will download concurrently from a single server. If your site contains a lot of small files, this can slow down your users' experience. One solution for this is to spread your files out between content delivery networks (CDNs). Another is to bundle your files together. Of course, you need to temper your actions with wisdom since having one gigantic file probably isn't going to be any better than a million little ones.

Minification

Like bundling, *minification* is designed to speed up load time for web pages. For CSS and JavaScript files to be readable, they are typically written with meaningful variable and function names, comments, and other formatting (at least they should be). The problem is that every bit getting sent over the wire counts, especially when dealing with mobile clients.

Minification is a process of replacing long names with short (sometimes just one-character) names, removing extra spaces, and making other formatting changes to reduce the size of the file. Most modern frameworks ship with two versions of their CSS and JavaScript files. Bootstrap is no different, shipping with bootstrap.css for use while developing your application and bootstrap.min.css for production.

FilterConfig

Filters are custom classes that provide a mechanism to intercept actions and requests. They can be applied at the action, controller, or global level. There are four types of filters in MVC, as listed in Table 29-6. Again, because of space limitations, filters are not covered in this chapter.

Table 29-6. *Filters in ASP.NET MVC*

Filter Type	Meaning in Life
Authorization	These implement IAuthorizationFilter and run before any other filter. Two examples are Authorize and AllowAnonymous. For example, the AccountController class is annotated with the [Authorize] attribute to require an authenticated user through Identity, and the Login action is marked with the [AllowAnonymous] attribute to allow any user.
Action	Implement IActionFilter and allow for interception of action execution with OnActionExecuting and OnActionExecuted.
Result	Implement IResultFilter and intercept the result of an action with OnResultExecuting and OnResultExecuted.
Exception	Implement IExceptionFilter and execute if an unhandled exception is thrown during the execution of the ASP.NET pipeline. By default, the HandleError filter is configured at the global level. This filter displays the error view page Error.cshtml located in the Shared\Error folder.

IdentityConfig

Identity.config.cs and Startup.Auth.cs are both used to support ASP.NET Identity. Identity is too big of a topic to be covered as part of this chapter. In fact, I could write a book on all the details around security and identity.

RouteConfig

Early versions of ASP.NET Web Forms defined the URLs of the site based on the physical folder structure of the project. This could be changed with HttpModules and HttpHandlers, but that was far from ideal. MVC from the start included routing, which enables you to shape the URLs to better suit your users. This will be covered in greater detail later in this chapter.

The Content Folder

The Content folder is designed to hold your site's CSS files, images, and other content that will be directly rendered. The default template creates a custom CSS file named Site.css that contains the initial CSS for the site.

Bootstrap

ASP.NET MVC ships with Bootstrap, a popular open source HTML, CSS, and JavaScript framework in use today for developing responsive, mobile-first web sites.

Microsoft started including Bootstrap with MVC 4 and continues to ship it with MVC 5, and the default project template for MVC 5 uses Bootstrap to style the scaffolded pages.

■ **Note** There isn't enough space in this book to cover Bootstrap, but you can learn more and see excellent examples at www.getbootstrap.org.

The Fonts Folder

Bootstrap ships with GlyphIcons-Halflings font sets, which you will use later in this chapter to enhance your application UI. The version of Bootstrap that ships with the MVC project template requires that its fonts are located in the Fonts folder.

The Scripts Folder

The Scripts folder is where JavaScript files are placed. Table 29-7 lists the files that ship with the default template and their use.

Table 29-7. *JavaScript Files in the ASP.NET MVC Project Template*

JavaScript File	Meaning in Life
bootstrap.js bootstrap.min.js	These are the JavaScript files for Bootstrap. The .min file is the minified version.
jquery-1.x.intellisense.js jquery-1.x.js jquery-1.x.min.js jquery-1.x.min.map	jQuery is a JavaScript framework for web developers. In addition to DOM manipulation capabilities, there are a host of frameworks that depend on jQuery, including the validation plug-in used in the MVC project template.
jquery.validate-vsdoc.js jquery.validate.js jquery.validate.min.js	The jQuery Validate plug-in makes client-side validation much simpler. The .vsdoc file is for Visual Studio IntelliSense, and the .min file is the pre-minified version.
jquery.validate.unobtrusive.js jquery.validate.unobtrusive.min.js	The Unobtrusive jQuery Validation plug-in works with jQuery Validation, leveraging HTML5 attributes for client-side validation.
modernizr-2.x.js	Modernizr contains a series of fast tests ("detects" in Modernizr parlance) to determine browser capabilities. This works directly against the browser instead of relying on browser capability files that may or may not be out-of-date.
respond.js respond.min.js	Respond.js is an experimental jQuery plug-in for building web sites with responsive content.

Update Project NuGet Packages

As you can see, there are *lots* of files and packages that comprise the core MVC project template, and many of them are open source frameworks. Open source projects get updated at a much more rapid pace than Microsoft can (or should) release updates to the Visual Studio templates. It's almost a guarantee that as soon as you create a new project, the packages are already out-of-date.

Fortunately, updating them is as simple as running the NuGet GUI, as you have done throughout this book. Right-click your project and select Manage NuGet Packages from the context menu. Once the NuGet package manager loads, click the "Updates menu" item, click the "Select all packages" check box, and click Update.

Update the Project Settings

By default, MVC apps are configured to run the currently selected page in Solution Explorer. It's usually best to always run the default route, and that is updated in the project properties.

Open the Project properties window, navigate to the Web option in the left sidebar, and change the Start Action setting to Specific Page, as shown in Figure 29-5.

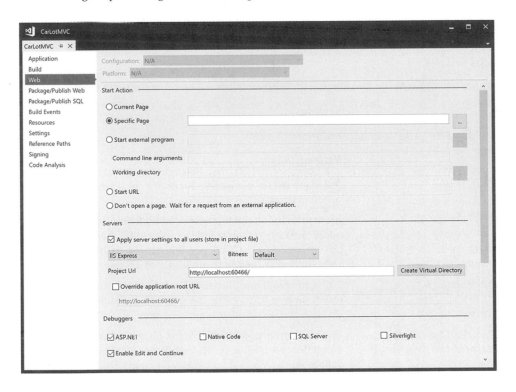

Figure 29-5. *Updating the Start Action setting*

Routing

Routing is the way MVC matches URL requests to controllers and actions in your application, instead of the original Web Forms mechanism of matching URLs to file structure. Run the CarLotMVC project, and notice the URL. It consists of the host and the port number, such as http://localhost:60466 (on your machine, the port number will most likely be different).

Now click the Contact link, and the URL changes to `http://localhost: 60466/Home/Contact`. Examining your solution, there isn't a folder path of `Home/Contact`. MVC routing uses URL patterns to determine the controller and action method to execute.

URL Patterns

Routing entries are composed of URL patterns comprised of variable placeholders and literals placed into an ordered collection known as the *route table*. Each entry defines a different URL pattern to match. Placeholders can be custom variables or from a predefined list.

Open `RouteConfig.cs` (located in the `App_Start` folder) and examine the contents, as shown here:

```
public class RouteConfig
{
  public static void RegisterRoutes(RouteCollection routes)
  {
    routes.IgnoreRoute("{resource}.axd/{*pathInfo}");

    routes.MapRoute(
      name: "Default",
      url: "{controller}/{action}/{id}",
      defaults: new { controller = "Home", action = "Index", id = UrlParameter.Optional }
    );
  }
}
```

The first line directs the routing engine to ignore requests that have an `.axd` extension, which denotes an `HttpHandler`. The `IgnoreRoute()` method passes the request back to the web server, in this case IIS. The `{*pathinfo}` pattern handles a variable number of parameters, extending the matches to any URL that includes an `HttpHandler`.

The `MapRoute()` method adds the entry into the route table. The call specifies a name, URL pattern, and any default values for the variables in the URL pattern. In the previous code sample, the predefined `{controller}` and `{action}` placeholders refer to a controller and an action method. The placeholder `{id}` is custom and is translated into a parameter (named `id`) for the action method.

When a URL is requested, it is checked against the route table. If there is a match, the proper code is executed. An example URL that would be serviced by this route is `Inventory/Delete/5`. This invokes the `Delete()` action method on the `InventoryController`, passing 5 to the `id` parameter.

The defaults specify how to fill in the blanks for URLs that don't contain all of the defined components. In the previous code, if nothing was specified in the URL (such as `http://localhost:60466`), then the routing engine would call the `Index()` action method of the `HomeController` class, without an `id` parameter. The defaults are progressive, meaning that they can be excluded from right to left. However, route parts can't be skipped. Entering a URL like `http://localhost:60466/Delete/5` will fail the `{controller}/{action}/{id}` pattern.

It is important to note that the process is serial and ordered. It checks the URL against the entries in the collection in the order that they were added. The process stops when the first match is found; it doesn't matter if a *better* match occurs later in the route table. This is an important consideration to keep in mind when adding route table entries.

Notice that the route doesn't contain a server (or domain) address. IIS automatically prepends the correct information before the defined route parameters. For example, if your site was running on `http://skimedic.com`, a correct URL for the route could be `http://skimedic.com/Inventory/Delete/5`.

Creating Routes for the Contact and About Pages

One of the advantages of routing is the ability to shape URLs to the benefit of your users. This means creating URLs that are easy to remember and find on search engines. For example, instead of http://skimedic.com/Home/Contact and http://skimedic.com/Home/About, it would be better to also be able to reach them with http://skimedic.com/Contact and http://skimedic.com/About (of course without losing the longer mapping). With routing, this is easy to accomplish.

Open RouteConfig.cs, and add the following line of code *after* the IgnoreRoutes call and *before* the default route:

```
routes.MapRoute("Contact", "Contact", new { controller = "Home", action = "Contact" });
```

This line adds a new entry named Contact into the route table that contains only one literal value, Contact. It maps to Home/Contact, not as defaults but as hard-coded values. To test this, run the app, and click the Contact link. The URL changes to http://localhost:60466/Contact (your port will be different), which is exactly what you wanted—an easy-to-remember URL for your customers.

Now update the URL to http://localhost:60466/Home/Contact/Foo. It still works! This is because the URL failed to match the first entry in the route table and fell through to the second route entry, which it matched. Now update the URL in the browser to http://localhost:60466/Home/Contact/Foo/Bar. This time it fails since it doesn't match any of the routes. Fix this by adding {*pathinfo} to the pattern. This allows any number of additional URL parameters. Update the Contact route entry to the following:

```
routes.MapRoute("Contact", "Contact/{*pathinfo}", new { controller = "Home",
action = "Contact" });
```

Now when you enter the URL http://localhost:60466/Contact/Foo/Bar, it still shows the Contact page. Mission accomplished. This is an easy-to-remember URL for your users, and even if they mess it up by adding a bunch of additional garbage on the end, they can still find your page.

To complete the exercise, add the following line immediately after the Contact entry to create a route for the About page:

```
routes.MapRoute("About", "About/{*pathinfo}", new { controller = "Home", action = "About" });
```

■ **Note**   MVC 5 also supports attribute routing, which isn't covered in this chapter but will be covered in Chapter 30.

Redirecting Using Routing

Another advantage of routing is that you no longer have to hard-code URLs for other pages in your site. The routing entries are used bidirectionally, not only to match incoming requests but also to build URLs for your site. For example, open the _Layout.cshtml file in the Views/Shared folder. Notice this line:

```
@Html.ActionLink("Contact", "Contact", "Home")
```

The ActionLink() HTML helper creates a hyperlink with the display text *Contact* for the Contact action in the Home controller. Just like incoming requests, the routing engine starts at the top and works down until it finds a match. This line matches the Contact route you added earlier in the chapter and is used to create the following link:

```
<a href="/Contact">Contact</a>
```

If you hadn't added the Contact route, the routing engine would have been created this:

```
<a href="/Home/Contact">Contact</a>
```

■ **Note**   This section introduced several new items that I haven't covered yet, such as the @ syntax, the Html object, and the _Layout.cshtml file. These are all covered in more detail soon enough. The main takeaway is that the routing table is used not only to parse incoming requests and send them to the appropriate resource for handling but also to create URLs based on the resources specified.

Adding AutoLotDAL

Applications need data, and CarLotMVC is no different. Start by copying the AutoLotDAL and AutoLotDAL. Models projects from Chapter 22 into the CarLotMVC folder (at the same level as the CarLotMVC solution file). You will be updating the data access library from what you built previously, so you can't just reference the DLLs.

Add the projects into your solution by right-clicking the CarLotMVC solution, selecting Add ➤ Existing Project, and navigating to the correct folders. Add a reference from CarLotMVC to both AutoLotDAL and AutoLotDAL.Models. Also confirm that the reference from AutoLotDAL to AutoLotDAL.Models is still there. If you add the AutoLotDAL.Models project first, it should retain the reference.

The next step is to add the Entity Framework (6.1.3) NuGet package to CarLotMVC. Once that is done, add the connection string into the Web.config file (in the root, not the one in the Views folder). Open the Web.config file and add the following values (your value might be slightly different than shown here):

```
<connectionStrings>
    <add name="AutoLotConnection" connectionString="data source=(localdb)\
    mssqllocaldb;initial catalog=AutoLot;integrated security=True;MultipleActive
    ResultSets=True;App=EntityFramework" providerName="System.Data.SqlClient" />
  </connectionStrings>
```

Finally, set the data initializer on application startup. Open Global.asax.cs and add the following using statements to the top:

```
using System.Data.Entity;
using AutoLotDAL.EF;
```

Next, in the Application_Start() method, add the following line of code:

```
Database.SetInitializer(new MyDataInitializer());
```

This will drop and re-create the database every time you run the application. This is a great feature for testing, but if you were to deploy this as a production application, you would want to double- and triple-check that you removed that line of code! This will also affect the startup time for your app, so if you are noticing it taking quite a bit of time to run, comment out the line you just added.

■ **Note**   You will need to complete Chapter 22 on Entity Framework to use the data access library. At the least, you need to get the code for the AutoLotDAL and AutoLotDAL.Models projects and execute the migrations.

Controllers and Actions

As discussed earlier, when a request comes in from the browser, it (typically) gets mapped to an action method for a specific controller class. While that sounds fancy, it's pretty straightforward. A controller is a class that inherits from one of two abstract classes, `Controller` or `AsyncController`. Note that you can also create a controller from scratch by implementing `IController`, but that is beyond the scope of this book. An action method is a public method in a controller class.

Action Results

Actions typically return an `ActionResult` (or `Task<ActionResult>` for async operations). There are several types that derive from `ActionResult`, and some of the more common ones are listed in Table 29-8.

Table 29-8. *Typical ActionResult-Derived Classes*

Action Result	Meaning in Life
ViewResult PartialViewResult	Returns a view (or a partial view) as a web page
RedirectResult RedirectToRouteResult	Redirects to another action
JsonResult	Returns a serialized JSON result to the client
FileResult	Returns binary file content to the client
ContentResult	Returns a user-defined content type to the client
HttpStatusCodeResult	Returns a specific HTTP status code

Adding the Inventory Controller

The best way to understand this is to add a new controller with actions using the built-in helpers in Visual Studio. Right-click the `Controllers` folder in your project, and select Add ➤ Controller, as shown in Figure 29-6.

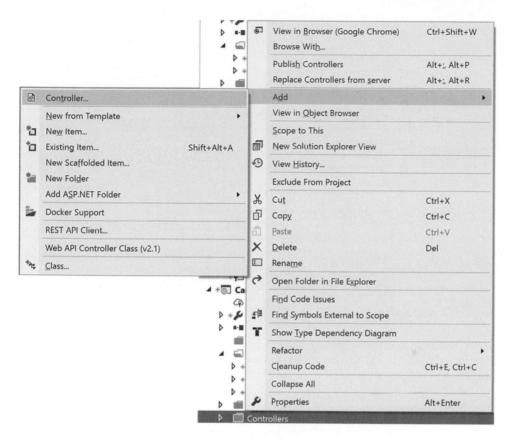

Figure 29-6. *Launching the Add New Controller scaffolding dialog*

This brings up the Add Scaffold dialog, as shown in Figure 29-7. There are several options available, and you want to choose the "MVC 5 Controller with views, using Entity Framework."

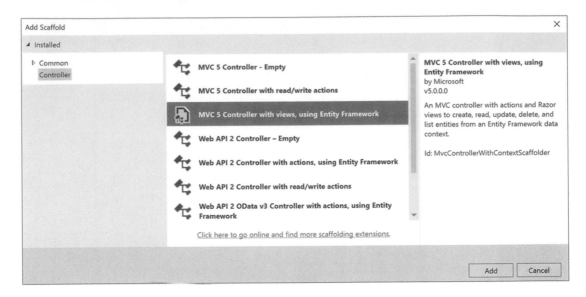

Figure 29-7. *The Add Scaffold dialog*

This will bring up an additional dialog (shown in Figure 29-8) that allows you to specify the types for your controller and action methods. The first question is to specify the model class, which determines the type for the controllers and action methods. Select the Inventory class from the drop-down.

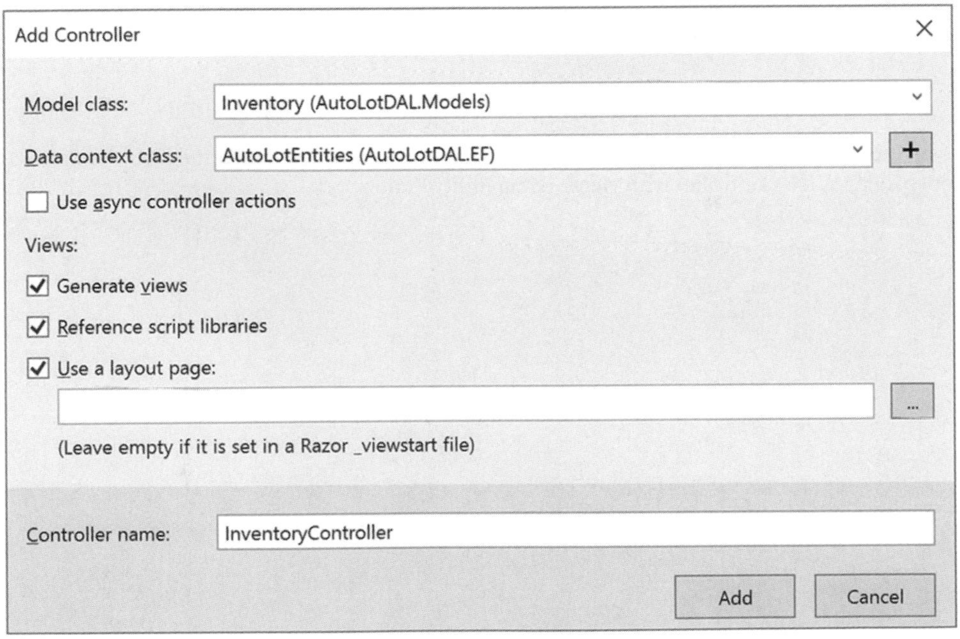

Figure 29-8. *Selecting the model, context, and other options*

The next question asks you to specify the context class. If you don't select one, the wizard will create one for you. For the data context, select AutoLotEntities. The next option is whether to use async controller action methods or not. Select the option that best meets your project needs. For this example, don't select it.

The "Generate views" option (selected by default) instructs the wizard to create a related view for each of the action methods. The "Reference script libraries" option instructs the wizard to include the relevant scripts into the views. The "Use a layout page" option will be discussed later in this chapter. Leave those three (Generate views, Reference script libraries, and Use a layout page) selected, and change the name to InventoryController (from InventoriesController).

This does several things for you. First, it creates an InventoryController class in the Controllers folder. It also creates an Inventory folder in the Views folder and adds five views under that folder. We will examine each of these in detail now.

■ **Note**   There are quite a few tooling aids in Visual Studio for MVC projects. You just saw the New Controller Wizard. If you right-click the Views folder, there is a menu item to add a new view. If you right-click an action, you can add a new view (which will be placed in the Views/Controller folder with the same name as the action), or you can navigate to the proper view. All of these features depend on the conventions discussed earlier, so if you follow the rules, life will be good!

Examine and Update the InventoryController

Open the InventoryController.cs class. Notice that it follows the convention of ending in the word *Controller*. It also derives from the abstract class Controller. There are a series of methods (actions) such as Index(), Edit(), and so on. You will examine each of these in turn, as well as the attributes decorating them. Finally, there is a Dispose() override that you can use to forcefully garbage collect any expensive resources (such as the EF Context class) used by the controller.

Using the Inventory Repository

The first line in the InventoryController class creates a new instance of AutoLotEntities, which is exactly what you told the wizard to use. You need to change this to use the InventoryRepo class. First, add the following using statements to the top of the file:

```
using AutoLotDAL.EF;
using AutoLotDAL.Models;
using AutoLotDAL.Repos;
using System.Data.Entity.Infrastructure;
```

Next, add an InventoryRepo instance variable at the top of the class like this and delete the AutoLotEntities variable:

```
private readonly InventoryRepo _repo = new InventoryRepo();
```

Next, dispose of the InventoryRepo in the Dispose override.

```
protected override void Dispose(bool disposing)
{
  if (disposing)
  {
    _repo.Dispose();
  }
  base.Dispose(disposing);
}
```

The Index Action

The Index action gets all the Inventory records and returns the data to the view. Update the call to use the InventoryRepo class like this:

```
// GET: Inventory
public ActionResult Index()
{
    return View(_repo.GetAll());
}
```

The View() call in the previous code snippet is an overloaded method in the Controller base class and returns a new ViewResult. When a view name is not passed in (as in the version you just saw), convention dictates that the view will be named after the action method and located in the folder named after the controller, in this case, Views/Inventory/Index.cshtml. You can also change the name of the view and pass the new name into the View() method. For example, if you named your view Foo.cshtml, you would call the View() method as follows:

```
return View("Foo", _repo.GetAll());
```

The Details Action

The Details() action method returns all the details for one Inventory record. A URL in the format http://mysite.com/Inventory/Details/5 will get mapped to the InventoryController's Details() action method with a parameter named id and a value of 5 passed in as the argument. Update this method to use the InventoryRepo class instead of AutoLotEntities directly, like this:

```
// GET: Inventory/Details/5
public ActionResult Details(int? id)
{
    if (id == null)
    {
        return new HttpStatusCodeResult(HttpStatusCode.BadRequest);
    }
    Inventory inventory = _repo.GetOne(id);
    if (inventory == null)
    {
        return HttpNotFound();
    }
    return View(inventory);
}
```

1198

There are a couple of interesting items in this simple-looking method. Remember from the route discussion that the id parameter is optional, so the URL /Inventory/Details will correctly map to this method. However, you can't get an Inventory record if there isn't an id value passed in to the method, so the method returns an HttpStatusCode 400 (Bad Request). Try this by running the app and entering Inventory/Details (leaving off the id part of the URL), and you should see an error screen. Likewise, if an inventory record cannot be found, the action method returns the HttpNotFound (404) status code.

Finally, if everything is good with the format of the URL and an Inventory record is found, then the Views/Inventory/Details.cshtml page is returned to the client.

A Word About Preventing Double Posts

A common problem of web sites is users clicking a submit button on a form twice, potentially duplicating whatever change the page supports. MVC adopts a pattern that severely mitigates this problem, but before discussing that, it's important to understand the two HTTP verbs used in MVC web applications.

HttpPost vs. HttpGet

While ASP.NET Web Forms largely ignored the difference between HttpGet and HttpPost, MVC uses the HTTP verbs appropriately. The Hypertext Transfer Protocol (HTTP) defines an HttpGet call as requesting data from the server and an HttpPost call as one that submits data to be processed to a specific resource.

In MVC, any action *without* an HTTP attribute (such as HttpPost) will be executed as an HttpGet operation. The Index() and Details() action methods covered earlier both use the HTTP Post protocol. To specify an HttpPost (an action where data will be submitted and potentially updated), you must decorate your action with the [HttpPost] attribute.

■ **Note** MVC does not use the HTTP DELETE or PUT verbs and sticks with just GET and POST, keeping in line with browser functionality. ASP.NET Web API (covered in Chapter 30) uses all four verbs.

The Post-Redirect-Get (PRG) Pattern

To prevent duplicate form submissions, MVC uses the Post-Redirect-Get (PRG) pattern. This pattern predates MVC and is commonly used by web developers. It consists of redirecting every successful Post action to a Get action, so if a user hits the submit button again, it just refreshes the page presented by the Get action and doesn't resubmit the Post.

You will see this pattern in the Create, Add, and Delete processes.

The Create Action

The Create process implements the PRG pattern using two Create() methods; one has an empty signature, and the second takes an Inventory object as a parameter.

The Get Version

The parameterless Create() method handles an HttpGet request and simply presents a page that allows for a user to add the information needed to create a record.

```
// GET: Inventory/Create
public ActionResult Create()
{
    return View();
}
```

The Post Version

The Create() overload that takes an Inventory object as its parameter has two method-level attributes, [HttpPost] and [ValidateAntiForgeryToken], and one parameter-level attribute, [Bind], as shown here:

```
[HttpPost]
[ValidateAntiForgeryToken]
public ActionResult Create([Bind(Include = "Make,Color,PetName")] Inventory inventory)
```

This version is executed when a user has clicked the submit button of the Create form (presuming all client-side validations pass). All of these items are covered in the next sections.

Model Binding

Model binding takes all of the name-value pairs from an HTML form (including form, query string, etc.) and attempts to reconstitute a specified type using reflection by matching the property names with the names from the name-value pairs and then assigning the values. If one or more value can't be assigned (e.g., because of data type conversion issues or validation errors), the model binding engine will indicate an error by setting the ModelState.IsValid property to false. If all matched properties are successfully assigned, it sets ModelState.IsValid = true.

In addition to the IsValid property, the ModelState is a ModelStateDictionary and contains error information for every property that failed, as well as model-level error information. If you want to add a specific error for a property, you would write code like this:

```
ModelState.AddModelError("Name","Name is required");
```

If you want to add an error for the entire model, use string.Empty for the property name, like this:

```
ModelState.AddModelError(string.Empty, $"Unable to create record: {ex.Message}");
```

There is explicit and implicit model binding. For explicit model binding, you call TryUpdateModel(), passing in an instance of the type. If the model binding fails, the TryUpdateModel() call returns false; it also adds any binding errors to the ModelState errors collection just like implicit model binding. For example, you could write the Create() method this way:

```
public ActionResult Create()
{
    var inv = new Inventory();
    if (TryUpdateModel(inv))
    {
        //Save the data
    }
}
```

For implicit model binding, you use the desired type as the parameter for the method. The model binding engine does the same operation with the parameter as it did with `TryUpdateModel()` in the previous example.

```
public ActionResult Create(Inventory inventory)
{
  if (ModelState.IsValid)
  {
    //Save the data;
  }
}
```

In the Create, Delete, and Edit views, if the `ModelState` is not valid, the user is returned to the same view to try again, with any previously entered data restored. If the `ModelState` is valid, the method should save the record to the database and then send the user to the `Index` action (a Get method).

AntiForgery Tokens

One of a number of weapons to fight hacking, the `AntiForgeryToken` attribute adds a special form value. This form value is then validated on the server side by MVC when an `HttpPost` request comes in (as long as the `[ValidateAntiForgeryToken]` attribute is present on the action method). While not a one-stop shop for security (web security is beyond the scope of this book), every form should add an `AntiForgeryToken`, and every `HttpPost` action should validate it.

The Bind Attribute

The `Bind` attribute in `HTTPPost` methods allows you to whitelist or blacklist properties to prevent over-posting attacks. When fields are *whitelisted*, they are the only fields that will be assigned through model binding. *Blacklisting* excludes properties from model binding. In the scaffolded `Create()` method, all of the fields on an Inventory record are whitelisted. Since you want only the `Make`, `Color`, and `PetName` properties on a Create action, remove the `Id` and `Timestamp` fields from the `Include` portion, as follows:

```
public async Task<ActionResult> Create([Bind(Include = "Make,Color,PetName")] Inventory
inventory)
```

Updating the Method to Use the InventoryRepo

Update the `Create()` method to use the `InventoryRepo` and add a model-level `ModelState` error if there is an issue while saving the record, like this:

```
[HttpPost]
[ValidateAntiForgeryToken]
public ActionResult Create([Bind(Include = "Make,Color,PetName")] Inventory inventory)
{
  if (!ModelState.IsValid) return View(inventory);
  try
  {
    _repo.Add(inventory);
  }
```

```
  catch (Exception ex)
  {
    ModelState.AddModelError(string.Empty,$@"Unable to create record: {ex.Message}");
    return View(inventory);
  }
    return RedirectToAction("Index");
}
```

The Edit Action

Just like the Create() action method, the edit process uses the PRG pattern as well, implemented using two
Edit() methods.

The Get Version

The first Edit() method takes an id, gets the inventory record, and returns the correct view. Other than
returning a different view (based on the name of the method), this is identical to the Details() method.
Make sure to change the method to use the Inventory repository instead of AutoLotEntities.

```
// GET: Inventory/Edit/5
public ActionResult Edit(int? id)
{
    if (id == null)
    {
        return new HttpStatusCodeResult(HttpStatusCode.BadRequest);
    }
    Inventory inventory = _repo.GetOne(id);
    if (inventory == null)
    {
        return HttpNotFound();
    }
    return View(inventory);
}
```

The Post Version

This version is executed when a user has clicked the submit button of the Edit form (presuming all client-
side validations pass). If the model state isn't valid, the method once again returns the Edit view, sending
the current values for the Inventory object. If the model state is valid, the Inventory object is sent to the
repository for an attempted save.

In addition to the general error handling (like you used in the Create() method), you need to add a
check for DbUpdateConcurrencyException, which will occur if another user has updated the record since the
user originally loaded it into the web page. If all is successful, the action method returns a RedirectToAction
result, sending the user to the Index() action method of the InventoryController.

```
[HttpPost]
[ValidateAntiForgeryToken]
public ActionResult Edit([Bind(Include = "Id,Make,Color,PetName,Timestamp")] Inventory
inventory)
```

```
{
  if (!ModelState.IsValid) return View(inventory);
  try
  {
    _repo.Save(inventory);
  }
  catch (DbUpdateConcurrencyException ex)
  {
    ModelState.AddModelError(string.Empty,
      $@"Unable to save the record. Another user has updated it. {ex.Message}");
    return View(inventory);
  }
    catch (Exception ex)
  {
    ModelState.AddModelError(string.Empty,$@"Unable to save the record. {ex.Message}");
    return View(inventory);
  }
  return RedirectToAction("Index");
}
```

■ **Note** For more information on `DbUpdateConcurrencyException`, refer to Chapter 22.

The Delete Action

The `Delete()` action method also uses the PRG pattern with two methods.

The Get Version

The first `Delete()` method takes an `id` and is identical to the `Details()` and `Edit()` `HttpGet` methods. Make sure to change the `HttpGet` version to use the `Inventory` repository instead of `AutoLotEntities`.

```
public ActionResult Delete(int? id)
{
  if (id == null)

    return new HttpStatusCodeResult(HttpStatusCode.BadRequest);
  }
  Inventory inventory = _repo.GetOne(id);
  if (inventory == null)
  {
    return HttpNotFound();
  }
  return View(inventory);
}
```

The Post Version

This version is executed when a user has clicked the submit button on the Delete form. The autogenerated version of this method takes only the id as a parameter, meaning it has the same signature as the HttpGet version of the method. Since you can't have two methods of the same name with the same signature, the wizard named this method DeleteConfirmed() and added the [ActionName("Delete")] attribute. Update the signature to the following (you can delete the ActionName attribute as well as long as you rename the method to Delete()):

```
[HttpPost]
[ValidateAntiForgeryToken]
public ActionResult Delete( [Bind(Include="Id,Timestamp")]Inventory car)
```

AutoLotDAL checks for concurrency conflicts and requires the Timestamp property in addition to the Id to delete a record. That is why you changed the int id parameter to Inventory inventory. The [Bind] attribute with the Include value of "Id,Timestamp" pulls just those values into the Inventory instance and ignores the rest of the values.

Finally, update the method to use the Inventory repository and add the error handling (the same as you did for the HttpPost version of the Edit() method). The final version of the code is as follows:

```
[HttpPost]
[ValidateAntiForgeryToken]
public ActionResult Delete([Bind(Include="Id,Timestamp")]Inventory inventory)
{
  try
  {
    _repo.Delete(inventory);
  }
  catch (DbUpdateConcurrencyException ex)
  {
    ModelState.AddModelError(string.Empty, $@"Unable to delete record. Another user updated
    the record. {ex.Message}");
  }
  catch (Exception ex)
  {
    ModelState.AddModelError(string.Empty, $@"Unable to create record: {ex.Message}");
  }
  return RedirectToAction("Index");
}
```

If you ran your project now and tried to delete an Inventory record, it wouldn't work because the view is not sending the Timestamp property, just the Id. You will fix that shortly.

Wrapping Up Controllers and Actions

This was a lot of information to cover, and I've only scratched the surface of everything that you can do in MVC controllers and action methods. To summarize, controllers are C# classes, and they should follow the <Name>Controller.cs naming convention. Actions are public methods in a controller class that return an ActionResult. Action methods can be decorated with an attribute that indicates if it's an HttpPost or an HttpGet (the default), and all HttpPost methods should use the AntiForgery token. Now, let's move onto views.

The Razor View Engine

Before covering views in detail, it's important to understand the Razor view engine and how to add server-side code to your views using Razor. The Razor view engine was designed as an improvement over the Web Forms view engine and uses Razor as the core language. Razor views don't extend `System.Web.Page` (there isn't any `Page` directive), which adds testability.

Razor is a template markup syntax that is interpreted to C# (or VB.NET code) on the server side. Using Razor in your views with HTML and CSS results in cleaner and easier-to-read markup, as you will soon see. The Razor view engine supports everything that the Web Forms view engine supports, so you aren't giving anything up by using Razor.

Razor also supports the creation of methods for code encapsulation in the form of HTML helpers, Razor functions, and Razor delegates. These can be created in a view for localized use or for general use by placing them in the `App_Code` folder or creating them using the `static` keyword.

■ **Note** While the Web Forms view engine is still supported in ASP.NET MVC 5, it is not supported in ASP.NET Core. If you've resisted the transition to Razor, this is a good time to make the change.

Razor Syntax

The first difference between the Web Forms view engine and the Razor view engine is that you add code with the @ symbol. There is also intelligence built into Razor that removes the need to add closing @ symbols, unlike the Web Forms view engine, which requires opening and closing "nuggets" (`<% %>`).

Statements, Code Blocks, and Markup

Single-line statements are prefixed with just an @ symbol, without any closing symbol, like this:

```
@ShowInventory(item)
```

Statement blocks open with an @ and are enclosed in braces, like this:

```
@foreach (var item in Model)
{
}
//or
@{
  ShowInventory(item);
}
```

Code blocks can intermix markup and code. Lines that begin with a markup tag are interpreted as HTML, while lines that begin with code are interpreted as code, like this:

```
@foreach (var item in Model)
{
  int x = 0;
  <tr></tr>
}
```

The @ sign in front of a variable is equivalent to `Response.Write()`, and by default HTML encodes all values. If you want to output unencoded data (i.e., potentially unsafe data), you have to use the `@Html.Raw(username)` syntax. Razor and markup can be used together, like this:

```
<h1>Hello, @username</h1>
```

The @: and `<text>` tags denote text that should be rendered as part of the markup, like this:

```
@:Straight Text
<div>Value:@i</div>
<text>
Lines without HTML tag
</text>
```

The @* and *@ indicate a multiline comment.

```
@* This is a comment that could go across multiple lines *@
```

Razor is also pretty smart about when it should be an @ sign versus a statement. E-mail addresses are a great example. If Razor encounters an e-mail address, it does not interpret that as code. If your code *looks* like an e-mail address, following that @ with parentheses informs Razor to treat the line as code. Here's an example:

```
someone@foo.com @* email address *@
someone@(foo).com @* foo is interpreted as Razor code and the variable foo is replaced by
its value*@
```

If you need to escape an @ sign, double them up, like the following, which outputs @foo to the view:

```
@@foo
```

Built-in HTML Helpers

There are many built-in HTML helpers, and many of the common ones are listed in Table 29-9. You will see many of these in action through the rest of this chapter.

Table 29-9. *Common HTML Helpers*

HTML Helper	Meaning in Life
`ActionLink`	Creates an anchor tag.

`TextBox[For]`
`TextArea[For]`
`CheckBox[For]`
`RadioButton[For]`
`DropDownList[For]`
`ListBox[For]`
`Hidden[For]`
`Password[For]`
`Label[For]`
	Each creates the same-named HTML Form control for the property on the model. The `For` versions are strongly typed.

`Display[For]`	Renders property as read-only based on a template. If no custom template is found, the default template (based on data type) is used. The `For` version is strongly typed.
`Editor[For]`	Renders property as form controls based on a template. If no custom template is found, the default template (based on data type) is used. The `For` version is strongly typed.
`DisplayForModel` `EditotForModel`	Renders display or editor markup for the entire model. Uses custom template if one exists; otherwise uses the default template.
`DisplayName[For]`	Gets the display name if one is assigned; otherwise displays the property name. The `For` version is strongly typed.
`ValidationSummary` `ValidationMessageFor`	Creates a validation summary or message when validation fails during client-side or server-side validation.
`@Html.BeginForm()`	Creates an HTML form tag, containing everything within the enclosing braces.
`@Html.AntiForgeryToken()`	Works in conjunction with the `ValidateAntiForgeryToken` action method attribute.

The templated helpers rely on default templates unless custom templates are created and in the correct location. You will see how to create custom templates shortly.

The Edit Templated HTML Helpers

While the display helpers simply display data, the editor helpers do a bit more than just create the relevant control. For example, the `EditorFor()` HTML helper creates an input field based on the data type of the property referenced in the lambda. For example, the following line:

```
@Html.EditorFor(model => model.Make, new { htmlAttributes = new { @class = "form-control" } })
```

creates this:

```
<input name="Make" class="form-control text-box single-line" id="Make" type="text" value=""
data-val-length-max="50" data-val-length="The field Make must be a string with a maximum
length of 50." data-val="true">
```

Let's examine this before moving on. The name and the id of the HTML element comes from the name of the property, the type comes from the data type of the property, and the class assignment comes from a combination of the HTML helper and the additional HTML attributes added through the helper.

The value of the control is set to the property's value. In this case, the value is set to the empty string since it's a new instance of Inventory. The validation code is generated by the data annotations and will be covered in more detail later in the chapter.

Adjusting the HTML Rendered by HTML Helpers

By themselves, the HTML helpers will render vanilla markup. If you want add styling or other attributes, you have to use one of the overloads. This sounds simple, but the syntax is a bit, well, to use a technical term, wonky.

You have to create a new anonymous object with name-value pairs of the HTML that should be rendered along with the base output. If the HTML attribute name is also a reserved word in C#, it must be escaped with an @ symbol. This seems backward since the @ symbol is used to mark an item as Razor code!

For example, if you want to set the CSS class on a label element, you would use this code:

```
@Html.LabelFor(model => model.Color, htmlAttributes: new { @class = "control-label col-md-2" })
```

This will then update the label markup to include the CSS class attribute.

Custom HTML Helpers

Razor HTML helpers render markup. There are many built-in helpers that you will use extensively, such as the @Html.ActionLink() HTML helper, which creates an anchor tag. In addition to the built-in helpers, you can create custom HTML helpers to reduce (or eliminate repetitive code).

For example, you can write a helper that outputs the details for an Inventory record. To do this, open the Index.cshtml view in the Views\Inventory folder, and place the following HTML helper code at the top of file (after the @model line), like this:

```
@using AutoLotDAL.Models
@helper ShowInventory(Inventory item)
{
  @item.Make<text>-</text>@item.Color<text>(</text>@item.PetName<text>)</text>
}
```

After the @foreach, add a call to ShowInventory(), like this:

```
@foreach (var item in Model)
{
    @ShowInventory(item)
    <!-- rest removed for brevity -->
}
```

Run the app and navigate to the Inventory/Index page; you will see the details for each record as one lone string. In a real HTML helper, you would add formatting and markup to be consistent with the look and feel of your site. Since this is just an example of how to create an HTML helper and not something you want to use in your site, comment out the line like this:

```
@*@ShowInventory(item)*@
```

Razor Functions

Razor functions do not return markup but instead are used to encapsulate code for reuse. To see this in action, add the following SortCars() function after the HTML helper in the Index.cshtml view page. The function takes a list of Inventory items and sorts them by PetName:

```
@functions
{
  public IList<Inventory> SortCars(IList<Inventory> cars)
  {
    var list = from s in cars orderby s.PetName select s;
    return list.ToList();
  }
}
```

Update the @foreach to call the function. The Model variable represents an IEnumerable<Inventory>, so you must add the ToList() method in that call, as follows:

```
@foreach (var item in SortCars(Model.ToList()))
{
    <!-- rest removed for brevity -->
}
```

Razor Delegates

Razor delegates work just like C# delegates. For example, add the following delegate code immediately after the SortCars() function in the Index.cshtml view file. This delegate makes the marked characters bold.

```
@{
  Func<dynamic, object> b = @<strong>@item</strong>;
}
```

To see this in action, add the following line of code immediately after the code block that defines the delegate:

```
This will be bold: @b("Foo")
```

Of course, this example is trivial, but more involved code that is repeated can benefit from being wrapped in a delegate. Essentially, all the same pros and cons for C# delegates apply. After running the app and navigating to the Inventory index page, you will see the word *Foo* in bold. Go ahead and comment out the call to the delegate since you don't need it for the rest of the samples.

MVC Views

Views in MVC represent the UI in MVC sites. MVC views are meant to be very lightweight, passing server-side processing to the controllers and client-side processing to JavaScript. Layout views are similar to master pages in Web Forms, views render within a layout, and partial views only render themselves (i.e., without a layout).

Layouts

Navigate to the Views/Shared folder and open the _Layout.cshtml file. It is a full-fledged HTML file, complete with <head> and <body> tags and a mix of HTML markup and Razor HTML helpers. Just like Web Forms master pages, the _Layout.cshtml page is the core of what will be presented to the user when views (that use the _Layout.cshtml page) are rendered.

There are two key items to keep in mind when working with layouts: body and sections. The body is where a view will be inserted when the view and layout are rendered and is positioned in the layout by the following line of Razor code:

```
@RenderBody()
```

Sections are areas of the layout page that layouts can fill in at runtime. They can be required or optional and are introduced into the layout page with the RenderSection() Razor function. The first argument names the section, and the second indicates whether the section is required. In _Layout.cshtml, the following line of code creates a section named scripts, which is optional for the view:

```
@RenderSection("scripts", required: false)
```

If you wanted to create a new section named Header that is required, you would code it like this:

```
@RenderSection("Header",required: true)
```

To render a section in from your view, you use the @section Razor block. For example, in the Edit.cshtml page under Views/Inventory, the following lines add the jQuery validation bundle to the rendered page:

```
@section Scripts {
  @Scripts.Render("~/bundles/jqueryval")
}
```

Choosing a Layout Page

MVC views can be based on a master layout to give the site a universal look and feel. Views can explicitly declare the layout view that they will be rendered in, or they can use the default layout view.

The default is declared in the _ViewStart.cshtml file. This file just has one Razor code block that sets the layout to a specific file. Open this file now to examine the contents, shown here:

```
@{
  Layout = "~/Views/Shared/_Layout.cshtml";
}
```

Any view at or below the level of this file will then be assigned that layout view if it doesn't specify one itself (excluding partial views, covered later).

Using a Specific Layout Page

In addition to relying on the default layout page, you can specify your views to use a specific page by adding a Layout line to the top of the view. Suppose you had a layout named _LayoutNew.cshtml. You would update your view to this:

```
@{
  ViewBag.Title = "Index";
  Layout = "~/Views/Shared/_LayoutNew.cshtml";
}
```

Update the Layout Menu Options

Layout views usually contain the site navigation, and this site is no different. In _Layout.cshtml, locate the line containing @Html.ActionLink(" Home", "Index","Home"). You need to add a menu for the new Inventory pages, so add the following just after that line:

```
<li>@Html.ActionLink("Inventory", "Index", "Inventory")</li>
```

Partial Views

Partial views are the same as regular views, except they do not use a layout view as their base and are useful for encapsulating UI. The difference between a partial view and a full view is how they are rendered. A full view (returned from a controller with the View() method) will use a layout page if one is specified, either as the default through _ViewStart.cshtml or through the Layout Razor statement. A view when rendered with the PartialView() method (or the Partial() HTML helper) does not use the default layout but will still use a layout if specified with a Layout Razor statement.

To demonstrate this, open the InventoryController.cs class and change the Index() action method to return a partial view instead of a view, as follows:

```
public ActionResult Index()
{
  return PartialView(_repo.GetAll());
}
```

Run the app and click the Inventory menu link. You will then see the same data as you did before, minus any layout.

Make sure to change the Index action method back to calling View() instead of PartialView().

In addition to rendering a view from an action method with the PartialView() method, you can pull a partial view into another view using an HTML helper. If you had a view named MyPartial.cshtml, you could bring that into another view like this:

```
@Html.Partial("MyPartial")
```

Sending Data to Views

As you learned in the discussion of the InventoryController.cs class, action methods can return data to the view. This was done by passing an object (or list of objects) into the View() method. The data passed into the View() method becomes the model for the view.

Strongly Typed Views and View Models

Views in MVC are typically strongly typed to the data they use. The type of data they expect is defined with the @model statement in the view. For example, the Index.cshtml view uses an IEnumerable<Inventory> as its data source:

```
@model IEnumerable<AutoLotDAL.Models.Inventory>
```

To access this data in the rest of the view, you use the Model keyword. Note the uppercase *M* in the Model keyword and the lowercase *m* in the @model line. When referring to the data contained in the view, you use Model (capital *M*), as in the following line, which iterates through each of the Inventory records:

```
@foreach (var item in Model)
{
  //Do something interesting here
}
```

ViewBag, ViewData, and TempData

The ViewBag, ViewData, and TempData objects are mechanisms for sending small amounts of data into a view. An example of this is in the top of each of the Inventory views with a line setting the ViewBag.Title property, like the following in the Index.cshtml view:

```
@{
    ViewBag.Title = "Index";
}
```

The ViewBag.Title property is used to send the title of a view to the layout to be used in the following line in _Layout.cshtml:

```
<title>@ViewBag.Title - My ASP.NET Application</title>
```

Table 29-10 lists details about all three mechanisms.

Table 29-10. Ways to Send Data to a View

Data Transport Object	Meaning in Life
TempData	This is a short-lived object that works during the current request and next request only.
ViewData	A dictionary that allows storing values in name-value pairs. Here's an example: ViewData["Title"] = "Foo".
ViewBag	Dynamic wrapper for the ViewData dictionary. Here's an example: ViewBag.Title = "Foo".

Now that you understand how data gets sent to the views, let's add some data annotations to clean up the models for MVC.

The Display Data Annotation

Many of the data annotations used by Entity Framework are also used by the MVC view engine for rendering markup and for validations. There are additional data annotations that are ignored by EF but used for MVC, such as the Display data annotation.

The Display data annotation informs MVC the name to use instead of the property name when the DisplayName or DisplayNameFor HTML helper is used in a view. The syntax is simple, as shown in the following example, which changes the display name from PetName (the property name) to Pet Name, a more readable display name:

```
[Display(Name="Pet Name")]
```

While I only cover the Display data annotation, there are many additional annotations that can be used in the same manner. Please consult the .NET Framework documentation to learn more.

Custom Metadata Files

While you can add additional data annotations to the model classes themselves, it is often beneficial to add them to a separate class to preserve the integrity of the model classes. Add a new folder named MetaData to the AutoLotDAL.Models project. In this folder, add a new class named InventoryMetaData.cs. Make the class public, and add the following using statement to the top of the file:

```
using System.ComponentModel.DataAnnotations;
```

Next, add a property of type string named PetName. To this property, add the [Display(Name="Pet Name")] attribute. Your class should look like this:

```
public class InventoryMetaData
{
    [Display(Name="Pet Name")]
    public string PetName;
}
```

Open the InventoryPartial.cs class, and update the using statements to the following:

```
using System.ComponentModel.DataAnnotations;
using System.ComponentModel.DataAnnotations.Schema;
using AutoLotDAL.Models.MetaData;
```

Next, add the [MetadataType] attribute to the class, as follows:

```
[MetadataType(typeof(InventoryMetaData))]
public partial class Inventory
{
    public override string ToString() =>
        $"{this.PetName ?? "**No Name**"} is a {this.Color} {this.Make} with ID {this.Id}.";
}
```

Metadata files are not full class definition files; they are used only to load attributes into another file. Therefore, you do not need to add the get/set syntax to this property, and in fact, you shouldn't. You might be asking how the framework knows that this class is supplying attributes to the Inventory class. Currently, it doesn't. You need to add a class-level attribute to the Inventory.cs class so the framework knows this class holds additional attributes for it. You'll make that change next.

Run the app now, click the Inventory link, and you will see that the PetName label is displayed as Pet Name, without changing any code in the view.

Razor Templates

Table 29-9 mentioned several HTML helpers that depend on templates, either custom or default. Razor supports two types of custom templates, display templates and editor templates. Templates are created as Razor view and must be located based on convention.

For display templates, they must be located in a folder named DisplayTemplates, either under the Views\Shared folder or under a controller-specific view folder, such as Views\Inventory. The same rules for views apply to templates; any templates under the Views\Shared folder are accessible throughout the application, and templates located in a controller-specific folder are accessible only from views for that controller. For editor templates, all of the same rules apply, except that the folder must be named EditorTemplates.

Templates can be invoked either explicitly or implicitly. To explicitly invoke a template, you reference it by name. For example, if you had a display template named InventoryList.cshtml, you invoke it like this:

```
@Html.DisplayFor(modelItem=>item,"InventoryList")
```

To implicitly invoke a template, name the template the same as the data type it should render. Then it will be invoked automatically when the data type of the property matches the name of the template. For example, if you name a template Inventory.cshtml, it would be invoked on an Inventory instance like this:

```
@Html.DisplayFor(modelItem=>item)
```

Create a Custom Display Template

To create a custom display template, start by creating a new folder under View\Inventory named DisplayTemplates. In that folder, add a new view by right-clicking the new folder, selecting Add ➤ View, and filling in the wizard screen, as shown in Figure 29-9.

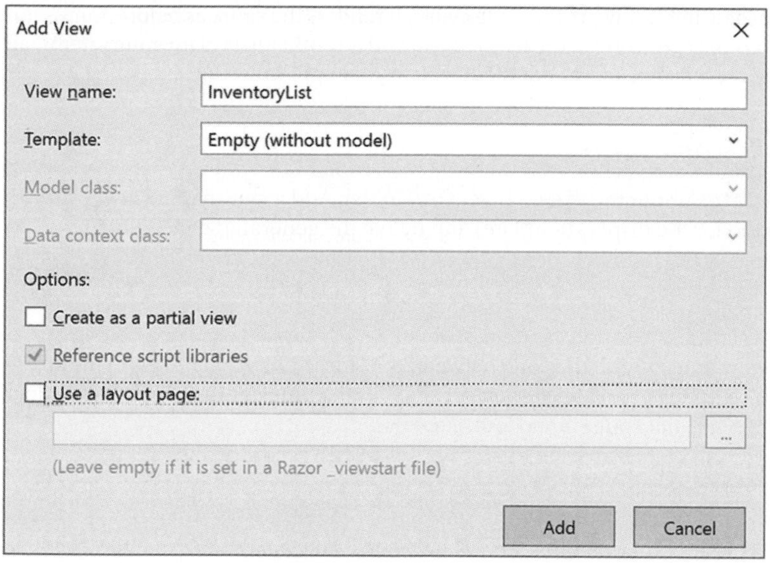

Figure 29-9. *Creating a display template*

This template will replace the code that is used to display each row in the Inventory Index view. Delete the code in the file and replace it with the following (notice the absence of the timestamp property):

```
@model AutoLotDAL.Models.Inventory

<tr>
  <td>@Html.DisplayFor(model => model.Make)</td>
  <td>@Html.DisplayFor(model => model.Color)</td>
  <td>@Html.DisplayFor(model => model.PetName) </td>
  <td>
        @Html.ActionLink("Edit", "Edit", new { id = Model.Id }) |
        @Html.ActionLink("Details", "Details", new { id = Model.Id }) |
        @Html.ActionLink("Delete", "Delete", new { id = Model.Id })
  </td>
</tr>
```

Now update the Index view's foreach statement to the following:

```
@foreach (var item in SortCars(Model.ToList()))
{
  @Html.DisplayFor(modelItem=>item,"InventoryList")
}
```

The last step is to remove the index header from the list page. Open the Index.cshtml file and *remove* the following code:

```
<th>
  @Html.DisplayNameFor(model => model.Timestamp)
</th>
```

When you run the app and navigate to the Inventory Index view, it renders the same as before, minus the timestamp property (which would just be confusing to the user). If you had any other lists of inventory items, all you need to do is use the template, and you will have a consistent look to your app, with a lot less typing.

Create a Custom Editor Template

Create a folder named EditorTemplates under the Views\Inventory folder. Add a view named Inventory.cshtml in this folder (just like you did for the display template) and delete the generated code. Add the following model:

```
@model AutoLotDAL.Models.Inventory
```

Next, open the Edit.cshtml view and copy all the code between the "form-horizontal" div (including the div itself). Paste that into the new editor template. Remove the div for the timestamp property and add a new hidden field for the timestamp. The final code should look like this:

```
@model AutoLotDAL.Models.Inventory
<div class="form-horizontal">
  <h4>Inventory</h4>
  <hr />
  @Html.ValidationSummary(true, "", new { @class = "text-danger" })
  <div class="form-group">
    @Html.LabelFor(model => model.Make,
      htmlAttributes: new { @class = "control-label col-md-2" })
    <div class="col-md-10">
      @Html.EditorFor(model => model.Make,
        new { htmlAttributes = new { @class = "form-control" } })
      @Html.ValidationMessageFor(model => model.Make, "",
        new { @class = "text-danger" })
    </div>
  </div>
  <div class="form-group">
    @Html.LabelFor(model => model.Color,
      htmlAttributes: new { @class = "control-label col-md-2" })
    <div class="col-md-10">
      @Html.EditorFor(model => model.Color,
        new { htmlAttributes = new { @class = "form-control" } })
      @Html.ValidationMessageFor(model => model.Color, "",
        new { @class = "text-danger" })
    </div>
  </div>
  <div class="form-group">
    @Html.LabelFor(model => model.PetName,
      htmlAttributes: new { @class = "control-label col-md-2" })
    <div class="col-md-10">
      @Html.EditorFor(model => model.PetName,
        new { htmlAttributes = new { @class = "form-control" } })
      @Html.ValidationMessageFor(model => model.PetName, "",
        new { @class = "text-danger" })
    </div>
  </div>
</div>
```

The final step is to clean up the `Edit.cshtml` view. Update the code to the following:

```
@using (Html.BeginForm())
{
    @Html.AntiForgeryToken()
  @Html.HiddenFor(model => model.Id)
  @Html.HiddenFor(model => model.Timestamp)

    @Html.EditorForModel()

  <div class="form-group">
    <div class="col-md-offset-2 col-md-10">
      <input type="submit" value="Save" class="btn btn-default" />
    </div>
  </div>
}
```

This significantly cleaned up the `Edit.cshtml` view and encapsulated thc markup for editing an Inventory record. Edit the `Create.cshtml` view to the following:

```
@using (Html.BeginForm())
{
  @Html.AntiForgeryToken()
  @Html.EditorForModel()
  <div class="form-group">
    <div class="col-md-offset-2 col-md-10">
      <input type="submit" value="Create" class="btn btn-default" />
    </div>
  </div>
}
```

The same template works in both places, significantly reducing the markup on both pages.

Working with Forms

Unless you are building a pure marketing site, getting data from the user through forms is a vital component of web development. With that in mind, you should take a closer look at the `BeginForm` and `AntiForgeryToken` HTML helpers.

The BeginForm() HTML Helper

The `BeginForm()` HTML helper creates a `<form>` tag in the HTML output. By default, the form's action property is the current URL, and the form's method property is `post` (each is customizable through different overloads of the `BeginForm()` method). The `using` block in Razor will encapsulate everything between the opening and closing braces within the generated opening and closing HTML `form` tags. For example, say you entered this Razor block into a view:

```
@using (Html.BeginForm())
{
  <input name="foo" id="foo" type="text"/>
}
```

If the URL for the HttpGet request was Inventory/Create, the Html.BeginForm() helper would create the following markup:

```
<form action="/Inventory/Create" method="post">
  <input name="foo" id="foo" type="text"/>
</form>
```

The AntiForgeryToken() HTML Helper

If you recall, the [ValidateAntiForgeryToken] attribute needs to be added to all the HttpPost action methods (and is by default when using the built-in scaffolding). The AntiForgeryToken() HTML helper creates the client-side value that is checked by the server-side validation. If they don't match properly, the request is denied.

Updating the Delete View

You also need to change the scaffolded Delete view. First, remove the Timestamp field display, which is meaningless (and potentially confusing) to the user. This view also doesn't create an inventory record; it relies entirely on URL parameters to reference the record to be deleted.

Update the form code to the following to pass in the required values to enable deletion of an inventory record:

```
@using (Html.BeginForm()) {
  @Html.AntiForgeryToken()
  @Html.HiddenFor(x => x.Id)
  @Html.HiddenFor(x => x.Timestamp)
  @Html.ValidationSummary(true, "", new { @class = "text-danger" })
  <div class="form-actions no-color">
    <input type="submit" value="Delete" class="btn btn-default" /> |
    @Html.ActionLink("Back to List", "Index")
  </div>
}
```

Validation

MVC applications have two layers of validation: server-side and client-side. You saw server-side validation earlier in the chapter, when you added errors to the ModelState, in addition to the errors that came from model binding failures. Client-side checking happens with JavaScript, and you'll look at that soon enough.

Displaying Errors

The ModelState errors get displayed in the UI by the HTML helpers ValidationMessageFor() and ValidationSummary(). The ValidationSummary() method will show ModelState errors that are not attached to a property as well as property errors (as long as the ValidationSummary.ExcludePropertyErrors property is set to false). Typically, you will display property errors alongside the properties and show only non-property-specific errors in the ValidationSummary(). For example, the following line (in the Create, Edit, and Delete views) will show all the model errors and none of the property errors in a red font:

```
@Html.ValidationSummary(true, "", new { @class = "text-danger" })
```

To show individual property errors, use the `ValidationMessageFor()` helper adjacent to a particular property in the view page, like this:

```
@Html.ValidationMessageFor(model => model.Make, "", new { @class = "text-danger" })
```

This produces the following markup:

```
<span class="field-validation-valid text-danger" data-valmsg-replace="true" data-valmsg-for="Make"></span>
```

To see the messages in action, run the project, navigate to the Inventory ➤ Create New page, and type something into the Make field that is longer than 50 characters. When you tab out of the control, the client-side validation raises an error that is then displayed by the `ValidationMessageFor` HTML helper.

Update the `ValidationSummary` to the following, specifying to show all errors, including property errors:

```
@Html.ValidationSummary(false, "", new { @class = "text-danger" })
```

Run the project again, create the same error, and notice that it *doesn't* show in the validation summary. This is because, unfortunately, the `ValidationSummary` and client-side validation don't get along. To see server-side validation in action, you need to disable client-side validation.

Disable Client-Side Validation

Fortunately, it is easy to disable client-side validation for MVC views. In the `Create.cshtml` view, change the `@section` code to the following:

```
@section Scripts {
    @*@Scripts.Render("~/bundles/jqueryval")*@
}
```

Run the app again, create the same error, and notice that it doesn't show when you tab out of the Make control. Click the Create button, and you will see the summary and the field-level message appear.

Make sure to reenable the jQuery bundle before moving on to the next section.

Client-Side Validation

Client-side validation is handled through the jQuery, jQuery validation, and jQuery validation unobtrusive libraries. The MVC framework works with jQuery by examining the attributes on the model and then adding the appropriate validations to the rendered HTML when using the editor HTML helpers. For example, the `EditorFor` HTML helper generates the following markup for the `Make` property:

```
<input name="Make" class="form-control text-box single-line input-validation-error"
id="Make" aria-invalid="true" aria-describedby="Make-error" type="text" value=""
data-val-length-max="50" data-val-length="The field Make must be a string with a maximum
length of 50." data-val="true">
```

The data attributes also support custom error messages. Open the `InventoryMetaData.cs` class in the `AutoLotDAL.Models` project, and add the following:

```
[StringLength(50, ErrorMessage = "Please enter a value less than 50 characters long.")]
public string Make;
```

Now run the app, repeat the test, and you will see the friendlier error message displayed.

■ **Note**   While this example showed that you can have the same attribute defined twice for a property, it is generally not a good idea to do so. Duplication of any kind in software is a code smell, and the better course of action would be to add the message directly on the Inventory class attribute.

The Final Word on ASP.NET MVC

The question I am often asked is this: "Web Forms or MVC?" The answer is not that simple when working with the full .NET Framework. If your dev team is more comfortable with the drag-and-drop nature of UI creation or they struggle with the stateless nature of HTTP, Web Forms is probably the better choice. If your team is more comfortable with having complete control of the UI (which also means less "magic" being done for you) and developing stateless applications that leverage the HTTP verbs (such as HttpGet and HttpPost), then MVC is probably a better choice. Of course, there are lots more factors to consider in your decision. These are just a few of them.

When building applications based on the full .NET Framework, you don't have to choose between Web Forms or MVC since they are both are based on System.Web and can be used together, even in the same application. When Microsoft introduced "One ASP.NET" in Visual Studio 2013, blending the two frameworks into a single project became much easier.

That being said, .NET Core and ASP.NET Core support only MVC-style applications, and there isn't much chance of Web Forms being rewritten for .NET Core. That might alter your decision on which framework you select when working with the full .NET Framework.

Admittedly, this chapter only scratches the surface of ASP.NET MVC. There is just too much to cover in one chapter. For a deeper look into all that MVC has to offer, *Pro ASP.NET MVC 5* by Adam Freemen (available on Apress at www.apress.com/9781430265290?gtmf=s) is an excellent book on the subject.

■ **Source Code**   You can find the CarLotMVC solution in the Chapter 29 subfolder.

Summary

This chapter examined many aspects of ASP.NET MVC. You began by examining the Model-View-Controller pattern and built your first MVC site. You learned about convention over configuration for the MVC framework and about all the files scaffolded for you as part of the new project template, as well as the folders that were created and their purpose. You examined each of the classes created in the App_Start folder and how they help you create MVC applications. You also learned about bundling and minification and how to turn them off if needed.

The next section went into routing and how requests are directed to your controllers and actions. You created new routes for the About and Contact pages and learned about redirecting users to other resources in your site using routing instead of hard-coded URLs.

Next, you created a controller for the Inventory pages and learned how the scaffolding built into Visual Studio creates base action methods and views. You learned about HttpGet and HttpPost requests and how they work with routing for even finer control of what action method gets called. You then updated the action methods to use AutoLotDAL, as well as updated the signatures and code to fit your business requirements.

Then you learned about the Razor view engine; the syntax; and Razor helpers, functions, and delegates. You also learned more about strongly typed views, partial views, and layouts. You learned to send data to a view using `ViewBag`, `ViewData`, and `TempData`.

After that, you modified each scaffolded view, updated the `InventoryController` actions as needed, and explored client-side and server-side validation.

Next you will learn about a very close relative of ASP.NET MVC, which is ASP.NET Web API.

CHAPTER 30

■ ■ ■

Introducing ASP.NET Web API

The previous chapter covered ASP.NET MVC, the pattern, and the .NET implementation. This chapter introduces you to the ASP.NET Web API, a service framework built largely on the chassis of MVC that shares many of the concepts, including routing, controllers, and actions. ASP.NET Web API allows you to leverage your MVC knowledge to build RESTful services without the configuration and plumbing that WCF (Chapter 23) requires. You will create a RESTful service called CarLotWebAPI that exposes all of the create, read, update, and delete (CRUD) functionality on the inventory records. Finally, you will finish the chapter by updating CarLotMVC to use `CarLotWebAPI` as the data source, instead of directly calling into the data access layer.

■ **Note**   This chapter will not repeat the content from the previous chapter but, instead, focuses on the specifics of creating a RESTful service with ASP.NET Web API projects. If you are new to ASP.NET MVC, I suggest you read Chapter 29 before continuing with this chapter.

Introducing ASP.NET Web API

As you learned in Chapter 23, Windows Communication Foundation (WCF) is a full-fledged framework for creating .NET-based services that can communicate with a wide range of clients. While WCF is extremely powerful, if all you need are simple HTTP-based services, creating WCF-based services may be more involved than you want or need. Enter ASP.NET Web API, another framework for building web APIs in .NET that can be accessed from any HTTP-aware client. As an MVC developer, Web API is a logical addition to your .NET toolbox. Web API is built on MVC and leverages many of the same concepts such as models, controllers, and routing. Web API was first released with Visual Studio 2012 as part of MVC 4 and updated to version 2.2 with Visual Studio 2013 Update 1.

Creating the Web API Project

Start by creating a Web API project named CarLotWebAPI. In the New Project dialog, select the Web grouping in the left side of the window and the ASP.NET Web Application (.NET Framework) template, as shown in Figure 30-1.

© Andrew Troelsen and Philip Japikse 2017
A. Troelsen and P. Japikse, *Pro C# 7*, https://doi.org/10.1007/978-1-4842-3018-3_30

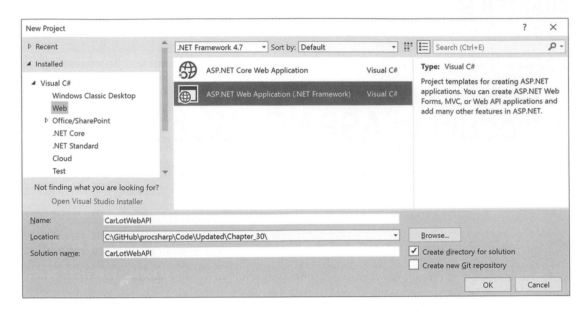

Figure 30-1. *Create a new ASP.NET web application*

By now you should be familiar with the next screen. However, this time, select the Empty template and select the Web API box under "Add folders and core references for" (as shown in Figure 30-2). If you select the Web API template, a lot of boilerplate and sample code (including MVC controllers and views) are added to the project, and all you need is the base Web API plumbing.

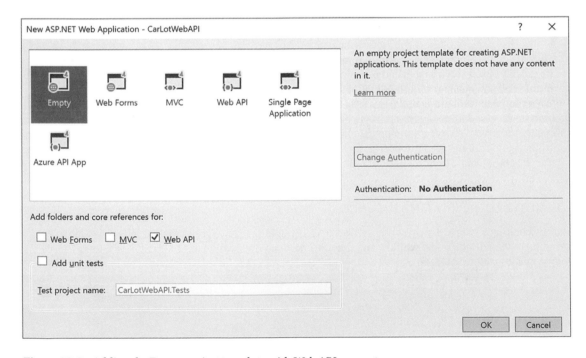

Figure 30-2. *Adding the Empty project template with Web API support*

Click OK, and the project is added to the solution.

Managing the NuGet Packages

As with the Web Forms and MVC projects, many of the included NuGet packages are out-of-date when you create a new project. Right-click the project in Solution Explorer, select Manage NuGet Packages, and change the filter to Upgrade Available. Upgrade all the packages that can be upgraded.

Change the filter back to Browse and install the AutoMapper and EntityFramework (6.1.3) packages.

Adding AutoLotDAL and AutoLotDAL.Models

Copy the AutoLotDAL and AutoLotDAL.Models projects from Chapter 29 into the CarLotWebAPI folder (at the same level as the CarLotWebAPI solution file). Add the projects into your solution by right-clicking the solution, selecting Add ➤ Existing Project, and navigating to the correct folders. Add a reference from CarLotWebAPI to both AutoLotDAL and AutoLotDAL.Models. Also confirm that the reference from AutoLotDAL to AutoLotDAL.Models is still there. If you add the AutoLotDAL.Models project first, it should retain the reference.

Finally, add the connection string to the Web.config file (your connection string may differ based on your installation path).

```
<connectionStrings>
  <add name="AutoLotConnection" connectionString="data source=(localdb)\mssqllocaldb;initial
    catalog=AutoLot;integrated security=True;MultipleActiveResultSets=True;App=EntityFramework"
    providerName="System.Data.SqlClient" />
</connectionStrings>
```

Creating the InventoryController Class

While there is support in Visual Studio for scaffolding in Web API projects (just like MVC projects), you are going to build up the class manually. Add a class named InventoryController.cs to the Controllers folder. Add the following using statements to the top of the file:

```
using System;
using System.Collections.Generic;
using System.Net;
using System.Threading.Tasks;
using System.Web.Http;
using System.Web.Http.Description;
using AutoLotDAL.Models;
using AutoLotDAL.Repos;
using AutoMapper;
```

Make the class public and inherit from ApiController.

```
public class InventoryController : ApiController
{
}
```

Routing

The WebApiConfig.cs file configures the project. It is called from the Global.asax.cs file. Open the WebApiConfig.cs file in the App_Start folder. The code starts with a line that enables attribute routing (covered next). The next bit of code adds the default route to the route table, just like ASP.NET MVC. The difference is that the default route starts with the api/ string literal.

```
public static class WebApiConfig
{
  public static void Register(HttpConfiguration config)
  {
    // Web API configuration and services
    // Web API routes
    config.MapHttpAttributeRoutes();
    config.Routes.MapHttpRoute(
        name: "DefaultApi",
        routeTemplate: "api/{controller}/{id}",
        defaults: new { id = RouteParameter.Optional }
    );
  }
}
```

Go ahead and delete (or comment out) the code that configures the default route since you will be using attribute routing for this project.

Attribute Routing

In attribute routing, routes are defined using C# attributes on controllers and their action methods. This can lead to more precise routing but can also increase the amount of configuration since all controllers and actions need to have routing information specified.

To demonstrate this, add the following route definition to the top of the controller:

```
[Route("api/Inventory/{id?}")]
public class InventoryController : ApiController
```

This is the same route definition that was created as the default route, with one major difference—the lack of the {controller} variable. When using attribute routing, the controller is inferred. With Web API 2.2, attribute routing is usually reserved for use on action methods, but there isn't anything wrong with using it on the controller. In fact, you could change the previous code to the following to change the URL to /Cars from /Inventory:

```
[Route("api/Cars/{id?}")]
public class InventoryController : ApiController
```

Now, add two action methods, as follows:

```
public IEnumerable<string> Get()
{
  return new string[] { "value1", "value2" };
}
```

```
// GET api/values/5
public string Get(int id)
{
  return id.ToString();
}
```

You might have noticed that neither the default route nor the attribute route defines an action. This is because the routing engine uses the HTTP verbs (GET, PUT, POST, DELETE) in place of specifying an action name. In Web API 2.2, the name of the action method directly translates to the methods. In this example, since both method names start with *Get*, they will be requested using an HTTPGet.

While this is a nice feature, it is deprecated in ASP.NET Core, so it's better to get used to specifying the proper verb. Update the methods and controller attribute to the following:

```
[RoutePrefix("api/Inventory")]
public class InventoryController : ApiController
{
  [HttpGet, Route("")]
  public IEnumerable<string> Get()
  {
    return new string[] {"value1", "value2"};
  }
  // GET api/values/5
  [HttpGet, Route("{id}")]
  public string Get(int id)
  {
    return id.ToString();
  }
}
```

There are a couple of items to discuss. First, the controller attribute was changed to RoutePrefix from Route. If you left it as Route, any Route attributes on the action methods override the controller attribute. The Get attribute defines the route as responding to an HTTP Get request, so you can then name the action method anything you want. The empty Route attribute on the Get() action method is required to complete the route since the RoutePrefix attribute denotes only the start of a route, not a complete route.

Changing the Start Page

Web API applications are headless services, meaning there isn't a user interface. So, the default project settings of starting the currently selected page in Solution Explorer doesn't make a lot of sense.

You can configure the application to do nothing on startup (the "Don't open a page. Wait for a request from an external application." option), or you can configure it to start a specific route. In this case, select the Specific Page option and enter api/Inventory, as shown in Figure 30-3. After doing this, it will run the default HTTP GET request for the Inventory controller.

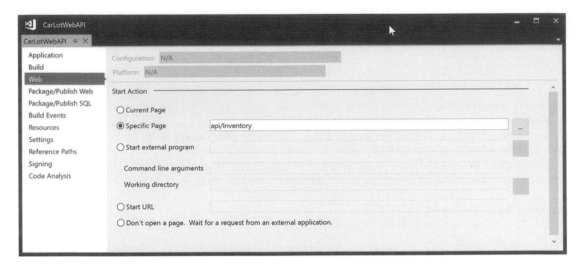

Figure 30-3. *Configuring the project startup for CarLotWebAPI*

Now, when you run the project, you should see the values from the Get() method displayed in your browser. Depending on your browser of choice, it will either just be the string or a more formal representation of the data.

JavaScript Object Notation

JavaScript Object Notation (JSON) is one way to transport data between services and has largely taken the place of XML as a data transport mechanism. It is a simple key-value text representation of objects and classes. For example, consider the following JSON representation of an Inventory item:

```
{"CarId":1,"Make":"VW","Color":"Black","PetName":"Zippy","Timestamp":"AAAAAAAAB9o=",
"Orders":[]}
```

Each JSON object starts and ends with braces, and property name and string values are quoted. JSON objects can also be nested. If the Make property wasn't a string but an object (with the properties Builder and Year), the JSON could resemble something like this:

```
{"CarId":1,"Make":{"Builder":"VW","Year":2015},"Color":"Black","PetName":"Zippy","Timestamp":
"AAAAAAAAB9o=","Orders":[]}
```

As you can see from the Orders property, lists are indicated by brackets ([ ]). If the service was sending a list of Inventory objects, the JSON might resemble this:

```
[{"CarId":1,"Make":"VW","Color":"Black","PetName":"Zippy","Timestamp":"AAAAAAAAB9o=","Orders":
[]},{"CarId":2,"Make":"Ford","Color":"Rust","PetName":"Rusty","Timestamp":"AAAAAAAAB9s=",
"Orders":[]}]
```

■ **Note** The Web API project template includes a free open source utility called Newtonsoft's Json.NET. It is a robust utility for creating JSON from objects, as well as creating objects from JSON. You will use Json.NET later in this chapter, and you can find more information (including documentation and examples) at www.newtonsoft.com/json.

Web API Action Results

Web API action methods can return one of four items.

- Void: Returns an HTTP 204 (no content)

- HttpResponseMessage: Converts directly into a standard HTTP response

- IHttpActionResult: Creates an HTTP response for return

- Some other type: Writes a serialized return value along with an HTTP OK (200)

The void option is self-explanatory, so I won't spend any time on it. The HttpResponseMessage response requires you to build up a message for return, as in the following example:

```
public HttpResponseMessage Get()
{
  HttpResponseMessage response = Request.CreateResponse(HttpStatusCode.OK, "value");
  response.Content = new StringContent("hello", Encoding.Unicode);
  response.Headers.CacheControl = new CacheControlHeaderValue()
  {
      MaxAge = TimeSpan.FromMinutes(20)
  };
  return response;
}
```

IHttpActionResult was introduced with Web API 2 and is essentially an HttpResponseMessage factory. Most commonly, the return is one of the implementations defined in the System.Web.Http.Results namespace, fully documented here: https://msdn.microsoft.com/en-us/library/system.web.http. results.aspx. The ApiController base class has many helper methods for your convenience, as you will see later in the chapter. For your reference, some of the more common ones are listed in Table 30-1.

Table 30-1. Typical IHttpActionResult-Derived Classes

Action Result	Meaning in Life
OkResult	Returns an HTTP 200 (OK)
RedirectResult RedirectToRouteResult	Redirects to another action or route
JsonResult	Returns a serialized JSON result to the client
BadRequestResult	Returns an empty bad request result
NotFoundResult	Indicates the requested item wasn't found
FormattedContentResult	Returns a formatted user-defined content type to the client
StatusCodeResult	Returns a specific HTTP status code

For all other response types, Web API uses a media formatter to serialize the return value, writes the value into the message body, and returns an HTTP OK (200). This is the format that will be used for returning Inventory records to the client.

Serialization Issues with EntityFramework

When you add a reference to another project (or assembly), you are free to pass instances of .NET classes around. The Web works differently, in that everything is serialized into another format, like JSON.

Chapter 20 covered serialization techniques, but the good news is that the Web API framework does most of the heavy lifting for you. However, there is a problem when using EF models: the navigation properties. Serialization walks the entire object model, attempting to serialize everything in its path. That means all the dependency objects as well. Your data could become very large, bringing back much more than anticipated. Or, it can fail if lazy loading is enabled.

When sending data as JSON (or XML) from a RESTful service, it's important to just send the data that you need. In this case, that is only the Inventory class itself and not the related objects. Fortunately, there is a great open source utility that you can use to fix this issue for you.

AutoMapper

AutoMapper (which you installed earlier in this section) is a free, open source utility for creating a new instance of a type from an instance of another type. It uses reflection to determine matching properties but can also be configured for special cases.

In the sample application, when you pull back an Inventory record, you want to strip any of the related objects. AutoMapper can create a new instance of the same type, which you will do here. Add a constructor into InventoryController.cs, and in that constructor, add the following code:

```
public InventoryController()
{
    Mapper.Initialize(
        cfg =>
        {
            cfg.CreateMap<Inventory, Inventory>()
            .ForMember(x => x.Orders, opt => opt.Ignore());
        });
}
```

This code creates a mapping between the Inventory type and itself (or collections of Inventory types), ignoring the Orders property. To convert an Inventory instance into a new one (or a List<Inventory> instances), you would use the following code (where inventory and inventories are the original items):

```
var newInv = Mapper.Map<Inventory, Inventory>(inventory)
var newList = Mapper.Map<List<Inventory>, List<Inventory>>(inventories)
```

■ **Note**   There isn't enough space in this chapter to go any deeper with AutoMapper, but it is an active and widely used utility for .NET developers. You should consider adding it to your standard toolbox. You can find more information, including documentation and examples, at the project home page at http://automapper.org.

Getting Inventory Data

Now that the foundation is in place, it's time to update the InventoryController to do real work. Start by adding a class-level variable for the inventory repository.

```
private readonly InventoryRepo _repo = new InventoryRepo();
```

Delete (or comment out) the two sample methods you created, and replace them with the following code:

```
// GET: api/Inventory
[HttpGet, Route("")]
public IEnumerable<Inventory> GetInventory()
{
  var inventories = _repo.GetAll();
  return Mapper.Map<List<Inventory>, List<Inventory>>(inventories);
}

// GET: api/Inventory/5
[HttpGet, Route("{id}", Name = "DisplayRoute")]
[ResponseType(typeof(Inventory))]
public async Task<IHttpActionResult> GetInventory(int id)
{
  Inventory inventory = _repo.GetOne(id);
  if (inventory == null)
  {
    return NotFound();
  }
  return Ok(Mapper.Map<Inventory, Inventory>(inventory));
}
```

The first method gets all of the Inventory records from the database and returns a list. This list will be returned as either XML or JSON, depending on the client. Chrome and Firefox return the data as XML, while Edge and Fiddler return the data as JSON. I'll cover Fiddler next. The route name will be used later in the controller.

The second method looks for a specific inventory record and, if not found, returns an HTTP 404 (Not Found). If it is found, it returns an HTTP 200 (OK) with the record as the content.

Adding the Dispose() Method

Dispose of the repo in the controller Dispose() method, as shown here:

```
protected override void Dispose(bool disposing)
{
    if (disposing)
    {
        _repo.Dispose();
    }
    base.Dispose(disposing);
}
```

Using Fiddler

Fiddler is a free tool from Progress software for creating and monitoring web requests. It's helpful when testing Web API applications, supporting all of the verbs that need testing (GET, POST, PUT, and DELETE). It can be downloaded from www.telerik.com/fiddler.

Once Fiddler is installed, open it up to the main window. In the main window, click the Compose button. You will see a place to enter the URI of the request and the type. Select Get and add the URI of your application (http://localhost:60710/api/Inventory in my case). This is shown in Figure 30-4.

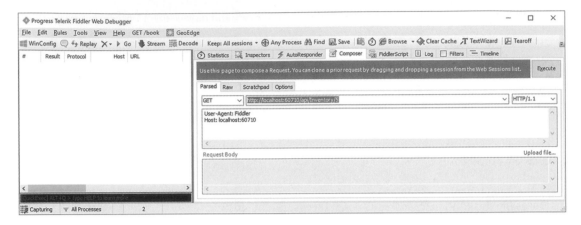

Figure 30-4. *Testing the Get All Inventory action with Fiddler*

Wirth the application running, click the Execute button and then locate the request in the left window. Double-click it, and you will see the results of the call in the right window. You can pick between XML or JSON, examine the headers, and look at all aspects of the request and response. This is shown in Figure 30-5.

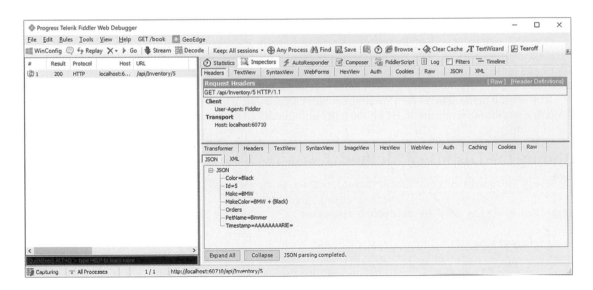

Figure 30-5. *Examining the response from the Web API application*

You will use Fiddler through the rest of the chapter.

Updating an Inventory Record (HttpPut)

Updating a record in HTTP is achieved with an HttpPut call. For this example, I am passing in the ID of the record to be updated and an Inventory instance by way of JSON. Web API uses model binding (just like Web Forms) to create an instance of the Inventory class with the values sent from the client in the body of the message.

Create a PutInventory() method that accepts an id and an Inventory object. The code is shown here and will be discussed after the listing:

```
[HttpPut, Route("{id}")]
[ResponseType(typeof(void))]
public IHttpActionResult PutInventory(int id, Inventory inventory)
{
  if (!ModelState.IsValid)
  {
    return BadRequest(ModelState);
  }
  if (id != inventory.Id)
  {
    return BadRequest();
  }
  try
  {
    _repo.Save(inventory);
  }
  catch (Exception ex)
  {
    //Production app should do more here
    throw;
  }
  return StatusCode(HttpStatusCode.NoContent);
}
```

In the body of the action method, the first check is to make sure ModelState is valid. If not, then it returns an HttpBadRequest (400). If it is valid, the method then checks that the value of the id parameter passed in through the URL matches the Id of the Inventory record (from the message body). This helps cut down (but doesn't eliminate) URL hacking by an unscrupulous user. The code then attempts to save the record and, if successful, returns an HTTP 204 (No content). If there is an exception, this example merely returns it to the client. In a production app, you would want to handle any and all exceptions accordingly.

Setting the Data Initializer

Before testing changes to the database, it's wise to use the data initializer to re-create the database every time the application is run. While this will add to the startup time of the app, it ensures a consistent experience while developing the application.

Open Global.asax.cs, and add the following using statements to the top of the file:

```
using System.Data.Entity;
using AutoLotDAL.EF;
```

Now, in the Application_Start() method, add the following line:

```
Database.SetInitializer(new MyDataInitializer());
```

Testing Put Methods

Open Fiddler, and in the Compose screen, add in the URI (for example, `http://localhost:60710/api/Inventory/5`), select Put as the method, and add the following to the top box:

```
Content-Type: application/json
```

In the bottom box, add the JSON for the record to be updated. Keep in mind that, with concurrency checking enabled, you need valid ID and timestamp values for a successful test.

■ **Note**   The easiest way to get the JSON is to execute a Get test with Fiddler, double-click the response, and then select TextView in the results pane. Copy the results into the request body for the Put request.

Figure 30-6 shows a sample request.

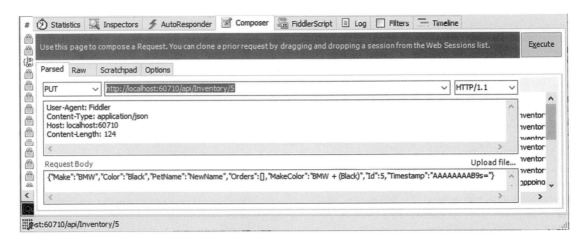

Figure 30-6.   *Creating a Put request with Fiddler*

After executing the request, you can execute a Get request with Fiddler to confirm the changes were accepted.

Adding Inventory Records (HttpPost)

Adding records in HTTP is achieved by using `HttpPost` calls and passing the object being added in the message body. The `PostInventory()` method also uses model binding to create an instance of the `Inventory` class from the message body. Add the following code, with the discussion after the listing:

```
// POST: api/Inventory
[HttpPost, Route("")]
[ResponseType(typeof(Inventory))]
public IHttpActionResult PostInventory(Inventory inventory)
{
```

```
if (!ModelState.IsValid)
{
  return BadRequest(ModelState);
}
try
{
  _repo.Add(inventory);
}
catch (Exception ex)
{
  //Production app should do more here
  throw;
}
return CreatedAtRoute("DisplayRoute", new { id = inventory.Id }, inventory);
}
```

The PostInventory() action is set to a ResponseType of type Inventory since it returns the added Inventory record, complete with the server-generated values. This action method also uses model binding to get the values from the message body, checks ModelState, and returns an HttpBadRequest (400) if there are issues in the model binding. If model binding is successful, the method then attempts to add the new record. If the add is successful, then the action returns an HttpCreated (201) with the new Inventory record in the body of the message. The CreatedAtRoute method adds the URI of this new item into the header so the client can use it if necessary.

Test this method the same way as you tested HttpPut. Make sure to change the type to Post, and leave the Id and Timestamp properties out of the JSON message body. When you execute the Post, examine the headers and the body of the response message.

You should see the following headers in the response (or at least something similar):

```
HTTP/1.1 201 Created
Cache-Control: no-cache
Pragma: no-cache
Content-Type: application/json; charset=utf-8
Expires: -1
Location: http://localhost:60710/api/Inventory/10
```

The text view shows you the full JSON of the created record, including the Id and Timestamp properties.

Deleting Inventory Records (HttpDelete)

The final action method to add is the DeleteInventory() method. Add two parameters, an integer id and an Inventory object, the latter which will get populated from the message body. Here is the code:

```
// DELETE: api/Inventory/5
[HttpDelete, Route("{id}")]
[ResponseType(typeof(void))]
public IHttpActionResult DeleteInventory(int id, Inventory inventory)
{
  if (id != inventory.Id)
  {
    return BadRequest();
  }
```

```
try
{
  _repo.Delete(inventory);
}
catch (Exception ex)
{
  //Production app should do more here
  throw;
}
return Ok();
}
```

As you can see, the pattern is the same as the previous methods.

Wrapping Up ASP.NET API

ASP.NET Web API leverages much of the ASP.NET MVC framework, and it allows you to leverage your knowledge of building web applications and RESTful services using ASP.NET.

There is much more you can do with Web API, but space in this book is limited. This chapter sent you well on your way, and you can learn more at https://docs.microsoft.com/en-us/aspnet/web-api/.

ASP.NET Web API can be used in a variety of ways—as a stand-alone service, as a back end for JavaScript front ends (like Angular or React), or as the back end for MVC applications. You will see that in action next.

■ **Source Code**   You can find the CarLotWebAPI solution in the CarLotWebAPIStandAlone directory of the Chapter 30 subfolder.

Updating CarLotMVC to Use CarLotWebAPI

The CarLotMVC ASP.NET MVC site from Chapter 29 uses the AutoLotDAL library for all of its CRUD operations. In this section, you will replace that with the CarLotWebAPI project you just built.

Adding the CarLotMVC Application

You can continue using the same solution from the beginning of the chapter. For your convenience, there are two solutions in the downloads; one is just the CarLotWebAPI project, and the second combines the CarLotMVC application.

Copy the CarLotMVC folder (from Chapter 29) into the CarLotWebAPI folder and add it into the solution. Set both the CarLotWebAPI and CarLotMVC projects as startup, in that order. You can access that menu by right-clicking the solution, choosing Select Startup Projects, and adjusting the dialog to match Figure 30-7.

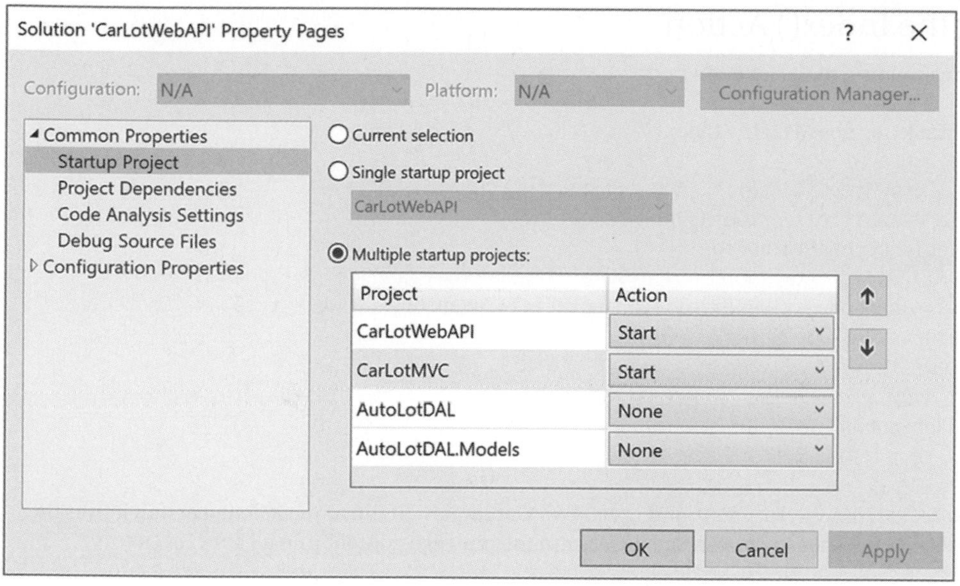

Figure 30-7. *Setting multiple startup projects*

Remove the references to the AutoLotDAL project from the CarLotMVC project. You will only need access to the models. Finally, open Global.asax.cs in the MVC project, and delete the line that sets the DatabaseInitializer, as well as the using AutoLotDAL.EF line.

Updating the MVC InventoryController

The InventoryController in the MVC project is using the InventoryRepo, and you will remove all references to that. Go ahead and remove the AutoLotDAL.Repos using statement and add the following:

```
using System.Collections.Generic;
using System.Net.Http;
using System.Threading.Tasks;
using AutoLotDAL.Models;
using Newtonsoft.Json;
using System.Text;
```

Also add a class-level variable to hold the base URL for the Web API site (make sure to update the port for your project).

```
private string _baseUrl = "http://localhost:60710/api/Inventory";
```

Each of the methods will be updated to call into the Web API service using the HttpClient class. The Web API methods return an IHTTPActionResult, which has two properties that you care about for this process: IsSuccessStatusCode and Content.

The IsSuccessStatusCode returns true if the call worked. This prevents you from having to check every possible code that could get returned since there are many that are considered successful depending on the type of call. The Content property provides access to the message body. Each of the methods must be updated to async and return Task<ActionResult>.

Updating the Index() Action

Update the Index method to the following:

```
public async Task<ActionResult> Index()
{
  var client = new HttpClient();
  var response = await client.GetAsync(_baseUrl);
  if (response.IsSuccessStatusCode)
  {
    var items = JsonConvert.DeserializeObject<List<Inventory>>(await response.Content.
    ReadAsStringAsync());
    return View(items);
  }
  return HttpNotFound();
}
```

This code creates a new HttpClient and executes a Get request. If the request is successful, it uses the Newtonsoft Json.NET package to convert the JSON from the message content into a List<Inventory>.

■ **Note**   None of these examples has the level of error handling needed for a production application. That decision was made to make sure the examples are clear and concise. You would want to take what you learned earlier in Chapter 7 to handle any and all exceptions gracefully.

Updating the Details() Action

The next step is to update the Details() action method. Update the code to the following:

```
// GET: Inventory/Details/5
public async Task<ActionResult> Details(int? id)
{
  if (id == null)
  {
    return new HttpStatusCodeResult(HttpStatusCode.BadRequest);
  }
  var client = new HttpClient();
  var response = await client.GetAsync($"{_baseUrl}/{id.Value}");
  if (response.IsSuccessStatusCode)
  {
    var inventory = JsonConvert.DeserializeObject<Inventory>(
      await response.Content.ReadAsStringAsync());
    return View(inventory);
  }
  return HttpNotFound();
}
```

The main change here (just like in the Index action) is to get the record using a new HttpClient instance. Again, check to make sure the call was successful, and if so, use Json.NET to deserialize the content of the message to an Inventory object. Finally, return the view.

Updating the Create() Action

The first Create() action method doesn't need to be updated since it loads a view without any database interaction. The HttpPost version does need to be updated. The entire action method is listed here, and the changes will be discussed after the listing:

```
[HttpPost]
[ValidateAntiForgeryToken]
public async Task<ActionResult> Create([Bind(Include = "Make,Color,PetName")] Inventory inventory)
{
  if (!ModelState.IsValid) return View(inventory);
  try
  {
    var client = new HttpClient();
    string json = JsonConvert.SerializeObject(inventory);
    var response = await client.PostAsync(_baseUrl,
            new StringContent(json, Encoding.UTF8, "application/json"));
    if (response.IsSuccessStatusCode)
    {
      return RedirectToAction("Index");
    }
  }
  catch (Exception ex)
  {
    ModelState.AddModelError(string.Empty, $"Unable to create record: {ex.Message}");
  }
  return View(inventory);
}
```

The PostAsync()method requires the body to be formatted a certain way. This is accomplished by first converting the Inventory object into JSON and then creating a new StringContent object. This is then passed into the PostAsync() method, along with the URI, to execute the call. If all succeeds, the user is redirected to the Index view.

Updating the Edit() Actions

Both of the Edit() action methods need to be updated. The HttpGet version gets changed in the same way that the Details() action was and is listed here:

```
public async Task<ActionResult> Edit(int? id)
{
  if (id == null)
  {
    return new HttpStatusCodeResult(HttpStatusCode.BadRequest);
  }
  var client = new HttpClient();
  var response = await client.GetAsync($"{_baseUrl}/{id.Value}");
  if (response.IsSuccessStatusCode)
```

```
  {
    var inventory = JsonConvert.DeserializeObject<Inventory>(
      await response.Content.ReadAsStringAsync());
    return View(inventory);
  }
  return new HttpNotFoundResult();
}
```

The HttpPost version is updated in much the same way as the Create() action method, except that it uses a PutAsync() call instead of a PostAsync() call.

```
[HttpPost]
[ValidateAntiForgeryToken]
public async Task<ActionResult> Edit([Bind(Include = "Id,Make,Color,PetName,Timestamp")]
Inventory inventory)
{
  if (!ModelState.IsValid) return View(inventory);
  var client = new HttpClient();
  string json = JsonConvert.SerializeObject(inventory);
  var response = await client.PutAsync($"{_baseUrl}/{inventory.Id}",
    new StringContent(json, Encoding.UTF8, "application/json"));
  if (response.IsSuccessStatusCode)
  {
    return RedirectToAction("Index");
  }
  return View(inventory);
}
```

■ **Note**   You might be wondering why the action method in the MVC controller is marked with the HttpPost attribute but the call to the web service is an HttpPut. The important takeaway is that the HTTP verb used to call MVC actions does not have to match the HTTP verb used to call Web API action methods. They are separate operations.

Updating the Delete() Actions

There are two Delete() action methods, and like the Edit() HttpGet version, the only change is to call the web service to get the data.

```
// GET: Inventory/Delete/5
public async Task<ActionResult> Delete(int? id)
{
  if (id == null)
  {
    return new HttpStatusCodeResult(HttpStatusCode.BadRequest);
  }
  var client = new HttpClient();
```

```
  var response = await client.GetAsync($"{_baseUrl}/{id.Value}");
  if (response.IsSuccessStatusCode)
  {
    var inventory = JsonConvert.DeserializeObject<Inventory>(await response.Content.
    ReadAsStringAsync());
    return View(inventory);
  }
  return new HttpNotFoundResult();
}
```

The HttpPost Delete() action method requires more work. As you might suspect, there is indeed a DeleteAsync() extension method on the HttpClient, but it doesn't accept any parameters for content in the message body. Using this method will cause the delete to fail since the timestamp value must be passed in as part of the concurrency check. Instead, you have to create the HttpRequestMessage by hand. Here is the code, and the discussion will follow:

```
[HttpPost]
[ValidateAntiForgeryToken]
public async Task<ActionResult> Delete([Bind(Include = "Id,Timestamp")] Inventory inventory)
{
  try
  {
    var client = new HttpClient();
    HttpRequestMessage request =
        new HttpRequestMessage(HttpMethod.Delete,$"{_baseUrl}/{inventory.Id}")
    {
      Content =
          new StringContent(JsonConvert.SerializeObject(inventory), Encoding.UTF8,
          "application/json")
    };
    var response = await client.SendAsync(request);
    return RedirectToAction("Index");
  }
  catch (Exception ex)
  {
    ModelState.AddModelError(string.Empty, $"Unable to create record: {ex.Message}");
  }
  return View(inventory);
}
```

The constructor for the HttpRequestMessage takes the HttpMethod as the first parameter and the URL as the second. Json.NET serializes the inventory object so that it can be added to a StringContent instance, which is part of the object initialization for the message. If all is successful, redirect the user back to the Index view.

■ **Source Code**   You can find the combined CarLotWebAPI and CarLotMVC solution in the CarLotWebAPI folder in the Chapter 30 directory.

Summary

This chapter examined many aspects of Web API. You created a new Web API project, added a controller, explored attribute routing, and looked at testing APIs with Fiddler. You also used AutoMapper to avoid some of the issues with serialization of Entity Framework models.

After finishing the `InventoryController` actions in the CarLotWebAPI project, you updated CarLotMVC to call into the CarLotWebAPI service's URLs, using Json.NET to serialize and deserialize records. You also learned how to make calls using the additional HTTP verbs used by the Web API.

This concludes your look at the 4.7 .NET Framework. In the next part, you will begin your exploration of .NET Core, Entity Framework Core, and ASP.NET Core.

PART IX

.NET CORE

CHAPTER 31

■ ■ ■

The Philosophy of .NET Core

On June 27, 2016, Microsoft announced the release of .NET Core version 1.0, a revolutionary new platform for .NET developers everywhere. This new platform was released simultaneously for Windows, macOS, and Linux, and it is based on C# and the .NET Framework that you have spent the last 30 chapters learning about. The initial release included the .NET Core runtime, ASP.NET Core, and Entity Framework Core. Since then there have been two additional releases: 1.1 and 2.0 (the current release).

In addition to the cross-platform deployment capabilities, another significant change was introduced. The .NET Core platform and related frameworks are completely open source. They are not just source in the open, where you can view and play with the code, but are full-fledged open source projects. Pull requests are accepted and, in fact, expected. There have been significant contributions from the development community, with more than 10,000 developers contributing to the initial release of .NET Core. What was a relatively small team of Microsoft developers building .NET and the related frameworks, now the broader development community can provide additional functionality, performance improvements, and bug fixes. This open source initiative covers not only the software but the documentation as well. In fact, the documentation links provided in the earlier chapters of this book all point to the new open source documentation platform at http://docs.microsoft.com.

This chapter introduces you to the philosophy of .NET Core. The remaining three chapters then cover Entity Framework Core (Chapter 32) and ASP.NET Core (Chapters 33 to 34).

From Project K to .NET Core

As stated by Rich Lander on the .NET Blog (https://blogs.msdn.microsoft.com/dotnet/2016/06/27/announcing-net-core-1-0/), Microsoft was receiving a significant number of requests for ASP.NET to run on non-Windows platforms. Out of these requests and parallel discussions with the Windows team regarding Windows Nano, Project K was born to target additional platforms.

The initial efforts were focused on ASP.NET. To run on other operating systems, the dependency on System.Web had to be removed. This ended up being nontrivial and became essentially a rewrite of the framework. Decisions had to be made as to what would be included, and in examining the different ASP.NET platforms (Web Forms, ASP.NET MVC, and ASP.NET Web API), it was determined that the best approach was to create one platform that could be used for web applications and RESTful services. MVC and Web API were finally completely merged into one framework (instead of the closely related siblings that they are in the full .NET Framework). The new web development platform was initially named ASP.NET 5.

The new web platform would need a data access layer, and the Entity Framework was the obvious choice. This would also be essentially a rewrite of EF 6, and the initial name chosen was Entity Framework 7.

In my honest opinion, those were the worst possible names that could have been selected. I can't tell you how much time I've spent explaining to customers and conference attendees that ASP.NET 5 isn't the next version of the full .NET Framework, even though 5 is greater than 4.6 (the version of the full .NET Framework at the time), and EF 7 isn't the next version of EF, even though 7 is greater than 6.

The good news is that it all got sorted out, and the cross-platform versions of the .NET platform were rebranded as "Core," as in .NET Core, ASP.NET Core, and Entity Framework Core. This distinction cleared up a lot (but, unfortunately, not all) of the confusion around the different frameworks and where they fit into the developer ecosystem.

The Future of the Full .NET Framework

What of the full .NET Framework and the related frameworks? Are they on life support? Do I have to rewrite all of my applications before support ends? Absolutely not, on both counts! If there is any doubt about the continued development of C# and .NET, this book should squash that. If .NET wasn't being updated, this book wouldn't have an eighth edition covering C# 7.1 and .NET 4.7.

Additional questions continue to come up about the future of different frameworks, such as WinForms, Web Forms, WPF, WFC, etc. Admittedly, there hasn't been much earth-shattering news related to many of the .NET frameworks, but that doesn't mean they have been abandoned. One could argue that those technologies are "done." WinForms and Web Forms are still widely used today, and the absence of them in the main chapters of this book doesn't mean I don't believe they are viable; there just isn't anything to report beyond the prior editions.

■ **Note**   The question still remains what the next major version of the full .NET Framework will be. The logical next version number is 5, but unfortunately, that card has been played. I'm sure it will all be revealed in time, and this book will be right there for you to cover it all.

The Goals of.NET Core

Running on additional operating systems other than Windows was a lofty enough goal, but that wasn't the only goal for the new platform. As a production framework, .NET has been around since 2002, and a lot has changed since then. Developers have gotten smarter, computers have gotten faster, the demands of users have increased, and mobile has become a dominant force (just to name a few).

The following are some of the goals of .NET Core:

- *Cross-platform support*: .NET Core can run on Windows, Linux, and macOS. .NET Core applications can be built across platforms using Visual Studio Code or Visual Studio for the Mac. Additionally, the inclusion of Xamarin adds iOS and Android to the supported deployment platforms.

- *Performance*: The performance of .NET Core is consistently near the top of all relevant performance charts, and each release brings additional improvements.

- *Portable class libraries usable across all .NET runtimes*: .NET Core introduced .NET Standard, a formal specification to establish uniformity for .NET runtime behavior.

- *Portable or stand-alone deployment*: .NET Core applications can be deployed alongside the framework or use the machine-wide installation of .NET Core.

- *Full command-line support*: .NET Core focuses on full command line support as a primary objective.

- *Open source:* As mentioned, .NET Core and its documentation are completely open source, complete with pull requests from the worldwide developer community.

- *Interoperability with the full .NET Framework:* The 2.0 release of .NET Core allows referencing .NET Framework libraries.

I'm sure Microsoft looked at the existing codebase in the full .NET Framework and, in considering the stated goals, realized that changing the full .NET Framework *and* keeping all the production apps still running just wasn't possible. This pretty much called for a complete rewrite of .NET, not just ASP.NET.

Now, let's take a look at each of these goals in greater detail.

Cross-Platform Support

As mentioned earlier, .NET Core applications are not limited to running on Windows-based operating systems. This opens a wide array of options for deploying (and developing) applications using .NET and C#. The initial release of .NET Core supported Windows (of course), macOS, and several distros of Linux, plus iOS and Android through Xamarin. Each subsequent release has included new distros and expanded version support on Linux. To see the latest supported OS list, refer to `https://github.com/dotnet/core/blob/master/roadmap.md#technology-roadmaps`.

You might be wondering how a cross-platform version of .NET will help you. After all, you are probably already dedicated to Windows and developing on a Windows machine (or on a Mac using virtualization technology).

Develop .NET Core Apps Anywhere

With .NET Core, you can build web and mobile applications anywhere. Visual Studio still runs on Windows (of course), but now there is Visual Studio for the Mac, so you can develop .NET Core applications straightaway on your Mac. And with the file-based project system (covered shortly), you can use cross-platform tools like Visual Studio Code for .NET Core development.

Additional Deployment Options

While experienced .NET developers already have their applications running on Windows, .NET Core brings additional deployment options to the table. Linux servers are typically cheaper to maintain than Windows servers, especially in the cloud, so being able to deploy your web applications and services to Linux can be a significant cost savings. This is especially advantageous for startups as well as companies that want to reduce the number of Windows servers.

Containerization

In addition to support for Linux distributions, .NET Core supports containerization of .NET Core applications. Popular container vendors, like Docker, significantly decrease the complexity of releasing applications to different environments (e.g., from development to test). The application and the necessary runtime files (including the OS) are all bundled together in one (pardon the circular reference) container. This container then gets copied from one environment to another, without worrying about installations. With Windows and Azure adding support for Docker, this story has gotten even better.

You can now develop in a Docker container, and when you are ready to move your application to integration/test, you just move the container from one environment to the other. No installs or complicated deploys! And when you are ready for production, you can just move the container to your production server. Gone are the days of production release problems while the developers proudly state, "It works on my machine!"

Performance

ASP.NET Core applications consistently score top marks in benchmark tests. This is because of performance being considered a first-class citizen when it comes to design goals. The full .NET Framework has grown extremely massive over the past 15 years, and squeezing performance out of hard-to-change code is difficult at best.

Since .NET Core is largely a rewrite of the platform and frameworks, the builders of .NET Core are able to think about optimization before and during, development, not just afterwards on platform. The most important part of that sentence is the *before*. Performance is now an integral part of architectural and development decisions.

Portable Class Libraries with .NET Standard

The .NET Standard library is a formal specification for .NET APIs that is available on all .NET runtimes. This is intended to establish greater uniformity in the .NET ecosystem. The following key scenarios are enabled via .NET Standard:

- Defines a uniform set of base class library APIs for all .NET implementations, independent of workload

- Enables developers to produce portable libraries usable across .NET implementations

- Reduces (or eliminates) conditional compilation of shared resources

Any assembly targeting a specific .NET Standard version will be accessible by any other assembly targeting that same .NET Standard version. The various .NET implementations target specific versions of .NET Standard. For more information about the .NET Standard Library and the full chart of compatibility across platforms, frameworks, and versions, see the chart at `https://docs.microsoft.com/en-us/dotnet/standard/net-standard`.

Portable or Stand-Alone Deployment Models

.NET Core supports true side-by-side installations of the platform, unlike the full .NET Framework. Installation of additional versions of the .NET Core framework does not affect existing installations or applications. This expands the deployment models for .NET Core applications.

Portable applications are configured to target a version of .NET Core installed on the target machine and include only application-specific packages in the deployment. This keeps the installation size small but requires the target framework version to be installed on the machine.

Stand-alone deployments contain all the application files as well as the required CoreFX and CoreCLR files for the target platform. This obviously makes the installation size larger but isolates the applications from any machine-wide issues (such as someone removing the required version .NET Core).

Full Command-Line Support

Realizing that not everyone will be using Visual Studio to develop .NET Core applications, the team decided to focus on command-line support first before Visual Studio tooling. For every release before .NET Core 2.0, the tooling has lagged behind what you could accomplish with a text editor and the .NET Core CLI.

The tooling has made great strides since the release of .NET Core 1.0 (when the tooling wasn't even RTM yet), but it still lags behind the Visual Studio tooling available for .NET Framework applications.

Open Source

As mentioned, Microsoft has released .NET Core and the related frameworks as true open source. The initial release had more than 10,000 members providing input and/or code, and that number continues to grow.

Interoperability with the .NET Framework

With the release of Visual Studio 15.3 and .NET Core 2.0, you can now reference .NET Framework libraries from .NET Standard libraries. This latest addition provides a better mechanism for moving existing code from existing applications to .NET Core.

There are some limitations, of course. The assemblies you are referencing can only use types that are supported in .NET Standard. While using an assembly that uses APIs that are not in .NET Standard might work, it's not a supported scenario, and you will need to conduct extensive testing.

The Composition of .NET Core

In general terms, .NET Core is comprised of four main parts.

- The .NET Core runtime

- A set of framework libraries

- SDK tools and the dotnet app host

- Language compilers

The .NET Core Runtime (CoreCLR)

This is the base library for .NET Core. It includes the garbage collector, JIT compiler, base .NET types, and many of the low-level classes. The runtime provides the bridge between the .NET Core framework libraries (CoreFX) and the underlying operating systems. Only types that have a strong dependency on the internal workings of the runtime are included. Most of the class library is implemented as independent NuGet packages.

CoreCLR tries to minimize the amount of implemented code, leaving specific implementations for many of the framework classes to CoreCLR. This provides a smaller, more agile codebase that can be modified and deployed quickly for bug fixes or feature addition. CoreCLR doesn't do much on its own. Any library code defined here compiles into the assembly System.Private.CoreLib.dll, which, as the name suggests, is not meant for consumption outside CoreCLR or CoreFX.

Additional tooling provided by CoreCLR are ILDASM and ILASM (the .NET Core versions of programs you used earlier in this book) as well as a test host, which is a small wrapper for running IL DLLs from the command line.

The Framework Libraries (CoreFX)

This is the set of .NET Core foundational libraries and includes classes for collections, file systems, the console, XML, async, and many other base items. These libraries build on CoreCLR and provide the interface points for other frameworks into the runtime. Other than the specific CoreCLR implementations contained in CoreFX, the rest of the libraries are runtime- and platform-agnostic. CoreCLR contains mscorlib.dll, the public face of CoreCLR. Together, CoreCLR and CoreFX compose .NET Core.

The SDK Tools and the dotnet App Host

Included in the SDK tools is the .NET command-line interface (CLI), used for building .NET Core applications and libraries. The dotnet app host is the general driver for running CLI commands, including .NET Core applications.

The CLI commands and .NET Core applications are launched using the dotnet application host. To see this in action, open a command window (it does not have to be a Visual Studio developer command prompt) and enter the following:

```
dotnet --version
```

This executes the dotnet app host and will show the currently installed and path-accessible version of the .NET Core SDK. There are many commands that come out of the box with the CLI, and the most commonly used commands are listed in Table 31-1.

Table 31-1. *Common .NET Core CLI Commands*

Command	Meaning in Life
--help	Shows the help information.
--version	Lists the version of the .NET Core SDK.
--info	Lists the version of the .NET Core command-line tools and the shared framework host.
new	Initializes a sample .NET Core console application.
restore	Restores the dependencies for a given application. With 2.0, it is implicit with the build and run commands.
build	Builds a .NET Core application.
clean	Cleans the output of a project.
publish	Publishes a .NET portable or self-contained application.
run	Runs the application from source.
test	Runs the tests using the specified test runner.
pack	Creates a NuGet package from source.

In addition to the built-in commands of the CLI, frameworks can add additional command-line options. For example, Entity Framework Core introduces a series of commands for migrations and database updates. You will use these in the next chapter.

The Language Compilers

The .NET Compiler platform ("Roslyn") provides open source C# and Visual Basic compilers with rich code analysis APIs. While *some* Visual Basic support was added to .NET Core with the 2.0 release, C# is still the primary language and supported in all .NET Core frameworks.

The .NET Core Support Lifecycle

.NET Core is supported by Microsoft, even though it's open source. Each release has a defined lifecycle and is divided into two categories, Long Term Support (LTS) and Current (previously called Fast Track Support). Each major and minor release will generally be supported for three years as long as the patches are kept current (e.g., 1.0.1), with some exceptions, as explained here.

LTS releases are

- Major release versions (e.g., 1.0, 2.0)

- Supported for three years after the general availability (GA) of an LTS release

- Or, supported for one year after the next LTS release (whichever is shorter)

Current releases are

- Minor release versions (e.g., 1.1, 1.2)

- Supported within the same three-year window as the parent LTS release

- Supported for three months after the GA release of a subsequent Current release

- Or, supported for one year after the GA of a subsequent LTS release

If this seems a bit convoluted and confusing, you won't find any argument from me. Licensing has never been simple with Microsoft products, and .NET Core doesn't seem to be any different. Make sure to send your legal team to `https://www.microsoft.com/net/core/support` for more information and ensure compliance.

■ **Note**   In the release notes for .NET Core 2.0, it is mentioned that .NET Core 1.1 has joined .NET Core 1.0 as a LTS support product, instead of Current.

Installing .NET Core 2.0

If you haven't already installed Visual Studio 2017, make sure you follow the instructions in Chapter 2, installing (at least) the following workloads:

- .NET desktop development

- ASP.NET and web development

- .NET Core cross-platform development

You must be running at least version 15.3 of Visual Studio 2017 to use .NET Core 2.0. Additionally, at the time of this writing, the .NET Core 2.0 SDK must be installed separately, and it can be downloaded from `https://dot.net/core`.

Once Visual Studio 15.3 and the .NET Core 2.0 SDK are installed, open a command prompt and execute the following:

```
dotnet -version
```

You should see 2.0.0 (if not higher, depending on when you are reading this book) in the console window. Next, execute the following:

```
dotnet --info
```

You should see the following in the console window:

```
.NET Command Line Tools (2.0.0)

Product Information:
 Version:            2.0.0
 Commit SHA-1 hash:  cdcd1928c9

Runtime Environment:
 OS Name:     Windows
 OS Version:  10.0.16257
 OS Platform: Windows
 RID:         win10-x64
 Base Path:   C:\Program Files\dotnet\sdk\2.0.0\

Microsoft .NET Core Shared Framework Host

  Version : 2.0.0
  Build   : e8b8861ac7faf042c87a5c2f9f2d04c98b69f28d
```

This will confirm that you have the proper versions installed for the final chapters of this book.

Comparison with the Full .NET Framework

While .NET Core uses C# and many of the same APIs that are in the full .NET Framework, there are some important differences, as follows:

- Expanded platform support

- Open source

- Reduced number of app models supported

- Fewer APIs and subsystems implemented

The first two items have been covered already in this chapter, so the following sections cover the remaining items.

Reduced Number of App Models Supported

As mentioned, .NET Core does not support all of the .NET Framework app models, especially the ones built directly on top of Windows technologies. Furthermore, all .NET Core applications distill down to either a console application or a class library. Even ASP.NET Core applications are just console applications that create a web host, as you will see in Chapters 33 and 34.

Fewer APIs and Subsystems Implemented

The full .NET Framework is absolutely massive, and attempting to change all of the APIs over at once would be a nearly impossible task. Following the agile principles, the developers of .NET Core determined what the minimal viable product was for supporting .NET Core 1.0 and released just enough to satisfy those requirements. Every subsequent release of .NET Core includes many more APIs from the full .NET Framework, with the 2.0 release implementing more than 32,000 APIs.

.NET Core implements only a subset of the subsystems from the full .NET Framework, with the goal of a simpler implementation and programming model. For example, while reflection is supported, Code Access Security (CAS) is not.

Summary

The point of this chapter was to lay the groundwork for the next three chapters by showing the similarities and differences between the full .NET Framework and .NET Core. As you will see in the next chapters, developing .NET Core applications is similar to developing .NET Framework applications. There are fewer frameworks to work with, and the number of raw APIs available is fewer, but other than that, it's just C# code.

There were many design goals for .NET Core, and the team (including the worldwide open source developer community) has done an incredible job in a short amount of time, providing .NET developers with an amazing set of tools that can be used for cross-platform development and deployment.

■ **Note**   The next three chapters, covering EF Core 2.0 (Chapter 32) and ASP.NET Core 2.0 (Chapters 33 and 34), are limited by space in how much can be covered. For a deeper exploration of these topics, as well as using JavaScript UI frameworks with .NET Core, I suggest another one of my books, *Building Web Applications with Visual Studio 2017*, which is available at `https://www.amazon.com/Building-Applications-Visual-Studio-2017/dp/1484224779/`.

CHAPTER 32

■ ■ ■

Introducing Entity Framework Core

Microsoft released Entity Framework Core along with .NET Core and ASP.NET Core. EF Core is a complete rewrite of EF, taking advantage of all the goodness that is .NET Core. However, being a rewrite, there wasn't time to re-create all of the features in EF 6 within the timeline of the release of .NET Core 1.0. Based on feature comparison, the first version was, well simply put, weak. There really weren't enough features to consider it a production-ready product.

That all changed with the release of EF Core 1.1. That release brought more features from EF 6 online and introduced new features as well. While still not complete, it was complete enough for ASP. NET developers to start using it in real projects. EF Core 2.0 brought even more features online, added performance improvements, and expanded the uses beyond just ASP.NET. If EF Core 1.1 wasn't feature rich enough for your needs, chances are EF Core 2.0 is.

■ **Note** This chapter assumes you have a working knowledge of Entity Framework 6. If you don't, please review Chapter 22 before proceeding.

The first part of this chapter compares the features of EF 6 and EF Core 2. The remainder of the chapter shows how to build the EF Core 2 version of AutoLotDAL, which you will use in the next two chapters covering ASP.NET Core 2.

Comparing Feature Sets

There are some features of EF 6 that will not be carried forward, others that are complete, and many more that are still in progress. There are also new features and performance enhancements introduced into EF Core.

As mentioned earlier, EF Core represents a whole new codebase for the framework. This has provided an opportunity for the team to add features that would have been too difficult or costly to implement in EF 6. But it also means the team has a lot to catching up to do.

■ **Note** New features are getting added with every release, and the team is doing a great job keeping the documents current. For a comparison of EF 6 versus EF Core, visit `https://docs.microsoft.com/en-us/ef/efcore-and-ef6/`. Additionally, the road map is publicly available on the GitHub site, located at `https://github.com/aspnet/EntityFrameworkCore/wiki/Roadmap`.

Features Not Replicated

Fortunately, this list is short. The main features not ported to EF Core are the EF visual designer and EDMX modeling features. While the visual designer filled a need in the early days of EF adoption, modern developers are moving to the Code First paradigm and away from designer-generated models. The amount of work to replace this feature that is waning in use would have prevented the team from releasing a significant number of other features. Therefore, EF Core supports only the Code First paradigm.

■ **Note** As discussed in Chapter 22, Code First does not mean you can't work with an existing database. It really means "code-centric." You can still scaffold all of your EF code from an existing database or create the database from your code.

Changes from EF 6

On the surface, many of the EF Core and EF 6 features look the same. However, there are some subtle (and not so subtle) changes in EF Core. EF has been in production since 2008, and the team has taken the opportunity of the rewrite to improve many features as they were ported to EF Core. Here are a few of the differences between EF Core and EF 6:

- `DbContext` creation and configuration are based on dependency injection and not simple inheritance.
- Installation is modular and provider-centric.
- Fewer data annotations are supported, and there is more reliance on the Fluent API.
- There are changes to the `DbSet<T>` and `Database` APIs, such as adding the `Update()` and `FromSql()` methods.
- There are major performance improvements through cleaner code as well as query improvements, such as batching.

You will examine each of these as you build the EF Core version of AutoLotDAL.

New Features in EF Core

EF Core 2.0 has several new features that weren't in EF 6. Some of the new features are listed in Table 32-1.

Table 32-1. *Some of the New Features in EF Core*

Feature	Meaning in Life
Shadow state properties	Properties that are not defined on the model but can be tracked and updated by EF Core. These are commonly used for foreign keys.
Alternate keys	Provides non-primary key targets for foreign keys.
Key generation: client	Allows for key values to be generated on the client side.
Global query filters	Allows for global query filters, such as soft-delete or tenant ID.
Backing fields/field mapping	EF can write to fields instead of properties.
Mixed client-server evaluation	Enables queries to run client-side code intermixed with server-side code.
Eager loading with `Include()` and `ThenInclude()`	Improved eager loading with `ThenInclude()` to make cleaner LINQ statements.
Raw SQL queries with LINQ	Return tracked entities with `FromSQL()`.
Batching of statements	Reduces chattiness of database interactions for higher performance.
Scalar function mapping	Maps scalar function to C# function for use in query statements.
SQL Server `LIKE` (provider-specific)	Adds "like" capabilities in LINQ statements.
`DbContext` pooling	With ASP.NET Core, pools `DBContext` instances for higher performance.
Explicitly compiled queries	Maps LINQ query to C# function for precompilation and higher performance.

For more information on all of these features, consult the documentation at `https://docs.microsoft.com/en-us/ef/#pivot=efcore`.

Usage Scenarios

EF Core can be used in any .NET application, even full .NET Framework apps. Even though EF Core is built on top of .NET Core, you are not limited to just .NET Core applications. EF Core can be used with ASP.NET MVC 5, Web API 2.2, and even Windows Presentation Foundation.

Why would you want to use EF Core with full .NET Framework apps? There are lots of reasons, including all of the new features shown in Table 32-1. But the main reason (in my honest opinion) is the performance aspect. I have used EF Core in production with MVC 5 applications, and I saw a significant increase in performance over EF 6.

That brings up the next point: EF 6 and EF Core can live happily in the same application. You need to place the EF 6 context and the EF Core context into different assemblies, but they can share the same models.

Creating AutoLotCoreDAL_Core2

It's time to build the .NET Core version of AutoLotDAL.

Creating the Projects and Solution

Start by creating a new .NET Core class library project named AutoLotDAL_Core2, as shown in Figure 32-1. Delete the default `Class1.cs` file.

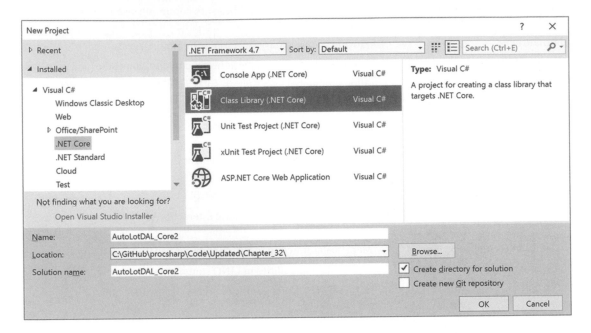

Figure 32-1. *Creating the initial .NET Core project and solution*

Add another .NET Core class library named AutoLotDAL_Core2.Models to the solution and delete the default `Class1.cs` file. Finally, add a .NET Core console app named AutoLotDAL_Core2.TestDriver to the solution. Set the AutoLotDAL.Core2.TestDriver project as the startup project.

Add a reference from AutoLotDAL_Core2 to AutoLotDAL_Core2.Models and add a reference from AutoLotDAL_Core2.TestDriver to AutoLotDAL_Core2 and AutoLotDAL_Core2.Models.

Adding the NuGet Packages

Starting with AutoLotDAL_Core2.Models, right-click the project and select Manage NuGet Packages. Click Browse in the top-left corner, and enter `Microsoft.AspNetCore.Mvc.DataAnnotations`. Install that package into the project. This package has the .NET Core version of the MVC-specific data annotations, including the updated `MetadataType` annotation, now called `ModelMetaDataType`.

Next, right-click the AutoLotDAL_Core2 project and select Manage NuGet Packages. Unlike EF 6, EF Core is a series of smaller packages. There are main packages that must be installed with any use of EF Core and the provider-specific packages. For this application, you are using the SQL Server provider, so install all of the following packages:

- `Microsoft.EntityFrameworkCore`

- `Microsoft.EntityFrameworkCore.Design`

- `Microsoft.EntityFrameworkCore.Relational`

- Microsoft.EntityFrameworkCore.SqlServer

- Microsoft.EntityFrameworkCore.Tools (optional; this enables using Package Manager Console for EF migrations)

That last one isn't required if you are going to use the .NET Core command-line interface (CLI) to do the migrations. The final change is to add the .NET Core version of Microsoft.EntityFramework.Tools to the project file. Unfortunately, this has to be done manually. Visual Studio makes this easier, by allowing for the direct editing of project files in the IDE. Right-click the project and select Edit AutoLotDAL_Core2.csproj. This will open the project file in the Visual Studio editor. Add the following markup to the project file (you must place it in its own ItemGroup). This enables running the EF commands directly from any command line.

```
<ItemGroup>
  <DotNetCliToolReference Include="Microsoft.EntityFrameworkCore.Tools.DotNet" Version="2.0.0" />
</ItemGroup>
```

Adding the Model Classes

I will be using the same model classes from the Chapter 29 version of the AutoLotDAL. If you have been following along with the book, you can copy the model classes from that project (make sure to change the namespaces), or you can pull them from the Chapter 32 download files. If you are using the Chapter 29 versions, there are some changes that need to be made for .NET Core. The full classes are listed in the next sections if you want to create them from scratch.

The EntityBase.cs Class

In the AutoLotDAL_Core2.Models project, create a folder named Base, and add a file named EntityBase.cs. Remove the initial code and add the following to the file:

```
using System.ComponentModel.DataAnnotations;
namespace AutoLotDAL_Core2.Models.Base
{
    public class EntityBase
    {
        [Key]
        public int Id { get; set; }
        [Timestamp]
        public byte[] Timestamp { get; set; }
    }
}
```

The primary key (Id) will be a sequence in SQL Server, and the Timestamp column will be used for concurrency checking. These work the same as their EF 6 versions.

The CreditRisk.cs Class

Add a new file named `CreditRisk.cs` into the Models project. Remove the existing code and replace it with the following:

```
using System.ComponentModel.DataAnnotations;
using AutoLotDAL_Core2.Models.Base;

namespace AutoLotDAL_Core2.Models
{
    public partial class CreditRisk : EntityBase
    {
        [StringLength(50)]
        public string FirstName { get; set; }
        [StringLength(50)]
        public string LastName { get; set; }
    }
}
```

Notice the removal of the Index data annotations from the Chapter 29 code. Multicolumn indexes cannot be configured with data annotations in EF Core; they must be configured with the Fluent API, which you will do shortly.

The Customer Class

Add a new file named `Customer.cs` class, clear out the existing code, and replace it with this:

```
using System.Collections.Generic;
using System.ComponentModel.DataAnnotations;
using System.ComponentModel.DataAnnotations.Schema;
using AutoLotDAL_Core2.Models.Base;
namespace AutoLotDAL_Core2.Models
{
    public partial class Customer : EntityBase
    {
        [StringLength(50)]
        public string FirstName { get; set; }
        [StringLength(50)]
        public string LastName { get; set; }
        public List<Order> Orders { get; set; } = new List<Order>();
        [NotMapped]
        public string FullName => $"{FirstName} {LastName}";
    }
}
```

Notice two changes from the EF 6 version. The first is that the `virtual` keyword is removed. The `virtual` keyword enabled EF 6 to lazy load data, and since lazy loading is not yet supported in EF Core, the modifier can be removed.

The second change is that the Orders property is defined as a List<Order> instead of an ICollection <Order>/HashSet<Order> combination. This is one of the subtle improvements in EF Core in that collections can be simple List<T> types.

The Inventory Class

Add a new file named Inventory.cs class, clear out the existing code, and replace it with this:

```
using System.Collections.Generic;
using System.ComponentModel.DataAnnotations;
using System.ComponentModel.DataAnnotations.Schema;
using AutoLotDAL_Core2.Models.Base;
namespace AutoLotDAL_Core2.Models
{
    [Table("Inventory")]
    public partial class Inventory : EntityBase
    {
        [StringLength(50)]
        public string Make { get; set; }
        [StringLength(50)]
        public string Color { get; set; }
        [StringLength(50)]
        public string PetName { get; set; }
        public List<Order> Orders { get; set; } = new List<Order>();
    }
}
```

Again, the Orders property is defined as a List<Order> instead of an ICollection<Order>/HashSet<Order> combination.

The InventoryMetaData Class

Add a new folder named MetaData, and in that folder add a new file named InventoryMetaData.cs. Once again, clear out the existing code, and replace it with this:

```
using System.ComponentModel.DataAnnotations;
namespace AutoLotDAL_Core2.Models.MetaData
{
    public class InventoryMetaData
    {
        [Display(Name = "Pet Name")]
        public string PetName;
        [StringLength(50, ErrorMessage = "Please enter a value less than 50 characters long.")]
        public string Make;
    }
}
```

The InventoryPartial Class

Back in the main directory of the project, add a new file named InventoryPartial.cs, clear out the existing code, and replace it with this:

```
using System.ComponentModel.DataAnnotations.Schema;
using AutoLotDAL_Core2.Models.MetaData;
using Microsoft.AspNetCore.Mvc;

namespace AutoLotDAL_Core2.Models
{
  [ModelMetadataType(typeof(InventoryMetaData))]
  public partial class Inventory
  {
    public override string ToString()
    {
      // Since the PetName column could be empty, supply
      // the default name of **No Name**.
      return $"{this.PetName ?? "**No Name**"} is a {this.Color} {this.Make} with ID {this.Id}.";
    }
    [NotMapped]
    public string MakeColor => $"{Make} + ({Color})";
  }
}
```

Notice the change of the attribute name to ModelMetadataType (from MetadataType) and the updated namespace of Microsoft.AspNetCore.Mvc that contains the annotation.

The Order Class

For the final model, add a new file named Order.cs, clear out the existing code, and replace it with this:

```
using System.ComponentModel.DataAnnotations.Schema;
using AutoLotDAL_Core2.Models.Base;

namespace AutoLotDAL_Core2.Models
{
    public partial class Order : EntityBase
    {
        public int CustomerId { get; set; }
        public int CarId { get; set; }
        [ForeignKey(nameof(CustomerId))]
        public Customer Customer { get; set; }
        [ForeignKey(nameof(CarId))]
        public Inventory Car { get; set; }
    }
}
```

The only change is the removal of the virtual modifier from the two navigation properties.

Creating the AutoLotContext

Create a new folder named EF in the AutoLotDAL_Core2 project. In that folder, add a new class named AutoLotContext.cs. Add the following using statements to the top of the file:

```
using System;
using AutoLotDAL_Core2.Models;
using Microsoft.EntityFrameworkCore;
using Microsoft.EntityFrameworkCore.Diagnostics;
```

Make the class public and inherit DbContext, as follows:

```
public class AutoLotContext : DbContext
```

There are some changes in how DbContext-derived classes work in EF Core, mostly around supporting dependency injection and configuration. Instead of a default constructor that passed the name of a connection string into the base class, DbContext-derived classes in EF Core are configured through DbContextOptions instances that are injected into the constructor. Create a new constructor like this:

```
public AutoLotContext(DbContextOptions options) : base(options)
{
}
```

The DbContextOptions instance is created by the DbContextOptionsBuilder class, and it allows you to specify the database provider, the connection string, and any provider-specific options. The fact that it is injected into the class allows for changing the provider at runtime. While this might not be practical to change from SQL Server to Oracle (since there are probably too many other considerations in play), this works great for changing to the new InMemory provider. This provider works great as a testing tool for your data access layer without needing to have a physical database.

In addition to the dependency injection (DI) support, there is a fallback mechanism built into the OnConfiguring() base method. This method exposes a DbContextOptionsBuilder that can be used to confirm that the context was configured and, if not, allow you to configure it. Add the following code (the discussion will follow):

```
protected override void OnConfiguring(DbContextOptionsBuilder optionsBuilder)
{
  if (!optionsBuilder.IsConfigured)
  {
    var connectionString = @"server=(LocalDb)\MSSQLLocalDB;database=AutoLotCore2;
        integrated security=True; MultipleActiveResultSets=True;App=EntityFramework;";
    optionsBuilder.UseSqlServer(connectionString, options => options.EnableRetryOnFailure())
        .ConfigureWarnings(warnings=>warnings.Throw(RelationalEventId.
        QueryClientEvaluationWarning));
  }
}
```

The IsConfigured property is set to true if the context was configured in the constructor, and it is set to false if not. The next two sections explain the configured settings.

■ **Note**   In Chapter 22, the connection string used data source and initial catalog instead of server and database. Either will work, but the new way is the recommended format moving forward.

Connection Resiliency

Enabling connection resiliency sets EF to automatically retry database operations if certain transient errors occur. These retry attempts happen a certain amount of times, with a set delay between each retry. This can improve your users' experience, cutting down on failures when there is a simple hiccup in the connection (for example).

You can create a custom execution strategy, but for SQL Server, you don't need to do this since the team has provided SqlServerRetryingExecutionStrategy for you. Additionally, the provider team has enabled a shortcut to add this execution strategy to your connection. By adding in the following DbContext option, transient SQL Server and/or SQL Azure errors will be retried up to six times (that number and the delay between each are configurable):

```
options => options.EnableRetryOnFailure())
```

The SqlServerRetryingExecutionStrategy can be configured to set the max retry limit, set the delay between each retry, and add additional errors for retry beyond the default errors.

If the retry limit is exceeded, EF will throw a RetryLimitExceededException. Trapping for this error in your repos enables you to act accordingly to the application requirements.

Mixed Client and Server Evaluation

Recall from Chapter 22 that EF 6 queries don't execute until they are iterated over by using First() or similar LINQ commands. Also recall that LINQ statements can't mix server-side and client-side processing. This is different in EF Core, starting with EF Core 1.0. Mixed client and server evaluation is a feature in EF Core that permits LINQ statements to utilize both server-side and client-side code.

With mixed query evaluation, if EF detects a client-side call, it will execute the server-side part of the query, returning the data resulting from that call, and then essentially use LINQ to Objects on the client side. While this can be beneficial, it can also cause problems if the order of your LINQ operations isn't correct.

For example, suppose you have a table that has a field defined as a GUID and you want to filter records based on that field. Now suppose that the parameter for the filter is a string and not a GUID. You might think (I know I did) that the following query would work just fine:

```
return Table.FirstOrDefault(x => x.TheGuid.ToString() == g)
```

And it does work, just not so fine. The engine that converts LINQ statements into SQL statements doesn't understand TheGuid.ToString() and doesn't translate that to SQL. Instead, it runs that code on the client side. That means all of the records from the table are retrieved, the GUID is converted to strings (one at a time), and then it compares them to the string g until it finds the first match.

A simple mistake like this can cripple your application, especially if you aren't thoroughly testing your data access code. To change this to server-side execution, change the parameter g into a GUID *before* the LINQ call, and then do the search, like this:

```
Guid g = Guid.Parse(guid);
return Table.FirstOrDefault(x => x.Guid == g);
```

That's a fairly subtle difference, and there are many other cases where you might be (unpleasantly) surprised about client-side evaluation. My suggestion is to stay away from mixed-mode evaluation unless you have a strong need for it and then test your data access code like there's no tomorrow!

Unfortunately, though, it can't be truly disabled. The best you can do is throw an exception when mixed-mode evaluation occurs. That is the final setting in the DbContextOptionsBuilder.

```
.ConfigureWarnings(warnings=>warnings.Throw(RelationalEventId.
QueryClientEvaluationWarning));
```

1264

With that setting enabled, you can at least trap when it occurs and update your queries appropriately. I leave this as the default for all of my applications, and if I find an instance where my app benefits from mixed mode, I merely inject in a different set of options that doesn't throw the error when client-side code is executed.

Adding the Parameterless Constructor

Later in the chapter, the AutoLotDAL_Core2.TestDriver project will use a parameterless constructor to create a new instance of AutoLotContext. When a context class is created using a parameterless constructor, the OnConfiguring() fallback is executed, setting the proper values on the context.

However, for the new DbContext pooling ASP.NET Core feature to be used, there can be only one constructor on your context class, and that's the one that takes a DbContextOptions instance. To satisfy both of these needs, create an internal parameterless constructor, like this:

```
internal AutoLotContext()
{
}
```

To use this constructor and leverage the OnConfiguring() event handler, you need to expose the internal items in AutoLotDAL_Core2 to the AutoLotDAL_Core2.TestDriver project. Right-click the AutoLotDAL_Core2 project and select Add New Item. Select Assembly Information File, and name it AssemblyInfo.cs. Clear out the existing code, and update it to just this:

```
using System.Runtime.CompilerServices;
[assembly: InternalsVisibleTo("AutoLotDAL_Core2.TestDriver")]
```

■ **Note**   At the time of this writing, Visual Studio will throw an error when adding this file. Just ignore it and continue.

Adding the Design-Time Context Factory

To run EF migrations, there needs to be a public parameterless constructor on your context class or an implementation of IDesignTimeDbContextFactory<TContext>. Since a public parameterless constructor prevents using DbContext pooling, you are going to need to add a class that implements the IDesign DbTimeContextFactory<TContext> interface. This interface has one method, CreateDbContext(). If the EF migrations engine finds an instance of this interface in the same assembly as the context being used, it will use the CreateDbContext() method to create the context and not the public constructor.

Add a new class named AutoLotContextFactory.cs to the EF directory in the AutoLotDAL_Core2 project. Clear out the template code, and replace it with the following:

```
using Microsoft.EntityFrameworkCore;
using Microsoft.EntityFrameworkCore.Design;
using Microsoft.EntityFrameworkCore.Diagnostics;

namespace AutoLotDAL_Core2.EF
{
  public class AutoLotContextFactory : IDesignTimeDbContextFactory<AutoLotContext>
  {
    public AutoLotContext CreateDbContext(string[] args)
```

```
    {
      var optionsBuilder = new DbContextOptionsBuilder<AutoLotContext>();
      var connectionString = @"server=(LocalDb)\MSSQLLocalDB;database=AutoLotCore2;
          integrated security=True; MultipleActiveResultSets=True;App=EntityFramework;";
      optionsBuilder.UseSqlServer(
        connectionString, options => options.EnableRetryOnFailure())
      .ConfigureWarnings(warnings => warnings.Throw(RelationalEventId.
       QueryClientEvaluationWarning));
      return new AutoLotContext(optionsBuilder.Options);
    }
  }
}
```

Adding the DbSet<T>s

Next, you add the tables that you want managed by EF, just like in EF 6. The difference, once again, is to not add the virtual modifier to the properties. Add the following code to the AutoLotContext.cs class:

```
public DbSet<AutoLotDAL_Core2.Models.CreditRisk> CreditRisks { get; set; }
public DbSet<AutoLotDAL_Core2.Models.Customer> Customers { get; set; }
public DbSet<AutoLotDAL_Core2.Models.Inventory> Cars { get; set; }
public DbSet<AutoLotDAL_Core2.Models.Order> Orders { get; set; }
```

■ **Note** Because of a bug in the ASP.NET Core scaffolding, if your context and models are in different assemblies, the types in the DbSet<T> properties must be namespace qualified, as in the preceding code. Any using statements are ignored. I presume this will be fixed soon, maybe even by the time you are reading this.

Using the Fluent API to Finish the Models

The Fluent API is another way to shape the models and the resulting database tables and columns. As mentioned earlier, there is less support for data annotations in EF Core than EF 6. You must use the Fluent API to create multicolumn indices. Add the OnModelCreating override, as follows:

```
protected override void OnModelCreating(ModelBuilder modelBuilder)
{
  //create the multi column index
  modelBuilder.Entity<CreditRisk>(entity =>
  {
    entity.HasIndex(e => new { e.FirstName, e.LastName }).IsUnique();
  });
  //set the cascade options on the relationship
  modelBuilder.Entity<Order>()
    .HasOne(e => e.Car)
    .WithMany(e => e.Orders)
    .OnDelete(DeleteBehavior.ClientSetNull);
}
```

The first block sets the multicolumn, unique index on the CreditRisk table. The second creates the one-to-many relationship between the Inventory and Order tables and then sets the cascade option to no action (the default).

Adding the GetTableName() Function

The final method to add is one that will return the SQL Server table name for a DbSet<T>. This is needed because the class and table names don't have to match, and you will need the SQL Server table name in the data initialization code (coming up later in the chapter).

Add the following method to the AutoLotContext.cs class:

```
public string GetTableName(Type type)
{
  return Model.FindEntityType(type).SqlServer().TableName;
}
```

This completes the AutoLotContext class.

Creating the Database with Migrations

Migrations have changed for the better in EF Core. EF 6 migrations created a hash of the database definition and stored that in the migration table in the database. If two developers made changes, there wasn't any way to consolidate the changes since hashes are one-way. This made using migrations in a team environment difficult at best.

EF Core has completely removed the hash from the process. All that is stored in the database is the name of the migration and the EF version number. The database definition is stored in a C# file named <contextname>ModelSnapshot.cs. Then developers can use a standard diff tool to work out any conflicting changes.

Migrations can be run using the Package Manager Console commands (e.g., add-migration, update-database, etc.) or using the new .NET Core CLI. The advantage of learning the .NET Core CLI version is that it can be run from any command line, and not just Package Manager Console.

Using the EF .NET CLI Commands

Before using the EF .NET CLI commands, your project file has to be configured with the correct package. This was done earlier in the chapter by adding the following item into the project file for the AutoLotDAL_Core2 project file:

```
<ItemGroup>
  <DotNetCliToolReference Include="Microsoft.EntityFrameworkCore.Tools.DotNet" Version="2.0.0" />
</ItemGroup>
```

You need to be in the same directory as the project file that defines the .NET Core CLI command options. Open a command prompt and navigate to the directory that contains the project file for AutoLotDAL_Core2.csproj. You can also execute these commands from Package Manager Console since it doubles as a command prompt. Just make sure to change to the correct directory. You can do this by using the following command (assuming you just opened up Package Manager Console):

```
cd .\AutoLotDAL_Core2
```

To see the full command list available for EF using the .NET CLI, execute the following at the command prompt:

```
dotnet ef
```

This will show the EF unicorn in ASCII art and the list of commands available. To get more information on any command, execute the command with the -h (or --help) option.

```
dotnet ef migrations -h
```

To add the migration to create your database, make sure to save all of the files, build the project (for safe measure), and then execute the following:

```
dotnet ef migrations add Initial --context AutoLotDAL_Core2.EF.AutoLotContext -o
EF\Migrations
```

The migration will be named Initial, using the fully qualified AutoLotContext, and will place the resulting migrations in the EF\Migrations directory. This creates the timestamped files (similar to EF 6 migrations) that are used to update the database and creates the AutoLotContextModelSnapshot.cs file, which stores the complete database model.

To apply this migration, simply execute the following command:

```
dotnet ef database update
```

Initializing the Database with Data

Missing from EF Core are the options to seed the database using migrations, or the base classes that drop and re-create the database. Fortunately, this functionality is easy to re-create manually. Start by creating a new folder named DataInitialization in the AutoLotDAL_Core2 project. In this folder, add a class named MyDataInitializer.cs.

Make the class public and static, and add the following using statements to the top of the file:

```
using System.Collections.Generic;
using AutoLotDAL_Core2.EF;
using AutoLotDAL_Core2.Models;
using Microsoft.EntityFrameworkCore;
```

Seeding the Database

Seeding the database simply means creating records in code and adding them using standard EF functions. Add the static InitializeData() method as follows (discussion to follow):

```
public static void InitializeData(AutoLotContext context)
{
  var customers = new List<Customer>
  {
    new Customer {FirstName = "Dave", LastName = "Brenner"},
    new Customer {FirstName = "Matt", LastName = "Walton"},
    new Customer {FirstName = "Steve", LastName = "Hagen"},
    new Customer {FirstName = "Pat", LastName = "Walton"},
```

```
    new Customer {FirstName = "Bad", LastName = "Customer"},
  };
  customers.ForEach(x => context.Customers.Add(x));
  context.SaveChanges();
  var cars = new List<Inventory>
  {
    new Inventory {Make = "VW", Color = "Black", PetName = "Zippy"},
    new Inventory {Make = "Ford", Color = "Rust", PetName = "Rusty"},
    new Inventory {Make = "Saab", Color = "Black", PetName = "Mel"},
    new Inventory {Make = "Yugo", Color = "Yellow", PetName = "Clunker"},
    new Inventory {Make = "BMW", Color = "Black", PetName = "Bimmer"},
    new Inventory {Make = "BMW", Color = "Green", PetName = "Hank"},
    new Inventory {Make = "BMW", Color = "Pink", PetName = "Pinky"},
    new Inventory {Make = "Pinto", Color = "Black", PetName = "Pete"},
    new Inventory {Make = "Yugo", Color = "Brown", PetName = "Brownie"},
  };
  context.Cars.AddRange(cars);
  context.SaveChanges();
  var orders = new List<Order>
  {
    new Order {Car = cars[0], Customer = customers[0]},
    new Order {Car = cars[1], Customer = customers[1]},
    new Order {Car = cars[2], Customer = customers[2]},
    new Order {Car = cars[3], Customer = customers[3]},
  };
  orders.ForEach(x => context.Orders.Add(x));
  context.SaveChanges();
  context.CreditRisks.Add(
    new CreditRisk
    {
      Id = customers[4].Id,
      FirstName = customers[4].FirstName,
      LastName = customers[4].LastName,
    });
  context.Database.OpenConnection();
  try
  {
    var tableName = context.GetTableName(typeof(CreditRisk));
    //In 2.0, must separate .NET string interpolation from SQL interpolation
    var rawSqlString = $"SET IDENTITY_INSERT dbo.{tableName} ON;";
    context.Database.ExecuteSqlCommand(rawSqlString);
    context.SaveChanges();
    rawSqlString = $"SET IDENTITY_INSERT dbo.{tableName} OFF";
    context.Database.ExecuteSqlCommand(rawSqlString);
  }
  finally
  {
    context.Database.CloseConnection();
  }
}
```

This is close to the EF 6 version, except for a few notable changes. First, there isn't an `AddOrUpdate()` method on the `DbSet<T>`, so all of the operations are `Add()` or `AddRange()`. Second is the syntax around enabling identity insert. The following code shows an example of enlisting an existing connection to execute multiple commands together. This can also be done with transactions.

```
context.Database.OpenConnection();
try
{
  var tableName = context.GetTableName(typeof(CreditRisk));
  //In 2.0, must separate .NET string interpolation from SQL interpolation
  var rawSqlString = $"SET IDENTITY_INSERT dbo.{tableName} ON;";
  context.Database.ExecuteSqlCommand(rawSqlString);
  context.SaveChanges();
  rawSqlString = $"SET IDENTITY_INSERT dbo.{tableName} OFF";
  context.Database.ExecuteSqlCommand(rawSqlString);
}
finally
{
    context.Database.CloseConnection();
  }
```

The final change is the effect of string interpolation on the raw SQL commands, covered next.

String Interpolation in Raw SQL Queries

New in EF Core 2.0 is the combination of C# string interpolation and parameterization of raw SQL queries when using `FromSql()` and `ExecuteSqlCommand()`. In EF 6 and EF Core prior to 2.0, the following statements were equivalent (presuming the value of `tableName` is `CreditRisk`):

```
context.Database.ExecuteSqlCommand($"SET IDENTITY_INSERT dbo.{tableName} ON;");
context.Database.ExecuteSqlCommand("SET IDENTITY_INSERT dbo.CreditRisk ON;");
```

In EF Core 2, the first query gets translated into a parameterized query, like this:

```
SET IDENTITY_INSERT dbo.@p0 ON
```

In most cases, the new method of handling interpolated strings is better. However, it's not true in this particular case, so if you don't want a parameterized query, then you must move C# string interpolation out of the raw SQL commands.

Clearing the Database and Resetting Sequences

In addition to loading the database, it's helpful during testing to reset the database to its original state. This was done in EF 6 with the `DropCreateDatabaseAlways<T>` base class. In EF Core, this needs to be done manually.

To delete the database and re-create it, there are some helper methods on the `Database` property of the context class. These are shown in Table 32-2.

Table 32-2. *The Database Helpers for Dropping and Creating Database*

Method	Meaning in Life
EnsureDeleted	Deletes the database if it exists; does nothing if it doesn't.
EnsureCreated	Creates the database based on the <context>ModelSnapshot code if it doesn't exist; does nothing if it exists. This is mutually exclusive of Migrate().
Migrate	Creates the database and executes all migrations if it doesn't exist; applies any missing migrations if it exists. This is mutually exclusive with EnsureCreated().

Unless you have specific code in migrations (e.g., creating stored procedures), EnsureCreated() and Migrate() result in the same condition, except for the population of the __EFMigrationsHistory table. The EnsureCreated() method never runs migrations and therefore doesn't populate the table. So if you attempt to run migrations after calling EnsureCreated(), they will fail since the objects in the migrations will already exist.

To drop and create the database, add the following static method to the MyDataInitializer class:

```
public static void RecreateDatabase(AutoLotContext context)
{
  context.Database.EnsureDeleted();
  context.Database.Migrate();
}
```

You might not always want to drop and create the database, so next you will create methods to delete the existing data and reset the sequences. Add the following code to do this:

```
public static void ClearData(AutoLotContext context)
{
  ExecuteDeleteSql(context, "Orders");
  ExecuteDeleteSql(context, "Customers");
  ExecuteDeleteSql(context, "Inventory");
  ExecuteDeleteSql(context, "CreditRisks");
  ResetIdentity(context);
}

private static void ExecuteDeleteSql(AutoLotContext context, string tableName)
{
  //With 2.0, must separate string interpolation if not passing in params
  var rawSqlString = $"Delete from dbo.{tableName}";
  context.Database.ExecuteSqlCommand(rawSqlString);
}

private static void ResetIdentity(AutoLotContext context)
{
  var tables = new[] { "Inventory", "Orders", "Customers", "CreditRisks" };
  foreach (var itm in tables)
  {
    //With 2.0, must separate string interpolation if not passing in params
    var rawSqlString = $"DBCC CHECKIDENT (\"dbo.{itm}\", RESEED, -1);";
    context.Database.ExecuteSqlCommand(rawSqlString);
  }
}
```

This completes the data initialization code.

Adding Repositories for Code Reuse

The repositories in the EF Core 2.0 version are slightly different than the ones from EF 6. They are changed to take advantage of the improvements in EF Core 2.0. Start by adding a new folder named Repos in the AutoLotDAL_Core2 project.

Adding the IRepo Interface

Add a new interface into the Repos folder named IRepo.cs. Update the using statements to the following:

```
using System;
using System.Collections.Generic;
using System.Linq.Expressions;
```

The full interface is listed here:

```
public interface IRepo<T>
{
  int Add(T entity);
  int Add(IList<T> entities);
  int Update(T entity);
  int Update(IList<T> entities);
  int Delete(int id, byte[] timeStamp);
  int Delete(T entity);
  T GetOne(int? id);
  List<T> GetSome(Expression<Func<T, bool>> where);
  List<T> GetAll();
  List<T> GetAll<TSortField>(Expression<Func<T, TSortField>> orderBy, bool ascending);
  List<T> ExecuteQuery(string sql);
  List<T> ExecuteQuery(string sql, object[] sqlParametersObjects);
}
```

In this version, the Add()/AddRange() and Update()/UpdateRange() methods have been converted to just Add() and Update(), respectively, with overloads. There is a new method, GetSome(), that takes an expression for the where clause, and there is an overload of GetAll() that takes an expression for the sort expression.

To see these in action, you would call the methods like this:

```
return GetSome(x=>x.Color == "Pink");
return GetAll(x=>x.PetName,true);
```

Adding the BaseRepo

Next, add another class to the Repos directory named BaseRepo. This class will implement the IRepo interface and provide the core functionality for type-specific repos. Update the using statements to the following:

```
using System;
using System.Collections.Generic;
using System.Linq;
```

```
using System.Linq.Expressions;
using AutoLotDAL_Core2.EF;
using AutoLotDAL_Core2.Models.Base;
using Microsoft.EntityFrameworkCore;
using Microsoft.EntityFrameworkCore.Storage;
```

Make the class public and generic, implement IRepo and IDisposable, and limit the generic types to be classes of EntityBase, as follows:

```
public class BaseRepo<T> : IDisposable,IRepo<T> where T:EntityBase, new()
```

Add two private readonly variables to hold the context and the DbSet<T>, and add one protected field to expose the context to any child classes.

```
private readonly DbSet<T> _table;
private readonly AutoLotContext _db;
protected AutoLotContext Context => _db;
```

The constructor needs to be updated. Add a new constructor that takes an instance of the AutoLotContext to take advantage of the dependency injection feature in ASP.NET Core. The parameterless constructor will chain it to the version that takes the context instance. The Dispose() method is the same as the EF 6 version. Add the following code to the class:

```
public BaseRepo() : this(new AutoLotContext())
{
}
public BaseRepo(AutoLotContext context)
{
  _db = context;
  _table = _db.Set<T>();
}
public void Dispose()
{
  _db?.Dispose();
}
```

The Add() methods are similar to the EF 6 version, except in this version I chose to just use Add() with overloads. But the underlying functionality works the same.

```
public int Add(T entity)
{
  _table.Add(entity);
  return SaveChanges();
}
public int Add(IList<T> entities)
{
  _table.AddRange(entities);
  return SaveChanges();
}
```

The Update() methods have changed, as EF Core has added Update() and UpdateRange() methods. Instead of having to change EntityState to EntityState.Modified, you just call Update()/UpdateRange() on the DbSet<T>.

```
public int Update(T entity)
{
  _table.Update(entity);
  return SaveChanges();
}
public int Update(IList<T> entities)
{
  _table.UpdateRange(entities);
  return SaveChanges();
}
```

The Delete(), GetOne(), and the empty GetAll() methods are the same as the EF 6 versions.

```
public int Delete(int id, byte[] timeStamp)
{
  _db.Entry(new T() {Id = id, Timestamp = timeStamp}).State = EntityState.Deleted;
  return SaveChanges();
}
public int Delete(T entity)
{
  _db.Entry(entity).State = EntityState.Deleted;
  return SaveChanges();
}
public T GetOne(int? id) => _table.Find(id);
public virtual List<T> GetAll() => _table.ToList();
```

The updated GetAll() and new GetSome() methods use the expressions to refine the queries. The GetAll() method changes the sort direction based on the value of the ascending parameter.

```
public List<T> GetAll<TSortField>(Expression<Func<T, TSortField>> orderBy, bool ascending)
  => (ascending? _table.OrderBy(orderBy) : _table.OrderByDescending(orderBy)).ToList();
public List<T> GetSome(Expression<Func<T, bool>> where)
  => _table.Where(where).ToList();
```

The remaining methods are covered in the next sections.

Retrieving Records with FromSql()

EF Core introduced a new method used for processing raw SQL queries. Currently, the FromSql() method can only populate a DbSet<T> property of the context. There is a backlog item to permit ad hoc class population, but there isn't a time table associated with it. This doesn't mean the class needs to be mapped to a database table; it just has to be in the context as a DbSet<T>. You could add an unmapped property to the context, as follows, and use it with FromSql():

```
[NotMapped]
public DbSet<MyViewModel> ViewModels {get;set;}
```

The query columns have to match the mapped columns on the model, all columns must be returned, and you cannot return related data (from the initial query). One of the great features of FromSql() is that you can add LINQ queries on top of the call. For example, if you wanted to return all Inventory records and the related Order and Customer records, you could write the following:

```
return Context.Cars.FromSql("SELECT * FROM Inventory").Include(x => x.Orders).ThenInclude
(x => x.Customer).ToList();
```

This also demonstrates the new ThenInclude() method to pull in related data after an Include().

■ **Note** As I stated in Chapter 22, you should be extremely careful running raw SQL strings against a data store, especially if the string accepts input from a user. Doing so makes your application ripe for SQL injection attacks. This book doesn't cover security, but I do want to point out the dangers of running raw SQL statements.

Implementing the SaveChanges() Helper Methods

The final method wraps the context's SaveChanges() method. The exception handlers for the SaveChanges() method on the DbContext are simply stubbed out. In a production application, you would need to handle any exceptions accordingly.

```
internal int SaveChanges()
{
  try
  {
    return _db.SaveChanges();
  }
  catch (DbUpdateConcurrencyException ex)
  {
    //Thrown when there is a concurrency error
    //for now, just rethrow the exception
    throw;
  }
  catch (RetryLimitExceededException ex)
  {
    //Thrown when max retries have been hit
    //Examine the inner exception(s) for additional details
    //for now, just rethrow the exception
    throw;
  }
  catch (DbUpdateException ex)
  {
    //Thrown when database update fails
    //Examine the inner exception(s) for additional
    //details and affected objects
    //for now, just rethrow the exception
    throw;
  }
```

```
  catch (Exception ex)
  {
    //some other exception happened and should be handled
    throw;
  }
}
```

■ **Note** Creating a new instance of the DbContext can be an expensive process from a performance perspective. ASP.NET Core 2 and EF Core 2 have added support for context pooling, which you will see in Chapter 33.

Creating the InventoryRepo

The final repo to build is InventoryRepo. This handles specific work on the Inventory table that isn't covered by the base repo. You will also need to create an IInventoryRepo interface to set you up for ASP.NET Core dependency injection.

Add a new interface named IInventoryRepo.cs to the Repos directory, and update the code to the following:

```
using System.Collections.Generic;
using AutoLotDAL_Core2.Models;
namespace AutoLotDAL_Core2.Repos
{
    public interface IInventoryRepo : IRepo<Inventory>
    {
        List<Inventory> Search(string searchString);
        List<Inventory> GetPinkCars();
        List<Inventory> GetRelatedData();
    }
}
```

Next, add a new class named InventoryRepo.cs to the Repos directory. Add the following using statements to the top of the file:

```
using System.Collections.Generic;
using System.Linq;
using AutoLotDAL_Core2.EF;
using AutoLotDAL_Core2.Models;
using Microsoft.EntityFrameworkCore;
using static Microsoft.EntityFrameworkCore.EF;
```

Make the class public, inherit from BaseRepo<Inventory>, and implement IInventoryRepo, like this:

```
public class InventoryRepo : BaseRepo<Inventory>, IInventoryRepo
```

Add a constructor that takes an AutoLotContext as the parameter and chain it to the base constructor. This will be used by the DI framework in ASP.NET Core to create the repository using one of the pooled AutoLotContext instances.

```
public InventoryRepo(AutoLotContext context) : base(context)
{
}
```

Add the GetAll() override and the GetPinkCars() methods, both of which have already been discussed.

```
public override List<Inventory> GetAll() => GetAll(x=>x.PetName,true).ToList();
public List<Inventory> GetPinkCars() => GetSome(x => x.Color == "Pink");
```

Executing a SQL LIKE Query

New in EF Core 2.0 is the EF.Functions property that can be used by database providers to implement specific operations. The first implementation released for the SQL Server provider is a .NET implementation of the SQL LIKE operator.

To see this in action, add the following code (note that you must add the % operator yourself):

```
public List<Inventory> Search(string searchString)
  => Context.Cars.Where(c => Functions.Like(c.PetName, $"%{searchString}%")).ToList();
```

This uses the Like function to create the following SQL query (presuming searchString == "foo":

```
SELECT * FROM Inventory WHERE PetName like '%foo%'
```

Using Include() and ThenInclude() for Related Data

The final method to add demonstrates the FromSql(), Include(), and ThenInclude() methods.

```
public List<Inventory> GetRelatedData()
  => Context.Cars.FromSql("SELECT * FROM Inventory")
             .Include(x => x.Orders).ThenInclude(x => x.Customer).ToList();
```

As discussed, ThenInclude() brings in related data from the current position in the relational tree.

Test-Driving AutoLotDAL_Core2

Before you can use your console app to test your data access code, you need to decide whether you plan on using full dependency injection in your tests or whether you will just create a new context using the parameterless constructor and use the fallback configuration in the OnConfiguring() method. For these examples, I am just going to use the fallback mechanism.

Open the Program.cs file in the AutoLotDAL_Core2_TestDriver project. Add the following using statements to the top of the file:

```
using System;
using System.Linq;
using AutoLotDAL_Core2.DataInitialization;
using AutoLotDAL_Core2.EF;
```

```
using AutoLotDAL_Core2.Models;
using AutoLotDAL_Core2.Repos;
using Microsoft.EntityFrameworkCore;
```

Update the Main() method to the following:

```
static void Main(string[] args)
{
  Console.WriteLine("***** Fun with ADO.NET EF Core 2 *****\n");
  using (var context = new AutoLotContext())
  {
    MyDataInitializer.RecreateDatabase(context);
    MyDataInitializer.InitializeData(context);
    foreach (Inventory c in context.Cars)
    {
      Console.WriteLine(c);
    }
  }
  Console.WriteLine("***** Using a Repository *****\n");
  using (var repo = new InventoryRepo())
  {
    foreach (Inventory c in repo.GetAll())
    {
      Console.WriteLine(c);
    }
  }
  Console.ReadLine();
}
```

Running this code first drops and creates the database (using the migrations), populates the data, and then retrieves the records, first using AutoLotContext and then using InventoryRepo.

Feel free to copy the additional test code from the Chapter 22 version to test the other features of the new data access layer.

■ **Source Code**   You can find the updated AutoLotDAL_Core2 example in the Chapter 32 subdirectory.

Summary

This chapter introduced you to the newest version of Entity Framework, EF Core 2.0. EF allows you to program against a conceptual model that closely maps to your business domain. While you can reshape your entities in any way you choose, the EF runtime ensures that the changed data is mapped to the correct physical table data.

You began the chapter learning about some of the differences between EF 6 and EF Core, and then you converted the EF 6 data access layer into a cross-platform version using EF Core 2.0. This new version will serve as the data access layer for the ASP.NET Core projects that you will build in Chapters 33 and 34.

CHAPTER 33

■ ■ ■

Introducing ASP.NET Core Web Applications

This is the first of the two chapters that introduce ASP.NET Core. As mentioned in Chapter 31, ASP.NET MVC and ASP.NET Web API have finally been fully combined into one framework with the release of ASP.NET Core. The subtle (and some not so subtle) differences between MVC 5 and Web API are gone. Coincidentally, so are the naming differences. It is just ASP.NET Core.

ASP.NET Core is built on top of .NET Core to provide cross-platform development and deployment of web applications and RESTful services using C# (and, of course, Razor, HTML, JavaScript, etc.). Like EF Core, ASP.NET Core isn't just a port; it's a rebuild. This allowed the team to clean up the codebase significantly, focusing on performance and feature enhancements.

This chapter starts by building the ASP.NET Core solution for the web application, then covers the features of ASP.NET Core, and finishes by flushing out the finishing touches of the CarLotMVC application.

■ **Note** This chapter assumes you have a working knowledge of ASP.NET MVC 5. If you don't, please review Chapter 28 before proceeding.

The ASP.NET Core Web App Template

Just like for ASP.NET MVC 5, Visual Studio ships with a rather complete project template for building ASP.NET Core web applications. In addition, there are templates for building projects that focus on Web API–style services, projects that use Razor Pages, and projects that use Angular, React, and React and Redux.

The New Project Wizard

To create the solution for this chapter, start by launching Visual Studio and selecting File ➤ New ➤ Project. In the left sidebar, select Web under Visual C#, select ASP.NET Core Web Application, and then change Name to AutoLotMVC_Core2, as shown in Figure 33-1.

© Andrew Troelsen and Philip Japikse 2017
A. Troelsen and P. Japikse, *Pro C# 7*, https://doi.org/10.1007/978-1-4842-3018-3_33

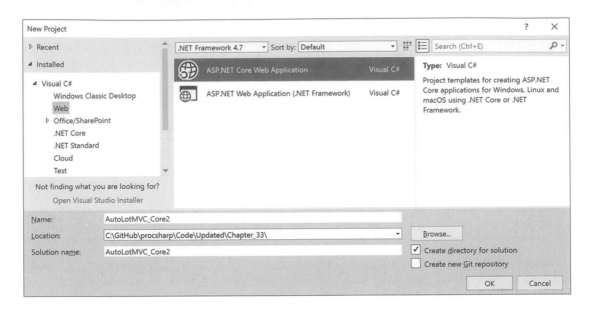

Figure 33-1. *Creating a new ASP.NET Core web application*

On the next screen, notice the new templates available with ASP.NET Core 2.0 and Visual Studio 2017 v15.3. These are listed in Table 33-1.

Table 33-1. *ASP.NET Core 2.0 Templates*

Option	Meaning in Life
Empty	An empty project template for creating ASP.NET Core applications.
Web API	A project template for creating RESTful services, with a sample controller. This can also be used for MVC applications.
Web Application	A project template for creating web applications using Razor Pages, with sample content.
Web Application (Model-View-Controller)	A project template for creating an ASP.NET Core application with views and controllers, with examples. This can also be used to build RESTful services.
Angular	A project template for creating an ASP.NET Core application with Angular.
React.js	A project template for creating an ASP.NET Core application with React.js.
React.js and Redux	A project template for creating an ASP.NET Core application with React.js and Redux.

Select the Web Application (Model-View-Controller) template. Leave Enable Docker Support deselected, and set the authentication to No Authentication, as shown in Figure 33-2.

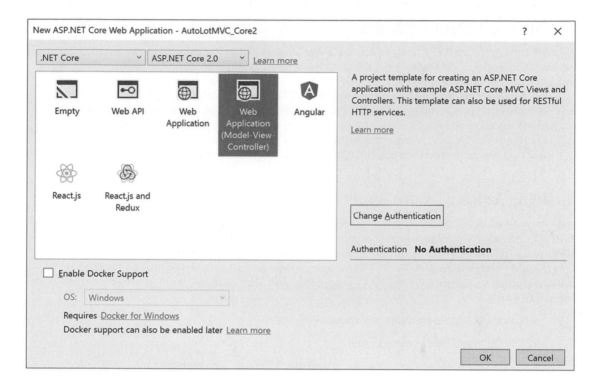

Figure 33-2. Selecting the Web Application (Model-View-Controller) project template

---

■ **Note** Docker is a containerization technology that is beyond the scope of this book. You can find more information at https://docs.microsoft.com/en-us/azure/vs-azure-tools-docker-hosting-web-apps-in-docker.

ASP.NET Core Project Organization

ASP.NET Core projects are structured differently than MVC 5 applications. The new structure is much improved, separating content from code. The wwwroot folder contains client-side content, such as CSS, JavaScript, images, and any other nonprogrammatic content.

Programming content (such as the models, views, controllers, etc.) lives outside the wwwroot directory and is structured as you would expect an MVC application to be.

Add the Data Access Library

Copy the AutoLotDAL_Core2 and AutoLotDAL_Core2.Models projects from Chapter 32 into the same folder as the AutoLotMVC_Core2 project. Right-click the AutoLotMVC_Core2 solution, select Add ➤ Existing Project, and add the two data access projects into the solution. If you add the Models project to the solution first, the reference between the DAL and the Models project should stay intact. Add references from the AutoLotMVC_Core2 project to the AutoLotDAL_Core2 and AutoLotDAL_Core2.Models projects.

Update the NuGet Packages

Right-click the AutoLotMVC_Core2 project, and select Manage NuGet Packages. Click the Installed link in the top menu, and you will see just two packages. One is the `Microsoft.NETCore.App` package that comes with all .NET Core applications.

The other is a new metapackage release with ASP.NET Core 2.0, `Microsoft.AspNetCore.dll`. This new package contains everything you need to create an ASP.NET Core web application, greatly simplifying the package selection process. In addition to containing everything you might need for ASP.NET web applications, the deployment process prunes the packages that your app doesn't need.

Click Updates in the top menu bar, and update any packages that need updating.

Running ASP.NET Core Applications

Previous versions of ASP.NET web applications were run from IIS (or IIS Express during development). The ASP.NET Core team has adopted Kestrel, an open source web server based on libuv, as the main execution platform. Kestrel presents a uniform development experience across all platforms.

The addition of Kestrel and the .NET Core command-line interface (CLI) has opened the door to additional options when running ASP.NET Core applications. They can now be run (during development) in one of four ways.

- From Visual Studio, using IIS Express

- From Visual Studio, using Kestrel

- From the Package Manager Console with the .NET CLI, using Kestrel

- From a command prompt with the .NET CLI, using Kestrel

The `launchsettings.json` file (located under the Properties node in Solution Explorer) configures how the application will run, both under Kestrel and under IIS Express. The `launchsettings.json` file is listed here for reference (your ports will be different):

```
{
  "iisSettings": {
    "windowsAuthentication": false,
    "anonymousAuthentication": true,
    "iisExpress": {
      "applicationUrl": "http://localhost:54471/",
      "sslPort": 0
    }
  },
  "profiles": {
    "IIS Express": {
      "commandName": "IISExpress",
      "launchBrowser": true,
      "environmentVariables": {
        "ASPNETCORE_ENVIRONMENT": "Development"
      }
    },
    "AutoLotMVC_Core2": {
      "commandName": "Project",
      "launchBrowser": true,
      "environmentVariables": {
```

```
      "ASPNETCORE_ENVIRONMENT": "Development"
    },
    "applicationUrl": "http://localhost:54472/"
  }
 }
}
```

The iisSettings node and the IIS Express node (under profiles) match the UI for the Debug section of the project properties page. Any changes to the UI get written to the launchSettings.json file, and any changes written to the file update the UI. The iisSettings section defines the settings for running the application using IIS Express as the web server. The most important settings to note are applicationUrl, which defines the port, and the environmentVariables block, which defines the runtime environment. This setting supersedes any machine environment setting.

The second profile (AutoLotMVC_Core2) defines the settings when running the application using Kestrel as the web server. The profile defines the applicationUrl setting and port, plus the environment.

■ **Note**   In earlier versions of .NET Core and ASP.NET Core, the launchSettings.json file was used only when running from Visual Studio. In the current release, the settings are used even from the .NET CLI.

The run command in Visual Studio allows for choosing either IIS Express or Kestrel, as shown in Figure 33-3.

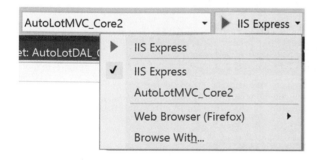

Figure 33-3. *The available Visual Studio debugging profiles*

Pressing F5 with the IIS Express profile opens a browser to the following URL (your port will be different):

http://localhost:54471/

When the Kestrel profile is selected, the Visual Studio debugger launches a browser with this URL (again, your port will be different):

http://localhost:54472/

The third way to run the application is from the Package Manager Console using the .NET CLI. To do this, enter the following command into the Package Manager Console:

dotnet run

■ **Note** At the time of this writing, there is an issue with using the .NET CLI from the Package Manager Console. It doesn't allow you to shut down the Kestrel server.

The final way is to open any command prompt (it does not have to be a developer command prompt), navigate to the folder containing the `AutoLotMVC_Core2.csproj` file, and enter the `dotnet run` command. To end the process, press Ctrl+C.

Deploying ASP.NET Core Applications

Prior versions of ASP.NET applications could be deployed to Windows servers only using IIS. ASP.NET Core can be deployed to multiple operating systems in multiple ways, including outside of a web server. The high-level options are as follows:

- On a Windows server (including Azure) using IIS

- On a Windows server (including Azure app services) outside of IIS

- On a Linux server using Apache

- On a Linux server using NGINX

- On Windows or Linux in a Docker container

The main steps, regardless of the deployment target, are as follows:

1. Publish the app to a folder on the hosting server.

2. Set up a process manager that starts the app when requests come in (making sure to restart it if the server crashes or reboots).

3. Set up a reverse proxy that forwards requests to the app.

The documentation covers each of these in great detail; see `https://docs.microsoft.com/en-us/aspnet/core/publishing/?tabs=aspnetcore2x`.

What's New in ASP.NET Core

ASP.NET MVC and ASP.NET Web API are still very successful platforms, widely in use today. So why the new platform? The first reason has already been discussed at length: the need for ASP.NET and Entity Framework to run on operating systems other than Windows. This was accomplished by removing the dependency on `System.Web`.

The other reason for the rewrite is that the codebases for ASP.NET MVC 5 and ASP.NET Web API 2.2 are getting old, at least in Internet time. When there is an aging codebase (or in this case two similar codebases) that must remain backward compatible, it can be difficult to innovate.

The decision to rebuild ASP.NET Core and to have just one framework (instead of separating MVC and Web API) has provided the opportunity for the team to innovate and improve the feature set and also to focus on performance as a primary concern. And, just like EF Core, ASP.NET Core is completely open source.

Here are some additional improvements and innovations:

- Unified story for building web applications and RESTful services

- Built-in dependency injection

- Cloud-ready, environment-based configuration system

- Can run on .NET Core or the full .NET Framework

- Lightweight, high-performance, and modular HTTP request pipeline

- Integration of modern client-side frameworks and development workflows

- Introduction of tag helpers

- Introduction of view components

These are covered in the next sections.

Unified Story for Web Applications and Services

Unlike MVC 5 and Web API 2.2, ASP.NET Core has only a single base controller type. The `Controller`, `ApiController`, and `AsyncController` types are all rolled into one class, `Controller`. Controller actions return an `IActionResult` (or `Task<IActionResult>` for async operations) or a class that implements `IActionResult`. The `IHTTPActionResult` from Web API 2.2 is rolled into the ASP.NET Core `IActionResult`.

Built-in Dependency Injection

Dependency injection (DI) is a mechanism to support loose coupling between objects. Instead of directly creating dependent objects or passing specific implementations into methods, classes and methods program to interfaces. That way, any implementation of the interface can be passed into methods and classes, dramatically increasing the flexibility of the application.

DI support is one of the main tenets in the rewrite of ASP.NET Core. Not only does the `Startup` class (covered later in this chapter) accept all of the configuration and middleware services through dependency injection, your custom classes can (and should) be added to the service container to be injected into other parts of the application.

The ASP.NET Core DI container is typically configured in the `ConfigureServices` method of the `Startup` class using the instance of `IServiceCollection` that itself is injected in. When an item is configured into the DI container, there are four lifetime options, as shown in Table 33-2.

Table 33-2. *Lifetime Options for Services*

Lifetime Option	Functionality Provided
Transient	Created each time they are needed.
Scoped	Created once for each request. Recommended for Entity Framework `DbContext` objects.
Singleton	Created once on first request and then reused for the lifetime of the object. This is the recommended approach versus implementing your class as a `Singleton`.
Instance	Similar to `Singleton` but created when `Instance` is called versus on first request.

You can find more information on DI and ASP.NET Core in the documentation at `https://docs.microsoft.com/en-us/aspnet/core/fundamentals/dependency-injection`.

Cloud-Ready Environment-Based Configuration System

This actually encompasses two improvements. The first is the capability of ASP.NET Core applications to leverage machine environment settings in the configuration process. The second is a greatly simplified configuration system.

1285

Determining the Runtime Environment

ASP.NET Core applications look for an environment variable named ASPNETCORE_ENVIRONMENT to determine the current running environment. The environment variable value is usually read from a settings file, from the development tooling (if running in debug mode), or through the environment variables of the machine executing the code. The names can be anything, but convention defines the different environments as Development, Staging, and Production.

Once the environment is set, there are many convenience methods available to developers to take advantage of the setting. For example, the following code enables logging for the development environment but not for the staging or production environment:

```
if (env.IsDevelopment())
{
  loggerFactory.AddConsole(Configuration.GetSection("Logging"));
  loggerFactory.AddDebug();
}
```

This environment-checking feature is used throughout ASP.NET Core. Prime examples of this are determining which configuration files to load; setting debugging, error, and logging options; and loading environment-specific JavaScript and CSS files. You will see each of these in action while building the AutoLotMVC_Core2 web application.

For more information on ASP.NET environments, reference the help at https://docs.microsoft.com/en-us/aspnet/core/fundamentals/environments.

Application Configuration

Previous versions of ASP.NET used the web.config file to configure services and applications, and developers accessed the configuration settings through the System.Configuration class. Of course, *all* configuration settings for the site, not just application-specific settings, were dumped into the web.config file making it a (potentially) complicated mess.

ASP.NET Core introduces a greatly simplified configuration system. By default, it's based on simple JSON files that hold configuration settings as name-value pairs. The default file for configuration is the appsettings.json file. The initial version of the appsettings.json file created by the Visual Studio 2017 template simply contains configuration information for the logging and is listed here:

```
{
  "Logging": {
    "IncludeScopes": false,
    "LogLevel": {
      "Default": "Warning"
    }
  }
}
```

The template also creates an appsettings.Development.json file. The configuration system works in conjunction with the runtime environment awareness to load additional configuration files based on the runtime environment. This is accomplished by instructing the configuration system to load a file named appsettings.{environmentname}.json after the appSettings.json file. When running under development, the appsettings.Development.json file is loaded after the initial settings file. If the environment is staging, the appsettings.Staging.json file is loaded. It is important to note that when more than one file is loaded, any settings that appear in both files are overwritten by the last file loaded; they are not additive.

Connection Strings

Connection strings typically vary by environment. The environment-based configuration system is tailored perfectly for that. Update the appsettings.Development.json file to include your connection string as follows (this should match the connection string used in Chapter 32):

```
{
  "Logging": {
    "IncludeScopes": false,
    "LogLevel": {
      "Default": "Debug",
      "System": "Information",
      "Microsoft": "Information"
    }
  },
  "ConnectionStrings": {
    "AutoLot": "server=(LocalDb)\\MSSQLLocalDB;database=AutoLotCore2;integrated security=True;
    MultipleActiveResultSets=True;App=EntityFramework;"
  }
}
```

Retrieving Settings

Once the configuration is built, settings can be accessed using the traditional Get family of methods, such as GetSection, GetValue, etc.

```
Configuration.GetSection("Logging")
```

There is also a shortcut for getting application connection strings.

```
Configuration.GetConnectionString("AutoLot")
```

Running on .NET Core or the Full .NET Framework

Just like EF Core, ASP.NET Core can be used in any .NET application, either full .NET Framework apps or .NET Core apps, as long as you are deploying to Windows. If you are deploying to macOS or Linux, then the only option is to use ASP.NET Core in .NET Core applications.

You might be asking why you would want to use ASP.NET Core in a full .NET Framework application. One answer is pretty simple: you want to take advantage of all the new features and improved performance in ASP.NET Core. An additional reason is reliance on existing service or middle-layer code (or even third-party libraries) that haven't been ported to .NET Core.

However, unlike EF Core and EF 6, ASP.NET Core and ASP.NET MVC cannot coexist in the same application. That means there needs to be more thought about moving existing MVC 5 or Web API 2.2 applications to ASP.NET Core. There also really isn't an "upgrade" path from MVC 5 (or Web API) to ASP. NET Core. It's more of a port. While a lot of the same code can be reused by copying and pasting into a new application, there isn't a magic button that you can push to suddenly have an ASP.NET Core application.

Lightweight and Modular HTTP Request Pipeline

Following along with the core principles of .NET Core, everything in ASP.NET Core is an opt-in process. By default, nothing is loaded into an application. As you will see later in this chapter, even the support of static files must be explicitly added.

This enables applications to be as lightweight as possible, improving performance and minimizing their surface area.

Integration of Client-Side Frameworks

As you saw in Figure 33-2, there are out-of-the-box templates for ASP.NET Core applications using Angular and React. The proliferation of client-side frameworks means any web application must be able to use their choice of JavaScript frameworks and not be locked into the Microsoft stack.

■ **Note** While this book doesn't cover using client-side JavaScript frameworks with ASP.NET Core, my other book on .NET Core covers using Angular and React with ASP.NET Core. You can find that book at `https://www.amazon.com/Building-Applications-Visual-Studio-2017/dp/1484224779/`.

Tag Helpers

Tag helpers are a new feature in ASP.NET Core that greatly improves the development experience and readability of MVC views. Unlike HTML helpers, which are invoked as Razor methods, tag helpers are attributes added to HTML elements. Tag helpers encapsulate server-side code that shapes the attached element. While HTML helpers are still supported, it is recommended that tag helpers be used for input controls in ASP.NET Core applications. If you are developing with Visual Studio, then there is the added benefit of IntelliSense for the built-in tag helpers.

To see the difference between HTML helpers and tag helpers, examine the following HTML helper that creates a label for the `FullName` property of the view model:

```
@Html.Label("FullName","Full Name:",new {@class="customer"})
```

This generates the following HTML:

```
<label class="customer" for="FullName">Full Name:</label>
```

You saw this (and many more HTML helpers) in action in Chapter 29. While HTML helpers are familiar for C# developers who have been working with ASP.NET MVC and Razor, the HTML helper syntax is not intuitive, especially for someone who works in HTML/CSS/JavaScript and not C#. The problem is focused on adding HTML attributes and route information (when needed) since you need to create anonymous objects to pass these in, and there isn't any IntelliSense support.

As a comparison, the following HTML snippet does the same thing as the previous HTML helper:

```
<label class="customer" asp-for="FullName">Full Name:</label>
```

Notice the cleanliness of this. You build the HTML tag as you normally would, with the addition of the `asp-for` tag, which is new. That tag is the tag helper. It references the same `FullName` property on the model, is discoverable with IntelliSense, and supports the `DisplayName` data annotation, just like the HTML helper. The additional HTML attributes don't have to be passed in with an anonymous object; they are simply added into the `label` HTML tag.

The preceding HTML and tag helper produce the same output as the HTML helper example, but it is much more readable, especially for designers who might not understand C# or HTML helpers.

There are many built-in tag helpers, and they are designed to be used instead of their respective HTML helpers. However, not all HTML helpers have an associated tag helper. Table 33-3 lists the available tag helpers, their corresponding HTML helper, and the available attributes. Each will be explained in the next sections, except for the **label** tag helper, which was already discussed.

Table 33-3. *Built-in Tag Helpers*

Tag Helper	HTML Helper	Available Attributes

Form	`Html.BeginForm`
	`Html.BeginRouteForm`
	`Html.AntiForgeryToken`
		`asp-route`: For named routes (can't be used with controller or action attributes).
		`asp-antiforgery`: Sets whether the antiforgery should be added (true by default).
		`asp-area`: Sets the name of the area.
		`asp-controller`: Sets the controller.
		`asp-action`: Sets the action.
		`asp-route-<ParameterName>`: Adds the parameter to the route (e.g., `asp-route-id="1"`).
		`asp-all-route-data`: Dictionary for additional route values.
		Note: This tag helper automatically adds the `antiforgery` token unless explicitly turned off using the `asp-antiforgery` tag helper.

Anchor	`Html.ActionLink`	`asp-route`: For named routes (can't be used with controller or action attributes). `asp-area`: Sets the name of the area. `asp-controller`: Defines the controller. `asp-action`: Defines the action. `asp-protocol`: Defines HTTP or HTTPS. `asp-fragment`: Defines a URL fragment. `asp-host`: Sets the host name. `asp-route-<ParameterName>`: Adds the parameter to the route (e.g., `asp-route-id="1"`). `asp-all-route-data`: Dictionary for additional route values.
Input	`Html.TextBox/TextBoxFor` `Html.Editor/EditorFor`	`asp-for`: A model property. Can navigate the model (`Customer.Address.AddressLine1`) and use expressions (`asp-for="@localVariable"`). The `id` and `name` attributes are autogenerated. Any HTML5 `data-val` attributes are autogenerated.
TextArea	`Html.TextAreaFor`	`asp-for`: A model property. Can navigate the model (`Customer.Address.Description`) and use expressions (`asp-for="@localVariable"`). The `id` and `name` attributes are autogenerated. Any HTML5 `data-val` attributes are autogenerated.

(continued)

Table 33-3. (*continued*)

Tag Helper	HTML Helper	Available Attributes
Label	Html.LabelFor	asp-for: A model property. Can navigate the model (Customer.Address.AddressLine1) and use expressions (asp-for="@localVariable").
Select	Html.DropDownListFor Html.ListBoxFor	asp-for: A model property. Can navigate the model (Customer.Address.AddressLine1) and use expressions (asp-for="@localVariable"). asp-items: Specifies the options elements. Autogenerates the selected="selected" attribute. The id and name attributes are autogenerated. Any HTML5 data-val attributes are autogenerated.
Validation Message (Span)	Html. ValidationMessageFor	asp-validation-for: A model property. Can navigate the model (Customer.Address.AddressLine1) and use expressions (asp-for="@localVariable"). Adds the data-valmsg-for attribute to the span.
Validation Summary (Div)	Html. ValidationSummaryFor	asp-validation-summary: Select one of All, ModelOnly, or None. Adds the data-valmsg-summary attribute to the div.
Link	N/A	asp-append-version: Appends version to file name. asp-fallback-href: Fallback file to use if primary is not available, usually used with CDN sources. asp-fallback-href-include: Globbed file list of files to include on fallback. asp-fallback-href-exclude: Globbed file list of files to exclude on fallback. asp-fallback-test-*: Properties to use on fallback test. Included are class, property, and value. asp-href-include: Globbed file pattern of files to include. asp-href-exclude: Globbed file pattern of files to exclude.
Script	N/A	asp-append-version: Appends version to file name. asp-fallback-src: Fallback file to use if primary is not available, usually used with CDN sources. asp-fallback-src-include: Globbed file list of files to include on fallback. asp-fallback-src-exclude: Globbed file list of files to exclude on fallback. asp-fallback-test: The script method to use in fallback test. asp-src-include: Globbed file pattern of files to include. asp-src-exclude: Globbed file pattern of files to exclude.
Image	N/A	asp-append-version: Appends version to file name.
Environment	N/A	name: One of Development, Staging, or Production.

In addition to the long list of supplied tag helpers, custom tag helpers can be created as well, which will be discussed after the built-in tag helpers.

The Form Tag Helper

The form tag helper replaces the `Html.BeginForm` and `Html.BeginRouteForm` HTML helpers. One advantage of the form tag helper over the HTML helper version is that the antiforgery token is included by default with all Form tag helpers.

For example, to create a form that submits to the HTTP POST version of the `Edit` action on the `InventoryController` with one parameter (`id`), use the following code:

```
<form method="post"
  asp-controller="Inventory"
  asp-action="Edit"
  asp-route-id="5">
<!-- Omitted for brevity -->
</form>
```

Like its `HTML.BeginForm` counterpart, the defaults can be omitted. Assuming that the route to the Edit page is `\Inventory\Edit\5` and the `HttpPost` should also go to the same route, the form tag could be written like this:

```
<form asp-action="Edit">
<!-- Omitted for brevity -->
</form>
```

Note that at least one tag helper must be included for ASP.NET Core to consider this an MVC form. This renders the following HTML for the view:

```
<form action="/Inventory/Edit/5" method="post" novalidate="novalidate">
  <input name="__RequestVerificationToken" value="CfDJ8MS41wJsL5BBhMUQM4d2aMQ2
  LWeBJhUL4IzlKM3LxaOr_NpB_QWvurqZybbBOtPXHVDME6M5bGOoR2aBkhitRt6mTl6fnctt2CP_
  kaHcVoiqcGNM4XcesnihpmEKOvyg8mFybqRMeU6ezvjOB6VIT5O" type="hidden">
  <!-- omitted for brevity -->
</form>
```

The Anchor Tag Helper

The anchor tag helper replaces the `Html.ActionLink` HTML helper. For example, to create a link to edit an item, use the following code:

```
<a asp-controller="Inventory" asp-action="Edit" asp-route-id="@Model.Id">Edit</a>
```

The tag helper creates the URL from the route table, using the `InventoryController`, `Edit` action method, and the current value for the `Id`. The anchor tag text is `Edit`, as you would expect. The resulting URL looks like this:

```
<a href="/Inventory/Edit/5">Edit</a>
```

The Input Tag Helper

The input tag helper is the most versatile of the tag helpers. In addition to autogenerating the HTML `id` and `name` attributes, as well as any HTML5 `data-val` validation attributes, the tag helper builds the appropriate HTML markup based on the data type of the target property. Table 33-4 lists the HTML type that is created based on the .NET type of the property.

Table 33-4. *HTML Types Generated from .NET Types Using the Input Tag Helper*

.NET Type	Generated HTML Type
Bool	type="checkbox"
String	type="text"
DateTime	type="datetime"
Byte, Int, Single, Double	type="number"

Additionally, the input tag helper will add HTML5 type attributes based on data annotations. Table 33-5 lists some of the most common annotations and the generated HTML5 type attributes.

Table 33-5. *HTML5 Type Attributes Generated from .NET Data Annotations*

.NET Data Annotation	Generated HTML5 Type Attribute
EmailAddress	type="email"
Url	type="url"
HiddenInput	type="hidden"
Phone	type="tel"
DataType(DataType.Password)	type="password"
DataType(DataType.Date)	type="date"
DataType(DataType.Time)	type="time"

For example, to display a text box for editing the Make value of a car, enter the following:

```
<input asp-for="Make" class="form-control" />
```

Presuming the value of the Make field is BMW, the following HTML gets generated:

```
<input class="form-control" data-val="true" data-val-length="The field Make must be a string
with a maximum length of 50." data-val-length-max="50" id="Make" name="Make" value="BMW"
type="text">
```

The id, name, value, and data-val attributes are all added automatically.

The TextArea Tag Helper

The textarea tag helper adds the id and name attributes automatically and any HTML5 validation tags defined for the property. For example, the following line creates a textarea tag for the Description property:

```
<textarea asp-for="Description"></textarea>
```

The resulting markup is this:

```
<textarea name="Description" id="Description" data-val="true" data-val-maxlength-max="3800"
data-val-maxlength="The field Description must be a string or array type with a maximum
length of '3800'.">This is the text that is shown in the text area control</textarea>
```

The Select Tag Helper

The select tag helper builds input select tags from a model property and a collection. As with the other input tag helpers, the id and name are added to the markup, as well as any HTML5 data-val attributes. If the model property value matches one of the select list item's values, that option gets the selected attribute added to the markup.

For example, take a model that has a property named Country and a SelectList named Countries, with the list defined as follows:

```
public List<SelectListItem> Countries { get; } = new List<SelectListItem>
{
  new SelectListItem { Value = "MX", Text = "Mexico" },
  new SelectListItem { Value = "CA", Text = "Canada" },
  new SelectListItem { Value = "US", Text = "USA"    },
};
```

The following markup will render the select tag with the appropriate options:

```
<select asp-for="Country" asp-items="Model.Countries"></select>
```

If the value of the Country property is set to CA, the following full markup will be output to the view:

```
<select id="Country" name="Country">
  <option value="MX">Mexico</option>
  <option selected="selected" value="CA">Canada</option>
  <option value="US">USA</option>
</select>
```

This just scratches the surface of the select tag helper. For more information, please refer to the documentation at https://docs.microsoft.com/en-us/aspnet/core/mvc/views/working-with-forms#the-select-tag-helper.

The Validation Tag Helpers

The validation message and validation summary tag helpers closely mirror the Html.ValidationMessageFor and Html.ValidationSummaryFor HTML helpers. The first is applied to a span HTML tag for a specific property on the model, and the latter is applied to a div tag and represents the entire model. The validation summary tag helper has the option of All errors, ModelOnly (excluding errors on model properties), or None.

The following code adds a validation message tag helper for the Make property of the model:

```
<span asp-validation-for="Make" class="text-danger"></span>
```

If there was an error on the Make property, the output would resemble this:

```
<span class="text-danger field-validation-error" data-valmsg-for="Make" data-valmsg-
replace="true"><span id="Make-error" class="">The field Make must be a string with a maximum
length of 50.</span></span>
```

Validation and model binding work the same as in ASP.NET MVC 5 and ASP.NET Web API 2.2.

The Link and Script Tag Helpers

The link and script tag helpers are used to improve the user experience. The `asp-append-version` adds a hash of the file being referenced to the `href` so the browser cache is invalidated when the file changes. This forces a reload, even though the actual name of the file didn't change. The following is an example of the `asp-append-version` attribute:

```
<link rel="stylesheet" href="~/css/site.css" asp-append-version="true"/>
```

The rendered code is as follows:

```
<link href="/css/site.css?v=v9cmzjNgxPHiyLIrNom5fw3tZj3TNT2QD7aOhBrSa4U" rel="stylesheet">
```

The `asp-fallback-*` attributes are typically used with content delivery network (CDN) file sources. For example, the following code attempts to load jquery from the Microsoft CDN. If it fails, it loads the local version.

```
<script src="https://ajax.aspnetcdn.com/ajax/jquery/jquery-3.1.1.min.js"
  asp-fallback-src="~/lib/jquery/dist/jquery.min.js"
  asp-fallback-test="window.jQuery">
```

The Image Tag Helper

The image tag helper provides the `asp-append-version` attribute, which works the same as described in the link and script tag helpers.

The Environment Tag Helper

The environment tag helper is used to conditionally load files based on the current environment that the site is running under. The following code will load the unminified files if the site is running in development and loads the minified versions if the site is not running in development:

```
<environment include="Development">
  <link rel="stylesheet" href="~/lib/bootstrap/dist/css/bootstrap.css" />
  <link rel="stylesheet" href="~/css/site.css" />
</environment>
<environment exclude="Development">
  <link rel="stylesheet" href="https://ajax.aspnetcdn.com/ajax/bootstrap/3.3.7/css/
  bootstrap.min.css"
    asp-fallback-href="~/lib/bootstrap/dist/css/bootstrap.min.css"
    asp-fallback-test-class="sr-only" asp-fallback-test-property="position" asp-fallback-
    test-value="absolute" />
  <link rel="stylesheet" href="~/css/site.min.css" asp-append-version="true" />
</environment>
```

■ **Note**   Prior to ASP.NET Core 2.0, instead of an `include` attribute, the environment tag helper used the `names` attribute, where each environment had to be specifically named. The 2.0 version uses `include` and `exclude` instead.

Enabling Tag Helpers

Tag helpers, like any other code, must be made visible to any code that wants to use them. The _ViewImports.html file contains the following line:

```
@addTagHelper *, Microsoft.AspNetCore.Mvc.TagHelpers
```

This makes all tag helpers in the Microsoft.AspNetCore.Mvc.TagHelpers assembly (which contains all of the built-in tag helpers) available to all of the views.

Custom Tag Helpers

Custom tag helpers can also be created. Custom tag helpers can help eliminate repeated code, such as creating mailto: links. Create a new folder named TagHelpers in the root of the AutoLotMVC_Core2 project. In this folder, create a new class named EmailTagHelper.cs and add the following using statement to the top of the file:

```
using Microsoft.AspNetCore.Razor.TagHelpers;
```

Next, make the class inherit TagHelper, as follows:

```
public class EmailTagHelper : TagHelper
{
}
```

Add two properties to hold the EmailName and the EmailDomain, as follows:

```
public string EmailName { get; set; }
public string EmailDomain { get; set; }
```

Any public properties on a custom tag helper are accessed as attributes of the tag helper, converted to lower-kebab-case. For the EmailTagHelper, they have values passed in like this:

```
<email email-name="blog" email-domain="skimedic.com"></email>
```

When a tag helper is invoked, the Process method is called. The Process method takes two parameters, a TagHelperContext and a TagHelperOutput. The TagHelperContext is used to get any other attributes on the tag and a dictionary of objects used to communicate with other tag helpers targeting child elements. The TagHelperOutput is used to create the rendered output.

Add the following method to the EmailTagHelper class:

```
public override void Process(TagHelperContext context, TagHelperOutput output)
{
  output.TagName = "a";    // Replaces <email> with <a> tag
  var address = EmailName + "@" + EmailDomain;
  output.Attributes.SetAttribute("href", "mailto:" + address);
  output.Content.SetContent(address);
}
```

Make Custom Tag Helpers Visible

Similar to using statements, the @addTagHelper command is used to make tag helpers visible for views to use. This can be added into each view that needs it, or you can use the new _ViewImports.chtml file to provide universal access to any view at or below the directory level of the _ViewImports.chtml file.

Open the _ViewImports.cshtml file in the root of the Views folder, and add the following line to make the EmailTagHelper visible to the views in the application:

```
@addTagHelper *, AutoLotMVC_Core2
```

The asterisk (*) indicates that all tag helpers in the AutoLotMVC_Core2 assembly should be available. You can also specific tag helpers if you need.

Use Custom Tag Helpers

Open the Contact.cshtml view, and notice the following lines that display e-mail addresses:

```
<address>
    <strong>Support:</strong> <a href="mailto:Support@example.com">Support@example.com</a><br />
    <strong>Marketing:</strong> <a href="mailto:Marketing@example.com">Marketing@example.com</a>
</address>
```

Replace those lines with the following code to take advantage of the new custom tag helper:

```
<address>
    <strong>Support:</strong><email email-name="Support" email-domain="example.com"/><br />
    <strong>Marketing:</strong><email email-name="Marketing" email-domain="example.com" />
</address>
```

View Components

View components are new in ASP.NET Core. They combine the benefits of partial views with child actions to render parts of the UI. Like partial views, they are called from another view, but unlike partial views by themselves, view components also have a server-side component. This combination makes them a great fit for functions such as creating dynamic menus, login panels, sidebar content, or anything that needs to run server-side code but doesn't qualify to be a stand-alone view. You will build a view component later in this chapter.

The Razor View Engine Changes

There is a slight difference between MVC 5 and ASP.NET Core when it comes to the Razor view engine. While most of the capabilities are replicated in ASP.NET Core, custom HTML helpers are not supported.

Building AutoLotMVC_Core2

Now that you have looked at the new features for ASP.NET Core, it's time to learn the rest of the framework by building the AutoLotMVC_Core2 application. You will do this by examining each of the pieces of ASP.NET Core in detail and updating the templated files as necessary.

The Program.cs File

ASP.NET Core applications are simply console applications that build a web server in the Main() method. The web server is built by using an instance of the WebHostBuilder class.

Open the Program.cs class and examine the contents, shown here for reference:

```
public class Program
{
  public static void Main(string[] args)
  {
    BuildWebHost(args).Run();
  }
  public static IWebHost BuildWebHost(string[] args) =>
    WebHost.CreateDefaultBuilder(args)
      .UseStartup<Startup>()
      .Build();
}
```

The CreateDefaultBuilder() method compacts the usual setup into one method call. This method is backed by the following code:

```
return new WebHostBuilder()
  .UseKestrel()
  .UseContentRoot(Directory.GetCurrentDirectory())
  .ConfigureAppConfiguration(
    (Action<WebHostBuilderContext, IConfigurationBuilder>) ((hostingContext, config) =>
    {
      IHostingEnvironment hostingEnvironment = hostingContext.HostingEnvironment;
      config.AddJsonFile("appsettings.json", true, true).AddJsonFile(
        string.Format("appsettings.{0}.json",
        (object) hostingEnvironment.EnvironmentName), true, true);
      if (hostingEnvironment.IsDevelopment())
      {
        Assembly assembly = Assembly.Load(new AssemblyName(hostingEnvironment.ApplicationName));
        if (assembly != (Assembly) null)
          config.AddUserSecrets(assembly, true);
      }
      config.AddEnvironmentVariables();
      if (args == null)
        return;
      config.AddCommandLine(args);
    }))
  .ConfigureLogging((Action<WebHostBuilderContext, ILoggingBuilder>) ((hostingContext,
   logging) =>
    {
      logging.AddConfiguration((IConfiguration) hostingContext.Configuration.
      GetSection("Logging"));
      logging.AddConsole();
      logging.AddDebug();
    }))
```

```
.UseIISIntegration()
.UseDefaultServiceProvider((Action<WebHostBuilderContext, ServiceProviderOptions>)
((context, options) => options.ValidateScopes = context.HostingEnvironment.
IsDevelopment())));
```

The preceding code demonstrates the modularity of ASP.NET Core and the opt-in nature of its services. After creating a new instance of the WebHostBuilder, the code enables just the features that the application needs. The Kestrel web server is enabled, and the root directory for content is set as the project directory. The next code block configures the application and demonstrates how to use the different JSON files based on the currently executing environment.

■ **Note** This is a change from the previous versions of ASP.NET Core, where all the configuration code was processed in the Startup.cs class and not in Main. It was moved to Main to make the Startup.cs class cleaner and hold closer to the single responsibility principle.

After configuring the application and logging, IIS integration is added (in addition to Kestrel). Finally, the default service provider for dependency injection is configured.

Back in the BuildWebHost() method, the UseStartup method sets the configuration class to Startup.cs and then builds the WebHostBuilder instance, fully configured for the application.

Back in the Main() method, the WebHostBuilder is given the Run() command to activate the web host.

Adding Data Initialization Support

The Program.cs file is where data initialization should occur. This is where the AutoLotDAL_Core2 data initializer will be executed. Start by adding the following using statements to the top of the Program.cs file:

```
using AutoLotDAL_Core2.DataInitialization;
using AutoLotDAL_Core2.EF;
using Microsoft.Extensions.DependencyInjection;
```

Now, update the code in the Main() method to the following:

```
var webHost = BuildWebHost(args);
using (var scope = webHost.Services.CreateScope())
{
  var services = scope.ServiceProvider;
  var context = services.GetRequiredService<AutoLotContext>();
  MyDataInitializer.RecreateDatabase(context);
  MyDataInitializer.InitializeData(context);
}
webHost.Run();
```

The code gets the scope of the DI container and uses that to get the AutoLotContext from the container. It then calls the methods to drop and re-create the database and then adds the test data.

■ **Note** If you try to run your project now, it will fail since the DI container hasn't been configured. This will be done next.

The Startup.cs File

The Startup class configures how the application will handle HTTP requests and responses, configures any needed services, and sets up the dependency injection container. The class name can be anything, as long as it matches the UseStartup<T> line in the configuration of the WebHostBuilder, but the convention is to name the class Startup.cs.

Open the Startup.cs file and update the using statements to the following:

```
using AutoLotDAL_Core2.EF;
using AutoLotDAL_Core2.Repos;
using Microsoft.EntityFrameworkCore;
using Microsoft.EntityFrameworkCore.Diagnostics;
using Microsoft.AspNetCore.Builder;
using Microsoft.AspNetCore.Hosting;
using Microsoft.Extensions.Configuration;
using Microsoft.Extensions.DependencyInjection;
```

Now that you have the proper using statements in place, it's time to learn about the available services in the Startup class.

Available Services for Startup

The startup process needs access to framework and environmental services and values, and these are injected into the class by the framework. There are five services available to the Startup class for configuring the application, listed in Table 33-6. The following sections show these in action.

Table 33-6. *Available Services in Startup*

Service	Functionality Provided
IApplicationBuilder	Defines a class that provides the mechanisms to configure an application's request pipeline.
IHostingEnvironment	Provides information about the web hosting environment an application is running in.
ILoggerFactory	Used to configure the logging system and create instances of loggers from the registered logging providers.
IServiceCollection	Specifies the contract for a collection of service descriptors. This is part of the dependency injection framework.
IConfiguration	This is an instance of the application configuration, created in the Main() method of the Program class.

The constructor takes an instance of IConfiguration and optional instance of IHostingEnvironment, although typical implementations use only the IConfiguration parameter. The Configure method must take an instance of IApplicationBuilder but can also take instances of IHostingEnvironment and/or ILoggerFactory. The ConfigureServices method takes an instance of IServiceCollection.

The templated Startup class with the services injected looks like this:

```
public class Startup
{
    public Startup(IConfiguration configuration)
    {
        Configuration = configuration;
    }

    public IConfiguration Configuration { get; }

    // This method gets called by the runtime. Use this method to add services to the container.
    public void ConfigureServices(IServiceCollection services)
    {
        services.AddMvc();
    }

    // This method gets called by the runtime. Use this method to configure the HTTP request
    pipeline.
    public void Configure(IApplicationBuilder app, IHostingEnvironment env)
    {
        if (env.IsDevelopment())
        {
            app.UseDeveloperExceptionPage();
            app.UseBrowserLink();
        }
        else
        {
            app.UseExceptionHandler("/Home/Error");
        }

        app.UseStaticFiles();

        app.UseMvc(routes =>
        {
            routes.MapRoute(
                name: "default",
                template: "{controller=Home}/{action=Index}/{id?}");
        });
    }
}
```

Each of the methods will be discussed in the next sections.

The Constructor

The constructor takes an instance of the IConfiguration interface that was created by the WebHost.CreateDefaultBuilder() method in the Program.cs file and assigns it to the Configuration property for use elsewhere in the class.

The Configure() Method

The Configure() method is used to set up the application to respond to HTTP requests. If the environment is set to development, then an enhanced exception page for debugging as well as Browserlink is enabled. If it's not development, then the standard exception route is used when there is an error:

```
if (env.IsDevelopment())
{
  app.UseDeveloperExceptionPage();
  app.UseBrowserLink();
}
else
{
  app.UseExceptionHandler("/Home/Error");
}
```

Next, support for static files is added. This is an example of the opt-in nature of ASP.NET Core. Only services that you need are explicitly added in.

```
app.UseStaticFiles();
```

The last line sets up all of the services needed to run an MVC application, including the default route:

```
app.UseMvc(routes =>
{
  routes.MapRoute(
    name: "default",
    template: "{controller=Home}/{action=Index}/{id?}");
});
```

Add the Additional Routes

ASP.NET Core supports traditional route tables as well as attribute routing. Update the app.UseMvc() code to include the Contact and About routes that you created for the MVC 5 version.

```
app.UseMvc(routes =>
{
  routes.MapRoute("Contact", "Contact/{*pathInfo}", new { controller = "Home", action = "Contact" });
  routes.MapRoute("About", "About/{*pathinfo}", new { controller = "Home", action = "About" });
  routes.MapRoute(name: "default",template: "{controller=Home}/{action=Index}/{id?}");
});
```

The ConfigureServices() Method

The ConfigureServices method is used to configure any services needed by the application and insert them into the dependency injection container. The default service is MVC.

```
services.AddMvc();
```

Configure the AutoLotContext and InventoryRepo for Dependency Injection

EF Core is configured using `IServiceCollection` as well. Configuring an EF `DbContext` class includes setting the required `DbContextOptions`, as well as adding it into the DI container. Configuration of the `AutoLot` context class was covered in depth in Chapter 32. Adding the `DbContext` into the DI container allows you to just specify a parameter of type `AutoLotContext` in the constructor of a class, and the DI container will create a configured instance for you. New in ASP.NET Core 2.0 and EF Core 2.0 is the ability to add a pool of instances, greatly improving performance. Add the following code after the call to `services.AddMvc()`:

```
services.AddDbContextPool<AutoLotContext>(
  options => options.UseSqlServer(Configuration.GetConnectionString("AutoLot"),
      o => o.EnableRetryOnFailure())
    .ConfigureWarnings(warnings => warnings.Throw(RelationalEventId.
    QueryClientEvaluationWarning)));
```

The `AddDbContextPool` command creates a pool of context classes into the DI framework. Since creating a `DbContext` instance can be a relatively expensive operation, pooling several instances can greatly improve an application's performance. While you could do something like this on your own in prior versions of ASP.NET Core and EF Core, the advantage of using the context pool is that the `DbChangeTracker` is reset for each instance as it is added back into the pool. This prevents any bleed-over from one user to another.

Add a new line after the `AutoLotContext` configuration to add the `InventoryRepo` into the DI container.

```
services.AddScoped<IInventoryRepo, InventoryRepo>();
```

Now any classes that have a parameter of `AutoLotContext` or `IInventoryRepo` in their constructor will have the appropriate instance created for it.

Package Management with Bower

Bower (`https://bower.io/`) is a powerful client-side library manager for web sites, containing thousands of packages. Its library is much more extensive than NuGet and managed by the web community at large. Bower is not a replacement for NuGet but should be considered a supplement. Visual Studio 2017 and ASP. NET Core use Bower to manage client-side packages.

The `.bowerrc` file is the configuration file for Bower. It is found underneath the `bower.json` file in Solution Explorer. It is used to set the relative path for the root location where packages are to be installed into the application and defaults to the `lib` directory under `wwwroot`, as follows:

```
{
  "directory": "wwwroot/lib"
}
```

Bower packages included in an ASP.NET Core application are managed through the `bower.json` file. You can edit this file directly to add/remove packages or use Visual Studio 2017's Bower Package Manager GUI. The Bower Package Manager works just like NuGet Package Manager and is accessed by right-clicking the project name in Solution Explorer and selecting Manage Bower Packages.

The `bower.json` file lists all the packages under the `dependencies` node. The Visual Studio 2017 template installs four packages, as shown here:

```
{
  "name": "asp.net",
  "private": true,
  "dependencies": {
```

```
    "bootstrap": "3.3.7",
    "jquery": "2.2.0",
    "jquery-validation": "1.14.0",
    "jquery-validation-unobtrusive": "3.2.6"
  }
}
```

Bower Execution

Visual Studio 2017 watches for the bower.json file to change, and when a change is detected, the packages are added or removed (based on the listed packages) into individual subdirectories under wwwroot\lib. You can force Visual Studio to update the packages by right-clicking the bower.json file and selecting Restore Packages.

Bundling and Minification

Bundling and minification are important tools for increasing your application's performance. Splitting custom JavaScript and CSS files into smaller, focused files increases maintainability, but doing this can cause performance issues. Browsers have built-in limits controlling how many files can be simultaneously downloaded from the same URL, so too many files (even if they are very small) can lead to slower page loads. Bundling is the process of combining smaller files into larger files. This gets around the browser file download limitation but must be done wisely since gigantic files can cause issues as well.

Minification is the process of reducing a file's size by renaming variable and function names to something much shorter, removing unnecessary white space, and removing line breaks. Its goal is to make the file as small as possible without hampering functionality.

The BundlerMinifier Project

Bundling and minification for .NET Core projects seemed to be in constant flux during the early versions. The ASP.NET Core team has settled on the BundlerMinifier project created by Mads Kristensen. It runs as both a Visual Studio extension and a NuGet package for the .NET Core CLI. You can find more information at https://github.com/madskristensen/BundlerMinifier.

■ **Note** Gulp, Grunt, WebPack, and many other build tools are still supported by .NET Core and Visual Studio 2017. Microsoft backed off of picking a specific open source framework as the default because of the longevity of support for templates (three years for LTS versions) and the rapid mood swings of the JavaScript community.

Configuring Bundling and Minification

The bundleconfig.json file configures the targets and the output files. The default configuration is listed here:

```
// Configure bundling and minification for the project.
// More info at https://go.microsoft.com/fwlink/?LinkId=808241
[
  {
    "outputFileName": "wwwroot/css/site.min.css",
```

```
  // An array of relative input file paths. Globbing patterns supported
  "inputFiles": [
    "wwwroot/css/site.css"
  ]
},
{
  "outputFileName": "wwwroot/js/site.min.js",
  "inputFiles": [
    "wwwroot/js/site.js"
  ],
  // Optionally specify minification options
  "minify": {
    "enabled": true,
    "renameLocals": true
  },
  // Optionally generate .map file
  "sourceMap": false
}
]
```

Each block of JSON has (at a minimum) definitions for input files (with globbing support) and the name and location of the output bundled and/or minified file. For example, the first block in the previous file listing takes the `site.css` file and creates the minified version named `site.min.css`. If there was more than one file in the `inputFiles` array (or if wildcards are used), then all of the files listed are bundled into the output file. The second block does the same thing for the `site.js` file and shows the optional `minify` and `sourceMap` parameters. Both of these parameters are optional. They are shown set to their respective default values for illustration purposes. The `sourceMap` option is for creating source map files from the input JavaScript files.

Visual Studio Integration

Check for the version of the `BundlerMinifier` extension installed in Visual Studio by selecting Tools ➤ Extensions and Updates and then selecting Installed on the left side of the dialog. If the extension is not installed, select Online ➤ Visual Studio Gallery. It should show up in the first page of the Most Popular extensions, but if not, search for it by using *Bundler* in the search box.

If there is an updated version from what is installed on your machine, it will show in the Updates section. Install or update the extension to the latest version, which at the time of this writing is 2.4.340. This might require a restart of Visual Studio.

Bundling on Change

To configure bundling and minification to watch for changes, right-click the project name in Solution Explorer and select Bundler & Minifier. Make sure Produce Output Files is selected, as shown in Figure 33-4.

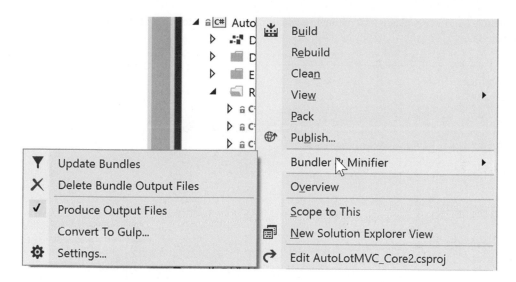

Figure 33-4. *Configuring the BundlerMinifier Visual Studio extension*

Checking this option adds a watcher to the files referenced in bundleconfig.json. To test this, navigate to the css directory under wwwroot, and delete the site.min.css file. Open the site.css file, make an inconsequential change to the file (such as adding a space or typing a character and then backspacing over it), and save the file. The site.min.css file is re-created.

Bundling on Build

There are two ways to enable bundling when Visual Studio 2017 builds your project. The first is to right-click the bundleconfig.json file, select Bundler & Minifier, and then select the "Enable bundle on build" option, as shown in Figure 33-5.

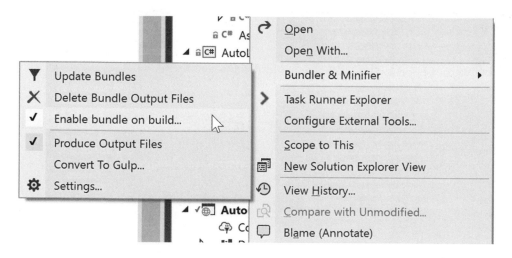

Figure 33-5. *Enabling bundling on build*

This downloads another NuGet package that hooks BundlerMinifier into the MSBuild process. You will have to confirm the install, as shown in Figure 33-6.

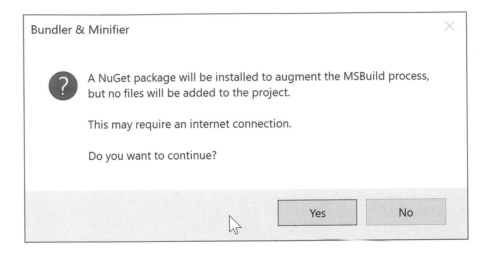

Figure 33-6. *Adding support for MSBuild integration*

Using the Task Runner Explorer

The second way is to use the Task Runner Explorer to bind the bundling tasks into the build process. The Task Runner Explorer is another Visual Studio extension created by Mads Kristensen but is now part of the standard install for Visual Studio 2017. It enables binding command-line calls into the MSBuild process. Open it by selecting Tools ➤ Task Runner Explorer. The left side of the Task Runner Explorer shows the available commands, and the right side shows the assigned bindings.

To assign the binding to update all the files after each build, right-click the command "Update all files," and select Bindings ➤ After Build, as shown in Figure 33-7.

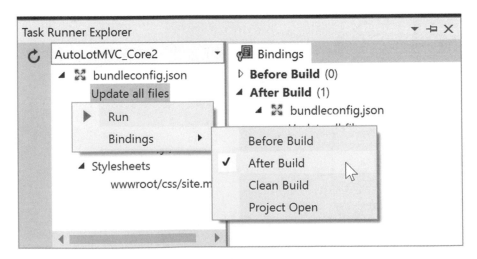

Figure 33-7. *Updating all files after each build*

For the "Clean output files" task, assign the Before Build and Clean bindings. This will remove the minified and bundled files before a build starts or when a Clean command is executed.

.NET Core CLI Integration

In addition to integrating with Visual Studio, BundlerMinifier also works with the .NET Core CLI by using the `BundlerMinifier.Core` NuGet package. Confirm the version available by opening the NuGet package manager and searching for `BundlerMinifier.Core`, but don't install it. The Visual Studio tooling (at the time of this writing) doesn't have built-in support for adding CLI package references into the project, so this must be done manually.

Open the `AutoLotMVC_Core2.csproj` file by right-clicking the project name in Solution Explorer and then selecting Edit AutoLotMVC_Core2.csproj. Add the package as a `DotNetCliToolReference` following the web generation tools, like this (make sure to use the current version):

```
<ItemGroup>
  <DotNetCliToolReference Include="Microsoft.VisualStudio.Web.CodeGeneration.Tools"
    Version="2.0.0" />
  <DotNetCliToolReference Include="BundlerMinifier.Core" Version="2.5.357" />
</ItemGroup>
```

This sets up execution of bundling and/or cleaning using the .NET CLI from either the Package Manager Console or a simple command prompt. Open the Package Manager Console, navigate to the directory containing the project file, and execute the following command:

```
dotnet bundle
```

To remove all generated files, enter the `clean` command, like this:

```
dotnet bundle clean
```

Client-Side Content (wwwroot Folder)

The `wwwroot` folder is designed to hold your site's CSS files, images, and other content that will be directly rendered. The default template creates four folders, `css`, `images`, `js`, and `lib`, that hold the client-side content. A custom CSS file (named `site.css`) and a custom JavaScript file (named `site.js`) contain the initial CSS and JavaScript, respectively, for the site. The `lib` folder is used by Bower to hold the client-side frameworks specified in the `bower.json` file.

Any additional JavaScript, CSS files, or images should be placed under here, as this is where the deployment process expects such content to live. Also remember to add any additional JavaScript and/or CSS files to the bundling and minification process.

The Models, Controllers, and Views Folders

These folders serve the same purpose as their counterparts in MVC 5. The only project-specific model in this application is `ErrorViewModel.cs`, used by the `HomeController` and the `Error.cshtml` view.

The controllers and views will be covered in their own sections later in this chapter.

Controllers and Actions

Just like MVC 5 and ASP.NET Web API, controllers and actions are the workhorses of an ASP.NET Core application. They were both covered in detail in the ASP.NET MVC 5 chapter, so I will just cover the specifics for ASP.NET Core.

The Controller Base Class

As mentioned already, ASP.NET Core unified ASP.NET MVC 5 and ASP.NET Web API. This combines the Controller, ApiController, and AsyncController base classes from MVC 5 and Web API 2.2 into one new base class, Controller.

There are also many helper methods for returning HTTP status codes in the controller base class. Table 33-7 lists some of the most commonly used helper methods that return HTTP status code results.

Table 33-7. *Some of the Helper Methods Provided by the Base Controller Class*

Controller Helper Method	HTTP Status Code Action Result	Raw Code Equivalent
NoContent	NoContentResult	204
Ok	OkResult	200
NotFound	NotFoundResult	404
BadRequest	BadRequestResult	400
Created CreateAtAction CreatedAtRoute	CreatedResult CreatedAtActionResult CreateAtRouteResult	201
Accepted AcceptedAtAction AcceptedAtRoute	AcceptedResult AcceptedAtActionResult AcceptedAtRouteResult	202

As an example, the following code returns a 400 Bad Request if the parameter value is null and a 404 Not Found if the record isn't found:

```
public IActionResult Edit(int? id)
{
  if (id == null)
  {
    return BadRequest();
  }
  var inventory = _repo.GetOne(id);
  if (inventory == null)
  {
    return NotFound();
  }
  return View(inventory);
}
```

Actions

ASP.NET Core actions return an IActionResult (or Task<IActionResult> for async operations) or a class that implements IActionResult, such as ActionResult. The most commonly used classes that implement IActionResult are described in the following sections.

Action Results

Some of the more commonly used types that derive from ActionResult are listed in Table 33-8.

Table 33-8. *Typical ActionResult-Derived Classes*

Action Result	Meaning in Life
ViewResult PartialViewResult	Returns a view (or a partial view) as a web page
RedirectResult RedirectToRouteResult	Redirects to another action
JsonResult	Returns a serialized JSON result to the client
FileResult	Returns binary file content to the client
ContentResult	Returns a user-defined content type to the client
HttpStatusCodeResult	Returns a specific HTTP status code

Formatted Response Results

To return an object (or object collection) formatted as JSON, wrap the object (or objects) in the Json object (or an ObjectResult object), which creates a JsonResult. An example of this is as follows:

```
public IActionResult GetAll()
{
  IEnumerable<Customer> customers = _repo.GetAllCustomers();
  return Json(customers);
}
```

Actions that return a type (or a strongly typed collection) do the same as the previous method. An alternate way to write the preceding action is as follows:

```
public IEnumerable<Customer> GetAll()
{
  return Repo.GetAll();
}
```

Formatted response results can be combined with HTTP status codes by wrapping the object result in one of the status code action results, as follows:

```
public IActionResult GetAll()
{
  return Ok(_repo. GetAllCustomers());
}
```

Redirect Results

The RedirectToActionResult redirects the users to another action. The following example redirects the user to the Index action of the current controller.

```
return RedirectToAction(nameof(Index));
```

Overloads exist for specifying a different controller as well as route values.

ViewResults

Just like MVC 5, a ViewResult is a type of ActionResult that encapsulates a Razor view. A PartialViewResult is a type of ViewResult that is designed to be rendered inside another view.

Add the Inventory Controller

With Visual Studio 2017 15.3 and ASP.NET Core 2.0, many of the helper features (such as scaffolding of controllers and views) have returned. Right-click the Controllers folder and select Add ➤ Controller, as shown in Figure 33-8.

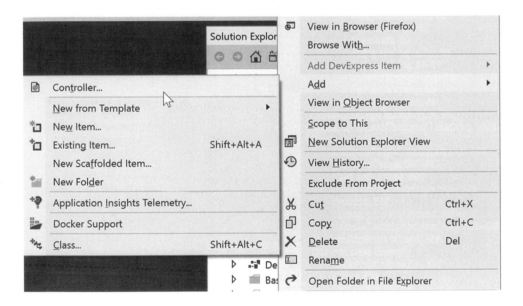

Figure 33-8. *Launching the Add New Controller scaffolding dialog*

If this is the first time you have done this for your project, you will be prompted to add the scaffolding dependencies, as shown in Figure 33-9. Select the Minimal Dependencies option and click Add.

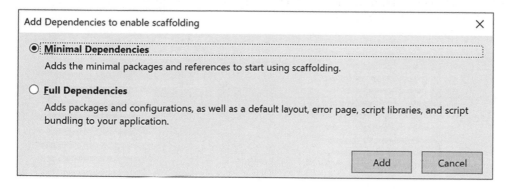

Add Dependencies to enable scaffolding   ✕

◉ **Minimal Dependencies**

   Adds the minimal packages and references to start using scaffolding.

○ **Full Dependencies**

   Adds packages and configurations, as well as a default layout, error page, script libraries, and script
   bundling to your application.

                                                                    Add   Cancel

Figure 33-9. *Adding scaffolding*

This creates a text file (named ScaffoldingReadMe.txt) that you can largely ignore since you have already done everything it suggests. It also updates the project file, adding the following package:

```
<PackageReference Include="Microsoft.VisualStudio.Web.CodeGeneration.Design" Version="2.0.0" />
```

Now that the dependencies are installed, once again right-click the Controllers folder and select Add ➤ Controller. This brings up the Add Scaffold dialog, as shown in Figure 33-10. There are several options available, and you want to choose "MVC Controller with views, using Entity Framework."

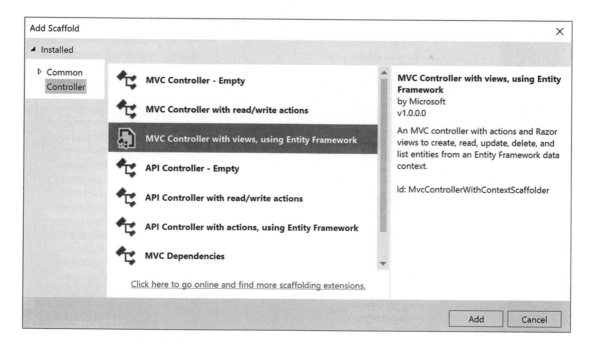

Add Scaffold   ✕

◢ Installed

   ▷ Common
     Controller

   MVC Controller - Empty   **MVC Controller with views, using Entity
                                                   Framework**
                                                   by Microsoft
   MVC Controller with read/write actions   v1.0.0.0

   MVC Controller with views, using Entity Framework   An MVC controller with actions and Razor
                                                   views to create, read, update, delete, and
                                                   list entities from an Entity Framework data
   API Controller - Empty   context.

   API Controller with read/write actions   Id: MvcControllerWithContextScaffolder

   API Controller with actions, using Entity Framework

   MVC Dependencies

   Click here to go online and find more scaffolding extensions.

                                                            Add   Cancel

Figure 33-10. *The Add Scaffold dialog*

This will bring up an additional dialog (shown in Figure 33-11) that allows you to configure your controller and views. The first task is to specify the model class, which determines the type for the controllers and action methods. Select the Inventory class from the drop-down.

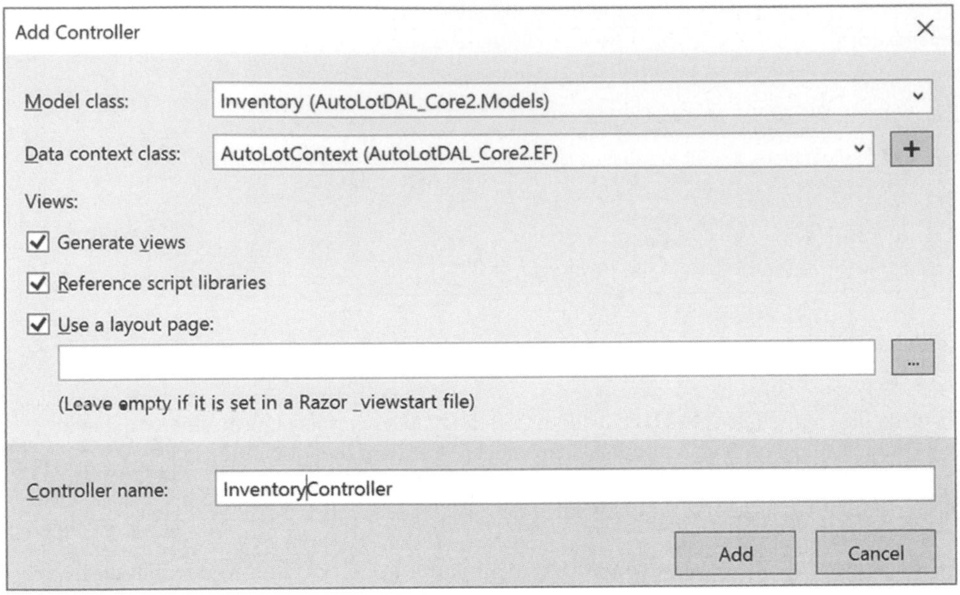

Figure 33-11. *Selecting the model, context, and other options*

The next question asks you to specify the context class. If you don't select one, the wizard will create one for you. For the data context, select AutoLotContext.

The "Generate views" option (selected by default) instructs the wizard to create a related view for each of the generated action methods. Just like the MVC 5 wizard, action methods and views for listing, adding, editing, and deleting records as well as showing the details of a single record are created.

Notice the absence of the check box for using async actions. By default, in ASP.NET Core, the scaffolding makes the action methods async. The "Reference script libraries" and "Use a layout page" work the same as the MVC 5 wizard. Leave these checked. Finally, change the name of the controller to InventoryController (from InventoriesController). The completed wizard is shown in Figure 33-11. Click Add to continue.

This did several things for you. First, it created an InventoryController class in the Controllers folder. It also created an Inventory folder in the Views folder and added five views under that folder.

Update the InventoryController

The brunt of the generated controller is similar to the MVC 5 version. In fact, you could use the bulk of the InventoryController class from Chapter 29 in this application with only minor tweaks. The main difference is the default use of async for the action methods. Another difference is the use of the new controller helper methods to return status codes instead of manually creating HTTStatusCodeResults. In the next sections, you will update the controller to use the AutoLotDAL_Core2 data access layer and, more specifically, the InventoryRepo. You will also change to their synchronous versions, returning IActionResults instead of Task<IActionResult>s.

■ **Note** I am not endorsing using synchronous over asynchronous methods. This book has covered the differences between the two in great detail, and I leave it up to you, the reader, to determine whether to sync or async action methods. Just make sure to thoroughly test your application, regardless of which version you decide to use.

At the end of the controller is a method named InventoryExists(). This can be deleted. It is used by the scaffolded code but will not be used by the updated code.

Update the using Statements

Start by updating the using statements to the following:

```
using System;
using System.Threading.Tasks;
using Microsoft.AspNetCore.Mvc;
using Microsoft.EntityFrameworkCore;
using AutoLotDAL_Core2.Models;
using AutoLotDAL_Core2.Repos;
```

Update the Constructor

In the Add Controller Wizard, you selected AutoLotContext for the source of the data. While this will work, you want to use the InventoryRepo repo instead. Update the private variable and the constructor to the following:

```
private readonly IInventoryRepo _repo;
public InventoryController(IInventoryRepo repo)
{
  _repo = repo;
}
```

All you need for the repo is the interface as the parameter, and the DI container will do the rest of the work in creating the instance of the InventoryRepo class. The DI container also creates the instance of the AutoLotContext class that is passed into the InventoryRepo using the constructor.

```
public InventoryRepo(AutoLotContext context) : base(context)
{
}
```

Update the Index() and Details() Action Methods

The Index() and Details() action method updates are a simple replacement of the AutoLotContext with the InventoryRepo instance, as follows:

```
// GET: Inventory
public IActionResult Index()
{
  return View(_repo.GetAll());
}
```

```
// GET: Inventory/Details/5
public IActionResult Details(int? id)
{
  if (id == null)
  {
    return BadRequest();
  }
  var inventory = _repo.GetOne(id);
  if (inventory == null)
  {
    return NotFound();
  }
  return View(inventory);
}
```

The Post-Redirect-Get Pattern

Just like MVC 5, ASP.NET Core uses the Post-Redirect-Get pattern to help reduce the issue with uses executing double posts. This is used for the Create(), Edit() and Delete() processes.

This was covered in Chapter 29, but as a refresher, it consists of redirecting every successful HTTP POST action to a HTTP GET action, so if a user hits submit again, it just refreshes the page presented by the GET action and doesn't resubmit the POST request.

Update the Create() Action Methods

The HTTP GET version of the Create () action method doesn't require any change.

```
// GET: Inventory/Create
public IActionResult Create()
{
  return View();
}
```

The HTTP POST Create() action method gets updated a bit from the default. Just like you did in Chapter 29, remove the Id and Timestamp fields from the Bind attribute. These are server-generated fields and won't be entered by the user when creating a new record. Change the signature to be synchronous, and update the code to use better error handling.

```
// POST: Inventory/Create
// To protect from overposting attacks, please enable the specific properties you want to
bind to, for
// more details see http://go.microsoft.com/fwlink/?LinkId=317598.
[HttpPost]
[ValidateAntiForgeryToken]
public IActionResult Create([Bind("Make,Color,PetName")] Inventory inventory)
{
    if (!ModelState.IsValid) return View(inventory);
    try
    {
        _repo.Add(inventory);
    }
```

```
    catch (Exception ex)
    {
        ModelState.AddModelError(string.Empty, $@"Unable to create record: {ex.Message}");
        return View(inventory);
    }
    return RedirectToAction(nameof(Index));
}
```

Update the Edit() Action Methods

The HTTP GET version of the Edit() action method gets updated to be synchronous and leverages the repository.

```
// GET: Inventory/Edit/5
public IActionResult Edit(int? id)
{
  if (id == null)
  {
    return BadRequest();
  }
  var inventory = _repo.GetOne(id);
  if (inventory == null)
  {
    return NotFound();
  }
  return View(inventory);
}
```

The HTTP POST version also gets updated to use the repository and is changed to synchronous.

```
// POST: Inventory/Edit/5
// To protect from overposting attacks, please enable the specific properties you want to
bind to, for
// more details see http://go.microsoft.com/fwlink/?LinkId=317598.
[HttpPost]
[ValidateAntiForgeryToken]
public IActionResult Edit(int id, [Bind("Make,Color,PetName,Id,Timestamp")] Inventory
inventory)
{
  if (id != inventory.Id)
  {
    return BadRequest();
  }
  if (!ModelState.IsValid) return View(inventory);
  try
  {
    _repo.Update(inventory);
  }
```

```
catch (DbUpdateConcurrencyException ex)
{
  ModelState.AddModelError(string.Empty,
    $@"Unable to save the record. Another user has updated it. {ex.Message}");
  return View(inventory);
}
catch (Exception ex)
{
  ModelState.AddModelError(string.Empty, $@"Unable to save the record. {ex.Message}");
  return View(inventory);
}
return RedirectToAction(nameof(Index));
}
```

Update the Delete() Action Methods

The HTTP GET version of the Delete() method is updated to use the repository, as follows:

```
// GET: Inventory/Delete/5
public IActionResult Delete(int? id)
{
  if (id == null)
  {
    return BadRequest();
  }
  var inventory = _repo.GetOne(id);
  if (inventory == null)
  {
    return NotFound();
  }
  return View(inventory);
}
```

The HTTP POST version gets the same overhaul that you did in Chapter 29: update the signature to take an Inventory record and change the name back to Delete() from DeleteConfirmed().

```
// POST: Inventory/Delete
[HttpPost]
[ValidateAntiForgeryToken]
public IActionResult Delete([Bind("Id,Timestamp")] Inventory inventory)
{
  try
  {
    _repo.Delete(inventory);
  }
  catch (DbUpdateConcurrencyException ex)
  {
    ModelState.AddModelError(string.Empty,
        $@"Unable to delete record. Another user updated the record. {ex.Message}");
  }
```

```
  catch (Exception ex)
  {
    ModelState.AddModelError(string.Empty, $@"Unable to create record: {ex.Message}");
  }
  return RedirectToAction(nameof(Index));
}
```

Wrapping Up Controllers and Actions

Someone with a strong background in ASP.NET MVC will notice how similar the preceding controller and action code is to what you have been using for years.

Views

While controllers and actions in ASP.NET Core should be familiar to MVC 5 developers, views leverage a host of new features. The MVC 5–style HTML helpers are still supported, but the new tag helpers (discussed earlier) are used heavily, making the views in ASP.NET Core much more HTML friendly.

The next sections cover updating the views and templates for the AutoLotMVC_Core2 application.

Update the View Imports File

Open the _ViewImports.cshtml file and add the following using statements:

```
@using AutoLotMVC_Core2
@using AutoLotMVC_Core2.Models
```

■ **Note**   Because of an apparent glitch in the framework at the time of this writing, the views aren't actually picking up the using statements in the _ViewImports.cshtml file. In addition to specifying the using statements in the _ViewImports.cshtml file, they are also specified in the views.

The Layout View

The _Layout.cshtml view (in the Views\Shared directory) is similar to the MVC 5 version, including using Bootstrap for styling and responsive design. The main differences are the tag helpers used. For example, the environment tag helper is used to determine which CSS and JavaScript files to load.

```
<environment include="Development">
  <link rel="stylesheet" href="~/lib/bootstrap/dist/css/bootstrap.css" />
  <link rel="stylesheet" href="~/css/site.css" />
</environment>
<environment exclude="Development">
  <link rel="stylesheet" href="https://ajax.aspnetcdn.com/ajax/bootstrap/3.3.7/css/
  bootstrap.min.css"
    asp-fallback-href="~/lib/bootstrap/dist/css/bootstrap.min.css"
```

```
    asp-fallback-test-class="sr-only" asp-fallback-test-property="position" asp-fallback-
    test-value="absolute" />
  <link rel="stylesheet" href="~/css/site.min.css" asp-append-version="true" />
</environment>
<!-- omitted for brevity -->
<environment include="Development">
  <script src="~/lib/jquery/dist/jquery.js"></script>
  <script src="~/lib/bootstrap/dist/js/bootstrap.js"></script>
  <script src="~/js/site.js" asp-append-version="true"></script>
</environment>
<environment exclude="Development">
  <script src="https://ajax.aspnetcdn.com/ajax/jquery/jquery-2.2.0.min.js"
    asp-fallback-src="~/lib/jquery/dist/jquery.min.js"
    asp-fallback-test="window.jQuery"
    crossorigin="anonymous"
    integrity="sha384-K+ctZQ+LL8q6tP7I94W+qzQsfRV2a+AfHIi9k8z8l9ggpc8X+Ytst4yBo/hH+8Fk">
  </script>
  <script src="https://ajax.aspnetcdn.com/ajax/bootstrap/3.3.7/bootstrap.min.js"
    asp-fallback-src="~/lib/bootstrap/dist/js/bootstrap.min.js"
    asp-fallback-test="window.jQuery && window.jQuery.fn && window.jQuery.fn.modal"
    crossorigin="anonymous"
    integrity="sha384-Tc5IQibO27qvyjSMfHjOMaLkfuWVxZxUPnCJA7l2mCWNIpG9mGCD8wGNIcPD7Txa">
  </script>
  <script src="~/js/site.min.js" asp-append-version="true"></script>
</environment>
```

In addition to the environment tag helper, the preceding code also uses the script and link tag helpers. The menu is built using the link tag helper. Add a new menu item for the Inventory pages, like this:

```
<div class="navbar-collapse collapse">
  <ul class="nav navbar-nav">
    <li><a asp-area="" asp-controller="Home" asp-action="Index">Home</a></li>
    <li><a asp-area="" asp-controller="Home" asp-action="About">About</a></li>
    <li><a asp-area="" asp-controller="Home" asp-action="Contact">Contact</a></li>
    <li><a asp-area="" asp-controller="Inventory" asp-action="Index">Inventory</a></li>
  </ul>
</div>
```

The Validation Scripts Partial View

While the ValidationScriptsPartialView.cshtml doesn't need to be changed, it's another great example of the environment and script tag helpers.

```
<environment include="Development">
  <script src="~/lib/jquery-validation/dist/jquery.validate.js"></script>
  <script src="~/lib/jquery-validation-unobtrusive/jquery.validate.unobtrusive.js"></script>
</environment>
<environment exclude="Development">
```

```
<script src="https://ajax.aspnetcdn.com/ajax/jquery.validate/1.14.0/jquery.validate.min.js"
    asp-fallback-src="~/lib/jquery-validation/dist/jquery.validate.min.js"
    asp-fallback-test="window.jQuery && window.jQuery.validator"
    crossorigin="anonymous"
    integrity="sha384-Fnqn3nxp3506LP/7Y3j/25BlWeA3PXTyT1l78LjECcPaKCV12TsZP7yyMxOe/G/k">
</script>
<script src="https://ajax.aspnetcdn.com/ajax/jquery.validation.unobtrusive/3.2.6/jquery.
    validate.unobtrusive.min.js"
    asp-fallback-src="~/lib/jquery-validation-unobtrusive/jquery.validate.unobtrusive.min.js"
    asp-fallback-test="window.jQuery && window.jQuery.validator && window.jQuery.validator.
    unobtrusive"
    crossorigin="anonymous"
    integrity="sha384-JrXK+k53HACyavUKOsL+NkmSesD2P+73eDMrbTtTkOh4RmOF8hF8apPlkp26JlyH">
</script>
</environment>
```

The Inventory Display Template

Just like MVC 5, ASP.NET Core supports display and editor templates. Create a new folder named
DisplayTemplates under the Views\Inventory folder. In this directory, add a new partial view named
InventoryList.cshtml. Clear out the templated code, and replace it with the following:

```
@using AutoLotDAL_Core2.Models
@model Inventory
<tr>
    <td>
        @Html.DisplayFor(model => model.Make)
    </td>
    <td>
        @Html.DisplayFor(model => model.Color)
    </td>
    <td>
        @Html.DisplayFor(model => model.PetName)
    </td>
    <td>
        <a asp-action="Edit" asp-route-id="@Model.Id">Edit</a> |
        <a asp-action="Details" asp-route-id="@Model.Id">Details</a> |
        <a asp-action="Delete" asp-route-id="@Model.Id">Delete</a>
    </td>
</tr>
```

As you can see from the preceding markup, HTML helpers are still an important part of ASP.NET Core
development, especially for displaying data. All of the same rules apply as with MVC 5.

The new markup uses the anchor tag helper, demonstrating the asp-action and
asp-route-<variablename> attributes.

The Inventory Editor Template

Create a new folder named `EditorTemplates` under the `Views\Inventory` folder. In this directory, add a new partial view named `Inventory.cshtml`. Clear out the templated code, and replace it with the following:

```
@using AutoLotDAL_Core2.Models
@model Inventory
<h4>Inventory</h4>
<hr />
<div asp-validation-summary="ModelOnly" class="text-danger"></div>
<div class="form-group">
  <label asp-for="Make" class="control-label"></label>
  <input asp-for="Make" class="form-control"/>
  <span asp-validation-for="Make" class="text-danger"></span>
</div>
<div class="form-group">
  <label asp-for="Color" class="control-label"></label>
  <input asp-for="Color" class="form-control"/>
  <span asp-validation-for="Color" class="text-danger"></span>
</div>
<div class="form-group">
  <label asp-for="PetName" class="control-label"></label>
  <input asp-for="PetName" class="form-control"/>
  <span asp-validation-for="PetName" class="text-danger"></span>
</div>
```

This template uses the validation and validation summary tag helpers, as well as the label and input tag helpers. For comparison to the MVC 5 version, this is the same template using Razor:

```
@model AutoLotDAL.Models.Inventory
<div class="form-horizontal">
    <h4>Inventory</h4>
    <hr />
    @Html.ValidationSummary(false, "", new { @class = "text-danger" })
    <div class="form-group">
        @Html.LabelFor(model => model.Make, htmlAttributes: new { @class = "control-label
        col-md-2" })
        <div class="col-md-10">
            @Html.EditorFor(model => model.Make, new { htmlAttributes = new { @class =
            "form-control" } })
            @Html.ValidationMessageFor(model => model.Make, "", new { @class = "text-danger" })
        </div>
    </div>
    <div class="form-group">
        @Html.LabelFor(model => model.Color, htmlAttributes: new { @class = "control-label
        col-md-2" })
        <div class="col-md-10">
            @Html.EditorFor(model => model.Color, new { htmlAttributes = new { @class =
            "form-control" } })
            @Html.ValidationMessageFor(model => model.Color, "", new { @class = "text-danger" })
        </div>
    </div>
```

```
    <div class="form-group">
        @Html.LabelFor(model => model.PetName, htmlAttributes: new { @class = "control-label
        col-md-2" })
        <div class="col-md-10">
            @Html.EditorFor(model => model.PetName, new { htmlAttributes = new { @class =
            "form-control" } })
            @Html.ValidationMessageFor(model => model.PetName, "", new { @class = "text-danger" })
        </div>
    </div>
</div>
```

This difference between the two code listings pretty clearly demonstrates the advantage of using tag helpers over HTML helpers. To be clear, the second listing will work in ASP.NET Core as well.

The Index View

The Index.cshtml file is updated to use the Razor function as well as the InventoryList.cshtml display template.

```
@using AutoLotDAL_Core2.Models
@model IEnumerable<Inventory>
@functions
{
  public IList<Inventory> SortCars(IList<Inventory> cars)
  {
    var list = from s in cars orderby s.PetName select s;
    return list.ToList();
  }
}
@{
  ViewData["Title"] = "Index";
}
<h2>Index</h2>
<p>
  <a asp-action="Create">Create New</a>
</p>
<table class="table">
  <thead>
    <tr>
      <th>@Html.DisplayNameFor(model => model.Make)</th>
      <th>@Html.DisplayNameFor(model => model.Color)</th>
      <th>@Html.DisplayNameFor(model => model.PetName)</th>
      <th></th>
    </tr>
  </thead>
  <tbody>
  @foreach (var item in SortCars(Model.ToList()))
  {
    @Html.DisplayFor(modelItem=>item,"InventoryList")
  }
  </tbody>
</table>
```

The Details View

The only change to the Details.cshtml view is to remove the display of the timestamp data. The updated file is listed here for your reference:

```
@model AutoLotDAL_Core2.Models.Inventory

@{
    ViewData["Title"] = "Details";
}

<h2>Details</h2>

<div>
  <h4>Inventory</h4>
  <hr />
  <dl class="dl-horizontal">
    <dt>@Html.DisplayNameFor(model => model.Make)</dt>
    <dd>@Html.DisplayFor(model => model.Make)</dd>
    <dt>@Html.DisplayNameFor(model => model.Color)</dt>
    <dd>@Html.DisplayFor(model => model.Color)</dd>
    <dt>@Html.DisplayNameFor(model => model.PetName) </dt>
    <dd>@Html.DisplayFor(model => model.PetName)</dd>
  </dl>
</div>
<div>
  <a asp-action="Edit" asp-route-id="@Model.Id">Edit</a> |
  <a asp-action="Index">Back to List</a>
</div>
```

The Create View

The Create.cshtml view combines HTML helpers and Razor editor templates with tag helpers to minimize the HTML needed. Update the view to the following:

```
@model AutoLotDAL_Core2.Models.Inventory
@{
    ViewData["Title"] = "Create";
}
<h2>Create</h2>
<div class="row">
  <div class="col-md-4">
    <form asp-action="Create">
      @Html.EditorForModel()
      <div class="form-group">
        <input type="submit" value="Create" class="btn btn-default"/>
      </div>
    </form>
  </div>
</div>
```

```
<div>
    <a asp-action="Index">Back to List</a>
</div>

@section Scripts {
    @{await Html.RenderPartialAsync("_ValidationScriptsPartial");}
}
```

Notice the use of the form tag helper and the lack of HTML.AntiforgeryToken(). Recall that the antiforgery token is provided by the form tag helper automatically.

The Edit View

The Edit.cshtml view follows the pattern of the Create.cshtml view, with the addition of two hidden fields, using the input tag helper. Update the markup to the following:

```
@model AutoLotDAL_Core2.Models.Inventory
@{
  ViewData["Title"] = "Edit";
}
<h2>Edit</h2>
<div class="row">
  <div class="col-md-4">
    <form asp-action="Edit">
      <input type="hidden" asp-for="Id"/>
      <input type="hidden" asp-for="Timestamp"/>
      @Html.EditorForModel()
      <div class="form-group">
        <input type="submit" value="Save" class="btn btn-default"/>
      </div>
    </form>
  </div>
</div>
<div>
  <a asp-action="Index">Back to List</a>
</div>
@section Scripts {
    @{await Html.RenderPartialAsync("_ValidationScriptsPartial");}
}
```

The Delete View

For the Delete.cshtml view, first remove the display for the Timestamp column. Next, add a hidden input for the Timestamp column inside the form tag. The final form is shown here:

```
@model AutoLotDAL_Core2.Models.Inventory
@{
  ViewData["Title"] = "Delete";
}
```

```
<h2>Delete</h2>
<h3>Are you sure you want to delete this?</h3>
<div>
  <h4>Inventory</h4>
  <hr />
  <dl class="dl-horizontal">
    <dt>@Html.DisplayNameFor(model => model.Make)</dt>
    <dd>@Html.DisplayFor(model => model.Make)</dd>
    <dt>@Html.DisplayNameFor(model => model.Color)</dt>
    <dd>@Html.DisplayFor(model => model.Color)</dd>
    <dt>@Html.DisplayNameFor(model => model.PetName)</dt>
    <dd>@Html.DisplayFor(model => model.PetName)</dd>
  </dl>
  <form asp-action="Delete">
    <input type="hidden" asp-for="Id" />
    <input type="hidden" asp-for="Timestamp" />
    <input type="submit" value="Delete" class="btn btn-default" /> |
    <a asp-action="Index">Back to List</a>
  </form>
</div>
```

Wrapping Up Views

ASP.NET Core introduced tag helpers as an alternative to using HTML helpers for many form-related tags. While the MVC 5 HTML helpers are still supported, the previous sections demonstrate the advantages of using tag helpers where you can. They result in cleaner and more readable markup, which ultimately makes the code more maintainable.

View Components

As mentioned earlier, view components are new in ASP.NET Core. The use case is anything that combines server-side code with UI markup that should not be an endpoint for a user action. A typical example is dynamically building a menu system based on records from the database. There isn't any reason a user should directly call that code. In this example, you are going to replace the Index.cshtml view with a view component.

Building the Server-Side Code

View components are composed of a server-side class that derives from ViewComponent and uses the naming convention <customname>ViewComponent. This code can live anywhere in your project, although I typically place them in a folder named (appropriately enough) ViewComponents. Create a new folder named ViewComponents in the root directory of the AutoLotMVC_Core2 project. Add a new class file named InventoryViewComponent.cs into this folder. Add the following using statements to the top of the file:

```
using System.Threading.Tasks;
using AutoLotDAL_Core2.Repos;
using Microsoft.AspNetCore.Mvc;
```

Change the class to public, and inherit from ViewComponent. View components don't have to inherit from the ViewComponent base class, but like the Controller base class, it is beneficial to do so. Update the class to this:

```
public class InventoryViewComponent : ViewComponent
{
}
```

To replicate the Index view from the InventoryController, this view component needs to call the GetAll() method on the InventoryRepo class. Fortunately, view components also leverage the DI container built into ASP.NET Core. Create a class-level variable to hold an instance of the IInventoryRepo interface, and create a constructor that receives an instance of the interface, as shown here:

```
public class InventoryViewComponent : ViewComponent
{
  private readonly IInventoryRepo _repo;
  public InventoryViewComponent(IInventoryRepo repo)
  {
    _repo = repo;
  }
}
```

View components are rendered from views by invoking the public method InvokeAsync. This method returns a Task<IViewComponentResult>, which is conceptually similar to an IActionResult. Add the following code to the InventoryViewComponent class:

```
public async Task<IViewComponentResult> InvokeAsync()
{
  var cars = _repo.GetAll(x => x.Make, true);
  if (cars != null)
  {
    return View("InventoryPartialView", cars);
  }
  return new ContentViewComponentResult("Unable to locate records.");
}
```

This method gets a list of all cars, sorted by Make (ascending) and, if successful, returns a ViewComponentResult using the View() helper method from the base ViewComponent class, passing in the list of Inventory records as the view model. If the list cannot be retrieved, the view component returns a ContentViewComponentResult with an error message.

The View helper method from the base ViewComponent class works similarly to the base Controller class method of the same name, except for a couple of key differences. The first difference is that the default View file name is Default.cshtml. As with the View() Controller method, another name can be used for the partial view by passing in the name for the first parameter. The second difference is that the location of the partial view to be rendered *must* be one of these two directories.

```
Views/<parent_controller_name_calling_view >/Components/<view_component_name>/<view_name>
Views/Shared/Components/<view_component_name>/<view_name>
```

The complete class is listed here:

```
public class InventoryViewComponent : ViewComponent
{
  private readonly IInventoryRepo _repo;
  public InventoryViewComponent(IInventoryRepo repo)
  {
    _repo = repo;
  }
  public async Task<IViewComponentResult> InvokeAsync()
  {
    var cars = _repo.GetAll(x => x.Make, true);
    return View("InventoryPartialView", cars);
  }
}
```

Building the Client-Side Code

Views rendered from view components are simple partial views. Create a new folder named `Components` under the `Views\Shared` folder. In this new folder, create another new folder named `Inventory`. This final folder name must match the name of the view component class created earlier, minus the `ViewComponent` suffix. In this folder, create a partial view named `InventoryPartialView.cshtml`.

Clear out the existing code and add the following markup:

```
@using AutoLotDAL_Core2.Models
@model IEnumerable<Inventory>
<table class="table">
  <thead>
  <tr>
    <th>@Html.DisplayNameFor(model => model.Make)</th>
    <th>@Html.DisplayNameFor(model => model.Color)</th>
    <th>@Html.DisplayNameFor(model => model.PetName)</th>
    <th></th>
  </tr>
  </thead>
  <tbody>
  @foreach (var item in Model.ToList())
  {
    <tr>
      <td>@Html.DisplayFor(modelItem => item.Make)</td>
      <td>@Html.DisplayFor(modelItem => item.Color)</td>
      <td>@Html.DisplayFor(modelItem => item.PetName)</td>
      <td>
<a asp-controller="Inventory" asp-action="Edit" asp-route-id="@item.Id">Edit</a> |
<a asp-controller="Inventory" asp-action="Details" asp-route-id="@item.Id">Details</a> |
<a asp-controller="Inventory" asp-action="Delete" asp-route-id="@item.Id">Delete</a>
      </td>
    /tr>
  }
  </tbody>
</table>
```

This markup should by now be familiar to you. View component views are just views in a designated location, built the same as partial views.

Invoking View Components

View components are typically invoked from a view (although they can be rendered from a controller action method as well). The syntax is straightforward: Component.Invoke(<string name of the view component>). Just like controllers, the ViewComponent suffix must be removed when invoking a view component.

```
@await Component.InvokeAsync("Inventory")
```

Invoking View Components as Custom Tag Helpers

New in ASP.NET Core 1.1, view components can be called as tag helpers. Instead of using Component.InvokeAsync, simply call the view component like this:

```
<vc:Inventory></vc:Inventory>
```

To use this method of calling view components, they must be added as tag helpers using the @addTagHelper command. This was already added to the _ViewImports.cshtml file earlier in this chapter to enable the custom Email view component. As a refresher, here is the line that was added:

```
@addTagHelper *, AutoLotMVC_Core2
```

Adding the View Component to AutoLotMVC_Core2

The InventoryViewComponent will replace the current Index view. Copy the Index.cshtml view in the Views\Inventory folder, and name the new view IndeixWithViewComponent.cshtml. Clear out the code in the new file, and replace it with this:

```
@{
    ViewData["Title"] = "Index";
}
<h2>Index</h2>

<p>
    <a asp-action="Create">Create New</a>
</p>
    <vc:Inventory></vc:Inventory>
```

Now, update the Index() action method in the InventoryController.cs class to the following:

```
public IActionResult Index()
{
  return View("IndexWithViewComponent");
}
```

Now, when you run the application and click Inventory in the main menu, the Index() method will call the simple view that renders the InventoryViewComponent and the InventoryPartialView.cshtml, showing all of the records from the Inventory table.

■ **Source Code**　You can find the AutoLotMVC_Core2 solution in the Chapter 33 subfolder.

Summary

This chapter examined many aspects of building web applications with ASP.NET Core. After seeing the new ASP.NET Core Web Application Template project in action, you learned about the new features in ASP.NET Core, including a new environment-based configuration system, built-in DI support, Kestrel, tag helpers, and much more. Finally, you took a deeper look into ASP.NET Core, building AutoLotMVC_Core2 along the way.

Next you will learn about building RESTful services using ASP.NET Core.

CHAPTER 34

■ ■ ■

Introducing ASP.NET Core Service Applications

The previous chapter covered ASP.NET Core in great detail while building the AutoLotMVC_Core2 web application. This chapter completes the coverage of ASP.NET Core by creating the AutoLotAPI_Core2 RESTful service.

You will begin by using the ASP.NET Core Web API template (yes, the template is still named Web API even though it's all one framework now) to create the solution and project. Then you will examine the project organization and startup options, update the NuGet packages, and add the AutoLotDAL_Core2 data access library from Chapter 32. Next, you will examine the changes from ASP.NET Web API 2.2 that haven't already been covered in Chapter 33 and then complete the RESTful service.

Finally, you will update the AutoLotMVC_Core2 web application to use the AutoLotAPI_Core2 service as the back-end data source instead of using AutoLotDAL_Core2.

■ **Note** This chapter assumes you already have a working knowledge of ASP.NET Web API 2.2 (from Chapter 30) and have already read and worked through Chapter 33 for ASP.NET Core. If that is not the case, please review Chapters 28 and 33 before proceeding.

The ASP.NET Core Web API Template

As discussed in Chapter 33, Visual Studio has separate templates for web applications (MVC style, using Razor Pages, or several JavaScript frameworks) and service applications. Since there is only one ASP.NET Core framework, the differences between the templates are semantic as opposed to structural. All the templates do in ASP.NET Core is to change the initial files that are created for you.

The New Project Wizard

To create the solution for this chapter, start by launching Visual Studio and selecting File ➤ New ➤ Project. In the left sidebar, select Web under Visual C#, select ASP.NET Core Web Application, and then change Name to AutoLotAPI_Core2, as shown in Figure 34-1.

© Andrew Troelsen and Philip Japikse 2017
A. Troelsen and P. Japikse, *Pro C# 7*, https://doi.org/10.1007/978-1-4842-3018-3_34

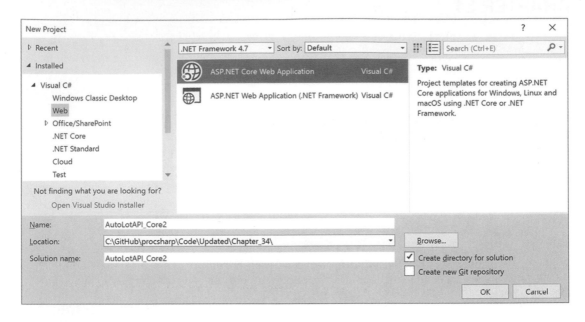

Figure 34-1. *Creating a new ASP.NET Core RESTful service*

On the next screen, select the Web API template. Leave the Enable Docker Support deselected and set the authentication to No Authentication, as shown in Figure 34-2.

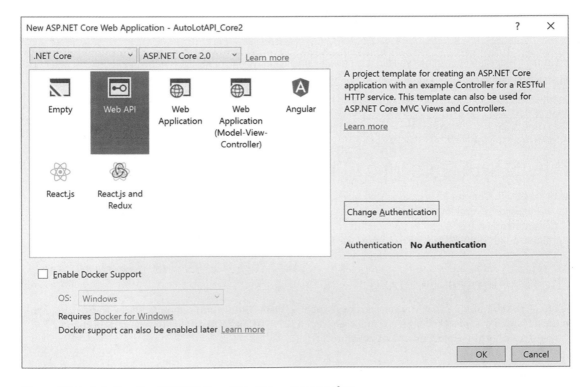

Figure 34-2. *Selecting the ASP.NET Core Web API project template*

■ **Note**   Docker is a containerization technology that is beyond the scope of this book. You can find more information at https://docs.microsoft.com/en-us/azure/vs-azure-tools-docker-hosting-web-apps-in-docker.

ASP.NET Core Server Project Organization

By now the new organization for ASP.NET Core projects should be familiar to you. The main difference between ASP.NET Core Web Application projects and Service projects is that the Service template creates the wwwroot folder but leaves it empty (as one would expect in a service application).

Add the Data Access Library

This is the same process you did in Chapter 33. As a refresher, copy the AutoLotDAL_Core2 and AutoLotDAL_Core2.Models projects from Chapter 32 into the same folder as the AutoLotAPI_Core2 Project, add references from the AutoLotAPI_Core2 project to the AutoLotDAL_Core2 and AutoLotDAL_Core2. Models projects, and confirm that the AutoLotDAL_Core2 project still references the AutoLotDAL_Core2. Models project.

Update and Add the NuGet Packages

Right-click the AutoLotAPI_Core2 project and select Manage NuGet Packages. Click Updates in the top menu bar, and update any packages that need updating.

   This application will use the AutoMapper NuGet package to transform the model classes and remove related instances, just like you did with the Web API 2.2 project in Chapter 30. To install it, click the Browse menu item at the top left of the NuGet Package Manager screen, enter **AutoMapper** in the search box, and install the package.

Run and Deploy Service Applications

Just like ASP.NET Core web applications, ASP.NET Core service applications can be run using Visual Studio (using IIS or Kestrel) and the command line (using Kestrel). All of the options are controlled by the settings in the launchsettings.json file.

   ASP.NET Core service applications also have the same deployment options as ASP.NET Core web applications.

What's Changed in ASP.NET Core Services

There are two potentially significant changes in ASP.NET Core service applications from ASP.NET Web API 2.2. The first is the format of JSON returned from action methods, and the second is the requirement for explicit routing of HTTP verbs.

Format for Returned JSON

Prior versions of ASP.NET Web API returned JSON formatted in *Pascal casing*. Pascal casing has the first letter capitalized and every subsequent separator character capitalized as well. This is the standard capitalization scheme for public .NET properties. For example, the following class has the properties FirstName and JobTitle Pascal cased:

```
public class Customer
{
    public string FirstName { get; set; }
    public string JobTitle { get; set; }
}
```

When an instance of this class was returned as JSON in Web API 2.2, it would be formatted like this:

```
{"FirstName":"Bob","JobTitle":"Boss"}
```

ASP.NET Core joined virtually the rest of the Internet and now returns data in a *camel cased* format (first letter lowercase and every subsequent separator character capitalized). If the same data is returned from an ASP.NET Core service, it is formatted like this:

```
{"firstName":"Bob","jobTitle":"Boss"}
```

The question you might be asking is "What's the big deal?" In a world where you are working entirely with the Microsoft stack, it's not a big deal. However, if your RESTful service is feeding data to frameworks that care about casing, this change can (and will) break your applications. The good news is that you can configure your service to work like Web API 2.2.

Open Startup.cs in the AutoLotAPI_Core2 application and add the following using statement to the top of the file:

```
using Newtonsoft.Json.Serialization;
```

Next, navigate to the ConfigureServices() method and update the services.AddMvc() line to the following:

```
services.AddMvc()
    .AddJsonOptions(options =>
    {
        //Revert to PascalCasing for JSON handling
        options.SerializerSettings.ContractResolver = new DefaultContractResolver();
    });
```

Now, the JSON returned from your service will be Pascal cased.

Explicit Routing for HTTP Verbs

ASP.NET Web API 2.2 allowed you to not specify the HTTP verb for a method if the name started with *GET*, *PUT*, *DELETE*, or *POST*. As I mentioned in Chapter 30, relying on this convention is generally considered a bad idea for Web API projects and has been removed in ASP.NET Core.

If an action method does not have an HTTP verb specified, it will be called using an HTTP Get.

Control Model Binding in ASP.NET Core

Model binding in ASP.NET Core, just like model binding in MVC 5 and Web API 2.2, looks for data in the posted form (if there is one), then the route data, and finally the query string parameters. This can be manipulated using attributes on the action method parameters, as listed in Table 34-1.

Table 34-1. *ASP.NET Core 2.0 Templates*

Attribute	Meaning in Life
BindingRequired	A model state error will be added if binding cannot occur.
BindNever	Tells the model binder to never bind to this parameter.
FromHeader FromQuery FromRoute FromForm	Used to specify the exact binding source to apply (HTTP header, querystring, route parameters, or form values).
FromServices	This value will be added using dependency injection.
FromBody	Binds data from the request body. The formatter is selected based on the content of the request (e.g., JSON, XML, etc.).
ModelBinder	Used to override the default model binder (for custom model binding).

For ASP.NET Core service applications, you will typically use the FromRoute and FromBody attributes.

Build AutoLotAPI_Core2

It's time to build AutoLotAPI_Core2. Nothing in this section should be a surprise to you. Everything you learned in Chapter 33 about ASP.NET Core project configuration, DI, controllers, and actions still applies. Much of this section will be similar to setting up the AutoLotMVC_Core2 project.

Add the Connection String

Open the appsettings.Development.json file to include your connection string as follows (this should match the connection string used in Chapters 32 and 33):

```
{
  "Logging": {
    "IncludeScopes": false,
    "LogLevel": {
      "Default": "Debug",
      "System": "Information",
      "Microsoft": "Information"
    }
  },
  "ConnectionStrings": {
    "AutoLot": "server=(LocalDb)\\MSSQLLocalDB;database=AutoLotCore2;integrated
    security=True;MultipleActiveResultSets=True;App=EntityFramework;"
  }
}
```

Update the Program.cs File for Data Initialization

Just like in AutoLotMVC_Core2, the Program.cs file is where the data initialization code is placed. Add the following using statements to the top of the Program.cs file:

```
using AutoLotDAL_Core2.DataInitialization;
using AutoLotDAL_Core2.EF;
using Microsoft.Extensions.DependencyInjection;
```

Now, update the code in the Main() method to the following:

```
var webHost = BuildWebHost(args);
using (var scope = webHost.Services.CreateScope())
{
  var services = scope.ServiceProvider;
  var context = services.GetRequiredService<AutoLotContext>();
  MyDataInitializer.RecreateDatabase(context);
  MyDataInitializer.InitializeData(context);
}
webHost.Run();
```

■ **Note**   If you try to run your project now, it will fail since the DI container hasn't been configured. This will be done next.

Update the Startup.cs File

There is less customization of the Startup.cs file in ASP.NET Core services than web applications. Some of the differences are fairly obvious; for example, anything having to do with a UI is removed. You will notice that the Configure() method doesn't create a route table. This is because service applications typically rely on attribute routing instead of route tables.

Open the Startup.cs file and update the using statements to the following:

```
using AutoLotDAL_Core2.EF;
using AutoLotDAL_Core2.Repos;
using Microsoft.EntityFrameworkCore;
using Microsoft.EntityFrameworkCore.Diagnostics;
using Microsoft.AspNetCore.Builder;
using Microsoft.AspNetCore.Hosting;
using Microsoft.Extensions.Configuration;
using Microsoft.Extensions.DependencyInjection;
```

Update the Constructor

The constructor can also take an instance of the IHostingEnvironment, which will be needed later in the chapter. Add a private readonly variable to hold this instance, and update the constructor to the following:

```
private readonly IHostingEnvironment _env;
public Startup(IConfiguration configuration, IHostingEnvironment env)
{
  _env = env;
  Configuration = configuration;
}
```

Update the ConfigureServices() Method

You've already updated the services.AddMVC() method call to use the Web API 2.2 JSON resolver, like this:

```
services.AddMvc()
    .AddJsonOptions(options =>
    {
        //Revert to PascalCasing for JSON handling
        options.SerializerSettings.ContractResolver = new DefaultContractResolver();
    });
```

The next task is to configure the AutoLotContext and add the IInventoryRepo to the DI container.

Configure the AutoLotContext and InventoryRepo for DI Support

ASP.NET Core services also support the pooling of DbContext classes. Add the following code after the call to services.AddMvc():

```
services.AddDbContextPool<AutoLotContext>(
  options => options.UseSqlServer(Configuration.GetConnectionString("AutoLot"),
      o => o.EnableRetryOnFailure())
    .ConfigureWarnings(warnings => warnings.Throw(RelationalEventId.
    QueryClientEvaluationWarning)));
```

Add a new line after the AutoLotContext configuration to add the InventoryRepo into the DI container:

```
services.AddScoped<IInventoryRepo, InventoryRepo>();
```

Add Application-wide Exception Handling

ASP.NET Core supports filters just like MVC 5 and Web API 2.2, and when creating service applications, it's helpful to add a global ExceptionFilter to encapsulate error handling for your service.

Add the AutoLotExceptionFilter

Right-click the AutoLotAPI_Core2 project, and add a new folder named Filters. In this folder, add a new class named AutoLotExceptionFilter. Update the using statements to match the following:

```
using Microsoft.AspNetCore.Hosting;
using Microsoft.AspNetCore.Mvc;
using Microsoft.AspNetCore.Mvc.Filters;
using Microsoft.EntityFrameworkCore;
```

Make the class public and implement the IExceptionFilter interface. The IExceptionFilter interface has one method, OnException(), that is fired when an unhandled exception is thrown. Update the class as follows:

```
public class AutoLotExceptionFilter:IExceptionFilter
{
  public void OnException(ExceptionContext context)
  {
  }
}
```

The goal of this filter is essentially to replicate the developer exception page in ASP.NET Core web applications. If the environment is development, then the filter should return the stack trace and full exception details as JSON. If the environment is not development, then the filter should return a friendly message without all of the technical details.

To determine the runtime environment, you will leverage an instance of the IHostingEnvironment interface, which will be passed in through constructor injection. This will be used to assign the value of a Boolean class-level variable named _isDevelopment. Add the variable and the constructor, as follows:

```
private readonly bool _isDevelopment;
public AutoLotExceptionFilter(IHostingEnvironment env)
{
    _isDevelopment = env.IsDevelopment();
}
```

In the OnException() method, retrieve the actual exception from the ExceptionContext. This allows you to get the stack trace and determine the exact error that occurred. In this example filter, you are going to check for a DbUpdateConcurrency exception as a special case and handle all other exceptions the same.

The rest of the method builds up an IActionResult as either a BadRequestObjectResult (for concurrency errors) or a generic ObjectResult (for all other errors). Update the method to the following:

```
public void OnException(ExceptionContext context)
{
  var ex = context.Exception;
  string stackTrace = (_isDevelopment) ? context.Exception.StackTrace : string.Empty;
  IActionResult actionResult;
  string message = ex.Message;
  if (ex is DbUpdateConcurrencyException)
  {
```

```
  //Returns a 400
  if (!_isDevelopment)
  {
    message = "There was an error updating the database. Another user has altered the
    record.";
  }
  actionResult = new BadRequestObjectResult(
      new { Error = "Concurrency Issue.", Message = ex.Message, StackTrace = stackTrace });
}
else
{
  if (!_isDevelopment)
  {
    message = "There was an unknown error. Please try again.";
  }
  actionResult = new ObjectResult(
        new { Error = "General Error.", Message = ex.Message, StackTrace = stackTrace })
    {
        StatusCode = 500
    };
}
context.Result = actionResult;
}
```

Register the Exception Filter

Now you need to register the filter with the MVC framework. Open the Startup.cs file, and add the following using statement:

```
using AutoLotAPI_Core2.Filters;
```

Next, navigate to the ConfigureServices() method, and update the services.AddMvc() call to the following:

```
services.AddMvc(config =>
  {
    config.Filters.Add(new AutoLotExceptionFilter(_env));
  })
.AddJsonOptions(options =>
  {
    //Revert to PascalCasing for JSON handling
    options.SerializerSettings.ContractResolver = new DefaultContractResolver();
  });
```

Now any unhandled errors in the application pipeline will be caught by the AutoLotExceptionFilter.

Add the Inventory Controller

Right-click the Controllers folder and select Add ➤ Controller, as shown in Figure 34-3.

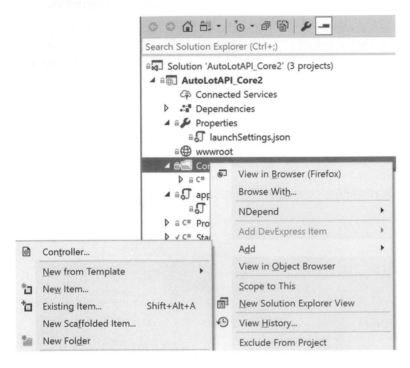

Figure 34-3. *Launching the Add New Controller scaffolding dialog*

Once again, if this is the first time you have done this for your project, you will be prompted to add the scaffolding dependencies, as shown in Figure 34-4. Select the Minimal Dependencies option and click Add.

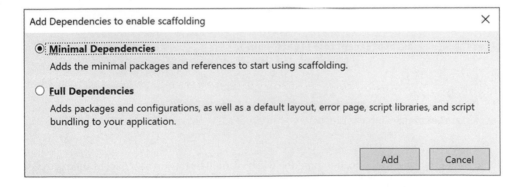

Figure 34-4. *Adding the scaffolding dependencies*

Just like with ASP.NET Core web applications, this wizard creates the ScaffoldingReadMe.txt file and adds the following package (if it isn't already in the project file):

```
<PackageReference Include="Microsoft.VisualStudio.Web.CodeGeneration.Design" Version="2.0.0" />
```

To add the controller, once again right-click the Controllers folder and select Add ➤ Controller. Select "API Controller with actions, using Entity Framework," as shown in Figure 34-5.

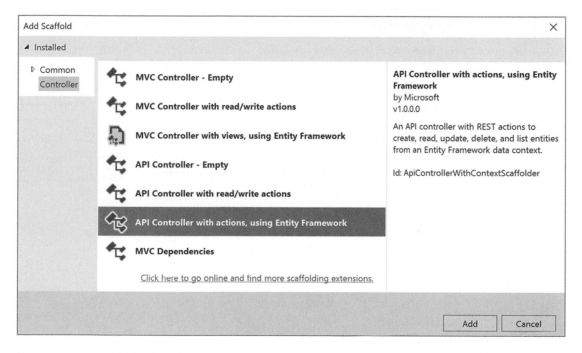

Figure 34-5. *The Add Scaffold dialog*

This will bring up the additional dialog to select the model and the context and name the controller. Figure 34-6 shows the completed wizard. Click Add to continue.

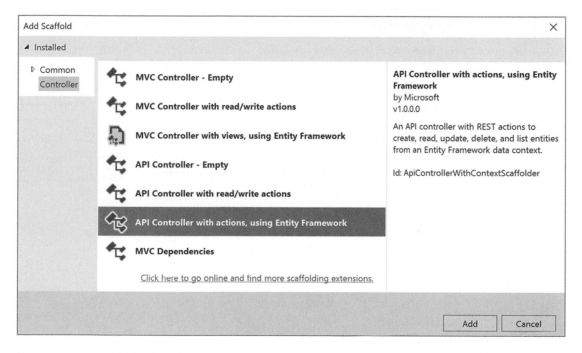

Figure 34-6. *Selecting the model and context and naming the controller*

Just like with the ASP.NET Core web application wizard, this created the InventoryController class in the Controllers folder.

Delete the InventoryExists( ) Method

This method is not used in your version of the code, so you can delete it from the controller.

Update the InventoryController

The wizard created a controller that codes directly against the AutoLotContext. The bulk of the changes to the controller involve replacing the AutoLotContext with the InventoryRepo.

Examine the attribute at the top of the controller:

```
[Produces("application/json")]
```

This is a filter that specifies all content returned from this controller will be formatted as JSON. ASP.NET Core defaults to JSON for data returned from a controller, but a client could overwrite that with an Accept header. The Produces attribute prevents clients from requesting another format.

The next attribute defines the route for this controller:

```
[Route("api/Inventory")]
```

Update the Using Statements

Add the following using statements to the top of the file:

```
using AutoLotDAL_Core2.Models;
using AutoLotDAL_Core2.Repos;
using AutoMapper;
using Newtonsoft.Json;
```

Update the Constructor

In the Add Controller Wizard, you selected the AutoLotContext for the source of the data. While this will work, you want to use the InventoryRepo instead. Update the private variable and the constructor to the following:

```
private readonly IInventoryRepo _repo;
public InventoryController(IInventoryRepo repo)
{
  _repo = repo;
}
```

Next, you need to configure AutoMapper to clean out any navigation properties, just as you did with the Web API 2.2 project in Chapter 30. Add the following code to the constructor:

```
Mapper.Initialize(
  cfg =>
    {
      cfg.CreateMap<Inventory, Inventory>().ForMember(x => x.Orders, opt => opt.Ignore());
    });
```

AutoMapper will be used in several of the action methods.

Update the GetCars() Action Methods

The GetCars() action method update is twofold. First, replace the call to the AutoLotContext with a call to the InventoryRepo GetAll() method. Second, you use AutoMapper to remove any instances of navigation properties. Remember that EF Core does not support lazy loading, so unless you specified to include the related data (which you didn't), you will have errors when the JSON serializer tries to return an Inventory record. For more information, refer to Chapter 30, where this was discussed in more detail. Update the method to the following:

```
// GET: api/Inventory
[HttpGet]
public IEnumerable<Inventory> GetCars()
{
  var inventories = _repo.GetAll();
  return Mapper.Map<List<Inventory>, List<Inventory>>(inventories);
}
```

Update the GetInventory() Action Method

The GetInventory() action method has several updates. First, name the route (this will be used later in the controller). In ASP.NET Core attribute routing, you name routes as part of the HTTP verb declaration. Update the attribute to this:

```
[HttpGet("{id}",Name= "DisplayRoute")]
```

Next, update the method to use the InventoryRepo and then return the cleaned Inventory record (using AutoMapper) as the content for an HTTP OK status message. Note that this uses one of the base Controller helper methods, the Ok() method. The full action method is listed here:

```
// GET: api/Inventory/5
[HttpGet("{id}",Name= "DisplayRoute")]
public async Task<IActionResult> GetInventory([FromRoute] int id)
{
  Inventory inventory = _repo.GetOne(id);
  if (inventory == null)
  {
    return NotFound();
  }
  return Ok(Mapper.Map<Inventory, Inventory>(inventory));
}
```

Note the use of the FromRoute parameter to make sure that the id is passed in from the route and not any other source.

Update the PutInventory() Action Method

In HTTP parlance, a PUT is an update of an existing record. The PutInventory() action method takes the id parameter of the record to be updated from the route and the values of the Inventory record (including the id parameter) from the body of the request message. The method checks to make sure the model state is valid (leveraging the validation system of the model binder) and then confirms that the id parameter from the route is the same as the id parameter of the Inventory record from the body of the message. If either of these checks fails, the method uses the BadRequest() helper method from the base Controller class to return the HTTP response.

The simple change to this method is to rip out the code that updates a record using the AutoLotContext and replace it with the Update() method of the InventoryRepo. The full method is shown here:

```
// PUT: api/Inventory/5
[HttpPut("{id}")]
public async Task<IActionResult> PutInventory([FromRoute] int id, [FromBody] Inventory
inventory)
{
  if (!ModelState.IsValid)
  {
    return BadRequest(ModelState);
  }
  if (id != inventory.Id)
  {
    return BadRequest();
  }
  _repo.Update(inventory);
  return NoContenl();
}
```

You removed the error handling code since the AutoLotExceptionFilter will catch any exceptions and handle them by returning the appropriate JSON (based on the environment).

Update the PostInventory() Action Method

The PostInventory() action method adds a new Inventory record into the database. If the model state isn't valid, it returns a BadRequest() with the errors in the body. If it is valid, it adds the inventory using the InventoryRepo. If that succeeds, it returns the URL of the GetInventory() action method as a header. The completed method is listed here:

```
// POST: api/Inventory
[HttpPost]
public async Task<IActionResult> PostInventory([FromBody] Inventory inventory)
{
  if (!ModelState.IsValid)
  {
    return BadRequest(ModelState);
  }
  _repo.Add(inventory);
  return CreatedAtRoute("DisplayRoute", new { id = inventory.Id }, inventory);
}
```

Update the DeleteInventory() Action Method

To delete a record using concurrency checking, you need the Id and the Timestamp. HTTP DELETE requests don't have a body, so this information must be added to the route. Update the route (inside the HttpDelete attribute) and the method signature to the following:

```
[HttpDelete("{id}/{timestamp}")]
public async Task<IActionResult> DeleteInventory([FromRoute] int id,[FromRoute] string timestamp)
```

The Timestamp property is (as you well know) an array of byte, which doesn't work in a URL as part of a route. Any calls to this action method must encode the Timestamp into a string, and you are going to use Newtonsoft's JSON.NET to do this. Later in the chapter you will encode the values; all you need to do here is turn the string back into a byte array. It's important to note that you have to add quotes into the string for the process to work correctly. The code to do that is listed here:

```
if (!timestamp.StartsWith("\""))
{
  timestamp = $"\"{timestamp}\"";
}
var ts = JsonConvert.DeserializeObject<byte[]>(timestamp);
```

Finally, the method calls Delete() on the InventoryRepo, passing in the Id and Timestamp values, and then returns an Ok(). The full action method is listed here:

```
// DELETE: api/Inventory/5
[HttpDelete("{id}/{timestamp}")]
public async Task<IActionResult> DeleteInventory([FromRoute] int id,[FromRoute] string timestamp)
{
  if (!timestamp.StartsWith("\""))
  {
    timestamp = $"\"{timestamp}\"";
  }
  var ts = JsonConvert.DeserializeObject<byte[]>(timestamp);
  _repo.Delete(id, ts);
  return Ok();
}
```

Once again, the error handling is covered by the AutoLotExceptionFilter.

Wrapping Up ASP.NET Core Service Applications

As you saw in this chapter, ASP.NET Core web applications and service applications leverage the same framework. Configuration, startup, controllers, filters, and all other aspects of ASP.NET Core (except for the UI, of course) are completely transferrable between web applications and RESTful services.

Update AutoLotMVC_Core2 to Use AutoLotAPI_Core2

Just like you updated the CarLotMVC ASP.NET MVC site to use CarLotWebAPI, now you will update AutoLotMVC_Core2 to use the AutoLotAPI_Core2 service instead of AutoLotDAL_Core2 as the back-end data access layer.

Copy and Add the AutoLotMVC_Core2 Application

Copy the AutoLotMVC_Core2 project folder (from Chapter 33) into the AutoLotAPI_Core2 solution folder. Add it into the solution by right-clicking the solution and selecting Add ➤ Existing Project. Set both the AutoLotAPI_Core2 and AutoLotMVC_Core2 projects as startup, in that order. You do this by right-clicking the solution, choosing Select Startup Projects, and adjusting the dialog that opens to match Figure 34-7.

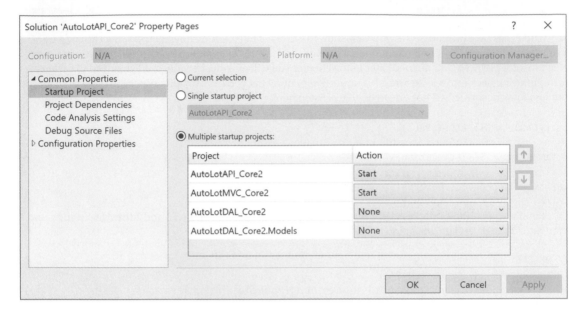

Figure 34-7. *Setting multiple startup projects*

Remove AutoLotDAL_Core2 from AutoLotMVC_Core2

You no longer need a reference to AutoLotDAL_Core2, but you will still need access to the models in AutoLotDAL_Models. Remove the reference to AutoLotDAL_Core2 by expanding the Dependencies\Projects node under the AutoLotMVC_Core2 project.

Update Program.cs

Open Program.cs, and remove the code that initializes the database. The Main() method will look like this after you are done:

```
public static void Main(string[] args)
{
    var webHost = BuildWebHost(args);
    webHost.Run();
}
```

Also, remove the extra using statements. All that you will need when you are done are these two:

```
using Microsoft.AspNetCore;
using Microsoft.AspNetCore.Hosting;
```

Update Startup.cs

Open `Startup.cs`. In the `ConfigureServices()` method, remove the code that initializes the `AutoLotContext`, and remove the line that adds the `InventoryRepo` into the DI container. The method will look like this when you are done:

```
public void ConfigureServices(IServiceCollection services)
{
    services.AddMvc();
}
```

You will also need to remove the two `using` statements that refer to `AutoLotDAL_Core2` database and remove the two `EntityFrameworkCore` using statements. Remove the following using statements:

```
using AutoLotDAL_Core2.EF;
using AutoLotDAL_Core2.Repos;
using Microsoft.EntityFrameworkCore;
using Microsoft.EntityFrameworkCore.Diagnostics;
```

Update the Settings File

You no longer need the connection string in the `appsettings.Development.json` file. Open the file and delete the `ConnectionStrings` node and replace it with base URL of the AutoLotAPI_Core2 service. Your file will resemble this (your port will be different):

```
{
  "Logging": {
    "IncludeScopes": false,
    "LogLevel": {
      "Default": "Debug",
      "System": "Information",
      "Microsoft": "Information"
    }
  },
  "ServiceAddress":"http://localhost:51714/api/Inventory"
}
```

To confirm your port, open the `launchSettings.json` file for the `AutoLotAPI_Core2` service. Determine whether you will use IIS or Kestrel to test, and select the appropriate port.

Create a New InventoryController

You are going to build up the new `InventoryController` from scratch. Delete the existing `InventoryController.cs` class, and create a new one with the same name. Add the following using statements to the top of the file:

```
using System;
using System.Collections.Generic;
using System.Net.Http;
using System.Text;
using System.Threading.Tasks;
```

```
using Microsoft.AspNetCore.Mvc;
using AutoLotDAL_Core2.Models;
using Microsoft.Extensions.Configuration;
using Newtonsoft.Json;
```

Create the Constructor

Next, make the class public and inherit from Controller. Add a private variable to hold the URL of the service and a constructor that takes an instance of the IConfiguration class. Use the IConfiguration instance to get the base URL from the settings file. Here is the class so far:

```
public class InventoryController : Controller
{
  private readonly string _baseUrl;
  public InventoryController(IConfiguration configuration)
  {
    _baseUrl = configuration.GetSection("ServiceAddress").Value;
  }
}
```

Create the GetInventoryRecord() Method

Next, you are going to create a private helper method to get a single inventory record from the service. The code will create a new HttpClient() and call the GetInventory() method of the InventoryController in AutoLotAPI_Core2. If the call succeeds, JSON.NET is used to create an instance of an Inventory record from the JSON returned. If the call does not succeed, the method returns null. Here is the method in full:

```
private async Task<Inventory> GetInventoryRecord(int id)
{
    var client = new HttpClient();
    var response = await client.GetAsync($"{_baseUrl}/{id}");
    if (response.IsSuccessStatusCode)
    {
        var inventory = JsonConvert.DeserializeObject<Inventory>(await response.Content.
        ReadAsStringAsync());
        return inventory;
    }
    return null;
}
```

Create the Index() Action

The Index() action method creates a new HttpClient and calls the default HTTP GET method on the service. The method is shown here:

```
public async Task<IActionResult> Index()
{
  var client = new HttpClient();
  var response = await client.GetAsync(_baseUrl);
  if (response.IsSuccessStatusCode)
```

```
  {
    var items = JsonConvert.DeserializeObject<List<Inventory>>(
        await response.Content.ReadAsStringAsync());
    return View(items);
  }
  return NotFound();
}
```

If you chose to use the version that leverages the InventoryViewComponent, then update the Index() action method to this:

```
public async Task<IActionResult> Index()
{
  return View("IndexWithViewComponent");
}
```

Either way, you will need to update the InventoryViewComponent since the current version is still referencing the AutoLotDAL_Core2 project.

Update the InventoryViewComponent

The InventoryViewComponent.cs class also needs to be updated to use the RESTful service instead of AutoLotDAL_Core2. Start by updating the using statements to the following:

```
using System.Collections.Generic;
using System.Net.Http;
using System.Threading.Tasks;
using AutoLotDAL_Core2.Models;
using Microsoft.AspNetCore.Mvc;
using Microsoft.AspNetCore.Mvc.ViewComponents;
using Microsoft.Extensions.Configuration;
using Newtonsoft.Json;
```

Next, update the constructor to take an instance of IConfiguration and get the root URL, just as you did for the InventoryController. Here is the updated code:

```
private readonly string _baseUrl;

public InventoryViewComponent(IConfiguration configuration)
{
    _baseUrl = configuration.GetSection("ServiceAddress").Value;
}
```

Finally, update the InvokeAsync() method to use a new instance of the HttpClient class to get the list of Inventory records to be passed into the partial view:

```
public async Task<IViewComponentResult> InvokeAsync()
{
    var client = new HttpClient();
    var response = await client.GetAsync(_baseUrl);
    if (response.IsSuccessStatusCode)
```

```
{
    var items = JsonConvert.DeserializeObject<List<Inventory>>(await response.Content.
    ReadAsStringAsync());
    return View("InventoryPartialView", items);
}
return new ContentViewComponentResult("Unable to return records.");
}
```

Create the Details() Action

The next step is to add the Details() action method. It first checks to make sure an id parameter was passed in and, if not, returns a BadRequest(). If there was an ID, then the GetInventoryRecord() method is used to return the Details.cshtml view with the Inventory record or return a NotFound() if the value returned from the GetInventoryRecord() method is null. Add the following code:

```
public async Task<IActionResult> Details(int? id)
{
    if (id -- null)
    {
        return BadRequest();
    }
    var inventory = await GetInventoryRecord(id.Value);
    return inventory != null ? (IActionResult) View(inventory) : NotFound();
}
```

Add the Create() Action Methods

The first Create() action method is the same as the previous version.

```
// GET: Inventory/Create
public IActionResult Create()
{
    return View();
}
```

The HTTP POST version of the Create() method checks the model state and then uses a new instance of the HttpClient to submit a POST request to the service. If it worked, the method redirects to the Index() action method. If it doesn't, the user is returned to the Create.cshtml view to correct any errors.

```
// POST: Inventory/Create
// To protect from overposting attacks, please enable the specific properties you want to
bind to, for
// more details see http://go.microsoft.com/fwlink/?LinkId=317598.
[HttpPost]
[ValidateAntiForgeryToken]
public async Task<IActionResult> Create([Bind("Make,Color,PetName")] Inventory inventory)
{
  if (!ModelState.IsValid) return View(inventory);
  try
```

```
  {
    var client = new HttpClient();
    string json = JsonConvert.SerializeObject(inventory);
    var response = await client.PostAsync(_baseUrl,
        new StringContent(json, Encoding.UTF8, "application/json"));
    if (response.IsSuccessStatusCode)
    {
      return RedirectToAction(nameof(Index));
    }
  }
  catch (Exception ex)
  {
    ModelState.AddModelError(string.Empty, $"Unable to create record: {ex.Message}");
  }
  return View(inventory);
}
```

Add the Edit() Action Methods

The HTTP GET version of the Edit() action method checks to make sure an ID was passed into the method and, if so, uses the GetInventoryRecord() method to get the Inventory instance and pass it into the Edit.cshtml view. The method is listed here:

```
// GET: Inventory/Edit/5
public async Task<IActionResult> Edit(int? id)
{
  if (id == null)
  {
    return BadRequest();
  }
  var inventory = await GetInventoryRecord(id.Value);
  return inventory != null ? (IActionResult)View(inventory) : NotFound();
}
```

The HTTP POST version of the Edit() action method operates much the same as the Create() action method, except that it creates a PUT request to the service. The full code is listed here:

```
// POST: Inventory/Edit/5
// To protect from overposting attacks, please enable the specific properties you want to bind to, for
// more details see http://go.microsoft.com/fwlink/?LinkId=317598.
[HttpPost]
[ValidateAntiForgeryToken]
public async Task<IActionResult> Edit(int id, [Bind("Make,Color,PetName,Id,Timestamp")]
Inventory inventory)
{
  if (id != inventory.Id) return BadRequest();
  if (!ModelState.IsValid) return View(inventory);
  var client = new HttpClient();
  string json = JsonConvert.SerializeObject(inventory);
  var response = await client.PutAsync($"{_baseUrl}/{inventory.Id}",
```

```
    new StringContent(json, Encoding.UTF8, "application/json"));
if (response.IsSuccessStatusCode)
{
  return RedirectToAction(nameof(Index));
}
return View(inventory);
}
```

Add the Delete() Action Methods

The GET version of the Delete() action method works much the same as the GET version of the Edit()
action method and is shown here:

```
// GET: Inventory/Delete/5
public async Task<IActionResult> Delete(int? id)
{
  if (id == null)
  {
    return BadRequest();
  }
  var inventory = await GetInventoryRecord(id.Value);
  return inventory != null ? (IActionResult)View(inventory) : NotFound();
}
```

The POST version uses Json.NET to convert the Timestamp property to a string so it can be added to the
route. It then uses the HttpClient to create a DELETE request. If all is successful, the user is redirected to the
Index action method.

```
// POST: Inventory/Delete/5
[HttpPost]
[ValidateAntiForgeryToken]
public async Task<IActionResult> Delete([Bind("Id,Timestamp")] Inventory inventory)
{
  var client = new HttpClient();
  var timeStampString = JsonConvert.SerializeObject(inventory.Timestamp);
  HttpRequestMessage request =
    new HttpRequestMessage(HttpMethod.Delete, $"{_baseUrl}/{inventory.Id}/
    {timeStampString}");
  await client.SendAsync(request);
  return RedirectToAction(nameof(Index));
}
```

Wrapping Up the Migration of AutoLotMVC_Core2

As you would expect, the changes made to AutoLotMVC_Core2 so it uses the RESTful service instead of
AutoLotDAL_Core2 were similar to the same exercise you did in Chapter 30. Much of the same code could
be used to communicate with the CarLotAPI project instead of AutoLotAPI_Core2.

■ **Source Code**   You can find the combined AutoLotAPI_Core2 and AutoLotMVC_Core2 solution in the
Chapter 34 directory of the download files.

Summary

This chapter completed your look into ASP.NET Core by building a RESTful service. After creating the
solution, you examined the additional differences between Web API 2.2 and ASP.NET Core that weren't
already covered in Chapter 33.

Next, you built the AutoLotAPI_Core2 application to handle the CRUD operations for Inventory
records. After adding the connection string to appsettings.development.json, you then updated the
Startup.cs and Program.cs files. You added the AutoLotExceptionFilter to handle exceptions in
application's action methods and registered the filter with the MVC framework.

You then added the InventoryController using the built-in scaffolding, and updated the controller to
use the InventoryRepo instead of the AutoLotContext. Finally, you updated AutoLotMVC_Core2 to call into
the AutoLotAPI_Core2 service's URLs, using JSON.NET to serialize and deserialize records.

Index

■ B

■ E

■ J, K

■ L

■ X, Y, Z

Get the eBook for only $5!

Why limit yourself?

With most of our titles available in both PDF and ePUB format, you can access your content wherever and however you wish—on your PC, phone, tablet, or reader.

Since you've purchased this print book, we are happy to offer you the eBook for just $5.

To learn more, go to http://www.apress.com/companion or contact support@apress.com.

Apress®